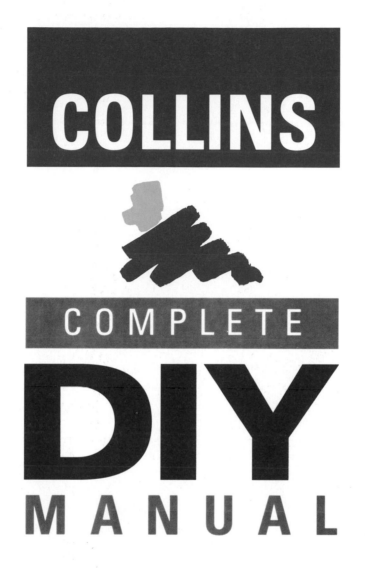

COLLINS

COMPLETE

DIY

MANUAL

COLLINS

COMPLETE

DIY
MANUAL

JACKSON·DAY

Colour
Library
Direct

CLD 21896

This edition was published in 2000
for Colour Library Direct Ltd,
New Mill, New Mill Lane,
Witney, Oxon OX8 5TF

Collins Complete DIY Manual
was first published in 1993
by HarperCollins*Publishers*, London
Reprinted 1994, 1995 (twice), 1996,
1997, 1998 (twice)

Copyright © 1993
HarperCollins*Publishers*

ISBN 0 00 760476 9

Conceived, edited and designed
by Jackson Day Jennings Ltd
trading as Inklink.

Text
Albert Jackson
David Day

Editorial director
Albert Jackson

Text editors
Diana Volwes
Peter Leek

Executive art director
Simon Jennings

Design and art direction
Alan Marshall

Additional design
Amanda Allchin

Production assistant
Simon Pickford

Illustrations editor
David Day

Illustrators
Robin Harris
David Day

Additional illustrations
Brain Craker
Michael Parr
Brian Sayers

Photographers
Neil Waving
Paul Chave
Peter Higgins
Simon Jennings
Albert Jackson
Shona Wood

Picture researchers
David Day
Anne-Marie Ehrlich
Hugh Olliff

Proofreaders
Mary Morton
Alison Turnball

Indexer
Susan Bosanko

Consultants
The authors are grateful to the
following consultants for their
contributions and assistance.

Paul Cookson
PLANNING AHEAD

John Dees
Bob Cole
ELECTRICITY

Roger Bisby
PLUMBING
HEATING

The CIP catalogue record for this
book is available from the British
Library

Text set in Univers Condensed and
Bodoni
by Inklink, London

Imagesetting by
TD Studio, London

Colour origination by
Colourscan, Singapore

Printed and bound by
Rotolito Lombarda, Italy

Picture sources

Key to photographic credits
L = Left, R = Right, T = Top,
TL = Top left, TR = Top right,
C = Centre, UC = Upper centre,
LC = Lower centre, CL = Centre Left,
CR = Centre right, B = Bottom,
BL = Bottom left, BC = Bottom centre,
BR = Bottom right

Acquisitions Fireplaces Ltd page 400B
allmilmö Ltd page 34TL
Aristocast Originals Ltd page 159C.
Tim Beddow/EWA page 74T.
Behr Furniture page 36C.
Blue Circle Industries Ltd pages 47B;
48T, B; 49; 75.
Pat Brindley pages 421CL; 465T.
John Carr (Joinery Sales) Ltd
page 198C.
Cement & Concrete Association
pages 175C, B; 459.
Paul Chave pages 26; 28T; 29T; 30; 82;
102; 298; 299; 300; 301; 303L; 305; 306;
309; 313L,R; 314; 315; 320; 321; 322; 323;
325; 326; 332; 335; 340; 407; 409; 435;
436L; 438B; 442; 460; 463.
Creda Ltd page 418.
Michael Crockett/EWA pages 27BL;
71BL.
Crown Berger Ltd pages 32BL; 33TR;
38BL; 67.
David Day pages 144; 198R; 214L,R.
Karl Dietrich-Buhler/EWA page 36B;
421B.
Michael Dunne/EWA pages 25BL; 27T;
31CL, CR; 37T; 38R; 70T; 72BL; 73BL.
Faber Blinds (GB) Ltd pages 25CR;
34BL; 36T.
Gaskell Carpets Ltd page 102T.
Jerry Harpur/EWA page 421T.
Robin Harris pages 303R; 308CL; 313C.
Brian Harrison/EWA page 73BR.
Clive Helm/EWA pages 32TL; 34BR.
Peter Higgins pages 71T, C; 72T,UC,
LC; 73T,C; 229.
Hörmann (UK) Ltd page 199.
Howard Ceilings page 150.
Hunter Douglas Ltd pages 216; 217.
Rodney Hyett/EWA pages 25TR; 32TR;
35BR.
Ed Ironside/EWA page 74BR.
Albert Jackson pages 25BR; 420TL,
TR, BR; 434T; 438TR, CL, CR; 464UC, B;
467.
Simon Jennings pages 44; 46; 47T, C;
48C; 52; 53; 54R; 56; 58; 60; 65; 255; 260;
269; 424; 425; 432; 433; 434UC, LC, B;
436R; 438TL; 499; 452; 462;464T, LC.
Ken Kirkwood pages 25TL; 72BR;
74BL.
Tom Leighton/EWA page 70B; 71BR.
Neil Lorimer/EWA page 28BR; 38TL.
Magnet Trade page 198L.
Alan Marshall page 423.
Minsterstone (Wharf Lane) Ltd
page 400T.
**The Original Box Sash Window
Company Ltd** page 475.
Patrick Fireplaces page 400C.
Pella Doors page 196.
Spike Powell/EWA pages 35TL; 37B.
Rentokil Ltd pages 252; 254; 255.
Arthur Sanderson and Sons Ltd. pages
29BL; 32BR; 33BL, BR.
Smallbone page 29BR; 33TL.
Harry Smith Collection pages 420BL;
421CR; 465B; 469; 472.
Tim Street-Porter page 27BR.
Jerry Tubby pages 31T; 34TR.
The Velux Company Ltd page 215.

Waterways Ltd/Dr D.W.Davison
page 474.
Neil Waving pages 54L; 63; 76; 77; 84;
92; 93; 101; 102C,B; 103; 114; 116; 117;
119; 163; 180; 185; 193R; 203; 224; 246;
256; 295; 304; 308R; 324; 327; 329; 330.
Peter Wolosynski/EWA pages 31B;
35BL.
Elizabeth Whiting & Associates
pages 35TR; 74BC.
Winther Browne & Co. Ltd page 226.
Shona Wood pages 62; 146; 159T;
175T; 193L; 224T.
Wrighton International Ltd.
page 28BL.

HOW TO USE THIS BOOK

Today's home improver enjoys the benefits of a highly sophisticated market that recognizes the way 'do it yourself' has developed over the years. He or she has become used to a ready supply of well-designed products and materials that are easy to use and produce first-class results which many a professional would be proud of. Any work of reference for this generation of home improvers must reflect the same high standards in its presentation,

depth of information and simplicity of use. No-one reads a book of this kind from start to finish like a novel in the hope of absorbing all the information in one go. Instead, every reader wants to refer to his or her particular interest or problem without having to extract it from page after page of continuous text. This book has been written and designed to make the location of specific information as easy as possible by dividing the subject matter into

clearly defined, colour-coded chapters for easy reference. Every chapter has its own contents list so that you can find the pages you are looking for, and every page is divided by specially designed features into digestible sections. The book has a detailed index, but to guide you quickly from chapter to chapter or from one section to another, each page contains a list of cross-references that refer you to other information related to the task in hand.

Colour-coding
Colour-coded tabs designate the extent of each chapter for easy identification.

Running heads
As a guide to the number of pages devoted to a particular subject, a running head identifies the broad outline of subject matter to be found on each page.

Numbers in text
A bold number in the text draws your attention to a particular illustration which will help to clarify the instructions at that point.

Tinted boxes
Tinted boxes are used to separate certain information from the main text. Your attention is drawn to special safety precautions by red-tinted boxes.

Banded headings
The main text is divided into sections by easily identifiable headings so that you can locate specific information or a single stage in the work. It is a useful feature when you want to refresh your memory without having to reread the whole page.

Main headings
Clearly defined headings introduce the main topic dealt with on a particular page.

Cross-references
There are few DIY projects that do not require a combination of skills. Decorating a single room, for example, might also involve modifying the plumbing or electrical wiring, installing ventilation or insulation, repairing the structure of the building and so on. As a result, you might have to refer to more than one section of this book. The list of cross-references in the margin will help you locate relevant sections or specific information related to the job in hand.

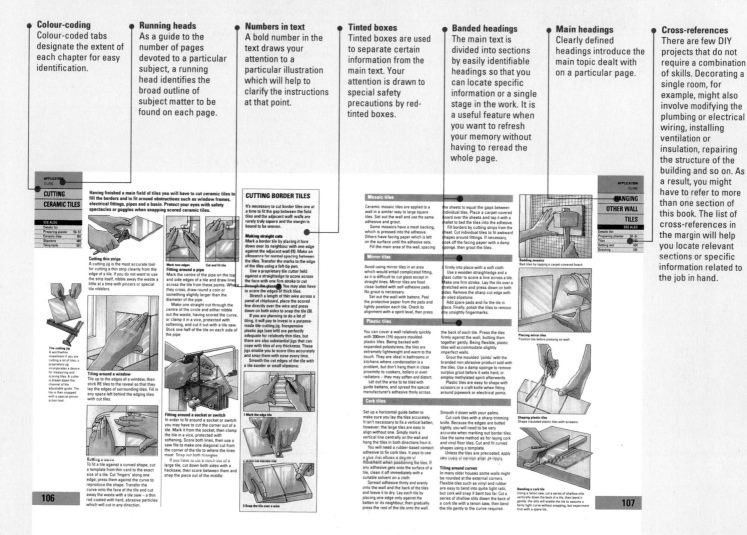

Dimensions
Although many trade suppliers use the metric system, some people are more familiar with imperial measurements. In this book, exact dimensions are given in metric followed by an approximate conversion to imperial for comparison. Do not mix imperial and metric dimensions when you are making a calculation.

CONTENTS

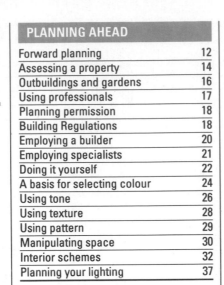

CONTENTS

CONTENTS

The authors and publishers wish to thank the following individuals and organizations for their help in the preparation of this book.

3M United Kingdom Plc, Bracknell, Berkshire
Addis Safety Ltd, Hertford, Herfordshire
Advanced Design & Manufacture Ltd, Bradford, Yorkshire
Airflow Developments Ltd, High Wycombe, Buckinghamshire
Akzo Coatings Ltd, Abingdon, Oxfordshire
Alumasc Ltd, Kettering, Northamptonshire
The Amtico Company Ltd, Coventry, Warwickshire
Aqualisa Products Ltd, Westerham, Kent
Aristocast Originals Ltd, Sheffield, Yorkshire
Armstrong World Industries Ltd, Uxbridge, Middlesex
Artex Ltd, Newhaven, Sussex
Asbestos Information Centre, Widnes, Cheshire
Axminster Carpets Ltd, Axminster, Devon
B & R Electrical Products Ltd, Harlow, Essex
B.E.L. Products Ltd, Birmingham, B24
Bamber Carpets Ltd, Preston, Lancashire
Banbury Homes and Gardens Ltd, Banbury, Oxfordshire
Barbee Ceramics Ltd, Erith, Kent
Belco Manufacturing Co Ltd, Basildon, Essex
A. Bell & Co Ltd, Northampton, NN2
Berger Paints Ltd, Darwen, Lancashire
Beta Naco Ltd, Bridgnorth, Shropshire
Blue Circle Cement, Aldermaston, Berkshire
Bonar & Flotex Ltd, Ripley, Derbyshire
Bondaglass-Voss Ltd, Beckenham, Kent
Bostik Ltd, Leicester, Leicestershire
Bowman Webber, Harlow, Essex
Bradstone Garden Products, Swindon, Wiltshire
C. Brewer & Sons Ltd, Surbiton, Surrey
Brian Hyde Ltd, Solihull, West Midlands
Bridisco Group, London, N17
Neil Briggs, British Gas, London, WC1
Brintons Ltd, Kidderminster, Worcestershire
British Board of Agrément, Watford, Hertfordshire
British Coal, Ashtead, Surrey
British Flat Roofing Council, Nottingham, NG1
British Flue and Chimney Manufacturers' Association, Bourne End, Buckinghamshire
British Gypsum Ltd, Loughborough, Leicestershire
British Red Cross, London, SW19
British Telecommunications Plc, London, EC1A
Campbell Marson & Co Ltd, London, SW17
Caradon Everest Ltd, Potters Bar, Hertfordshire
Caradon Mira Ltd, Cheltenham, Gloucestershire
The Carpet Bureau, London, SW1
Carvall Group Ltd, London, N15
Castle Nails, Cardiff, South Glamorgan
Catnic Ltd, Caerphilly, Mid Glamorgan
Cavity trays Ltd, Yeovil, Somerset
Celcon Blocks Ltd, London, WC1V
Ciba Geigy Plastics, Cambridge, CB2
Clam-Brummer Ltd, Boreham Wood, Hertfordshire
Clos-o-Mat (GB) Ltd, Sale, Cheshire
Colas Building Products Ltd, Basildon, Essex
Commtel Consumer Electronics Plc, Manchester, M30
The Computer Shower Company Ltd, Sidcup, Kent
Comyn Ching Ltd, London, EC1Y
Cranleigh Clark Ltd, Abingdon, Oxfordshire
Creda Ltd, Stoke-on-Trent, Staffordshire
Crown Berger Ltd, Darwen, Lancashire
Cuprinol Ltd, Frome, Somerset
Dixon Wallcoverings Ltd, London, SE1
DIY Plastics Plc, Faringdon, Oxfordshire
Douglas Kane Ltd, Atherstone, Warwickshire
Draught Proofing Advisory Association Ltd, Haslemere, Surrey
Dunlop Adhesives, Birmingham, B35
Earlex Ltd, Godalming, Surrey
ECC Building Products Ltd, Swindon, Wiltshire
Electropatent Ltd, Hansworth, Middlesex
Energy Efficiency Office, London, SW1E
Energy Ways, Standon, Hertfordshire
English Abrasives & Chemicals Ltd, Stafford, ST16
Eswa Ltd, London, SE11
Eternit UK Ltd, Meldreth, Hertfordshire
Evode Ltd, Stafford, ST16
Excel Industries Ltd, Ebbw Vale, Gwent
External Wall Insulation Association, Haslemere, Surrey
Feb Ltd, Swinton, Manchester
Ferham Products, Sheffield, Yorkshire
Fernox Manufacturing Co Ltd, Clavering, Essex
Frazer Pipestock, Peckleton, Leicestershire
Freudenberg LP, Lutterworth, Leicestershire
G&B Electrical Co, London, SW20
Gaskell Carpets Ltd, Blackburn, Lancashire

GE Lighting Ltd, Mitcham, Surrey
Georgian Carpets Ltd, Kidderminster, Worcestershire
Glass and Glazing Federation, London, SE1
Glen Co. Enterprises, Georgia, U.S.A
Greenwood Airvac, Rustington, Sussex
Gyproc Insulation Ltd, Runcorn, Cheshire
Halls Homes & Gardens (Trading) Ltd, Tonbridge, Kent
Harlequin Wallcoverings Ltd, Loughborough, Leicestershire
Haslimann Taylor Buckingham Ltd, Birmingham, B74
P.C. Henderson Ltd, Romford, Essex
Henkel Ltd, Winsford, Cheshire
Hepworth Building Products, Sheffield, Yorkshire
Hepworth Heating Ltd, Belper, Derbyshire
Heuga UK Ltd, Aylesbury, Buckinghamshire
Martyn Hocking, Practical Householder Magazine, London, NW1
Homeguard UK Ltd, Daventry, Northamptonshire
Hörmann (UK) Ltd, Whetstone, Leicestershire
Humbrol Ltd, Kingston upon Hull, Humberside
Hunter Building Products Ltd, London, SE28
Hunter Douglas Ltd, Larkhall, Lanarkshire
Hunting Specialised Products Ltd, Prudhoe, Northumberland
Mike Hurley
ICI Paints, Slough, Berkshire
Ideal-Standard Ltd, Kingston upon Hull, Humberside
IMI Range Ltd, Staybridge, Cheshire
Insulgard Ltd, Horsham, Sussex
Internal Climate Control, Cobham, Surrey
International Paint Ltd, Southampton, Hampshire
International Seamless Gutters Ltd, London, W3
IPPEC Heating Systems, Birmingham, B5
JB Weld Company, Slough, Berkshire
John Carr Joinery Sales Ltd, Sheffield, Yorkshire
John Guest Ltd, West Drayton, Middlesex
John Myland Ltd, London, SE27
H & R Johnson Tiles Ltd, Stoke-on-Trent, Staffordshire
E. Jones & Son, Erith, Kent
Joseph Tipper Ltd, Darlaston, West Midlands
Kopex International Ltd, Slough, Berkshire
Langlow Products Ltd, Chesham, Buckinghamshire
Laura Ashley Contract Services, Maidenhead, Berkshire
Lectros International Ltd, Kettering, Northamptonshire
Loctite UK, Welwyn Garden City, Hertfordshire
London & Lancashire Rubber Co Ltd, London, N18
London Brick Company Ltd, Stewartby, Bedfordshire
Luxcrete Ltd, London, NW10
M C D London, Rochester, Kent
M C Flooring, London, SE9
Macpherson Paints, Haverhill, Suffolk
J. Manger & Son Ltd, Irchester, Northamptonshire
Marflex International Ltd, Cowbridge, South Glamorgan
Marley Extrusions Ltd, Maidstone, Kent
Marley Floors Ltd, Maidstone, Kent
Marshalls Plc, Halifax, Yorkshire
Maxview Ltd, King's Lynn, Norfolk
McAlpine & Co Ltd, Glasgow, G52
Metex Ceilings Ltd, Hayes, Middlesex
MK Electric Ltd, London, N9
Motivation Security Systems, Great Bookham, Surrey
National Approval Council for Security Systems, Maidenhead, Berkshire
National Association of Loft Insulation Contractors, Haslemere, Surrey
National Cavity Insulation Association, Haslemere, Surrey
Nettlefolds Ltd, Wednesbury, West Midlands
New Cosmos Electric UK Ltd, Peterborough, Cambridgeshire
NewTeam Ltd, Corby, Northamptonshire
Oracstar Ltd, Brackmills, Northamptonshire
Pegler Ltd, Doncaster, Yorkshire
Pella Doors, London, SW1
Permoglaze Paints Ltd, Kingston upon Hull, Humberside
Pilkington Glass Ltd, St Helens, Lancashire
Pilkington Insulation Ltd, St Helens, Lancashire
Plasplugs Ltd, Burton-on-Trent, Staffordshire
Plasti-Kote Ltd, Stortford, Hertfordshire
Plastic Padding Ltd, High Wycombe, Buckinghamshire
Plastica Ltd, Hastings, Sussex
Polycell Products Ltd, Welwyn Garden City, Hertfordshire
Polypipe Plc, Doncaster, Yorkshire
Producta Ltd, Stillingfleet, Yorkshire

Racal-Chubb Products Ltd, Wolverhampton, West Midlands
Rapitest Ltd, Corwen, Clwyd
Redland Plasterboard Ltd, Reigate, Surrey
Redland Roof Tiles Ltd, Reigate, Surrey
Redring Electric Ltd, Peterborough, Cambridgeshire
REGA Metal Products, Sandy, Bedfordshire
Rentokil Ltd, East Grinstead, Sussex
Renubath Services, Cirencester, Gloucestershire
Richard Burbidge Ltd, Oswestry, Shropshire
Ruberoid Building Products Ltd, Welwyn Garden City, Hertfordshire
Rustins Ltd, London, NW2
Arthur Sanderson and Sons Ltd, London, W1
SEAC Ltd, Leicester, Leicestershire
SF Detection Ltd, Poole, Dorset
Sikkens UK Ltd, Didcot, Oxfordshire
Siroflex Group Ltd, Leeds, Yorkshire
Slottseal Plc, Corby, Northamptonshire
Smiths Industries Environmental Controls Co Ltd, London, NW2
Snowcem PMC Ltd, Croydon, CR9
Solaglas, Coventry, Warwickshire
Sommer Allibert (UK) Ltd, Droitwich, Worcestershire
Stapeley Water Gardens, Nantwich, Cheshire
Sterling Roncraft, Barnsley, Yorkshire
Stovax Ltd, Exeter, Devon
Swish Products Ltd, Tamworth, Staffordshire
Taymar Ltd, Stockport, Cheshire
Tetrosyl (Building Products) Ltd, Bury, Lancashire
Thermoflue Systems Ltd, Cowbridge, South Glamorgan
Thomas Dudley Ltd, Dudley, West Midlands
Thoro System Products Ltd, Redditch, Worcestershire
Tintawn Carpets Ltd, Leatherhead, Surrey
Tor Coatings Ltd, Chester le Street, Durham
Treetex Ceilings Ltd, West Bromwich, West Midlands
Triton Plc, Nuneaton, Warwickshire
Truline Building Products Ltd, Chelmsford, Essex
Turner Wallcoverings Ltd, London, N7
Vaillant Ltd, Rochester, Kent
Vallance & Co Ltd, Leeds, Yorkshire
Vencel Resil Ltd, Dartford, Kent
Ventlane Ltd, Bolton, Lancashire
Watermill Products Ltd, Oxted, Surrey
Wavecare Ltd, Oakham, Leicestershire
Western Cork Ltd, Cardiff, South Glamorgan
Western Hyde Products Ltd, Hyde, Cheshire
WhiteSeal Stairways Ltd, Chatham, Kent
Wicanders (Great Britain) Ltd, Crawley, Sussex
Willan Building Services Ltd, Sale, Cheshire
Winn & Coals (Denso) Ltd, London, SE27
Winther Browne, London, N1
Xpelair Ltd, Birmingham, B6
Yale Security Products Ltd, Willenhall, West Midlands

The authors are indebted to the companies listed below who generously supplied samples of their materials and products for artist's reference and photography.

Carpets
Axminster Carpets Ltd, Axminster, Devon
Bamber Carpets Ltd, Preston, Lancashire
Brintons Ltd, Kidderminster, Worcestershire
The Carpet Bureau, London, SW1
Gaskell Carpets Ltd, Blackburn, Lancashire
Georgian Carpets Ltd, Kidderminster, Worcestershire
M C D London, Rochester, Kent
M C Flooring, London, SE9
Tintawn Carpets Ltd, Leatherhead, Surrey
Carpet tiles
Bonar & Flotex Ltd, Ripley, Derbyshire
Heuga UK Ltd, Aylesbury, Buckinghamshire
Ceiling tiles
Vencel Resil Ltd, Dartford, Kent
Ceramic tiles
Barbee Ceramics Ltd, Erith, Kent
Carvall Group Ltd, London, N15
H & R Johnson Tiles Ltd, Stoke-on-Trent, Staffordshire
Cork tiles/wood flooring
Western Cork Ltd, Cardiff, South Glamorgan
Wicanders (Great Britain) Ltd, Crawley, Sussex
Door furniture
Comyn Ching Ltd, London, EC1Y
Door locks
Yale Security Products Ltd, Willenhall, West Midlands
Electrician's skate
Brian Hyde Ltd, Solihull, West Midlands
Floor and ceiling tiles
Armstrong World Industries Ltd, Uxbridge, Middlesex
Glass blocks
Luxcrete Ltd, London, NW10
Immersion heaters
Redring Electric Ltd, Peterborough, Cambridgeshire
Light fittings
GE Lighting Ltd, Mitcham, Surrey
Racal-Chubb Products Ltd, Wolverhampton, West Midlands
Linebox
British Telecommunications Plc, London, EC1A
Mirror tiles
Bowman Webber, Harlow, Essex
Pipe-freezing equipment
Wavecare Ltd, Oakham, Leicestershire
Plumbing fittings
Frazer Pipestock, Peckleton, Leicestershire
McAlpine & Co Ltd, Glasgow, G52
Pegler Ltd, Doncaster, Yorkshire
Watermill Products Ltd, Oxted, Surrey
Rubber floor tiles
Freudenberg LP, Lutterworth, Leicestershire
Telephone fittings
Bridisco Group, London, N17
Testers
Rapitest Ltd, Corwen, Clwyd
Textured paint
Plasti-Kote Ltd, Stortford, Hertfordshire
Tiling tools
Plasplugs Ltd, Burton-on-Trent, Staffordshire
Vinyl flooring
Marley Floors Ltd, Maidstone, Kent
Wallcoverings
C. Brewer & Sons Ltd, Surbiton, Surrey
Crown Berger Ltd, Darwen, Lancashire
Dixon Wallcoverings Ltd, London, SE1
Harlequin Wallcoverings Ltd, Loughborough, Leicestershire
Arthur Sanderson and Sons Ltd, London, W1
Turner Wallcoverings Ltd, London, N7
Western Hyde Products Ltd, Hyde, Cheshire
Waterproof connectors
Stapeley Water Gardens, Nantwich, Cheshire
Wood finishes
Rustins Ltd, London, NW2
Wood flooring
Campbell Marson & Co Ltd, London, SW17 E. Jones & Sons, Erith, Kent
Wood mouldings
Winther Browne, London, N1

CHAPTER 1

PLANNING AHEAD

FORWARD PLANNING

SEE ALSO
Details for:
What is involved?   13

Carrying out a substantial scheme of home improvement can be either an enjoyable and stimulating experience or a nightmare. If you plan each step carefully before you begin work you are more likely to make real improvements that will benefit your family while adding to the value of your property. On the other hand, if you buy a property that is unsuitable for your needs, or launch into an ambitious project without thinking through the consequences, you could waste time and money.

Check lists

Buying a house or flat is an exciting event – and when you find one that seems to be just what you have been searching for it can be such a heady moment that it is all too easy to get carried away and forget to check the essentials. Your first impressions can be so misleading that the shortcomings of what seemed to be your dream home may begin to emerge only after you have moved in. Consequently, it is a good idea to arm yourself with a checklist of salient points when you visit a prospective house so that you are less likely to discover later that it is going to cost a great deal to bring the building up to the required standard.

In some ways, assessing the potential of your present home can be even more difficult. Everything fits like an old glove and it is hard to be objective about possible improvements. Try to step back and take a fresh look at it by using the same sort of checklist as you would if you were considering the purchase of a new house.

No single property is ever absolutely ideal, but forward planning will provide you with the means to make the best of what any house has to offer.

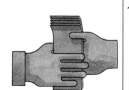

Before you buy
Buying a home will probably be your largest-ever single investment, so don't be misled by first impressions. Check your list of essential points carefully so that you can consider the property fully before investing in professional surveys.

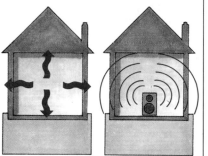

Structural condition

Before you make up your mind to buy a house or flat the building should be inspected by a professional surveyor to make sure it is structurally sound, but make some spot checks yourself before spending money on a survey. A pair of binoculars will help you inspect the building from ground level.

Look out for cracks in the walls, both inside and out. Cracked plaster may simply be the result of shrinkage, but if the fault is visible on the outside it may indicate deformation of the foundations.

Inspect chimney stacks for faults. A loose stack could cause considerable damage if it were to collapse.

Check the condition of the roof. A few loose slates can be repaired easily, but if a whole section appears to be misplaced it could mean a new roof.

Ask if the house has been inspected or treated for rot or insect infestation. If so, is there a guarantee? Don't rely upon your own inspection, but if the skirting boards look distorted or a floor feels unduly springy expect trouble.

Look for signs of damp. In hot weather the worst effects may have disappeared, but stained wallpapers or even poor pointing of the brickwork should make you suspicious.

Insulation

Ask what form of insulation, if any, has been installed. Extensive cavity-wall or external-wall insulation should carry a guarantee. You may not want to inspect loft insulation yourself, but study any surveyor's report to be certain that it is adequate by current standards.

HOME SECURITY

Check whether all doors and windows are secured with good-quality locks and catches. You will probably want to change the front-door lock anyway. A burglar alarm is an advantage only if it is reliable and intelligently installed. Make sure that there is adequate provision for escape in the event of fire, especially in a block of flats where access routes are shared.

Services

An estate agent's written details of the property will describe recent rewiring, but in the absence of such assurance try to determine the likely condition of the installation. The presence of old-fashioned switches and sockets may indicate out-of-date wiring, but new equipment is no guarantee at all that the cables themselves have been replaced. The age of the wiring around the consumer unit will be your best indication. Check that there are enough sockets in every room for your needs. Is the lighting well planned? Pay particular attention to safe lighting over stairs.

Is the plumbing of an age and type that can be extended easily to take new fittings? Extensive lead pipework will need to be replaced. Take note of the size of the hot-water cylinder to make sure it can supply enough hot water, and check that it is insulated.

If the house is only partially centrally heated, check that the boiler is large enough to cope with additional radiators or you may later find yourself faced with the unexpected expense of buying a new one. Is the heating system fitted with proper thermostatic controls to keep costs down? Ask whether flues and fireplaces are in working order.

● Flats

When buying a flat make additional checks on the condition of the access, whether it is by stairs or lift. Ask about shared facilities like laundry and waste disposal, and joint responsibilities such as maintenance of public areas and drains. In buildings that have been converted to flats check adequacy of fire-escape routes and confirm with the local authority that all necessary permissions have been granted for the conversion. Also check whether sound insulation has been installed.

Decoration/improvements

Decorative condition

Is the house decorated to a high standard inside and out, both to protect the structure and enhance the appearance of the building? The decorative condition of the house is reflected in the price and the chances are that you will be expected to pay the same whether the work is up to a good professional standard or shoddily applied. It is up to you to point out the difference to the vendor.

Improvements

Make up your own mind whether 'improvements' have been carried out tastefully. Ask yourself if you can live in a house where the original doors and windows have been replaced with alternatives that are at odds with the style of the architecture. The advantages claimed for certain types of stone cladding are very dubious, and stripping painted brickwork can be both time-consuming and costly. The neighbouring houses will probably give you an idea of the original appearance of the one you are considering.

What is involved?

Having checked the condition of the building, refer to other sections of this book to ascertain how much work is involved to correct any faults you have noticed. This will help you to decide whether to do the work yourself, hire a professional or look elsewhere.

PLANNING FOR PEOPLE

Function, comfort and appearance should take equal priority when you are planning your home. The best designers build their concepts around the human frame, using statistics from research into the way people use their home and working environments.

Anthropometrics

Although human stature varies a great deal, the study of anthropometrics, as it is called, has determined the optimum dimensions of furniture and the spaces that surround it to accommodate people of average build. These conclusions have been adopted by both designers and manufacturers so that most shop-bought fittings for kitchens, bathrooms and living and dining areas are now built to standardized dimensions.

This is especially true of kitchen units, which are designed for compatibility with appliances such as cookers and fridges to make a scheme which fits together as an integrated, functional whole. The standard worktop height allows fridges, dishwashers and washing machines to fit beneath it, while cookers are designed to fit flush with counter tops and base units. Designers adopt the same criteria for other items of furniture; standard-size chairs, tables and desks allow most people to work and eat comfortably.

An appreciation of anthropometrics cuts down on accidents; correctly positioned shelves and worktops in the kitchen preclude climbing on to a chair to reach the top shelf, for instance. It also helps you to choose appropriate furniture around the home, avoiding low-level easy chairs and soft beds that offer no support to the back.

Using available space

As well as the size and function of the furniture itself, its positioning within the room falls within the province of anthropometrics. An efficient use of floor area is an essential ingredient of good planning, providing people with freedom of action and sufficient room to make use of furniture and appliances with ease.

Whether you are buying furniture or just planning the furnishings and fittings for your home, you should familiarize yourself with the dimensions shown on the following pages. They will help you buy wisely and make the best use of available space.

13

ASSESSING POTENTIAL

Assuming the structural condition of the house is such that you are willing to take on the work involved, check out those points that a structural surveyor won't be looking for. Is it the right home for you and your family? It takes a bit of imagination to see how a room might look when it has been divided in two or when a wall has been removed, but it is even more difficult to predict what your lifestyle might be in five or ten years' time. Unless you intend to live in the house for only a couple of years before moving on, you must try to assess whether it will be able to evolve with you.

You will need to take measurements before you can make some decisions, so carry a tape measure with you.

MEASURING A ROOM

If you think that you might want to change the shape of a room, or you suspect there may be a problem with fitting certain items of furniture into it, measure the floor area and the ceiling height so that you can make a scale drawing later to clarify your thoughts. Take the main dimensions, including alcoves, the chimney breast and so on. Make a note of which way the doors swing and the positions of windows, radiators and fixed furniture. Transfer the measurements later to squared paper with each square representing a set dimension.

When you have drawn your plan of the room cut out pieces of paper to represent your furniture, using the same scale measurements. Rearrange them until you find a satisfactory solution.

Draw a measured plan on squared paper

The hallway

When you are invited into the house, you will be able to gauge whether the entrance hall is large enough to receive visitors comfortably. Will there be room to store coats, hats, boots, umbrellas and so on? Is the staircase wide enough to allow you to carry large pieces of furniture to the bedrooms?

If all the family tend to be out in the daytime, it is an advantage if there is some facility for deliveries to be stored outside but safely under cover when the house is unoccupied. Check also whether you will be able to identify visitors before you open the door to them, especially after dark.

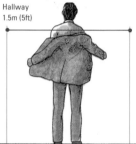

Hallway
1.5m (5ft)

Removing a coat
When planning a hallway, allow 1.5m (5ft) to remove a coat or jacket.

Headroom
2m (6ft 6in)

▲
Staircase headroom
A headroom of 2m (6ft 6in) above a staircase will allow you to carry a wardrobe up to the next floor.

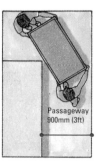

Passageway
900mm (3ft)

Negotiating a bend
You can turn a large piece of furniture around a bend in a 900mm (3ft) wide passageway.

Living rooms

How many reception rooms are there in the house? More than one living room will make it possible for members of the family to engage in different pursuits without inconveniencing each other. If there is one living room only, make sure there are facilities elsewhere for private study, music practice or hobbies that take up a lot of space or make intrusive noise.

Is the living room large enough to accommodate the seating arrangement you have in mind, or will you have to remove a wall to incorporate extra space? If you do, it is worth considering folding doors so that you can divide the area again when it suits you.

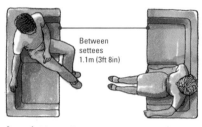

Between settees
1.1m (3ft 8in)

Arranging two settees
Allow a minimum of 1.1m (3ft 8in) between two settees facing each other.

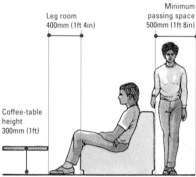

Minimum passing space
500mm (1ft 8in)

Leg room
400mm (1ft 4in)

Coffee-table height
300mm (1ft)

Low seating
The density of upholstery and the dimensions of the seat and back vary so much that it is impossible to suggest a standard, but make certain your back is supported properly and you can get out of a chair without help. If you place a coffee table in front of a settee, try to position the latter so that people can reach it from each end in order to avoid treading on the toes of someone seated.

ASSESSING POTENTIAL

Dining room

Is there a separate dining room for dinner parties? Estimate whether there will be sufficient space for guests to circulate freely once your table and chairs are in the room.

A dining room should be positioned close to the kitchen so that meals arc still warm when they get to the table. You may have to consider installing a serving hatch.

If the dining area is part of the kitchen, efficient ventilation will be necessary to extract cooking odours. Some cooks prefer a kitchen that is screened from visitors. Are the present arrangements suitable for your needs?

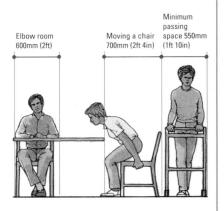

Elbow room 600mm (2ft)
Moving a chair 700mm (2ft 4in)
Minimum passing space 550mm (1ft 10in)

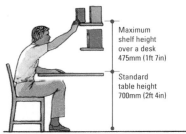

Maximum shelf height over a desk 475mm (1ft 7in)

Standard table height 700mm (2ft 4in)

Sitting at a table
Sitting at a dining table, desk or dressing table requires the same area. Arrange dining-room furniture so that people are able to get in and out of a chair while leaving enough room behind it for a trolley to be pushed past.

Breakfast bar
A 900mm (3ft) high breakfast bar aligns with a worktop.

Minimum knee room 250mm (10in)

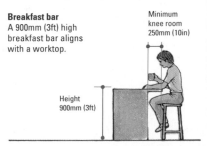

Height 900mm (3ft)

Bedrooms

The number of rooms may be adequate for your present needs, but what about the future? There may be additions to the family, and although young children can share a room for a while individual accommodation will be required eventually. You may want to put up a guest from time to time or have elderly relatives to stay for extended periods – in which case, will they be able to cope with stairs? It might be possible to divide a large room with a simple partition, or perhaps a room on the ground floor can double as a bedroom. As a long-term solution, you could plan for an extension or loft conversion.

Are all the bedrooms of an adequate size? As well as a bed or bunks, a bedroom must accommodate clothes storage and, in some cases, books, toys and facilities for homework or pastimes. A guest room may have to function as a private sitting room, possibly with provision for preparing snacks and hot drinks. You could dismantle or move a dividing wall, or possibly incorporate part of a large landing provided it does not interfere with access to other rooms or obstruct an escape route in case of fire. Try not to rely on using a bedroom which only has access via another room. This arrangement is fine when you want to be close to a young child, but a connected room might otherwise be suitable only as a dressing room or *en-suite* bathroom.

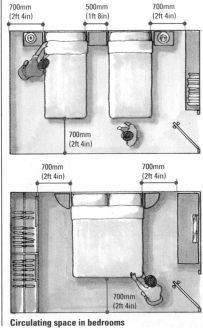

700mm (2ft 4in)
500mm (1ft 8in)
700mm (2ft 4in)

700mm (2ft 4in)

700mm (2ft 4in)
700mm (2ft 4in)

700mm (2ft 4in)

Circulating space in bedrooms

The bathroom

If the bathroom does not provide the amenities you require, estimate whether there is space for extra appliances, even if this means rearranging the existing layout or perhaps incorporating an adjacent toilet. Is there a separate toilet for use when the bathroom is occupied? Can a ground-floor toilet be installed for the disabled or elderly?

You should investigate the possibility of installing a second bathroom or shower cubicle elsewhere if the present bathroom is not accessible to all the bedrooms. Alternatively, consider plumbing a basin in some bedrooms.

Make a note of electrical installations in the bathroom. If they do not comply with accepted recommendations they must be replaced with new units.

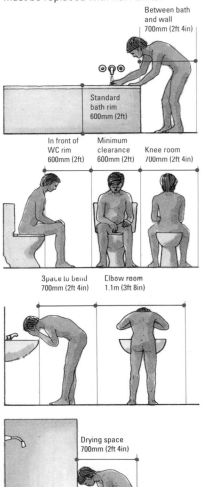

Between bath and wall 700mm (2ft 4in)

Standard bath rim 600mm (2ft)

In front of WC rim 600mm (2ft)
Minimum clearance 600mm (2ft)
Knee room 700mm (2ft 4in)

Space to bend 700mm (2ft 4in)
Elbow room 1.1m (3ft 8in)

Drying space 700mm (2ft 4in)

SEE ALSO

Details for:	
Official permission	19
Moving a door	128–129
Removing walls	130–136
Dividing a room	137–143
Fire precautions	250
Extractor fans	287–288, 290
Cooker hoods	289
Plumbing a WC	371–372
Plumbing a basin	373–376
Plumbing a bath	377–378
Plumbing a shower	379–384
Plumbing a bidet	385

Between bath and wall
Allow sufficient room between bath and wall to dry yourself with a towel. You can bend in the same amount of space in order to clean the bath.

WC and bidet
Allow for the same space in front of a WC or bidet, but provide extra leg room on each side of a bidet. The same spaces provide room to maintain and clean an appliance.

Using a basin
Allow generous space so you can bend over the basin and have plenty of elbow room when washing hair. The same space will also give you room to wash a child.

Drying after a shower
This is the minimum space required to dry yourself in front of an open cubicle. If the cubicle is screened, allow an extra 300mm (1ft) of clearance.

ASSESSING
POTENTIAL

The kitchen

The quality of kitchen furniture and fittings varies enormously, but every well-designed kitchen should incorporate the following features.

A labour-saving layout

Preparing meals is a chore unless the facilities for the preparation of food, cooking and washing up are grouped in a layout which avoids unnecessary movement. To use designer's parlance, the kitchen must form an efficient work triangle. In ideal conditions, the sides of the triangle combined should not exceed 6 to 7m (20 to 22ft) in length.

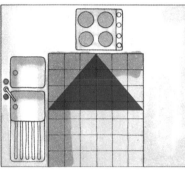

Work triangle
A typical work triangle links washing, cooking and preparation areas.

Storage

Whether you are building storage into a kitchen, workshop, bedroom or lounge, make sure every item is within easy reach and ensure there is room to open drawers and doors without backing into a wall or injuring others.

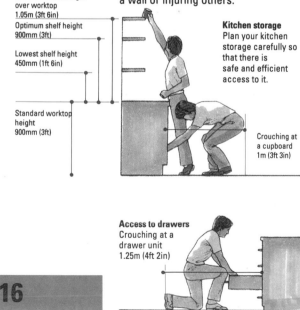

Maximum shelf height over worktop
1.05m (3ft 6in)

Optimum shelf height
900mm (3ft)

Lowest shelf height
450mm (1ft 6in)

Standard worktop height
900mm (3ft)

Kitchen storage
Plan your kitchen storage carefully so that there is safe and efficient access to it.

Crouching at a cupboard
1m (3ft 3in)

Access to drawers
Crouching at a drawer unit
1.25m (4ft 2in)

Storage and appliances

If the work triangle is to be effective, a kitchen must incorporate enough storage space in each area. The fridge and foodstuffs should be close to where the meals are prepared, and adequate work surfaces must be provided. A freezer could be housed elsewhere, but should be somewhere conveniently close to the kitchen.

The hob and oven should be grouped together, with heat-proof surfaces nearby to receive hot dishes. Cooking equipment should be within easy reach.

Appliances that require plumbing are best grouped together with the sink on an outside wall. In a small house the kitchen area may contain a dishwasher, washing machine and tumble dryer, although a separate laundry room is really the ideal solution.

KITCHEN SAFETY

Check the layout of the kitchen with a view to safety. A cramped kitchen can lead to accidents, so make sure that more than one person at a time can circulate in safety.

- If possible, avoid an arrangement that encourages people to use the working part of the kitchen as a through passage to other parts of the house or the garden.
- Make sure children cannot reach the hob and construct a barrier that will keep small children right outside the work triangle.
- Placing the hob or cooker in a corner or at the end of a run of cupboards is not advisable. Try to plan for a clear worktop on each side. Don't place it under a window, either; a draught could extinguish a gas pilot light and someone will eventually get burned trying to open the window.

A dangerously placed cooker
Do not position cookers under windows

OUTBUILDINGS AND GARDENS

Garage and workshop

Is the garage large enough for your car or cars? Is there also enough space to use it as a workshop?

If the garage is too small for the latter purpose, you could possibly fit out a cellar provided there is storage space for materials and you can deliver them without disruption or damaging the decorations and furniture.

A new shed or outbuilding is another solution, provided there is room in the garden or beside the house and a utilitarian building will not spoil the outlook of the property.

Long-term storage is always a problem. Every household accumulates bulky items like camping or sports equipment which have to be stored for much of the year. Once again a garage or outbuilding is ideal, but if necessary can you use the loft for storage? Check the size of the hatchway, and decide whether you might need to board over the joists or reposition insulation.

The garden

If you are not a keen gardener you will not want a large garden requiring a lot of attention. If you are, does the garden receive enough sunlight for the type of plants you want to grow ?

Check the outlook. When climbers, trees and shrubs are bare of foliage will you be confronted with an eyesore that is screened during the summer months?

Make sure the fences or walls are high enough to provide privacy. If you view a house at the weekend, ask whether there are any factories, workshops or playgrounds nearby that may disturb your peace and quiet during the week.

It is an advantage if the garden has access for building materials and equipment as otherwise they will need to be carried through the house.

Can children play safely in the garden without supervision? Make sure that gates are secure and high enough to prevent them wandering out of the garden and out of sight.

USING PROFESSIONALS

Why pay someone to do a job when you can do it perfectly well yourself? There are plenty of skilled amateurs who can tackle just about any job to a high standard. However, it usually takes them longer than it would a professional specialist, and for most of us time is at a premium.

There are certain jobs it is worth paying to have done quickly and efficiently – ones that are holding up a series of other projects, for example, or that call for techniques with which you do not feel sufficiently confident. You may prefer to ask an electrician to do major wiring or a plumber to install a new bathroom, although you plan to carry out all the peripheral labouring and finishing yourself. Then there are certain skills that will require time and practice before you become really proficient at them. In a house of average size you might develop the knack of plastering as the work is coming to an end, but you probably will not need to plaster another wall until you buy your next house.

Essential professional advice

You must seek professional advice to obtain planning permission and Building Regulation approval, and if you need a mortgage the bank or building society will insist on the building being professionally surveyed. If the surveyor's report highlights a serious defect the mortgage company will want the fault rectified by a specialist firm who will guarantee the work.

The surveyor

When you apply for a mortgage the bank or building society will appoint a surveyor who is trained to evaluate a property in order to protect the mortgage company's investment. His or her job is to check that the building is structurally sound and to pinpoint anything that needs attention. You will have to pay for the service, but the surveyor will report directly to the mortgage company. There was a time when the bank or building society was not obliged to show you the report but simply told you what work had to be carried out in order to secure your mortgage. Mortgage companies are now more lenient, however, and will give you a copy of the surveyor's report.

A survey may consist of a basic evaluation, a home-buyer's report or a full structural survey. For complete peace of mind it is best to obtain the latter. Unless you are buying a fairly new property this type of report makes depressing reading; if the surveyor has done a thorough job it will list everything that needs attention, from peeling paintwork to dry rot. No surveyor will take responsibility for guaranteeing the condition of areas of the house that were inaccessible at the time of inspection. For example, if the house is occupied, fitted carpets make it difficult to examine thoroughly the condition of the floors. The report will point out that these areas cannot be guaranteed as sound, but that does not necessarily imply that there is likely to be a problem.

Study the report for specific references to serious faults that may be expensive to put right, such as damage to the foundations, dry or wet rot, woodworm, severe damp or a badly deteriorating roof. Also take note of points which could lead to trouble in the future. If the survey refers to leaking guttering which is soaking a wall, for example, urgent repair will be required to avoid penetrating damp.

If you are not satisfied with the mortgage company's report, commission your own survey before you finally commit yourself. Contact the Royal Institution of Chartered Surveyors or the Incorporated Association of Architects and Surveyors.

Royal Institution of Chartered Surveyors,
12 Great George Street,
London, SW1P 3AD
Telephone 071-222 7000

Incorporated Association of Architects and Surveyors,
Jubilee House,
Billing Brook Road,
Weston Favell,
Northampton,
NN3 4NW
Telephone 0604-404121

The architect

If you are planning ambitious home improvements, especially ones that will involve major structural alterations or extensions, you should consult a qualified architect. He or she is trained to design buildings and interiors which are not only structurally sound but aesthetically pleasing. An architect will prepare scale drawings of the development for submission to the authorities for planning permission and Building Regulation approval. You can even employ the same architect to supervise the construction of the building to ensure that it meets the required specifications. You and your architect must work as a partnership. Brief him or her by discussing the type of development you have in mind, how you plan to use it, how much you want to spend and so on.

You can contact the Royal Institute of British Architects for a list of professionals working in your area, but a personal recommendation from a friend or colleague is far more valuable. Arrange to meet the architect and to see some recent work before you commit yourself to engaging him or her.

Royal Institute of British Architects,
66 Portland Place, London, W1N 4AD
Telephone 071-580 5533

OFFICIAL PERMISSION

Before you undertake certain developments you are obliged to obtain the approval of local-government authorities. Many people are reluctant to cooperate, fearing that the authorities are likely to be obstructive, but in fact their purpose is to protect all of us from irresponsible builders and developers and they are most sympathetic and helpful to any householder who seeks their advice and sets out to comply with the statutory requirements. People confuse the two main controls that exist – planning permission and Building Regulation approval. Receiving planning permission does not automatically confer Building Regulation approval and vice versa; you may require both before you can proceed. There may be variation in the planning requirements, and to some extent the Building Regulations, from one area of the country to another. Consequently, the information given on the following pages should be considered as a guide only and not as an authoritative statement of the law. If you live in a listed building of historical or architectural interest, or your house is in a conservation area, seek advice before considering any alterations.

SEEKING
APPROVAL

Planning permission

Planning controls exist primarily to regulate the use and siting of buildings and other constructions as well as their appearance. What might seem to be a minor development in itself could have far-reaching implications you had not considered: a structure which obscured drivers' vision at a junction, for instance, might constitute a danger to traffic. Equally, the local authority might refuse permission on the grounds that the planned scheme does not blend sympathetically with its surroundings.

The actual details of planning requirements are complex but, in broad terms, with regard to domestic developments the planning authority is concerned with construction work such as an extension to the house or the provision of new outbuildings such as a garage. Structures like walls and fences fall into the same category because their height or siting might infringe the rights of other members of the community. The authority will also want to approve any change of use such as converting a house into flats or running a business from premises previously occupied as a dwelling only.

Your property may be affected by legal restrictions such as a right of way which might prejudice planning permission. Examine the deeds of your house or consult a solicitor.

Applying for planning permission

You can obtain the necessary application form from the planning department of your local council; it is laid out simply, with guidance notes to help you fill it in. Alternatively, ask a builder or architect to apply on your behalf. This is sensible if the development you are planning is in any way complicated, because you will have to include measured drawings with the application form. In all probability, you will have to prepare a plan showing the position of the site in question (site plan) so that the authority can determine exactly where the building is located. You must submit another, larger-scale, plan to show the relationship of the building to other premises and highways (block plan). In addition, you should supply drawings which give a clear idea of what the new proposal will look like, together with details of both the colour and the kind of materials you intend to use. You may prepare the drawings yourself, provided you are able to make them accurate.

Under normal circumstances you will have to pay a fee in order to seek planning permission, but there are exceptions. The planning department will advise you.

Before preparing detailed plans, you can make an outline application furnishing information on the size and form of the development. Assuming permission is granted under these circumstances, you will then have to submit a further application in greater detail. In the main, this applies to large-scale developments only and you will be better off making a full application in the first place.

Do not be afraid to discuss the proposal with a representative of the planning department before you submit your application. He or she will do his or her best to help you comply with the requirements and will always grant planning permission unless there are very sound reasons for refusal, in which case the department must explain the decision to you so that you can amend your plans accordingly and resubmit them for further consideration. A second application is normally exempt from a fee. As a last resort, however, you can appeal against a decision to the Secretary of State for the Environment. The planning authority will supply you with the necessary appeal forms. If you were to proceed without approval, you might find yourself obliged to restore the property to its original condition.

You can expect to receive a decision from the planning department within eight weeks and, once granted, planning permission is valid for five years. If the work is not begun within that time, you will have to apply for planning permission again.

Building Regulations

Even when planning permission is not required, most building works, including alterations to existing structures, are subject to minimum standards of construction to safeguard public health and safety. The Building Regulations are designed to ensure structural stability and to promote the use of suitable materials to provide adequate durability, fire and weather resistance, and the prevention of damp. The Regulations also stipulate the minimum amount of ventilation and natural light to be provided for habitable rooms.

Building standards are enforced by your local Building Control Officer, but for matters concerning drainage or sanitary installations, consult the Technical Services Department.

Obtaining approval

You, as the builder, are required to fill in an application form and return it, along with basic drawings and relevant information, to the Building Control Office at least two days before work commences. Alternatively, you may submit fully detailed plans for approval. Whatever method you adopt, it may save time and trouble if you make an appointment to discuss your scheme with the Building Control Officer well before you intend to carry out the work. He or she will be happy to discuss your intentions, including proposed structural details and dimensions, together with a list of the materials you intend to use so that he or she can point out any obvious contravention of the Regulations before you make an official application for approval. At the same time he or she can suggest whether it is necessary to approach other authorities to discuss planning, sanitation, fire escapes and so on. The Building Control Officer will ask you to inform the office when crucial stages of the work are ready for inspection by a surveyor in order to make sure the work is carried out according to your original specification. Should the surveyor be dissatisfied with any aspect of the work, he or she may suggest ways to remedy the situation.

If you wish, you can appoint a builder, or preferably an architect, to handle everything for you, but do not be bullied into ignoring the surveyor's request to inspect the site or you could incur the cost and inconvenience of exposing covered work at a later stage. Failure to submit an application form or detailed plans could result in a substantial fine as well as wasted time. You will be expected to pay certain fees to the local council for the services you have received from the surveyor. These fees are not extortionate and you can obtain an estimate of the amount before building begins.

When the building is finished you must notify the council, and it would be to your advantage to ask for written confirmation that the work was satisfactory as this will help to reassure a prospective buyer when you come to sell the property.

WILL YOU NEED APPROVAL?

If you live in a single-family house you may undertake certain developments without planning permission. This chart is intended to help you decide whether you need to seek planning permission or Building Regulation approval before starting work. However, always check with the relevant authority for confirmation. If your dwelling has been converted to flats, all external alterations will require planning permission.

	TYPE OF WORK	●	PLANNING PERMISSION		BUILDING REGULATION APPROVAL	
	Decorations or repairs inside and outside	39 121	NO	Unless it is a listed building.	NO	
	Replacing windows and doors	188 200	NO	Unless they project beyond the foremost wall of the house facing a highway. Or: The building is listed or is in a conservation area.	Possibly	Consult your Building Control Officer
	Electrical work	292	NO		NO	But it must comply with IEE Regulations.
	Plumbing	347	NO		NO YES	No for replacements, but consult the Technical Services Department for any installation which alters present internal or external drainage. Yes for an unvented hot-water system.
	Central heating	404	NO		NO	
	Oil-storage tank		NO	Provided it is in the garden and has a capacity of not more than 3,500 litres (778 gallons). And: No point is more than 3m (9ft 9in) high. And: No part projects beyond the foremost wall of the house facing a highway.	NO	
	Structural alterations inside	121	NO	As long as the use of the house is unchanged.	YES	
	Loft conversion	157 273	NO YES	No provided the volume of the house is unchanged, and the highest part of the roof is not raised. Yes for front-elevation dormer windows or rear ones over a certain size.	YES	
	Building a garden wall or fence	424 434	YES	If it is more than 1m (3ft 3in) high and is a boundary enclosure adjoining a highway. Or: If it is more than 2m (6ft 6in) high elsewhere.	NO	
	Planting a hedge		NO	Unless it obscures view of traffic at a junction or access to main road.	NO	
	Laying a path or driveway	458	NO	Unless it provides access to main road.	NO	
	Felling or lopping trees	423	NO	Unless the trees are protected or you live in a conservation area.	NO	
	Installing a swimming pool	474	Possibly	Consult your planning department.	YES	For an indoor pool.
	Constructing a small outbuilding	121 434	Possibly	SEE MARGIN NOTE (RIGHT)	YES	If area exceeds 30sq m (35.9sq yd). If it is within 1m (3ft 3in) of a boundary, it must be built from incombustible materials.
	Building a porch	121 434	NO	Unless: The floor area exceeds 3sq m (3.6sq yd). Or: Any part is more than 3m (9ft 9in) high. Or: Any part is less than 2m (6ft 6in) from a boundary adjoining a highway or public footpath.	NO	If under 30sq m (35.9sq yd) in area.
	Building a conservatory	475	Possibly	Treat as an extension	NO	If under 30sq m (35.9sq yd) in area.
	Building a garage	121 434	YES	If within 5m (16ft 6in) of house, treat like an extension, otherwise treat as an outbuilding.	Possibly	Consult your Building Control Officer.
	Hardstanding for a car	454	NO	Provided it is within your boundary and is not used for a commercial vehicle.	NO	
	Building an extension	121 434	Possibly	You can extend your house up to certain permitted limits without planning permission (see margin note). However, the total of both previous and new extensions cannot exceed the permitted volume, or permission is required.	YES	
	Demolition		YES	Particularly if it is listed or in a conservation area. And: If the whole house is to be demolished. Seek advice for partial demolition.	NO YES	No for a complete, detached house. Yes for a partial demolition to ensure that the remaining part or adjoining buildings are structurally sound.
	Converting a house to flats		YES	Including bedsitters	YES	
	Converting a house to business premises		YES		YES	

● Refer to these pages for further information

● OUTBUILDINGS
You can build an outbuilding up to 10cu m (13.08cu yd) in volume without planning permission if it is within 5m (16ft 3in) of the house or an extension. Further away than this, it can be up to half the area of the garden, but the height must not exceed 4m (13ft).

● EXTENSIONS
Planning permission is required if:
Volume
The extension results in an increase in volume of the original house by whichever is the greater of the following amounts. For terraced houses 50cu m (65.5cu yd) or 10 per cent up to a maximum of 115cu m (150.4cu yd). Other houses 70cu m (91.5cu yd) or 15 per cent up to a maximum of 115cu m (150.4cu yd). In Scotland General category 24sq m (28.7sq yd) or 20 per cent.
Height
Any part is higher than the highest part of the house roof.
Projections
Any part projects beyond the foremost wall of the house facing a highway.
Boundary
Any part within 2m (6ft 6in) of a boundary is more than 4m (13ft) high.
Area
It will cover more than half the original area of the garden.
Dwelling
It is to be an independent dwelling.

19

EMPLOYING A BUILDER

● **Estimates and quotations**
A builder's estimate is an approximate price only. Before you engage him or her, ask for a written quotation which is a firm statement of the current market price.

Federation of Master Builders
14 Great James Street, London, WC1N 3DP
071 242 7583

The search for a builder who is reliable and proficient can be frustrating. You will hear many stories of clients being overcharged for shoddy work or being left with a half-completed job for months on end. It is not that good builders do not exist, but that there are unscrupulous individuals who masquerade as professional tradesmen and give the whole industry a bad name.

Choosing a builder

Recommendation is the only safe way to find a builder. If someone whose opinion you respect has found a professional who is skilful, reliable and easy to communicate with, then the chances are you will enjoy the same experience. Even so, you should inspect the builder's work yourself before you make up your mind. If a recommendation is hard to come by, choose a builder who is a member of a reputable association such as the Federation of Master Builders. To be represented by the Federation, a builder must have a good reputation and supply bank and insurance references.

A good builder will be booked up for months ahead, so allow plenty of time to find someone who will be free when you need him or her to start work. If a builder is very highly recommended you might feel you do not want to look elsewhere, but unless you get two or three firms to estimate for the same job you will not know whether the price is fair; a builder who is in demand might suggest a high price because he really does not need the work. On the other hand, an inexperienced builder might submit a price that seems tempting but then cut corners or ask for more money later because he or she had not anticipated all the problems that might arise before the job is completed.

SUB-CONTRACTORS

Unless a builder is a 'jack of all trades' he will have to employ electricians, plumbers, plasterers or whatever. The builder is responsible for the quality of the sub-contracted work unless you agree beforehand that you will appoint the specialists yourself. Agree to discuss anything concerning sub-contracted work with the builder himself. A sub-contractor must receive clear instructions from one person only or there is bound to be confusion.

Writing a specification

Many of the disagreements that arise between builder and client are as a result of insufficient briefing before the work was started. Do not give a builder vague instructions; he may do his best to provide the kind of work he thinks you want, but this might be wide of the mark. Also, he cannot possibly quote an accurate price unless he knows exactly what you require. You do not have to write a legal document, nor do you have to tell the builder how to do his job; just write a detailed list of the work you want him to carry out and, as far as possible, the materials you want him to use. If you have not yet made up your mind about the wallcovering you want or the exact make of bathroom fitting, then at least say so in the specification. You can always discuss it with the builder before he submits a quotation. Read the relevant sections in this book to find out what a particular job involves, or, if the work is complicated, employ an architect to write a specification for you.

The specification should include a date for starting the work and an estimate of how long it will take to complete. You will have to obtain that information from the builder when he submits his estimate, but make sure it is added to the specification before you both agree to the terms and price. There may be legitimate reasons why a job does not start and finish on time, but at least the builder will be left in no doubt that you expect him to behave in a professional manner.

Getting an estimate

When you ask several builders to tender for the work you will receive their estimates of costs. These will be based on current prices and the amount of information you have supplied at the time. If you take a long time to make up your mind, or alter the specification in the meantime, prices may change. Before you officially engage a builder, ask him for a firm quotation with a detailed breakdown of his costs. Part of that quotation may still be estimated. If you still have not decided on certain items you can both agree on a provisional sum to cover them, but make it clear that you are to be consulted before that money is spent. Also, a builder might have to employ a specialist for some of the work, and that

---

fee might be estimated. Try to get the builder to firm up on the price before you employ him and certainly before the work begins.

Agree on a method of payment. Many builders will complete the work before any money changes hands; others will ask for stage payments to cover the cost of materials. If you agree to stage payments it must be on the understanding that you will pay for work completed or that at least the materials will have been delivered to the site. Never agree to an advance payment. Provided you make it clear to the builder before he accepts the contract, you can retain a figure for an agreed period after the work is completed to cover the cost of faulty workmanship. Between five and ten per cent of the overall cost is a reasonable sum to retain.

Neither you nor the builder can anticipate all the problems that might arise. If something unexpected occurs which affects the price for the job, ask the builder for an estimate of costs before you decide what course of action to take. Similarly, if you change your mind or ask for work that is extra to the specification, you must expect to pay for any resulting increase in costs – but make sure you agree the amount at the time rather than trying to negotiate it at the end of the job.

Working with your builder

Most people find they get a better job from a builder if they create a friendly working atmosphere. You must provide access to electricity and water if they are required for the job, and somewhere to store materials and tools. A certain amount of mess is inevitable, but a builder should leave the site fairly tidy at the end of a working day, and you should not have to put up with mud in areas of the house that are not part of the building site.

Unless you have an architect to supervise the job, keep your eye on the progress of the work. Disagreements will occur if you constantly interrupt the builder, but inspect the job when the workers have left the site at the end of the day to satisfy yourself on the standard of the workmanship and that the builder is keeping to schedule.

EMPLOYING SPECIALISTS YOURSELF

SEE ALSO
Details for:
Crime Prevention
Officer   244
Fire Prevention Officer   244

Hiring a specialist tradesperson is no different from contracting a general builder. Provide a detailed specification, then obtain several estimates and a firm quotation. Personal recommendation is the best guarantee of finding a reliable professional, but there are certain organizations you can approach.

Decorators

British Decorators Association,
32 Coton Road, Nuneaton,
Warwickshire, CV11 5TW
0203 353776

Scottish Decorators Federation,
41A York Place, Edinburgh, EH1 3HT
031-557 9345

Plasterers

Federation of Master Builders,
14 Great James Street,
London, WC1N 3DP
071-242 7583

Roofers

Builders' Merchants Federation
15 Soho Square, London W1V 5FB
071-439 1753

National Federation of Roofing Contractors,
24 Weymouth Street, London W1N 3FA
071-436 0387

Asbestos specialists

Asbestos Information Centre Ltd,
PO Box 69, Widnes, Cheshire,
WA8 9GW
051-420 5866

Concrete specialists

British Ready Mixed Concrete Association,
The Bury, Church Street, Chesham,
Buckinghamshire, HP5 1JE
0494 791050

Home security

Local Crime Prevention Officer
Refer to your local directory

Local Fire Prevention Officer
Refer to your local directory.

National Approval Council for Security Systems,
Queensgate House, 14 Cookham Road,
Maidenhead SL6 8AJ
0628 37512

Master Locksmiths Association,
Units 4–5, Woodford Halse Business Park, Great Central Way, Woodford Halse, Daventry, NN11 6PZ
0327 62255

British Security Industry Association,
Security House, Barbourne Road,
Worcester WR1 1RS
0905 21464

Damp, rot, infestation

British Wood Preserving & Damp Proofing Association,
Building No. 6, The Office Village, 4 Romford Road, Stratford,
London, E15 4EA
081-519 2588

English Nature,
Northminster House, Northminster Road, Peterborough PE1 1VA
0733 340345

Countryside Council for Wales,
Plaspenrhos, Penrhos Road, Bangor,
Gwynedd, LL57 2LQ
0248 370444

Scottish Natural Heritage,
12 Hope Terrace, Edinburgh, EH9 2AS
031-447 4784

Local Department of Environmental Health
Refer to your local directory

Glazing specialists

Glass and Glazing Federation,
44–48 Borough High Street,
London SE1 1XB
071-403 7177

Insulation installers

Draught Proofing Advisory Association Ltd,
External Wall Insulation Association,
National Cavity Insulation Association,
National Association of Loft Insulation Contractors,
PO Box 12, Haslemere,
Surrey GU27 3AH
0428 654011

Ventilation

Heating and Ventilating Contractors Association,
Esca House, 34 Palace Court,
London W2 4JG
071-229 2488

Electricians

National Inspection Council for Electrical Installation Contracting,
37 Albert Embankment,
London SE1 7UJ
071-582 7746

Plumbers

Institute of Plumbing,
64 Station Lane, Hornchurch,
Essex RM12 6NB
0708 472791

National Association of Plumbing, Heating and Mechanical Services Contractors,
Ensign House, Ensign Business Centre,
Westwood Way, Coventry, CV4 8JA
0203 470626

Heating installers

British Gas Regional Office
Refer to your local directory.

Electricity Supply Company
Refer to your local directory.

British Coal Corporation,
Hobart House, Grosvenor Place,
London, SW1X 7AE
071-235 2020

Heating and Ventilating Contractors Association,
Esca House, 34 Palace Court,
London W2 4JG
071-229 2488

National Association of Plumbing, Heating and Mechanical Services Contractors,
Ensign House, Ensign Business Centre,
Westwood Way, Coventry, CV4 8JA
0203 470626

Fencing erectors

Fencing Contractors Association,
St John's House, 304–310 St Albans Road, Watford, WD2 5PE
0923 248895

DOING IT YOURSELF

SEE ALSO
Details for:
Sealing to contain dust 132

In the majority of cases you will save money by doing most of the work yourself. You will probably have to pay more for materials than a tradesperson who benefits from discounts, but you will save the labour costs that account for a large part of the professional's bill. You will also gain personal satisfaction from producing good-quality work, whereas a tradesperson must equate the time he or she spends with the price for the job and may not be able to devote as much time attending to details.

Planning work priorities

Although forward planning might not be so important when you are doing all the work yourself, careful forethought will reduce disruption to the household to a minimum and will avoid spoiling finished decor and carpets with dust generated in other parts of the building. Work out a schedule, listing the jobs in order of priority. Some may need to be carried out urgently to safeguard the structure of the house or because the prospect of bad weather dictates the order of work, but your schedule should mostly follow a sequence that will avoid your having to backtrack because you forgot to complete an earlier stage.

Planning your time

An important aspect to consider is the amount of time you can devote to the work, because that can determine how you tackle a long-term project. Unless you can work full-time for periods of weeks or even months on end, it will take several years to completely renovate even a small house. Therefore, you have to decide whether you and your family are prepared to put up with the inconvenience caused by tackling the entire house in one go or whether it would be better to divide up the work so that part of the house is still relatively comfortable. Just how you plan the work will depend on the layout of the building. If you have more than one entrance it may be possible to seal off one section completely while you work on it. If the house is built on several floors, work out a sequence whereby you are not treading dust and dirt from a work site on an upper level through finished and carpeted areas below. Leave linking areas such as stairs, landings and hallways undecorated until the last moment.

WORKING TO A SEQUENCE

No two homes or family circumstances are identical, but the chart will help you plan your own sequence of events. You should always tackle first those measures which will arrest deterioration, and it is usually best to repair and decorate the exterior before the interior to make sure the house is weatherproof. In practice, you will find that it is very difficult to stick rigidly to your schedule. Unexpected problems will dictate a change of plan, and family pressures or financial restraints often demand that a task be given priority or left to a later stage even though logic would suggest another solution.

PRIORITY WORK

URGENT REPAIRS

Attend to faults mentioned in a professional survey (these repairs are often insisted upon by a mortgage company). Repair anything in a dangerous condition or which is damaging to the structure of the building and getting rapidly worse. This may include:
● Dry rot, rising damp, penetrating damp.
See pages 255, 256–264.
● Seriously cracked or loose masonry.
See pages 46–47, 49, 423.
● Woodworm infestation.
See pages 252–253.
● Faulty plumbing, downpipes and drains.
See pages 348–394, 240–242.
● Faulty electrical wiring.
See pages 292–346.
● Unstable garden walls.
See pages 434–451.
● Roof repairs.
See next column and pages 227–239.

SECURITY

● Fit locks to all vulnerable doors and windows.
See pages 246–249.
● Change front-door lock if you have just moved in to a new house – you cannot know who has a key.
See pages 246–247.
● Install smoke detector, fire extinguisher and fire blanket.
See page 250.

APPROVAL

● Seek planning permission and Building Regulation approval from your local authority for any work likely to require official permission.
See pages 17–19.

ROOF WORK

ROOF COVERING

● Repair or replace damaged or missing slates or tiles.
See pages 229–233.
● Repair faulty flashings.
See pages 238–239.

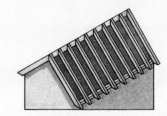

ROOF TIMBERS

● Treat or replace rotten or damaged roof timbers. You may have to hire a professional.
See pages 20–21, 228, 252, 255.

ROOF INSULATION

● Insulate and ventilate the roof space.
See pages 271–273, 285–286.

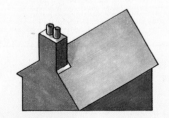

CHIMNEY STACK

● Repoint chimney stack.
See pages 45, 238.
● Repair cracked flaunching.
See page 402.
● Secure loose chimney pots.
See pages 399, 402.

SEE ALSO

Details for:

Assessing a property 12-16

Using professionals 17-21

INDOOR WORK

ALTERATIONS

Undertake major interior structural changes such as:
- Building or removing dividing walls.
See pages 125, 130–136, 137–143, 448.
- Lowering ceilings.
See pages 146–150.
- Opening up or closing off doors and hatches.
See pages 126–129.
- Replacing or removing fire surrounds.
See pages 398–399.

SERVICES

PLUMBING
- Undertake new plumbing and heating work.
See pages 348–394, 396–418.

ELECTRICS
- Wire new electrical sockets and appliances.
See pages 292–346.

INSULATION

FLOOR INSULATION
- Insulate below groundfloor level.
See page 276.

DOUBLE GLAZING
- Install double glazing.
See pages 277–280.

VENTILATION

- Provide adequate ventilation.
See pages 283–290.

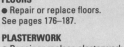

REPAIRS AND RENOVATIONS

FLOORS
- Repair or replace floors.
See pages 176–187.

PLASTERWORK
- Repair or replace plasterwork.
See pages 50–51, 152–171.

WOODWORK
- Fit new skirtings.
See page 185.
- Fit new door architraves.
See page 189.

FURNITURE
- Build in cupboards and fitted storage.
See page 16.

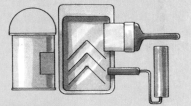

DECORATION

CEILINGS
- Paint or paper ceilings.
See pages 67–69,100.

WALLS
- Paint walls at this stage.
See pages 67–74.

FINISH WOODWORK
- Paint or varnish woodwork.
See pages 76–86.

WALLCOVERINGS
- Hang wallpapers and wallcoverings.
See pages 92–99.

FLOORCOVERINGS
- Lay carpets and floorcoverings.
See pages 57, 62, 109–120.

CURTAINS AND BLINDS
- Make and fit new drapes.
See pages 216-217

OUTDOOR WORK

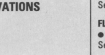

OUTSIDE WALLS

REPAIRING WALLS
- Repoint brickwork.
See pages 45.
- Patch damaged rendering.
See pages 47, 172–175.
- Repair damaged masonry.
See page 46.

INSULATING WALLS
- Consider installing external or cavity-wall insulation at this stage.
See pages 275–276.

WEATHERPROOF WALLS
- Waterproof or paint masonry walls.
See pages 46, 48, 64–66.

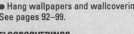

WINDOWS AND DOORS

- Repair or replace doors and windows.
See pages 188–215.
- Refit locks and catches.
See pages 246–249.

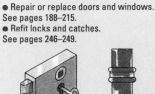

WOOD AND METAL

- Paint or varnish all wood and metalwork.
See pages 53, 76–86, 87–88.

GARDEN WORK

WALLS AND FENCES
- Repair or build garden walls and fences.
See pages 424–433, 434–451.

PAVING AND STEPS
- Lay paving.
See pages 458–466.
- Build steps.
See pages 467–468.

PONDS AND WATERGARDENS
- Construct garden ponds and waterfalls.
See pages 469–473.

ROCKERY
- Build a rockery before planting.
See page 473.

CONSERVATORIES
- Planning and building.
See pages 475–476

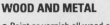

A BASIS FOR SELECTING COLOUR

Developing a sense of the 'right' colour is not the same as learning to paint a door or hang wallpaper. There are no 'rules' as such, but there are guidelines that will help. In magazine articles on interior design and colour selection you will find terms such as 'harmony' and 'contrast'; colours are described as tints or shades, and as cool or warm. These terms form a basis for developing a colour scheme. By considering colours as the spokes of a wheel, you will see how they relate to each other and how such relationships create a particular mood or effect.

Primary colours
All colours are derived from three basic 'pure' colours – red, blue and yellow. They are known as the primary colours.

Secondary colours
When you mix two primary colours in equal proportions, a secondary colour is produced. Red plus blue makes violet, blue with yellow makes green and red plus yellow makes orange. When a secondary colour is placed between its constituents on the wheel, it sits opposite its complementary colour – the one primary not used in its make-up. Complementary colours are the most contrasting colours in the spectrum and are used for dramatic effects.

Tertiary colours
When a primary is mixed equally with one of its neighbouring secondaries, it produces a tertiary colour. The complete wheel illustrates a simplified version of all colour groupings. Colours on opposite sides are used in combination in order to produce vibrant contrasting schemes, while those grouped on one side of the wheel form the basis of a harmonious scheme.

Warm and cool colours
The wheel also groups colours with similar characteristics. On one side are the warm red and yellow combinations, colours we associate with fire and sunlight. A room decorated with warm colours feels cosy or exciting depending on the intensity of the colours used. Cool colours are grouped on the opposite side of the wheel. Blues and greens suggest vegetation, water and sky, and create a relaxed airy feeling when used together.

A basic colour wheel
A colour wheel shows the relationship of basic primary, secondary and tertiary colours. Warm and cool colours are grouped on opposite sides of the wheel.

RED BLUE YELLOW

VIOLET GREEN ORANGE

PRIMARY TERTIARY SECONDARY

COOL WARM

A BASIS FOR SELECTING COLOUR

Bold treatment for a sitting room
(Top left)
A deep-red wall is made all the more striking by the use of a blue-painted ceiling and blue colouring in the curtains and upholstery.

A child's playroom
(Bottom left)
Primary and secondary colours, used in stylized and geometric forms, create a lively interior for a playroom.

Coloured equipment
(Top right)
Basic appliances such as sinks and radiators are now produced in a range of colours and play an important part in a colour scheme.

Adding colour with window blinds
(Centre right)
Coloured or patterned curtains are fairly commonplace, but fewer people choose from the available range of brightly coloured Venetian blinds. Strong sunlight contributes to the colourful effect.

Using colour outside
(Bottom right)
Most buildings do not lend themselves to being painted in bright colours. In areas of the country where colour is traditionally acceptable, a bold treatment can be very exciting.

USING TONE
FOR SUBTLETY

Pure colours can be used to great effect for both exterior and interior colour schemes, but a more subtle combination of colours is called for in most situations. Subtle colours are made by mixing different percentages of pure colour, or simply by changing the tone of a colour by adding a neutral.

Neutrals

The purest forms of neutral are black and white, from which colour is entirely absent. The range of neutrals can be extended by mixing the two together to produce varying tones of grey. Neutrals are used extensively by decorators because they do not clash with any other colour, but in their simplest forms they can be either stark or rather bland. Consequently, a touch of colour is normally added to a grey to give it a warm or cool bias so that it can pick up the character of another colour with which it harmonizes or provide an almost imperceptible contrast with a range of colours.

Tints

Changing the tone of pure colours by adding white creates pastel colours or tints. Used in combination, tints are safe colours; it is difficult to produce anything but a harmonious scheme whatever colours you use together. The effect can be very different, however, if a pale tint is contrasted with dark tones to produce a dramatic result.

Shades

The shades of a colour are produced by adding black to it. Shades are rich, dramatic colours which are used for bold yet sophisticated schemes. It is within this range of colours that browns appear – the interior designer's stock-in-trade. Brown blends so harmoniously into almost any colour scheme that it is tantamount to a neutral.

1 Neutrals

2 Tints

3 Shades

1 Neutrals
A range of neutral tones introduces all manner of subtle colours.

2 Tints
A composition of pale tints is always harmonious and attractive.

3 Shades
Use darker tones, or shades, for rich, dramatic effects.

USING TONE FOR SUBTLETY

White makes a spacious room
(Top)
Gloss white paint on the boarded ceiling and wall provides a light and refreshing dining room that is enhanced by the bright greens of the garden foliage beyond.

Using tints creatively
(Bottom left)
Pale colours are often used when a safe harmonious scheme is required, but you can offset them with the introduction of a strong neutral tone such as provided by the black cabinets on each side of this sofa.

Dark, dramatic tones
(Bottom right)
The very dark tone used for walls, ceiling and floors in this room is relieved by a painted frieze and white accessories. Gloss paint will reflect some light even when such a dark colour is used.

TAKING TEXTURE INTO ACCOUNT

Natural and man-made textures
(Right)
Many people are not conscious of the actual texture of materials. This selection ranges from the warmth of wood and coarsely woven materials to the smooth coolness of marble, ceramics, plastic and metal.

Textural variety
(Below)
It is relatively simple to achieve interesting textural variety with almost any group of objects. Here, a few stylish kitchen artefacts contrast beautifully with a patterned-tile splashback and warm oak cupboards.

Colour is an abstraction, being merely the way we perceive reflected wavelengths of light, yet we are far more aware of the colour of a surface than its more tangible texture, which we almost take for granted. Texture is a vital ingredient of any decorative scheme and merits careful thought.

The visual effect of texture is also created by light. A smooth surface reflects more light than one that is rough. Coarse textures absorb light, even creating shadows if the light falls at a shallow angle. Consequently, a colour will look different according to whether it is applied to a smooth surface or a textured one.

Even without applied colour, texture adds interest to a scheme. You can contrast bare brickwork with smooth paintwork, for instance, or use the reflective qualities of glass, metal or glazed ceramics to produce some stunning decorative effects.

Texture can be employed to make an impression, the source of which we may not even be consciously aware of. Cork, wood, coarsely woven fabrics and rugs add warmth, even a sense of luxury, to an interior, while smooth, hard materials such as polished stone, stainless steel, ceramic tiles, vinyl or even a black-lacquered surface give a clean, almost clinical feeling to a room.

Carefully chosen textures *(Right)*
Soft and hard textures have been selected with care for this cool, sophisticated environment.

USING PATTERN FOR EFFECT

Recent purist approaches to design have made us afraid to use pattern boldly. Our less inhibited forefathers felt free to cover their homes with pattern and applied decoration with spectacular results, creating a sense of gaiety and excitement which is difficult to evoke in any other way.

A well-designed patterned wallpaper, fabric or rug can provide the basis for the entire colour scheme and a professional designer will have chosen the colours to form a pleasing combination. There is no reason why the same colours should not look equally attractive when applied to the other surfaces of a room, but perhaps the safest way to incorporate a pattern is to use it on one surface only to contrast with plain colours elsewhere.

Combining different patterns can be tricky, but a small, regular pattern normally works well with large, bold decoration. Also, different patterns with a similar dominating colour can coordinate well even if you experiment with contrasting tones. Another approach is to use the same pattern in different colourways. You should also select patterns according to the atmosphere you want to create. Simple geometric shapes are likely to be more restful than bold, swirling motifs.

Be bold with pattern
(Left)
There is no reason to be afraid of using pattern when you consider that manufacturers have done most of the thinking for you. Well-designed materials are available to clad just about any surface in your home.

Coordinated pattern
(Bottom left)
The colours used for the striped curtain and furniture fabrics are the basis of this coordinated colour scheme.

A profusion of pattern
(Bottom right)
This bedroom combines a wealth of pattern with the rich colour of natural-mahogany furniture. It shows what can be achieved if one has the courage to opt for the bold approach.

29

MANIPULATING
SPACE

There are nearly always areas of a house that feel uncomfortably small or, conversely, so spacious that one feels isolated, almost vulnerable. Perhaps the first reaction is to consider structural alterations like knocking down a wall or installing a false ceiling. In some cases such measures will prove to be the most effective solution, but there is no doubt that they will be more expensive and disruptive than the alternative ways of manipulating space by using colour, tone and pattern.

Our eyes perceive colours and tones in such a way that it is possible to create optical illusions that apparently change the dimensions of a room. Warm colours appear to advance, so that a room painted brown or red, for example, will give the impression of being smaller than the same room decorated in cool colours such as blue or green which have a tendency to recede.

Tone can be used to modify or reinforce the desired illusion. Dark tones, even when you are using cool colours, will advance, while pale tones will open up a space visually.

The same qualities of colour and tone will change the proportion of a space. Adjusting the height of a ceiling is an obvious example. If you paint a ceiling a darker tone than the walls it will appear lower. If you treat the floor in a similar way, you can almost make the room seem squeezed between the two. A long, narrow passageway will feel less claustrophobic if you push out the walls by decorating them with pale, cool colours which will, incidentally, reflect more light as well.

Using linear pattern is another way to alter our perception of space. Vertically striped wallpaper or woodstrip panelling on the walls will counteract the effect of a low ceiling. Venetian blinds make windows seem wider, and stripped wooden floors are stretched in the direction of the boards. Any large-scale pattern draws attention to itself and will advance like warm, dark colours, while from a distance small patterns appear as an overall texture so have less effect.

Practical experiments *(Right)*
A model will help to determine whether an optical illusion will have the desired effect.

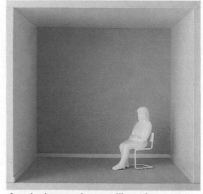
Warm colours appear to advance

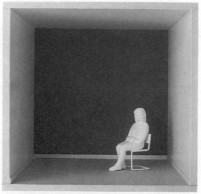
A cool colour or pale tone will recede

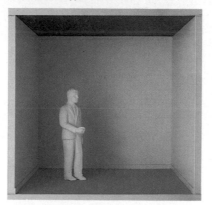
A dark ceiling will appear lower

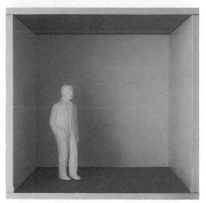
A dark floor and ceiling make a room smaller

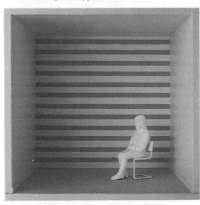
Horizontal stripes make a wall seem wider

Vertical stripes increase the height

Large-scale patterns advance

A small, regular pattern recedes

VERIFYING YOUR SCHEME

Before you spend money on paint, carpet or wallcoverings, collect samples of the materials you propose to use in order to gauge the effect of one colour or texture on another.

Collecting samples

Make your first selection from the more limited choice of furniture fabrics or carpets. Collect offcuts of the other materials you are considering, or borrow sample books or display samples from the suppliers to compare them at home. As paint charts are printed you can never be absolutely confident they will match the actual paint. Consequently, some manufacturers produce small sample pots of paint so you can make test patches on the wall or woodwork.

Making a sample board

Professional designers make sample boards to check the relative proportions of materials as they will appear in the room. Usually a patch of carpet or wallcovering will be the largest dominating area of colour, painted woodwork will be proportionally smaller and accessories might be represented by small spots of colour. Make your own board by gluing your assembly of materials to stiff card, butting one piece against another to avoid leaving a white border around each sample which would change the combined effect.

Incorporating existing features

Most schemes will have to incorporate existing features such as a bathroom suite or kitchen units. Use these items as starting points, building the colour scheme around them. Cut a hole in your sample board to use as a window for viewing existing materials or borrowed examples against those on the card.

Checking your colour selection
View your completed sample board in natural and artificial light to check your colour selection.

Using mirrors
(Top)
Mirrored wardrobe doors fitted from floor to ceiling provide the illusion of a larger space.

Lowering a ceiling
(Centre left)
A dark-tone ceiling reduces the apparent height of the room and also helps disguise supporting beams.

Creating space in a hallway
(Centre right)
A trompe l'oeil glazed door with a garden vista beyond creates an illusion of space in a confined area.

Creating space with pattern
(Bottom)
The linear effects of patterned carpet and pictures ranged across the wall help to make this room seem larger.

31

SCHEMES FOR LIVING ROOMS

In most homes the living room is the largest area in the house. It is where you spend most of your leisure time and entertain your friends, and the room upon which most money is spent in terms of furnishings, curtains and carpets, not to mention expensive hi-fi units, the television set and so on. For all these reasons, you will want to make sure that the living-room decor has lasting appeal. After all, you are unlikely to replace costly furniture and materials frequently.

Unless you are lucky enough to have more than one reception or living room, it is an area that must feel comfortable during the day, relaxing in the evening and lively enough for the occasional party. If the room receives very little sunlight, a warm colour scheme is often the best in order to create a cosy atmosphere. Dark, cool tones will produce a similarly snug result under artificial light, but very deep tones can have the opposite effect by creating dark, shadowy areas. Neutral colour schemes or a range of browns and beiges will be easy to change in the future by simply swapping the accessories without having to spend money on replacing essentials. Natural textures are

equally versatile.

Patterned carpets or rugs are less likely to be ruined by the inevitable spillages than plain colours, but very dark tones are almost as difficult to keep clean as pale colours.

Curtains and blinds provide the perfect solution to a change of mood. During the day they are pulled aside or rolled up and therefore contribute very little to the general appearance of the room, but in the evening they can become a wall of colour or pattern which can transform the scheme.

Sheer curtains or blinds can also be used to screen the view through the window while allowing daylight to fill the room with a soft light that will not damage upholstery fabrics.

Sympathetic style
(Top left)
A surviving period living room deserves appropriate styling.

Simple styling suits a modern house
(Top right)
A modern home can be treated successfully with restrained colours and natural textures.

An adaptable scheme
(Bottom left)
A safe yet comfortable scheme lends itself to change by swapping the accessories.

Typically traditional
(Bottom right)
Pink-washed walls and floral patterns suit a typical country cottage.

SCHEMES FOR BEDROOMS

A bedroom is first and foremost a personal room. Its decor should reflect the character of its occupant and the functions to which the room is put. At night, a bedroom should be relaxing, even romantic. Much depends on the lighting, but pattern and colour can in themselves create a luxurious and seductive mood.

Few people ever use pattern on a ceiling yet a bedroom provides the ideal opportunity, especially as you are unlikely to spend much of your waking life there and can consequently afford to be adventurous with the decor. Bedroom carpet is invariably of inferior quality because it need not be hardwearing, but you could give the colour scheme a real lift by investing in an expensive rug or deep-pile carpet knowing that it will come to no harm. If a bedroom faces south early sunlight will provide the necessary stimulus to wake you up, but a north-facing room will benefit from bright, invigorating colours.

Some bedrooms may have to serve a dual function. A teenager's bedroom, for example, may have to double as a study or a private sitting room so needs to be stimulating rather than restful. A child's bedroom will almost certainly function as a playroom as well. The obvious choice would be for strong, even primary colours, but as most children accumulate large numbers of brightly coloured toys, books and pictures you might select a neutral background to the colourful accessories. The smallest bedrooms are usually reserved for guests, but they can be made to appear larger and more inviting by the judicious manipulation of the proportions with colour or tone.

An elegant master bedroom
(Top left)
This elegant bedroom has a peaceful character, created from a basically neutral scheme warmed very slightly by a hint of cream and pale yellow.

Bright and refreshing
(Top right)
The combination of bright yellow and white makes for a cheerful and lively start to the day.

Dual-purpose room
(Bottom left)
When a bedroom doubles as a sitting room it needs to be stimulating during the day and cosy at night.

A guest room
(Bottom right)
A guest room should make a visitor feel at home immediately. The warmth of stripped pine makes this room very inviting.

DECOR FOR COOKING AND EATING

Kitchens need to be functional areas capable of taking a great deal of wear and tear, so the materials you choose will be dictated largely by practicalities. However, that does not mean you have to restrict your use of colour in any way. Kitchen sinks and appliances are made in bright colours as well as the standard stainless steel and white enamel, while tiled worktops and splashbacks, vinyl floor coverings and melamine surfaces offer further opportunity to introduce a range of colours.

Textures are an important consideration with a range of possibilities. Natural timber remains a popular material for kitchen cupboards and will provide a warm element which you can either echo in your choice of paint, paper or floorcovering or contrast with cool colours and textures. Some people prefer to rely entirely on plastic, ceramic and metallic surfaces which give a clean and purposeful character.

If the kitchen incorporates a dining area you may decide to decorate the latter in a fashion more conducive to relaxation and conversation. Softer textures such as carpet tiles, cork flooring and fabric upholstery absorb some of the clatter that is generated by kitchen utensils. You could also decorate the walls in a different way to change the mood, perhaps using darker tones or a patterned wallcovering to define the dining area.

A functional kitchen
(Top left)
This simple kitchen, laid out to form a perfect work triangle, looks extremely functional without feeling clinical.

A family kitchen
(Top right)
Some people like the kitchen to be part of an informal sitting and dining area where the family can relax.

A breakfast room
(Bottom left)
A sunny alcove linked to the kitchen makes an ideal area for a breakfast room.

A kitchen extension
(Bottom right)
Colourful fabric blinds shade this kitchen extension from direct sunlight.

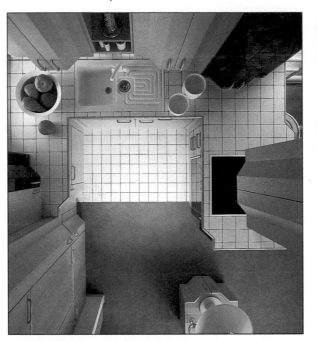

BATHROOMS

Bathrooms, like kitchens, must fulfil quite definite functions, but they should never look clinical. Even when a bathroom is centrally heated a cold, uninviting colour scheme would not be a wise choice as enamelled and tiled surfaces are inevitable. Coloured bathroom appliances are commonplace, but choose carefully as they are likely to remain the dominating influence on any future colour schemes.

Like the bedroom, the bathroom is an area where you can afford to be inventive with your use of colour or pattern. A bold treatment which might become tiresome with overexposure can be highly successful in a room used only for brief periods. Try to introduce some sound-absorbing materials such as ceiling tiles, carpet or cork flooring to avoid the hollow acoustics associated with old-fashioned tiled bathrooms. If you want to use delicate materials that might be affected by steam, make sure that the bathroom is

properly ventilated. Bathrooms are usually small rooms with relatively high ceilings, but painting a ceiling a dark tone that might improve the proportion of a larger room can make a bathroom feel somewhat like a box. A more successful way to counter the effect of a high ceiling is to divide the walls with a dado rail, using a different colour or material above and below the line.

If your home is in a hard-water area, avoid dark-coloured bathroom suites which will inevitably emphasize ugly lime-scale deposits.

Changing the proportion
(Top left)
The use of a wood-panelled dado reduces the apparent height of this bathroom and introduces a warm, attractive texture to the interior.

Pure white
(Top right)
A woven-cane chair and delicate potted plants relieve the stark qualities of this all-white bathroom.

Warm and luxurious
(Bottom left)
There is no reason why your bathroom should not be designed and furnished in the style of an elegant sitting room.

Fashionable styling
(Bottom right)
The blue stained glass of the original window has been used as the basis for the colour scheme of this period-style bathroom.

SINGLE ROOMS AND SMALL FLATS

An open-plan flat
(Top)
Create a sense of
space with a fitted
carpet and white-
painted walls. Vertical
louvred blinds can be
used to screen one
area from another.

One large room
(Centre)
A warm colour
scheme makes a large
room feel cosier. Fold-
away furniture is an
advantage when you
live in one room.

Dividing a single room
(Bottom)
Custom-built storage
divides this floor space
into specific areas,
while the continuous
ceiling retains the
impression of a
spacious interior.

When you live in one room every
activity takes place in the same
area, so its decor must be versatile.
However, much depends on your
lifestyle. If you are out at work
during the day you may decide to
concentrate on creating a mood for
the evening. On the other hand, if
you work at home, your priority
will be to provide a daytime
environment that is stimulating but
not too distracting.

Ideally, you should attempt to design an
interior that can be changed at will to
suit the time of day or your disposition.
While curtains or blinds can be used to
greater effect after dark, more positive
measures are required to make the
room as adaptable as possible.
    Some means of screening off a
sleeping alcove is always an
advantage. Floor-length curtains hung
from a ceiling-mounted track can form
a soft wall of colour or texture, or you
can use vertical louvred blinds so that
with the flick of a pull cord you can let
in the sunlight. A concertina-folding
wall of panels or louvred shutters gives
the impression of a permanent screen
during the day, and provides the
opportunity to introduce natural or
stained timber to a scheme.
Alternatively, construct a portable
screen from flat panels which you can
decorate to suit yourself.
    Dividing the floor area will define
areas of activity: soft rugs for seating,
polished boards or tiling for cooking or
eating. You can even change the floor
level with a simple wooden dais
covered in carpet. Areas of wall can be
sharply defined to pick up the theme,
using different finishes.
    A small open-plan flat suggests other
options. Prevailing natural light might
persuade you to treat areas differently,
either freshening up a dark corner or
cooling down an area that is constantly
sunlit. You can create the impression of
greater space by running the same
flooring throughout the flat, and white or
pastel-painted walls will have a similar
effect. Picking out some walls with
strong colour or pattern will lead the
eye into another area. You could play
with the ceiling level by using colour or
tone, possibly pulling it down over a
cosy sitting area or bedroom while
apparently increasing the volume of
another space by painting the ceiling
with a pale neutral or pastel tint.

PLANNING YOUR LIGHTING

Successful lighting must be functional so you can work, read or study without eyestrain; it must brighten areas of potential danger and provide general background illumination. However, the decorative element of lighting is equally important. It can create an atmosphere of warmth and wellbeing, highlight objects of beauty or interest and transform the character of an interior with areas of light and shadow.

Living areas

For the living areas of the house the accent should be on versatility, creating areas of light where they are needed most, both for function and dramatic effect. Seating areas are best served by lighting placed at a low level so that naked bulbs are not directed straight into the eyes, and in such a position that a book or newspaper is illuminated from beside the reader. Choose lighting which is not so harsh as to cause glare from white paper and supplement it with additional low-powered lighting to reduce the effects of contrast between the page and the darker areas beyond.

Working at a desk demands similar conditions, but the light source must be situated in front of you to avoid throwing your own shadow across the work. Choose a properly shaded desk lamp or conceal lighting under wall storage or bookshelves above the desk.

Similar concealed lighting is ideal for a wall-hung hi-fi system, but you may need extra lighting in the form of ceiling-mounted downlighters to illuminate the shelves themselves. Alternatively, use fittings designed to clip on to the shelves or wall uprights.

Concealed lighting in other areas of the living room can be very attractive. Strip lights placed on top and at the back of high cupboards will bounce light off the ceiling. Hide lighting behind pelmets to accentuate curtains, or put it along a wall to light pictures. Individual artworks can be picked out with specially designed strip lights placed above them, or use a ceiling spot light that is adjustable so you can place the pool of light exactly where it is required. Do not direct lights at pictures protected by glass (unless it is the special non-reflective type) as reflections will destroy the desired effect. Use lighting in an alcove or recess to give maximum impact to an attractive display of items.

Concealed lighting
(Top)
Interesting effects are created by concealing the actual source of artificial lighting, using it to throw dramatic shadows or provide accents of light in specific areas.

Atmospheric lighting
(Bottom)
Mellow illumination from table lamps and picture lighting provides an atmosphere of warmth and wellbeing.

PLANNING YOUR LIGHTING

Sleeping areas

Bedside lamps are essential requirements in any bedroom, or better still, use concealed lighting above the bedhead. Position the fitting low enough to prevent light falling on your face as you lie in bed. Install two lights behind the baffle over a double bed, each controlled individually so that your partner can sleep undisturbed if you want to read into the early hours. A dressing table needs its own light source placed so that it cannot be seen in the mirror but illuminates the person using it. Wall lights or downlighters in the ceiling will provide atmospheric lighting, but install two-way switching so that you can control them from the bed and the door. Make sure bedside light fittings in a child's room are completely tamper-proof and, preferably, double-insulated. A dimmer switch controlling the main room lighting will provide enough light to comfort a child at night but can be turned to full brightness when he or she is playing in the evening.

Dining areas/kitchens

A rise-and-fall unit is the ideal fitting to light a dining table because its height can be adjusted exactly. If you eat in the kitchen, have separate controls for the table lighting and work areas so that you can create a cosy dining area without having to illuminate the rest of the room. In addition to a good background light, illuminate kitchen worktops with strip lights placed under the wall cupboards but hidden from view by baffles along the front edges. Place a track light or downlighters over the sink so that your own shadow is not cast over it as you work.

Bathrooms

Safety must be your first priority when lighting a bathroom. Fittings must be designed to protect electrical connections from moisture and steam, and they must be controlled from outside the room or by a ceiling-mounted switch. It can be difficult to create atmospheric lighting in a bathroom, but concealed light directed on to the ceiling is one solution as long as you provide another source of light over the basin mirror.

Staircases

Light staircases from above so that the treads are illuminated clearly, throwing the risers into shadow. This will define the steps clearly for anyone with poor eyesight. Place a light over each landing or turn of the staircase. Two-way or even three-way switching is essential to be certain that no-one has to negotiate the stairs in darkness.

Workshops

Plan workshop lighting with efficiency and safety in mind. Light a workbench like a desk and provide individual, adjustable fittings for machine tools. Fluorescent lighting can create the optical illusion that moving machinery such as a woodturning lathe is stationary, especially when it is slowing down after being switched off.

Bedside lamps
(Top left)
You can expend a great deal of thought on planning the lighting in your bedroom only to find that two simple bedside lamps are the perfect solution.

An improvised lampshade
(Bottom left)
This Oriental sunshade throws a diffused light on the table while bouncing extra light off the ceiling.

Concentrating areas of illumination
(Right)
Discreet lighting mounted above the worktops makes for an efficient and attractive kitchen.

DECORATING

MEANS OF ACCESS

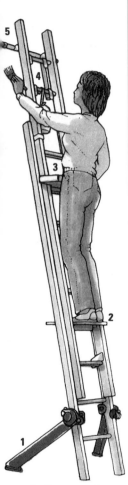

Ladder accessories
Kit out your ladder with a range of helpful devices to make working easier and safer. This ladder features stabilizers (1) for uneven ground, a foot rest for comfort (2), a tool tray (3), a paint-can hook (4) and a stay (5) to hold the top away from eaves or gutters.

BEFORE YOU BEGIN

Timing, weather and the condition of the site are important factors to consider before you decorate outside. Indoors, you have the problem of what to do with a room full of furniture and furnishings while you work.

Outside the house

Plan your work so that you can begin the decoration of the house exterior in late summer and autumn when the previous warm weather will have dried out the fabric of the building sufficiently.

The best weather for decorating is a warm but overcast day. Avoid painting on rainy days or in direct sunlight, as both rain and sun can ruin new paintwork. On a sunny day, follow the sun around the house so that its warmth will have dried out the night's dew on the woodwork before you apply paint.

Do not work on windy days or dust will be blown on to the paint. Sprinkle water or spray it with a houseplant spray around doors and windows before you paint to settle dust which would otherwise be churned up by your feet.

Clear away any rubbish around the house, as it will slow your progress and may even cause accidents. Cut back overhanging foliage from trees and shrubs. Protect plants and paving with dustsheets in the work area.

Inside the house

Before you decorate a room inside, carry out all repairs necessary and have the chimney swept if you use an open fire: a soot fall would ruin your decorations. Clear as much furniture from the room as possible, and group what is left under dustsheets. Lift rugs or carpets, then spray water on the floor and sweep it to collect dust before you begin to paint. Protect finished wood or tiled floors with dustsheets.

Remove all furnishings such as pictures and lampshades, and unscrew fingerplates and door handles. Keep the access door handle in the room with you in case you accidentally get shut in.

What to wear

Do not wear woollen garments when decorating as they tend to leave hairs sticking to paintwork. Overalls with loops and large pockets for tools are ideal for decorating and other work.

Whether you are decorating inside or out, you must provide adequate means of reaching the area on which you are working. Using inefficient equipment and makeshift structures is dangerous; even if you do not want to buy suitable ladders, you can hire them quite cheaply. Safety and comfort while working are important considerations, and there is a range of devices and accessories to make the job that much easier.

Types of ladders and access equipment

Stepladders are essential for interior decoration. Traditional wooden stepladders are still available, but they have been largely superseded by lightweight aluminium-alloy types. You should have at least one that stands about 2m (6ft 6in) high so that you can reach a ceiling without having to stand on the top step. A second shorter ladder might be more convenient for other jobs and you can use both, with scaffold boards, to build a platform.

Outdoors you will need ladders to reach up to the eaves. Double and triple wooden extension ladders are very heavy, so consider a metal one.

Some doubles and most triples are operated by a rope and pulley so that they can be extended single-handed.

To estimate the length of ladder you need, add together the ceiling heights of your house. Add at least 1m (3ft 3in) to the length to allow for the angle and access to a platform.

There are many versions of dual-purpose or even multi-purpose ladders which convert from stepladder to straight ladder. A well-designed, versatile ladder is a good compromise.

Sectional scaffold frames can be built up to form towers at any convenient height for decorating inside and outside. Wide feet prevent the tower sinking into the ground, and adjustable versions allow you to level it. Some models have locking castors, which enable you to move the tower.

Towers are ideal for painting a large expanse of wall outdoors. Indoors, smaller platforms made from the same scaffold components bring high ceilings within easy reach.

Accessories for ladders

● **Ladder stay** A stay holds the ladder away from the wall. It is an essential piece of equipment when painting overhanging eaves and gutters: you would otherwise be forced to lean back, risking overbalancing.
● **Tool tray and paint-can hook** You should always support yourself with one hand on a ladder, so use a wire or bent-metal hook to hang a paint can or bucket from a rung. A clip-on tray is ideal for holding a small selection of tools.

● **Clip-on platform** A wide flat board, which clamps to the rungs, provides a comfortable platform to stand on while working for long periods.
● **Stabilizers** Bolt-on accessories that prevent the ladder from slipping and compensate for uneven ground.

Alloy stepladder   Dual-purpose ladder   Scaffold tower   Extending ladder

When you buy or hire a ladder, either wooden or metal, bear in mind that:

● Wooden ladders should be made from straight-grained, knot-free timber.
● Good-quality wooden ladders have hardwood rungs tenoned through the upright stiles and secured with wedges.
● Wooden rungs with reinforcing metal rods stretched under them are safer than ones without.
● End caps or foot pads are an advantage to prevent the ladder from slipping on hard ground.
● Adjustability is a prime consideration. Choose a ladder that will enable you to gain access to various parts of the building and will convert to a compact unit for storage.
● The rungs of overlapping sections of an extension ladder should align or the gap between the rungs might be too small to secure a good foothold.
● Choose an extension ladder with a rope and pulley, plus an automatic latch that locks the extension to its rung.
● Check that you can buy or hire a range of accessories (see opposite) to fit your make of ladder.
● Choose a stepladder with a platform at the top to take cans and trays.
● Treads should be comfortable to stand on. Stepladders with wide, flat treads are the best choice.
● Stepladders with extended stiles give you a handhold at the top of the steps.
● Wooden stepladders often have a rope to stop the two halves sliding apart. A better solution used on most metal stepladders is a folding stay, which locks in the open position.

Is the ladder safe to use?

Check ladders regularly and before you use them after a winter's break. Inspect a hired ladder before use.

Look for splits along the stiles and check that there are no missing or broken rungs and that the joints are tight. Sight along the stiles to make sure they are aligned, or the ladder could rock when leant against a wall.

Inspect wooden ladders for rot or woodworm. Even a small amount of sponginess or a few holes could signify serious damage below the surface. Test that the wood is sound before using the ladder and treat it with a preserver or woodworm fluid. If in doubt, scrap the ladder for safety's sake.

Check that fixings for hinges and pulleys are secure and lubricate them. Inspect the pulley rope for fraying and renew if necessary.

Oil or varnish wooden ladders regularly to stop them drying out. Apply extra coats to the rungs, which take most wear. Do not paint a ladder as this may hide serious defects.

How to handle a ladder

Ladders are heavy and unwieldy; handle them properly so that you do not damage property or injure yourself.

Carry a ladder upright, not slung across your shoulder. Hold the ladder vertically, bend your knees slightly, then rock the ladder back against your shoulder. Grip one rung lower down while you support the ladder at head height with your other hand, then straighten your knees.

To erect a ladder, lay it on the ground with its feet against the wall. Gradually raise it to vertical as you walk towards the wall. Pull the feet out from the wall so that the ladder is resting at an angle of about 70 degrees – if the ladder extends to 8m (26ft) for example, its feet should be 2m (6ft 6in), or one-quarter of its height, from the wall.

Raise an extending ladder to the required height while holding it upright. If it is a heavy ladder, get someone to hold it while you operate the pulley.

Handling a ladder
Carry the ladder upright, leaning back against your shoulder; grip one rung low down, another at head height. When erected, the base of the ladder should be one-quarter of its height away from the wall so that it is correctly balanced.

WORKING WITH LADDERS

SEE ALSO	
Details for:	
Work platforms	42
Varnishing	84
Oiling wood	86
Woodworm	252–253
Dealing with rot	255–256

HOW TO USE A LADDER SAFELY

More accidents are caused by the unwise use of ladders than by faulty equipment. Erect the ladder safely before you ascend it and move it when the work is out of reach – never lean to the side or you will overbalance. Follow these simple, commonsense rules:

Securing the ladder

If the ground is soft, spread the load of the ladder by placing a wide board under the feet; screw a batten across the board to wedge the ladder in place. On hard ground, make sure the ladder has anti-slip end caps and lay a sandbag (or a tough polyethylene bag filled with earth) at the base.

Secure the stiles near the base with rope tied to timber stakes driven into the ground at each side and just behind the ladder (1). When you extend a ladder the sections should overlap by at least one-quarter of their length. Do not lean the top against gutters, soil pipes, drainpipes and, especially, glass as they may give way.

Anchor the ladder near the top by tying it to a stout timber rail, held across the inside of the window frame. Make sure that the rail extends about 300mm (1ft) on each side of the window and pad the ends with old cloth to protect the wall from any damage (2).

It is a good idea to fix ring bolts at regular intervals into the masonry just below the fascia board: this is an excellent way to secure the top of a ladder as you will have equally good anchor points wherever you choose to position it. Alternatively, fix large screw eyes to the masonry or a sound fascia board and attach the ladder to them.

Safety aloft

Never climb higher than four rungs from the top of the ladder or you will not be able to balance properly and there will be no handholds within reach. Keep both your feet on a rung and your hips centred between the stiles. Avoid a slippery foothold by placing a sack or doormat at the foot of the ladder to dry your boots before you ascend.

Unless the manufacturer states otherwise, do not use a ladder to form a horizontal walkway, even with a scaffold board lying on it.

Stepladders are prone to topple sideways. Clamp a strut to the stile on uneven floors (3).

1 Staking a ladder
Secure the base of the ladder by lashing it to stakes in the ground.

2 Securing the top
Anchor the ladder to a batten held inside the window frame.

3 Supporting a stepladder
Clamp a strut to the stile to prop up a pair of stepladders.

41

ERECTING
WORK
PLATFORMS

A lot of work can be carried out by moving a ladder little by little as the work progresses. However, this can become tedious and may lead to an accident as you try to reach just a bit further before having to move along; you will find it more convenient to build a work platform that allows you to tackle a large area without moving the structure. You can hire decorators' trestles and bridge a pair with a scaffold board, or make a similar structure with two pairs of stepladders **(1)**.

Clamp or tie the board to the rungs and use two boards, one on top of the other, if two people need to use the platform at once.

An even better arrangement is to use scaffold-tower components to make a mobile platform **(2)**. One with locking castors is the ideal solution for painting or papering ceilings.

2 Mobile platform
An efficient structure made from scaffold-tower frames.

Gaining access to a stairwell

Stairwells present particular problems when you are building work platforms. The simplest method is to use a dual-purpose staircase ladder, which can be adjusted to stand evenly on a flight **(3)**. Anchor the steps with rope through a couple of large screw eyes fixed to the stair risers; the holes will be concealed by carpet later. Rest a scaffold board between the ladder and the landing to

form a bridge. Screw the board to the landing and tie the other end.

Alternatively, construct a tailor-made platform from ladders and boards to suit your staircase **(4)**. Make sure the boards and ladders are clamped or lashed together, and that the ladders cannot slip on the treads. If necessary, screw wooden battens to the stairs to prevent the foot of the ladder moving.

1 Improvised platform
A simple yet safe platform made from stepladders and a scaffold board.

ERECTING
PLATFORMS OUTSIDE

Scaffolding is by far the best method of building a work platform to decorate the outside of a house. Towers made from slot-together frames are available for hire. Heights up to about 9m (30ft) are possible; the tallest ones require supporting 'outriggers'.

Build the lower section of the frame first and level it with adjustable feet before erecting a tower on top. As you build, climb up and stand on the inside of the tower.

Erect a proper platform at the top with toe boards all round to prevent tools and materials being knocked off and extend the framework to provide hand rails all round. Secure the tower to the house by tying it to ring bolts fixed into the masonry, as with ladders.

Some towers incorporate a staircase inside the scaffold frame; floors with trapdoors enable you to ascend to the top of the tower. If you cannot find such a tower, the safest access is via a ladder. Make sure it extends at least 1m (3ft 3 in) above the staging so that you can step on and off safely.

It is difficult to reach windows and walls above an extension with just a ladder. With a scaffold tower, however, you can construct a cantilevered section fixed to the main tower which rests on the roof of the extension.

Stair scaffold
Erect a platform with scaffold frames to compensate for the slope of a staircase.

Cloths protect wall

Boards lashed together

Screwed to box

Battens screwed to landing

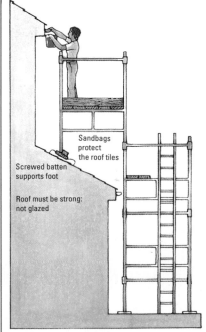

Sandbags protect the roof tiles

Screwed batten supports foot

Roof must be strong: not glazed

3 Dual-purpose ladder
Use a stair ladder to straddle the flight with a scaffold board to give a level work platform.

4 Tailor-made platform
Build a network of scaffold boards, stepladders, ladders and boxes to suit your stairwell layout.

Erecting a cantilevered platform
Rest cantilever section on a board to spread the load.

PREPARATION

AND PRIMING

Thorough preparation of all surfaces is the vital first step in redecorating. If you neglect this stage, subsequent finishes will be rejected. Preparation means removing dirt, grease and loose or flaking finishes, as well as repairing serious deterioration such as cracks, holes, corrosion and decay. It is not just old surfaces that need attention: new timber and metalwork must be sealed for protection, and priming is necessary to ensure a surface is in a suitable condition to accept its finish. Consult the charts on this page for details of primers and sealers for all the materials you are likely to encounter in and around the home, then read the following sections, which examine each material in detail.

TYPES OF PRIMERS AND SEALERS

There are numerous primers and sealers to suit a variety of materials.

Stabilizing primer
Used to bind powdery or flaky materials. A clear or white liquid.

Wood primer
Standard solvent-based pink or white primer prevents other coats of paint soaking in.

Acrylic wood primer
Fast-drying water-based primer. Some types can be used for undercoating.

Aluminium wood primer
Used to seal oily hardwoods, it will also cover creosote.

General-purpose primer
Seals porous building materials and covers patchy walls and ceilings.

Metal primers
Essential to prevent corrosion in metals and to provide a key for paint. Special rust-inhibitive primers both treat rust and prevent its recurrence.

PVA bonding agent
A general-purpose liquid adhesive for many building materials. An excellent primer and sealer when diluted, even for bituminous paints.

Water repellent
A liquid which dries colourless and is used to seal masonry against water penetration.

Alkali-resistant primer
Used to prevent the alkali contents of some materials attacking oil paints.

Aluminium spirit-based sealer
Formulated to obliterate materials likely to 'bleed' through subsequent coatings. Effective over bituminous paints, metallic paints, creosote and nicotine.

SEE ALSO

Details for:	
Priming brickwork	46
Waterproofing masonry	46
Priming flaky paint	48
Priming plaster	50
Priming wood	53
Priming man-made boards	54
Priming metal	60-61

● Black dot denotes that primer and surface are compatible.

● Red dot denotes metal primers

● **Lead content in paint**
Lead, which is a poison, was widely used in the past as a dryer in solvent-based paints, including primers. (Emulsions, which are water-based, have never contained lead). Most solvent-based paints are now made without lead. If possible, choose one labelled 'no lead added' or similar. Do not let children chew old painted surfaces, which may have a high lead content.

PRIMERS AND SEALERS: SUITABILITY, DRYING TIME AND COVERAGE

SUITABLE FOR	Stabilizing primer	Wood primer	Acrylic wood primer	Aluminium wood primer	General-purpose primer	Zinc-phosphate primer	Fast-drying metal primer	Rust-inhibitive primer	PVA bonding agent	Water repellent	Alkali-resistant primer	Aluminium spirit-based sealer
Brick	●				●				●	●	●	
Stone	●				●				●	●	●	
Cement rendering	●				●				●	●	●	
Concrete	●				●				●	●	●	
Plaster	●				●				●		●	
Plasterboard	●				●						●	
Distemper	●											
Limewash	●											
Cement paint	●											
Bitumen-based paints									●			●
Asbestos cement	●				●				●		●	
Softwoods/hardwoods		●	●	●	●							
Oily hardwoods				●								
Chipboard		●	●	●	●							
Hardboard		●	●	●	●							
Plywood		●	●	●	●							
Creosoted timber				●								●
Absorbent fibre boards	●										●	
Ferrous metals (inside)						●	●	●				
Ferrous metals (outside)						●	●	●				
Galvanized metal						●						
Aluminium						●						
DRYING TIME: HOURS												
Touch dry	3	4-6	0.5	4-6	4-6	4	2	2	3	1	4	0.25
Recoatable	16	16	2	16	16	16	5-6	6	16	16	16	1
COVERAGE (Sq m per litre)												
Smooth surface	6	12	12	13	12	13	8	8	9	3-6	10	4
Rough/absorbent surface	7	10	10	11	9	10	6	6	7	2-3	7	3

CLEANING BRICK AND STONE

Before you decorate the outside of your house, check the condition of the brick and stonework and carry out any necessary repairs. Unless you live in an area of the country where there is a tradition of painting brick and stonework, you will probably want to restore painted masonry to its original condition. Although most paint strippers cannot cope with deeply textured surfaces, there are thick-paste paint removers that will peel away layers of old paint from masonry walls.

Stained brickwork

Organic growth

Efflorescence

Treating new masonry

New brickwork or stonework should be left for about three months until it is completely dry before any further treatment is considered. White powdery deposits called efflorescence may come to the surface over this period, but you can simply brush them off with a stiff-bristle brush or a piece of dry sacking. Masonry is weatherproof and therefore requires no further treatment, except that in some areas of the country you may wish to apply paint.

Cleaning organic growth from masonry

There are innumerable species of mould growth and lichens which first appear as tiny coloured specks or patches on masonry. They gradually merge until the surface is covered with colours that range from bright orange to yellow, green, grey and black.

Moulds and lichen will only flourish in damp conditions, so try to cure the source of the problem before treating the growth. If one side of the house always faces away from the sun, for example, it will have little chance to dry out. Relieve the situation by cutting back any overhanging trees or shrubs to increase ventilation to the wall.

Make sure the damp-proof course (DPC) is working adequately and is not being bridged by piled earth or debris.

Cracked or corroded rainwater pipes leaking on to the wall are another common cause of organic growth. Feel behind the pipe with your fingers or slip a hand mirror behind it in order to locate the leak.

Removing the growth
Brush the wall vigorously with a stiff-bristle brush. This can be an unpleasant, dusty job, so wear a facemask. Brush away from you to avoid debris being flicked into your eyes.

Microscopic spores will remain even after brushing. Kill these with a solution of bleach or, if the wall suffers from persistent fungal growth, use a proprietary fungicide, available from most DIY stores.

Using a bleach solution
Mix 1 part household bleach with 4 parts water and paint the solution on to the wall with an old paintbrush. Wash the surface with clean water, using a scrubbing brush, 48 hours later. Brush on a second application of bleach solution if the original fungal growth was severe.

Using a fungicidal solution
Dilute the fungicide with water according to the manufacturer's instructions and apply it liberally to the wall with an old paintbrush. Leave it for 24 hours, then rinse the wall with clean water. In extreme cases, give the wall two washes of fungicide, allowing 24 hours between applications and a further 24 hours before washing it down with water.

Removing efflorescence from masonry

Soluble salts within building materials such as cement, brick, stone and plaster gradually migrate to the surface along with the water as a wall dries out. The result is a white crystalline deposit called efflorescence.

The same condition can occur on old masonry if it is subjected to more than average moisture. Efflorescence itself is not harmful, but the source of the damp causing it must be identified and cured before decoration proceeds.

Regularly brush the deposit from the wall with a dry stiff-bristle brush or coarse sacking until the crystals cease to form. Do not attempt to wash off the crystals – they will merely dissolve in the water and soak back into the wall. Above all, do not attempt to decorate a wall which is still efflorescing, because this is a sign that it is still damp.

When the wall is completely dry, paint the surface with an alkali-resistant primer to neutralize the effect of the crystals before you apply an oil paint. Masonry paints and clear sealants that let the wall breathe are not affected by the alkali content of the masonry, so can be used without applying a primer.

REPOINTING
MASONRY

CLEANING OLD MASONRY

Improve the appearance of unpainted masonry by washing it with clean water. Starting at the top of the wall, play a hose gently on to the masonry while you scrub it with a stiff-bristle brush (1). Scrub heavy deposits with half a cup of ammonia added to a bucketful of water, then rinse again.

Removing unsightly stains
Soften tar, grease and oil stains by applying a poultice made from fuller's earth or sawdust soaked in paraffin or a proprietary grease solvent. Follow manufacturers' instructions and wear protective gloves.

Dampen the stain with solvent, then spread on a 12mm (½in) thick layer of poultice and leave it to dry out and absorb the stain. Scrape off the dry poultice with a wooden or plastic spatula and scrub the wall with water.

Stripping spilled paint
Remove a patch of spilled paint from brickwork with a proprietary paint stripper. Follow manufacturers' recommendations with regard to protective clothing. Stipple the stripper on to the rough texture (2). After about 10 minutes, remove the softened paint with a scraper and scrub the residue out of the deeper crevices with a stiff-bristle brush and water. Finally, rinse the wall with clean water.

1 Remove dirt and dust by washing

2 Stipple paint stripper on to spilled paint

A combination of frost action and erosion tends to break down the mortar pointing between bricks and stonework. The mortar eventually falls out, exposing the open joints to wind and rain that eventually drive dampness through the wall to the inside. Replacing pointing is straightforward, but time-consuming. Tackle a small, manageable area at a time, using a ready-mixed mortar or your own mix.

Applying the mortar

Rake out the old pointing with a thin wooden lath to a depth of about 12mm (½in). Use a cold chisel or a special plugging chisel and a club hammer to dislodge sections that are firmly embedded, then brush out the joints with a stiff-bristle brush.

Spray the wall with water to make sure the bricks or stones will not absorb too much moisture from the fresh mortar. Mix up some mortar in a bucket and transfer it to a hawk. If you are mixing your own mortar, use the proportions 1 part cement : 1 part lime : 6 parts builders' sand.

Pick up a little sausage of mortar on the back of a small pointing trowel and push it firmly into the upright joints. This can be difficult to do without the mortar dropping off, so hold the hawk under each joint to catch it. Try not to smear the face of the bricks with mortar as it will stain. Repeat the process for the horizontal joints. The actual shape of the pointing is not vital at this stage.

Once the mortar is firm enough to retain a thumbprint it is ready for shaping. Match the style of pointing used on the rest of the house (see below). When the pointing has almost hardened, brush the wall to remove traces of surplus mortar.

Shaping the mortar joints

The joints shown here are commonly used for brickwork. Rubbed joints are best for most stonework. Leave the pointing of dressed-stone ashlar blocks to an expert.

Flush joints
The easiest profile to produce, a flush joint is stippled with a stiff-bristle brush to expose the sand aggregate.

Rubbed (concave) joints
Bricklayers make a rubbed or rounded joint with a tool shaped like a sled runner with a handle: the semi-circular blade is run along the joints. Improvise by bending a length of metal tube or rod; use the curved section only or you will gouge the mortar. Once the mortar is shaped, stipple it so that it matches the weathered pointing.

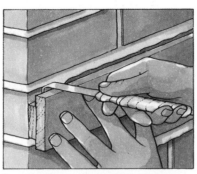

Use a Frenchman to trim weatherstruck joints

Raked joints
A raked joint is used to emphasize the type of bonding pattern of a brick wall. It is not suitable for soft bricks or for a wall that takes a lot of weathering. Scrape out a little of the mortar, then tidy up the joints by running a 9mm (⅜in) lath along them.

Weatherstruck joints
The sloping profile is intended to shed rainwater from the wall. Shape the mortar with the edge of a pointing trowel. Start with the vertical joints and slope them in either direction, but be consistent. During the process, mortar will tend to spill from the bottom of a joint as surplus is cut off. Bricklayers use a tool called a 'Frenchman' to neaten the work: It has a narrow blade with the tip bent at right angles. Make your own tool by bending a thin metal strip and binding insulating tape round the other end to form a handle, or bend the tip of an old kitchen knife after heating it in the flame of a blowtorch or cooker burner.

You will find it easiest to use a wooden batten to guide the blade of the Frenchman along the joints, but nail scraps of plywood at each end of the batten to hold it off the wall. Align the batten with the bottom of the horizontal joints, then draw the tool along it, cutting off the excess mortar.

● **Mortar dyes**
Liquid or powder additives are available for changing the colour of mortar to match existing pointing. Colour matching is difficult and smears can stain the bricks permanently.

Flush joint

Rubbed joint

Raked joint

Weatherstruck joint

REPAIRING MASONRY

Cracked masonry may simply be the result of cement-rich mortar being unable to absorb slight movements within the building. However, it could also be a sign of a more serious problem – subsiding foundations, for example. Do not just ignore the symptoms but investigate immediately and put the necessary repairs in hand.

Filling cracked masonry

If a brick or stone wall has substantial cracks, consult a builder or your local Building Control Officer to ascertain the cause. If a crack proves to be stable you can carry out repairs yourself.

Cracked mortar can be removed and repointed in the normal way, but a crack that splits one or more bricks cannot be repaired neatly and the damaged

masonry should be replaced in the same manner as spalled brickwork (see right).

Cracks across a painted wall can be filled with mortar that has been mixed with a little PVA bonding agent to help it to stick. Before you effect the repair, wet the damaged masonry with a hose to encourage the mortar to flow deeply into the crack.

Crack may follow pointing only

Cracked bricks could signify serious faults

Priming brickwork for painting

Brickwork will only need to be primed if it is showing signs of efflorescence or spalling. An alkali-resistant primer will guard against the former and a stabilizing solution will both bind crumbling masonry and help to seal it.

If you are planning to paint the wall for the first time with masonry paint, you may find that the first coat is difficult to apply due to the suction of the dry, porous brick. Thin the first coat slightly with water or solvent.

Waterproofing masonry

1 Replacing a spalled brick
Having mortared the top and one end, slip the new brick into the hole you have cut.

Colourless water-repellent fluids are intended to make masonry impervious to water without colouring it or stopping it from breathing, which is important in order to allow moisture within the walls to dry out.

Prepare the surface thoroughly before applying the fluid: make good any cracks in bricks or pointing and remove organic growth, then allow the wall to dry out thoroughly.

Apply the fluid generously with a large paintbrush and stipple it into the joints. Apply a second coat as soon as the first has been absorbed to ensure that there are no bare patches where water could seep in. So that you can be sure you are covering the wall properly,

use a sealant containing a fugitive dye which will disappear gradually after a specified period.

Carefully paint up to surrounding woodwork; if you accidentally splash sealant on to it, wash it down immediately with a cloth dampened with white spirit.

The fumes from the fluid can be dangerous if inhaled, so be sure to wear a proper respirator as recommended by the manufacturer. If you need to treat a whole house, it might be worth hiring a company which will undertake spraying on the sealant. Make sure their workmen rig up plastic-sheet screens to prevent overspray drifting across to your neighbour's property.

REPAIRING SPALLED MASONRY

Moisture that has penetrated soft masonry will expand in icy weather, flaking off the outer face of brickwork and stonework. The process, known as spalling, not only looks unattractive but also allows water to seep into the surface. Repairs to spalled bricks or stones can be made, though treatment depends on the severity of the problem.

If spalling is localized, cut out the bricks or stones and replace them with matching ones. The sequence below describes doing this with brickwork, but the process is similar for a stone wall.

Spalled bricks caused by frost damage

Where spalling is extensive, the only practical solution is to accept its less-than-perfect appearance, repoint the masonry and apply a clear water repellent that will protect the wall from any further damage while at the same time allowing it to breathe.

Replacing a spalled brick
Use a cold chisel and club hammer to rake out the pointing surrounding the brick, then chop out the brick itself. If the brick is difficult to prise out, drill numerous holes in it with a large-diameter masonry bit, then slice up the brick with a cold chisel and hammer: it should crumble, enabling you to remove the pieces easily.

To fit the replacement brick, first dampen the opening and spread mortar on the base and one side. Butter the dampened replacement brick with mortar on the top and one end and slot it into the hole (1). Shape the pointing to match the surrounding brickwork.

If you can't find a replacement brick of a suitable colour, remove the spalled brick carefully, turn it round to reveal its undamaged face and reinsert it.

REPAIRING

RENDER

Brickwork may be clad with a smooth or roughcast cement-based render, both for improved weatherproofing and to give a decorative finish. Often the render is susceptible to the effects of damp and frost, which can cause cracking, bulging and staining. Before you redecorate a rendered wall make good any damage and clean off surface dirt, mould growth and flaky material in order to achieve a long-lasting finish.

Cracked render allows moisture to penetrate

Blown pebbledash parts from the masonry

Leaky guttering causes rust stains

Repairing defective render

Before you repair cracked render, correct any structural faults that may have contributed to it. Apply a stabilizing solution if the wall is dusty.

Ignore fine hairline cracks if you intend to paint the wall with a reinforced masonry paint. Rake out larger cracks with a cold chisel, dampen with water and fill them flush to the surface with an exterior filler. Fill any major cracks with a render made of 1 part cement : 2 parts lime : 9 parts builder's sand, plus a little PVA bonding agent to help it adhere to the masonry.

Bulges in render normally indicate that the cladding has parted from the masonry. Tap gently with a wooden mallet to find the extent of these hollow areas and hack off the material to sound edges. Undercut the perimeter of each hole except for the bottom edge, which should be left square.

Brush out debris, then apply a coat of PVA bonding agent. When it becomes tacky, trowel on a 12mm (½in) thick layer of 1 : 1 : 6 render and leave it to set firm. Scratch it to form a key and, the next day, fill flush with a slightly weaker 1 : 1 : 9 mix. Smooth the surface with a wooden float, using circular strokes.

Reinforcing a crack in render

To prevent a crack in render opening up again, reinforce the repair with a glass-fibre membrane embedded in a bitumen base coat. Rake out the crack to remove any loose material, then wet it. Fill just proud of the surface with a mortar mix of 1 part cement : 4 parts builders' sand. When this has stiffened scrape it flush with the render.

When the mortar has hardened, brush on a generous coat of bitumen base coat, making sure it extends at least 100mm (4in) on both sides of the crack. Embed strips of fibre-glass scrim (sold with the base coat) into the bitumen, using a stippling and brushing action (1). While it is still wet, feather the edges of the bitumen with a foam roller (2), bedding the scrim into it. After 24 hours the bitumen will be hard, black and shiny. Apply a second coat, feather with a roller and, when it has dried, apply two full coats of a compatible reinforced masonry paint.

1 Embed the scrim

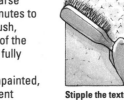

2 Feather with roller

Patching pebbledash

Pebbledash comprises small stones stuck to a thin coat of render over a thicker base coat. If damp gets behind pebbledashing, one or both layers may separate. Hack off any loose render to a sound base and seal it with stabilizer. If necessary, repair the scratchcoat of render. Simulate the texture of pebbledash with a thick paste made from PVA bonding agent. Mix 1 part cement-paint powder with 3 parts clean sharp (plastering) sand. Stir in 1 measure of bonding agent diluted with 3 parts water to form a thick, creamy paste. Load a banister brush and scrub the paste on to the bare surface.

Apply a second generous coat of paste, stippling it to form a coarse texture. Leave for about 15 minutes to firm up then, with a loaded brush, stipple it to match the texture of the pebbles. Let the paste harden fully before painting.

To leave the pebbledash unpainted, make a patch using replacement pebbles. The result may not be a perfect match, but could save you having to paint the entire wall. Cut back the blown area and apply a scratchcoat followed by a buttercoat. While this is still wet, fling pebbles on to the surface from a dustpan; they should stick to the soft render, but you may have to repeat the process until the coverage is even.

Stipple the texture

Removing rust stains

Faulty plumbing will often leave rusty streaks on a rendered wall. Before decorating, prime the stains with an aluminium spirit-based sealer or they will bleed through. Rust marks may also appear on a pebbledashed wall, well away from any metalwork: these are caused by iron pyrites in the aggregate. Chip out the pyrites with a cold chisel, then seal the stain.

PAINTED
MASONRY

Painted masonry inside the house is usually in fairly good order, and apart from a good wash down to remove dust and grease and a light sanding to give a key for the new finish, there is little else you need to do. Outside, however, it is a different matter; the exterior surface, subjected to extremes of heat, cold and rain, is likely to be affected to some degree by stains, flaking and chalkiness.

A chalky surface needs stabilizing

Strip flaky paintwork to a sound surface

Chimney stained by tar deposits from the flue

Curing a chalky surface

Rub the palm of your hand lightly over the surface of the wall to see if it is chalky. If the paint rubs off as a powdery deposit, treat the wall before you redecorate. Brush the surface with a stiff-bristle brush, then paint the whole wall liberally with a stabilizing primer, which will bind the chalky surface so that paint will adhere to it. Use a white stabilizing primer, which can also act as an undercoat. Clean splashes of the fluid from surrounding woodwork with white spirit. If the wall is very dusty, apply a second coat of stabilizer after about 16 hours. Wait a further 16 hours before painting over.

Dealing with flaky paintwork

Flaking is often a result of poor surface preparation or incompatible paint and preparatory treatments. Damp walls will also cause flaking, so remedy this and let the wall dry out before further treatment. A further cause could be too many previous coats of paint.

Subsequent coats of paint will not bind to a flaky surface, so this must be removed before you start painting. Use a paint scraper and stiff-bristle brush to remove all loose material. Coarse glasspaper should finish the job or at least feather the edges of any stubborn patches. Stabilize the surface as for chalky walls before repainting.

If the flaking is as a result of spalled brickwork, stabilize the affected bricks with a bitumen base coat. Feather the edges with a foam roller, leave the bitumen to harden for 24 hours, then paint the wall with two coats of reinforced masonry paint.

Treating a stained chimney

A painted brick chimney stack with the outline of courses showing clearly through the paint as brown staining is caused by a breakdown of the internal rendering (known as 'pargeting') of the chimney; this allows tar deposits to migrate through the mortar to the outer paintwork. To solve the problem, first fit a flue liner in the chimney, then treat the brown stains with an aluminium spirit-based sealer before applying a fresh coat of paint.

STRIPPING PAINTED MASONRY

In the past, even sound brickwork was often painted simply to 'brighten up' a house. In some areas of the country where painted masonry is traditional, there is every reason to continue with the practice. Indeed, houses with soft, inferior brickwork were frequently painted when they were built in order to protect them from the weather, and to strip them now could have serious consequences. However, one painted house in an otherwise natural-brick terrace spoils the entire neighbourhood, and painting one half of a pair of semi-detached houses has an equally undesirable effect.

Restoring painted brickwork to its natural condition is not an easy task. It is usually a messy business, involving the use of toxic materials that have to be handled with care and disposed of safely. Extensive scaffolding may be required and, most importantly, getting the masonry entirely clean demands considerable experience. For all these reasons, it pays to hire professionals to do the work for you.

Applying the stripper

Special ready-mixed paste strippers will remove practically any combination of paints. The paste is trowelled on to the masonry and then covered with a laminated sheet of fibrous tissue and plastic. This poultice is left in place for up to 48 hours, during which time the paint softens and is absorbed into the fibrous material.

When the time is right the poultice is peeled away, taking the paint with it. The residue of paint adhering to the wall is carefully washed away and the wall is left to dry out for several days.

Other applications

The same type of poultice stripper can be used to remove paint from plasterwork (including moulded cornices and ceiling roses), woodwork and metal. It is perfectly possible to tackle a smaller project such as this yourself, but make sure you follow the manufacturer's health-and-safety recommendations to the letter. Before buying a stripper, check that it is suitable for the particular material you want to restore.

Concrete is used in and around the house as a surface for solid floors, drives, paths and walls. In common with other building materials, it suffers from the effects of damp – spalling and efflorescence – and related defects such as cracking and crumbling. Repairs can usually be made in much the same way as for brickwork and render, although there are some special considerations you should be aware of. If the damage is widespread, however, it is quite straightforward to resurface the concrete prior to decorating.

Sealing concrete

New concrete has a high alkali content and efflorescence can develop on the surface as it dries out. Do not use any finish other than a water-thinned paint until the concrete is completely dry. Treat efflorescence on concrete in the same manner as for brickwork.

A porous concrete wall should be waterproofed with a clear sealant on the exterior. Some reinforced masonry paints will cover bitumen satisfactorily, but it will bleed through most paints unless you prime it with a PVA bonding agent diluted 50 per cent with water. Alternatively, use an aluminium spirit-based sealer.

Cleaning dirty concrete

Clean dirty concrete as you would brickwork, but where a concrete drive or garage floor is stained with patches of oil or grease, apply a proprietary oil-and-grease remover. Soak up fresh spillages immediately with dry sand or sawdust to prevent them becoming permanent stains.

Binding dusty concrete

Concrete is trowelled when it is laid in order to give a flat finish. If this is overdone, cement is brought to the surface and when the concrete dries out this thin layer begins to break up within a short time, producing a loose, dusty surface. It is not worth your while applying any decorative finish to concrete in this condition.

Treat a concrete wall with stabilizing primer, but paint a dusty floor with a concrete-floor sealer.

Repairing cracks and holes

Rake out and brush away loose debris from cracks and holes in concrete. If the crack is less than 6mm (¼in) wide, open it up a little with a cold chisel so that it will accept a filling. Undercut the edges to form a lip so the filler will grip.

To fill a hole in concrete, add a fine aggregate such as gravel to the sand-and-cement mix. Make sure the fresh concrete sticks in shallow depressions by priming the damaged surface with 3 parts bonding agent : 1 part water. When the primed surface is tacky, trowel in the concrete and smooth it.

Treating spalled concrete

When concrete breaks up, or spalls, due to the action of frost, the process is accelerated as steel reinforcement is exposed and begins to corrode. Fill the concrete as described above, but paint the metalwork first with a rust-inhibitive primer. If spalling recurs, particularly in exposed conditions, protect the wall with a bitumen base coat and a compatible reinforced masonry paint.

Spalling concrete
Rusting metalwork causes concrete to spall.

REPAIRING A CONCRETE FLOOR

An uneven or pitted concrete floor must be made flat and level before you apply any form of floorcovering. You can do this fairly easily yourself, using a proprietary self-levelling screed, but first of all you must ensure the surface is free from dampness.

Testing for dampness
Do not lay any sheet floorcoverings or tiles (or apply a levelling screed) to a floor that is damp. If the floor is new it must incorporate a damp-proof membrane; however, a new floor should be left to dry out for six months before an impermeable covering is added.

If you suspect an existing floor is damp, make a simple test by laying a small piece of polyethylene on the concrete and sealing it all round with self-adhesive parcel tape. After one or two days, inspect it for any traces of moisture on the underside.

For a more accurate assessment, hire a moisture meter. This device will read the moisture content of a suspect surface when you hold its contact pins against it. If the moisture reading does not exceed 6 per cent, you can proceed with covering or levelling the floor.

If either test indicates treatment is necessary, paint the floor with a bitumen-based waterproofer. Prime the surface first with a slightly diluted coat, then brush on two full-strength coats, allowing each to dry between applications. If necessary you can then lay a self-levelling screed over the waterproofer.

Applying a self-levelling compound
Fill holes and cracks deeper than about 3mm (⅛in) by first raking them out and undercutting the edges (**1**), then filling them with mortar mix.

Self-levelling compound is supplied as a powder which you mix with water. Make sure the floor is clean and free from damp, then pour some of the compound in the corner that is furthest away from the door. Spread the compound with a trowel (**2**) until it is about 3mm (⅛in) thick, then leave it to seek its own level. Continue across the floor, joining the area of compound until the entire surface is covered. You can walk on the floor after about one hour without damaging it, but leave the compound to harden for a few days before laying permanent floorcovering.

SEE ALSO

Details for:	
Primers	43
Efflorescence	44
repairing brickwork	46
Repairing render	47
Priming metal	60–61
Masonry paints	65
Damp-proof membrane	186
Curing damp	257–264
Mixing concrete	453

● **Cement-based exterior filler**
As an alternative for patching holes and rebuilding broken corners in concrete, use a proprietary cement-based exterior filler. When mixed with water, the filler remains workable for 20 minutes. Just before it sets hard, smooth or scrape the filler level.

1 Rake out cracks

2 Apply compound
Spread self-levelling compound with a trowel.

49

PLASTERWORK: MAKING GOOD

Plaster is used to finish the inner surfaces of the walls and ceilings in most houses. Ceilings are traditionally clad with slim wood laths which are then plastered over: the plaster grips between the laths. Walls are usually covered directly with a backing (floating) coat of plaster and a smooth finish coat, various grades of plaster being used to suit the condition and quality of the masonry. An old house might have lath-and-plaster walls and ceilings; in modern houses, plasterboard is used instead. A plastered or boarded surface can be decorated with paint, paper or cladding such as tiles, the preparation being similar for each. Whatever you intend to use as a decorative finish, the plastered wall or ceiling must be made good by filling cracks and holes.

Smooth finish
Smooth the surface of small repairs with a wet brush or knife in order to reduce the amount of sanding required later.

PREPARING TO DECORATE

New plaster

Before you decorate new plaster, allow efflorescence to form on the surface, then wipe it off with sacking; repeat periodically until it ceases to appear.

For brand-new interior surfaces use new-plaster emulsion only; standard vinyl emulsions are not sufficiently moisture-vapour permeable. Always leave fresh plaster to dry out thoroughly before decorating with wallpaper or any paint other than new-plaster emulsion. Use an alkali-resistant primer first if you are applying solvent-based paints. Size new, absorbent plaster before hanging wallpaper or the water will be sucked too quickly from the paste, which will result in poor adhesion. Use either a proprietary size or a heavy-duty wallpaper paste. If you are hanging vinyl wallcovering, make sure that the size contains fungicide as vinyl cannot breathe like a plain paper can.

For tiling, no further preparation is needed once the plaster is dry.

Old plaster

Apart from filling minor defects and dusting down, old, dry plaster needs no further preparation. If the wall is patchy, apply a general-purpose primer.

If the surface is friable apply a stabilizing solution before you decorate.

Do not decorate damp plaster; cure the fault, then let the plaster dry out.

Plasterboard

Fill all joints between newly fixed plasterboard, then, whether you are painting or papering the board, daub all nail heads with zinc-phosphate primer.

Before you paint plasterboard with oil paint, prime it with one coat of general-purpose primer. One coat of thinned emulsion may be needed on an absorbent board before the normal full-strength coats are applied.

Prior to hanging wallcovering, seal plasterboard with a general-purpose primer thinned with white spirit. After 48 hours, apply a coat of size. This allows wet-stripping without disturbing the board's paper facing.

Painted plaster

Wash sound paintwork with a sugar-soap or detergent solution. Use water and medium-grade wet-and-dry abrasive paper to key the surface of gloss paint, particularly if covering with emulsion. Prime and allow to dry.

If the ceiling is severely stained by smoke and nicotine, prime it with an alkali-resistant primer or an aluminium spirit-based sealer. Sealers are sold in aerosol cans for treating isolated stains.

If you want to hang wallcovering on oil paint, key then size the wall. Cross-line the wall with lining paper before hanging a heavy embossed paper.

Remove flaking materials with a scraper or stiff-bristle brush. Feather off the edges of the paintwork with wet-and-dry abrasive paper. Treat bare plaster patches with a general-purpose primer. If the edges of old paintwork continue to show, prime those areas again, rubbing down afterwards. Apply stabilizing primer if the paint is friable.

Apply tiles over sound paintwork after removing any loose material.

Cracks in solid plaster

Special flexible emulsions and textured paints are designed to cover hairline cracks, but larger ones will reappear in a relatively short time if they are not filled adequately.

Rake loose material from a crack with the blade of a scraper or filling knife (1). Undercut the edges of larger cracks in order to provide a key for the filling. Mix up interior-grade cellulose filler to a stiff consistency or use a pre-mixed filler.

Dampen the crack with a paintbrush, then press the filler in with a filling knife. Drag the blade across the crack to force the filler in, then draw it along the crack (2) to smooth the filler. Leave the filler standing slightly proud of the surface ready for rubbing down smooth and flush with abrasive paper.

Fill shallow cracks with one application but build up the filler in stages in deep ones, letting each application set before adding more.

Cracks sometimes appear in the corner between walls or a wall and ceiling; fill these by running your finger dipped in filler along the crack. When the filler has hardened, rub it down with medium-grade abrasive paper.

Fill and rub down small holes and dents in solid plasterwork in the same way as for filling cracks.

1 Rake out loose material

2 Press filler into crack

Large gaps can open up between skirting boards and the wall plaster. Cellulose filler simply falls into the cavity behind, so bridge the gap with a roll of press-in-place butyl sealant.

SEE ALSO

Details for:	
Primers	43
Stripping painted masonry	48
Finish plaster	161
Floats and trowels	494

A lath-and-plaster wall

If the laths are intact, plaster up the holes as for solid plasterwork. A hole under 75mm (3in) wide can simply be packed out with a ball of wet newspaper dipped in plaster. Fill flush to the surface with cellulose filler.

If some laths are broken, reinforce the repair with a piece of fine expanded-metal mesh. Rake out loose plaster and undercut the edge of the hole with a bolster chisel. Use tinsnips to cut the metal to the shape of the hole, but a little larger (1). The mesh is flexible, so you can easily bend it in order to tuck the edge behind the sound plaster all round (2). Flatten it against the laths with light taps from a hammer and, if possible, staple the mesh to a wall stud to hold it (3).

Gently apply one thin coat of backing plaster (4) and let it dry for about one hour before you continue patching.

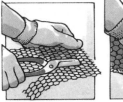
1 Cut with tinsnips

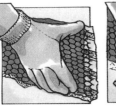
2 Tuck mesh into hole

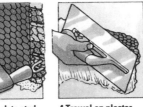
3 Staple mesh to stud

4 Trowel on plaster

A plasterboard wall or ceiling

A large hole punched through a plasterboard wall or ceiling cannot be patched with wet plaster only. Cut back the damaged board to the nearest studs or joists at each side (1), using a sharp trimming knife against a straightedge. Cut a new panel of plasterboard to fit snugly within the hole and nail it to the joists or studs using galvanized plasterboard nails. Use a steel trowel to spread finish plaster over the panel, forcing it well into the edges (2). Allow the plaster to stiffen, then smooth it with a dry trowel. You may have to add another layer to bring the patch to the level of the wall or ceiling.

1 Cut damaged panel to nearest supports

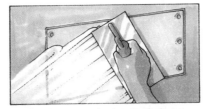
2 Nail on the new panel and coat with plaster

A small hole in plasterboard

For very small holes in plasterboard use cellulose filler instead of plaster. Use plasterer's glass-fibre patching tape for holes up to about 90mm (3½in) across. Stick on the self-adhesive strips in a star shape over the hole, then apply filler and feather the edges (1).

Alternatively, use an offcut of plasterboard just larger than the hole yet narrow enough to slot through. Bore a hole in the middle and thread a length of string through. Tie a galvanized nail to one end of the string (2). Butter the ends of the offcut with filler, then feed it into the hole. Pull on the string (3) to force it against the back of the cladding, then press filler into the hole so that it is not quite flush with the surface. When the filler is hard, cut off the string and apply a thin coat of filler for a flush finish.

1 Fill and feather the patch

2 Fix string to offcut

3 Pull on string

DEALING WITH DISTEMPER

Distemper was once a popular finish, so you may have to deal with it if your house is old. It is basically powdered chalk or whiting, mixed with glue size and water. It makes a poor base for decorating: when wet it redissolves and comes away from the surface along with the new decorations.

Brush away all loose material and apply a stabilizing primer to bind any traces left on the surface.

Many delicate plaster mouldings have been obliterated over time with successive coats of distemper. As it is water-soluble, you can remove it with care and patience. Work on a small area at a time, wetting it through with water. Remove the distemper with a toothbrush until the detail of the moulding is clear, then scrape out the softened paint with pointed sticks such as wooden skewers. Wash the moulding and apply a stabilizing primer.

Alternatively, hire a specialist to strip distemper with steam.

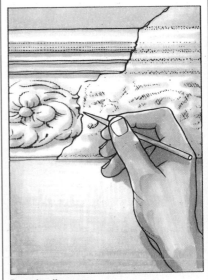
Removing distemper
Scrub with a toothbrush, then scrape out the softened paint with a pointed stick.

Limewash and cement paints

Other water-thinned paints such as limewash and cement paints are less likely to cause problems when you need to overpaint them unless they are in poor condition. Scrape and brush down with a stiff-bristle brush, then wipe the surface with white spirit to remove grease (it is best not to use water on these paints). Ensure the surface is sound by applying a stabilizing primer.

External corners
Dampen the chipped corner, then use a filling knife to scrape the filler on to the damaged edge, working from both sides of the angle (1). Let the filler stiffen, then shape it with a wet finger so it closely resembles the original profile (2).

1 Use filler knife

2 Shape with finger

● **Lath-and-plaster ceiling**
If the laths are sound, plaster over as for solid plasterwork. If the laths are broken, cut back to the nearest joist and secure with galvanized nails. Fit a panel of plasterboard and spread on a coat of bonding plaster followed by a coat of finish plaster.

PREPARING
WALLCOVERINGS

2 Steam stripper
You can hire a large industrial model or buy a lightweight steam stripper with its own built-in reservoir. Hold the sole plate against the wall until the steam penetrates and softens the paper, then remove it with a scraper. Wash the wall to remove traces of paste.

52

ERADICATING MOULD GROWTH

If damp conditions are present mould can develop, usually in the form of black specks. The cause of the damp must be remedied before you begin to treat the walls or ceiling.

Sterilize the mould growth before you carry out any other preparatory work to avoid distributing spores into the atmosphere. Apply a liberal wash of a solution made from 1 part household bleach : 16 parts water. (Do not make the solution any stronger as it may damage the wall decoration.) Leave the solution for at least four hours, then carefully scrape off the mould, wipe it on to newspaper and burn it outside.

Wash the wall again with the solution, then leave it for three days in order to sterilize the wall completely. When the wall is dry, paint it with a stabilizing primer thinned with white spirit. If you plan to hang wallpaper, size the wall using a size containing a fungicide solution.

Where mould growth is affecting wallpaper, soak the area in a warm water-and-bleach solution, then scrape off the contaminated paper and burn it. Wash the wall with a fresh bleach solution to remove paste residue.

Apply a liberal wash of similar solution to sterilize the wall and leave it for at least three days, but preferably one week, to make sure no further growth occurs. When the wall is completely dry, apply a stabilizing primer thinned with white spirit, followed by a coat of size if you plan to repaper the wall.

Mould growth
Mould, typified by black specks, will grow on damp plaster or paper.

When you are faced with a previously papered surface the best solution is to strip it completely before hanging new wallcovering. However, if the paper is perfectly sound, you can paint it with emulsion or oil paints (but be warned: it will be more difficult to remove in the future). If the paper has strong reds, greens or blues or metallic inks in the pattern these may show through the paint; mask them by applying an aluminium spirit-based sealer. Do not paint vinyl wallcovering, except for blown vinyl. If you opt for stripping off the old covering, the method you use will depend on the material and how it has been treated.

Stripping wallpaper

Soak the paper with warm water with a little washing-up liquid or proprietary stripping powder or liquid added to soften the adhesive. Apply the water with a sponge or houseplant sprayer. Repeat and leave the water to penetrate for 15 to 20 minutes.

Use a wide metal-bladed scraper to lift the softened paper, starting at the seams. Take care not to dig the points of the blade into the plaster. Resoak stubborn areas of paper and leave them for a few minutes before stripping. Electricity and water are a lethal combination: where possible, dry-strip around switches and sockets. If the paper cannot be stripped dry, switch off the power at the consumer unit when you come to strip around electrical fittings. Unscrew the faceplates so that you can get at the paper trapped behind. Do not use a sprayer near electrical accessories.

Collect all the stripped paper in plastic sacks, then wash the wall with warm water containing a little detergent. From then on, treat the wall as for plaster.

Scoring washable wallpaper

Washable wallpaper has an impervious surface film, which you must break through to allow the water to penetrate to the adhesive.

Use a toothed perforating wheel, a wire brush or a serrated scraper to score the surface, then soak it with warm water and stripper. It may take several applications of the liquid before the paper begins to lift.

Peeling off vinyl wallcovering

Vinyl wallcovering consists of a thin layer of vinyl fused with a paper backing. It is possible to peel off the vinyl, leaving the backing paper on the wall; the latter can then be either painted or used as a lining for a new wallcovering.

To remove the vinyl, lift both bottom corners of the top layer of the wallcovering, then pull firmly and steadily away from the wall. Either soak and scrape off the backing paper or, if you want to leave it as a lining paper, smooth the seams with medium-grade abrasive paper, using very light pressure to avoid wearing a hole.

Stripping painted wallcoverings

Wallcoverings which have been painted can be difficult to remove. If the paper is sound, simply prepare it in the same way as painted plaster and decorate over it.

To strip it, use a wire brush or home-made scraper (1) to score the surface, then soak with warm water plus a little paper stripper. Painted papers (and washables) can easily be stripped using a steam stripper. Hold the stripper plate against the paper until the steam penetrates, then remove the soaked paper with a wide-bladed scraper (2).

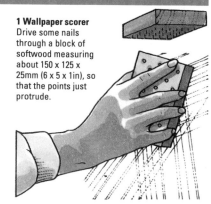

1 Wallpaper scorer
Drive some nails through a block of softwood measuring about 150 x 125 x 25mm (6 x 5 x 1in), so that the points just protrude.

PREPARING WOODWORK

The wooden joinery in our homes needs redecorating long before any other part of the house, particularly bargeboards and fascias and the exterior of windows and doors. The cause is in the nature of the wood itself, which swells when it becomes moist, then shrinks again when the sun or central heating dries it out. Paint will not adhere for long under these conditions, nor will any other finish. Wood is also vulnerable to woodworm and various forms of rot caused primarily by damp, so careful preparation is essential to preserve most types of timber.

Treating new timber

A lot of new joinery is primed at the factory, but check that the primer is in good condition before you begin work: it may be quite some time since the timber was delivered from the factory. If the primer is satisfactory, rub it down lightly with fine-grade abrasive paper, dust it off, then apply a second coat of wood primer to areas that will be inaccessible after installation. Do not leave the timber uncovered outside, as primer is not sufficient protection against prolonged exposure to the weather.

To prepare bare timber, make sure it is dry, then sand the surface in the direction of the grain, using a fine-grade glasspaper (wrap it round a wood block for flat surfaces and a piece of dowel or a pencil for moulded sections).

Once you have removed all raised grain and lightly rounded any sharp edges, dust the wood down. Finally, rub it over with a tack rag (an impregnated cloth to which dust will stick) or with a rag moistened with white spirit.

Seal resinous knots with shellac knotting

Knots and other resinous areas of the wood must be treated to prevent them staining subsequent paint layers. Pick off any hardened resin, then seal the knots by painting them with two coats of shellac knotting if you plan to paint with pale finishing colours; if you will be using darker paints, seal the knots and prime the timber in one operation with aluminium primer.

Alternatively, paint bare softwood with a solvent-based wood primer or a quick-drying water-thinned acrylic primer. Apply either primer liberally, taking care to work it well into the joints

and particularly the end grain (which will require at least two coats to give it adequate protection).

Wash oily hardwoods with white spirit immediately prior to priming with an aluminium primer. Use standard wood primers for other hardwoods, thinning them slightly to encourage penetration into the grain.

When the primer is dry, fill open-grained timber with a fine surface filler. Use a piece of coarse cloth to rub it well into the wood, making circular strokes followed by parallel strokes in the direction of the grain. When the filler is dry, rub it down with a fine abrasive paper to a smooth finish.

Fill larger holes, open joints, cracks and similar imperfections with flexible interior or exterior wood filler. Press the filler into the holes with a filling knife, leaving it slightly proud of the surface so that it can be sanded flush with fine-grade abrasive paper once it has set. Dust down ready for painting. If you find a hole you have missed just before you start applying the undercoat, fill it with putty; unlike other fillers, you can paint straight over putty without having to wait for it to dry, although you should wait until it forms a skin.

Using grain filler

If you plan to clear-finish an open-grained timber, apply a proprietary grain filler after sanding. Use a natural filler for pale timbers: for darker wood, buy a filler that matches the timber. Rub the filler across the grain with a coarse rag, leave to harden for several hours, then rub off the excess along the grain with a clean coarse rag.

Apply grain filler with a coarse rag

Preparing for a clear finish

There is no need to apply knotting when you intend to finish the timber with a clear varnish or lacquer. Sand the wood in the direction of the grain using progressively finer grades of abrasive paper, then seal it with a slightly thinned coat of the intended finish.

If the wood is in contact with the ground or in proximity to previous outbreaks of dry rot, treat it first with a liberal wash of clear timber preserver. Check with the manufacturer's recommendations that the liquid is compatible with the finish.

Cellulose filler would show through a clear finish, so use a proprietary stopper to fill imperfections: these are thick pastes made in a range of colours to suit the type of timber. You can adjust the colour further by mixing the stopper with wood dyes. As stoppers can be oil-based or water-based, make sure you use a similar-based dye. Where possible, use an oil-based stopper outside. Fill the blemishes as before and rub down when the stopper hardens.

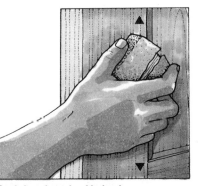

Sand along the grain with abrasive paper

MAN-MADE BOARDS

Versatile and relatively inexpensive, man-made boards are used extensively in the home – most typically for levelling floors, cladding walls, building units for the kitchen and bedroom and for shelving. The type of preparatory treatment that is required before decoration depends upon the nature of the board.

1 Plywood
2 Blockboard
3 Chipboard
4 MDF
5 Hardboard back
6 Hardboard face
7 Fibreboard

Preparing man-made boards for decoration

Wallboards such as plywood, MDF, chipboard, blockboard, hardboard and softboard are all made from timber, but they must be prepared differently from natural timber. Their finish varies according to the quality of the board: some are compact and smooth and may even be presealed ready for painting; others must be filled and sanded before a smooth finish is achieved.

As a rough guide, no primer will be required when using acrylic paints other than a sealing coat of the paint itself, slightly thinned with water. However, any nail or screw heads must be driven below the surface and coated with zinc-phosphate primer to prevent rust stains.

If you are using solvent-based paint, prime the boards first with a general-purpose primer or, for porous softboard, a stabilizing primer. Where possible, you should prime both sides of the board. If the boards are presealed, apply undercoat directly to the surface.

BLEACHING BOARD AND TIMBER

Unevenly coloured or stained board and timber can be bleached before the application of wood dyes and polishes. If possible, try to bleach the entire area rather than an isolated part to avoid a light patch in place of the discoloration.

Two-part bleach
To use a proprietary two-part wood bleach, brush one part on to the wood and apply the second part over the first 10 to 20 minutes later. The bleach is then left to work on the discoloration.

After three to four hours the bleach should have removed the discoloration. Wash it off with water or a mild acid such as white vinegar, according to the manufacturer's instructions.

Bleaching timber
Apply a solution of bleach to stained wood using a paintbrush and leave until the discoloration has disappeared, then wash off with water or vinegar.

A sanded wooden floor sealed with a clear finish that highlights its grain is a most attractive feature for many rooms. Although straightforward, the job is laborious, dusty and extremely noisy. Considerable patience is also required in order to achieve an even, scratch-free and long-lasting finish.

Repairing the floorboards

There is no point in spending time and money sanding floorboards which are in poor condition, so examine them first. Look for any boards with signs of woodworm infestation. If the beetle is still active, treat the remaining boards and joists below with a proprietary woodworm fluid. Even if the beetle has been eradicated, replace any boards that have more than a few holes in them: beneath the surface there may well be a honeycomb of tunnels made by the woodworm larvae. As the process of sanding will remove a lot of timber, these tunnels may be revealed on the surface of the boards.

If you find signs of dry or wet rot when you lift up a floorboard, have it treated straightaway before you make a start on the sanding.

Examine the floor for boards which have been lifted previously by electricians and plumbers. Replace any that are split, too short or badly jointed. Try to find second-hand boards to match the rest of the floor, but if you have to use new wood, stain or bleach it after the floor has been sanded to match the colour of the old boards. Drive all nail heads below the surface with a punch and hammer: a raised head will rip the abrasive paper on the sander's drum.

Sink nail heads below the surface

Filling gaps between the floorboards

What you do about gaps between boards depends on how much they bother you. Many people simply ignore them, but you will end up with a superior job as well as improved draughtproofing if you make the effort to fill them invisibly or close them up.

Closing up
Over a large area, the quickest and most satisfactory solution is to lift the boards a few at a time and re-lay them butted side by side, filling in the final gap with a new board.

Filling with papier mâché
If there are a few gaps only, make up a stiff papier-mâché paste with white newsprint and wallpaper paste, plus a little water-based wood dye to colour it to match the sanded floor. Scrape out dirt and wax from between the boards and press the paste into the gap with a filling knife. Press it well below the level likely to be reached by the sander and fill flush with the floor surface. Run the blade along the gap to smooth it.

Inserting a wooden lath
Large gaps can be filled by a thin wooden lath planed to fit tightly between the boards. Apply a little PVA adhesive to the gap and tap the lath in with a hammer until it is flush with the surface. Skim with a plane if necessary. Do not bother to fill several gaps this way: it is easier to close up the boards and fill one gap with a new floorboard.

Force papier mâché between the boards

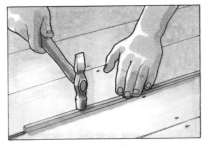
Wedge a wooden lath into a wide gap

CHOOSING A SANDING MACHINE

The area of a floor is far too large to contemplate sanding with anything but an industrial sanding machine. You can obtain such equipment from the usual tool-hire outlets, which also supply the abrasive papers. You will need three grades of paper: coarse, to level the boards initially, followed by medium and fine to achieve a smooth finish.

It is best to hire a large upright drum sander for the main floor area and a smaller rotary sander for tackling the edges. You can use the rotary sander only for smaller rooms such as bathrooms and WCs.

Some companies also supply a scraper for cleaning out inaccessible corners, but do make sure it is fitted with a new blade when you hire it.

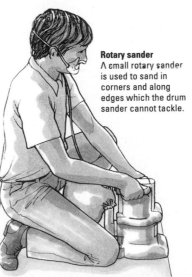

Drum sander
An upright drum sander is used for sanding the main floor area with coarse, medium then fine-grade abrasive papers for a smooth finish.

Rotary sander
A small rotary sander is used to sand in corners and along edges which the drum sander cannot tackle.

SEE ALSO

Hook scraper
Use a small hook scraper for removing paint spots from the floor, and for reaching into spaces that are inaccessible to the rotary sander. The tool cuts on the backward stroke; various sizes and blade shapes are available to deal with most situations.

Fitting the abrasive sheet

Precise instructions for fitting abrasive paper to sanding machines should be included with the hired kit. If they are not, ask the hirer to demonstrate what you need to do. Never attempt to change abrasive papers while a machine is plugged into a socket.

With most machines the paper is wrapped round the drum and secured with a screw-down bar (1). Ensure that the paper is wrapped tightly around the drum: if it is slack it may slip from its clamp and will be torn to pieces.

Rotary sanders take a disc of abrasive, usually clamped to the sole plate by a central nut (2).

1 Drum sander   **2 Rotary sander**

Operating a drum sander

Stand at the beginning of a run with the drum sander tilted back so that the drum itself is clear of the floor. Drape the electric lead over one shoulder to make sure it cannot become caught in the sander.

Switch on the machine, then gently lower the drum on to the floor. There is no need to push a drum sander: it will move forward under its own power. Hold the machine in check so that it proceeds at a slow but steady walking place along a straight line. Do not hold it still for even a brief period as it will rapidly sand a deep hollow in the floorboards. Take care you do not let go of it, either, as it will run across the room on its own, probably damaging the floorboards in the process.

When you reach the other side of the room tilt the machine back, switch off and wait for it to stop before lowering it to the floor.

If the abrasive paper rips, tilt the machine on to its back castors and switch off. Wait for the drum to stop revolving, disconnect the power, then change the paper.

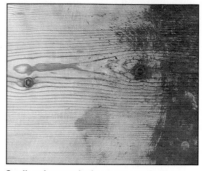

Sanding cleans and rejuvenates wooden floors

Using a rotary sander

Hold the handles on top of the machine and drape the flex over your shoulder. Tilt the sander on to its back castors to lift the disc off the floor. Switch on and lower the machine. As soon as you contact the boards, sweep the machine in any direction, but keep it moving. As soon as it comes to rest the disc will score deep, scorched swirl marks in the wood which are difficult to remove. There is no need to press down on the machine. When you have finished, tilt back the machine and switch off, leaving the motor to run down.

1 Sand diagonally across the floorboards

Sanding procedure

A great deal of dust is produced by sanding a floor, so before you begin empty the room of furniture and take down curtains, lampshades and pictures. Seal around the room door with masking tape and stuff folded newspaper under it. Open all windows. Wear old clothes and a dust mask.

Sweep the floor to remove grit and other debris. Old floorboards will most likely be curved across their width (cupped), so the first task is to level the floor across its entire area.

With coarse paper fitted in the drum sander, sand diagonally across the room (1). At the end of the run, tilt the machine, pull it back and make a second run parallel to the first. Allow each pass to overlap the last slightly.

When you have covered the floor once, sand it again in the same way, but this time across the opposite diagonal of the room (2). Sweep the sawdust from the floor after each run is completed.

Once the floor is flat and clean all over, change to a medium-grade paper and sand parallel to the boards (3). Overlap each pass as before. Finally, switch to the fine-grade paper in order to remove all obvious scratches and give a smooth finish, working parallel to the boards and overlapping each pass again. Each time you change the grade of paper on the drum sander, put the same grade on the rotary sander and sand the edges of the room so that they are finished to the same standard as the main area (4).

Even the rotary sander cannot clean right up to the skirting or into the corners; finish these small areas with a scraper, or fit a flexible abrasive disc in a power drill.

Vacuum the floor and wipe it over with a cloth dampened with white spirit ready for finishing.

2 Sand across the opposite diagonal

3 Sand parallel to the floorboards

4 Finish the edges with the rotary sander

PREPARATION
WOODWORK

LEVELLING
A WOODEN
FLOOR

SEE ALSO

Details for:	
Laying floor tiles	110–113
Laying parquet	114–115
Laying carpet	118
Laying sheet vinyl	120
Ventilation	284
Coping saw	480

Tiles, sheet vinyl and carpet should not be laid directly on to an uneven suspended timber floor; the undulations would cause the tiles or covering to lift or even crack. The solution is to panel over the floorboards with 3mm (⅛in) thick hardboard or, preferably, 6mm (¼in) plywood. The method is identical whichever board you use.

Conditioning boards

Before you seal your floor with plywood or hardboard, make sure that the underfloor ventilation is efficient in order to prevent problems with damp or dry rot. Bear in mind, too, that once the floor is sealed you will not have ready access to underfloor pipework and electric cables, so make sure that these are in good order.

It is important to match the moisture content of the board and the humidity of the room or the board will buckle after it has been laid. If the house is not regularly heated, wet the textured back of hardboard or both sides of plywood with warm water, then leave the sheets stacked back-to-back in the room for 24 hours. If central heating has been in use for some time there is no need to dampen the board: just stack the sheets on edge in the room for 48 hours so that they can adjust to the atmosphere.

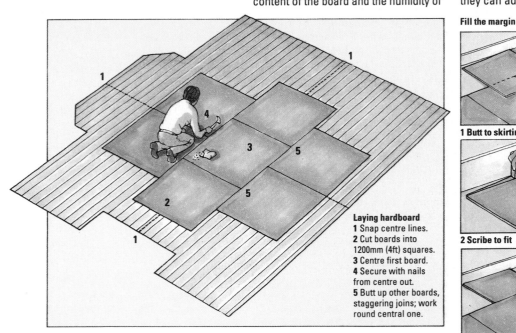

Laying hardboard
1 Snap centre lines.
2 Cut boards into 1200mm (4ft) squares.
3 Centre first board.
4 Secure with nails from centre out.
5 Butt up other boards, staggering joins; work round central one.

Nail hardboard over floorboards
Secure from centre outwards, then fill margin.

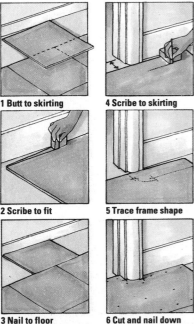

Fill the margin

1 Butt to skirting

2 Scribe to fit

3 Nail to floor

Fit to a doorway

4 Scribe to skirting

5 Trace frame shape

6 Cut and nail down

LAYING A BASE
FOR CERAMIC TILES

A concrete platform is the most suitable base for ceramic floor tiles, but you can lay them on a suspended wooden floor provided the joists are perfectly rigid so that the floor cannot flex. The space below must be adequately ventilated with air bricks to prevent rot. Level the floor using 12mm (½in) plywood and screw it down every 300mm (1ft) for a firm fixing.

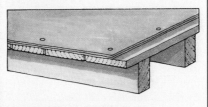

Using plywood over floorboards

Laying the boards

Cut the boards to form 1200mm (4ft) squares. Nail loose floorboards, plane off high points, then sink the nail heads.

Use chalked string to snap two centre lines across the room, crossing at right angles. Lay the first board on the centre, adjusting it so that its edges do not align with the gaps between the floorboards. Unless the flooring manufacturer's instructions state otherwise, lay hardboard rough-side up as a key for the adhesive. Loose-lay the boards in both directions: if the margins will be narrow, reposition them.

Nail the first board to the floor with 20mm (¾in) hardboard pins. Start near the centre of the board and fix it every 150mm (6in) until you get within 25mm (1in) of the edge, then nail around the edge every 100mm (4in). Nail other boards butted up to the first (see above).

To cut edge strips to fit the margin, lay the board on the floor touching the skirting but square to the edges of the nailed boards (**1**). Hold the board firmly and use a block of softwood to scribe along it to fit the skirting (**2**). Cut the scribed line and butt it up to the skirting, then mark the position of the nailed boards on both sides of the edge strip. Join the marks, then cut along this line. Nail the board to the floor (**3**).

To fit into a doorway, butt a board up to the frame and measure to the doorstop. Cut a block of softwood to this size and scribe to the skirting (**4**). Use the same block to trace the shape of the architrave (**5**) and cut the shape with a coping saw. Slide the board into the doorway, mark and cut the other edge to meet the nailed boards, then nail it to the floor (**6**).

● **Shortening a door**
If you level a floor with hardboard or ply, you may have to plane the bottom of the door to provide a new clearance. Take it off its hinges and plane towards the centre from each end. Your carpet supplier will recommend a carpenter who can trim the door *in situ*, using a special circular saw.

Most of the joinery in and around your house will have been painted or varnished at some time and provided it is in good condition it will form a sound base for new paintwork. However, when too many coats of paint have been applied, the mouldings around doorframes and window frames begin to look poorly defined and the paintwork has a lumpy and unattractive appearance. In such a case it is best to strip off all the old paint down to bare wood and start again. Stripping is also essential where the paintwork has deteriorated and is blistering, crazing or flaking.

Liquid sander
You can prepare sound paintwork with a liquid sander; wipe it on to the surface with a cloth or sponge and leave it to soften the top layer of paint slightly, leaving a matt finish. It is an ideal surface on which to apply the new top coat of paint. The chemical cleans and degreases the paintwork, too.

● **Flexible acrylic filler**
An acrylic filler is ideal for filling large cracks or gaps in painted woodwork. It is squeezed into the gap from a cartridge gun and smoothed with a damp cloth – no sanding is required. You can overpaint one hour later.

Dry, flaky paintwork

Heavily overpainted woodwork

Badly weathered varnish

Preparing sound paintwork

Wash the paintwork from the bottom upwards with a solution of warm water and sugar soap or detergent. Pay particular attention to the areas around the door handles and window catches, where dirt and grease will be heaviest. Rinse with fresh water from bottom to top to prevent runs of dirty liquid staining the surface.

Rub down gloss paintwork with fine-grade wet-and-dry abrasive paper dipped in water in order to provide a key for the new finish coat and to remove any blemishes. Prime bare patches of wood. Build up these low spots gradually with undercoat, rubbing down between each application.

Fill open joints or holes with filler and rub down when set. Renew crumbling putty and seal around window frames and doorframes with mastic, then proceed with undercoat and top coat.

Preparing unsound paintwork or varnish

Unsound paintwork or varnish such as the examples pictured left must be stripped to bare wood. There are several methods you can use, but always scrape off loose material first.

In some cases, where the paint is particularly dry and flaky, dry-scraping may be all that is required, using a proprietary hook scraper and finishing with a light rub down with abrasive paper. Where most of the paint is stuck firmly to the woodwork, remove it using one of the methods described below and on the facing page.

Stripping paint and varnish with a blowtorch

The traditional method for stripping old paint is to burn it off with a blowtorch fuelled with liquid gas from a pressurized canister, but you can also obtain more sophisticated blowtorches that are connected by a hose to a metal gas bottle of the type used for camping or in caravans. This type of gas torch is finely adjustable, so is useful for other jobs such as brazing and soldering.

To reduce the risk of fire, take down curtains and pelmets and, outside, rake out old birds' nests from behind your roof fascia board and soffit.

It is only necessary to soften the paint with a flame to scrape it off, but it is all too easy to heat the paint so that it is actually burning. Deposit scrapings in a metal paint kettle or bucket as you remove them.

Start by stripping mouldings from the bottom upwards. Never direct the flame at one spot but keep it moving all the time so that you do not scorch the wood. As soon as the paint has softened, use a shavehook to scrape it off. If it is sticky or hard, heat it a little more then try scraping again.

Having dealt with the mouldings, strip flat areas of woodwork, using a wide-bladed stripping knife. When you have finished stripping, sand the wood with medium-grade abrasive paper to remove hardened specks of paint and any accidental light scorching.

It may prove impossible to sand away heavy scorching without removing too much wood. Sand or scrape off loose blackened wood fibres, fill any hollows and repaint the woodwork, having primed the scorched areas with an aluminium wood primer.

Shavehook, used for mouldings

Scraper, used for flat surfaces

SELECTING AND USING CHEMICAL STRIPPERS

An old finish can be removed using a stripper that reacts chemically with paint or varnish. There are general-purpose strippers that will soften both solvent-based and water-based finishes, including emulsions and cellulose paints, as well as strippers that are formulated to react with a specific type of finish such as textured paint or varnish. Dedicated strippers achieve the desired result more efficiently than general-purpose ones, but at the cost of you having to acquire a whole range of specialist products.

Traditionally, strippers have been manufactured from highly potent chemicals that have to be handled with care. Working with this type of stripper means having to wear protective gloves and safety glasses, and possibly a respirator too. The newer generation of so-called 'green' strippers do not burn your skin nor do they exude harmful fumes. However, removing paint with these milder strippers is a relatively slow process. Whichever type of stripper you decide to use, always follow the manufacturer's health-and-safety recommendations and if in doubt err on the side of caution.

Before you opt for a particular stripper, you should also consider the nature of the surface you intend to strip. The thick, gel-like paint removers that will cling to vertical surfaces such as doors and wall panelling are perfect for all general household joinery. Strippers made to a thinner consistency are perhaps best employed on delicately carved work. For good-quality furniture, especially if it is veneered, make sure you use a stripper that can be washed off with white spirit as water will raise the grain and may soften old glue.

Working with chemical strippers

Lay polyethylene sheets or plenty of newspaper on the floor, then apply a liberal coat of stripper to the paintwork, stippling it well into any mouldings. Leave it for 10 to 20 minutes, then try scraping a patch to see if the paint has softened through to the wood. (You might have to leave one of the milder strippers in contact with the paint for 45 minutes or longer.) Do not waste your time removing the top coats of paint only, but apply more stripper and stipple the partially softened finish back down with a brush so the stripper will soak through to the wood. Leave it for another 5 to 10 minutes.

Once the chemicals have completed their work, use a stripping knife to scrape paint from flat surfaces and a shavehook to remove it from mouldings.

Wipe the paint from deep carvings with fine wire wool, except when stripping oak; use small pieces of coarse sacking for the latter as particles of metal can stain the wood.

Having removed the bulk of the paint, clean off residual patches with a wad of wire wool dipped in fresh stripper. Rub with the grain, turning the wad inside out to present a clean face as it becomes clogged with paint. Neutralize the stripper by washing the wood with white spirit or water, depending on the manufacturer's advice.

Let the wood dry out thoroughly, then prepare it as if it were new timber.

Industrial stripping

Any portable woodwork can be taken to a professional stripper, who will immerse the whole thing in a tank of stripping solution of hot caustic soda which must then be washed out of the wood by hosing down with water. It is an efficient process (which incidentally kills woodworm at the same time), but it risks splitting panels, warping the wood and opening up joints. At best, you can expect a reasonable amount of raised grain, which you will have to sand before refinishing.

Some companies use a cold chemical dip, which does little harm to solid timber and raises the grain less. However, this treatment is likely to prove more expensive than the caustic-soda process.

Most stripping companies will collect; many will rehang a door for you, and some offer a finishing service, too.

Never submit veneered items to industrial treatment: veneers were formerly applied with animal glues, which may be dissolved by the chemical so that the veneer peels off. Instead, strip the items with a chemical stripper and finish off by wiping them with white spirit.

Using a hot-air stripper

Although stripping paint with a flame is fast and efficient, there is always the risk that you will burn the wood. Scorching can be covered with paint, but if you want to varnish the stripped wood scorch marks will mar the finish.

Electrically-heated guns – like powerful hair dryers – work almost as quickly as a blowtorch but with less risk of scorching or fire. They operate at an extremely high temperature: under no circumstances test the stripper by holding your hand over the nozzle.

Some guns come with variable heat settings and a selection of nozzles for various uses (see below). Hold the gun about 50mm (2in) from the surface of the paintwork and move it slowly backwards and forwards until the paint blisters and bubbles. Immediately remove the paint with a shavehook or scraper. Aim to heat the paint just ahead of the scraper so you develop a continuous work action.

Fit a shaped nozzle on to the gun when stripping glazing bars to deflect the jet of hot air and reduce the risk of cracking the glass.

Old primer can sometimes be difficult to remove with a hot-air stripper. This is not a problem if you are repainting the timber; just rub the surface down with abrasive paper. For a clear finish, remove residues of paint from the grain with wads of wire wool dipped in chemical stripper (see left).

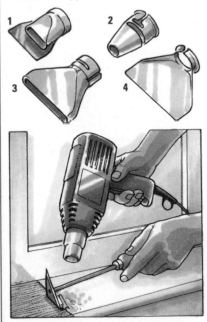

With a hot-air gun there is less risk of scorching

Nozzles for hot-air guns
Hot-air strippers come with a standard wide mouth for general usage. Most manufacturers offer optional extras, typically a push-on nozzle with an integral scraper (1), a conical nozzle to concentrate the heat on a small area (2), a flared nozzle to spread the heat (3) and a nozzle that protects the glass when you strip glazing bars (4).

METALWORK: IRON AND STEEL

Metals are used extensively for window frames, railings, gutters, pipework, radiators and door furniture in both modern and period homes. Areas of metal that are exposed to the elements, or are in close proximity to water, are usually prone to corrosion. Many paints on their own do not afford sufficient protection against corrosion, so special treatments and coatings are often required to prolong the life of the metal.

Cast-iron railings deeply pitted with rust

Flaking casement window as a result of rust

Severely corroded cast-iron drainpipe

What is rust?

Rust is a form of corrosion that affects ferrous metals – notably iron and steel – due to the combination of water, oxygen and carbon dioxide. Although most paints slow down the rate at which moisture penetrates, they do not bar it altogether; primers are needed to complete the protection, and the type you use depends on the condition of the metal and how you plan to decorate it. Make your preparation thorough or the job will be ruined.

Treating bare metal

Remove light deposits of rust by rubbing with wire wool or wet-and-dry abrasive paper dipped in white spirit. If the rust is heavy and the surface of the metal pitted, use a wire brush or, for extensive corrosion, a wire wheel or cup brush in a power drill. Wear goggles while wire-brushing in order to protect your eyes from flying particles.

Use a zinc-phosphate primer to protect metal inside the house. You can use the same primer outdoors, too, but if you are painting previously rusted metal, especially if it is in a very exposed location, use a high-performance rust-inhibitive primer.

Work primers into crevices and fixings, and make sure sharp edges and corners where corrosion often begins are coated generously.

Preparing previously painted metal

If the paint is perfectly sound wash it with sugar soap or a detergent solution, then rinse and dry it. Rub down gloss paint with fine wet-and-dry abrasive paper to provide a key.

If the paint film is blistered or flaking where water has penetrated and corrosion has set in, remove all loose paint and rust with a wire brush or a wire wheel or cup brush in a power drill. Apply rust-inhibitive primer to bare patches, working it well into joints, bolt heads and other fixings. Prime bare metal immediately as rust can re-form very rapidly.

When you are preparing cast-iron guttering, brush out dead leaves and other debris and wash it clean. Coat the inside with a bitumen paint. If you want to paint over old bitumen paint, use an aluminium primer first to prevent it bleeding to the surface.

Stripping painted metal

Delicately moulded sections – on fire surrounds, garden furniture and other cast or wrought ironwork – will often benefit from stripping off old paint and rust which is masking fine detail. They cannot easily be rubbed down with a wire brush and a hot-air stripper cannot be used here as the metal dissipates the heat before the paint softens. A gas blowtorch can be used to strip wrought ironwork, but cast iron might crack if it becomes distorted by localized heating.

Chemical stripping is the safest method, but before you begin check that what appears to be a metal fire surround is not in fact made from plaster mouldings on a wooden background: the stripping process can play havoc with soft plasterwork. Tap the surround to see if it is metallic, or scrape an inconspicuous section.

Paint the bare metal with a rust-inhibitive primer or, alternatively, a proprietary rust-killing jelly or liquid which will remove and neutralize rust: usually based on phosphoric acid, they combine with the rust to leave it quite inert in the form of iron phosphate. Some rust killers will deal with minute particles invisible to the naked eye and are self-priming so that no additional primer is required.

Alternatively, if the metalwork is portable, you can take it to a sandblaster or an industrial stripper. None of the disadvantages of industrial stripping apply to metal.

Clean the stripped metal with a wire brush, then wash it with white spirit before applying a finish.

Corrosion in aluminium

Aluminium does not corrode to the same extent as ferrous metals. Indeed, modern aluminium-alloy window frames and doorframes are designed to withstand weathering without a coat of protective paint. Nevertheless, in adverse conditions, aluminium may corrode to a dull grey and even produce white crystals on the surface.

To remove the corrosion, rub the aluminium with a fine wet-and-dry abrasive paper, using white spirit as a lubricant, until you get back to bright, but not gleaming, metal. Wipe the metal with a cloth dampened with white spirit to remove metal particles and traces of grease. When dry, prime the surface with a zinc-phosphate primer. Never use a primer containing lead on aluminium, as there is likely to be an adverse chemical reaction between the metals in the presence of moisture.

Painting galvanized metal

Galvanized iron and steel has a coating of zinc applied by hot dipping. When new, this provides a poor key for most paints. Leaving the galvanizing to weather for six months will remedy this, but in many cases the manufacturer of galvanized metalwork will have prepared it chemically for instant priming. Check when you purchase it.

Treating chipped galvanizing
Any small rust spots caused by accidental chipping of the zinc coating should be removed by gentle abrasion with wire wool, but take care not to damage the surrounding coating. Wash the area with white spirit, then allow the surface to dry. Prime with zinc-phosphate primer.

Protecting corrugated iron
For long-term protection of corrugated iron, first remove rust deposits, then prime with a bitumen base coat before finishing with a compatible reinforced masonry paint.

Maintaining brass and copper

Ornamental brassware – typically door knobs, fingerplates and other door furniture – should not be painted, especially as there are clear lacquers available which protect it from the elements. Strip painted brass with a chemical stripper; deal with corroded brass as described right.

Copper – mainly plumbing pipework and fittings – does not require painting for protection, but visible pipe runs are usually painted so they blend in with the room decor (it is possible to make a feature of them by polishing, but it is a chore to keep them looking pristine).

Do not just paint on to the bare pipes: degrease and key the surface first with fine wire wool lubricated with white spirit. Wipe away any metal particles with a cloth dampened with white spirit. Apply undercoat and top coats: no primer is required.

Painting over lead

Before decorating old lead pipework, scour the surface first with wire wool dipped in white spirit; no further preparation is required before the application of paint.

Advanced lead corrosion
The cames (grooved retaining strips) of stained-glass windows can become corroded, producing white stains.

Unless the glass is etched, clean the lead with a soap-filled wire wool pad. Wipe the lead clean and wash the glass with warm soapy water.

Darken the lead with a touch of black grate polish on a shoe brush. Brush across the cames, not along them.

Key lead pipes with wire wool before painting

REMOVING CORROSION FROM BRASS FITTINGS

Brass corrodes to a dull brown colour, but the corrosion is normally easy to remove with a standard metal polish. However, if exterior brass door fittings have been left unprotected, deposits build up until they are hard to polish off.

Mix one level tablespoonful each of salt and vinegar in 275ml (½ pint) of hot water. Soften the corrosion by applying liberal washes of the solution to the brass using very fine wire wool.

Wash the metal in hot water containing a little detergent, then rinse and dry it before polishing.

Clean brass with salt-and-vinegar solution

Removing verdigris
Badly weathered brass can develop green deposits called verdigris. This heavy corrosion may leave the metal pitted, so clean it as soon as possible.

Line a plastic bowl with ordinary aluminium cooking foil. Attach a piece of string to each item of brassware, then place in the bowl on top of the foil. Dissolve a cup of washing soda in 2.2 litres (4 pints) of hot water and pour it into the bowl to cover the metalware.

Leave the solution to fizz and bubble for a couple of minutes, then lift out the brass items with the string. Replace any that are still corroded. If necessary, the process can be repeated using fresh solution and new foil.

Rinse the brass with hot water, dry it with a soft cloth, then polish.

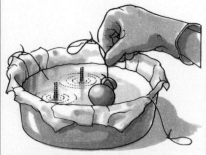
Remove verdigris with a washing-soda dip

TILED
SURFACES

Tiles are used to clad walls, floors and ceilings. They are made in a vast range of materials – ceramic, cork, vinyl and polystyrene being popular – and in a number of different surface textures and finishes. If they are looking shabby it is possible to either revive their existing finish or decorate them with paint or wallcoverings. With some it is even feasible to stick new tiles on top for a completely new look.

Washing maintains the colour of a tiled floor

CLEANING AN OLD QUARRY-TILED FLOOR

Old quarry tiles are absorbent, and the floor becomes ingrained with dirt and grease. If normal washing with detergent fails to revitalize their colour and finish, try one of the industrial preparations available to cleaning and maintenance companies. Suppliers of industrial tile-cleaning materials are listed in the telephone directory. Describe the type and condition of the tiles to the supplier, who will be able to suggest the appropriate cleaner.

Loosen stubborn grimy patches by scrubbing with a plastic scouring pad.

Removing ingrained dirt
Scrub stubborn patches of grime with a plastic scouring pad.

Removing ceramic or quarry tiles
To remove old tiles, first chop out at least one of them with a cold chisel, then prise the others off the surface by driving a bolster chisel behind them. Chop away any remaining tile adhesive or mortar with the bolster.

Ceramic wall and floor tiles

Ceramic tiles are stuck to the wall or floor with a special adhesive or, in the case of quarry tiles, mortar. Removing them in their entirety in order to redecorate the wall is messy and time-consuming, but it is often the most satisfactory long-term solution.

Provided a ceramic-tiled wall is sound, you can paint it with a general-purpose primer followed by a solvent-based paint. Wash the surface thoroughly with sugar-soap or detergent solution. Glazed tiles do not provide a good key for paintwork and you may find that the new surface chips easily.

You can lay new tiles directly over old ones, but make sure the surface is perfectly flat – check by holding a long spirit level or straightedge across the surface. Tap the tiles to locate any loose ones and either glue them firmly in place or chop them out with a cold chisel and club hammer, then fill the space with mortar. Wash the wall to remove grease and dirt.

It is also possible to tile over old quarry or ceramic floor tiles in the same way. Treat an uneven floor with a self-levelling compound.

It is not practicable to paper over old ceramic wall tiles as the adhesive cannot grip on the shiny surface.

Polystyrene ceiling tiles

Polystyrene tiles are stuck directly on to the surface with an adhesive that can be difficult to remove. The adhesive was commonly applied in five small dabs, but this method is no longer approved due to the risk of fire. Manufacturers normally recommend a complete bed of adhesive, which makes it even more difficult to detach them.

Remove the tiles by prising them off with a wide-bladed scraper, then prise off the adhesive dabs. On stubborn patches, try to soften the adhesive with warm water, wallpaper stripper or even paint stripper (but wear goggles and PVC gloves: it is difficult to avoid splashes). For larger areas of adhesive try a solution of ammonia (see below).

One way to give these tiles a facelift is to paint them. Never use a solvent-based paint, which would increase the risk of fire spreading across the tiles. Brush the tiles to remove dust, then apply emulsion paint.

Vinyl floor tiles

Vinyl floor tiles are not a good foundation, so resurface or remove them completely. Soften the tiles and their adhesive with a thermostatically controlled hot-air stripper on a low setting and use a scraper to prise them up. Remove traces of old adhesive by applying a solution of half a cup of household ammonia and a drop of liquid detergent stirred into a bucket of cold water. When the floor is completely clean, rinse it with water.

If vinyl tiles are firmly glued to the floor, clean them and then resurface the floor with a latex self-levelling screed. Before you try this method, however, check the recommendations of your floorcovering manufacturer: this treatment may not make a suitable surface for your new covering.

Cork floor and wall tiles

Dense prefinished wall tiles can be painted directly provided they are clean and firmly attached to the wall. Prime very absorbent cork first with a general-purpose primer before painting over it or thin down emulsion or water-based acrylic paint with water for your first coat in order to reduce absorption.

Unless the tiles are textured or pierced they can be papered over, but size the surface with commercial size or heavy-duty wallpaper paste, then line them horizontally with lining paper to prevent joins showing through.

The advice given above for vinyl floor tiles applies to cork tiles also.

Mineral-fibre ceiling tiles

Acoustic-fibre tiles can be painted with water-based acrylic or emulsion paints. Wash them with a mild detergent, but do not soak the tiles as they are quite absorbent. Conceal stains with an acrylic undercoat before decorating.

In decorating terms, a finish means a liquid or semi-liquid substance which sets, dries or cures to protect and sometimes colour materials such as wood or masonry. Apart from paint, other finishes for wood include stains, varnishes, oil, wax and French polish, all of which are used specifically where you want to display the grain of the timber for its natural beauty.

The make-up of paint

Paint is made from solid particles of pigment suspended in a liquid binder or medium. The pigment provides the colour and body of the paint, while the medium allows the material to be brushed, rolled or sprayed and, once applied, forms a solid film binding the pigment together and adhering to the surface. Binder and pigment vary from paint to paint, but the two most common types are solvent-based (sometimes known as oil-based) and water-based.

COMMON PAINT FINISHES AND ADDITIVES

The type of paint you choose depends on the finish you want and the material you are decorating. Various additives adapt the paint's qualities.

Solvent-based (oil) paints

The medium for solvent-based paints (commonly called oil paints) is a mixture of oils and resin. A paint made from a natural resin is slow-drying, but modern paints contain a synthetic resin such as alkyd, which makes for a faster-drying finish. Various pigments determine the colour of the paint.

Water-based paints

Emulsion is perhaps the most familiar type of water-based paint. It, too, is manufactured with a synthetic resin, usually vinyl, which is dispersed in a solution of water.

Water-based acrylic paints are primarily intended for finishing interior or exterior woodwork. They tend to dry with a semi-matt sheen rather than a full gloss.

Additives in paint

No paint is made simply from binder and pigment; certain additives are included during manufacture to give the paint qualities such as faster drying time, high gloss, easy flow or longer pot life, or to make it non-drip.
● **Thixotropic** paints are the typical non-drip types; they are thick, almost jelly-like in the can, enabling you to pick up a brushload without it dripping.
● **Extenders** are added as fillers to strengthen the paint film. Cheap paint contains too much filler, reducing its covering power.

Paint thinners

If a paint is too thick it cannot be applied properly and must be thinned before it is used. Some finishes, such as low-odour paints, require special thinners provided by the manufacturer, but most oil paints can be thinned with white spirit, and emulsions with water. Turpentine will thin oil paint, but has no advantages over white spirit for household paints and is much more expensive.

Gloss or matt finish?

The proportion of pigment to resin affects the way the paint sets. A gloss (shiny) paint contains approximately equal amounts of resin and pigment, whereas a higher proportion of pigment produces a matt (dull) paint. By adjusting the proportions, it is possible to make satin or eggshell paints. Matt paints tend to cover best due to their high pigment content, while the greater proportion of resin in gloss paints is responsible for their strength.

Applying a paint system

Unless you are using one of the specially formulated one-coat finishes, it is necessary to apply successive layers to build up a paint system.

● Painting walls requires a simple system, comprising two or three coats of the same paint.
● Painting woodwork and metalwork usually involves a more complex system, using paints with different qualities. A typical paint system for woodwork is illustrated below.

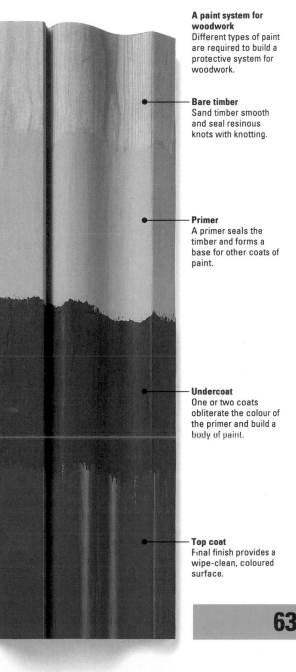

A paint system for woodwork
Different types of paint are required to build a protective system for woodwork.

Bare timber
Sand timber smooth and seal resinous knots with knotting.

Primer
A primer seals the timber and forms a base for other coats of paint.

Undercoat
One or two coats obliterate the colour of the primer and build a body of paint.

Top coat
Final finish provides a wipe-clean, coloured surface.

PAINTING
EXTERIOR
MASONRY

Strain old paint
If you're using leftover paint, filter it through a piece of muslin or old tights stretched over the rim of a container.

Resealing the lid
Wipe the rim of the can clean before you replace the lid, then tap it down all round with a hammer over a softwood block.

SAFETY WHEN PAINTING

DECORATING WITH SOLVENT-BASED PAINT IS NOT DANGEROUS PROVIDED YOU TAKE SENSIBLE PRECAUTIONS.

● Ensure good ventilation indoors while applying a finish and when it is drying. Wear a respirator if you suffer from breathing disorders.
● Do not smoke while painting or in the vicinity of drying paint.
● Contain paint spillages outside with sand or earth and don't allow any paint to enter a drain.
● If you splash paint in your eyes, flush them with copious amounts of water with your lids held open; if symptoms persist, visit a doctor.
● Always wear barrier cream or gloves if you have sensitive skin. Use a proprietary skin cleaner to remove paint from your skin or wash it off with warm soapy water. Do not use paint thinners to clean your skin.
● Keep any finish and thinners out of reach of children. If a child swallows a substance, do not make any attempt to induce him or her to vomit – seek medical treatment instead.

PREPARING THE PAINT

Whether you're using newly purchased paint or leftovers from previous jobs, there are some basic rules to observe before you apply it.
● Wipe dust from the paint can, then prise off the lid with the side of a knife blade. Don't use a screwdriver: it only buckles the edge of the lid, preventing an airtight seal and making subsequent removal difficult.
● Gently stir liquid paints with a wooden stick to blend the pigment and medium. There's no need to stir thixotropic paints unless the medium has separated; if you have to stir it, leave it to gel again before using.
● If a skin has formed on paint, cut round the edge with a knife and lift out in one piece with a stick. It's a good idea to store the can on its lid, so that a skin cannot form on top of the paint.
● Whether the paint is old or new, transfer a small amount into a paint kettle or plastic bucket. Old paint should be filtered at the same time, tying a piece of muslin or old nylon tights across the rim of the kettle.

The outside walls of houses are painted for two major reasons: to give a clean, bright appearance and to protect the surface from the rigours of the climate. What you use as a finish and how you apply it depends on what the walls are made of, their condition and the degree of protection they need. Bricks are traditionally left bare, but may require a coat of paint if previous attempts to decorate have resulted in a poor finish. Rendered walls are often painted to brighten the naturally dull grey colour of the cement; pebbledashed surfaces may need a colourful coat to disguise previous conspicuous patches. On the other hand, you may just want to change the present colour of your walls for a fresh appearance.

Working to a plan

Before you embark upon painting the outside walls of your house, plan your time carefully. Depending on the amount of preparation that is required, even a small house will take a few weeks to complete.

It is not necessary to tackle the whole job at once – although it is preferable, as the weather may change to the detriment of your timetable. You can split the work into separate stages with days (even weeks) in between, provided you divide the walls into manageable sections. Use window frames and doorframes, bays, downpipes and corners of walls to form break lines that will disguise joins.

Start at the top of the house, working from right to left if you are right-handed and vice versa.

● Black dot denotes compatibility. All surfaces must be clean, sound, dry and free from organic growth.

FINISHES FOR MASONRY

	Cement paint	Water-based masonry paint	Reinforced masonry paint	Solvent-based masonry paint	Textured coating	Floor paint
SUITABLE TO COVER						
Brick	●	●	●	●	●	●
Stone	●	●	●	●	●	●
Concrete	●	●	●	●	●	●
Cement rendering	●	●	●	●	●	●
Pebbledash	●	●	●	●	●	●
Emulsion paint		●	●	●	●	●
Solvent-based paint			●	●		●
Cement paint	●	●	●	●	●	●
DRYING TIME: HOURS						
Touch dry	1–2	1–2	2–3	4–6	6	2–3
Recoatable	24	4–6	24	16	24–48	3–16
THINNERS: SOLVENTS						
Water	●	●	●		●	●
White spirit			●	●		●
NUMBER OF COATS						
Normal conditions	2	2	1–2	2	1	1–2
COVERAGE: DEPENDING ON WALL TEXTURE						
Sq metres per litre		4–10	3–6.5	6–16	2	5–10
Sq metres per kg	1–6				1–2	
METHOD OF APPLICATION						
Brush	●	●	●	●	●	●
Roller	●	●	●	●		●
Spray gun	●	●	●	●		

SUITABLE PAINTS FOR EXTERIOR MASONRY

There are various grades of paint suitable for decorating and protecting exterior masonry which take into account economy, standard of finish, durability and coverage. Use the chart opposite for quick reference.

Cement paint

Cement paint is supplied as a dry powder, to which water is added. It is based on white cement, but pigments are added to produce a range of colours. Cement paint is one of the cheaper paints suitable for exterior use. Spray new or porous surfaces with water before applying two coats.

Mixing cement paint
Shake or roll the container to loosen the powder, then add 2 volumes of powder to 1 of water in a clean bucket. Stir it to a smooth paste, then add a little more water until you achieve a full-bodied, creamy consistency. Mix up no more than you can use in one hour, or it will start to dry.

Adding an aggregate
When you are painting a dense wall or one treated with a stabilizing solution so that its porosity is substantially reduced, it is advisable to add clean sand to the mix to give it body. It also provides added protection for an exposed wall and helps to cover dark colours. If the sand changes the colour of the paint, add it to the first coat only. Use 1 part sand to 4 parts powder, stirring it in when the paint is still in its paste-like consistency.

Masonry paints

When buying weather-resistant exterior-masonry paints you have a choice between a smooth matt finish or a fine granular texture.

Water-based masonry paint
Most masonry paints are water-based, being in effect exterior-grade emulsions with additives that prevent mould growth. They are supplied ready for use, but in fact it pays to thin the first coat on porous walls with 20 per cent water. Follow up with one or two full-strength coats, depending on the colour of the paint.

Water-based masonry paints must be applied during fairly good weather. Damp or humid conditions and low temperatures may prevent the paint drying properly.

Solvent-based masonry paints
Some masonry paints are thinned with white spirit or with a special solvent, but unlike most oil paints they are moisture-vapour permeable so that the wall is able to breathe. It is often advisable to thin the first coat with 15 per cent white spirit, but check with the manufacturer's recommendations .

Solvent-based paints can be applied in practically any weather conditions, provided it is not actually raining.

Reinforced masonry paint
Masonry paint that has powdered mica or a similar fine aggregate added to it dries with a textured finish that is extremely weatherproof. Reinforced masonry paints are especially suitable in coastal districts and in industrial areas – where dark colours are also an advantage in that dirt will not show up so clearly as on a pale background. Although large cracks and holes must be filled prior to painting, reinforced masonry paint will cover hairline cracks and crazing.

Textured coating

A thick textured coating can be applied to exterior walls to form a thoroughly weatherproof, self-coloured coating which can also be overpainted to match other colours. The usual preparation is necessary and brickwork should be pointed flush. Large cracks should be filled, although a textured coating will cover fine cracks. The paste is brushed or rolled onto the wall, then left to harden, forming an even texture. However, if you prefer, you can produce a texture of your choice using a variety of simple tools. It is an easy process, but put in some practice on a small section first.

Concrete floor paints

Floor paints are specially prepared to withstand hard wear. They are especially suitable for concrete garage or workshop floors, but they are also used for stone paving, steps and other concrete structures. They can be used inside for playroom floors.

The floor must be clean, dry and free from oil or grease. If the concrete is freshly laid, allow it to mature for at least a month before painting. Prime powdery or porous floors with a proprietary concrete sealer.

The best way to paint a large area is to use a paintbrush around the edges, then fit an extension to a paint roller for the bulk of the floor.

Apply paint with a roller on an extension

Paint in manageable sections
You can't hope to paint an entire house in one session, so divide each elevation into manageable sections to disguise the joins. The horizontal moulding divides the wall neatly into two sections, and the raised door and window surrounds are convenient break lines.

65

TECHNIQUES
FOR PAINTING
MASONRY

1 Cut in with a gentle scrubbing motion

3 Use a banister brush
Tackle deeply textured wall surfaces with a banister brush, using a scrubbing action.

4 Use a roller
For speed in application, use a paint roller with a deep pile for heavy textures and a medium pile for light textures and smooth wall surfaces.

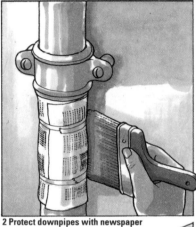

2 Protect downpipes with newspaper

5 Spray onto the apex of external corners

6 Spray internal corners as separate surfaces

Using paintbrushes

Choose a 100 to 150mm (4 to 6in) wide paintbrush for walls; larger ones are heavy and tiring to use. A good-quality brush with coarse bristles will last longer on rough walls. For a good coverage, apply the paint with vertical strokes, criss-crossed with horizontal ones. You will find it necessary to stipple paint into textured surfaces.

Cutting in

Painting up to a feature such as a doorframe or window frame is known as cutting in. On a smooth surface, you should be able to paint a reasonably straight edge following the line of the feature, but it's difficult to apply the paint to a heavily textured wall with a normal brush stroke. Don't just apply more paint to overcome the problem; instead, touch the tip of the brush only to the wall, using a gentle scrubbing action (1), then brush excess paint away once the texture is filled.

Wipe splashed paint from window frames and doorframes with a cloth dampened with the appropriate thinner.

Painting behind pipes

To protect rainwater downpipes, tape a roll of newspaper around them. Stipple behind the pipe with a brush, then slide the paper tube down the pipe to mask the next section (2).

Painting with a banister brush

Use a banister brush (3) to paint deep textures such as pebbledash. Pour some paint into a roller tray and dip the brush in to load it. Scrub the paint onto the wall using circular strokes to work it well into the uneven surface.

Using a paint roller

A roller (4) will apply paint three times faster than a brush. Use a long-pile roller for heavy textures and a medium-pile for lightly textured or smooth walls. Rollers wear out very quickly on rough walls, so have a spare sleeve handy. Vary the angle of the stroke when using a roller to ensure an even coverage, and use a brush to cut into angles and obstructions.

A paint tray is difficult to use at the top of a ladder unless you fit a tool support, or, better still, erect a flat platform from which to work.

Using a spray gun

Spraying is the quickest and most efficient way to apply paint to a large expanse of wall, but you will have to mask all the parts you do not want to paint, using newspaper and masking tape, and erect plastic screening to prevent overspray. Thin the paint by about 10 per cent and set the spray gun according to the manufacturer's instructions to suit the particular paint. It is advisable to wear a respirator.

Hold the gun about 225mm (9in) away from the wall and keep it moving with even, parallel passes. Slightly overlap each pass and try to keep the gun pointing directly at the surface – tricky while standing on a ladder. Trigger the gun just before each pass and release it at the end of the stroke.

When spraying a large, blank wall, paint it with vertical bands, overlapping each band by 100mm (4in).

Spray external corners by aiming the gun directly at the apex so that paint falls evenly on both surfaces (5). When two walls meet at an internal angle, treat each surface separately (6).

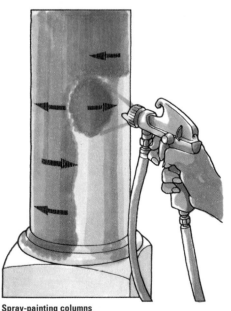

Spray-painting columns
Columns (such as those forming part of a front door portico, for example) should be painted in a series of overlapping vertical bands. Apply the bands by running the spray gun from side to side as you work down the column.

Unless the house has been recently built, most of the interior walls and ceilings will be plastered and probably papered or painted too. Preparation varies, but the methods for painting them are identical and they can be considered smooth surfaces in terms of paint coverage. A matt paint is usually preferred, but there's no reason why you shouldn't use a gloss or satin finish.

Finishes for bare masonry

Some interior walls are left unplastered, either for the sake of a decorative appearance or because it is considered unnecessary to clad the walls of certain rooms such as the basement, workshop or garage. Some have been deliberately stripped for effect – a brick or stone chimney breast, for example, acts as an attractive focal point in a room, and an entire wall of bare masonry can make a dramatic impression.

If you want to finish brick, concrete or stone walls, follow the methods described for exterior walls. However, because in this case they do not have to withstand any weathering, you can use paint designed for interiors. Newly stripped masonry will require sealing first with a stabilizing primer in order to bind the surface.

SELECTING PAINTS FOR INTERIOR SURFACES

Emulsion paint is most people's first choice for internal decorations: it is relatively cheap, practically odourless and there are several qualities of paint to suit different circumstances. However, some situations demand a combination of paints to provide the required degree of protection or simply to achieve a pleasing contrast of surface textures.

Emulsion paints

Vinyl emulsions are the most popular and practical paints for walls and ceilings. They are available in liquid or thixotropic consistencies, with matt or satin (semi-gloss) finishes. A satin emulsion is less likely to show fingerprints or scuffs, and non-drip thixotropic paints have obvious advantages when painting ceilings.

One-coat emulsion
You will need to apply two coats of standard emulsion to avoid a patchy, uneven appearance, perhaps thinning the first coat slightly when decorating porous surfaces. A one-coat high-opacity emulsion is intended to save you time, but you will not get satisfactory results if you try to spread the paint too far, especially when overpainting strong colours.

New-plaster emulsion
New-plaster emulsions are specially formulated for new interior walls and ceilings to allow moisture vapour to escape. Standard vinyl emulsions are not sufficiently permeable.

Gloss and satin paints

Paints primarily intended for woodwork can be applied to walls and ceilings that require an extra degree of protection, and similar paints are ideal for decorating the disparate elements of a period-style dado – wooden rail, skirting and embossed wallcovering.

Gloss paints tend to accentuate uneven wall surfaces, so most people prefer a satin (eggshell) finish.

You can use any of the standard spirit-thinned paints on walls and ceilings, but for a faster drying time choose water-based acrylic paints.

Textured paints

Provided the masonry or plaster is basically sound, you can obliterate any unsightly cracks with just one coat of textured paint. A coarse high-build paint will cover cracks up to 2mm (1⁄16in) wide, but there are also fine-texture paints for areas where people may brush against the wall. Available with a matt or satin finish, the paint is normally applied with a coarse-foam roller, but you can use a synthetic-fibre roller if you want to create a finer texture.

Cement paint

Cement paint is an inexpensive exterior finish which is ideal for a utilitarian area indoors, such as a cellar, workshop or garage. Sold in dry-powder form, it must be made up with water and dries to a matt finish.

A painted decorative dado adds character to an old house

Paints for walls and ceilings
Emulsion paint, in its many forms, is the most practical finish for interior walls and ceilings, but use an acrylic or solvent-based paint on wall-fixed joinery like skirtings and picture rails. The example above illustrates the advantage of contrasting textures: matt emulsion for the walls up to the cornice; gloss paint for the dado rail and skirting; satin emulsion for the embossed dado.

USING BRUSHES, PADS AND ROLLERS

Applying paint by brush

Choose a good-quality brush for painting walls and ceilings. Cheap brushes tend to shed bristles, which is both infuriating and less economical in the long run. A brush about 200mm (8in) wide will give the quickest coverage, but if you are not used to handling a brush your wrist will soon tire; you may find a 150mm (6in) brush, plus a 50mm (2in) brush for the edges and corners, more comfortable to use, although the job will take longer.

Loading the brush
Don't overload a brush with paint; it leads to messy work and ruins the bristles if the paint is allowed to dry in the roots. Dip no more than the first third of the brush into the paint, wiping off excess on the side of the container to prevent drips (1). When using thixotropic paint, load the brush and apply paint without removing excess.

Using a brush
You can hold the brush whichever way feels comfortable to you, but the 'pen' grip is the most versatile, enabling your wrist to move the brush freely in any direction. Hold the brush handle between your thumb and forefinger, with your fingers on the ferrule (metal band) and your thumb supporting it from the other side (2).

Apply the paint in vertical strokes, then spread it at right angles to even out the coverage. Emulsion paint will not show brush marks when it dries, but finish oil paints with light upward vertical strokes for the best results.

1 Dip only the first third of bristles in paint

2 Place fingers on ferrule, thumb behind

Applying paint by roller

A paint roller with interchangeable sleeves is an excellent tool for applying paint to large areas. Choose a roller about 225mm (9in) long for painting walls and ceilings. Larger ones are available, but they become tiring to use.

There are a number of different sleeves to suit the type of paint and texture of the surface. Long-haired sheepskin and synthetic-fibre sleeves are excellent on textured surfaces, especially with emulsion paint. Choose a shorter pile for smooth surfaces, and with gloss or satin paints.

Disposable plastic-foam rollers can be used to apply some specialist paints, but they soon lose their resilience and have a tendency to skid across the wall.

Special rollers
Rollers with long detachable extension handles are ideal for painting ceilings without having to erect a work platform.

Narrow rollers for painting behind radiators are invaluable if the radiators cannot be removed from the wall.

Loading a roller
You will need a special paint tray to load a standard roller. Having dipped the sleeve lightly into the paint reservoir, roll it gently onto the ribbed part of the tray to coat the roller evenly (1).

Using a roller
Use zig-zag strokes with a roller (2), painting the surface in all directions to achieve an even coverage. Keep the roller on the surface at all times. If you let it spin at the end of a stroke it will spatter paint onto the floor or adjacent surface. When applying oil paint, finish in one direction, preferably towards prevailing light.

1 Dip roller in paint, roll onto ribbed tray

2 Apply in zig-zags, finish in one direction

Applying paint by pad

1 Loading a paint pad
Load the pad evenly by drawing it across the integral roller on the tray without squeezing.

Paint pads for large surfaces have flat rectangular faces covered with a short mohair pile. A plastic-foam backing gives the pad flexibility so that the pile will always be in contact with the wall, even on a rough surface.

The exact size of the pad will be determined by the brand you choose, but one about 200mm (8in) long is best for applying paint evenly and smoothly to walls and ceilings. You will also need a small pad or paintbrush for cutting in at corners and ceilings.

Loading a pad
Load a pad from its own special tray, drawing the pad across the captive roller so that you pick up an even amount of paint (1).

Using a pad
To apply the paint consistently, keep the pad flat on the wall and sweep it gently and evenly in any direction (2). Use criss-cross strokes for emulsion, but finish oil paints with vertical strokes to prevent streaking.

2 Sweep pad gently in any direction

APPLYING PAINT TO WALLS AND CEILINGS

SEE ALSO

Details for:	
Work platforms	42
Primers	43
Preparing masonry	44–46
Preparing paint surfaces	48, 50
Preparing concrete	49
Preparing plaster	50–51
Stripping wallpaper	52
Consumer unit	304

Even the most experienced decorator can't help dripping a little paint, so always paint the ceiling before the walls. Erect a work platform so you can cover as much of the surface as possible without changing position: you will achieve a better finish and will be able to work in safety. Choose your tools wisely and follow a strict working routine for the best effects. Refer to the chart below for professional results.

● Black dot denotes compatibility.
All surfaces must be clean, sound, dry and free from organic growth.

FINISHES FOR INTERIOR WALLS & CEILINGS

	Emulsion	One-coat emulsion	New-plaster emulsion	Solvent-based paint	Acrylic paint	Textured paint	Cement paint
SUITABLE TO COVER							
Plaster	●	●	●	●	●	●	●
Wallpaper	●	●	●	●	●		
Brick	●	●	●	●	●	●	●
Stone	●	●	●	●	●	●	●
Concrete	●	●	●	●	●	●	●
Previously painted surface	●	●	●	●	●	●	
DRYING TIME: HOURS							
Touch dry	1-2	3–4	1–2	2–4	1–2	24	1–2
Recoatable	4		4	16–18	4		24
THINNERS: SOLVENTS							
Water	●	●	●		●		●
White spirit				●			
NUMBER OF COATS							
Normal conditions	2	1	2	1–2	1–2	1	2
COVERAGE: APPROXIMATE							
Sq metres per litre	9–15	8 -	11	15–16	10–14	2–3	
Sq metres per kg							1–6
METHOD OF APPLICATION							
Brush	●	●	●	●	●	●	●
Roller	●	●	●	●	●	●	●
Spray gun	●	●	●	●	●		

Painting the walls

Use a small brush to paint the edges, starting at a top corner of the room. If you are right-handed work from right to left and vice versa. Paint an area of about 600mm (2ft) square at a time. When using emulsion, paint in horizontal bands (1), but with gloss paints use vertical strips (2) as the junctions are more likely to show unless you blend in the wet edges quickly. Always finish a complete wall before you take a break as otherwise a change of tone will show between separate painted sections.

1 Paint emulsion in horizontal bands

2 Apply oil paints in vertical strips

Painting the ceiling

Start in a corner near the window and carefully paint along the edges with a small paintbrush.

Paint around the edges first

Working from the wet edges, paint in 600mm (2ft) wide bands, working away from the light. Whether you use a brush, pad or a roller, apply each fresh load of paint just clear of the previous application, then blend in the junctions for even coverage.

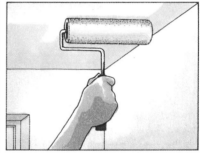

Blend in the wet edges

Electrical fittings

Unscrew a ceiling-rose cover so that you can paint right up to the backplate with a small brush. Loosen the faceplate or mounting box of sockets and switches to paint behind them.

Remember: switch off at the mains before exposing electrical connections.

Unscrew rose cover to keep it clean

69

DECORATIVE
EFFECTS

Decorative effects with paint, once common practice, can be applied to walls, ceilings, furniture and joinery to give an individual look to a scheme. Some of the more complex effects – traditionally the domain of the skilled craftsman – are made easier to achieve using modern materials.

The importance of practice
Although some of the techniques are easy, it is worth practising them on a piece of flat board before you tackle a whole room. The texture of the actual wall might influence the finished effect, but at least you will be familiar with the basic techniques. If the result is not to your satisfaction, don't worry – you can always paint or paper over it.

Applying a basecoat
Although many decorative effects can be applied successfully to woodwork, some are best when applied to a flat plaster surface, and thorough preparation is essential as with any decoration. Any of the following finishes require a flat basecoat in your choice of colour. This initial coat is applied by brush, roller or paint pad and left to dry.

Decorated walls and woodwork
(Top)
The use of pattern and painted textures give this period interior a unique character.

Decorated walls
(Bottom)
The walls of this cottage have been transformed by the application of painted swirls and stencilled borders.

SPATTERING AND SPONGE STIPPLING

SEE ALSO

Details for:	
Paints	67
Brushes	498

Spattering

Achieve a speckled effect by spattering two or three contrasting colours onto an emulsion background. When planning your colour scheme, consider the background as your dominant colour. Cover the floor with dustsheets and mask doors, windows and electrical fittings.

For the spatter colours, use acrylic or solvent-based paints thinned to the required consistency; this is best achieved by trial and error on your practice board. Don't make the paint too thin or your speckled effect will become a mass of runs. If an accident occurs, blot the paint immediately with absorbent paper and allow it to dry. Obliterate the mistake by dabbing with a sponge dipped in the base colour.

Take a stiff-bristle banister brush, and dip only the tips of the bristles into the paint. Holding the brush about 100mm (4in) from the wall, drag a ruler towards you, across the bristles: this flicks tiny drops of paint onto the surface (1). Produce an even or random coverage as you prefer, but avoid concentrating the effect in one place. When the first spatter coat is dry, apply other colours in turn.

You can decorate furniture, picture frames and other small objects with speckled paint sprayed from an aerosol can. Having achieved the required coverage and texture, seal and protect the colour by overspraying with the transparent acrylic top coat that is supplied with the kit.

The speckled effect of spattering

1 Spatter paint
Produce a speckled effect by drawing a ruler across a stiff-bristle brush.

Sponge stippling

Stipple textures onto an emulsion background with a natural sponge. Use a dark-toned emulsion paint to stipple over a lighter base colour for a two-tone effect. When selecting the paint, remember that the base colour will be the dominant colour in the room.

Dampen a natural sponge with water until it swells to its full size. Squeeze out excess water to leave it moist. Pour a tablespoonful of paint into a shallow tray and dip the sponge into it. Touch off

excess paint onto a piece of plain scrap paper until it leaves the required mottled effect, then apply the sponge lightly to the wall (2).

Do not press hard or the sponge will leave a patch of almost solid paint. Group the impressions closely to form an even texture across the wall. If any area appears too dark when dry, stipple base colour over it to tone it down.

When the first stipple coat has dried, sponge another tone or colour over it.

Subtle textures with sponge stippling

2 Sponge stipple
Apply a delicate stipple texture by patting a paint-dampened sponge on the wall.

Spattered paintwork
(Bottom left)
The walls and radiator have been treated with the spattering technique to unify them into the general colour scheme.

Sponge stippling
(Bottom right)
Sponged blue walls harmonize with the colours in the print and table setting.

STIPPLING, BAG GRAINING & RAG ROLLING

SEE ALSO

Details for:	
Colour schemes	24–37
Preparing plaster	50–51
Paints	67
Painting walls	67–69

1 Rag stipple
Create vivid stipple textures using a crumpled cotton rag.

2 Stipple off with a rag-filled plastic bag

3 Rag rolling
Roll off a dark finish to reveal the paler basecoat.

Bag graining
(Bottom left)
The textured paintwork makes an impressive feature of this alcove fitting.

Rag rolling
(Bottom right)
Subtle colouring and textures suit a period-style interior.

Rag stippling

Although the technique is similar, stippling with cotton rag instead of a sponge produces a more vivid effect. Crumple a piece of rag into a ball and dip it into the paint until it is saturated. Squeeze it out and stipple a creased part of the ball onto scrap paper. When you achieve the required effect, apply the rag lightly to the wall **(1)**.

Use different parts of the ball as you work across the wall and refold it to vary the pattern. Stipple out mistakes using a clean rag dipped in base colour once the first stipple coat is dry.

Bag graining

Bag graining removes paint from the wall instead of applying it. Use a darker paint over a pale emulsion background. It is more convenient if two people work together, one to apply the paint while the other patterns it.

Dilute emulsion paint with about 50 per cent water, mixing enough paint to cover at least one complete wall at a time. Before you start, use newspaper and masking tape to cover areas you don't want to paint.

Use a wide brush to apply the diluted paint over the base colour. Take care to avoid runs. After you have applied a band of paint about 600mm (2ft) wide, take a plastic bag half-filled with rags and use it to stipple the wet paint **(2)**. Overlap each impression to produce an overall effect. As paint builds up on the bag, wipe it off onto a piece of rag.

Your helper should work just ahead of you, applying fresh paint so that you can texture it before it dries.

Rag rolling

Also known as scumbling, rag rolling is a technique similar to bag graining. You will need a helper to paint bands of diluted colour ahead of you. The best results are achieved with a basecoat of pale satin solvent-based paint overlaid with a darker satin solvent-based paint diluted by 50 per cent.

Fold a piece of rag into quarters, then twist it into a roll. Starting at the bottom of the wall, roll the rag upwards to remove wet paint, producing a texture resembling watered silk **(3)**.

As you reach the ceiling, use the roll to stipple the margin. If you blot the ceiling, remove paint immediately with a clean rag dampened with white spirit.

Start the next band of texturing at the bottom again, but don't attempt to produce straight strips of pattern. Change direction constantly to overlap and blend with previous impressions. Remake the rolled rag each time it becomes impregnated with paint.

Rag stippling creates a vivid effect

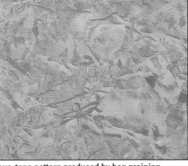

Two-tone pattern produced by bag graining

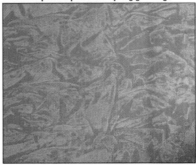

Rag rolling resembles watered silk

Mottling and veining

Producing a marble-like effect with paint is not an easy technique to master, so be prepared to experiment on a practice board until you achieve a convincing result. Study some examples of marble, taking note of the basic colours and tones involved, then choose a limited colour range which you can mix to produce a variety of similar hues.

Artist's oil paints are the best materials to use for marbling as they take a long time to dry (it's necessary to work the whole effect with wet paint) and they blend extremely well. Student oils are relatively cheap, but if you want to marble a large area you may prefer to use ordinary solvent-based paints instead: satin paints are probably best.

Starting with an oil glaze

A transparent oil glaze, obtainable from a specialist paint supplier, is the best material to use for the basecoat and as a medium for the marbling paints. Dip a clean lint-free rag into the glaze and rub it evenly over the surface of the wall. A light coating is usually quite sufficient to achieve the best effect.

Applying a mottled pattern

Mix up one or two colour washes using oil paints and glaze. Use a 25mm (1in) paintbrush to paint uneven patches onto the wet glazed surface.

Space them randomly, overlapping colours and tones. Take the rag used to apply the glaze and stipple the patches to blend them and lose any distinct edges.

Complete the mottled effect with a clean, soft-bristled paintbrush, sweeping it very gently back and forth across the paintwork to produce delicately softened areas of shaded colour. Adjust the tone of areas that are too dark by applying small patches of lighter paint on top, then blend them in again.

Forming the veining

Use an artist's paintbrush to draw on the veins using colour washes mixed as for mottling. Veins are best freely painted with varying thicknesses of line. Note carefully the branching lines typical of marble veining.

Blot any thick paint carefully with an absorbent tissue, then blur the veins by brushing back and forth with a soft paintbrush until they appear as subtle, soft-edged lines.

Sealing with varnish

Allow the marbled paintwork to dry thoroughly, then paint on a coat of semi-gloss polyurethane varnish. When the varnish has set hard, burnish the wall with a soft cloth to raise a delicate sheen. If necessary, you can modify the finish by applying a little wax polish.

Mottled effects suggest some types of marble

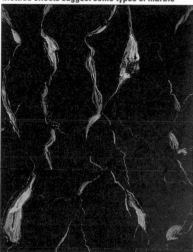

Freely painted strokes resemble veining

Mottled marbling
(Bottom left)
Dramatic marbling endows this interior with a sense of opulence.

Veined marbling
(Bottom right)
Veined marbling is an appropriate treatment for a bathroom in an old house.

STENCILLING AND MASKING

1 Cutting a stencil

2 Stippling with paint

3 Paint a clean edge
Use masking tape to define a line; brush paint away from the tape to avoid a thick edge forming.

4 Striping tape
Paint bands of colour with striping tape.

Stencilling

Ready-made paper stencils for painting patterns or motifs onto a wall are available from artists' suppliers. If you cannot find a stencil which suits your purpose, buy blank sheets of stencil paper from the same outlets and cut your own design with a sharp scalpel (**1**). Design your stencil with thin strips that hold the shapes together.

Ordinary emulsion paint is ideal for stencilling, but you will need a special stencil brush. It has short stiff bristles and is used with a stippling action (**2**).

Mark out the wall lightly to position the stencil accurately. At the same time, make small marks to indicate the position of repeat patterns. Use small pieces of masking tape to hold the stencil on the wall.

Spoon a little paint onto a flat board. Take a stencil brush and touch the tips of the bristles into the paint. Stipple excess paint onto waste paper until it deposits paint evenly, then transfer it to the wall.

Hold the stencil flat against the wall. Stipple the edges of the motif first, then fill in the centre. If necessary, apply a second coat immediately to build up the required depth of colour. When the motif is complete, hold the stencil perfectly still while you slowly peel it away from the wall. Wipe traces of paint from the back of the stencil before repositioning it to repeat the motif.

If paint has crept under the stencil, try dabbing it off with a piece of absorbent paper rolled into a thin taper, and touch in with background paint. Alternatively, allow the paint to become touch-dry, then scrape it carefully away with a scalpel blade.

A random repeat pattern of stencilled birds and butterflies creates an illusion of open skies

Masking straight edges

Use low-tack masking tape when you want to paint two areas of colour, or even a coloured band, perhaps, to finish off a painted dado. This tape can be peeled off without removing the painted surface below. Don't use ordinary transparent adhesive tape.

Marking the line
Draw straight horizontal lines, using a batten and a spirit level as a guide. Vertical lines can be marked on a wall by snapping a chalked plumb line against the surface.

Painting the edge
Run masking tape along one side of the marked line, taking care not to stretch or curve the tape. Using a small brush, paint away from the tape so that you do not build a thick edge of paint against it, which could peel off with the tape (**3**). Complete the rest of the wall with a roller or brush.

Peel off the tape when the paint is touch-dry. Pull back and away from the edge to leave a clean line. If you happen to pull away specks of paint, touch in with an artist's paintbrush.

Painting a band of colour
To paint a band of colour, complete the background, then mask the top and bottom of the band. Apply the paint and when touch-dry, remove both tapes.

Alternatively, use striping tape designed to paint lines on car bodies. Once the tape is applied to the wall, the centre section is peeled away, leaving a gap between two masked edges, which you fill in with paint (**4**).

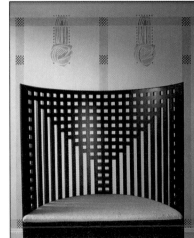

Stencilled Art Nouveau motifs with masked border

Stencilled floral borders brighten this hallway

Masked borders simulate panel mouldings

TEXTURED
COATINGS

APPLYING TEXTURED COATING

You can apply the coating with either a roller or broad wall brush: finer textures are possible using the latter. Buy a special roller if recommended by the coating manufacturer.

With a well-loaded roller, apply a generous coat in a 600mm (2ft) wide band across the ceiling or down a wall. Do not press too hard and vary the angle of the stroke.

If you decide to brush on the coating, do not spread it out like paint. Lay it on with one stroke and spread it back again with one or two strokes only.

Texture the first band, then apply a second band and blend them together before texturing the latter. Continue in this way until the wall or ceiling is complete. Keep the room ventilated until the coating has hardened.

Painting around fittings
Use a small paintbrush to fill in around electrical fittings and along edges, trying to copy the texture used on the surrounding wall or ceiling. Some people prefer to form a distinct margin around fittings by drawing a small paintbrush along the perimeter to give a smooth finish.

Creating a texture
You can experiment with a variety of tools to make any number of textures. Try a coarse expanded-foam roller or one made with a special surface to produce diagonal or diamond patterns; alternatively, apply a swirling, ripple or stipple finish with improvised equipment, as shown on the right.

Textured coatings can be obtained as a dry powder for mixing with warm water or in a ready-mixed form for direct application from the tub. They are available in a range of standard colours, but if none of them suit your decorative scheme you can use ordinary emulsion as a finish. Textured coatings are suitable for both exterior and interior walls.

Using rollers, scrapers or improvised tools, you can produce a variety of textures. It pays to restrict distinctly raised textures with sharp edges to areas where you are unlikely to rub against the wall. Create finer textures for children's rooms, small bathrooms and narrow hallways.

Preparing for textured coatings

New surfaces will need virtually no preparation, but joints between plasterboard must be reinforced with tape. Strip any wallcoverings and key gloss paint with glasspaper. Old walls and ceilings must be clean, dry, sound and free from organic growth. Treat friable surfaces with stabilizing solution.

Although large cracks and holes must be filled, a textured coating will conceal minor defects in walls and ceilings by filling small cracks and bridging shallow bumps and hollows.

Masking joinery and fittings
Use 50mm (2in) wide masking tape to cover doorframes and window frames, electrical fittings, plumbing pipework, picture rails and skirting boards. Lay dust sheets over the floor.

1 Diamond pattern

2 Stipple effect

3 Swirl design

4 Combed arcs

5 Tree-bark simulation

6 Stucco finish

1 Geometric patterns
Use a roller with diamond or diagonal grooves: load the roller and draw lightly across the textured surface.

2 Stippled finish
Pat the coating with a damp sponge to create a pitted profile. Rinse out frequently. Alter your wrist angle and overlap sections.

3 Random swirls
Twist a damp sponge on the textured surface, then pull away to make a swirling design. Overlap swirls for a layered effect.

4 Combed arcs
A toothed spatula sold with the finish is employed to create combed patterns: arcs, criss-cross patterns or wavy scrolls.

5 Imitation tree bark
Produce a bark texture by applying parallel strokes with a roller, then lightly drawing the straight edge of a spatula over it.

6 Stucco finish
Apply parallel roller strokes, then run the rounded corner of a spatula over it in short straight strokes.

FINISHING
WOODWORK

Paint is the usual finish for woodwork in and around the house, offering as it does a protective coating in a choice of colours and surface finishes. However, stains, varnishes and polishes can also be used to give an attractive, durable finish to joinery. They enable you to add colour to woodwork without obliterating the natural beauty of its grain, while transparent finishes are a good alternative where you don't want to alter the natural wood colour. Bear in mind the location of the woodwork and the amount of wear it is likely to get when choosing a finish.

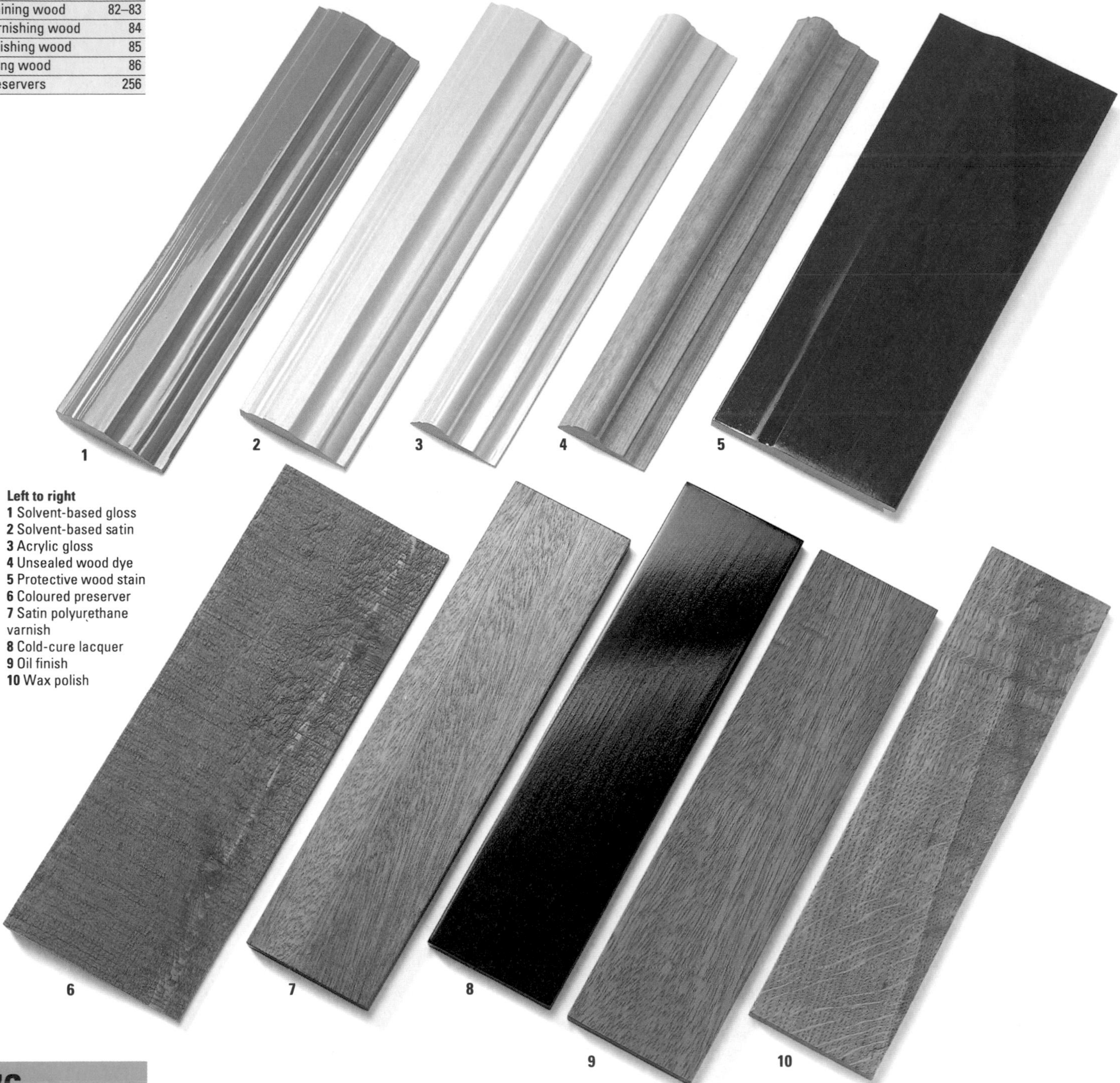

Left to right
1 Solvent-based gloss
2 Solvent-based satin
3 Acrylic gloss
4 Unsealed wood dye
5 Protective wood stain
6 Coloured preserver
7 Satin polyurethane varnish
8 Cold-cure lacquer
9 Oil finish
10 Wax polish

The list below gives a comprehensive range of finishes for decorating and protecting woodwork. Each has qualities which render it suitable for a particular purpose, although many can be employed simply for their attractive appearance rather than for any practical considerations. However, this does depend on the location of the timberwork, as some finishes are much more durable than others.

WOOD FINISHES

Solvent-based paints
Traditional solvent-based paints (oil paints) are available as high-gloss and satin finishes with both liquid and thixotropic consistencies. Indoors, they last for years with only the occasional wash down to remove finger marks. One or two undercoats are essential, especially outside where durability is reduced considerably by the action of sun and rain: you should consider redecorating every three to four years.

A one-coat paint, with its creamy consistency and high-pigment content, can protect primed wood or obliterate existing colours without undercoating. Apply it liberally and allow it to flow freely rather than brushing it out like a conventional oil paint.

Low-odour solvent-based finishes have largely eradicated the smell and fumes associated with drying paint.

Acrylic paints
Acrylic paints have several advantages over conventional oil paint. Being water-based, they are non-flammable, practically odourless, and constitute less of a risk to health and the environment. They also dry very quickly, so that a job can often be completed in one day. However, this means you have to work swiftly when decorating outside in direct sunlight to avoid leaving brush marks in the rapidly drying paintwork.

Provided they are applied to adequately prepared wood or keyed paintwork, acrylic paints form a tough yet flexible coating that resists cracking and peeling. However, in common with other water-borne finishes, acrylic paints will not dry satisfactorily if they are applied on a damp or humid day. Even under perfect conditions, don't expect to achieve a high-gloss finish.

Wood dyes
Unlike paint, which after the initial priming coat rests on the surface of timber, a dye penetrates the wood. Its main advantage is to enhance the natural colour of the woodwork or to unify the slight variation in colour found in even the same species.

Water-based or oil-based dyes are available ready for use, and powdered pigments are available for mixing with methylated spirit. None of these dyes will actually protect the timber and you will have to seal them with a clear varnish or polish.

Protective wood stains
The natural colour of wood can be enhanced with protective wood stains. Being moisture-vapour permeable, they allow the wood to breathe while providing a weather-resistant satin finish that resists flaking and peeling.

Protective wood stains are invariably brushed onto the wood. Some manufacturers recommend two to three coats, while others offer a one-coat finish. Some ranges include a clear finish for redecorating previously stained woodwork without darkening the existing colour. Generally, water-based stains tend to dry faster than those thinned with a spirit solvent.

Coloured preservers
Sawn-timber fencing, wall cladding and outbuildings look particularly unattractive when painted, yet they need protection. Use a wood preserver, which penetrates deeply into the timber to prevent rot and insect attack. There are clear preservers, plus a range of natural-wood colours.

Traditional preservers, especially creosote, have a strong, unpleasant smell and are harmful to plants, but most modern low-odour solvent-based and water-based preservers are perfectly safe, even for greenhouses and propagators.

Varnishes
Varnish is a clear protective coating for timber. Most modern varnishes are made with polyurethane resins to provide a waterproof, scratchproof and heat-resistant finish. Most are ready to apply, although some are supplied with a catalyst which must be added before the varnish is used. They come in high-gloss, satin or matt finishes.

An exterior-grade varnish is more weather-resistant. Yacht varnish, which is formulated to withstand even salt water, would be an ideal finish for exterior woodwork in a coastal climate.

Some varnishes are designed to provide a clear finish with a hint of colour. They are available in the normal wood shades and some strong colours. Unlike a wood dye a coloured varnish does not sink into the timber, so there may be loss of colour in areas of heavy wear or abrasion unless you apply additional coats of clear varnish.

Fast-drying acrylic varnishes have an opaque, milky appearance when applied, but are clear and transparent when dry.

Cold-cure lacquer
Cold-cure lacquer is a plastic coating which is mixed with a hardener just before it is used. It is extremely durable (even on floors) and is resistant to heat and alcohol. The standard type dries to a high gloss, which can be burnished to a lacquer-like finish if required. There is also a matt-finish grade, but a smoother matt surface can be obtained by rubbing down the gloss coating with fine steel wool dipped in wax. Cold-cure lacquer is available in clear, black or white.

Oil
Oil is a subtle finish which soaks into the wood, leaving a mellow sheen on the surface. Traditional linseed oil remains sticky for hours, but a modern oil will dry in about an hour and provides a tougher, more durable finish. Oil can be used on softwood as well as open-grained oily hardwoods, such as teak or afrormosia. It is suitable for interior and exterior woodwork.

Wax polishes
Wax can be used to preserve and maintain another finish or as a finish itself. A good wax should be a blend of beeswax and a hard polishing wax such as carnauba. Some contain silicones to make it easier to achieve a high gloss.

Wax polish may be white or tinted various shades of brown to darken the wood. Although it is very attractive, it is not a durable finish and should be used indoors only.

SEE ALSO

Details for:	
Primers	43
Wood flooring	114
Preservers	256

French polish
French polish is a specialized wood finish made by dissolving shellac in alcohol. It is easily scratched and alcohol, even water, will etch the surface, leaving white stains. Consequently, it can be used only on furniture unlikely to receive normal wear and tear.

There are several varieties. Reddish-brown button polish is the best-quality standard polish. It is bleached to make white polish for light-coloured woods and if the natural wax is removed from the shellac, a transparent polish is produced. For mahogany, choose a dark-red garnet polish.

1 Button polish
2 Garnet polish
3 White polish

PAINTING WINDOW FRAMES

● **Clean windows first**
Clean the glass in your windows before decorating to avoid picking up particles of dust in the paint.

Cutting-in brush
Paint glazing bars with a cutting-in brush. The bristles are cut at an angle to enable you to work right up to the glass.

● **Painting French windows**
Although French windows are really glazed doors, treat them like large casement windows.

PROTECTING THE GLASS

When painting the edge of glazing bars, overlap the glass by about 2mm (⅟₁₆in) to prevent rain or condensation seeping between the glass and woodwork.

If you find it difficult to achieve a satisfactory straight edge, use a proprietary plastic or metal paint shield held against the edge of the frame to protect the glass.

Alternatively, run masking tape around the edges of the window pane, leaving a slight gap so that the paint will seal the join between glass and frame. When the paint is touch-dry, carefully peel off the tape. Don't wait until the paint is completely dry or the film may peel off with the tape.

Once it has set, scrape off any paint that has accidentally dripped onto the glass with a sharp blade. Many DIY stores sell plastic handles to hold blades for this purpose.

Using a paint shield
A plastic or metal paint shield enables you to paint a straight edge up to glass.

KEEPING THE WINDOW OPEN

With the catch and stay removed there's nothing to stop the frame closing. Make a stay with a length of stiff wire, hook the other end and slot it into one of the screw holes in the frame.

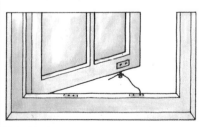

Temporary stay
Wind wire around a nail driven in the underside of the frame and use it as a stay.

Like doors, window frames need to be painted in strict order so that the various components will be evenly treated and so that you can close them at night. You also need to take care not to splash window panes with paint or apply a crooked line around the glazing bars – the mark of poor workmanship.

Painting a casement window

A casement window hinges like a door, so if you plan to paint each side a different colour, follow a similar procedure to that described for painting doors and frames.

Remove the stay and catch before you paint the window. So that you can still operate the window during decorating without touching wet paint, drive a nail into the underside of the bottom rail as a makeshift handle.

Painting sequence
First paint the glazing bars (**1**), cutting into the glass on both sides. Carry on with the top and bottom horizontal rails (**2**) followed by the vertical stiles (**3**). Finish the casement by painting the edges (**4**), then paint the frame (**5**).

Painting sequence for casement window ▶

Painting a sash window

Sash windows are the most difficult type to paint, as the two panes slide vertically, overlapping each other.

The following sequence describes the painting of a sash window from the inside. To paint the outside face, use a similar procedure, but start with the lower sash. If you are using different colours for each side, the demarcation lines are fairly obvious: when the window is shut, all the visible surfaces from one side should be the same.

Painting sequence
Raise the bottom sash and pull down the top one. Paint the bottom meeting rail of the top sash (**1**) and the accessible parts of the vertical members (**2**). Reverse the position of the sashes, leaving a gap top and bottom, and complete the painting of the top sash (**3**). Paint the bottom sash (**4**), then the frame (**5**) except for the runners in which the sashes slide.

Leave the paint to dry, then paint the inner runners (**6**) plus a short section of the outer runners (**7**), pulling the cords aside to avoid splashing paint on them as this will make them brittle, shortening their working life. Make sure the window slides before the paint dries.

Raise bottom sash and pull down top

Reverse the position of the sashes

Lower both sashes for access to runners

PAINTING FIXED JOINERY

Staircase

Paint banisters first, making sure that you do not precipitate runs by stroking the brush against the edges or mouldings. Start at the top of the stairs, painting the treads, risers and strings together to keep the edges of the paintwork fresh.

If there is any chance that the paint will not dry before the staircase is used again, paint all the risers, but alternate treads only. The next day, paint the remaining treads.

Skirting boards

The only problem with painting a skirting board is to protect the floor from paint and at the same time avoid picking up dust on the wet paintbrush.

Slide strips of thin card under the skirting as a paint shield (don't use newspaper; it will tear and remain stuck to the skirting).

PAINTING EXTERIOR WEATHERBOARDING

Start at the top of the wall and apply paint to one or two boards at a time. Paint the under-edge first, then the face of the boards; finish parallel with the edge. Make sure you coat exposed end grain well, as it is more absorbent and requires extra protection.

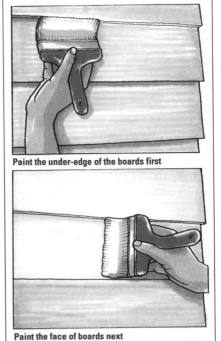

Paint the under-edge of the boards first

Paint the face of boards next

Graining is a technique for simulating natural wood with paint which was once used extensively on cheap softwood joinery to imitate expensive hardwoods. Doors and panels can look attractive treated in this way. The basic method is simple to describe, but practice on a flat board is essential before you can achieve convincing results. A skilled grainer can simulate actual species of timber, but just try to suggest wood grain rather than attempt to produce a perfect copy.

Equipment and preparation for graining

The simplest graining effects can be achieved by removing dark paint to reveal a paler basecoat below. The traditional way to carry out this effect is to use a special hog's-hair or squirrel-hair brush called a mottler or grainer. To compromise, try trimming a soft-bristled paintbrush or even a dusting brush. You can also buy steel, rubber or leather combs from decorator's suppliers to achieve similar effects.

Applying a base coat (ground)

Prepare the base coat as normal paintwork, finishing with a satin oil paint. It should represent the lightest colour of the timber you want to reproduce and is normally beige or olive green. The base coat will look more convincing if it is slightly dull rather than being too bright.

Choosing the graining colour

Translucent, flat-drying paints are produced especially for graining in a range of appropriate colours. These paints must be thinned with a mixture comprising 2 parts white spirit : 1 part raw linseed oil to make a graining glaze. The quantity of thinner controls the colour of the graining, so add it to the paint sparingly until you achieve the required result. Try the method on a practice panel first.

Producing the effect

Paint an even coat of glaze onto the ground with a 50mm (2in) paintbrush. After only two or three minutes, lightly drag the tip of the mottler or comb along the line of the rail or panel, leaving faints streaks in the glaze.

When two rails meet at right angles, mask the joint with a piece of card to prevent the simulated grain being disturbed on one rail while you paint a rail next to it.

The grain does not have to be exactly parallel with the rail. You can vary the pattern by allowing the comb or mottler to streak out the glaze at a slight angle and over the edge of some of the rails.

Leave the graining to dry overnight, then apply one or two coats of clear varnish to protect and seal the effects.

Steel graining comb

Rubber or leather comb

Bristle grainer

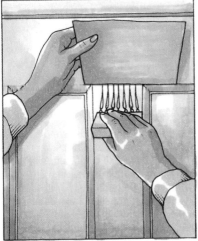

Masking meeting rails
Hold a piece of card over the joint between two meeting rails – for example, where muntins meet cross rails on a panelled door – to avoid spoiling the graining on one while treating the other.

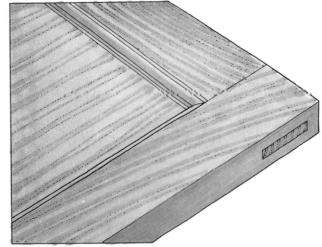

Applying graining patterns
To produce graining patterns that are convincing, run the streaks more or less parallel to the timber, simulating natural wood grain by occasionally running the pattern off at an angle.

81

VARNISHING WOODWORK

Varnish serves two main purposes: to protect the wood from knocks, stains and other marks, and to give it a sheen that accentuates the beautiful grain pattern. In some cases, it can even be used to change the colour of the wood to that of another species – or to give it a fresh, new look with a choice of bright primary colours.

The effect of varnish
The examples below demonstrate how different varnishes affect the same species of wood. From top to bottom: untreated softwood; matt clear varnish; gloss clear varnish; wood-colour varnish; satin tinted varnish; pure-colour varnish.

How to apply varnish

Use paintbrushes to apply varnish in the same way as paint. You will need a range of sizes for general work: 12, 25 and 50mm (½, 1 and 2in) are useful widths. For varnishing floors, use a 100mm (4in) brush for quick coverage. Whatever size of brush you use, always make sure that it is spotlessly clean; any remaining traces of paint on it may spoil the finish.

Load a brush with varnish by dipping the first third of the bristles into the liquid, then touch off the excess on the side of the container. Don't scrape the brush across the rim of the container as it causes bubbles in the varnish, which can spoil the finish if transferred to the woodwork.

You can employ a soft cloth pad, or rubber, to rub a sealer coat of varnish into the grain. While it's not essential to use a rubber it is a convenient method, especially if you are coating shaped or turned pieces of wood.

Applying the varnish

Thin the first sealer coat of varnish by 10 per cent and rub it well into the wood with a cloth pad in the direction of the grain. Brush on the sealer coat where the rubber is difficult to use.

Apply the second coat of varnish within the stipulated time. If more than 24 hours have elapsed, lightly key the surface of solvent-based gloss varnish with fine abrasive paper. Wipe it over with a cloth dampened with white spirit in order to remove dust and grease, then brush on a full coat of varnish in the same manner as for paint.

Apply a third coat if the surface is likely to take hard wear.

Using coloured varnish

A wood stain can only be used on bare timber, but you can use a coloured varnish to darken or alter the colour of woodwork that has been varnished previously without having to strip the finish. Clean the surface with wire wool and white spirit mixed with a little linseed oil. Dry the surface with a clean cloth, then apply the varnish.

Apply tinted varnish in the same way as the clear type. It might be worth making a test strip to see how many coats you will need to achieve the depth of colour you want.

Varnishing floors

Varnishing a floor is no different from finishing any other woodwork, but if you are using a solvent-based finish the greater area can produce an unpleasant concentration of fumes in a confined space. Open all windows to provide maximum ventilation and wear a respirator.

Start in the corner furthest from the door and work back towards it. Brush the varnish out well to make sure it does not collect in pools.

DEALING WITH DUST PARTICLES

Minor imperfections and particles of dust stuck to the varnished surface can be rubbed down with fine abrasive paper between coats. If your top coat is to be a high-gloss finish, take even more care to ensure that your brush is perfectly clean.

If you are not satisfied with your final finish, wait until it is dry, then dip very fine wire wool in wax polish and rub the varnish with parallel strokes in the direction of the grain. Buff the surface with a soft duster. This treatment removes a high gloss, but it leaves a pleasant sheen on the surface with no obvious imperfections.

Produce a soft sheen with wire wool and wax

FRENCH POLISHING

The art of French polishing has always been considered the province of the expert, to be left well alone by amateurs. It is true that an expert will make a better job of the polishing and work much faster than an amateur, but there's no reason why anyone cannot produce a satisfactory finish with a little practice.

Woodwork must be prepared immaculately before polishing as every blemish will be mirrored in the finish, so spoiling the effect. The grain should be filled, either with a proprietary filler or with layers of polish, which are rubbed down and recoated until the pores of the wood are eventually filled flush.

Always work in a warm, dust-free room: a low temperature will make the polish go cloudy (bloom) and dust will mar the finish.

Make sure you work in a good light so that you can glance across the surface in order to gauge the quality of the finish you are applying.

BRUSHING FRENCH POLISH

If you haven't the time to practise applying shellac with a rubber, use a special French polish that can be brushed onto the surface. It contains an agent that retards the drying process so that brush marks can flow out before the polish begins to set.

The technique for applying this brushing polish is easy to master. Use a soft paintbrush to apply an even coat, then, after 15 to 20 minutes, rub down lightly with silicon-carbide paper. Paint on two more coats, rubbing down between applications. When the shellac has set, dip a ball of 0000 grade wire wool in soft wax polish and rub it gently up and down the panel, using overlapping parallel strokes.

Leave the wax to harden for five minutes, then burnish vigorously with a soft duster.

Apply an even coat with a paintbrush

Traditional French polishing

With the rubber open in the palm of your hand, pour shellac onto the cotton wool until it is fully charged, but not absolutely saturated. Fold the fabric over the cotton wool and press the rubber against a scrap board to squeeze out the polish, distributing it evenly across the sole or base of the pad. Dip your fingertip in linseed oil and spread it across the sole to act as a lubricant.

Applying the polish

To apply French polish to a flat panel, first make overlapping circular strokes with the rubber, gradually covering the whole surface with shellac. Go over the same surface again, this time using figure-of-eight strokes – varying the strokes ensures an even coverage. Finish with straight, overlapping strokes parallel with the grain.

Very little pressure is required with a freshly charged rubber, but you need to increase the pressure gradually as the work proceeds. Recharge the cotton wool with polish as necessary, adding another spot of linseed oil to the sole when the rubber starts to drag.

Keep the rubber on the move, sweeping it on and off the wood at the beginning and end of each complete coverage. If you stop with the rubber in contact with the work the pad will stick to the polish, leaving a scar. In this event, let the shellac harden thoroughly and rub it down with very fine self-lubricating silicon-carbide paper.

Assuming the first complete application is free from blemishes, leave it to dry for 30 minutes, then repeat the process. Build up four to five coats in the same way and leave the polish to harden overnight.

Next day, sand out any dust, runs or rubber marks with silicon-carbide paper before applying four or five coats of polish. In all, 10 to 20 coats will be needed to build a protective coating with the required depth of colour.

Spiriting-off

The linseed-oil lubricant leaves streaks in the polish that have to be removed with a rubber that is practically empty of shellac, but with a few drops of methylated spirit on the sole. Apply the rubber to the polished surface, using straight parallel strokes only, gliding on and off the panel at the beginning and end of each stroke. Recharge the rubber with more methylated spirit as soon as it begins to drag. Leave the work for a minute or two, and repeat the process if the streaks reappear. Spiriting off not only removes streaking but eventually burnishes the French polish to a glass-like finish.

Half an hour later, buff the surface with a soft duster, then leave it to harden for at least a week.

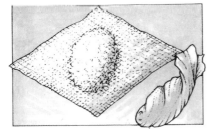

Making a rubber
Traditionally, French polish is applied with a soft pad known as a rubber. To make one, take a handful of cotton wool and squeeze it roughly egg-shaped, then place it in the centre of a 300mm (1ft) square of white linen. Fold the fabric over the cotton wool, gathering the loose material in the palm of your hand. Smooth out any wrinkles across the sole of the pad.

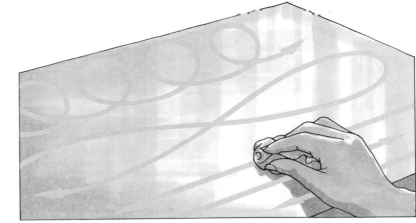

Using the rubber
Apply the polish with a combination of circular and figure-of-eight strokes so that every part of the surface is covered. When you finish each coat, run the rubber in long straight strokes, parallel to the wood grain. Keep your rubber pliable by storing it in a screw-top jar overnight.

85

COLD-CURE LACQUER

Due to its chemical composition, careful preparation is essential or cold-cure lacquer will take days to cure instead of only two hours. It must be applied to a clean, grease-free surface, which has been sanded smooth. Strip the old finish, but do not use a caustic stripper, as this will react against the coating.

Clean old wax polish from the wood. You must remove every trace, even from the pores of the timber. Wash it with white spirit, using a ball of fine wire wool in the direction of the grain. When the wood is dry, scrub it with water and detergent, then rinse the surface with clean water with a little white vinegar added.

If you use wood dye, make sure it is made by the manufacturer of the lacquer, otherwise it might change colour. Use the same manufacturer's stopping to fill cracks and holes and never use plaster or plastic fillers.

Mixing cold-cure lacquer

In most cases using a paintbrush is the best method of applying plastic coating, although you can use a plastic-foam roller instead, especially for large areas of woodwork.

When you are ready to apply the lacquer, mix the coating and hardener in a glass or polyethylene container. Use the proportions recommended by the manufacturer. Mix just enough for your needs, as it will set in two to three days in an open dish. Don't be tempted to try to economize by pouring the mixed lacquer back into its original container as the hardener will completely ruin any remaining substance therein.

Applying the lacquer

Cold-cure lacquer must be applied in a warm atmosphere. Use a well-loaded applicator and spread the lacquer onto the wood. There is no need to brush out the liquid as it will flow unaided and even a thick coat will cure thoroughly and smoothly. The lacquer dries quickly and will begin to show brush marks if it is disturbed after 10 to 15 minutes, so you should work swiftly in order to pick up the wet edges.

After two hours, apply the second coat. If necessary, rub down the hardened lacquer with fine abrasive paper to remove blemishes, then add a third coat. You will achieve better adhesion between the layers if you can apply all the coats in one day, as long as each has time to dry.

Burnishing lacquer

If you want a mirror finish, wait for 24 hours, then use a proprietary burnishing cream. Rub down the lacquer with very fine abrasive paper or wire wool, then rub the cream onto the surface with a soft cloth. Burnish it vigorously with a clean soft duster to achieve the required depth of sheen.

Matting lacquer

To produce a subtle satin coat, rub the hardened lacquer along the grain with fine wire wool dipped in wax polish. The grade of the wire wool will affect the degree of matting. Use fine 000 grade for a satin finish and a coarse 0 grade for a fully-matted surface. Polish with a clean, soft duster.

SAFETY WHEN USING LACQUER

Although cold-cure lacquer is safe to use, take care when applying it to a large surface such as a floor as there will be a concentration of fumes.

Open all windows and doors if possible for ventilation – but remember the necessity for a warm atmosphere, too – and take the extra precaution of wearing a respirator to prevent you breathing in the fumes. The hardener is acidic, so wash thoroughly with water if you spill any on your skin.

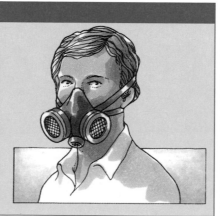

- **Spontaneous combustion**
  It is essential to dispose of oily rags immediately you have finished with them as they have been known to burst into flames.

OILING AND WAXING WOODWORK

Applying the oil

Clean and prepare the wood for oiling. Remove previous finishes carefully so that oil can penetrate the grain.

The most efficient way to apply a finishing oil is to rub it into the wood with a soft, lint-free rag in the form of a rubber. Don't store oily rags: keep them in a sealed tin while the job is in progress, then unfold them and leave them outside to dry before throwing them away.

A brush is a convenient way to spread oil liberally over large surfaces and into carvings or deep mouldings.

Rub or brush a generous coating of oil into the wood grain. Leave it to soak in for a few minutes, then rub off excess oil with a clean cloth. After about six hours, coat the wood with oil once more. The next day, apply a third and final coat; raise a faint sheen by burnishing with a soft duster.

Wax-polishing timber

If you want to wax-polish new timber, seal the wood first with one coat of clear varnish (or French polish on fine furniture). This will stop the wax being absorbed too deeply into the wood and provides a slightly more durable finish. Before waxing an old clear finish, clean it first to remove deposits of dirt and possibly an old wax dressing.

To remove dirty wax, mix up white spirit with 25 per cent linseed oil. Use the liquid to clean the surface vigorously with a coarse cloth. If there is no obvious improvement, try dipping very fine wire wool into the cleaner and rub in the direction of the grain. Don't press too hard as you want only to remove wax and dirt without damaging the finish below. Wash the cleaned surface with a cloth dipped in white spirit and leave to dry before refinishing.

Wax polish can be applied with a soft cloth, but when using liquid wax it's best to employ a paintbrush to seal the wood with it first. Then pour the liquid wax onto a cloth pad and rub it in with a circular motion, followed by strokes parallel with the grain. Make this first coat a generous one.

Buff up the wax after one hour, then apply a second, thinner coat in the direction of the grain only. Burnish this coat lightly and leave for several hours to harden. Bring to a high gloss by burnishing vigorously with a soft duster.

SEE ALSO

Details for:	
Preparing wood	53
Sanding floors	55–56
Stripping wood	58–59
Protective stains	77
Painting a door	79
Removing putty	202
Wood preservers	256

Ferrous metals that are rusty will shed practically any paint film rapidly, so the most important aspect of finishing metalwork is thorough preparation and priming to prevent this corrosion from returning; after that, applying the finish is virtually the same as painting woodwork.

When you are choosing a finish for metalwork in and around the house, make sure it fulfils your requirements (see chart below and table overleaf for suitable types). Many of the finishes listed are easy to apply to metal, but the ability of some to withstand heavy wear is likely to be poor.

Methods of application

Most of the finishes suggested for use on metalwork can be applied with a paintbrush. The exception is black lead. In general, use the standard techniques for painting woodwork, except that bitumen-based paints should be laid on only and not brushed out as are conventional coatings.

Remove metal door and window fittings for painting, suspending them on wire hooks to dry. Make sure that sharp edges are coated properly, as the finish can wear thin relatively quickly.

Some paints can be sprayed, but there are few situations where this is advantageous, except perhaps in the case of intricately moulded ironwork such as garden furniture, which you can paint outside. Indoors, ventilation is a necessity.

A roller is suitable for large flat surfaces. Pipework requires its own special V-section roller, which is designed to coat curved surfaces.

● Black dot denotes compatibility.
All surfaces must be clean, sound, dry and free from organic growth.

FINISHES FOR METALWORK

	Solvent-based paint	Hammered-finish paint	Metallic paint	Bitumen-based paint	Security paint	Radiator enamel	Black lead	Lacquer	Bath Paint	Non-slip Paint
DRYING TIME: HOURS										
Touch-dry	4	0.5	4	1–2		2–6		0.25	6–10	4–6
Recoatable	14	1–3	8	6–24		7–14			16–24	12
THINNERS: SOLVENTS										
Water				●						
White spirit	●		●	●	●		●		●	●
Special		●				●				
Cellulose thinners								●		
NUMBER OF COATS										
Normal conditions	1–2	1	1–2	1–3	1	1–2	Variable	1	2	2
COVERAGE										
Sq metres per litre	12–16	3–5	10–14	6–15	2.5	13	Variable	18	13–14	3–5
METHOD OF APPLICATION										
Brush	●	●	●	●	●	●	●	●	●	●
Paint pad	●	●		●						
Spray gun	●	●		●				●		
Cloth pad (rubber)							●			

PAINTING RADIATORS AND PIPES

Leave radiators and hot-water pipes to cool before you paint them. The only problem with decorating a radiator is how to paint the back: the best solution is to remove it completely or, if possible, swing it away from the wall. After you have painted the back, reposition the radiator and paint the front.

If this is inconvenient, use a special radiator brush with a long metal handle (see right). Use the same tool to paint in between the leaves of a double radiator. It is difficult to achieve a perfect finish even with the brush, so aim at covering areas you are likely to see when the radiator is fixed in position rather than a complete application.

Don't paint over radiator valves or fittings or you will not be able to operate them afterwards.

Paint pipework lengthwise rather than across, or runs are likely to form. The first coat on metal piping will be streaky, so be prepared to apply two or three coats. Unless you are using radiator enamel, allow the paint to harden thoroughly before turning on the heat, or it may blister.

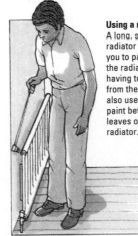

Using a radiator brush
A long, slim-handled radiator brush enables you to paint the back of the radiator without having to remove it from the wall. You can also use this brush to paint between the leaves of a double radiator.

METALWORK

1 Protect wall
Use card behind a downpipe when painting behind it.

2 Apply lacquer
Use a large, soft artist's paintbrush.

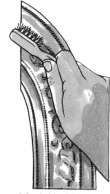

3 Apply black lead
Scrub cream into intricate surfaces using an old toothbrush.

Gutters and downpipes

It is best to coat the inside of gutters with a bitumen-based paint for thorough protection against moisture, but you can finish the outer surfaces with oil paint or security paint.

To protect the wall behind a downpipe, slip a scrap of card between while painting the back of the pipe (1).

Metal casement windows

Paint metal casement windows using the sequence described for wooden casements, which allows you to close the frame at night without spoiling a freshly-painted surface.

Lacquering metalwork

Polish the metal to a high gloss, then use a nail brush to scrub it with warm water containing some liquid detergent. Rinse the metal in clean water, then dry it thoroughly with an absorbent cloth.

Paint on acrylic lacquer with a large, soft, artist's brush (2), working swiftly from the top. Let the lacquer flow naturally, and work all round the object to keep the wet edge moving.

If you do leave a brush stroke in partially-set lacquer, finish the job, then warm the metal (by standing it on a radiator if possible). As soon as the blemish disappears, remove the object from the heat and allow it to cool gradually in a dust-free atmosphere.

Blacking cast iron

Black lead produces an attractive finish for cast iron. It is not a permanent or durable finish and will have to be renewed periodically. It may transfer if rubbed hard.

Black lead is supplied in a toothpaste-like tube. Squeeze some onto a soft cloth and spread it onto the metal. Use an old toothbrush (3) to scrub it into decorative ironwork for best coverage.

When you have covered the surface, buff it to a satin sheen with a clean, dry cloth. Build up several applications of black lead to give a patina and a moisture-resistant finish.

SUITABLE FINISHES FOR METALWORK

Solvent-based paints

Conventional solvent-based paints are perfectly usable on metal. Once it has been primed, interior metalwork will need at least one undercoat plus a top coat. Add an extra undercoat to protect exterior metalwork.

Hammered-finish paint

A combination of heat-hardened glass flakes, aluminium particles and resins, hammered-finish paint is applied as one coat only. There's no need for primer or undercoat, even when painting previously rusted metal. A smooth-finish paint with the same properties is also available.

Metallic paints

For a metallic-like finish, choose a paint containing aluminium, copper, gold or bronze powders. These paints are water-resistant and are able to withstand very high temperatures – up to about 100°C (212°F).

Bitumen-based paints

Bitumen-based paints give economical protection for exterior storage tanks and piping. Standard bituminous paint is black, but there is also a limited range of colours, plus 'modified' bituminous paint, which contains aluminium.

Security paints

Non-setting security paint, primarily for rainwater and waste downpipes, remains slippery to prevent intruders from scaling the wall via the pipe. Restrict it to pipework over about 2m (6ft) above the ground.

Radiator enamels

Radiator enamel is a heat-stoving acrylic paint that is applied in two thin coats. A choice of satin and gloss finishes is available.

Radiator enamel can be used over emulsion or oil paints as long as these have not been recently applied (don't rub them down first). Apply a compatible metal primer over new paint or factory priming to stop solvents in the enamel reacting with the previous coating (this does not apply to water-based radiator enamel). A special thinner is normally required for brush cleaning.

Finish the radiator in position, then turn the heating on (set to maximum) for a minimum of two hours to bake the enamel onto the metal. Apply a second coat six to eight hours later.

You can also use radiator enamel to repaint boiler cabinets, refrigerators, cookers and washing machines.

Black lead

A cream used for cast ironwork, black lead is a mixture of graphite and waxes. It is reasonably moisture-resistant, but is not suitable for exterior use.

Lacquer

Virtually any clear lacquer can be used on polished metalwork without spoiling its appearance, but many polyurethanes yellow with age. A clear acrylic metal lacquer will protect chrome-plating, brass and copper – even outside.

Non-slip paints

Designed to provide good foot-holding on a wide range of surfaces, including metal, non-slip paint is ideal for painting metal staircase treads and exterior fire escapes. The surface must be primed before application.

Walls that are in poor condition – except those that are damp – can be covered with panelling to conceal them and to provide a decorative surface. Panelling can be practical in other ways, too, if used in conjunction with insulation. There are various types of decorative panelling for walls, notably solid-wood planking and decorative wallboards faced with various patterns.

Tongue-and-groove boards

Solid-wood panelling is made from planks with a tongue along one edge and a matching groove on the other. The main function of this design is to provide room for movement resulting from atmospheric changes, but it also allows for secret nailing to fix the planks to the wall. The meeting edges of some planks – called tongued, grooved and V-jointed (TGV) boards – are machined to produce a decorative V-shaped profile, accentuating the shape of each board. Other types have more decorative profiles. Shiplap has a rebate on the back face, which holds down the coved front edge of the next board.

A few hardwoods are available as panelling, but the majority is made from softwood, typically knotty pine, which is unsuitable for joinery because of the large number of knots it contains.

Buy boards in one batch

Make sure you buy enough TGV boards to complete the work. Boards from another batch may not be compatible because the machine used to shape their edge joints may have been set to slightly different tolerances.

Wallboards

Manufactured sheet wallboards are made to various standard sizes and in thicknesses ranging from 4 to 6mm (3/16 to 1/4in). Plywood or hardboard panels are faced with real-timber veneers or paper printed to simulate wood grain, and there are plastic-faced boards in various colours. Typical surfaces include embossed brick, stone, plaster or tiled effects.

Wall panels made from wood-fibre boards are 12mm (1/2in) thick and can be bought with cork, grass and fabric surfaces; they reduce sound penetration and are heat-insulating.

CONSTRUCTING A FRAMEWORK FOR PANELLING

If a wall is flat you can glue thick wallboards directly to the surface, but as most walls are fairly uneven, it is best to construct a frame from softwood battens, called furring strips. For TGV boarding and thin wallboards, this is the only practical solution. You can pin any type of panelling directly to the studs and noggings of a stud-partition wall.

Before you start, carefully prise off the skirting boards, picture rails and coving, so that you can refix these on the panelling, if required. If fixing to a solid wall, erect the framework using 50 x 25mm (2 x 1in) planed or sawn softwood. Treat the timber with proprietary wood preserver.

To prevent condensation, line an external wall with a polyethylene vapour barrier before you attach the furring strips. The simplest way to do this is to tack the polyethylene sheets to the wall, using masonry nails, then secure them with the battens.

You can also insulate the wall by sandwiching a layer of glass-fibre insulation material between it and the panelling. If you do this, fix the polyethylene vapour barrier over the furring strips.

The battens should be fixed 400mm (1ft 4in) apart with 50mm (2in) masonry nails or screws and wallplugs. Use a builder's spirit level to align each batten with its neighbour in order to produce a vertical, flat plane. Pack out any hollows behind the strips with card or with thin strips of hardboard.

Wallboards are fixed vertically to the framework, but TGV boards can be arranged in a variety of patterns – vertically, horizontally, diagonally, or even in a zig-zag fashion for a really individual effect.

To fix vertical TGV panelling, run the furring strips horizontally. The lowest strip should be level with the top of the skirting, with short vertical strips below it for fixing the skirting to. For horizontal boards, run the furring strips from floor to ceiling. Nail offcuts of panelling to the bottom of the strips as spacers to support the skirting board at the new level. Stagger the joints between boards on alternate rows. Fix diagonal boards to strips running horizontally and stagger the joints also.

To fix wallboards, centre vertical furring strips on the edges of each wallboard. Fill in with horizontal strips every 400mm (1ft 4in).

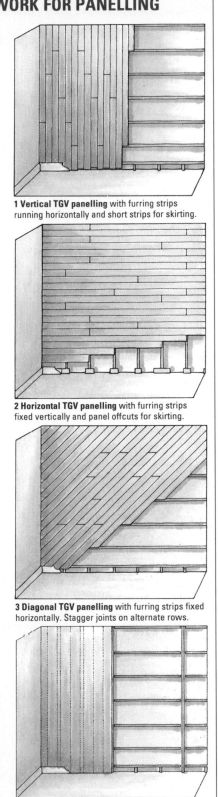

1 Vertical TGV panelling with furring strips running horizontally and short strips for skirting.

2 Horizontal TGV panelling with furring strips fixed vertically and panel offcuts for skirting.

3 Diagonal TGV panelling with furring strips fixed horizontally. Stagger joints on alternate rows.

4 Wallboards need vertical furring strips at the edges and horizontal strips between.

Tongue-and-groove boards
Solid-wood tongue-and-groove planks are sold by timber merchants in various lengths up to 3m (10ft); nominal dimensions are 100 x 12mm (4 x 1/2in). Prepacked kits of TGV boards are available from specialists. Packs contain six 2.4 or 2.7m (8 or 9ft) lengths. Various profiles are made: tongued, grooved and V-jointed **(1)**, rebated shiplap **(2)**, moulded TGV **(3)**.

ATTACHING
STRIP-WOOD
PANELLING

SEE ALSO
Details for:
Turning off power 302

Fixing vertical panelling

Mark out and cut the boards to length, using a tenon saw. Sand all the boards before fixing them (unless they are in a kit). With the grooved edge against the left-hand wall, plumb the first board with a spirit level. Nail it to the battens through the centre of the face, using 25mm (1in) panel pins. Use 36mm (1½in) pins when fixing to a stud-partition wall.

Slide the next board onto the tongue and protect the edge while you tap it in place with a hammer. Fix to the battens using the secret-nailing technique: drive a pin through the inner corner of the tongue, at an angle (**1**). Sink the head below the surface with a nail set. Slide on the next board to hide the fixing, and repeat to cover the wall (**2**).

Use up short lengths of boarding by butting them end to end over a furring strip, but stagger such joints across the wall to avoid a continuous line.

When you reach the other end of the wall, cut the last board down its length to fit the gap. Nail it through the face. If it is a tight fit, spring the last two boards in at the same time: slot them together, slot the penultimate board's groove onto the exposed tongue, then push both into the wall. Pin a small quadrant cover strip down the edges, nail the skirting in place and fit a ceiling coving to conceal the edges of the boards.

Metal clips
Some prepacked boards are attached to the battens with metal clips, which locate in the groove of a board, leaving a tab which takes the pin. With this type of fixing, plane the tongue from the first board and place that edge against the left-hand side wall (or the ceiling). The clips are concealed by the next board.

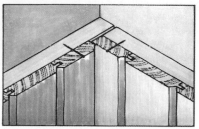

1 Secret nailing

HORIZONTAL FURRINGS

Fix boards tongue outwards

SKIRTING BATTENS

2 Fixing vertical TGV boards

Metal-clip flange slots into groove

An alternative method of fixing boards

Fixing horizontal panelling

Follow the same procedure as for vertical cladding, but position the first board just below skirting level, with its groove at the bottom.

Panelling around doors and windows

Remove the architrave and sill mouldings and nail furring strips (**1**) close to the frame. Fix the panelling (**2**) and cover the edge with a thin wooden strip (**3**) so that it is flush with the inner face of the frame. Refit the mouldings (**4**) on top of the panelling.

Adapting the mouldings
Follow the numbered sequence to adapt mouldings around doors and windows.

PANELLING INTO CORNERS

To panel adjacent walls, shape solid-wood strips to make neat internal or external corners.

Internal corners
Scribe a butt joint using a block of wood and a pencil, then plane a chamfer on one board. Pin the chamfered board to the furring strips through its face. The detailing is similar for vertical or horizontal boards.

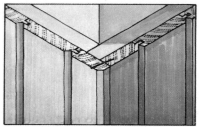

Fit chamfered board to make internal corner

External corners
To join vertical boards, lap one with another and pin them together. Plane a bevel on the outer corner (**1**). For horizontal boards, pin on a bevelled moulding to cover the end grain (**2**).

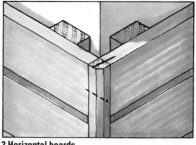

1 Vertical boards

2 Horizontal boards

Panelling a ceiling

It is relatively straightforward to panel a ceiling with TGV boards, following the methods described for cladding a wall. First locate the joists, then nail or screw the furring strips across them.

ATTACHING
SHEET
PANELLING

SEE ALSO

Details for:	
Varnishing	77, 84
Furring strips	89
Preserving wood	252–253, 256
Nail set	488

DEALING WITH ELECTRICAL FITTINGS

Existing socket outlets and light switches must be adapted to fit the newly panelled wall. You can either refix surface-mounted fittings on the face of the new panelling or leave the fittings where they are and simply panel around them so that their faceplates project through the panelling. Flush-mounted ones should be brought forward and set flush with the new surface.

Flush-mounted fittings

Turn off the power at the mains, then unscrew and disconnect the faceplate. There should be enough slack in the cable for you to be able to extract the metal mounting box and move it slightly to one side. Screw the box to the wall so that it will lie flush with the finished panelling, and nail short fixing battens all round **(1)**.

Alternatively, fix the mounting box to the panelling itself, using metal-box mounting flanges intended for use on hollow partition walls. These flanges resemble small 'ears' that project from two sides of the box. By tightening the faceplate-fixing screws, the panelling is clamped between the flanges and the rim of the faceplate.

Surface-mounted fixings

Nail short battens on each side of the cable to take the screws holding the fitting to the wall **(2)**. Drill a hole in the panelling, pass the cable through and screw the mounting box over it. Wire and fit the faceplate.

If you don't want to surface-mount the fitting, frame it with short battens nailed to the wall, then cut the panelling to fit around it.

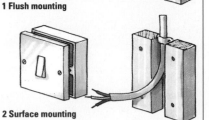

1 Flush mounting

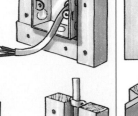

2 Surface mounting

Pinning wallboards

Scribe the first board to the left-hand side wall and ceiling. Cut the boards with a panel saw, face-side uppermost to avoid splitting the grain.

Use a footlifter to hold the panel off the floor **(1)** and pin it through the grooves. Tap the pins just below the surface with a fine nail set ready for filling later.

Butt-join subsequent panels. The edges are bevelled to make a matching V-groove. Cut the last board to fit against the opposite wall, then fit a cover strip and moulding.

Gluing on wallboards

Wood-fibre boards can be pinned to the furring strips, but nail heads may spoil the appearance. For a better result, use a proprietary wallboard adhesive to glue the boards to the framework. If the panels are narrower than standard wallboards, reduce the spacing of the furring strips accordingly.

Fit the first board to the wall and ceiling. Use a sharp knife to cut the panel as a saw tends to fray the edges. Follow the manufacturer's instructions to apply the glue. Some recommend applying it in patches or continuous bands, before pressing the panels in place. Strike the edges with the side of your fists to spread the glue.

Contact adhesive can also be used to fix the boards. Apply the adhesive to the strips, then press the board against the framework; peel it off again to leave glue on both surfaces. Wedge a batten under the bottom edge **(2)** to maintain its position relative to the wall. When the glue is touch-dry, press the panel in place again for an immediate bond.

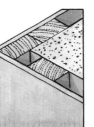

Pin external corners
Nail softwood blocks to one furring strip to support the edges of the board. Add adhesive to the blocks, then pin the boards along a groove. Bevel one board at the corner and stain the exposed core.

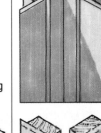

Pin internal corners
Butt-join the wallboards at an internal corner. For the sake of neatness, you can conceal the join by gluing a matching cover strip into the angle.

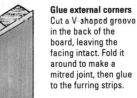

Glue external corners
Cut a V-shaped groove in the back of the board, leaving the facing intact. Fold it around to make a mitred joint, then glue to the furring strips.

Glue internal corners
Cut through the wallboard as far down as the face material, then fold it – face to face – to fit the corner and glue it to the furring strips.

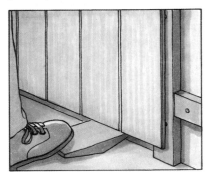

1 Using a footlifter

GLUED FURRING STRIPS

BATTEN

2 Using contact adhesive
Having peeled a board off the glued strips, wedge it against the ceiling until the adhesive is touch-dry.

Joining grooved boards
Some boards are grooved along the vertical edges to accept a fillet joint strip. Nail or staple along the joint, covering the fixing with the fillet.

Butt-jointing boards
Square-edged boards can be butt-jointed or left with a slight gap between; stain or paint the furring strip behind as a decorative feature.

Fitting a cover strip
The third method of concealing the joins between wallboards is to leave a slight gap between butted boards and glue on a rounded cover strip.

WALLCOVERINGS

Top right
1 Expanded polystyrene
2 Lining paper
3 Woodchip

Bottom left
4 Hand-printed
5 Machine-printed

Bottom right
6 Lincrusta
7 Embossed-paper wallcovering
8 Blown vinyl

Although wallcoverings are often called 'wallpaper', only a proportion of the wide range available is made solely from wood pulp. There is a huge range of paper-backed fabrics from exotic silks to coarse hessians; other types include natural textures such as cork or woven grass on a paper backing. Plastics have widened the choice of wallcoverings still further: there are paper-backed or cotton-backed vinyls, and plain or patterned foamed plastics. Before wallpaper became popular fabric wall hangings were used to decorate interiors and this is still done today, using unbacked fabrics glued or stretched across walls.

Ensuring a suitable surface

Although many wallcoverings will cover minor blemishes, walls and ceilings should be clean, sound and smooth. Eradicate damp and organic growth before hanging any wallcovering. Consider whether you should size the walls to reduce paste absorption.

COVERINGS THAT CAMOUFLAGE

Although a poor surface should be repaired, some coverings hide minor blemishes as well as providing a foundation for other finishes.

Expanded-polystyrene sheet
Thin polystyrene sheet is used for lining a wall before papering. It reduces condensation and also bridges hairline cracks and small holes. Polystyrene dents easily, so don't use where it will take a lot of punishment. There is a patterned version for ceilings.

Lining paper
A cheap, buff-coloured wallpaper for lining uneven or impervious walls prior to hanging a heavy or expensive wallcovering. It also provides an even surface for emulsion paint.

Woodchip paper
Woodchip or ingrain paper is a relief covering made by sandwiching particles of wood between two layers of paper. It is inexpensive, easy to hang (but a problem to cut), and must be painted.

Printed wallpapers
One advantage of ordinary wallpaper is the superb range of printed colours and patterns, which is much wider than for any other covering. Most papers – the cheapest – are machine-printed.

The more costly hand-printed papers are prone to tearing when wet and the inks have a tendency to run if you smear paste on the surface. They are not really suitable for walls exposed to wear or condensation. Pattern matching can be awkward, because hand-printing isn't as accurate as machine printing.

Relief papers
Relief papers with deeply embossed patterns hide minor imperfections. Reliefs are invariably painted with emulsion, satin-finish oil paints or water-based acrylics.

The original embossed wallcovering, Lincrusta, consists of a solid film of linseed oil and fillers fused onto a backing paper before the pattern is applied with an engraved steel roller. It is still available, though many people prefer embossed-paper wallcoverings or the superior-quality versions made from cotton fibres. Lightweight vinyl reliefs are also popular. During manufacture, they are heated in an oven which 'blows' or expands the vinyl, creating deeply embossed patterns.

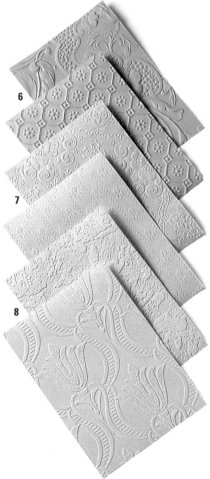

WALLCOVERINGS

Washable papers

These are printed papers with a thin impervious glaze of PVA to make a spongeable surface. Washables are suitable for bathrooms and kitchens. The surface must not be scrubbed or the plastic coating will be worn away.

Vinyl wallcoverings

A base paper, or sometimes a cotton backing, is coated with a layer of vinyl upon which the design is printed. Heat is used to fuse the colours and vinyl. The result is a durable, washable wallcovering ideally suited to bathrooms and kitchens. Many vinyls are sold ready-pasted for easy application.

Foamed-polyethylene covering

This is a lightweight wallcovering made solely of foamed plastic with no backing paper. It is printed with a wide range of patterns, colours and designs. You paste the wall instead of the covering. It is best used on walls that are not exposed to wear.

Flock wallcoverings

Flock papers have the major pattern elements picked out with a fine pile produced by gluing synthetic or natural fibres (such as silk or wool) to the backing paper: the pattern stands out in relief, with a velvet-like texture.

Standard flock papers are difficult to hang, as contact with paste will ruin the pile. Vinyl flocks are less delicate, can be hung anywhere, and may even come ready-pasted.

You can sponge flock paper to remove stains, but brush to remove dust from the pile. Vinyl flocks can be washed without risk of damage.

Grass cloth

Natural grasses are woven into a mat and glued to a paper backing. While these wallcoverings are very attractive, they are fragile and difficult to hang.

Cork-faced paper

This is surfaced with thin sheets of coloured or natural cork. It is not as easily spoiled as other special papers.

Paper-backed fabrics

Finely woven cotton, linen or silk on a paper backing must be applied to a flat surface. They are expensive, not easy to hang, and you must avoid smearing the fabric with adhesive. Most fabrics are delicate, but some are plastic-coated to make them scuff-resistant.

Unbacked fabrics

Upholstery-width fabric – typically hessian – can be wrapped around panels which are then glued or pinned to the wall.

Left to right
1 Washable papers
2 Textured and patterned vinyls
3 Foamed polyethylene
4 Flock papers
5 Paper-backed fabric
6 Grass-cloth mats
7 Cork-faced paper

WALLCOVERINGS: ESTIMATING QUANTITIES

Calculating the number of rolls of wallcovering you will need to cover your walls and ceiling depends on the size of the roll – both length and width – the pattern repeat and the obstructions you have to avoid. Because of variations in colour between batches, you must take into account all these points – and allow for wastage, too. A standard roll of wallcovering measures 520mm (1ft 9in) wide and 10.05 metres (33ft) long. Use the two charts on this page to estimate how many rolls you will need for walls and ceilings.

Estimating non-standard rolls

If the wallcovering is not cut to a standard size, calculate the amount you need in this way:

Walls

Measure the height of the walls from skirting to ceiling. Divide the length of the roll by this figure to find the number of wall lengths you can cut from a roll.

Measure around the room, excluding windows and doors, to work out how many widths fit into the total length of the walls. Divide this number by the number of wall lengths you can get from one roll to find how many rolls you need.

Make an allowance for short lengths above doors and under windows.

Ceilings

Measure the length of the room to determine one strip of paper. Work out how many roll widths fit across the room. Multiply the two figures and divide the answer by the length of a roll to find out how many rolls you need. Check for waste and allow for it.

Checking for shading

If rolls of wallcovering are printed in one batch, there should be no problem with colour matching one roll to another. When you buy, look for the batch number printed on the wrapping.

Make a visual check before hanging the covering, especially for hand-printed papers or fabrics. Unroll a short length of each roll and lay them side by side. You may get a better colour match by changing the rolls around, but if colour difference is obvious, ask for a replacement roll.

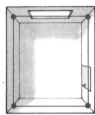

Measuring walls for standard rolls
You can include windows and doors in your estimate.

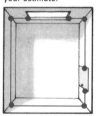

Measuring walls for non-standard rolls
Do not include doors and windows when estimating for expensive materials. Allow for short lengths afterwards.

Walls:
Standard rolls
Measure your room, then look down height column and across wall column to assess number of standard rolls required.

WALLS	HEIGHT OF ROOM IN METRES FROM SKIRTING — NUMBER OF ROLLS REQUIRED FOR WALLS							
MEASUREMENT IN METRES AROUND WALLS, INCLUDING DOORS AND WINDOWS	2–2.25m	2.25–2.5m	2.5–2.75m	2.75–3m	3–3.25m	3.25–3.5m	3.5–3.75m	3.75–4m
10m	5	5	6	6	7	7	8	8
10.5m	5	6	6	7	7	8	8	9
11m	5	6	7	7	8	8	9	9
11.5m	6	6	7	7	8	8	9	9
12m	6	6	7	8	8	9	9	10
12.5m	6	7	7	8	9	9	10	10
13m	6	7	8	8	9	10	10	10
13.5m	7	7	8	9	9	10	10	11
14m	7	7	8	9	10	10	11	11
14.5m	7	8	8	9	10	10	11	12
15m	7	8	9	9	10	11	12	12
15.5m	7	8	9	9	10	11	12	13
16m	8	8	9	10	11	11	12	13
16.5m	8	9	9	10	11	12	13	13
17m	8	9	10	10	11	12	13	14
17.5m	8	9	10	11	12	13	14	14
18m	9	9	10	11	12	13	14	15
18.5m	9	10	11	12	12	13	14	15
19m	9	10	11	12	13	14	15	16
19.5m	9	10	11	12	13	14	15	16
20m	9	10	11	12	13	14	15	16
20.5m	10	11	12	13	14	15	16	17
21m	10	11	12	13	14	15	16	17
21.5m	10	11	12	13	14	15	17	18
22m	10	11	13	14	15	16	17	18
22.5m	11	12	13	14	15	16	17	18
23m	11	12	13	14	15	17	18	19
23.5m	11	12	13	15	16	17	18	19
24m	11	12	14	15	16	17	18	20
24.5m	11	13	14	15	16	18	19	20
25m	12	13	14	15	17	18	19	20
25.5m	12	13	14	16	17	18	20	21
26m	12	13	15	16	17	19	20	21
26.5m	12	14	15	16	18	19	20	22
27m	13	14	15	17	18	19	21	22
27.5m	13	14	16	17	18	20	21	23
28m	13	14	16	17	19	20	21	23
28.5m	13	15	16	18	19	20	22	23
29m	13	15	16	18	19	21	22	24
29.5m	14	15	17	18	20	21	23	24
30m	14	15	17	18	20	21	23	24

Ceilings:
Standard rolls
Measure perimeter of ceiling. Number of standard rolls required are shown next to overall dimensions.

Dimensions
All dimensions are shown in metres (1m = 39in).

CEILINGS: NUMBER OF ROLLS REQUIRED							
Measurement around room	Number of rolls	Measurement around room	Number of rolls	Measurement around room	Number of rolls	Measurement around room	Number of rolls
11m	2	16m	4	21m	6	26m	9
12m	2	17m	4	22m	7	27m	10
13m	3	18m	5	23m	7	28m	10
14m	3	19m	5	24m	8	29m	11
15m	4	20m	5	25m	8	30m	11

TRIMMING AND CUTTING TECHNIQUES

Most wallcoverings are machine-trimmed to width so that you can butt adjacent lengths accurately. Some hand-printed papers are left untrimmed. These are usually expensive, so don't attempt to trim them yourself: ask the supplier to do this for you.

Cutting plain wallcoverings

Measure the height of the wall at the point where you will hang the first 'drop'. Add an extra 100mm (4in) for trimming top and bottom. Cut several pieces from your first roll to the same length and mark the top of each one.

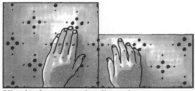

Allowing for patterned wallcoverings
You may have to allow extra on alternate lengths of patterned wallcoverings to match patterns.

CHOOSING PASTE

Most wallpaper pastes are supplied as powder or flakes for mixing with water.

All-purpose paste

Standard wallpaper paste is suitable for most lightweight to medium-weight papers. With less water added, it can be used to hang heavyweight papers.

Heavy-duty paste

Specially prepared to hang embossed papers, paper-backed fabrics and other heavyweight wallcoverings.

Fungicidal paste

Most pastes contain a fungicide to prevent mould growth under impervious wallcoverings such as vinyls, washable papers and foamed-plastic coverings.

Ready-mixed paste

Tubs of ready-mixed, thixotropic paste are specially made for heavyweight wallcoverings such as fabric.

Stain-free paste

For use with delicate papers that could be stained by conventional pastes.

Repair adhesive

Sticks down peeling edges and corners. It even glues vinyl to vinyl.

You can use any wipe-clean table for pasting, but a narrow fold-up pasting table is a good investment if you are doing a lot of decorating. Lay several cut lengths of paper face down on the table to keep it clean. Tuck the ends under a length of string tied loosely round the table legs to stop the paper rolling up while you are pasting.

Applying the paste

Use a large, soft wall brush or pasting brush to apply the paste. Mix the paste in a plastic bucket and tie string across the rim to support the brush, keeping its handle clean while you hang the paper.

Align the wallcovering with the far edge of the table so there will be no paste on the table to be transferred to the face of the wallcovering. Apply the paste by brushing away from the centre. Paste the edges and remove any lumps.

If you prefer, apply the paste with a short-pile paint roller. Pour the paste into a roller tray and roll in one direction only towards the end of the paper.

Pull the covering to the front edge of the table and paste the other half. Fold the pasted end over – don't press it down – and slide the length along the table to expose an unpasted part.

Paste the other end, then fold it over to almost meet the first cut end: the second fold is invariably deeper than the first, a good way to denote the bottom of patterned wallcoverings. Fold long drops concertina-fashion.

Hang vinyls and lightweight papers immediately; drape other coverings over a broom handle spanning two chair backs and leave them to soak. Some heavy or embossed coverings may need to soak for 15 minutes.

Pasting the wall

Hang exotic wallcoverings by pasting the wall instead to reduce the risk of marking their delicate faces. Apply a band of paste just wider than the length of covering, so that you will not have to paste right up to its edge for the next length. Use a brush or roller.

Ready-pasted wallcoverings

Many wallcoverings come precoated with adhesive, activated by soaking a cut length in a trough of cold water. Mix ordinary paste to recoat dry edges.

SEE ALSO

Details for:	
Wallcoverings	92–93
Ready-pasted paper	98

1 Lay several drops face down on the pasting table, their ends retained with string ties.

2 Align covering with far edge of table; apply paste by brushing away from centre, covering the edges.

3 Pull covering to front of table, paste other half, then fold over. Slide length on and paste as before.

4 For long drops, as on a stairwell, fold paper concertina-fashion and leave to soak. Carry drop draped over your arm.

95

PAPERING A WALL

● **Hide a join in a corner**
When you are using a wallcovering with a large pattern, try to finish where it will not be noticeable if the pattern does not quite match.

Sticking down the edges
Ensure that the edges of the paper adhere firmly by running a seam roller along the butt joint.

Losing air bubbles
Slight blistering usually flattens out as wet paper dries and shrinks slightly. If you find that a blister remains, either inject a little paste through it and roll it flat, or cut across it in two directions, peel back the triangular flaps and paste them down.

LINING A WALL

Lining a wall prior to decorating is only necessary if you are hanging embossed or luxury wallcoverings, or if the wall has imperfections that might show through a thin paper. Hang lining paper horizontally so that the joints cannot align with those in the top layer. Work from right to left if you are right-handed and vice versa.

Mark a horizontal line near the top of the wall, one roll-width from the ceiling. Holding the concertina-folded length in one hand, start at the top right-hand corner of the wall, aligning the bottom edge with the marked line. Smooth the paper onto the wall with a paperhanger's brush, working from the centre towards the edges.

Work along the wall gradually, unfolding the length as you do so. Take care not to stretch or tear the wet paper. Use the brush to gently stipple the edge into the corner at each end.

Use the point of a pair of scissors to lightly mark the corner, peel back the paper and trim to the line. Brush the paper back in place. You may have to perform a similar operation along the ceiling if the paper overlaps slightly. Work down the wall butting each strip against the last, or leave a tiny gap between the lengths.

Trim the bottom length to the skirting. Leave the lining paper to dry out for 24 hours before covering.

Lining prior to painting

If you line a wall for emulsion painting, hang the lining paper vertically as you would with other wallcoverings as the joints will hardly show.

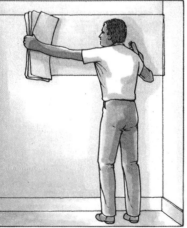

Hanging lining paper horizontally
Hold the concertina-folded paper in one hand and smooth onto the wall from top right, butting strips.

Where to start

Don't apply any type of wallcovering until all the woodwork has been painted or varnished and the ceiling has been painted or papered.

The traditional method for papering a room is to hang the first length next to a window close to a corner, then work in both directions away from the light, but you may find it easier to paper the longest uninterrupted wall to get used to the basic techniques before tackling corners or obstructions.

If your wallcovering has a large regular motif, centre the first length over the fireplace for symmetry. You could also centre this first length between two windows, unless you will be left with narrow strips each side, in which case it's best to butt two lengths on the centre line.

Centre a large motif over fireplace

Butt two lengths between windows

Hanging on a straight wall

The walls of an average room are rarely truly square, so use a plumb line to mark a vertical guide against which to hang the first length of wallcovering. Start at one end of the wall and mark the vertical line one roll-width away from the corner, minus 12mm (½in) so the first length will overlap the adjacent wall.

Allowing enough wallcovering for trimming at the ceiling, unfold the top section of the pasted length and hold it against the plumbed line. Using a paperhanger's brush, work gently out from the centre in all directions to squeeze out any trapped air.

When you are sure the paper is positioned accurately, lightly draw the point of your scissors along the ceiling line, peel back the top edge and cut along the crease. Smooth the paper back and stipple it down with the brush. Unpeel the lower fold of the paper, smooth it onto the wall with the brush, then stipple it into the corner. Crease the bottom edge against the skirting, peel away the paper, then trim and brush it back against the wall.

Hang the next length in the same manner. Slide it with your fingertips to align the pattern and produce a perfect butt joint. Wipe any paste from the surface with a damp cloth. Continue to the other side of the wall, allowing the last drop to overlap the adjoining wall by 12mm (½in).

1 Mark first length
Use a roll of paper to mark the wall one width away from the corner – less 12mm (½in) for an overlap onto the return wall – then draw a line from ceiling to skirting, using a plumb line.

2 Hang the first drop
Cut the first drop of paper, allowing about 50mm (2in) at each end for trimming, paste and allow to soak. Hang the top section against the plumbed line and brush out from the centre, working down.

3 Trim at ceiling
When the paper is smoothly brushed on, run the tip of your scissors along the ceiling angle, peel away the paper, cut off the excess, then brush back onto the wall.

4 Trim at skirting
Unfold the lower section of paper. At the skirting, tap your brush into the top edge, peel away the paper and cut along the folded line, then brush back.

SEE ALSO

Details for:	
Preparing plaster	50–51
Wallcoverings	92–93
Turning off power	302
Radiator roller	499

Papering around doors and windows

Hang the length next to a door frame, brushing down the butt joint to align the pattern and allowing the other edge to loosely overlap the door.

Make a diagonal cut in the excess towards the top corner of the frame (1). Crease the waste down the side of the frame with scissors, peel it back, trim off then brush back. Leave a 12mm (½in) strip for turning on the top of the frame. Fill in with short strips above the door.

Butt the next full length over the door and cut the excess diagonally into the frame so that you can paste the rest of the strip down the other side of the door. Mark and cut off the waste.

When papering up to flush window frames, treat them like a door. Where a window is set into a reveal, hang the length of wallcovering next to the window and allow it to overhang the opening. Make a horizontal cut just above the edge of the window reveal. Make a similar cut near the bottom, then fold the paper around to cover the side of the reveal. Crease and trim along the window frame and sill.

Cut a strip of paper to match the width and pattern of the overhang above the window reveal. Paste it, slip it under the overhang and fold it around the top of the reveal (2). Cut through the overlap with a smooth, wavy stroke, remove the excess paper and roll down the joint (3).

To continue, hang short lengths on the wall below and above the window, wrapping top lengths into the reveal.

1 Cut the overlap diagonally into the frame

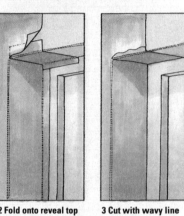

2 Fold onto reveal top   **3 Cut with wavy line**

Papering around a fireplace

Paper around a fireplace as for a door. Make a diagonal cut in the waste overlapping the fireplace, up to the edge of the mantel shelf, so that you can tuck the paper in all round for creasing and trimming to the surround.

To cut to an ornate surround, paper the wall above the surround. Cut strips to fit under the mantel at each side, turning them around the corners of the chimney breast. Gently press the wallcovering into the moulding, peel it away and cut round the impression with nail scissors. Brush the paper back.

Papering internal and external corners

Turn an internal corner by marking another plumbed line so that the next length of paper covers the overlap from the first wall. If the piece you trimmed off at the corner is wide enough, use it as your first length on the new wall.

To turn an external corner, trim the last length so that it wraps around it, lapping the next wall by about 25mm (1in). Plumb and hang the remaining strip with its edge about 12mm (½in) from the corner.

12mm (½in) OVERLAP

Internal corner

25mm (1in) OVERLAP

12mm (½in) FROM CORNER

External corner

● **Papering archways**
Arrange strips to leave even gaps between arch sides and the next full-length strips. Hang strips over face of arch, cut curve leaving 25mm (1in) margin. Fold it onto underside, snipping into margin to prevent creasing. Fit a strip on the underside to reach from floor to top of arch. Repeat on opposite side of arch.

Papering behind radiators

If you cannot remove a radiator, turn off the heating and allow it to cool. Use a steel tape to measure the positions of the brackets along the radiator to the wall. Transfer these measurements to a length of wallcovering and slit it from the bottom to the top of the bracket. Feed the pasted paper behind the radiator, down both sides of the brackets. Use a radiator roller to press it to the wall. Crease and trim to the skirting board.

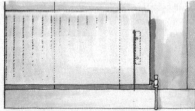

Slit to top of bracket behind radiator

Papering around switches and sockets

Turn off the electricity at the mains. Hang the wallcovering over the switch or socket. Make diagonal cuts from the centre of the fitting to each corner and tap the excess paper against the edges of the faceplate with the brush. Trim off the waste, leaving 6mm (¼in) all round. Loosen the faceplate, tuck the margin behind and retighten it. Don't switch the power back on until the paste is dry.

Trim off the waste

STAIRWELLS

The only real problem with papering a stairwell is having to handle the extra-long drops on the side walls. You will need to build a safe work platform over the stairs. Plumb and hang the longest drop first, lapping the head wall above the stairs by 12mm (½in).

Carrying the long drops of wallcovering – sometimes as much as 4.5m (15ft) long – is awkward: paste the covering liberally so that it's not likely to dry out while you hang it, then fold it concertina-fashion. Drape it over your arm while you climb the platform. You will need an assistant to support the weight of the pasted length while you apply it. Unfold the flaps as you work down the wall.

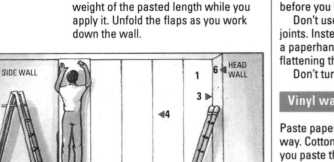

Papering sequence
Follow the sequence for papering a stairwell.
1 Hang the longest drop.
2 Crease it into the angled skirting and trim to fit.
3 Lap the paper onto the head wall.
4 & 5 Work away from the first drop in both directions.
6 Paper the head wall.

Crease and cut the bottom of the paper against the angled skirting. Don't forget to allow for this angle when first you cut the length; work to the longest edge measurement. Work away from this first length in both directions, then paper the head wall.

Where the banister rail is let into the stairwell wall, try to arrange the rolls so that the rail falls between two butted drops. Hang the drops to the rail and cut horizontally into the edge of the last strip at the centre of the rail, then make radial cuts so the paper can be moulded around the rail. Crease the flaps, peel away the wallcovering and cut them off. Smooth the covering back.

Hang the next drop at the other side of the rail, butting it to the previous piece, and make similar radial cuts.

SPECIAL TECHNIQUES FOR WALLPAPERING

No matter what kind of wallcovering you may be using, the standard wallpapering techniques previously explained hold good. However, there are some additional considerations and special techniques involved in applying some types of covering.

Relief wallcoverings

When hanging embossed-paper wallcoverings, line the wall first and use a heavy-duty paste. Apply the paste liberally and evenly, but try not to leave too much paste in the depressions. Allow it to soak for 10 minutes (or, for cotton-fibre wallcoverings, 15 minutes) before you hang it.

Don't use a seam roller on the butt joints. Instead, tap the paper down with a paperhanger's brush to avoid flattening the pattern.

Don't turn a relief wallcovering around corners. Measure the distance from the last drop to the corner and cut your next length to fit. Trim and hang the offcut to meet at the corner. Fill external corners with cellulose filler once the paper has dried thoroughly.

Lincrusta is available in a limited range of original Victorian patterns for re-creating period-style decorative schemes. Hanging this expensive material requires special techniques that are difficult to master, and it pays in the long run to leave it to an expert.

Vinyl wallcoverings

Paste paper-backed vinyls in the normal way. Cotton-backed vinyl hangs better if you paste the wall and then leave it to become tacky before you apply the wallcovering. Use fungicidal paste.

Hang and butt-join lengths of vinyl, using a sponge to smooth them onto the wall rather than a brush. Crease a length top and bottom, then trim it to size with a sharp knife.

Vinyl will not normally stick to itself, so when you turn a corner use a knife to cut through both pieces of paper where they overlap. Peel away the excess and rub down the vinyl to produce a perfect butt joint. Alternatively, glue the overlap, using a tube of repair adhesive.

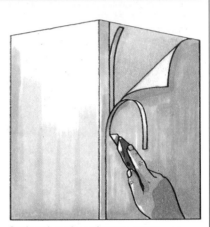

Cut through overlap and remove excess

Ready-pasted wallcoverings

Place the trough of cold water next to the skirting at the position of the first drop. Roll a cut length loosely from the outside. Immerse the roll in the trough for the prescribed time, according to the manufacturer's instructions.

Take hold of the cut end and lift the paper, allowing it to unroll naturally and draining the surface water back into the trough at the same time. Hang and butt-join in the usual way, using a sponge to apply vinyls and a paperhanger's brush for other coverings.

Hanging a long wet length can be difficult if you follow the standard procedure. Instead, roll the length from the top with the pattern outermost. Place it in the trough and immediately reroll it through the water. Take it from the trough in roll form and drain excess water, then unroll the strip as you proceed to hang it.

Pull paper from trough and hang on the wall

SPECIAL TECHNIQUES FOR WALLPAPERING

Foamed polyethylene

A foamed-plastic wallcovering can be hung straight from the roll onto a pasted wall. Sponge in place and trim it top and bottom with scissors.

Flock paper

Protect the flocking with a piece of lining paper as you remove air bubbles with a paperhanger's brush. Cut through both thicknesses of overlapping strips and remove the surplus; press back the edges to make a neat butt joint.

Fabrics and special coverings

Try to keep paste off the face of paper-backed fabrics and any other special wallcoverings. There are many different types of wallcovering, so check with the supplier which paste to use for the one you have chosen.

In order to avoid damaging a delicate surface, use a felt or rubber roller to press the covering in place or stipple gently with a brush.

Most fabric coverings will be machine-trimmed, but if the edges are frayed, overlap the joints and cut through both thicknesses, then peel off the waste to make a butt joint. Make a similar joint at a corner.

Many fabrics are sold in wide rolls: even one cut length will be heavy and awkward to handle. Paste the wall, then support the rolled length on a batten between two stepladders. Work from the bottom upwards.

PASTE WALL

BATTEN SUPPORT

FABRIC ROLL

Supporting heavy fabric

Expanded polystyrene

Paint or roll special ready-mixed adhesive onto the wall. Hang the covering straight from the roll, smooth gently with the flat of your hand, then roll over it lightly with a dry paint roller.

If the edge is square, butt adjacent drops. If it is crushed or crumbled, overlap the join and cut through both thicknesses with a sharp trimming knife, peel away the offcuts and rub the edges down. Unless the edges are generously glued, they will curl apart. Trim top and bottom with a knife and straightedge. Allow to dry for 72 hours, then hang a subsequent wallcovering using a thick fungicidal paste.

Hang the wallcovering straight from the roll

If you want to apply a plain-coloured medium-weight fabric, you can glue it directly to the wall. However, it can be difficult to align a pattern if the fabric stretches.

For more control, stretch the fabric onto 12mm (½in) thick panels of lightweight insulation board (you will then have the added advantage of insulation and a pin-board). Stick the boards directly onto the wall.

Using paste

Test an offcut of fabric to make sure the adhesive will not stain it. Use a ready-mixed paste and roll it onto the wall.

Wrap a cut length of fabric around a cardboard tube (from a carpet supplier) and gradually unroll it on the surface, smoothing it down with a dry paint roller. Take care not to distort the weave. Overlap the joins, but do not cut through them until the paste has dried in case the fabric shrinks. Reapply paste and close the seam.

Press the fabric into the ceiling line and skirting, then trim away the excess with a sharp trimming knife when the paste has set.

Making wall panels

Cut the insulation board to suit the width of the fabric and the height of the wall. Stretch the fabric across the panel, wrap it around the edges, then use latex adhesive to stick it to the back. Hold it temporarily with drawing pins while the adhesive dries.

Either use wallboard adhesive to glue the panels to the wall or pin them, tapping the nail heads through the weave of the fabric to conceal them.

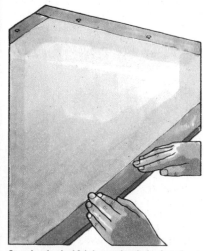

Stretch unbacked fabric over insulation board

PAPERING
A CEILING

Working from a ladder
If you have to work from a stepladder, an assistant can support the paper on a cardboard tube taped to a broom.

Papering a ceiling isn't as difficult as you may think: the techniques are basically the same as for papering a wall, except that the drops are usually longer and more unwieldy to hold while you brush the paper into place. Set up a sensible work platform – it's virtually impossible to work from a single stepladder – and enlist a helper to support the folded paper while you position one end, progressing backwards across the room. If you have marked out the ceiling first, the result should be faultless.

Setting out the ceiling

Arrange your work platform before you begin to plan out the papering sequence for the ceiling. The best type of platform to use is a purpose-made decorator's trestle, but you can manage with a pair of scaffold boards spanning two stepladders.

Now mark the ceiling to give a visual guide to positioning the strips of paper. Aim to work parallel with the window wall and away from the light, so you can see what you are doing and so that the light will not highlight the joints between strips. If the distance is shorter the other way, hang the strips in that direction for ease.

Mark a guideline along the ceiling, one roll-width minus 12mm (½in) from the side wall, so that the first strip of paper will lap onto the wall.

Putting up the paper

Paste the paper as for a wallcovering and fold it concertina-fashion. Drape the folded length over a spare roll and carry it to the work platform. You will find it easier if a helper supports the folded paper, leaving both your hands free for brushing it into place.

Hold the strip against the guideline, using a brush to stroke it onto the ceiling. Tap it into the wall angle, then gradually work backwards along the scaffold board, brushing on the paper as your helper unfolds it.

If the ceiling has a cornice, crease and trim the paper at the ends. Otherwise, leave it to lap the walls by 12mm (½in) so that it will be covered by the wallcovering. Work across the ceiling in the same way, butting the lengths of paper together. Cut the final strip roughly to width, and trim into the wall angle.

Papering a ceiling
The job is much easier if two people work together.
1 Mark a guideline on the ceiling.
2 Support the folded paper on a tube.
3 Brush on the paper from the centre outwards.
4 The overlap is eventually covered by wallpaper.
5 Use a pair of boards to support two people.

LIGHTING FITTINGS AND CENTREPIECES

Unlike walls, where you have doors, windows and radiators to contend with, there are few obstructions on a ceiling to make papering difficult. The only problem areas occur where there is a pendant light fitting or a decorative plaster centrepiece.

Cutting around a pendant light
Where the paper passes over a ceiling rose, cut several triangular flaps so that you can pass the light fitting through the hole. Tap the paper all round the rose with a paperhanger's brush and continue on to the end of the length. Return to the rose and cut off the flaps with a knife.

Papering around a centrepiece
If you have a decorative plaster centrepiece, work out the position of the strips so that a joint will pass through the middle. Cut long flaps from the side of each piece so that you can tuck it in all round the plaster moulding.

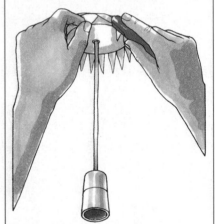

Cut off triangular flaps when paste is dry

Cut long strips to fit around moulding

CHOOSING

TILES

Tiling is a popular method of decorating a surface, with an almost inexhaustible range of colours, textures and patterns to choose from depending on the degree of durability required. Tiling provides the facility of finishing a surface with small, regular units which can be cut and fitted into an awkward shape far more easily than can sheet materials.

Glazed ceramic tiles

Hard ceramic tiles, usually glazed and fired, are made for walls and floors. Unglazed tiles are available to provide a surer grip for flooring; a textured surface reduces the risk of accidents where a floor might become wet. All ceramic tiles are durable and waterproof but, where appropriate, be sure to use special tiles that are resistant to heat or frost. Do not use wall tiles on the floor as they cannot take the weight of traffic or furniture.

The majority of tiles are square, the dimensions varying according to use and the manufacturer's preference. Rectangular and more irregularly shaped tiles are also available: typical shapes include hexagons, octagons, diamonds and interlocking units with curved, elaborate edges, as well as slim rectangles with either pointed (pic) or slanted (cane) ends. Use them in combination to produce patterned floors and walls.

Mosaic tiles

Mosaic tiles are small versions of the standard ceramic tiles. To lay them individually would be time-consuming and lead to inaccuracy, so they are usually joined by a paper covering, or a mesh background, into larger panels. Square tiles are common, but rectangular, hexagonal and round mosaics are also available. Because they are small, mosaics can be used on curved surfaces, and will fit irregular shapes better than large ceramic tiles.

Quarry tiles

Quarry tiles are thick, unglazed ceramic tiles which are used for floors which need a hardwearing, waterproof surface. The colours are limited to browns, reds, black and white. Machine-made tiles are regular in size and even in colour but hand-made ones are variable, producing a beautiful mottled effect. Quarry tiles are difficult to cut, so do not contemplate using them where you will have to try to fit them against a complicated shape. Round-edge quarry tiles can be used as treads for steps, and skirting tiles are available for finishing a floor.

Stone and slate flooring

A floor laid with real stone or slate tiles will be exquisite but expensive. Sizes and thicknesses vary according to the manufacturer – some will even cut to measure. A few materials are so costly that you should consider hiring a professional to lay them, otherwise treat cheaper ones like quarry tiles.

Standard tile sections
A range of sections is produced for specific functions:

Field tile for general tiling with spacing lugs moulded onto it.

Rounded-edge (RE) tile for edging the field.

REX tile with two adjacent rounded edges.

Universal tile with two glazed, square edges for use in any position.

Tile selection
The examples shown left are a typical cross-section of commercially available ceramic tiles.
1 Glazed ceramic
2 Shape and size variation
3 Mosaic tiles
4 Quarry tiles
5 Slate and stone

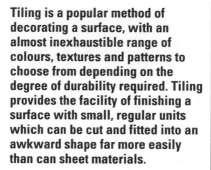

CHOOSING

TILES

Stone and brick tiles

Thin masonry facing tiles can be used to simulate a stone or brick wall as a feature area for a chimney breast, for example, or to clad a whole wall. Stone tiles are typically made from reconstituted stone in moulds, and most look unconvincing as an imitation of the real thing. Colour choice is intended to reflect local stone types, and is typically white, grey or buff. Some 'weathered' versions are also made.

Brick tiles look much more authentic. The best ones are actually brick 'slips' – slivers cut from kiln-produced bricks. A very wide range of traditional brick colours is available.

Brick tiles
For the best result, use fired-clay slips.

Carpet tiles

Carpet tiles have advantages over wall-to-wall carpeting. An error is less crucial when cutting a single tile to fit, and, being loose-laid, a worn, burnt or stained tile can be replaced instantly. However, you can't substitute a brand-new tile several years later, as the colour will not match. Buy several spares initially and swap them around regularly to even out the wear and colour change. Most types of carpet are available as tiles, including cord, loop and twist piles in wool as well as a range of man-made fibres. Tiles are normally plain in colour, but some are patterned to give a grid effect. Some tiles have an integral rubber underlay.

Carpet tiles make hardwearing floorcoverings

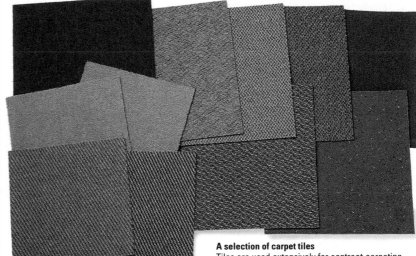

A selection of carpet tiles
Tiles are used extensively for contract carpeting, but they are equally suitable as a hardwearing floorcovering in the home.

Vinyl tiles

Vinyl tiles are among the cheapest and easiest floorcoverings to use. Vinyl can be cut easily, and provided the tiles are firmly glued, with good joints, the floor will be waterproof. However, it will still be susceptible to scorching. A standard coated tile has a printed pattern between a vinyl backing and a harder, clear-vinyl surface. Solid-vinyl tiles are made entirely of the hardwearing plastic. Some vinyl tiles have a high proportion of mineral filler. As a result they are stiff and must be laid on a perfectly flat base. Unlike standard vinyl tiles, they will resist some rising damp in a concrete sub-floor. Most tiles are square or rectangular, but there are interlocking shapes and hexagons. There are many patterns and colours to choose from, including embossed vinyl which represents ceramic, brick or stone tiling.

Vinyl tiles can simulate other flooring materials

Polystyrene tiles

Although expanded-polystyrene tiles will not reduce heat loss from a room by any significant amount, they will prevent condensation as well as mask a ceiling in poor condition. Polystyrene cuts easily provided the trimming knife is very sharp. For safety in case of fire, choose a self-extinguishing type and do not overpaint with an oil paint. Wall tiles are made, but they will crush easily and are not suitable for use in a vulnerable area. Polystyrene tiles may be flat or decoratively embossed.

Mineral-fibre tiles

Ceiling tiles made from compressed mineral fibre are dense enough to be sound-insulating and heat-insulating. They are normally fitted into a suspended grid system that may be exposed or concealed depending on whether the tile edges are rebated or grooved. Fibre tiles can also be glued directly to a flat ceiling. A range of textured surfaces is available.

Mirror tiles

Square and rectangular mirror tiles are attached to walls by means of a self-adhesive pad in each corner. There is a choice of silver or bronze finish. Don't expect these tiles to produce a perfect reflection unless they are mounted on a completely flat surface.

Plastic tiles

Insulated plastic wall tiles inhibit condensation. Provided you don't use abrasive cleaners on them they are relatively durable, but they will melt if subjected to direct heat. A special grout is applied to fill the 'joints' moulded across the 300mm (1ft) square tiles.

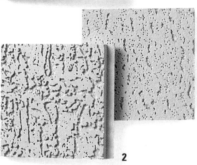

Rubber tiles

Rubber tiles were originally made for use in shops and offices, but they are equally suitable for the home, being hardwearing yet soft and quiet to walk on. The surface is usually studded or textured to improve the grip.

Cork tiles

Cork is a popular covering for walls and floors. It is easy to lay with contact adhesive and can be cut to size and shape with a knife. A wide range of textures and warm colours is available. Presanded but unfinished cork will darken in tone when you varnish it. Alternatively, you can buy ready-finished tiles with various plastic and wax coatings. Soft, granular insulating cork is suitable as a decorative finish for walls only. It crumbles easily, so should not be used where it will be exposed on external corners.

Left to right
1 Polystyrene tiles
2 Mineral-fibre tiles
3 Mirror tiles
4 Plastic tiles
5 Rubber tiles
6 Cork floor tiles

103

SETTING OUT
FOR WALL TILES

Setting out
The setting-out procedure described on this page is applicable to the following tiles: cork, mosaics, ceramic, mirror and plastic.

Using a gauge stick
Hold a home-made gauge stick firmly against the wall and mark the positions of the tiles on the surface.

Setting out for tiling
Plan different arrangements of wall tiles as shown right, but first plot the symmetry of the tile field with a gauge stick to ensure a wide margin all round.
1 Temporarily fix a horizontal batten at the base of the field.
2 Mark the centre of the wall.
3 Gauge from the mark, then fix a vertical batten to indicate the side of the field.
4 Start under a dado rail with whole tiles.
5 Use a row of whole tiles at sill level.
6 Place cut tiles at back of a reveal.
7 Support tiles over window while they set.

Whatever type of tiles you plan to use, the walls must be clean, sound and dry. You cannot tile over wallpaper, and flaking or powdery paint must be treated first to give a suitable stable base for the tiles. It is important that you make the surface as flat as possible so the tiles will stick firmly. Setting out the prepared surface accurately is vital to hanging the tiles properly.

MAKING A GAUGE STICK

First make a gauge stick (a tool for plotting the position of tiles on the wall) from a length of 50 x12mm (2 x ½in) softwood. Lay several tiles along it, butting together those with lugs, or add spacers for square-edged tiles, unless they are intended to be close-butted. Mark the position of each tile on the softwood batten.

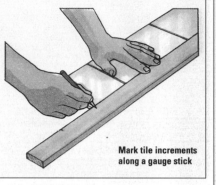

Mark tile increments along a gauge stick

Setting out a plain wall

On a plain uninterrupted wall, use the gauge stick to plan horizontal rows starting at skirting level. If you are left with a narrow strip at the top, move the rows up half a tile-width to create a wider margin. Mark the bottom of the lowest row of whole tiles. Temporarily nail a thin guide batten to the wall aligned with the mark **(1)**. Make sure it is horizontal by placing a level on top.

Mark the centre of the wall **(2)**, then use the gauge stick to set out the vertical rows at each side of it. If the border tiles measure less than half a width, reposition the rows sideways by half a tile. Use a spirit level to position a guide batten against the last vertical line and nail it to the wall **(3)**.

Plotting a half-tiled wall

If you are tiling part of a wall only (up to a dado rail, for example) set out the tiles with a row of whole tiles at the top **(4)**.

This is even more important if you are using RE tiles which are used for the top row of a half-tiled wall.

Arranging tiles around a window

Use a window as your starting point so that the tiles surrounding it are equal in size, but not too narrow. If possible, begin a row of whole tiles at sill level **(5)**, and position cut tiles at the back of a window reveal **(6)**. Fix a guide batten over a window to support a row of tiles temporarily **(7)**.

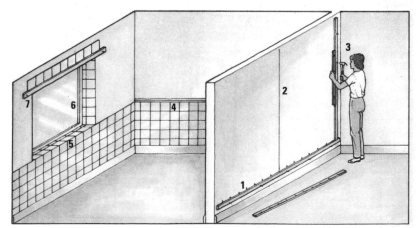

RENOVATING TILES

A properly tiled surface should last for many years, but the appearance is often spoiled by one or two damaged tiles (particularly the lifting of cork, vinyl or polystyrene tiles) and by discoloured grouting between ceramic tiles. There is usually no need to redecorate as most problems can be solved fairly easily.

Renewing the grouting
It's not necessary to rake out old, drab grouting: use a renovator to brighten it up instead. This liquid colourant forms a water-resistant bond with grout but does not adhere to ceramic surfaces. Wash the tiles with sugar soap and let them dry overnight. Paint the renovator along the joints and leave it to dry for a couple of hours. Wet the whole tiling with a plant spray and after three minutes wipe off excess colourant with a damp sponge. Dry and polish the tiles with a soft cloth or paper towel.

Replacing a cracked ceramic tile
Scrape the grout from the damaged tile, then use a fine cold chisel to chip out the tile, working from the centre. Take care not to dislodge its neighbours.

Scrape out the remains of the adhesive and vacuum the recess. Butter the back of the replacement tile with adhesive, then press it firmly in place. Wipe off excess adhesive, allow it to set, then renew the grouting.

Lifting a cork or vinyl floor tile
Try to remove a single tile by chopping it out from the centre with a wood chisel. If the adhesive is firm, warm the tile with a domestic iron (or a hot-air gun on a very low setting, but take care not to damage the surrounding tiles). Scrape the old adhesive from the floor and try the new tile for fit. Trim it if necessary. Spread adhesive on the floor, then place one corner of the tile in position. Gradually lower the tile into place, then press with your fingertips to squeeze out any air bubbles, place a heavy weight on it and leave overnight.

Removing a ceiling tile
Loosen a polystyrene tile by picking it out from the centre with a sharp knife and paint scraper. Don't lever it out or you will crush the adjoining tile. Stick the replacement tile on a complete bed of special adhesive. Remove a stapled ceiling tile by cutting through the tongues all round.

Choosing the correct adhesive

Most ceramic-tile adhesives are sold ready-mixed, although a few need to be mixed with water. The tubs or packets will state the coverage.

A standard adhesive is suitable for most applications, but use a waterproof type in areas likely to be subjected to running water or splashing. If the tiles are to be laid on a wallboard, use a flexible adhesive and make sure that it is heat-resistant if you are tiling above worktops or around a fireplace. Some adhesives can also be used for grouting the finished wall. A notched plastic spreader is usually supplied with each tub, or you can use a serrated trowel.

Hanging the tiles

Spread enough adhesive on the wall to cover about 1 metre square (about 3ft 3 in square). Press the teeth of the spreader against the surface and drag it through the adhesive so that it forms horizontal ridges (1).

Press the first tile into the angle formed by the setting out battens (2) until it is firmly fixed, then butt up tiles on each side. Build up three or four rows at a time. If the tiles do not have lugs, place proprietary plastic spacers between them to form the grout lines.

Wipe away adhesive from the surface with a damp sponge.

Spread more adhesive, and tile along the batten until the first rows of whole tiles are complete. From time to time, check that your tiling is accurate by holding a batten and spirit level across the faces and along the top and side edges. When you have completed the entire field, scrape adhesive from the border and allow the rest to set before removing the setting-out battens and proceeding with the grouting.

Grouting tiles and sealing joins

Use a ready-mixed paste called grout to fill the gaps between the tiles. Standard grouts are white, grey or brown, but there is also a range of coloured grouts to match or contrast with the tiles. Alternatively, to match a particular colour, mix pigments with dry, powdered grout before adding water.

Waterproof grout is essential for showers and bath surrounds, and you should use an epoxy-based grout for worktops to keep them germ-free.

Leave the adhesive to harden for 24 hours, then use a rubber-bladed spreader to press the grout into the joints (3). Spread it in all directions to make sure all joints are well filled.

Wipe grout from the surface of the tiles with a sponge before it sets and smooth the joints with a blunt-ended stick – a sharpened dowel will do. When the grout has dried, polish the tiles with a dry cloth.

Do not use a tiled shower for about seven days to make sure the grout hardens thoroughly.

Sealing around bathroom fittings

Don't use grout or ordinary filler to seal the gap between a tiled wall and shower tray, bath or basin: the fittings can flex enough to crack a rigid seal, and frequent soakings will allow water to seep in, create stains and damage the floor and wall. Use a silicone-rubber caulking compound to fill the gaps; it remains flexible enough to accommodate any movement.

Packed in cartridges, sealants are available in a choice of colours to match popular tile and sanitaryware colourways. They can cope with gaps up to 3mm (⅛in) wide. Alternatively, use a strip of press-in-place sealant.

If you are using a cartridge, trim the end off the plastic nozzle (the amount you cut off dictates the thickness of the bead) and press the tip into the joint at an angle of 45 degrees. Push forward at a steady rate while squeezing the applicator's trigger or the base of the cartridge itself to apply a bead of sealant (4). Smooth any ripples with the back of a wetted teaspoon.

Ceramic coving or quadrant tiles are made for edging a bath or shower unit, and there are glue-on plastic coving strips which you cut to length.

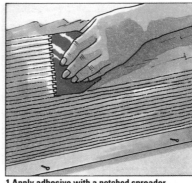
1 Apply adhesive with a notched spreader

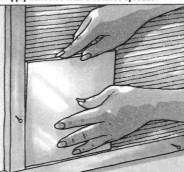
2 Stick first tile in angle of setting-out battens

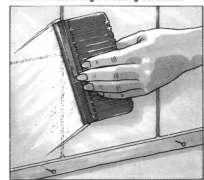
3 Press grout into joints with rubber spreader

4 Seal between tiles and fittings with sealant

Ceramic coving tiles

Quadrant
Used to fill the joint between bath and wall.

Mitred tile
Use at the end if you want to turn a corner.

Bullnose tile
Use this tile to finish the end of a straight run.

● **Tiling around pipes and fittings**
Check with the gauge stick how the tiles will fit round socket outlets and switches, pipes and other obstructions. Make slight adjustments to the position of the main field to avoid difficult shaping around these features.

105

CUTTING
CERAMIC TILES

Tile-cutting jig
A worthwhile investment if you are cutting a lot of tiles, a proprietary jig incorporates a device for measuring and scoring tiles. A cutter is drawn down the channel of the adjustable guide. The tile is then snapped with a special pincer-action tool.

Having finished a main field of tiles you will have to cut ceramic tiles to fill the borders and to fit around obstructions such as window frames, electrical fittings, pipes and a basin. Protect your eyes with safety spectacles or goggles when snapping scored ceramic tiles.

Cutting thin strips
A cutting jig is the most accurate tool for cutting a thin strip cleanly from the edge of a tile. If you do not want to use the strip itself, nibble away the waste a little at a time with pincers or special tile nibblers.

Tiling around a window
Tile up to the edges of a window, then stick RE tiles to the reveal so that they lap the edges of surrounding tiles. Fill in any space left behind the edging tiles with cut tiles.

Cutting a curve
To fit a tile against a curved shape, cut a template from thin card to the exact size of a tile. Cut 'fingers' along one edge; press them against the curve to reproduce the shape. Transfer the curve onto the face of the tile and cut away the waste with a tile saw – a thin rod coated with hard, abrasive particles which will cut in any direction.

Mark two edges   **Cut and fit tile**

Fitting around a pipe
Mark the centre of the pipe on the top and side edges of a tile and draw lines across the tile from these points. Where they cross, draw round a coin or something slightly larger than the diameter of the pipe.

Make one straight cut through the centre of the circle and either nibble out the waste, having scored the curve, or clamp it in a vice, protected with softening, and cut it out with a tile saw. Stick one half of the tile on each side of the pipe.

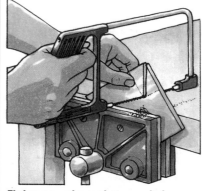

Fitting around a socket or switch
In order to fit around a socket or switch you may have to cut the corner out of a tile. Mark it from the socket, then clamp the tile in a vice, protected with softening. Score both lines, then use a saw file to make one diagonal cut from the corner of the tile to where the lines meet. Snap out both triangles.

If you have to cut a notch out of a large tile, cut down both sides with a hacksaw, then score between them and snap the piece out of the middle.

CUTTING BORDER TILES

It's necessary to cut border tiles one at a time to fit the gap between the field tiles and the adjacent wall: walls are rarely truly square and the margin is bound to be uneven.

Making straight cuts
Mark a border tile by placing it face down over its neighbour with one edge against the adjacent wall (**1**). Make an allowance for normal spacing between the tiles. Transfer the marks to the edge of the tiles using a felt-tip pen.

Use a proprietary tile cutter held against a straightedge to score across the face with one firm stroke to cut through the glaze (**2**). You may also have to score the edges of thick tiles.

Stretch a length of thin wire across a panel of chipboard, place the scored line directly over the wire and press down on both sides to snap the tile (**3**).

If you are planning to do a lot of tiling, it will pay to invest in a purpose-made tile-cutting jig. Inexpensive plastic jigs (see left) are perfectly adequate for relatively thin tiles, but there are also substantial jigs that can cope with tiles of any thickness. These jigs enable you to score tiles accurately and snap them with ease every time.

Smooth the cut edges of the tile with a tile sander or small slipstone.

1 Mark the edge tile

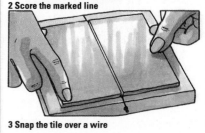

2 Score the marked line

3 Snap the tile over a wire

APPLICATION
TILING

HANGING

OTHER WALL

TILES

SEE ALSO

Mosaic tiles

Ceramic mosaic tiles are applied to a wall in a similar way to large square tiles. Set out the wall and use the same adhesive and grout.

Some mosaics have a mesh backing, which is pressed into the adhesive. Others have facing paper which is left on the surface until the adhesive sets.

Fill the main area of the wall, spacing the sheets to equal the gaps between individual tiles. Place a carpet-covered board over the sheets and tap it with a mallet to bed the tiles into the adhesive.

Fill borders by cutting strips from the sheet. Cut individual tiles to fit awkward shapes around fittings. If necessary, soak off the facing paper with a damp sponge, then grout the tiles.

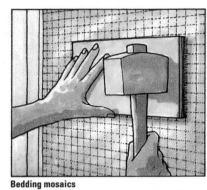

Bedding mosaics
Bed tiles by tapping a carpet-covered board.

Mirror tiles

Avoid using mirror tiles in an area which would entail complicated fitting, as it is difficult to cut glass except in straight lines. Mirror tiles are fixed close-butted with self-adhesive pads. No grout is necessary.

Set out the wall with battens. Peel the protective paper from the pads and lightly position each tile. Check its alignment with a spirit level, then press it firmly into place with a soft cloth.

Use a wooden straightedge and a glass cutter to score a line across a tile. Make one firm stroke. Lay the tile over a stretched wire and press down on both sides. Remove the sharp cut edge with an oiled slipstone.

Add spare pads and fix the tile in place. Finally, polish the tiles to remove any unsightly fingermarks.

Placing mirror tiles
Position tile before pressing on wall.

Plastic tiles

You can cover a wall relatively quickly with 300mm (1ft) square moulded-plastic tiles. Being backed with expanded polystyrene, the tiles are extremely lightweight and warm to the touch. They are ideal in bathrooms or kitchens where condensation is a problem, but don't hang them in close proximity to cookers, boilers or even radiators – they may soften and distort.

Set out the area to be tiled with guide battens, and spread the special manufacturer's adhesive thinly across the back of each tile. Press the tiles firmly against the wall, butting them together gently. Being flexible, plastic tiles will accommodate slightly imperfect walls.

Grout the moulded 'joints' with the branded non-abrasive product sold with the tiles. Use a damp sponge to remove surplus grout before it sets hard, or employ methylated spirit afterwards.

Plastic tiles are easy to shape with scissors or a craft knife when fitting around pipework or electrical points.

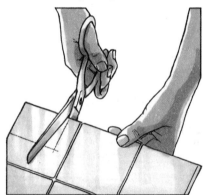

Shaping plastic tiles
Shape insulated plastic tiles with scissors.

Cork tiles

Set up a horizontal guide batten to make sure you lay the tiles accurately. It isn't necessary to fix a vertical batten, however; the large tiles are easy to align without one. Simply mark a vertical line centrally on the wall and hang the tiles in both directions from it.

You will need a rubber-based contact adhesive to fix cork tiles. It pays to use a glue that allows a degree of movement when positioning the tiles. If any adhesive gets onto the surface of a tile, clean it off immediately with a suitable solvent on a cloth.

Spread adhesive thinly and evenly onto the wall and the back of the tiles and leave it to dry. Lay each tile by placing one edge only against the batten or its neighbour, then gradually press the rest of the tile onto the wall.

Smooth it down with your palms.

Cut cork tiles with a sharp trimming knife. Because the edges are butted tightly, you will need to be very accurate when marking out border tiles. Use the same method as for laying cork and vinyl floor tiles. Cut and fit curved shapes using a template.

Unless the tiles are precoated, apply two coats of varnish after 24 hours.

Tiling around curves
In many older houses some walls might be rounded at the external corners. Flexible tiles such as vinyl and rubber are easy to bend into quite tight radii, but cork will snap if bent too far. Cut a series of shallow slits down the back of a cork tile with a tenon saw, then bend the tile gently to the curve required.

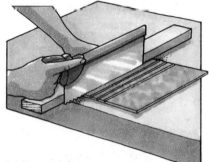

Bending a cork tile
Using a tenon saw, cut a series of shallow slits vertically down the back of a tile, then bend it gently: the slits will enable the tile to assume a fairly tight curve without snapping, but experiment first with a spare tile.

107

FIXING
BRICK TILES

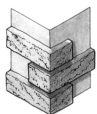

Applying adhesive
Butter the tile back using a notched spreader.

Corner tiles
Start with three preformed corner tiles at each end of a run.

Fixing brick tiles
Follow this procedure when fixing brick tiles to your wall.
1 Plot the tile courses vertically and horizontally with two gauge sticks. Allow joint spaces between each tile.
2 Use preformed tiles at external corners.
3 Set a course of tiles on end above a window as a brick lintel.
4 Set the bottom row of tiles on the skirting or substitute with a row of brick tiles set on end.
5 Leave a gap for ventilating the flue in a blocked-off fireplace.
6 Fix tiles from the bottom up, staggering the vertical joints.

Brick tiles can look quite authentic if they are laid in any of the standard brick-bond patterns, especially if you point them carefully with mortar.

You can either leave the skirting in place and start the first course of tiles just above it, or remove the skirting and replace it just lapping over the bottom course of tiles for an authentic appearance. Alternatively, remove the skirting and set a row of brick tiles on end.

Setting out the wall

Make two gauge sticks, one for the vertical coursing and another to space the tiles sideways. Allow 10mm (⅜in) spacing between each tile for the mortar joints, but adjust this slightly if need be so there will be a full-width tile top and bottom.

Work out your spacing side to side so that, if possible, you have one course of whole tiles, alternating with courses containing a half tile at each end.

If you are using corner tiles at each end, work out your spacing from them towards the middle of a wall, and place cut tiles centrally.

Fitting around a window
Lay tiles vertically above a window in a 'soldier course' to simulate a brick lintel. Use prefabricated corner tiles to take the brickwork into a window reveal for the most realistic effect.

Cutting brick tiles
Most brick tiles can be cut with a hacksaw, but if a cut edge looks too sharp, round it over by rubbing with a scrap piece of tile. You can also cut tiles using a club hammer and bolster chisel; the thinnest type can even be cut with scissors.

Gluing on the tiles

You can use mortar to stick brick tiles to the wall, but most types are sold with a compatible adhesive. Use a notched spreader to coat the back of each tile, then press it on the wall. (Some manufacturers recommend spreading the adhesive onto the wall rather than the tile – check instructions.)

If you are using preformed corner tiles, fix them first, three at a time, alternating headers and stretchers to resemble real brickwork. Using a batten and spirit level, check that they are level at each side of the wall.

Fill in one row at a time, using small 10mm (⅜in) wooden offcuts to space the tiles: alternatively, the polystyrene packing that comes with some tiles can be cut into pieces to use as spacers. Every third course, check the alignment of the tiles with a spirit level and adjust them if necessary.

Pointing the joints
After 24 hours, use a ready-mixed mortar to point the wall as if it were real brickwork. Brush mortar from the face of the tiles with a stiff-bristle brush.

STONE TILES

Stone tiles are laid in the same way as brick tiles. Coursed stones should be arranged with a selection of small and large tiles for the most authentic look: lay the tiles on the floor to plan the setting out, then transfer them to the wall one by one.

Irregularly-shaped stones can be laid in any pattern you want, but again, it's best to set them out on the floor to achieve a good balance of large and small sizes for realism.

With some stone tiles you have to coat the wall with a special mortar-coloured adhesive which gives an overall background, then stick the individual tiles on by buttering their backs with adhesive.

FIXING POLYSTYRENE CEILING TILES

Where to use the tiles
Polystyrene tiles can be used in virtually any room in the house except the kitchen, where they would be directly over a source of heat.

Setting out the ceiling
Remove any friable material and make sure the ceiling is clean and free from grease. Snap two chalked lines which cross each other at right angles in the centre of the ceiling. Hang the tiles to the chalked lines, checking their alignment frequently.

Applying the tiles
Use a proprietary polystyrene adhesive or a heavy-duty wallpaper paste. Spread the adhesive across the back of the tile to cover all but the very edge.

Press the first tile into one of the angles formed by the marked lines. Use the flat of your hand: fingertip pressure can crush polystyrene. Proceed with subsequent tiles to complete one half of the ceiling, then the other.

Cutting the tiles
Mark the border tiles, then, on a flat piece of board, cut through them with a single stroke, using a sharp trimming knife with a long blade. Clean up the edges, but take care not to rub them too hard or the polystyrene granules will crumble away.

Mark out curves with a card template, then follow the marked line freehand with a trimming knife.

SETTING OUT FOR DIAGONAL TILING

Arranging tiles diagonally can create an unusual decorative effect, especially if your choice of tiles enables you to mix colours. Setting out and laying the tiles off centre is not complicated – it's virtually the same as fixing them at right-angles, except that you will be working towards a corner instead of a straight wall. Mark a centre line, and bisect it at right-angles using an improvised compass (see right). Draw a line from opposite diagonal corners of the room through the centre point. Dry-lay a row of tiles to plot the margins (see below right). Mark a right angle to the diagonal. Fix a batten along one diagonal as a guide to laying the first row of tiles.

SETTING OUT FOR SOFT FLOOR TILES

Vinyl, rubber, cork and carpet tiles are relatively large, so you can complete the floor fairly quickly. Some vinyl tiles are self-adhesive, and carpet tiles are loose-laid, both of which speed up the process still further. Soft tiles such as these can be cut easily with a sharp trimming knife or even scissors, so fitting to irregular shapes is easier.

Marking out the floor

It is possible to lay soft tiles onto either a solid-concrete or suspended wooden floor, provided the surface is level, clean and dry. Most soft tiles can be set out in a similar way: find the centre of two opposite walls and snap a chalked string between them to mark a line across the floor (1). Lay loose tiles at right angles to the line up to one wall (see below left). If there is a gap of less than half a tile-width, move the line sideways by half a tile in order to give a wider margin.

To draw a line at right angles to the first, use string and a pencil as an improvised compass to scribe arcs on the marked line, at equal distances each side of the centre (2).

From each point, scribe arcs on both sides of the line (3), which bisect each other. Join the points to form a line across the room (4). As before, lay tiles at right angles to the new line to make sure border tiles are at least half-width. Nail a guide batten against one line to align the first row of tiles.

If the room is noticeably irregular in shape, centre the first line on the fireplace or the door opening (see below right).

SEE ALSO

Details for:
Levelling concrete	49
Levelling floors	57
Floor tiles	102–103

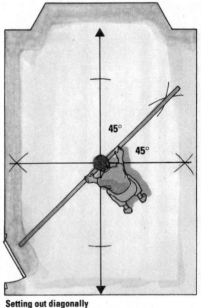

Setting out diagonally
Bisect the quartered room at 45 degrees.

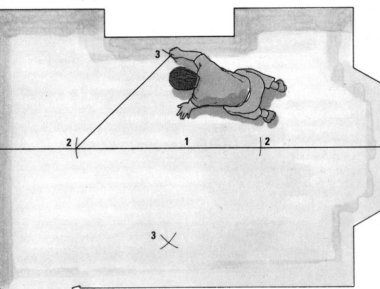

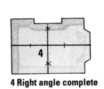

Setting out
A quartered room ensures that the tiles are laid symmetrically. This method is suitable for the following tiles: vinyl, rubber, cork and carpet.

4 Right angle complete

Plotting margin width (near right)
Lay loose tiles to make sure there is a reasonable gap at the margins. If not, move the line half a tile-width to the left.

Plotting an odd-shaped room (far right)
When a room is not a single rectangle, set out the lines using the fireplace and door as focal points.

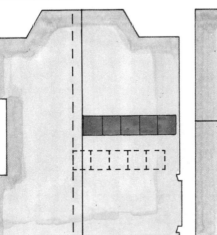

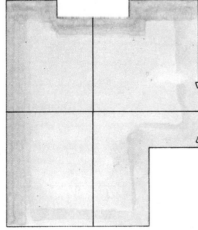

LAYING VINYL
FLOOR TILES

Tiles precoated with adhesive can be laid quickly and simply, and there is no risk of squeezing glue onto the surface. If you are not using self-adhesive tiles, however, follow the tile-manufacturer's instructions concerning the type of adhesive to use.

Fixing self-adhesive tiles

Stack the tiles in the room for 24 hours before you lay them so they become properly acclimatized.

If the tiles have a directional pattern – some have arrows printed on the back to indicate this – make sure you lay them the correct way.

Remove the protective paper backing from the first tile prior to laying (**1**), then press the edge against the guide batten. Align one corner with the centre line (**2**). Gradually lower the tile onto the floor and press it down.

Lay the next tile on the other side of the line, butting against the first one (**3**). Form a square with two more tiles. Lay tiles around the square to form a pyramid (**4**). Continue in this way to fill one half of the room, remove the batten and tile the other half.

1 Peel paper backing from self-adhesive tiles

GLUING VINYL TILES

Spread adhesive thinly but evenly across the floor, using a notched spreader and covering an area for two to three tiles only. Lay the tiles carefully and wipe adhesive from their faces.

Apply bed of adhesive with notched spreader

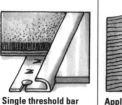

Single threshold bar

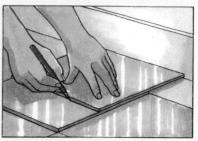

2 Place first tile in angle of intersecting lines

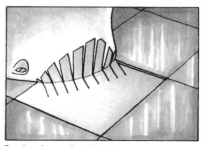

3 Butt up next tile on other side of line

4 Lay tiles in a pyramid, then complete half room

Finishing off the floor

As soon as you have laid all the floor tiles, wash over the surface with a damp cloth to remove any finger marks. It is not often necessary to polish vinyl tiles, but you can apply an emulsion floor polish if you wish.

Fit a straight metal strip (available from carpet suppliers) over the edge of the tiles when you finish at a doorway. When the tiles butt up to an area of carpet, fit a single threshold bar onto the edge of the carpeting (see left).

CUTTING TILES TO FIT

Trimming border tiles
Edges are rarely square, so cut border tiles to the skirting profile. To make a border tile, lay a loose one exactly on top of the last full tile. Place another tile on top, but with its edge touching the wall. Draw along the edge of this tile with a pencil to mark the tile below. Remove the marked tile and cut along the line, then fit the cut-off portion of the tile into the border.

Cutting irregular shapes
To fit curves and mouldings, make a template for each tile out of thin card. Cut fingers which can be pressed against the object to reproduce its shape. Transfer the template to a tile and cut it out. You can also use a profile gauge to mark tiles when you are cutting complex curves.

Fitting around pipes
Mark the position of the pipe on the tile using a compass. Draw parallel lines to the edge of the tile, taken from the perimeter of the circle. Measure halfway between the lines and cut a straight slit to the edge of the tile. Fold back the slit and slide the tile in place.

Carpet tiles

Carpet tiles are laid as for vinyl tiles, except that they are not usually glued down. Set out centre lines on the floor, but don't fit a guide batten: simply aligning the row of tiles with the marked lines is sufficient.

Carpet tiles have a pile which must be laid in the correct direction. This is sometimes indicated by arrows marked on the back of each tile.

Some tiles have ridges of rubber on the back which mean they will slip easily in one direction, but not in another. The non-slip direction is typically denoted by an arrow on the back of the tile. It is usual to lay the tiles in pairs so that one prevents the other from moving. In any case, stick down every third row of tiles using double-sided carpet tape, and tape squares in those areas where there is likely to be heavy traffic.

Cut and fit carpet tiles as described for vinyl tiles.

Checking direction of pile
Some carpet tiles have arrows on the back to indicate the direction in which they should be laid.

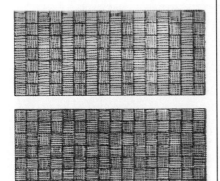

Using pile for decoration
Two typical arrangements of tiles, using the pile to make decorative textures.

Cork tiles

Use the methods described for laying vinyl tiles to cut and fit cork tiles, but use a contact adhesive: thixotropic types allow a degree of movement as you position the tiles.

Make sure the tiles are level by tapping down the edges with a block of wood. Unfinished tiles can be sanded lightly to remove minor irregularities.

Vacuum then seal unfinished tiles with two to three coats of clear varnish.

Bedding cork tiles
Bed the edges of cork tiles with a woodblock.

Rubber tiles

Use the same methods for laying rubber tiles as for vinyl types. Use a latex flooring adhesive.

Laying rubber tiles
Lay large rubber tiles by placing one edge and corner against neighbouring tiles before lowering onto a bed of adhesive.

NEAT DETAILING FOR SOFT FLOOR TILES

Covering a plinth
Create the impression of a floating bath panel or kitchen base units by running floor tiles up the face of the plinth. Hold carpet tiles into a tight bend with gripper strip (1) or glue other tiles in place for a similar detail. Glue a plastic moulding, normally used to seal around the edge of a bath, behind the floor covering to produce a curved detail which makes cleaning the floor a lot easier (2).

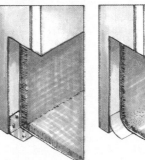

1 Sharp bend with gripper strip **2 Curved detail for easy cleaning**

Cutting holes for pipes
With most soft floor tiles you can cut neat holes for central-heating pipes using a home-made punch: cut a 150mm (6in) length of the same diameter pipe and sharpen the rim on the inside at one end with a metalworking file. Plot the position for the hole on the tile, then place the punching tool on top. Hit the other end of the punch with a hammer to cut through the tile cleanly. With some carpet tiles you may have to cut round the backing to release the cut-out and prevent fraying with tape.

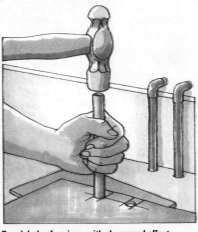

Punch holes for pipes with sharpened offcut

LAYING OTHER TYPES OF SOFT FLOOR TILES

SEE ALSO

Details for:	
Levelling concrete	49
Levelling floors	57
Carpet tiles	102
Cork tiles	103
Rubber tiles	103
Setting out	109

● **Access to plumbing**
If you are covering a bath panel with tiles, remember to make a lift-off section in the panel to gain access to pipes and tap fittings beneath the bath tub.

LAYING CERAMIC FLOOR TILES

● **Battens on concrete**
Use masonry nails to hold battens onto a concrete floor.

Ceramic floor tiles make a durable, hard surface that can also be extremely decorative. Laying the tiles on a floor is similar to hanging them on a wall, except that because floor tiles are somewhat thicker than wall tiles you have to be especially careful when cutting them to fit in order to achieve neat and accurate results.

Setting out

To lay ceramic tiles on a suspended wooden floor, cover it first with 12mm (½in) plywood to make a solid, level surface that will not flex. A flat, dry concrete floor is an ideal base in itself.

Mark out the floor as for soft floor tiles and work out the spacing to achieve even, fairly wide border tiles. Nail two softwood guide battens to the floor, set at a right angle and aligned with the last row of whole tiles on two adjacent walls farthest from the door. Even a small error will become obvious by the time you reach the other end of the room, so check the angle by measuring three units from one corner along one batten and four units along the other. Measure the diagonal between the marks: it should measure five units if the battens form an angle of 90 degrees. Make a final check by dry-laying a square of tiles in the angle.

Laying the tiles

Use a proprietary floor-tile adhesive that is waterproof and slightly flexible when set. Spread it on with a plain or notched trowel, according to the manufacturer's recommendations. The normal procedure is to apply adhesive to the floor for the main area of tiling and to butter the backs of cut tiles.

Spread enough adhesive on the floor for about 16 tiles. Press the tiles into the adhesive, starting in the corner. Work along both battens, then fill in between to form the square. Few floor tiles have spacing lugs, so use plastic spacers.

Check the alignment of the tiles with a straightedge and make sure that they are lying flat by checking them with a spirit level. Work your way along one batten, laying squares of 16 tiles each time. Tile the rest of the floor in the same way, working back towards the door. Leave the adhesive to dry for 24 hours before you walk on the floor to remove the guide battens and fit the border tiles.

Cutting ceramic floor tiles

Measure and cut the tiles to fit the border as described for wall tiles. Because they are thicker, floor tiles will not snap quite so easily, so if you have a large area to fill, use a tile-cutting jig.

Alternatively, make your own device by nailing two scraps of 12mm (½in) thick plywood to 50 x 25mm (2 x 1in) softwood battens, leaving a parallel gap between them which is just wide enough to take a tile. Hold the device on edge, insert a scored tile into the gap, up to the scored line – which should be uppermost – and press down on the free end (see below right). Snap thin strips from the edge in this way. Saw or nibble curved shapes.

● **Grouting the joints**
Grout the tiles as for walls, but fill the joints almost flush rather than indenting them. A dark grout is less likely to look dirty after a time.

Setting out for tiling
Mark out the floor as for soft floor tiles, then set out the field with battens.
1 Fix temporary guide battens at the edge of the field on the two adjacent walls farthest from the door.
2 Ensure that the battens are at true right angles by measuring the diagonal.
3 Dry-lay a square of 16 tiles in the angles as a final check.

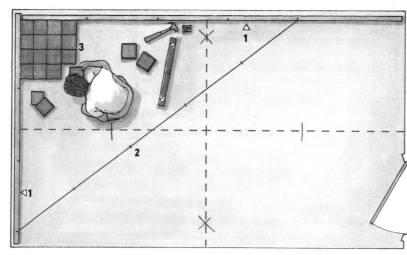

LAYING MOSAIC FLOOR TILES

Set out mosaic floor tiles as for ceramic floor tiles. Spread on the adhesive, then lay the tiles, paper-facing uppermost, with spacers that match the gaps between individual pieces. Press the sheets into the adhesive, using a block of wood to tamp them level. Twenty-four hours later, remove the spacers and soak off the facing with warm water. Grout as normal.

If you have to fit a sheet of mosaic tiles around an obstruction, remove individual mosaic pieces as close to the profile as possible. Fit the sheet (**1**), then cut and replace the pieces to fit around the shapes.

If you are using mosaics in areas of hard wear, such as patio steps, protect vulnerable edges with a nosing of ordinary ceramic floor tiles to match or contrast with the main field of tiles (**2**).

1 Remove mosaic pieces to fit around pipe

2 Lay a nosing of ceramic tiles on step treads

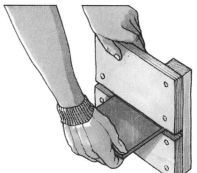

Using a home-made jig
It is essential to ensure that the marked line is positioned parallel to the edge of the plywood or the tile will not snap accurately. Protect your eyes with goggles.

Quarry tiles, being tough and hardwearing, are the best choice for floors that will receive heavy use. However, they are relatively thick and making even a straight cut is not easy. Reserve them for areas that don't require a lot of complex shaping.

Don't lay quarry tiles on a suspended wooden floor; replace the floorboards with 18 or 22mm (¾ or 1in) exterior-grade plywood to provide a sufficiently flat and rigid base. A concrete floor presents no problems, as long as it is free from damp. Provided the floor is reasonably flat, the mortar bed on which the tiles are laid will take care of fine levelling.

Setting out for tiling

Set out two guide battens in a corner of the room at right angles to each other, as described for ceramic floor tiles, opposite. The depth of the battens should measure about twice the thickness of the tiles to allow for the mortar bed. Fix them temporarily to a concrete floor with long masonry nails. The level of the battens is essential, so check with a spirit level; pack out under the battens with scraps of hardboard or card where necessary. Mark tile widths along each batten, leaving 3mm (⅛in) gaps between for grouting, as a guide to positioning.

Dry-lay a square of 16 tiles in the angle, then nail a third batten to the floor, butting against the tiles and parallel with one of the other battens. Level and mark it as before.

Bedding down the tiles

Lay quarry tiles on a bed of mortar made from 1 part cement : 3 parts builder's sand. When water is added, the mortar should be stiff enough to hold an impression when squeezed.

Soak quarry tiles in water prior to laying to prevent them absorbing water from the mortar too rapidly, causing poor adhesion. Cut a stout board to span the parallel battens: this will be used to level the mortar bed and tiles. Cut a notch in each end to fit between the battens (see right). In depth, each notch should match the thickness of a tile less 3mm (⅛in).

Spread the mortar to a depth of about 12mm (½in) to cover the area of 16 tiles. Level the mortar by dragging the notched side of the board across it.

Dust dry cement on the mortar, then lay the tiles along three sides of the square against the battens. Fill in the square, spacing the tiles by adjusting them with a trowel.Tamp down the tiles gently with the un-notched side of the board until they are level with the battens. If the mortar is too stiff, brush water into the joints. Wipe mortar from the faces of the tiles before it hardens.

Fill in between the battens, then move one batten back to form another bay of the same size. Level it to match the first section. Tile section-by-section until the main floor is complete. When the floor is hard enough to walk on, lift the battens and fill in with border tiles.

SEE ALSO
Details for:
Damp floors	49
Levelling concrete	49
Levelling floors	57
Mixing mortar	174

CUTTING QUARRY TILES

Quarry tiles are so thick that the only practicable method for cutting them is to use a robust jig. Choose one that is designed to cut tiles up to 18mm (¾in) thick. It should also incorporate a tungsten-carbide cutting wheel and an adjustable fence to facilitate fast and accurate work.

Having scored the cut line once only, locate the tile in the jaws of the tool and press down on the long lever arm to snap the tile cleanly.

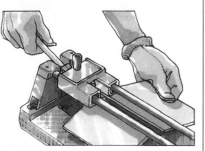

Snap thick quarry tiles with a tile-cutting jig

Levelling the mortar
With a notch located over each guide batten, drag the levelling board towards you.

Notching the levelling board
Cut matching notches at each end of the board for levelling the mortar.

TILE LESS 3mm
MORTAR
BATTEN

Levelling border tiles
Use a notched piece of plywood to level the mortar and tamp down the tiles with a block.

● **Finishing off the quarry tiling**
Grout quarry tiles as for ceramic floor tiles, using cement or proprietary waterproof grout. Clean it off the surface by sprinkling sawdust onto it and wiping off with a cloth. Wash the finished floor with a soapless detergent.

Setting out a quarry-tiled floor
Tho mothod for laying quarry tiles is similar to the one used for glazed ceramic tiles.
1 Fix two guide battens – about twice the tile thickness – at right angles to each other.
2 Fix a third batten parallel with one of the others.
3 Dry-lay 16 tiles between the battens to check their accuracy, then proceed with tiling.

PARQUET FLOORING

1 Strip flooring
These short sections of flooring illustrate a few of the beautiful woods used for this type of parquet. They are available as plywood or solid-wood strips, and some are pre-finished.

2 Hardwood parquet panels
Solid-wood strips make up flat panels for gluing to the floor.

3 Timber-faced cork
This type of flooring is easy to lay. Cut to fit with a sharp knife.

Parquet flooring is a relatively thin covering of decorative timber which is laid in the form of panels or narrow strips. Hardwoods such as oak, birch and cherry are used for their beautiful grain patterns and rich colouring, which can be further highlighted by applying one of the many waxes, polishes and varnishes that are available.

Types of parquet flooring

The type of flooring you choose will be determined by the range of timbers offered by the manufacturer, the price and, of course, your own preference. Laying any type of parquet is as easy as tiling a floor, but you will need to take into consideration the nature of the sub-floor.

Strip flooring
Wooden floors can also be constructed from tongue-and-groove (T&G) and square-edged strips or tiles, either machined from solid timber or made from veneered plywood. They can be nailed to a wooden floor or left as floating parquetry by gluing just the jointed edges together. Tiles and strips range in thickness from 9 to 18mm (⅜ to ¾in). Fix them either as parallel strips or arrange them in various combinations to make herringbone or woven patterns.

Hardwood panels
Perhaps the most common form of

hardwood flooring is a 450mm (1ft 6in) square panel made by gluing 8mm (⅜in) solid-wood fingers into herringbone or basketweave patterns. The panels are presanded and sometimes prefinished as well. Some have a bitumen-impregnated backing to protect them from rising damp (although the floor itself must include a damp-proof membrane). Hardwood panels can be glued to wooden or concrete floors, their edges butted like floor tiles: some are self-adhesive.

Timber-faced cork
This is not a conventional parquet flooring, being a composite tile made from a layer of cork backed with vinyl and surfaced with a natural or stained hardwood veneer. The timber is protected by a clear-vinyl coating. The tiles are available in 900 x 150mm (3ft x 6in) strips.For setting out, fitting and cutting timber-faced cork, see the section on vinyl and cork tiles.

PREPARING THE SUB-FLOOR

Whether the sub-floor is concrete or wooden, it must be clean, dry and flat before parquet flooring is laid. Level wooden floors with hardboard panels and screed a concrete base.Some manufacturers recommend that a building paper or thin plastic-foam underlay is laid for floating parquetry. To reduce the risk of warping, leave parquet panels or strips in the room where they will be laid for several days so that they adjust to the atmosphere.

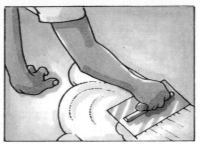

Preparation for solid floors
When laying parquet flooring on a solid-concrete base, ensure the floor is completely dry and damp-proof (impervious to rising damp), make good, and screed the surface with a proprietary self-levelling compound.

1

2

3

CUTTING WOOD-STRIP & PANEL FLOORING

Cutting curves

Mark out curved shapes with cardboard templates, transfer them to the strip or panel, then cut along the line with a coping saw.

Fitting into a doorway

If the parquetry is to run through two rooms, use a piece of the flooring to support the blade of a panel saw in order to cut off the bottom of the door frame. The parquetry will fit neatly under the frame. This is easier than trying to fit to the moulded architrave.

If the flooring is to change at the door, fit a hardwood threshold the same thickness as the panels and the full depth of the frame. Cut the bottom of the door frame to take the threshold, then screw or nail it to the floor.

Fitting around a pipe

Measure and mark the position of a pipe projecting from the floor, or use a profile gauge. Drill a hole slightly larger than the pipe, then cut out a tapered section of the tile to accommodate the pipe; retain the offcut. Glue the tile to the floor and fit the wedge-shaped offcut behind the pipe.

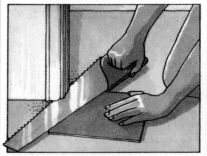

Cutting away a door frame
Professional fitters cut away the bottom of the frame to the thickness of the flooring.

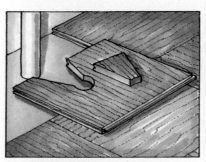

Accommodating a pipe
Fit the notch over the pipe, locate the tongue, then lower the panel into place.

Laying hardwood panels

Set out the floor to calculate the position of the panels in the same way as described for vinyl tiles, but instead of fixing a guide batten to the floor, stretch a length of string between nails that mark the edge of the last row of whole panels next to the wall furthest from the door.

Use a notched trowel to spread the recommended adhesive onto the floor to cover a strip next to the string. Align the first row of hardwood panels with the string, levelling them with a softwood block and hammer. Check the alignment with a straightedge. Lay subsequent panels butted against the preceding row, working from the centre in both directions.

Cutting border panels

Measure and mark border panels as described for vinyl tiles, but deduct 12mm (½in) to provide an expansion gap along the skirting. Cut the panels with a tenon saw.

Glue the border panels in place, then cover the gap with quadrant moulding pinned to the skirting. Don't pin the moulding to the flooring, as it would part from the skirting and serve no useful purpose.

Finishing the flooring

Sand any slight irregularities between tiles, then vacuum the floor. Seal the parquetry with three or four coats of clear finish.

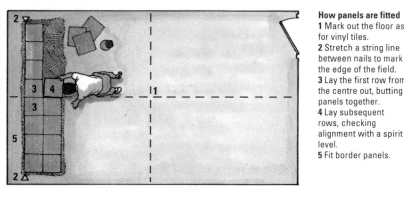

How panels are fitted
1 Mark out the floor as for vinyl tiles.
2 Stretch a string line between nails to mark the edge of the field.
3 Lay the first row from the centre out, butting panels together.
4 Lay subsequent rows, checking alignment with a spirit level.
5 Fit border panels.

Laying strip flooring

Decide on the direction of the strip flooring, then snap a chalked line about 12mm (½in) from a skirting which runs parallel with it.

Place the grooved edge of the first strip against the line and nail it through the face with panel pins. Tap the next strip onto the tongue, using a scrap strip to protect the edge.

Nail through the inner angle of the tongue every 200mm (8in) up to 35mm (1½in) from the ends. Use a nail set and hammer to drive the nail heads below the surface.

Proceed across the floor, cutting each strip 12mm (½in) short of the skirting board. At the far end of the room the gap will allow you to lever the last strip in place and nail it through the face. Nail a cover moulding all round the perimeter of the room.

Finish strip flooring with three or four coats of clear varnish in the same way as panel flooring.

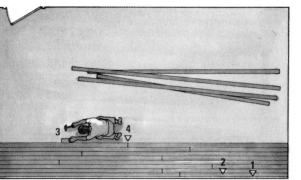

How strips are fixed
Flooring strips are fixed across the floor from the skirting.
1 Snap a chalked string line parallel with the skirting.
2 Nail a strip through its face, tongue outwards, against the chalk guideline.
3 Slot on subsequent strips and nail through the tongues.
4 Stagger the end-to-end joints.

SEE ALSO

Edge detail
An expansion gap is necessary around a parquet-tiled floor, but you can conceal it by nailing a strip of quadrant moulding to the skirting.

Fitting the last strip
Lever in the last strip using a crowbar with an offcut of board to protect the paintwork.

● **Floating parquet flooring**
Instead of nailing the strips to the floor, you can glue them edge-to-edge by applying a little PVA adhesive to each groove, as they are tapped in place. Place wedges between the parquet flooring and the skirting to maintain the 12mm (½in) expansion gap until the moulding is fixed.

115

CARPETS

SEE ALSO
Details for:
Laying carpet 118
Estimating carpet 119

Originally, piled carpets were made by knitting strands of wool or other natural fibres into a woven foundation but gradually, with the introduction of machine-made carpets and synthetic fibres, a very wide variety of different types has been developed. There is a good choice available for virtually all areas of the house, whether the need is for something luxurious or practical and hardwearing.

When selecting carpet, consider your options carefully; the floor area is an important element in the style of an interior and the wrong choice could be an expensive mistake.

A good-quality, well-laid carpet will last for many years, so unless you can afford to change your floorcovering as regularly as you redecorate take care to choose one that you can live with after changing your colour scheme or furnishings. Neutral or earthy colours are easiest to accommodate. Plain colours and small repeat patterns are suitable for rooms of any size; large, bold designs are best reserved for spacious interiors.

If you are planning to carpet adjoining rooms, consider using the same carpet to link the floor areas. This provides a greater sense of space and harmony.

You can use patterned borders in combination with plain carpet to create a distinctive made-to-measure floorcovering in specific areas.

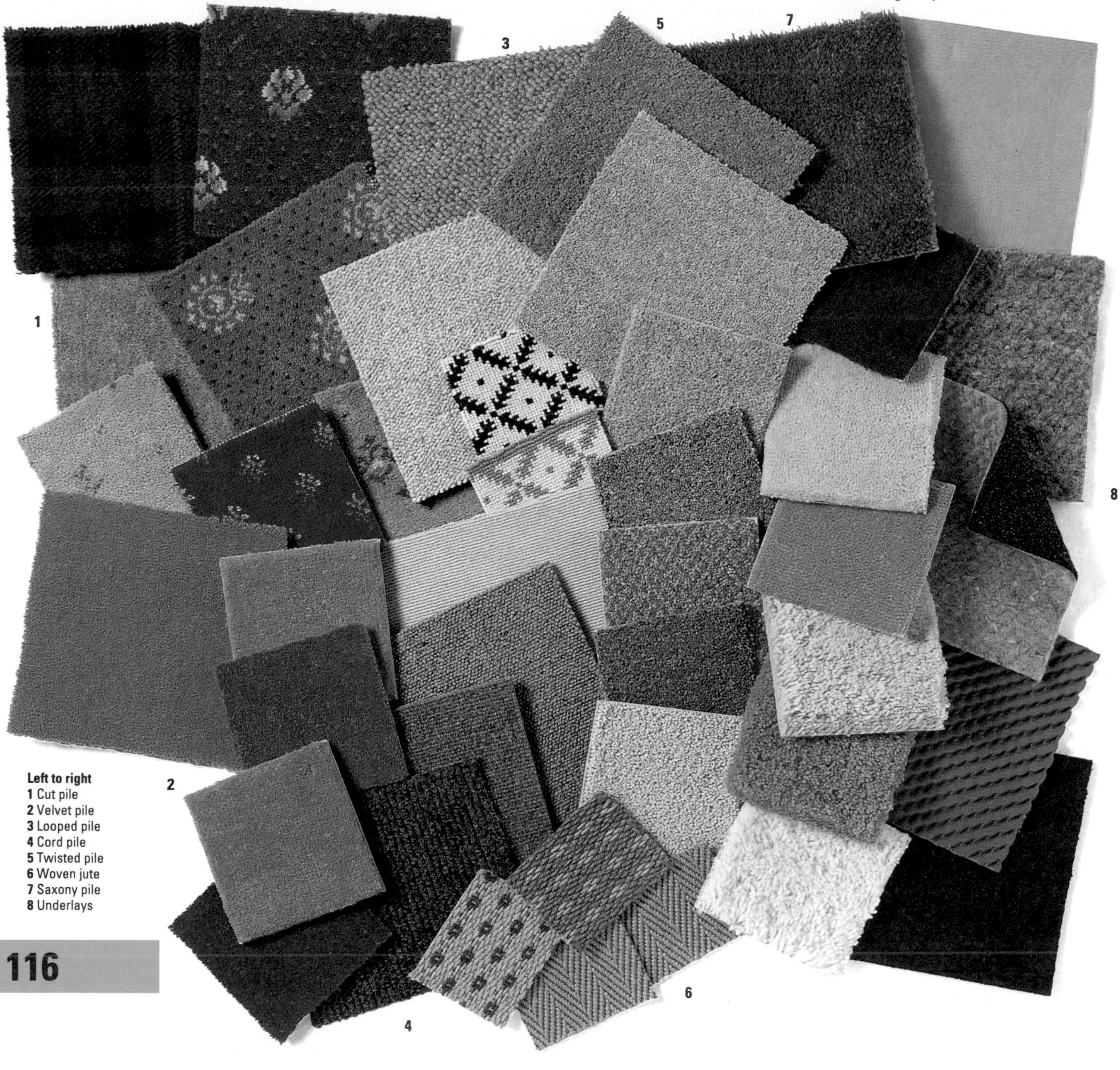

Left to right
1 Cut pile
2 Velvet pile
3 Looped pile
4 Cord pile
5 Twisted pile
6 Woven jute
7 Saxony pile
8 Underlays

CHOOSING
CARPET

When you are shopping for carpeting, there are various factors to consider, including fibre content, type of pile and durability. Although wool carpet is luxurious, don't look down on the synthetic versions widely available – they have a lot to offer in terms of comfort underfoot, finish, texture and value for money.

How fibre content affects the carpet

The best carpets are made from wool or a mixture of wool plus a percentage of man-made fibre. Wool carpets are expensive, so manufacturers have experimented with a variety of fibres to produce cheaper but durable and attractive carpets. Materials such as nylon, polypropylene, acrylic, rayon and polyester are all used for carpet-making, either singly or in combination.

Synthetic-fibre carpets were once inferior substitutes, often with an unattractive shiny pile and a reputation for building up a charge of static electricity that produced mild shocks when anyone touched a metal doorknob. Nowadays, manufacturers have largely solved the problem of static, but you should still seek the advice of the supplier before you buy.

As far as appearance is concerned, a modern carpet made from good-quality blended fibres is hard to distinguish from one made from wool. Certain combinations produce carpets that are so stain-resistant that they virtually shrug off spilled liquids. To their disadvantage, synthetic fibres tend to react badly to burns, shrivelling rapidly from the heat, whereas wool tends only to smoulder.

Rush, sisal, coir and jute are natural vegetable fibres used to make coarsely-woven rugs or strips.

Which type of pile?

The nature of the pile is even more important to the feel and appearance of a carpet than the fibre content. Piled carpets are woven or tufted. Axminster and Wilton are names used to describe two traditional methods of weaving the pile simultaneously with the foundation so that the strands are wrapped around and through the warp and weft threads.

With tufted carpets, continuous strands are pushed between the threads of a prewoven foundation. Although it is secured with an adhesive backing, tufted pile is not as permanent as woven pile. Consult the box, right, for the various ways tufted and woven piles are created. Where durability is important, see below.

The importance of underlay

An underlay can be a thick felt or a layer of foamed rubber or plastic. It is false economy to try to save on the cost of underlay. Without it, carpet wears faster and is not as comfortable underfoot. Eventually, the lines of floorboards will begin to show as dirty marks on a pale carpet as dust from the gaps begins to emerge. In theory, rubber-backed or foam-backed carpets need no additional underlay, but floorboards can still show through cheaper qualities.

As a precaution, it is worth laying rolls of brown paper over the floor to stop dust and grit working its way into an underlay and to prevent rubber-backed carpet sticking to the floor.

CHOOSING A DURABLE CARPET

Whether it is woven, tufted or bonded, a hardwearing carpet must have a dense pile. When you fold the carpet and part the pile you should not be able to see the backing to which it is attached.

Fortunately, the British Carpet Classification Scheme categorizes floorcoverings according to their ability to withstand wear. If the classification is not stated on the carpet, ask the supplier how it is categorized.

● **Light domestic**	Bedrooms
● **Medium domestic**	Light traffic only, e.g. dining room, well-used bedroom
● **General domestic**	Living rooms
● **Heavy domestic**	Hallways and stairs

HOW CARPETS ARE MADE

Tufted and woven carpet pile is treated in a number of ways to give some different qualities of finish: with some types the strands are left long and uncut; with others the looped pile is twisted together to give a coarser texture; very hardwearing types have their looped pile pulled tight against the foundations; and cut, velvety and shaggy types have the top of their loops removed to leave single-fibre strands.

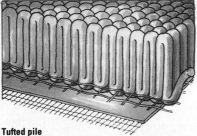

Tufted pile
Continuous strands pushed into a woven foundation secured on an adhesive backing.

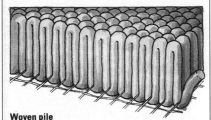

Woven pile
Continuous strands woven onto the warp and weft threads of the foundation.

1 Looped pile
Ordinary looped pile gives a smooth feel.

2 Twisted pile
Looped pile twisted for a coarser texture.

3 Cord pile
Loops are pulled tight against the foundation.

4 Cut pile
Loops are cut, giving a velvety texture pile.

5 Velvet pile
Loops are cut short for a close-stranded pile.

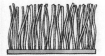

6 Saxony pile
A long cut pile up to 38mm (1½in) long.

Fibre-bonded pile
Fibre-bonded pile, the most modern method of carpet production, consists of synthetic fibres packed tightly together and bonded to an impregnated backing. The texture is like coarse felt.

Fibre-bonded pile
A tough low-cost carpet mostly used for commercial interiors.

117

LAYING
CARPET

Fixing carpet
Use one of three ways:

Fold tacked to floor

Double-sided tape

Gripper strip

Joining at a doorway
Use one of the bars below:

Double threshold bar

Single threshold bar

Some people prefer to loose-lay carpet, relying on the weight of furniture to stop it moving around. However, a properly stretched and fixed carpet looks much better, and isn't difficult to accomplish. There are three main methods of fixing, as detailed right.

Laying a standard width

The only special tool required for laying carpet is a knee kicker for stretching it. It has a toothed head, which is pressed into the carpet while you nudge the end with your knee. You can hire a knee kicker from a carpet supplier.

A knee kicker, used to stretch carpet to fit

Join the underlay with short strips of carpet tape or secure it with a few tacks to stop it moving. Roll out the carpet, butting one machine-cut edge against a wall, and fix that edge. (If the carpet is patterned, it should run parallel to the main axis of the room.)

Stretch the carpet to the wall directly opposite and temporarily fix it with tacks, or slip it onto gripper strips. Don't cut it yet. Work from the centre towards each corner, stretching and fixing. Do the same at the other sides of the room.

Cut the corners like sheet vinyl to allow the carpet to lie flat. Adjust it until it is stretched evenly, then fix it permanently. When you are using tape or strips, press the carpet into the angle between skirting and floor with a bolster chisel; trim with a knife held at 45 degrees to the skirting. Tuck the cut edge behind the strip with the bolster.

Cutting to fit
Cut and fit carpet into doorways and around obstacles like sheet vinyl. Join carpets at a doorway with a single or double-sided threshold bar.

Joining carpet
Don't join expensive woven carpets; they should be sewn by a professional. Glue straight seams with latex adhesive or, for rubber-backed carpet, adhesive tape. Use as described for sheet vinyl.

Methods of fixing

Tacks
A 50mm (2in) strip of carpet is folded under and nailed to a wooden floor with improved cut tacks about every 200mm (8in). Lose the head in the pile by rubbing the pile with your fingertips. Underlay should be laid 50mm (2in) short of the skirting to allow the carpet to lie flat along the edge.

Double-sided tape
For rubber-backed carpets only. Stick 50mm (2in) tape around the perimeter of the room. When you are ready to fix the carpet, peel off the protective paper layer from the adhesive tape.

Gripper strips
These wooden or metal strips have fine metal teeth which grip the woven foundation. They are not really suitable for rubber-backed carpets, although they are used. Nail the strips to the floor 6mm (¼in) from the skirting with the teeth angled towards the wall. Cut short strips to fit doorways and alcoves. Glue the strips to a concrete floor. Cut underlay up to the edge.

Carpeting a staircase

If possible use one of the narrow standard widths of carpet for a staircase. Order an extra 450mm (1ft 6in) to the required length so that the carpet can be moved at a later date to even out the wear. This allowance is turned under onto the bottom step.

You can fit staircarpeting across the entire width of the treads or stop short to reveal a border of polished or painted staircase. If you adopt the latter style of carpeting, you can use traditional metal or wooden stair rods to hold the carpet against the risers. Fixing the rods is simply a matter of screwing brackets on each side of the stairs.

Alternatively, you can tack the carpet to the stairs every 75mm (3in) across the treads. Push the carpet firmly into the angle between riser and tread with a bolster chisel while you tack the centre, then work outwards to each side.

Provided the carpet is not rubber-backed, you can use angled gripper strip to fix the run in place.

Fitting the underlay
Cut underlay into separate pads for each tread. Secure each pad next to the riser with tacks or gripper strip, and tack the front edge under the nosing.

Laying a straight run
The pile of the carpet should face down the stairs. Rub your palm along the carpet in both directions; it will feel smoother in the direction of the pile.

Start at the bottom of the staircase with the carpet laid face down on the first tread. Fix the back edge with tacks or nail a strip over it. Stretch the carpet over the nosing and fix it to the bottom of the riser by nailing through a straight strip. Run the carpet up the staircase, pushing it firmly into each gripper strip with a bolster. Nail the end of the carpet against the riser on the last tread, then bring the landing carpet over the top step to meet it.

Carpeting winding stairs
To carpet the winding section of a staircase, keep the carpet in a continuous length, but fold the excess under and secure it to the riser with a stair rod. Alternatively, fold the slack against the riser and tack through the three thicknesses of carpet. To install fitted carpet, cut a pattern for each step and carpet it individually.

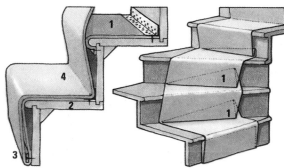

Straight run   **Winding stairs**

Carpeting stairs
1 Tack underlay pads.
2 Tack carpet face down on first treat.
3 Pull over nosing and tack to base of riser.
4 Run carpet upstairs, fixing to grippers.

Carpeting winding stairs
1 Don't cut the carpet, but fold the excess under and fix to riser with stair rod or long carpet tacks.

ESTIMATING SHEET VINYL AND CARPET

Measure the floor area and draw a freehand plan, including the position of doors, window bay, alcoves and so on, plus the full width of the doorframe. Make a note of the dimensions on the plan and take it to the flooring supplier, who will advise you on the most economical way to cover the floor.

The ideal solution is to achieve a seamless wall-to-wall covering, but this is often impossible, either because a particular width is unobtainable or because the room is such an irregular shape that there would be too much wastage if it were cut from one piece. Carpet or sheet-vinyl widths have to be butted together in these circumstances, but try to avoid seams in the main walkways. You also have to consider matching the pattern and the direction of carpet pile; it must run in the same direction or each piece of carpet will look different. Remember to order 75mm (3in) extra all round for fitting.

Standard widths

Most manufacturers produce carpet or vinyl to standard widths. Some can be cut to fit any shape of room, but the average wastage factor is reflected in the price. Not all carpets are available in the full range of widths and you may have difficulty in matching a colour exactly from one width to another, so ask the supplier to check. Carpet and vinyl are made to metric sizes, but the imperial equivalent is normally quoted.

Available Widths	
Carpet	**Vinyl**
*0.69m (2ft 3in)	2m (6ft 6in)
0.91m (3ft)	3m (9ft 10in)
2.74m (9ft)	4m (13ft)
3.66m (12ft)	
*4m (13ft)	
*4.57m (15ft)	

*rare

Carpet widths of 2.74m (9ft) and over are called broadlooms; narrower widths are called body or strip carpets.

Carpet squares

Carpet squares, not to be confused with tiles, are large rectangular loose-laid rugs. Simply order whichever size suits the proportion of your room. Carpet squares should be swapped round from time to time to even out wear.

Sheet flooring fits wall-to-wall. The coverings most often used today are sheet vinyl (the modern equivalent of linoleum) and carpet in all its forms. Included in the cost of an expensive floorcovering should be an allowance for having it professionally laid – and even if there's an additional charge, you would be well advised to spend that little extra to avoid the risk of spoiling costly carpet or vinyl. On the other hand, there's no reason why you shouldn't lay the cheaper ranges, where cost-saving makes more sense.

Types of sheet floorcovering

There are many types of vinyl flooring: choose according to durability, colour and pattern.

Unbacked vinyl

Sheet vinyl is made by sandwiching the printed pattern between a base of PVC and a clear protective PVC covering. All vinyls are relatively hardwearing, but some have a thicker, reinforced protective layer to increase their durability; ask the supplier which type would suit your needs . There is a vast range of colours, patterns and textures from which to choose.

Backed vinyl

Backed vinyl has similar properties to the unbacked type, with the addition of a resilient underlay to make it softer and warmer to walk on. The backing may be felt or, more often, a cushion of foamed PVC.

Vinyl carpet

Vinyl carpet, a cross between carpet and sheet vinyl, was originally developed for contract use but is now available for domestic installation. It has a velvet-like pile of fine nylon fibres embedded in a waterproof, expanded-PVC base. It's popular for kitchens as spillages are washed off easily with water and a mild detergent. It comes in 2m (6ft 7in) wide rolls.

Vinyl flooring
Being hardwearing and waterproof, sheet vinyl is one of the most popular floorcoverings for bathrooms and kitchens. Vinyl carpet has a pile but is equally suitable in those areas.
Left to right
1 Unbacked vinyl
2 Backed vinyl
3 Vinyl carpet

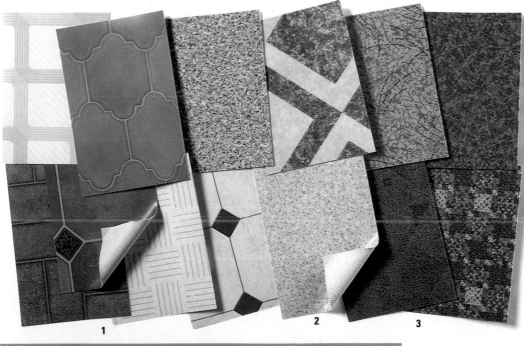

1   2   3

Preparing the floor for floorcovering

Before you lay a sheet covering make sure the floor is flat and dry. Vacuum the surface and nail down any loose floorboards. Take out any unevenness by screeding or hardboarding the floor.

A concrete floor must have a DPM and a ground-level wooden floor must be ventilated below. Don't lay vinyl over timber that has recently been treated with preserver.

119

LAYING
SHEET VINYL

Sheet vinyl is ideal wall-to-wall floorcovering for kitchens, utility rooms and bathrooms, where you are bound to spill water from time to time. There are numerous colours, patterns and embossed effects available, and you will find most types straightforward to lay if you follow a systematic routine.

Leave the vinyl in a room for 24 to 48 hours before laying, preferably opened flat or at least stood on end, loosely rolled. Assuming there are no seams, start by fitting against the longest wall first. Drive a nail through a wooden lath about 50mm (2in) from one end.

Pull the vinyl away from the wall by approximately 35mm (1½in). Make sure it is parallel with the wall or the main axis of the room. Use the nailed strip to scribe a line following the skirting (**1**). Cut the vinyl with a knife or scissors and slide the sheet up against the wall.

To get the rest of the sheet to lie as flat as possible, cut a triangular notch at each corner. Make a straight cut down to the floor at external corners. Remove as much waste as possible, leaving 50 to 75mm (2 to 3in) turned up all round.

Press the vinyl into the angle between skirting and floor with a bolster. Align a metal straightedge with the crease and run along it with a sharp knife held at a slight angle to the skirting (**2**). If your trimming is less than perfect, nail a cover strip of quadrant moulding to the skirting.

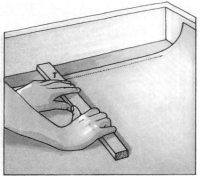
1 Fit to first wall by scribing with a nailed strip

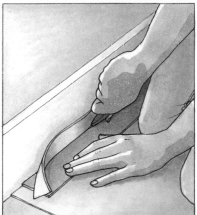
2 Press the edge to the skirting and cut

Trimming and gluing vinyl sheet

Trimming to fit a doorway
Work around the doorframe moulding making straight cuts and removing triangular notches at each change of angle as if they were miniature corners. Crease the vinyl against the floor and trim the waste. Make a straight cut across the opening and fit a threshold bar over the edge of the sheet.

Cutting around an obstruction
To fit around a WC pan or basin pedestal, fold back the sheet and pierce it with a knife just above floor level. Draw a blade up towards the edge. Make triangular cuts around the base, gradually working around the curve until the sheet can lie flat on the floor (**3**). Crease and cut off the waste.

Sticking the sheet
Modern vinyls can be loose-laid but you may prefer to glue the edges, especially along a door opening. Peel back the edge and spread a band of the recommended flooring adhesive with a toothed spreader (**4**) or use a 50mm (2in) wide double-sided adhesive tape.

Making a join
If you have to join widths of vinyl, scribe one edge as described above, then overlap the free edge with the second sheet until the pattern matches exactly. Cut through both pieces with a knife, then remove the waste strips.

Without moving the sheets, fold back both cut edges, apply tape or adhesive and press the join together.

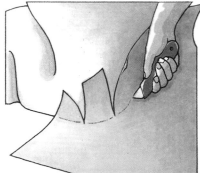
3 Make triangular cuts around a curve

Positioning the vinyl
Aligning the vinyl sheet squarely on the floor is essential.
1 Fit to the longest, uninterrupted wall.
2 Cut triangular notches at each external and internal corner so the sheet will lie flat.
3 Allow folds of about 75mm (3in) all round for scribing to fit accurately.
4 Make a straight cut against the door opening so a threshold bar can be fixed.

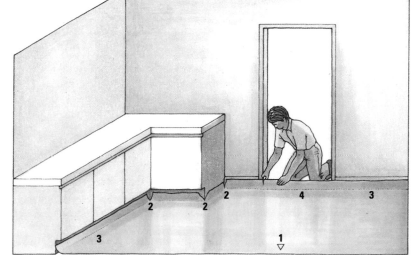

4 Secure butting edges on a bed of adhesive

CHAPTER 3

REPAIRS & IMPROVEMENTS

BRICK HOUSE
CONSTRUCTION

Foundations
The foundations carry the whole weight of the house. The type, size and depth are determined largely by the loadbearing properties of the subsoil.

Strip foundation
A continuous strip of concrete set well below ground.

Trench foundation
Similar to the strip type, but concrete fills the trench.

Raft foundation
A concrete slab covers the whole ground area.

Brick-built houses follow a long tradition of styles and methods of construction. The brickwork gives the building character and is the main loadbearing element. If you have to repair and renovate your home it is useful to understand the basic principles of its construction.

Support for the house

To support the weight of the structure, most brick-built buildings are supported on a solid base called foundations (see diagrams left).

Wall formation

External walls are loadbearing, supporting roof, floors and internal walls. Cavity walls comprise two leaves braced with metal ties; older houses have solid walls at least 225mm (9in) thick. Bricks are laid with mortar in overlapping bonding patterns to give the wall rigidity. A damp-proof course (DPC) just above ground level prevents moisture rising. Window and door openings are spanned above with rigid supporting beams called lintels.

Internal walls are either non-loadbearing divisions which are made from lightweight blocks, manufactured boards or timber studding, or loadbearing structures of brick or block.

Solid and timber floors

Ground floors are either solid concrete or suspended timber types. A damp-proof membrane (DPM) is laid between walls where a floor is concrete. With timber floors, sleeper walls of honeycomb brickwork are built on oversite concrete between the base brickwork; a timber sleeper plate rests on each wall and timber joists are supported on them. Their ends may be similarly supported, let into the brickwork or suspended on metal hangers. Floorboards are laid at right angles to joists. First-floor joists are supported by the masonry or hangers.

Pitched-roof construction

Pitched (sloping) roofs comprise angled rafters fixed to a ridge board, braced by purlins, struts and ties and fixed to wall plates bedded on top of the walls. Roofs are usually clad with slates or tiles to keep the rain out.

TYPICAL COMPONENTS OF A BRICK-BUILT HOUSE

1 Tiles or slates	**9** Lath-and-plaster stud partition	**15** Brick loadbearing internal wall	**22** Sleeper wall
2 Ridge board	**10** Internal brick wall	**16** Lintel	**23** Damp-proof course
3 Tile battens	**11** Brick cavity wall	**17** Block partition	**24** Oversite concrete
4 Roofing felt	**12** Suspended joists	**18** Staircase	**25** Strip foundation
5 Purlin	**13** Herringbone bracing	**19** Floorboards	**26** Ground
6 Rafters	**14** Plaster ceiling	**20** Ground-floor joists	
7 Ceiling joists		**21** Timber sleeper plate	
8 Wall plate			

TIMBER-FRAMED HOUSE CONSTRUCTION

Timber is an excellent all-purpose material for building and has been used in house construction for centuries. Modern timber-framed houses differ from their brick-built counterparts in that the main structural elements are timber frames, irrespective of whether the walls of the building are clad with brickwork, timber boarding or tiles.

Foundations

A timber-framed house is built on sound concrete foundations. These are usually of 'strip' or 'raft' construction to spread weight to firm ground.

Wall assembly

Modern timber-framed house walls are constructed of vertical timber studs with horizontal top and bottom plates nailed to them. The frames, which are erected on a concrete slab or a suspended timber platform supported by cavity brick walls, are faced on the outside with plywood sheathing to stiffen the structure. Breather paper is fixed over the top to act as a moisture barrier. Insulation quilt is used between studs. Rigid timber lintels at openings carry the weight of the upper floor and roof.

Brick cladding is typically used to cover the exterior of the frame. It is attached to the frame with metal ties. Weatherboarding often replaces the brick cladding on upper floors.

Floor construction

Floors in a timber-framed house are either solid concrete or suspended timber, as with a masonry house. In some cases, a concrete floor may be screeded or surfaced with timber or chipboard flooring. Suspended timber floor joists are supported on wall plates and surfaced with chipboard.

Prefabricated roof

Timber-framed houses usually have trussed roofs — prefabricated triangulated frames which combine the rafters and ceiling joists — which are lifted into place and supported by the walls. The trusses are joined together with horizontal and diagonal ties. A ridge board is not fitted, nor are purlins required. Roofing felt, battens and tiling are applied in the usual way.

Foundation problems
Consult your Building Control Officer when dealing with problems or new work involving foundations.

Settlement
Settlement cracks in walls are not uncommon. If they have stabilized and are not too wide they are not a serious problem.

Subsidence
Subsidence caused by weak or shallow foundations or excessive moisture-loss from the ground can be more serious. Widening cracks from window or door openings are an indication of subsidence.

Heave
Weak foundations can also be damaged by ground swell, or 'heave'.

Light foundations
The walls of extensions or bays with lighter or shallower foundations than the house may show cracks where the two meet as a result of differential movement.

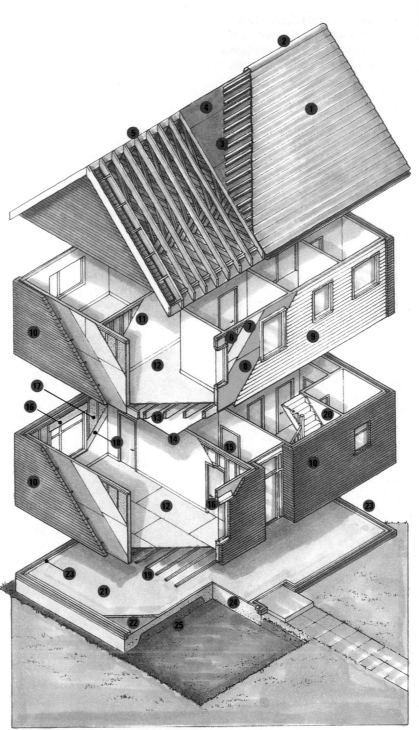

TYPICAL COMPONENTS OF A TIMBER-FRAMED HOUSE

1 Tiles or slates	8 Breather paper	15 Loadbearing	22 Damp-proof
2 Ridge tiles	9 Weatherboarding	internal stud wall	membrane
3 Tile battens	10 Brick cladding	16 Lintel	23 Timber sole plate
4 Roofing felt	11 Stud partition	17 Insulation	24 Concrete slab
5 Trussed rafters	12 Chipboard floor	18 Vapour barrier	25 Ground
6 Timber-framed	13 First-floor platform	19 Floor battens	
loadbearing wall	14 Plasterboard	20 Staircase	
7 Plywood sheathing	ceiling	21 Concrete screed	

WALLS: EXTERNAL WALLS

Solid walls provide good sound insulation but poor thermal insulation. There are three basic types, made from brick, block or natural stone. Cavity walls, a relatively modern form of construction, are more effective in preventing moisture penetration and heat loss than solid walls.

How solid walls are made

Solid walls are mainly constructed from bonded brickwork or concrete blocks, although local natural stone is also used in certain areas. They are usually at least 225mm (9in) thick — the length of a standard brick — but are frequently a brick and a half thick if they are to be exposed to severe weather conditions.

Moisture resistance
Moisture is prevented from penetrating to the inside surface of the wall by evaporation; rainwater absorbed by the bricks is normally drawn out before it reaches the inner surface. Moisture is prevented from being absorbed from

the ground by an impervious damp-proof course (DPC), usually of bituminous felt, set in a bed joint of the brickwork at least 150mm (6in) — two brick courses — from ground level.

Weatherproofing qualities
Many solid walls are cement-rendered or otherwise clad to weatherproof the brickwork. Exterior-grade concrete blocks 225mm (9in) thick can be left exposed, but their appearance is improved by rendering. Natural stone walls are usually left bare and weatherproofing relies solely on the thickness and density of the material.

Solid walls
Traditional brick and stone walls will vary in thickness according to the age and size of the building. Concrete blocks are now common.

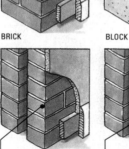

BRICK   BLOCK   STONE

Cavity walls
These have replaced solid walls in modern houses. A combination of brick, block and timber frame may be used to construct a cavity wall; brick is usually used for the outer leaf.

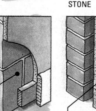 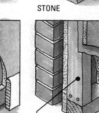

BRICK INNER LEAF   BLOCK INNER LEAF   TIMBER INNER LEAF

How cavity walls are made

Typical cavity walls consist of two 100mm (4in) thick walls or 'leaves', separated by a 50mm (2in) gap. They may be constructed from bricks, concrete blocks, hollow clay bricks or timber framing, or a combination of these. The stretcher-bonded leaves must be tied together with metal wall ties (see left) to make them stable.

For the cavity to work as a moisture barrier, it is essential that the gap is not bridged. This can happen if mortar collects on the ties during construction.

Where openings occur at a doorway or window, the cavity is closed and a DPC is provided to stop moisture seeping in. Weep holes — unmortared vertical joints between every third or fourth brick — are usually provided in

the outer leaf above lintels and below the main DPC. Their function is to drain any moisture from the cavity that penetrates the outer leaf.

Thermal-insulating panels are sometimes included as a cavity wall is built. Alternatively, the cavity is filled with an insulating material later on.

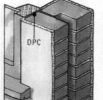 

Vertical DPC at window opening in cavity wall.

Weep holes are formed below main DPC.

Cavity ties
Cavity-wall ties are laid in the bed joints at 900mm (3ft) spacings horizontally and 450mm (1ft 6in) vertically. They are staggered on alternate brick courses.

Wire butterfly tie

Sheet-metal tie

IDENTIFYING LOADBEARING AND NON-LOADBEARING WALLS

The external walls of the house transmit the loads of suspended timber floors, most of the roof and other structures to the foundations. Usually all the external walls are loadbearing. The floor and ceiling joists and other internal walls might also be carried on loadbearing internal walls.

Not all internal walls are loadbearing, or 'structural'. Those that are can be identified by their position in the structure and the materials used in their construction.

A wall that carries the floor joists will have the floorboards running parallel with it. Check at each floor level, as a wall that passes through the centre of the house may carry the first floor but not the ground floor. Floor joists usually run in the direction of the shortest span. Check roof braces, which may bear on an internal wall.

Loadbearing walls are usually made of brick or loadbearing concrete blocks. Occasionally, wooden stud walls are used to carry some weight. A wall may also be termed loadbearing or structural where it is not actually carrying a load but is adding to the stability of the structure.

Non-loadbearing walls
Walls that divide the floor space into rooms and are not intended to support the structure are known as non-loadbearing. They may be made of brick, lightweight concrete blocks, timber studding or cellular-core wallboard, and are usually only a single storey in height. If the floorboards run under the wall it is likely that the wall is non-loadbearing.

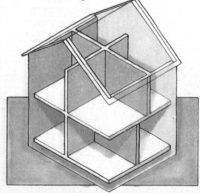

Non-loadbearing walls
These walls divide the internal space into smaller rooms and are relatively lightweight.

INTERNAL
WALLS

There are two types of internal wall: structural party walls, which divide houses built side by side, and partition walls, which divide up the space within a house and may be loadbearing or non-loadbearing.

Party wall construction

Party walls, or separating walls, are shared solid walls which divide houses built side by side. Party walls separate the properties over the entire height of the building to prevent the spread of fire and provide good sound insulation.

Partition walls

Internal partition walls can be loadbearing or non-loadbearing, but are usually relatively lightweight and not more than one brick thick. Partition walls for houses may be made from brick, concrete blocks, hollow clay blocks, timber framing or cellular-core wallboard (see below). A plaster finish is usually applied to brick or block walls for a smooth surface.

Stud-partition walls

Timber-framed partitions called stud walls are common in new and old houses. They are usually made from 100mm (4in) wide sawn softwood. The vertical timbers, called studs, are placed 400mm (1ft 4in) or 600mm (2ft) apart from centre to centre. Diagonal braces may be included for strength.

Laths – thin strips of wood nailed horizontally to the studs – are used as a key for plaster in old houses, although plasterboard has now replaced lath-and-plaster on this type of wall. Stud walls are usually non-loadbearing, but they can carry a lateral load.

Stud walls offer a convenient duct for running services such as wiring, but because of their hollow construction special fixings are required when attaching anything to the surface.

Lath-and-plaster stud partition

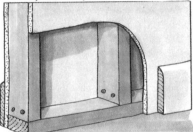

Plasterboarded stud partition

Lightweight concrete blocks

Blocks are widely used for modern partition walls. They are made to course with bricks and are nominally 150 to 225mm (6 to 9in) high and 450 or 600mm (1ft 6in or 2ft) long.

The most common size used is 450 x 225mm (1ft 6in x 9in) and a range of thicknesses from 50 to 300mm (2 to 12in) is available – use the 100mm (4in) wide block for a partition wall. This size corresponds to standard brick bonding, being equal to three courses high and two bricks long. Blocks are grey in colour and are made from cement and lightweight aggregate. Their large size makes building a wall quick and simple. They provide good sound and thermal insulation and are fireproof. Fixings can be made at any point on the wall using special plugs, and services can be channelled into the surface. Blocks are cut easily with a bolster chisel.

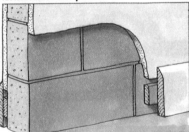

Plastered concrete-block partition

Hollow clay blocks

Clay blocks are red in colour, may be smooth-faced or horizontally grooved as a key for a plaster coating, and are hollow. They make a lightweight wall that has good sound and thermal insulation properties and is fireproof.

Hollow clay blocks do not take nails well; fixings should be made with screws and suitable cavity fixings. Where nailing is required – for fixing skirtings or door linings, for example – solid blocks should be incorporated.

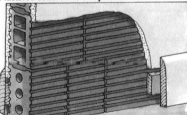

Plastered hollow clay-block partition

Cellular-core wallboard

This manufactured wall panel is made from two sheets of plasterboard with a gridded cardboard core bonded between them. It is available in similar sizes to standard plasterboard sheets, and 57 or 63mm (2¼ or 2½in) thick. The cell structure makes a light but rigid partitioning that is simple to install and can be decorated directly or finished with plaster. All fixings to this type of wall require a screwed cavity device unless wooden plugs are fitted during erection. The plugs are short lengths of the battening used to fix the panels together. It is necessary to preplan the placing of the fixtures before the plugs are driven into the core from the edge. The face of the board is marked to indicate the positions of the plugs before the partition is assembled. Clear channels for cable or pipe runs before beginning assembly.

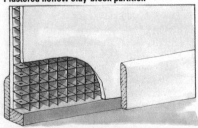

Cellular-core wallboard partition

Glass blocks

Hollow glass blocks can be used for non-loadbearing feature walls. Made in square and rectangular shapes and a range of surface patterns and colours, they can be either laid in mortar or dry-fixed. Get advice on methods of installation from your supplier.

SPANNING
OPENINGS
IN WALLS

Stone and timber

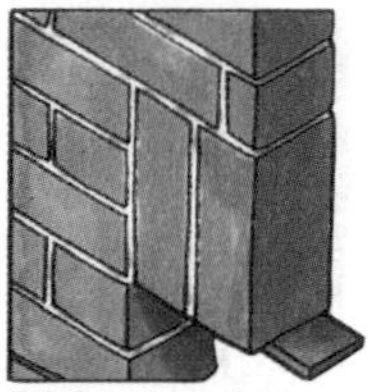

Brick and steel

Reinforced concrete

Pressed steel

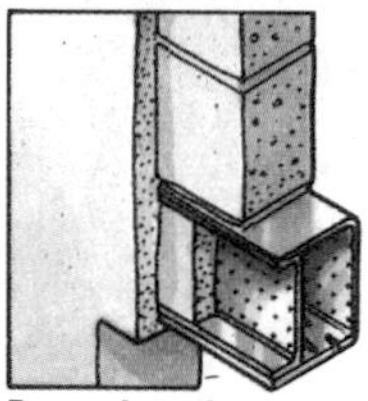

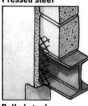
Rolled steel

TYPES OF LINTEL

A lintel bridges the gap above an opening. The type used will depend on the size of the opening and availability.

Wood
Wooden lintels were commonly built into the brick walls of older houses, often in exterior walls, behind a stone lintel or brick arch. They can suffer from rot due to penetrating damp, but are still used in timber-framed houses.

Brick
Brick lintels are used with wood, steel or concrete lintels over external openings, but are not strong. Some are supported by a flat or angled metal bar.

Stone
Stone is not strong in tension and cannot be used for wide spans. The stone lintels seen in older houses do not normally support the full thickness of the wall – timber lintels are used behind them.

Concrete
Concrete lintels are used for interior and exterior openings. Concrete is good in compression but not in tension. To overcome this, metal rods are embedded in the lower portion of the beam to reinforce it. Concrete lintels are made in a range of sizes to match brick and block courses and to suit various wall thicknesses. Though they are capable of spanning large openings, their weight can make handling awkward. Prestressed concrete lintels, reinforced with wire strands set in the concrete under tension, are lighter.

Steel
Galvanized pressed-steel lintels are widely used for internal and external openings. They are designed for cavity and solid walls of brick and block or timber-framed construction. The versions for cavity walls include a tray which channels moisture to the outside. Standard sections and lengths are available. They are fairly light in weight and some are perforated so they can be plastered direct.

Heavyweight rolled-steel joists (RSJs) are mainly used when making two rooms into one. The supplier will cut the I-section beam to length.

To create a doorway or window an opening must be made in the wall. In a loadbearing wall, the top of the opening must carry the structure above. Even cutting a hole in a partition necessitates propping the masonry.

Where supports are required

Doorframes and window frames are not designed to carry superimposed loads, so the load from floors above must be supported by a rigid beam called a lintel, which transmits the weight to the sides where the bearings are firm. Wider openings call for stronger beams, such as rolled-steel joists (RSJs). There are numerous beams, but all work in the same way.

The forces on a beam

When a load is placed at the centre of a beam supported at each end, the beam will bend. The lower portion is being stretched and is in 'tension'; the top portion is being squeezed and is in 'compression'. The beam is also subjected to 'shear' forces where the vertical load is trying to sever the beam at the points of support. A beam must be able to resist these forces. This is achieved by the correct choice of material and the depth of the beam in relation to the imposed load and the span of the opening.

Calculating lintel size

The purpose of a lintel is to form a straight bridge across an opening which can carry the load of the structure above it. The load may be relatively light, being no more than a number of brick or block courses, but it is more likely that other loads from upper floors and the roof will also bear on the lintel.

The lintel must be of suitable size for the job it has to do. The size should be derived from calculations based on the weight of the materials used in the construction of the building. Calculation for specifying a beam is, strictly speaking, a job for an architect or structural engineer. Tables relating to the weight of the materials are used to establish the figures.

In practice, for typical situations, a builder can use his experience to help you decide on the required size of lintel. A Building Control Officer may be happy to accept this type of specification, but he can insist that proper calculations are submitted with your application for Building Regulations approval.

When to support a wall

If you are creating a door, window or hatchway which is no wider than 900mm (3ft) across in a non-loadbearing wall, you can cut the hole without having to support the walling above provided the wall is properly bonded and sound. The only area of brickwork that is likely to collapse is roughly in the shape of a 45-degree triangle directly above the opening, leaving a self-supporting stepped arch of brickwork. This effect is known as self-corbelling. Do not rely on the self-corbelling effect to support the wall if you plan to make an opening which is more than 900mm (3ft) wide – provide temporary support for the wall as if it were loadbearing.

Before you make any opening in a loadbearing wall you will need to erect adjustable props as temporary supports, not only for the weight of the masonry but also for the loads that bear on it from floors, walls and roof above.

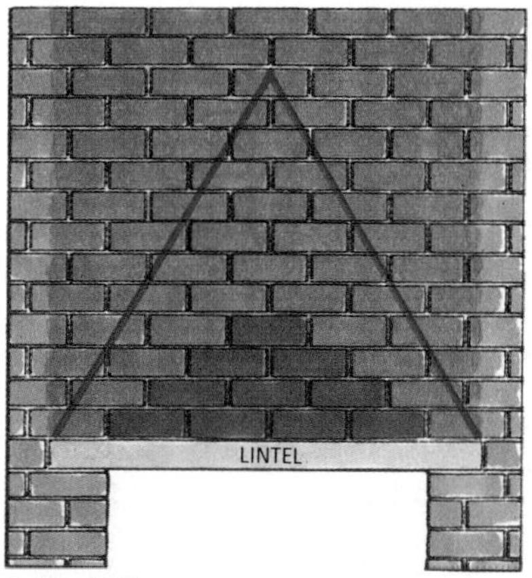

Self-corbelling
The darkest bricks are the only ones that may fall before the lintel is installed because of the self-corbelling effect of the bricks above. In theory the lintel supports the weight of materials within the 60-degree triangle plus any superimposed floor or roof loading, but when the side walls (piers) are narrow the load on the lintel is increased to encompass the area of the rectangle.

MAKING A HATCHWAY

RIGGING UP ADJUSTABLE PROPS

To remove part of a loadbearing wall it is necessary to provide support for the wall above the opening. Hire adjustable steel props and scaffold boards to spread the load across the floor. Where the brickwork will remain below the ceiling level, you will also need 'needles' to spread the load. Needles must be of sawn timber at least 150 x 100mm (6 x 4in) in section and about 1.8m (6ft) long.

For a hatchway or door opening, one needle and two props will suffice: place the needle centrally over the opening about 150mm (6in) above the lintel position. For wider openings, or where a load is great, space two needles and four props no more than 900mm (3ft) apart across the width of the opening.

Chop a hole in the wall for each needle and slot them through. Support each end with a prop, which works like a car jack. Stand the props on scaffold boards no more than 600mm (2ft) from each side of the wall.

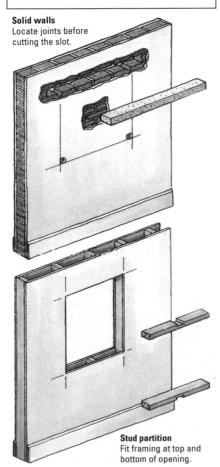

Solid walls
Locate joints before cutting the slot.

Stud partition
Fit framing at top and bottom of opening.

A serving hatch is a convenient opening in a wall, usually between a kitchen and dining area, through which you can pass food, drinks and equipment. If you are blocking off a doorway, or making a stud wall, it may be advantageous to allow for a hatch. Alternatively, you may want to make a hatchway in an existing wall.

Planning the size and shape

Ideally, the bottom of the opening should be an extension of the kitchen worktop or at least flush with a work surface: 900mm (3ft) is a comfortable working height and the standard height for kitchen worktops. For practicality – for passing through a tray and serving dishes, for instance – it should not be narrower than 740mm (2ft 6in).

Hatches should be fitted with some means of closing the opening for privacy, for preventing cooking smells from drifting and, in some cases, so that they act as a fire-check (see right).

Creating the opening

You can make a hatchway in either a loadbearing or a solid non-loadbearing wall in much the same way: the main requirement with the former is temporary support for the masonry above and the load imposed on the wall. Mark the position for the hatch on the wall. Align the hole with the vertical and horizontal mortar courses between the bricks to save having to cut too many of the latter – hack off a square of plaster at the centre to locate the joints.

Drill through at the corners of the opening and mark out the shape and position of the hatch on the other side of the wall. Make the hole about 25mm (1in) oversize to allow for fitting a lining frame. Mark the lintel position.

Set up adjustable props and needles if you are working on a loadbearing wall (see left), then chop a slot for the lintel with a club hammer and bolster chisel on a brick wall this will probably be a single course of bricks deep; on a block wall, remove a whole course of blocks and fill the gap with bricks. Set the lintel in mortar trowelled on to the bearings. Use a spirit level to check that the lintel is perfectly horizontal – pack under it with pieces of slate if necessary. Replace any bricks above the lintel that have dropped. Leave for 24 hours to set, then remove the props and needles and hack away the masonry below.

Making a hatchway in a stud wall

Cutting an opening in a stud-partition wall is simpler than making one in a solid wall, but if the wall bears some weight you will need to support the floor or ceiling above with props, using planks to spread the load.

Mark out, then cut away the plasterboard or lath-and-plaster covering from each side to expose the studs. For a hatch the same width as the distance between the studs (up to 550mm/1ft 10in), just skew-nail a nogging between them at the top and bottom of the opening. If it is to be wider, make the opening span three studs. Cut away part of the middle stud at the height you want the hatch, allowing for a horizontal frame member at top and bottom. Make the framing from studding timber and cut to fit between the two studs on each side of the cut one. Fit and check for level.

Fitting a lining frame

Line the hatch opening with 25mm (1in) thick planed softwood joined at the corners with butt joints or bare-faced tongue-and-groove joints for a neater result. The frame can either finish flush with the plaster wall surface and be covered with an architrave, or project beyond the plaster to form a lip or shelf.

The sides of the opening in a masonry wall are likely to be rough – it is not easy to chop a clean line. Make and fit the frame, then pack out the gap between masonry and lining with offcuts of wood. The frame must be truly square within the opening – check this with a spirit level before proceeding. Screw the frame to the masonry using fixing plugs, fitted when the frame is positioned. Make good with mortar all round it. Rake back the surface of the mortar and, when it has set, finish flush with plaster.

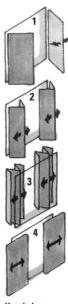

Hatch doors
1 Double-hinged
2 Twin bi-fold
3 Concertina
4 Horizontal-sliding

Finishing the frame
Use an architrave to cover the joint between the lining and wall or let the frame project to mask it.

Fit an architrave

Let frame project

CUTTING AN INTERNAL DOORWAY

1 Fix galvanized ties

2 Nail to wedges

Making a doorway in an existing wall may be necessary if you are changing the use of the room or improving its layout: this is often required as part of the process of converting a kitchen, where fitted units dictate the positions of access and exit doors. As with fitting a hatchway, it is necessary to install a lintel to ensure the stability of the wall itself and any other load which bears on it.

Preparing a brick or block wall

First check whether the wall is non-loadbearing or loadbearing. If the latter, seek approval from the Building Control Officer (BCO). Begin by marking the opening on one side of the wall, then examine the coursing of the bricks or blocks by exposing a small area; move the opening if necessary to align the perimeter with the vertical joints.

The height of the opening should allow for the height of the door plus 9mm (⅜in) tolerance, the thickness of the soffit lining and a new concrete or steel lintel. The width should be the width of the door plus 6mm (¼in) tolerance and twice the thickness of the door-jamb lining. Allow a further 12mm (½in) for fitting the lining.

Carefully prise off the skirtings from both sides of the wall. They can be cut and reused. Prop the wall and fit the lintel (see right) before cutting out the bulk of the masonry. Leave overnight for the bearings to set hard. The next day, starting from the top just below the lintel, chop out individual bricks, using a club hammer and bolster chisel. At the sides of the opening, cut the half or three-quarter bricks protruding into the doorway. Chop downwards where you can. If the wall is built from lightweight blocks, use a universal hand saw or a masonry saw to slice through the bonding. At the bottom, chop out the brickwork to just below floor level so that you can continue the flooring.

Bag up the rubble frequently in stout polyethylene sacks and stack whole bricks out of the way for reuse. Spray the area with water from a plant sprayer in order to settle the dust.

Fitting the door lining
You will have to fit a timber frame within the new doorway to which you can attach the stop-bead, door and decorative architrave. Make the frame from planed timber 25mm (1in) thick and the width of the wall. Fit the lining to the sides of the opening with galvanized-metal frame cramps (1) mortared into slots cut in the brickwork, or fit wooden wedges in the mortar joints and nail the frame to them (see diagram (2) left).

Dealing with a stud wall

First locate the positions of the studs, then prise off the skirting. Mark out the position for the opening on the wall, then remove the plasterwork. For lath-and-plaster walls, chop through to the laths with a bolster chisel and saw them off. For a plasterboard wall, saw through the cladding or use a sharp knife. If there are studs on each side of the opening, cut the plasterboard or laths flush with them. If the position of the hole does not correspond with the studs, cut back to the centre of the nearest stud on each side. Cut one or two studs to the right height – that is, the height of the door plus 9mm (⅜in) tolerance, the lining thickness and a 50mm (2in) head member.

Level up and and skew-nail the head member to the remaining studs at each end. Also dovetail-nail it to the ends of the cut studs. Saw through and remove the floor plate to the width of the door, plus 6mm (¼in) tolerance and twice the thickness of the door lining. Cut and nail the new studs, which will form the door jambs, to fit between the head and sill. Fit noggings between the new and original stud or studs. Cut and nail plasterboard to fill the gaps between the original wall surface and the new studs. Make and fit the door lining. Finish the surfaces with plaster, fit the architraves and replace the skirting.

Alternatively, cut the cladding from floor to ceiling and refit the studding flush with the cut edge. Mark the width of the opening, saw through the plaster from both sides of the wall then strip the plasterwork and knock out the exposed studs and noggings. Cut the floor sill level with the plaster and remove. Drive the studs into the cut edges until flush. Nail them at top and bottom. Fit a door-head member between them and a short vertical stud above it. Cover the space above the doorway with plasterboard.

INSTALLING THE LINTEL

Draw the position for the lintel, allowing a margin for fitting tolerance. Chop a groove around the perimeter of the opening with a club hammer and bolster chisel, then hack off the plaster. Fit adjustable metal props and needles, then cut a slot for the lintel. Bed a concrete lintel in a mortar mix of 1 part cement : 3 parts sand on bearings no narrower than 150mm (6in) at each side of the slot, and set level. Pack underneath the lintel with pieces of slate until it is horizontal. Replace loose bricks and fill any gaps with the same mortar mix.

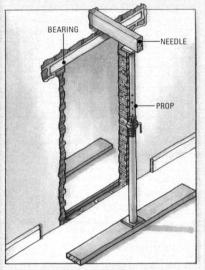

BEARING

NEEDLE

PROP

Fit a needle supported by props

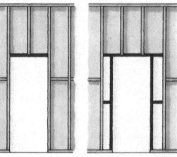

Door aligns with studs   **Door is misaligned**

Making the frame
The method you adopt for the frame will depend on the positions of the studs. The diagrams illustrate typical solutions.

Studs repositioned

FILLING AN OPENING IN A STUD PARTITION

Strip the door lining as described (see right). Trim the lath-and-plaster or plasterboard back to the centre line of the door-jamb studs and head member with a sharp trimming knife. Lever out the old nails with a claw hammer. Nail the new cut edge all round.

Nail a matching sill to the floor between the studs. Nail a new stud centrally between head and sill. Cut and nail noggings between the studs across the opening. Cut plasterboard 3mm (⅛in) less all round and fix to each face of the opening. Apply plaster or fill and tape the joints, then finish as required.

Nail the sill, stud and noggings

If you are making a new opening in a wall, you may also have to block off the original one. Obviously you will want the patch to be invisible, which takes careful plastering or filling of plasterboard joints.

Choosing the right materials

It is generally better to fill in the opening with the same materials used in the construction of the wall to prevent cracks forming due to movements in the structure (you can consider bricks and blocks to be the same). You could use a wooden stud frame with a plasterboard lining and plaster finish to fill an opening in a brick wall, but it would not have the same acoustic properties as a solid infill and cracks are difficult to prevent or disguise.

Removing the woodwork

Remove the architraves, then saw through the door-jamb linings close to the top and prise them away from the brickwork with a wrecking bar. If the linings were fitted before the flooring, the ends could be trapped: cut them flush with the floor. Next, prise the soffit board away from the top.

Bricking up the opening

Cut back the plaster about 150mm (6in) all round the opening. It need not be an even outline; unevenness helps to disguise the shape of the doorway.

To bond the new brickwork into the old, cut out a half-brick on each side of the opening at every fourth course, using a club hammer and bolster chisel. For a block wall, remove a quarter of a block from alternate courses.

It is not vital to tooth-in the infill if you are using blocks (which are easy and quick to lay) as it will require more cutting to fit. Instead, 100mm (4in) cut clasp nails driven dovetail fashion into the bed joints of the side brickwork **(1)** can be used to tie the masonry together.

Galvanized-metal frame cramps can also be used to save cutting into the bricks **(2)** – screw them to the wall, resting on every fourth brick.

Lay the bricks or blocks in mortar, following the original courses. If a wooden suspended floor runs through the opening, lay the bricks on a timber sole plate nailed across the opening. When the mortar has set, spread on a base coat of plaster, followed by a finishing coat. Fit two complete lengths of new matching skirting, or add to the original. When making up the skirting from old pieces, make sure the joints do not occur in the same place as the original opening.

1 Nail ties

2 Frame cramp

Cut out half-bricks

Lay bricks into the courses

Cut blocks to match bonding

CONVERTING TWO ROOMS INTO ONE

Making a through room is the best way to improve access between areas frequently used – the dining and living rooms, for example – and provides an opportunity for redesigning your living space. The job uses similar principles to making a hatchway or a new doorway, although on a much larger scale. Removing a dividing wall – whether it is structural or simply a non-loadbearing partition – is a major undertaking, but it need not be daunting. Provided you follow some basic safety rules, much of the job is straightforward, if messy and disruptive. Before you start, plan out your requirements and consult the at-a-glance flow chart, right, for a break-down of just what is involved.

Do you want a through room?

Before you go ahead and demolish the wall between the two rooms, consider first just how the new space might function, its appearance, the time it will take you to carry out the work, and the cost you will incur.

Ask yourself the following questions: Will the shape and size of the new room suit your needs? (If you have a young family, remember that your needs are likely to change as they grow up.)

Will most of the family activities be carried out in the same room (eating, watching TV, playing music, reading, conversation, playing with toys, pursuing hobbies, doing homework)?

Will removing the wall deprive you of privacy within the family, or from passers-by in the street?

Will the new room feel like one unit and not a conversion? For example, do the skirtings and mouldings match? Are the fireplaces acceptable when seen together, or should one be removed? If the doorways are close together, should one be blocked off?

Will the loss of a wall make the furniture arrangements difficult – particularly if central-heating radiators are in use and take up valuable wall space elsewhere?

Will the heating and lighting need to be modified?

Will the proposed shape of the opening be in character with the room and of the right proportion?

● **Hiring professionals**
If in doubt, hire a professional builder: to save costs, you may be able to work as a labourer or do preparation and clearing work.

130

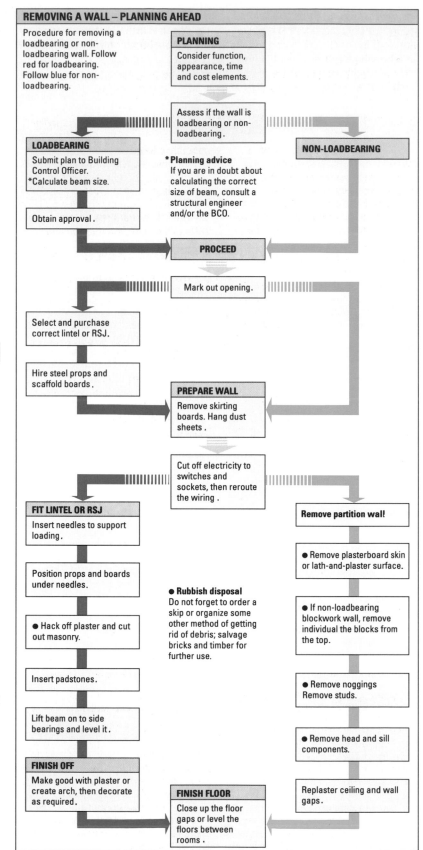

REMOVING A WALL – PLANNING AHEAD

Procedure for removing a loadbearing or non-loadbearing wall. Follow red for loadbearing. Follow blue for non-loadbearing.

PLANNING
Consider function, appearance, time and cost elements.

Assess if the wall is loadbearing or non-loadbearing.

LOADBEARING
Submit plan to Building Control Officer.
*Calculate beam size.

Obtain approval.

NON-LOADBEARING

* **Planning advice**
If you are in doubt about calculating the correct size of beam, consult a structural engineer and/or the BCO.

PROCEED

Mark out opening.

Select and purchase correct lintel or RSJ.

Hire steel props and scaffold boards.

PREPARE WALL
Remove skirting boards. Hang dust sheets.

Cut off electricity to switches and sockets, then reroute the wiring.

FIT LINTEL OR RSJ
Insert needles to support loading.

Position props and boards under needles.

● Hack off plaster and cut out masonry.

Insert padstones.

Lift beam on to side bearings and level it.

FINISH OFF
Make good with plaster or create arch, then decorate as required.

● **Rubbish disposal**
Do not forget to order a skip or organize some other method of getting rid of debris; salvage bricks and timber for further use.

Remove partition wal!

● Remove plasterboard skin or lath-and-plaster surface.

● If non-loadbearing blockwork wall, remove individual the blocks from the top.

● Remove noggings Remove studs.

● Remove head and sill components.

Replaster ceiling and wall gaps.

FINISH FLOOR
Close up the floor gaps or level the floors between rooms.

Once you are satisfied that the opening will be an improvement to your home's layout, consider the practical problems. First, determine whether the wall is loadbearing or a non-loadbearing partition: bear in mind that a loadbearing wall will need a beam spanning the opening with at least 150mm (6in) bearings at each end. Mark out the proposed opening on the wall with chalk to help you visualize its size and proportion.

Choosing a beam

The most suitable beam is usually a rolled-steel joist (RSJ), although this type of beam will require preparation before it can be plastered over. Reinforced and prestressed concrete lintels can be used for openings up to about 3m (10ft), but, over a wide span, their weight makes them difficult to handle; prestressed types are lighter, but better for single door or hatch openings rather than wide spans. Pressed-steel box lintels – available in lengths up to 5.4m (about 18ft) – are lighter and can be plastered directly.

What size beam?
You can use the following rule of thumb for specifying an RSJ, although exact details depend on the location, and the result must be approved by the Building Control Officer. For pressed-steel lintels, refer to the manufacturer for sizes:

CALCULATING THE SIZE OF A BEAM
A rule-of-thumb guide used by builders.
Make beam 25mm (1in) deep for every 300mm (1ft) span.

Height of the opening

The height of the opening is to some extent determined by the height of the ceiling and the depth of the beam. The latter is determined by the width of the opening the beam has to span, and the load it must carry. Consult an architect or structural engineer who, for a fee, can calculate this for you. The beam can be positioned directly under the ceiling joists of a low ceiling.

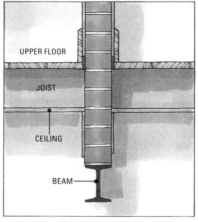

Brickwork supported below ceiling level

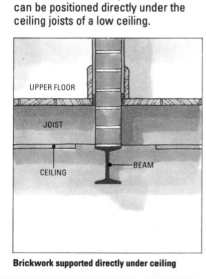

Brickwork supported directly under ceiling

Applying for permission

Before any work is started on a loadbearing wall you must seek approval from your local authority's Building Control Officer. He will require a drawing showing the proposed opening, its overall height and width and how the structure above the opening is to be supported. This need not be drawn up by a professional, but it should be clear. Approval is unlikely to be withheld provided the work complies with the Building Regulations. The BCO must be satisfied that the removal of the wall will not weaken the structure of the house, or any buildings attached to it, and that it will not encourage the spread of fire. Where a party wall is involved, it will be necessary to get written approval (a party award) from your neighbour. The BCO will advise you.

HOW A BEAM IS SUPPORTED

The supports are usually brick piers, which are in effect columns attached to the side walls and formed from the remainder of the old wall. Concrete padstones are required on which to sit the beam. The BCO may want the piers increased in thickness to give sufficient support to the beam and the side walls.

Ideally, it would be better if no piers were used as they interrupt the line of the side walls running through. It might be possible to run the ends of the beam into the walls, eliminating the need for piers, but this is subject to Building Regulations approval. It requires a horizontal concrete beam called a spreader to be set in the wall and distribute the load across more of the wall.

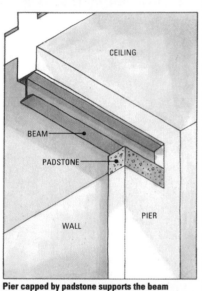

Pier capped by padstone supports the beam

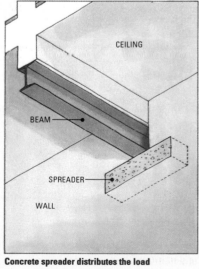

Concrete spreader distributes the load

REMOVING
THE WALL

Supporting the wall
1 When removing a wall up to ceiling level, support the upper floor with scaffold boards and props alone when the joists pass through the brickwork to support the wall. Otherwise, in addition, use needles on jacks placed directly above the props.
2 Normally brickwork projects below the ceiling level and is supported on needles passing through holes in the wall.

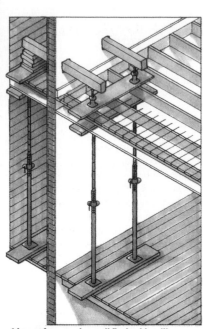

1 Layout for removing wall flush with ceiling

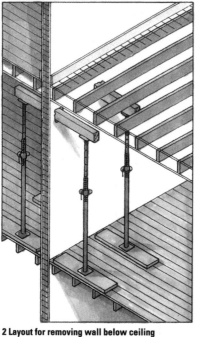

2 Layout for removing wall below ceiling

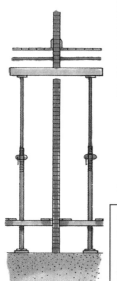

Props passing through the suspended floor

TRANSFER THE LOAD TO THE SUBFLOOR

If the floor appears to spring when you jump on it, check with a builder that the floor can carry the weight imposed; you may have to lift some floorboards and support the props on the foundations. In older houses, where there is no concrete below the floor, scaffold boards must be placed under the props to spread the load over the ground.

To remove part of a loadbearing wall you must temporarily support the walling above the opening. You will need to hire adjustable steel props and scaffold boards on which to support them. Where the beam is to be placed at ceiling level, hire extra boards to support the ceiling (**1**). Generally you will have to fit needles through the wall to transfer the load to the props (**2**). The needles must be at least 150 x 100mm (6 x 4in) in section.

Hire sufficient props to space them not more than 900mm (3ft) apart across the width of the opening. Buy the beam after the Building Control Officer's inspection. It can then be supplied to your exact requirements.

Preparation and marking out
First remove the skirting boards from both sides of the wall. On one side of the wall, mark the position of the beam in pencil. Use a steel tape measure, spirit level and straightedge for accuracy.

Hang dust sheets around the work area on the opposite face of the wall to help contain much of the inevitable airborne dust; attach them with battens nailed over them at the top. Seal gaps around all doors with masking tape to prevent the dust from travelling throughout the house. Open windows in the rooms you are working in.

Inserting the needles
Mark the positions for the needles on the wall, then cut away the plaster locally and chisel a hole through the brickwork at each point. Finish level with the bottom of one course of bricks. Make the holes slightly oversize so you can easily pass the needles through. Position a pair of adjustable props under each needle not more than 600mm (2ft) from each side of the wall. Stand the props on scaffold boards in order to spread the load over the floor.

Adjust the props to take the weight of the structure and nail their base plates to the supporting boards to prevent them being dislodged.

Supporting the ceiling
If the ceiling needs supporting, stand the props on scaffold boards at each side of the wall and adjust them so they run virtually to ceiling height – they should be placed 600mm (2ft) from the wall. Place another plank on top of the pairs of props and adjust simultaneously until the ceiling joists are supported.

Removing the wall
Hack off the plaster using a club hammer and bolster chisel, then start to cut out the brickwork, working from the top. Once you have removed four or five courses, cut the bricks at the side of the opening. Chop downwards with the bolster pointing in towards the wall to cut the bricks cleanly. Remove all the brickwork down to one course below the floorboards. As you work, load the rubble into stout polyethylene sacks; it may be worth hiring a skip. The job is laborious, but you can make it easier by using a hired power brick-cutting saw (see below). Only use this method if you have experience with machine tools.

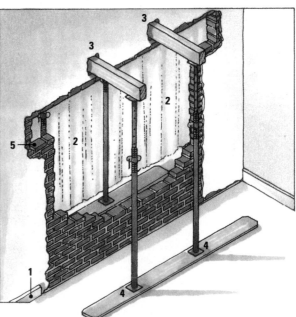

Cutting the opening
1 Remove or cut back the skirting and mark the beam's position.
2 Hang dust sheets around the work area.
3 Cut openings and insert needles.
4 Stand props on scaffold boards and adjust them to support the needles.
5 Cut away the plaster, then chisel out the bricks starting from the top of the opening.

Brick-cutting saw
Use with great care, following the suppliers' instructions.

Building piers

If the wall you are removing is deemed unsuitable as a basis for the supporting piers, you have two other choices. Where the adjacent wall is double thickness you may be able to cut a hole to take the end of the beam, allowing the weight to be distributed to the existing foundation. If this is not possible, you will have to build new piers with their own foundations. The piers must be built below the floor on concrete padstones cast on hardcore; they must include a DPC – engineering bricks may suffice – and must themselves be bonded in single or double brick thickness and toothed at every fourth course into the brickwork of the adjoining wall. The BCO will tell you the size for the piers.

Installing the beam

Make two wooden forms or boxes from thick plywood or softwood and cast concrete padstones on which to bed the RSJ to the size required by the BCO. Mix the concrete to the proportions 1 part cement : 2 parts sand : 4 parts aggregate. When the concrete has set, bed the padstones in mortar at the top of each pier. A large padstone may be better cast *in situ*. Set up formwork at the required height on each side and check the level between the two.

Build a work platform by placing doubled-up scaffold boards between steady stepladders, or hire scaffold-tower sections. You will need help to lift the beam into position.

Apply mortar to the padstones, then lift and set the RSJ in place. Pack pieces of slate between the beam and the brickwork above to fill out the gap. Alternatively, 'dry-pack' the gap with a mortar mix of 1 part cement : 3 parts sand, which is just wet enough to bind it together. Work it well into the gap with a bricklaying trowel and compact it with a wooden batten and a hammer. Where the gap can take a whole brick or more, apply a bed of mortar and rebuild the brickwork on top of the beam. Work the course between the needles so that when the timbers are removed the holes can be filled in to continue the bonding. Allow two days for the mortar to set, then remove the props and the needles and fill in the holes.

When the beam is fitted against ceiling joists you can use a different method. Support the ceiling with props and a board to spread the load (see opposite) on each side of the wall. Cut away the wall, then lift the beam into position and fit a pair of adjustable props under it. Apply mortar to the top of the beam and screw up the props to push it against the joists and brickwork above. Bed padstones in mortar or build formwork at each end and cast them.

FINISHING THE BEAM

A steel beam should be enclosed to provide protection from fire (which would cause it to distort) and to give a flat surface that can be decorated. Wet plaster, plasterboard or a specially made fireproof board can be used.

Cladding with plaster
Clad an RSJ with galvanized expanded-metal mesh to provide a key for the plaster. Fold the mesh around the beam, then lap it up on to the brickwork above and secure with galvanized nails.

Alternatively, wedge shaped wooden blocks (soldiers) into the recessed sides of the beam and nail the expanded metal to these. It is a good idea to prime the cut edges of the mesh to prevent corrosion which may stain the plaster.

Apply metal-lathing plaster or a stiff mix of bonding undercoat plaster in 9mm (⅜in) layers. Bond metal beading along the edges to reinforce the corners and cover with finishing plaster flush with the original surface.

Making good with plasterboard
To box in the beam with plasterboard or fireproof board you will need to fit shaped wooden blocks, wedged into the sides. To these, fix wooden battens nailed together to make fixings for the plasterboard panels (if you plan to install a folding-door system in the opening, you can nail the door lining directly to these same fixings). Set the board about 3mm (⅛in) below plaster level to allow for a skim coat to finish flush with the surrounding wall. Fill and seal the corner joints with tape.

Plaster the piers, then finish the beam and piers together.

● **Finishing a pressed-steel beam**
Pressed-steel box-profile beams are made with perforated faces to provide a key for the plaster.

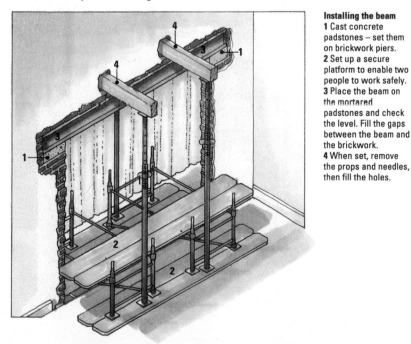

Installing the beam
1 Cast concrete padstones – set them on brickwork piers.
2 Set up a secure platform to enable two people to work safely.
3 Place the beam on the mortared padstones and check the level. Fill the gaps between the beam and the brickwork.
4 When set, remove the props and needles, then fill the holes.

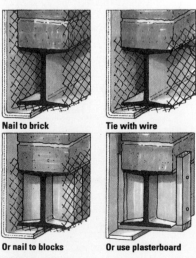

Nail to brick   Tie with wire

Or nail to blocks   Or use plasterboard

FITTING

ARCHES

Arch-formers
Expanded-metal mesh arch-formers are made in standard shapes and are easy to install. The shapes can be modified by adding a soffit strip.

Semi-circular

Oriental

Tudor

Spanish

Removing a dividing wall – to create a through living-and-dining room, for example – leaves you with a rectangular opening formed by the RSJ and its piers. If you prefer a curved archway, you can buy ready-made metal formers that are fitted in the opening and plastered over. Alternatively , design the archway yourself, construct your own formers and cover them with wet plaster or plasterboard.

Deciding on the arch profile

It is advisable to plan for the installation of an arch before you begin to make your opening. Choose the style of arch carefully: the shape will effectively lower the height of the opening at the sides, which may be impracticable and poorly proportioned for the room.

Corner arches round off the angle and do not encroach on headroom; semi-circular types give a full, rounded shape, but eat into headroom at the sides; pointed arches make a distinctive shape without taking up headroom at the middle of the opening.

Metal mesh arch-formers

Expanded-metal mesh arch-formers are available from builders' merchants. Various profiles are made – typically semi-circles, corner quadrants and ellipses, although Spanish, Oriental and Tudor styles are also available.

One-piece mesh frames are sold, but they are suitable only for walls 112mm (4½in) thick. Segmented formers – half the face and half the soffit (underside) – are more versatile; some have a separate soffit strip and can fit any wall.

Fitting the former
Wedge a batten across the top of the opening, to which you can attach the mesh with nails. Hold the former in position and set it squarely, using a spirit level (**1**). Secure the mesh to the piers with galvanized masonry nails – you may have to hack off a margin of plaster at the sides so the mesh can be fixed flat against the bricks. Hold a spirit level diagonally against the fold of mesh

at the curves and the hard plaster surface on the pier to check that it is set at the correct depth (**2**).

If you are fitting mesh segments, fit one half then the other (**3**) and tie the soffit strips together with galvanized or copper wire to prevent the mesh sagging under the weight of the plaster. On a thick wall, insert a soffit strip and tie it to the side pieces.

Mix up some metal-lathing plaster and spread a rough key coat on to the soffit with a plasterer's steel trowel, working from bottom to top from both sides (**4**). Do not press too hard or excess plaster will be forced through the mesh. Apply plaster to the face of the arch, scraping it off level with the hard plaster edge on the pier and the rigid mesh fold on the arch curve. When the plaster has stiffened, after about 15 minutes, apply a thin coat of ordinary finish plaster. Apply a second coat immediately and trowel smooth.

1 Set former square

2 Check it is level

3 Tie former soffits

4 Apply plaster

Fibrous-plaster arches

Prefabricated decorative archways made from fibrous plaster are available. These are normally fixed with screws to wooden battens at the top and sides of the opening. The joints between the fibrous-plaster mouldings and the wall

plaster are filled after installation. To complete an authentic-looking period interior, there are ornate fibrous-plaster accessories such as corbels (supporting brackets), pillars and pilasters with which to clad the piers.

MAKING A CUSTOMIZED ARCH

If you cannot find an arch former in the profile you require, make your own in one of two ways.

Using wet plaster
The arch may be a single curve, or it may incorporate intricate curves and points. Cut 12mm (½in) plywood ribs to the contour of the arch shape, but make them 12mm (½in) less than the finished size. Nail or screw them to the beam fixings and piers. Nail softwood spacer battens between the ribs.

Cut and fix expanded-metal mesh sheeting across the faces and edge of the shape, moulding it around the curves (**1**). You may have to snip the mesh with tinsnips to enable you to fold it around tight shapes.

Make up plastering guides from hardboard. Cut these to the finished shape you require. Temporarily nail them, smooth side inwards, over the mesh with packing pieces behind. The packing should equal the finished thickness of the plaster. Set the edges of the guide to overlap the underside of the arch by 12mm (½in), the required thickness of plaster. Spread plaster on to the underside of the arch between the overlapping edges. When this has set, remove the guides and plaster the wall faces, using the hard plaster edge as a level. Finally, apply finish plaster.

1 Fix mesh to ribs

2 Fit plasterboard

Using plasterboard
You can use plasterboard to make an arch to your own design. Cut the sheet to the required profile and nail it over the framework (**2**). Cut a thin strip of hardboard or thin plywood for the soffit, and pin it to the frame to form the underside of the arch. Fix hardboard textured side out. Bed paper scrim in plaster over the joins to prevent cracking due to slight movement. Apply a skim coat of finish plaster to all the surfaces. Alternatively, pin a strip of metal mesh to the soffit and apply a base coat and finish coat of plaster.

Lightweight partition walls which are not loadbearing can be removed without consulting the authorities for approval, and without the need to add temporary supports. You must, however, be certain that the wall is in fact not structural, as some partitions do offer partial support.

Dismantling a stud partition

Remove the skirting boards from both sides of the wall, plus any picture-rail mouldings: it is a good idea to save these for possible reuse or repairs in the future. If any electrical switches or socket outlets are attached to the wall, they must be disconnected and the wiring rerouted before work begins.

Removing the plasterwork
Use a claw hammer or wrecking bar to hack off the plaster and laths or plasterboard covering the wall frame. Once the framework is stripped, remove the vertical studs. Bag up the debris and remove it.

Removing the framework
First knock away any nailed noggings from between the studs. If the studs are nailed to the head and sill, they can be knocked apart. If they are housed or mortised in place, saw through them (at an angle to prevent the saw jamming). If you make the cut close to the joint, you will be left with a handy length of reusable timber.

Prise off the head and sill members from the ceiling joists and floor. If the end studs are fixed to the walls, prise them away with a wrecking bar.

Finishing off
Replaster the gap left in the ceiling and walls; you may need to fit a narrow strip of plasterboard. Fit floorboarding to close the gap in the floor if the boards are not continuous.

Dismantling a blockwork wall

Partition walls are sometimes made using lightweight concrete blocks. To remove the wall, start to cut away the individual units from the top with a bolster chisel and club hammer. Work from the middle out towards the sides.

Chop off an area of plaster first so that you can locate the joints between blocks, then drive your chisel into these to lever them out.

METHODS OF CLOSING A FLOOR GAP

When you remove a dividing wall that penetrates the floor, you are left with a gap between the floors on each side. The floorboards may run parallel with, or at right angles to, the line of the wall. Filling the gap with new floorboards is straightforward.

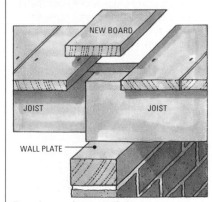

NEW BOARD
JOIST
JOIST
WALL PLATE

Boards running parallel
When the boards are parallel with the wall the supporting joists may rest on a wall plate built into the lower wall. Cut a board matching the thickness of the floorboards to fill the gap. Nail the board to the joist.

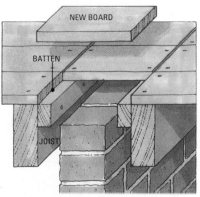

NEW BOARD
BATTEN
JOIST

Boards at right angles
When the boards are at right angles to the gap, the ends will be supported on joists running parallel with the wall and about 50mm (2in) from it.

Cut the ends of the board flush with the joists. Nail 50 x 25mm (2 x 1in) sawn softwood battens to the sides of the joists, level with the underside of the boards. Cut short lengths of matching floorboards to bridge the gap and nail them to the batten.

● **Making a room divider in an old house**
Create a room divider by stripping the plasterwork from the studding to reveal the timber framework. Once it is clean, paint or stain the frame to suit your interior decorative scheme.

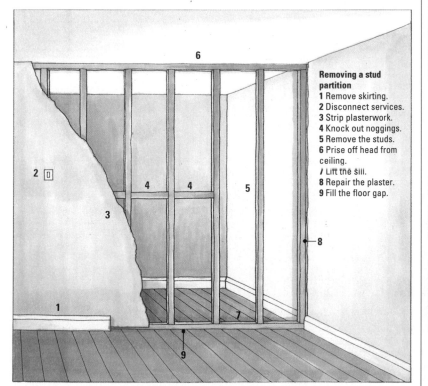

Removing a stud partition
1 Remove skirting.
2 Disconnect services.
3 Strip plasterwork.
4 Knock out noggings.
5 Remove the studs.
6 Prise off head from ceiling.
7 Lift the sill.
8 Repair the plaster.
9 Fill the floor gap.

When the joists run parallel with a wall that has been removed, you may find that one floor is not level with the other. This may have been caused by slight movement in parts of the building or it may be that the floors were never intended to be aligned. Depending on the difference between the floors, a slope or step will provide a satisfactory solution to the problem of misalignment.

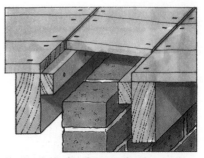

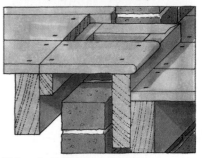

Fit short sloping boards across the gap

Packing and trimming

When the joists of the two floors are supported on the same wall plate, the chances are that both floors will be at the same level. Because wood can shrink or warp, however, it may be necessary to pack or trim the top of one or two joists slightly to allow for the infill board to sit properly between the floors.

Dealing with misalignment

A misalignment up to 18mm (¾in) can be accommodated by the short lengths of floorboards cut to span the gap. Although probably acceptable, the slope will be apparent. Where the difference in level is large, it may be necessary to create a single step or make a gradual slope. The latter should be less noticeable, but cannot satisfactorily run across a door opening.

Make a step if difference in level is large

Making a step

Trim the ends of the floorboards on the high side flush with the joists and nail a batten to it. Trim the boards on the low side in the same way, but screw a 38mm (1½in) thick planed softwood riser to the side of the joist to finish level with the batten on the higher floor (see right).

If the floors are to be covered, cut and nail short lengths of floorboards to form the step tread. Where you want a bare-wood floor, a single board running the width of the step would look better.

In this case, skew-nail noggings flush with and between the riser and adjacent joists at approximately 750mm (2ft 6in) centres – necessary for a wide board that is weak across its width.

Where a floor has been raised, make a shallow threshold step at a doorway. Prepare a hardwood threshold board to fit between the door linings and finish flush with the raised floor. Nail it to the lower floor. Trim the door to clear the step and refit it on its hinges.

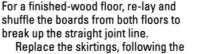

Fit a threshold at a doorway

Making a gradual slope

Cut the floorboards flush with the joist on the high side, and nail a batten to the joist as before. Remove the skirting boards from the side walls and lift the floorboards from the room with the lowest floor. Rest one end of a stout straightedge on the batten nailed to the higher floor and the other end on one of the joists of the lower floor to make a gradual slope (1).

Take measurements between each joist and the underside of the straight-edge. Set an adjustable bevel to the angle between the side of each joist and the board. With a power saw, cut lengths of 50mm (2in) wide softwood at the required angle to fill these gaps. Nail the prepared packing to the tops of the joists in descending order (2).

Re-lay the floorboards, butting their ends against the boards of the higher floor. Insert new floorboards where necessary to fill any gaps.

For a finished-wood floor, re-lay and shuffle the boards from both floors to break up the straight joint line.

Replace the skirtings, following the line of the floor, and nail to the wall.

Setting the slope
Measure gap between a straightedge and each joist, and set an adjustable bevel to the angle. Cut packing strips to fit and nail in place, followed by the floorboards.

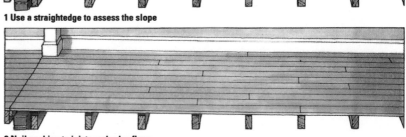

1 Use a straightedge to assess the slope

2 Nail packing to joists and relay floor

Building a partition to divide a large area into two smaller ones is quite straightforward to do, using a frame of timber studs. You can clad the wall and plaster it so the new addition looks an integral part of the house. Before you can go ahead, however, you may first need to seek approval from your local authority.

Complying with the Regulations

Before you begin to build a partition wall, check with your local authority to make sure that the space you are creating complies with the Regulations.

These state that if a new room is to be 'habitable' – a living room, dining room or bedroom (but not a WC, bathroom or kitchen) – it must meet requirements relating to ventilation.

The regulations stipulate that an open space must be available on the outside of the window to provide sufficient ventilation to the room. The openable area of the windows to each room must be not less than a twentieth of the room's floor area. (To check this, divide the area of the floor by the area of the window's sash or top vent.) Also, part, if not all, of the top vent must be 1.75m (5ft 9in) above the floor.

Alternative and additional means of ventilation may be provided by a mechanical ventilator direct to the open air. It may be permissible for a fanlight to connect to a vented lobby.

If you plan to partition a large bedroom to make an *en-suite* shower or WC on an internal wall, natural light will not be required, but ventilation will. Consider the positioning of the new room in relation to the existing plumbing and the means of ventilation.

Bear in mind the size and shape of the rooms in relation to the furniture – for example, should you plan to make a large bedroom into two smaller units, allow sufficient space for the beds to be made without difficulty. You will also need to create a corridor to make the two rooms self-contained.

Constructing a stud partition

Timber-framed non-loadbearing walls can be built relatively easily. The frame is usually made from 100 x 50mm (4 x 2in) or 75 x 50mm (3 x 2in) sawn softwood. The partition comprises a head or ceiling plate, which forms the top of the wall and is fixed to the ceiling joists; a matching length, nailed to the

floor, which forms the sill, or sole plate; studs which fit between the plates, equally spaced – about 400mm (1ft 4in) centre to centre – and fixed with nails; and short noggings which are nailed between the studs to make the structure rigid. Noggings are required where horizontal joints occur in the panelling.

Positioning the partition

If the new partition is to run at right angles to the floor and ceiling joists, it can be fitted at any point. Each joist will share the load and provide a solid fixing.

If the wall is to run parallel with the joists, it must stand directly over one of

them: this may mean altering the overall dimensions of your planned rooms. Locate the floor joist in question and check whether stiffening is required. If so, reinforce it by fixing an additional joist on each side (see right).

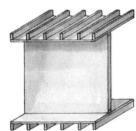

Right angle
A partition set at right angles to joists is well supported.

Parallel
A partition parallel with the joists must be supported by one of them.

Reinforcing
The floor joist may need stiffening to bear the extra weight of the partition (see right).

REINFORCING A JOIST

Remove the skirting and lift the floorboards. Temporarily lay some of the boards to walk on while working. Screw metal joist hangers to the walls at each end, using 50mm (2in) long screws, to support the reinforcing joists flush with the original joist. Cut two reinforcing joists to fit between the hangers. Allow not more than 6mm (¼in) for tolerance.

Use 12mm (½in) diameter coachbolts to clamp the joists together. Drill the holes for them slightly larger than their diameter and spaced not more than 900mm (3ft) apart, working from the centre. Place large plain washers under the head and nut.

Alternatively, you can use 75mm (3in) diameter double-sided timber connectors between the meeting faces instead of joist hangers. If you have room, and a drill bit long enough, drill through all three joists while they are held together with cramps. If not, clamp one in place and drill through the two. Remove the reinforcing joist and clamp the other on the opposite side. Drill through it using the hole in the original joist as a guide. Bolt the reinforcing joists together.

Replace the floorboards on which to erect the partition (see below).

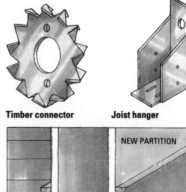

Timber connector   **Joist hanger**

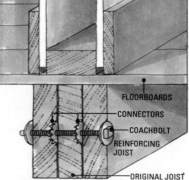

NEW PARTITION
FLOORBOARDS
CONNECTORS
COACHBOLT
REINFORCING JOIST
ORIGINAL JOIST

Stiffening the joist

SEE ALSO

Details for:	
Planning a room	15
Building Regulations	18–19
Suspended floors	176
Joist hangers	174
Ventilation	283–284
Plumbing	348–385

Parts of a stud partition
1 Head plate
2 Sole plate (sill)
3 Wall stud
4 Studs
5 Noggings

Fitting a partition between joists
Fit timber bearers between the floor joists and ceiling joists to support the stud partition.

BUILDING
A STUD
PARTITION

Making a stud-partition wall is the easiest way to divide a room into two: you can construct a plain wall or add a doorway, serving hatch or glazed area to 'borrow' light from an existing window. You can build the partition directly on to the floorboards, or on to the joists below so that the flooring will be independent of the partition. The sides of the partition can be set against the plaster surface or set in channels to provide a better fixing to the masonry and make any unevenness easier to fill.

Marking out and spacing the studs

With chalk, mark the width of the sill for the new wall on the floor, using the sill member – a length of 100 x 50mm (4 x 2in) sawn softwood – as a guide to draw the line. Continue the guidelines up the walls at each side, using a spirit level and straightedge or a plumb line and bob. Make guidelines on the ceiling by snapping a distinct chalk line on to the surface with a taut string **(1)**.

Spacing the studs

Lay the sill and head members together with their face sides uppermost. Mark the position of the studs at 400mm (1ft 4in) or 600mm (2ft) centres, working from the middle. Square the lines across both members, using a try square **(2)**. Use the 400mm (1ft 4in) spacing to support thin board materials and 9.5mm (⅜in) thick plasterboard, and the 600mm (2ft) spacing for 12.5mm (½in) plasterboard and tongue-and-groove (T&G) boards.

Marking out a doorway

If you require a doorway in the wall, make an allowance for the opening. The studs that form the sides of the opening must be spaced apart by the width of the door plus a 6mm (¼in) tolerance gap and the thickness of both door linings. Mark the width of the opening on the head plate, then mark the positions for the studs, working from the opening. Take the dimensions for the two sills from the head and cut both plates to length **(3)**. The door studs overlap the ends of the sills, which must be cut back to allow for them.

Fixing the framework

Secure the sill to the floor on each side of the door opening, using 100mm (4in) long nails or 75mm (3in) long No10 countersunk woodscrews. Use the head plate as a guide to keep both parts of the sill in line. Prop the head plate against the ceiling on its line **(4)** and check the stud marks are true with the sill, using a plumb line. Nail or screw the head plate to the joists.

Measure the distance between the head and sill at each end and cut the outer wall studs to length: they should be a tight fit between the sill and head plate. Drill and plug the walls if you are fixing the studs with screws, or use 75mm (3in) long masonry nails.

Fixing door studs

Cut the door studs to fit between the head plate and floor. Wedge them in place, but do not fix them yet. Add together the door height and the thickness of the head lining, plus 9mm (⅜in) for tolerance, then mark the position of the underside of the door head on the edge of one stud. Hold a spirit level on this mark and transfer it accurately to the other door stud.

Fixing the door head

Remove the studs, then mark and cut a 12mm (½in) deep housing to receive the 50mm (2in) door head. Reposition and skew-nail the door studs to the head plate and dovetail-nail into the ends of the sills. Locate the door-head member in its housing and dovetail-nail it through the studs **(5)**. Fit a short stud between the head plate and door head.

Alternative fixing for door studs

An alternative method for fixing the door studs is to cut them to the required door height and double up with a stud between the sill and head plate. Support the door head and nail it to the top of the door studs. Cut a short length of studding to fit vertically between the centre of the head plate and door head. Secure in place by dovetail-nailing. Make sure when nailing all the parts together that their faces are flush.

Double door studs
1 Door-height studs
2 Full-height studs
3 Door head

1 Snap a chalk line on the ceiling

2 Mark the sill and head plate together

3 Mark a door opening on the head plate first

4 Prop the head plate against the ceiling

5 Nail the studs to the door head

Fixing studs and noggings

Measure and cut each full-length stud and fix in turn (see right). Cut noggings to fit between the studs and, working from the wall, skew-nail the first end to the wall stud, then dovetail-nail through the next stud into the end of the nogging. One or two rows of noggings may be required: if you are going to fit plasterboard horizontally, place the centre of the noggings at 1.2m (4ft), working from the ceiling. When the boards are to be fitted vertically, space the line of noggings evenly, staggering them to make the fixing easier.

Space studs equally and nail top and bottom

Nail noggings between studs to stiffen them

Fixing to an existing stud wall

Stud partitions are commonly used for internal walls of rooms on the first-floor level. If your new partition meets a timber-framed wall, align it with the existing solid-frame members.

Where possible, fix the first stud of the new partition to one of the studs in the existing wall. Locate the stud by tapping, then drill a series of small holes through the plaster to find its centre.

When the new partition falls between studs, fix its first stud to the noggings, head and sill of the original wall. Construct the new wall as above but, in this instance, cut the wall stud to fit between the floor and the ceiling and fix it before the sill and head plate are nailed or screwed into place.

Fixing plasterboard vertically

Start at the doorway with the edge of the first board flush with the stud face. Before fixing, cut off a 25mm (1in) wide strip, running from the top edge of the board down to the bottom of the door-head member. Fix the board with 30mm (1¼in) or 40mm (1½in) plasterboard nails not more than 150mm (6in) apart. Fit the boards on both sides of the doorway, then cut and fit a section above the opening. Allow a 3mm (⅛in) gap at the cut joint. Fit the remaining boards.

Fixing plasterboard horizontally

Plasterboard can be fitted horizontally where it is more economical or convenient to do so. First nail the top line of boards in place, so that if it is necessary to cut the bottom run of boards the cut edge will fall behind the skirting. Cut a strip from the edge of the boards on each side of the doorway to allow for the boarding over the door to be fixed to the studs.

Temporarily nail a horizontal support batten to the studs 3mm (⅛in) below the centre line of the noggings. Sit a board on the batten and nail it to the studs. Fit the remainder of the top boards in this way; then fit the bottom row. Stagger the vertical joints.

A second person should assist you by holding the plasterboard steady. If you have to work alone, use a length of timber to prop the board while you work. Nail from the centre of the board.

NAILING TECHNIQUES

Use two 100mm (4in) round wire nails to skew-nail each butt joint, driving one through each side. Temporarily nail a batten behind the stud to prevent it moving sideways when you are driving in the first nail. Battens cut to fit between each stud can be permanently nailed in place to form housings for extra support.

Alternative stud-fixing method
For a particularly rigid fixing, set the studs into 12mm (½in) deep housings notched into the head and sill plates before nailing them.

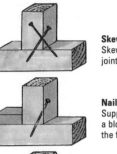

Skew-nailing
Skew-nail a butt joint with two nails.

Nailing technique
Support the stud with a block while driving the first nail.

Supporting joint
Battens fixed to each side brace the joint.

Housing joints
Housing joints ensure a true and rigid frame.

Fixing vertically
Work away from a doorway or start at one end.

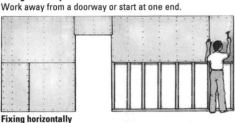

Fixing horizontally
Fix the top row first; stagger the joints on the next.

SEE ALSO

Details for:
Stud partition   138–139
Nail fixing   163
Plasterboarding a wall   163
Scribing plasterboard   164
Finishing
plasterboard   168–169

BUILDING A STAGGERED PARTITION

Building the wall
1 Mark out partitions.
2 Transfer the marks to the ceiling.
3 Cut and fix the sills to the floor.
4 Fix the head plates to the ceiling.
5 Make corners from three studs.
6 Fix the other studs at required spacing.
7 Fit noggings, then fix the boarding.
8 Fit doorframe and complete the boarding.
9 Fit door lining, door and mouldings.

A stud wall can be built to divide a room into two and provide alcoves for storage at the same time. The method of construction is the same as described for the straight partition, but also includes right-angle junctions. Constructing a staggered partition with a door at one end and a spacious alcove, as shown below, makes sensible use of available space.

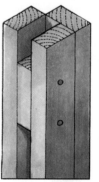

A staggered partition forms storage alcoves on each side, one for each room

Positioning the wall

First mark out the thickness of the main partition across the floor, then mark the position of the 'recessed' partition parallel with it. For clothes storage, set them apart by 600mm (2ft).

Calculate the length of the partitions by setting them out on the floor. Starting from the wall adjacent to the doorway, measure off the thickness of a stud, the door lining, the width of the door, a second door lining and a second stud. Also add 6mm (¼in) for clearance around the door. This takes you to the face of the first short partition that runs parallel to the wall. Measure from this point to the other wall and divide the dimension in two. This gives you the line for the other short partition. Set out their thicknesses at right angles to the main partitions.

Fixing the sill and head plates

Mark the positions for the head plates on the ceiling. Use a straightedge and spirit level or a plumb line to ensure that the marks exactly correspond with those marked on the floor.

Cut and fix the sill and head plates to the floor and ceiling respectively, as for erecting a straight partition. Cut and fit the studs at the required spacing to suit the thickness of the cladding.

CONSTRUCTING THE CORNERS

The right-angled corners and the end of the short partition, which supports the doorframe, need extra studs to provide a fixing for the plasterboard. Make up a corner from three studs arranged and nailed in place. Fit short offcuts of studding to pack out the gap. Fix the offcuts level with the noggings. Fit the boards with one edge overlapping the end of the adjoining panel. For the end of the short partition, fit two studs 50mm (2in) apart with nailed offcuts between. Nail the board to the two faces of the partition. Leave the end exposed until the doorframe is fitted.

Measure and cut the door studs, head plate and door head to length. Nail the head plate to the ceiling, and fix one stud to the room wall and one to the stud wall. Ensure they are square and flush with the end of the partition. Fit the door head and a short vertical stud above it. Plasterboard above the doorway and to the side faces of the studs, including the end of the wall.

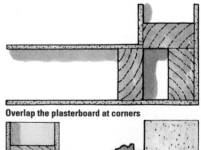

Corner post
Use three studs at the partition corners.

End post
Use two studs at the end of the partition.

Overlap the plasterboard at corners

Fix one door stud to the partition

Screw-fix the other stud to the wall

Unlike solid walls of brick or block, stud walls are mainly hollow, presenting problems when wall fixtures are to be hung. Wherever possible these should be fixed directly to the structural stud members for maximum support, but if the positions of fixtures are preplanned, extra studding, noggings or mounting boards can be incorporated before the wall lining is applied.

Mounting a hand basin

A wall-mounted hand basin will need a sound enough fixing to carry its own weight and that of someone leaning on it when it is in use.

Buy the basin before building the wall – or work from the manufacturer's literature, which usually specifies the distance between centres for fixing the brackets – and position two studs to take the fixing screws. Mark the centre lines of the studs on the floor before applying the wall lining so that you can eventually transfer the marks to the face of the lining. Measure the height from the floor for the basin brackets and fix them securely with wood screws.

If you plan wall-mounted taps above the basin make a plywood mounting board to fit between a pair of standard-spaced studs to carry both the basin and the taps. Use exterior-grade plywood at least 18mm (¾in) thick. Plywood is tougher and more stable than softwood and chipboard does not hold screws well.

Screw 50 x 50mm (2 x 2in) battens to the inside faces of the studs, set back from their front edges by the thickness of the board. Cut the board to size with enough height to support basin and taps, then screw it to the battens to lie flush with the two studs.

Apply the lining to the side of the wall that will carry the basin, leaving the other side open for plumbing in the appliances. Drill clearance holes and fit the taps; fix the basin-support brackets, preferably with bolts.

To hide the plumbing within the wall, pass the waste downpipe through a hole drilled in the wall-sill member and run it under the floor. If the wastepipe must run sideways in the wall, notch the studs (see below).

Fitting a wall cupboard

It is not always possible to fix to the studs because walls tend to be put up well before furnishings are considered. If there are no studs just where you want them, you will have to use cavity fixings instead. Choose a type that will adequately support the cabinet.

Hanging shelving

Wall-mounted bookshelves have to carry a considerable weight and must be fixed securely, especially to stud partitions. Use a shelving system which has strong metal uprights into which adjustable brackets are slotted. The uprights spread the load across all the wall fixings. Screw into studs if you can, otherwise use suitable cavity fixings (see below right).

When the studs are spaced at 400mm (1ft 4in) centres, fix the shelving uprights to alternate studs. For 600mm (2ft) spaced studs fix to each in turn.

As an alternative, fix individual shelves along their back edges with extruded-aluminium shelf-supports screwed horizontally across the studs.

Hanging small fixtures

Load-carrying fixtures with a small contact area can crush the plaster and strain the fixings. Mount coat hooks, for example, on a board to spread the load and screw the boards to studs.

Hang small pictures on picture hooks secured with steel pins, larger ones on a double-pin type, preferably fixed to a stud. Use mirror plates fixed to the frame to screw a large mirror or picture to the wall. Suspend heavy frames from stranded wire, not twine.

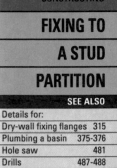

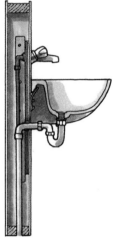

Mounting a basin
Fix a wall-mounted hand basin and taps to an exterior-grade plywood board.

FITTING SERVICES IN STUD PARTITIONS

It is easy to plan and fit services in a stud-partition wall before lining it. To guard against future occupants drilling into service runs, set horizontal cables or pipes no more than 150mm (6in) above floor level.

Plumbing
Plan the runs of pipes by marking the faces of the vertical studs or the noggings that brace them. Remember that a wastepipe must have a slight fall. When you are satisfied with the layout cut notches in the timbers for the pipework (see right).

Transfer the marked lines to the sides of the studs or noggings and drill holes for the pipes close to their front edges. Cut in to the holes to make notches. If cut at a slight angle they will hold the pipes while they are being fitted.

Notches cut for wastepipes must be reinforced to prevent them weakening the studs. Drill the holes in the centres of the studs, following the pipe run.

Before cutting in to the holes cut housings for 300mm (12in) lengths of 50 x 25mm (2 x1in) softwood to bridge the notches. Make the notches, set the wastepipe in place, then screw the bridging pieces into their housings flush with the fronts of the studs.

Noggings need not be braced, but fit one under a pipe bend as a support.

Running electric cable
Drill 12 to 18mm (½ to ¾in) holes at the centres of the studs for level runs of cable and in noggings for vertical runs. Fit extra noggings to carry mounting boxes for sockets and switches. For a flush-mounted fitting, inset the noggings to the depth of the box so that its front edge lies flush with the lining. Run the cable. With the lining in place, mark and cut an opening for the box and pull the cable through. If you have omitted a mounting board during construction, you can use dry-wall fixing flanges to hold the metal box to the lining.

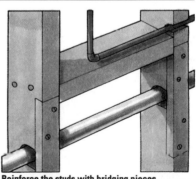

Reinforce the studs with bridging pieces

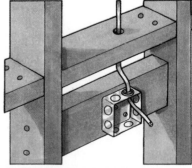

Fit metal boxes to a mounting board

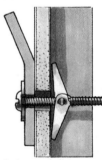

Spring-toggle fixing

Cavity fixings
Various cavity fixings are available for insertion into holes and securing with screws or bolts. Some expand to grip the lining as a screw is tightened; some are held in place by a toggle that springs out behind the lining.

141

BUILDING A DRY-PARTITION WALL

For a lightweight non-loadbearing partition, cellular-core dry-partitioning is easy to construct. Made from two sheets of plasterboard with a cardboard core, it makes a rigid wall when installed. The panels can be purchased from larger builders' merchants, but will probably have to be ordered. Tapered-edge panels for decorating and square-edged panels for plastering are available. The panels provide a reasonable level of sound insulation, but gaps between boards reduce their performance. Acoustic sealant can be applied to all the jointing surfaces during erection.

Fixing the framing

The panels are fixed to a lightweight timber frame. Mark out the floor, walls and ceiling in the same way as for a stud partition. Nail to the floor a 50mm (2in) planed (PAR) softwood sill, which matches the thickness of the partitioning. Plane 18mm (¾in) thick softwood ceiling and wall battens to make a snug fit in the gap between the plasterboard sheets. Remove the arris from the outside long edges of the battening and then nail or screw the battening to the wall and ceiling. To locate the bottom of the partition, cut a point on a 150mm (6in) locating block cut from wall battening, and nail it to the sill with its square end against the wall batten. Use 50mm (2in) wire nails.

Fixing the panels

Using a saw, cut the panels to fit between the sill and the ceiling with a 3mm (⅛in) tolerance . Rip out the cardboard core with the claw of a hammer to the depth of the battens – about 18mm (¾in) – along the top and two long edges. Also remove 150mm (6in) of the core from each end of the bottom edge. Use a wood chisel to trim away any lumps of glue.

Drive 150mm (6in) lengths of battening into the core at the bottom of the partitioning approximately 400mm (1ft 4in) apart. These plugs are used to fix skirtings. Mark the position of each plug on the surface of the partition for future reference.

Lift and locate the top of the first panel over the ceiling batten about 200mm (8in) from the wall. Swing the panel into the vertical position and locate it on the floor sill. Slide the panel carefully along the sill to locate over the locating block and wall batten. Cut an intermediate locating block 300mm (1ft) long and taper each end. Tap half of its length into the bottom corner of the panel's core and nail it to the sill.

Cut a length of square-section vertical joint batten to fit between the ceiling batten and intermediate locating block. Tap the batten halfway into the edge of the panel and then skew-nail it at the top and bottom. Fix the boards to the framework with galvanized nails at 225mm (9in) centres.

Prepare the other panels and secure them in the same way. Butt the edges of the tapered panels, but leave a 3mm (⅛in) gap between square-edged ones.

JOINTS AND JUNCTIONS

Joints

To make a T-joint, nail a vertical wall batten to one of the joint battens or to plugs cut from the joint battening and driven into the core of the corresponding partition. Fit the 150mm (6in) long plugs horizontally, about 600mm (2ft) apart, before erecting the partition. Hammer them into the edge, following a line of cells. Use a spare length of battening to drive the plugs further in if required. Always mark the position of the plugs on the surface.

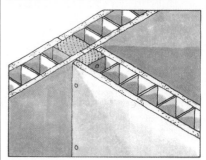

Fixing to joint batten

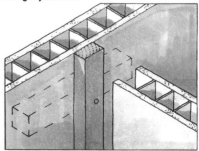

Fixing to batten plugs

Junctions

Right-angle corners are made by cutting away the inside face of the plasterboard and core to form a rebate for the full width of the adjoining panel. A batten must be fitted into each panel for nailing.

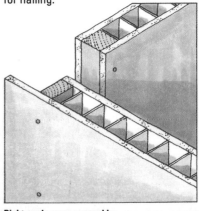

Right-angle corner assembly

Partition components
1 Softwood sill at base of panel.
2 Wall batten (hidden inside long edge of panel).
3 Ceiling batten.
4 Locating block (hidden).
5 Cellular-core panel.
6 Intermediate locating block.
7 Vertical joint batten.
8 Skirting-fixing plug.

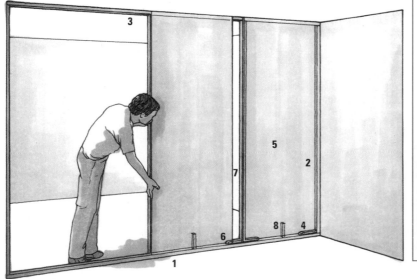

Making a door opening

Mark the position of the doorway on the floor. Make allowances for the width of the door and door linings. Mark out the width of the panels, working from the opening to each wall. Fit the ceiling and wall battens. Cut the sill to stop at the opening and fix it to the floor. Fit the panels, working from the wall towards the opening and starting with any cut panels. At the opening, remove the core from the vertical edges of the panels and insert vertical battens flush with the edges. Skew-nail at top and bottom and fix the plasterboard with galvanized nails at 225mm (9in) intervals.

Measure and cut a panel to fit above the door opening. Nail a length of wall batten, with one end tapered, to the vertical batten on each side of the opening. The battens should be about 75mm (3in) shorter than the depth of the cut panel. Ensure they are set true.

Clear the core from all round the panel, allowing enough room at the bottom to accommodate a length of joint battening. Slide the panel over the side battens and nail it in place with a 3mm (⅛in) gap at the top.

Fit the horizontal head batten into the core, flush with the bottom edge, and nail it to the vertical battens at each end, then nail the door linings to the stud framework.

If you fit a ready-made doorframe, treat it as a panel and build it in as the other partitions are erected. When assembling the partition, remember to omit a section of the sill at the doorway.

Slide the panel over the side battens

Fitting a partition between walls

Working from one wall, mark out the width of the full panels across the floor. Inevitably, you will have to cut the last panel to fit. Measure and cut it to the required width, less 6mm (¼in). Fix the framing to the floor, ceiling and both walls. Fit the bottom locating batten.

Prepare and fit the cut panel at one end and then proceed from each end towards the centre. Clean out the core from the panels on each side of the opening to allow a jointing batten to be set in flush. Make three equally spaced wide saw cuts in the edges of the panels. Cut the vertical battens so that they fit loosely between the ceiling batten and sill. Set them flush into the prepared edges of the panel. Insert 50mm (2in) screws part way into the centre of the battens at each saw cut. Lift the last panel into position, then tap the screws sideways to drive half the vertical batten into the edge of it. Skew-nail the vertical batten to the top and bottom frames through the board. Fix the panels and remove the screws.

Insert last panel then tap batten sideways

SEE ALSO

Details for:
Door casings   189, 194
Dry-wall fixings   315

Fixing details

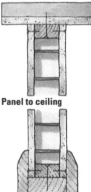

Panel to ceiling

Panel to floor

Panel to wall

FITTING FIXTURES AND INSTALLING SERVICES

Fixtures

Lightweight loads such as pictures, small or medium-size mirrors, clocks and display shelving may be fitted to a dry-partition wall with cavity-wall fixings. Heavy loads, for example storage units, should be screwed to wooden plugs installed in the core before assembly. Shelving systems with metal uprights can be screwed directly to the plugs; a surface-mounted board screwed to a pair of plugs will help to spread the load of a heavy cabinet.

Services

Electric cable can be passed horizontally through the core as panels are erected. Use a 25mm (1in) diameter pipe to clear a path for the cable. A permanent length of plastic conduit running through the core may help you to feed the cable through as the panels are fitted. Vertical cable runs can also be made, provided they occur next to a joint in the panel and do not infringe Wiring Regulations.

Cut accurate openings in the face of the partitioning for switches and socket-mounting boxes, and fit them with partition-wall flanges.

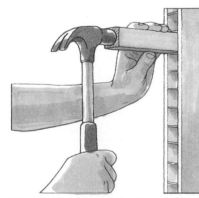

Drive wooden plugs in from the edge

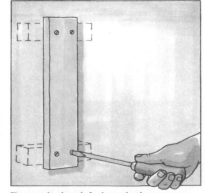

Fix mounting boards for heavy loads

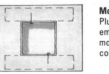

Mounting boxes
Plugs can also be employed for fixing mounting boxes in the core cavity.

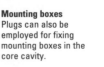

SHELVING

Pressed-steel fixed brackets

Aluminium-extrusion shelf support

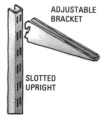

ADJUSTABLE BRACKET

SLOTTED UPRIGHT

ADJUSTABLE BRACKET

GROOVED UPRIGHT

Adjustable bracket systems
Each type can be fitted with a choice of brackets.

Wooden stiffeners
1 Wooden batten
2 Plywood strip
3 Rebated batten
4 Half-round lipping

Metal stiffeners
5 Screwed angle
6 Grooved T-section
7 Grooved angle
8 Screwed T-section

Depending on where it is and what it is to be used for, shelving can be anything from a set of planks on functional-looking brackets in a garage to elegant spans of solid wood or plate glass on apparently delicate supports of light alloy. Whatever its form or context, shelving is the cheapest, simplest and most economical kind of storage.

Wall-hung shelves

Shelves can be fixed into an alcove on support battens or cantilevered off a wall with any one of a wide range of shelving brackets. The brackets may be made from pressed, cast or wrought steel or extruded alloy.

There are many systems on the market with brackets that slot or clip into metal upright supports which are screwed to the wall. Most uprights have holes or slots at close intervals that take lugs on the rear of the bracket. In one system, the upright has a continuous groove over its entire length so that the brackets may be placed at any level.

One advantage of such systems is that the weight and stress of loaded shelves are distributed down the supporting uprights. Another factor in their favour is that, once the uprights are in place, shelving arrangements can be changed easily and further shelves added as the need arises without the necessity for more fixings.

Use the cheap and functional pressed-metal types for utilitarian shelving such as that in a garage or workshop and choose the more expensive and attractive brackets for your storage needs around the house.

Shelf span

Sagging occurs when the span of a shelf between two supports is too long in relation to its thickness or load, or both. On this score solid timber or blockboard with its core running lengthways are best for sturdy shelving. Veneered chipboard, though popular because of its low cost, availability and appearance, will eventually sag under relatively light loads, so it needs support at closer intervals than timber does.

A shelf with supports at each end will sag more than one with the supports placed about a quarter of the shelf length in from the ends as this helps distribute the load. The chart shows recommended maximum spans for shelves of different materials. If you want to increase the length of the shelf, either position the supports in from the ends, add a bracket, use thicker material or support the edges.

RECOMMENDED SHELF SPANS

Material	Thickness	Light load	Medium load	Heavy load
Solid wood	18mm (¾in)	800mm (2ft 8in)	750mm (2ft 6in)	700mm (2ft 4in)
Blockboard	18mm (¾in)	800mm (2ft 8in)	750mm (2ft 6in)	700mm (2ft 4in)
Chipboard	16mm (⅝in)	750mm (2ft 6in)	600mm (2ft)	450mm (1ft 6in)
MDF	18mm (¾in)	800mm (2ft 8in)	750mm (2ft 6in)	700mm (2ft 4in)
Glass	6mm (¼in)	700mm(2ft 4in)	Not applicable	Not applicable

Stiffening a shelf

Wooden battens, lippings or metal extrusions can be applied to the underside or front edges of a shelf to increase its stiffness. A wall-fixed batten may also be used to support the back edge in some cases. A deep wooden front rail will also conceal a strip-light fitting, while metal reinforcement can be slimmer and less noticeable.

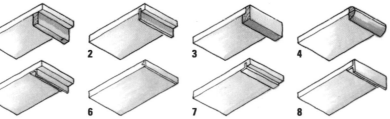

1 2 3 4

5 6 7 8

Built-in shelves
The simplest way to make built-in open shelves is to fit them into alcoves such as those flanking a chimney breast. However, the surface of the walls is unlikely to be perfectly regular and some trimming of the shelves may be needed to make them a good fit.

Fitting fixed shelves
Mark the height of the shelves. Space them apart to suit the items to be stored. Draw levelled lines from the marks using a spirit level.

Cut wooden support battens to suit the depth of the shelves. If the shelves are not fitted with a deep lipping, cut the front ends of the supports to a 45-degree angle (**1**). However, it looks better if you lip the shelves to cover the supports (**2**). For a more refined look, use metal supports (**3**).

Adjustable shelf unit
You can erect a bank of built-in shelves using side panels. The screw-fixed panels overcome problems with uneven walls and allow adjustable shelf fittings to be used.

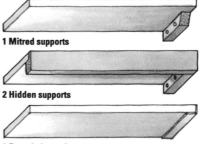

1 Mitred supports

2 Hidden supports

3 Extruded-metal supports

FIXING TO WALLS

SHELVING MATERIALS

Ready-cut shelves, in a wide variety of sizes, are usually made from solid wood or man-made boards, but shelves manufactured from glass or painted pressed steel are also available. Man-made board shelves are painted or finished with wood or plastic veneer. If the standard range of shelves does not meet your requirements you can make your own using the following materials.

Solid wood
Softwoods such as pine usually contain knots unless specially selected. Parana pine is generally knot-free and available in wide boards, but is more expensive.

Hardwoods such as oak, beech, ash and possibly mahogany and teak are available from some timber merchants, but their high cost limits their use to special features and furniture.

Blockboard
Blockboard is a stable man-made board constructed from strips of softwood glued and sandwiched between two layers of plywood-grade veneer.

The board is as strong as solid wood provided the shelving is cut with the core running lengthways. You will need to lip the edges with veneer or solid wood to cover the core.

Plywood
Plywood is built up from veneers with their grain alternating at right angles to one another for improved strength and stability. The edge can be left exposed or covered as for blockboard.

Chipboard
The cheapest man-made board is most often used as the core for manufactured veneered shelving. Chipboard shelves are liable to bend under load.

Medium-density fibreboard
Medium-density fibreboard (MDF) is a dense and stable man-made board that machines and works like solid wood. It finishes smoothly on all edges and does not need to be lipped. It provides an ideal surface for painting or veneering.

Glass
Plate glass is an elegant material for display shelving. Use toughened glass, available to special order. Have it cut to size and the edges ground and polished by the supplier. Textured and wired glass can be used for added interest.

The construction of the wall will to some extent determine the type of fixing and the positioning of shelves. On masonry walls, shelf supports can be placed almost anywhere; on a timber-framed wall, shelves should ideally be fixed to the studs or noggings, but you can use special cavity fixings provided the loads are not excessive.

A load cantilevered on brackets from a wall imposes great stress on the fixing screws, especially the top ones. If the screws are too small in gauge, or if the wall plugs are inadequate, the fixing may be torn out. This is even more likely when you are erecting deep shelves. The fixings of a shelf with its ends supported on battens within a masonry alcove are not so highly stressed.

For most ordinary shelving, brackets fixed to a wall of masonry with 50mm (2in) screws and wall plugs should be adequate. Deep shelves intended for a heavy load such as a television set or stack of records may need more robust fixings such as wall bolts, though extra brackets to prevent the shelf sagging will also share the weight. Brackets must be long enough to support almost the whole depth of the shelf.

Fixing individual shelf brackets
When fixing pairs of individual brackets to a solid wall, first mark two vertical guidelines. Hold one bracket at the required height and mark the wall through the fixing holes. Drill into the wall with a masonry bit, insert wall plugs and screw the bracket in place. Using a shelf and spirit level, position the second bracket, then mark and fix it in the same way.

When fixing brackets to a timber-framed wall, locate the studs and drill pilot holes for the screws. Lightly lubricate screws that are difficult to insert. If you use cavity-wall fixings, drill appropriate clearance holes through the plaster lining for the fittings.

When you are erecting a bank of shelving, fix all the brackets first and simply place the shelves on them. Use a plumb line or spirit level to align the ends of the shelves before you fix them to the brackets.

Fitting shelving systems
The upright supports must be vertical, and the best way of ensuring this is to fix each one lightly to the wall by its top screw, then, holding it vertical with the aid of a spirit level, mark the position of the bottom screw (1). With that screw in place you can check that the upright is vertical in its other plane, not sloping outwards because the wall is out of true. If necessary, place packing behind the upright to correct it (2). Also insert packing wherever hollows occur close to fixing points.

Clip one bracket to the upright, then another to the second upright while you hold it against the wall. Get a helper to lay a shelf across the brackets, then use a spirit level to check that the shelf is horizontal. Mark the top hole of the second upright, and fix that upright as you did the first one.

Locate the brackets in the uprights and fix the shelves to them. The gap between the back of the shelves and the wall provides a useful space for cables leading to lamps or equipment.

1 Plumb the upright support
Use a spirit level to plumb the upright, then mark the bottom fixing hole on the wall.

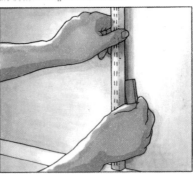

2 Packing out the upright support
Push strips of packing behind the metal upright until it is vertical.

Masonry wall
Use wall plugs as wall fixings.

Partition wall
Screw directly into the studs.

145

From a practical point of view, a high ceiling can be a liability. It incurs greater heating bills, and decorating costs will be higher as more material is required to cover the walls. Lowering the ceiling can help solve these problems as well as providing a distinctive feature in a room.

High ceilings are generally found in older houses. Some are ornately moulded, while many have more simple yet attractive cornice mouldings. These should be preserved to maintain the character of the house, but where a room is plain and the ceiling needs attention, or where the proportions of the room would benefit from alteration, a lowered ceiling can be an improvement. It can be used to hide ducting, improve sound and heat insulation and provide a space for flush or concealed lights.

Changing the character of a room

A room's character is largely determined by the relation of its area to its ceiling height. Low cottage ceilings are considered charming and cosy, while tall rooms are felt to be very imposing when they are altogether large in scale. However, small rooms with high ceilings often feel rather 'uncomfortable'.

The sense of cosiness or otherwise may be based on practical experience. For example, a cottage room is smaller in volume than a room with the same floor area but with a higher ceiling, so it is easier to heat evenly – and a room with an even temperature feels more comfortable than one where the temperature varies due to rising and falling currents of air. Also, the acoustics in a small room may be better, inducing a relaxed atmosphere. Yet the qualities of light and space in a room are often due to a high ceiling, and if that were lowered, drastically changing the room's proportions, tall windows may look awkward and the sense of space be lost.

Making a model

Making a card model of a room is a good way to check that planned alterations will suit the room before you spend time and money on the real thing.

Measure the length, width and height of the room and the height, width and positions of the windows and doors. Mark out and cut rectangular pieces of

The lowered ceiling is sloped to accommodate the tall window

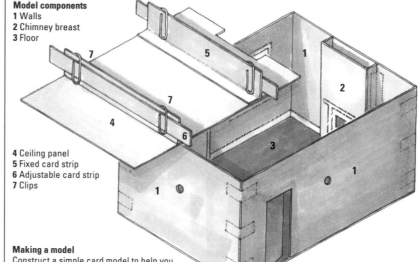

Model components
1 Walls
2 Chimney breast
3 Floor

4 Ceiling panel
5 Fixed card strip
6 Adjustable card strip
7 Clips

Making a model
Construct a simple card model to help you visualize the final room proportions.

stiff cardboard for the floor and walls to a scale of 1 : 10 (1mm = 1cm) or, in the imperial measure, 1 : 12 (1in = 1ft).

Mark the positions of the doors and windows on the cardboard walls and cut out the openings with a craft knife. Hinge a card door in its opening, using self-adhesive tape. Draw lines on the walls to represent the skirting and architraves around the doors and windows. You can colour these details to make them more realistic. Draw the fireplace to the same scale. If necessary, make a projecting chimney breast from card and glue it in place.

Punch a small peep-hole in each wall at a height scaled to the average eye level, and assemble the floor and walls, using glue or self-adhesive tape.

Cut a cardboard panel, representing the ceiling, to fit closely between the

walls. If the proposed ceiling is to be the suspended type, with lighting round its edges, cut the model ceiling panel smaller to provide the equivalent gaps at the sides of the room.

Cut two strips of card about 50mm (2in) wide and as long as the width of the ceiling piece, then glue them on edge across the back of the ceiling. Cut two strips a little longer, and use clips to attach these to the shorter ones. With the longer strips bridging the walls, adjust the paper clips to set the card ceiling at various heights. Check the effect on the room by viewing the interior space through the peepholes, and the door and window openings.

To simulate an illuminated grid-system ceiling, make a balsa-wood framework to the same scale and cover it with tracing paper.

LOWERING A CEILING: OPTIONS

You might want to lower a ceiling for practical reasons or simply to change the style of the interior – but whatever the reason, consider your options carefully because the outcome is liable to be expensive.

Timber-framed ceilings are heavy, but they can be tailor-made to suit the room, using basic wood-working skills.

Proprietary suspended-ceiling systems are relatively lightweight and particularly easy to install. Manufacturers offer a wide choice of materials for the panelling, but a strong grid pattern is unavoidable.

Use the chart (right) to help you consider a number of projects in advance and to compare one system with another.

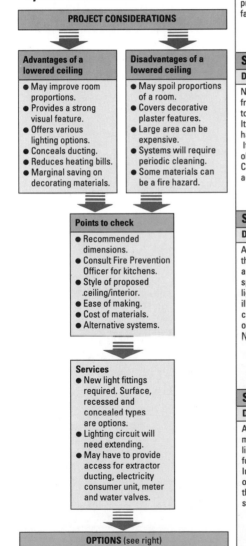

PROJECT CONSIDERATIONS

Advantages of a lowered ceiling
- May improve room proportions.
- Provides a strong visual feature.
- Offers various lighting options.
- Conceals ducting.
- Reduces heating bills.
- Marginal saving on decorating materials.

Disadvantages of a lowered ceiling
- May spoil proportions of a room.
- Covers decorative plaster features.
- Large area can be expensive.
- Systems will require periodic cleaning.
- Some materials can be a fire hazard.

Points to check
- Recommended dimensions.
- Consult Fire Prevention Officer for kitchens.
- Style of proposed ceiling/interior.
- Ease of making.
- Cost of materials.
- Alternative systems.

Services
- New light fittings required. Surface, recessed and concealed types are options.
- Lighting circuit will need extending.
- May have to provide access for extractor ducting, electricity consumer unit, meter and water valves.

OPTIONS (see right)

LOWERED CEILING

Design features	Planning the scheme	Type of construction	Covering/finishes
Will change the room proportions. Will conceal old ceiling and services. Least likely to appear a conversion. Can be fitted with cornice mouldings. Without a hatch, it prevents access to the void above.	Make initial sketches of the proposed interior, then draw scale plans on graph paper to detail and cost the scheme. Make a scale model to visualize the effect of the ceiling.	This type of structure uses new ceiling joists that span the room in the shortest direction. The joists are notched over battens fixed to the walls. Ties and hangers are used for spans over 2.4m (8ft).	Materials: Plasterboard. Fire-resistant building board. Veneered board. Tongue-and-groove boarding. Mineral-fibre tiles. Finishes; papered, painted, varnished or ready-finished.

PART-LOWERED CEILING

Design features	Planning the scheme	Type of construction	Covering/finishes
Similar to the full lowered ceiling above, but has added interest in the form of a split-level. The end 'drop' can be vertical or sloped, the latter being preferable when it faces a window.	As for lowered ceiling (see above). Consider the line of the 'drop' in relation to a window. It should not cut across a window when viewed from the opposite side of the room.	Timber-frame construction as for lowered ceiling (see above). The end framework is formed from ties and hangers. The hangers are set at the required angle for a sloped end.	As for lowered ceiling (see above).

SLATTED CEILING

Design features	Planning the scheme	Type of construction	Covering/finishes
Not a true ceiling but a framework that appears to be continuous. It is most effective in a hallway or passage. It does not seal off the old ceiling. Can be dismantled for access to services.	As for lowered ceiling (see above). The spacing and depth of the slats can be varied: you should not be able to see between the slats when looking straight ahead.	Edge-on-plank construction using no sub-structure. Perimeter planks are housed and fixed to the wall; the slats are slotted into them.	No covering is used. The ceiling and walls above the slats are painted a dark colour. Finish for woodwork: light-coloured stain, clear varnish or paint.

SUSPENDED CEILING

Design features	Planning the scheme	Type of construction	Covering/finishes
As it is not attached to the walls, the ceiling appears to float in space: concealed lighting enhances this illusion. It is modern in character and masks old ceiling and services. Not demountable.	As for lowered ceiling (see above). Locate original ceiling joists and set out their position on your plan drawing: design the structure around them.	This is a timber-frame construction, using ties that are fixed to ceiling joists and carry hangers from which the new frame is suspended. The main components are bolted together.	As for lowered ceiling (see above).

SUSPENDED-CEILING SYSTEMS

Design features	Planning the scheme	Type of construction	Covering/finishes
A grid system manufactured from lightweight materials for self-assembly. Individual translucent or opaque panels sit in the grid framework. The system is demountable.	As for lowered ceiling (see above). Draw a plan of the room on graph paper and set out a symmetrical grid.	Lightweight aluminium T-section bearers are suspended from angle sections screwed to the walls. Bearers are loose-fitted.	Metal: anodized. Panel materials: plain, textured or coloured translucent plastic; opaque plastic; mineral fibre.

SEE ALSO

Details for:	
Drawing a plan	14
T&G boarding	89–90
Decorating ceilings	100
Mineral-fibre tiles	103
Making a hatch	151
Lighting circuits	331–339
Wood joints	501

Vapour checks
Provide a vapour check to prevent condensation problems in an unventilated space above a lowered ceiling. Use a vapour-check plasterboard, an impervious sealer or polyethylene sheeting. The gaps between the boards or sheets of polyethylene must be sealed effectively.

Plasterboard
Bed joints in mastic

Polyethylene sheeting
Fold and staple edges

CONSTRUCTING A LOWERED CEILING

You can build a new ceiling at any practical height. However, the height of window openings may limit your choice. About 2.4m (8ft) is a useful height for a lowered ceiling; it is a common room height for modern houses and relates to standard wallboard sheet sizes. Most manufacturers of built-in furniture adopt it as a standard height for ceilings.

Planning the layout

Making a lowered ceiling requires a considerable amount of timber for the framework and boarding to cover it. Work out your material requirements by drawing a plan to establish the most economical way to construct the ceiling. If you intend to use plasterboard, choose a vapour-check type. Arrange the panels with the paper-covered edges set at right angles to the timber supports. Stagger the end joints between each row of boards and arrange them so that they fall on a joist.

If you plan to use tongue-and-groove boarding buy it in lengths that can be cut economically to suit your joist arrangement, as short offcuts are wasteful. From time to time you will have to join boards end to end, using butt joints. Stagger short boards so that two adjacent joints do not coincide.

Materials for the framework

Make a cutting list of the materials you will need to make up the structure. Use 75 x 50mm (3 x 2in) sawn softwood for the ceiling joists. Calculate the number of joists you will need; they should span the room in the shortest direction and should be spaced at 400mm (1ft 4in) or 600mm (2ft) centres according to the thickness of the plasterboard. These dimensions are also suitable for other types of boarding.

You will need extra joist timber for the noggings fitted between the joists, plus 50 x 25mm (2 x 1in) sawn softwood for wall battens to run round the perimeter of the room.

Support spans of over 2.4m (8ft) with hangers and ties, made from timber not less than 50 x 50mm (2 x 2in) and fixed to the original ceiling above. Support the joists at about the middle of their span.

It is possible to use more hangers and reduce the section of the joists from 75 x 50mm (3 x 2in) to 50 x 50mm (2 x 2in). In this case place the hangers about 900mm (3ft) apart.

● **Cutting list**
A cutting list is your shopping guide. It will enable you to establish your requirements and help your supplier in making up your order. List the individual parts of the structure, and, under separate columns, fill in the quantity, length, width, thickness and material required.

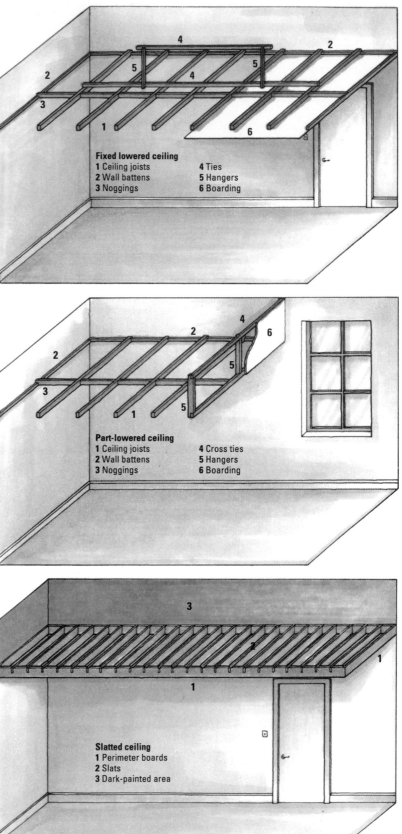

Fixed lowered ceiling
1 Ceiling joists   4 Ties
2 Wall battens   5 Hangers
3 Noggings   6 Boarding

Part-lowered ceiling
1 Ceiling joists   4 Cross ties
2 Wall battens   5 Hangers
3 Noggings   6 Boarding

Slatted ceiling
1 Perimeter boards
2 Slats
3 Dark-painted area

Constructing the ceiling

Mark the height of the new ceiling, including the thickness of the boarding, on one wall. Draw a horizontal line across the wall at this level, using a straightedge and spirit level for accuracy. Continue the line around the room at this height. Cut the 50 x 25 mm (2 x 1in) wall battens to length. Nail or screw them to the walls at 400mm (1ft 4in) intervals, with the bottom edge level with the line.

Cut the 75 x 50mm (3 x 2in) ceiling joists to length. Notch the ends to sit over the wall battens to bring the bottom edges flush. Skew-nail the joists to the wall battens. Cut and fit hangers and ties to prevent long joists sagging (see opposite). These supports also stiffen the structure.

Cut and nail noggings between the joists to support the edges of the plasterboard. Nail tapered-edge plasterboard to the joists, noggings and wall battening. Fill and tape the joints between boards and walls.

Lowering part of a ceiling

You can lower part of a ceiling to overcome problems with tall window openings or to create a split-level effect. Follow the method for constructing a ceiling as described above, but enclose the end drop with plasterboard nailed to hangers suspended from a cross-tie member fixed above the last joist.

Making a slatted ceiling

Planed softwood planks 150 x 25mm (6 x 1in) in size, set on edge and spaced apart, can create a simple yet effective slatted ceiling. Smaller sections can be used where the span is short, as with a narrow hallway.

Cut four lengths of planking for the perimeter of the slatted ceiling. Before nailing or screwing them at the required height, mark and cut housings in two opposite planks. Space the housings 225mm (9in) apart. For boards less than 150mm (6in) wide, space the housings about 100 to 150mm (4 to 6in) apart. Cut notches in the ends of the 'slat' boards to sit in the housings so that the bottom edges finish flush.

Before fitting the slats, paint the walls and ceiling above the perimeter boards with a dark emulsion paint. Paint ducting or plumbing to disguise it. Finish the slats with varnish, stain or paint.

MAKING A SUSPENDED CEILING

A suspended ceiling is a framed panel that gives the impression that it is floating away from the walls. Fluorescent lights can be placed around the edge of the panel to enhance the floating effect and provide wall-washing illumination. Cover the panel with plasterboard, decorative veneered ply or mineral-fibre ceiling tiles.

Locate the position of the ceiling joists by noting the direction of the floorboards of the room above; the joists run at right angles to them. Pinpoint the joists from below by drilling pilot holes through the ceiling, then mark the centre of each joist.

Setting out the grid

Measure the lengths of the walls and draw a scaled plan of the room on graph paper. Set out the shape of the ceiling panel on the drawing with its edges approximately 200mm (8in) from each wall. Then set out the position of the 50 x 50mm (2 x 2in) softwood ceiling ties. The ties should run at right angles to the joists of the ceiling above. The ends of the ties and sides of the two outer ones should be about 300mm (1ft) from the walls. The number of ties you need depends on the size of the ceiling, but three should be a minimum. They should be spaced not more than 900mm (3ft) apart for adequate support.

Constructing the ceiling

Counterbore and securely screw the ties in position to each of the joists they cross. Cut 50 x 50mm (2 x 2in) softwood hangers to the required length and fix them to the ties with coach bolts not more than 900mm (3ft) apart.

Cut additional ties to the same length as the planned ceiling panel. Bolt them across the ends of the hangers with an equal space at each end.

Cut the required number of 50 x 50mm (2 x 2in) planed softwood furring battens to suit the spacings necessary to support the boards or tiles used as a covering. Their length should be the span of the ceiling panel less two 50 x 25mm (2 x 1in) capping battens. Space the furring battens equally and screw them to the tie members. Counter-sink the screw heads.

Mark off the positions of the furring battens along the sides of each capping batten. Drive 50mm (2in) nails into, but not quite through, the cappings at these points. Apply woodworking adhesive and nail the cappings to the ends of the furring battens.

Finishing the assembly

Run electrical wiring for the fluorescent lights. Cover the underside of the frame with plasterboard, decorative veneered boarding or ceiling tiles. Fill and finish the surface and edges of a plasterboard ceiling panel. Finish the exposed edges of the frame to match the other materials as required.

Wire up slim fluorescent light fittings and fix them to loose boards that rest on top of the projecting frame. The light fittings can then be removed easily for servicing at any time. Provide enough spare electrical flex to allow the lights to be lifted clear.

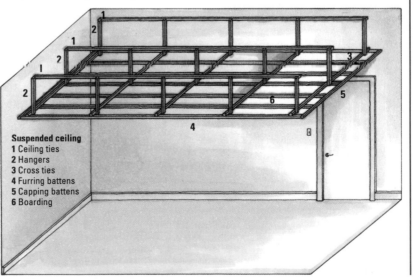

Suspended ceiling
1 Ceiling ties
2 Hangers
3 Cross ties
4 Furring battens
5 Capping battens
6 Boarding

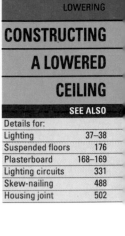

Setting out
Set out the panel on graph paper with a 200mm (8in) gap all round. Inset the ties about 300mm (1ft).

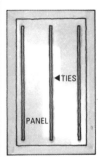

Light fitting
Fix a fluorescent light to a removable board for servicing.

149

SUSPENDED-CEILING SYSTEMS

Panel layouts

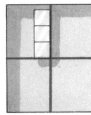

1 Main bearer centred

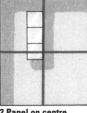

2 Panel on centre

3 Cross bearer centred

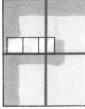

4 Panel on centre

5 Best grid arrangement

Manufactured suspended-ceiling systems are made from slim metal sections, which provide a fairly lightweight structure for acoustic or translucent panels. They are quick and easy to fit and do not require specialist tools.

Manufactured systems
Manufacturers offer a choice of finishes for the framing as well as textured, translucent and opaque panels.

The lightweight alloy framework is made from three basic elements: an angle section, which is fixed to the walls; a main-bearer section, which spans the shortest direction; and a lighter T-section cross bearer, which bridges the space between the main bearers.

The loose panels sit on the flanges provided by the bearers. They can be lifted out easily to provide access to ducting or for servicing light fittings concealed behind them. You need at least 200mm (4in) above the framework in order to fit the panels.

Setting out the grid

Normally, 600mm (2ft) square panels are used for suspended-ceiling systems. Before fitting the framework, draw a plan of the ceiling on squared graph paper to ensure that the borders are symmetrical (see far left). Draw a plan of the room with two lines taken from the halfway point on each wall to bisect at the centre. Lay out the grid on your plan with a main bearer centred on the short bisecting line (1), then lay it out again with a line of panels centred on the same line (2). Use the grid that provides the widest border panels.

Plot the position of the cross bearers in the same way, using the other line (3,4). Try to get the border panels even on opposite sides of the room (5).

Fitting the framework

Before building a suspended ceiling with translucent panels, remove flaking materials and make good any cracks in the plaster ceiling above. Paint the ceiling with white emulsion to improve reflectivity if concealed fluorescent lighting is to be used.

Fix fluorescent light fittings to the joists, spacing them evenly across the ceiling: 16 watts per square metre is recommended for a suitable level of light in most rooms.

Mark the height of the suspended ceiling on the walls with a continuous levelled line. Hacksaw two lengths of angle section to fit the longest walls. Remove burrs from the ends with a file. Drill screw holes at 600mm (2ft) intervals. Drill and plug the walls, using the angle as a guide, and screw the components in place (1).

Next cut lengths of angle to fit the shorter walls. Their ends should fit on the angles already fitted. Screw-fix them in the same way.

Mark the positions of the bearers along two adjacent walls, as set out on the graph paper. Cut the main bearers to span the room. Sit them on the wall angles (2). Use a ceiling panel to check they are parallel and at right angles to the wall and each other. Cut the border cross bearers to fit between the end main bearers and wall angles. Set them in line with the points marked on the wall. Position the remainder of the cross bearers following the same line.

Working from the centre, drop in the full-size panels. Measure and cut the border panels to fit and then drop them into place.

Spanning wide rooms
If the size of the room is such that it exceeds the maximum length of the main bearer, join two or more pieces together. A joint-bridging piece is provided if the ends of the bearers are not made to lock together.

For spans exceeding 3m (10ft), support the main bearers with wire hangers. Fix each wire, spaced not more than 1.5m (5ft) apart, through a hole in the bearer and hang it from a screw eye in a furring strip or joist in the ceiling.

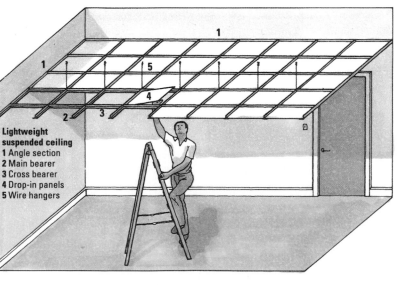

Lightweight suspended ceiling
1 Angle section
2 Main bearer
3 Cross bearer
4 Drop-in panels
5 Wire hangers

1 Screw the angle to the wall

2 Position the main bearers

INSTALLING A FOLDING LOFT LADDER

Access to the roof space is safer and more convenient if you install a folding loft ladder. Some are complete with built-in hatch cover, frame and fittings, ready to install in a new opening. Normally, the length of the ladders suits ceiling heights of 2.3 and 2.5m (7ft 6in and 8ft 3in), although some can extend to 2.9 to 3m (9ft 6in to 10ft).

Concertina ladder
To fix a concertina ladder, screw the fixing brackets of the ladder to the framework of the opening. Fit the retaining hook to the framework to hold the ladder in the stowed position. Operate the ladder with a pole that hooks over the bottom rail. Fit the hatch door to the frame with a continuous hinge and fix a push-to-release latch to the edge of the hatch door.

Ready-to-install folding ladder
Cut the opening and trim the joists to the size specified by the manufacturer. Insert the casing with built-in frame in the opening and screw it to the joists.

A concertina ladder is simple to install.

Folding ladders are easy to deploy.

Many houses have a hatch in the ceiling that provides access to the roof space for servicing water cisterns and maintaining the roof structure. Should your house have a large roof space without access, installing a hatch could provide you with extra room for storage. Although the procedure is basically straightforward, it does entail cutting away part of the roof structure.

In older houses this is not a problem as the timbers are substantial. In modern houses, however, lightweight timber is used to make strong triangulated trussed-roof structures. These are designed to carry the weight of the roof with each member playing an important part, so any alteration may weaken the structure. If your house is relatively new you should check with the company that built it, or with a local builder, that it is safe to proceed.

If you have a choice, site the hatch over a landing (although not too close to the stairs) so that lowering the access ladder will not cause disruption to the occupants, furniture or function of a room. Take into consideration the pitch of the roof, as you will need headroom above the hatch.

Making the opening
If you are planning to fit a special folding loft ladder, the size of the new opening will be specified by the manufacturer. In general, aim to cut no more than one ceiling joist: these are usually spaced 350mm (1ft 2in) apart.

Locate three joists by drilling pilot holes in the ceiling. Mark out a square for the opening between the two outer joists. Cut an inspection hole inside the marked area to check that there are no obstacles in the way of the cutting line. Saw through the ceiling plasterwork and strip it away.

Pass a light into the roof space and climb up into it between the joists. Lay a board across the joists to support yourself. Saw through the middle joist, cutting it back 50mm (2in) from each edge of the opening. Cut two new lengths of joist timber – called trimmers – to fit between the joists. Allow for a 12mm (½in) deep square housing at each end **(1)**. Nail the housed joints, and the butt joints between the trimmers and joists. Use two 100mm (4in) round wire nails to secure each joint.

Nail the ceiling laths or plasterboard to the underside of the trimmers. Cut timber linings to cover the joists and the edges of the plaster. Make good the damaged edges of the plaster with filler. When set, nail mitred architrave moulding around the opening. Make a drop-in or hinged panel of 18mm (¾in) plywood or blockboard. If you plan to use the loft mainly for storage, fix chipboard panels over the joists. Cut the panels beforehand to ensure they will pass through the opening.

MAKING A LOFT-ACCESS HATCH

SEE ALSO

Details for:	
Repairing plaster	50–51
Patching a ceiling	158
Chipboard flooring	180
Laying chipboard	183
Pitched roofs	227

Alternative ways to install hatch covers

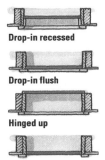

Drop-in recessed

Drop-in flush

Hinged up

Hinged down

Hatch opening
1 Ceiling joists
2 Trimmed joist
3 Trimmers

1 Housing joints
A housing joint will give better support to the trimmer joist than nails alone.

151

INTERIOR PLASTERWORK

Storing plaster
Keep an open bag of plaster in a plastic sack sealed with adhesive tape.

Plasterwork is used to provide internal walls and ceilings with a smooth, flat surface suitable for decorating with paint or paper. Plaster also provides sound and thermal insulation as well as protection from fire. Decorative mouldings – a feature of walls and ceilings in many older houses – are also made of plaster and are still available for renovations. There are basically two methods of providing a plaster finish: the traditional one is wet-plastering, while the modern method uses plasterboard and is known as 'dry-lining'.

Traditional plastering techniques

Traditional plastering uses a mix of plastering materials and water which is spread with a trowel over the rough background in one, two or even three layers and levelled accordingly. When set, the plaster forms an integral part of the wall or ceiling. The background may be masonry or timber-framed walls and ceilings finished with lath-and-plaster. Laths are thin strips of wood nailed to the timber framework to support plaster, which, forced between the laths, spreads to form nibs that grip on the other side. Traditional plastering takes practice before the plasterer can achieve a smooth, flat surface over a large area. With care, an amateur can produce satisfactory results, provided the right tools and plaster are employed and the work is divided into manageable sections. All-purpose one-coat plasters are now available to make traditional plastering easier for amateurs.

Dry-lining with plasterboard

Manufactured boards of paper-covered plaster are widely used to dry-line the walls and ceilings in modern homes and during renovations. Plasterboard obviates the drying-out period required for wet plasters and requires less skill to apply. The large, flat boards are nailed or bonded to walls and ceilings to provide a separate finishing layer. The surface may be decorated directly once the boards are sealed, or covered with a thin coat of finish plaster.

BUYING AND STORING PLASTER

Plaster powder is normally sold in 50kg (1cwt) paper sacks. Smaller sizes, including 2.5kg (5½lb) bags, are available from DIY stores for repair work. It is generally more economical to buy the larger sacks, but this depends on the scale of the work. Try to buy only as much plaster as you need – although it is better to overestimate to allow for wastage and to avoid running out of it at an inconvenient moment.

Store plaster in dry conditions. If it is to be kept in an outbuilding for some time, cover it with plastic sheeting to protect it from moisture. Keep the paper bags off a concrete floor by placing them on boards or plastic sheeting. Open bags are more likely to absorb moisture, which can shorten the setting time and weaken the plaster, so keep an opened bag in a plastic sack sealed with self-adhesive tape. Discard plaster which contains lumps.

Ready-to-use plaster is available in plastic tubs. It can be more expensive to buy, but it is easier for amateurs to use and will keep for a long time, provided the airtight lid is sealed well.

Traditional plastering
(Right)
The construction of a lath-and-plaster ceiling and plastered masonry wall.
1 Brick background
2 Ceiling joists
3 Lath background
4 Rendering coat
5 Floating coat
6 Finishing coat
7 Cornice moulding

Dry-lining
(Far right)
The construction of a modern dry-lined wall and ceiling.
1 Block background
2 Batten fixing
3 Ceiling joists
4 Noggings
5 Plasterboard
6 Coving
7 Tape
8 Filler

Traditional plastering

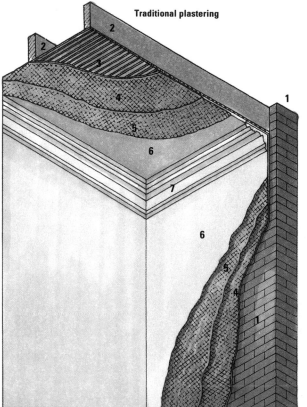

Dry-lining

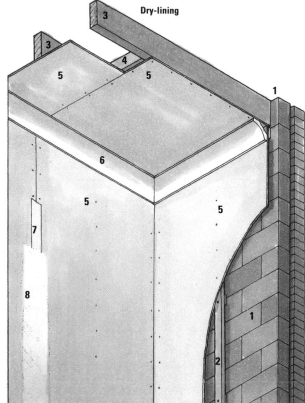

TYPES OF PLASTER

Plastering is carried out using modern gypsum plasters or mixes based on cement, lime and sand. By varying the process and introducing additives, a range of plasters can be produced within a given type to suit different background materials.

Plasters are basically produced in two grades – one as a base or 'floating' coat, the other for finishing coats. Base-coat gypsum plasters are premixed types which contain lightweight aggregates. Base-coat sanded plasters that are based on cement or cement/lime have to be mixed on site with a suitable grade of clean, sharp sand. Fine-powdered finish plasters only require the addition of water before they are ready to use.

The following information deals only with those materials that are suitable for domestic work.

CHOOSING PLASTERS FOR DOMESTIC WORK

Gypsum plasters

Most plasters in common use are produced from ground gypsum rock by a process that removes most of the moisture from the rock and results in a powder that sets hard when mixed with water. Setting times are controlled by the use of retarding additives which give each of the several types of plaster a setting time suitable to its purpose.

Gypsum plasters are intended for interior work only; they should not be used on permanently damp walls. They must not be remixed with water once they start to set.

Plaster of Paris

This quick-setting non-retarded gypsum plaster gives off heat as it sets. It is white or pinkish, and is mixed to a creamy consistency with clean water. It is unsuitable for general plastering, but good for casting, and can be used for repairs to decorative mouldings.

Carlite plaster

Carlite refers to a range of retarded gypsum plasters which are premixed with a lightweight aggregate and only need water adding to prepare them for use. The undercoat bonds well to most backgrounds, and this, coupled with their light weight – about half that of plasters mixed with sand – makes Carlite plasters fairly easy to use. The lightweight aggregate also gives some degree of thermal insulation. The average setting time for Carlite plasters is about two hours.

Four types of Carlite undercoat plasters – 'browning', 'browning HSB', 'bonding' and 'metal-lathing' – are available, each formulated to suit a background of a particular surface texture and suction. Browning is generally used for solid backgrounds with average suction (such as brickwork), while the higher impact-resistant HSB type is for high-suction backgrounds. Bonding undercoat is best for low-suction surfaces like dense brick or concrete blocks. Metal-lathing plaster is less commonly used and is primarily for an expanded-metal background.

When more than one undercoat layer is required to build up a thickness, the same plaster should be used for all layers to ensure compatibility.

There is only one Carlite finishing plaster; it can be used over all the undercoats, being applied as soon as the undercoat has set.

Thistle plasters

Thistle is the brand name of a range of building plasters used for a variety of conditions and backgrounds.

'Hardwall' is an undercoat plaster which provides superior impact and efflorescence resistance. It is suitable for most backgrounds.

There are two types of finishing plaster, both mixed with water only: multi-finish plaster, for use over sanded and hardwall undercoats, and board-finish plaster, used for finishing plasterboard surfaces.

Two special 'renovating' plasters are used on walls with residual dampness. The undercoat is a premixed gypsum plaster with special additives, and the finish plaster, formulated specially for use with the undercoat, contains a fungicide. These plasters are for damp walls that are slow to dry out, such as new exposed building work or in old houses where new damp-proof courses have been installed. This type of plaster is not itself a damp-proofing material, but it does allow the background material to breathe and dry out without letting the moisture show on the surface. Deal with the cause before you apply the plaster.

Sanded plasters

Before the advent of modern gypsums, lime and sand for undercoats and neat lime for finishes were employed in traditional wet plastering, often with animal hair added to the undercoat mix to act as a binder. Lime plasters are generally less strong than gypsum and cement-based plasters.

Lime is still used, but mainly as an additive to improve the workability of a sand-and-cement plaster or rendering. Cement-based sanded-plaster undercoats may be required by some authorities for kitchen and bathroom walls constructed on timber and expanded-metal lathing. These undercoats can also be used on old brickwork or where a strong impact-resistant covering is required.

Single-coat plasters

A universal one-coat plaster can, as its name implies, be used in a single application on a variety of backgrounds, and trowelled to a normal finish. The plaster is sold in 40kg (88lb) bags and only water need be added to prepare it for use. It will stay workable for up to an hour and some types can be built up to a thickness of 50mm (2in) in one coat.

One-coat plaster is also available in small packs, either ready-mixed or contained in mixing tubs. These are ideal for small repairs. For larger areas it is more economical to buy bigger bags and mix the plaster on a board in the usual way.

Ready-mixed plasters

A brush-on skim plaster is also available. It is applied up to 3mm (⅛in) thick with a wide brush, and smoothed with a spreader or trowel. When firm it is polished with a damp sponge.

Fillers

Fillers are fine plaster powders used for repairs. Some, reinforced with cellulose resin, are sold in small packs and need only mixing with clean water for use. They are non-shrinking, adhere well and are ideal for filling cracks and holes in plaster and wood.

● **Avoiding old plaster**
Plaster may deteriorate if stored for more than two months so suppliers try to ensure it is sold in rotation. The paper sacks in which plaster is supplied are usually date-stamped by the manufacturer. If you are buying from a self-service supplier, choose a sack with the latest date.

TYPES OF
SURFACE

● **Providing a 'key'**
Rake out mortar joints to help plaster and cement renderings adhere to the surface.

A well-prepared background is the first step to successful plastering. New surfaces of block or brickwork may need only dampening or priming with a bonding agent, depending on their absorbency. Old plastered surfaces needing repair should be thoroughly checked. If the plaster has 'blown', hack it off back to sound material, then treat the surface and replaster the area.

Background preparation and absorbency

Brush down the surface of a masonry background to remove loose particles, dust and efflorescent salts. Test the absorption of the background by splashing on water; if it stays wet, consider the surface 'normal'. This means that it will only require light dampening with clean water prior to applying the plaster.

A dry background that absorbs the water immediately will take too much water from the plaster, making it difficult to work. It will also prevent the plaster from setting properly and may result in it cracking. Soak the masonry with clean water applied with a brush.

High-absorbency surfaces

For very absorbent surfaces, such as aerated concrete blocks, prime the background with 1 part PVA bonding agent : 5 parts clean water. When dry, apply a bonding coat of 3 parts bonding agent : 1 part water. Apply the plaster when the bonding coat is tacky.

Low-absorbency surfaces

Prime low-absorption smooth brickwork or concrete with a solution of 1 part bonding agent : 5 parts water. Allow to dry. Apply a second coat of 3 to 5 parts bonding agent : 1 part water, and trowel on the plaster when the bonding coat is tacky. Alternatively, allow it to dry for no more than 24 hours before plastering.

Non-absorbent surfaces

Glazed tiles and painted walls are considered non-absorbent and will require a coating of neat bonding agent to enable the plaster to stick. The plaster is applied while the agent is tacky. An alternative for glazed tiles is to apply a slurry of 2 parts sharp sand : 1 part cement mixed with a solution of 1 part bonding agent : 1 part water. Apply the slurry with a stiff-bristle brush to form a stippled coating. Allow to dry for 24 hours, then apply the plaster.

Another option is to chip off the old tiles, using a hammer and cold chisel.

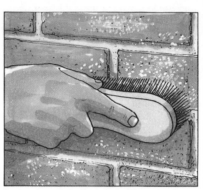
Remove loose particles with a stiff brush

Prime porous surfaces to control the suction

A bonding agent improves adhesion

Smooth tiles can be 'keyed' with a slurry

MAKING FILLER AND MORTAR BOARDS

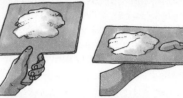

Filler board
You can make a useful board for mixing and working with filler from 6mm (¼in) exterior-grade plywood. Cut out a 300mm (1ft) square with a projecting handle, or make a thumb hole as in an artist's palette. Seal the surface with a polyurethane varnish or apply a plastic laminate for a smooth finish.

Mortar board
Cut a piece of 12mm (½in) or 18mm (¾in) thick exterior-grade plywood, approximately 900mm (3ft) square. Round off the corners and chamfer the edges all round. Screw three lengths of 50 x 25mm (2 x 1in) softwood across the underside, spread equally apart. Make a 600mm (2ft) square 'spotboard' in a similar way.

Using a stand
You will find it easier to handle plaster with the mix at table height.

Using a stand
Use a stand to support the mortar board at table height, about 700mm (2ft 4in) from the ground. This enables the plaster to be picked up on a hawk by placing the latter under the edge of the board and drawing the plaster on to it.

Construct a folding stand, using 50 x 38mm (2 x 1½in) softwood for the legs and 75 x 25mm (3 x 1in) softwood for the rails. Make one leg frame to fit inside the other and bolt them securely together at the centre.

A portable Workmate bench can be used to support the mortar board instead of a stand: grip the centre batten in the vice jaws.

SEE ALSO

Details for:
Repairing plaster   50–51
Builder's tools   504–506

With the background prepared, the next step is to make a good mix. It pays to mix your plaster close to the work site, as it can be a messy job. Cover the floor with plastic dust sheets or old newspapers, and remember to wipe your feet when leaving the room.

Plaster that is mixed to the correct consistency will be easier to apply. Use a plastic bucket to measure the cement, lime and sand or plaster accurately. For large quantities of plaster, simply multiply the number of bucket measures. For small quantities, just use half-bucket measures or less.

Old, hard gypsum plaster stuck to your equipment can shorten the setting time and reduce the strength of the newly mixed plaster. Do not try to rework plaster that has begun to set by adding more water: discard it and make a fresh batch. Mix only as much plaster as you will need. For larger areas, mix as much as you can apply in about 20 minutes – judge this by practice.

BONDING AGENTS

Bonding agents modify the suction of the background or improve the adhesion of the plaster. When you are using a bonding agent, do not apply the base-coat plaster any thicker than 9mm (³⁄₈in) at a time. If you need to build up the thickness, scratch the surface to provide an extra key and allow at least 24 hours between coats.

Bonding agents can be mixed with plaster or sand and cement to fill cracks. Brush away any loose particles and then apply a solution of 1 part agent : 3 to 5 parts water with a brush.

Mix the plaster or sand and cement with 1 part bonding agent : 3 parts water to a stiff mix. Apply the filler with a trowel, pressing it well into the crack.

Wash tools and brushes thoroughly in clean water. It may be necessary to rinse out the brushes as the work progresses on a large job.

Wash agent from brushes before it sets

Undercoat plasters

Mix undercoat plasters on a mortar board (see opposite). For sanded plasters, measure out each of the materials and thoroughly dry-mix them with a shovel, or a trowel for small quantities. Make a well in the heaped plaster and pour in some clean water. Turn in the plaster, adding water to produce a thick, creamy consistency.

Just add water to premixed gypsum plasters (which already contain an aggregate). Mix them on the board in the same way. Always wash down the board after you have finished using it.

You can mix small quantities of premixed plaster in a bucket. Pour the plaster into the water and stir to a creamy consistency; 1kg (2lb 4oz) of plaster will need about 0.75 of a litre (1⅓ pints) of water.

Finish plaster

Mix finish plaster in a clean plastic bucket. Pour not more than 2 litres (4 pints) of water into the bucket, then sprinkle the plaster into the water and stir it with a stout length of wood until it reaches a thick, creamy consistency. Tip the plaster out on to a clean, damp mortar board ready for use. Wash the bucket out with clean water before the plaster sets in it.

PLASTER TYPES, APPLICATION AND COVERAGE

Type	Background	Type of coat	Coat thickness	Average coverage (m³ per 50kg) (sq yd per 50kg)
CARLITE				
Browning *Normal suction*	Brick walls	Undercoat	9mm (³⁄₈in)	6.5–7.5 sq m (7¾–9 sq yd)
	Block walls	Undercoat	9mm (³⁄₈in)	6.5–7.5 sq m (7¾–9 sq yd)
Browning HSB *High suction*	Concrete bricks	Undercoat	9mm (³⁄₈in)	6.5–7.5 sq m (7¾–9 sq yd)
	Coarse concrete	Undercoat	9mm (³⁄₈in)	6.5–7.5 sq m (7¾–9 sq yd)
Bonding *Low suction*	Brick walls	Undercoat	9mm (³⁄₈in)	5.0–8.25 sq m (6–9¾ sq yd)
	Block walls	Undercoat	9mm (³⁄₈in)	5.0–8.25 sq m (6–9¾ sq yd)
	Concrete bricks	Undercoat	9mm (³⁄₈in)	5.0–8.25 sq m (6–9¾ sq yd)
	Smooth precast concrete	Undercoat	8mm (⁵⁄₁₆in)	5.0–8.25 sq m (6–9¾ sq yd)
	Plasterboards (Greyface)	Undercoat	8mm (⁵⁄₁₆in)	5.0–8.25 sq m (6–9¾ sq yd)
	Polystyrene	Undercoat	9mm (³⁄₈in)	5.0–8.25 sq m (6–9¾ sq yd)
Metal-lathing	Expanded metal	Undercoat	9mm (³⁄₈in)	3.0–3.5 sq m (3½–4 sq yd)
Finish	Carlite undercoats	Finish top coat	2mm (¹⁄₁₆in)	20.5–25.0 sq m (24½–30 sq yd)
THISTLE				
Hardwall	See Carlite undercoats	Undercoat	9mm (³⁄₈in)	5.7 sq m (6¾ sq yd)
Multi-finish	Sanded undercoats	Top coat	2mm (¹⁄₁₆in)	17.5–22.5 sq m (21–27 sq yd)
Board-finish	Plasterboards (Greyface)	Top coat	5mm (³⁄₁₆in)	8.0–8.5 sq m (9½–10 sq yd)
Renovating *Normal suction*	Brick walls	Undercoat	9mm (³⁄₈in)	6.0 sq m (7 sq yd)
	Block walls	Undercoat	9mm (³⁄₈in)	6.0 sq m (7 sq yd)
	Concrete walls	Undercoat	9mm (³⁄₈in)	6.0 sq m (7 sq yd)
Renovating-finish	Renovating plaster	Top coat	2mm (¹⁄₁₆in)	19.0–21.0 sq m (22¾–25 sq yd)
ONE COAT				
	All types	Undercoat/finish	12mm (½in)	4.5 sq.m. (5½ sq yd)

Plaster fillers

Pour out a small heap of cellulose filler on to a flat board or tile. Scrape a hollow in the centre with your filling knife and pour in water. Gradually drag the powder into the centre until it absorbs all the water, then stir the mix to a creamy thickness; if it seems too runny add a little more powder. Begin to fill deep holes and cracks with a stiff mix, but finish off with creamy filler.

APPLYING PLASTER

Plastering can seem a daunting business to the beginner, yet it has only two basic requirements: that the plaster should stick well to its background and that it should be brought to a smooth, flat finish. Good preparation, the careful choice of plaster and use of the right tools should ensure good adhesion, but the ability to achieve the smooth, flat surface will come only after some practice. Most plasterer's tools are somewhat specialized, but their cost may prove economical in the long term if you are planning several jobs.

Problems to avoid

Uneven surfaces
Many amateurs tackle plastering with the idea of levelling the surface by rubbing it down when it has set. This approach is very dust-creating and laborious, and invariably produces a poor result. If a power sander is used the dust is unpleasant to work in and permeates other parts of the house, making more work. It is far better to try for a good surface as you put the plaster on, using wide-bladed tools to spread the material evenly. Ridges left by the corners of a trowel or filling knife can be carefully shaved down afterwards with the knife – not with abrasive paper.

When covering a large area with finishing plaster it is not always easy to see if the surface is flat as well as smooth. Look obliquely across the wall or shine a light across it from one side to detect any irregularities.

Crazing
Fine cracks in finished plaster may be due to a sand-and-cement undercoat still drying out and therefore shrinking. Such an undercoat must be fully dry before the plaster goes on, though if the plaster surface is sound the fine cracks can be wallpapered over.

Top coat and undercoat plaster can also crack if made to dry out too fast. Never heat plaster to dry it.

Loss of strength
Gypsum and cement set chemically when mixed with water. If they dry out before the set takes place they do not develop their full strength, and become friable. Should this happen you may have to strip the wall and replaster.

PLASTERING TECHNIQUES

Picking up

Hold the edge of the hawk below the mortar board and scrape a manageable amount of plaster on to the hawk, using the trowel (**1**). Take no more than a trowelful to start with.

Tip the hawk towards you and, in one movement, cut away about half of the plaster with the trowel, scraping and lifting it off the hawk and on to the face of the trowel (**2**).

1 Load the hawk   **2 Lift the plaster**

Application

Hold the loaded trowel horizontally and tilted at an angle to the face of the wall (**1**). Apply the plaster with a vertical upward stroke, pressing firmly so that plaster is fed to the wall. Flatten the angle of the trowel as you go (**2**), but never let its whole face come into contact with the plaster as suction can pull it off the wall again.

1 Tilt the trowel   **2 Apply the plaster**

Levelling up

Build a slight extra thickness of plaster with the trowel, applying it as evenly as possible. Use a rule to level the surface, starting at the bottom of the wall, with the rule held against original plaster or wooden screeds nailed on at either side. Work the rule upwards while moving it from side to side, then lift it carefully away, taking the surplus with it. Fill in any hollows with more plaster from the trowel, then level the surface again. Allow the plaster to stiffen before you smooth it finally with the trowel.

Work the rule up the wall to level the surface

Finishing

Apply the finishing coat to a gypsum-plaster undercoat as soon as it is set. A cement-based sanded plaster must dry thoroughly, but dampen its surface to adjust suction before finish-plastering. The grey face of plasterboard is finished immediately without wetting.

Apply the finish with a plasterer's trowel, spreading it evenly no more than 2 to 3mm (1/16 to 1/8in) thick, judging this by eye. Plasterboard requires two coats to build a 5mm (3/16in) thickness.

As the plaster stiffens, brush or lightly spray it with water, then trowel the surface to consolidate it and produce a smooth matt finish. Avoid pressing hard and overworking the surface. Sponge off surplus water.

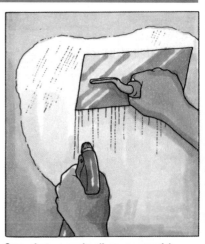

Spray plaster occasionally as you smooth it

REPAIRING PLASTERWORK

REINFORCING A CORNER

When damage to a corner extends along most of the edge, you can reinforce the repair plasterwork with a metal corner beading (1). As well as strengthening the new corner it will considerably speed up the repair work because it dispenses with the need to use a board as a guide. You can obtain beading from any good builders' merchant or DIY store. Cut it to length with snips and a hacksaw. It has a protective galvanized coating, and the cut ends must be sealed with a metal primer or bituminous paint.

Cut back the old plaster from the damaged edge, wet the brickwork and apply patches of undercoat plaster each side of the corner. Press the wings of the beading into the plaster patches (2), using your straightedge to align its outer nose with both original plaster surfaces. Alternatively, check for plumb with a builder's level. Allow the plaster to set.

Build up the undercoat as before, but this time scrape it back to 2mm (1/16in) below the old finished level (3).

Apply the finishing coat, using the beading as a level to achieve flush surfaces. Take care not to damage the beading's galvanized coating with your trowel; rust can come through later and stain wallcoverings. To be on the safe side, brush metal primer over the new corner before decorating.

OLD PLASTER
NEW UNDERCOAT PLASTER
MASONRY
TOP-COAT PLASTER
METAL BEADING

1 Section through a repaired corner

2 Set in plaster   **3 Trim undercoat back**

Every decorator will at some time have to fill small holes and cracks with plaster or filler as part of normal preparations, and these should present few problems. However, once you start tackling more ambitious jobs like removing fireplaces and taking down walls, you will need to develop some of the professional plasterer's skills in order to handle larger areas.

Plastering over a fireplace

A bricked-in fireplace provides an area large enough to give the amateur good practice without the work becoming unmanageable. Jobs of this kind can be done with a one-coat plaster, or you can apply an undercoat plaster followed by a top coat of finishing plaster.

Using a one-coat plaster
Prepare the background by cutting away any loose plaster above and around the brickwork. Remove dust and loose particles with a stiff brush.

Mix the plaster in a tub according to the manufacturer's instructions.

Dampen the background with clean water and place a strip of hardboard below the work area to help you to pick up dropped plaster cleanly.

Tip the mixed plaster on to a dampened mortar board, then scoop some on to a hawk and, with a trowel (or the spreader provided), apply the plaster to the brickwork.

Work in the sequence shown (1), starting at the bottom of each section and spreading the plaster vertically. Work each area in turn, blending the edge of one into the next, then level with a rule. Fill any hollows and level again.

Leave the plaster to stiffen for about 45 minutes, when firm finger pressure should leave no impression, then lightly dampen the surface with a close-textured plastic sponge. Wet a trowel or spreader and give the plaster a smooth finish. Use firm pressure, sweeping the trowel from side to side, then up and down until you have 'polished' the surface. Keep the tool wet.

Let the plaster dry thoroughly for about six weeks before decorating.

Two-coat plastering
Apply undercoat and finish-coat plasters as described above, scraping back the undercoat to allow for the thickness of the finishing coat.

1 Plastering sequence
Divide the area into manageable portions and apply the plaster in the sequence shown.

Repairing a chipped corner

When part of the external corner of a plastered wall has broken away to reveal the brickwork behind, rebuild it with one-coat or two-coat plaster. Use a 100mm (4in) wide board as a guide to achieve a straight corner.

With a bolster, cut the plaster back from the damaged edge to reveal about 75mm (3in) of brickwork on each side of the corner.

If you are using two-coat plaster, place the guide board against the old plaster, set back about 3mm (1/8in) from the surface of the plaster on the other side of the corner (1). Fix the board temporarily with masonry nails, placing them well away from the corner.

Mix up the undercoat plaster, wet the brickwork and the edge of the old plaster, then fill one side of the corner flush with the edge of the board but not the wall (2). Scratch-key the new plaster with the trowel.

When the plaster is stiff, remove the board, pulling it straight from the wall to prevent the plaster breaking away. The exposed edge represents the finished surface, so scrape it back about 3mm

(1/8in) with the trowel and straightedge (3) to allow for the top coat.

For such a job a professional would simply hold the board over the new repair and fill the second side of the corner immediately – but this leaves only one hand to lift and apply the plaster, a difficult trick for the amateur. An easier, though slower, method is to let the new plaster harden, then nail the board in place before applying and keying fresh plaster as before (4). Or, if the new plaster is set hard, you can use the scraped edge as a guide.

Let the undercoat set, then nail the board to the wall as before, but this time set it flush with the corner and level off with finishing plaster. Dampen the undercoat if necessary to help the top coat to stick.

When both sides are firm, polish the new plaster with a wet trowel, rounding over the sharp edge slightly, then leave it to dry out.

If you choose to carry out the repair with a one-coat plaster you must set the board flush with the corner before applying the material.

1 Set board back

2 Fill flush with board

3 Scrape back edge

4 Fill second side

2 Cut an opening

3 Nail in noggings

4 Nail in battens

PATCHING A PLASTERBOARD CEILING

A misplaced foot in the attic, a roof leak that has gone unnoticed, a leaking water pipe – any of these will damage a plaster ceiling. Fortunately serious damage is usually localized and is easily patch-repaired.

Before starting work, turn off the electricity supply at the mains. The next job is to check the direction in which the ceiling joists run and whether there is any electrical wiring close to the damaged area. If the damaged ceiling is below a floor, you can usually carry out the inspection from above by raising a floorboard. Alternatively, knock an inspection hole through the centre of the damage with a hammer. You will find that it is possible to look along the void with the help of a torch and a mirror (**1**).

1 Use a mirror and torch to inspect a void

Mark out a square or rectangle on the ceiling, enclosing the damaged area. Cut away an area of the plasterboard slightly larger than the damage, working up to the sides of the nearest joists (**2**). Use a padsaw or, if there is wiring nearby, a craft knife which will just penetrate the thickness of the plasterboard.

Cut and skew-nail 50mm (2in) noggings between the joists at the ends of the cut-out, with half their thickness projecting beyond the cut edges of the plasterboard (**3**).

Nail 50 x 25mm (2 x 1in) softwood battens to the sides of the joists, flush with their bottom edges (**4**).

Cut a plasterboard patch to fit the opening with a 3mm (⅛in) gap all round, and nail it to the noggings and battens. Fill and tape over the joints to give a flush surface.

Minor damage
Use cellulose filler to make minor repairs to plasterboard the next time you decorate the room.

When the plaster of a lath-and-plaster wall deteriorates with age it often loses its grip on the laths. The plaster will probably bulge and may crack in places. It will sound hollow when tapped and tends to yield when you press against it. Loose plaster should be replaced.

Repairing a wall

Cut out loose plaster with a bolster and hammer (**1**). If the laths are sound you can replaster over them. Dampen the laths and plaster edges (**2**) round the hole and apply a one-coat plaster with a plasterer's trowel, pressing it firmly between the laths (**3**). Build up the coating flush with the original plaster and level with a rule. Let the plaster stiffen and smooth it with a damp sponge and a trowel. Alternatively, apply it in two coats. Scratch-key the first coat and let it set (**4**), then apply the second coat and finish as before. For large repairs, use two coats of premixed lightweight bonding undercoat or metal-lathing plaster followed by a finishing plaster. For a small patch repair use a cellulose filler, pressing it on and between the laths.

If laths are damaged cut them out and replace them, or cover the studs with plasterboard and finish with plaster. When using plasterboard nail it in the opening with the grey side towards you.

1 Cut away loose or damaged plaster

2 Dampen edges of old sound plaster

3 Apply plaster, pressing it between the laths

4 Scratch-key the undercoat

Repairing a ceiling

A water leak above a lath-and-plaster ceiling will cause localized damage to the plaster. Repair the ceiling with metal-lathing plaster, finishing with a top-coat gypsum plaster.

Carefully cut back the plaster to sound material. Dampen the background and apply the undercoat (**1**). Do not build up a full thickness. Key the surface and let it set. Give the ceiling a second coat, then scrape it back 3mm (⅛in) below the surface and lightly key it. When set, finish-coat the ceiling using a plasterer's trowel (**2**).

1 Apply a thin first coat with firm pressure

2 Level top coat over keyed undercoat

Most Victorian and Edwardian houses of any quality had moulded cornices and centrepieces in at least some of their rooms. Many of them were destroyed in comparatively recent times when they were thought to be unfashionable, but with the renewed appreciation of period-style plasterwork, damaged mouldings are being restored or replaced.

Restoring original centrepieces

A ceiling centrepiece, or 'rose', is a decorative plaster moulding placed at the centre of a ceiling, usually with a pendant light fitting hanging from it. Original mouldings of this kind are often caked in distemper that tends to mask the fine detail. Restore them whenever possible by cleaning away the layers of old paint with water or paint stripper and by repairing any cracks and chipped details with filler.

Fine detail can be obscured by paint

Fitting a reproduction centrepiece

Replace an original ceiling moulding that is beyond repair with one of the excellent reproduction mouldings made from fibrous plaster. They are available in a range of sizes and period styles.

If there is a light fitting attached to the ceiling, turn off the power supply at the mains before you disconnect and remove the entire fitting.

Use a hammer and cold chisel to carefully chip away the old damaged moulding back to the ceiling plaster. Make good the surface with plaster and leave it to dry.

Find the exact centre of the ceiling, using lengths of string stretched diagonally from corner to corner – the point where they cross is the centre. Mark the point and drill a hole for the lighting cable. If the new centrepiece lacks a hole for the cable, drill one through its centre.

Apply a proprietary ceramic-tile adhesive to the back of the moulding and press it firmly into place after first passing the lighting cable through the hole in the centre. On a flat ceiling, suction should be sufficient to hold the moulding in place, but as a precaution prop it until the adhesive sets.

Reinforce larger mouldings with brass screws driven into the joists above. Cover the screwheads with filler to follow the contour of the moulding.

Wipe away surplus adhesive from round the edges of the moulding with a damp brush or sponge.

When the adhesive has set, attach the light fitting. You may need longer screws than before in order to make a really secure fixing.

Fibrous-plaster reproduction centrepiece

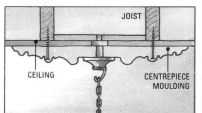

Reinforce larger mouldings with screws

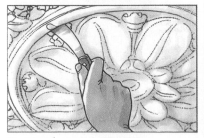

Cover the screw, using a filling knife

REPAIRING MOULDED CEILINGS

Sagging plaster on a traditional moulded ceiling can, if it is left unchecked, develop into an expensive repair job, requiring the services of a professional. But if part of the plaster has broken away from its lath background, yet is otherwise intact, it can be refixed and prevented from collapsing.

Screw repair
First lift the sagging portion of the ceiling, using wide boards propped in place with lengths of timber or hired screw props.

Drive countersunk plated screws fitted with galvanized or plated washers through the plaster and into the ceiling joists. The washers should be about 25mm (1in) in diameter and the fixings should be spaced about 300mm (12in) apart. The screwheads will bed themselves into the plaster and can then be concealed with filler.

Plaster repair
A laborious but more substantial repair to a sagging ceiling can be made by using plaster of Paris to bond the plaster back to the laths.

Prop up the ceiling as for the screw repair, then lift the floorboards in the room above – this is not usually necessary in an attic – so that you can get at the back of the ceiling.

Use a vacuum cleaner to remove dust and loose material. If the groundwork is not clean the plaster of Paris will not adhere properly.

Wet the back of the ceiling with clean water, then mix the plaster of Paris to a creamy consistency and spread it fairly quickly over the whole of the damaged area, covering both the laths and the plasterwork (**1**).

Plaster of Paris sets very quickly, but leave the props in place until it has dried quite hard.

1 Spread plaster over laths and old plaster

REPAIRING
CORNICE
MOULDINGS

Cornice mouldings are decorative plaster features running round the perimeter of a room in the angles between the walls and the ceiling. They are often damaged as a result of the 'settling down' of a house over a long period of time. Cracks can easily be made good with filler, but missing sections of mouldings have to be re-created. Small pieces of straight mouldings can be formed *in situ*, but longer sections are often made on a bench and then fixed in place with adhesive. In either case, clean all the old paint off the remaining moulding before starting so as to regain the well-defined modelling of the shape and make a better repair.

Running a cornice

First, temporarily nail a straight guide batten to the wall, tucked up against the lower edge of the moulding (**1**) and spanning the missing section.

Now make a template of the moulding profile, including the guide batten (**2**). Use a profile gauge (needle template) to make a copy of the moulding, then transfer it to a piece of stiff aluminium sheet or plastic laminate. Cut along the line with a tile saw and finish the edge with variously shaped files, regularly checking its fit against an intact section of moulding.

Contact-glue and screw the template to a plywood backing board that has been cut to follow the same shape but with its contoured edge cut to an angle of about 45 degrees (**3**).

Screw a straight-edged baseboard to the template so that it just touches the wall when the template is in position. Make sure that the template is at 90 degrees to the edge of the baseboard. Screw a triangular brace to the back edge of the template and to the baseboard to make the whole assembly rigid. Finally, fix a 'fence' batten to the baseboard on each side of the template and level with the shaped edge. When the template is in use, the fence runs along the face of the guide batten (**4**).

Clear away any loose material and dampen the area to be restored. Mix plaster of Paris to a creamy consistency and spread it over the damage. Build the thickness up gradually with progressive layers of plaster, running the template along the guide batten to form the shape as the plaster stiffens. Include pieces of jute scrim in the thick sections to reinforce the plaster.

1 Fix a batten to wall

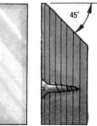

2 Make a template

3 Bevel backing board

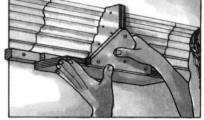

4 Run fence along guide batten

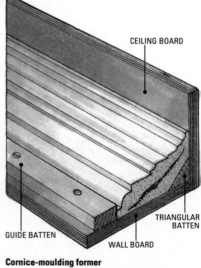

Template assembly
1 Guide batten
2 Template
3 Backing board
4 Baseboard
5 Triangular brace
6 Fence batten

MAKING A NEW LENGTH OF MOULDING

Make long sections of cornice moulding on the bench in a former constructed by screwing two lengths of board together to represent the angle between the wall and the ceiling. Glue a triangular batten into the angle between them. Measure the height of the existing cornice and fix a guide batten to the board representing the wall at that distance from the 'ceiling' board. Next paint and wax all the interior surfaces of the former.

Take the profile of the cornice and make up a template assembly (see left). Mix up the plaster and spread it on to the faces of the former while working the template carefully along the guide batten. Build up the cornice, gradually forming the shape as you add layers of plaster. Reinforce the thicker parts of the moulding with pieces of jute scrim. When the moulding is hard and dry, remove it from the former.

Cut back the old and damaged cornice to sound material, making square cuts with a fine-toothed saw. Clean out any broken pieces from the angle with a hammer and chisel. Cut the new section of moulding to fit, apply a proprietary ceramic-tile adhesive to its back and top, then press the moulding into place. A very heavy section should have the additional support of brass screws driven into the ceiling joists. Hide the screwheads with filler.

Scrape away any surplus adhesive and fill the joints where the sections butt together, then wipe down with a damp brush or sponge.

CEILING BOARD

TRIANGULAR BATTEN

GUIDE BATTEN

WALL BOARD

Cornice-moulding former
Run the template assembly along guide batten.

PLASTERING A WALL

The plastering of a complete wall is not likely to be required in many households. New work is more easily carried out with plasterboard, but there are times when repairs arising from problems with damp or resulting from alterations such as the moving of a doorway leave fairly large areas to be plastered. Plastering of this sort can be tackled by the non-professional, although some previous experience, such as patching up damaged plaster, would be an advantage. The key to success is to divide the wall into manageable areas.

Applying the plaster

Using the face of a plasterer's trowel, scrape a couple of trowel-loads of plaster on to the hawk and start undercoat-plastering at the top of the wall, holding the trowel at an angle to the face of the wall and applying the plaster with vertical strokes. Work from right to left if you are right-handed and vice versa if you are left-handed.

Using firm pressure to ensure good adhesion, apply a thin layer first and then follow this with more plaster, building up the required thickness. If the final thickness of the plaster needs to be greater than 9mm (⅜in), key the surface with a scratcher and let it set, then apply a second or 'floating' coat.

Fill the area between two screed battens. It is not necessary to work tight up against them. Level the surface with a rule laid across the battens, sliding the tool from side to side as you work from the bottom upwards. Fill in any hollows and then level the plaster again. Scratch the surface lightly to provide a key for the finishing coat and let the plaster set. Work along the entire wall in this way, then remove the battens. Fill the gaps left by the battens, again levelling the plaster with the rule.

With gypsum plasters the finishing coat can be applied as soon as the undercoat is set. Cement undercoats must be left to dry for at least 24 hours because of shrinkage, then wetted when the top coat is applied.

PREPARING TO PLASTER

In addition to specialized plasterer's tools, you need a spirit level and some lengths of 9mm (⅜in) thick planed softwood battening. The battens – known as screeds – are nailed to the wall to act as guides when it comes to levelling the plaster. Professional plasterers form 'plaster screeds' by applying bands of undercoat plaster to the required thickness. These can be laid vertically or horizontally.

Prepare the background and fix wooden screeds vertically to the wall with masonry nails. Driving the nails fully home will make it easier for you to work the trowel, but it can also make it more difficult to remove the screeds afterwards. The screens should be spaced no more than 600mm (2ft) apart. Use the spirit level to get them truly plumb, packing them out with strips of hardboard or wood as necessary.

Mix the undercoat plaster to a thick, creamy consistency and measure out two bucketfuls to begin with, though you can increase this to larger amounts when you become more proficient.

Plumb the screeds
Pack out the screed battens at the fixing points as required.

Finishing

Cover the undercoat with a thin layer of finishing plaster, working from top to bottom and from left to right (see left) using even, vertical strokes. If you are left-handed, work from right to left. Hold the trowel at a slight angle so that only one edge is touching.

Make sweeping horizontal strokes to level the surface further. You can try using the rule to get the initial surface even, but you may risk dragging the finish coat off. Use the trowel to smooth out any slight ripples.

Wet the trowel and work over the surface with firm pressure to consolidate the plaster. As it sets, trowel it to produce a smooth matt finish, but do not overwork it. Wipe away any plaster slurry which appears with a damp sponge.

The wall should be left to dry out for some weeks before decorating.

The order for applying plaster by a right-handed person

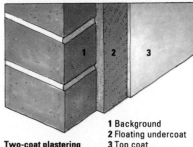

Two-coat plastering
1 Background
2 Floating undercoat
3 Top coat

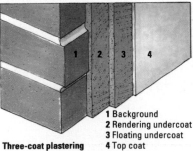

Three-coat plastering
1 Background
2 Rendering undercoat
3 Floating undercoat
4 Top coat

Plaster layers
Plaster is applied in layers to build up a smooth, level surface. Two or three coats may be used.

PLASTERBOARD

Plasterboard provides a relatively quick and simple method of cladding walls or ceilings and providing a smooth surface for decorating. It also offers good sound insulation as well as fire protection. It is quite easy to cut and to fix, either by bonding or by nailing it into place.

A range of dry-lining plasterboards is available from builders' merchants. The boards are all made with a core of aerated gypsum plaster and covered on both sides with a strong paper liner. A grey paper facing is for finishing with plaster while the ivory-coloured paper is for direct decorating with wallpaper or paint.

Plasterboard is made in a range of thicknesses and sheet sizes, usually with square or tapered edges. Tapered edges are invariably on the ivory-coloured side of a sheet (see below), whereas the edges on the grey side are always square.

STORING AND CUTTING PLASTERBOARD

Plasterboard is fragile, having very little structural strength. Nevertheless, the sheets are quite heavy, so always get someone to help you carry one. Always carry it vertically on edge – there is a serious risk of breaking it if you carry a board face up.

Manufacturers and suppliers of plasterboard store it flat in stacks, but this is usually inconvenient at home and is anyway not necessary for a small number of sheets. Store them on edge instead, leaning them at a slight angle against a wall, their ivory-coloured faces together to protect them.

Stack the sheets carefully to avoid damaging their edges.

Cutting plasterboard
You can cut plasterboard with a saw or with a stiff-blade craft knife.

Support a sheet face-side up on lengths of wood laid across trestles. First mark the cutting line on it with the aid of a straightedge. When sawing, hold the saw at a shallow angle to the surface of the plasterboard. If the offcut is a large one, ask a helper to support it as you approach the end of the cut in order to prevent the board breaking.

When slicing plasterboard with a knife, cut fairly deeply into the material following a straightedge, then snap the board along the cutting line over a length of wood. Cut through the paper facing on the other side to separate the two pieces.

Employ a keyhole saw, a power jigsaw or a craft knife to make openings in plasterboard for switches and other electrical fittings.

Remove any ragged paper after cutting by rubbing down the edges with an abrasive paper.

Tapered edge

Square edge

Duo edge

Types of edge
Tapered edges are filled and taped for smooth, seamless jointing. The duo type provides a tapeless option. Square-edged boards can be filled and taped, or plastered over.

PLASTERBOARD SPECIFICATIONS

PLASTERBOARD: TYPES AND USAGE	WIDTHS	LENGTHS	THICKNESS	EDGE FINISH
Standard wallboard and plank				
This material is generally used for the dry-lining of walls and ceilings. It is produced in a range of lengths, and though most suppliers stock only a limited selection, other sizes can be ordered. One side is ivory-coloured for direct decoration and the other is grey for plastering.	600mm (2ft) 900mm (3ft) 1.2 (4ft)	1.8m (6ft) to 3.6m (12ft) *Commonly stocked in 2.43m (8ft) and 3.0m (10ft) lengths*	9.5mm (⅜in) 12.5mm (½in) 12.5mm (½in) 15mm (⅝in)	Tapered, duo or square
	Plank 600mm (2ft)	2.35m (7ft 8½in) to 3m (10ft)	19mm (¾in)	Square
Baseboard				
Baseboard is a square-edged plasterboard that is lined with grey paper and is produced as a backing for a plaster finish. It is used mainly for plastered ceilings. It is also available as vapour-check grade (see below).	900mm (3ft)	1.2m (4ft) 1.22m (4ft) 1.37m (4ft 6in)	9.5mm (⅜in)	Square
Lath board				
Lath board is used similarly to baseboard, but its long edges are rounded.	400mm (1ft 4in)	1.2m (4ft) 1.22m (4ft) 1.35m (4ft 5in) 1.37m (4ft 6in)	9.5mm (⅜in) 12.5mm (½in)	Round
Thermal-insulation board				
Thermal-insulation boards are standard sheets of plasterboard with a backing of expanded-polystyrene or urethane laminate. The paper surface may be ivory-coloured for direct decoration or grey for plastering.	1.2m (4ft)	2.4m (7ft 10½in) 2.7m (8ft 10¼in)	25mm (1in)* 30mm (1⅛in) 32mm (1¼in)* 35mm (1⅜in) 40mm (1⅝in)* 45mm (1¾in) 50mm (2in)	Tapered or square
Vapour-check plasterboard				
These boards have a tough metallized polyester-film backing which is vapour-resistant and provides reflective thermal insulation. They are used as an internal lining to prevent warm moist air condensing on or inside structural wall or ceiling materials.	900mm (3ft) 1.2m (4ft)	*Stocked in similar lengths to standard board.*	*Stocked in same thicknesses as standard wallboard.*	Tapered or square

N.B. Metric sizes actual, imperial sizes approximate   *Urethane-backed

Plasterboard can be nailed directly on to the timber framework of a stud partition or on to wooden battens fixed to a masonry wall. It can also be bonded straight on to solid walls with plaster or an adhesive. The boards can be fitted horizontally if it is more economical to do so, but generally they are placed vertically. All of the edges should be supported. When plasterboarding a ceiling and walls, cover the ceiling first.

Methods of fixing plasterboard

Nailing to a stud partition
Timber-framed partition walls may simply be plain room-dividers or they may include doorways. Start fitting boards from one corner when you are plasterboarding a plain wall; if the wall includes a doorway, work away from it towards the corners of the room.

Starting from a corner
Using a footlifter, try the first board in position. Mark and scribe the edge that meets the adjacent wall if this is necessary, then nail the board into position (see far right), securing it to all the frame members.

Fix the rest of the boards in place, working across the partition. Butt the edges of tapered-edge boards, but leave a gap of 3mm (⅛in) between boards that are going to be coated with a board-finishing plaster.

If necessary, scribe the edge of the last board to fit the end corner before nailing it into place.

Cut a skirting board, mitring the joints at the corners or scribing the ends of the new board to the original. Fit the skirting board.

Starting from a doorway
Using the footlifter, hold a board flush with the door stud and mark the position of the underside of the door head on the edge of the board. Between this mark and the top edge of the board, cut out a 25mm (1in) wide strip. Reposition the board and fix it in place, nailing it to all the frame members (see right).

Fix the rest of the boards in place, working towards the corner. Butt the edges of tapered-edge boards, but leave a 3mm (⅛in) gap between boards that you intend to coat afterwards with a board-finishing plaster.

If necessary, scribe the last board to fit any irregularities in the corner before fixing it in place.

Cover the rest of the wall on the other side of the doorway in a similar way, starting by cutting a 25mm (1in) wide strip from the first board between its top edge and a mark indicating the lower side of the door head.

Cut a plasterboard panel to go above the doorway, butting into the cutouts in the boards on each side of the door. Sand away the ragged edges of paper before fitting the panel.

Clad the other side of the partition with plasterboard in the same way.

When all of the plasterboard is in place, fill and finish the joints. Cut and fit solid-wood door linings and cover the edges with an architrave moulding.

Cut and fit skirting boards, nailing through the plasterboard into alternate studs behind.

NAIL FIXING
Use special galvanized plasterboard nails of lengths appropriate to the thickness of the plasterboard, as shown in the table below.

Space the nails 150mm (6in) apart and place them not less than 9mm (⅜in) from the paper-covered edge and 12mm (½in) from the cut ends. Drive the nails in straight so that their heads sink just below the surface without tearing through the paper lining.

Board thickness	Nail length
9.5mm (⅜in)	32mm (1¼in)
12.5mm (½in)	40mm (1⅝in)
15mm (⅝in)	40mm (1⅝in)
19mm (¾in)	50mm (2in)
25mm (1in)	50mm (2in)
30mm (1⅛in)	65mm (2½in)
32mm (1¼in)	65mm (2½in)
35mm (1⅜in)	65mm (2½in)
40mm (1⅝in)	65mm (2½in)
45mm (1¾in)	75mm (3in)
50mm (2in)	75mm (3in)

Types of nail used with plasterboard

Fixing to metal studs
Some modern houses may have metal-stud partition walls. If you need to fix into these studs, use special self-tapping drywall screws.

Plasterboard nails
1 Galvanized nails
2 Ring-shank nails
3 Nailable plugs
4 Jagged nails

Using a footlifter
Cut the board about 16mm (⅝in) below room height to clear the footlifter, a simple tool that holds the board against the ceiling leaving both hands free for nailing. You can make one from a 75mm (3in) wide block of wood.

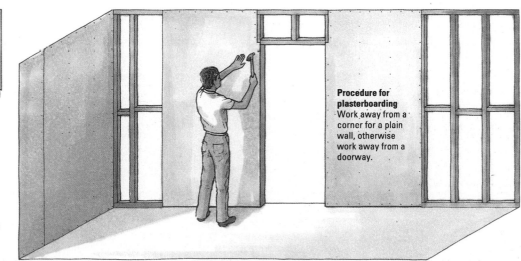

Procedure for plasterboarding
Work away from a corner for a plain wall, otherwise work away from a doorway.

Distances between stud centres
When providing new supports it is cheaper to use 12.5mm (½in) thick board on studs set 600mm (2ft) apart. Maximum distance between stud centres: for 9.5mm (⅜in) board, 450mm (1ft 6in); for 12.5mm to 50mm (½ to 2in) thick board, 600mm (2ft).

SCRIBING
PLASTERBOARD

If the inner edge of the first sheet of plasterboard butts against an uneven wall, or its other edge does not fall on the centre of the stud, the board must be scribed to fit.

Scribing the first board

Try the first board in position (**1**). The illustration shows an uneven wall pushing the plasterboard beyond the stud at the other edge of the sheet of plasterboard.

Reposition the board (**2**) so that its inner edge lies on the centre of the stud and hold it at the required height, using a footlifter. Tack it in place with plasterboard nails driven partway into the intermediate studs.

With a pencil and a batten (cut to the width of the board) trace a line down the face of the wall, making sure you keep the batten level.

Take the board down and use a craft knife or saw to trim the waste away from the scribed edge. Replace the board in the corner and fix it to the studs with plasterboard nails (**3**).

Scribing the last board

Temporarily nail the board to be scribed over the last fixed board (**4**), ensuring that their edges lie flush.

Using a batten and a pencil as above, trace a pencil line down the face of the board, using the batten as a guide and carefully keeping it level.

Remove the marked board, cut along the scribed line, then nail the board to the studs (**5**).

Fill and tape the joints or apply finish plaster as required.

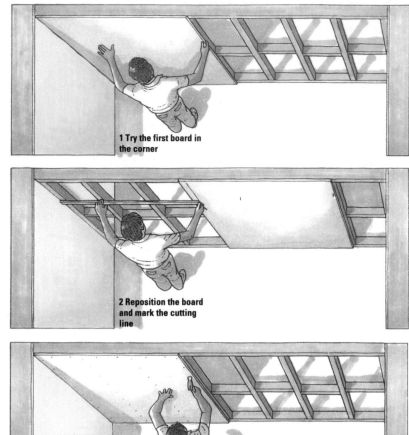

1 Try the first board in the corner

2 Reposition the board and mark the cutting line

3 Cut the board to size and nail in place

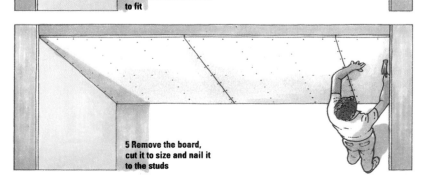

4 Temporarily nail the last board and scribe it to fit

5 Remove the board, cut it to size and nail it to the studs

Plasterboard cannot be nailed directly to masonry walls, so battens of sawn timber known as furring strips are used to provide a good fixing for the nails and to counter any unevenness of the wall surface. These should be treated with a wood preserver. You can cover old plaster if it is sound, but if not strip it back to the brickwork. If damp has damaged the original plaster, it must be treated and, if possible, the area should be allowed to dry out before lining. Fix any plumbing pipe runs, electrical conduit or cable to the wall before the battens are fixed to conceal them.

Marking out

Use a straightedge to mark the position of the battens on the wall with vertical chalk lines. The lines should be placed at 400mm (1ft 4in), 450mm (1ft 6in) or 600mm (2ft) centres according to the width and thickness of the plasterboard being used. Bear in mind that sheets of plasterboard must meet on the centre lines of the battens. Work away from any door or window opening and allow for the thickness of the battens and plasterboard at the reveals.

Fixing the battens

Cut the required number of furring battens from 50 x 32mm (2 x 1¼in) sawn softwood. The vertical battens should be cut 155mm (6¼in) less than the height of the wall. Horizontal battens should be made to run along the tops and bottoms of the vertical ones and any short vertical infill battens above and below openings (see below).

Nail the vertical furring battens on first, setting their bottom ends 100mm (4in) above the floor. Fix them with masonry nails or cut nails, with the face of each batten level with the guideline (see right), and check with a straightedge and spirit level that they are also flat and plumb, packing them out as necessary.

Now nail the horizontal battens across the tops and bottoms of the vertical members, inserting packing to bring them all to the same level.

Fixing the plasterboard

To fix plasterboard to furring battens, follow the procedure described for nailing to a stud partition. However, the boards at the sides of windows and doors need not be notched to receive panels above or below the openings. The procedure for filling and finishing joints between the boards is identical. Cut the skirting board to length and nail it through the plasterboard to the bottom horizontal furring batten. If it is a high moulded skirting of the type used in period houses, it can be nailed to the vertical battens.

LEVELLING THE FURRING BATTENS

Masonry walls are often uneven and, if the lining is to finish straight and flat, this must be taken into account. To check if the wall is flat, hold a long straightedge horizontally against it at different levels. If it is uneven, mark the vertical chalk line already drawn on the wall which is the closest to the point where the wall bulges most **(1)**.

Hold a straight furring batten vertically on the marked chalk line keeping it plumb with a straightedge and spirit level, then mark the floor **(2)** where the edge of the batten falls. Draw a straight guideline across the floor **(3)**, passing through this mark and meeting the walls on each end at right angles. Align all furring battens with this line.

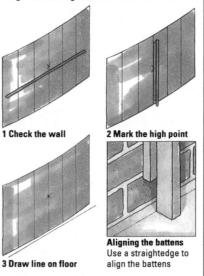

1 Check the wall

2 Mark the high point

3 Draw line on floor

Aligning the battens
Use a straightedge to align the battens

Attaching furring battens to a wall
1 Mark batten positions.
2 Fix vertical battens.
3 Attach horizontal battens.
4 Fix short pieces over doors and windows and offset the short vertical ones.
5 Nail boards in place, working away from a door or window.

BONDING TO
A SOLID WALL

As an alternative to using batten fixing for dry-lining a solid wall, tapered-edge plasterboard can be bonded directly to the wall with dabs of plaster or adhesive. Rectangular pads about 100 x 50mm (4 x 2in) cut from remnants of plasterboard are used for levelling the wall. The pads are bonded to the wall in lines as substitutes for battens and allowed to set. Dabs of plaster are then applied between the pads and the plasterboard is temporarily nailed to the pads while the plaster sets.

Boards 900mm (3ft) wide are normally used for this technique. The wall must be prepared in the usual way.

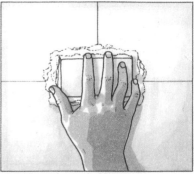

1 Bond first pad on marked intersection

Fixing the pads

Set out vertical chalk lines on the wall 450mm (1ft 6in) apart, working from one corner or from an opening (see below). Draw a horizontal line 225mm (9in) from the ceiling, one 100mm (4in) from the floor and another centred between them. If the wall is more than 2.4m (8ft) high, divide the space between the top and bottom equally with two lines. The pads are placed where the horizontal and vertical lines intersect.

Using a spirit level and a straightedge that is almost the full height of the wall, check at each vertical line, noting high spots at the intersections of the lines.

Bond a pad on the most prominent intersection point (**1**), using a bonding-coat plaster or a proprietary tile adhesive, and press it in place. This pad forms the datum point from which the rest of the pads are levelled.

Bond and plumb the other pads on the same vertical line, then complete a second vertical row, two lines from the first. Check these pads for level vertically then diagonally with the first row. Work across the wall in this way, then fix the remaining pads on the other intersections. Allow two hours for the adhesive to set.

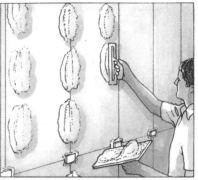

2 Apply thick dabs of plaster between the pads

Fixing the plasterboard

Apply thick dabs of bonding plaster to the wall with a trowel (**2**) over an area for one board at a time. Space the dabs 75mm (3in) apart vertically. Do not let the plaster overlap the area of the next board. Using the straightedge to press it evenly and a footlifter to position it, press the board firmly against the pads so that the plaster spreads out behind it.

Check the alignment, then fix the board with plasterboard nails driven

into the pads round the edge. Do not drive the nails in fully. Fix the next board in the same way, butting it to the first, and work on across the wall, scribing the last board into the internal angle. When the plaster has set, remove the nails with pincers or a claw hammer, protecting the plasterboard surface (**3**).

Work round angles and openings (see opposite) and, when all surfaces are covered, fill and finish the joints.

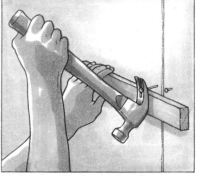

3 Pull out the nails when the plaster has set

Bonding plasterboard to a wall
1 Mark pad positions.
2 Stick the pads over the intersections.
3 Apply dabs of plaster to the wall.
4 Place plasterboard and nail temporarily. Remove nails when plaster has set.

ANGLES AND OPENINGS

WINDOW OPENINGS

Cut plasterboard linings to fit the soffit and window reveals, and attach them before you apply the boards that line the wall. Align the front edges of the window linings with the faces of the battens or allow for dabs of plaster.

Apply evenly spaced dabs of plaster adhesive to the back of the soffit lining, press it into place (1) and prop it there while the adhesive sets. If the lining bridges a wide span, support it with a wooden board before you prop it. Fit the reveal linings in the same way (2).

Working away from the window, fix the wall linings so that the paper-covered edge of the board laps the cut edge of the reveal lining.

The panels for above and below the window are cut and fitted last. Sand off rough edges of paper and leave a 3mm (⅛in) gap between boards for filling.

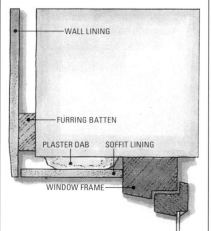

1 Soffit lining
Fix a soffit lining with dabs of plaster adhesive and prop in place until set.

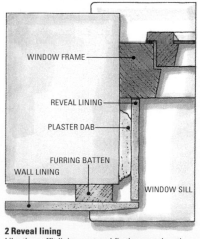

2 Reveal lining
Like the soffit lining, cut and fix the reveal so the wall lining overlaps its cut edge.

Internal angle

Fix wooden furring battens or plasterboard pads close to the corner. Whenever possible, place the cut edges of the plasterboard lining into an internal corner.

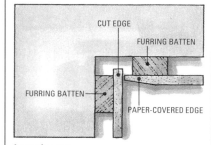

Internal corner
Set cut edges into the angle.

External angle

Attach furring battens or plasterboard pads as close to the corner as possible. Use screws and wall plugs to fix the battens so as to prevent the corner breaking away. At least one board should have a paper-covered edge, which should lap the other.

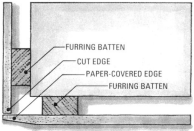

External corner
A paper-covered edge should lap the outer edge.

Door openings

Line the reveals and soffits of doorways in exterior walls as described for window openings (see far left).
In the case of interior door openings, screw-fix timber furring battens or bond plasterboard pads level with the edge of the wall, then nail the plasterboard linings in place.

Fit a new door lining (or modify the old one) and cover the joint with an architrave moulding.

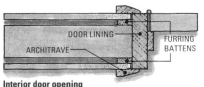

Interior door opening
Fit a new lining or widen the old one and cover the joint between the lining and plasterboard with an architrave moulding.

Electrical fittings

Depending on the type of fitting, chase the wall or pack out the mounting box for an electrical switch or socket outlet so that it finishes flush with the face of the plasterboard lining. Screw-fix short lengths of furring batten at each side of the box or use dabs of adhesive.

Cut the opening for the box before fixing the board. If you find it difficult to mark the opening accurately by transferring measurements, remove the fitting from its mounting box and take an impression by placing the board in position and pressing it against the box.

Fix the plasterboard panel in place and replace the electrical fitting.

Electrical fittings
Turn off the power before you dismantle electrical fittings. Chase the wall or pack out the mounting box to set it flush with the plasterboard.

Lining door and window openings
1 Fit soffit lining.
2 Fit reveal lining.
3 Fit boards, working away from window.
4 Fit panels above and below window.
5 Fit boarding, working away from doorway.
6 Cut and fit panel above doorway.
7 Cut openings for electrical fittings.

FINISHING
PLASTERBOARD

All joints between boards and indentations left by nailing must be filled and smoothed before the ivory-coloured surface of plasterboard is ready for decorating. You will need jointing tape, filler and a special plaster-based 'finish' that leaves a smooth feathered joint.

Tools and materials

The filler and finish are prepared for use by being mixed with water. The paper jointing tape is 53mm (2⅛in) wide with feathered edges, and is creased along its centre. It is used for reinforcing flat joints and internal angles. A special paper jointing tape is available for covering and reinforcing external angles. This tape has thin metal strips on each side of its central crease which strengthen the corners.

Professional plasterers use purpose-made tools for finishing joints, but you can use medium and wide filling knives, a plasterer's trowel and a close-textured plastic sponge.

Covering nails

Fill the indentations that have been left by nailing, using a filling knife to apply then smooth the filler. When the filler has set, apply a thin coating of joint finish and feather it off at the edges with a damp sponge.

Filling tapered-edge joints

Mix joint filler to a creamy consistency and apply a continuous band of it about 60mm (2½in) wide down the length of each joint.

Press the paper tape into the filler, using a medium-size filling knife to bed it in well and exclude air bubbles **(1)**. Follow this with another layer of filler applied over the tape to level the surface, this time using the wide filling knife. When the filler has stiffened slightly, smooth its edges with the damp sponge, then let it set completely before filling any remaining small hollows.

When all the filler has set, coat it with a thin layer of joint finish. Mix the finish thoroughly to the consistency of thick cream and apply it in a broad band down the joint, using a wide filler knife or trowel **(2)**. Before it sets, feather its edges with a dampened sponge.

After the joint finish has set, apply another thin but wider band over the first application, again feathering the edges with the sponge, working with a circular motion **(3)**.

1 Press tape into filler

2 Apply finish in a wide band

3 Feather edge with a sponge

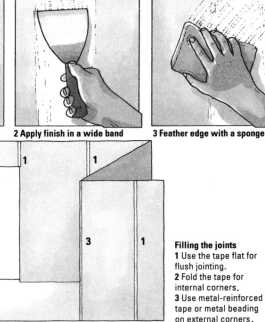

Filling the joints
1 Use the tape flat for flush jointing.
2 Fold the tape for internal corners.
3 Use metal-reinforced tape or metal beading on external corners.

CUT EDGES

When a square-cut edge of plasterboard butts against a tapered-edge board, fill the joint flush before you apply the jointing tape **(1)**.

Where two cut edges meet **(2)**, press filler into the 3mm (⅛in) gap to finish flush. When the filler has set, apply a thin band of joint finish to it and press the paper tape tight against the board. Cover this with a wide but thin coat of finish and feather the edges. Finish off as before.

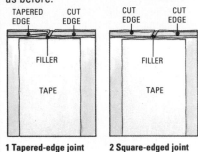

1 Tapered-edge joint   **2 Square-edged joint**

GLASS-FIBRE TAPE

A self-adhesive glass-fibre mesh tape can be used instead of traditional paper tape for jointing new plasterboard or for making patch repairs. The 50mm (2in) wide tape is a strong binder and does not need prior application of filler to bond it in place. The tape is applied first, then joint filler is pressed through the mesh.

Applying the tape
Ensure that the jointing edges of the plasterboard are dust-free. If the edges of boards have been cut, burnish them with the handle of your filling knife to remove all traces of rough paper.

Starting at the top, centre the tape over the joint, then unroll it and press it in place as you work down the wall. Cut it off to length at the bottom. Butt the ends rather than overlap them if you have to make a join in the tape.

Mix the filler and press it through the tape into the joint with a filling knife, then level off the surface so that the mesh of the tape is visible. Allow the filler to set.

Complete the joint with plaster-based joint finish, as with paper tape.

Applying filler
Press the filler through the tape with a flexible filling knife.

Internal corners

The internal corners of dry-lined walls are finished by a method similar to that used for flat joints. Any gaps are first filled flush with filler and if necessary a band of PVA bonding agent is applied to the original ceiling or wall plaster to reduce its suction.

Cut the paper tape to length and fold it down its centre. Brush a thin band of finish on to each side of the corner and press the tape into it while it is still wet. Use a square-section length of wood to press down both sides at once to remove air bubbles (1).

With a filling knife, apply a 75mm (3in) wide band of finish to both sides of the corner immediately and feather the edges with a damp sponge (2). When the finish has set, apply a second, wider coat and feather the edges again.

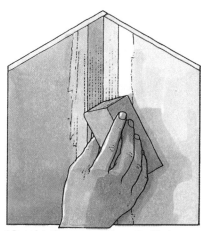

1 Press into the corner with a wooden block

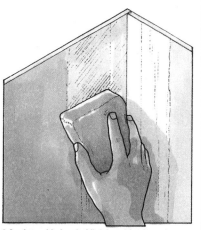

2 Apply a wide band of finish and feather edge

External corners

When finishing an external-corner joint, use metal-reinforced corner tape. Cut it to length, fold it down its centre, then apply a 50mm (2in) wide band of filler down both sides of the corner and press the tape onto it, using a wide filling knife to keep the corner straight. Press the tape down well so that the metal strips are bedded firmly against the face of the plasterboard. If you have used tapered-edge board, however, square up the corner with filler before you apply the tape (1). Apply two coats of joint finish, feathering the edges as described for internal corners.

Protect a vulnerable corner with a length of metal angle bead. Apply a coating of filler to each side of the corner, then bed the angle bead in it, smoothing the filler flush with a knife before leaving it to set (2).

Apply a second coat of filler to both sides in a wide band and feather it off with a damp sponge.

When the filler has set, apply two coats of finish, feathering off as before.

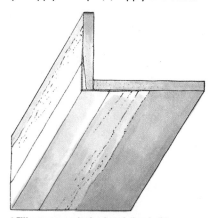

1 Fill out a tapered-edge board, then bed tape

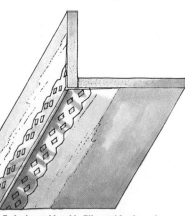

2 Embed metal bead in filler and feather edge

PREPARING FOR DECORATION

Finishing with plaster
As an alternative to direct decoration of the ivory-coloured side of plasterboard, apply a thin coat of board-finish plaster to the grey face.

Applying a thin finishing coat is not an easy technique to master, but with some practice you may be able to tackle the walls. However, it pays to leave the plastering of ceilings to a professional, though you can still prepare the plasterboard (see below) and have it ready for the tradesman. If you decide to attempt the plastering yourself, study the section on plastering thoroughly before you begin.

Preparing the background
First fill flush with the surface all joints and gaps between boards and at the corners. Reinforce them with strips of jute scrim pressed into a thin band of plaster. Rolls of jute scrim, 90mm (3½in) wide, are available from the majority of builders' merchants.

Let the plaster set, but not dry out thoroughly, before applying a coat of finishing plaster.

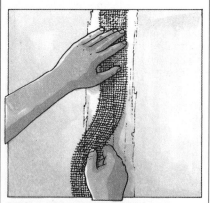

Reinforce joints with scrim before plastering

Decorating directly
Before the ivory-coloured side of plasterboard can be decorated it must be given a uniform surface by the application of a sealer. Brush or sponge-apply a thin coating of joint finish mixed to a thin consistency. If you paint it on, follow up with the sponge, working with a light circular motion over the entire surface. Alternatively, use a proprietary ready-mixed top coat which can be applied with a brush or roller and is suitable for all decorative treatments. Two coats will also provide a vapour barrier.

PLASTER-
BOARDING
A CEILING

Plasterboard is usually employed to make new ceilings, but it can also be used to replace an old lath-and-plaster ceiling which has deteriorated beyond repair.

Fixing the plasterboard in place and finishing its surface ready for decorating can be tackled by a competent amateur, but applying wet-plaster to a boarded ceiling should be left to a skilled tradesman – it is strenuous work and extremely difficult to perfect.

Preparing an old ceiling

Start by stripping away all the old and damaged plaster and laths, and pull out all the nails.

This is a messy job, so wear protective clothing, a pair of goggles and a face mask while working. It is also a good idea to seal the gaps round doors in the room to prevent dust escaping into the rest of the house. You will need to dispose of a surprising amount of waste material, so have a number of strong plastic sacks available to make it easier to handle, and hire a skip to have it removed.

If necessary, trim back the top of the wall plaster so that the edge of the ceiling plasterboard can be tucked in.

Inspect and treat the exposed joists for any signs of woodworm or rot.

FITTING NEW BOARDING

Measure the area of ceiling and select the most economical size of boards to cover it.

The boards should be fitted with their long paper-covered edges running at right angles to the joists. The butt joints between the ends of the boards should be staggered on each row and supported by a joist in every case.

Skew-nail perimeter noggings between the joists against the walls, and fit intermediate ones in lines across the ceiling to support the long edges of the boards. It is not always necessary to fit intermediate noggings if the boards are going to be plastered, but they will ensure a sound ceiling. The intermediate noggings should be at least 50mm (2in) thick and should be fitted so that the edges of the boards will fall along their centre lines.

If necessary, trim the length of the boards to ensure that their ends fall on the centre lines of the joists.

Start fixing the boards, working from one corner of the room. Plasterboard is a relatively heavy material and it normally takes two people to support a large and awkward sheet while it is being fixed (see below). However, if you have to work on your own, use support battens and props, called 'dead-men', to hold the boards in place while you are nailing them (see far left).

Make a pair of props that are slightly longer than the overall height of the room (1) from 50 x 50mm (2 x 2in) softwood. Nail a cross piece and braces to one end of each prop. You will need to nail a 50 x 25mm (2 x 1in) temporary batten close to the top of the wall to support the long edges of the first row of boards (2). Support the next row with a batten that overlaps the edges of the first boards and is nailed to the joists (3). Fit packing under the batten to provide the necessary clearance for the new boards.

Use galvanized plasterboard nails to fix each board, working from the middle outwards and nailing at 150mm (6in) centres. This prevents the boards from sagging in the middle, which is likely to happen if their edges are nailed first.

If the boards are to be plastered, leave 3mm (⅛in) gaps between the cut ends and the paper-covered edges. For direct decoration, however, butt the paper-covered edges, but leave 3mm (⅛in) gaps at the ends of each board.

Finish the joints, using the method described for plasterboard walls.

Working single-handedly

1 Support the boards with simple T-shaped props called dead-men.

2 Nail a batten to the wall to give temporary support to the long edge of the board.

3 Nail a temporary support batten to the ceiling joists when butting boards.

Boarding a ceiling
1 Cut and fit perimeter noggings against the wall.
2 Nail intermediate noggings between the joists to suit the width of the boarding.
3 Fix the first board in one corner. Start nailing from the centre of the board.
4 Butt the side joints for direct decoration or leave a 3mm (⅛in) gap if plastering over.
5 Stagger the end joints, leaving a 3mm (⅛in) gap in all cases.

Coving and cornices

A plaster cornice or a simple coving are used to finish the edges of a ceiling where it meets the walls. Ready-made gypsum coving is widely available, generally in a fairly limited range of profile sizes and in various lengths. However, you can buy any number of period-style fibrous-plaster cornices, many of which are exact copies of Georgian and Victorian originals.

Templates are sometimes provided by the makers which are intended to be used as guides when you are cutting the internal and external mitre joints.

Fitting a cornice or coving

This sequence describes how to make a coved ceiling, but you can use the same method to fit a cornice.

Start by marking parallel lines along the wall and ceiling, setting them off from the angle at the distance specified in the manufacturer's instructions, then scratch the plastered surfaces within the lines in order to provide a good key for the adhesive (1).

Measure the wall and cut the coving to fit, using the template to saw the mitre (see right). Remember that when you are cutting mitres for outside corners, the coving must be longer than the wall, and must extend up to the line of the return angle drawn on the ceiling. Cut the coving with a fine-toothed saw, sawing from the face side.

Prepare the special adhesive by mixing the powder with clean water and stirring it to a creamy consistency. The adhesive should remain usable for about 30 minutes, but it is best to aim at making just enough for one length of coving at a time. Use a filling knife to apply the adhesive liberally to the back faces of the coving which will be in contact with the wall and ceiling.

Dry, bare plaster must be dampened just before the coving is put in place. Press it into the angle and level it with the guidelines (2). If a piece of coving is more than about 2m (6ft 6in) long, two people should fit it. Should it tend to sag when in place, support it with a couple of nails driven temporarily into the wall under its bottom edge and remove them when the adhesive has set.

Scrape away any beads of surplus adhesive before it sets and use it to fill the mitre joints as the work progresses. Use your finger to apply the adhesive to internal mitres if you find it easier, but finish off all joints with a filling knife to leave a sharp corner (3).

Wipe along the edges of the coving with a damp brush or sponge to remove any traces of adhesive. When it dries, prime the coving for painting.

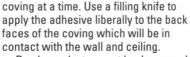

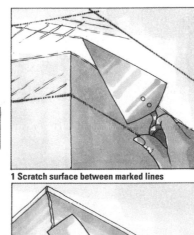

Fitted coving at external and internal corner

2 Press the coving into angle, level with the lines

1 Scratch surface between marked lines

3 Finish off with a filling knife

CUTTING THE MITRES

Using a template

Some makers of plaster coving and cornice supply a cardboard template with their product, which enables you to cut mitred corners more easily.

Mark the coving or cornice to length on one edge, bearing in mind whether you are mitring for an external corner or an internal one. Trim and fold the template and place it over the coving in line with the measured mark, then press it down so that it moulds itself to the curve of the material. Use the appropriate edge of the template – for an external or an internal mitre – and, with a soft pencil, draw the cutting line along it or the face and edges of the coving, tracing the template's edge.

Cut the mitre with a fine-toothed saw, following the marked angle.

Using a jig

If you use plaster coving or cornice right through the house, it is worth making a mitre block as a jig to help you cut the joints accurately.

Cut a baseboard from 18mm (¾in) plywood or chipboard about 200mm (8in) wide and 450mm (1ft 6in) long. Cut a piece of 100 x 50mm (4 x 2in) planed softwood to the same length for a fence.

Glue the fence to the baseboard flush with one long edge. When the adhesive has set, mark out and make three saw cuts, one at right angles to the face of the fence and two at 45 degrees in opposite directions. Nail a stop batten to the baseboard at a distance from the fence which will allow the coving to fit snugly between them for cutting.

The baseboard of the mitre block represents the ceiling and the fence represents the wall. Lay the coving in the jig with the end to be cut in the right direction for either an external or an internal mitre (see right).

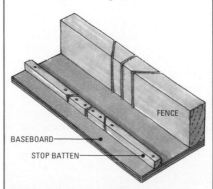

BASEBOARD
STOP BATTEN
FENCE

Make a mitre block for cutting joints accurately

Cornice profile

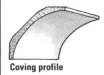

Coving profile

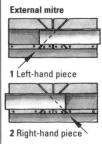

External mitre

1 Left-hand piece

2 Right-hand piece

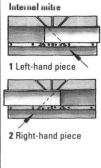

Internal mitre

1 Left-hand piece

2 Right-hand piece

171

EXTERIOR RENDERING

Rendering is the application of a relatively thin layer of cement or cement-and-lime mortar to the surfaces of exterior walls to provide a decorative and weather-resistant finish.

Any such treatment of exterior walls should be carefully considered beforehand, because the finished outer surface should always harmonize with the character of a building and not look ill at ease with those of its neighbours. This is particularly important in the case of terraced housing, where the fronts of the houses form an unbroken run of wall.

Planning ahead
Except for listed buildings or houses in a conservation area, there are no regulations controlling the change of colour or texture of exterior walls. Consequently, houses are often made conspicuous by their individualistic decorative treatment.

Re-rendering a wall is always acceptable as it is merely a case of renewing what is already there. Rendering old brickwork might improve its weather-resistance, but at the considerable cost of destroying the appearance of the building. Here it would be better to rake out the mortar joints, repoint them and, if necessary, treat the brickwork with a clear sealant.

Rendering techniques
The technique used in rendering is virtually the same as in plastering, for which cement and lime are also sometimes used. It generally involves using the same tools, though a wooden float is better than a plasterer's trowel for finishing cement rendering. The wood leaves a finely textured surface that looks better than the very smooth one produced with a metal trowel.

Rendering the walls of a house is really a job for a professional, as it involves covering a large area evenly, and also requires the ability to colour-match the batches of mortar, which is critical if the finished job is not to look patchy.

While a non-professional can undertake repairs to rendering, it is still difficult to match the colour of the new work to the old. You might consider painting the rendered wall.

For new work, divide the wall into manageable panels with screed battens as for plastering. However, colour-matching the mortar will still be a problem, and 'losing' the joints can be difficult. It might pay to concentrate on getting the rendering flat and then disguising any patchiness with paint, but once again you should consider the character of the house.

Before attempting to render a large wall, practise if possible on a smaller project, such as a garden wall.

BINDERS FOR EXTERIOR RENDERING

Mortar

Mortar is a mixture of sand, cement and clean water. The sand gives the mix bulk and the cement binds the particles. A cement mix will bond to any ordinary masonry material and to metals. Mortars of various strengths are produced by adjusting the proportions of sand and cement, or by adding lime.

A mortar should not be stronger than the materials on to which it is being applied. A cement-and-sand mix can be applied to a wall of dense hard bricks, for example, but a weaker mix of cement, sand and lime is more appropriate for soft bricks or blocks.

Cement sets by a chemical reaction with water known as hydration, and begins as soon as the water is added. Cement does not need to dry out in order to set, and the more slowly it dries out the stronger it will be.

Normally an average mix will stay workable for at least two hours. It will continue to gain strength for a few days after its initial set, reaching full strength in about a month.

Hot weather will reduce the workable time and can affect the set of the mortar by making it dry out too fast. In these conditions the work should be kept damp by being lightly sprayed with water or by being covered with polyethylene sheeting to retain the moisture and slow the drying time.

Cement

Cement made from limestone or chalk and clay is generally called Portland cement. Various types are made by adding other materials or by modifying the production methods.

Ordinary Portland cement (OPC)
This common light grey cement is mixed with aggregates for concrete and mortars. It is available in 50kg (110lb) bags and in smaller amounts.

Sulphate-resistant Portland cement
This is used in areas where soluble sulphates cause degrade problems.

White Portland cement
Similar to ordinary Portland but is more expensive. It makes light-coloured mixes for bricklaying, concrete and rendering. Pigment powders are available for colouring mortar mixes. The materials must be carefully proportioned for the batches to match.

Quick-setting cement
This cement is mixed with water and sets hard in 30 minutes. It is non-shrinking and waterproof and is useful for small repair jobs.

Masonry cement
This grey cement is specially made for rendering and bricklaying.

Lime

Lime is made from limestone or chalk. When it leaves the kiln it is called quicklime, and may be non-hydraulic or hydraulic. Non-hydraulic lime, in general use, sets by combining with carbon dioxide from the air as the water mixed with it dries out. Hydraulic lime has similar properties to cement; it sets when water is added and so can be used under water. When quicklime – the non-hydraulic type especially– is 'slaked' (mixed with water) it expands and gives off heat.

Lime must be properly slaked before use, and at one time a batch would have been soaked in a tub for weeks before it was used. This soaked lime was called lime putty.

Preslaked non-hydraulic lime powder, or hydrated lime, is sold by builders' merchants. It can be used at once, but is often soaked for 24 hours before use to make lime putty. The lime is mixed with water to a creamy consistency or with sand and water and left to stand as lime mortar called 'coarse stuff'. This can be kept for some days without setting if it is heaped up and covered with polyethylene sheet to prevent the water evaporating.

The less active hydraulic lime is dry-mixed with the sand like cement powder and the slaking process takes place when water is added.

AGGREGATES

SEE ALSO	
Details for:	
Storing plaster	152
Mixing mortar	174

Mortars are mixed with the finest aggregate, sand. Sand is graded by the size and shape of its particles; a well-graded sand will have particles of different sizes rather than ones that are uniformly large or small.

Types of sand

Sharp sand is used with coarse aggregates for making concrete and floor screeds. Plasterers' sharp sand is of a finer grade, and is used for rendering. Builders' sand, also known as bricklayers' or soft sand, has smoother particles and is used for masonry work. Use well-washed sand, as impurities can weaken a mortar and affect the set. A good sand should not stain your hand if you squeeze it.

Most aggregates may be bought from builders' merchants by the cubic metre; some suppliers sell it in small packs.

Stone chippings

Specially prepared crushed stone in various colours is used for pebble-dash rendering. Order enough for the whole job in hand (your supplier should be able to advise you) as additional stones bought later may not match the colour of the original batch. If you do run short, stop work at a corner rather than partway across a wall. The extra stones can be mixed with the remaining ones and a subtle change of colour is less likely to show on the adjacent wall.

Dry-mixed mortar

Prepacked sand-and-cement mortar mixes are sold by builders' merchants and DIY shops in large and small packs. They are ready-proportioned for different kinds of application and require only water to be added. As sand and cement 'settle out', a whole bag should be used and mixed well before adding the water.

Premixed and self-coloured one-coat renders are also available as an alternative to the traditional two-coat variety. The available colours are white, ivory, cream, stone, grey and pink.

STORING SAND AND CEMENT

Storing the materials should not normally be necessary because it is best to buy them as required and use them up by the end of the job.

However, if you are held up for a time after taking delivery, store powder or premixed materials as recommended for plaster. Store sand in a neat heap on a board or a plastic sheet and protect it from windblown dirt and rain with plastic sheeting.

Storing sand
Dirty sand can affect the set of the cement. Keep it covered with plastic sheeting.

ADDITIVES

Proprietary additives which modify the properties of mortar are added to the mix in precise proportions according to manufacturers' instructions. Their functions vary. Waterproofers, which make mortar impervious by sealing its pores, may be used when rendering on exposed walls. Plasticizers (additives which make a mortar easier to work) can be used instead of lime.

MORTAR MIXES FOR TWO-COAT RENDERING

The mix for a mortar will depend upon the strength of the material that is being rendered as well as the degree of exposure. The mix for the undercoat should not be stronger than the background, and the top coat should be no stronger than the undercoat.

Though these considerations are hardly ever critical for the majority of DIY work, when a situation does dictate that a precise mix is required, the proportions of the materials must be measured quite accurately.

Measure the material by volume, using a bucket. Loose cement and damp sand tend to 'bulk up' when loaded. Encourage cement powder to settle by tapping the bucket, and then top it up. Damp sand will not settle, so increase the measure by 25 per cent. Dry sand and saturated sand will settle to a normal measure.

TYPE OF BACKGROUND	TYPE OF MIX	PARTS BY VOLUME			
		AVERAGE EXPOSURE		SEVERE EXPOSURE	
		UNDERCOAT	TOP COAT	UNDERCOAT	TOP COAT
Low-suction backgrounds: Hard, dense clay bricks Dense concrete blocks Stone masonry Normal ballast concrete	Cement : lime : sand	1 : ½ : 4½	1 : 1 : 6*	1 : ½ : 4½	1 : 1 : 6
	Cement : sand & plasticizer	1 : 4	1 : 6*	1 : 4	1 : 6
	Masonry cement : sand	1 : 3½	1 : 5*	1 : 3½	1 : 5
Normal-absorption backgrounds: Most average-strength bricks Clay blocks Normal concrete blocks Aerated concrete blocks	Cement : lime : sand	1 : 1 : 6	1 : 2 : 9*	1 : 1 : 6	1 : 1 : 6
	Cement : sand & plasticizer	1 : 6	1 : 8*	1 : 6	1 : 6
	Masonry cement : sand	1 : 5	1 : 6½*	1 : 5	1 : 5

*Suitable mixes for interior plastering undercoats

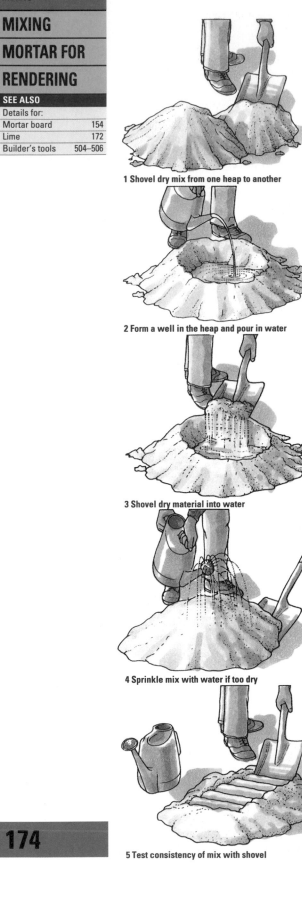

1 Shovel dry mix from one heap to another

2 Form a well in the heap and pour in water

3 Shovel dry material into water

4 Sprinkle mix with water if too dry

5 Test consistency of mix with shovel

Mix only as much mortar as you can use in an hour and, if the weather is very hot and dry, shorten this to half an hour. Keep all your mixing tools and equipment thoroughly washed so that no mortar sets on them.

Measure the required level bucketfuls of sand on to the mortar board or, for larger quantities, on to a smooth, level base such as a concrete drive.

Using a second dry bucket and shovel, kept exclusively for cement powder, measure out the cement, tapping the bucket to settle the loose powder and topping it up as needed. Tip the cement over the heaped-up sand and mix the sand and cement together by shovelling them from one heap to another and back again (**1**). Continue to turn this dry mix (the sand will actually be damp) until the whole takes on a uniform grey colour.

Form a well in the centre of the heap and pour in some water (**2**) – but not too much at this stage.

Shovel the dry mix from the sides of the heap into the water until the water is absorbed (**3**). If you are left with dry material, add more water as you go until you achieve the right firm, plastic consistency in the mortar, turning it repeatedly to mix it thoroughly to an even colour. It is quite likely that you will misjudge the amount of water at first, so if after turning the mix is still relatively dry, sprinkle it with water (**4**). Bear in mind, though, that too much water will weaken the mix.

Draw the back of your shovel across the mortar with a sawing action to test its consistency (**5**). The ribs formed in the mixture should not slump back or crumble. That would indicate that the mortar is either too wet or too dry respectively. The back of the shovel should leave a smooth texture on the surface of the mortar.

Make a note of the amount of water used in proportion to the dry materials so that further mixes will be consistent.

For cement-lime-sand mixes, the lime powder can be added with the cement and dry-mixed as described above. Otherwise lime putty can be mixed with the sand before the cement is added, or the cement can be added to prepared 'coarse stuff'. When you have finished, hose down and sweep clean the work area, particularly if it is a driveway, as any remaining cement slurry will stain the surface.

MIXING MORTAR BY MACHINE

You can hire a small-capacity electric or petrol-driven cement mixer. Such a mixer can save you a great deal of time and effort, especially on big jobs, and is quite easy to use.

Set the machine as close as possible to the work area and place a board under the drum to catch any spilt materials. If it is an electric-powered machine, take all due precautions with the power supply and keep the cables well clear of the work.

Load the drum with half the measure of sand and add a similar proportion of cement, and lime if required. Dry-mix them by running the mixer, then add some water.

Load the remainder of the materials in the same sequence, adding a little water in between.

Run the mixer for a couple of minutes to mix the materials thoroughly, then stop the machine and test some of the mix for consistency.

Generally, it pays to make a rendering mix somewhat stiffer for blockwork than for brickwork. However, this depends to some extent on the absorbency of the background.

It is advisable to wash out the drum of the mixer after each mix and to scour it out with water and some coarse aggregate at the end of the working day. If you return the machine with dry or drying mortar in its drum you may be charged extra.

Cement mixer
Hire an electric or petrol-driven mixer when a large batch of mortar is required.

TEXTURED RENDERINGS

It is possible to use tools to texture rendering while it is still damp, but it is more usual to apply a coarse aggregate. This is a fairly skilled procedure (see below for details). Try to reproduce a texture when patch-repairing.

Roughcast rendering
For this rendering, mix aggregate no more than 9mm (⅜in) in size with the top-coat mortar. Add about half as much as the amount of sand used, with enough water for a sticky mix. Flick it on the wall to build up an even coat.

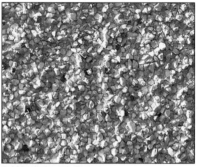

Pebble-dash rendering
Crushed-stone aggregate gives pebble dash its colour, and an even distribution of the chippings is necessary in order to avoid patchiness. A 9 to 12mm (⅜ to ½in) top coat is applied and the stones are thrown at it while it is soft, then pressed with a float to bed them in.

Tyrolean finish
A fine cement mix is sprayed from a hand-cranked 'Tyrolean machine' to build up a decorative texture over a dry undercoat rendering. Doors, windows, gutters and so on must be masked beforehand. Tyrolean machines may be hired.

Preparing the surface

Using a hammer and chisel, neatly chop away the old loose coating on areas of cracked or blistered rendering. Rake out the mortar joints in the exposed brickwork if necessary and brush the area down. Clean off any organic growth such as lichen or algae that may be present and apply a fungicide.

Work platform

Set up a safe work platform from which to do the rendering. You will need both hands free to use the tools, so it cannot be done from a ladder. Pairs of steps with a scaffold board between them can be used for working on ground-floor walls, but for upper walls you will need a scaffold tower.

Two-coat work

Set up 9mm (⅜in) vertical screed battens spaced no more than 900mm (3ft) apart, fixing them with masonry nails into the mortar joints of the brickwork. Check them for level and pack them out where necessary.

Apply undercoat rendering between two battens, using a firm pressure to make it bond well on to the dampened background. Build up the rendering to the thickness of the screed battens.

Level the mortar with a straightedge laid across the battens, working upward with a side-to-side movement, then scratch the surface of the mortar to provide a key for the top coat and leave it to set for a week.

You can fill in the panels between the battens in sequence or alternately. Allow the rendering to set before you remove the battens.

Apply top-coat rendering about 6mm (¼in) thick, either freehand or with the aid of screed battens as before. Use a straightedge for levelling the render, then finish it with a wooden float.

One-coat work

Set out 16mm (⅝in) vertical screed battens, spaced as for two-coat work. Apply the render to the brickwork in a single coat. Level the surface and allow the render to stiffen, then finish with a wooden float or texture the surface with a proprietary scraper, working it in a circular motion.

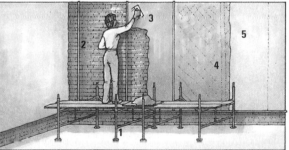

Patch repairs

Use a metal plasterer's trowel to apply the rendering and finish the top coat with a wooden float.

Take a trowelful of mortar from your hawk and spread it on the wall with an upward stroke, applying firm pressure (**1**). Level the surface of a one-coat render with a straightedge laid across the surfaces of the surrounding rendering and worked upward with a side-to-side motion. Finish with a float.

For two-coat work, build up the undercoat layer no more than two-thirds the thickness of the original rendering or 9mm (⅜in), whichever is the thinner.

Level the mortar with a straightedge that fits within the cut-out of the area being patched, then key the surface for the top coat (**2**). Leave the undercoat to set and strengthen for a few days.

Before applying the top coat, dampen the undercoat rendering to even out the suction. Finally, level the top coat with a straightedge and finish with a float.

Applying two-coat rendering
1 Set up a safe work platform.
2 Divide the wall with vertical screeds.
3 Apply the undercoat between all screeds or on alternate panels.
4 Remove screeds and fill in gaps or panels.
5 Apply top coat over keyed undercoat.

1 Use firm pressure

2 Key the surface

175

FLOORS: SUSPENDED FLOORS

Floor construction in the majority of buildings is based on timber beams known as joists. These are rectangular in section, placed on edge for maximum strength, usually about 400mm (1ft 4in) apart, and supported at the ends by the walls.

Such 'suspended floors' contrast with concrete 'solid floors' – supported over their whole area by the ground – which are usually to be found in basements and commonly at ground level in modern houses.

Traditional suspended floors are usually boarded with tongue-and-groove or plain-edged planks, though in modern houses flooring-grade chipboard is used on both types of floor.

Ground floors

The joists of a suspended ground floor are usually made from 100 x 50mm (4 x 2in) sawn softwood. Their ends and centre portions are nailed to lengths of 100 x 75mm (4 x 3in) softwood called wall plates that distribute the load from the joists to the walls, which support the weight of the floor.

In older houses, various methods were employed for supporting the wall plates. At one time it was common for the ends of the joists to be slotted into the walls and set on wall plates that were built into the brickwork.

Alternatively, the brickwork was formed so as to provide ledges – known as offsets – to support the wall plates. However, when the damp-proof courses laid beneath the wall plates broke down, the wood was affected by penetrating and rising damp in the brickwork. As a result, such floor timbers frequently suffer from decay.

The relatively lightweight joists tend to sag in the middle and are therefore usually supported by additional wall plates set on three or four courses of honeycombed brickwork known as sleeper walls. The spaces left in the brickwork allow air to circulate under the floor. Sleeper walls are usually spaced at intervals of about 2m (6ft), and are sometimes used to support the ends of the joists.

Beneath a fireplace in a room with a suspended floor will be found a solid brick wall, built to the same height as the sleeper walls. It retains and supports the concrete hearth. This fender wall carries a wall plate along its top edge to support the ends of the floor joists that run up to it.

UPPER FLOORS

The first-floor joists and those of other upper floors can be supported only at their ends, so they are usually laid in the direction of the shortest span. Also, as they can have no intermediate support, such joists are made deeper to give them greater rigidity. These 'bridging joists' are usually 50mm (2in) thick, but their depth will be determined by the distance they must span. The joists supporting the floor of an average-size upper room would be about 225mm (9in) deep.

Where floor joists cannot run right through – as around a fireplace or at a stairway opening – a thicker joist is used to bear the extra load of the short joists. This load is transferred to the thicker joist by crosspieces jointed at right angles (see left). The thicker joist is known as a 'trimming joist', the short ones parallel to it are 'trimmed joists' and the crosspieces joining them together are known as 'trimmers'.

In older properties the upstairs joists may be supported on wall plates which are built into solid walls; the problems of damp and decay are less critical here. With modern cavity-wall construction the ends of the joists may also be built in, but in this case they rest directly on the inner skin of blockwork. The joist-ends should not project into the cavity itself, and they must be treated with a preserver to guard against the risk of timber decay.

Components of the first floor

1 Joists
2 Trimming joist
3 Trimmed joist
4 Trimmer
5 Herringbone strutting

Components of the ground floor

6 Oversite concrete
7 Sleeper walls
8 Wall plate
9 Fender wall
10 Floor joists

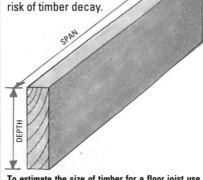

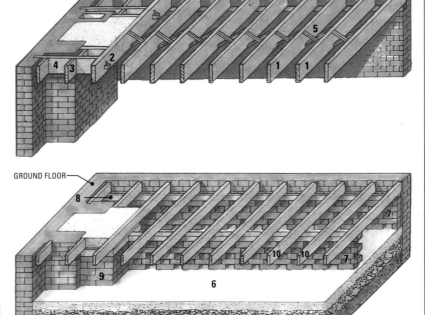

FIRST FLOOR

GROUND FLOOR

To estimate the size of timber for a floor joist use the following rule of thumb as a guide.

Depth in units of 25mm (1in) =

$$\frac{\text{Span of joist in units of 300mm (1ft)}}{2} + 2$$

Examples:

Metric.

Joists span 3m divided by 300mm = 10 units

$$\frac{10 \text{ units}}{2} + 2 = 5 + 2 = 7 \text{ units} \times 25\text{mm} = 175\text{mm}$$

Imperial.

$$\frac{\text{Joist span 10ft}}{2} + 2 = 5 + 2 = 7 \text{inches}$$

BRACING FLOORS

For extra stiffness the joists of an upper floor are braced with 'solid strutting' – solid sections of timber nailed between them **(1)** – or with diagonal wooden braces called 'herringbone strutting' **(2)**.

The traditional herringbone strutting, of 50 x 25mm (2 x 1in) softwood, is preferable because it can compensate for timber shrinkage. Folded wedges or packing blocks are placed in line with the strutting between the outer joists and the walls to keep the joints tight.

Modern herringbone strutting is carried out with ready-made metal units **(3)** which are usually equipped with a drilled flange at each end for nailing to joists set at 400, 450 or 600mm (1ft 4in, 1ft 6in or 2ft) centres.

A solid ground floor is essentially a concrete slab laid on a sub-stratum of coarse rubble, or hardcore. To lay such a floor the topsoil is first removed and the hardcore then laid to consolidate the ground and level up the site. The rough surface of the hardcore is filled (blinded) with a thin layer of sand which is rolled flat. This sand layer prevents the cement draining out of the concrete and into the hardcore, which would cause the concrete to be weakened.

The concrete slab is usually about 100 to 150mm (4 to 6in) thick and is either laid over or covered by a continuous layer of moisture-resistant material, the damp-proof membrane, or DPM. This membrane may be a thick sheet of polyethylene or the more traditional liquid coating of asphalt or bituminous material. However it is laid, the DPM must be joined to the damp-proof course (DPC) set in the walls.

A concrete raft foundation can either form a solid floor on which the walls are built, or, where strip or trench foundations are used, the slab can be laid over the ground contained within the brickwork walls.

The floor must first be covered with a smooth screed of sand and cement before it can be overlaid with a floorcovering. When the DPM is below the concrete slab the screed can be 44mm (1¾in) thick, but when a membrane is laid over the slab the screed should be at least 63mm (2½in) in thickness.

A suspended solid floor is a recent type that uses precast concrete beams set on sleeper walls at DPC level and infilled with concrete blocks.

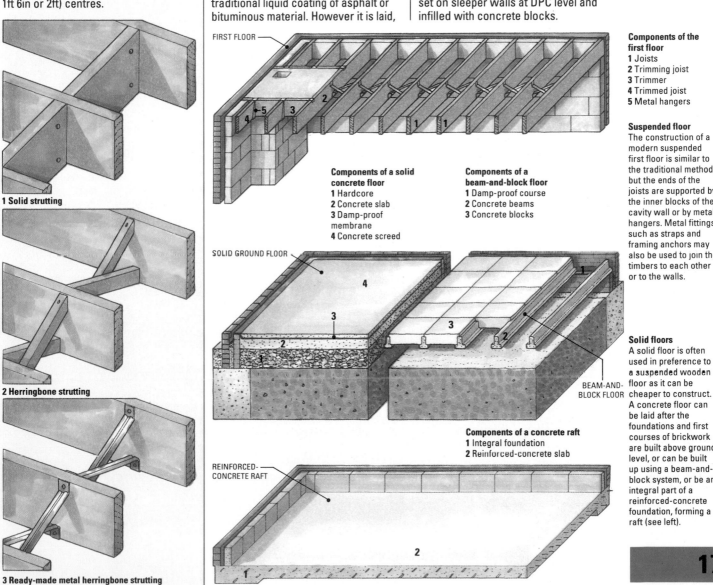

1 Solid strutting

2 Herringbone strutting

3 Ready-made metal herringbone strutting

FIRST FLOOR

Components of the first floor
1 Joists
2 Trimming joist
3 Trimmer
4 Trimmed joist
5 Metal hangers

Suspended floor
The construction of a modern suspended first floor is similar to the traditional method, but the ends of the joists are supported by the inner blocks of the cavity wall or by metal hangers. Metal fittings such as straps and framing anchors may also be used to join the timbers to each other or to the walls.

Components of a solid concrete floor
1 Hardcore
2 Concrete slab
3 Damp-proof membrane
4 Concrete screed

Components of a beam-and-block floor
1 Damp-proof course
2 Concrete beams
3 Concrete blocks

SOLID GROUND FLOOR

BEAM-AND-BLOCK FLOOR

Solid floors
A solid floor is often used in preference to a suspended wooden floor as it can be cheaper to construct. A concrete floor can be laid after the foundations and first courses of brickwork are built above ground level, or can be built up using a beam-and-block system, or be an integral part of a reinforced-concrete foundation, forming a raft (see left).

Components of a concrete raft
1 Integral foundation
2 Reinforced-concrete slab

REINFORCED-CONCRETE RAFT

177

METAL FITTINGS FOR FLOORS

Floor construction is one of the many areas in which modern builders have been able to substitute the use of factory-made fittings for traditional methods of construction.

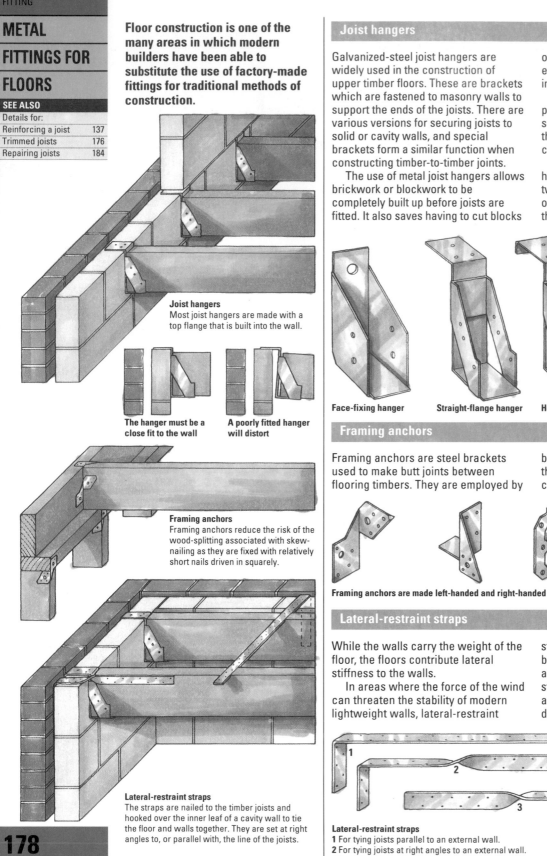

Joist hangers
Most joist hangers are made with a top flange that is built into the wall.

The hanger must be a close fit to the wall

A poorly fitted hanger will distort

Framing anchors
Framing anchors reduce the risk of the wood-splitting associated with skew-nailing as they are fixed with relatively short nails driven in squarely.

Lateral-restraint straps
The straps are nailed to the timber joists and hooked over the inner leaf of a cavity wall to tie the floor and walls together. They are set at right angles to, or parallel with, the line of the joists.

Joist hangers

Galvanized-steel joist hangers are widely used in the construction of upper timber floors. These are brackets which are fastened to masonry walls to support the ends of the joists. There are various versions for securing joists to solid or cavity walls, and special brackets form a similar function when constructing timber-to-timber joints.

The use of metal joist hangers allows brickwork or blockwork to be completely built up before joists are fitted. It also saves having to cut blocks or bricks in order to infill between the ends of joists that are built into the inner leaf of a wall.

The hangers should be fitted properly, with the top flange sitting squarely on the bricks or blocks, and the rear face of the bracket fitting closely against the face of the masonry.

The ends of the joists are fixed into hangers with 32mm (1¼in) sherardized twisted nails or plasterboard nails, one or two being driven through the holes in the side gussets.

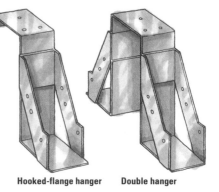

Face-fixing hanger   **Straight-flange hanger**   **Hooked-flange hanger**   **Double hanger**

Framing anchors

Framing anchors are steel brackets used to make butt joints between flooring timbers. They are employed by builders to fix trimmed joists to save them having to cut complicated time-consuming joints.

Framing anchors are made left-handed and right-handed

Lateral-restraint straps

While the walls carry the weight of the floor, the floors contribute lateral stiffness to the walls.

In areas where the force of the wind can threaten the stability of modern lightweight walls, lateral-restraint straps are used to provide ties between the walls and the floor. They are simply rigid strips of galvanized steel that are perforated for nail fixing and bent in various ways to suit the direction of the floor joists.

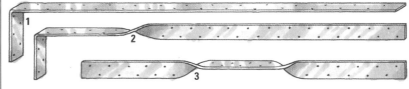

Lateral-restraint straps
1 For tying joists parallel to an external wall.
2 For tying joists at right angles to an external wall.
3 For tying joists on either side of an internal wall.

BOARDED
SOLID FLOORS

Most floorcoverings, including woodblock flooring, can be bonded directly to a dry, smooth, screeded floor, but floorboards cannot be directly bonded and so must be fixed by other means.

The boards are nailed down to 50 x 50mm (2 x 2in) softwood battens, or bearers. These battens are embedded in the concrete while it is wet or are fixed to metal clips which are already implanted in the concrete. In either case the timber must be treated with a wood preserver. A damp-proof membrane (DPM) must be incorporated, usually in the form of a continuous coat of bituminous material sandwiched within the slab.

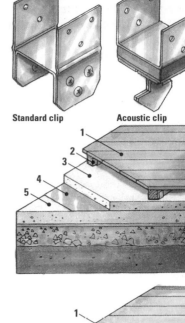

Standard clip   **Acoustic clip**

The clip method

This means of fixing requires the slab to be level and relatively smooth. The flanges of the clips are pressed into the surface of the concrete before it sets, while a marked guide batten is used to space the clips and align them in rows. The rows are normally set 400mm (1ft 4in) apart to centres, starting 50mm (2in) from one wall. When the concrete is completely dry the 'ears' of the clips are raised from their folded position with a claw hammer. The battens, having been cut to length and their ends treated with a preserver, are nailed in place through the holes in the clips. The boards are nailed to the battens.

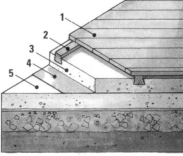

1 Clip method
Composition of floor
1 Floorboards
2 Clipped battens
3 Concrete screed
4 DPM
5 Concrete slab

Embedded battens

These are splayed in section so as to key into the concrete slab. Again, the slab is built up in two layers with the DPM sandwiched between them. Before the top layer or screed is laid, the treated battens are positioned at 400mm (1ft 4in) centres and levelled on dabs of concrete. Strips of wood are nailed across them temporarily to hold them in position. When the dabs of concrete are set and the battens firmly held, the wood strips are removed and the top layer of concrete is poured and compacted. It is levelled with a rule that is notched to fit over the battens. As the rule is drawn along the battens, it finishes the concrete 12mm (½in) below their top edges. When the concrete layer is fully dry the boards are nailed on the battens in the conventional way.

2 Embedded battens
Composition of floor
1 Floorboards
2 Embedded battens
3 Concrete screed
: DPM
5 Concrete slab

Chipboard floating floor

Flooring-grade chipboard is a relatively recent innovation as a material for boarding over a solid floor. It is quicker and cheaper to lay than a floor made of boards. Chipboard flooring is also more stable and it can be laid without being fixed to the concrete slab.

This technique produces a floor of the type known as a 'floating floor'. The simplest floor of this kind is laid with 18mm (¾in) tongue-and-groove chipboard, either the standard grade or the moisture-resistant type.

First a sheet of insulating material such as rigid polystyrene or fibreboard is laid on the concrete slab; then a vapour barrier of polyethylene sheet is laid above the polystyrene. The vapour barrier must be a continuous sheet, with its edges turned up and trapped behind the skirting boards. The chipboard, glued edge to edge, is then laid on the vapour barrier.

The chipboard flooring is held in place by its own weight and by the skirting boards, which are nailed to the walls round its edges. The skirting boards also cover a 9mm (⅜in) gap between the chipboard and the walls, allowing for expansion across the floor.

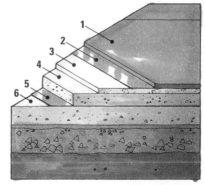

3 Chipboard floating floor
1 Chipboard flooring
2 Vapour barrier
3 Polystyrene insulation
4 Concrete screed
5 DPM
6 Concrete Slab

Battened floating floor

Battens can be incorporated in a floating floor. Lengths of 50 x 50mm (2 x 2in) softwood, treated with a preserver, are spaced at 400mm (1ft 4in) intervals for 18mm (¾in) chipboard; for heavy-gauge 22mm (⅞in) material they are spaced 600mm (2ft) apart. A quilt-type sheet of insulating material is laid on the concrete slab, then covered with a polyethylene vapour barrier. The battens are positioned on the insulation, held together temporarily with strips of wood nailed across them. Tongue-and-groove chipboard is laid at right angles to the battens and glued at the edges before it is nailed down.

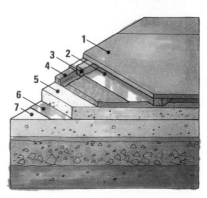

4 Battened floating floor
1 Chipboard flooring
2 Vapour barrier
3 Battens
4 Insulation
5 Concrete screed
6 DPM
7 Concrete slab

FLOORING

Flooring is the general term used to describe the boarding which is laid over the floor's structural elements – the timber floor joists or the concrete slab. This boarding consists of hardwood or softwood planks, or man-made boards.

Floorboards

Floorboards are usually made from softwoods and sold planed all round (PAR) with square or tongue-and-groove edges. Standard sizes are specified as 125 x 25mm (5 x 1in) or 150 x 25mm (6 x1in) nominal.

However, boards as narrow as 75mm (3in) and others as wide as 280mm (11in) may be found in some houses. The narrow boards produce superior floors because they make any movement due to shrinkage less noticeable. Installation costs are high, and consequently they tend to be used in more expensive houses only. Hardwoods, such as oak or maple, are also used for high-grade flooring but are even more costly.

The best floorboards are quarter sawn (1) from the log, a method that diminishes distortion due to shrinkage. However, since this method is wasteful of timber, boards are more often cut tangentially (2) for reasons of economy. Boards cut in this way tend to bow, or 'cup', across their width and they should be fixed with the concave side facing upwards, as there is a tendency for the grain of the other side to splinter. The cut of a board – tangential or quarter cut – can be checked by looking at the annual-growth rings on the end grain.

The joint on tongue-and-groove boards is not at the centre of their edges but closer to one face, and these boards should be laid with the offset joint nearer to the joist. Though tongue-and-groove boards are nominally the same sizes as square-edged boards, the edge joint reduces their floor coverage by about 12mm (½in) per board.

In some old buildings you may find floorboards bearing the marks left by an adze on their undersides. Such old boards have usually been trimmed to a required thickness only where they sit over the joists.

1 Quarter-sawn boards
Shrinkage does not distort these boards

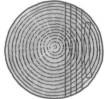

2 Tangentially sawn boards
Shrinkage can cause these boards to 'cup'

Types of flooring
1 Square-edged softwood board
2 T & G softwood board
3 Square-edged chipboard
4 T & G chipboard
5 Square-edged plywood
6 T & G plywood
7 Square-edged MDF

SHEET FLOORING

Softwood and hardwood boards not only provide a tough flooring; when sealed and polished they will also take on an attractive colour. Sheet materials such as flooring-grade plywood or particle boards are merely functional, however, and are usually used as a sub-base for other floor surfaces.

Plywood
Any exterior-grade plywood – known as WPB bonded plywood – can be used for flooring. Those sold as flooring-grade boards are square-edged or tongued and grooved on all four edges.

Plywood flooring laid directly over the joists should be 16 to 18mm (⅝ to ¾in) thick, though boards laid over an existing floor surface (to level it or to provide an underlay for tiles) can be 6 to 12mm (¼ to ½in) in thickness. Plywood floors are laid in the same way as chipboard ones.

Chipboard
Chipboard is a commonly available particle board made from bonded chips of wood. Only proper flooring-grade chipboard, which is compressed to a higher density than standard material, should be used for flooring. It is available in square-edged and tongue-and-groove boards. The square-edged boards measure 2.4 x 1.22m (8 x 4ft) and are 18mm (¾in) thick. Tongue-and-groove boards are available in two grades: flooring-standard and moisture-resistant. Both grades come in sheets measuring 2.4m x 600mm (8 x 2ft) and 22mm (⅞in) thick. The moisture-resistant type should always be used where damp conditions may occur, such as in bathrooms or kitchens.

The 18mm (¾in) thick boards are suitable for laying on joists spaced no more than 400mm (1ft 4in) apart. Where the joists are at 600mm (2ft) intervals, 22mm (⅞in) boarding should be used.

Medium-density fibreboard
Medium-density fibreboard (MDF) is a dense sheet material made from fine compressed wood fibres. It is produced in standard, moisture-resistant and exterior grades, and is suitable for flooring where a plain, smooth finish is required. Available in 2.4 x 1.22m (8 x 4ft) square-edged sheets in a wide range of thicknesses, it is more expensive than chipboard.

TONGUE-AND-GROOVE BOARDING

Check whether your floorboards are tongued and grooved by trying to push a knife into the gap between them.

To lift a tongue-and-groove board it is necessary first to cut through the tongue on each side of the board. Saw carefully along the line of the joint with a dovetail or tenon saw (1) held at a shallow angle. A straight wooden batten temporarily nailed along the edge of the floorboard may help you to keep the saw on a straight line.

With the tongue cut through, saw across the board and lift it as you would a plain square-edged one.

If the original flooring has been 'secret nailed' (2), use lost-head nails (3) to fix the boards back in place and conceal the nail heads with a matching wood filler.

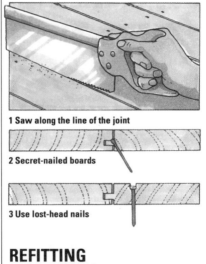

1 Saw along the line of the joint

2 Secret-nailed boards

3 Use lost-head nails

REFITTING A CUT BOARD

The butted ends of floorboards normally meet over a joist (1). A board that has been cut flush with the side of a joist must be supported from below when it is replaced (2).

Cut a piece of 50 x 50mm (2 x 2in) softwood and screw it to the side of the joist, flush with the top edge. Screw the end of the floorboard to the support.

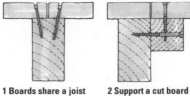

1 Boards share a joist   **2 Support a cut board**

Floorboarding is produced in lengths that are intended to run from wall to wall. In practice this rarely happens because odd, shorter lengths are often laid to save on materials. When lifting floorboards, start with these shorter pieces if possible. In many older homes one or two boards will probably have been lifted already for access to services.

Square-edged boards

Tap the blade of a bolster into the gap between the boards close to the cut end (1). Lever up the edge of the board, but try not to crush the one next to it. Fit the bolster into the gap at the other side of the board and repeat the procedure.

Ease the end of the board up in this way, then work the claw of a hammer under it until there is room to slip a cold chisel under the board (2). Lift the next pair of nails, proceeding in the same fashion along the board until it is free.

1 Lever up board with bolster chisel

2 Place cold chisel under board

Lifting a continuous board

Floorboards are nailed in place before the skirting boards are fixed, so the ends of a continuous board are trapped under them. You will have to cut the board in half before you can lift it.

Prise up the centre of the floorboard with a bolster until you can slip a cold chisel under it to keep it bowed. Remove the nails and, with a tenon saw, cut through the board (1) over the centre of the joist. You can then lift the two halves of the board, using the method described above.

A board that is too stiff to be bowed upwards, or is tongued and grooved, will have to be sawn *in situ*. This means cutting it flush with the side of the joist instead of over its centre.

Locate the side of the joist by passing the blade of a padsaw (2) vertically into the gaps on both sides of the board (the joints of tongue-and-grooved boards will also have to be cut beforehand). Mark both edges of the board where the blade stops, and draw a line between these points representing the side of the joist. Make an access slot for the padsaw blade by drilling three or four 3mm (⅛in) diameter holes close together near one end of the line marked across the surface.

Work the tip of the blade into the hole and start making the cut with short strokes. Gradually tilt the blade to a shallow angle to avoid cutting into any cables or pipes that may be hidden below. Lever up the board with a bolster chisel as described above.

Freeing the end of a board

To release the end of a floorboard that is trapped under the skirting, lift the board until it is almost vertical, then pull it straight out of the gap between the skirting and the joist (1).

A floorboard that runs beneath a partition wall must be cut close to the skirting before you can raise it (2). Drill an access hole so that you can insert the blade of a padsaw. Alternatively, you can hire a special saw (3) that can be used for cutting floorboards. It has a curved cutting edge that allows you to saw through a board without lifting it completely.

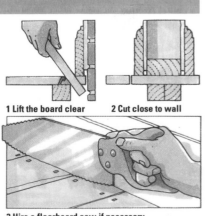

1 Lift the board clear   **2 Cut close to wall**

3 Hire a floorboard saw if necessary

1 Saw across the board

2 Find the joist's side

RE-LAYING
A FLOOR

Though floors take more wear and tear than any other interior surface, it is usually fire damage, timber decay – which would also affect the joists – or simply large gaps in the boarding caused by shrinkage that require the floor to be re-laid, or even entirely renewed.

If the floor is to be renewed, measure the room and buy your materials in advance. Leave floorboards or sheet materials to acclimatize – ideally in the room where they are to be laid – for at least a week before fixing.

Removing the flooring

To lift the complete flooring you must first remove the skirting boards from the walls. If you intend to re-lay the boards, number them with chalk before starting to raise them. Lift the first few boards as described, starting from one side of the room, then prise up the remainder by working a bolster chisel between the joists and the undersides of the boards. When lifting tongue-and-groove boards, carefully ease them up two or three at a time to avoid breaking the joints, then pull them apart.

Pull all the nails out of the boards and joists, and scrape any accumulated dirt from the tops of the joists. Clean the edges of the boards similarly if they are to be reused. Check all timbers for rot or insect infestation and treat or repair them as required.

● **Closing gaps**
You can re-lay floorboards without removing all the boards at once. Lift and renail about six boards at a time as you work across the floor. Finally cut and fit a new board to fill the last gap.

Laying floorboards
Working from a platform of loose boards, proceed in the following order.
1 Fix the first board parallel to the wall.
2 Cut and lay up to six boards, clamp them together and nail.
3 Lay the next group of boards in the same way, continue across the floor and cut the last board to fit.

Laying new floorboards

Though these instructions describe the fixing of tongue-and-groove boarding, the basic method applies equally to square-edged floorboarding.

First lay a few loose floorboards together to act as a work platform. Measure the width or the length of the room – whichever is at right angles to the joists – and cut your boards to stop 9mm (⅜in) short of the walls at each end. Lay four to six boards at a time.

Where two shorter floorboards are to be butted end to end, cut them so that the joint will be centred over a joist, but it pays to arrange several boards so that you are not left with butt joints occurring side by side.

Fix the first board with its grooved edge no more than 9mm (⅜in) from the wall and nail it in place with cut floor brads or lost-head nails that are at least twice as long as the thickness of the board.

Place the nails in pairs, one about 25mm (1in) from each edge of the board and centred on the joists. Use a nail punch to drive them about 2mm (¹⁄₁₆in) below the surface. When 'secret nailing', drive nails diagonally through the tongued edge instead.

Lay the other cut boards in place and clamp them up to the fixed one so as to close the edge joints. Special floorboard cramps can be hired for this, but wedges cut from 400mm (1ft 4in) offcuts of board will work just as well (**1**). To clamp the boards with wedges, temporarily nail another floorboard just less than a board's width away from them. Insert pairs of wedges in the gap, resting on every fourth or fifth joist, and with two hammers tap the wedges toward each other. Nail the clamped floorboards in place as before, then remove the wedges and repeat the procedure with the next group of boards, continuing in this way across the room.

At the far wall, cut the last board to fit by removing the tongued edge. It should be cut to leave a gap equal to the width of the tongue or 9mm (⅜in), whichever is less. If you cannot slide the groove onto the tongue, cut away the bottom section of the grooved edge so that it will drop into place (**2**).

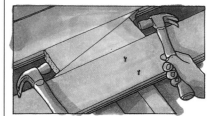

1 Make wedges to clamp boards

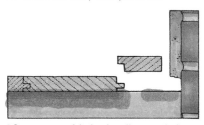

2 Cut away part of the last board's grooved edge

FLOORBOARD CRAMP

This special tool automatically grips the joist over which it is placed by means of two toothed cams. A screw-operated ram applies pressure to the floorboards when the tommy bar is turned.

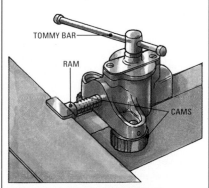

Hire a special cramp to re-lay floorboards

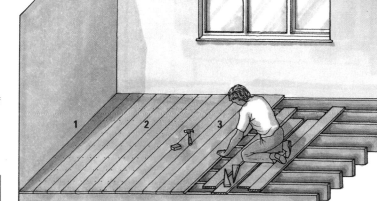

For a floor that is going to be invisible beneath some kind of covering – vinyl, cork, fitted carpet or whatever – chipboard is an excellent material. It can be laid relatively quickly and is much cheaper than an equivalent amount of timber flooring. It comes square-edged or tongued and grooved. Each has its own laying technique.

CUTTING TO FIT

Square-edged boards
The widths of the boards may have to be cut down (1) so that their long edges will butt on the joists' centre lines.

Tongue-and-groove boards
Only the last boards need cutting in order to fit against the wall (2).

1 Square-edged boards   2 T&G boards

Square-edged boards

All the edges of square-edged sheet flooring must be supported. Lay the boards with their long edges along the joists and nail 75 x 50mm (3 x 2in) softwood noggings between the joists to support the ends of the boards. The noggings against the wall can be inserted in advance; those supporting joints between boards must be nailed into place as the boards are laid.

Start with a full-length board in one corner and lay a row of boards the length of the room, cutting the last one to fit as required. Leave an expansion gap of about 9mm (⅜in) between the outer edges of the boards and the walls. The boards' inner edges should fall on the centre line of a joist. If necessary cut the boards to width, but remove the waste from the edges closest to the wall, preserving the machine-cut edges to make neat butt joints with the next row of boards. Nail down the boards, using 50mm (2in) ring-shank nails spaced about 300mm (1ft) apart along the joists and noggings. Place the nails about 18mm (¾in) from the board edges.

Cut and lay the remainder of the boards with the end joints staggered on alternate rows.

Tongue-and-groove boards

Tongue-and-groove boards are laid with their long edges running across the joists. Noggings are required only to support the outer edges close to the walls. The ends of the boards are supported by joists.

Working from one corner, lay the first board with its grooved edges about 9mm (⅜in) from the walls and nail it in place. Apply PVA wood adhesive to the joint along the end of the first board, then lay the next one in the row. Knock it up to the first board with a hammer for a good close joint, protecting the edge with a piece of scrap wood. Nail the board down as before, then wipe any surplus adhesive from the surface before it sets, using a damp rag.

Continue in this way across the floor, gluing all of the joints as you go. Cut boards to fit at the ends of rows or to fall on the centre of a joist, and stagger end joints on alternate rows.

Finally, fit the skirting boards, which will cover the expansion gaps around the perimeter of the floor.

If you wish to, you can seal the surface of the chipboard with two coats of clear polyurethane varnish to protect it from dirt.

1 Square-edged boards
Lay the boards with their long edges resting on a joist and their ends supported by noggings.

2 Tongue-and-groove boards
Lay boards crosswise with their ends falling on a joist.

1 Arrangement for laying square-edged boards

2 Arrangement for laying T&G boards

FLOOR JOISTS

Fitting services
1 Make holes for cables within the red line.
2 Place notches for pipes within red area

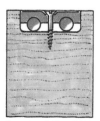

Accommodating pipes
Drill and saw notches for pipes and cover them with a protector.

Repairing a joist
The stages for replacing a joist are combined in the illustration.
1 Cut away old joist.
2 Cut out wall plate.
3 Fit new wall plate.
4 Cut and fit new joist and brace the joint with bolted joist timbers.

As all floor joists are loadbearing, their size and spacing in new structures must satisfy a Building Control Officer. However, for most domestic repairs calculations are not usually necessary – matching new timber for old should suffice.

Use 'structurally graded' timber, which has been expertly examined or machine-tested. SS is the grade mark of 'special structural timber', used for joists; GS, 'general structural timber', is for general framing as well as joists. Purple colour-coded MSS and green MGS denote machine-graded timber to the same specification.

Fitting services

Service runs like heating pipes and electric cables can run in the void below a suspended ground floor, but those running at right angles to the joists in upper floors must pass through the joists, which are covered by flooring above and a ceiling below.

So as not to weaken the structure, bore holes for cables through the centre of a joist, or at least 50mm (2in) below the top edge to clear floor nails. Try to place the holes within the middle two-thirds of the joist's length **(1)**.

Notches for pipe runs in the top edge should ideally be no deeper than one-eighth the depth of the joist and within a quarter of the joist's length at each end **(2)**. Make a notch by drilling through the joist, then saw down to the hole.

Repairing joists

Floor joists which have been seriously attacked by wet rot, dry rot or insect infestation have to be cut out and replaced. Such attack usually occurs at ground-floor level because of its proximity to the damp soil. If the damage is extensive, or the upper floors are also affected, you should call in an expert to do the job. However, if it is localized and not too serious you can probably deal with it yourself.

Remove the skirtings and lift the floorboards over the infected area until you reach a sleeper wall. Test the condition of the wood – joists, floorboards and skirting boards – by spiking it with a sharp knife. If the blade penetrates easily the wood will have to be replaced. Sound wood can be treated with chemical preserver to kill rot spores or woodworm larvae.

Preparation

The damp conditions which have caused the outbreak of wet or dry rot must themselves be identified and corrected before any remedial work on the timbers is carried out.

All infected timbers must be removed in an area extending at least 450mm (1ft 6in) beyond the last visible signs of attack, and all surrounding masonry must be treated with a fungicide. Burn all the infected timber. The following assumes that the end of a joist and perhaps also the wall plate are affected.

Saw through and remove the infected end of the joist, cutting it back to the centre of the nearest sleeper wall. If the wall plate which has been supporting the joist is also affected, cut it away. If the wall plate is built into the brickwork, drill a series of holes into its edge and finish cutting it away with a wood chisel and mallet, trimming the remaining ends square. Wall plates on sleeper walls can be cut with a saw.

Replacement

Cut a new length of wall-plate timber to fill the gap and treat it thoroughly with wood preserver.

If the original mortar bed joint and damp-proof course are undamaged, apply a coating of liquid bituminous damp-proofing over it and put the new section of wall plate into place.

If necessary, re-lay the bed joint and insert a new length of DPC, making sure that its ends overlap the ends of the old one, if present, by at least 150mm (6in). Then reseat the wall plate.

Now cut a length of new joist to sit on the repaired wall plate and meet the cut end of the old joist on the sleeper wall. Treat it well with timber preserver. To ensure that it is level with the other joists, trim its underside or pack it with DPC felt.

Brace the joint with two 900mm (3ft) lengths of joist timber – also treated – on each side and bolt through with four coach bolts and two timber connectors for each bolt.

Finally, replace all the floorboards and skirtings.

FITTING JOIST HANGERS

Sections of infected wall plate which have had to be removed can be replaced with metal joist hangers to support the ends of the repaired joists.

Having removed the damaged joist and section of wall plates (see above), lay bricks in the resulting slot. Before laying the mortar, check on the condition of the DPC and reinforce it with an extra layer of DPC felt or a liquid damp-proofing material if you think it necessary.

Set the flange of the joist hanger in mortar at the required level, then allow the mortar to harden before fitting the new section of joist as indicated above.

SKIRTINGS

Skirtings are protective 'kick boards', usually moulded to form a decorative border between the floor and walls. Modern skirtings are relatively small and simply formed, with a rounded or bevelled top edge.

Skirtings found in older houses can be as much as 300mm (1ft) wide and quite elaborately moulded, but those in most homes are about 175mm (7in) wide and of 'ovolo' or 'torus' design. These can still be bought from timber merchants. Some will supply more elaborate designs to special order. Skirtings can be nailed directly on to plastered brickwork or to battens, known as 'grounds', which have been fixed during the plastering stage. Skirting boards on partition walls are nailed to timber studs.

Removing the skirting

Remove a skirting by levering it away from the wall with a crowbar or bolster chisel. Where a skirting butts against a door architrave or an external corner it can be levered off easily enough, but a continuous length whose ends are mitred into internal corners may have to be cut before it can be removed.

Tap the blade of the bolster between the skirting and the wall, and lever the top edge away sufficiently to insert the chisel end of the crowbar behind it. Place a thin strip of wood behind the crowbar to protect the wall, then tap the bolster in again a little to one side, working along the skirting in this way as the nails loosen until the board is free.

With the board removed, pull the nails out through the back of the skirting to avoid splitting the face.

Cutting a long skirting

A long stretch of skirting may bend sufficiently for you to cut it in place. Lever it away at its centre and insert blocks of wood (1), one on each side of the proposed cut, to hold the board about 25mm (1in) from the wall.

Make a vertical cut with a panel saw held at about 45 degrees to the face of the board (2) and work with short strokes, using the tip of the saw.

1 Prise skirting away from wall and pack out

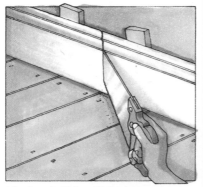

2 Cut through skirting with tip of saw

Fitting new skirting

A damaged skirting should be restored if possible, particularly if it is an unusual moulding for which there is no modern replacement; otherwise you could try making one up yourself from various moulded sections (see right). Standard mouldings are readily available.

Measure the length of each wall, bearing in mind that most skirtings are mitred at the corners.

Mark the length on the plain bottom edge of the skirting board, mark a 45-degree angle for the mitre, and extend the marked line across the face of the board, using a try square. Clamp the board on edge in a vice and carefully saw down the line at that angle.

Sometimes moulded skirting boards are scribed and butt-jointed at internal corners. To achieve the required profile, cut the end off one board at 45 degrees as for a mitre joint (1) and, with a coping saw, cut along the contour line on the moulded face so that it will 'jig-saw' with its neighbour (2).

Fix skirting boards with cut-clasp nails or masonry nails when nailing to brickwork, but use lost-head nails when attaching a skirting to wooden grounds or stud partitions.

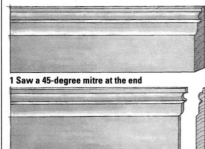

1 Saw a 45-degree mitre at the end

2 Cut the shape following the contour line

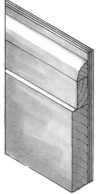

Making a skirting
If you are unable to buy a length of skirting to match your original, have one machined specially or make one up from various sections of wood.

SKIRTING MOULDINGS

Most standard skirting mouldings are made in softwood ready for painting. Hardwood is not so common and is usually reserved for special decorative skirtings. Hardwoods are coated with a clear finish. 'Moulded-reverse' skirtings are machined with a different profile on each side of the board.

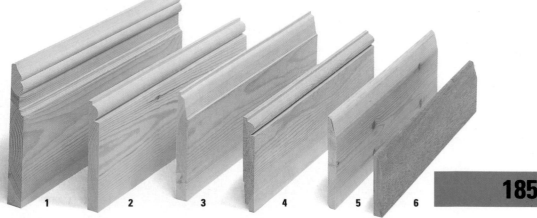

Selection of skirting mouldings
1 Bolection mould skirting **2** Torus skirting
3 Ovolo skirting **4** Torus/ovolo reverse skirting
5 Bevelled/rounded reverse skirting **6** Bevelled hardwood skirting

185

● **Damp-proof membrane**
A continuous DPM of polyethylene can be inserted beneath the concrete slab (see right) or it can be placed between the slab and screed, in which case the screed should be at least 65mm (2½in) thick. Alternatively, apply a thick mastic DPC on top of the concrete; this can be in the form of a bituminous flooring adhesive.

REPAIRING A CONCRETE FLOOR

Concrete floors sometimes shrink and crack. Usually it is only the screed that has cracked and it can be repaired easily, but a cracked floor that is also uneven may be a sign of settlement in the sub-base and you should have it checked by a surveyor or by a Building Control Officer, who will advise you on what steps to take.

Filling a crack
Clean all dirt and loose material out of the crack and, if necessary, open up narrow parts with a cold chisel to allow better penetration of the filler.

Prime the crack with a solution of 1 part bonding agent : 5 parts water and let it dry. Make a filler of 3 parts sand : 1 part cement mixed with equal parts of bonding agent and water, or use a ready-mixed quick-setting cement. Apply the filler with a trowel, pressing it thoroughly into the crack.

Laying pipes in a concrete floor
House conversions or installations like central heating sometimes call for pipework to be run across a room. If the floor is solid that means either running it round the walls or setting it into the concrete. Although the latter method was common practice for plumbing, water bylaws now stipulate that pipes must not be embedded in a solid-concrete wall or floor. However, it is possible to conceal pipes in internal partition walls provided the water can be turned off in the event of a leak.

Another way to comply with these requirements is to run pipes inside moulded-plastic ducting laid in the solid floor. A plywood or a chipboard cover panel is screwed to the lipping of the duct to finish flush with the floor after the pipework has been fitted and tested. Any decorative floorcovering should ideally be loose-fitted or detailed to provide easy access.

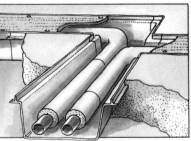

Plastic ducting for floor-run pipes

A suspended timber floor which has been seriously damaged by rot or insect infestation can be replaced with a solid concrete floor, provided the space below it needs no more than 600mm (2ft) of infill material. If it requires more, a concrete floor would be liable to damage through settlement of the infill, so a new suspended floor would have to be fitted.

Before taking any action consult your local Building Control Officer, because the converting of one floor can affect the ventilation of another and insulation may also be required.

If the work involves the electrical supply main or the supply pipes for gas or water you should check with the appropriate authority.

Wiring and heating pipes should be rerun before the infill is laid.

Preparing the ground

Strip out and burn all the old infected timbers and remove the door of the room. Treat the ground and all the surrounding masonry thoroughly with a strong fungicide. Fill in any recesses in the walls left by the timbers with bricks and mortar.

Mark the walls with a levelled chalk line to indicate the finished floor level, making allowance for the floorcovering if you intend to use a thick material such as quarry tiles or wood blocks. About 50mm (2in) below this line, mark another one, the space between them representing the thickness of the screed. Then mark a third chalk line a further 100mm (4in) down, indicating the thickness of the slab, followed by an allowance for 50mm (2in) thick polystyrene insulation board.

The infill

Lay the infill material to the required depth in layers of no more than 225mm (9in) at a time, compacting each layer thoroughly and breaking larger pieces with a sledgehammer **(1)**. You can use brick and tile rubble or, better still, gravel rejects (coarse stones from quarry waste). If you are using second-hand rubble, discard any fragments of plaster (which can react unfavourably with cement) and pieces of wood.

Bring the surface up to within 25mm (1in) of the chalk line for the insulation and 'blind' the surface with a layer of sand, tamped or rolled flat.

Spread a polyethylene damp-proof membrane of 1000-gauge (0.010in) minimum thickness over the surface of the sand, turning its edges up all round and lapping it up the walls to form a tray. Make neat folds at the corners and hold them temporarily in place with paper clips. If the floor needs more than one sheet of polyethylene to cover it, the sheets must overlap by at least 200mm (8in) and the joints should be sealed with a special waterproof tape available from builders' merchants.

1 Preparing the ground
Mark the walls with chalk lines for the finished floor level, thickness of the screed, thickness of the concrete slab and insulation. Fill the floor area with hardcore to within 25mm (1in) of the first line, compacting it well with a sledgehammer. Cover the hardcore with sand up to the line and lay a damp-proof membrane over it.

CONCRETE
FLOORS

Laying the concrete

Lay closely butted insulation board on the DPM and tape the joints. Provide strips of insulant around the edges up to screed level. Mix a medium-strength concrete of 1 part cement : 2½ parts sand : 4 parts aggregate. Do not add too much water; the mix should be a relatively stiff one.

Lay the concrete progressively in bands about 600mm (2ft) wide. The direction of the bands will depend on the door because you will have to work in such a way as to finish at the doorway. Tamp the concrete with a length of 100 x 50mm (4 x 2in) timber to compact it and finish level with the chalked line (2). As you go along, check the overall surface with a spirit level and straightedge and fill in any hollows, though slight unevenness will be taken up by the screed. Leave it to cure for at least three days under a sheet of polyethylene to prevent shrinkage caused by rapid drying.

Laying the screed

Mix the screed from 3 parts sharp sand : 1 part Portland cement. Dampen the floor and prime with a cement grout mixed to a creamy consistency with water and bonding agent in equal parts. Working from one wall, apply a 600mm (2ft) band of grout with a stiff brush.

Apply a bedding of mortar at each end of the grouted area to take 38 x 38mm (1½ x 1½in) 'screed battens'. True them with a spirit level and straightedge so that they are flush with the surface-level line on the walls.

Lay mortar between the battens and tamp it down well (3). Level the mortar with a straightedge laid across the battens, then smooth it with a wooden float. Lift out the battens carefully, fill the hollows with mortar and level with the float.

Repeat the procedure, working your way across the floor in bands 600mm (2ft) wide. Cover the finished floor with a sheet of polyethylene and leave it to cure for about a week. As soon as the floor is hard enough to walk on, trim the damp-proof membrane to within 25mm (1in) of the floor and fit the skirtings to cover its edges (4).

The floor will not be fully dry for about six months. Allow a month for every 25mm (1in) of thickness and in the meantime do not lay an impermeable floorcovering.

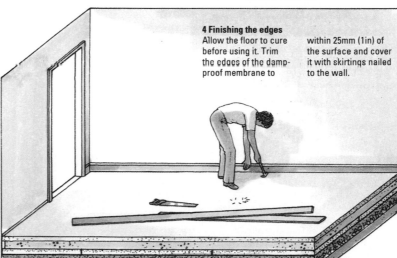

2 Laying the concrete
Working towards a doorway, lay concrete in bands not more than 600mm (2ft) wide.

Tamp the concrete to consolidate it and bring it level with the second chalk line.

3 Laying the screed
Apply a 600mm (2ft) wide band of cement grout to the concrete base and set levelled screed battens in mortar at each end. Lay the screed in

bands not more than 600mm (2ft) wide and level it with a straight-edge and float. Lift out the battens and fill the hollows left by them, then lay the next band.

4 Finishing the edges
Allow the floor to cure before using it. Trim the edges of the damp-proof membrane to

within 25mm (1in) of the surface and cover it with skirtings nailed to the wall.

● **Insulating the floor**
The degree of thermal insulation required varies according to the area of the floor and its construction. Check with your local BCO or ask an architect to calculate whether insulation is required.

187

DOORS: TYPES AND CONSTRUCTION

At first glance there appears to be a great variety of doors to choose from, but in fact most of the differences are simply stylistic. They are all based on a small number of construction methods.

The wide range of styles can sometimes tempt householders into buying doors that are inappropriate for the houses they live in. When replacing a front door you should be careful to choose one that is not incongruous with the architectural style of your house.

Buying a door

Internal and external doors in softwood and hardwood are available, the latter being the more expensive and normally reserved for special rooms or entrances where the natural features of the wood can be appreciated. Softwood doors are for more general workaday use and are intended to be painted. However, some people prefer a clear finish.

Glazed doors are often used for front and rear entrances. Traditionally, these are of wooden-frame construction, though modern aluminium-framed and uPVC plastic doors can be bought in standard sizes, complete with double glazing and fitments.

Wooden-frame and panel doors are supplied in unfinished wood, and mostly require trimming, glazing and fitting out with hinges, locks and letter plates.

Door sizes

Doors are made in several standard sizes to meet most domestic needs. The range of heights is usually 2m (6ft 6in), 2.03m (6ft 8in) and occasionally 2.17m (7ft). Widths range from 600mm (2ft) to 900mm (3ft) in steps of about 75mm (3in). Thicknesses vary from 35mm (1⅜in) to 44mm (1¾in).

Older houses often have relatively large doors to the main rooms on the ground floor, but modern homes tend to have standard-size joinery throughout. The standard is usually 2m x 762mm (6ft 6in x 2ft 6in), except for front-entrance doors which are invariably larger in order to harmonize with the proportions of the façade.

When replacing a door in an old house, where the openings may well be of non-standard sizes, have a door made to measure or buy one of the nearest available size and trim it to fit, removing an equal amount from each edge to preserve the frame's symmetry.

External flush door
A central rail is fitted to take a letter plate.

Planted moulding

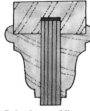

Bolection moulding

Panel doors have hardwood or softwood frames made with mortise and tenons or dowel joints. The frames are rebated or grooved to house the panels, which can be of solid wood, plywood or glass. Cheaper doors, constructed from moulded-hardboard panels fixed to a lightweight frame, are also available.

1 Muntins
These are the central vertical members of the door. They are jointed into the three cross rails.

2 Panels
These may be of solid wood or of plywood. They are held loosely in grooves in the frame to allow for shrinkage without splitting. They stiffen the door.

3 Cross rails
Top, centre and bottom rails are tenoned into the stiles. In cheaper doors the mortise-and-tenon joints are replaced with dowel joints.

4 Stiles
These are the upright members at the sides of the door. They carry the hinges and door locks.

Panel-door mouldings
The frame's inner edges may be plain or moulded to form a decorative border. Small mouldings are machined on the frame before assembly or pinned to the inside edge. An ordinary planted moulding (see far left) can shrink away from the frame, making cracks in the paintwork. A bolection moulding which laps the frame overcomes this problem.

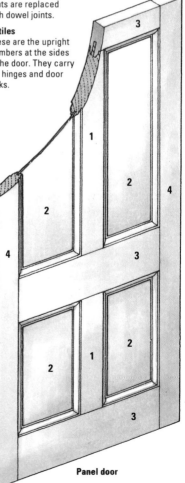

Panel door

Flush doors have softwood frames faced on both sides with sheets of plywood or hardboard, and infilled with a core material. Used mainly internally, they are lightweight, cheap and simple, but lacking in character. External flush doors have a central rail to take a letter plate. Firecheck doors are a special fire-retardant grade.

1 Top and bottom rails
These are tenoned into the stiles (side pieces).

2 Intermediate rails
These lighter rails, jointed to the stiles, are notched to allow the passage of air to prevent the panels sinking.

3 Lock blocks
A softwood block to take a mortise lock is glued to each stile.

4 Panels
The plywood or hardboard panels are left plain for painting or finished with a wood veneer. Metal-skinned doors may be ordered specially.

Core material
Paper or cardboard honeycomb is usually sandwiched between the panels. A solid fire-retardant material forms the core of firecheck doors.

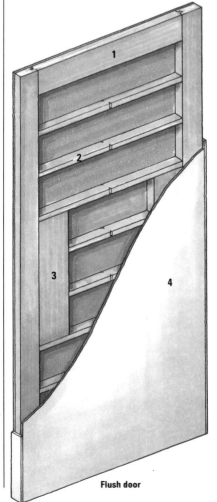

Flush door

Ledged and braced doors

These doors have a rustic look and are often found in old houses, outbuildings and garden walls. They are strong, secure and cheap, though sometimes a little crude. A superior framed version is tenon-jointed or dowelled instead of being merely nailed or stapled.

1 Battens
Tongue-and-groove boards are nailed to the ledges.

2 T-hinges
Butt hinges will not hold in the end-grain of the ledges, so long T-hinges take the weight.

3 Braces
These diagonals, notched into the ledges, transmit the weight to the hinges and stop the door sagging.

4 Ledges
These are the cross rails to which the battens are nailed.

Framed, ledged, braced and battened door

Ledged, braced and battened door

DOORFRAMES AND CASINGS

External frames

An exterior door is typically fitted into a wooden frame consisting of the head (**1**) at the top, the sill (**2**), with a water-repellent weather bar, at the bottom and, mortised and tenoned between them, two rebated side posts (**3**).

The horns, 50mm (2in) projections (**4**) of the head on each side, support the joints and are built into the brickwork to hold the frame in place. The pallets (**5**) are wooden plates, also built into the brickwork, for nail-fixing the frame.

Metal brackets (**6**) can provide an alternative way of fixing the doorframe.

Aluminium and uPVC door sets are supplied with an extruded frame and separate sill. The components are fixed to the masonry with frame fixings, and the doorframe to the sill with self-tapping screws.

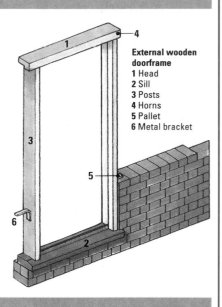

External wooden doorframe
1 Head
2 Sill
3 Posts
4 Horns
5 Pallet
6 Metal bracket

Internal casings

Internal doors are hung in a timber lining frame (see below) made up from three members: the soffit casing (**1**) at the top and jamb casings (**2**) on both sides of the opening. They are jointed together at the corners with bare-faced tongue-and-groove joints (**3**). The jamb casings are nailed to pallets, wooden plugs (**4**) in the brickwork, at 600mm (2ft) intervals. Casings may also be nail-fixed directly to block walls. An architrave (**5**) covers the joints between the casings and wall. The door closes

against applied doorstops (**6**) which form a rebate.

In better-quality buildings hardwood casings are often nailed to softwood grounds (see below). These are rough-sawn lengths of timber which are nailed in place to form a frame around the door opening. The soffit grounds (**7**) are nailed to the front of the lintel and the jamb grounds (**8**) to wooden plugs in the brickwork. The grounds provide a level for the wall plaster and a good fixing for the architrave moulding.

Internal door casing
1 Soffit casing
2 Jamb casing
3 Bare-faced T&G joint
4 Pallet
5 Architrave
6 Doorstop

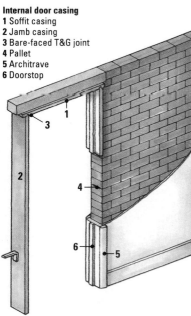

Internal hardwood casing
7 Soffit grounds
8 Jamb grounds

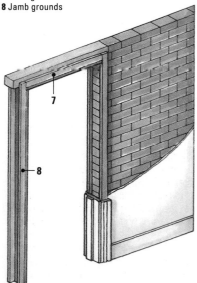

Whatever the style of door you wish to fit the procedure is similar, with only minor differences to contend with. Two good-quality 100mm (4in) butt hinges are enough to support a standard door, but if you are hanging a fire door or a heavy hardwood one you should add a third, central hinge.

As you will have to try a door in its frame several times to get the perfect fit, it pays to have someone working with you.

Fitting a door

Before attaching the hinges to a new door make sure that it fits nicely into its frame. It should have a clearance of 2mm (1/16in) at the top and sides and should clear the floor by at least 6mm (1/4in). As much as 12mm (1/2in) may be required for a carpeted floor.

Measure the height and width of the door opening and the depth of the rebate in the frame into which the door must fit. Choose a door of the right thickness and, if you cannot get one that fits the opening exactly, select one large enough to be trimmed down.

Cutting to size
New doors are often supplied with 'horns', extensions to their stiles which prevent the corners being damaged while the doors are in storage. Cut these off with a saw (1) before starting to trim the door to size.

Transfer the measurements from the opening to the door, making allowance for necessary clearances all round.

To reduce the width of the door support it on edge, latch-stile up, in a portable bench, then plane the stile down to the marked line. If a lot of wood has to be removed, take some off each stile– this is especially important in the case of panel doors in order to preserve their symmetry.

If you need to take off more than 6mm (1/4in) to reduce the height of the door, remove it with a saw and finish off with a plane. Otherwise plane the waste off (2). The plane must be extremely sharp to deal with the end grain of the stiles. Work from each corner towards the centre of the bottom rail to avoid 'chipping out' the corners.

Try the door in the frame, supporting it on shallow wedges (3). If it still does not fit take it down and remove more wood where appropriate.

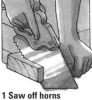

1 Saw off horns

2 Plane to size

3 Wedge the door

The upper hinge is set about 175mm (7in) from the door's top edge and the lower one about 250mm (10in) from the bottom. They are cut equally into the stile and doorframe. Wedge the door in its opening and, with the wedges tapped in to raise it to the right floor clearance, mark the positions of the hinges on both the door and frame.

Stand the door on edge, hinge stile uppermost, open a hinge and, with its knuckle projecting from the edge of the door, align it with the marks and draw round the flap with a pencil (1). Set a marking gauge to the thickness of the flap and mark the depth of the housing. With a chisel, make a series of shallow cuts across the grain (2) and pare out the waste to the scored line. Repeat the procedure with the second hinge, then, using the flaps as guides, drill pilot holes for the screws and fix both hinges into their housings.

Wedge the door in the open position, aligning the free hinge flaps with the marks on the doorframe. Make sure that the knuckles of the hinges are parallel with the frame, then trace the housings on the frame (3) and cut them out as you did the others.

Adjusting and aligning
Hang the door with one screw holding each hinge and see if it closes smoothly. If the latch stile rubs on the frame you may have to make one or both housings slightly deeper. If the door appears to strain against the hinges it is said to be 'hinge bound'. In this case insert thin cardboard beneath the hinge flaps to pack them out. When the door finally opens and closes properly drive in the rest of the screws.

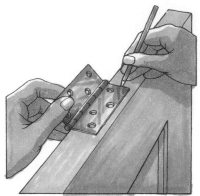

1 Mark round the flap with a pencil

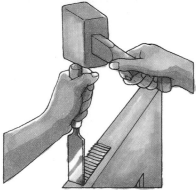

2 Cut across the grain with a chisel

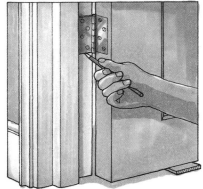

3 Mark the size of the flap on the frame

MEASUREMENTS

A door that fits well will open and close freely and look symmetrical in the frame. Use the figures given as a guide for trimming the door and setting out the position of the hinges.

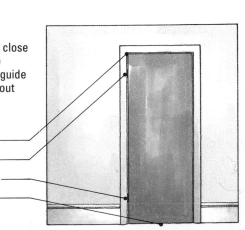

2mm (1/16) clearance at top and sides

Upper hinge 175mm (7in) from the top

Lower hinge 250mm (10in) from the bottom

6 to 12mm (1/4 to 1/2in) gap at the bottom

CLEARANCE AND WEATHER-PROOFING

SEE ALSO

Details for:	
Door construction	188
Power saw	481
Router	484
Plug cutter	488

Rising butt hinges

Rising butt hinges lift a door as it is opened and are fitted to prevent it dragging on thick pile carpet.

They are made in two parts: a flap with a fixed pin which is screwed to the doorframe, and another flap with a single knuckle which is fixed to the door. The knuckle pivots on the pin.

Rising butt hinges must be fixed one way up only, and are therefore made specifically for left-hand or right-hand opening. The countersunk screwholes in the fixed-pin flap indicate the side to which it is made to be fitted.

Fitting

Trim the door and mark the hinge positions (see opposite), but before fitting the hinges plane a shallow bevel at the top outer corner of the hinge stile so that it will clear the frame as it opens. As the stile runs through to the top of the door, plane from the outer corner towards the centre to avoid splitting the wood. The top strip of the doorstop will mask the bevel when the door is closed.

Fit the hinges to the door and frame, then lower the door on to the hinge pins, taking care not to damage the architrave above the opening.

Left-hand opening   **Right-hand opening**

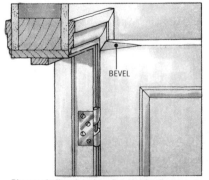

Plane a shallow bevel to clear the doorframe

Weatherproofing a door

Fitting a weatherboard

A weatherboard is a special moulding which is fitted to the bottom of an external door to shed rainwater away from the threshold. To fit one, measure the width of the opening between the doorstops and cut the moulding to fit, cutting one end at a slight angle where it meets the doorframe on the latch side. This will allow it to clear the frame as the door swings open.

Use screws and a waterproof glue to attach a weatherboard to an unpainted door. When fitting one to a door that is already finished, apply a thick coat of primer to the back surface of the weatherboard to make a weatherproof seal, then screw the moulding in place while the primer is still wet. Fill or plug the screw holes before you prime and finish the weatherboard.

Allowing for a weather bar

Though a rebate cut into the head and side posts of an external doorframe provides a seal round an inward-opening door, a rebate cut into the sill at the foot of the door would merely encourage water to flow into the house.

Unless protected by a porch, a door in an exposed position needs to be fitted with a weather bar to prevent rainwater running underneath. This is a metal or plastic strip which is set into the step or sill. If you are putting in a new door and wish to fit a weather bar, use a router or power saw to cut a rebate across the bottom of the door in order to clear the bar.

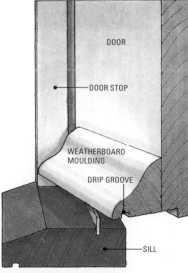

Door fitted with a weatherboard

ADJUSTING BUTT HINGES

Perhaps you have a door catching on a bump in the floor as it opens. You can, of course, fit rising butt hinges, but the problem can be overcome by resetting the lower hinge so that its knuckle projects slightly more than the top one. The door will still hang vertically when closed, but as it opens the out-of-line pins will throw it upwards so that the bottom edge will clear the bump.

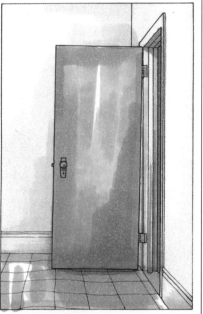

Resetting the hinge
You may have to reset both hinges to the new angle to prevent binding.

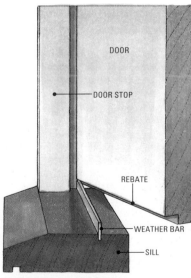

Sill fitted with weather bar

REPAIRS AND
IMPROVEMENTS

SEE ALSO

Details for:	
Painting doors	79
Wood stains	82–83
Door construction	188
Hinge bolts	247
Wood preserver	256
Saws	479

Repairing a battened door

The battens, or tongue-and-groove boards, of a ledged and braced door tend to rot first along the bottom edge of the door because the end grain absorbs moisture. Nailing a board across the bottom of the door is not the easy solution it may appear because moisture will be trapped behind the board and will increase the rot.

Remove the door and cut back the damaged boards to sound material. Where a batten falls on a rail, use the tip of a tenon saw, held at a shallow angle, to cut through most of it, then finish off the cut with a chisel. Use a padsaw or a power jigsaw where the blade can pass clear of the rail. When replacing the end of a single batten

make the cut at right angles (**1**). When a group of battens is to be replaced, make 45-degree cuts across them (**2**). In this manner the interlocking of the tongued and grooved edges between the old and new sections is better maintained.

When cutting new pieces of boarding to fit, leave them over length. Apply an exterior woodworking adhesive to the butting ends of the battens, but take care not to get any on the tongue-and-groove joints. Tap the pieces into place and nail each to the rail with two, staggered lost-head nails. Cut off the ends of the repaired battens in line with the door's bottom edge, then treat the wood with a preserver to prevent any further damage.

1 Cut the end of a single batten square

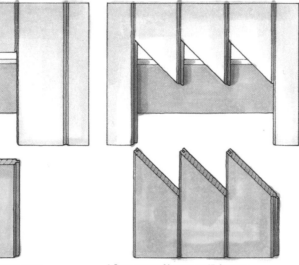

2 Cut a group of battens to 45 degrees

Easing a sticking door

If the bottom corner of a door rubs against the frame, take it off its hinges and shave the corner with a plane. If the top corner is rubbing check the hinges before planing. After years of use, hinges wear and the pins become slack, allowing the door to drop. In this case fit new hinges or, as a cheaper alternative, swap the old hinges, top for bottom, which reverses the wear on the pins.

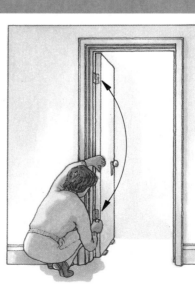

Swopping hinges
Swop worn hinges, top for bottom, for a cheap and convenient repair.

REPAIRING A PANEL DOOR

A panel door is commonly used for the main entrance to a house. Unless subjected to serious neglect this type of door should give good service over the life of the building. However, even sound doors can be seriously damaged when a housebreaker uses brute force to gain entry. Although relatively strong, practically any entrance door can be kicked in or smashed open with a sledgehammer, the weakest point often being down the hinged edge rather than on the well-fortified lock side.

When the frame or panels are badly splintered the easiest course is to replace the whole door. However, if the door is unique and therefore worth preserving, insert pieces of new wood to repair the damage.

Rebuilding the edge
If the hinge stile has been split, the wood will have failed in the vicinity of the hinge screws and broken out from the front face of the door. If the splintered wood can be clamped back into place, glue the break with exterior wood adhesive. Cover the repair with a piece of polyethylene sheeting and place wooden blocks under the cramp heads to spread the forces over the damaged area. You will also need to glue wooden plugs into the old screw holes for refixing the door. Clean up the repair with a plane and fill any hollows with a wood filler prior to repainting.

However, it is likely that the split wood is beyond repair, in which case replace the damaged material with new wood. Use a chisel to cut back the damaged stile to sound wood, forming a regular recess. Undercut the ends to 45 degrees (see below).

Shape a block of similar wood to fit the length of the recess, but leave it oversize in width and thickness. Glue it in place and, when set, plane the block flush. Cut the housings for the hinges.

Rehang the door and fit hinge bolts to the door stile and frame to help prevent it happening again.

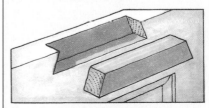

Glue a shaped block into the recess

DOOR
FURNITURE

Fitting a door pull

A period brass door knob, kept well polished, or one of black iron can be an attractive feature on a panelled door. Such knobs are reproduced in many traditional styles and patterns.

An external door knob (door pull) is usually fitted on the centre line of a panel door. If a letter plate occupies the middle rail, place the knob above it on the muntin.

Drill a counterbored hole from the inside of the door to take the head of the screw that is used for fixing the knob; the clearance hole for the threaded shank passes right through the door.

The backplate of the knob has a locating peg on the reverse which stops the knob turning when the screw is tightened. Drill a shallow recess for the peg. Fit the knob and tighten the screw.

For a neat finish, plug the counter-bored hole on the inside to conceal the screw head.

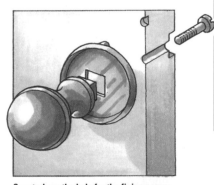
Counterbore the hole for the fixing screw

Choose fittings to suit the door style

Fitting a door knocker

A complete set of reproduction exterior-door furniture in the traditional manner comprises a letter plate, a door knob and a knocker. Being the most ornate item in the set, a door knocker is more often regarded as an optional decorative feature rather than an essential item. Electric door bells have made door knockers virtually obsolete.

On a panel door, fit a knocker to the muntin at about shoulder height. Mark a vertical centre line on the muntin at the required height and drill a counterbored clearance hole for the fixing screw as described for fixing a door pull (see left). Plug the counterbored hole on the inside after fixing the backplate.

Reproduction brass fittings are usually finished at the factory with a clear lacquer to prevent tarnishing. If not, you can always apply a water-clear acrylic lacquer yourself.

Fitting a letter plate

Letter plates are designed for horizontal or vertical fitting. They are available in a variety of styles and materials – solid brass, stainless steel, plated, cast iron and aluminium. The fitting of a horizontal letter plate is described here, but the method used is applicable to both versions.

Mark out the rectangular opening on the centre of the cross rail. The slot must be only slightly larger than the hinged flap on the letter plate (**1**).

Drill a 12mm (½in) access hole in each corner of the rectangle for the blade of a padsaw or power jigsaw. Cut out the slot, trim the corners with a chisel and clean up the edges.

Mark and drill the fixing holes, then attach the letter plate (**2**). You may have to shorten the screws to suit a thin door. Plug or fill the counterbored holes that house the screw heads.

Better still, fit an internal flap cover. Made from metal or plastic, they are held in place with small wood screws. A flap cover reduces draughts, looks neat and allows the letter plate to be removed easily if it is to be machine-polished from time to time.

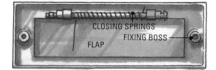
CLOSING SPRINGS
FLAP
FIXING BOSS

1 Sizing the opening
Take dimensions from the flap and make the opening slightly larger

SEE ALSO

Details for:	
Metalwork	60–61, 87–88
Door construction	188
Door bells	328
Padsaw	480
Power jigsaw	481

2 Counterbore the door for the plate and bolts

Fitting finger plates
Finger plates, used to protect the paintwork on interior doors, are screwed to each side of the lock stile just above the centre rail.

Reproduction door furniture
1 Brass 'Georgian' letterplate
2 Brass 'Georgian' knocker
3 Brass 'Georgian' door knob
4 Black-iron door knob
5 Black-iron knocker
6 Black-iron letter plate

193

RENEWING A DOORFRAME

External doorframes are built into the brickwork as it is erected, so replacing one inevitably damages the plaster or rendering.

In older houses the frames are recessed into the brickwork, the inside face of the frame flush with the plasterwork and the architrave covering the joint. Modern houses may have frames close to or flush with the outer face of the brickwork. Work from whichever side the frame is closer to.

Measure the door and buy a standard frame to fit, or make one from standard frame sections.

Removing the old frame

Chop back the plaster or rendering with a chisel to expose the back face of the doorframe (**1**).

With a universal saw (**2**) cut through the three metal fixings holding the frame in the brickwork on each side, one about 225mm (9in) from both the top and bottom and one halfway up.

Saw through the jambs halfway up (**3**), and if necessary cut the head member and the sill. Lever the frame members out with a crowbar.

Clear any loose material from the opening and repair a vertical DPC in a cavity wall with gun-applied mastic to keep moisture out of the gap between inner and outer layers of brickwork.

Fitting the new frame

Fitting a frame is easier with its horns removed, but this weakens it. If possible fit the frame with horns shaped like the old ones (see right).

Wedge the frame in position, checking that it is central, square and plumb. Drill three counterbored clearance holes in each jamb for the fixing screws, positioned about 300mm (1ft) from the top and bottom with one halfway. Try to avoid drilling into mortar joints. Run a masonry drill through the clearance holes to mark their positions on the brickwork.

Remove the frame, drill the holes in the brickwork and insert No12 wall plugs. Replace the frame and fix it with 100mm (4in) No12 steel screws. Plug the counterbored holes. Alternatively, use nailable-plug frame fixings.

Pack any gap under the sill with mortar. Make good the brickwork, rendering or plasterwork and apply mastic sealant round the outer edge of the frame to seal any small gaps.

When fitting an aluminium or uPVC frame, first level the sill on a bed of mortar and screw-fix it in place. Insert and plumb the frame, then fasten it to the walls and sill. Seal all the joints with frame sealant.

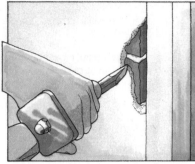

1 Cut back to expose the back of the frame

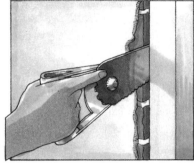

2 Cut through the frame fixings

3 Saw through the frame to remove it

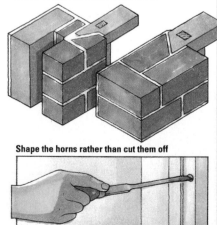

Shape the horns rather than cut them off

Screw the frame to the plugged wall

FIXING A DOOR CASING

A new internal door opening will need a casing to finish it. These are usually of board, 25mm (1in) thick where the applied doorstop is used or 38mm (1½in) when rebated to take the door. The width of the casing should equal the thickness of the finished wall.

Door casings are sold by joinery suppliers as unassembled kits for standard door sizes. If your door is not standard you can make a lining, using a bare-faced tongue-and-groove joint (**1**).

Wedge the assembled and braced frame in position in the opening (**2**) and, if necessary, place hardboard or plywood packing between the lintel and the soffit casing at each end. Check that the edges project equally from both faces of the wall and nail the soffit casing with two 75mm (3in) oval nails.

Plumb one jamb casing with a straightedge and spirit level, then pack it in place (**3**). Start nailing about 75mm (3in) from the bottom and work upwards, checking for true as you go. Place the nails in pairs 450mm (1ft 6in) apart.

Cut a 'pinch rod' to fit closely between the jamb casings at the top of the frame, then place it across the bottom and pack out the unfixed jamb to fit (**4**). Check that the jamb is plumb. Nail the casing in place and use the pinch rod to check the distance between the jamb casings at all levels.

Finish the wall surface round the opening and cover the joint with a mitred architrave moulding. Hang the door and fit the doorstop battens to the inside of the casing.

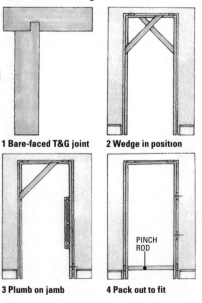

1 Bare-faced T&G joint   **2 Wedge in position**

3 Plumb on jamb   **4 Pack out to fit**

PINCH ROD

The great majority of external doorframes are constructed of softwood, and this, if it is regularly maintained with a good paint system, will give years of excellent service. However, the ends of door sills and the frame posts are vulnerable to wet rot if they are subject to continual wetting. This can happen when the frame has moved because the timber has shrunk, or where old pointing has fallen out and left a gap where water can penetrate. Alternatively, old and porous brickwork or an ineffective damp-proof course can be the cause of wet-rot damage.

Prevention is always better than cure, so check round the frame for any gaps and apply a mastic sealant where necessary. Keep all pointing in good order. A minor outbreak of wet rot can be treated with the aid of a proprietary repair kit and a chemical preserver.

It is possible for the sill to rot without the doorposts being affected, in which case just replace the sill. But if the posts are also affected, repair them at the same time (see right). In some cases the post ends are tenoned into the sill and fitted as a unit.

Replacing a sill

You can buy 150 x 50mm (6 x 2in) softwood or hardwood door-sill sections which can be cut to the required length. If your sill is not of a standard-shaped section, you can have a replacement made to order. A hardwood such as oak will be relatively expensive, but will prove more economical in the long run as it lasts much longer.

Taking out the old sill
First measure and note down the width of the door opening, then remove the door. The posts are usually tenoned into the sill, so split the sill lengthways with a wood chisel in order to dismantle the joints. A saw-cut across the centre of the sill makes the job easier.

The ends of the sill are set into the brickwork on each side of the opening. To release the sill, use a plugging chisel to chop out the mortar joints carefully, then pull out a brick from each side. Keep them for replacing later.

The new sill has to be inserted from the front so that it can be tucked under the posts and into the brickwork. Cut off the tenons level with the shoulders of the posts (1). Mark and cut shallow housings for the ends of the posts in the top of the new sill, spacing them apart as previously noted. The housings must be deep enough to take the full width of the posts (2) which may mean the sill being slightly higher than the original one, so you will have to trim a little off the bottom of the door.

Fitting a new sill
Try the new sill for fit and check that it is level. Before fixing it, apply two coats of all-purpose wood preserver to its underside and to both ends, and, as a precaution against rising or penetrating

damp, apply two or three coats of bitumen latex emulsion to the brickwork in contact with the sill.

When both treatments are dry, glue the sill to the posts, using an exterior-grade woodworking adhesive. Wedge the underside of the sill with pieces of roofing slate to push it up against the ends of the doorposts. Skew-nail the posts to the sill and leave it for the adhesive to set.

Pack the gap between the underside of the sill and the masonry with a stiff mortar of 3 parts sand : 1 part cement, then rebond and point the bricks. Finish by treating the wood with a preserver and seal any gaps around the doorframe with mastic.

1 Cut tenons off level with the joint's shoulder

2 Cut a housing to receive the post

REPAIRING DOORPOSTS

Rot can attack the ends of doorposts where they meet stone steps or are set into concrete, especially in a doorway that is regularly exposed to driving rain.

If the damage is not too extensive the rotten end can be cut away and replaced with a new piece, either scarf-jointed or halving-jointed into place. If your sill is made from wood, combine the following information with that given for replacing a sill (see left).

First remove the door, then saw off the end of the affected post back to sound timber. For a scarf joint make the cut at 45 degrees to the face of the post (1); for a halving joint cut it square. If the post is located on a metal dowel set into the step, chop out the dowel with a cold chisel.

Measure and cut a matching section of post to length, allowing for the overlap of the joint, then cut the end to 45 degrees or mark and cut both parts of the post to form a halving joint (2).

Drill a hole in the end of the new section for the metal dowel if it is still usable. If not, make a new one from a piece of galvanized-steel gas pipe and prime it to prevent corrosion. Treat the new wood with a preserver and insert the dowel. Set the dowel in mortar and glue and screw the joint (3).

If a dowel is not used, fix the post to the wall with counterbored screws. Place hardboard or plywood packing behind it if necessary and plug the screw holes.

Apply a mastic sealant to the joints between the door post, wall and base.

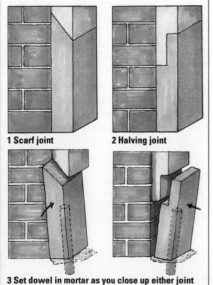
1 Scarf joint   2 Halving joint

3 Set dowel in mortar as you close up either joint

FITTING
ROOM-DIVIDING
DOORS

It is quite common for new houses to be built with large open-plan living rooms, and many owners of older properties have adopted the style by having two small rooms knocked into one. However, there are occasions when two rooms would be preferable in the interests of greater privacy within the family group.

A reasonable compromise is to install a door system which allows the living space to be used either way. It is a compromise because any door system will in some way intrude into an otherwise uncluttered room and when closed it is not as sound-proof as a solid wall. Sliding (1), bi-fold (2) or multi-fold (3) doors are the most suitable for this kind of installation.

Complete door systems, ready for fitting, are available; alternatively, you can buy the door mechanism only and fit doors of your choice.

MEASURING THE OPENING

Before ordering a made-to-measure door system, measure the opening carefully – and then double-check, for your money will probably not be refunded if you make an error. If you use a steel tape measure, get a helper to keep it taut and avoid a false reading. Measure the width at the top and bottom of the opening and the height at both ends. Take the smaller dimension in each case.

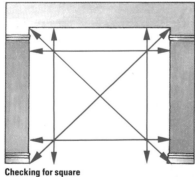

Checking for square
If you are fitting a system in an old house check that the opening is square by measuring across both the diagonals, as the house may have settled unevenly. If they are not the same you may have to true up the frame or pack out the new system.

Glazed folding doors
Glazed room-dividing doors, such as this multi-fold system, will provide an attractive screen when closed, while allowing extra daylight into a north-facing room.

1 Sliding doors
Sliding doors are hung from a track and are most useful where floor space is limited, but they will require clear wall space on one or both sides of the opening.

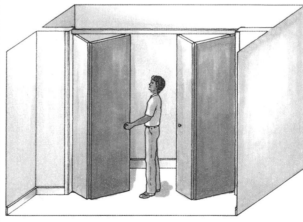

2 Bi-fold doors
Tracked systems are easy to operate and offer an attractive means of dividing a room while not requiring as much clear floor space as conventional hinged doors.

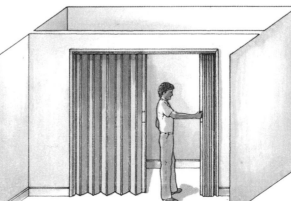

3 Multi-fold doors
Like the bi-fold doors, these operate on a tracked system, but have narrow door panels which enable the door to be stowed within the thickness of the wall.

SEE ALSO	
Details for:	
Door types	188
Door casing	189, 194
Plumb line	504, 510

Sliding doors

A sliding-door system is a good space-saver. Whereas a hinged door needs clear floor space, an arc at least as wide as the door itself, a sliding door occupies practically no floor space though it does require a clear stretch of wall to the side of the opening. Apart from accommodating such fixtures as radiators this is rarely a problem as the door can slide behind furniture placed close to the wall.

A range of door-track sets is available for light, medium and heavy doors. The doors themselves can range in size from 330mm (1ft 1in) to 2m (6ft 6in) in width, and from 16mm (⅝in) to 50mm (2in) in thickness, depending on the type chosen. Two separate sets are required for a pair of sliding doors.

Though designs vary, all track systems for sliding doors have adjustable hanger brackets which are fixed to the top edge of the door and attached to the rollers. A track screwed to the wall above the opening carries and guides the rollers. When the door is closed it should overlap the opening by about 50mm (2in) at each side.

Fitting the system
Following the maker's instructions, set out the hangers and screw them to the top edge of the door. Plug and screw a packing batten for the track to the wall above the doorway. The batten must be as long as the track and equal in thickness to the skirting boards and the architrave. Sometimes it is possible to replace the top section of the architrave with the packing batten.

Screw the track to the packing batten, levelling it at the same time.

Assemble the hangers and rollers and suspend the door from the track, then adjust the hangers to level if necessary. Fit the door guide to the floor, and then the stops to the track.

Make a pelmet twice as long as the door's width to cover the whole track system and fix it to the top edge of the packing batten or use metal brackets.

Bi-fold doors

Bi-fold doors offer a reasonable way of providing a door without intruding too much on the room space. The doorway should be lined in the normal way and fitted with an architrave. The top section of the architrave can be lowered in order to cover the packing pieces on each side of the track.

The pivot hinge and track gear is available in standard sets for two or four doors of equal width. However, up to six doors can be hung from one track, in which case a bottom guide track must also be fitted. For extra-wide openings more than one door set can be used. The doors range in thickness between 20mm (¾in) and 40mm (1⅝in), and in height up to 2.4m (8ft). Maximum width is 600mm (2ft) per door.

Fitting the system
Following the maker's instructions, fit the pivot hinges into the top and bottom edges of the end door, then fit the pivoting hangers in the top edges of alternate doors, working away from the pivoted end door.

Hinge the doors together. They will swing to one side of the wall or the other according to which way the hinge knuckles face. Set them up to suit the layout of your room.

Locate the top pivot plate on the track, then fit the doors on the track before you screw it to the underside of the opening. Fix the bottom pivot to the floor so that it is exactly plumb with the top one. Fit the door pivots in their plates and adjust them for level.

Multi-fold doors

Multi-fold or concertina folding doors are designed to fold up and stack within the depth of the door opening. They are made up from narrow panels, hinged to each other and hung by sliders from a track in the top of the opening. No bottom track is necessary.

The panels are quite slim so that they will stack in the opening with a minimum of bulk. For this reason they do not provide much in the way of sound insulation.

The doors are available for fitting in standard door openings or can be made to measure to fit larger ones – for example, where two rooms have been knocked into one. They are supplied in kits, ready for fitting.

Fitting the system
Screw the lightweight track to the underside of the wall opening between two rooms or, where the opening is to full room height, fix it to the ceiling. It is possible to inset the track flush with a plastered ceiling, but it is much easier to face-mount it and add a cover moulding on each side.

Fit the track over the rollers of the stacked panels and screw it in place (1). Screw the cover moulding in place (2) to fill the gap between the soffit and the top of the door.

Screw the end-fixing panel of the door to the jamb (3) and the latch plate on the opposite side (4) to complete the installation of the system.

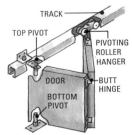

TRACK
ROLLER HANGER
DOOR GUIDE

TRACK
TOP PIVOT
PIVOTING ROLLER HANGER
DOOR
BUTT HINGE
BOTTOM PIVOT

Bi-fold-door system

1 Fit and screw track in place

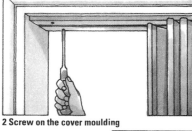

2 Screw on the cover moulding

3 Screw the door to the jamb

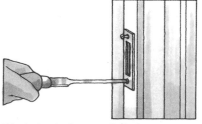

4 Fix the door latch on opposite jamb

FIRE-RESISTANT DOORS

Fire-resistant doors and door sets – doors with frames – are designed to prevent the spread of fire for a certain minimum length of time. They are commonly referred to as half-hour or one-hour firecheck doors, but under a modified system their ratings are now designated by their integrity performance (resistance to penetration by flames or smoke through splits or gaps) with a prefix FD. For example, under this system an FD30 door has a 30-minute rating.

Fire-resistant doors: types and construction

Fire-resistant doors are generally flush doors made from wood with a core of solid board material. They are available in standard sizes and in thicknesses of 44mm (1¾in) for the FD20 or FD30 grade or 54mm (2⅛in) for the FD60 type. A simulated panel door, faced with moulded hardboard, is available. Doors with window openings must be glazed with wired glass that is bedded in intumescent material.

Fire-resistant doorframes have an integral stop in the form of a deep rebate whose inside face is fitted with an intumescent strip **(1)** that swells when it is heated and in so doing seals the gaps round the door.

Moulded-panel door

A fire door is required for an attached garage

1 Doorframe
A fire-resistant doorframe member is machined from one piece of wood and has an intumescent strip set in the rebate.

Fitting a door

A fire-resistant interior door can be fitted in place of a standard door to help prevent the spread of fire, but if it is to be effective the frame must be upgraded. The simplest way to do this is to strip off the old oil paint and finish the frame with a flame-retardant paint. The addition of a band of intumescent paste in a groove cut round the edge of the door will also help. This can be applied with a gun, then planed and sanded smooth when it is dry.

Alternatively, remove the old lining altogether and replace it with a new fire-resistant frame with an integral intumescent strip. This framing is not usually as wide as standard door lining and will need an extra section of lining glued to it **(2)**. Fill the gap between the new woodwork and the walling with plaster or with fire-resistant mineral-wool packing under the architrave.

Trim the new door to be a good fit in the opening and hang it on steel rising butt hinges to make it self-closing. Alternatively, use steel butt hinges and fit a door closer. Fit the smallest mortise lock and latch available, as a large mortise cut in the stile will reduce the door's fire resistance.

2 Extended frame lining

● **Hinges**
Fire-door hinges must have a melting point of at least 800°C. Light-alloy or plastic hinges are not suitable.

BUILDING REGULATIONS

The Building Regulations stipulate that certain doors in domestic buildings must meet the FD20 level of fire-resistance and must be self-closing.

These regulations normally concern dwellings of three or more storeys, and are designed to prevent fire spreading to staircases or other escape routes.

They can also apply to the entrance door of a flat or a maisonette that leads from a common area. A door between a house and an attached garage must also meet the required standard.

Before installing a new door in any of these situations you should consult your local Fire Prevention Officer.

GARAGE DOORS

Traditionally, wide garage doors were hung on heavyweight hinges of the kind known as 'bands and hooks'. The doors are normally constructed from softwood on the ledged, braced and battened principle, and may be solid or fitted out with windows.

Two standard sizes are available: 2.13m (7ft) wide x 1.98m (6ft 6in) high; and 2.13m (7ft) wide x 2.13m (7ft) high.

Traditional hinged garage doors

These doors give long service if they are painted regularly, but they have a tendency to weaken after a time due to their excessive weight; the frame drops and the doors begin to bind. If the face-fixed battens scrape on the ground, they absorb moisture which inevitably leads to wet rot.

A modern alternative is up-and-over doors. These are manufactured as single panels in a wide range of styles.

The up-and-over door is counter-balanced, usually by springs, and is lifted upwards to clear the opening. A system of tracks and levers at each side guides the door up and back into the garage. Depending on the design of the mechanism, the door may retract fully into the garage when it is opened or remain partly projecting out of the doorframe. The latter type is known as a canopy up-and-over door. The vertically tracked canopy-type door is usually the simplest to install as it involves no horizontal guide tracks. A non-protruding type should be used where the garage opening is level with your boundary line.

Another type is the sectional overhead door. This is made up of horizontal sections, hinged together, which run on wheels on a continuous track from the vertical closed position to horizontal. These doors lift vertically and so are suitable for situations where the door must not swing out; they can be opened even when there is a car parked close to them.

Garage-door sizes

Up-and-over doors are manufactured in a range of standard sizes, specified in terms of the size of the garage opening – the distance between the frame posts and the height measurement between the floor and the head member, including a tolerance for fitting.

Most up-and-over doors require a wooden frame to provide a solid fixing as well as clearance for the mechanism at the sides and top. Some companies also produce doors complete with a metal frame that simply needs screwing to the brickwork. When a frame is included, the dimensions of the opening and overall frame are specified.

If you are replacing old timber doors with an up-and-over door your frame may not be a standard size, but most firms supply made-to-measure doors.

Fixing arrangements

Most types of up-and-over garage doors can have their frame posts, or jambs, fitted between the walls or set behind them (**1**). In the same way the head member of the frame can be fitted behind the lintel or underneath it (**2**).

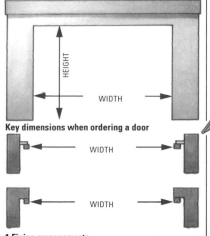

Key dimensions when ordering a door

1 Fixing arrangements
Doors are set between the walls or behind them.

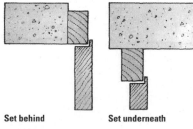

Set behind   Set underneath

2 Head fixing
There is more headroom if the frame is set behind the opening than underneath it.

Up-and-over garage doors are made from wood or metal in a range of styles

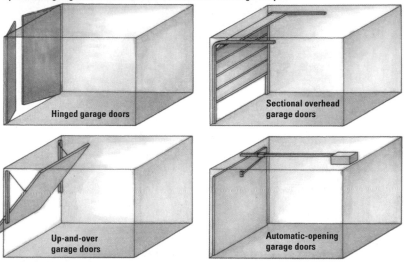

Hinged garage doors

Sectional overhead garage doors

Up-and-over garage doors

Automatic-opening garage doors

AUTOMATIC-OPENING GARAGE DOORS

An automatic door opening system is available for most types of up-and-over garage doors. The system allows the electrically operated mechanism to be worked by remote control, from inside the car, using a hand-held push-button radio transmitter.

The electric-motor housing, which is installed inside the building, normally incorporates a light that automatically switches on as the garage door opens and, with most systems, turns itself off after a few minutes.

The door mechanism has a personal coding system that enables it to be set to different combinations. It is activated only by a transmitter set to the same frequency. A switch fixed to the garage wall also operates the door mechanism, and a manual override is a common safeguard in case there should be a power failure.

The system also incorporates an automatic safety device which will stop or reverse the action immediately if the door should come into contact with an obstacle left in the doorway.

Automatic doors should not be regarded as merely a novel luxury. They can save you time and provide easier, safer access to a garage that faces a busy or narrow road.

Hinged doors
Traditional hinged doors require considerable floor space in which to open.

Sectional overhead garage door
A sectional overhead door retracts within its own space and can be used on a boundary where a door must not swing out.

Up-and-over door
These counter-balanced doors are tracked vertically or horizontally and are fully or partially retracting.

Automatic opening garage door
Remote-controlled automatic door-opening mechanisms can be attached to most up-and-over garage doors.

Traditionally, windows have been referred to as 'lights', and the term 'fixed light' is still used to describe a window or part of a frame that does not open. The section that opens for ventilation, the 'sash', is a separate frame that slides vertically or is hinged from its side, top or bottom edge. Windows of the hinged type are commonly referred to as casement windows. A pane of glass can also be pivoted horizontally as a single sash, or several can be grouped together to make up a louvre window.

Most frames and sashes are made up from moulded sections of solid wood. Mild steel and, more recently, aluminium or rigid plastic are also used, though such frames are usually fixed to the brickwork by means of wooden sub-frames.

Casement windows

Window frames with hinged sashes – casement windows – are the most common and are now produced in the widest range of materials and styles.

A traditional wooden window frame and its hinged sash are constructed in much the same way as a door and its frame. A jamb at each side is joined with mortise and tenons to the head member at the top and into a sill at the bottom (see below). The frame may be divided vertically by a 'mullion', or horizontally by a 'transom' (1).

The sash, which fits within the frame, has its top and bottom rails jointed into its side stiles. Glazing bars – relatively lightweight moulded sections – are used to sub-divide the glazed area for smaller panes (2).

Side-hung sashes are fitted on butt hinges or sometimes, for better access to the outside of the glass, on 'easy clean' extension hinges. A lever fastener, or 'cockspur', for securing the sash is screwed to the middle of the stile on the opening side, while a casement stay on the bottom rail holds the sash in various open positions and also acts as a locking device when the sash is closed. Top-hung sashes, or vents, are secured with a stay only.

Galvanized mild-steel casement windows (3) were once popular for houses and blocks of flats. They are made in the same format as wooden hinged windows, but have a slimmer framework. The joints of the metal sections are welded.

Mild-steel windows are strong and long-lasting but vulnerable to rust unless protected by galvanized plating or sound paintwork. Rusting is caused both by weathering outside and condensation on the inside.

1 Casement window

TRANSOM
MULLION

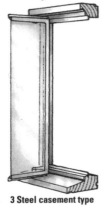

2 Glazing bars

3 Steel casement type

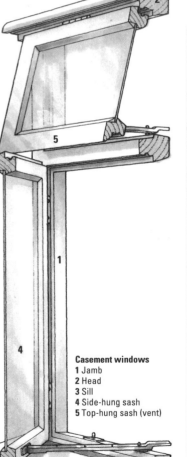

Casement windows
1 Jamb
2 Head
3 Sill
4 Side-hung sash
5 Top-hung sash (vent)

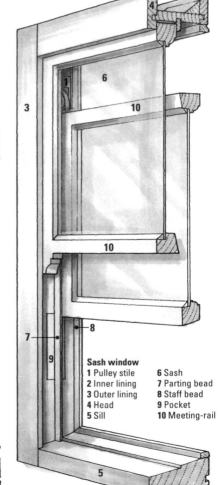

Sash window

1 Pulley stile	6 Sash
2 Inner lining	7 Parting bead
3 Outer lining	8 Staff bead
4 Head	9 Pocket
5 Sill	10 Meeting-rail

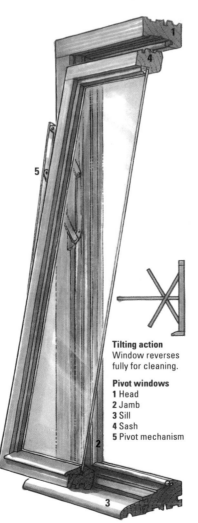

Tilting action
Window reverses fully for cleaning.

Pivot windows
1 Head
2 Jamb
3 Sill
4 Sash
5 Pivot mechanism

Sash windows

Vertically sliding windows are commonly known as sash windows. When both the top and bottom sashes can be opened they are referred to as 'double-hung' sash windows.

The traditional wooden sash window (see opposite) is constructed with a 'box frame' in which the jambs are made up from three boards: the pulley stile and the inner and outer lining. A back completes the box that houses the sash counterweights. The head is made up in a similar way but without the back lining, and the sill is of solid wood. The pulley stiles are jointed into the sill and the linings are set in a rebate.

The sashes of a double-hung window are held in tracks formed by the outer lining, a parting bead and an inner staff bead. The beads can be removed for servicing the sash mechanism. Each sash is counterbalanced by two cast-iron weights – one at each side – which are attached by strong cords or chains that pass over pulleys in the stiles. Access to the weights is through 'pockets' – removable pieces of wood – set in the lower part of the stiles.

The top sash slides in the outer track and overlaps the inner bottom sash at their horizontal 'meeting-rails'. The closing faces of the meeting-rails are bevelled, and their wedging action helps to prevent the sashes rattling. It also provides better clearance when the window is opened, and improves security when it is locked. The sashes are secured by two-part fasteners of various types fitted on the meeting-rails.

Spiral balances

Modern wooden or aluminium vertically sliding sashes have spring-assisted spiral balances which do not need a deep box construction. Rather than being concealed, the slim balances are fitted on the faces of the stiles.

Spiral balances
The balances are usually fixed to the faces of the frame stiles and set in grooves in the sash stiles.

Pivot windows

Wooden-framed pivot windows (see opposite) are constructed in a similar way to casement windows, but the sash is held on a pair of hinge mechanisms which allow the window to be tilted right over to provide for easy cleaning from inside. A safety catch is fitted which locks the frame open at 100mm (4in) and fully reversed.

Pivoting roof windows are available for pitched roofs with slopes from 15 to 90 degrees. Like the vertical pivoting windows, they can be fully reversed for cleaning. The windows are supplied double-glazed with sealed units, and ventilators are incorporated in the frame or sash. The timbers are protected on the outside by a metal covering, and flashing kits are supplied for fitting to tile or slate roofs.

Louvre windows

A louvre window is another form of pivot window. The louvres are unframed 'blades' of glass, 6mm (¼in) thick, which have their long edges ground and polished. The louvres are held at each end in moulded plastic carriers which pivot on an alloy upright member, and this is screwed to a wooden frame. One side of the window is fitted with an opening and locking mechanism which links the louvres together so that they all operate as one.

Louvre windows are effective as ventilators but they do not provide good security unless they are fitted with bonded blade locks.

Where an opening is more than 1.07m (3ft 6in) wide it is best to use two sets of louvres, with the central pair of uprights set back to back and linked with coupling blocks to form a mullion.

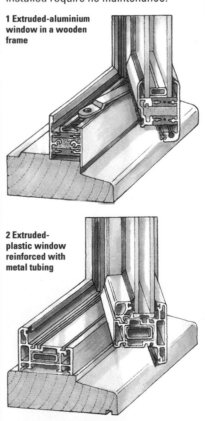

Use two sets of louvres for a wide opening

ALUMINIUM AND PLASTIC WINDOW FRAMES

Aluminium windows

These are often used in new houses or as replacements for old wooden or metal windows. The aluminium is extruded into complex sections (1) to hold double-glazed sealed units and draught strips and, finished in white, satin silver, black or bronze, requires no maintenance. These highly engineered windows come complete with concealed projection hinges and lockable fasteners. They need no stays to hold them open.

To combat condensation the latest designs incorporate a 'thermal break' of insulating material in the hollow sections of the frame.

Most aluminium windows designed for replacement work are purpose-made and fitted by specialist companies. They usually need wooden sub-frames.

Plastic windows

Rigid plastic windows (2) are rather similar to aluminium ones, but are thicker through their sections. They are manufactured in white plastic and once installed require no maintenance.

1 Extruded-aluminium window in a wooden frame

2 Extruded-plastic window reinforced with metal tubing

201

HOW WINDOWS ARE FITTED

Solid walls

In older houses it is usual to find the window-frame jambs set in recesses on the inside of the brickwork. The openings were formed before the windows were fitted and the frames were nailed or screwed into wooden plugs in the brickwork. No vertical damp-proof courses were fitted; evaporation was relied upon to keep the walls dry.

The frames in a 225mm (9in) thick wall were set flush with the inside. In a 340mm (1ft 1½in) wall they were set back from the inner surface. All required sub-sills, usually of stone, outside.

Brickwork above the opening in a traditional brick wall might be supported by a brick arch or a stone lintel. Flat or shallow-curved arches were generally used, their thickness being the width of one brick. Wooden lintels were placed behind them to support the rest of the wall's thickness. Semi-circular arches were usually as thick as the wall.

Many stone lintels were carved to make decorative features. As with arches, an inner lintel shared the weight. Such openings were never wide because of the relative weaknesses of the materials. The wide windows of main rooms had several openings divided by brick or stone columns.

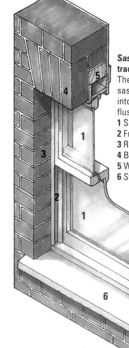

Sash windows – traditional method
The box frame of a sash window is set into the brickwork and flush on the inside.
1 Sashes
2 Frame
3 Reveal
4 Brick arch
5 Wooden lintel
6 Stone sub-sill

Cavity walls

The window frames in modern houses are usually installed while the brickwork is in the process of being erected. They are fixed into place with metal brackets known as 'frame cramps'; these are screwed to the jambs of the frame and set in the mortar bed joints. There are three such cramps on each side of the window frame.

Cavity walls must have a vertical damp-proof course. This is sandwiched between the external brick leaf of the wall and the cavity-closing bricks of the inner leaf. The window frame is set forward in the opening and covers the joint. Sometimes the damp-proof courses are fastened to the frames.

With a window frame in this position a good deal of the wall's thickness is exposed on the inside of the house. The sides of the opening, known as 'reveals', are finished off with plaster, as is the top or soffit.

The ledge at the bottom is finished with a window board which is tongued into a groove along the back of the frame sill and also screwed or nailed down to the brickwork. Quarry tiles are sometimes used to form the inner sill.

Sash windows – modern method
The brickwork is built around the window frame and includes a vertical DPC.
1 Frame
2 DPC
3 Concrete lintel
4 Wooden sill
5 Frame cramp

CONCRETE AND STEEL LINTELS

Modern lintels are made from reinforced concrete or galvanized steel or a combination of both. These extremely strong lintels can support brickwork over a considerable span, enabling large picture windows to be installed without additional support.

A damp-proof course must be provided above the window opening in order to prevent any moisture within the cavity permeating the inner leaf of masonry or the window frame, though some metal lintels can be installed without additional damp-proof material.

The front face of a concrete 'through-the-wall' or 'boot' lintel can be seen above the opening. Where a brick facing is required a steel lintel is used and the bricks are laid on the relatively thin metal edge in bonded courses or on their ends to simulate a brick arch.

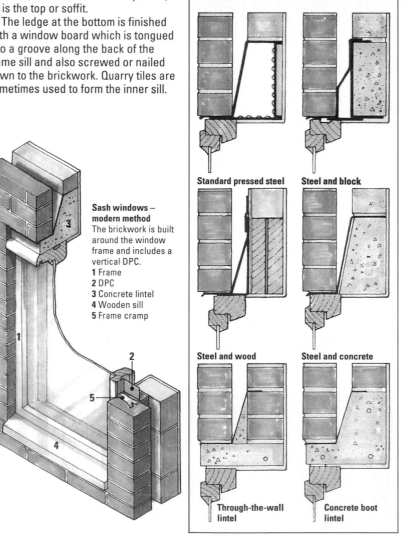

Standard pressed steel **Steel and block**

Steel and wood **Steel and concrete**

Through-the-wall lintel **Concrete boot lintel**

TYPES OF GLASS

Glass is made from silica sand, which is heated with such additives as soda, lime and magnesia until it is molten in order to produce the raw material. The type and quality of glass produced for windows is determined by the method by which it is processed at the molten stage. Ordinary window glass is known as annealed glass. Special treatments during manufacture give glass particular properties, such as heat-resistance or extra strength.

Float glass

Float glass is generally used for glazing windows. It is made by floating the molten glass on a bath of liquid tin to produce a sheet with flat, parallel and distortion-free surfaces. It has virtually replaced plate glass, which was a rolled glass ground and polished on both sides.

Clear float glass is manufactured in a range of thicknesses from 3mm (⅛in) up to 25mm (1in), but it is generally stocked in only three: 3mm (⅛in), 4mm (⁵⁄₃₂in) and 6mm (¼in).

Patterned glass

Patterned glass has one surface embossed with a texture or a decorative design. It is available in clear or tinted sheets in thicknesses of 3mm (⅛in), 4mm (⁵⁄₃₂in), and 6mm (¼in).

The transparency of the glass depends to a large extent on the density of the patterning. Such 'obscured' glass is used where maximum light is required while maintaining privacy, such as for bathroom windows. Patterned safety glass – toughened or laminated – should be used for bath or shower screens.

Solar-control glass

Special glass which reduces the heat of the sun is often used for roof-lights. This tinted glass, which can be of the float, laminated or textured type, also reduces glare, though at the expense of some illumination. Solar-control glass is available in thicknesses ranging from 4mm (⁵⁄₃₂in) to 12mm (½in), depending on the type. The 6mm (¼in) thick glass is the one most commonly used.

Low-emissivity glass

Low-E glass is a clear float glass with a special coating on one surface. It is primarily used for the inner pane of double glazing with the coating facing the cavity to produce an efficient unit that retains warmth in the room while keeping the cold out. It provides good light transmission and optimizes the heat from the sun. The outer pane of the unit can be of any other type of glass.

Non-reflective glass

This type of glass is 2mm (¹⁄₁₆in) thick with a slightly textured surface, and is much used for glazing picture frames. When placed within 12mm (½in) of the picture surface, the glass appears completely transparent yet eliminates the surface reflections associated with ordinary polished glass.

Safety glass

Glass which has been strengthened by means of reinforcement or a toughening process is known as safety glass. It should be employed whenever the glazed area is relatively large or where its position makes it vulnerable to accidental breakage. In domestic situations, safety glass should be considered for glazed doors, low-level windows and shower screens.

Wired glass

Wired glass is a 6mm (¼in) thick roughcast or clear annealed glass with a fine steel wire mesh incorporated in it during its manufacture. Glass with a 13mm (½in) square mesh is known as Georgian wired glass. The mesh stops the glass disintegrating in the event of breakage. The glass itself is not special and is no stronger than ordinary glass of the same thickness.

Wired glass is regarded as a fire-resistant material with one-hour rating. Though the glass may break, its wire reinforcement helps to maintain its integrity and prevent the spread of fire.

Toughened glass

Toughened glass is ordinary glass that has been heat-treated to improve its strength. It is sometimes referred to as tempered glass. The process of treatment renders the glass about four to five times stronger than an untreated glass of similar thickness. In the event of its breaking it merely shatters into relatively harmless granules.

Toughened glass cannot be cut. Any work required, such as holes drilled for screws, must be done before the toughening process. Joinery suppliers of doors and windows usually stock standard sizes of toughened glass to fit standard frames.

Laminated glass

Laminated glass is made by bonding together two or more layers of glass with a clear tear-resistant plastic film sandwiched between. This glass absorbs the energy of an object hitting it, so preventing the object penetrating the pane. The plastic interlayer also binds broken glass fragments together and reduces the risk of injury from fragments of flying glass.

It is made in a range of thicknesses from 4mm (⁵⁄₃₂in) up to 8mm (⁵⁄₁₆in), depending on the type of glass used. Clear, tinted and patterned versions are all available.

Etched glass

Following the increased interest in the renovation of older houses, traditional acid-etched decorative glass is now available. It is produced in 4mm (⁵⁄₃₂in) and 6mm (¼in) thicknesses and in four designs. It can be toughened or laminated for safety.

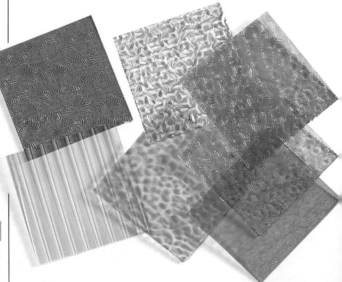

Patterned and tinted glass
Clear and tinted glass can be used for restoring windows in older houses as well as new installations.

203

WORKING WITH GLASS

BUYING GLASS

You can buy most types of glass from your local stockists. They will advise you on thickness, cut the glass to your measurements and deliver larger sizes and amounts.

The thickness of glass, once expressed by weight, is now measured in millimetres. If you are replacing old glass, measure its thickness to the nearest millimetre, and, if it is slightly less than any available size, buy the next one up for the sake of safety.

Though there are no regulations about the thickness of glass, for safety reasons you should comply with the recommendations set out in the British Standard Code of Practice. The required thickness of glass depends on the area of the pane, its exposure to wind pressure and the vulnerability of its situation – for example, in a window overlooking a play area. Tell your supplier what the glass is needed for – a door, a window, a shower screen – to ensure that you get the right type.

Measuring up

Measure the height and width of the opening to the inside of the frame rebate, taking the measurement from two points for each dimension. Also check that the diagonals are the same length. If they differ markedly, indicating that the frame is out of square, make a cardboard template of it. In any case, deduct 3mm (⅛in) from the height and width to allow a fitting tolerance. When making a template, allow for the thickness of the glass cutter.

When you order patterned glass, specify the height before the width. This will ensure that the glass is cut with the pattern running in the right direction. Alternatively, take a piece of the old glass with you (which you may need to do in any case to match the pattern).

For an asymmetrically shaped pane of patterned glass supply a template, marking the surface that represents the outside face. This ensures that the glass will be cut with its smooth surface to the outside and will therefore be easier to keep clean.

Always carry panes of glass on edge to stop them bending, and use stout work gloves to protect your hands from sharp edges. Wear the same gloves and protect your eyes with goggles when removing broken glass from a frame. Wrap it up in thick layers of newspaper if you have to dispose of it in your dustbin, but check first with your local glazier to see if he might be willing to add it to his offcuts, which are usually sent back to the manufacturers for recycling.

Basic glass-cutting

It is usually unnecessary to cut glass at home as suppliers are willing to do it, but you may have some surplus glass that you wish to cut yourself. Diamond-tipped cutters are available, but the type with a steel wheel is cheaper and quite adequate for normal use.

Cutting glass successfully is largely a matter of practice and confidence. If you have not done it before, you should make a few practice cuts on waste pieces of glass and get used to the 'feel' before doing a real job.

Lay the glass on a flat surface covered with a blanket. (Patterned glass is placed patterned side downwards and cut on its smooth side.) Clean the surface with methylated spirit.

Set a T-square the required distance from one edge, using a steel measuring tape (**1**). If you are working on a small piece of glass or do not have a T-square, mark the glass on opposing edges with a felt-tipped pen or wax pencil and use a straightedge to join up the marks and guide the cutter.

Lubricate the steel wheel of the glass cutter by dipping it in thin oil or paraffin. Hold the cutter between middle finger and forefinger (**2**) and draw it along the guide in one continuous stroke. Use even pressure throughout and run the cut off the end. Slide the glass forward over the edge of the table (**3**) and tap the underside of the scored line with the back of the cutter to initiate the cut. Grip the glass on each side of the score line with gloved hands (**4**), lift the glass and snap it in two. Alternatively, place a pencil under each end of the scored line and apply even pressure on both sides until the glass snaps.

1 Measure the glass with a tape and T-square

2 Cut glass with one continuous stroke

3 Tap the underside to initiate the cut

4 Snap the glass in two

Cutting a thin strip of glass

A pane of glass may be slightly oversize due to inaccurate measuring or cutting or to distortion of the frame.

Remove a very thin strip of glass with the aid of a pair of pliers. Nibble away the edge by gripping the waste with the tip of the jaws close to the scored line.

Nibble away a thin strip with pliers

CUTTING CIRCLES AND DRILLING HOLES

Fitting items such as an extractor fan may involve cutting a circular hole in a pane of glass. This can be done with a beam-compass glass cutter.

Cutting a circle in glass

Locate the suction pad of the central pivot on the glass, set the cutting head at the required distance from it and score the circle round the pivot with even pressure. Now score another, smaller, circle inside the first one (1). Remove the cutter and score across the inner circle with straight cuts, then make radial cuts about 25mm (1in) apart in the outer rim. Tap the centre of the

scored area from underneath to open up the cuts (2) and remove the inner area. Next tap the outer rim and nibble away the waste with pliers if necessary.

To cut a disc of glass, scribe a circle with the beam-compass cutter, then score tangential lines from the circle to the edges of the glass (3). Tap the underside of each cut, starting close to the edge of the glass.

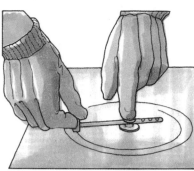

1 Score the circle with even pressure

Smoothing the edges of cut glass

You can grind down the cut edges of glass to a smooth finish using wet-and-dry paper wrapped round a wooden block. It is fairly slow work, though just how slow will depend on the degree of finish you require.

Start off with medium-grit paper wrapped tightly round the block. Dip the block, complete with paper, in water and begin by removing each 'arris' (the

sharp corners along the edge) with the block, holding it at 45 degrees to the edge. Keep the abrasive paper wet.

Follow this by rubbing down the actual edge to remove any nibs and go on to smooth it to a uniform finish. Repeat the process with progressively finer grit papers. Finally, polish the edge with a wet wooden block coated with pumice powder.

2 Tap the centre of the scored area

3 Cutting a disc
Scribe the circle then make tangential cuts from it to the edge of the glass.

Using a glass-cutting template

Semi-circular windows and glazed openings above Georgian-style doors have segments of glass mounted between radiating glazing bars.

Modern windows with semi-circular openings and reproductions of period doors can be glazed with ready-shaped panes available from joinery suppliers, but it is necessary to cut panes of glass to fit an old glazed door or window.

The pieces of glass are segments of a large circle, beyond the scope of a standard beam-compass glass cutter (see above), so make a cardboard template to serve as a guide for scoring with an ordinary cutter.

Remove the broken glass, clean up

the rebate, then tape a sheet of paper over the opening and, using a wax crayon, take a rubbing of the shape (1). Remove the paper pattern and tape it to a sheet of thick cardboard. Make the actual template about 3mm (⅛in) smaller all round than the pattern to provide a tolerance for fitting between glazing bars, and to allow for the thickness of the glass cutter.

Fix the template to the glass with double-sided tape, score round it with the glass cutter (2), running all cuts to the edge, and snap the glass in the normal way. Any slight irregularities will be hidden by the glazing-bar rebates and putty.

1 Take a rubbing of the shape with a crayon

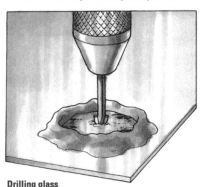

2 Cut round the template, using even pressure

Drilling a hole in glass

There are special spear-point drilling bits available for drilling holes in glass. As glass should not be drilled at high speed, use a hand-held brace or power drill set to run at a low speed.

Mark the position for the hole, no closer than 25mm (1in) to the edge of the glass, using a felt-tipped pen or a wax pencil. On mirror glass work from the back (the coated surface).

Place the tip of the bit on the marked centre and, with light pressure, twist it

back and forth so that it grinds a small pit and no longer slides off the centre. Form a small ring with putty round the pit and fill the inner well with a lubricant such as white spirit, paraffin or water.

Work the drill at a steady speed and pressure – too much pressure may chip the glass. When the tip of the drill just breaks through, turn the glass over and drill from the other side. Drilling straight through from one side risks breaking out the surface round the hole.

Drilling glass
Always run the drill in a lubricant to reduce friction.

● **Plastic glazing**
As an alternative to glass, cut acrylic plastic with a fret saw to fit awkward shapes.

205

REPAIRING A BROKEN WINDOW

A cracked window pane, even when no glass is missing, is a safety hazard. Smashed panes are a security risk and are no longer weatherproof, so replace them promptly.

Temporary repairs

For temporary protection from the weather a sheet of polyethylene can be taped or pinned with battens over the outside of the window frame. If the window is merely cracked it can be temporarily repaired with a special clear self-adhesive waterproof tape. Applied to the outside, the tape gives an almost invisible repair.

Safety with glass

The method you use to remove the glass from a broken window will to some extent depend on conditions. If the window is not at ground level, it may be safest to take out the complete sash to do the job. However, a fixed window will have to be repaired on the spot, wherever it is.

Large pieces of glass should be handled by two people and the work done from a tower rather than ladders. Avoid working in windy weather and always wear protective gloves and spectacles for this work.

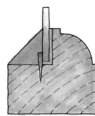

Glass fixed with putty

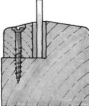

Wooden bead fixing
Some wooden frames feature screwed-on beading bedded into mastic to hold the panes in place. Unscrew beading and scrape out mastic. Bed new glass in fresh mastic and replace beading.

Repairing glass in wooden frames

In wooden window frames the glass is set into a rebate cut in the frame's moulding and bedded in putty. Small wedge-shaped nails known as sprigs are also employed to hold the glass in place. Linseed-oil putty is used for glazing traditional softwood frames. A more flexible putty compound is made to accommodate movement in modern softwood or hardwood frames finished with paints or stains that are moisture-vapour permeable.

Removing the glass

If the glass in a window pane has shattered, leaving jagged pieces set in the putty, grip each piece separately (wearing gloves) and try to work it loose (**1**). It is always safest to start working from the top of the frame.

Old putty that is dry will usually give way, but if it is strong it will have to be cut away with a glazier's hacking knife and a hammer (**2**). Alternatively, use a blunt wood chisel. Work along the rebate to remove the putty and glass. Pull out the sprigs with pincers (**3**).

If the glass is cracked but not holed, run a glass cutter round the perimeter of the pane about 25mm (1in) from the frame, scoring the glass (**4**). Fasten strips of self-adhesive tape across the cracks and scored lines, then tap each piece of glass until it breaks free and is held only by the tape (**5**). Carefully remove individual pieces of glass, working from the centre of the pane.

Clean remnants of old putty out of the rebates, then seal the wood with wood primer. Measure the height and width of the opening to the inside of the rebates and have your new glass cut 3mm (⅛in) smaller on each dimension to provide a tolerance for fitting.

Fitting new glass

Purchase new sprigs and enough putty for the frame. Your glass supplier should be able to advise you on this but, as a guide, 500g (1lb) of putty will fill an average-sized rebate of about 4m (13ft) in length.

Knead a palm-sized ball of putty to an even consistency. Very sticky linseed-oil putty is difficult to work with, so wrap it briefly in newspaper to absorb some of the oil. You can soften putty that is too stiff by adding linseed oil.

Press a fairly thin, continuous band of putty into the rebate all round with your thumb. This is the bedding putty. Lower the edge of the new pane on to the bottom rebate, then press it into the putty. Press close to the edges only, squeezing the putty to leave a bed about 2mm (⅛in) on the inside, then secure the glass with sprigs about 200mm (8in) apart. Tap them into the frame with the edge of a firmer chisel so that they lie flat with the surface of the glass (**1**). Trim the surplus putty from the back of the glass with a putty knife.

Apply more putty to each rebate on the outside. With a putty knife (**2**), work the putty to a smooth finish at an angle of 45 degrees. Wet the knife with water to prevent it dragging and make neat mitres in the putty at the corners. Let the putty set and stiffen for about three weeks, then apply a paint or stain finish as required. Before painting, clean any putty smears from the glass with methylated spirit. Let the paint lap the glass slightly to form a weather seal.

A self-adhesive plastic foam can be used instead of the bedding putty. Run it round the back of the rebate in a continuous strip, starting from a top corner, and press the glass into place on the foam. Secure it with sprigs, then apply putty on the outside as described above. Alternatively, apply a second strip of foam round the outside of the glass and cover it with a wooden beading, then paint.

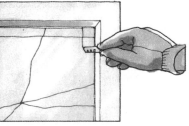

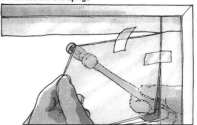

1 Work loose the broken glass

2 Cut away the old putty

3 Pull out the old sprigs

4 Score glass before removing a cracked pane

5 Tap the glass to break it free

1 Tap in new sprigs

2 Shape the putty

LEADED-LIGHT WINDOWS

Leaded lights are windows glazed with small pieces of glass joined by strips of lead called cames. The cames are used to create sinuous patterns enclosing coloured glass or a lattice of lead with rectangular or diamond-shaped panes of clear glass. Sometimes areas of glass are hand-painted.

SUPPORTING A LEADED LIGHT

Leaded lights are relatively weak and they can sag with age. If you have such a window and it is bowing you can support it with the help of a 6mm (¼in) mild steel rod.

Drill a 6mm (¼in) hole on each side of the window frame, placing the holes about halfway up the sides close to and in line with the lead strips and drilling one hole twice as deep as the other. Flatten the window carefully with the palm of a gloved hand or with a board to spread the load.

Solder a few short lengths of tinned copper wire to the back of the came(s), or use small tinplate strips cut from a food can. Set them in line with the supporting rod.

The length of the rod should equal the distance across the inside of the window frame, plus twice the depth of the shallowest hole drilled in the frame.

Locate the rod in the holes, inserting it in the deeper hole first. Twist the wires – or crimp the tinplate strips – round the rod so that the window is tied to it. Finish the rod with black paint and, if necessary, form a waterproof seal on both sides of the window by brushing putty into the cames (see right).

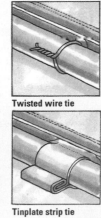

Support a sagging leaded light with a metal rod

Twisted wire tie

Tinplate strip tie

Replacing broken glass in leaded lights

It is always easier to replace a piece of glass with the window out of its frame, but as leaded lights are rather fragile it is sometimes safer to carry out the repair with the window still in place. If the complete unit does have to be removed, carefully hack out the putty and support the whole of the panel on a board as it is taken out.

Cut the cames around the broken pane at each joint, using a sharp knife (1). If possible, make the cuts on the inside of the window.

With a putty knife, lift the edges of the cames holding the glass and prise the lead up until it is at right angles to the face of the glass (2). Lift or tap out the broken pieces and scrape away the old putty cement. If you are working with the leaded light in place, support it from behind with your hand or with a board fixed across the window frame during this procedure.

Take a paper rubbing of the open cames to help give you the shape and size of the glass needed. Lay the new glass over the rubbing and follow the shape with a glass cutter and straightedge, keeping the cut a little inside the line (3). Try the glass for fit and, if necessary, rub down corners and edges with wet-and-dry paper.

Mix some black grate polish into a ball of ordinary linseed-oil putty, apply it to the open cames and bed the glass into it with even pressure.

Fold the edges of the cames over to secure the glass and burnish them flat with a piece of wood.

Thoroughly clean the cut joints in the cames with fine wire wool and resolder them (4), using an electric soldering iron and resin-cored solder.

Use your thumbs to press coloured putty under the edges of the cames on the inside of the window. Run a pointed stick against the cames to remove excess putty, then consolidate it by brushing across the glass panes in all directions with a small bristle brush.

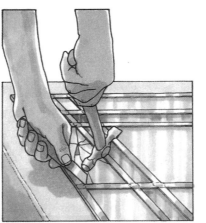

1 Cut the cames with a sharp knife

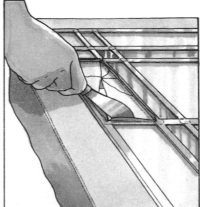

2 Prise the lead up with a putty knife

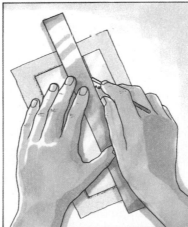

3 Cut the glass following a paper rubbing

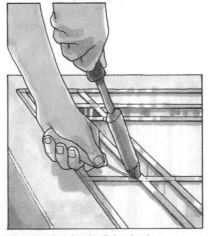

4 Resolder the joint after fitting the glass

Came styles

Round came

Flat came

Beaded came

207

DOUBLE-GLAZING UNITS

Using putty
Follow this sequence when fitting stepped double glazing.
1 Set the packing in bedding putty.
2 Fit the glazing and secure with sprigs.
3 Weatherproof the glass with putty.

Using beading
Set square-edged units in a non-setting compound.
1 Set the packing and spacers in compound.
2 Fit the unit, apply more compound and place spacers behind the screw-fixing points for the beading.
3 Press the beading against the spacers and fix in place with screws.

Using putty

Set stepped sealed units in putty in the same way as for fitting new glass but place packing pieces of resilient material (supplied with the units) in the putty to support the greater weight of the double glazing.

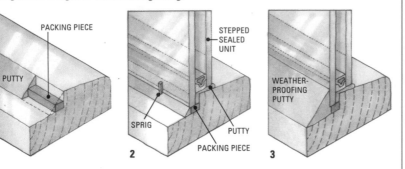

Using beading

Square-edged units are set in a non-setting glazing compound and held in place with wooden beading, a type of fixing that is normally used for hardwood or metal window frames which are meant to be maintenance-free, i.e. not painted.

Apply two coats of sealer to the rebate of a hardwood frame, and when it is dry lay a bed of the non-setting compound. Place the packing on the bottom of the rebate and the spacers against the back of it to prevent the glass moving in the compound. Set the spacers about 50mm (2in) from the corners and 300mm (1ft) apart, directly behind a screw-fixing point for the wooden beading.

Set the sealed unit into the rebate and press it in firmly. Apply an outer layer of the non-setting compound and another set of spacers against the glass, positioned as before.

Cut the beading to length, making mitred ends, press it against the spacers and screw it in place with countersunk brass or plated screws. Countersink the holes in the beading or use countersunk screw cups to give a neat finish.

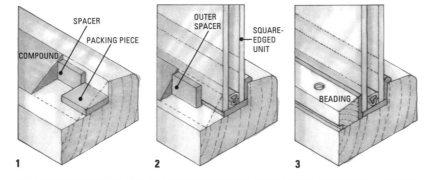

Metal-framed windows

Mild-steel window frames are made with galvanized-metal sections that form a rebate for the glass. This type of window is glazed in much the same way as a wooden-framed window, but a special metal-frame or universal putty is required for installation. The glass is secured in the frame with spring clips **(1)** which are set in putty and locate in holes in the frame. Replace glass in a metal frame following the sequence described for wooden frames, but use clips instead of sprigs. Treat any rust and apply a metal primer before fitting the glass.

Modern aluminium and plastic double-glazed frames use a dry-glazing system which involves synthetic-rubber gaskets. These are factory-installed and should be maintenance-free. If you break a pane in a window of this type you should consult the manufacturers, as they usually have their own patent repair system.

RELIEVING STICKING WINDOWS

The sashes of wooden casement windows are liable to swell in wet weather, and this causes them to bind in the frame. If the windows have not been painted properly it may be sufficient to wait for a period of dry weather which will allow the wood to shrink, then apply a good paint system.

The persistent sticking of a casement window in all weathers may be due to a heavy build-up of paint. In this case, strip the old paint from the meeting edges of the sash and/or the frame rebate and apply fresh paint. You may also have to plane the edge a little.

Unless a window was kept open when it was last painted, it is likely to be glued shut by the paint. Free it by working a wallpaper scraper or thin knife between the sash and the frame.

The tolerances on wooden vertically sliding sashes are such that they do not stick unless they have been painted while shut or the staff or parting beads have been badly positioned.

CURING RATTLING WINDOWS

The rattling of a casement window is usually caused by an ill-fitting lever fastener. If the fastener is worn you should either replace it with a new one or reset the plate on the frame into which the fastener locates.

Old wooden sash windows are notorious for rattling. The cause is usually a sash (generally the bottom one) being a loose fit in its stile tracks. Remove and replace the inner staff bead with a new length so that it makes a close fit against the sash. Rub candle wax on both sliding surfaces.

Pack out a rattling top sash and adjust the position of the catch to pull the sashes together.

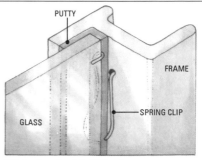

1 Use spring clips to hold the glass

Inevitably, old wooden casements and sash windows will have deteriorated to some extent, but regular maintenance and prompt repairs will preserve them almost indefinitely. New frames, or frames which have been stripped, should always be treated with a clear wood preserver before they are painted.

Regular maintenance

The bottom rail of a softwood sash is most vulnerable to rot, particularly if it is left unprotected. Rainwater seeps in behind old shrunken putty and moisture is gradually absorbed through cracked or flaking paintwork. Carry out an annual check and deal with any faults. Cut out old putty that has shrunk away from the glass and replace it. Remove flaking paint, make good any cracks in the wood with flexible filler and repaint. Do not forget to paint the underside of the sash.

Replacing a sash rail

Where rot is well advanced and the rail is beyond repair it should be cut out and replaced. This should be done before the rot spreads to the stiles, otherwise you will eventually have to replace the whole sash frame.

Remove the sash by unscrewing the hinges or, if it is a double-hung sash window, by removing the beading.

With a little care the repair can be carried out without removing the glass, though if the window is large it is safer to do so. In any event, cut away the putty from the damaged rail.

The bottom rail is tenoned into the stiles (1), but it can be replaced, using bridle joints. Saw down the shoulder lines of the tenon joints (2) from both faces of the frame and remove the rail.

Make a new rail, or buy a length of moulding if it is a standard section, then mark and cut it to length with a full-width tenon at each end. Set the positions of the tenons to line up with the mortises of the stiles. Cut the shoulders to match the rebated sections of the stiles (3) or, if there is a decorative moulding, pare the moulding from the stile to leave a flat shoulder (4). Cut slots in the ends of the stiles to receive the tenons.

Glue the new rail securely into place with a waterproof resin adhesive and reinforce the two joints with pairs of 6mm (¼in) stopped dowels. Drill the stopped holes from the inside of the frame and stagger them.

When the adhesive is dry, plane the surface as required and treat the new wood with a clear preserver. Reputty the glass and apply paint as soon as the putty is firm.

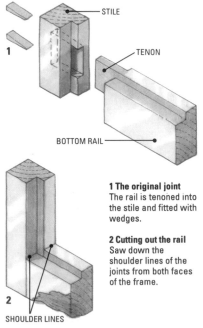

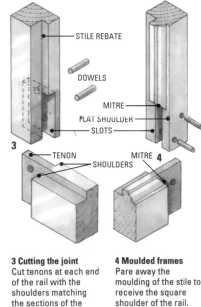

1 The original joint
The rail is tenoned into the stile and fitted with wedges.

2 Cutting out the rail
Saw down the shoulder lines of the joints from both faces of the frame.

3 Cutting the joint
Cut tenons at each end of the rail with the shoulders matching the sections of the stiles.

4 Moulded frames
Pare away the moulding of the stile to receive the square shoulder of the rail. Mitre the moulding.

REPLACING A FIXED-LIGHT RAIL

The frames of some fixed lights (windows) are made like sashes, but are screwed permanently to the jamb and mullion. Such a frame can be repaired in the same way as a sash (see left) after its glass is removed and it is unscrewed from the window frame. Where this proves too difficult you will have to carry out the repair *in situ*.

First remove the putty and the glass, then saw through the rail at each end, close to the stile. Use a chisel to pare away what remains of the rail and chop out the tenons from the stiles. Cut a new length of rail to fit between the stiles and cut housings in its top edge at both ends to take loose tenons (1). Place the housings so that they line up with the mortises and make each housing twice as long as the depth of the mortise.

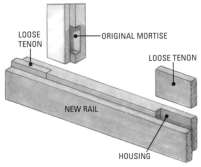

1 Cut housings at each end for loose tenons

Cut two loose tenons to fit the housings and two packing pieces. The latter should have one sloping edge (2).

Apply an exterior woodworking adhesive to all of the jointing surfaces, place the rail between the frame members, insert the loose tenons and push them sideways into the mortises. Drive the packing pieces behind the tenons to lock them in place. When the adhesive has set, trim the top edges, treat the new wood with clear preserver, replace the glass and reputty. Repaint once the putty is firm.

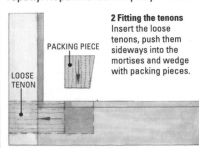

2 Fitting the tenons
Insert the loose tenons, push them sideways into the mortises and wedge with packing pieces.

● **Removing glass**
Removing glass from a window frame in one piece is not easy, so be prepared for it to break. Apply adhesive tape across the glass to bind the pieces together if it should break. Chisel away the putty to leave a clean rebate, then pull out the sprigs. Work the blade of a putty knife into the bedding joint on the inside of the frame to break the grip of the putty. Steady the glass and lift it out when it is freed.

REPAIRING ROTTEN SILLS

The sill is a fundamental part of a window frame, and if one is afflicted by rot it can mean major repair work.

A casement-window frame is constructed in the same way as a doorframe and can be repaired in a similar way. All the glass should be removed first. The window board may also have to be removed, then refitted level with the replacement sill.

Make sure that the damp-proofing of the joint between the underside of the sill and the wall is maintained. Modern gun-applied mastics have made this particular problem easier to overcome. Some traditional frames have a galvanized-iron water bar between the sill and sub-sill. When replacing a sill of this type without removing the whole frame you may have to discard the bar and rely on mastic sealants to keep the water out.

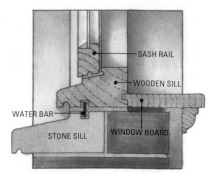

Traditional frame with stone sub-sill

Replacing a wooden sill

Do not simply replace a sill by cutting through it and fitting a new section between the jambs. Even if you seal the joints with mastic, any breakdown of the sealant will allow water to penetrate the brickwork and end grain of the wood, and you may find yourself doing the job all over again.

Serious rot in the sill of a sash window may require the whole frame to be taken out. Make and fit a new sill, using the old one as a pattern. Treat the new wood with a preserver and take the opportunity to treat the old wood which is normally hidden by the brickwork. Apply a bead of mastic sealant to the sill, then replace the complete frame in the opening from inside. Make good the damaged plaster.

It is possible to replace the sill from the inside with the frame in place (see right). Saw through the sill close to the jambs and remove the centre portion. Cut away the bottom ends of the inner lining level with the pulley stiles and remove the ends of the old sill. Cut the ends of the new sill to fit round the outer lining, and under the stiles and inner lining. Fit the sill and nail or screw the stiles to it.

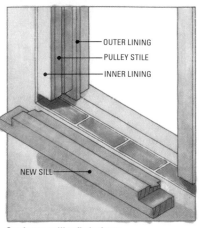

Cut the new sill to fit the frame

Repairing a stone sub-sill

The traditional stone sills that feature in older houses may become eroded by the weather if they are not protected with paint. They are also liable to crack if the wall subsides.

Repair cracks and eroded surfaces with a ready-mixed quick-setting waterproof mortar. Rake out the cracks to clean and enlarge them. Dampen the stone with clean water and work the mortar well into the cracks, finishing flush with the top surface.

Undercut any depressions caused by erosion to help the mortar adhere – a thin layer of mortar simply applied to a shallow depression in the surface will not last for long. Use a cold chisel to cut away the surface of the sill at least 25mm (1in) below the finished level and remove all traces of dust.

Make a wooden former to the shape of the sill and temporarily nail it to the brickwork. Dampen the stone, trowel in the mortar and tamp it level with the former, then smooth it out. Leave mortar to set for a couple of days before removing the former. Allow it to dry thoroughly before applying paint.

Make a wooden former to the shape of the sill

CASTING A NEW SUB-SILL

Cut out what remains of the old stone sill with a hammer and cold chisel. Make a wooden mould with its end pieces shaped to the same section as the old sill. The open top of the mould represents the underside of the sill.

Fill two-thirds of the mould with fine-aggregate concrete, tamped down well. Add two lengths of mild-steel reinforcing rod, judiciously spaced to share the volume of the sill, then fill the remainder of the mould. Set a narrow piece of wood such as a dowel into notches cut in the ends of the mould. This is to form a 'throat' or drip groove in the underside of the sill.

Cover the concrete with polyethylene sheeting or dampen it regularly for two to three days to prevent rapid drying. When the concrete has set (allow about seven days), remove it from the mould and lay the new sill in the wall on a bed of mortar, packed from underneath with slate to meet the wooden sill.

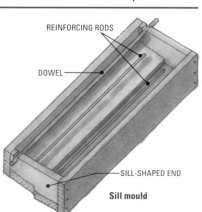

Sill mould

SEE ALSO

Details for:	
Craft knife	511

In time, the sash cords from which the sashes are suspended will wear and eventually break. Replace both cords even if only one has broken.

Waxed sash cording is normally sold in standard hanks, although some suppliers sell it by the metre. Each sash requires two lengths of cord, measuring about three-quarters the height of the window. Do not cut it to length beforehand.

Removing the sashes

Lower both sashes and cut through the cords with a knife to release the weights. Hold on to the cords and lower the weights as far as possible before allowing them to drop.

Use a wide-bladed paint scraper to prise off the side staff beads from inside the frame, bending them in the middle until their mitred ends spring out.

Lean the inner sash towards you and mark the ends of the cord grooves on the face of the sash stiles (1). Reposition the sash and carry the marks on to the pulley stiles. The sash can now be pulled clear of the frame.

Carefully prise out the two parting beads from their grooves in the stiles. You can then remove the top sash, after marking the ends of the grooves as before. Place the sashes safely aside.

To gain access to the weights, take out the pocket pieces which were trapped by the parting bead and lift the weights out through the openings.

Pieces of thin wood known as parting strips are usually suspended inside the box stiles to separate each pair of weights. Push the strips aside to reach the outer weights.

Remove the old sash cords from the weights and sashes, and clean up the wood ready for the new cords.

Fitting the sashes

The top sash is fitted first, but not before all the sash cords and weights are in place. Clean away any build-up of paint from the pulleys. Tie a length of fine string to one end of the hank of sash cording. Weight the other end of the string with small nuts or a piece of chain. Thread the weight, known as a mouse, over a pulley (2) and pull the string through the pocket opening until the cord is pulled through. Attach the end of the cord to the weight with a special knot (see below left).

Pull on the cord to hoist the weight up to the pulley, then let it drop back about 100mm (4in). Hold it temporarily in this position with a nail driven into the stile just below the pulley. Cut the cord level with the mark on the pulley stile (3). Repeat this procedure for the cord on the other side, and similarly for the bottom sash.

Replace the top sash on the sill, lean it towards you and locate its cords in the grooves in the stiles. Nail the cords in place, using three or four 25mm (1in) round wire nails. Nail only the bottom 150mm (6in), not all the way up (4). Lift the sash to check that the weights do not touch bottom.

Replace the pocket pieces and pin the parting beads in their grooves. Fit the bottom sash in the same way. Finally replace the staff beads, taking care to position them accurately or you may trap the bottom sash.

The workings of a double-hung sash window

1 Pulleys	5 Parting bead
2 Bottom sash	6 Bottom-sash weight
3 Staff bead	7 Pocket
4 Top sash	8 Top-sash weight

HOW TO TIE A SASH-WEIGHT KNOT

Make a loop about 75mm (3in) from the end of the cord. Take the end round the back of the cord to form a figure of eight and pass it through the first loop.

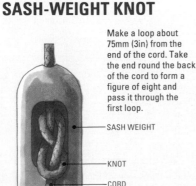

SASH WEIGHT

KNOT

CORD

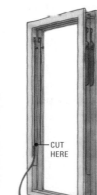

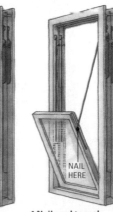

MARK HERE

STRING

CORD

MOUSE

CUT HERE

NAIL HERE

1 Mark cord grooves   **2 Pull cord through**   **3 Cut cords at mark**   **4 Nail cord to sash**

SPIRAL
BALANCES

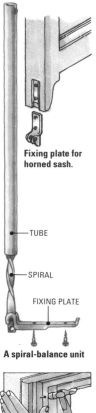

**Fixing plate for
horned sash.**

— TUBE

— SPIRAL

FIXING PLATE

A spiral-balance unit

Fit top-limit stop

Fit bottom-limit stop

Instead of counterweights and cords, modern sash windows use spiral balances which are mounted on the faces of the frame stiles, eliminating the need for traditional box frames. Pairs of balances are made to match the size and weight of individual glazed sashes and can be ordered through builders' merchants or by post from the manufacturers.

Spiral-balance components

Each balance consists of a torsion spring and a spiral rod housed in a tube. The top end is fixed to the frame stile and the inner spiral to the bottom of the sash. The complete unit can be housed in a groove in the sash stile or in the window frame.

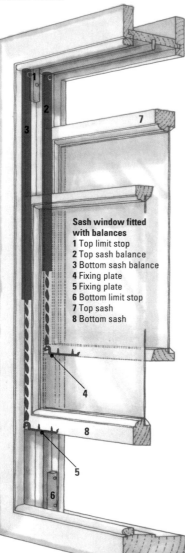

**Sash window fitted
with balances**
1 Top limit stop
2 Top sash balance
3 Bottom sash balance
4 Fixing plate
5 Fixing plate
6 Bottom limit stop
7 Top sash
8 Bottom sash

You can fit spiral sash balances to replace the weights in a traditionally constructed sash window.

Remove the sashes and weigh them on your bathroom scales. Place your order, giving the weight of each sash together with its height and width, plus the height of the window frame. Refit the sashes temporarily until the balances arrive, then take them out again and remove the pulleys.

Plug the holes and paint the box-frame stiles. Cut grooves, as specified by the manufacturers, in the stiles of each sash to take the balances (**1**). Also cut a housing at each end of their bottom edges to receive the spiral-rod fixing plates. Fit the fixing plates with screws (**2**).

Sit the top sash in place, resting it on the sill, and fit the parting bead. Take the top pair of balances, which are shorter than those for the bottom sash, and locate each in its groove (**3**). Fix the top ends of the balance tubes to the frame stiles with the screw nails provided (**4**) and set the ends tight against the head.

Lift the sash to its full height and prop it with a length of wood. Hook the wire 'key' provided by the makers into the hole in the end of each spiral rod and pull each one down about 150mm (6in). Keeping the tension on the spring, add three to five turns anti-clockwise (**5**). Locate the end of each rod in its fixing plate and test the balance of the sash. If it drops, add another turn on the springs until it is perfectly balanced. Take care not to overwind the balances.

Fit the bottom sash in the same way, refitting the staff bead to hold it in place. Fit the stops that limit the full travel of the sashes in their respective tracks (see far left).

RENOVATING
SPIRAL BALANCES

In time the springs of spiral balances may weaken. Re-tension them by unhooking the spiral rods from their fixing plates, then turn the rods anti-clockwise once or twice.

The mechanisms can be serviced by releasing the tension and unwinding the rods from the tubes. Wipe them clean and apply a little thin oil, then rewind the rods back into the tubes and tension them as described above.

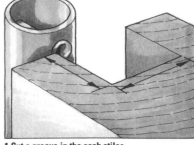

1 Cut a groove in the sash stiles

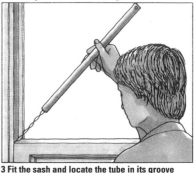

2 Fix the plates in their housing with screws

3 Fit the sash and locate the tube in its groove

4 Nail the top end of the tube to the stile

5 Tension the springs with the key provided

READY-MADE WINDOWS

Joinery suppliers offer a range of ready-made window frames in both hardwood and softwood. Some typical examples are shown below.

Manufactured wooden frames are treated with preserver and some are ready-primed for painting or prestained for final finishing. With the increased awareness of energy conservation, most frames are rebated to take double-glazed sealed units as well as traditional single glazing.

In addition to the stays and fasteners supplied with the frames, some windows also have the top rail of the opening sash, or the frame itself, slotted to take a ventilator kit to comply with Building Regulations for background ventilation in habitable rooms.

Self-assembly kits composed of machined framing are available to make frames of any size to fit non-standard window openings.

Casement windows

Vertical sliding sash windows

The style of the windows is important to the appearance of any house. If you are replacing windows in an older dwelling it is preferable – and not necessarily more expensive – to have new wooden frames made to measure rather than change to modern windows of aluminium or plastic.

Planning and Building Regulations
Window conversions do not normally need planning permission as they come under the heading of house improvement or home maintenance, but if you plan to alter your windows significantly – for example by bricking one up or making a new window opening, or both – you should consult your local Building Control Officer.

All authorities require minimum levels of ventilation to be provided in the habitable rooms of a house, and this normally means that the openable part of windows must have an area at least one-twentieth that of the room. Also, part if not all of a top vent must be 1.75m (5ft 9in) above the floor. Trickle ventilators with a 4000mm² (6½ sq in) opening are also required for new installations.

If you live in a listed building or in a conservation area, you should also check with your local authority before making any changes to your windows.

Buying replacement windows
Try to maintain the character of an older house by preserving the original joinery. If you have to replace the window, copy the original style – specialist joinery firms will make up wooden frames to fit. Specify an appropriate hardwood or, for a painted finish, softwood impregnated with a timber preserver.

Alternatively, you can approach a replacement-window company, though this is likely to limit your choice to aluminium or plastic frames. Ready-glazed units can be fitted to your old timber sub-frames or to new hardwood ones supplied by the installer. Most replacement-window companies also fit the windows they supply, and their service includes disposing of the old windows and debris.

This method saves time and effort, but you should carefully consider the compatibility of such windows with the style of your house. Choose a frame that reproduces the proportions and method of opening of the original window as closely as possible.

Measure the width and height of the window opening. If the replacement window needs a timber sub-frame (and the existing one is in good condition), take your measurements from inside the frame. Otherwise, take them from the brickwork. You may have to cut away some of the rendering or internal plaster first in order to obtain accurate measurements. Order your replacement window accordingly.

Remove the old window by first taking out the sashes and then the panes of glass in any fixed light. Unscrew exposed fixings, such as may be found in a metal frame, or chisel away the plaster or rendering and cut through the fixings with a hacksaw. It should be possible to knock the frame out in one piece, but if not, saw through it in several places and lever the pieces out with a crowbar **(1)**. Clean up the exposed brickwork with a bolster chisel to make a neat opening.

1 Lever out the pieces of the old frame

Cut the horns off the new frame, then wedge the frame in the window opening and check it is plumb **(2)**. Drill screw holes through the stiles into the brickwork **(3)**, then remove the frame and plug the holes or use frame fixings. Attach a bituminous-felt damp-proof course to the jambs and sill and refit the frame, checking again that it is plumb before screwing it firmly in place.

Make good the wall with mortar and plaster. Gaps of 6mm (¼in) or less can be filled with mastic. Glaze the new frame as required.

2 Fit the new frame   **3 Drill fixing holes**

REPLACEMENT WINDOWS

Joining frames
A flexible sealant is used for joining standard frames. The frames are screwed together to fit the opening.

Bay windows

A bay window is a combination of window frames built out from the face of the building. The side frames may be set at 90- or 45-degree angles to the front of the house. Curved bays are also made with equal-sized frames set at a very slight angle to each other to form a faceted curve.

The brick structure that supports the window frames may continue up through all storeys, finishing with a gable roof. Alternatively, the bay might have a brick base only, or be supported on brackets, with a flat or pitched roof.

Bay windows can break away from the main wall as a result of subsidence caused by poor foundations or differential ground movements. Damage from slight movement can be repaired once it has stabilized by repointing the brickwork and applying mastic sealant to gaps round the woodwork. However, any damage from extensive or persistent movement should be dealt with by a builder. Consult your local Building Control Officer and inform your insurance company.

Fitting the frame

Where the height of the original window permits, fit standard window frames to make up a replacement window. Various combinations of frames can be joined with shaped hardwood corner posts to set the side frames at an angle of 90 or 45 degrees. A sealant is used to weatherproof the joints between the posts and frames.

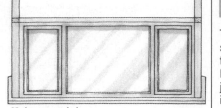

90-degree-angle bay

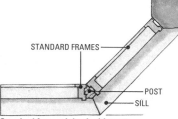

45-degree-angle bay

STANDARD FRAMES

POST

SILL

Standard frames joined with posts

Modern angled bay with decorative lead flashing

Bow windows

These windows are constructed on a shallow curve and normally project from a flat wall. Complete hardwood bow-window frames are available from joinery suppliers, ready for installation in a brickwork opening. A flat-topped canopy of moulded plastic is made for finishing the top of the window in place of a traditional lead-sheet covering.

Fitting the frame

Tack damp-proof-course material to the sides of the frame and the underside of the sill, then fit both the frame and the canopy into the wall opening, the outer edges of the frame set flush with the wall. Screw the frame to the brickwork. The vertical damp proofing should overlap any damp-proof course built into the wall.

Weatherproof the canopy with a lead flashing cut into the wall and dressed over the upturned rear edge of the canopy. Use mastic to seal the joints between the frame and the brickwork.

Attractive bow window that suits an older house

REPLACING A SASH WINDOW

Traditional boxed-sash windows fitted with cords and counterweights can be home-made or supplied by specialists who can also fit them for you. Alternatively, an old vertically sliding sash window can be replaced with a new frame with spiral-balance sashes.

Remove the sashes, then take out the old frame from inside the room. Prise off the architrave, then the window boards, and chop away the plaster as necessary. Most frames are wedged in their openings, and you can loosen one by simply hitting the sill on the outside with a heavy hammer and a wood block. Lift out the frame (**1**) and remove any debris from the opening.

Fit a traditional sash-window frame exactly like the original, making sure the wood is treated with preserver.

Set a new spring-balance type (which has a thinner frame) centrally in the window opening. Check the frame for plumb and wedge the corners at the head and sill. Make up the space left by the old box stiles with mortared brickwork (**2**).

Metal brackets screwed to the new frame's jambs can also be set in the mortar joints to secure the frame.

When the mortar has set, replaster the interior wall and replace the architrave. Glaze the sashes and apply a mastic sealant to the joints between the exterior brickwork and the frame to keep rainwater out.

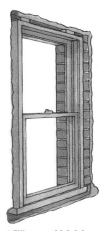

1 Lift out old frame   **2 Fill gaps with brick**

SEE ALSO

Details for:
Plasterboard   162–163
Roofs   227–232, 238–239

Double-glazed roof windows are becoming increasingly popular for the modernizing of old attic skylights and as part of a loft conversion. They are supplied ready-glazed and fully equipped with catches and ventilators. Flashing kits to fit the frame and to suit high-profile or low-profile roofing material are also available.

Centre-pivoting sashes can be used for roofs with pitches between 15 and 90 degrees. Top-hung windows are available for pitched roofs between 15 and 75 degrees. A combined top-hung and central-pivot variant is also available to provide a large opening that can be used as an emergency exit.

Roof windows are relatively easy to fit, using ordinary woodworking tools. They can usually be installed from inside the roof space and the glass can be cleaned conveniently from inside. Accessories such as remote-opening devices and blinds are also available.

Roof windows used in a traditional building

Internal and external blinds are available

Choosing the size

Cost is always a consideration when choosing roof windows, but take into consideration also the total area of glass that will be necessary to provide a suitable level of daylight in the room. The manufacturers of roof windows offer a standard range of sizes.

The height of the window is also quite important and is largely determined by the pitch of the roof. Manufacturers produce charts which give the recommended dimensions according to roof pitch. Ideally, if the window is to provide a reasonable outlook; the bottom rail should not obstruct the view from normal seat height, nor should it cut across the line of sight of someone standing. Broadly speaking, this means that the shallower the pitch of the roof, the taller the window needs to be. However, the top of the window should always remain within comfortable reach.

Standard-size windows can be set side-by-side or placed one above the other to create a larger window; the widest single window available measures 1.34m (4ft 4¼in). When deciding on the size of a window, bear in mind its proportions and position in relation to the building's appearance.

You probably will not need planning permission to install this type of window, but check if you live in a listed building or in a conservation area. However, the structural alterations will require Building Regulations approval, and so will a complete loft conversion.

The manufacturers of roof windows supply fixing instructions to suit installation in all situations. Below is a summary of one type of window fitted in a slate-covered roof. The frame for a tiled roof has a different flashing kit.

Fitting a window

Start by stripping off the roof covering material over the area which is to be occupied by the window. The final placing of the frame will be determined by the position of the rafters and the roofing. Start by setting the bottom of the window frame at the specified distance above the nearest full course of slates and try to position it so as to have half or whole slates on each side.

Cut through the slating battens, roofing felt and rafters to make the opening, following the dimensions that are given by the manufacturer. Cut and nail horizontal trimmers between the rafters to set the height of the opening, and a vertical trimmer or trimmers to set the width.

With the glazed sash removed, screw the window frame in place with the brackets provided. A guideline is clearly marked round the frame, and you must set this level with the surface of the roofing battens. Check that the frame is square by measuring across its diagonals to be sure they are equal.

Complete the outside work by fitting the slates and flashing kit, working up from the bottom of the frame. Replace the glazed sash.

Cut and nail plasterboard to the sides of the rafters on the inside and close the top and bottom of the opening with plasterboard nailed in the groove provided in the frame and to the timbers of the roof structure.

Finish off the joints with filler and tape, ready for decoration.

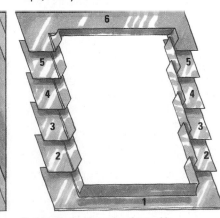

Cut the opening and fit trimmers

HORIZONTAL TRIMMER

RAFTER

VERTICAL TRIMMER

CUT RAFTER

RAFTER

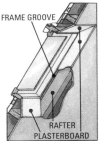

Flashing kit showing order of assembly

Window height
The height should enable someone sitting or standing to see out of the window with ease.

FRAME GROOVE

RAFTER
PLASTERBOARD

Lining the opening with plasterboard
Section through a window seen from the inside, showing the lining on the side, top and bottom of the opening. Prefabricated linings are also available.

CURTAINS
AND BLINDS

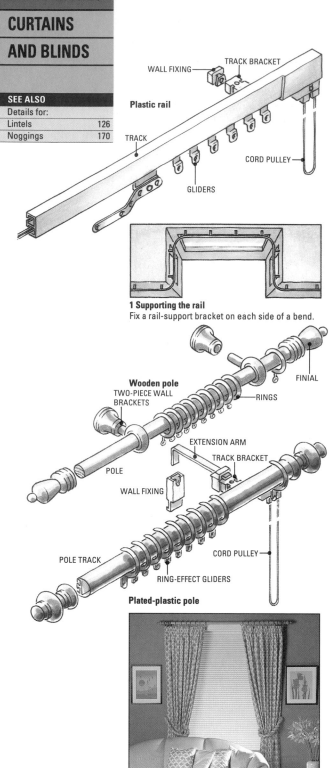

Plastic rail

WALL FIXING
TRACK BRACKET
TRACK
CORD PULLEY
GLIDERS

1 Supporting the rail
Fix a rail-support bracket on each side of a bend.

Wooden pole
TWO-PIECE WALL BRACKETS
FINIAL
RINGS
POLE
EXTENSION ARM
TRACK BRACKET
WALL FIXING
POLE TRACK
CORD PULLEY
RING-EFFECT GLIDERS

Plated-plastic pole

Curtains combined with a blind create an attractive window treatment

Window treatments play an important part in the design of an interior. Although the overall size and shape of any window is fixed, you can emphasize or modify its proportions by careful dressing with blinds or curtains.

Curtain rails

Curtains provide privacy while also insulating the room from the sun, cold draughts and noise. They can be bought ready-made in a variety of fabrics and sizes, or you can make your own. The choice of materials and the methods for hanging them all contribute to the decorative style.

Modern rails are made from plastic, aluminium or painted steel. They are available in various styles and lengths and come complete with fixing brackets and glider rings or hooks. Some are supplied ready-corded, which makes drawing curtains easier and protects them from hand soiling.

Although typically used in straight lengths, most rails can be shaped to fit a bay window. More brackets may be required when fitting a plastic rail into a bay than for metal types, depending on the tightness of the radius. Rails vary in rigidity, which dictates the minimum radius to which they can be bent. Plastic bends more easily when warm.

Curtain poles

The curtain poles that were a feature of heavily draped Victorian interiors have become a popular alternative to the low-key track systems of modern times. Made from metal, plastic or wood, they come in a range of plated, painted or polished finishes. Traditional poles are supported on decoratively shaped brackets and fitted with end-stop finials and large curtain rings. Some designs now conceal corded tracks to provide the convenience of modern rails while retaining old-world charm.

Two wall-mounted decorative brackets are normally used to support curtain poles, but a central bracket may be required to support heavy fabrics. Modern plated-plastic, tracked versions with ring-effect gliders are available in a range of lengths and are mounted on angle brackets. Light-weight slim poles are also made for sheer curtains or nets. These are fitted with side-fixing or face-fixing sockets.

Fixing to the ceiling

Joists that run at right angles to the wall provide a convenient fixing for placing the track at any distance from the wall (1). Drill pilot holes into the joists and screw the brackets in place.

Joists that run parallel to the wall need noggings nailed between them at the required fixing points (2). Skew-nail the noggings flush with the ceiling.

If the required position is close to the original joist, nail a 50 x 50mm (2 x 2in) batten to the face of the joist to provide fixing points (3).

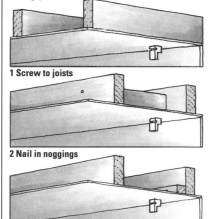

1 Screw to joists

2 Nail in noggings

3 Nail on a batten

Fixing to the wall

Draw a guideline at a suitable height above the opening. Plot the positions for the brackets along the line. Drill fixing holes and fit wall plugs when you are fixing into masonry walls. The screws must penetrate right into the structural material, not just into the plaster. Screw directly into wood framing, and use self-tapping screws or cavity fixings for metal lintels.

If it proves difficult to get a secure fixing at all the marked positions, screw a 25mm (1in) thick batten to the wall on which to mount the brackets. This can be painted or covered with wallpaper.

The architrave of a traditional sliding sash window provides a convenient fixing rail in some cases.

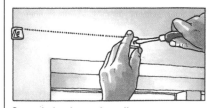

Screw the brackets to the wall

Blinds provide simple, attractive and sophisticated ways of screening windows. Most are available in standard sizes, but they can be made to measure or cut to size at home. Although simple in appearance, some incorporate refined opening-and-closing mechanisms.

Roller blinds

Low-cost roller blinds can be bought in a range of fabric designs and colours, ready-made or in kit form. A kit consists of a wooden roller with two end caps, one of them spring-loaded to work the blind; two support brackets; a narrow lath; and a pull cord with a knob (**1**). You can buy the fabric separately and cut it to width and length. The rollers come in several lengths. Unless you find one that fits your window exactly, get the next largest size and cut it down.

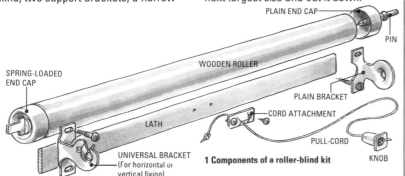

PLAIN END CAP
PIN
WOODEN ROLLER
SPRING-LOADED END CAP
PLAIN BRACKET
CORD ATTACHMENT
LATH
PULL-CORD
UNIVERSAL BRACKET (for horizontal or vertical fixing)
KNOB

1 Components of a roller-blind kit

Cutting to size
A blind can be hung within the window recess or across the front of it. If fitting the roller inside, place the brackets in the top corners of the frame. Remove the right-hand end cap by pulling out the round pin from the roller. Cut the roller to fit between the brackets, replace the cap and drive in the pin.

If fitting the roller outside a window recess, cut the roller 100mm (4in) longer than the width of the opening. Fit the brackets by drilling and plugging the wall, using the roller as a guide.

Fitting the fabric
The fabric must be non-fraying to avoid hems and cut exactly rectangular or it will not run evenly on the roller. Cut the width to fit between the two end caps, and the length to cover the window plus an extra 200mm (8in). Make a bottom hem 6mm (¼in) wide, then turn it up to form a sleeve for the lath. Glue and tack the other end of the fabric to the roller, taking care to align the top edge with the roller's axis. Fix the pull cord to the lath with small screws provided.

Tensioning the spring
Holding the roller with its flat spring-loaded peg on the left, roll the fabric up so that it hangs from the roller's far side. Place the roller in the brackets and pull down on the blind. Now make it return by giving it a slight pull to release the spring catch. If it returns sluggishly it needs more tension. Pull it halfway down, carefully lift it off the brackets, roll it up fully by hand and replace it. If it now flies back too violently take the rolled-up blind off the brackets, unwind it a little and replace it.

Vertical blinds

Like Venetian blinds, vertical blinds suit simple modern interiors and work well with large glazed openings such as patio doors. The blinds consist of an aluminium headtrack that houses the mechanism and which is fixed to brackets screwed to the wall or ceiling; the vanes are simply clipped into hooks on the headtrack and linked together by short chains at the bottom. Weights fitted into bottom pockets ensure the vanes hang straight.

Fixing the track
Mark a guide line on the wall, ceiling or soffit. Allow sufficient clearance for the rotating vanes to clear obstacles such as handles. Drill, plug and screw the mounting brackets in place and clip the track into the brackets.

Hang the preassembled vanes on the headtrack hooks, first checking that the hooks are facing the same way and that you are attaching the vanes with the seams in the same direction.

Venetian blinds used in a modern setting

Venetian blinds

Horizontal blinds, or Venetian blinds as they are more often called, provide a stylish treatment for most windows. They come in a range of standard sizes, and can be made to measure. They are usually made of metal and are available in a range of coloured finishes, including special effects such as mirror, marble and perforated slats. Wooden-slat versions are also made.

Fitting a blind
If the blind is to be fitted into a window recess, measure the width at the top and bottom of the opening. If the dimensions differ, use the smaller one. Allow about 9mm (⅜in) clearance at each end. Screw the brackets in place so that the blind, when hanging, will clear any handles or catches. Set the end brackets about 75mm (3in) in from the ends of the headrail.

Mount the headrail in the brackets. Some are simply clamped, while others are locked in place by a swivel catch on each bracket (**1**). Raise and lower the blind to check the mechanism is working freely. To lower the blind, pull the cord across the front of the blind to release the lock mechanism and let it slide through your hand. Tilt the slats by rotating the control wand.

Fitting at an angle
Venetian blinds can be specified for use on a sloping window. Thread the guide lines that prevent the blind sagging through holes punched in the slats. These lines are fixed at each end to the headrail and are held taut by fixing brackets at the bottom (**2**).

1 Locate headrail on brackets

2 Fix guide-line brackets to the wall

STAIRS

In functional terms a stair is a series of steps that link one floor with another, but a staircase – traditionally the stair combined with that part of the building which surrounds it – can also be a powerful expression of the style of the house itself. By its location, its sometimes impressive scale and its interesting shape or decorative features, the staircase is an important element in the character of a domestic interior.

Elaborate examples of the joiner's art can be found in the staircases of some older houses, but unfortunately joinery nowadays has lost much of the character of earlier periods. However, the spacious and airy quality of modern open-tread stairways, although they are simply constructed, makes them attractive in their own right.

An old, worn or creaking stair can be repaired, and though its decorative elements may be laborious to restore the end result is worth the effort.

Types of stair

The simplest stair is a straight flight of steps. This type of stair requires the greatest 'going', that is, the horizontal distance between the face of the bottom-step riser and the riser of the top step (1). In houses with limited space, shorter flights are used, an intermediate landing making a turn and linking one flight with another. There are various combinations of stairs and landings – the dog-leg, the open-well, the quarter-turn and the half-turn staircase.

Most domestic stairs use newel posts for their support and are known as newel stairs. The posts are a prominent feature, the newel at the foot of the stair often being larger and rather more decorative than those above. Stairs of this type usually have straight treads, though tapered treads known as winders are used at the top or bottom of a stair where the going is restricted.

Winders may be used exclusively, forming a sweeping curved or helical stair. This type, known as a geometric stair, does not have newel posts. A spiral staircase is a helical stair constructed round a central column which can be used where space is limited. Reproductions of old spiral stairs and modern styles in wood, steel and concrete are made.

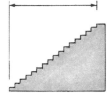

1 The going
The going of the stair is the horizontal measurement between the bottom and top riser.

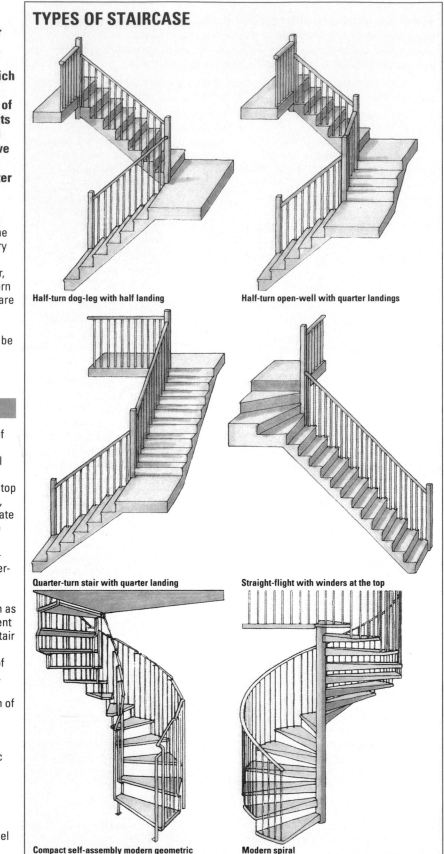

TYPES OF STAIRCASE

Half-turn dog-leg with half landing

Half-turn open-well with quarter landings

Quarter-turn stair with quarter landing

Straight-flight with winders at the top

Compact self-assembly modern geometric

Modern spiral

Softwood is most commonly used for the construction of traditional stairs. Expensive hardwoods such as oak, teak and mahogany are usually reserved for better-quality houses, though hardwood is sometimes combined with softwood for such features as newel posts and handrails.

Stone and metal are also used, though they are less often found in ordinary domestic contexts other than in spiral staircases or basements.

Steps

Each step of an ordinary straight flight of wooden stairs is made from two boards: the vertical riser that forms the front of the step and the horizontal tread on which you walk. The riser is a stiffening member and is fixed between two treads, giving support to the front edge of one and the rear of the other.

Treads and risers may be jointed in a number of ways (see below right), but there are always triangular blocks glued into the angles between risers and treads to provide greater stiffness.

Open-tread stairs have thick treads and no risers. To comply with the Building Regulations, metal tie rods must be fitted across the stair in the gaps between the treads.

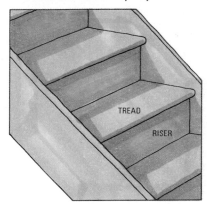

Each step of the common stair has a tread and riser

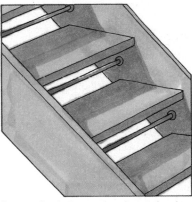

Open-tread stairs have no risers but use tie rods

Strings

Steps are carried at their ends by wide boards known as strings which are set on edge. These are the main structural members that run from one floor level to another. A wall string is an inner one that is fixed to the wall, while the string on the open side of the stair is called the outer string.

The appearance of the stair is affected by the style of the strings, of which there are two types: the closed string has parallel long edges, while the cut or open string has its top edge cut away to the shape of the steps. The closed version is used for the wall string of a stair to pick up the line of the skirting. The outer string can be either the simple closed type, preferred in modern houses, or the cut type that is generally found in older dwellings.

The closed string has long parallel edges

The open string is cut to the shape of the steps

Step/string joints

The treads and risers of stairs are set in housings cut into the face of a closed string and secured with glued wedges. The wedges are driven in from the underside to make a tight joint.

In the case of an open string, the outer ends of the risers are mitred into the vertical cut edges and the treads are nailed onto the horizontal edges. The nosing – the rounded projecting edge – of this type of tread, which usually has a scotia moulding beneath it, is 'returned' by a matching moulding that covers the tread's end grain.

Additional decorative features of fretted wood may be pinned and glued to the side of the string underneath the tread mouldings.

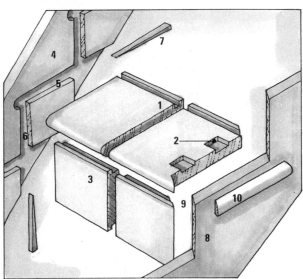

Step assembly showing typical stair joints
1 Grooved tread
2 Baluster housing
3 Tongued riser
4 Wall string
5 Tread housing
6 Riser housing
7 Wedge
8 Open string
9 Mitred butt joint
10 Moulding

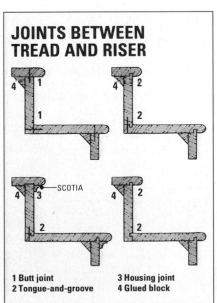

JOINTS BETWEEN TREAD AND RISER

1 Butt joint
2 Tongue-and-groove
3 Housing joint
4 Glued block

STAIR CONSTRUCTION

Storage space
The area below a stair is usually enclosed to provide storage space.

Stair components
1 Wall string
2 Outer string
3 Newel
4 Handrail
5 Balusters
6 Spandrel
7 Carriage piece
8 Floor plate
9 Birdsmouth joint
10 Rough brackets
11 Tread
12 Riser

Newels

The wall string is screwed to the wall at points underneath the treads and the outer string is tenoned into the newels at each end. Newel posts are at least 100 x 100mm (4 x 4in) in section. They give support to the stair while securing it to the floor at the bottom and to the structural trimmer of the floor or landing above. The newel at the top of a stair, or the central newel on a stair with a landing, is usually continued down to the floor. The handrail is nailed or tenoned into the newels.

The balustrade

The space between the handrail and the outer string may be filled with traditional balusters, modern balustrade rails or framed panelling. The assembly is known as the balustrade, or banisters. There are some fairly rigorous stipulations about balustrades under the Building Regulations (see right).

Storage space

The space underneath a stair is often enclosed to make a cupboard and provide extra storage space. The triangular infilling between the outer string of the stair and the floor is known as the spandrel. It may be a plastered surface or one of wood panelling. It is not structural and can be removed if and when required. You should think twice before opening up this area as the understair cupboard is a sensible use of a space that is otherwise of little value. Many families find it a good place for keeping such things as vacuum cleaners and folded pushchairs.

The central bearer

Traditional stairs, 900mm (3ft) in width, should be supported on their underside by a central bearer or 'carriage piece'. This is a length of 100 x 50mm (4 x 2in) timber which is fixed with birdsmouth joints to a 100 x 50mm (4 x 2in) floor plate at the bottom and the floor joist at the top. Short lengths of 25mm (1in) thick board known as rough brackets are nailed to alternate sides of the bearer to support each tread.

If the finished underside of the stair, or soffit, is of lath and plaster, the central bearer also provides support for the laths. The ends of the laths are nailed to the edges of the strings or to additional bearers beside them.

When central bearers are fitted, relatively wide strings are required to clear them. Such a string may be cut from a single wide board or made up from two narrower ones. In the latter case the extra bottom board is tongued and grooved into the lower edge of the actual step-bearing string.

In some cases, where no bearer is used and the underside of the stair is of lath and plaster, the laths are nailed longitudinally to the under-edges of the treads, following the angle of the stair.

BALUSTRADE BUILDING REGULATIONS

Current Building Regulations relating to balustrades stipulate that the height of a stair balustrade should be not less than 900mm (3ft) and not more than 1m (3ft 3in), the measurement being taken vertically (1) from the pitch line, the line of the stair nosings (2). A balustrade protecting a landing or floor (3) should be no less than 900mm (3ft) high.

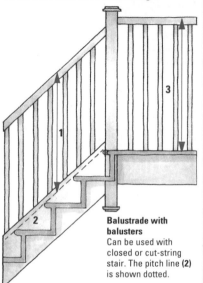

Balustrade with balusters
Can be used with closed or cut-string stair. The pitch line (2) is shown dotted.

The spaces between balusters or balustrade rails must not be so wide as to allow a 100mm (4in) ball to pass between them at any point (4). Children should not be able to climb the barrier.

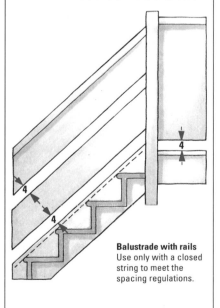

Balustrade with rails
Use only with a closed string to meet the spacing regulations.

CURING CREAKING STAIRS

Stairs creak when joints become loose and start rubbing. The slight gaps that allow this movement are often the result of the timber having shrunk, though wear and tear will also contribute to the problem.

The method you choose for dealing with it will depend on whether you have access to the backs of the treads. A better repair can be carried out from below, but if that means cutting into the plaster of a soffit it will be more convenient to work from above.

Working from underneath

If it is possible to get to the underside of the stairs, have someone walk slowly up the steps, counting them out loud. From your position under the stair, note any loose steps and mark them with chalk. Have your assistant step on and off the loose treads while you inspect them to discover the source of the creaking.

Loose housing joint
If the tread or the riser is loose in its string housing, the glued wedge may have worked loose. Remove the wedge (1), clean it up, apply PVA woodworking adhesive and rewedge the joint. If the wedge is damaged, make a new one from hardwood (2).

Loose blocks
Check the triangular blocks that fit in the angle between the tread and riser. If the adhesive has failed on any of the faces, remove the blocks and clean off the old adhesive. Before replacing the blocks, prise the shoulder of the tread-to-riser joint slightly open with a chisel, apply new adhesive to it (3), then pull the joint up tight, using 38mm (1½in) countersunk screws sunk below the surface of the wood.

Rub-joint the glued blocks into the angle (4). If suction alone proves to be insufficient, use panel pins to hold the blocks in place while the adhesive sets (try to avoid treading on the repaired steps in the meantime).

If some of the blocks are missing, make new ones from a length of 50 x 50mm (2 x 2in) softwood. Set the wood upright in a vice and, sawing diagonally across the end, cut down the grain for about 175mm (7in). Remove the wood from the vice, hold it on a bench hook and saw off 75mm (3in) long triangular blocks.

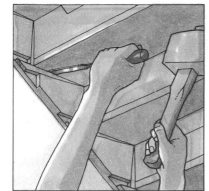
1 Prise out the old wedge with a chisel

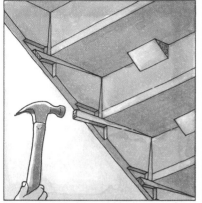
2 Apply glue to the joint and drive in new wedge

3 Prise open the joint and inject adhesive

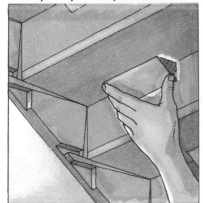
4 Rub-joint the glued blocks into the angle

Working from above

To identify where problems occur, remove the stair carpet and walk slowly up the stairs. When you reach a creaking tread, shift your weight to and fro to discover which part is moving and mark it with chalk.

Nosing – loose joint
To cure a loose tongue-and-groove joint between the riser and tread nosing, drill clearance holes for 38mm (1½in) countersunk screws into the tread, centring on the thickness of the riser (1). Inject fresh PVA woodworking adhesive into the holes and work the joint a little to encourage the adhesive to spread into it, then pull the joint up tight with the screws. If the screws cannot be concealed by stair carpet, counterbore the holes so as to set the screw heads below the surface of the tread, then plug the holes with matching wood.

Riser – loose joint
A loose joint at the back of the tread cannot be repaired easily from above. You can try working water-thinned PVA woodworking adhesive into the joint, but you cannot use wood screws to pull the joint together.

As an alternative, reinforce the joint by gluing a section of 12 x 12mm (½ x ½in) triangular moulding into the angle between the tread and the riser (2). This is viable only if it does not leave the remaining width of the tread below the minimum Building Regulation specification of 220mm (8¾in). Unless the stair carpet covers the full width of the treads, cut the moulding slightly shorter than the width of the carpet. Another option is to glue a similar moulding to each step, and apply a wood dye to unify the colour.

1 Screw joint tight

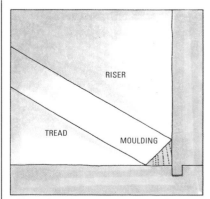
2 Glue a triangular moulding into the angle

REPAIRING WORN STAIRS

Old softwood stairs that have not been protected by a floor covering are inevitably worn in places. Worn treads and nosings are dangerous and should be repaired promptly. If all the treads are badly worn, have the stair replaced by a builder.

Treads fitted between closed strings can be replaced only from below. If the soffit of the stair is enclosed with lath and plaster, or with plasterboard, you will have to cut an opening to reach the worn-out tread. Where a central bearer has been used the work can be extensive, and in such a case you should again seek the advice of a builder.

Renewing a nosing

Wear on a nosing is usually concentrated around the centre of the step, and you can repair it without having to renew the whole tread.

Mark three cutting lines just outside the worn area, one parallel with the edge of the nosing and the other two at right angles to it (1). Adjust the blade depth of a portable circular saw to the thickness of the tread. Pin a batten the required distance from, and parallel to, the long cutting line to guide the edge of the saw's baseplate.

Cutting out the waste

Position the saw, switch on, then make the cut by gradually lowering the blade into the wood (2). Try not to overrun the short end lines. Having made the cut, remove the guide batten.

Use a tenon saw to make the end cuts at 45 degrees to the face of the tread (3) Try not to saw beyond the kerf left by the circular saw.

Cut away the waste with a chisel, working with the grain and taking care to avoid damaging the riser tongue and triangular reinforcing blocks. Pare away the waste that remains in the uncut corners (4).

Replacing the nosing

Plane a groove in the underside of a new section of nosing to receive the tongue of the riser, and cut its ends to 45 degrees. Check its fit in the opening, then apply PVA wood adhesive to all meeting surfaces and fix it in place. Clamp it down with a batten screwed at each end to the tread (5). Place a packing strip of hardboard under the batten to concentrate the pressure, and a piece of polyethylene to prevent the hardboard sticking.

Drill and insert 6mm (¼in) diameter, glued dowels into the edge of the nosing to reinforce the butt joint and, when the adhesive has set, plane and sand the repair flush. Refix any blocks that may have fallen off.

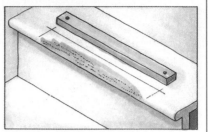
1 Mark the cutting lines around the worn area

2 Make the cut with a saw guided by a batten

3 Make 45-degree cuts at each end

4 Pare away the waste from the corners

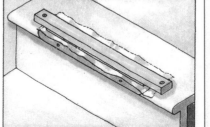
5 Clamp new section of nosing with a batten

REPLACING TREADS

Most stairs have tongue-and-groove joints between their risers and treads, though in some cases the tops of the risers are housed into the undersides of the treads and in others simple butt joints are secured with nails or screws.

You can determine which type of joint you are faced with by trying to pass a thin knife blade between the shoulders of the joint. It will help if you first remove any nails or screws. A butt joint will allow the blade to pass through, while a housed or a tongue-and-groove joint will obstruct it.

As the joints effectively lock the treads and risers together, those in contact with the damaged tread must be freed before the tread can be removed. A butt joint is relatively easy to dismantle, whereas a housed or a tongue-and-groove joint has to be cut.

Dismantling a butt joint

To take a butt joint apart first take out the nails or screws and, if adhesive has been used, give the tread a sharp tap to break the hardened adhesive, or prise it up with a chisel. Remove the triangular glued blocks in a similar way.

Cutting a tongue

Cut the tongue of a riser jointed into the underside of a tread, working from the front of the step; where the riser's tongue is jointed into the top of the tread it must be cut from the rear (1). If there is a scotia moulding fitted under the nosing, try to prise it away first with an old wood chisel.

Before cutting a tongue, remove any screws, nails and glued reinforcement blocks, then drill a line of 3mm (⅛in) holes just below the shoulder of the joint into which you can insert the blade of a padsaw (2). Begin the saw cut and when the kerf is long enough continue with a panel saw, using the underside of the tread to guide the blade.

The method you use to remove the tread depends on whether it is fitted between closed strings or has an open string at one end (see opposite).

1 Cut the tongue from the front or rear

2 Initiate the cut with a padsaw

Closed-string stair

Working from the underside of the stair, chisel out the retaining wedges from the string housings at the ends of the tread (**1**), then free the joints by giving the tread a sharp tap from above with a hammer and block.

Next drive the tread backwards and out of its two housings, alternately tapping one end and then the other (**2**).

Make a tread to fit, shaping its front edge to match the nosing of the other steps, and cut a new pair of wedges. Slide the new tread and wedges into place from underneath, measure the gaps left by the sawcuts at its front and back (**3**) and cut wooden packing strips or pieces of veneer to fill them.

Remove the tread, apply PVA wood adhesive and replace it, along with the wedges and packing pieces. Secure the tread with 38mm (1½in) countersunk wood screws into the risers.

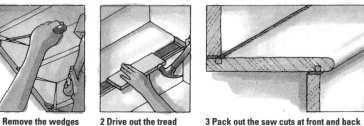

1 Remove the wedges   **2 Drive out the tread**   **3 Pack out the saw cuts at front and back**

Open-string stair

Use a chisel to prise off the moulding that covers the end grain of the tread, taking care not to split it (**1**), then remove the two balusters.

Chisel the wedge out of the wall-string housing to free the inner end of the tread, then drive the tread out from the rear of the stair, using a hammer and a wood block on its back edge (**2**). In this way the end of the tread fitted to the outer string is released while the inner end is still partly engaged in its housing.

You will have to cut through or extract any nails that fix the tread to the outer string before it can be pulled completely clear.

Use the original tread as a template and mark its shape out on a new board, then cut the board accurately to size. Take care to preserve the exact shape of the nosing, which must follow that of the return moulding.

Mark out and cut the housings for the balusters (**3**) and make a new hardwood wedge for the inner-tread housing. Treat new wood with a preserver.

Fit the tread from the front, insert packing strips, then glue and screw it, following the method described for a closed-string tread (see above).

Apply adhesive to the balusters and replace them. Finally, pin and glue the return moulding to the end of the tread and replace any scotia moulding.

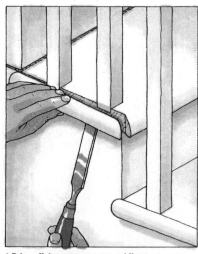

1 Prise off the return cover moulding

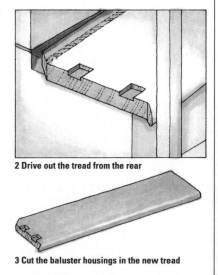

2 Drive out the tread from the rear

3 Cut the baluster housings in the new tread

REPAIRING A RISER

Risers take much less wear and tear than treads and will not ordinarily have to be replaced. Should a riser become weak through woodworm infestation it can be reinforced from behind by gluing and screwing a new board to it, but treat the old and new wood with a chemical preservative to eradicate insects. A riser seriously affected by woodworm should be replaced.

Closed-string stair

In the case of a closed-string stair, remove the tread below the damaged riser using the method described (see left), but also saw through the tongue at the top of the riser. Knock the wedges out of the riser housings, then knock or prise out the riser (**1**).

Measure the distance between the strings and from the underside of one tread to the top of the other, then cut a new riser to fit. Though you could make tongue-and-groove joints for the new riser it is easier to join it to the treads with glued butt joins (**2**).

Glue and wedge the new riser into the string housings (**3**), then glue and screw the upper tread to its top edge.

If yours is a 'show-wood' staircase – one in which the steps are not carpeted – counterbore the screw-holes and use wood plugs to conceal the screws. Another way to secure a glued butt joint is to screw and glue blocks to both parts underneath.

Refit the tread as previously described (see left), but note that you need pack out only the front saw cut as the new riser has been made to fit. Glue and screw the tread to the lower edge of the new riser.

Open-string stair

First remove any scotia moulding that is fitted under the nosing, then saw through the tongues at the top and bottom of the infected riser and remove the wedge from its wall-string housing.

Knock apart the mitred joint between the end of the riser and the outer string by hammering it from behind. Once the mitred joint is free, pull the inner end of the riser out of its housing.

Make a new riser to fit between the treads, mitring its outer end to match the joint in the string. Apply adhesive and fit the riser from the front. Re-wedge the inner housing joint, screw the treads to the riser, nail the mitred end and replace the scotia moulding.

1 Prise out the riser

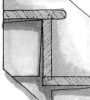

2 Cut riser to fit

3 Wedge the riser

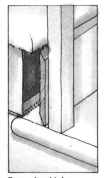

Free mitred joint

REPAIRING BALUSTERS

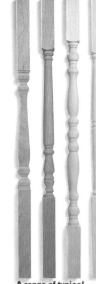

A range of typical hardwood and softwood balusters

A broken baluster is potentially dangerous and it should be repaired or replaced promptly. If the baluster is a decorative one it should be preserved if possible; damage that is not too extensive can be repaired *in situ*. Otherwise, if the damage is beyond repair, a new baluster can be made to replace it.

A traditional staircase featuring turned balusters

Buying balusters

Ready-turned balusters of various patterns are available from joinery suppliers. They can be used to re-create an acceptable balustrade when made-to-measure replicas of the originals would prove too expensive. They also make suitable replacements for old square balusters, adding character to what may be a rather utilitarian staircase.

Baluster joints
1 Housed **2** Housed and nailed **3** Housed **4** Stub-tenoned **5** Nailed

How balusters are fixed

Balusters are usually housed or stub-tenoned into the underside of the handrail and into the edge of a closed string or the treads of an open-stringed stair. Sometimes they are simply butt-jointed and secured with nails, or are housed at the bottom but nailed at the top (see above). You can detect a nail fixing by examining or feeling the surface of the baluster at the back, where you will find a slight bump or hollow. If the wood is stripped the fixing will be obvious. A light shone across the joint can also reveal a nail fixing.

HANDRAIL REGULATIONS

Current Building Regulations require a stair in a private residential dwelling to have two handrails, one at each side, if the stair is 1m (3ft 3in) or more in width. If the stair is less than a metre wide and has tapered treads (winders) a handrail must be provided on the side of the stair where the treads are widest. This usually means the wall-string side, in which case two handrails are still required because the outer-string balustrade must always have a handrail.

Though these requirements concern new building work there is good reason for you apply them also to existing buildings wherever possible. Tapered steps can be very hazardous, and it makes good sense to follow the guidelines for your own and your family's safety.

Handrails in hardwood and softwood, including vertical and horizontal curved sections, are available from joinery suppliers. Their various parts are bolted together with special steel handrail screws and are fixed to the wall with brass, iron, stainless-steel or anodized-aluminium handrail brackets. The size of a bracket is given as the distance from the wall to the centre of the rail-fixing plate. Some handrail brackets are made with cupped fixing plates to support round handrails.

Replacing a baluster

A damaged baluster that is butt-jointed and nailed can be knocked out by driving its top end backwards and its bottom end forwards. If it is housed at the bottom it can be pulled out of the housing once the top has been freed.

A baluster housed at both ends can be removed only by first cutting through the shoulder line of the joint on the underside of the handrail. It can then be pulled out of the lower housing.

When a baluster is fitted into an open string, remove the moulding that covers the end of the tread. Knock the bottom end of the baluster sideways out of its housing, then pull it down to disengage it from the handrail housing.

Fitting a baluster

Mark the required length on the new baluster, then mark out and cut the ends, using the old baluster as a pattern. Alternatively, take the angle of the handrail and string by setting an adjustable bevel on an adjacent baluster, then use the bevel to mark the new baluster for cutting. Fit and fix the new baluster in the reverse order to the way in which the old one was taken out.

To replace a baluster which is housed at both ends in a closed-string stair, first trim off the back corner of the top tenon (**1**), place the bottom tenon in its housing and then swing the top end of the baluster into position (**2**).

1 Trim back the corner of the tenon   **2 Swing into place**

Mending a baluster

A baluster that has split along the grain can be repaired *in situ*. Work PVA glue into the split, squeeze the parts together and wipe any surplus glue from the surface with a damp rag. Bind the repair with waxed string or self-adhesive tape until the glue sets (see right). Remove the binding and sand the repair smooth.

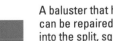

Mending a baluster Apply glue and tape the split

FITTING A HANDRAIL

Measuring and marking out

Mark a line on the wall to represent the top of the handrail, setting the height in accordance with the Building Regulations. Where there are tapered treads, some relaxation of the rules may be necessary, but you should check with your local Building Control Officer.

Set out the line by marking a series of points measured vertically from the nosing of each tread on a straight flight. Where tapered treads occur, take the same measurement from the central 'kite winder' tread and landing (**1**).

Marking tips and techniques
Marking the points can be greatly simplified if you first cut a straight batten to the required height and use it as a guide. Ring the points with your pencil as you make them so that you can find them easily later.

Marking out procedure
Using a straightedge, join up the marks to produce the line of the handrail, then draw a second line below and parallel to it at a distance equal to the thickness of the handrail. Where the rail changes direction draw lines across the intersections (**A**) to find the angles at which the components must be cut (**2**).

Measure the run of the handrail and buy the required lengths, including such special sections as turns, ramps and the opening rise (see right). Also buy enough handrail brackets for them to be spaced at about 1m (3ft 3in) intervals.

Assembling and fitting

Cut the components to the correct lengths and angles, then dowel and glue short sections together, or use special handrail screws. These require clearance holes in the ends of each part and housings cut in the undersides for the nuts. When using handrail screws you must also fit locating dowels (**3**) to stop the sections rotating as they are pulled together. Assemble the rail in manageable sections.

Screw the brackets to the rail and hold it against the wall while a helper marks the fixing holes. Drill and plug the wall and screw the rail in place with No10 or No12 screws at least 63mm (2½in) long to make a secure fixing in the brickwork and not just into the plaster (**4**).

Rub down the handrail and finish it with clear varnish or paint.

KITE-WINDER TREAD

1 Setting out
Mark the wall above each tread and join the marks with a straightedge.

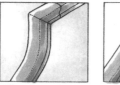

2 Changing angles
The junction of a sloping handrail with a horizontal one can either be made with special components (see right) or a simple mitre joint.

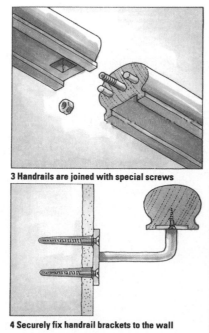

3 Handrails are joined with special screws

4 Securely fix handrail brackets to the wall

FIXING A LOOSE BALUSTRADE

When the whole balustrade, including the handrail and newel post, feels loose it usually indicates a breakdown of the joints between the steps and the outer string. You should attend to it as soon as possible before someone leans heavily against the balustrade and the whole structure collapses.

Refix a loose string and newel to the steps by first removing the wedges from the tread and riser housings and then, working along the face of the string with a hammer and wood block, knock it back into place to reseat the joints (**1**).

If the string tends to spring away, hold it in place with lengths of timber braced between it and the opposite wall (**2**). Secure the joints by driving in glued hardwood wedges.

Reinforce the joint between the bottom step and the newel post with glued blocks rubbed into the angle on the underside of the stair. Alternatively, screw metal angle plates into the corners (**3**).

1 Reseat loose joints with a hammer and block

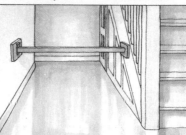

2 Brace the string against the opposite wall

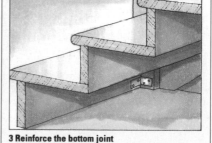

3 Reinforce the bottom joint

SEE ALSO	
Details for:	
Wood finishes	77
Stair construction	219-220
Building Regulations	220
Loose housing	221
Adjustable bevel	478
Dowel joints	502-503
Wall fixings	516

Handrail components
In addition to normal handrail mouldings, special matched components are available, such as turns, ramps and open rise. These are joined with special handrail screws or dowels.

Horizontal cap turn

Horizontal turn

Opening rise

Concave ramp

Goose neck

225

REPLACING A
BALUSTRADE

While the staircase contributes greatly to the character of a house, the character of the staircase itself is largely determined by the design of its balustrade.

A mahogany balustrade constructed from a kit

Balustrade components
1 Newel base
2 Newel centre
3 Decorative knob
4 Turned balusters
5 Handrail
6 Base rail
7 Spacer fillets
8 Metal brackets
9 Cover buttons

Older houses, including those in mass-produced terraces, were often fitted with attractive decorative features such as turned newel posts and balusters, but over the years many of these old balustrades have been 'modernized'. Sometimes this has been done by simply panelling over the open balusters, sometimes by replacing turned ones with straight ones, and sometimes even by cutting away the whole assembly to achieve an 'open-plan' appearance (which, aesthetics apart, does not comply with the Building Regulations; a new balustrade should be fitted for your own safety).

Using a kit to replace a balustrade

A kit of parts is available which enables you to reinstate a balustrade with a choice of traditional styles . Each kit consists of newel posts made up of three parts – a base section (**1**), a turned centre section (**2**) and a decorative knob (**3**) – plus turned balusters (**4**) with a handrail (**5**) and machine-grooved base rail (**6**) in which to fit them. Spacer fillets (**7**) are also provided to make the fitting and finishing of the balusters a straight-forward job, and there are special metal brackets (**8**) for joining the ends of the handrails to the posts. You can use all or any of the parts to meet the demands of most types of wooden staircase, but below a straight-flight stair is taken as a typical example.

Preparation
Remove all old hardboard or plywood panelling, and cut away, knock out or unscrew all old balusters, balustrade rails and handrails.

Fitting the newels
The simplest way to replace a damaged or modified newel is to cut it off, leaving intact the joints between its base and the outer string.

Saw through the base of the bottom newel, about 260mm (10¼in) above the pitch line – the stair nosing line – where it crosses the centre of the post. Cut the top newel 183mm (7¼in) above the pitch line and cut the base of any intermediate newel to a height of 251mm (10in) above the nosing. Mark diagonal lines across

the cut ends to find their centres, then drill out central holes, 50mm (2in) in diameter, to receive the centre spigots of the new newel posts. Use a special hole saw and spade bit in a power drill or an expansion bit in a hand brace. Shape the cut ends of the old newel posts to a slightly convex contour and set the new newels in position, but do not glue them yet.

Fitting the rails
With an adjustable bevel, take the angle of the stair string where it meets the newel base. Hold the balustrade base rail against the stair, following the angle of the string exactly, and make a mark at each end where it meets the newels. Mark the cutting lines at these points, using the bevel and a try square, and cut the rail to length.

Mark and cut the handrail in the same way, or use the base rail as a guide if it is the same length. Screw the base rail to the string, then fix the special bolted handrail brackets to the newels and take up the slack with a spanner. Check that the newels are upright and that the rails fit properly, then glue the newels in place. Use a PVA woodworking adhesive or, if the joints are slack, a gap-filling synthetic-resin glue. Tighten the handrail-bracket bolts, and when the adhesive has set, fit cover buttons (**9**) to conceal the nuts.

Fitting the balusters
Calculate the number of balusters you need, allowing the equivalent of two per tread and one for the tread adjacent to the newel. In any event, none of the elements should be spaced more than 100mm (4in) apart at any point.

To find out how many infill fillets will be required, double the number of balusters and add four.

Measure the vertical distance between the groove in the handrail and the groove in the base rail, then transfer this dimension to a baluster. Mark it out, using the adjustable bevel to achieve the exact angle. Cut the baluster to size and check it for fit, then cut the others to suit. Space the balusters equally, using the precut fillets to even out the spacing over the total run.

Pin and glue the balusters and fillets in place, and when the adhesive has set rub them down and finish the bare wood with coloured stain and clear varnish or paint as required.

Most pitched roofs were once built on site from individual lengths of timber, but to save time and materials, most builders now use prefabricated frames called trussed rafters. These are specifically designed to meet the loading requirements of a given house and, unlike traditional roofs, are not usually suitable for conversion because to remove any part of the structure can cause it to collapse.

Close-couple roof
A roof structure which has its rafters joined by joists. A variation is the collar roof where the joists (collars) are set at a higher level.

Basic construction

The framework of an ordinary pitched roof is based on a triangle, the most rigid and economical form for a loadbearing structure. The weight of the roof covering is carried by the sloping members, the 'common rafters', which are set in opposing pairs whose heads meet against a central 'ridge board'. The lower ends, or feet, of the rafters are fixed to timber wall plates which are bedded on the exterior walls and distribute the weight uniformly.

To stop the roof's weight pushing the walls out, horizontal joists (ties) are fixed to the ends of each pair of rafters and the wall plates, forming a simple structure called a close-couple roof. The joists usually support the ceiling plaster; the rafters are also linked by roof-tiling battens.

TYPES OF PITCHED ROOF

Single roofs

Any roof, pitched or flat, with unbraced rafters – except for the pitched roof's joists – is called a single roof (**1**), and is only suitable for light coverings and short spans. For a wide span or heavy covering, the design would need unduly large roof timbers.

Double roofs

In double roofs, horizontal beams called purlins support the rafters (**2**), linking them either midway between foot and ridge or 2.5m (8ft) apart. This reduces the span of the rafters and allows light-weight timber to be used, 100 x 50mm (4 x 2in) being common. The cross section of a purlin depends to a great extent on the weight of the roof covering, but it usually exceeds that of the rafters; 200 x 50mm (8 x 2in) is normal. The ends of the purlins are supported on the brickwork of a gable wall or, in a hipped roof, by hip rafters.

To keep the size of the purlins to a minimum, struts are set in opposing pairs to brace them diagonally at every fourth or fifth pair of rafters. Struts transfer some weight back to the centre of the ceiling joists, which are supported there by a loadbearing dividing wall at right angles to them. The ends of the struts are jointed to a horizontal 'binder' fixed to the joists directly above the supporting wall. Where ceiling joists are fairly lightweight and the span could make

them sag, vertical timber 'hangers' are suspended from the top of every third and fourth rafter or from adjacent purlins at like intervals. At the bottom, hangers are fixed to a binder running at right angles across the joists.

Trussed roofs

Some traditional roofs embody trusses, rigid triangular frames that allow for a wider span, dispensing with loadbearing partition walls. Trusses carry the purlins, which in turn support the rafters and form a 'triple' or 'framed' roof. The trusses are spaced at 1.8m (6ft) or more, depending on the purlins' section or the roof covering's weight. As main bearers for the roof, they transmit weight to the exterior walls. Few trussed roofs can be converted and you should not try to cut into them.

'Trussed rafters' are now used in all new housing (**3**). Computer-designed for economy plus rigidity, the trusses are prefabricated of planed softwood 38mm (1½in) thick and up to 150mm (6in) wide, depending on roof loading. Each truss combines two common rafters, a joist and strut bracing in one frame; the members are butt-jointed and fixed with special nailed plate connectors.

The trusses are spaced a maximum 600mm (2ft) apart, linked horizontally with bracing members nailed to the struts. Such roofs are relatively lightweight, and are usually fixed to the walls with steel anchor straps to resist wind pressure.

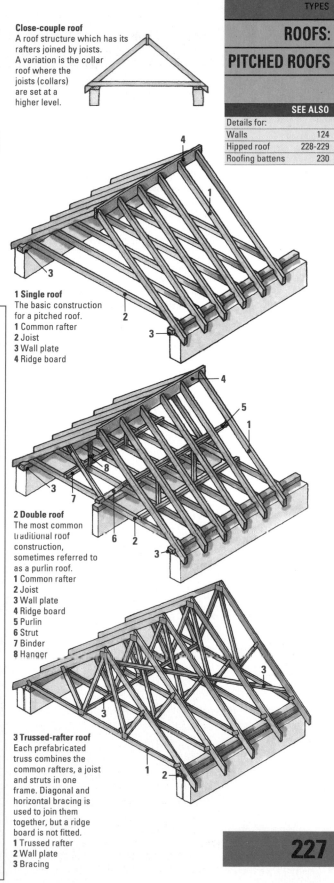

1 Single roof
The basic construction for a pitched roof.
1 Common rafter
2 Joist
3 Wall plate
4 Ridge board

2 Double roof
The most common traditional roof construction, sometimes referred to as a purlin roof.
1 Common rafter
2 Joist
3 Wall plate
4 Ridge board
5 Purlin
6 Strut
7 Binder
8 Hanger

3 Trussed-rafter roof
Each prefabricated truss combines the common rafters, a joist and struts in one frame. Diagonal and horizontal bracing is used to join them together, but a ridge board is not fitted.
1 Trussed rafter
2 Wall plate
3 Bracing

227

Hips and valleys

All the components mentioned earlier are found in ordinary gable roofs. One with a hipped end or valleys has even more parts, but all serve to fulfil similar functions. Below, a double roof is used to illustrate the components.

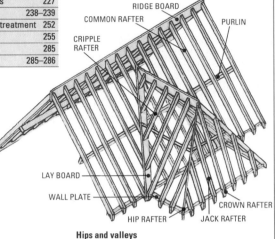

RIDGE BOARD
COMMON RAFTER
PURLIN
CRIPPLE RAFTER
LAY BOARD
WALL PLATE
CROWN RAFTER
HIP RAFTER
JACK RAFTER

Hips and valleys

Eaves

That part of a roof where the rafters meet the exterior walls is known as the eaves. When rafters are cut flush with the walls, a fascia board is nailed horizontally across their ends to protect them and support the guttering (**1**).

1 Flush eaves

Open eaves

The ends of projecting rafters can be left exposed (**2**), with gutter-fixing brackets screwed either to their sides or to their top edges.

2 Open eaves

Closed eaves

Projecting rafters can also be clad with a fascia that is grooved to take a soffit board, enclosing the eaves (**3**). The soffit board can be at 90 degrees to the wall or slope with the rafters. If the loft is insulated, a roof with closed eaves must be ventilated with soffit vents.

3 Closed eaves

The verge

The verge is the sloping edge of the roof. It can end flush with the gable wall or project past it. With a flush verge, the end rafter fits inside the wall, but the roof covering extends over it (**4**). A projecting verge is constructed with the roof timbers extending beyond the wall to carry an external rafter with a 'barge board' fixed to it. There is often a soffit board behind the barge board to enclose a projecting verge (**5**).

ROOF-STRUCTURE PROBLEMS

A roof structure can fail as a result of timber decay caused by poor weatherproofing, condensation or insect attack. It can also suffer from overloading, especially if the timbers were inadequate in the first place. It is important to check that new roofing is not too heavy and to ensure that a window opening is braced properly. A sagging roof is often visible from street level, but it pays to inspect the roof structure closely from inside.

Inspection

The roof should be inspected annually to check that it is still weatherproof and that there is no woodworm infestation. If your loft has no natural lighting, buy a powerful torch or rig up a mains-powered extension lead with a caged lamp. In an unboarded attic, place planks across the joists to walk on.

Rot and infestation

Rot in roof timbers is a serious problem which should rectified by experts, and its cause should be identified and dealt with promptly. Rot is the result of damp conditions that encourage wood-rotting fungi to grow. Inspect the roof covering closely for loose and damaged slates or tiles in the vicinity of the rot; on a pitched roof water may be penetrating the covering at a higher level, so the leak may not be immediately obvious. If the rot is close to a gable wall you should suspect the flashing. Rot can also be the result of condensation. Better ventilation is the usual remedy.

If you employ contractors to treat the rot, it is better to have them make all the repairs. Their work is covered by a guarantee which may be invalidated if you attempt to deal with the cause yourself to save money.

Wood-boring beetle infestation should also be treated by professionals if it is serious. Severely infected wood may have to be replaced, and the whole structure will have to be sprayed.

Strengthening the roof

A sagging roof may not require bracing as long as the structure is sound, stable and weatherproof. Old houses with slightly sagging roof lines are often considered attractive, but consult a surveyor if you suspect a roof is weak.

The walls under the eaves should be inspected for bulging and checked with a plumb line. Bulging tends to occur where window openings are close to the eaves, making a wall relatively weak. However, bulging is sometimes caused by an inadequately braced roof structure that is spreading and pushing the walls outwards. If this proves to be the case, call in a builder or roofing contractor to do the repair work.

A lightly constructed roof can be strengthened by adding extra timbers. The exact method depends on the type of roof, its span, loading and condition. It may be possible to add sufficient bracing from inside the roof, provided the new timbers are not too large. If not, at least some of the roof covering will have to be stripped off.

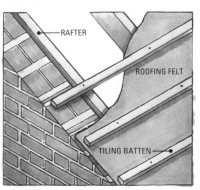

RAFTER
ROOFING FELT
TILING BATTEN

4 Flush verge

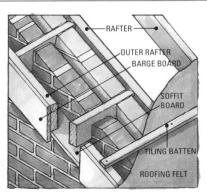

RAFTER
OUTER RAFTER
BARGE BOARD
SOFFIT BOARD
TILING BATTEN
ROOFING FELT

5 Projecting verge

TYPES OF ROOFING

Roof coverings are manufactured by moulding clay or concrete into various profiles or by cutting natural materials such as slate into flat sheets.

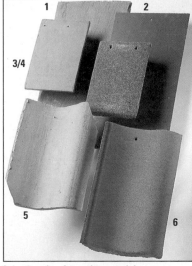

Selection of roof-covering materials
1 Natural slate. 2 Machine-made slate. 3 Plain tile (clay). 4 Plain tile (concrete). 5 Plain pantile (clay). 6 Interlocking pantile (concrete).

Coverings for domestic pitched roofs follow a long tradition, and despite the developments in new materials the older ones and the ways of using them have not changed radically.

Like most early building materials those used for roofing were generally of local origin, which led to a diversity of roof coverings, including tiles, slates and timber shingles. For centuries they were hand-made and had their own characteristics, visible in various regional styles.

During the last century the more durable roof coverings, such as tiles and slates, became more widely adopted.

Most roofing materials are laid across the roof in rows called courses so that the bottom of each overlaps the top of the one below. This means they are laid working from the eaves up the slope of the roof to the ridge.

Specially shaped tiles are used for capping the ridge or hips so as to weatherproof the junctions of the slopes. Where the covering meets a chimney or a wall it is protected with flashing, usually made of lead or mortar

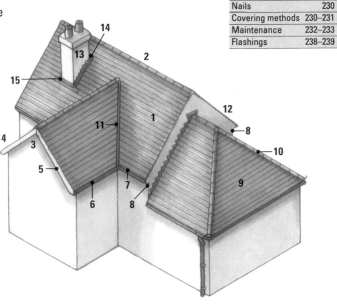

Roof-covering components for a pitched roof.

1 Tile or slate covering	9 Hipped end
2 Ridge tile	10 Hip tile
3 Gable end	11 Valley
4 Projecting verge	12 Flush verge
5 Barge board	13 Lead stepped
6 Eaves	flashing
7 Fascia	14 Back gutter
8 Soffit	15 Apron

TYPICAL COVERINGS FOR PITCHED ROOFS

Material	Common sizes	Finish	Colour	Fixing	Weight* kg/m² (lb/sq yd)	Minimum pitch in degrees
TYPE OF COVERING						
SLATE Split metamorphic sedimentary rock	Lengths: 300 to 600mm (1ft to 2ft) Widths: 180 to 350mm (7in to 1ft 2in)	Natural	Natural Blue Grey Green	Two nails	27.5 to 70 (51 to 129)	17½°
MACHINE-MADE SLATE Fibre cement Asbestos cement (now rarely used)	Lengths: 400, 500, 600mm (1ft 4in, 1ft 8in, 2ft) Widths: 200, 250, 300mm (8in, 10in, 1ft)	Acrylic coating	Grey Blue/black Brown Russet Mottled	Two nails plus copper-disc rivet	18.5 to 22 (34 to 40)	20°
STONE Split sandstone or limestone sedimentary rock Machine made	Random and as natural slate Lengths: 200 to 550mm (8in to 1ft 9½in) Widths: 100 to 500mm (4in to 1ft 8in)	Natural	Natural Yellow Grey Green	Two nails	90 (166) 84 to 110 (155 to 203)	20°
SHINGLES Split or sawn red cedar	Length: 400mm (1ft 4in) Widths: 75 to 300mm (3in to 1ft)	Natural	Natural Brown Grey	Two nails	7 (13)	20°
PLAIN TILES Hand-moulded or machine-moulded clay or machine-made concrete	Length: 265mm (10½in) Width: 165mm (6½in)	Sanded Smooth	Brown Red Grey Blue Green	Two nails or loose laid on nibs	76 to 87 (140 to 160)	40° clay 35° concrete
INTERLOCKING TILES Hand-moulded or machine-moulded clay or machine-made concrete	Lengths: 380, 410, 430mm (1ft 3in, 1ft 4½in, 1ft 5in) Widths: 220, 330, 380mm (9in, 1ft 1in, 1ft 3in)	Sanded Smooth Glazed	Red Brown Grey Blue Green	Loose laid on nibs, nailed or clipped	40 to 57 (74 to 105) depending on profile	22½° clay 17½° to 30° concrete

*Approx

229

Tile clip

Nailed tile clip

Eave clip (flat)

Eave clip (contoured)

Verge clip (flat)

Copper rivet

TYPES OF ROOF COVERING

Double-lap coverings

Plain tiles, slates, stone 'slates' and wooden shingles are all double-lap coverings. They are basically flat – with the exception of plain tiles, which have a slight camber and nibs – and are laid with their side edges butting together, not overlapping. To prevent water penetrating the joints each course is lapped in part by the two courses above it. The joints are staggered, or 'broken jointed', on alternate courses like courses of bricks in a wall.

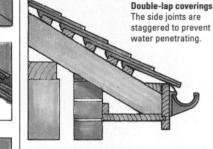

Double-lap coverings
The side joints are staggered to prevent water penetrating.

Single-lap coverings

Nearly all tiles of moulded clay and concrete are single-lap coverings, which means that each tile is profiled so as to interlock with the next one by means of a single lap on its side, and each course is laid with only a single lap at the head.

Early single-lap examples, such as clay pantiles, simply used the curved shape of the tile to form the overlap, but modern machine-made tiles of clay or concrete incorporate systems of grooves and water bars which prevent water penetrating the lap. These tiles have nibs at their top back edges which hook on to the battens. They are held in place by their own weight or are fixed with nails or clips.

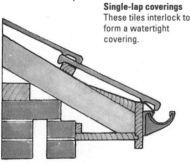

Single-lap coverings
These tiles interlock to form a watertight covering.

If you intend to make repairs yourself you will need some knowledge of the roof-covering system used on a common pitched roof. It will also help you if you have to commission contractors, either for repairs or reroofing work, as you will benefit from a better understanding of the work that is being carried out.

Underlay

To comply with current Building Regulations, new and re-covered pitched roofs must have a weather-resistant underlay of some kind.

This underlay, sometimes called sarking, should be a reinforced bituminous felt, Type 1F, or a suitable tear-resistant plastic material like polyethylene. These are sold in rolls to be cut to length as required.

The sheet material provides a barrier to any moisture that may penetrate the outer covering. It also improves the insulation value of the roof.

Like the tiles themselves, the sarking is laid horizontally, working upwards from the eaves, each strip overlapped by the one above it.

Battens

The roof covering is supported on sawn softwood battens which are nailed across the rafters, over the sarking (**1**). They are pretreated with a preserver. When the roof is close-boarded there should be vertical counter-battens under the horizontal battens (**2**) to provide some ventilation under the tiles and to allow any moisture to drain freely down the roof.

1 The battens are nailed over the sarking

2 Close-boarded roofs should have vertical counter-battens

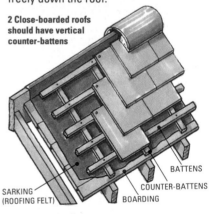

BATTENS

SARKING (ROOFING FELT)

SARKING (ROOFING FELT)

BOARDING

BATTENS

COUNTER-BATTENS

Fixings

Most roof coverings are fixed with nails or clips. Slates and shingles are fixed individually with nails, normally two placed halfway up, though some are nailed at the top. Fibre-cement slates are centre-nailed with copper rivets to hold down the tails (see left).

Tiles have nibs that hook over the battens, keeping them in place, and some types need nothing more. Others are held with nails or clips.

The fixings are determined by the type and size of tile, the pitch of the roof and the exposure of the building.

● Black dot denotes that nail type and roof covering are compatible.

TYPE OF ROOF COVERING						
TYPE OF NAIL	Slate	Fibre-cement slate	Clay tiles	Concrete tiles	Shingles	Felt
COPPER	●	●	●	●	●	
ALUMINIUM-ALLOY	●		●	●	●	
SILICON-BRONZE	●	●	●	●	●	
GALVANIZED-STEEL					●	●
STAINLESS-STEEL	●	●	●	●	●	

GENERAL CONSTRUCTION

ROOF SAFETY

Working on a roof can be hazardous, and if you feel insecure working at that height, you should hire a contractor. If you decide to do it yourself, do not use ladders alone to reach the roof; hire a sectional scaffold tower and scaffold board to provide a safe working platform complete with toe boards.

Roof coverings are fairly fragile and may not bear your weight – hire crawl boards or special roof ladders to gain access. A roof ladder should reach from the scaffold tower to the ridge of the roof and hook over the latter. Wheel the ladder up the slope and then turn it over to engage the hook (**1**).

Roof ladders are made with rails that keep the treads clear of the roof surface and spread the load (**2**), but if you think it necessary you can place additional padding of paper-stuffed or sand-filled sacks to help spread the load further.

Carry your tools in a special belt and only put them down within the roof-ladder framework. Make sure you bring every tool down from the roof when you have finished work.

1 Engage the hook of the ladder over the ridge

2 A roof ladder spreads the load

It is important for the overall appearance and performance of the roof that the covering is well finished at the verge, eaves and valley edges.

Verges

In the interest of neatness the verge is normally formed by first laying an undercloak of plain tile or slate bedded on the brickwork or – in the case of an overhanging verge – nailed to the timber frame. The roof covering is then bedded in mortar on top of the undercloak and finished flush. The verge of a slate or plain tiled roof is set to slope inwards slightly to prevent rainwater running down the walls, but single-lap tiles are laid flat.

Special dry-fixed verge tiles are available for use with single-lap concrete tiles and fibre-cement slates.

Eaves

The detail of the roof covering at the eaves depends on the type of covering. Plain tiling begins with a course of short under-tiles, nailed to a batten and projecting 38 to 50mm (1½ to 2in) over the gutter. The first course of whole tiles is laid with staggered joints over the under-tiles with their tail edges flush (**1**).

Some single-lap tiles, such as pantiles, also use an undercloak of plain tiles, the first course being bedded in mortar that fills up the hollow rolls. As an alternative there are special eaves tiles with blocked ends or overhangs.

Single-lap low-profile tiles are normally laid directly over, and supported by, the fascia board (**2**).

When the roof covering is natural slate, a double course is laid at the eaves. A course of short slates is nailed to the first batten and covered by a course of full slates with their tails flush and their joints staggered.

Three courses are used for fibre-cement slates to support the tail rivets used with this type of covering.

Valleys

Traditional double-lap roof coverings of plain tiles may embody special valley tiles, or, as with slate, may be formed into 'swept' or 'laced' valleys. The latter call for great skill and are expensive to make. Most valleys are formed as open gutters using sheet metal.

Single-lap roofing may use sheet valleys or special trough units.

An undercloak course projects slightly and gives a neat finish to the verge

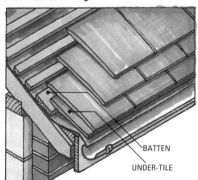

BATTEN

UNDER-TILE

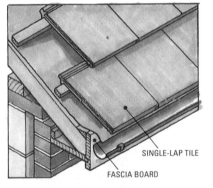

SINGLE-LAP TILE

FASCIA BOARD

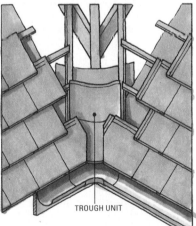

TROUGH UNIT

Verge detail at ridge
The ridge tile is set flush with the verge and filled with bedding mortar.

1 Plain tiles
The eaves under-tiles are nailed to a batten. The joints between them are covered with full tiles.

2 Single-lap low-profile tiles
Not all interlocking tiles need under-tiles at the eaves, but the fascia must support the eaves course at the correct angle.

Valley tiles
Modern roofs may have trough units instead of the traditional lead sheeting.

ROOF
MAINTENANCE

The roof and upper parts of a building, such as chimneys and parapet walls, must be kept in sound condition if they are to remain weatherproof. Failure of the roof covering can cause expensive deterioration of the underlying timber structure, interior plaster and decorative finishes.

All roof coverings have a limited life, the length depending on the quality of materials used, the workmanship and exposure to severe weather. An average roof covering might be expected to give good service for 40 to 60 years, and some materials can last for 100 years or more, though some deterioration of the fixings and the flashings will take place. Reuse the old materials if you can.

Patch repairs may prove to be of only temporary value and can look unsightly. If patching becomes a recurrent chore it is time for the roof to be re-covered. This involves stripping off the original material and possibly reusing it, or perhaps replacing it with a new covering similar to the old. Major roof work is not something you should tackle yourself. A contractor will do it more quickly and will guarantee the work.

Reroofing work may qualify for a discretionary improvement grant from your local authority, so check with them before carrying out any work if you think you are eligible. You will not require planning permission unless you live in a listed building or a conservation area.

Inspecting the roof
The roofs of older houses are likely to show their age and should be checked at least once a year.

Start by taking a general look at the whole roof from ground level. Slipped or disjointed tiles or slates should be spotted easily against the regular lines of the undisturbed covering. The colour of any newly exposed and unweathered slate will also pinpoint a fault. Look at the ridge against the sky to check for misalignment and gaps in the mortar jointing. Follow this with a closer inspection through binoculars, checking the state of the flashings at abutments and around the chimney brickwork.

From inside an unlined roof you can spot chinks of daylight that indicate breaks in the covering. Use a torch to check the roof timbers for water stains; they may show as dark or white streaks. Trace the stain to find the source.

1 Pull out nails

2 Nail strip to batten

Removing and replacing a slate

A slate may slip out of place because the nails have corroded or because the slate itself has broken. Whatever the cause, slipped or broken slates should be replaced as soon as possible before a high wind strips them off the roof.

Use a slater's ripper to remove the trapped part of a broken slate. Slip the tool under the slate and locate its hooked end over one of the fixing nails **(1)**, then pull down hard on the tool to extract or cut through the nail. Remove the second nail in the same way. Even where an aged slate has already slipped out completely you may have to remove the nails in the same way to allow the replacement slate to be inserted.

You will not be able to nail a new slate in place. Instead, use a plastic clip or cut a 25mm (1in) wide strip of lead or zinc to the length of the slate lap plus 25mm (1in). Attach the strip to the batten by driving a nail between the slates of the lower course **(2)**, then slide the new slate into position and turn back the end of the lead strip to secure it **(3)**.

3 Fold strip over edge

Cutting natural slate

You may have to cut a second-hand slate to fit the gap in your roof. With a sharp point, mark out the required size on the back of the slate. Place the slate, bevelled side down, on a bench. Align the cutting line with the edge of the bench, then chop the slate with the edge of a bricklayer's trowel. Work from both edges towards the middle, using the edge of the bench as a guide. Drill nail holes or punch them out with a masonry nail – a punched hole leaves a recess for the head of a roofing nail.

Fibre-cement slates
Having scribed the lines, break a fibre-cement tile over a straightedge or cut it to size with a universal saw. If you saw asbestos-cement slates, wear a mask, keep the dust damped down and sweep it into a plastic bag for disposal. Make nail holes with a drill.

Cut from each edge

REPLACING A TILE

Individual tiles can be difficult to remove on two accounts: the retaining nibs on their back edges and their interlocking shape which holds them together.

Remove a broken plain tile by lifting it so that the nibs clear the batten on which they rest, then draw it out. This is easier if the overlapping tiles are first lifted with wooden wedges inserted at both sides of the tile that is to be removed **(1)**. If the tile is also nailed, try rocking it loose. If this fails you will have to break it out carefully. You may then have to use a slater's ripper to extract or cut any remaining nails.

Use a similar technique for a single-lap interlocking tiles, but in this case you will also have to wedge up the tile to the left of the one being removed **(2)**. If the tile has a deep profile you will have to ease up a number of surrounding tiles to achieve the required clearance.

If you are removing a tile to put in a roof vent, you can afford to smash it with a hammer, taking care not to damage any of the adjacent tiles. The remaining tiles should be easier to remove once the first is out.

1 Lift the overlapping tiles with wedges

2 Lift interlocking tiles above and to the left

CUTTING TILES

To cut tiles use an abrasive cutting disc in a power saw or hire an angle grinder for the purpose. Always wear protective goggles and a mask when cutting with a power tool.

To save money, use a tungsten-grit blade in a hacksaw frame to cut a few tiles. Trim the edges of a tile with pincers, but score the cutting line first with a tile cutter.

SHEET

ROOFING

REBEDDING RIDGE TILES

When the old lime mortar breaks down, a whole row of ridge tiles can be left with practically nothing but their weight holding them in place.

Lift off the ridge tiles and clear all the crumbling mortar from the roof and from the undersides of the tiles. Give the tiles a good soaking in water before starting to fix them.

Mix stiff mortar from 1 part cement : 3 parts sand. Load a bucket about half full and carry it on to the roof.

Dampen the top courses of roof tiles or slates, and lay a thick bed of mortar on each side of the ridge, following the line left behind by the old mortar **(1)**. Lay mortar for one or two tiles at a time.

Press a ridge tile firmly into the mortar and use a trowel to slice off mortar that has squeezed out. Try not to smear any on the ridge tile.

Build up a bed of mortar to fill the hollow end of each ridge tile, inserting pieces of tile or slate to prevent the mortar slumping **(2)**. Press the next tile in place, squeezing out enough mortar to fill the end joint flush. Build a similar mortar joint between ridge tiles and a wall or chimney stack.

1 Apply bands of bedding mortar on each side

2 Insert pieces of slate in joint bedding mortar

HALF-ROUND   HOG-BACK   ANGLE

Typical ridge tile shapes

The commonest sheet materials for roofing are made from fibre cement or rigid plastic (PVC). Aluminium, steel and corrugated bitumen sheeting are used for roofing, but not often for domestic work.

Sheet roofing is used mainly for outbuildings such as garages and garden sheds, and translucent plastic is used for lean-to extensions.

Consult your local Building Control Officer when considering a plastic roof to ensure that it complies with the fire regulations.

Corrugated-sheet roofing

Corrugated sheets are produced in standard profiles of 32mm (1¼in) and 75mm (3in) for plastic, and 75mm (3in) and 150mm (6in) for fibre cement.

When calculating the number of corrugated sheets you need, make an allowance for the side overlap. Small-profile sheets should overlap by at least two corrugations **(1)**, while larger ones require an overlap of one only **(2)**. The ends should overlap by at least 150mm (6in) in sheltered locations for roofs with pitches of about 22 degrees or more. For pitches of less than this, allow a 300mm (1ft) overlap.

Corrugated sheets are supported by purlins. They are of wood in most domestic buildings, though some system-built garages embody steel sections. Wood screws or drive screws fix the roofing to wooden purlins **(3)** and hooked bolts are used with metal ones **(4)**. There are special plastic washers and caps for sealing the heads of the screws or bolts.

Cutting corrugated plastic

Mark the cutting lines on thin plastic sheet with a felt-tipped pen, then cut with a tenon saw. Support the sheeting between two boards on trestles and use the top board as a guide for your saw.

When cutting sheets to length, saw across the peaks of the corrugations with the saw held at a very shallow angle. Cut halfway through, then turn the sheet over and finish cutting from the other side.

When cutting to width, make the cut along the peak of a corrugation, again working with the saw at a shallow angle. Support a flexible sheet on two planks, one on each side of the line.

Cutting corrugated fibre cement

Lay the sheet on boards supported by trestles. As the material is fairly thick you will not need a top supporting board and you can saw the sheet without turning it over. Use a sheet saw or universal saw and wear a mask. Damp down dust from asbestos-fibre sheet and sweep it into a plastic bag. Seal the bag with adhesive tape ready for disposal. Damp newspaper under the trestles will help contain the dust.

Laying corrugated sheet

You can work from stepladders inside the structure or from above on boards, depending on the pitch of the roof.

Start at the eaves and work from left to right or vice versa.

Plastic sheet

Position the first sheet and drill oversized clearance holes for the fixing screws on the centre lines of the wooden purlins. Drill the holes in the crowns of the corrugations and space them at about every third or fourth corrugation. Never place fixings in the troughs of the sheeting.

Do not make holes where the next sheet will overlap the first. Instead, lay the second sheet with corrugations overlapping and drill through both sheets. Lay and fix the rest of the row of sheets in the same way.

Start the next row on the same side as the first one **(1)**, overlapping the ends by at least 150mm (6in), and drill and fix through both layers.

Finally, fit the protective plastic caps over the fixing washers.

Laying fibre-cement sheet

Corrugated fibre-cement sheet is laid smooth side up. It is a fairly thick material, so cut some of the corners away to form mitres **(2)** in order to reduce the bulk of four thicknesses at the end laps. Draw the angle of the mitre between two points representing the length of the end lap and the width of the side lap.

Fix the sheets using the same method as for plastic sheet. For large-profile sheets use only two fixings to each purlin, placing them adjacent to the side laps. The end laps are fixed through both layers.

1 Small-profile lap

2 Large-profile lap

3 Wood purlin fixing

4 Metal purlin fixing

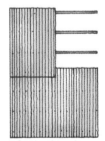

1 Overlap the ends

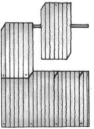

2 Mitre the corners

233

FLAT ROOFS

Timber-framed flat roofs are used for main roofs, rear extensions and outbuildings. Most have joists carrying stiff wooden decking, and these usually cross the shorter span, spaced at 400mm (1ft 4in), 450mm (1ft 6in) or 600mm (2ft) between centres. Herringbone or solid strutting is required for a span of more than 2.5m (8ft) to prevent the joists buckling. Their ends may be fixed to wall plates on loadbearing walls or, as on an extension, they are set in metal hangers or into the brickwork of the wall. Metal restraint straps tie the ends of the timbers down to the walls.

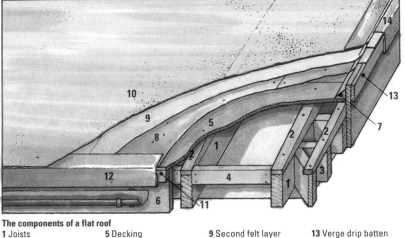

The components of a flat roof

1 Joists	5 Decking	9 Second felt layer	13 Verge drip batten
2 Furring	6 Fascia board	10 Third felt layer	14 Felt verge drip
3 Return-joist	7 Angle fillet	11 Eaves drip batten	
4 Nogging	8 First felt layer	12 Felt eaves drip	

Fall

Furring methods

1 Tapered furrings fixed in line with joist.

2 Furrings of decreasing size fitted across fall.

3 Tapered furrings fixed across joists.

The fall of a flat roof should be at least 1:80 for smooth surfaces like metal or plastic, and 1:60 for rougher materials. The fall is designed to shed water, but puddles may form if it is too shallow. The action of sun or frost can break down the roof covering and let the standing water through.

Sloping joists provide a fall, but this means that any ceiling below also slopes. To achieve a flat ceiling, tapered 'furrings' are nailed to the tops of the joists (1). Otherwise, joists may be set across the line of the fall with parallel furring pieces of decreasing thickness nailed to them (2) or tapered furrings are fixed across them (3). The latter provides better cross-ventilation.

Decking

Chipboard or plywood decking is fixed to the joists to make a flat base for the final covering. Older flat roofs were decked with square-edged or tongue-and-groove boards which were laid with their joints running with the fall of the roof to shed water efficiently.

Plywood and chipboard panels, normally 18mm (¾in) thick, are laid with their long edges across the joists and their ends centred over supporting joists. Noggings may be fitted between the joists to give extra support to the long edges of the panels, depending on their thickness and joist spacing.

If you want a felted roof you might consider using prefelted chipboard. This material is laid with 3mm (⅛in) gaps between the boards to allow for thermal expansion, and fixed down with either nails or screws.

If you are unable to apply the final layer of felt sheeting immediately, you can make prefelted decking temporarily waterproof by filling the gaps between the boards with a cold-bonding mastic and then sealing the joints with 100mm (4in) wide roof-sealing tape. This is not a viable option for other types of decking.

Covering the deck

Whatever decking is used, it must be waterproofed with either mastic asphalt or roofing felt (see right).

In addition, the roof can be covered with a 12mm (½in) thick layer of pale-coloured chippings to reflect some of the sun's heat.

FLAT-ROOF COVERINGS

Bitumen-based coverings fall into two types: asphalt and bituminous felt. Felts are much better than they once were and are now generally used on domestic buildings instead of the lead, zinc or copper seen on older houses.

Mastic asphalt

This waterproof material, made from either natural or synthetic bitumen, weathers very well. It is melted in a cauldron and spread over the roof hot, to set in an impervious layer. Two layers are applied with a float to a combined thickness of 18mm (¾in) on a layer of sheathing felt covering the decking. Laying hot asphalt is a skilled job.

Roofing felts

These bitumen-impregnated sheet materials are applied in layers to produce 'built-up' roofing, bonded with hot or cold bitumen. Making such a roof with hot bitumen is a professional job.

Several felts are available, and the choice will affect a roof's cost and longevity. Traditional British Standard felts are classified by their reinforcing base material and finish, indicated by a number and letter. A colour strip identifies the base material. These felts are less tough than modern high-performance ones. The latter are based on glass tissue reinforced with polyester or polyester fabric, some with modified bitumen for greater flexibility.

Bonding felts

Plywood and chipboard decks need partial bonding of the first layer, using a perforated underlay either applied loose or bonded with bands of bitumen about 500mm (1ft 8in) wide around the edges. The first layer is then partially bonded by the hot bitumen penetrating through the holes. On solid timber, the first layer is secured with clout nails. Subsequent layers are fully bonded by applying hot or cold bitumen with a trowel or a notched spreader over the whole surface.

Butyl roofing

Butyl roofing is a single-ply flexible membrane that is nailed over a single layer of underfelt. It provides a strong, maintenance-free covering.

ABUTMENTS
AND PARAPETS

Leaks can occur wherever a flat roof abuts a house or parapet wall, so the roof covering is usually turned up the wall to form a 'skirting' which is tucked into the mortar bed of the brickwork, or covered by flashing.

Parapet walls are prone to damp, being exposed on both sides. Their top edges are usually finished with brick, stone or tile coping which should overhang the wall faces to throw off rainwater. Damp-proof courses of lead, bituminous felt or asphalt must be set in the mortar bedding beneath copings (1).

A parapet wall no more than 350mm (1ft 2in) high may have an asphalt skirting taken up the face and continued under the full width of the coping (2). Alternatively, the roof covering is taken up two courses of bricks only and is built into the wall to form a damp-proof course (3).

A flexible damp-proof course like bituminous felt or lead is often set in the bed joint before the roofing is laid and then dressed down to form a flashing over the skirting (4).

Cavity parapet walls also need a damp-proof course. Water penetrating from the roof side must be prevented from running down the cavity to damage the interior walls. The damp-proof course is stepped up from the inside leaf across the cavity to the outer leaf to form a cavity tray (5).

Cladding a parapet with cement rendering is not an entirely satisfactory solution as movement in the wall causes cracks that let in water.

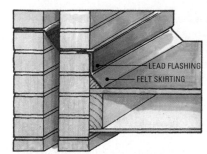

LEAD FLASHING
FELT SKIRTING

A dressed flashing normally laps the skirting

1 Solid and cavity walls need DPC under coping

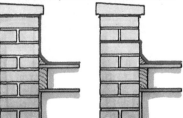

2 Full-height skirting   **3 Continuous covering**

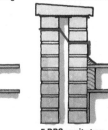

4 DPC flashing   **5 DPC cavity tray**

FITTING A NEW CAVITY TRAY

A cavity wall abutted by an extension roof needs a cavity tray to protect it from damp. Normally it would be built-in, but for existing buildings with new extensions, special trays – moulded units of polypropylene – can be inserted from outside by removing a course of bricks. A single tray, which equals two bricks in length, can also be used where a cavity is bridged by an extractor.

Inserting the tray
Remove three bricks, two courses above the proposed roof level. Do not let rubble fall into the cavity. On the cleaned bricks, lay a length of flashing wide enough to project 50mm (2in) into the wall and cover the roof skirting by 75mm (3in) when dressed down. Trap the flashing with the first tray unit, pushing it into one end of the opening (1). Use mortar to lay two bricks in the tray (2). Pack out the top joint with slate and fill it with mortar. Rake out a weep hole at the base of the middle joint to drain moisture from the cavity.

Cut out two more bricks, leaving a three-brick opening (3), roll out the flashing and insert a second tray. Join the trays with the clip provided, fitting it over the meeting ends to make a watertight joint (4). Lay two more bricks in the opening. Continue until the tray is the required length. You need only remove one brick at the end to make a two-brick opening for the last unit.

When the mortar is firm, point the new work to match the existing wall.

SEE ALSO	
Details for:	
Flashings	238–239
Ventilators	285
Builder's tools	504–506

Moulded cavity tray
Straight and angled sections are available from most builders' merchants.

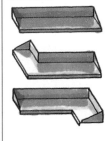

1 Trap the flashing

2 Lay two bricks

3 Cut out two bricks

4 Join the trays

TYPES OF BITUMINOUS FELTS FOR FLAT ROOFS					
Felt type British Standard Ref	Base	Surface Finish	Colour code	Weight kg/per roll	Properties and uses
BS 747 **1B**	Fibre	Sand	White	36kg (79lb)	Least expensive type. Relatively weak. Good for roofing outbuildings.
BS 747 **1E**	Fibre	Mineral	White	38kg (84lb)	
BS 747 **3B**	Glass fibre	Sand	Red	36kg (79lb)	Rot-proof, inexpensive, unsuitable for nailing. Good for 2- or 3-layer systems.
BS 747 **3E**	Glass fibre	Mineral	Red	28kg (62lb)	
BS 747 **3G**	Glass fibre	Grit underside Sand topside	Red	32kg (70lb)	Perforated first layer for partial bonding systems using hot bitumen.
HIGH-PERFORMANCE FELTS					
NO	Glass/polyester	Sand		36kg (79lb)	Rot-proof, tough, good weathering, can be nailed. Use for 2- or 3-layer systems.
BS NUMBERS	Glass/polyester	Mineral		28kg (62lb)	
BS 747 **5U, 5B**	Polyester	Sand	Blue	18.42kg (40.93lb)	More expensive than glass/polyester, but better performance. Use for 2- or 3-layer systems. Excellent for house extensions.
BS 747 **5E**	Polyester	Mineral	Blue	47kg (104lb)	
Elastomeric	Polyester	Sand		32kg (70lb)	Most expensive, but superior durability makes it long lasting and cost effective. Use for 2- or 3-layer systems. The best type for house extensions.
	Polyester	Mineral		40kg (88lb)	
	Polyester	Mineral		38kg (84lb)	

RENEWING A
FELT ROOF

Built-up felt system
Lap the edges of the felt strips and stagger the joints in alternate layers.

1 Nail first layer

2 Bond second layer

3 Lap eaves drip

Covering flat roofs, or stripping and re-covering them, should usually be left to professionals. A built-up felt system using hot bitumen or torching – using a gas-powered torch to soften bitumen-coated felt – is beyond the amateur. However, a competent person can confidently replace perished felt on a garage roof, using a cold-bitumen adhesive. The following example assumes a detached garage with a solid-timber decking covered with three layers of felt.

Replacing perished felt

Wait for dry weather, then strip the old felt. Pull out any clout nails and check the deck for distorted or rotten boards. Lift and replace unsound ones with new boards, using galvanized wire nails punched below the surface.

Cutting to stagger joints
For a three-layer build-up, start at one edge with a strip of felt about one-third of the roll width. The second layer starts with two-thirds width, the top layer with a full width. A two-layer roof starts with half a roll width, then with a full one. You can modify this to suit your roof and avoid having a strip that is too narrow at the other edge. If, for economy or ease of handling, you decide to use short lengths of felt, their ends should overlap by at least 100mm (4in), the lower piece always lapped by the higher one as you work up the slope.

First layer
Cut the strips for the first felt layer slightly longer than the slope of the roof and allow for an overlap of at least 50mm (2in) at the long edges. Cut the first narrow strip as described above.

Nail down the felt, using 18mm (¾in) clout nails 50mm (2in) apart down the centres of the laps and 150mm (6in) apart overall (1). Tuck and trim the felt into the corners of the verge upstand to achieve mitred butt joints. Trim the felt

flush at the eaves and verges, then form and fit the drip at the eaves (see right).

Second layer
Cut strips for the second layer, put the side piece in place, then roll it back halfway from the eaves end. Brush or trowel cold-bitumen adhesive on the felt below but not on the verge upstand. Re-lay the felt and press it down. Roll back the other half and repeat, ensuring that the adhesive is continuous.

Fold and tuck the felt into the corner of the verge upstand and trim it to a mitred butt joint. Turn it back from the verge, apply adhesive and press it into place against the upstand. Trim the end to butt against the edge of the felt eaves drip (see right) and trim the other edges flush with the verge. Place the next length overlapping the first by at least 50mm (2in) and again roll back each half in turn (2), applying the adhesive. Repeat across the roof, then cut and tuck the felt at the other verge corner.

Third layer
Cut and lay the mineral-felt top layer or 'capsheet' in the same way as the second layer, but this time lap the eaves drip and not the verge upstands (3).

Cut strips of mineral felt to form verge drips (see right), then nail and bond the strips into place around the side and rear edges.

MAINTAINING A FLAT ROOF

Whatever the material used for covering your flat roof, it is sensible to carry out a routine inspection at least once a year.

Wear soft-soled shoes when you climb on to the roof, preferably soon after it has rained when you can see if there are standing puddles.

Remove old leaves, twigs and litter. Brush off any silt deposits that have built up, but take care you do not inadvertently lift the lapped edges of roofing felt. Note the positions of puddles because, although they may not present an immediate problem, you will

have a better idea of where to look if the roof springs a leak later on. You should also note any blisters or ripples on a roof covered with felt or asphalt. Check the overlapping joints on a felted roof to make sure they are still well-bonded.

Also make a close inspection of the vulnerable edges of the roof. Check the soundness of the covering at the verges and eaves and the flashings at abutments.

You should also inspect the condition of the gutters and downpipes, and remove any blockages.

MAKING DRIPS

Eaves
Cut 1m (3ft 3in) long strips from the length of a roll of felt. Calculate the width of the strips by measuring the depth of the drip batten and add 25mm (1in). Double this figure and add at least 100mm (4in).

Cut 50mm (2in) from one corner to enable the ends to be overlapped and make folds in the strips, using a straightedge. Nail the drip sections to the drip batten with galvanized clout nails, fold each strip back on itself and bond it over the first layer of felt (1).

Cutting the corners
Where the drip meets the verge, cut the corners to cover the end of the upstand (2). If necessary, make a paper pattern before cutting the felt. You may need an extra-wide strip to allow for a tall upstand. Fold the tabs and bond into place, except the end one, which is left free to be tucked into the verge drip.

Verge drips
Cut and fix the verge drips in place after the top layer of roofing. Cut the strips 1m (3ft 3in) long and calculate their width as with the eaves drip, but allow extra for the top edge and slope of the upstand. Working from the eaves, notch the ends of the strips where they overlap, as for eaves. Cut and fold the end of the first strip where it meets the eaves (3), nail the strip to the batten and bond the remainder in place (4).

At the rear corners, cut and fold the strip covering the side verge (5). Cover the rear verge last, cutting and folding the corners to lap the side pieces and finishing with neat mitres (6).

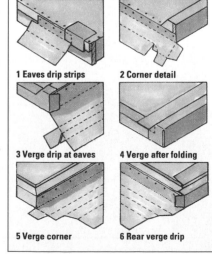

1 Eaves drip strips   **2 Corner detail**

3 Verge drip at eaves   **4 Verge after folding**

5 Verge corner   **6 Rear verge drip**

FLAT-ROOF
REPAIRS

FAULT-FINDING

Damp patches
Damp patches on a ceiling are a clear sign that the roof needs attention, but the source of the problem is not always so obvious. If, however, the patches are close to a wall against which the roof abuts, you can be pretty sure the flashing has broken down.

Locating the leak
A leak anywhere else in the roof may be hard to find, as the water can run downhill from its entry point before dripping on to the ceiling. Measure the distance between the patch and the edges of the ceiling, then locate the point on the roof surface and work from there up the slope to find the source.

Splits and blisters
Splits and blisters on the smooth surface of an asphalt or bitumen felt covering may be obvious, but chippings on a covering tend to obliterate the cause of the leak. Use a blowtorch or hot-air paint stripper to soften the bitumen so you can scrape the chippings away. The surface must be smooth if it is to be patch-repaired.

Splits in the covering caused by movement of the substrate can be recognized by the lines they follow. Blisters formed by trapped moisture or air should be pressed to locate any weaknesses in the covering, which will show as moisture is expelled. These must be sealed with patches. They may be a result of moisture permeating the substrate from below and, heated by the sun, expanding under the covering. You can leave an undamaged blister for the time being, but deal with the cause as soon as possible.

Damp and condensation
Damp near a wall may be caused by porous brickwork above the flat roof, lack of pointing or damp-proof course, slipped or inadequate coping on parapet walls and/or a breakdown of flashings, which should be made good as required. Condensation also causes dampness, and can be a more serious problem. If warm, moist air permeates the ceiling, the vapour condenses under the cold roof and encourages rot in the structural timbers. In such a case, upgrade the ceiling with a vapour barrier and fit some type of ventilation. Otherwise, have the roof re-covered and include better insulation.

The best approach for repairing a flat roof depends on its general condition and age and the extent of the damage. If the surface of the covering has decayed, as may happen to some bitumen felts, it may be best to call in a contractor and have the roof re-covered.

Patch repairs

Such localized damage as splits and blisters can be patch-repaired with the aid of proprietary repair kits but, as their effectiveness is only as good as their adhesion to the background, take care when cleaning the surface. Kill any lichen or moss spores with fungicide or bleach before starting the repair work.

A patched roof, if visible from above, can be rather an eyesore. This can be corrected with a finishing coat of bitumen and chippings or reflective paint to unify the surface area. Work on a warm day, preferably after a spell of dry weather.

Dealing with splits

You can use most self-adhesive repair tapes to patch-repair splits in all types of roof coverings.

First remove any chippings (see left), then clean the split and its surrounding surface thoroughly. Fill a wide split with a mastic compound before taping. Apply the primer supplied over the area to be covered and leave it for an hour.

Where a short split has occurred along a joint in the board substrate, prepare the whole line of the joint for covering with tape.

Peel back the protective backing of the tape and apply it to the primed surface (1). If you are working on short splits cut the tape to length first. Otherwise work from the roll, unrolling the tape as you work along the repair.

Press it down firmly and, holding it in place with your foot, roll it out and tread it into place as you go, then cut it off at the end of the run. Go back and ensure that the edges are sealed (2).

1 Apply the tape

2 Press tape firmly

Dealing with blisters

Any blisters in asphalt or felted roofs should be left alone unless they have caused the covering to leak or they contain water.

To repair a blister in an asphalt roof, first heat the area with a blow torch or hot-air stripper and, when the asphalt is soft, try to press the blister flat with a block of wood. If water is present cut into the asphalt to open the blister up and let the moisture dry out. Apply gentle heat before pressing the asphalt back into place. Work mastic into the opening before closing it, then cover the repair with a patch of repair tape.

Make two intersecting cuts across a blister on a felted roof and peel back the covering. Heating the felt will make this easier. Dry and clean out the opening, apply bitumen adhesive and when it is tacky nail the covering back into place with galvanized clout nails (3).

Cover the repair with a patch of roofing felt, bonded on with the bitumen adhesive. Cut the patch so as to lap at least 75mm (3in) all round. Alternatively, you can use repair tape.

Treating the whole surface

A roof which has already been patch-repaired and is showing general signs of wear and tear can be given an extra lease of life by means of a liquid waterproofing treatment.

The treatment consists of a thick layer of cold-applied bitumen-based liquid waterproofer which can also be reinforced with an open-weave glass-fibre membrane.

First sweep the roof free of all dirt and litter, then treat the surface with a fungicide to kill off any traces of lichen and moss.

Following the manufacturer's instructions, apply the first coat of waterproofer with a brush or broom (4), then lay the glass-fibre fabric into the wet material and stipple it with a loaded brush. Overlap the edges of the fabric strips by at least 50mm (2in) and bed them down well with the waterproofer. Clean the brush with soapy water before the coating sets.

Let the first coat dry thoroughly before laying the second and allow that one to dry before applying the third and last coat. When the last coat becomes tacky cover it with fine chippings or clean sharp sand to provide it with a protective layer.

3 Nail cut edges
Use bitumen adhesive to glue a felt patch over the repair.

4 Brush on first coat

FLASHINGS

Flashings are used to weatherproof the junctions between a roof and the other parts of the building, which are usually at the abutments with walls and chimneys and where one roof meets another.

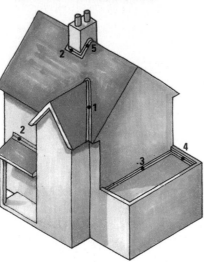

Where flashing is used
Typical types of flashing for pitched and flat roofs.
1 Valley
2 Apron
3 Wall abutment
4 Parapet abutment
5 Chimney abutment

Flashing materials

The most common flashing materials are lead, zinc, roofing felt and mortar fillets. Of all these, lead is by far the best because it weathers well, is easily worked – though shaping it is generally a craft skill – and can be applied to any situation and roof covering.

Zinc is a cheaper substitute for lead, but is not so long-lasting or so easy to work into shape. Consider using lead when zinc flashings need replacing – the extra cost buys a flashing that lasts considerably longer.

Bitumen felt may be used for flashings on felted roofs, but this material cannot be manipulated easily and is normally used for the more simple cover flashings that overlap the skirtings of felt roofs.

Mortar flashings, sometimes with inset cut tiles, are common on the pitched roofs of older houses. Although they tend to shrink and cause problems later, mortar flashings are still used as they are cheap and easy to apply.

FLASHING CONSTRUCTION

The design of a given flashing is determined by the particular details at the junction and to some extent by the materials used. Typical situations and methods are described here, using lead for the flashings.

1 Double-lap flashing

2 Single-lap flashing

3 Valley flashing

Abutments

A flashing is used to seal the joints between the sloping edge of a pitched roof and abutting walls. The type of flashing is determined by the pitch and the nature of the roof covering.

Double-lap flashing

Slate or plain-tiled roofs with a pitch of 30 degrees or more normally use soakers and a cover flashing. Soakers are lead or zinc pieces, equal in length to a tile's overlap, folded at right angles lengthways. The part that lies on the tiles should be at least 100mm (4in) wide and the upstand 75mm (3in). The back edge turns down over the tile's top edge, so add 12 to 25mm (½ to 1in) to the length of the soaker. A soaker is laid over the end tile or slate as a course is laid. The upstand lies flat against the brickwork and is lapped by a stepped flashing dressed down over it. The flashing's top edges are turned into the bed joints, held by lead wedges and pointed with mortar **(1)**.

Single-lap flashing

Contoured single-lap tiles can be treated at abutments with a one-piece flashing. The lead is tucked into the brick wall using the stepped method, and dressed down over the tile. The amount of overlap depends on tile contour and roof pitch. On a shallow pitch it should be at least 150mm (6in). The lead is dressed to the tile's shape and the step at each course, and its free edge is carried over the nearest raised tile contour **(2)**.

Valley flashing

Some tiled roofs have valley tiles that take the tiling into the angle, but most tiled and slated roofs have metal valley flashings made by laying a lead lining on boarding that runs from eaves to ridge, following the angle of the valley. The lead is dressed over wood fillets nailed to the boarding to form an upstand **(3)**. Where two valleys meet at the ridge, a lead saddle is formed. The edges of the tiles or slates are cut to follow the angle of the valley and to leave a gap of no less than 100mm (4in) between them.

Slate coverings should overhang the supporting valley fillet by 50mm (2in) and contoured tiles should be bedded in mortar and finished flush with the edge of the tiles to form a watertight gutter.

Apron flashing

The head of a lean-to roof is weatherproofed with a lead apron flashing, its top edge pointed into a mortar joint two courses above the roof. The lead is dressed down on to the roof and overlaps the the roof covering by 150mm (6in) or more.

Special moulded flashing units are available for use with corrugated-sheet roofing of plastic or fibre cement. These are shaped to fit the contour of the roofing and have flat hinged upstands which can be adapted to fit any roof slope. The upstand is lapped with a conventional flashing or is sealed with self-adhesive tape.

Moulded apron flashing for corrugated roofing

Chimney flashing

The flashing where a roof meets the side of a chimney is similar to that at an abutment, but there are also junctions at the front and back of the chimney.

An apron flashing is fitted in front. The upstand is returned on to the sides of the stack and its top edge is set in a joint in the brickwork. The apron, extending beyond the chimney sides, is dressed to the tile contour.

Single-lap or double-lap stepped flashings are fitted to the side of the chimney. At the back there is a timber-supported gutter. The front edge of the lead is turned up the brick face; its ends are folded over the side flashings. A separate cover flashing is dressed over the upstand at the rear of the chimney. The back of the gutter follows the roof slope and is lapped by the tiles, which are fitted last.

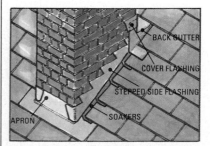

Chimney flashing for a slate roof

FLASHING
REPAIRS

There are many problems associated with flashings, usually as a result of the flashing material corroding or because the joints between different materials fail due to erosion or thermal movement.

A perished flashing should be stripped out and replaced. If this requires craft skills, the work should be done by a specialist contractor, but in many cases leaks are caused by shrinkage cracks which you can repair with self-adhesive flashing materials.

Caulking compound

Cement fillets often shrink away from wall abutments. If the fillets are otherwise sound, fill the gap with a gun-applied flexible caulking compound. Choose a colour that matches the fillet. Brush the surfaces to remove any loose material before injecting the compound.

Flashing tape

Prepare the surfaces by removing all loose and organic material. A broken or crumbling cement fillet should be made good with mortar.

Ensure that the surfaces are dry and if necessary apply a primer – it is supplied with some tapes – about one hour before using the tape (1).

Cut the tape to length and peel away the protective backing as you press the tape into place. Work over the surface with a cloth pad, applying firm pressure to exclude any air trapped beneath the tape (2).

1 Apply a primer with a 50mm (2in) paintbrush

2 Press tape with a pad to exclude air bubbles

Repointing flashing

Metal flashings which are tucked into brickwork may have worked loose where the old mortar is badly weathered. If the flashing is otherwise sound rake out the mortar joint, tuck the lead or zinc into it and wedge it there with rolled strips of lead spaced about 500mm (20in) apart. Then repoint the joint. While you have the roof ladders and scaffolding in place, rake out and repoint all of the mortar joints if they are in poor condition.

Rake out joint and repoint with fresh mortar

Patching lead

Lead will not readily corrode but splits can occur in it where it has buckled through expansion and contraction over the years. Flashing tape can be used but it is possible to patch lead by soldering or, for a more substantial repair, cutting away a weak or damaged portion and joining on a new piece by lead 'burning' or welding. This is not a job you can easily do yourself and it should be handed over to a professional. It should be done only when there is no risk of fire and it is more economical to have the old lead repaired than to have a new flashing fitted.

SEALED GLAZED ROOFS

Traditional porches, greenhouses and timber-framed conservatories all tend to suffer from leaks caused by a breakdown of the seal between the glass and glazing bars. Minor leaks should be dealt with promptly because trapped moisture can lead to timber decay and expensive repairs.

Using aluminium tape
You can waterproof glazing bars with self-adhesive aluminium tape simply cut to length and pressed in place.

Clean out old putty from both sides of the glazing bars, let the wood dry out and apply wood primer or linseed oil. When the primer is dry fill the rebates with putty or mastic.

The tape must be wide enough to cover each glazing bar and lap the glass on each side by about 18mm (¾in).

Start at the eaves and work up the roof, moulding the tape to each glazing bar and excluding air bubbles.

At a step in the glass, cut the tape and make an overlap. Mould the cut end over the stepped edge, then start a new length, lapping the stuck-down end by 50mm (2in).

At the ridge you may cut the tape to butt against the framework or lap on to it. Cover the ends with tape applied horizontally. Where a lean-to roof has an apron flashing tuck the tape under it.

Self-adhesive aluminium tape can be painted to match the woodwork or left its natural colour.

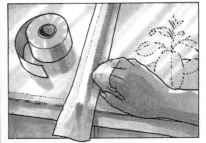

Mould the tape over the glazing bar

Clear tape
Make a temporary repair to cracked glass with clear self-adhesive waterproofing tape.

Clean the glass and apply the tape over the crack on the outside. It will make an almost invisible repair if applied promptly.

You can also use this tape for sealing the overlap on translucent corrugated-plastic roofing.

SEE ALSO	
Details for:	
Primers	43
Glazing	204–206
Pointing	444
Mastic gun	507

239

GUTTERING

Gutter sizes
Sizes are generally specified by their overall width in cross-section and sometimes by their depth as well.

Guttering collects rainwater that runs down a roof and leads it to a downpipe through which it discharges into a drain. Good rainwater disposal is vital in preventing damp developing in the fabric of a house.

Roof drainage

The size and layout of a roof drainage system should enable it to discharge efficiently all the water from a given roof area. Manufacturers of rainwater goods usually specify the maximum area for a given size and profile of gutter based on a rainfall rate of 75mm/hr (3in/hr). If you need to replace an old gutter, make sure you install one of the same size or perhaps slightly larger.

Very simple alterations can affect the performance of a drainage system quite dramatically. A system with a central downpipe, for example, can serve double the roof area of one with an end outlet. Conversely, a right-angle bend near the outlet can reduce the flow capacity by about 20 per cent.

In practice, unless you are working on an extension or a new garage, the positions of drains and downpipes are probably already fixed.

TYPICAL PROFILES AND SIZES OF GUTTERING

Half-round	Ogee (OG)	Moulded (OG)	Box
75mm (3in)			
100mm (4in)	100mm (4in)	100 x 75mm (4 x 3in)	100 x 75mm (4 x 3in)
112mm (4½in)	112mm (4½in)		
125mm (5in)	125mm (5in)	125 x 100mm (5 x 4in)	125 x 100mm (5 x 4in)
150mm (6in)	150 x 100mm (6 x 4in)	150 x 100mm (6 x 4in)	

EAVES-GUTTER SYSTEMS

Eaves-gutter systems are fabricated in cast iron, cast-aluminium, rolled-sheet aluminium, asbestos cement and a rigid uPVC plastic. With the exception of roll-formed aluminium types, the systems are made up from basic lengths of gutter and downpipes with a range of fittings (see diagram).

Moulded or cast gutters have a socket at one end into which the plain spigot end of the next section is jointed.

Gutters that are not symmetrical in section, such as an OG, require components that are left-handed or right-handed, and you will have to note this when ordering replacement parts.

Traditional cast-iron and modern aluminium guttering may be compatible should you wish to extend your system or renew part of it, but check carefully before purchasing. Patented plastic drainage systems, though superficially similar in style, are not always interchangeable.

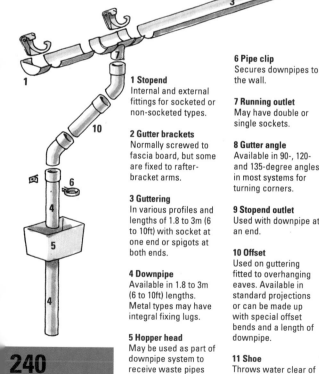

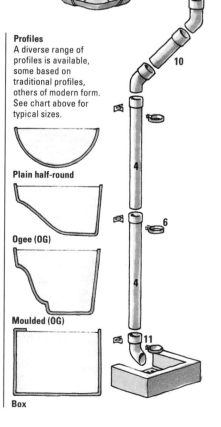

1 Stopend
Internal and external fittings for socketed or non-socketed types.

2 Gutter brackets
Normally screwed to fascia board, but some are fixed to rafter-bracket arms.

3 Guttering
In various profiles and lengths of 1.8 to 3m (6 to 10ft) with socket at one end or spigots at both ends.

4 Downpipe
Available in 1.8 to 3m (6 to 10ft) lengths. Metal types may have integral fixing lugs.

5 Hopper head
May be used as part of downpipe system to receive waste pipes from another source.

6 Pipe clip
Secures downpipes to the wall.

7 Running outlet
May have double or single sockets.

8 Gutter angle
Available in 90-, 120- and 135-degree angles in most systems for turning corners.

9 Stopend outlet
Used with downpipe at an end.

10 Offset
Used on guttering fitted to overhanging eaves. Available in standard projections or can be made up with special offset bends and a length of downpipe.

11 Shoe
Throws water clear of a wall into open gulley.

Types of guttering

The guttering on domestic buildings is adapted in various ways to suit the design of the roof.

Eaves gutters
Gutters that are fixed to fascia boards along the eaves of the roof are the most common form of guttering. They are made in many materials and a number of designs (see right).

Parapet gutters
Parapet gutters are generally found in older houses and may serve a flat or pitched roof set between two parapet walls. This type is generally purpose-made as part of the original structure of the roof and is usually covered with a metal or bituminous roofing material.

Valley gutters
Valley gutters are a form of flashing used at the junctions between sloping roofs. They are not gutter systems in themselves but they direct the rainwater into eaves or parapet gutters.

Profiles
A diverse range of profiles is available, some based on traditional profiles, others of modern form. See chart above for typical sizes.

Plain half-round

Ogee (OG)

Moulded (OG)

Box

MAINTENANCE

Cast-iron, cast-aluminium and asbestos-cement guttering are all rigid and may support a ladder, but it is much safer to use a ladder stay. Never prop a ladder against either plastic or roll-formed aluminium gutters.

Inspect and clean out the interior of gutters regularly. Gutters concentrate the dirt, and sometimes sand washed down from the tiles by the rain. This builds up quickly if the flow of water is restricted by leaves or twigs. Birds' nests also can effectively block the guttering or downpipes.

The weight of standing water can distort plastic guttering, and if a blockage causes the gutter to overflow, it leads to damp soaking through the wall below.

Removing debris

First block the gutter outlet with rag. With a shaped piece of plastic laminate scrape the silt into a heap, scoop it out of the gutter with a garden trowel and deposit it in a bucket hung from the ladder. Sweep the gutter clean with a stiff hand brush. Remove the rag and flush the gutter down with a bucket of water. Fit a wire or plastic 'balloon' in the end of the downpipe to prevent birds' nests or debris blocking the pipe.

Snow and ice

Plastic guttering can be badly distorted and even broken by snow and ice building up in it. Dislodge the build-up with a broom from an upstairs window if you can reach it safely. Otherwise, climb a ladder to remove it.

If snow and ice become a regular seasonal problem, fit a snow board made from 75 x 25mm (3 x 1in) planed softwood treated with a wood preserver and painted. Design it to stand about 25mm (1in) above the eaves tiles, using 25mm x 6mm (1 x ¼in) steel straps bent as required.

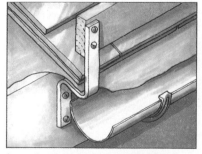

A snow board protects gutters or glazed roofs

GUTTERING MATERIALS

Cast iron

The cast-iron rainwater systems common on old houses are mostly of the OG type. They are fixed to the fascia board with short mushroom-headed screws that pass through the back of the gutter above the water line.

Each 1.8m (6ft) standard length of the guttering has a socket end into which the plain spigot end of the next piece fits **(1)**. Short bolts secure the joint and a bedding of putty forms a seal when they are tightened **(2)**.

1 A standard gutter has a socket at one end

2 The joint is sealed with putty then bolted

Cast iron is heavy and brittle, and installing or dismantling such a system needs two people. The iron can be cut with a hacksaw and drilled with twist drills in a power tool.

The guttering needs regular painting, and a bituminous paint applied inside helps to preserve the metal. If it is left unprotected it will rust, usually along the back edge, around the screws. Badly rusted guttering should be replaced, as it is likely to collapse.

Cast aluminium

Cast-aluminium guttering comes in a wide range of profiles. It is assembled in a similar way to cast-iron guttering with bolted joints, but a flexible mastic is used instead of putty to make the seals. The guttering may be fitted to the fascia with screws through the back, or with gutter brackets. The fixings should be sherardized or plated with zinc or cadmium. Cast aluminium is about one-third the weight of cast iron and can be left unpainted. However, in some situations it will corrode, and if it is used as part of a cast-iron system all the aluminium surfaces must be protected with zinc phosphate or with bituminous paint. It can be worked with ordinary metal-working tools.

Fibre cement

Fibre-cement guttering is of the socket-and-spigot type. The joints are secured with galvanized-iron bolts and the seals are made with a mastic jointing compound. The guttering is produced in half-round profiles in a range of several sizes. It is fixed to the house fascia board with gutter brackets, and these should not be spaced more than 900m (3ft) apart.

Fibre cement has good weathering properties and does not need to be painted. It can be cut with a hacksaw and drilled normally.

Rolled-sheet aluminium

Rolled-sheet aluminium guttering is a moulded lightweight OG system made from thin, prepainted flat-sheet aluminium which is roll-formed to the gutter shape by a portable machine. This is done on site by the suppliers, and continuous lengths are made to measure. The end stops and angles are supplied as separate items, crimped to the ends of the gutter sections. Outlets are formed by punching holes in the bottom. Simple metal fixing brackets are clipped to the front and back edges of the guttering and fixed to the fascia with drive screws. The system needs no maintenance, but can be painted.

Unplasticized PVC

Unplasticized PVC (uPVC) is now the most widely used guttering, both for new buildings and for replacing old systems. In many profiles and sizes, it is self-coloured in brown, black, grey and white. It needs no painting.

Most uPVC systems use clip-fastened joints with synthetic-rubber gaskets to form the seals. Some use a solvent cement to weld the joints. Downpipes may be a push fit, and are solvent-welded or sealed with an O-ring. The guttering is usually supported by brackets, but some systems employ screws to attach outlets and corner fittings for easier installation.

SCREW

Cast-iron OG gutter

SCREW

Cast aluminium

RAFTER BRACKET

FASCIA BRACKET

Gutter brackets

DRIVE SCREW

Sheet aluminium

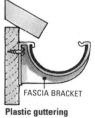

FASCIA BRACKET

Plastic guttering

241

FITTING NEW GUTTERING & DOWNPIPE

When your old gutter system reaches the end of its useful life you should replace it. Try to do so with a system in the same style or, at least, one that complements the style of your house. If you plan to install the guttering yourself a plastic system is probably the best choice, being the easiest to handle.

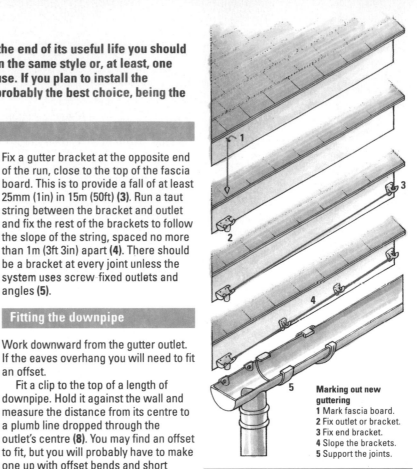

Marking out new guttering
1 Mark fascia board.
2 Fix outlet or bracket.
3 Fix end bracket.
4 Slope the brackets.
5 Support the joints.

Installing guttering

Measure round the base of the house to find the total length of gutter needed, and note the number and type of fittings to be ordered.

Use a plumb line to mark the position of the gutter outlet – directly over the existing drain – on the fascia board (1). Screw the outlet or its support bracket – depending on the system – to the fascia, no more than 50mm (2in) below the tile level (2).

Fix a gutter bracket at the opposite end of the run, close to the top of the fascia board. This is to provide a fall of at least 25mm (1in) in 15m (50ft) (3). Run a taut string between the bracket and outlet and fix the rest of the brackets to follow the slope of the string, spaced no more than 1m (3ft 3in) apart (4). There should be a bracket at every joint unless the system uses screw-fixed outlets and angles (5).

Fitting the gutter

Tuck the back edge of a length of gutter under the roofing felt and into the rear lips of the brackets. Attach the front of each bracket in turn (6).

Fit the second length in the same way, with its spigot end pushed into the socket of the first length. You will need to apply pressure to compress the rubber seal. Leave a 6mm (¼in) gap between the end of the spigot and the shoulder of the socket to allow for expansion.

6 Clip the guttering into the brackets

Cutting the gutter
Cut the gutter squarely with a hacksaw. You can snap a clip or bracket over it first to provide rigidity and guide the saw. Smooth rough edges with a file. Some systems require notches for the clips in the gutter's front and back edges; these can be made with a file.

Connecting to existing guttering
Renewing guttering on a terraced house may mean joining your system to your neighbour's. There are left-hand and right-hand adaptors for this purpose.

Remove your old guttering to the nearest joint between the houses, bolt the adaptor on, sealing the joint with mastic, and fix the new plastic gutter with the clip provided (7).

7 Use an adaptor to join different systems

Fitting the downpipe

Work downward from the gutter outlet. If the eaves overhang you will need to fit an offset.

Fit a clip to the top of a length of downpipe. Hold it against the wall and measure the distance from its centre to a plumb line dropped through the outlet's centre (8). You may find an offset to fit, but you will probably have to make one up with offset bends and short lengths of pipe. Use a solvent cement and assemble it on a table so that the bends lie in the same plane.

Fit the offset to the outlet spigot and the pipe to the offset. Adjust the pipe so that the clip's back plate falls on a mortar joint (9). Trim the offset spigot if necessary.

Mark the fixings, drill and plug the wall and fix the pipe and clip with plated round-head screws.

Mark and fix the lower lengths of pipe in the same way, with a 6mm (¼in) expansion gap between each pipe and the socket shoulder. Fit extra clips at the centre of pipes longer than 2m (6ft 6in).

Cut the bottom pipe to length and fit a shoe in the same way (10). If the pipe is jointed into a gulley trap (11) or a drain socket you may have to work upwards from the bottom.

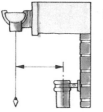

8 Drop a plumb line

9 Fit an offset

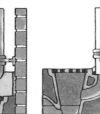

10 Finish with a shoe

11 Fit into gulley

REPAIRING GUTTERS AND DOWNPIPES

It is always better to replace a damaged part of a gutter system than to repair it, but a neat repair that stays watertight can tide you over.

Mending a crack
All types of chipped or cracked guttering or downpipes can be repaired with a sprayable asphalt mastic.

Brush off loose material and spray on one or two coats from a distance of 300 to 400mm (12 to 16in) to seal the leak. Mask off the area around the repair. For large breaks, apply a coat of mastic and cover with a patch of fine glass-fibre matting or gauze. Spray on a coating of mastic to complete the repair.

Using epoxy putty
You can build up the chipped edge of a cast-iron gutter with epoxy putty. Tape a waxed or polyethylene-lined piece of card across the outside of the broken edge and bend it to follow the contour of the gutter. Mix the two-part putty, fill the gap with it and remove the cardboard 'former' when the putty sets.

CHAPTER 4

HOME SECURITY

HOME SECURITY

The vulnerable areas of a house

1 The Front door
Inadequate locks invite forced entry.

2 Darkened porch
Makes identification of callers difficult.

3 Back or side doors
Often fitted with minimal locks.

4 French windows
Can be sprung with one well-placed blow.

5 Downstairs windows
A common means of entry if unlocked.

6 Upstairs windows
Vulnerable if they can be reached and opened easily.

7 Louvred windows
Their design permits silent entry.

8 Trap door to attic
The only way to enter a house from the loft.

9 Skylight
A possible means of entry for a burglar if accessible from an adjacent building.

10 Coal chute
A child can squeeze through a small chute.

11 Unlocked gate
Provides a convenient exit for a burglar removing bulky items.

All responsible householders will want to take reasonable precautions to protect themselves, their families and their property against the risks of fire and burglary. The cost and effort involved is small compared with the possible expense of replacement or even rebuilding – not to mention the grief caused by personal injury or the loss of items of sentimental value.

How a burglar gains entry

Many people innocently believe that they are unlikely to be burgled because they are not conspicuously wealthy. But statistics prove that most intruders are opportunists in search of one or two costly items, such as electrical hardware (typically the video, CD player and television set), jewellery or cash.

The average burglar takes only a few minutes to break into a house – often in broad daylight. Consequently, no house is immune to attack, especially one that affords an open invitation to thieves.

It's virtually impossible to prevent a determined burglar from breaking in, but you can do a great deal to make it difficult for the inexperienced criminal. The illustration below indicates the vulnerable areas of an average house, and the points listed opposite suggest methods for safeguarding them. Check out each point and compare them with your own home to make sure your security is up to the minimum standard recommended.

12 Garage or shed
A potential source of housebreaking tools.

13 Ladders
An available ladder can provide access to upstairs windows

14 Downpipe
As good as a ladder to an agile burglar.

15 Glass
Weak putty allows a thief to remove glass silently.

16 Burglar alarm
A valuable deterrent.

SEEKING EXPERT ADVICE

If, after reading this chapter, you require further details, you can obtain free advice tailored to your needs.

Crime Prevention Officer
Local police authorities appoint a full-time Crime Prevention Officer (CPO) who is responsible for advising commercial establishments and private individuals on ways to improve the security of their premises. Telephone your nearest police station to arrange for a confidential visit from the CPO, who will discuss any aspect of home security about which you need advice.

Fire Prevention Officer
Contact the Fire Prevention Officer (FPO) at your local fire-brigade headquarters for advice on how to balance security measures against the need to provide escape routes in case of fire. He will also explain the merits of simple fire-fighting equipment available to the home owner.

Insurance companies
Check with your insurance company that your home and its contents are adequately covered against fire and theft. Most policies are now index-linked, which means that each year the company automatically adjusts the premiums to allow for inflation.

You can also opt for a 'new-for-old' policy that will guarantee the full replacement cost of lost or destroyed property. In some circumstances, an insurance company may insist on certain precautions, but they may also be willing to reduce your premium if you provide adequate security.

You can reduce the risk of burglary by adopting security-conscious habits. Discourage opportunist burglars by closing and locking all windows and doors, even if you will be absent for a short time only. Burglaries have been known to occur while the whole family is watching television – so lock up before sitting down for the evening. When you leave the house at night, close the curtains and leave a light on in a living room. Alternatively, fit automatic time switches.

Don't open your front door to callers unless you know them or they have made a prior appointment. Even then, don't be afraid to ask for identification. Bona fide gas or electricity officials will expect to be challenged, so keep your security chain attached till you are satisfied that the identification is perfectly genuine.

When you go on holiday, cancel milk and paper deliveries. If possible, ask a trusted neighbour to switch lights on and off for you to give the impression that the house is still occupied. Remove an internal letterbox basket so that mail won't pile up. It is also a good idea to inform the police you are away and that a neighbour has a key. Deposit your valuables with a bank.

Engrave or etch your full post code plus your house number on your possessions, or use an invisible marker. Such measures help the police identify your belongings if they are recovered. Photograph jewellery, paintings or other valuables that are difficult to mark, and keep a record at the bank in case of fire. You can buy a strong yet compact floor or wall safe for storing valuables and important documents.

A CHECK LIST FOR SAFEGUARDING YOUR HOME

1 Front door
If there is no answer when an intruder rings the doorbell, he may be tempted to force an entry. Install a strong dead-locking bolt that conforms to BS 3621, and fit a bolt top and bottom on the inside of your front door.

Attach a security chain or similar fitting to prevent an intruder bursting in as you open the door a fraction. It is also worth fitting a peephole door viewer so you can identify callers.

If you live in a flat or apartment where the entrance door is the only vulnerable spot, consider having a multi-point lock fitted: it throws bolts into all four sides simultaneously.

2 Darkened porch
Fit a porch light so that a peephole door viewer is usable after dark. Security lighting may also make an intruder think twice before attempting to break in.

3 Back or side doors
A burglar can often work unobserved at the rear or side of a house. Consider additional security lighting, and fit mortise locks and bolts similar to those described for the front door. If the door opens outwards, fit hinge bolts – which will hold the door firmly in its frame even if the hinge pins are driven out.

4 French windows
Insecure French windows can be sprung by a heavy blow or kick. It is therefore essential to fit rack bolts top and bottom.

5 Downstairs windows
These are always vulnerable, particularly at the back and side of the house. Fit locks and catches to suit the material and style of the window.

6 Upstairs windows
If they can only be reached by ladder it is probably safe enough to use a standard catch, but fit a cheap key-operated lock to be absolutely sure. Windows accessible by scaling drain-pipes, flat roofs or walls should be secured in the same way as similar windows downstairs.

7 Louvred windows
Each individual pane of glass can be removed silently simply by bending the aluminium-alloy holders. Use an epoxy adhesive to glue each one into its fitting or fix a grille.

8 Trap door to attic
Put a bolt on the trap door leading to your attic or roof space. Some terraced and semi-detached houses have common lofts – and burglars have sometimes been known to break through dividing walls between houses.

9 Skylights
Windows at roof level are at risk only if they can be reached easily by drainpipes or from an adjacent building, but it is advisable to fit a lock or a sturdy bolt to deter thieves.

10 Coal chute
Burglars with a child accomplice can gain access to a cellar through a small coal chute. Seal the chute if it is no longer required.

11 Side gate
Lock a side gate to prevent burglars carrying bulky items from your house. Fitting a lightweight trellis above the gate will discourage them from trying to vault over it.

12 Garages and sheds
Keep outbuildings locked to protect the contents and to prevent burglars using your own tools to break into your house. Fit a standard lock or a padlock with a close-fitting or concealed shackle so that it cannot be easily cut. Choose a design that covers the fixing screws. If possible, substitute bolts for screws to prevent the lock being prised off.

13 Ladders
Lock up your ladders, even if you have to chain them outside – to a garage wall, for example. A loose, accessible ladder provides burglars with an easy way to reach upstairs windows.

14 Downpipes
Paint downpipes with security paint to dissuade burglars from climbing them. The substance remains slippery, making it difficult to get a good grip.

15 Glass
Most people accept the risk that glass can be broken or cut. However, you can fit laminated glass or cover ordinary glass with a metal grille. A sliding grille on the inside can be concealed by curtains or a pelmet when not in use.

Keep window putty in good repair so that it cannot be picked out with a pen-knife to expose the fixings and remove a pane of glass.

Lead cames holding stained glass can be peeled silently and the glass removed. The only way to prevent this is to fit a metal grille or a secondary layer of laminated glass.

16 Burglar alarm
Although an alarm is a useful deterrent, it cannot be considered a sufficient safeguard on its own.

SECURING DOORS

SEE ALSO
Details for:
Fitting a porch light   340

Doors are vulnerable to forcing and are often used by an intruder as a quick means of exit, even if entry has been gained through a window. It makes good sense to fit strong locks and bolts. Don't just rely on the old-fashioned night latch, which offers no security at all – it is only as strong as the screws holding it to the door, and a thief can easily break a pane of glass to operate it or simply slide back the bolt with a credit card. Front doors and back doors need different locking arrangements, and there are various mechanisms to choose from.

Night latch
This type of lock alone does not provide adequate security.

Mortise sashlock
Suitable for back and side doors that are used frequently.

● **Changing locks**
If your key is lost or stolen there is no need to buy a new lock. Simply take the old one to a locksmith who will swap the internal mechanism for one that comes complete with a different set of keys.

The choice of door locks

The door by which you leave the house – usually the front door – needs a particularly strong lock because it can't be bolted from inside except when you are at home. Back and side doors need bolts top and bottom to prevent entry if they are smashed in from outside, plus a lock to stop thieves making an easy getaway with their spoils. The basic choice of locks is between mortise and rim types.

Deadlocking cylinder rim locks

A deadlocking cylinder rim lock can be fitted to a final-exit door as an alternative to a mortise lock: it locks automatically as the door is closed, so that the bolt cannot be forced back without a key except by turning the knob on the inside. One complete turn of the key prevents the lock being operated even from inside, so an intruder cannot walk out of the front door with your property. The staple should be fixed into the edge of the frame with screws or a metal stud; if it is screwed to the face, a well-placed kick may rip out the screws.

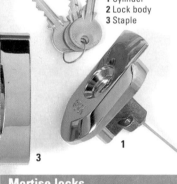

Deadlocking cylinder rim lock
1 Cylinder
2 Lock body
3 Staple

Mortise locks

A mortise lock is fitted into a slot cut in the edge of the door, where it cannot easily be tampered with. There are various patterns to suit the width of the door stile and the location of the door.

A mortise sashlock is suitable for back and side doors. It has a handle on each side to operate a springbolt, and a key-operated deadbolt which can't be pushed back once the door is closed.

Purely key-operated mortise locks are best for final-exit doors, where no handle is necessary. Any exterior-door lock should conform to BS 3621: this ensures that the lock has a minimum of 1000 key variations, is proof against 'picking' and is strong enough to resist drilling, cutting or forcing. Some locks are intended for right-hand or left-hand opening doors.

Mortise lock
1 Striking plate
2 Faceplate
3 Lock body

USING AUTOMATIC TIME SWITCHES

You can give the impression that someone is at home by using an automatic time switch plugged into an ordinary wall socket to control a table lamp or radio. Set the programme to switch the light or radio on and off several times over a period of 24 hours, or buy a more sophisticated switch that will turn the lighting on and off at different times every day of the week. Some programmes also provide for random switching.

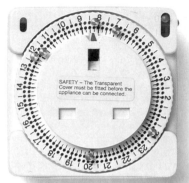

SAFETY – The Transparent Cover must be fitted before the appliance can be connected.

24-hour time switch

INSTALLING A DOOR VIEWER

A peephole door viewer enables you to identify callers before admitting them. Select a viewer with as wide an angle of vision as possible: you should be able to see someone standing to the side of the door or even crouching below the viewer. Choose one that is adjustable to fit any thickness of door.

Drill the recommended-size hole – usually 12mm (½in) – right through the centre of the door at a comfortable eye level. Insert the barrel of the viewer into the hole from the outside, then screw on the eyepiece from inside.

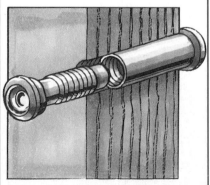

A telescopic viewer fits any size of door

Fitting a mortise lock

Scribe a line centrally on the edge of the door with a marking gauge, and use the lock body as a template to mark the top and bottom of the mortise (**1**). Choose a drill bit that matches the lock-body thickness and drill out the majority of the waste wood within marked lines.

Square up the edges of the mortise with a bevel-edge chisel (**2**) until the lock fits snugly in the slot. Mark around the edge of the faceplate with a knife (**3**), then chop a series of shallow cuts across the waste with a chisel. Pare out

the recess until the faceplate is flush with the edge of the door.

Hold the lock against the face of the door and mark the centre of the keyhole with a bradawl (**4**). Clamp a block of scrap timber to the other side of the door over the keyhole position and drill right through on the centre mark: the block prevents the drill bit splintering the face of the door as it bursts through on the other side. Cut out the keyhole slot on both sides with a padsaw, or use a power jigsaw.

1 Mark the mortise   **2 Chop out the waste**   **3 Mark the faceplate**   **4 Mark the keyhole**

Screw the lock into its recess and check its operation; screw on the coverplate and then the escutcheons over each side of the hole (**5**). With the door closed, operate the bolt; it may incorporate a marking device to gauge the position of the striking plate on the

door frame. If it doesn't have a marking device, shoot the bolt fully open, then push the door to and draw round the bolt on the face of the frame (**6**).

Mark out and cut the mortise and recess for the striking plate (**7**) as described for the lock itself.

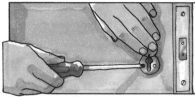 

5 Screw on escutcheon to cover the keyhole   **6 Mark bolt on frame**   **7 Fit striking plate**

Fitting a cylinder rim lock

Although fitting instructions vary from model to model, the following method shows how easy it is to fit a cylinder rim lock. Using the templates provided with the lock, mark then drill the holes for the cylinder (**1**). Hold the lock body against the door so that you can mark and cut a recess for its flange (**2**). Pass the cylinder into the hole from the outside and check the required length of the flat connecting bar. If need be, cut it to size

with a hacksaw (**3**). Bolt the cylinder to the door.

Screw the lock mounting plate on the inside of the door (**4**) and attach the lock body to it. Cut a recess in the edge of the door and screw the lock's flange into it, making sure it lies flush.

Use the fitted lock as a guide for positioning the staple on the door frame. Chisel out a shallow recess for the staple, then screw it to the frame.

  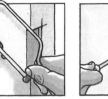 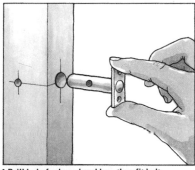

1 Mark cylinder centre   **2 Draw round flange**   **3 Cut connecting bar**   **4 Fit mounting plate**

FITTING RACK BOLTS

There are many types of bolt for securing a door from the inside, but rack bolts can be fitted into the edge of the door and have the advantage of being unobtrusive as well as secure.

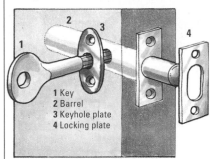

1 Key
2 Barrel
3 Keyhole plate
4 Locking plate

The components of a standard rack bolt

Drill a hole – usually 16mm (⅝in) in diameter – for the barrel of the bolt in the edge of the door. Use a try square to transfer the centre of the hole to the inside face of the door. Mark the keyhole, drill it with a 10mm (⅜in) bit, and insert the bolt (**1**).

With the key in position, mark the recess for the faceplate (**2**); then pare out the recess with a chisel. Screw the bolt and keyhole plate to the door. Operate the bolt to mark the frame, then drill a 16mm (⅝in) diameter hole to a depth that matches the length of the bolt. Fit the locking plate over the hole.

1 Drill hole for barrel and key, then fit bolt

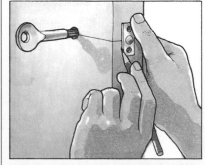

2 With the key in place, draw round the faceplate

Fitting hinge bolts
Fit at least two bolts per door and position them near the hinges. Drill a hole in the edge of the door for the bolt and another in the door frame. Recess the locking plate in the frame.

Attaching a security chain
No special skills are needed to fit a security chain. Simply screw the fixing plates to the door and frame. Fit a security chain just below the lock.

SECURING WINDOWS

Windows are a common means of entry for burglars, so make sure they are adequately secured, especially if they are in vulnerable locations. There are numerous types of lock for wooden and metal windows, including some that lock automatically when you close the window. Locks for metal frames are rather more difficult to fit, as you have to cut threads for the screw fixings.

How windows are locked

The type of lock suitable for a window depends on how the window opens. Sliding sashes are normally secured by locking the sashes together, whereas casements – which open like doors – should be fastened to the outer frame or locked by rendering the catches and stays immovable. Whichever type of lock you choose, it makes sense to buy the best you can afford for the more vulnerable windows and to spend less on ones that are difficult to reach.

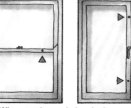
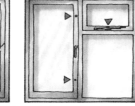

Where to place window locks
The black dots indicate the best positions for bolts or window locks

Window locks must be strong enough to resist forcing and have to be situated correctly for optimum security. On small windows, fit a single lock as close to the centre as possible; on larger windows, two locks are needed, spaced apart.

Locks that can only be released by a removable key are the most secure. Some keys will open any lock of the same design (an advantage in that you need fewer keys, although some burglars may carry a range of standard keys). With other locks, there are several key variations.

Wooden windows need to be fairly substantial to accommodate mortise locks, so surface-mounted lock are often used. These are quite adequate and, being visible, act as a deterrent.

If the fixing screws are not concealed when the lock is in place, drill out the centre of the screws once fitted so that they cannot be withdrawn.

Fitting sash-window locks

Installing dual screws
Cheap but effective, a dual screw consists of a bolt that passes through both meeting rails so that the sashes are immobilized. The screw is operated by a special key, and there is little to see when the window is closed.

To fit a dual screw, with the window shut and the catch engaged, drill through the inner meeting rail into the outer one. Tape the drill bit to gauge the depth. Slide the sashes apart and tap the two bolt-receiving devices into their respective holes. Close the window and insert the threaded bolt with the key until it is flush with the window frame. If need be, saw the bolt to length.

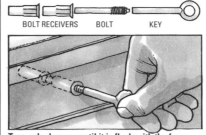

BOLT RECEIVERS   BOLT   KEY

Turn a dual screw until it is flush with the frame

Fitting a key-operated sash lock
These are simple key-operated locks that screw to the top surface of the two meeting rails, effectively clamping the rails together.

Using sash stops
When the bolt is withdrawn with a key, a sash stop fitted to each side of a window allows it to be opened slightly for ventilation. As well as deterring burglars, they prevent small children from opening the window any further.

To fit a stop, drill a hole in the upper sash for the bolt, then screw the face-plate over it (on close-fitting sashes, you will have to recess the faceplate). Screw the protective plate to the top edge of the lower sash.

Extract sash stop with a key to secure window

Lock for metal sash windows
To secure an aluminium sash window, fit the type of lock described for securing fanlight windows.

Locking casement windows

Fitting rack bolts
On large casement windows, fit rack bolts – as described for doors.

Fitting a casement lock
A locking bolt can be fitted to a wooden window frame: the bolt is engaged by turning a simple catch, but it can only be released with a key.

With the lock body screwed to the part of the window that opens, mark and cut a small mortise in the fixed frame for the bolt; then screw on the coverplate.

A similar device for metal windows, is a clamp which, when fixed to the opening part of the casement, shoots a bolt that hooks over the fixed frame.

A good casement lock has a removable key

Locking a cockspur handle
A cockspur handle, which secures the opening edge of the casement to the fixed frame, can be locked by means of an extending bolt that you screw to the frame below the handle. However, ensure that the handle is not worn or loose – otherwise the lock may be ineffective.

Lockable handles that will allow you to secure a window left ajar for ventilation can be substituted in place of a standard handle.

An extending bolt stops the handle turning

Securing pivot windows

If a pivot window is not supplied with an integral lock, use rack bolts or locks recommended for casement windows. Alternatively, fit the screw-mounted lock suggested for a fanlight window.

Securing fanlight windows

You can buy a variety of casement locks, as well as devices that secure the stay to the window frame. The simplest kind is screwed below the stay arm to receive a key-operated bolt passed through one of the holes in the stay arm. Purpose-made lockable stays are also available.

The device bolts the stay to the window frame

A better alternative is a device that clamps the window itself to the surrounding frame. Attach the lock first, then use it to position the staple.

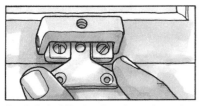

Attach the lock first in order to locate the staple

Securing French windows

French windows and other glazed doors are vulnerable to forcing — a burglar only has to break a pane to reach the handle inside. Key-operated locks are essential to prevent a break-in.

Each door of a French window needs a rack bolt at the top and bottom, positioned so that one bolt shoots into the upper frame and the other into the threshold below. It is necessary to take each door off its hinges in order to fit the lower bolt; if that is difficult, fit a lockable surface-mounted bolt instead.

Locking sliding doors

If you have aluminium sliding patio doors, fit additional locks at the top and bottom to prevent the sliding frame from being lifted off its track. These locks are costly, but they offer at least 1000 key variations and provide good security.

Fit a lock to the top and bottom of a sliding door

Although they are no substitute for good locks and catches, an alarm system provides an extra sense of security and may deter an intruder if there are other less well-protected premises nearby. The system itself must be reliable, and you and your family need to be disciplined in its use. If your neighbours are constantly subjected to false alarms, they are less likely to call the police in an emergency. Give the local police a record of two alarm-key holders that they can contact if your alarm goes off. Choose burglar alarms and installers with care, as the best are not always the most expensive.

A typical system

Alarm systems differ greatly, but there are two basic categories: passive systems that detect the presence of an intruder inside the house, and perimeter systems that guard all likely means of entry. The best systems incorporate a combination of features in case perimeter detectors are by-passed.

Control unit

The control unit is the heart of the system, and all the detectors are connected to it. From it, the signal is passed to a bell or siren. The control unit has to be set to allow sufficient time for legitimate entry and exit. If it has a zone-monitoring option, you can activate door contacts or sensors in part of the house – to permit freedom of movement upstairs at night, for example, while entry doors and down-stairs areas are fully guarded.

The control unit must be tamper-proof, so that it will trigger the alarm if disarming is attempted by any means other than a key or the correct digital code. It is usually wired directly to the mains-power consumer unit, but it should also have a rechargeable battery in case of power failure.

Detectors

Entrances can be fitted with magnetic contacts that trigger the alarm when broken by someone opening a door or window. Other types of detector sense vibrations caused by an attempted entry, including breaking glass. They must be accurately placed and set to distinguish between an intrusion and vibration from external sources.

Scanning devices

Infra-red sensors can be strategically positioned so they scan a wide area. The height of the beam can be adjusted to ignore small pets. This type of detector is usually connected to a central control unit, but there are independent battery-operated sensors for protecting a single room.

The alarm

Most alarms have a bell or siren mounted on an outside wall. These switch off automatically after a set period, but some alarms are designed to continue signalling with a flashing light and some will automatically rearm themselves. Many systems transmit a warning directly to a monitoring centre for swift response to a break-in. Whichever type you choose, it is important that the alarm is triggered by any attempt to tamper with it by dis-mantling or by cutting wires.

Personal-attack button

With most systems you can have a 'panic button' installed beside entry doors or elsewhere in the house to press in the event of an attack. Pressing a personal-attack button trips the alarm even when the system is switched off.

DIY systems

If you want to avoid the cost of pro-fessional installation, there are several DIY alarm systems that are quick and easy to install. However, you may need expert advice from the supplier of the equipment or your CPO on the choice and siting of sensors and detectors. You should also consult your insurance company to check whether your choice of alarm affects your policy in any way.

Make sure the system will enable you to select the type and number of detectors you require, and that it incorporates a reliable tamper-proof control unit.

Wireless systems, which use secure coded radio signals to trigger the alarm, avoid the need for extensive wiring and can be extended to monitor sheds and garages. They are easily dismantled, so can be taken with you when you move.

BURGLAR
ALARM
SYSTEMS
SEE ALSO

Details for:
Crime Prevention
Officer   244
Rack bolts   247
Consumer unit   304
Woodworker's
tools   478-489
Metalworker's
tools   502-507

• **British standards for burglar alarms**
Professionally installed alarm systems should comply with BS 4737. If you decide to install a DIY system, make sure that it complies with BS 6707. In addition, check that a wireless alarm has Department of Trade and Industries approval (MPT 1340), which will ensure that it operates on an approved frequency.

PROTECTING YOUR HOUSE AGAINST FIRE

Fire blanket and extinguisher
Portable extinguishers should comply with BS 5423, and fire blankets with BS 6575. Extinguishers must be serviced regularly.

Smoke detector
A detector provides an early warning of a fire. Choose only those that comply with BS 5446 Part 1.

No one needs to be reminded about the potential risk of fire – yet nearly all domestic fires are caused by careless disregard of the dangers. Many fires could be prevented by simple awareness and sensible precautions.

Avoiding the risks

Make sure your electrical installations and equipment are safe and in good order. Remove all plugs from sockets at night, especially the one connected to the television set. Don't overload power sockets with adaptors: fit more sockets instead. Don't trail long extension leads and flexes under carpets or rugs: if the wiring becomes damaged it could over-heat and start a serious fire.

Never leave fires or heaters unguarded, especially when there are children in the house. Don't dry clothes in front of a fire, since they could easily fall onto the elements or flames.

Take particular care with smoking materials. Empty ashtrays at night, but dampen the contents before discarding them. Don't rest ashtrays on chair arms: a burning cigarette's centre of gravity shifts as it burns, which may cause it to topple off and ignite the upholstery. Never smoke in bed: many fires are caused by smokers falling asleep and setting light to the bedclothes.

Keep your workshop or garage clear of shavings and rubbish – especially oily rags, which can ignite spontaneously. If possible, store flammable chemicals and paints in an outbuilding away from the house.

As a means of fighting a fire, install an all-purpose fire extinguisher in a prominent position, preferably on an escape route. Mount a fire blanket close to but not directly above the cooker. Your local Fire Prevention Officer will be able to recommend equipment for domestic use. Don't buy inferior items – they may not work in an emergency.

Providing escape routes

Your first responsibility is to ensure that your family can escape safely if your house should catch fire. Before you go to bed, close internal doors – which will help to contain a fire – but don't lock them. Locked internal doors rarely deter burglars, anyway.

Although you should not leave a key in an external lock, keep it close by but out of reach of the door or window. Make sure everyone in the house knows where the key is kept, and always return it to the same place after use.

Keep stairs and hallways free from obstructions: they may be difficult to see in dense smoke. Avoid using an oil heater to warm these areas in case it is knocked over during an escape and spreads the fire further. Communal stairs to flats are especially important, so try to persuade neighbours to keep them clear.

In the event of a fire, get everyone out of the building quickly, alert neighbours and call the fire brigade. If it is safe to do so, close doors and windows as you leave, but never open a door that feels warm – it could be protecting you from a dangerous smouldering fire.

Tackling a fire

Don't attempt to tackle a fire yourself unless you discover it early – and then only with the right equipment. Make sure that everyone in your family knows what to do in the event of a fire.

Fat fire
Cooking oil ignites when it reaches a certain temperature. Unattended chip pans are one of the most common causes of domestic fires. Don't attempt to move a burning pan:
● Turn off the source of heat.
● Smother the fire with a close-fitting lid or a fire blanket. Alternatively, quickly soak a towel in water, wring it out, and drape it over the pan.
● Let the pan cool for half an hour.
● If you aren't able to extinguish the fire immediately, call the fire brigade.

Chimney fire
If there is a blaze in a chimney, phone the fire brigade, then stand a fireguard on the hearth. Remove hearth rugs in case burning material drops onto them.

Clothes on fire
If someone's clothes catch fire, throw the person onto the ground and roll him or her in a blanket or rug. Seek medical attention in the event of burns.

INSTALLING A SMOKE DETECTOR

A smoke detector will identify the presence of smoke and fumes, even before flames start, and will sound a shrill warning. Although detectors can be incorporated into an alarm system, self-contained battery-operated units are easier to fix yourself. Make sure you change the battery at least once a year.

There are two basic types of smoke detector. Photo-electric devices detect smoke from smouldering or slow-burning fires, whereas ionization types are more attuned to hot blazing fires. There are also detectors that combine both systems to give good all round performance.

Siting a smoke detector
The best place for a smoke detector is on the ceiling, at least 300mm (1ft) away from any wall or light fitting. If it has to be wall mounted, make sure it is 150 to 300mm (6in to 1ft) below the ceiling. Don't install a detector in a kitchen or bathroom as steam can trigger the alarm, and don't fix one directly above a heater or an air-conditioning vent.

If you live in a bungalow, fit a smoke detector in the hallway between the bedrooms and living areas. For a two-storey home, fit at least one detector in the hallway, directly above the bottom of the stairs. If possible, fit a second alarm on the landing. Some alarms can be linked with bell wire – if one detects smoke, they are all triggered at once.

GAS DETECTORS

There are devices that warn you before escaping gas reaches dangerous concentrations. They are normally designed to detect natural gas, so are usually screwed to a wall no more than 300mm (1ft) below the ceiling of the kitchen or the room where the main gas appliance is installed. A gas detector must be wired directly to an unswitched fused connection unit containing a 3amp fuse. Make sure that any gas detector you install for natural gas complies with BS 7348.

If the alarm sounds, extinguish naked flames, including cigarettes, and don't operate electrical switches. Turn off the gas supply at the meter, and open doors and windows. Then, unless there's an obvious reason for the alert (such as a pilot light blown out or a gas tap turned on) call the Gas Emergency Service.

CHAPTER 5

DAMP, ROT & INFESTATION

WOODWORM

ATTACK

Our homes and surroundings are sometimes invaded by voracious insect pests. Some of them are quite harmless, although they cause a great deal of annoyance and even alarm, but certain insects can severely weaken the structure of a building and they often go unnoticed until the damage is done. At the first signs of infestation, try to identify and eradicate the pests as quickly as possible – before they seriously damage your home.

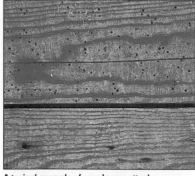

A typical example of woodworm attack

Attack by woodworm

Furniture beetle

Woodworm is the term used to describe all kinds of wood-boring insects.

The most common of these pests is the furniture beetle. The adult insect is a brown beetle about 3mm (⅛in) long, but the damage is caused by its larvae, which feed on the sapwood of most household timbers. The beetle, which is most active in early summer, lays its eggs in the crevices of bare timber. When the grubs hatch, they burrow into the wood for up to three years, then pupate just below the surface. The new adult emerges by chewing its way out, leaving the familiar round flight hole. These tiny holes are about 1 to 2mm (¹⁄₁₆in) in diameter and are generally the first signs of infestation, but there may be several generations of woodworm active inside the timber.

Other types of woodworm

The furniture beetle is said to inhabit about three-quarters of British homes – and most outbreaks of woodworm are certainly caused by this pest. However, there are other wood-boring insects that can create even greater damage.

The deathwatch and house longhorn beetles bore much larger holes – from 3 to 6mm (⅛ to ¼in) in diameter. Authorities are anxious to control the spread of these rarer insects, so contact your local Environmental Health Department if you suspect their presence in your

home. Another common insect pest is the weevil, which attacks wood at two stages in its life cycle. Both the adults and the grubs burrow into all types of timber – but only when it is already decaying and in a very moist condition.

Locating woodworm

Check the unfinished parts of your furniture, particularly plywood drawer bottoms and backs of cabinets, as woodworm has a taste for the glues used in their manufacture. The wooden frames of upholstered furniture are another favourite habitat of the pest; so is any form of wickerwork.

The structural timbers of your house are the place where woodworm can do most harm. Inspect roof timbers, stairs, floorboards and joists. The unpainted underedges of doors and skirtings are also common breeding grounds, as is the upper edge of picture rails.

Where the flight holes are dark in colour, the timber may have received treatment already; but clean holes, especially when surrounded by the fine dust known as frass, are signs of recent activity. If the signs are extensive, push a knife blade into the infected timbers. If the wood crumbles, the infestation is serious and you should seek the advice of a specialist contractor immediately, as the woodwork needs to be cut away and replaced. You can, nevertheless, treat basically sound timber yourself.

Wood-boring insects
(Not to scale)
These can destroy the timbers and furniture in your home.
Eradicate immediately!

Furniture beetle

Deathwatch beetle

House longhorn beetle

Weevil

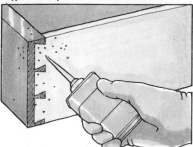

Inject fluid into flight holes

Spray fluid into confined spaces

Treating woodworm

If woodworm is located by a surveyor when inspecting a house that you are thinking of buying, a mortgage company will insist that you hire a reputable specialist to eradicate the pest, since their work carries a 30-year guarantee. Similarly, if you detect woodworm in your present home it is wise at least to have it inspected by a specialist firm who will advise you on the extent of the damage (which may not be obvious to the untrained eye) and quote a price for treating the infested timber. There is normally no charge for this service.

Any but the most serious infestation

can be treated easily, using a chemical insecticidal eradicator. Most of these fluids are flammable; so don't smoke when applying them, and extinguish any naked lights. Wear strong protective gloves and, while you are spraying the timbers, a respirator and goggles. The initial smell of solvent-based fluid can be unpleasant, but it will gradually fade.

Water-based low-odour woodworm eradicators are solvent-free and non-flammable. These eradicators will do little harm to building materials such as bitumen and expanded polystyrene, and are also suitable for use in bat roosts.

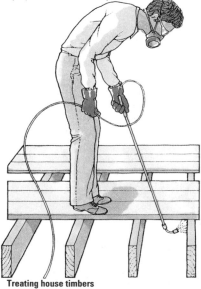

Treating house timbers
Hire a spray lance and compressor to treat woodworm in structural timbers. Lift several floorboards and use the lance to treat the joists and undersides of the boards. Spray the boards you have removed before replacing them.

Dealing with a minor outbreak

Treating woodworm in furniture is a fairly simple task. Use either a can with a pointed nozzle or a special aerosol applicator to inject woodworm fluid into the flight holes every 75 to 100mm (3 to 4in). As the tunnels are connected, that will be enough to penetrate deeply.

Continue the treatment by painting all unfinished timber with fluid. There's no need to paint polished surfaces, although the fluid will not harm them.

Use either a pump-action spray can or an aerosol to coat wickerwork or the inside of confined spaces.

After treatment, flight holes can be filled with cellulose filler; or use wax crayons to match the colour of show-wood. Melt the wax into a tin, and then press it into the holes with a filling knife.

Treating structural timbers

It's possible to treat timbers by flooding on the fluid using a brush, but it's more effective to spray them. Hire a sprayer that will produce a coarse spray; you will also need an extended lance in order to reach under floors and up into roof timbers. Open windows to provide as much ventilation as possible.

Remove insulating material from between ceiling joists, and vacuum the dust so that the fluid can penetrate the wood. Cover the water cistern, and check that electrical wiring is sound and clipped securely.

All exposed timbers must be soaked; but take care not to leave puddles in an attic, as they might stain the ceiling below. Should this happen, let it dry and prime the stain with aluminium sealer.

To treat a floor, lift every fourth floorboard so that you can spray all the joists and the undersides of the boards. Spray the tops of the boards, as well. The timber will dry out in two to three weeks, but you shouldn't lay impervious floorcoverings for about six months.

Preventative treatment

Any new timber can be treated with a chemical preserver to prevent attack. Once dry, it can be decorated in the normal way. Furniture can be protected with an insecticidal polish – if you buy or are given an old piece of furniture, it pays to treat it with an eradicator if there are any signs of infestation, to prevent the outbreak from spreading.

If you have to lift a door off its hinges for any reason, take the opportunity to paint the bottom edge, as woodworm does not attack painted timber.

ERADICATING OTHER INSECTS PESTS

Insecticides can be dangerous if they are allowed to contaminate food (they are also harmful to honey bees), so follow the manufacturers' instructions carefully when using them to eradicate insect pests of any kind.

Ants

The common black ant will enter a house in order to forage for food. Once established, the workers follow well-defined trails. In summer, great numbers of winged ants emerge from the nest to mate, but the swarming is over in a matter of hours, and the ants themselves are harmless. If winged ants stray into the house, they can be overcome with an insecticidal spray.

To locate the nest, follow the trail of ants. It will be situated under a path, at the base of a wall, in the lawn or under a flat stone, perhaps 6m (20ft) from the house. Destroy the nest by pouring boiling water into the entrances. If this is likely to damage plants, use an insecticidal dust or spray.

Wasps

Wasps are beneficial in spring and the early summer, as they feed on garden pests; but later in the year they destroy soft fruit. They have also been known to kill bees and raid hives for honey.

Trap foraging wasps in open jam jars containing a mixture of jam, water and detergent. Flying wasps can be killed with an aerosol fly spray. You can destroy wasps at the nest by depositing insecticidal powder near and around the entrances; tie a spoon to a cane to extend your reach. Alternatively, where there is no risk of fire, you can light a smoke-generating pellet, place it in the entrance and seal the opening.

Wasps sting when they are aroused or frightened. Treat a wasp sting with a cold compress soaked in witch hazel or use an antihistamine cream or spray.

Flies

Depending on the species, flies breed in rotting vegetables, manure, and decaying meat and offal. They can carry the eggs of parasitic worms, and spread disease by leaving small black spots of vomit and excreta on foodstuffs.

Cover food, and keep refuse in a bin liner inside a garbage bin with a tight lid. Gauze screens fitted over windows and bead curtains in open doorways will help to keep flies out of the house.

An aerosol fly spray will deal with small numbers; but for swarming flies – in a roof space, for example – use an insecticidal smoke generator (available from a hardware store or chemist). Large numbers in a living room can be sucked into a vacuum cleaner; then suck up some insecticidal powder and wait for a few hours before emptying.

Cockroaches

It is fairly rare to find cockroaches in domestic buildings, but they are sometimes attracted by warmth and a ready supply of food and water. Cockroaches are unhygienic, and smell unpleasant. Being nocturnal feeders, they tend to hide during the day in crevices in walls, behind cupboards, and above all in warm places – under cookers or fridges, for example, or near heating pipes.

A serious outbreak should be dealt with by professionals, but you can lay a finely dusted barrier of insecticidal powder between suspected daytime haunts and food supplies – taking care not to sprinkle it near the food itself. Use a paintbrush to stipple powder into crevices and under skirting boards. Once you have eradicated the pests, fill cracks and gaps to prevent a return.

Silver fish

Silver fish are tapered, wingless insects about 12mm (½in) long. They like the moist conditions found in bathrooms, kitchens and cellars. You may discover them behind wallpaper (where they feed on the paste) or in bookshelves, as they also eat paper. Use an insecticidal spray or powder in these locations.

SEE ALSO

Details for:
Aluminium sealer   43

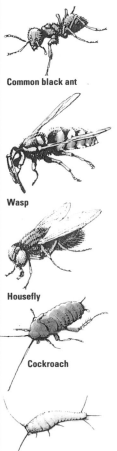

Typical household pests
(Not to scale)
The insects shown below are more of a nuisance and a health hazard than a threat to the structure of your house.

Common black ant

Wasp

Housefly

Cockroach

Silverfish

MICE, RATS AND BATS

Domestic mouse
Not a serious threat
to health, but it is an
unhygienic rodent.

Common rat
A serious health risk.
Seek expert advice.

Bat
Bats are completely
harmless and should
not be disturbed.

Rat damage to plug

Rat damage to electric cable

Rat damage to pipework

Insects are not the only pests that invade buildings. Mice and rats can be a menace, especially in houses that offer plenty of underfloor runs, where they are able to live and prosper uninterrupted and find a plentiful supply of food by invading your living quarters. Mice are a nuisance, but rats present a positive health hazard; eradication is therefore essential. Bats sometimes shelter inside houses too, usually occupying the roof space. Although you may not relish sharing your home with them, they are harmless and are now protected by law.

Mice

Mice are attracted by fallen scraps of food, so the easiest remedy is to keep floors spotlessly clean. However, mice can move from house to house, through roof spaces or wall cavities and under floors, so may be difficult to eradicate. Consult your local Environmental Health Department if they persist.

You can obtain ready-poisoned bait, which should be sprinkled onto a piece of paper or card, so uneaten bait can be easily removed. Keep pets and children away from the bait. If signs of mice are still evident after three weeks, resort to traps. Humane traps capture mice alive in a cage, enabling you to deposit them elsewhere. Although less humane, you can also use spring-loaded snap-traps.

Most people do not set enough traps. If possible, position them every 2m (6ft) across mouse runs. The best place is against the skirting, facing towards the wall. Bait traps with flour, porridge oats, or chocolate moulded onto the bait hook. Dispose of the bodies by burying, burning, or flushing them down the WC.

Rats

Serious rat infestation occurs rarely in the average domestic situation, but rats can be a problem in rural and inner-city areas or near rivers, canals and docks. They can be killed with anti-coagulant poisons; but as rats are a health hazard, always contact the Environmental Health Department for expert advice.

Bats

Bats prefer to roost in uninhabited structures such as barns, caves, mines and tunnels, but occasionally they take up residence in houses. They do not present a health hazard (their droppings are dry insect skeletons), nor do they gnaw at wood or paintwork. In fact, they are an advantage in a roof space, as they feed on woodworm beetles.

Bats are becoming very rare and are now a protected species. It is illegal to kill or injure a bat, or disturb its roosting place or block its means of access. If you are alarmed by their presence, contact your local authority for advice. You must inform the same authority if you plan to spray wood preservers or insect eradicators in a roof space inhabited by bats, since certain chemicals will harm them.

If a bat should fly into a room, try to keep calm. It will avoid you if it can – and it won't become entangled in your hair, as old wives' tales suggest. Open all the doors and windows immediately, so it is able to escape. A crawling bat can be carefully picked up in gloved hands and gently put outside.

HANDLING POISONS SAFELY

Poisons designed to kill rodents are deadly to humans too, so it is vital to follow manufacturers' handling and storage instructions to the letter. Make sure poisons are always well out of reach of children, and store them where pets and other animals cannot get at them. Never store them under the kitchen sink, where they could easily be mistaken for household products, or anywhere where they might contaminate food. If poison is accidentally consumed by humans or animals, keep the container so that the poison can be readily identified by a doctor or vet. Some containers are colour-coded specifically for this purpose. Always wear protective gloves when you handle poisons and chemicals.

Wear protective gloves when handling poisons

Rot occurs in unprotected household timbers, fences and outbuildings that are subject to damp. Fungal spores, which are always present, multiply and develop in these conditions until eventually the timber is destroyed. Fungal attack can cause serious structural damage and requires immediate attention if costly repairs are to be avoided. The two most common scourges are wet rot and dry rot.

Recognizing rot

Signs of fungal attack are easy enough to detect – but certain strains are much more damaging than others, and so it is important to be able to identify them.

Mould growth
White furry deposits or black spots on timber, plaster or wallpaper are mould growths. Usually, these are the result of condensation. When they are wiped or scraped off, the structure shows no sign of physical deterioration apart from staining. Cure the source of the damp conditions, and treat the affected area with a fungicide or a solution of 16 parts warm water : 1 part bleach.

Wet rot

Wet rot only occurs in timber that has a high moisture content. Once the cause of the moisture is eliminated, further deterioration is arrested. Wet rot often attacks the framework of doors and windows that have been neglected, allowing rainwater to penetrate joints or between brickwork and adjacent timbers. The first sign is often peeling paintwork. Stripping the paint reveals timber that is spongy when wet, but dark brown and crumbly when dry. In advanced stages the grain splits, and thin dark-brown fungal strands will be evident on the timber. Always treat wet rot as soon as practicable.

Dry rot

Once it has taken hold, dry rot is a most serious form of decay. Urgent treatment is essential. It will attack timber with a much lower moisture content than wet rot, but only in badly ventilated confined spaces indoors – unlike wet rot, which thrives outdoors as well as indoors .

Dry rot exhibits different characteristics depending on the extent of its development. It spreads by sending out fine pale-grey strands in all directions (even through masonry) to infect drier timbers and will even pump water from damp wood. The rot can progress at an alarming rate. In very damp conditions, these 'tubules' are accompanied by white growths resembling cotton wool. These are known as mycelium. Once established, dry rot develops wrinkled, pancake-shaped fruiting bodies, which produce rust-coloured spores that are expelled to rapidly cover surrounding timber and masonry. Infested timber becomes brown and brittle, with cracks across and along the grain, causing it to break up into cube-like pieces. You may detect a strong, musty, mushroom-like smell, produced by the fungus.

Wet rot – treat it at the earliest opportunity.

Dry rot – urgent treatment is essential.

TREATING ROT

Dealing with wet rot
Once you have eliminated the cause of the damp, cut away and replace badly damaged wood, then paint the new and surrounding woodwork with three liberal applications of chemical wet-rot eradicator. Brush the liquid well into the joints and end grain.

Before decorating, you can apply a wood hardener to reinforce slightly damaged timbers, then six hours later use wood filler to rebuild the surface. Repaint as normal.

Paint rotted timbers with wood hardener

Dealing with dry rot
Dry rot requires more drastic action and should be treated by a specialist contractor unless the outbreak is minor and self-contained. The fungus is able to penetrate masonry, so look under the floorboards in adjacent rooms and check cavity walls for signs of rot.

Eliminate the source of dampness and ensure that there is adequate ventilation in roof spaces or under the floors by unblocking or installing air bricks. Cut out all infected timber up to at least 450mm (1ft 6in) beyond the last visible sign of rot. Chop plaster from nearby walls, following the strands. Continue for another 450mm (1ft 6in) beyond the extent of the growth. Collect all debris in plastic bags and burn it.

Use a chemical dry-rot eradicator to kill any remaining spores. Wire-brush the masonry, then apply three generous brushcoats to all timber, brickwork and plaster within 1.5m (5ft) of the infected area. An alternative method is to hire a coarse sprayer and go over the same area three times.

If a wall has been penetrated by strands of dry rot, drill regularly spaced, staggered holes into it from both sides. Angle the holes downwards, so the fluid will collect in them to saturate the wall internally. Patch holes after treatment.

Coat all replacement timbers with eradicator and immerse the end grain in a bucket of fluid for five to ten minutes. When you come to make good the wall, apply a zinc-oxychloride plaster.

PREVENTATIVE
TREATMENT

Since fungal attack can be so damaging, it is well worth taking precautions to prevent it occurring. Regularly decorate and maintain doorframes and window frames (where water can easily penetrate) and seal around them with mastic. Provide proper ventilation between floors and ceilings, and also in the loft. Check and eradicate sources of damp, such as plumbing leaks; and (the most important precaution of all, perhaps) apply a chemical preserver to unprotected timbers during routine maintenance.

Looking after timberwork

Treat new and existing timbers with a chemical preserver. Brush and spray two or three applications on standing timbers, paying particular attention to joints and end grain.

Immersing timbers
Timber in contact with the ground will benefit from prolonged immersion in preserver. Stand fence posts on end in a bucket of fluid for 10 minutes. For smaller timbers, make a shallow bath from loose bricks and line it with thick polyethylene sheet. Fill the trough with preserver and immerse the timbers, weighing them down with bricks to prevent them from floating (1). To empty the bath, sink a bucket at one end of the trough, then remove the bricks at that end so the fluid will pour out (2).

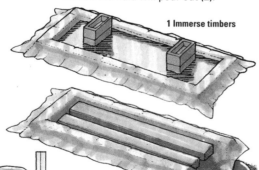

1 Immerse timbers

2 Drain into a bucket

Protecting timber frames
To protect timber frames, insert preserver in solid-tablet form into holes drilled at regular 50mm (2in) intervals in a staggered pattern. If the timber becomes wet, the tablets dissolve, placing preserver exactly where it is needed. Fill the holes with wood filler and paint as normal.

Protecting joints
Place preservative tablets close to the joints of a frame.

WOOD PRESERVERS

Water-based preservers are odourless and can safely be used on horticultural timbers. Most modern solvent-based products are also harmless to plants when dry, but it makes sense to check before you buy.

Clear preservatives

You can use clear liquid preservers that protect timber from dry or wet rot only. Alternatively, use an all-purpose fluid that will also provide protection against wood-boring insects. Clear preservers are useful when you want to retain the appearance of natural timber – oak beams or hardwood doors, for example – and you can usually paint or varnish the surface once the wood has dried.

Green preserver

There is also a green solvent-based preserver that is traditionally used for horticultural timbers. Being coloured, it helps to identify treated timbers for the future. However, the colour is due to the presence of copper, which is not a permanent colouring agent when used outdoors. Nevertheless, its protective properties are unaffected, even when the colour is washed out by heavy rain.

Wood-coloured preservers

Tinted preservers are formulated to protect sound exterior timbers against fungal and insect attack while staining the wood at the same time.

There is a choice of brown shades intended to simulate the most common hardwoods, and one that is designed specifically to preserve the richness of cedarwood. Solvent-based preservers are made with light-fast pigments that inhibit fading. They do not penetrate as well as a clear preserver, but generally offer slightly better protection than the coloured water-based preservers.

Clear   Coloured   Green

SAFETY WITH PRESERVERS

Solvent-based preservers are flammable, so do not smoke while using them and extinguish any naked lights. Wear protective gloves and goggles when applying preservers, together with a respirator when using these liquids indoors. Provide good ventilation while working, and do not sleep in a freshly treated room for 48 hours or so – in order to allow time for the fumes to dissipate completely. Wash spilt preserver from your skin and eyes with water immediately, and do not delay seeking medical advice if irritation persists.

DAMP
CAUSES

TYPES OF
DAMP

SEE ALSO
Details for:
Wet and dry rot   255–256

The symptoms of damp can be most distressing both in terms of your health and the condition of your home. Try to locate the source of the problem as quickly as possible, before it promotes its even more damaging side effects – wet and dry rot. Unfortunately, this is sometimes easier said than done, as one form of damp may be obscured by another, or may appear in an unfamiliar guise. The three main categories to eliminate are penetrating damp, rising damp and condensation.

Principal causes of penetrating damp
1 Broken gutter
2 Leaking downpipe
3 Missing roof tiles
4 Damaged flashing
5 Faulty pointing
6 Porous bricks
7 Cracked masonry
8 Cracked render
9 Blocked drip groove
10 Defective seals around frames
11 Missing weatherboard
12 Bridged cavity

Principal causes of rising damp
● Missing DPC or DPM
● Damaged DPC or DPM
● DPC too low
● Bridged DPC
● Earth piled above DPC

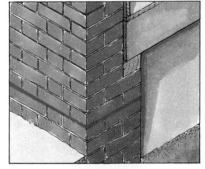

Penetrating damp

Penetrating damp is the result of water permeating the structure of the house from outside. The symptoms only occur during wet weather. After a few dry days, the damp patches dry out, often leaving stains.

As isolated patches are caused by a heavy deposit of water in one area, you should be able to pinpoint their source fairly accurately. General dampness usually indicates that the wall itself has become porous, but it could equally well be caused by some other problem.

Penetrating damp occurs most frequently in older homes, which have solid walls. Relatively modern houses built with a cavity between two thinner brick skins are less likely to suffer from penetrating damp, unless the cavity is bridged in one of several ways.

Rising damp

Rising damp is caused by water soaking up from the ground into the floors and walls of the house. Most houses are protected by an impervious barrier built into the walls and under concrete floors so that water cannot permeate above a certain level.

If the damp-proof course (DPC) in the walls or the membrane (DPM) in a floor breaks down, water is able to seep into the upper structure. Alternatively, there may be something forming a bridge across the barrier so that water is able to flow around it. Some older houses were built without a DPC.

This type of damp is confined to solid floors and the lower sections of walls. It is a constant problem – even during dry spells – and becomes worse with prolonged wet weather.

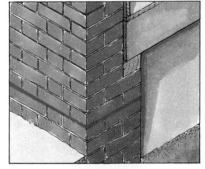

DPC in a solid wall
A layer of impervious material is built into a joint between brick courses, 150mm (6in) above the ground.

DPC and DPM in a cavity-wall structure
The damp-proof membrane in a concrete floor is linked to the DPC protecting the inner leaf of the wall. The outer leaf has its own damp-proof course.

DAMP: PRINCIPAL CAUSES

PENETRATING DAMP: PRINCIPAL CAUSES

CAUSE	SYMPTOMS	REMEDY
Broken or blocked gutter Rainwater overflows, typically at the joints of old cast-iron gutters, and saturates the wall directly below, preventing it from drying out normally.	Damp patches appearing near the ceiling in upstairs rooms, and mould forming immediately behind the leak.	Clear leaves and silt from the gutters. Repair the damaged gutters, or replace a faulty system with maintenance-free plastic guttering.
Broken or blocked downpipes A downpipe that has cracked or rusted douses the wall immediately behind the leak. If leaves lodge behind the pipe at the fixing brackets, that will eventually produce a similar effect.	An isolated patch of damp, often appearing halfway up the wall. Mould growth behind the downpipe.	Repair the cracked or corroded downpipe; or replace it, substituting a maintenance-free plastic version. Clear the blockage.
Loose or broken roof tiles Defective tiles allow rainwater to penetrate the roof.	Damp patches appearing on upstairs ceilings, usually during a heavy downpour.	Replace the faulty tiles, renewing any damaged roofing felt.
Damaged flashing The junction between the roof of a lean-to extension and the side wall of the house, or around a chimney stack emerging from the roof, is sealed with flashing strips (usually of lead or zinc) or sometimes with a mortar fillet. If the flashing or fillet cracks or parts from the masonry, water trickles down inside the building.	Damp patch on the ceiling extending from the wall or chimney breast; also on the chimney breast itself. Damp patch on the side wall near the junction with the lean-to extension; damp patch on the lean-to ceiling itself.	If the existing flashing appears to be intact, refit it securely. If it is damaged, replace it using similar material or a self-adhesive flashing strip.
Faulty pointing Ageing mortar between bricks in an exterior wall is likely to crack or fall out; water is then able to penetrate to the inside of the wall.	Isolated damp patches or sometimes widespread dampness, depending on the extent of the deterioration.	Repoint the joints between bricks, then treat the entire wall with water-repellent fluid.
Porous bricks Bricks in good condition are weather-proof, but old, soft bricks become porous and often lose their faces. As a result, the whole wall is eventually saturated, particularly on an elevation that faces prevailing winds, or where a fault with the guttering develops.	Widespread damp on the inner face of exterior walls. A noticeable increase in damp during a downpour. Mould growth appearing on internal plaster and decorations.	Repair bricks that have spalled, and waterproof the exterior with a clear water-repellent fluid.
Cracked brickwork Cracks in a brick wall allow rainwater (or water from a leak) to seep through to the inside face.	An isolated damp patch – on a chimney breast, for example, due to a cracked chimney stack.	Fill cracked mortar and replace damaged bricks.
Defective render Cracked or blown render encourages rainwater to seep between the render and the brickwork behind it. The water is prevented from evaporating and so becomes absorbed by the wall.	An isolated damp patch, which may become widespread. The trouble can persist for some time after rain ceases.	Fill and reinforce the crack. Hack off extensively damaged or blown render and patch it with new sand-cement render, then weatherproof the wall by applying exterior paint.
Damaged coping If the coping stones on top of a roof parapet are missing or the joints are open, water can penetrate the wall.	Damp patches on ceiling, near to the wall immediately below the parapet.	Bed new stones on fresh mortar and make good the joints.

PENETRATING DAMP: PRINCIPAL CAUSES

CAUSE	SYMPTOMS	REMEDY
Blocked drip groove Exterior windowsills should have a groove running longitudinally on the underside. When rain runs under the sill, the water falls off at the groove before reaching the wall. If the groove is bridged by layers of paint or moss, the water soaks the wall behind.	Damp patches along the underside of a window frame. Rotting wooden sill on the inside and outside. Mould growth appearing on the inside face of the wall below the window.	Rake out the drip groove. Nail a batten to the underside of a wooden sill to deflect drips.
Failed seals around windows and doorframes Timber frames often shrink, pulling the pointing from around the edges so that rainwater is able to penetrate the gap.	Rotting woodwork and patches of damp around the frames. Sometimes the gap is obvious where mortar has fallen out.	Repair the frame, and seal around the edges with mastic.
No weatherboard An angled weatherboard across the bottom of a door should shed water clear of the threshold and prevent water running under the door.	Damp floorboards just inside the door. Rotting at the base of the doorframe.	Fit a weatherboard, even if there are no obvious signs of damage. Repair rotted wood at the base of the doorframe.
Bridged wall cavity Mortar inadvertently dropped onto a wall tie connecting the inner and outer leaves of a cavity wall allows water to bridge the gap.	An isolated patch of damp appearing anywhere on the wall, particularly after a heavy downpour.	Open up the wall and remove the mortar bridge, then waterproof the wall externally with paint or clear repellent.

RISING DAMP: PRINCIPAL CAUSES

CAUSE	SYMPTOMS	REMEDY
No DPC or DPM If a house was built without either a damp-proof course or damp-proof membrane, the walls are able to soak up water from the ground.	Widespread damp up to about 1m (3ft) above skirting level. Damp concrete floor surface.	Fit a new DPC or DPM.
Damaged DPC or DPM If the DPC or DPM has deteriorated, water will penetrate at that point.	Damp at skirting level (possibly isolated but spreading).	Repair or replace the DPC or DPM.
DPC too low If the DPC is lower than the necessary 150mm (6in) above ground level, heavy rain is able to splash above the DPC and soak the wall surface.	Damp at skirting level, but only where the ground is too high.	Lower the level of the ground outside. If it's a path or patio, cut a 150mm (6in) wide trench and fill with gravel, which drains rapidly.
Bridged DPC If exterior render has been taken below the DPC or mortar has fallen within a cavity wall, moisture is able to cross over to the inside.	Widespread damp at and just above skirting level.	Hack off render to expose the DPC. Remove several bricks and rake out debris from the cavity.
Debris piled against wall A flower bed, rockery or area of paving built against a wall will bridge the DPC. Building material and garden refuse left there will also act as a bridge.	Damp at skirting level in area of bridge only, or spreading from that point.	Remove the earth, paving or debris and allow the wall to dry out naturally.

SEE ALSO
Details for:
Waterproofing bricks	46
New DPM	186, 264
Weatherboard	191
Repairing frames	194–195, 209–210
Bridged cavity	260
Drip batten	260
Sealing frames	260
New DPC	262–263

DPC too low

Render bridges DPC

Earth piled over DPC

1 Water drips to ground

2 A bridged groove

3 Drip moulding

Apply mastic with an applicator gun

CURING DAMP

Remedies for different forms of damp are suggested in the charts on the previous pages; where damp conditions are attributable to factors such as poor ventilation or deteriorating decoration, you will find detailed remedies in other sections of the book. The information below supplements these instructions by providing advice on measures relating solely to the eradication of damp.

Waterproofing walls

Applying a water repellent to the outside of a wall not only prevents water infusion but also reduces the possibility of interstitial condensation. This occurs when water vapour from the inside of the house penetrates an external wall until it reaches the damp, colder interior of the brickwork, where the vapour condenses. The moisture eventually migrates back to the inner surface of the wall, causing stains and mould.

Proprietary damp-proofing liquids are available for painting the inside of walls, but they should be considered a temporary measure only, as they do not treat the source of the problem.

Remove wallcoverings and make sure that the wall surfaces are sound and clean. Treat any mould growth with a fungicide. Apply two full brushcoats over an area appreciably larger than the present extent of the damp. Once the wall is dry, you can decorate it with paint or a wallcovering.

If any of your walls show signs of efflorescence, apply the appropriate treatment, then paint with heavy-duty moisture-curing polyurethane.

Providing a drip moulding

Because water cannot flow uphill, a drip moulding on the underside of an external windowsill forces rainwater to drip to the ground before it reaches the wall behind (1). When redecorating, scrape out old paint or moss from drip grooves before it forms a bridge (2).

If a wooden windowsill does not have a pre-cut drip groove, it is worth adding a drip moulding by pinning and gluing a 6mm (¼in) square hardwood strip 35mm (1½in) from the front edge of the sill (3). Paint or varnish the drip moulding to match the sill itself.

Sealing around window frames

Scrape out old or loose mortar from around the frame. Fill deep gaps with expanding-foam filler or rolled paper, then seal all around the frame with a flexible mastic. Mastic is available in cartridges, some designed for use with an applicator gun. Cut the end off the nozzle of the cartridge and run it along the side of the frame to form an even continuous bead. If the gap's very wide, fill it with a second bead once the first has set. Most sealants form a skin and can be overpainted after a few hours, but are waterproof without painting.

Bridged cavity

A bridged wall cavity allows water to cross over to the inner leaf. The easiest way to deal with it is simply to apply a water repellent to the outer surface.

However, this does not address the cause, which may lead to further dampness in the future. When it is convenient, during repointing perhaps, remove two or three bricks from the outside in the vicinity of the damp patch by chopping out the mortar around them. Use a small mirror and a torch to inspect the cavity. If you locate mortar lying on a wall tie, rake or chip it off with an opened wire coat hanger or a metal rod, then replace the bricks.

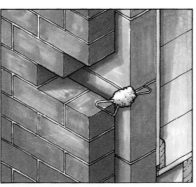

Exposing a bridged wall tie
Remove a few bricks in order to rake or chip the mortar from a wall tie.

Air carries moisture as water vapour, but its capacity depends on its temperature. As air becomes warmer, it absorbs more water, rather like a sponge. When water-laden air comes into contact with a surface that is colder than itself, it cools until it can no longer hold the water it has absorbed and (just like a sponge being squeezed) it condenses, depositing water in liquid form onto the surface.

Conditions for condensation

The air in a house is normally warm enough to hold water without reaching saturation point, but a great deal of moisture is also produced by cooking and using baths and showers, and even by breathing. In cold weather, when the low temperature outside cools the external walls and windows below the temperature of the heated air inside, all the extra water runs down window panes and soaks into the wallpaper and plaster. Matters are made worse in the winter by sealing off windows and doors so that fresh air cannot replace humid air before it condenses.

Damp in a fairly new house that is in good condition is almost invariably due to condensation.

The root cause of condensation is rarely simple, as it is a result of a combination of air temperature, humidity, poor ventilation and thermal insulation. Tackling just one of these problems in isolation may transfer condensation elsewhere or even exaggerate the symptoms. However, the chart opposite lists major factors that contribute to the total problem.

Condensation appears first on cold glazing

CONDENSATION: PRINCIPAL CAUSES

CAUSE	SYMPTOMS	REMEDY
Insufficient heat In cold weather the air in an unheated room may be close to saturation point. (Raising the temperature increases the ability of the air to absorb moisture without condensing.)	General condensation.	Heat the room – but do not use an oil heater (which produces moisture).
Oil heaters An oil heater produces as much water vapour as the paraffin it burns, causing condensation to form on cold windows, exterior walls and ceilings.	General condensation in rooms where oil heaters are used.	Substitute another form of heating.
Uninsulated walls and ceilings Moist air readily condenses on cold ceilings and exterior walls.	Widespread damp and mould. The line of ceiling joists is picked out because mould grows less well along the joists, which are relatively warm.	Install efficient loft insulation and/or line the ceiling with insulating tiles or polystyrene lining. Alternatively, apply anti-condensation paint.
Cold bridge Even when a wall has cavity insulation, there can be a cold bridge across the lintel over windows and the solid brick down the sides.	Damp patches or mould surrounding the window frames.	Line the walls and window reveals with expanded-polystyrene sheeting or foamed polyethylene.
Unlagged pipes Cold-water pipes attract condensation. The problem is often wrongly attributed to a leak when water collects and drips from the lowest point of a pipe run.	A line of damp on a ceiling or wall, following the pipework. An isolated patch on a ceiling, where water drops from plumbing. Beads of moisture on the underside of a pipe.	Insulate your cold-water pipes, either with plastic-foam lagging tubes or with mineral-fibre wrapping.
Cold windows When exterior temperatures are low, windows usually show condensation before any other feature, because the glass is thin and they are constantly exposed to the elements.	Misted window panes, or water collecting in pools at the bottom of the glass.	Double-glaze your windows. If condensation occurs inside a secondary system, place some silica-gel crystals (which absorb moisture) in the cavity between the panes.
Sealed fireplace If a fireplace opening is blocked up, the air trapped inside the flue cannot circulate and therefore condenses on the inside, eventually soaking through the brickwork.	Damp patches appearing anywhere on the chimney breast.	Ventilate the chimney by inserting a grille or airbrick at a low level in the part of the fireplace that has been blocked-up. Treat the chimney breast with damp-proofing liquid.
Loft insulation blocking airways If loft insulation blocks the spaces around the eaves, air cannot circulate in the roof space, and condensation is able to form.	Widespread mould affecting the timbers in the roof space.	Unblock the airways and, if possible, fit a ventilator grille in the soffit or install tile/slate vents.
Condensation after building or repairs If you have carried out work involving new bricks, mortar and especially plaster, condensation may be the result of these materials exuding moisture as they dry out.	General condensation affecting walls, ceiling, windows and solid floors.	Wait for the new work to dry out, then review the situation before decorating or other treatment.

● **Anti-condensation paint**
This paint contains minute hollow glass beads that act as insulators, as well as a fungicide to inhibit mould growth. It can be overpainted with emulsion to suit your colour scheme.

INSTALLING A DAMP-PROOF COURSE

SEE ALSO
Details for:
Rising damp   257

When an old damp-proof course (DPC) has failed, or where none exists, the only certain remedy is to insert a new one. Of the options available, chemical injection is the only method you should attempt yourself. Even then, consider whether it is cost-effective in the long run. Rising damp can lead to other expensive repairs unless it is completely eradicated, so hiring a reputable company may prove to be a wise investment. (They normally provide a 30-year guarantee.) Ask for a detailed specification – known as an Agrément certificate – to ensure that the work is carried out to approved standards. Also, check that the guarantee is fully covered by insurance in case the company goes out of business.

Checking for rising damp

There's no substitute for a professional survey to determine the cause of rising damp, but you can use an inexpensive electronic moisture meter to check the condition of your walls.

Working on the inside, take readings at regular intervals along the entire length of a wall, not just in one spot. Systematically check an area extending from floor level to about 1m (3ft) above the floor. If rising damp is present, the meter should indicate a high moisture reading that drops sharply due to natural evaporation above that level. Penetrating damp or condensation tend to show up as isolated patches or even as dampness that extends right up the wall. Even if you suspect rising damp, check that there is nothing bridging a perfectly sound damp-proof course before committing yourself to major works on the DPC itself.

It is sometimes possible to detect symptoms of rising damp even after the installation of a new DPC. This is due to old salt-contaminated plaster, which should be removed and replaced with special renovating plaster.

Use a moisture meter to test for rising damp

A physical DPC

A traditional DPC consists of a layer of impervious material built into the wall at about 150mm (6in) – or two to three brick courses – above ground level. It is possible to install a DPC in an existing wall by cutting out a mortar joint with a chain saw or a grinding disc. Copper sheet, polyethylene or bituminous felt is then inserted and the joint wedged and filled with fresh mortar. Experience is needed in order to avoid weakening the wall, and there's always a risk of cutting into a pipe or electric cable. Although a physical DPC is expensive to install, it is considered the most reliable method.

Electro-osmosis

This method utilizes the principle that a minute electrical charge will prevent

A physical DPC A joint is removed to insert an impervious layer.

Electro-osmosis A copper electrode is planted in the wall.

water rising by capillary action. A length of titanium wire is inserted in a continuous chase cut all round the building; anode points bent in the wire are then inserted into holes drilled in the masonry at regular intervals. The wire is connected to an earthing rod buried in the ground, and the system's power unit plugs into a standard 13amp socket. The holes and chase are filled with mortar to protect the wire. This type of system can be placed internally or externally, and has to be installed by a professional fitter.

Porous tubes

Porous clay tubes are inserted into a row of closely spaced holes to increase the rate of evaporation so that moisture will not rise to too high a level. This is a simple and cheap method.

INJECTING A CHEMICAL DPC

The most widely practised method is to inject a waterproofing chemical, usually silicone-based, to form a continuous barrier throughout the thickness of the wall. Suitable for brick or stone walls up to 600mm (2ft) thick, it is straightforward to install yourself using hired equipment.

Preparing the wall for injection

If you want to carry out the work yourself, use a hired pressure-injection machine. You will need 68 to 90 litres (15 to 20 gallons) of DPC fluid for every 30m (100ft) of a wall 225mm (9in) thick.

Remove skirtings and hack off plaster and render to a height of 450mm (1ft 6in) above the line of visible damp. Repair and repoint the brickwork.

Drilling the injection holes

Drill a row of holes about 150mm (6in) above external ground level, but below a suspended wooden floor or just above one made of solid concrete. If the wall has an old DPC, set the new course just above it and take care not to puncture it when drilling. Use a masonry drill about 18 to 25mm (¾ to 1in) in diameter – but not smaller than the injecting nozzles of

the machine. If possible, drill a row of identical holes from both sides of a wall 225mm (9in) or more thick to provide a continuous DPC.

When you are drilling a 225mm (9in) solid-brick wall, the holes should be at 112mm (4½in) centres, about 25mm (1in) below the upper-edge of a brick course. Angle them downwards slightly. Drill 75mm (3in) deep, unless the treatment is to be limited to one side only – in which case you should drill to a depth of 190mm (7½in). Treat each leaf of a cavity wall separately, drilling to a depth of 75mm (3in) in each leaf.

If the wall is made of impervious stone, you will need to drill into the mortar course around each stone block at the proposed DPC level, spacing the holes every 75mm (3in).

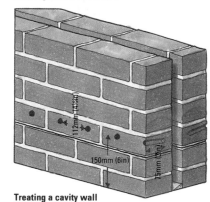
Treating a solid-brick wall

Treating a cavity wall

● **Chemical-injection kit**
As an alternative to hiring equipment, you can buy a DIY kit that contains all the essential materials, tools and specialized equipment, together with full instructions.

Injecting the fluid

Although there are various kinds of injection pump available, most of them work in basically the same way. With most types, the pump's filtered suction hose is inserted into a drum containing chemical. Make sure that the valves controlling the injection nozzles are closed, then connect the pump to the mains electrical supply.

Pressure injection machines usually have three to six nozzles. Connect the nozzles to the ends of the hoses and push them into the holes in the wall; if you are treating a thick wall, drill holes 75mm (3in) deep to begin with and start with the shorter nozzles.

Tighten the wing nuts sufficiently to secure the nozzles and form a seal – but don't overtighten them, or you may damage the expansion nipples at their tips. Open the control valves on all the nozzles except for the one at the far end, then switch on the pump so the fluid will circulate through the machine.

By opening its valve, bleed off some fluid through the remaining nozzle into a container to expel air from the system. Switch off the pump and insert the nozzle in the wall. Reopen the valve and allow the fluid to be injected until it wets the surface of the bricks. Maintain the pressure at about 100psi (pounds per square inch) by adjusting the valve

on the pump body.

Close off all valves, then move the nozzles to the next series of holes and repeat the procedure. When you reach the other end of the wall, switch off the pump, then return to the starting point and drill the same holes to 190mm (7½in) deep. Swap the short injection nozzles for the longer 190mm (7½in) ones (you may need to wrap PTFE sealing tape round the threads), slot them into the wall, tighten their nuts, and inject the fluid. Flush the machine through with white spirit after use to clean out all traces of fluid.

Treating an impervious-stone wall

At least one third thickness. Seek local professional advice.

Hiring equipment
Any tool-hire firm will supply you with all the materials and equipment necessary for injecting a chemical DPC yourself. It is an economical method that requires careful work rather than experience. Flush the machine thoroughly before you return it.

TREATING
A BASEMENT
OR CELLAR

SEE ALSO

Details for:	
Bonding agent	43
Efflorescence	44
Cleaning concrete	49
Repairing concrete	49
Rendering	172–175
New DPM	186
Rising damp	257
Condensation	260–261
Ventilation	283–290

Being at least partly below ground level, the walls and floors of a cellar or basement invariably suffer from damp to some extent. Because the problem cannot be tackled from the outside in the normal way, you will have to seal out the damp by treating the internal surfaces. Rising damp in concrete floors, whatever the situation, can be treated as described below, but penetrating or rising damp in walls other than in a cellar should be cured at source – since merely sealing the internal surfaces may encourage the damp eventually to penetrate elsewhere. In addition, ensure a treated cellar is properly ventilated and, if need be, even heat it to avoid condensation in the future.

Treating the floor

When laying a new concrete floor, incorporate a damp-proof membrane (DPM) during its construction. If the DPM was omitted or has failed in an existing floor, seal it with a heavy-duty, moisture-curing polyurethane.

Preparing the surface
Make sure that the floor is clean and grease-free. Fill any cracks and small holes by priming them with one coat of urethane, then one hour later applying a mortar made from 6 parts sand : 1 part cement, plus sufficient urethane to produce a stiff paste. Although it is possible to apply urethane to a damp or dry surface, it will penetrate a dry floor better; so force-dry an excessively damp cellar with a fan heater before treatment. Remove all heaters from the room before you begin damp-proofing.

Applying urethane
Apply the first coat of urethane with a broom, using 1litre to cover about 5sq m (50sq ft). If you are damp-proofing a room with a DPC in the walls, take the urethane coating up behind the skirting to meet it. Two or three hours later, apply a second coat (further delay may result in poor inter-coat adhesion). Apply three or four coats in all. After three days, you can lay a conventional floorcovering or use the floor as it is.

Treating a wall with bitumen-latex emulsion
1 Skim coat of mortar
2 Coat of bitumen latex
3 Blinded coat of latex
4 Plaster or dry lining

Moisture-curing polyurethane
Damp-proof a floor with three or four coats of urethane applied with a broom.

Patching active leaks

Before you damp-proof a cellar, patch any cracks that are active water leaks, using a quick-drying hydraulic cement. Supplied in powder form, ready for mixing with water, the cement expands as it hardens, sealing out the moisture.

Undercut a crack or hole, using a chisel and club hammer. Mix some cement and hold it in a gloved hand until it is warm, then push it into the crack. Keep it in place with your hand or a trowel for three to five minutes, until it is hard.

TREATING THE WALLS

Moisture-cured polyurethane can be used to completely seal the walls of a cellar or basement, as well as the floor.

If you have decided to paint the walls, decorate with emulsion paints within 24 to 48 hours after treatment for maximum adhesion.

If you want to hang a wallcovering, apply two coats of emulsion first and use a heavy-duty paste. (Don't hang an impervious wallcovering, such as vinyl, as it's vital that the wall can breathe.)

Bitumen-latex emulsion
Where you plan to plaster or dry-line the basement walls, you can seal out the damp by using a relatively cheap bitumen-latex emulsion. However, it is not suitable as an unprotected covering, either for walls or floors, although it is often used as an integral DPM under the top screed of a concrete floor and as a waterproof adhesive for some tiles and for wooden parquet flooring.

Hack off old plaster to expose the brickwork, then apply a skim coat of mortar to smooth the surface. Paint the wall with two coats of the bitumen emulsion, joining with the DPM in the floor. Before the second coat dries, imbed some clean, dry sand (blinding) into it to provide a key for the coats of plaster (see below left).

Cement-based waterproof coating
In a cellar or basement where there is severe damp, apply a cement-based waterproof coating. Hack off old plaster or rendering in order to expose the wall.

To seal the join between a concrete floor and the wall, cut a chase about 20mm (¾in) wide by the same depth. Brush out the debris and fill the channel with hydraulic cement (see left), finishing it off neatly as an angled fillet.

Mix the powdered cement-based coating with an acrylic solution, following the manufacturer's instructions, then apply two coats to the wall with a bristle brush. However, when brick walls are damp, they bring salts to the surface in the form of white crystals known as efflorescence – so before treating with waterproof coating, apply a salt-inhibiting render made of 1 part sulphate-resisting cement : 2 parts clean rendering sand. Add 1 part liquid bonding agent : 3 parts of the mixing water. Apply a thin trowelled coat to a rough wall, or brush it onto a relatively smooth surface. Then leave it to set.

INSULATION & VENTILATION

INSULATING YOUR HOME

No matter what fuel you use, the cost of heating a home has risen dramatically over recent years – and there's no reason to suppose it won't continue to rise, perhaps at an even faster rate. Saving money is a major consideration, but of equal importance is the need to conserve energy in order to protect the environment. And even if such considerations could be ignored, the improved comfort and health of your family would more than justify the effort and expense of installing adequate insulation in your home.

Local-authority grants

Because home insulation is of benefit to the economy, the Government has made discretionary grants available through local authorities to encourage people to insulate their lofts, storage tanks and pipework. You may also be eligible for a grant towards the cost of cavity-wall insulation, draughtproofing and double glazing. To qualify for a grant, you must obtain local-authority approval before carrying out the work or purchasing insulation materials.

Specifications for insulation

When comparing thermal insulating materials, you are likely to encounter certain technical specifications.

U-values

Elements of a house's structure and the insulation itself are often assigned a U-value. This is a measurement of thermal transmittance that represents the rate at which heat travels from one side to the other. The U-value is an expression of watts of energy per square metre per °C ($W/m^2/°C$). If a solid brick wall is specified as having a U-value of 2.0, it means that 2 watts of heat are conducted from every square metre of the wall for every °C difference in the temperature on each side of the wall. If the temperature outside is 10° lower than inside, each square metre of wall will conduct 20 watts of heat. The lower the U-value, the better the insulation.

R-values

A material may be given an R-value, which indicates the resistance to heat flow of a specified thickness. Materials with superior insulating qualities have the highest R-values.

CHOOSING INSULATION PRIORITIES

To many people the initial expense of total insulation seems prohibitive, even though they will concede that it is cost-effective in the long term. Nevertheless, you will find that it is worth embarking on an insulation programme as soon as practicable, since every measure will achieve some saving.

Most authorities suggest that in an average house 35 per cent of lost heat escapes through the walls, 25 per cent through the roof, 25 per cent through draughty doors and windows, and 15 per cent through the floor. At best, this is no more than a rough guide, as it is difficult to define an 'average' home in order to estimate the rate of heat loss.

A terraced house, for instance, will lose less than a detached house of identical size, even though their roofs have the same area and are in similar condition. And other factors are relevant, too – for example, large ill-fitting sash windows permit far greater heat loss than small tightly-fitting casements.

Although these statistics identify the major routes for heat loss, they don't necessarily indicate where you should begin your insulation programme in order to achieve the quickest return on your investment – or, for that matter, the most immediate improvement in terms of comfort. In fact, it is best to start with relatively inexpensive measures.

1 Hot-water cylinder and pipes

Begin by lagging the hot-water storage cylinder and any exposed pipework running through unheated areas of your house. This treatment will constitute a considerable saving in a matter of only a few months.

2 Radiators

Fit a foil-faced lining behind radiators against an external wall – so the heat is reflected back into the room, instead of being absorbed by the wall.

3 Draughtproofing

Eliminate heat loss around all windows and doors, including draughts between sashes. In return for a modest outlay, draughtproofing helps reduce heating costs and provides increased comfort. It is also easy to accomplish.

4 Roof

Tackle the insulation of your roof next. This is a very economical proposition – in addition to a significant reduction in domestic fuel bills, you may be eligible for a local authority grant towards the cost of roof insulation (see left).

5 Walls

Depending on the construction of your house, insulating the walls may be a sound investment. However, it's likely to be a relatively expensive operation. It will therefore take several years for you to recoup your initial outlay.

6 Floors

Floorcoverings such as carpets, tiles or parquet offer some degree of insulation. Whether you install extra insulation is likely to depend on the level of comfort you require and whether you need to carry out other improvements to a floor. Floor insulation is a mandatory requirement for all new dwellings.

7 Double glazing

Contrary to the typical advertisements, double glazing will produce only a slow return on your investment, especially if you choose one of the more expensive glazing systems. However, it may help to increase the value of your property, and a double-glazed room is definitely cosier. In addition, you will be troubled by less noise from outside, especially if you choose to install triple glazing.

LAGGING PIPES, CYLINDERS AND RADIATORS

SEE ALSO

Details for:	
Wallpaper paste	95
Cylinders	392-394
Radiator roller	499

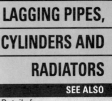

Insulating a hot-water cylinder

Many people think that an unlagged cylinder has the advantage of providing a useful source of heat in an airing cupboard – but in fact it squanders a surprising amount of energy. Even a lagged cylinder should provide ample heat in an enclosed airing cupboard; if not, an uninsulated pipe will do so.

Proprietary water-cylinder jackets are made from segments of mineral-fibre insulation, 80 to 100mm (3¼ to 4in) thick, wrapped in plastic. Measure the approximate height and circumference of the cylinder to choose the right size.

If need be, buy a jacket that is too large, rather than one that is too small. Make sure the quality is adequate by checking that it is marked with the British Standard kite mark (BS 5615).

Thread the tapered ends of the jacket segments onto a length of string and tie it round the pipe at the top of the cylinder. Distribute the segments evenly around the cylinder and wrap the straps or tapes provided around it to hold the jacket in place.

Spread out the segments to make sure the edges are butted together, and tuck the insulation around the pipes and the cylinder thermostat.

If you should ever have to replace the cylinder itself, consider substituting a pre-insulated version, of which there are various types on the market.

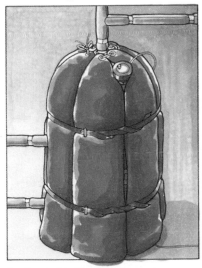

Lagging a hot-water cylinder
Fit a jacket snugly around the cylinder and wrap foamed-plastic tubes (see above right) around the pipework, especially the vent pipe directly above the cylinder.

Lagging pipe runs

You should insulate hot-water pipes in those parts of the house where their radiant heat is not contributing to the warmth of the rooms, and cold-water pipes in unheated areas of the building (where they could freeze). You can wrap pipework in lagging bandages (there are several types, some of which are self-adhesive), but it is generally more convenient to use foamed-plastic tubes designed for the purpose. This is especially true for pipes close to a wall, which may be awkward to wrap.

Foamed-plastic tubes are produced to fit pipes of different diameters: the tube walls vary in thickness from 12mm to 20mm (½in to ¾in). More expensive varieties incorporate a metallic-foil backing that reflects some of the heat back into hot-water pipes.

Most tubes are pre-slit along their length so that they can be sprung over the pipe (1). Butt successive lengths of tube end-to-end, and seal the joints with PVC adhesive tape.

At a bend, cut small segments out of the split edge so that it bends without crimping. Fit it around the pipe (2) and seal the closed joints with tape. If two pipes are joined with an elbow fitting, mitre the ends of the two lengths of tube, butt them together (3) and seal with tape. Cut lengths of tube to fit snugly around a tee-joint, linking them with a wedge-shaped butt joint (4), and seal with tape as before.

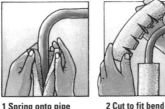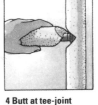

1 Spring onto pipe   **2 Cut to fit bend**   **3 Mitre over elbows**   **4 Butt at tee-joint**

Reflecting heat from a radiator

As much as 25 per cent of the radiant heat from a radiator against an outside wall may be lost to the wall behind it. You can reclaim maybe half this wasted heat by applying a foil-faced expanded-polystyrene lining to the wall behind the radiator, to reflect the heat back into the room. The material is available as rolls, sheets or tiles; and although it is easiest to apply it to the wall when the radiator is removed for decorating, that is certainly not essential.

Turn off the radiator and measure it, including the position of the brackets.

Use a sharp trimming knife or scissors to cut the lining to size, so it is slightly smaller than the radiator all round. Cut narrow slots, as need be, to fit over the fixing brackets (1).

Apply heavy-duty fungicidal wallpaper paste to the back of the material and then slide it behind the radiator (2). Smooth it onto the wall with a radiator roller or wooden batten. Allow the paste to dry before turning the radiator on again. Alternatively, you can fix the lining in place with double-sided adhesive pads.

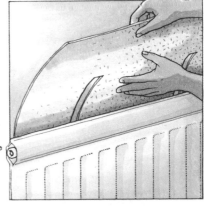

1 Cut slots to align with wall brackets   **2 Slide lining behind radiator and press to wall**

A certain amount of ventilation is desirable for a healthy environment and to keep water vapour at an acceptable level; it's also essential to enable some heating appliances to operate properly and safely. But using uncontrolled draughts to ventilate a house is not the most efficient way to solve the problem. Draughts account for quite a large proportion of the heat lost and are also responsible for a good deal of discomfort. It is therefore worth expending a little money and effort to exclude them from your home.

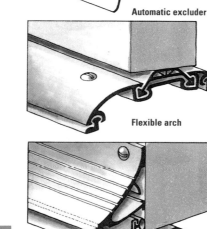

Flexible strip

Brush seal

Automatic excluder

Flexible arch

Complete kit

Locating and curing draughts

Tackle exterior doors and windows first, and seal only those interior doors which are the worst offenders (there should be some 'trickle' ventilation from room to room). Check other possible sources of draughts, such as spaces between floorboards, gaps in skirtings, fireplace openings, loft hatches, and the overflow pipes from sanitaryware.

Locate draughts by running the flat of your hand along likely gaps. If you dampen your skin, that will enhance its sensitivity to cold. Otherwise, wait for a very windy day to conduct your search.

Draught excluders are made by a variety of manufacturers, and there are so many variations that it is impossible to describe every type. Nevertheless, the following examples illustrate the principles that are commonly employed. Choose the best you can afford, and – more important, perhaps – try to select the type of excluder best suited to your particular requirements.

THRESHOLD DRAUGHT EXCLUDERS

If the gap between a door and the floor is very large, so that it admits fierce draughts, use a threshold excluder to seal the gap. If a threshold excluder is to be used on an exterior door, make sure it is suitable for that purpose. Buy a device that fits the opening exactly, or cut it to fit from a larger size.

Flexible-strip excluders

The simplest form of threshold excluder is a flexible strip of plastic or rubber that sweeps against the floorcovering to form a seal. The most basic versions are self-adhesive strips that are simply pressed along the bottom of the door, but other types have a rigid-plastic or aluminium extrusion screwed to the door to hold the strip in contact with the floor. This kind of excluder is rarely suitable for exterior doors and quickly wears out. However, it is inexpensive and easy to fit. Most types work best over smooth flooring.

Brush seals

A long nylon-bristle brush set into either a metal or plastic extrusion can be used to exclude draughts under doors. This kind of excluder is suitable for slightly uneven or textured floorcoverings, and can be fitted to hinged or sliding doors.

Automatic excluder

The plastic strip and its extruded clip are spring-loaded, so they lift from the floor as the door is opened. When you close the door, the excluder is pressed against the floor by a stop screwed to the doorframe. Suitable for both interior and exterior doors, automatic excluders inflict little wear on floorcoverings.

Flexible arch

The aluminium extrusion with its arched vinyl insert presses against the bottom edge of the door. As it has to be nailed or screwed to the floor, it is difficult to use a flexible-arch excluder on a solid-concrete floor. If you plan to fit one on an external door, buy a version that has additional underseals to prevent rain from seeping beneath it. You may have to plane the bottom of the door.

Door kits

The best solution for an exterior door is a kit combining an aluminium weather trim designed to shed rainwater, which is fitted to the door, and a weather bar with a tubular rubber or plastic draught excluder for screwing to the threshold.

A well-fitting door requires a gap of 2mm (⅛in) at top and sides so that it can be operated smoothly. However, a gap this large loses a great deal of heat. There are several ways to seal it, some of which are described here. The cheaper excluders have to be renewed regularly.

Foam strips

The most straightforward excluder is a self-adhesive foam-plastic strip, which you stick around the rebate: the strip is compressed by the door, forming a seal. The cheapest polyurethane foam will be good for one or two seasons (although it's useless if painted) and is suitable for interior doors only. The better-quality vinyl-coated polyurethane, rubber or PVC foams are more durable and do not perish on exposure to sunlight, as their cheaper counterparts do. Don't stretch foam excluders when applying them, as that reduces their efficiency. The door may be difficult to close at first, but the excluder soon adjusts.

Flexible-tube excluders

A small vinyl tube held in a plastic or metal extrusion is compressed to fill the gap around the door. The cheapest versions have an integrally moulded flange, which can be stapled to the doorframe, but they are not as neat.

Spring strip

Thin metal or plastic strips that have a sprung leaf are either pinned or glued to the doorframe. The top and closing edges of the door brush past the sprung leaf, sealing the gap, while the hinged edge compresses a leaf on that side of the door. This type of draught excluder cannot cope with uneven surfaces unless a foam strip is incorporated on the flexible leaf.

V-strip

A variation on the spring strip, the leaf is bent right back to form a V-shape. The strip can be mounted to fill the gap around the door or attached to the door stop so that the door closes against it. Most types are cheap and unobtrusive.

Draughtproofing sealant

In order to seal gaps, a bead of flexible sealant can be squeezed onto the door stop; a low-tack tape is applied to the surface of the door to act as a release agent. As the door is closed, it flattens the bead, filling the gap perfectly. When the sealant has set, the parting layer of tape is peeled from the door. You can also buy flexible tubing for bonding with sealant to compensate for movement.

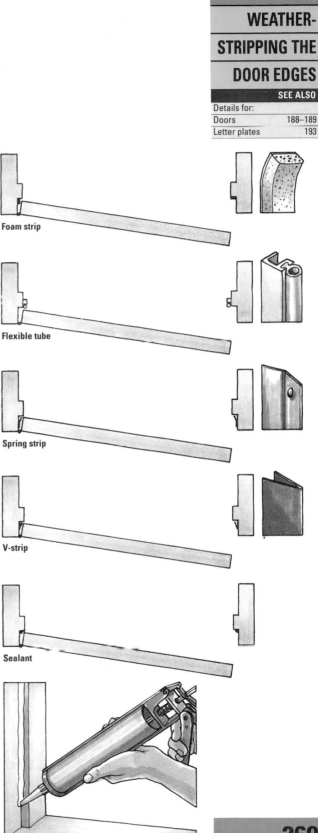

Foam strip

Flexible tube

Spring strip

V-strip

Sealant

Sealant fills uneven gaps perfectly

SEALING KEYHOLES AND LETTER BOXES

Make sure the external keyhole for a mortise lock is fitted with a pivoting cover plate to seal out draughts during the winter.

You can buy a hinged flap that screws onto the inner side of the door to cover a letter box. Some types have a brush seal behind the flap to reduce draughts.

Keyhole cover plate
The cover plate is part of the escutcheon.

Letter-box flap
A hinged flap neatly draughtproofs a letter box.

GENERAL DRAUGHT-PROOFING

Hinged casement windows are straightforward to seal, using any of the draught excluders suggested for fitting around the edge of a door (see previous page); but draught-proofing a sliding sash-window presents a more complex problem.

Sealing a sash window

The top and bottom closing rails of a sash window can be sealed with any form of compressible excluder. The sliding edges admit fewer draughts, but they can be sealed with a brush seal fixed to the frame – inside for the lower sash, outside for the top one.

A springy V-strip or a compressible plastic strip can be used to seal the gap between the sloping faces of the central meeting rails of a traditional sash window. For square rails, use a blade seal.

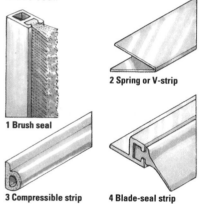

1 Brush seal

2 Spring or V-strip

3 Compressible strip

4 Blade-seal strip

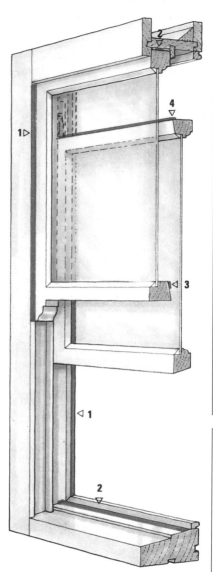

Sealing a pivot window

When you close a pivot window, the movable frame comes to rest against fixed stops. The stops for the top half of the window are on the outside of the house. Seal these exterior stops, at least, with draught excluders that are weatherproof. Use either compressible spring or V-strip draughtproofing, or a good-quality flexible-tube strip.

DRAUGHTY FIREPLACES

A chimney can be an annoying source of draughts. If you want to retain the appearance of an open fireplace, cut a sheet of thick polystyrene to seal the throat of the chimney, but leave a hole about 50mm (2in) across to provide ventilation. When you want to use the fireplace again, don't forget to remove the polystyrene, which is flammable.

Sealing large gaps

Large gaps left around newly fitted doorframes and window frames will be a source of draughts and allow noise to penetrate into your home. The same is true of a hole made for pipework or an air vent. Use an expanding-foam filler to seal these gaps. When the filler has set, repoint the masonry on the outside.

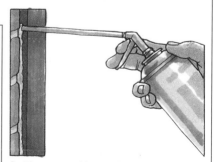

Seal large gaps with expanding foam

DRAUGHTPROOFING FLOORS AND SKIRTINGS

The ventilated void below a suspended wooden floor is a common source of draughts that penetrate through large gaps between floorboards and under the skirting. Fill between floorboards or cover them with hardboard panels.

Seal the gap between the skirting board and the floor with mastic applied with an applicator gun or in the form of caulking strips. For a neat finish, pin a quadrant moulding to the skirting to cover the sealed gap.

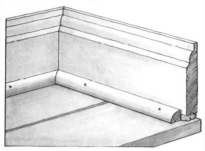

Seal the gap with mastic and wooden quadrant

DRAUGHT FROM OVERFLOW PIPES

Overflow pipes leading directly from a lavatory cistern or cold-water storage tank frequently provide a passage for serious draughts when there is a strong wind, and may cause pipes to freeze in harsh conditions.

Covering the opening
The simplest solution is to cut the neck off a balloon and stretch it over the end of the pipe. It hangs down to cover the opening, but gushing water will be able to pass through safely. Alternatively, fit a tee joint on the end of the pipe.

Fitting a cover flap
Another cure is to cut a cover flap from a rustproof lightweight metal such as zinc or aluminium. Make a simple pivot from the same metal and attach the flap to the end of the tube with a pipe clip.

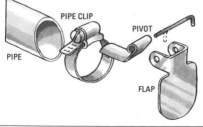

Approximately a quarter of the heat lost from an average house goes through the roof, so preventing this should be one of your priorities when it comes to insulating your home. Provided that you are able to gain access to your loft space, reducing heat loss through the roof is just a matter of laying insulating material between the joists, which is cheap, quick and effective. If you want to use your attic, insulating the sloping surface of the roof is a quite straightforward alternative.

Treating a flat roof

A flat roof – perhaps on an extension – may also need insulating, but the only practical remedy for most house-holders is to apply a layer of insulation to the ceiling surface. It is not a particularly difficult task, providing the area is not too large, but you will have to relocate lighting and take into consideration any features, such as windows or fitted cupboards, that extend to the ceiling. Fixing ceiling tiles is an alternative, but their insulation value is minimal.

Preparing the loft

On inspection, you may find that your roof space has existing but inadequate insulation – at one time even 25mm (1in) of insulation was considered to be acceptable. It is worth installing extra material to bring the insulation up to the recommended thickness of 150mm (6in). Check roof timbers for woodworm or signs of rot, so they can be treated first. Make sure that all the electrical wiring is sound, and lift it clear so that you can lay insulation beneath it.

The plaster or plasterboard ceiling below will not support your weight. You therefore need to lay a plank or two, or a chipboard panel, across the joists so you can move about safely.

If there is no permanent lighting in the loft, rig up an inspection lamp on an extension lead and move it wherever it is needed – or hang the lamp high up to provide an overall light.

Most attics are very dusty, so wear old clothes and a gauze face mask. It is also wisest to wear protective gloves, especially if you're handling glass-fibre batts or blanket insulation, which may irritate sensitive skin.

TYPES OF INSULATION

There's a wide range of insulating materials available, so it is important to check the recommended types with your local authority before applying for a grant.

Blanket insulation

Blanket insulation, which is made from glass fibre, mineral fibre or rock fibre, is widely available in the form of rolls that fit snugly between the joists. The same material, cut to shorter lengths, is also sold as 'batts'. A minimum thickness of 150mm (6in) is recommended for loft insulation. Blanket insulation may be unbacked, or paper-backed to improve its tear-resistance, or it may have a foil backing that serves as a vapour barrier (see below).

The unbacked type is normally used for laying on the loft floor. The blankets are usually either 100mm (4in) or 150mm (6in) thick. Some 100mm blankets can be split into two for topping up existing insulation. The rolls are typically 6 to 8m (20 to 25ft) long and 400mm (1ft 4in) wide in order to be suitable for standard joist spacing. For wider-than-usual joist spacing, choose a roll 600mm (2ft) wide.

If you want to fit blanket insulation to the sloping part of a roof, buy it with a lip of backing along each side to staple to the rafters. Both mineral fibre and glass fibre are non-flammable, and are proofed against damp, rot and vermin.

Loose-fill insulation

Loose-fill insulation in pellet or granular form is poured between the joists, up to the recommended depth of 150mm. This will inevitably bury some joists, but you can nail strips of wood to the tops of the joists that support walkway boarding.

Exfoliated vermiculite, made from the mineral mica, is the most common form of loose-fill insulation – but other types, such as mineral wool, cork granules or cellulose fibre (made from recycled paper), may be available. Loose-fill is supplied in 10 or 20kg (22 or 44lb) bags. A 10kg (22lb) bag covers about 1.6sq m (17sq ft) to a depth of 150mm (6in).

It's not advisable to use loose-fill in a draughty, exposed loft, as high winds can cause it to blow about. On the other hand, it is convenient to use if the joists are irregularly spaced.

Blown-fibre insulation

Fibrous inter-joist insulation is blown through a large hose by a professional contractor. It may not be suitable for a house in a windy location, but seek a contractor's advice. An even depth of at least 150mm (6in) is required.

Rigid and semi-rigid sheet insulation

Sheet insulation, such as semi-rigid batts of glass fibre or mineral fibre, can be fixed between the rafters. They tend to perform better than lightweight rolls, so relatively thin sheets can be used, especially if covered with plasterboard. However, it pays to install the thickest insulation possible, allowing sufficient ventilation between it and the roof tiles or slates to avoid condensation.

VAPOUR BARRIERS

Installing roof insulation has the effect of making the uninsulated parts of the house colder than before, so increasing the risk of condensation either on or within the structure itself. In time, this could reduce the effectiveness of the insulation – and also promote a serious outbreak of dry rot in the roof timbers.

One way to prevent this happening is to provide adequate ventilation for the areas which are outside the insulation. Another solution is to install a vapour barrier on the warm (inner) side of the insulation to prevent moisture-laden air passing through. The vapour barrier is usually a plastic or metal-foil sheet, and is sometimes supplied along with the insulation. It is vital that the barrier is continuous and undamaged; otherwise its effectiveness is greatly reduced.

TYPES OF ROOF INSULATION

SEE ALSO

Details for:	
Ceiling tiles	103, 108
Woodworm	252-253
Dry and wet rot	255
Condensation	260
Roof ventilation	285–286

ESTIMATING FOR BLANKET INSULATION
150 X 400mm wide rolls

Approx. loft area		
Square metres	Square feet	No. of rolls
30	332	17
34	366	20
38	409	22
42	452	25
46	495	27
50	538	29
54	581	32
58	624	34
62	667	36
66	710	39
70	753	41
74	796	43

Allows for average joist widths of 50mm (2in)

● **Ventilating the loft**
Laying insulation between the joists increases the risk of condensation in an unheated roof space – but provided there are adequate vents or gaps at the eaves, there will be enough air circulating to keep the loft dry.

271

Laying blanket insulation

Before starting to lay blanket insulation, seal gaps around pipes, vents or wiring entering the loft with flexible mastic.

Remove the blanket wrapping in the loft (the insulation is compressed for storage and transportation, but swells to its true thickness when released), and begin by placing one end of a roll into the eaves. Make sure you don't cover the ventilation gap (trim the end of the blanket to a wedge-shape so that it does not obstruct the airflow), or fit eaves vents.

Unroll the blanket between the joists, pressing it down to form a snug fit – but don't compress it. If you have bought a roll that's slightly wider than the joist spacing, allow it to curl up against the timbers on each side.

Continue at the opposite side of the loft with another roll. Cut it to butt up against the end of the first one, using either a large kitchen knife or a pair of long-bladed scissors. Continue across the loft till all the spaces are filled. Trim the insulation to fit odd spaces.

Do not cover the casings of light fittings that protrude into the loft space. Also, avoid covering electrical cables, as there is a risk that that could cause overheating. Instead, lay the cables on top of the blanket or clip them to the sides of the joists above it.

Do not insulate the area immediately below a cold-water cistern (the heat rising from the room below will help to prevent freezing during the winter).

Cut a piece of blanket to fit the cover of the entrance hatch, and attach it with PVA adhesive or with cloth tapes and drawing pins. Fit foam draught excluder around the edges of the hatch.

Laying loose-fill insulation

When laying loose-fill insulation, take precautions against condensation similar to those described for blanket insulation (see above). To avoid blocking the eaves, wedge strips of plywood or thick cardboard between the joists before laying the insulant.

Pour insulation between the joists and distribute it roughly with a broom. Level it with a spreader cut from hardboard. If the joists are shallow, nail on lengths of wood to build up their height to at least 150mm (6in), if only to support walkway boarding in specific areas of the loft. To insulate the entrance hatch, screw battens around the outer edge of the cover, then fill with granules and pin on a hardboard lid to contain them.

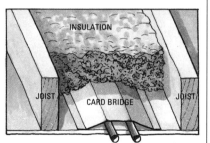

Insulating pipes between joists

Insulating cisterns
To comply with current bylaws, your cold-water-storage cistern must be insulated. It's simplest to buy a Bylaw 30 kit, which includes a cylinder jacket and all the other equipment that is required. Insulate your central-heating expansion tank at the same time.

Buy a ready-made jacket to insulate a cistern

Insulating pipes
If there are cold-water pipes running between the joists, lay the blanket insulation over them to prevent them from freezing. If that is not practical, insulate each pipe run separately.

Before pouring loose-fill insulation, lay a bridge made from thin card over cold-water pipes running between the joists, so they will benefit from warmth rising from the room below. If the joists are shallow, cover the pipes with foam sleeves before pouring the insulation.

Laying blanket insulation
(Left)
Seal all gaps around pipes, vents and wiring (**1**). Place end of roll against eaves and trim ends (**2**) or fit eaves vents (**3**). Press rolls between joists (**4**). Insulate cistern and cold-water pipes (**5**).

Spreading loose-fill insulant
(Right)
Seal gaps to prevent condensation (**1**). Use strips of plywood to prevent insulant from blocking ventilation (**2**) or fit eaves vents (**3**). Cover the cold-water pipes with a cardboard bridge (**4**), then use a spreader to level the insulant (**5**). Insulate and draughtproof the hatch cover (**6**).

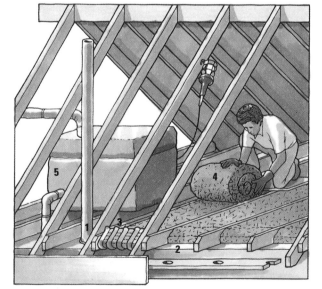

Insulating between the rafters

If the attic to be used, you will need to insulate the sloping part of the roof in order to heat the living space. Repair the roof covering first, so the insulation won't be soaked by leaks (it will also be difficult to spot leaks after insulating).

Condensation often causes serious problems after installing insulation between the rafters, as the undersides of the roof tiles become very cold. It is therefore vital to provide a 50mm (2in) gap between the insulant and the tiles, to promote sufficient ventilation to keep the space dry (this also determines the maximum thickness of insulation you can install). The ridge and eaves must be ventilated, and you should include a vapour barrier on the warm side of the insulation – either by fitting foil-backed blanket or by stapling polyethylene sheet to the lower edges of the rafters to cover unbacked insulation.

After installing any type of insulation, you can cover the rafters with sheets of plasterboard as a final decorative layer. Your choice of panels will be limited by the maximum size you can pass through the hatchway of your loft. Fix the panels to the rafters with plasterboard nails or screws, staggering the joints.

An alternative is to provide insulation and surface finish together by fitting insulated (thermal) plasterboard to the underside of the rafters.

Fixing blanket insulant

Unfold the side flanges from a roll of foil-backed blanket and staple them to the underside of the rafters. As you fit adjacent rolls, make sure you overlap the edges of the vapour barrier in order to provide a continuous layer.

Attaching sheet insulant

The most satisfactory method is to cut sheet insulation accurately in order to ensure a wedge-fit between the rafters. If need be, screw battens to the sides of the rafters so you can fix the insulating sheets to them (treat the battens with preserver first). Install a polyethylene-sheet vapour barrier over the rafters, double-folding the joints before stapling them in place.

INSULATING AN ATTIC ROOM

If an attic room was built as part of the original dwelling, you will probably not be able to insulate the pitch of the roof unless you are prepared to hack off the old plaster before insulating between the rafters (see left). It may therefore be simpler to insulate from the inside (as for a flat roof), although you won't have a lot of headroom. Insulate the short vertical wall of the attic from inside the crawlspace, making sure the vapour barrier faces the warm inner side of the partition. At the same time, insulate between the joists of the crawlspace.

Fit blankets with vapour barrier facing the room

Insulating a room in the attic
Surround the room itself with insulation, but leave the floor uninsulated so that the attic will benefit from heat rising from the rooms directly below.

Insulating an attic from the inside
Fit either blanket or sheet insulation between the rafters.
1 Minimum gap of 50mm (2in) between insulation and tiles for ventilation.
2 Blanket or batts.
3 Vapour barrier with double-folded joints stapled to rafters.
4 Sheet insulant fixed to battens.
5 Plasterboard nailed over vapour barrier.
6 Tile battens.
7 Tiles or slates.
8 Roof felt (sarking).

INSULATING FLAT ROOFS AND WALLS

Insulating a flat roof from outside
Expert contractors can insulate the roof from above.

Warm-roof system
1 Roof deck
2 Waterproof covering
3 New vapour barrier
4 Insulation
5 New waterproof covering

Protected-membrane system
1 Roof deck
2 Waterproof covering
3 Insulation
4 Paving slabs

Treatment from above

One way of insulating a flat roof is to lay rigid insulating board on the original deck. The bonded 'warm roof' system incorporates a vapour barrier – possibly just the old covering – that is laid under the insulation, which is then protected with a new waterproof covering. With a protected-membrane system, the insulation is laid over the covering and is held in place with paving slabs or a layer of pebbles. Both systems are best installed by contractors. Get them to check that the roof is weatherproof and can support the additional weight.

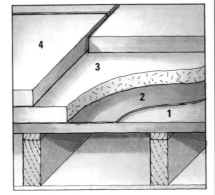

Warm-roof system

Protected-membrane system

Treatment from below

Another option is to insulate the ceiling below a flat roof. Very often the space within the roof structure has little or no ventilation. It is therefore essential to include a vapour barrier on the warm side of the ceiling, below the insulation, in order to prevent condensation.

Nail thermal plasterboard to the joists, or install fire-retardant expanded polystyrene, 50mm (2in) thick, between softwood battens screwed to the joists every 400mm (1ft 4in) across the ceiling. Fit the first batten against the wall at right-angles to the joists, then fit one at each end of the room. Butt the poly-styrene against the first batten; coat the back of the material with polystyrene adhesive, then glue it to the ceiling.

Continue with alternate battens and panels until you reach the other side of the room, finishing with a batten against the wall. Install a polyethylene vapour barrier, double-folding the joints and stapling them to convenient battens. Fix plasterboard panels to the battens with galvanized plasterboard nails. Stagger the joins between the panels, then fill the joins and finish ready for decorating as required. A double coat of oil paint is a vapour barrier itself.

Insulating the ceiling
Insulate a flat roof by fixing insulant to the ceiling.
1 Existing plasterboard or lath-and-plaster ceiling.
2 Softwood battens screwed to joists.
3 Insulation glued to existing ceiling.
4 Polyethylene vapour barrier stapled to battens.
5 Plasterboard nailed to battens.
6 If possible, provide cross ventilation by installing vents equal to 0.4 per cent of roof area.

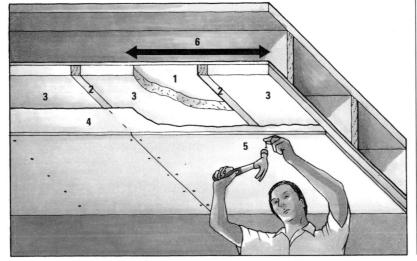

How you insulate the walls of your home is likely to be determined by several factors. Firstly, the type of construction. Houses built after 1920, and certainly after 1950, usually have cavity walls – two skins of brick, or one of brick and one of concrete block, with a gap between them through which air circulates to reduce the likelihood of water penetration. Although heat loss is slightly slower through a cavity wall than one of solid brick, that does not substantially reduce the cost of home heating. However, filling the cavity with insulation prevents circulation, trapping the air in millions of tiny air pockets within the material. This can reduce heat loss through the wall by as much as 65 per cent.

Solid walls require different treatment. You can either employ a contractor to insulate the external face of the walls or line the inner surfaces yourself.

Advantages and disadvantages

With cavity filling every exterior wall must be treated simultaneously, so it is most cost-effective for homes that are heated throughout for long periods and have a properly controlled system. Heating without controls will simply increase the temperature inside instead of saving on fuel bills. This type of insulation is not practical for flats or apartments unless the whole building is insulated at the same time.

Walls made of solid brick or stone have to be insulated in some other way. Cladding the exterior of the house with insulation is expensive and also ruins the appearance of most buildings. The suggestions concerning the manner of heating and effective controls to make cavity filling worthwhile apply equally to exterior-wall insulation.

Another method – suitable for solid and cavity walls – is to line the inner surfaces of the walls with insulation. This may involve a great deal of effort, depending on the amount of alteration required to joinery, electrical fittings and plumbing – but it does provide an opportunity for selective insulation, concentrating on those rooms which are likely to benefit most. It is also the only form of wall insulation that can be carried out by the householder.

When constructing a new house, a builder will include a layer of insulation between the two masonry leaves of exterior walls – a simple measure that greatly increases the thermal insulation of the building. To insulate an existing wall is a different matter. It requires a skilled and experienced contractor to introduce an insulant through holes cut in the outer brick leaf and to fill the cavity in such a way that a substantial reduction of heat loss is achieved, while avoiding the undesired side effect of damp penetrating to the inner leaf.

It's advisable to hire contractors that are approved by the Agrément Board or registered with the British Standards Institution, or belong to the National Cavity Insulation Association.

You should expect the contractor to carry out a thorough initial survey of the building to make sure that the walls are structurally fit for filling and that there is no evidence of frost damage or failed pointing. An approved company will also make the necessary application to the local authority before commencing installation, in order to comply with the Building Regulations. This is particularly important if you live in an area of the country where your house is exposed to severe driving rain or blizzards for prolonged periods, since not all cavity fillings are suitable for such extreme weather conditions.

Do not hire a contractor who does not provide a long-term guarantee that is transferable with ownership of the house. It should state that the insulant will be effective throughout the period of the guarantee and that it is rot-proof

and vermin-proof. Most important of all perhaps, check that the contractor's guarantee unequivocally states that damp resulting from faulty material or installation will be cured free of charge.

You are most likely to be offered one of three insulants. Urea-formaldehyde foam is the cheapest and most widely used material, despite its reputation for releasing unpleasant odours as the foam cures. In fact this happens in very few instances, and it is then usually due to a poor survey that has failed to detect that the walls of the house are not in a fit condition for filling.

Mineral or glass fibre treated with a water repellent are the next most popular cavity insulants. Both materials are completely inert and, if properly installed, will form a stable insulation that will neither settle nor shrink once inserted into the cavity.

Expanded-polystyrene beads form the third most commonly used insulant. Some of them are lightly coated with adhesive at the moment of injection, so that the fill does not settle over a period of time. If polystyrene is treated and properly installed, it does not affect the fire resistance of a masonry wall.

Whatever process you choose, the work should take no more than two to three days to complete and all of it is carried on outside the house, where holes are drilled at regular intervals in the brickwork (1). The insulant is either injected or blown through a hose (2), then the insertion holes are plugged. If the work is done properly, the holes should be virtually invisible, except perhaps on close inspection.

DRY LINING FROM THE INSIDE

If you're planning to dry line an external wall with some form of panelling, it is worth taking the opportunity to include blanket or sheet insulation between either the wall battens or the furring strips. Fix a polyethylene-sheet vapour barrier over the insulation by stapling it to the furring strips before nailing the panelling in place. Alternatively, use a metallized plastic-backed plasterboard, which has the advantage of requiring no additional vapour barrier.

Any form of panelling can be applied over mineral-fibre or glass-fibre blanket insulation, but plasterboard should be used to cover expanded-polystyrene insulant. A somewhat simpler method is to glue insulated (thermal) plasterboard directly onto a sound plaster surface. This type of wall insulation is made from standard plasterboard backed by either a layer of expanded-polystyrene or rigid-polyurethane foam. An integral vapour barrier is incorporated in both boards (see below).

Using a notched applicator, apply a band of the manufacturer's adhesive, 200mm (8in) wide, to the wall so as to coincide with the vertical edges of the panel and its centre line (1). Spread horizontal bands top and bottom. Press the panel against the adhesive and tamp it down with a heavy straightedge, then secure it to the wall with nine nailable plugs (2) in three rows. Position the plugs 50mm (2in) from all edges of the panel, and place one in the centre. Use a fine-toothed saw to cut a panel to fit into a corner. At a cut edge, allow for a 3mm (⅛in) gap for filling after the panel is fixed. Tape and fill all joints.

Details regarding door and window mouldings can be found in the section on wall panelling, but bed the skirting board onto a bead of mastic sealant applied to the floor and plasterboard. Fix the skirting board through the panel to the wall behind.

SEE ALSO
Details for:
Furring strips	89
Panelling	89–91
Taping joints	168

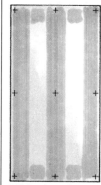

1 Fixing thermal plasterboard
Spread adhesive along the bands shown in the diagram above. The crosses indicate the centres of nailable fixing plugs.

2 Nailable plug
Used to fix insulated plasterboard to the wall. Push the plug into a hole drilled through the board, then drive in the nail to expand the plug and grip the masonry.

275

1 Drilling holes in the outer leaf
A professional contractor will begin by drilling large-diameter holes through the outer skin of brickwork to gain access to the cavity.

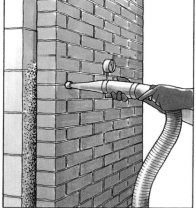

2 Introducing the insulant
A hose is then inserted into each hole and the insulant is injected or blown into the cavity under pressure, filling it from the base. Afterwards, the holes are plugged with colour-matched mortar.

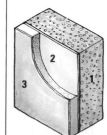

1 Insulant (either expanded polystyrene or foamed polyurethane)
2 Integral vapour barrier
3 Plasterboard lining

The structure of insulated plasterboard

INSULATING WALLS AND FLOORS

INSULATING AN EXTERNAL WALL

External-wall insulation should only be undertaken after careful consideration of the benefits – and the pitfalls. The techniques involve the application of a thermal insulant, plus a weatherproof cladding that also provides a decorative finish. The thickness of the insulation will be determined by U-value calculations based on the structure of the existing wall.

Expert installation is required, and it makes sense to use a contractor who is a registered member of the External Wall Insulation Association, which has a vested interest in promoting a high standard of workmanship.

Planning permission may have to be obtained before work commences, in case it is totally unsuitable for the style of the building. In particular, treatment of the doors and windows needs to be sensitively detailed in order to preserve the character of the house; and strict regulations apply to listed buildings and houses situated in Conservation Areas. In addition, downpipes, ventilators, and telephone and TV cables will have to be relocated. Exterior cladding inevitably involves a great deal of labour, as well as a considerable amount of materials, and these factors are reflected in the high cost of the work.

Apart from reducing heat loss, the main advantage of insulating the outside of your house is weatherproofing. If you are faced with the expense of tackling severe penetrating damp, then you may find that it is economical to choose external insulation as a solution to both problems. However, it will have no effect on rising damp, which must be remedied before work begins.

One method of exterior insulation that is currently available involves the application of an insulating render of cement and polystyrene beads. This is trowel-applied to a maximum thickness of 80mm (3¼in), then decorated with a suitable waterproof finish. Alternatively, polystyrene, mineral-fibre or glass-fibre slabs are mechanically fixed or glued to the walls. Once they are in place, the insulation is covered with a glass-fibre or wire mesh before rendering.

Yet another method sometimes used for insulating the exterior walls of a house is to apply either wall-hung tiles or weatherboarding over a wooden framework that incorporates blanket or slab insulation.

Building Regulations stipulate that new floors must be insulated. It's possible to upgrade an existing concrete surface by applying an insulated floating floor. A suspended wooden floor loses heat to the crawlspace below, which must be ventilated to keep it free from rot. You can reduce draughts by lining the floor with hardboard covered with carpet and underlay, but really effective insulation requires additional measures.

Methods of treatment

If you're prepared to lift the floorboards, then you can lay a substantial amount of insulation between the joists. Staple some plastic netting to the sides of the joists as support for blanket insulation. Alternatively, nail battens to the joists to support panels cut from sheet insulant.

If you are able to gain access to the joists from below, it is easier to push insulating material between them and then staple plastic netting or wire mesh to the undersides to hold it in place.

Insulating from above
Lift the floorboards and staple plastic netting (1) to the sides of the joists (2). Lay blanket insulation (3) between the joists. Alternatively, nail battens (4) to the sides of the joists to support sheet insulation (5).

Insulating from below
If you have a cellar or basement below the room you want to insulate, it makes sense to press batts between the joists (1) and hold them in place by stapling netting to the timbers (2). Line with plasterboard for a neat finish.

SEE ALSO

Details for:
Double-glazed units   208

A double-glazed window consists of two sheets of glass separated by an air gap. The air gap provides an insulating layer, which reduces heat loss and sound transmission. Condensation is also reduced because the inner layer of glass remains warmer than the glass on the outside. Factory-sealed units and secondary glazing are the two methods commonly used for domestic double glazing. Both will provide good thermal insulation. Sealed units are unobtrusive, while secondary glazing offers improved noise insulation. Choose the type that suits your requirements best.

What size air gap?

For heat insulation, a 20mm (¾in) gap will give the optimum level of efficiency. If the gap is less than 12mm (½in), the air can conduct a proportion of the heat across it. If it's greater than 20mm (¾in), there is no appreciable gain in thermal insulation, and air currents can transmit heat to the outside layer of glass. For noise insulation, an air gap of 100 to 200mm (4 to 8in) is more effective. A combination of a sealed unit coupled with secondary glazing, known as triple glazing, provides the ideal solution.

Double glazing will help to cut your fuel bills, but the benefit that you will be aware of immediately is the elimination of draughts. The cold spots associated with a large window, which are most noticeable when you are sitting still, will also be reduced.

In terms of saving energy, the heat lost through windows is relatively small – around 10 to 12 per cent – compared to the heat loss for the whole house, but the installation of double glazing can halve this amount.

Double glazing will improve security against forced entry, particularly when sealed units or toughened glass have been installed. However, make sure that some accessible part of the windows can be opened to afford an emergency escape route in case of fire.

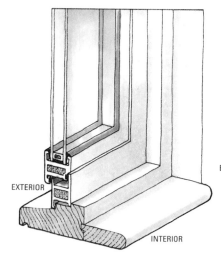

Factory-sealed unit
A complete frame system installed by a contractor.

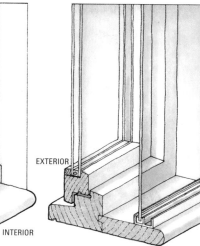

Secondary double glazing
Fitted in addition to an ordinary glazed window.

Triple glazing
A combination of secondary and sealed units.

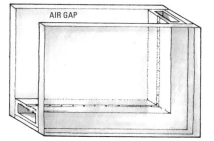

Double-glazed sealed units

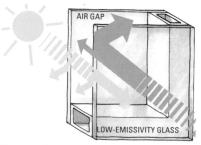

Heat-retentive sealed unit

Double-glazed sealed units

Double-glazed sealed units consist of two panes of glass that are separated by a spacer and hermetically sealed all round. The cavity between the glass may be 6, 9, 12 or 20mm (¼, ⅜, ½ or ¾in) wide. The gap may contain dehydrated air – which eliminates condensation between the two panes of glass – or inert gases, which also improve thermal and acoustic insulation.

The thickness and type of glass used are determined by the size of the unit. Clear float glass or toughened glass is commonly employed. When obscured glazing is required to provide privacy, patterned glass is used. Heat-retentive sealed units, incorporating special low-emissivity glass, are supplied by some double-glazing companies,

Generally, factory-sealed units are produced and installed by suppliers of ready-made double-glazed replacement windows. You can also buy sealed units that are suitable for self-fixing from some joinery suppliers, or have them made to order by specialists. Square-edged units are available for frames with a deep rebate, and stepped units for window frames that were originally intended for single glazing.

Double-glazed sealed units with PVC or aluminium frames are rarely suitable for older houses. A secondary system that leaves the original window intact is generally more appropriate – especially if you have attractive leaded windows, which need to be preserved (a sealed unit with fake glazing bars or a modern interpretation of leaded lights is not an adequate substitute for the real thing).

SECONDARY DOUBLE GLAZING

SEE ALSO
Details for:
Draughtproofing   270

● **Providing a fire escape**
If you fit secondary glazing, make sure there is at least one window in every occupied room that can be opened easily.

Secondary double glazing comprises a separate pane of glass or plastic sheet fitted over an ordinary single-glazed window. It is normally fitted on the inside of the existing window, and is one of the most popular methods of double glazing as it is relatively easy to install yourself – usually at a fraction of the cost of other systems.

How the glazing is fixed

Secondary glazing can be fastened to the sash frames (**1**) or window frame (**2**), or across the window reveal (**3**). The method depends on the ease of fixing, the type of glazing chosen, and amount of ventilation required.

Glazing fixed to the sash will reduce heat loss through the glass and provide accessible ventilation, but it won't stop draughts – whereas glazing fixed to the window frame has the advantage of cutting down heat loss and eliminating draughts at the same time. Glazing fixed across the reveal offers improved noise insulation too, since the air gap can be wider. Any system should be readily demountable, or preferably openable, to provide a change of air if the room does not have any other form of ventilation.

A rigid-plastic or glass pane can be fitted to the exterior of the window if secondary glazing fitted on the inside would look unsightly. Windows set in a deep reveal, such as the sliding-sash type, are generally the most suitable ones for external secondary glazing (**4**).

Glazing with renewable film

Quite effective double glazing can be achieved using double-sided adhesive tape to stretch a thin flexible sheet of plastic across a window frame. The taped sheet can be removed at the end of the winter.

Clean the window frame (**1**) and cut the plastic roughly to size, allowing an overlap all round. Apply double-sided tape to the edges of the frame (**2**), then peel off the backing paper.

Attach the plastic film to the top rail (**3**), then tension it onto the tape on the sides and bottom of the window frame (**4**). Apply only light pressure until you have positioned the film, and then rub it down onto the tape all round.

Remove all creases and wrinkles in the film, using a hair dryer set to a high temperature (**5**). Starting at an upper corner, move the dryer slowly across the film, holding it about 6mm (¼in) from the surface. When the film is taut, cut off the excess plastic (**6**).

GLAZING POSITIONS

Secondary double glazing is particularly suitable for DIY installation. It's possible to fit a secondary system to almost any style or shape of window.

1 Sash-fixed
Glazing fixed to the opening window frame.

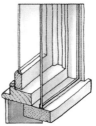

2 Frame-fixed
Glazing fixed to the structural frame.

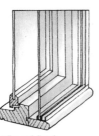

3 Reveal-fixed
Glazing fixed to the reveal and interior windowsill.

4 Exterior-fitted
Glazing fixed to the reveal and exterior windowsill.

1 Wipe woodwork to remove dust and grease

2 Apply double-sided tape to the fixed frame

3 Stretch the film across the top of the frame

4 Pull the film tight and fix to sides and bottom

5 Use a hair dryer to shrink the film

6 Trim the waste with a sharp knife

SEE ALSO

Details for:
Woodworking tools 478–489

Demountable systems

A simple method of interior secondary glazing uses clear-plastic film or sheet. These lightweight materials are held in place by self-adhesive strips or rigid moulded sections, which form a seal. Most strip fastenings use magnetism or some form of retentive tape, thus allowing the secondary glazing to be removed for cleaning or ventilation. The strips and tapes usually have a flexible-foam backing, which takes up slight irregularities in the woodwork. This type of glazing can be left in place throughout the winter and removed for storage during the summer months.

Fitting a demountable system

Clean the windows and the surfaces of the window frame. Cut the plastic sheet to size. Place the glazing on the window frame and mark around it **(1)**. Working with the sheet on a flat table, peel back the protective paper from one end of the self-adhesive strip. Apply the strip to the surface of the plastic, flush with one edge. Cut it to length and repeat on the other edges. Cut the mating parts of the strips and apply them to the window frame following the guide lines. Press the glazing into place **(2)**.

When using rigid moulded sections, cut the sections to length with mitred corners. To fit an extruded clip-type moulding **(3)**, stick the base section to the frame, then insert the outer section to retain the glazing.

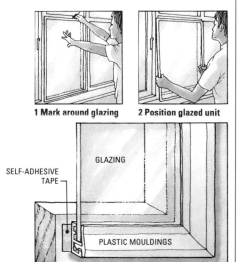

1 Mark around glazing **2 Position glazed unit**

SELF-ADHESIVE TAPE

GLAZING

PLASTIC MOULDINGS

3 Rigid plastic mouldings support the glazing

PLASTIC MATERIALS FOR DOUBLE GLAZING

To reduce costs or for safety, plastic materials can be used in place of glass to provide lightweight double glazing. They are available as clear, thin flexible film and as clear, textured or coloured rigid sheets.

Unlike glass windows, plastic glazing has a high impact-resistance and does not splinter when broken. Depending on its thickness, plastic can be cut with scissors, drilled, sawn, planed or filed.

The clarity of new plastics is as good as glass, but they are easily scratched. They are also liable to degrade with age and are prone to static. To clean plastic sheet, wash with a liquid-soap solution. Slight abrasions can be rubbed out with metal polish.

Film and semi-rigid plastics are sold by the metre or in rolls. Rigid sheets are available in a range of standard sizes or can be cut to order.

Rigid-plastic sheets are generally supplied with a protective covering of paper or thin plastic on both faces. To avoid scratching the surface of the sheets, only peel off the covering after cutting and shaping.

Polyester film

Polyester film is a form of plastic often used for inexpensive secondary double glazing. It can be trimmed with scissors or a knife, and fixed with self-adhesive tape or strip fasteners. Since polyester is tough, virtually tearproof and very clear, it is an ideal plastic for glazing living-room windows. It is sold in 5, 10 and 25m (32, 64 and 160ft) rolls, 1143mm (3ft 9in) and 1270mm (4ft 2in) wide.

Polystyrene

Polystyrene is an inexpensive clear or textured rigid plastic. Clear polystyrene doesn't have the clarity of glass and degrades in strong sunlight – so should not be used for south-facing windows or if a distortion-free view is desirable. Depending on the climate, the life of polystyrene is estimated to be between three and five years. Its working life can be extended if the glazing is removed for storage in summer. It is available in thicknesses of 2mm ($\frac{1}{16}$in), 3mm ($\frac{1}{8}$in) and 4mm ($\frac{5}{32}$in), and in sheet sizes up to 1372 x 2440mm (4ft 6in x 8ft).

Acrylic

Acrylic is a good-quality rigid plastic. It is up to ten times stronger than glass, but without any loss in clarity.

Although acrylic costs about twice as much as polystyrene, its working life is estimated to be at least 15 years and it is manufactured in a useful range of translucent and opaque colours.

The thicknesses commonly available for clear glazing are 2.5mm ($\frac{3}{32}$in) and 3mm ($\frac{1}{8}$in). It is produced in sheet sizes up to 1220 x 2440mm (4ft x 8ft).

Polycarbonate

A lightweight vandal-proof glazing with a high level of clarity, polycarbonate is most commonly available as twin-wall sheeting for glazing conservatory roofs, although a triple-wall version is also produced. The hollow ribbed section gives it exceptional rigidity, at the same time keeping heat loss and weight to a minimum. Polycarbonate is available in 4, 6, 8, 10 and 16mm ($\frac{1}{8}$, $\frac{1}{4}$, $\frac{5}{16}$, $\frac{3}{8}$ and $\frac{5}{8}$in) thicknesses, and is sold in sheet sizes up to 4000 x 1250mm (13 x 4ft 1in).

PVC glazing

PVC is available as a flexible film or rigid sheet that is ultraviolet-stabilized and therefore unaffected by sunlight. PVC film provides inexpensive glazing where a high degree of clarity is not essential (for example, in a bedroom).

Rigid PVC, which is 3mm ($\frac{1}{8}$in) thick, is produced in sheet sizes up to 1220mm x 2440mm (4ft x 8ft). It can be used to glaze conservatories and carport roofs.

OPENABLE
SECONDARY
GLAZING

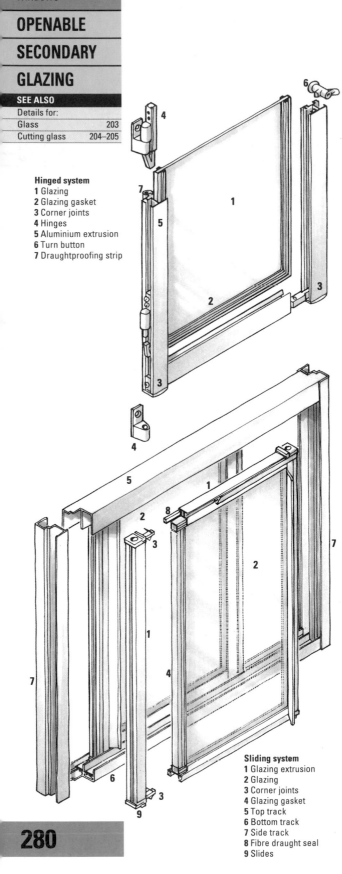

Hinged system
1 Glazing
2 Glazing gasket
3 Corner joints
4 Hinges
5 Aluminium extrusion
6 Turn button
7 Draughtproofing strip

Sliding system
1 Glazing extrusion
2 Glazing
3 Corner joints
4 Glazing gasket
5 Top track
6 Bottom track
7 Side track
8 Fibre draught seal
9 Slides

You can buy hinged or sliding secondary-glazing systems in kit form for home assembly; sliding systems are also made and installed by glazing companies. Both types are intended to be permanent fixtures.

Types of glass used

Normally 4mm ($\frac{5}{32}$in) glass is used in an openable secondary-glazing system.

For sliding windows, no pane should exceed 1.85sq m (20sq ft). In side-hung hinged sections the panes should be no more than 1.1sq m (12sq ft), but panes that are top-hung can be 1.65sq m (18sq ft). The height of each pane should not exceed 1.5m (5ft), nor should the height be more than twice the width.

For low windows or those that are at risk from impact, use toughened glass.

Hinged system

Hinged systems incorporate aluminium extrusions to form a frame for the glass or rigid-plastic sheet. The glazing sits in a flexible gasket lining the extrusions. Screw-fixed corner joints hold the sides of the frame together, and pivot hinges are inserted into one of the extrusions to make side-hung or top-hung units. Hinged units are fitted to the face of a wooden window frame and secured by turn buttons. A flexible draughtproofing strip is fixed to the back of the frame. A self-locking stay can be fitted to keep the window open to provide ventilation.

Sliding systems

A horizontally sliding glazing system is normally used for casement windows, whereas a vertically sliding system is more suitable for tall windows such as double-hung sashes. Both rigid-plastic and aluminium versions are available. Each of the panes is framed by a light-weight extrusion, which is jointed at the corners, and the glass is sealed into its frame with a gasket.

A horizontal system has two or more sliding panes, the number depending on the width of the window. They are held in a tracked frame, which is screwed to the window frame or the reveal. Fibre seals are fitted to the sliding-frame members to prevent draughts between the moving parts. The glazing is opened with an integral handle, and each pane can be lifted out for cleaning.

A vertically sliding system has much the same form of construction, but the frame incorporates ratchet catches to hold the panes open at any height.

Fixing a horizontally sliding system

Measure your window opening, and buy a kit of parts slightly larger than the opening. After cutting the vertical track members to size using a junior hacksaw (**1**), plug and screw them to either the reveal or the inside face of the window frame. Then cut the horizontal track members and screw them in place (**2**).

Measure the opening for the glazing and have it cut to size, following the manufacturer's instructions regarding tolerances. Arrange the system so that the overlapping members of the sliding frames coincide with vertical window mullions. Cut and fit the components of the glazing frame, including the gaskets and seals. Join the four sides together, usually with screw-fixed corner joints (**3**), and lift the glazing into the sliding tracks to complete the installation (**4**).

1 Cut track to length

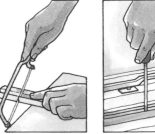

2 Screw it to the frame

3 Assemble the frame

4 Fit it into the tracks

Noise generated by road and air traffic, industrial processes, or thoughtless neighbours can make life distinctly unpleasant, if not intolerable. Although it is difficult to block out unwelcome sounds completely, it is possible to reduce noise levels in almost any home.

Sound is produced as a vibration that sets up pressure waves. These are transmitted to different elements in a house, which in turn resonate, making the noise 'echo' through the building.

The materials that make up the house react differently to sound waves. Carpets and curtains, for example, act as insulators – whereas hard surfaces such as ceramic tiles and plastered walls reflect sound, and thin materials offer little resistance. In addition, loose-fitting doors and windows, holes in the roof, and gaps between the floorboards and under skirtings all contribute to the problem of penetrating noise.

What's required is an airtight barrier that has sufficient mass to be resistant to vibration – but lightweight modern housing materials, though thermally efficient, are not as soundproof as the denser materials used in the construction of older, traditionally built houses.

Party and partition walls

Noise can only too easily penetrate a shared wall between houses. Although neighbourly courtesy ought to rule out noise problems, in practice neighbours aren't always so considerate.

Sealing gaps
Sealing gaps in the party wall is one obvious way to reduce airborne noise. If necessary, remove skirtings and floorboards close to the party wall so you can repoint poor mortar joints and fill any gaps around joists that are built into the masonry. After replacing the skirting and floorboards, seal any gaps between them with a flexible mastic. It may also be worth repointing the wall in the loft and plastering it to add mass.

Cladding a partition wall
To reduce the amount of noise that passes from room to room in your own home, line both sides of stud partitions with plasterboard 12.5mm (½in) thick; then fill and tape the joints and refix the skirting. When building a new partition, clad it with two layers of plasterboard and include blanket insulation.

SOUNDPROOFING A PARTY WALL

The soundproofing of a party wall can be greatly improved by the installation of a detached insulated lining, although its effectiveness will depend to some extent on the construction of the party wall, whether or not there is a fireplace, the location of electrical or plumbing fittings, and the proximity of windows.

The lining – constructed in a similar way to an ordinary stud partition – is fixed to the floor, ceiling and side walls, but not to the party wall itself. The gap between the lining and the party wall is filled with glass-fibre or mineral-fibre blanket insulation, and the lining is clad with two layers of plasterboard.

Adding a lining to the party wall of an older house may mean having to modify a moulded-plaster cornice; and the size of the room will be reduced, whatever the age of the house. Nevertheless, the benefits are likely to compensate for the disadvantages and effort involved.

Setting out
Switch off the electrical supply at the consumer unit, and replace any fittings attached to the party wall with junction boxes in readiness for relocating the fittings on the new lining. Remove the skirting carefully for reuse. Mark a line on the ceiling 100mm (4in) from the party wall. Drop a plumb line and make a similar mark on the floor below.

Fixing the lining sole plate to the floor presents few problems; but if the ceiling joists run parallel to the party wall, then you may have to nail noggings between

them to provide secure fixing points for the lining head plate.

Erecting the lining
Nail a 75 x 50mm (3 x 2in) softwood head plate and sole plate in position, with their front edges on the marked lines – which will leave a 25mm (1in) gap between them and the wall. Nail matching vertical studs between them at 600mm (2ft) intervals. Mark the position of the studs on the floor and ceiling to help you relocate them when fixing the plasterboard.

Hang floor-to-ceiling lengths of 100 x 600mm (4in x 2ft) insulating blanket between the studs, tucking the edges behind the framework. Skew-nail noggings between studs to serve as fixing points for shelving or electrical mounting boxes. Check that the power is still switched off, then run short lengths of cable from junction boxes to the new mounting-box locations.

Cover the framework with plasterboard 12.5mm (½in) thick. Fill the joints and seal around the outer edges with mastic. Nail a second layer of tapered-edge boards over the first, staggering the joints and placing the nails about 150mm (6in) apart.

Fill and tape the joints as you would for a stud-partition wall, then nail the skirting board in place. Mount and wire the electrical fittings, sealing around the edges of flush-mounted electrical mounting boxes with mastic. Seal the lower edge of the skirting board, too.

Detached insulated lining
1 Head plate
2 Sole plate
3 Studs
4 Insulating blanket
5 Nogging
6 First layer of plasterboard
7 Second layer of plasterboard
8 Electrical fitting

SOUNDPROOFING FLOORS AND CEILINGS

Sand pugging
1 Dry sand provides soundproofing.
2 Stiff-plywood platform lined with polyethylene.
3 Supporting batten, screwed to joist.

Insulated floating floor
1 Floorboards screwed through plasterboard to metal channel.
2 Plasterboard rests on metal flanges.
3 Metal channel rests on resilient strip.
4 Clip locates channel on joist.
5 Additional layer of plasterboard supported by battens screwed to joists.
6 Insulating blanket.
7 Floor joist.
8 Existing plaster ceiling.

Suspended ceiling with blanket insulation
1 Grid hangs from cables attached to original ceiling.
2 Lightweight insulating blanket.
3 Proprietary metal-channel system.
4 Loose-laid acoustic panels.

Framework lined with plasterboard
1 Glass-fibre insulation laid across joist.
2 New softwood ceiling joists.
3 Wall batten screwed to wall.
4 Double layer of plasterboard.

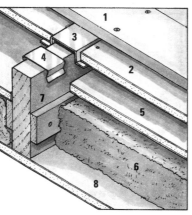

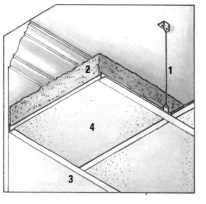

Resilient floorcoverings, such as cork tiling and carpet with underlay, are normally sufficient to deaden noise transmission between the floors of a house. However, more drastic measures may be needed when a building has been converted into flats. The most radical solutions require the cooperation of neighbours, but it is often possible to improve the situation, to some extent at least, unilaterally.

Sand pugging
In older houses where the dimensions of the building's components are fairly generous, a layer of sand can be laid beneath the floorboards to soundproof the room below. However, adding sand across a wide area imposes quite a lot of extra weight on the floor joists; the structure must therefore be checked by a surveyor beforehand.

Nail softwood battens to the sides of the floor joists to support strips of stiff plywood, then staple polyethylene between the joists to contain a 50mm (2in) layer of dry sand poured on top.

Insulated floating floor
You can buy a manufactured system for soundproofing a suspended wooden floor from a builders' merchant. The system includes a glass-fibre insulating blanket, 100mm (4in) thick, which is laid under the floor. The insulation does not significantly increase the floor's weight.

A metal channel with an integral resilient strip clips over the floor joists and supports strips of plasterboard, 19mm (¾in) thick, fitted on each side; the floorboards are screwed on top. If you fit a second layer of plasterboard, supported by battens screwed to the sides of the floor joists, that will provide additional acoustic insulation.

Independent ceilings
If you are unable to gain access to the floor above, you may want to consider introducing soundproofing in the form of a lowered ceiling. It's often possible to recreate a moulded-plaster cornice and central rose on the new ceiling, and it is worth obtaining expert advice before you proceed.

A proprietary suspended-grid system with acoustic panels is one relatively simple solution. Insulate the new ceiling with fibre blanket 150mm (6in) thick.

Another alternative is to construct an independent timber frame below the original ceiling. Provide new joists fixed to hangers or battens screwed to the walls. Lay insulation across the joists, then nail two layers of plasterboard over a polyethylene vapour barrier stapled to the framework. Fill and tape all joints in the plasterboard.

SOUNDPROOFING DOORS AND WINDOWS

Doors
To muffle noise from outside, draught-proof exterior doors and fit secondary double glazing to vestibule windows, perhaps incorporating toughened glass to improve security. The joints between the surrounding doorframe and the masonry should be sealed with mastic.

Draughtproofing your interior doors will have a similarly beneficial effect; and replacing lightweight hollow-core doors with heavy, solid doors may help to reduce sound transmission between neighbouring flats.

Windows
Traditional single-glazed windows form the most likely point in the fabric of a house for sound to enter. Not only does sound penetrate through gaps around the sashes (good draughtproofing is required to make them airtight), but it also passes directly through the thin panes of glass. Double glazing will improve matters, but there must be a gap of at least 100mm (4in) between the panes for satisfactory sound insulation. This can be achieved by installing an airtight secondary-glazing system, or triple glazing (which includes a sealed unit) provides the optimum solution.

Make sure a secondary system can be opened to provide an escape route in case of fire. If the window is the only source of ventilation, install a ventilator elsewhere in the room – preferably not connected directly to the outside. If that is not feasible, make sure the ventilator has a baffle that interrupts incoming sound. If you opt for a mechanical fan, choose one with a shutter that closes automatically when the fan is switched off. If possible, mount it away from the outside wall, connecting it with ducting.

VENTILATION

Ventilation is essential for a comfortable atmosphere, but it has a more important function with regard to the structure of our homes. It wasn't a problem when houses were heated with open fires, drawing fresh air through all the natural openings in the structure; but with central heating and thorough insulation and draughtproofing, well-designed ventilation is vital. Without a constant change of air, centrally heated rooms become stuffy, and the moisture content of the air soon becomes so high that water is deposited as condensation – often with serious consequences. There are various ways to provide ventilation – some extremely simple, others much more sophisticated, giving total control.

Initial considerations

Whenever you plan an improvement to your home that involves insulation in one form or another, take into account how it's likely to affect your existing ventilation. It may change conditions sufficiently to create a problem in areas outside the habitable rooms, so that damp and its side effects are able to develop unnoticed under floorboards or in the loft. If there is any likelihood that damp conditions might occur, provide additional ventilation.

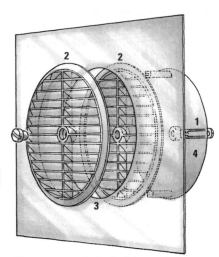

The components of a fixed window vent
1 Fixing bolt
2 Louvred grilles
3 Hole in the glass
4 Wind shield

Fitting a fixed window vent

You can provide continuous ventilation by installing an inexpensive fixed vent in a window. Well-designed ventilators of this kind allow a free flow of air without causing draughts (they usually have a wind shield on the outside), and are totally reliable as there are no moving parts to break down or produce those irritating squeaks that are associated with wind-driven fans.

Have a glazier cut the recommended size of hole in the glass. Then fit one of the vent's louvred grilles on each side of the window (clamping them together with the central fixing bolt), and bolt the plastic windshield to the outer grille.

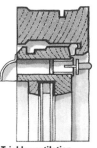

Trickle ventilation
Replacement windows can be supplied with a slot (either at the top of the fixed frame or in the movable sash) for a controllable trickle ventilator. This type of ventilator can also be fitted to an existing window in order to provide background ventilation when the window is closed.

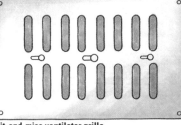

Hit-and-miss ventilator grille

Ventilating a fireplace

An open fire needs oxygen to burn well. If the air supply is reduced by thorough draughtproofing or double glazing, then the fire smoulders and the slightest downdraught will blow smoke into the room. There may be other reasons why a fire burns poorly – such as a blocked chimney flue – but if you find that the fire picks up within a few minutes of partially opening the door to the room, you can be certain that inadequate ventilation is the cause of the problem.

The most efficient solution is to cut a hole in the floorboards on each side of the hearth and cover the hole with a ventilator grille. Although cheap plastic grilles are just as effective, brass or aluminium ones look more attractive in a living room. Choose a hit-and-miss ventilator, which you can close to seal off draughts when the fire is not in use. If you have a fitted carpet, cut a hole in it and screw the grille on top.

If the room has a solid floor, a simple alternative is to fit a grille over the door or above a window. An aperture at that height won't create a draught, because cold air will disperse across the room and will warm up as it falls.

Ventilating an unused fireplace
A fireplace that has been blocked with brickwork, blockwork or plasterboard should be ventilated so air can flow up the chimney to dry out condensation or penetrating damp. Some people believe a vent from a warm interior aggravates the problem by introducing moist air to condense on the cold surface of the flue. However, so long as the chimney is uncapped, the updraught should draw moisture-laden air to the outside.

An airbrick cut into the flue from outside is a safer solution, although it is much more difficult to accomplish – and quite impossible if you live in a terraced house. Moreover, the airbrick will have to be either blocked or replaced should you later decide to reopen the fireplace.

To ventilate the fireplace from inside the room, either remove a single brick, make an aperture in the blocks, or cut a hole in the plasterboard used to block off the fireplace. Screw a face-mounted ventilator over the hole, or use one that is designed for plastering in (the thin flange for screw-fixing the ventilator to the wall will be covered as you plaster up to the slightly protruding grille).

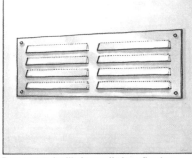

Face-mounted grille for ventilating a fireplace

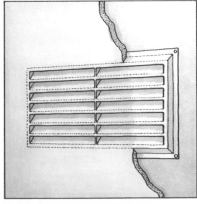

Hide the fixings of a grille with plaster

VENTILATING
BELOW FLOORS

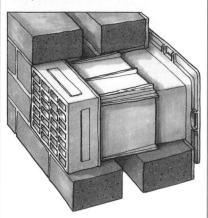

Single ceramic brick

Double-size plastic airbrick

Ventilating the space below a suspended wooden floor
The illustration (right) shows a cross-section through a typical cavity-wall structure with a wooden floor suspended over a concrete base. A house with solid-brick walls is ventilated in a similar way.
1 Airbrick fitted with telescopic sleeve.
2 Sleeper wall built with staggered bricks in order to allow air to circulate.
3 Floorboards and joists are susceptible to dry rot caused by poor ventilation.

Perforated openings known as airbricks are built into the external walls of a house to ventilate the space below suspended wooden floors. If they become clogged with earth or leaves, there's a strong possibility of dry rot developing in the timbers, so check their condition regularly. Clear a blocked airbrick as soon as you discover it – and if the original ones are inadequate, replace them with larger new ones.

Checking out the airbricks

Ideally there ought to be an airbrick every 2m (6ft) along an external wall, but in a great many buildings there is less provision for ventilation without ill effect – in fact sufficient airflow is more important than the actual number of openings in the wall.

Floor joists that span a wide room are supported at intervals by low sleeper walls of brick. Sometimes these are perforated to facilitate an even air-flow throughout the space – but in other cases there are merely gaps left by the builder between sections of solid wall. This method of constructing sleeper walls can lead to pockets of still air in corners where draughts never reach.

Even when all the airbricks are clear, dry rot can break out in areas that don't receive an adequate change of air. If you suspect that there are 'dead' areas under your floor – particularly if there are signs of damp or mould growth – fit an additional airbrick in a wall nearby.

Old ceramic airbricks do get broken, and are often ignored because there is no detrimental effect on the ventilation. However, even a small hole provides access for vermin. Don't be tempted to block the opening, even temporarily, but replace the broken airbrick with a similar one of the same size. You can choose from single or double-size airbricks, made in ceramic or plastic.

Installing or replacing an airbrick

Use a masonry drill to excise the mortar surrounding the brick you are removing, and a cold chisel to chop out the brick itself. You may have to cut some bricks to install a double-size vent. Having cut through the wall, spread mortar on the

base of the hole and along the top and both sides of the new airbrick. Push it into the opening, keeping it flush with the face of the brickwork, then repoint the mortar to match the profile used on the surrounding wall.

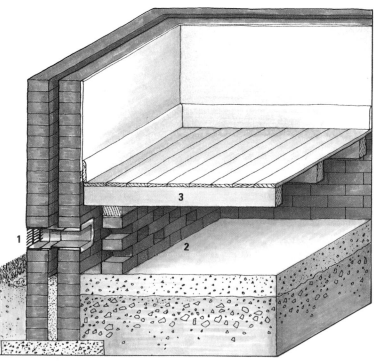

BRIDGING A CAVITY WALL

To build an airbrick into a cavity wall, bridge the gap with a plastic telescopic unit, which is mortared into the hole from both sides. If need be, a ventilator grille can be screwed to the inner end of the telescopic unit.

Where an airbrick is inserted above the DPC, you must fit a cavity tray over the telescopic unit to prevent water from percolating to the inner leaf of the cavity wall.

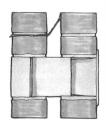

Airbrick with telescopic sleeve
Bridge a cavity wall with this type of unit.

Cavity tray
A cavity tray sheds any moisture that penetrates the cavity above the unit. It is necessary only when the airbrick is fitted above the DPC.

VENTILATING AN APPLIANCE

A fuel-burning appliance with a flue must have an adequate supply of air to function efficiently and safely. If any alteration or improvement interferes with that supply, then you must provide alternative ventilation. If you plan to block a vent, or alter a window or install an extractor fan in the same room as the appliance, consult a professional fitter. He will tell you whether the alteration is advisable, what type and size of vent to install, and where it should be positioned for best effect. An appliance with a balanced flue draws air directly from outside the house, so will not be affected by internal alterations.

VENTILATING
THE ROOF
SPACE

SEE ALSO

Details for:	
Plastering	161
Cutting glass	205
Condensation	260–261
Insulation	266–280
Airbricks	284
Sealed fireplace	399

When loft insulation first became popular as an energy-saving measure, householders were recommended to tuck insulant right into the eaves to keep out draughts. What people failed to recognize was that a free flow of air is necessary in the roof space to prevent moisture-laden air from below condensing on the structure. Inadequate ventilation can lead to serious deterioration: wet rot develops in the roof timbers and water drops onto the insulant, eventually rendering it ineffective as insulation. If water builds up into pools, the ceiling below becomes stained and there is a risk of short-circuiting the electrical wiring in the loft. For these reasons, efficient ventilation of the roof space is essential in every home.

Ventilating the eaves

The regulations applicable to new housing insist on ventilation equivalent to continuous openings of 10mm (⅜in) along two opposite sides of a roof with a pitch (slope) of 15 degrees or more. If the pitch of the roof is less than 15 degrees, ventilation should amount to the equivalent of 25mm (1in) continuous openings. It also makes sense to adopt similar standards when refurbishing a house of any age.

The simplest method of ventilating a standard pitched roof is to fit round soffit vents made with integral insect screens. The spacing is determined by the size of opening provided by the particular vent. Push the vents into openings cut with a hole saw.

If the opening at the eaves is likely to be restricted by insulation, insert a plastic or cardboard eaves vent between each pair of joists. Push the vent into the angle between the rafters and the joists, with the ribbed section uppermost. Vents can be cut to length with scissors for an exact fit. When installing blanket or loose-fill insulation, push it up against the vent.

Slate and tile vents

Certain types of roof construction do not lend themselves to ventilation from the eaves only, but the structure can be ventilated successfully by replacing strategic tiles or slates with specially designed roof vents. A range of colours and shapes is available to blend with various roof coverings.

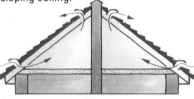

Ventilating the eaves
1 Fit plastic vents in the soffit board.
2 Push eaves vents between the rafters and joists to stop insulation blocking the flow of air.

WHEN ROOF VENTS ARE ESSENTIAL

Eaves-to-eaves ventilation normally keeps the roof space dry, but it is sometimes necessary to fit tile or slate vents to draw air through the roof space.

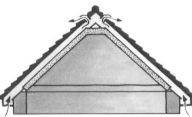

An attic space
If you insulate the slope of your roof, you must provide a minimum 50mm (2in) airway between the insulant and roof-covering. Fit soffit vents at the eaves, plus slate or tile vents near the ridge of the roof.

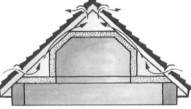

A room in the roof
Where a room is built into the attic, fit vents near the eaves and ridge to draw air through the narrow spaces over the sloping ceiling.

A fire or party wall
A solid wall built across the loft space prevents eaves-to-eaves ventilation. Fit slate or tile vents to ventilate each side of the wall independently. Use the same arrangement to ventilate a mono-pitch roof over an extension or lean-to.

A flat roof
An insulated flat roof can be ventilated by fitting over-fascia ventilators at the eaves and at the wall abutment. Some modification of the wall flashing will be necessary on an existing roof.

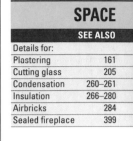

Soffit vent

Slate/tile vents
Roof vents are made to resemble a variety of roof coverings.

Double Roman tile vent

Slate vent

Double pantile vent

Over-fascia ventilator

285

FITTING
ROOF VENTS

Installing a slate or tile vent

If you are having the roof of your house replaced, it is worth getting the roofing contractor to incorporate vents at the same time – but it is possible to install roof vents yourself. Fitting instructions for individual models will vary in detail, but the description below for a double pantile vent demonstrates the principle.

As each vent must be fitted between rafters, you need to select the approximate position for a vent and remove just enough tiles to expose the felt and locate the heads of the nails holding the tile-support battens to the roof. The nails indicate the position of the rafters.

Centre the template supplied by the manufacturer between the rafters, and mark the position of the hole on the roof felt by scratching the corners with a knife **(1)**. Cut the diagonals of the opening and bend back the flaps **(2)**. Cut a slit in the felt, 100mm (4in) above and centred on the opening, and insert the tail of the undercloak of the vent **(3)**; then align the edge of the undercloak with the opening **(4)**. Plug the extension sleeve onto the underside of the cowl **(5)**, then insert the sleeve into the hole in the felt and nail the cowl to the support batten above the opening **(6)**. Replace the surrounding tiles, using hook clips to hold them in position.

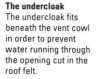

The undercloak
The undercloak fits beneath the vent cowl in order to prevent water running through the opening cut in the roof felt.

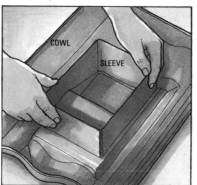

1 Scratch the corners of the hole with a knife

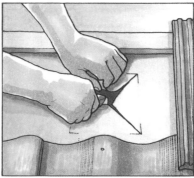

2 Slice the felt diagonally to make four flaps

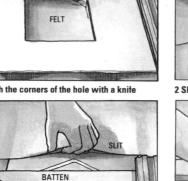

3 If need be, put undercloak under batten

4 Position the undercloak to align with hole

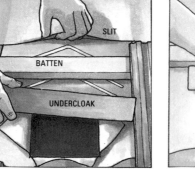

5 Plug sleeve onto the bottom of the vent cowl

6 Nail the vent to the tile batten

CALCULATING AIR-FLOW CAPACITY

All vents positioned near the eaves should provide the equivalent of a 10 or 25mm (⅜ or 1in) continuous gap, the size depending on the pitch of the roof. The ones near the ridge should provide airflow to suit the roof's construction.

To calculate how many vents will be needed, divide the specified airflow capacity of the type of vent you wish to use into the recommended continuous gap. If you are in doubt, provide slightly more ventilation than is indicated.

Position eaves vents in the fourth or fifth course of slates or tiles; place the higher vents a couple of courses below the ridge. Space all vents evenly along the roof, to ensure that there aren't any areas of 'dead' air.

CLEARING THE OPENING

When replacing tiles or slates with a vent you may have to cut through a tile-support batten to clear the opening. Nail a short length of batten above and below the opening to provide additional support. Because roofing slates overlap each other by a considerable amount, you'll find that you have to cut away the top corners of the lapped lower slates.

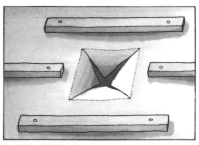

Providing additional support
Cut a tile batten that obstructs a hole, then place battens above and below to support the vent.

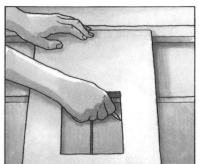

Marking slates that obstruct the hole
When slates cover the opening for a vent, use the template to mark the corners, then remove them.

SEE ALSO

Since kitchens and bathrooms are particularly prone to condensation, it is important to have some means of expelling moisture-laden air together with unpleasant odours. An electrically driven extractor fan freshens a room faster than if you have to rely on natural ventilation and without creating draughts. This type of fan is now mandatory in new kitchens and bathrooms.

Positioning an extractor fan

The best place to site a fan is either in a window or on an outside wall, but its exact position is more critical than that. Stale air extracted from the room must be replaced by fresh air – normally through the door leading to other areas of the house. But if the fan is sited close to the source of replacement air, it will promote local circulation while having little effect on the rest of the room. The ideal position for it is directly opposite the source of replacement air, as high as possible, to extract the hot air (1). In a kitchen, try to locate the fan adjacent to the cooker, so that cooking smells and steam will not be drawn across the room before being expelled (2).

If the room contains a fuel-burning appliance with a flue, you must ensure there is an adequate supply of fresh air at all times. The only exception is an appliance with a balanced flue, which takes its air directly from outside.

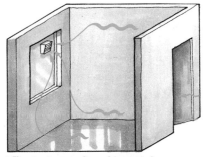

1 Fit extractor opposite replacement air source

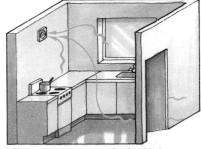

2 Place extractor near a cooker in a kitchen

Types of extractor fan

Many fans have an integral switch. If not, a switched connection unit can be wired into the circuit when you install the fan. Some types incorporate a built-in controller to regulate the speed of extraction and a timer that switches off the fan automatically after a certain interval. Axial fans can be installed in a window; and with the addition of a duct, some models will extract air through a solid or cavity wall (to overcome the pressure resistance in a long run of ducting, a centrifugal fan is required). To prevent backdraughts, choose a fan with external shutters that close when the fan is not in use.

Window-mounted axial fan
1 Inner casing
2 Motor assembly
3 Interior clamping plate
4 Glass
5 Grille-clamping plate
6 Exterior grille

Wall-mounted axial fan
1 Motor assembly
2 Interior backplate
3 Duct
4 Exterior grille

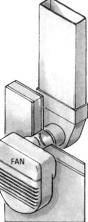

DUCTING TO EXTERIOR

FAN

Centrifugal fan

Choosing the size of a fan

The size of a fan, or to be accurate, its capacity, should be determined by the type of room in which it is installed and the volume of air it has to move.

A fan installed in a kitchen must be capable of changing the air completely ten to fifteen times per hour. A bathroom requires six to eight air changes per hour, and a WC six to ten. A living room normally requires about four to six changes per hour, but it's best to fit a fan with a slightly larger capacity in a smoky environment.

To determine the capacity of the fan you require, calculate the volume of the room (length x width x height) and multiply the volume by the recommended number of air changes per hour. Choose a fan that has at least that capacity (a slightly larger capacity is in fact best).

CALCULATING THE CAPACITY OF A FAN FOR A KITCHEN

Size			
Length	**Width**	**Height**	**Volume**
3.35m (11ft)	3.05m (10ft)	2.44m (8ft)	24.93cu m (880cu ft)
Air changes			
Per hour	**Volume**	**Fan capacity**	
15 x	24.93cu m (800cu ft)	= 374cu m per hour (13,200cu ft)	

Metal detector
Detect buried pipes or cables by placing a hired electronic sensor against the plaster.

1 Hold panel in place with plank

2 Seal plate spigot

3 Insert duct in hole

4 Screw-fix grille

FITTING A WALL-MOUNTED UNIT

Satisfy yourself there is no plumbing or electrical wiring buried in the wall, using an electronic sensor (see left). Make sure there are no drainpipes or other obstructions.

Cutting the hole

Wall-mounted fans are supplied with a length of plastic ducting for inserting in a hole cut through the wall. Plot the centre of the hole and draw its diameter on the inside of the wall. Use a long-reach masonry drill to bore a central hole right through. To prevent the drill breaking through the brickwork or rendering on the outside, hold a stout plywood panel against the wall and wedge it with a strong plank supported by stakes driven into the ground (**1**).

Before cutting the brick, drill holes close together around the inner edge of the hole. With a cold chisel, cut away the plaster using the holes as a guide, then continue to cut away the brickwork (try to avoid debris falling inside a cavity wall). When you reach the centre of the wall, remove the panel, then use the same technique to finish the hole from the outside face.

Fitting the fan

Wall fans are mostly fitted in a similar manner, but check the instructions beforehand. Separate the components of the fan, then attach a self-adhesive foam sealing strip to the spigot on the backplate to receive the duct (**2**).

Insert the duct in the hole so that the backplate fits against the wall (**3**). Mark the length of the duct on the outside, remembering to allow for fitting the spigot on the outer grille. Cut the duct to length with a hacksaw. Reposition the backplate and duct in order to mark the fixing holes on the wall. Drill and plug the holes, then feed the electrical supply cable into the backplate before screwing it to the wall. Stick a foam sealing strip inside the spigot on the grille. Position it on the duct, then mark, drill and plug the wall-fixing holes. Use a screwdriver to stuff scraps of loft insulation between the duct and the cut edge of the hole (or use a sprayed expanding foam), then screw on the exterior grille (**4**). If the grille doesn't fit flush with the wall, seal the gap with mastic. Wire the fan according to the manufacturer's instructions, then attach the motor assembly to the backplate.

An extractor fan can only be installed in a fixed window. If you want to fit one in a sash window, then you will need to secure the top sash, in which the fan is installed, and to fit a sash stop on each side of the window in order to prevent the lower sash damaging the casing of the fan, should it be raised too far.

If you plan to install an extractor fan in a hermetically sealed double-glazing system, ask the manufacturer to supply a special unit with a precut hole, which is sealed around the edges, to receive the fan. Some manufacturers supply a kit for adapting a fan so you can install it in a window with secondary double glazing. It allows the inner window to be opened without dismantling the fan.

Cutting the glass

Every window-mounted fan requires a round hole to be cut in the glass. The size is specified by the manufacturer. It is possible to cut a hole in an existing window, but stresses in the glass will sometimes cause it to crack. And while the glass is removed for cutting, there is always a security risk, especially if you decide to take it to a glazier. All things considered, it is generally better to fit a new pane, which will be easier to cut and can be installed as soon as the old one has been removed.

Cutting a hole in glass is not easy, and you may find it's more economical to have it cut by a glazier. You will need to supply exact dimensions, including the size and position of the hole. Use 4mm ($\frac{5}{32}$in) glass – either plain or obscured, to match the existing glazing.

Installing the fan

The exact assembly may vary, but the following sequence is a typical example of how a fan is installed in a window. Take out the existing window pane and clean up the frame, removing retaining sprigs and traces of old putty; then fit the new pane with the precut hole as you would any other window glass.

From outside, fit the exterior grille by locating its circular flange in the hole (**1**). Attach the plate on the inside, to clamp the grille to the glass. Tighten the fixing screws in rotation to achieve a good seal and even clamping force on the glass (**2**). Screw the motor assembly to the clamping plate (**3**). Wire up the fan in accordance with the maker's instructions. Fit the inner casing over the motor assembly (**4**). Switch on the fan to check that the mechanism runs smoothly, and that the backdraught shutter opens and closes automatically when the unit is switched on and off.

> **WARNING**
>
> Never make electrical connections until the power has been switched off at the consumer unit.

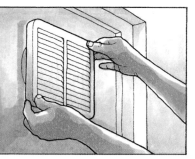

1 Place grille in the hole from outside

2 Clamp the inner and outer plate together

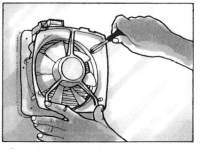

3 Screw the motor assembly to the plate

4 Attach the inner casing to cover the assembly

Window-mounted and wall-mounted fans are primarily intended for overall room extraction, but the most effective way to rid your kitchen of steam and greasy cooking smells is to mount an extracting hood – which is specifically designed for this purpose – directly over your cooker.

Where to mount the cooker hood

Unless the maker's recommendations indicate otherwise, an extracting hood should be positioned between 600mm (2ft) and 900mm (3ft) above a gas or electric hob or about 400mm (1ft 4in) to 600mm (2ft) above an eye-level grill.

Depending on the model, a cooker hood may be cantilevered from the wall or, alternatively, screwed between or beneath fitted kitchen cupboards. Some kitchen-unit manufacturers produce a special cooker-hood housing unit that matches the style of their cupboards (when the unit is opened, that operates the fan automatically). Most cooker hoods have two or three speed settings, and a built-in light fitting to illuminate the hob or cooker below.

Installing trunking

When a cooker hood is mounted on an external wall, air is extracted through the back of the unit into a straight duct passing through the masonry.

But if the cooker is situated against an interior wall, you'll need to connect the extracting hood to the outside by means of fire-resistant plastic trunking. The straight and curved components of the trunking – which simply plug into one another – form a continuous shaft running along the top of the cupboards fitted on the wall.

To fit the trunking, begin by plugging the female end of the first component over the outlet spigot attached to the top of the cooker hood. Cutting each of the components to length, as required, with a hacksaw or tenon saw, piece the rest of the trunking together, making the same female-to-male connections along the shaft. Some manufacturers print airflow arrows on the trunking to ensure each component is orientated correctly. If you should accidentally reverse a component somewhere along the shaft, then air turbulence may be created around the joint, reducing the effectiveness of the extractor. At the outside wall, cut a hole through the masonry for a straight piece of ducting and fit an external grille (see opposite).

Fitting a cooker hood

Recycling and extracting hoods are hung from wall brackets supplied with the machines. Screw-fixing points are provided for attaching them to the wall or to a cupboard. Cut a ducting hole through the wall, as for a wall-mounted fan (see opposite), and wire the cooker hood following the maker's instructions.

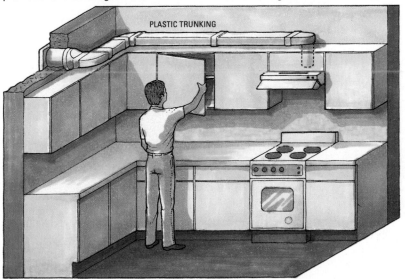

PLASTIC TRUNKING

RECIRCULATION OR EXTRACTION?

The most important difference between one cooker hood and another is what they do with the stale air they capture. Some hoods filter out the odours and grease then return the air to the room. Others dump stale air outside through a duct in the wall, in much the same way as a wall-mounted extractor fan. Since the air is actually changed, extraction is the more efficient method.

In order to install an extracting hood, it is necessary to cut a hole through the wall then fit ducting and an external grille. Cooker hoods that recycle the air are much simpler to install – but they do not expel moisture from the room, nor do they filter out all the grease and cooking odours; it is also essential to clean and change the filters regularly to keep a recirculation hood working at peak efficiency.

Recirculation hood returns filtered air to room

Extraction hoods suck air outside via trunking

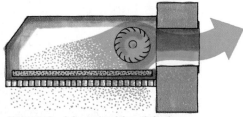

Alternatively, air is extracted through ducting

Running trunking outside
When a cooker is placed against an inside wall, run plastic trunking from the extractor hood along the top of wall-hung cupboards.

SEE ALSO	
Details for:	
Kitchen planning	16
Condensation	260–261

HEAT-RECOVERY VENTILATION

SEE ALSO
Details for:
Condensation   260–261

It is estimated that more than half the energy produced by burning fossil fuels is used simply to keep our homes warm. Although the installation of efficient insulation reduces heat loss to a minimum, a great deal of heat is still wasted as a result of necessary ventilation.

Heat-recovery ventilators are designed to balance the requirements of conserving energy and the need for a constant supply of clean fresh air. They range in size from compact airbrick-size units for continuous low-volume ventilation of individual rooms to whole-house ducted systems.

How heat-recovery ventilators work

This type of ventilator contains two low-noise electric fans. Stale air from the interior is extracted by one fan through a highly efficient heat exchanger. This absorbs up to 70 per cent of the heat that would otherwise be wasted, and transfers it to a flow of fresh air drawn into the room by the second fan. Since the two airflows don't mingle, odours and water vapour are not transferred along with the heat.

Self-contained heat-recovery ventilators can be fitted in exteriors wall or windows. The extraction unit of a larger ducted systems is usually mounted in the loft or a cupboard, and the cooker hood is normally connected to a whole-house system.

Designed for straightforward regular maintenance, both the air filters and the heat exchanger can be removed easily and washed in soapy water.

DEHUMIDIFIERS CONTROL CONDENSATION

To combat condensation, you can either remove the moisture-laden air by ventilation or warm it so that it is able to carry more water vapour before it becomes saturated. A third possibility is to extract the water itself from the air, using a dehumidifier.

A dehumidifier works by drawing air from the room into the unit and passing it over a set of cold coils, so that the water vapour condenses on them and drips into a reservoir. The cold but now dry air is then drawn by a fan over heated coils before being returned to the room as additional convected heat.

The process is based on the simple refrigeration principle that gas under pressure heats up – and when the pressure drops, the temperature of the gas drops too. In a dehumidifier, a compressor delivers pressurized gas to the 'hot' coils, in turn leading to the larger 'cold' coils, which allow the gas to expand. The cooled gas then returns to the compressor for recycling.

A dehumidifier for domestic use is built into a cabinet resembling a large hi-fi speaker. It contains a humidistat that automatically switches on the unit when the moisture content of the air reaches a predetermined level.

Working components of a dehumidifier
The diagram illustrates the layout of a typical domestic dehumidifier.
1 Incoming damp air
2 Cold coils
3 Water reservoir
4 Compressor
5 Hot coils
6 Fan
7 Dry warm air
8 Capillary tube where gas expands

When the reservoir is full, the unit shuts down in order to prevent overflowing, and an indicator lights up to remind you to empty the water in the container.

When a dehumidifier is installed in a damp room, it should extract the excess moisture from the furnishings and fabric within a week or two. After that, it will monitor the moisture content of the air to maintain a stabilized atmosphere. A portable version can be wheeled from room to room, where it is plugged into a standard wall socket.

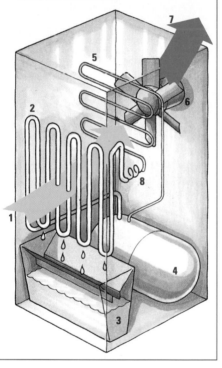

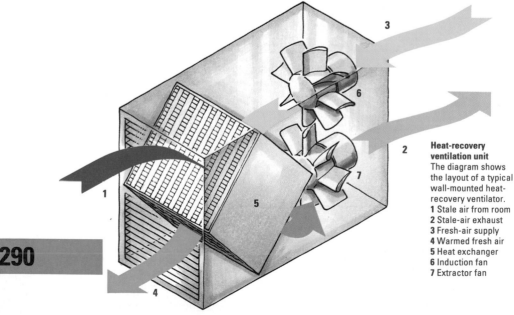

Heat-recovery ventilation unit
The diagram shows the layout of a typical wall-mounted heat-recovery ventilator.
1 Stale air from room
2 Stale-air exhaust
3 Fresh-air supply
4 Warmed fresh air
5 Heat exchanger
6 Induction fan
7 Extractor fan

Fitting a heat-recovery ventilator

Site a heat-recovery ventilator on an external wall, close to the ceiling and in a position where it will extract air most efficiently. Although typically set into a standard solid or cavity wall, you can install one in a thicker wall with the aid of a telescopic metal sleeve. The more compact units can be fitted in windows and single-leaf walls.

After marking out the aperture, cut away the brickwork, as described in the section on fitting a standard extractor fan. Fit the unit into the hole and make good the masonry and plasterwork, sealing any gaps around the unit with a gun-applied sealant. Finally, wire up the controls of the ventilator, following the manufacturer's instructions.

ELECTRICITY

REDUCING ELECTRICITY BILLS

Pressures from all sides urge us to conserve energy – and this applies just as much to electricity as to fossil fuels such as coal, oil and gas. But even without such encouragement, our quarterly electricity bills would provide stimulus enough to make us find ways of using less power.

Nobody wants to live in a poorly heated, dismally lit house without the comforts of hot water, refrigerators, television and other conveniences – but it is often possible to identify where energy is wasted and then find ways to reduce waste without compromising your comfort or pleasure.

Avoid false economy

Whether you do your own wiring or employ a professional, don't attempt to economize by installing fewer sockets than you really need. When you rewire a room, fit as many as you may possibly use. The inconvenience and expense later on of running extra cable and disturbing decoration will far outweigh the cost of an extra socket or two.

Similarly, don't restrict your use of lighting unnecessarily. It uses relatively little power, so it isn't worth risking accidents – for example, on badly lit stairs. Nor need you strain your eyes in the glare from a single light hanging from the ceiling, when extra lighting can provide comfortable and attractive background illumination where needed.

Fitting controls to save money

As the chart opposite clearly shows, heating is by far the biggest consumer of domestic power. One way to reduce your electricity bills is to fit devices that regulate the heating in your home to suit your life style, maintaining comfortable but economic temperatures.

Thermostats
Most modern heating has some form of thermostatic control – a device that will switch power off when surroundings reach a certain temperature. Many thermostats are marked out simply to increase or decrease the temperature, in which case you have to experiment with various settings to find the one that suits you. If the thermostat settings are more precise, try 18°C (65°F) for everyday use – although elderly people are more comfortable at about 21°C (70°F).

As well as saving you money, an immersion-heater thermostat prevents your water from becoming dangerously hot. Set it at 60°C (140°F). (For Economy 7 setting, see right.)

Time switches
Even when thermostatically controlled, heating is expensive if run continuously – but an automatic time switch can turn it on and off at preset times, so that you get up in the morning and arrive home in the evening to a warm house. Set it to turn off the heating about half an hour before you leave home or go to bed, as the house will take time to cool down.

A similar device will ensure that your water is at its hottest when needed.

Recording consumption
Keep an accurate record of your energy saving by taking weekly readings. Note the dates of any measures taken to cut power consumption and compare the corresponding drop in meter readings.

Digital meters
Modern meters display a row of figures or digits that represent the total number of units consumed since the meter was installed. To calculate the number of units used since your last electricity bill, simply subtract the 'present reading' shown on your bill from the number of units now shown on the meter. Make sure that the bill gives an actual reading and not an estimate (which is indicated by the letter 'E' before the reading).

● **Insulation**
Measures taken to save energy will have little effect unless you insulate your house as well as the hot-water cylinder and pipework. You can do most of the work yourself without much cost or effort.

ECONOMICAL OFF-PEAK RATES

Electricity is normally sold at a general-purpose rate, every unit used costing the same; but if you warm your home with storage heaters and heat your water electrically, then you can take advantage of the economical off-peak tariff. This system, called Economy 7, allows you to charge storage heaters and heat water at less than half the general-purpose rate for seven hours, starting between midnight and 1 a.m. Other appliances used during that time get cheap power too, so more savings can be made by running the dishwasher or washing machine after you've gone to bed. Each appliance must, of course, be fitted with a timer. The Economy 7 daytime rate is higher than the general-purpose one, but the cost of running 24-hour appliances such as freezers and refrigerators is balanced since they also use cheap power for seven hours.

For full benefit from off-peak water heating use a 182 to 227 litre (40 to 50 gallon) cylinder, to store as much cheap hot water as possible. You will need a twin-element heater or two separate units. One heater, near the base of the cylinder, heats the whole tank on cheap power; another, about half way up, tops up the hot water during the day. Set the night-time heater at 75°C (167°F), the daytime one at 60°C (140°F).

The Electricity Companies provide Economy 7 customers with a special meter to record daytime and night-time consumption separately, plus a timer that automatically switches the supply from one rate to the other.

HOW TO READ DIAL METERS

The principle of a dial meter is simple. Ignore the dial marked 1/10, which is only for testing. Start with the dial indicating single units (kWh) and, working from right to left, record the readings from the 10, 100, 1000 and finally 10,000 unit dials. Note the digits the pointers have passed. If a pointer is, say, between 5 and 6, record 5. If it is right on a number, say 8, check the next dial on the right: if that pointer is between 9 and 0, record 7; if it's past 0, record 8. Also, remember that adjacent dials revolve in opposite directions, alternating along the row.

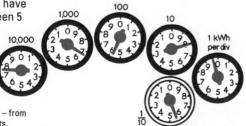

Reading a dial meter
Write down your reading in reverse order – from right to left. This meter records 76,579 units.

Apart from the standing charge and any hire-purchase payments, your electricity bill is based on the number of units of electricity you have consumed during a given period. Each unit represents the amount used in one hour by a 1kW appliance. An appliance rated at 3kW will use the same amount of energy in 20 minutes.

TYPICAL RUNNING COSTS

Appliance	Typical usage	No. of units	Appliance	Typical usage	No. of units
Cooker	Cooks 1 day's meal for four people.	2½	Iron	In use for 2 hours.	1
Microwave	Cooks 2 joints of meat.	1	Vacuum cleaner	Works for 1½–2 hours.	1
Slow cooker	Cooks for 8 hours.	1	Cooker hood	Runs for 24 hours continuously.	2
Storage heater (2kW)	Provides 1 day's heating.	11	Extractor fan	Runs for 24 hours continuously.	1
Bar fire or fan heater (2kW)	Provides heat for 1 hour.	2	Hair dryer	Runs for 2 hours.	1
Immersion heater	Supplies 1 day's hot water for a family of four.	9	Shaver	Gives 1800 shaves.	1
Instant water heater	Heats 2 to 3 bowls of washing-up water.	1	Single overblanket	Warms the bed for 1 week.	2
Instant shower	Gives 1 to 2 showers.	1	Single underblanket	Warms the bed for 1 week.	1
Dishwasher	Washes 1 full load.	2	Power drill	Works for 4 hours.	1
Automatic washing machine	Washes 1 full load with prewash.	2½	Hedge trimmer	Trims for 2½ hours.	1
Tumble dryer	Dries 1 full load.	2½	Cylinder lawn mower	Cuts grass for 3 hours.	1
4 cu ft refrigerator	Keeps food fresh for 1 week.	7	Hover mower	Cuts grass for 1 hour.	1
6 cu ft freezer	Maintains required temperature for 1 week.	9	Stereo system	Plays for 8 hours.	1
Heated towel rail	Warms continuously for 4 hours.	1	Colour TV	Provides 6 hours' viewing.	1
Electric kettle	Boils 40 cups of tea.	1	VCR	Records for 10 hours.	1
Coffee percolator	Makes 75 cups of coffee.	1	100W bulb	Gives 10 hours' illumination.	1
Toaster	Toasts 70 slices of bread.	1	40W fluorescent strip light	Provides 20 hours' illumination.	1

● **Typical running costs**
The table shows how much electricity is used on average by common household appliances that have different kilowatt (kW) ratings. For example, a 100W light bulb can give you 10 hours of illumination before it uses up a 1kW unit, whereas a 3kW bar fire will give off heat for only 20 minutes for the same 1kW.

UNDERSTANDING
THE BASICS

Many people imagine that working on the electrical circuits of a house is an extremely complicated business – but the circuitry is, in fact, based on very simple principles.

For any electrical appliance to work, the power must have a complete circuit – the electricity must be able to flow along a wire from its source (a battery, for instance) to the appliance (say a light bulb) and then back to the source along another wire. If the circuit is broken at any point, the appliance will stop working – the bulb will go out.

Breaking the circuit – and restoring it as required – is what a switch is for. When the switch is in the 'on' position, the circuit is complete and the bulb or other appliance operates. Turning the switch off makes a gap in the circuit, so the electricity stops flowing. Although a break in either of the two wires would stop the power flow, a switch must always be wired so that it interrupts the

live wire – the one that takes power to the appliance. In this way the appliance is completely dead when the switch is off. If the switch is wired to interrupt the neutral wire, which takes the electricity back to its source, the appliance will stop working but elements in it will still remain 'live' – which can be dangerous.

Although mains electricity is much more powerful than that produced by a battery, it operates in exactly the same way, flowing through a live or 'phase' wire linked to every socket outlet, light and fixed electrical appliance in your home. For purposes of identification the covering of live wires is coloured red or brown. The covering of the neutral wires, which take the current back out of the house, is either black or blue.

Identifying conductors ▶
The insulation used to cover the conductors in electrical cable and flex is colour-coded to indicate live, neutral and earth.

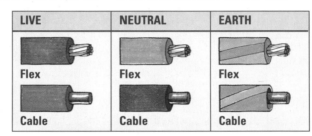

LIVE	NEUTRAL	EARTH
Flex	Flex	Flex
Cable	Cable	Cable

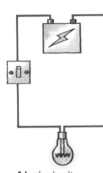

A basic circuit
Electricity runs from the source (battery) to the appliance (bulb) and then returns to the source. A switch breaks the circuit to interrupt the flow of electricity.

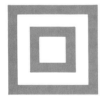

Double insulation
A square within a square either printed or moulded on an appliance means it is double-insulated and its flex does not need an earth wire.

Earthing

Any material through which electricity can flow is known as a conductor. Most metals conduct electricity well – which is why metal (most often copper, as it is probably the most efficient conductor of electricity) is used for electrical wiring.

However, the earth itself, the ground on which we stand, is also an extremely good conductor. In fact, it is an even better conductor than the wiring that's used for electrical circuits – which is why electricity will always flow into the earth, if it has an opportunity to do so, by the shortest available route. This means that if you were to touch a live conductor, the current would divert and take the short route through your body to the earth – perhaps with fatal results.

A similar thing can occur if a live wire comes accidentally into contact with any exposed metal component of an appliance, including its casing. To prevent this, a third wire is included in the wiring system and connected to the earth, usually via the outer casing of the Electricity Company's main service cable. This third wire – called the earth

wire – is attached to the metal casing of some appliances and to special earth terminals in others, providing a direct route to the ground should a fault occur. This sudden change of route by the electricity – known as an earth fault – causes a fuse to blow or circuit breaker to operate, cutting off the current.

Appliances that are double-insulated – which usually means they have a non-conductive plastic casing that insulates the user from metal parts that could become live – must not be be earthed with a third wire.

The earth wire either has a green-and-yellow covering or is a bare copper wire sandwiched between the insulated live and neutral wires in an electrical cable. Whenever a bare earth wire is exposed for linking to socket outlets or lighting fittings, it should be covered with a green-and-yellow sleeve.

Metal pipes must also be connected to the earthing system by a separate cable to ensure they do not precipitate an accident during the time it would take for a fault to blow a fuse.

DIY WIRING

Many householders are reluctant to undertake any but the simplest jobs involving electricity, no matter how competent they may be in other areas of home improvement.

To some extent this attitude is quite justifiable. After all, it is sensible to have a healthy respect for anything as potentially dangerous as electricity, and it would be very foolhardy of anyone to jump in at the deep end and undertake a major installation before gaining some experience on less ambitious jobs.

In the end, though, many of us are driven to doing our own house wiring simply by the prohibitive cost of hiring professionals. Nobody minds paying for expert skill and knowledge, but the truth is that much of the expert's time is taken up lifting floorboards, chopping out and repairing plaster, and drilling holes in walls and timbers to run the cable – all jobs that most people would be happy to do themselves.

The electrician's 'bible'
What unnerves the householder is the possibility of making mistakes with the connections or with the choice of equipment. Fortunately, in Britain we are guided by detailed rules laid down by the Institution of Electrical Engineers in a document known as the IEE Wiring Regulations. This is the professional electrician's 'bible', and it covers every aspect of electrical installation. If you follow its recommendations carefully, then you can feel confident that your wiring work will be safe.

You can buy a copy of the Wiring Regulations, or you may be able to borrow one from your public library. However, the Regulations themselves are notoriously difficult to understand, and it has even proved necessary to publish a 'guide to the guide' so that electricians can find their way through this exacting reference book.

The methods suggested in these pages comply with the Regulations, so you should have no need to refer to the originals unless you plan to undertake a job beyond the scope of this book.

Nevertheless, take the trouble to read all the relevant information in this chapter so that you fully understand what you are doing – and if at any time you feel unsure of your competence, then don't hesitate to ask a professional electrician for help or advice.

FUSES AND CIRCUIT BREAKERS

A conductor will heat up if an unusually powerful current flows through it. This can damage electrical equipment and create a serious fire risk if it is allowed to continue in any part of the domestic wiring system. As a safeguard, weak links are included in the wiring to break the circuit before the current reaches a dangerously high level.

The most common form of protection is a fuse, a thin wire that's designed to break the circuit by melting at a specific current. This varies according to the part of the system that the fuse is protecting – an individual appliance, a single power or lighting circuit, or the entire domestic wiring system.

Alternatively, a special switch called a circuit breaker is used that trips and cuts off the current as soon as an overload on the wiring is detected.

A fuse will 'blow' in the following circumstances:

- If too many appliances are operated on a circuit simultaneously, then the excessive demand for electricity will blow the fuse in that circuit.
- If the current reroutes to earth due to a faulty appliance, the flow of power increases in the circuit and blows the fuse (this is known as an earth fault).

WARNING: The original fault must be dealt with before the fuse is replaced.

Measuring electricity

Watts measure the amount of power used by an appliance when working. The wattage of an electrical appliance is normally marked on its casing.

One thousand watts (1000W) equal one kilowatt (1kW).

Amps measure the flow of current that is necessary to produce the required wattage for an appliance.

Volts measure the 'pressure' provided by the generators of the Electricity Company that drives the current along the conductors to the various outlets. In Britain 240 volts is standard.

If you know two of these measurements, you can determine the other one:

$\dfrac{\text{Watts}}{\text{Volts}}$ = Amps	Amps x Volts = Watts
Use this method to determine what kind of fuse or flex is safe.	Indicates how much power is needed to operate an appliance.

Throughout this chapter you will find many references to the need for safety while working on any part of your electrical system, but it cannot be stressed too strongly that you must also take every step possible to safeguard yourself and others who will later be using the system. Faulty wiring and appliances are dangerous, and can be lethal. Whenever you are dealing with electricity, the rule must be 'safety first'.

- Never inspect or work on any part of an electrical installation without first switching off the power at the consumer unit and removing the relevant circuit fuse.
- Always unplug a portable electrical appliance or light fitting before doing any work on it.
- Always double-check all your work (especially connections) before you turn the electricity on again.

- Always use the correct tools for an electrical job, and use good-quality equipment and materials.
- Fuses are vital safety devices. Never fit one that's rated too highly for the circuit it is to protect – and never be tempted to use any other type of wire or metal strip in place of proper fuses or fuse wire.
- Wear rubber-soled shoes when you're working on an electrical installation.

Using professionals

Always seek the advice and/or help of a professional electrician if you don't feel competent to handle a particular job yourself – especially if you discover or even only suspect that some part of an installation is out of date, or that it may be dangerous for some other reason.

Make sure that any professional you hire is fully qualified. Check whether he or she is registered with the NICEIC (the National Inspection Council for Electrical Installation Contracting). To be a member of this association an electrician has to be fully cognizant of the Wiring Regulations – published by the Institution of Electrical Engineers – and must ensure that his or her work complies with them.

Testing an installation

Any significant rewiring, especially new circuits, must be tested by a competent electrician – indeed, when you apply for connection to the mains supply you have to submit a certificate to the Electricity Company confirming that the new wiring complies with the Wiring Regulations.

For a fee, the Electricity Company will test DIY wiring at the time of connection. Never attempt to make connections to the meter or Company's earth terminal yourself. If you aren't sure whether new wiring requires testing, contact your local Electricity Company for advice.

IS THE POWER OFF?

Having turned off the power, you can make doubly sure that a particular accessory is safe to work on by using an electronic two-probe mains-voltage tester to check whether terminals or wires are live before tampering with them. Always make sure the tester itself is functioning properly before and after you use it by testing it on a circuit you know to be live.

Following the maker's instructions, put one probe on the neutral terminal and the other on the live terminal to be tested; if the bulb lights up, the circuit is live. If it does not illuminate, test again between the earth terminal and each of the live and neutral terminals. If the bulb still doesn't light up, you can assume the circuit isn't live – providing that you have checked the tester.

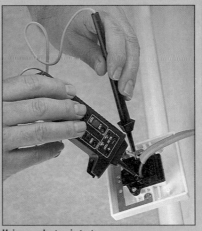

Using an electronic tester
Touch the neutral terminal with one probe and the live terminal with the other. The circuit is live if the indicator illuminates.

BATHROOM
SAFETY

● **Supplementary bonding in a kitchen**
Supplementary-bonding regulations apply to kitchens as well as bathrooms. Bond metal sink units, metallic supply and wastepipes, radiators and central-heating pipework. Space and water heaters must be bonded as for bathrooms.

296

Because water is a highly efficient conductor of electric current, water and electricity form a very dangerous combination. For this reason, bathrooms are potentially the most dangerous areas in your home in terms of electricity. Where there are so many exposed metal pipes and fittings, combined with wet conditions, stringent regulations must be observed if fatal accidents are to be avoided.

GENERAL SAFETY

● No socket outlets should be fitted in a bathroom – except for special ones that are approved for electric shavers and which conform to BS 3535.

● The IEE Wiring Regulations stipulate that any standard light switches in bathrooms must be well out of reach of anyone who is using a shower, bath or washbasin. The best way to comply with this requirement is to fit only ceiling-mounted pull-cord switches.

● Any bathroom heater must comply with the IEE Wiring Regulations.

● If you have a shower unit in a bedroom, it must be not less than 2.5m (8ft) from any socket outlet.

● Light fittings must be well out of reach and shielded, so fit a close-mounted ceiling light, properly enclosed, rather than a pendant fitting.

● Never use a portable fire or other electrical appliance, such as a hair dryer, in a bathroom, even if plugged into a socket outside the room.

WARNING

Have supplementary bonding tested by a qualified electrician. If you have not had any previous experience of wiring and making electrical connections, have supplementary bonding installed by a professional.

Supplementary bonding

In any bathroom there are many non-electrical metallic components, such as metal baths and basins, supply pipes to bath and basin taps, metal wastepipes, radiators, central-heating pipework and so on – all of which could cause an accident during the time it would take for an electrical fault to blow a fuse or operate a miniature circuit breaker (MCB). To ensure that no dangerous voltages are created between metal parts, the Wiring Regulations stipulate that all these metal components must be connected one to another by a conductor which is itself connected to a terminal on the earthing block in the consumer unit. This is known as supplementary bonding and is required for all bathrooms – even when there is no electrical equipment installed in the room and even though the water and gas pipes are bonded to the consumer's earth terminal near the consumer unit.

When electrical equipment such as a heater or shower is fitted in a bathroom, that too must be supplementary-bonded by connecting its metalwork – such as the casing – to the nonelectrical metal pipework, even though the appliance is connected to the earthing conductor in the supply cable.

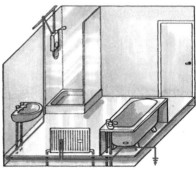

Supplementary bonding in a bathroom

Making the connections

The Wiring Regulations specify the minimum size of earthing conductor that can be used for supplementary bonding in different situations, so that large-scale electrical installations can be costed economically. In a domestic environment, use 6mm² single-core cable insulated with green-and-yellow PVC for supplementary bonding. This is large enough to be safe in any domestic situation. For a neat appearance, plan the route of the bonding cable to run from point to point behind the bath panel, under floorboards, and through basin pedestals. If necessary, run the cable through a hollow wall or under plaster like any other electrical cable.

Connecting to pipework

An earth clamp (1) is used for making connections to pipework. Clean the pipe locally with wire wool to make a good connection between the pipe and clamp, and scrape or strip an area of paintwork if the pipe has been painted.

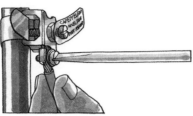

1 Fit an earth clamp to pipework

Connecting to a bath or basin

Metal baths or basins are made with an earth tag. Connect the earth cable by trapping the bared end of the conductor under a nut and bolt with metal washers (2). Make sure the tag has not been painted or enamelled.

If an old metal bath or basin has not been provided with an earth tag, drill a hole through the foot of the bath or through the rim at the back of the basin and connect the cable with a similar nut and bolt with metal washers.

2 Connect to bath or basin earth tag

Connecting to an appliance

Simply connect the earth to the terminal provided in the electrical appliance (3) and run it to a clamp on a metal supply pipe nearby.

3 Fix to the earth terminal in an appliance
The appliance's own earth connection may share the same terminal.

SEE ALSO

Details for:	
Safety tips	295

DEALING WITH ELECTRIC SHOCK

If someone in your presence receives an electric shock and is still in contact with its source, turn off the current at once either by pulling out the plug or by switching off at the socket or consumer unit. If this is not possible, don't take hold of the person – or the current may pass through you too. Pull the victim free with a scarf or dry towel or something like that, or knock their hand free of the electrical equipment with a piece of wood. As a last resort, free the victim by taking hold of their loose clothing – but without touching the body.

Don't attempt to move anyone who has fallen as a result of electric shock – except to place them in the recovery position (see right) – as they may have sustained other injuries. Wrap them in a blanket or coat to keep them warm until they can move themselves.

Once the person can move and is no longer in contact with the electrical equipment, treat their electrical burns by reducing the heat of the injury under slowly running cold water. Then apply a dry dressing and seek medical advice.

Isolating the victim
If a person sustains an electric shock, turn off the supply of electricity immediately, either at the consumer unit or at a socket (**1**). If this is not possible, pull the victim free with a dry towel, or knock their hand free of the electrical equipment (**2**) with a piece of wood or a broom.

Severe electric shock can make a person stop breathing. Once you have freed them from the electricity supply (without grasping the victim's body directly – see left), revive them by means of artificial ventilation.

Clear the airway
First, clear the victim's airway. To do this, loosen the clothing round the neck, chest and waist, make sure that the mouth is free of food, and remove loose dentures (**1**).

1 Clear the mouth of food or loose dentures

Lay the person on his or her back and carefully tilt the head back by raising the chin (**2**). This prevents the victim's tongue blocking the airway and may in itself be enough to restart the person's breathing. If it doesn't succeed in doing so quickly, try more direct methods of artificial ventilation.

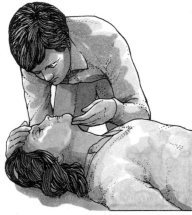

2 Tip the head back to open the airway

Mouth-to-mouth
Keeping the victim's nostrils closed by pinching them between thumb and forefinger, cover the mouth with your own, making a seal all round (**3**). Blow firmly and look for signs of the chest rising. Remove your lips and allow the chest to fall. Repeat this procedure, breathing rhythmically into the mouth every six seconds. After ten breaths, phone the emergency services. Continue with the artificial ventilation till normal breathing resumes or expert help arrives.

Mouth-to-nose
If injuries to the face make mouth-to-mouth ventilation impossible, follow a similar procedure but keep the victim's mouth covered with one hand and blow firmly into the nose (**4**).

3 Mouth-to-mouth   **4 Mouth-to-nose**

Reviving a baby
If the victim is a baby or small child, cover both the nose and the mouth at the same time with your own mouth (**5**) and proceed as for mouth-to-mouth ventilation (see left), but breathe every three seconds.

5 Cover a baby's nose and mouth

Recovery
Once breathing has started again, put the victim in the recovery position. Turn him or her face down with the head turned sideways and tilted up slightly. This keeps the airway open and will also prevent vomit being inhaled if the person is sick.

Lift one leg out from the body and support the head by placing the person's left hand, palm down, under his or her cheek (**6**). Keep the casualty warm with blankets until help arrives.

6 Recovery position

SIMPLE
REPLACEMENTS

You can carry out many repairs and replacements without having to concern yourself with the wiring system installed in your home. Many light fittings and appliances are supplied with electricity by means of flexible cords that plug into the system – so provided that they have been disconnected, there can be no risk of getting an electric shock while working on them.

WARNING

Never attempt to carry out electrical repairs without first unplugging the appliance or switching off the power supply at the consumer unit.

Flexible cord (flex)

All portable appliances and some of the smaller fixed ones, as well as pendant and portable light fittings, are connected to your home's permanent wiring system by means of conductors in the form of flexible cord, normally called 'flex'.

Each of the conductors in any type of flex is made up of numerous fine wires twisted together, and each conductor is insulated from the others by a covering of plastic insulation. So that the conductors can be identified easily, the insulation is usually colour-coded (brown = live; blue = neutral; and green-and-yellow = earth).

Further protection is provided on most flexible cords in the form of an outer sheathing of insulating material enclosing the inner conductors.

Heat-resistant flex is available for enclosed light fittings and appliances whose surfaces will become hot.

COILED FLEX

A coiled flex that stretches and retracts can be a convenient way of connecting a portable lamp or appliance.

Coiled flex is sold as a standard length

TYPES OF ELECTRICAL FLEX

Parallel twin

Parallel twin flex has two conductors insulated with PVC (polyvinyl chloride) running side by side. The insulation material is joined between the two conductors along the length of the flex. This kind of flex should only be used for extra-low-voltage (bell) wiring or inside certain types of light fitting. The wires are hardly ever colour-coded.

Twisted twin

This is similar to parallel twin flex, but the PVC-insulated conductors are twisted together for extra strength. It was once used to support hanging light fittings, but nowadays must be replaced with a two-core sheathed flex when wiring pendant lights. Also, any old rubber-insulated flex with braided-cotton covering, which is still found in some homes, should be replaced.

Flat twin sheathed

Flat twin sheathed flex has colour-coded live and neutral conductors inside a PVC sheathing. This flex is used for double-insulated light fittings and small appliances.

Two-core circular sheathed

This has colour-coded neutral and live conductors inside a PVC sheathing that is circular in its cross section. It is used for wiring certain pendant lights and some double-insulated appliances.

Three-core circular sheathed

This is like two-core circular sheathed flex, but it also contains an insulated and colour-coded earth wire. This flex is perhaps the most commonly used for all kinds of appliances.

Unkinkable braided

This flex is used for appliances such as kettles and irons, which are of a high wattage and whose flex must stand up to movement and wear. The three rubber-insulated conductors, plus the textile cords that run parallel with them, are all contained in a rubber sheathing that is bound outside with braided material. This type of flex can be wound round the handle of a cool electric iron.

Although the spacing of terminals in plugs and appliances varies, the method of stripping and connecting the flex is the same.

Stripping the flex

If the flex is sheathed, slit the sheath lengthwise with a sharp knife **(1)**, being careful not to cut into the insulation covering the individual conductors. Divide the conductors of parallel twin flex by pulling them apart before you expose their ends.

Peel the sheathing away from the conductors, then fold it back over the knife blade and cut it off **(2)**.

Separate the conductors, crop them to length and, using wire strippers, remove about 12mm (½in) of insulation from the end of each one **(3)**.

MULTI-PURPOSE TOOL

A multi-purpose tool will crop and strip any size of cable or flex.

Stripping flex with a multi-purpose tool

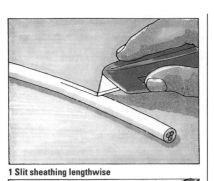

1 Slit sheathing lengthwise

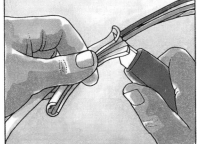

2 Fold sheathing over the blade and cut it off

3 Strip insulation from conductors

Connecting the conductors

Twist together the individual filaments of each conductor to make them neat.

If the plug or appliance has post-type terminals, fold the bared end of wire **(1)** before pushing it in the hole. Make sure the insulation butts against the post and that all the wire filaments are enclosed within the terminal. Then tighten the clamping screw, and pull gently on the wire to make sure it is held quite firmly.

1 Post terminal

When you're connecting to clamp-type terminals, wrap the bared wire round the post clockwise **(2)**, then screw the clamping nut down tight on the wire. After tightening the nut, check that the conductor is held securely.

2 Clamp terminal

CHOOSING A FLEX

Not only is the right type of flex for the job important; the size of its conductors must suit the amount of current that will be used by the appliance.

Flex is rated according to the area of the cross section of its conductors, 0.5mm² being the smallest for normal domestic wiring. The flex size required is determined by the flow of current that it can handle safely. Excessive current will make a conductor overheat, so the size of the flex must be matched to the power (wattage) of the appliance which it is feeding.

Manufacturers frequently fit 1.25mm² flex to appliances of less than 3000W (3kW), since it is safer to use a larger conductor than necessary if a smaller flex might be easily damaged. Adopt the same procedure when replacing flex.

Conductor	Current rating	Appliance
0.5mm²	3amp	Light fittings up to 720W
0.75mm²	6amp	Light fittings and appliances up to 1440W
1.0mm²	10amp	Appliances up to 2400W
1.25mm²	13amp	Appliances up to 3120W
1.5mm²	15amp	Appliances up to 3600W
2.5mm²	20amp	Appliances up to 4800W
4.0mm²	25amp	Appliances up to 6000W

● **Flex for immersion heaters**
Because they generate relatively high background temperatures, 3kW immersion heaters are wired with 2.5mm² heat-resistant flex (see WIRING AN IMMERSION HEATER).

EXTENDING FLEXIBLE CORD

When you plan the positions of socket outlets, try to ensure there will be enough, all conveniently situated, so that it is never necessary to extend the flexible cord of a table lamp or other appliance. But if you do find that a flex will not reach a socket, extend it so that it is not stretched taut, which can cause an accident. Never join two lengths of flex by twisting the bared ends of wires together, even if you bind them with insulating tape. People often do this as a temporary measure then neglect to make a proper connection later, which can have fatal consequences.

Flex connectors

If possible, fit a longer flex, wiring it into the appliance itself. But if you can't do this or don't want to dismantle the appliance, use a flex connector. There are two-terminal and three-terminal connectors, which you should match to the type of flex you are using. Never join two-core flex to three-core flex.

Strip off just enough sheathing so that the conductors can reach the terminals and the sheathed part of each cord will be secured under the cord clamp at each end of the connector.

Cut the conductors to length with engineer's pliers. Strip and connect the conductors; connect the live conductor to one of the outer terminals, the neutral to the other, and the earth wire (if present) to the central one. Make sure that matching conductors of the two cords are connected to the same terminals, then tighten the cord clamps and screw the cover in place.

In-line switches

If you plan to fit a longer continuous length of flex you can install an in-line switch that will allow you to control the appliance or light fitting from some distance away – a great advantage for the elderly or bed-ridden. Some in-line switches are fluorescent.

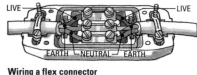

Wiring a flex connector

Wiring an in-line switch

Extension leads

If you fit a long flex to a power tool it will inevitably become tangled and one of the conductors will eventually break, perhaps causing a short circuit. The solution is to buy an extension lead or make one yourself.

The best type of extension lead to be had commercially is wound on a drum. There are 5amp ones – but it's safer to buy one with a 13amp rating, so that you can run a wider range of equipment without danger of overloading. If you use such a lead while it is wound on the drum it may overheat, so develop the habit of fully unwinding it each time (see left). The drums of these leads have a built-in 13amp socket to take the plug of the appliance; the plug on the lead is then connected to a wall socket.

You can make an extension lead from a length of 1.5mm^2 three-core flex with a standard 13amp plug on one end and a trailing socket on the other. Use those with unbreakable rubber casings. A trailing socket is wired in a similar way to a 13amp plug (see opposite). Its terminals are marked to indicate which conductors to connect to them.

'Multi-way' trailing sockets will take several plugs and are ideal for hi-fi systems or computers with individual components that need to be connected to the mains supply. Using a multi-way socket, the whole system is supplied from a single plug in the wall socket.

You can also extend a lead by using a lightweight two-part flex connector. One half has three pins that fit into the other half of the connector.

Unwind a lead
Always fully unwind a 13amp extension lead before you plug in an appliance rated at 1kW or more.

WARNING

When wiring a two-part flex connector never attach the part with the pins to the extension lead. The exposed pins will become live – and dangerous – when the lead is plugged into the socket. In fact nothing electrical should ever be wired so that a plug can become live other than when its pins are concealed in a socket.

TYPES OF FLEX EXTENDER

Below are illustrated four of the devices available for extending the flexible cords of electrical appliances.

Drum-type extension lead

13amp plug and trailing socket

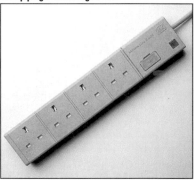

Multi-way trailing socket

Two-part flex connector

In the past there were many types of plug, but today standard 13amp square-pin plugs are used for all portable appliances and light fittings. They are available with rigid plastic or unbreakable rubber casings. Some have integral neon indicators to show when they are live, and some have pins insulated for part of their length to prevent the user getting a shock from a plug pulled partly from the socket.

Safety standards and fuses
Use only plugs marked BS 1363, which conform to British Standards. Square-pin plugs have to have a small cartridge fuse to protect the appliance. Use a 3amp (red) fuse for appliances of up to 720W, and a 13amp (brown) fuse for those of 720 to 3000W (3kW). There are also 2, 5 and 10amp fuses, but these are less often used in the home.

Wiring a 13amp plug

Loosen the large screw between the pins and remove the cover. Position the flex on the open plug to gauge how much sheathing to remove (remember that the cord clamp must grip sheathed flex, not the conductors).

Strip the sheathing and position the flex on the plug again, so that you can cut the conductors to the right length. These should take the most direct routes to their terminals and lie neatly in the channels of the plug.

Strip and prepare the ends of the wires, then secure each to its terminal. If you are using two-core flex, wire to the live and neutral terminals, leaving the earth terminal empty.

Tighten the cord clamp to grip the end of the sheathing and secure the flex (one type of plug has a sprung cord grip that tightens if the flex is pulled hard). Check that a fuse of the correct rating is fitted, then replace the plug's cover and tighten up the screw.

Wiring older plugs

If your home still has old round-pin sockets, they will only take round-pin plugs, which are not fused. Use 2amp plugs for lighting only; 5amp plugs for appliances of up to 1kW; and 15amp plugs for appliances between 1kW and 3kW. Have your wiring upgraded as soon as possible, so that you can use modern fused square-pin plugs.

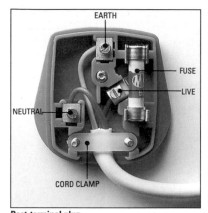
Post-terminal plug

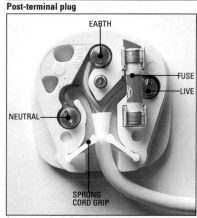
Clamp-terminal plug

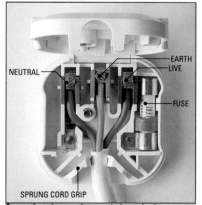
Some plugs have colour-coded terminals

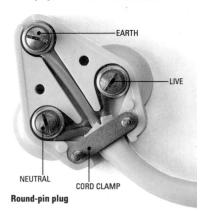
Round-pin plug

REPLACING A PENDANT LAMPHOLDER

Because they are not easy to inspect, damaged pendant lampholders often go unnoticed, so check their condition from time to time and replace any that look suspect before they become dangerous.

Pendant lampholders, which hang on flex from the ceiling, are in a stream of hot air rising from the bulb, and in time this can make plastic holders brittle and more easily cracked or broken. On a metal lampholder, the earth wire can become detached or corroded so that the fitting is no longer safe.

Types of lampholder
Plastic lampholders are the most common. These have a threaded skirt that screws onto the actual holder, the part that takes the bulb, and some versions have an extended skirt for fitting in bathrooms. You should fit heat-resistant plastic holders if you use a close-fitting or badly ventilated shade.

Plastic holders are designed to take two-core flex only. Never fit one on a three-core flex, as there is no place to attach the earth wire.

Metal lampholders are similar in their construction, but they must be wired with three-core flex so that they can be connected to earth. Never fit a metal lampholder in a bathroom, and never attach one to a two-core flex, which has no earth conductor.

Fitting a lampholder
Before commencing work, remove the circuit fuse or circuit breaker from the consumer unit so that no-one can turn the power on. Unscrew the old holder's cap – or the retaining ring if it's a metal one – and slide it up the flex to expose the terminals. Loosen their screws and pull the wires out. If some wires are broken or brittle, cut back slightly to expose sound wires before fitting the new holder.

Slide the cap of the new fitting up the flex and attach it temporarily with adhesive tape. Fit the live wire into one of the terminals, and the neutral wire into the other. Then loop the conductors round the supporting lugs of the holder, to take the weight off the terminals, and screw the cap down.

On a metal holder, pass the earth wire through the hole in the cap before you secure it. Connect the earth wire to the earth terminal, then secure the cap with the retaining ring.

WIRING PLUGS AND PENDANT LAMPHOLDERS

SEE ALSO

Details for:	
Flex	298
Connecting flex	299
Switching off	302

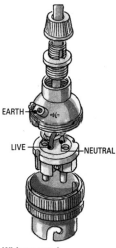

Wiring a plastic pendant lampholder

Wiring a metal pendant lampholder

MAIN SWITCH EQUIPMENT

Electricity flows because of a difference in 'pressure' between the live wire and the neutral one, and this difference in pressure is measured in volts.

Domestic electricity in Britain is supplied at 240 volts 'alternating current' by way of the Electricity Company's main service cable, which normally enters your house underground, although in some areas electricity is distributed by overhead cables.

The service head

The main cable terminates at the service head, or cutout, which contains the service fuse. This fuse prevents the neighbourhood's supply being affected if there should be a serious fault in the circuitry of your house. Cables connect the cutout to the meter, which registers how much electricity you consume. Both the meter and cutout belong to the Electricity Company and must not be tampered with. The meter is sealed in order to disclose interference.

If you use cheap night-time power for storage heaters and hot water, a time switch will be mounted between the cutout and the meter.

Consumer units

● **Main isolating switch**
Not all main isolating switches operate in the same way. Before you need to use it, check whether the main switch on your consumer unit should be up or down for 'off'.

Electricity is fed to and from the consumer unit by 'meter leads', thick single-core insulated-and-sheathed cables made up of several wires twisted together. The consumer unit is a box that contains the fuseways which protect the individual circuits in the house. It also incorporates the main isolating switch, which you operate when you need to cut off the supply of power to the whole house.

In a house where several new circuits have been installed over the years, the number of circuits may exceed the number of fuseways in the consumer unit, so an individual switchfuse unit – or more than one – may have to be mounted alongside the main unit. Switchfuse units comprise a single fuseway and an isolating switch. They too are connected to the meter by means of meter leads.

If your home is heated by off-peak storage heaters, then you will have an Economy 7 meter and a separate consumer unit for the circuits that supply the heaters.

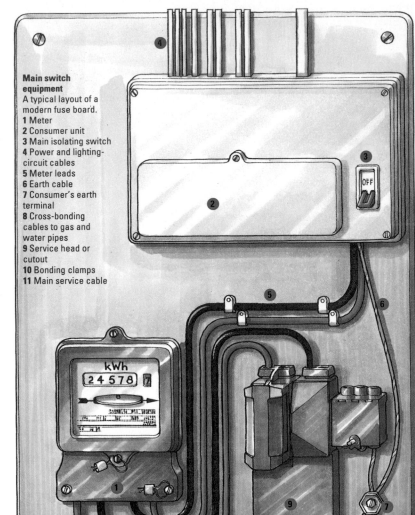

Main switch equipment
A typical layout of a modern fuse board.
1 Meter
2 Consumer unit
3 Main isolating switch
4 Power and lighting-circuit cables
5 Meter leads
6 Earth cable
7 Consumer's earth terminal
8 Cross-bonding cables to gas and water pipes
9 Service head or cutout
10 Bonding clamps
11 Main service cable

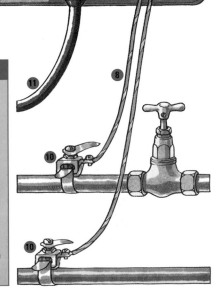

SWITCHING OFF THE POWER

In an emergency, switch off the supply of electricity to the entire house by operating the main isolating switch on the consumer unit.

Before working on any part of the electrical system of your home, always operate the main isolating switch and then remove the individual circuit fuse or miniature circuit breaker (MCB) that will cut off the power to the relevant circuit. That circuit will then be safe to work on, even if you restore the power to the rest of the house by operating the main switch again.

The earthing system

All of the individual earth conductors of the various circuits in the house are connected to a metal earthing block in the consumer unit. A single cable with a green-and-yellow covering runs from this earthing block to the consumer's earth terminal, which is mounted next to the cutout. In most urban houses a connection is provided from inside the cutout to an external earth-connection block, which is also wired to the consumer's earth terminal. This provides an effective path to earth – the current will pass along the sheath of the main service cable to the Electricity Company's substation, where it is solidly connected to earth.

In the past, most domestic electrical systems were earthed to the cold-water supply, so that earth-leakage current passed out along the metal water pipes into the ground in which they were buried. But nowadays more and more water systems use nonmetallic, nonconductive pipes and fittings, so that means of earthing is no longer reliable. Despite this, you will find that your gas and water pipework is connected to the consumer's earth terminal. This ensures that both water and gas piping systems are cross-bonded so that earth-leakage current passing through either system will run without hindrance to the main earth without creating dangerously high voltages. The cross-bonding clamps must be as close as possible to the point where the pipes enter the house but on the consumer's side (within 600mm) of the stopcock or gas meter.

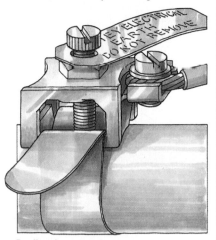

Bonding clamp
This type of clamp (BS951) is used to make connections to gas and water pipes. It should not be removed under any circumstances.

PME

Sometimes, especially in country areas, the Electricity Company provides a different method of earthing the system, called 'protective multiple earth' (PME), by which earth-leakage current is fed back to the substation along the neutral return wire, and so to earth.

Regulations regarding the earthing of this system are particularly stringent. Cross-bonding cables to gas and water services are generally required to be larger with PME. Check this with your Electricity Company.

RCDs

Although the local Electricity Company normally provides effective earthing for the electrical system of your home, safe earthing is actually the consumer's own responsibility. With this in mind, it is worth installing a residual current device (RCD) into the house circuitry.

When conditions are normal, the current flowing out through the neutral conductor is exactly the same as that flowing in through the live one. Should there be an imbalance between the two caused by an earth leakage, the RCD will detect it immediately and isolate the circuitry.

An RCD can be either installed as a separate unit or incorporated into the consumer unit together with the main isolating switch.

A separate unit containing an RCD

RECOGNIZING AN OLD FUSE BOARD

Domestic wiring systems were once very different from the ones used today. Besides lighting, water-heating and cooker circuits, each socket outlet had its own circuit and fuse, while further circuits would usually be installed from time to time as the needs of the household changed. Consequently, an old house may have a mixture of 'fuse boxes' attached to a fuse board along with the meter. The wiring itself may be haphazard and badly labelled, with the serious danger that you may not safely isolate a circuit you're going to work on. Furthermore, you will not be able to tell whether a particular fuse is correctly and safely rated unless you know what type of circuit it is protecting.

If your home still has such an old-style fuse board, have it inspected and tested by a qualified electrician before you attempt to work on any part of the system. He or she can advise you as to whether your installation needs to be replaced with a modern consumer unit; and if it is in good working condition, he or she can label the various circuits clearly to help you in the future.

An old-fashioned fuse board
This type of installation is out of date. A professional electrician may advise you to replace at least some of the components.

SEE ALSO

Details for:	
Supplementary bonding	296
RCDs	340

● **RCD**
An RCD – residual current device – is sometimes referred to as a residual current circuit breaker. It was formerly known as an ELCB – earth-leakage circuit breaker.

CONSUMER
UNIT

The consumer unit is the heart of your electrical installation, for every circuit in the house has to pass through it. There are several different types and styles of consumer unit, but all of them are based on similar principles.

Every consumer unit has a large main isolating switch, which can turn off the entire electrical system of the house. On some of the more-expensive units, the switch is in the form of an RCD that can be operated manually but will also 'trip' automatically should any serious fault occur, isolating the whole system in much less time than it would take for the Electricity Company's fuse to blow in a similar emergency.

Some consumer units are designed so that it is impossible to remove the outer cover without first turning off the main isolating switch. Even if yours is not of this type, you should always switch off before exposing any of the elements within the consumer unit.

Having turned off the main switch, remove the cover or covers so that you can see how the unit is arranged. The cover must be replaced before the unit is switched on again. Also, remember that even when the unit is switched off the cable connecting the meter to the main switch is still live – so take care.

Take note of the cables that feed the various circuits in the house. Ideally they should be spaced apart to prevent overheating. The black-insulated neutral wires run to a common neutral block where they are attached to their individual terminals. Similarly, the green-and-yellow earth wires run to a common earth block. The red-covered live conductors are connected to terminals on individual fuseways or circuit breakers.

Some wires will be twisted together in a single terminal. These are the two ends of a ring circuit, and that is how they should be wired.

CIRCUIT CABLES

FUSE CARRIER REMOVED FROM BELL CIRCUIT

EARTH BLOCK

NEUTRAL BLOCK

OFF

SPARE FUSEWAY (UNCONNECTED) BELL CIRCUIT LIGHTING CIRCUITS

RING CIRCUITS

MAIN SWITCH

COOKER CIRCUIT

IMMERSION-HEATER CIRCUIT

METER LEADS

EARTH LEAD

A typical cartridge-fuse consumer unit
Your consumer unit may have different circuits.

In the consumer unit there is a fuseway for each circuit. Into the fuseway is plugged a fuse carrier, which is essentially a bridge between the main switch and that particular circuit. When the fuse carrier is removed from the consumer unit, the current cannot pass across the gap.

Identifying a fuse

Pull any of the fuse carriers out of the unit to see what kind of fuse it contains. At each end of the carrier you will see a single-bladed or double-bladed contact. A rewirable carrier will have a thin wire running from one contact to the other, held by a screw terminal at each end. Fuse wire is available in various thicknesses, carefully calculated to melt at given currents when a circuit is substantially overloaded, thus breaking the 'bridge' and isolating the circuit. Alternatively, the carrier may contain a

cartridge fuse similar to those used in 13amp plugs, though circuit fuses are larger, varying in size according to their rating. The cartridge is a ceramic tube containing a fuse wire packed in fine sand. The wire is connected to metal caps at the ends of the cartridge that snap into spring clips on the contacts of the fuse carrier. Cartridge fuses provide better protection since they blow faster than ordinary fuse wire; it is therefore advisable to use cartridge-fuse carriers wherever possible.

Fuse ratings

Whatever the type of fuses used in the consumer unit, they are rated in the same way. Cartridge fuses are colour-coded and marked with the appropriate amp rating for a certain type of circuit. Fuse wire is bought wrapped round a card which is clearly labelled.

Never insert fuse wire that is heavier than the gauge intended for the circuit. To do so could result in a dangerous fault going unnoticed because the fuse wire fails to melt. And it is even more dangerous to substitute any other type

of wire or metal strip; these provide no protection at all.

When you need to change a fuse, do not automatically replace it with one of the same rating. Check first that it is the correct type of fuse for the circuit. The fuse carrier should be marked and/or colour-coded. You can also look at the list of circuits printed on the inside of the consumer-unit cover to identify the carriers and their required ratings.

Keep spare fuse wire or cartridge fuses in or close to the consumer unit.

FUSE RATINGS

Circuit		Fuse	Colour coding
Doorbell		5amp	White
Lighting		5amp	White
Immersion heater		15amp	Blue
Storage heater		15amp	Blue
Radial circuits – 20sq m maximum floor area 50sq m maximum floor area		20amp 30amp	Yellow Red
Ring circuits – 100sq m maximum floor area		30amp	Red
Shower unit		45amp	Green
Cooker		30amp	Red

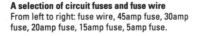

A selection of circuit fuses and fuse wire
From left to right: fuse wire, 45amp fuse, 30amp fuse, 20amp fuse, 15amp fuse, 5amp fuse.

FUSE CARRIERS AND MCBs

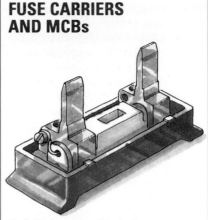

Single-bladed carrier with wire fuse

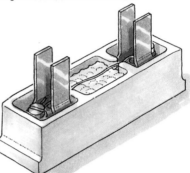

Double-bladed carrier with wire fuse

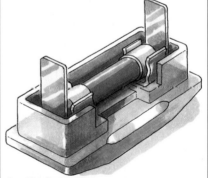

Cartridge-fuse carrier

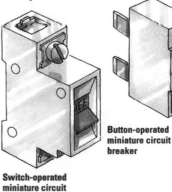

Switch-operated miniature circuit breaker

Button-operated miniature circuit breaker

● **MCB ratings**
In order to conform to European standards, MCB ratings tend to vary slightly from circuit-fuse ratings. (See CIRCUITS: MAXIMUM LENGTHS.) However, it is perfectly acceptable if you have MCBs that match the slightly smaller ratings shown for circuit fuses.

● **Selecting miniature circuit breakers**
Instead of fuses, MCBs (miniature circuit breakers) are sometimes used to protect circuits. There are many types of MCB on the market, but only buy ones that are made to the required standards of construction and safety. Make sure that any MCB you use is marked BS 3871 (this is the relevant British Standard). There are also different classes of MCB, so look for Type 2 or Type B. And lastly, MCBs are classified according to the largest potential fault current they can clear; ask for M6 or M9, as these will clear any potential current likely to be met in a domestic situation. If for any reason these MCBs are unavailable, ask your Electricity Company if they will accept alternatives.

305

CHANGING
A FUSE

When everything on a circuit stops working, first of all check the fuse to see if it has blown. Turn off the main switch on the consumer unit, take off the cover and look for the failed fuse. To identify the fuse, look at the list of circuits inside the cover. If there is no list, inspect the most likely circuits. If, for example, the lights blew when you switched them on, you need check only the lighting circuits, which are usually colour-coded white.

Checking a cartridge fuse

The simplest way to check a suspect cartridge fuse is to replace it with a new one and see if the circuit works. Alternatively, you can check the fuse with a metal-cased torch. Remove the bottom cap of the torch and touch one end of the fuse to the base of the battery while resting its other end against the torch's metal casing. If the torch bulb lights up, the fuse is sound.

Using a continuity tester
You can check a suspect cartridge fuse with a continuity tester. Place one of the tester's probes on each of the fuse's metal caps and then press the appropriate circuit-test button. If the bulb of the tester doesn't illuminate, the fuse has blown.

Testing a cartridge fuse
With the torch switched on, hold the fuse against the battery and the metal casing.

Checking a rewirable fuse

On a blown rewirable fuse, a visual check will usually detect the broken wire and scorch marks on the fuse carrier. If you cannot see the whole length of the fuse wire, pull gently on each end of the wire with the tip of a small screwdriver to see if it's intact.

Pull the wire gently with a small screwdriver

HOW TO REPLACE FUSE WIRE

To replace blown fuse wire, loosen the two terminals holding the old wire and extract the broken pieces. Wrap one end of a new length of the correct type of fuse wire clockwise round one of the terminals and tighten the screw **(1)**. Then run the wire across to the other terminal, leaving it slightly slack, and attach it in the same way **(2)**. Cut off any excess wire from the ends.

If the wire passes through a tube in the fuse carrier, it has to be inserted before either terminal is tightened **(3)**.

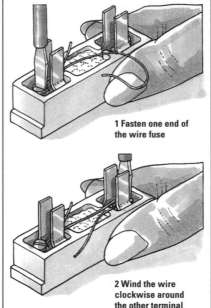

1 Fasten one end of the wire fuse

2 Wind the wire clockwise around the other terminal

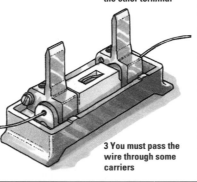

3 You must pass the wire through some carriers

IF THE FUSE BLOWS AGAIN

If a replaced fuse blows again as soon as the power is switched on, then there is either a fault or an overload (too many appliances plugged in) on that circuit and it must be detected and rectified before another fuse is inserted.

Miniature circuit breakers

In some consumer units you will find miniature circuit breakers (MCBs) instead of fuse carriers. Their current ratings tend to differ very slightly from fuse ratings, but the main difference is that circuit breakers switch to the 'off' position automatically, so a faulty circuit is obvious as soon as you inspect the consumer unit.

Turn the consumer unit's main switch off, then simply close the switch on the miniature circuit breaker to reset it. There is no fuse to replace. If the MCB switch or button will not stay in the 'on' position when power is restored, then there is still a fault on the circuit which must be rectified.

With the main switch off, reset the MCB

Checking out a fault

An electrician can test a circuit for you with special equipment, but first carry out some simple tests yourself.

Before inspecting any part of the circuit, turn off the consumer unit's main switch, remove the relevant fuse carrier or MCB, and keep it in your pocket so that no one can replace it while you are working.

Unplug all appliances on the faulty circuit to make sure that it is not simply overloaded, then switch on again. If the circuit is still faulty, switch off again and inspect the relevant socket outlets and light fittings to see if a conductor has worked loose and is touching one of the other wires or terminals or the outer casing, causing a short circuit.

If none of this enables you to find the fault, call in an electrician.

TYPES OF DOMESTIC ELECTRICAL CIRCUITS

Running from the consumer unit are the cables which supply the various fixed wiring circuits in your home. Not only are the sizes of the cables different; the circuits themselves also differ, depending on what they are used for and also, in some cases, how old they happen to be.

Ring circuits

The most common form of 'power' circuit for feeding socket outlets is the ring circuit, or 'ring main'. With this method of wiring, a cable starts from terminals in the consumer unit and goes round the house, connecting socket to socket and arriving back at the same terminals. This means that power can reach any of the socket outlets or fused connection units from both directions, which reduces the load on the cable.

Ring mains are always run in 2.5mm^2 cable and are protected by 30amp fuses or 32amp MCBs. Theoretically there is no limit to the number of socket outlets or fused connection units that can be fitted to one ring circuit provided that it does not serve a floor area of more than 100sq m (120sq yd) – a limit based on the number of heaters which would be adequate to warm that space. However, in practice two-storey houses usually have one ring main for the upper floor and another one for downstairs.

Spurs
The number of sockets on a ring main can be increased by adding extensions or 'spurs'. A spur can be either a single 2.5mm^2 cable connected to the terminals of an existing socket or fused connection unit or it can run from a junction box inserted in the ring.

It is good practice to have each spur serving one fused connection unit for a fixed appliance or one single or double socket outlet. You can have as many spurs on a ring circuit as there were sockets on it originally, and for this calculation a double socket is counted as two. The 30amp fuse that protects the ring main remains unchanged, no matter how many spurs are connected to the circuit.

Radial circuits

A radial power circuit feeds a number of sockets or fused connection units but, unlike a ring circuit, its cable terminates at the last outlet. The size of cable and the fuse rating depend on the size of the floor area to be supplied by the circuit. In an area of up to 20sq m (24sq yd), the cable should be 2.5mm^2, protected by a 20amp MCB or a 20amp fuse of any type. For a larger area, up to 50sq m type. For a larger area, up to 50sq m (60sq yd), you should use 4mm^2 cable with a 30amp cartridge fuse or 32amp MCB; a rewirable fuse is not permitted.

Any number of socket outlets can be supplied by one of these circuits, and spurs can be added if required. The circuits are known as multi-outlet radial circuits, but a powerful appliance such as a cooker or shower unit must have its own radial circuit.

Lighting circuits

Domestic lighting circuits are of the radial kind, but there are two systems currently in use.

The loop-in system simply has a single cable that runs from ceiling rose to ceiling rose, terminating at the last one on the circuit. Single cables also run from the ceiling roses to the various light switches.

The older system – known as the junction-box system – incorporates a junction box for each light. The boxes are situated conveniently on the single supply cable. A cable runs from each junction box to the ceiling rose, and another from the box to the light switch.

In practice, most lighting systems are a combination of the two methods.

A single circuit of 1mm^2 cable can serve the equivalent of twelve 100W light fittings. Check the load by adding together the wattage of all the light bulbs on the circuit. If it comes to more than 1200W, the circuit should be split. In any case, it makes sense to have two or more separate lighting circuits running from the consumer unit. If your house is large, requiring very long cable runs, use 1.5mm^2 two-core-and-earth cable instead of 1mm^2.

Lighting circuits must be protected by 5amp fuses or 6amp MCBs.

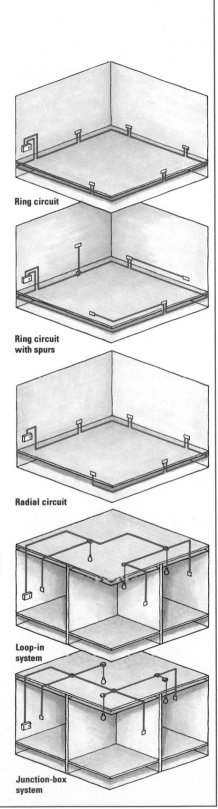

Ring circuit

Ring circuit with spurs

Radial circuit

Loop-in system

Junction-box system

TYPES OF CABLE

Two-core-and-earth cable

Cable for the fixed wiring of electrical systems normally has three conductors: the insulated live and neutral ones and the earth conductor lying between them, which is uninsulated except for the sheathing that encloses all three conductors. Cable up to 2.5mm² has solid single-core conductors; but larger sizes (up to 10mm²) wouldn't be flexible enough if they had solid conductors, so each one is made up of seven strands. The live conductor is insulated with red PVC, and the neutral one with black. If an earth conductor is exposed, as in a socket outlet, it should be covered with a green-and-yellow sleeve. You can buy sleeving from any electricians' supplier.

Heat-resistant sleeving is available for covering the conductors in an enclosed light fitting where the temperature could adversely affect the normal PVC insulation.

The PVC sheathing on the outside of the cable is usually white or grey.

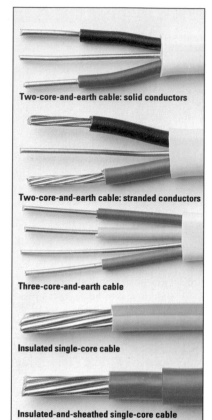

Two-core-and-earth cable: solid conductors

Two-core-and-earth cable: stranded conductors

Three-core-and-earth cable

Insulated single-core cable

Insulated-and-sheathed single-core cable

Three-core-and-earth cable

This type of cable is used for a two-way lighting system, which can be turned on and off at different switches – at the top and bottom of a staircase, for example, so that you never have to use the stairs in the dark. It contains three insulated conductors – with red, yellow and blue coverings – and a bare earth wire.

Single-core cable

Insulated single-core cable is used in buildings where the electrical wiring is run in metal or plastic conduit – a type of installation rarely found in domestic buildings. The cable is colour-coded in the normal way: red for live, black for neutral, and green-and-yellow for earth.

Single-core 16mm² cable insulated in a green-and-yellow PVC covering is used for connecting the consumer unit to the earth. Single-core cable of the same size is used for connecting the consumer unit to the meter. The meter leads are insulated and sheathed in red for the live conductor and black for the neutral one.

OLD CABLE

Houses which were wired before World War II may still have old cable that is sheathed and insulated in rubber, and some of them may even have old cable sheathed in lead.

Rubber sheathing is usually a matt black. It is more flexible than modern PVC insulation – unless it has deteriorated, in which case it will be crumbly.

This type of cable may be dangerous

STRIPPING CABLE

When cable is wired to an accessory, some of the sheathing and insulation must be removed.

Slit the sheathing lengthwise with a sharp knife, peel it off the conductors, then fold it over the blade and cut it off.

Take about 12mm (½in) of insulation off the ends of the conductors, using wire strippers.

Cover the uninsulated earth wire with a green-and-yellow plastic sleeve, leaving 12mm (½in) of the wire exposed for connecting to the earth terminal.

If more than one conductor is to be inserted in the same terminal, twist the exposed ends together with strong pliers to ensure the maximum contact for all of the wires.

Slip colour-coded sleeving over the earth wire

● **Cable sizes**
The chart on the right gives the basic sizes of cables used for wiring domestic circuits. For details of the maximum permitted lengths for circuits, see CIRCUITS: MAXIMUM LENGTHS.

If the Company fuse is larger than 60amps, 25mm² meter leads are required, but consult your local Electricity Company for advice.

CIRCUIT-CABLE SIZES		
Circuit	**Size**	**Type**
Fixed lighting	1.0mm² & 1.5mm²	Two-core-and-earth
Bell or chime transformer	1.0mm²	Two-core-and-earth
Immersion heater	2.5mm²	Two-core-and-earth
Storage heater	2.5mm² & 4.0mm²	Two-core-and-earth
Ring circuit	2.5mm²	Two-core-and-earth
Spurs	2.5mm²	Two-core-and-earth
Radial – 20amp	2.5mm²	Two-core-and-earth
Radial – 30amp	4.0mm²	Two-core-and-earth
Shower unit	10.0mm²	Two-core-and-earth
Cooker	4.0mm² & 6.0mm²	Two-core-and-earth
Consumer earth cable	16.0mm²	Single core
Meter leads	16.0mm²	Single core

RUNNING CABLE

SEE ALSO
Details for:
Repairing plaster 51
Nogging 137, 139
Switching off 302

INSIDE A HOLLOW WALL

To install a short cable run in a lath-and-plaster wall, hack the plaster away, fix the cable to the studs, and then plaster over again in the normal way.

Although you can run cable through the space between the two claddings of a stud partition wall, there is no way of doing this without some damage to the wall and the decoration. Drill a 12mm (½in) hole through the top wall plate above the spot where you are planning to position the switch, and then tap the wall directly below the hole to locate the nogging. Cut a hole in the lath-and-plaster to reveal the top of the nogging, then drill a similar hole through it.

Pass a lead weight on a plumb line through both of the holes and down to the location of the switch. Tie the cable to the line and pull it through.

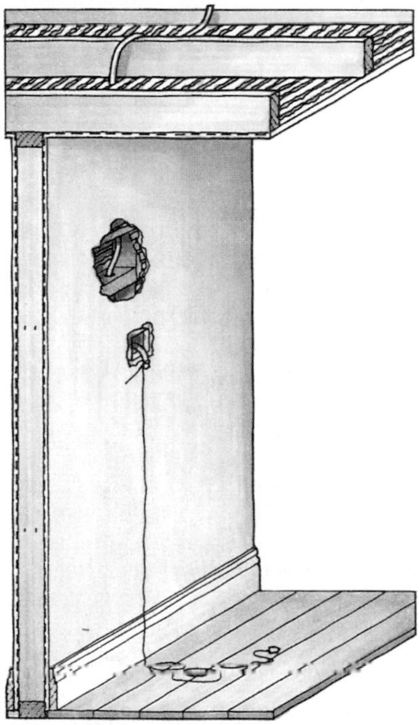

Running a cable through a hollow wall
If a nogging prevents you running cable directly to a switch, cut away some of the lath-and-plaster to drill a hole through the timber.

Long runs of cable are necessary to carry electricity from the consumer unit to all the sockets, light fittings and fixed appliances in the home. The cable must be fixed securely to the structure of the house along its route, except in confined spaces to which there is normally no access such as voids between floors and inside hollow walls. There are accepted ways of running and fixing cable, depending on particular circumstances.

Surface fixing

PVC-sheathed cable can be fixed to the surface of a wall or ceiling without any further protection. Fix it with plastic cable clips **(1)** or metal buckle clips **(2)** every 400mm (1ft 4in) on vertical runs, and every 250mm (10in) on horizontal runs. Try to keep the runs straight, and avoid kinks in the cable by keeping it on the drum as long as possible. If you do have to remove kinks, pull the cable round a thick dowel held in a vice.

If a cable seems vulnerable, you can cover it with an impact-resistant plastic channel **(3)**. Having secured the cable with clips, you simply nail the channel in place over it.

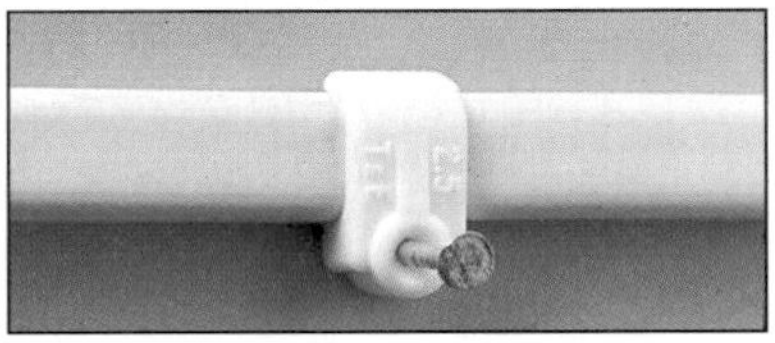

1 Plastic cable clip

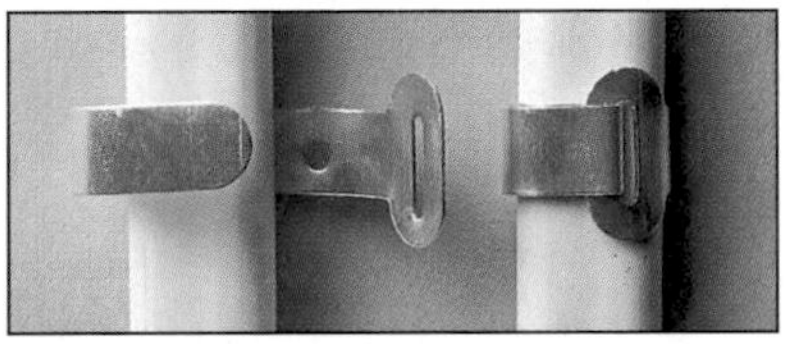

2 Metal buckle clip

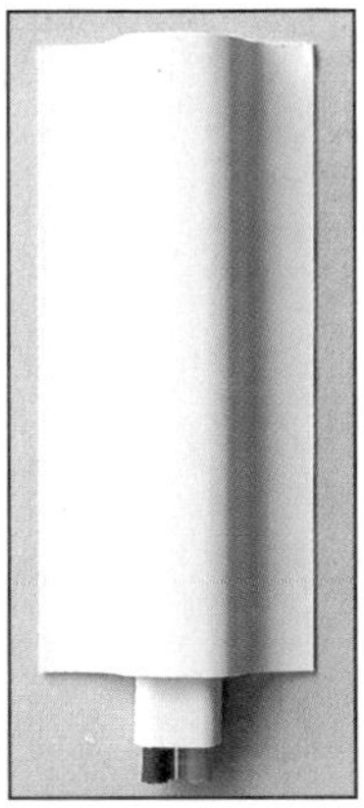

3 Impact-resistant plastic channel

Concealed fixing

While surface-fixed cable is acceptable in a cellar or in a garage or workshop, you wouldn't want to see it running across your living room walls or ceiling. From a decorative point of view it's better to bury it in the plaster or hide it in a wall void, and sheathed cable can be buried without further protection.

Where possible, run cable vertically to accessories such as switches or sockets, to avoid dangerous clashes with wall fixtures installed later. If that is not possible, you are permitted to run cable horizontally directly from the switch or socket. However, if a cable is not connected to a switch or socket on a wall in which it is concealed, then the cable must be within 150mm (6in) of the vertical or horizontal edges of the wall. Never, in any circumstances, run a buried cable diagonally across a wall.

Some people cover all buried cable with a channel, but this isn't required by the IEE Wiring Regulations.

Cable that is buried in light plastic conduit can, if necessary, be withdrawn later without disturbing decorations, but the need very rarely arises in a house.

Mark out your cable runs on the plaster, making allowance for a 'chase' or channel about 25mm (1in) wide for single cable. Cut both sides with a bolster and club hammer, and then hack out the plaster between the cuts with a cold chisel. Normally, plaster is thick enough to conceal cable, but you may have to chop out some brickwork to get the depth. Clip the cable in the channel **(1)** and, when you have checked that the installation is working satisfactorily, plaster over it. To avoid electric shock, ensure that the power to that circuit is turned off before you use wet plaster round a switch or socket outlet **(2)**.

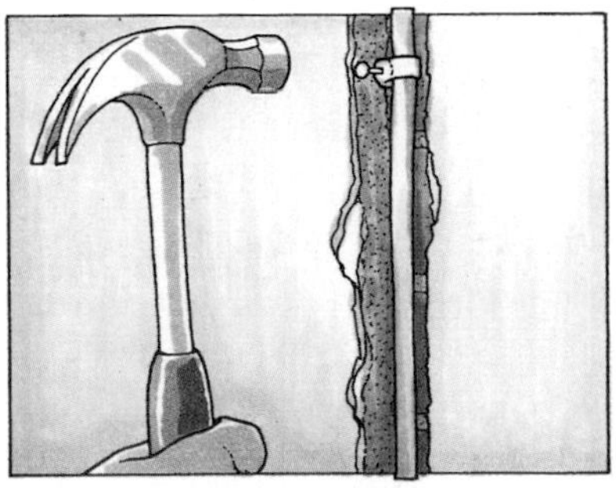

1 Nail plastic clips over the cable

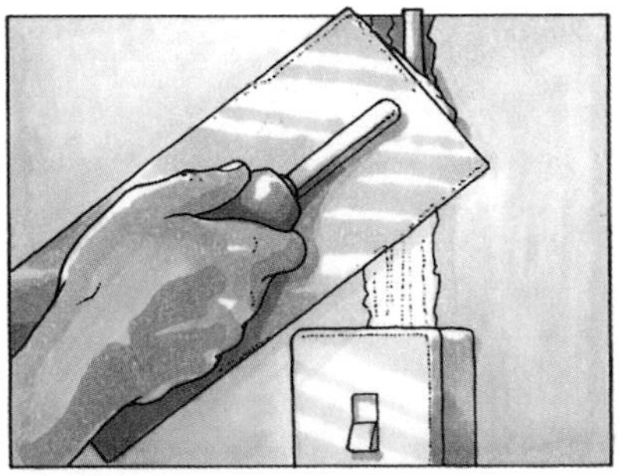

2 Repair the plaster up to the switch

RUNNING
CABLE
UNDER FLOORS

Cutting a full-length board
Cut a full-length board in two directly over a floor joist.

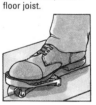

Using a skate
Run the disc of an electrician's skate between tongue-and-groove boards.

Power and lighting circuits are often concealed beneath floors if access is possible. It isn't necessary to lift every floorboard to run a cable from one side of a room to the other: by lifting a board every 2m (6ft) or so, you should be able to pass the cable from one gap to the next with the help of a length of stiff wire bent into a hook at one end. Look for boards that have been taken up before, as they will be fairly easy to lift and you will therefore damage fewer boards.

Lifting floorboards

Lifting square-edged boards
Drive a wide bolster chisel between two boards about 50mm (2in) from the cut end of one of them (**1**). Lever that board up with the bolster, then do the same on its other edge, working along the board until you have raised it far enough to wedge a cold chisel under it (**2**). Proceed along the board, raising it with the chisel, till the board is loose.

Full-length boards
If you have to lift a board that runs the whole length of the floor from one skirting to the other, start somewhere near the middle of the board, close to

one of the floor joists. (The nail heads indicate the positions of joists.) Lever the board up and make a sawcut through it centred on the joist, then lift the board in the normal way.

Lifting tongue-and-groove boards
You cannot lift a tongue-and-groove floorboard until you have cut through the tongues along both sides of the board with a floorboard saw, which has a blade with a rounded tip.

Alternatively, use an electrician's 'skate', made with a cutting disc that fits between the boards. Run the tool back and forth with one foot.

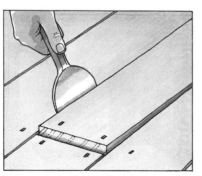

1 Prise up the floorboard with a bolster

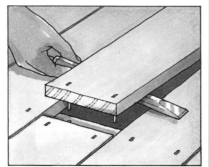

2 Wedge the raised end with a cold chisel

CUTTING A BOARD NEXT TO A SKIRTING

A joist that is fitted close to a wall may make it impossible to lift a floorboard in the normal way without damaging the bottom edge of the skirting.

In such a case, drill a starting hole through the floorboard alongside the joist, insert the blade of a padsaw in the hole, and cut across the board flush

with the side of the joist (**1**).

To support the cut end afterwards, nail a length of 50 x 50mm (2 x 2in) softwood to the joist. Hold the batten tightly against the undersides of the adjacent floorboards while you are fixing it, to ensure that the cut board will lie flush with the others (**2**).

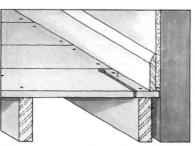

1 Cut through a trapped board with a saw

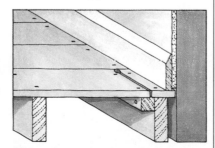

2 Support the cut board with a nailed batten

Solid floors

In a new concrete floor you can lay conduit and run cable through it before the concrete is poured.

In an existing solid floor you can cut a channel for conduit, although it's hard work without an electric hammer and chisel bit; and if the floor is tiled, you will not want to spoil it for one or two socket outlets. An alternative is to drop spur cables, buried in the wall plaster, from the ring circuit in the upper floor. Another way is to run cable through the wall from an adjacent area and channel it horizontally in the plaster just above the skirting. Yet another is to remove the skirting, clip the cable to the wall, and cover it with protective channel – but be sure to note the position of the cable, so you avoid piercing it when you nail back the skirting board.

In the roof space

In the roof space all wiring can be surface-run, but as people may enter it occasionally you must make sure that the cable is clipped securely to the joists or rafters. Run it through holes in the normal way, especially where joists are to be boarded over or in areas of access – around water tanks and near the entrance hatch, for example. If short lengths must run on top of a joist, add mechanical protection.

Wiring overlaid by roof-insulation material has a slightly higher chance of heating up. Lighting circuits do not present a problem, but circuits on which there are heaters, cookers or shower units, for example, are more critical. Wherever possible, run cable over thermal insulation. If you cannot avoid running it under the material, use a heavier cable, but consult a qualified electrician to be on the safe side.

When expanded-polystyrene insulation is in contact with electrical cable for a long time, it affects the plasticizer in the PVC sheathing on the cable. The plasticizer moves to the surface of the sheathing, reacts with the polystyrene, and forms a sticky substance on the cable. This becomes a dry crust which cracks if the cable is lifted out of the roof insulation and bent. It gives the impression that the cable insulation is cracking, but scientific testing has shown that the cracking is merely in the surface crust. On balance, however, it is best to keep cable away from polystyrene.

Running cable through the house structure
Use the most convenient method to run cable to sockets and switches.
1 Clip cable to battens nailed to roof timbers in the loft.
2 Junction boxes must be fixed securely.
3 Run cable through holes in the joists near the hatch.
4 Run cable over loft insulation.
5 To avoid damaging a finished floor, you can run a short spur through the wall from the next room.
6 When cable needs to run across the line of joists, drill holes 50mm (2in) below the joists' top edges.
7 When cable needs to run parallel to the joists, it can lie on the ceiling below.
8 Let cable drape onto the base below a suspended floor.
9 If it's impractical to run cable through a concrete floor, you can drop a spur from the floor above.

Burying cable in concrete
When you are laying a new concrete floor, take the opportunity to bury conduit for cable.

Running the cable

On the ground floor the cable can rest on the earth or on the concrete platform below the joists, providing there won't normally be access to the space. Allow enough slack, so that the cable is not suspended above the platform, which might put a strain on fixings to junction boxes or socket outlets. For the same reason, beside junction boxes or other accessories, secure cable with clips to the side of the joist. Never attach circuit cable to gas or water pipes; and don't run it next to heating pipes, as the heat could melt the insulation.

When laying cable between a floor and the ceiling below, it can rest on the ceiling without any other fixing provided it runs parallel with the joists. If it runs at right angles to the joists, drill a series of 12mm (½in) holes, one through each joist along the intended cable run. The holes must be at least 50mm (2in) below the tops of the joists, so that floorboard nails cannot at some time be hammered through the cable. Similarly holes must be at least 50mm (2in) from the bottom edge of ceiling joists, to be certain nails driven from below cannot pierce the cable. The space between the joists is limited, but you can cut down a spade bit and use it in a power drill.

Having marked out the position of a socket or fused connection unit, cut a channel from it down to the skirting board and, with an extra-long masonry drill in a power tool, remove the plaster from behind the skirting board. By using the drill at a shallow angle you can loosen much of the debris, but you will probably have to finish the job with a slim cold chisel. Raking the debris out from below with the same chisel also helps to dislodge it.

Pass a length of stiff wire with one end formed into a hook down behind the skirting board. Hook the cable and pull it through, at the same time feeding it from below with your other hand.

Preventing the spread of fire
Every time you cut an opening in the structure of the house for a cable, you are creating a potential route for fire to spread. After you have installed the cable, fill any holes between floors or rooms using plaster or some other non-flammable material (not asbestos). Even where you pass a cable into a mounting box you must fit a 'blind' grommet and cut a hole through it that is only just large enough for the cable.

SEE ALSO

Details for:	
Cable clips	309
Concealing cable	309
Fitting a grommet	315
Running a spur	317
Spade bit	488

Drilling the joists
Shorten a spade bit so that your drill fits between the joists.

Drilling behind skirting
Use an extra-long masonry drill to remove plaster behind a skirting board.

Fitting a grommet
There should be only just enough room for a cable to pass through a grommet into a mounting box for a switch or socket.

ASSESSING YOUR INSTALLATION

Inspect your electrical system to ensure that it is safe and adequate for your future needs. But remember, you should never examine any part of it without first switching off the power at the consumer unit.

If you are in doubt about any aspect of the installation, do not hesitate to ask a qualified electrician for an opinion. If you get in touch with your local Electricity Company, they will arrange for someone to test the whole system for you. There is usually a charge for this service.

QUESTIONS	ANSWERS
Do you have a modern consumer unit or a mixture of old 'fuse boxes'?	Old fuse boxes can be unsafe and should be replaced with a modern unit. Seek professional advice about this.
Is the consumer unit in good condition?	Replace a broken casing or cracked covers. Check that all the fuse carriers are intact and that they fit snugly in the fuseways.
Are the fuse carriers for the circuits clearly labelled?	If you cannot identify the various circuits, have an electrician test the system and label the fuses.
Are all your circuit fuses of the correct ratings?	Replace any fuses of the wrong rating. If an unusually large fuse is protecting one of the circuits, don't change it without getting professional advice – it may have a special purpose. Any wire other than proper fuse wire found in a fuse carrier should be replaced at once.
Are the cables that lead from the consumer unit in good condition?	The cables should be fixed securely, with no bare wires showing. If the cables appear to be insulated with rubber, have the whole installation checked as soon as possible. Rubber insulation has a limited life, so yours could already be dangerous.
Is the earth connection from the consumer unit intact and in good condition?	If the connection seems loose or corroded, have the Electricity Company check on whether the earthing is sound. You can check an RCD by pushing the test button to make sure it is working mechanically.
What is the condition of the fixed wiring between floors and in the loft or roof space?	If the cables are rubber-insulated, have the system checked by a professional, but first examine each of the circuits, as they may not all have been renewed at the same time. If cable is run in conduit, it can be hard to check on its condition – but if it looks doubtful where it enters accessories, have the circuit checked professionally. Wiring should be fixed securely and sheathing should run into all accessories, with no bare wire in sight. Junction boxes on lighting circuits should be screwed firmly to the structure and should have their covers in place.
Is the wiring discreet and orderly?	Tidy all surface-run wiring into straight properly-clipped runs. Better still, bury the cable in the wall plaster or run it under floors and inside hollow walls.
Are there any old round-pin socket outlets?	Make sure their wiring is adequate. Replace old radial circuits with modern wiring and 13amp square-pin sockets as soon as possible.
Are the outer casings of all accessories in good condition and fixed securely to the structure?	Replace any cracked or broken components and secure any loose fittings.
Do switches on all accessories work smoothly and effectively?	If the switches are not working properly, replace the accessories.
Are all the conductors inside accessories connected securely to their terminals?	Tighten all loose terminals and ensure that no bare wires are visible. Fit green-and-yellow sleeves to earth wires if they have not been fitted.

ASSESSING YOUR INSTALLATION

QUESTIONS	ANSWERS
Is insulation around wires inside any accessories dry and crumbly?	If so, it is rubber insulation in advanced decomposition. Replace the covers carefully and have a professional check the system as soon as possible.
Do any sockets, switches or plugs feel warm? Is there a burning smell, or scorch marks on sockets or around the base of plug pins? Does a socket outlet spark when you pull out a plug? Or a switch when you operate it?	These symptoms mean loose connections in the accessory or plug, or a poor connection between plug and socket. Tighten loose connections and clean all fuse clips, fuse caps and plug pins with silicon-carbide paper, then wipe them with a soft cloth. If the fault persists, try a new plug. If that fails to cure the problem, replace the socket or switch.
Is it difficult to insert a plug in a socket?	The socket is worn and should be replaced.
Are your sockets in the right places?	Sockets should be placed conveniently round a room so that you need never have long flexes trailing across the floor or under carpets. Add sockets to the ring circuit by running spurs.
Do you have enough sockets?	If you have to use plug adaptors, you need more sockets. Replace singles with doubles, add spurs, or extend the ring circuit.
Is there old braided twin flex hanging from some ceiling roses?	Replace it with PVC-insulated-and-sheathed flex. Also check that the wiring inside the rose is PVC-insulated.
Are there earth wires inside your ceiling roses?	If not, get professional advice on whether to replace the lighting circuits
Is your lighting efficient?	Make sure you have two-way switching on stairs, and consider extra sockets or different light fittings to make the lighting more effective or atmospheric.
Is there power in the garage or workshop?	Detached outbuildings need their own power supply.

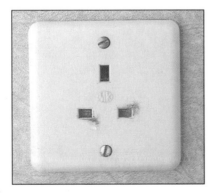

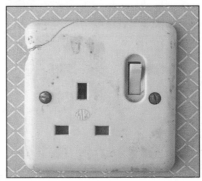

From left to right:

Scorch marks
Scorch marks on a socket or round the base of plug pins indicates poor connections.
Overloaded socket
If you have to use adaptors to power your appliances, you should fit extra sockets.
Unprotected connections
Sheath any bare earth wires and make sure covers or faceplates are fitted to all accessories.

From left to right:

Incorrect fuse
Replace improper wire with fuse wire.
Round-pin socket
Replace old round-pin sockets with 13amp square-pin sockets.
Damaged socket
Replace cracked or broken faceplates.

313

SURFACE-MOUNTED SOCKETS

Whatever the type of circuits in your home, use only standard 13amp square-pin sockets. All round-pin sockets are now out of date; and although they may not be actually dangerous at the moment, you should have them checked and consider changing your wiring to accommodate 13amp sockets.

Before you start work on any socket, switch the power off at the consumer unit and remove the fuse for the relevant circuit – then test the socket with an appliance that you know to be working, in order to make sure that the socket has been switched off properly.

Triple sockets
Triple sockets are useful where several electrical appliances are grouped together.

TYPES OF 13AMP SOCKET

Although all sockets are functionally very similar, there are several variations of the basic component.

There are single and double sockets, and both are available either switched or unswitched and with or without neon indicators so you can see at a glance whether the socket is switched on. All of these are wired in the same way.

Another basic difference is in how the sockets are mounted. They can be surface-mounted (screwed to the wall in a plastic box) or flush-mounted in a metal box buried in the wall with only its faceplate visible.

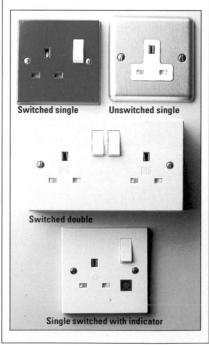

Switched single   **Unswitched single**

Switched double

Single switched with indicator

Positioning socket outlets

Choose the most convenient positions for television, hi-fi, table lamps and so on, and position your socket outlets accordingly. To avoid using adaptors or long leads, distribute the sockets evenly round living rooms and bedrooms, and wherever possible fit doubles rather than singles. Don't forget sockets for running the vacuum cleaner in hallways and on landings.

The optimum height for a socket is 225 to 300mm (9in to 1ft) above the floor. This will clear most skirting boards and leave ample room for flexible cord (flex) to hang from a plug, but is high enough not to be in danger of getting struck by the vacuum cleaner.

In the kitchen, fit at least four double sockets 150mm (6in) above the work-tops, or more if you have a lot of small appliances. In addition, fit sockets for floor-standing appliances such as your refrigerator and dishwasher.

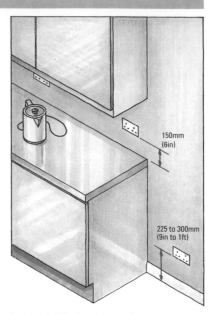

150mm (6in)

225 to 300mm (9in to 1ft)

Optimum heights for socket outlets

Surface-mounting socket outlets

First break out the thin plastic webs that cover the fixing holes in the back of a plastic mounting box. The best tool to use for this is an electrician's screwdriver. Two fixings should be sufficient. The fixing holes are slotted to enable easy adjustment.

Hold the mounting box firmly against a masonry wall, levelling it at the same time with a small spirit level, and mark the position of the fixing holes on the wall with a bradawl through the holes in the back of the box. Drill and plug the holes with No 8 wall plugs.

With a larger screwdriver and pliers, break out the plastic web covering the most convenient cable-entry hole in the box. For surface-run cable this will be in the side; for buried cable it will be the one in the base.

Feed the cable into the mounting box to form a loop about 75mm (3in) long (**1**), and then fix the box to the wall with 32mm (1¼in) countersunk woodscrews. Finally, wire and fit the socket.

Fixing to a hollow wall
On a dry-partition or lath-and-plaster wall, a surface-mounted box is fixed with any of the standard fixings used for hollow walls. Alternatively, use ordinary woodscrews if you are able to position the box over a stud – in which case, make sure you can feed the cable into the mounting box past the stud (**2**).

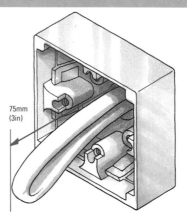

75mm (3in)

1 Leave a 75mm (3in) loop of cable at the box

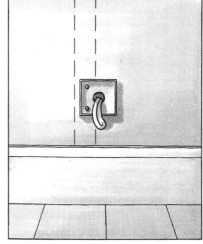
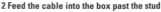

2 Feed the cable into the box past the stud

FLUSH-MOUNTED SOCKETS

Fixing to masonry

Hold the metal box against the wall and draw round it with a pencil (1), then mark a 'chase' (channel) running up from the skirting to the box's outline.

Using a bolster or a cold chisel, cut away the plaster, down to the brickwork (2), within the marked area.

With a masonry drill, bore several rows of holes down to the required depth (3) across the recess for the box, then with a cold chisel cut away the brick to the depth of the holes so that the box will lie flush with the plaster.

Try the box in the recess. If it fits in snugly, mark the wall through the fixing holes in its back, then drill the wall for the screw plugs. If you have made the recess too deep or the box rocks from side to side, apply some filler in the recess and press the box into it, flush with the wall and properly positioned. After about 10 minutes ease the box out carefully and leave the filler to harden so that you can mark, drill and plug the fixing holes through it.

Knock one or more of the blanked-off holes in the box out to accommodate the cable. Fit a grommet into each hole to protect the cable's sheathing from the metal edges (4), feed the cable into the box, and screw the box to the wall.

Plaster up to the box and over the cable chased into the wall; then, when the plaster has hardened, wire and fit the socket itself.

Fixing to plasterboard

In order to fit a flush socket to a wall made of plasterboard over wooden studs, trace the outline of the metal box in position on the wall and drill a hole in each corner of the outline. Then cut out the recess for the box with a padsaw.

Punch out the blanked-off entry holes in the box and fit rubber grommets, then feed the cable into the box.

Clip dry-wall fixing flanges to the sides of the box (5). These will hold it in place by gripping the wall from inside. Ease one side of the box, with flange, into the recess; and then, holding the screw-fixing lugs so as not to lose the box, manoeuvre it until both flanges are behind the plasterboard and the box sits snugly in the hole. (See also right.)

Finally, wire and fit the socket. As you tighten up the fixing screws, the plasterboard will be gripped between the flanges and the faceplate.

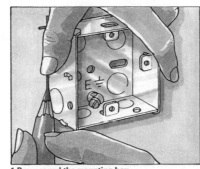
1 Draw round the mounting box

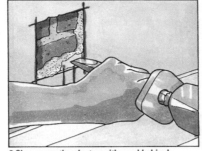
2 Chop away the plaster with a cold chisel

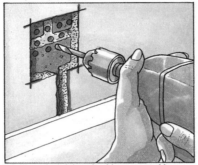
3 Drill out the brickwork with a masonry bit

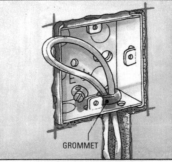
4 Fit a soft grommet in the cable-entry hole

GROMMET

5 Dry-wall fixing flanges clipped to a box

FLUSH MOUNTING TO LATH-AND-PLASTER

If you want to fit a flush socket outlet in a lath-and-plaster wall, try to locate it over a stud or nogging.

Mark the position of the metal box, cut out the plaster, and saw away the laths with a padsaw. Try the box for fit, and if necessary chop a notch in the woodwork until the box lies flush with the wall surface (1). Feed in the cable, and screw the box to the stud before wiring and fitting the socket.

If you cannot position the socket on a stud, cut away enough plaster and laths to make a slot in the wall running from one stud to the next. Between the studs, screw or skew-nail a softwood nogging to which you can fix the box. If necessary, set the batten back from the front edges of the studs, in order to make the box lie flush with the wall surface (2). Feed the cable into the box and make good the surrounding plaster before you wire and fit the socket.

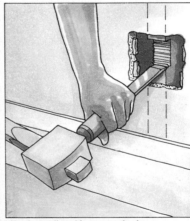
1 Notch a wall stud for a mounting box

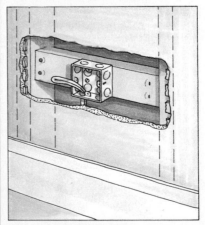
2 Nail a nogging between studs
Cut away wall plaster and laths when you have to fix a mounting box between wall studs.

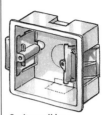
Cavity-wall box
Instead of fitting dry-wall fixing flanges to a standard mounting box, you can use a special cavity-wall box with integral hinged flanges that you push through the sides of the box after it is fitted.

315

REPLACING SOCKET OUTLETS

If you need to replace a broken or faulty socket outlet, there are several options worth considering before you embark on the job.

Simple replacement

Replacing a damaged socket with a similar one is a fairly straightforward job. A socket of any style will fit a metal mounting box, but check carefully when you substitute a socket that screws to a surface-mounted plastic box. Although it will fit and function perfectly well, square corners and edges on either will not suit rounded ones on the other. In such a case you may also have to buy a new, matching box.

An unswitched socket outlet can be replaced with a switched one without any change to the wiring or fixing.

Switch off the power at the consumer unit and take out the circuit fuse, then remove the fixing screws from the face-plate and pull the socket out of the box.

Loosen the terminals to free the conductors. Check that all is well inside the box, then connect the conductors to the terminals of the new socket. Fit the faceplate, using the original screws if those supplied with the new socket don't match the thread in the box.

Surface to flush

If you have to renew a socket, you may want to take the opportunity to replace a surface-mounted box with a flush one.

Turn off the power, remove the old socket and box, and then recess the new metal box into the wall, taking care not to damage the cable.

Replacing a single socket with a double

One way to increase the number of socket outlets in a room is to substitute doubles for singles. Any single socket on a ring circuit can be replaced with a double without making any changes to the wiring. Similarly, you can replace a single socket on a spur with a double socket outlet. Consider using switched sockets; they are safer than unswitched ones and the wiring is identical.

Surface to surface

Replacing a surface-mounted single socket with a surface-mounted double is quite easy. Having removed the old socket, simply fix the new, double box to the wall in the same place.

Flush to surface

Although flush-mounted socket outlets are neater, you may want to avoid the disturbance to decor that's involved in installing a double one. Instead, you can fit a double surface-mounted socket over the buried box of a single one (**1**). Switch off the power and remove the socket, leaving the metal box and the wiring in place, then knock out the cable-entry hole in the double plastic box and feed the cable through it. When the plastic box is centred over the old metal one, two fixing holes will line up with the fixing lugs on the buried box. Break out the plastic webs and fix the new box to the lugs with the screws that held the old socket in place. Wire up the new double socket and fit it.

Flush to flush

Switch off the power to the circuit, and remove the old single socket and its metal box. Then try the new double box over the hole. You can centre the box over the hole or align it with one end (**2**), whichever is more convenient. Trace the outline of the box on the wall and cut out the brickwork.

Use a similar procedure to substitute a double socket for a single one in a hollow wall, installing the socket by whichever method is most convenient.

Surface to flush

To replace a single surface-mounted socket with a flush double, cut a recess for the metal box in the normal way.

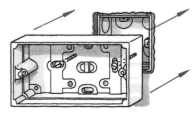

1 Fixing a surface-mounted box over a flush one

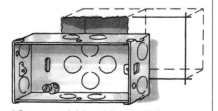

2 Cut out extra brickwork for a double box

CONNECTING UP TO A SOCKET

When a single cable is involved, strip off the sheathing in the normal way and connect the wires to the terminals: the black wire to neutral – N, the red one to live – L, and the earth wire, which you should insulate yourself with a sleeve, to earth – E (**1**). If necessary, fold the stripped ends over so that no bare wire protrudes from a terminal.

When connecting to a ring circuit, cut through the loop of cable, strip the sheathing from each half and twist together the bared ends of matching wires – live with live and so on – after slipping sleeves on the earth wires (**2**).

Cable is stiff, and can make it difficult to close the socket faceplate, so bend each conductor until it folds into the mounting box. Locate both fixing screws and tighten them gradually in turn until the plate fits firmly in place against the wall or box.

1 Wiring a socket outlet

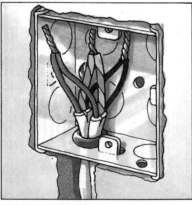

2 Twist cut wires together

If you need more sockets in a room, you can run 2.5mm² spur cables from a ring circuit and have as many spurs as there are sockets already on the ring. A spur can feed one single or one double socket.

A spur cable can be connected to any socket or fused connection unit on the ring circuit, or to a new junction box inserted in the circuit. If running a spur cable from an existing socket would mean disturbing the plaster, it will be more convenient to use a junction box. And if there is no socket outlet within easy reach of the proposed new one, using a junction box may save cable.

If the cable is surface-run and you want to extend a row of sockets – behind a workbench, for example – then it will be simpler to connect the spur to a socket.

Examine the socket. If it is fed by a single cable, it is probably already on a spur; and if there are three cables in the socket, then it's already feeding a spur itself. What you need to look for is a socket that has two cables.

Connecting to an existing socket

Fix the new socket, then wire it up in the normal way (see opposite) and run its spur cable to the existing socket outlet. Switch off the electricity and remove the existing socket. You may have to enlarge the entry hole or knock out another one to take the spur cable. Feed the cable into the box, prepare the conductors, and twist their bared ends together with those of the matching conductors of the ring circuit. Insert the wires in their terminals (red – L; black – N; and green-and-yellow – E) and replace the socket. Then switch the power on and test the new socket.

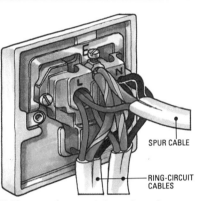

SPUR CABLE

RING-CIRCUIT CABLES

Taking a spur from an existing socket outlet

CONNECTING TO A JUNCTION BOX

You will need a 30amp junction box with three terminals to connect to a ring circuit. It will have either knock-out cable-entry holes or a special cover that rotates to blank off unneeded holes. The cover must be screw-fixed.

Lift a floorboard close to the new socket, where you can connect to the ring-circuit cable without stretching it.

Fix a platform for the box by nailing battens near the bottoms of two joists (see right) and screwing a 100 x 25mm (4 x 1in) strip of wood between the joists and resting on the battens. Loop the ring-circuit cable over the platform before fixing it, so that the cable need not be cut for connecting up. Remove the cover, screw the junction box to the platform, and break out two cable-entry holes. If you do forget to loop the cable over the platform, simply cut the cable when you come to connect it up.

Turn off the power at the consumer unit, then rest the ring-circuit cable across the box and mark the amount of sheathing to remove. Slit it lengthwise and peel it off the conductors. Don't cut the live and neutral conductors, but slice away just enough insulation on each to expose a section of bare wire that will fit into a terminal (see right). Cut the earth wire and fit insulating sleeves on the two ends.

Remove the screws from all three of the terminals and lay the wires across them – with the earth wire in the middle terminal, and the live and neutral ones on each side. Push the wires home with a screwdriver.

Having fitted and wired the new spur socket, run its cable to the junction box. Cut and prepare the ends of the wires, and break out an entry hole so that the spur wires can be fitted to the terminals of the box (see right). Take care that only colour-matched wires from both cables share terminals.

Replace the fixing screws, starting them by hand as they are easily cross-threaded, then tighten them up with a screwdriver. Check that all of the wires are secured and that the cables all fit snugly in their entry holes, with the sheathing running into the box, then fit the cover on the box.

Fix each cable to a nearby joist with cable clips, to take the strain off the terminals, then replace the floorboards.

Switch the power back on and test the new socket.

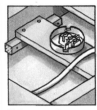

Make a wooden platform for a junction box

RING-CIRCUIT CABLE

SPUR CABLE

RING-CIRCUIT CABLE

Taking a spur from a junction box

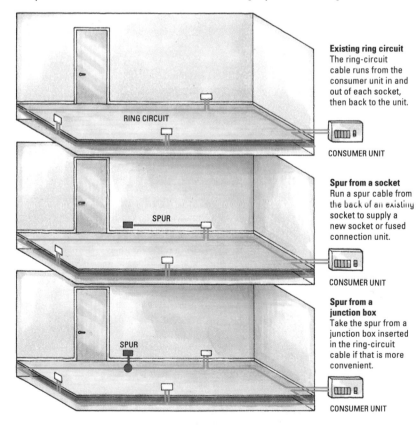

RING CIRCUIT

CONSUMER UNIT

Existing ring circuit
The ring-circuit cable runs from the consumer unit in and out of each socket, then back to the unit.

SPUR

CONSUMER UNIT

Spur from a socket
Run a spur cable from the back of an existing socket to supply a new socket or fused connection unit.

SPUR

CONSUMER UNIT

Spur from a junction box
Take the spur from a junction box inserted in the ring-circuit cable if that is more convenient.

317

EXTENDING
A RING CIRCUIT

There are times when it is better to extend a ring circuit than to fit spurs. For example, if you want to wire a room that isn't adequately serviced, or all of the conveniently placed sockets already have spurs running from them. You can break into the ring at an existing socket or via junction boxes. Either way, switch off the power to the circuit before you break into it.

Using an existing socket

Disconnect one in-going cable from a socket on the ring circuit and take it to the first new socket. Do this via a junction box if the cable won't otherwise reach. Continue the extension with a new section of cable from socket to socket, finally running it from the last new one back to the socket where you broke into the ring. Joining the new cable to the old one within the socket completes the circuit.

Using junction boxes

Cut the ring cable and connect each cut end to a junction box, then run a new length of cable from one box to the other, looping it into the new sockets.

Running the extension

No matter how you plan to break into the ring, always install the new cable first and then connect it up to the circuit at the last moment. This allows you to use power tools to run the extension – but don't forget to switch the power off just before connecting up.

Decide positions for the new sockets and plan your cable run (an easy route is better than a shorter, more difficult one). Allow some slack in the cable.

Cut out the plaster and brickwork for sockets and cable, then fit the boxes for the sockets. Now run the cable, leaving enough spare for joining to the ring circuit, and take it up behind the skirting to the first socket. Leave a loop hanging near the box (see right), then take the cable on to the next one, and so on until all the new sockets are supplied. Take the excess cable on to the point where you plan to join the ring.

Fit the new sockets, then switch off the electricity, break into the ring, and connect the extension to it. Switch the power on and test all the new sockets separately. Make good the plasterwork.

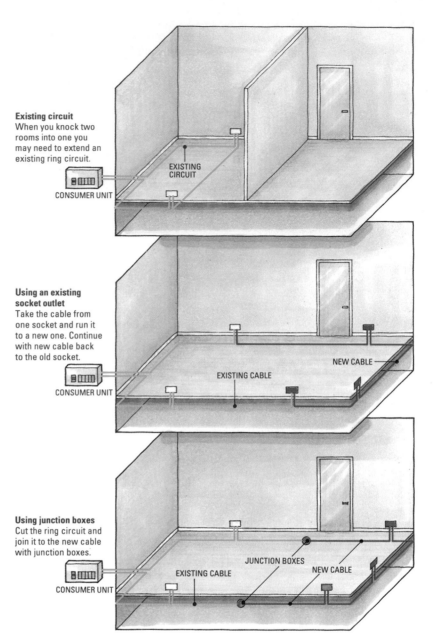

Existing circuit
When you knock two rooms into one you may need to extend an existing ring circuit.

EXISTING CIRCUIT

CONSUMER UNIT

Using an existing socket outlet
Take the cable from one socket and run it to a new one. Continue with new cable back to the old socket.

NEW CABLE

EXISTING CABLE

CONSUMER UNIT

Using junction boxes
Cut the ring circuit and join it to the new cable with junction boxes.

JUNCTION BOXES

NEW CABLE

EXISTING CABLE

CONSUMER UNIT

LEAVE SOME SLACK
IN THE CIRCUIT

Don't pull the cable too tight when you are running a new circuit. It places a strain on the connections and makes it difficult to modify the circuit at a later stage, should that become necessary.

Leave a generous loop of cable at each of the new socket positions till you have run the complete circuit. At that stage you can pull the loop back ready for connecting to the socket.

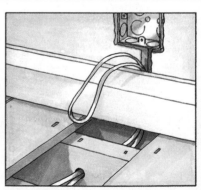

Leave ample cable above the skirting

CONVERTING A RADIAL CIRCUIT

If you have a radial circuit, you may want to convert it to a ring circuit, particularly if you wish to supply a larger area. Before starting work, switch off at the consumer unit.

Checking cable and fuse

If the radial circuit is wired with 2.5mm^2 cable (solid conductors), continue the circuit back to the consumer unit with the same size cable, but substitute a 30amp fuse and fuseway in place of the 20amp fuse. Even if the circuit is wired with 4mm^2 cable (stranded conductors), you can complete the ring with 2.5mm^2 cable. Check there's a 30amp fuse. See also CIRCUITS: MAXIMUM LENGTHS.

The extra cable is run in exactly the same way as described for extending a ring circuit (see opposite). Join the new cable at the last socket on the radial circuit and run it to all the new sockets. From the last socket, run the cable to the consumer unit.

Connecting to the consumer unit

You should examine your consumer unit and familiarize yourself with it. Even when the unit is switched off, the cable that connects the meter to the main switch is still live – so take great care. First locate the terminals to which the radial circuit is connected. The live (red wire) terminal is on the fuseway (or MCB) from which you removed the circuit fuse prior to starting work. The neutral (black wire) terminal is on the neutral block, to which all of the black wires are connected. You can usually trace the black wire you are looking for by working along from the sheathed part of the cable – and the earth terminal similarly, by tracing the green-and-yellow-insulated conductor. Pass the new cable into the consumer unit close to the original radial-circuit cable. Cut it to length, strip off the sheathing and prepare the conductors.

Disconnect the live (red) conductor from its terminal and, having checked for continuity (see far right), twist its end together with that of the red wire from the new cable, then reconnect both conductors in the same terminal. Do the same for the black wires and then the green-and-yellow ones – but slip a sleeve over the new earth wire.

Check that the circuit fuse is of the correct rating, then replace the fuse carrier. Close the consumer unit, switch on the power, and test the circuit.

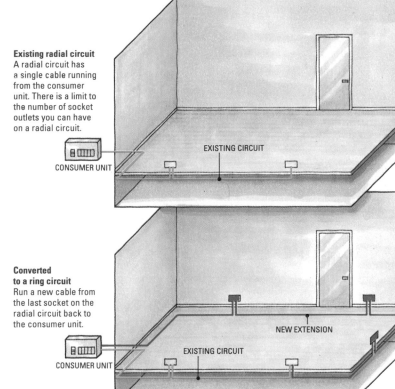

Existing radial circuit
A radial circuit has a single cable running from the consumer unit. There is a limit to the number of socket outlets you can have on a radial circuit.

CONSUMER UNIT

EXISTING CIRCUIT

Converted to a ring circuit
Run a new cable from the last socket on the radial circuit back to the consumer unit.

NEW EXTENSION

CONSUMER UNIT

EXISTING CIRCUIT

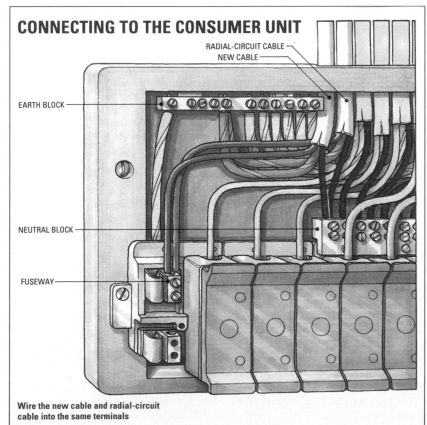

CONNECTING TO THE CONSUMER UNIT

RADIAL-CIRCUIT CABLE
NEW CABLE

EARTH BLOCK

NEUTRAL BLOCK

FUSEWAY

Wire the new cable and radial-circuit cable into the same terminals

● **Testing for continuity**
Check the continuity of the new ring circuit before you twist the conductors together and connect them to their terminals in the consumer unit. Using a continuity tester, place one of its probes on the red conductor at one end of the circuit cable and its other probe on the red conductor at the other end. Press the tool's test button and, if the circuit is complete, the tester's light will illuminate. Carry out the same test for the black conductors and then the earth wires.

319

13amp sockets are designed to enable appliances to be moved from room to room, with one socket used for different appliances at different times. But many electrical appliances, both large and small, are fixed to the structure of the house, or stand in one position permanently. Such appliances may therefore just as well be wired into your electrical installation permanently. For some there is no alternative, and they may even require radial circuits of their own direct from the consumer unit.

FUSED CONNECTION UNITS

A fused connection unit is basically a device for joining the flex (or sometimes cable) of an appliance to circuit wiring. The connection unit incorporates the added protection of a cartridge fuse similar to that found in a 13amp plug. If the appliance is connected by a flex, choose a unit that has a cord outlet in the faceplate.

Some fused connection units are fitted with a switch, and some of these have a neon indicator that shows at a glance whether they are switched on. A switched connection unit allows you to isolate the appliance from the mains.

All fused connection units are single (there are no double versions available) with square faceplates that fit metal boxes for flush mounting or standard surface-mounted plastic boxes.

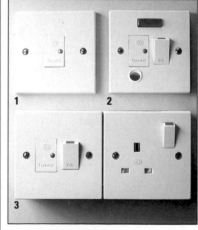

Changing a fuse
With the electricity turned off, remove the retaining screw in the face of the fuse holder. Take the holder from the connection unit; prise out the old fuse and fit a new one; then replace the holder and the retaining screw.

Fused connection units
1 Unswitched connection unit.
2 Switched unit with cord outlet and indicator.
3 Connection unit and socket outlet in a dual mounting box.

Small appliances

Small permanent electrical appliances with ratings of up to 3000W (3kW) – wall heaters, cooker hoods, heated towel rails and so on – can be wired into a ring or radial circuit by means of fused connection units.

Although such appliances could be connected by means of 13amp plugs to socket outlets, the electrical contact would not be so good – and there is also some risk of fire with that type of permanent installation.

Before wiring a fused connection unit to the house circuitry, always remember to switch off the power at the consumer unit.

Mounting a fused connection unit

A fused connection unit is mounted in the same type of box as an ordinary socket outlet, and the box is fixed to the wall in exactly the same way. The unit can also be mounted in a dual box that is designed to hold two single units – for example, a standard socket outlet beside a connection unit. The socket is wired to the ring circuit, and the two units are linked together inside the box by a short 2.5mm² spur.

A dual mounting box

Wiring a fused connection unit

Fused connection units can be supplied by a ring circuit, a radial circuit or a spur. Some appliances are connected to the unit with flex, others with cable. Either way, the wiring arrangements inside the units are the same. Units with cord outlets have clamps to secure the connecting flex.

An unswitched connection unit has two live (L) terminals, one marked 'Load' for the brown wire of the flex, and the other marked 'Mains' for the red wire from the circuit cable. The blue wire from the flex and the black wire from the circuit cable go to similar neutral (N) terminals; and both earth wires are connected to the unit's earth (E) terminal or terminals (**1**).

Switched connection unit
A fused connection unit with a switch also has two sets of terminals. Those marked 'Mains' are for the spur or ring cable that supplies the power; the terminals marked 'Load' are for the flex or cable from the appliance.

Wire up the flex side first, connecting the brown wire to the L terminal and the blue one to the N terminal, both on the 'Load' side. Connect the green-and-yellow wire to the E terminal (**2**) and tighten the cord clamp.

Attach the circuit conductors to the 'Mains' terminals – red to L and black to N, then sleeve the earth wire and take it to the E terminal (**2**).

If the fused connection unit is on a ring circuit, you must fit two circuit conductors into each 'Mains' terminal and the earth terminal. Before securing the unit in its box with the fixing screws, make sure the wires are held firmly in the terminals and can fold away neatly.

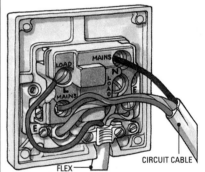

1 Wiring a fused connection unit

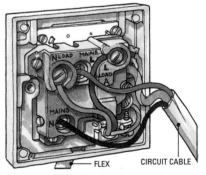

2 Wiring a switched fused connection unit

WIRING
HEATERS

When installing a skirting heater, wall-mounted heater or oil-filled radiator, wire the appliance to a fused connection unit mounted nearby at a height of about 150 to 300mm (6in to 1ft) from the floor. Whether the connection to the unit is by flex or cable will depend on the type of appliance. Follow the manufacturer's instructions for wiring, and fit the appropriate fuse in the connection unit.

In a bathroom, a fused connection unit must be mounted out of reach. Any heater that is mounted near the floor of a bathroom must therefore be wired to a connection unit installed outside the room. If the appliance is fitted with flex, mount a flexible-cord outlet (1) next to the appliance – and then run a cable from the outlet to the fused connection unit outside the bathroom and connect it to the 'Load' terminals in the unit.

The flexible-cord outlet is mounted on a standard surface-mounted box or flush on a metal box. At the back of the faceplate are three pairs of terminals to take the conductors from the flex and the cable (2).

Radiant wall heaters for use in bathrooms must be fixed high on the wall, out of reach from the bath or shower. A fused connection unit fitted with a 13amp fuse (or a 5amp fuse for a heater of 1kW or less) must be mounted at the same level, and the heater must be controlled by a double-pole pull-cord switch (the type that works by breaking both live and neutral contacts). Many heaters have a built-in double-pole switch; otherwise you must fit a ceiling-mounted 15amp double-pole switch between the fused connection unit and the heater. Switch terminals marked 'Mains' are for the cable on the circuit side of the switch; those marked 'Load' are for the heater side. The earth wires are connected to a common terminal on the switch box.

If it is not possible to run a spur to the fused connection unit from a socket outside the bathroom, don't be tempted to connect a radiant wall heater to the lighting circuit. Instead, run a separate radial circuit from the connection unit to a 15amp fuseway in the consumer unit, using 2.5mm² cable.

Heated towel rail

The Wiring Regulations covering other kinds of heater also apply to a heated towel rail situated in a bathroom. As the towel rail is mounted near the floor, run a flex from it to a flexible-cord outlet, which must in turn be wired to a fused connection unit outside the bathroom. For a towel rail of 1kW or less, fit a 5amp fuse; otherwise, fit a 13amp fuse.

If a heated towel rail is installed in a bedroom, the fused connection unit can be mounted alongside it.

Heat/light unit

Heat/light units, which are sometimes fitted in bathrooms, incorporate a radiant heater and a light fitting in the one appliance. Although they are ceiling-mounted, usually in the position of the ceiling rose, these units must never be connected to lighting circuits.

To install a heat/light unit in this position, turn off the power and, having identified the lighting cables, remove the rose and withdraw the cables into the ceiling void. Fit a junction box to a nearby joist and terminate the lighting cables at that point (3). Don't connect the switch cable, as it won't be needed.

Run a 2.5mm² two-core-and-earth spur cable from an unswitched fused connection unit mounted outside the bathroom to a ceiling-mounted 15amp double-pole switch, and from there to the heat/light unit.

Connect up to the fused connection unit (see opposite), then wire the heat/light unit according to the maker's instructions and fit a 13amp fuse in the connection unit.

SEE ALSO

Details for:	
Bathroom safety	296
Switching off	302
Running cable	309–311
Double-pole ceiling switch	331
Ceiling-rose connections	332

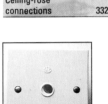

1 Flexible-cord outlet

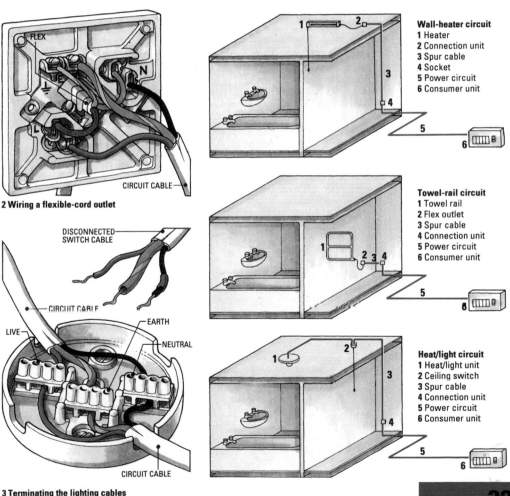

2 Wiring a flexible-cord outlet

3 Terminating the lighting cables
Join the circuit cables in a junction box. Label the disconnected switch wire for future reference.

Wall-heater circuit
1 Heater
2 Connection unit
3 Spur cable
4 Socket
5 Power circuit
6 Consumer unit

Towel-rail circuit
1 Towel rail
2 Flex outlet
3 Spur cable
4 Connection unit
5 Power circuit
6 Consumer unit

Heat/light circuit
1 Heat/light unit
2 Ceiling switch
3 Spur cable
4 Connection unit
5 Power circuit
6 Consumer unit

WIRING
SMALL
APPLIANCES

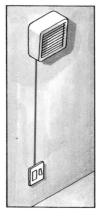

Wall-mounted fan
Run a 1.5mm^2 cable from a fused connection unit to a wall-mounted extractor fan.

Kitchen equipment circuits
1 Connection units
2 Flex outlets
3 Socket outlets

Extractor fan

To install an extractor fan in a kitchen, mount a fused connection unit 150mm (6in) above the worktop and run a cable to the fan or to a flexible-cord outlet next to it. If the fan has no integral switch, use a switched connection unit to control it. Fit a 3 or 5amp fuse as recommended by the manufacturer.

If the fan's speed and direction are controllable, it may have a separate control unit – in which case you need to wire the connection unit to the control unit, following the maker's instructions.

To fit an extractor fan in a bathroom, mount the fused connection unit outside the room and run the cable to the fan or flex outlet via a ceiling-mounted double-pole switch.

Fridges, dishwashers and washing machines

There is no reason why you cannot plug an appliance like a fridge, dishwasher or washing machine into a standard socket outlet – except that in a modern kitchen such appliances are installed under worktops, and sockets mounted behind them are difficult to reach.

It's therefore generally more convenient to mount a switched fused connection unit 150mm (6in) above the worktop, then connect it to the ring circuit and run a spur – using 2.5mm^2 cable – from the connection unit to a socket outlet mounted behind the appliance.

Cooker hood

Either mount a fused connection unit (fitted with a 3amp fuse) close to the cooker hood or mount the connection unit at worktop height and then run a 1mm^2 cable from the unit to a flexible-cord outlet beside the hood.

Instantaneous water heater

You can install an instantaneous water heater above a sink or washbasin in order to provide on-the-spot hot water. Join a 3kW model by heat-resistant flex to a switched fused connection unit mounted out of reach of anyone who is using the water.

If the heater is for use in a bathroom, wire it via a flex outlet to a ceiling pull-switch and then to the connection unit outside the bathroom. The connection unit must be fitted with a 13amp fuse.

Wire a 7kW water heater in the same way as a shower. If it is situated in the kitchen, you can use a double-pole wall switch to control it.

Waste-disposal unit

A waste-disposal unit is housed in the cupboard unit below the sink. Mount a switched fused connection unit 150mm (6in) above a worktop near the sink, but well out of reach of small children and anyone using the sink. From the unit, run a 1mm^2 cable to a flex outlet next to the waste-disposal unit. Clearly label the connection unit 'WASTE DISPOSAL' to avoid accidents. Fit a 13amp fuse.

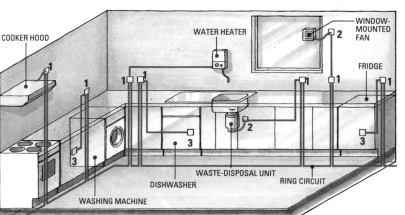

SHAVER SOCKETS

Special shaver socket outlets are the only kind of electrical socket allowed in bathrooms. They contain transformers that isolate the user side of the units from the mains, reducing the risk of an electric shock. This type of socket has to conform to the exacting British Standard BS 3535.

However, there are shaver sockets that do not have isolating transformers and therefore don't conform to BS3535. These are quite safe to install and use in a bedroom, but this type of socket must not be fitted in a bathroom.

You can wire a shaver socket from a junction box on an earthed lighting circuit or from a fused connection unit, fitted with a 3amp fuse, on a ring-circuit spur. If you are installing the shaver socket in a bathroom, then the fused connection unit must be positioned outside the room. Run 1mm^2 two-core-and-earth cable from the connection unit to the shaver socket; then connect the conductors: red to L and black to N (**1**). Sheath the earth wire with a green-and-yellow sleeve and connect it to E.

Shaver unit for use in a bathroom

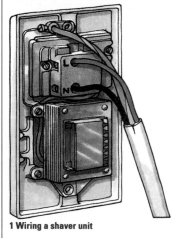

1 Wiring a shaver unit

Powerful appliances such as cookers that have a power load greater than 3000W (3kW) must have their own radial circuits connected directly to the consumer unit, with separate fuses protecting them.

Cookers

Small table cookers and separate ovens that rate no more than 3000W (3kW) can be connected to a ring circuit by a fused connection unit or even by means of a 13amp plug and socket. But most cookers are much more powerful, and must be installed on their own circuits.

The radial circuit

Cookers up to 14kW can be connected on a 30amp radial circuit. Provided that the cooker control unit does not include a 13amp socket outlet, cookers up to 18kW can be connected to a similar circuit. Depending on the length of the relevant circuit, you can use 4mm² or 6mm² two-core-and-earth cable (see CIRCUITS: MAXIMUM LENGTHS).

A separate radial circuit has to have its own fuseway. You can either use a spare fuseway in your consumer unit or, alternatively, fit an individual switchfuse unit – which performs a similar function to the consumer unit but for a single appliance. Ideally buy a switchfuse unit with a 32amp MCB; failing that, one with a 30amp cartridge fuse.

Cooker control units

The cable from the consumer unit runs to a cooker control unit situated within 2m (6ft 6in) of the cooker. The control unit is basically a double-pole isolating switch, but it may also incorporate a single 13amp switched socket outlet that can be used for appliances such as an electric kettle. Nowadays, when more homes have a number of socket outlets installed at worktop height, the extra one on the cooker control unit is not usually important; and it is in fact safer not to have a control unit with a built-in socket if it is to be situated near the hob – so as to avoid the risk of flex trailing across one of the hotplates.

Cooker control units can be either surface-mounted or flush-mounted. The control unit must be easily accessible, so don't install it inside a cupboard or under a worktop.

A single control unit can serve both sections of a split-level cooker, with separate cables running to the hob and the oven, provided that the control unit is within 2m (6ft 6in) of both parts. If this isn't possible with your cooker, you will need to install a separate control unit for each part. The connecting cables must be of the same size as the cable used in the radial circuit.

Because a freestanding cooker has to be moved from time to time for cleaning round and behind it, it should be wired with sufficient cable to allow it to be moved well out from the wall. The cable is connected to a terminal outlet box, which is screwed to the wall about 600mm (2ft) above floor level. A fixed cable runs from the outlet box to the cooker control unit.

1 Cooker control unit with socket
2 Basic control unit **3** Terminal outlet box

Cooker circuit
1 Cooker
2 Terminal outlet box
3 Control unit
4 Radial circuit
5 Consumer unit

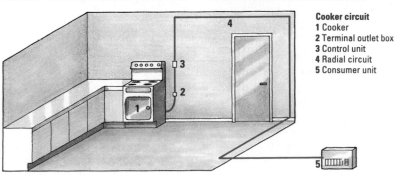

WIRING THE CONTROL UNIT

Having decided on the position for your control unit, if it's to be surface-mounted knock out the cable-entry holes in the mounting box and screw it to the wall. If it's to be flush-mounted, cut a hole in the plaster and brickwork for the metal box.

Running cable

Run and fix the cable, taking the most economical route to the cooker from the switchfuse unit or the consumer unit. Cut a chase in the wall up to the cooker control unit if you are going to bury the cable in the plaster, then cut similar chases for cables running to the separate hob and oven of a split-level cooker or for a single cable running to a terminal outlet box.

Connecting up the control unit

Feed the circuit cable and cooker cable into the control unit, then strip and prepare the conductors for connection. There are two sets of terminals in the control unit: one marked 'Mains' for the circuit conductors, and the other marked 'Load' for the cooker cable. Run the red wires to the L terminals and the black ones to the terminals marked N. Put green-and-yellow sleeves on both earth conductors and connect them to the E terminal (**1**). Screw the faceplate to the mounting box.

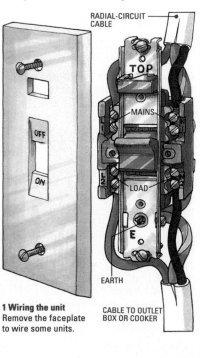

1 Wiring the unit
Remove the faceplate to wire some units.

● **Positioning cooker control units**
Place the control unit to the right or left of the cooker but never directly above it.

CONNECTING THE COOKER

Wiring to the cooker

Connect the cable to the hob and the oven following the manufacturer's instructions exactly.

For a freestanding cooker, run the cable down the wall from the cooker control unit to the terminal outlet box, which has terminals for connecting both of the cables. Strip the wires of the control-unit cable and insert them in the terminals (**1**), then insert the wires of the cooker cable in the same terminals, matching colour for colour, and secure it with the clamp. Screw the plastic faceplate onto the outlet box.

Wiring the switchfuse unit

If you are wiring to a fuseway in your consumer unit, run the red wire to the terminal on the fuseway, the black one to the neutral block, and – having first sleeved it – the earth wire to the earth block. All other connections will already have been made. Don't forget to switch off the power before starting this work, and remember that even then the cable connecting the meter to the main switch is still live.

Here we will assume that the cooker circuit is to be run from a switchfuse unit. Screw the unit to the wall close to the consumer unit, feed the cooker-circuit cable into it, and prepare the conductors for connection. Fix the red wire to the live terminal on the fuseway or MCB, the black wire to the neutral terminal, and the sleeved earth wire to the earth terminal (**2**).

Prepare the meter leads, one black and one red, from PVC-sheathed-and-insulated 16mm² single-core cable. (Use 10mm² cable if 16mm² cable is too thick for the switchfuse-unit terminals, but keep the meter leads as short as possible.) Bare about 25mm (1in) of each cable and connect them to their separate terminals on the main isolating switch, red to L and black to N (**2**). For an earth lead, prepare a similar length of the same size single-core cable sheathed in green-and-yellow PVC and attach it to the earth terminal in the switchfuse unit (**2**) in readiness for connection to the consumer's earth terminal. Don't make the connection to the Company's earth yourself.

Fit the appropriate fuse, then plug in the fuse carrier. Finally, label the carrier to indicate which circuit is run from the unit and fit the cover.

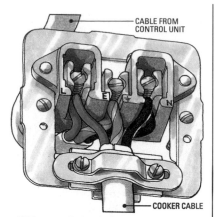

1 Wiring a terminal outlet box

2 Wiring a switchfuse unit for the cooker

CONNECTING TO THE MAINS

A new circuit must be tested by a competent electrician and a certificate stating that the wiring complies with the Wiring Regulations must be submitted to the Electricity Company to apply for connecting to the mains. Do not attempt to make this connection (which has to be made via the meter) yourself.

It may not be possible to attach both sets of meter leads – from consumer unit and switchfuse unit – to the meter, and you may have to install a connector block that has enough terminals to accommodate all the conductors. The Electricity Company will do this for a fee (before starting it's advisable to consult the Company about these matters).

Water in a storage cylinder can be heated by an electric immersion heater, providing a central supply of hot water for the whole house. The heating element is rather like a larger version of the one that heats an electric kettle. It is normally sheathed in copper, but more expensive sheathings of incoloy or titanium will increase the life of the element in hard-water areas.

Adjusting the water temperature
A thermostat to control the maximum temperature of the water is set by adjusting a screw inside the plastic cap that covers the terminal box (**1**).

Types of immersion heater
An immersion heater can be installed from the top of the cylinder or from the side, and top-entry units can have single or double elements. In the single-element top-entry type of heater the element extends down almost to the bottom of the cylinder, so that all of the water is heated whenever the heater is switched on (**2**).

For economy, one of the elements in the double-element type is a short one for daytime top-up heating, while the other is a full-length element that heats the entire contents of the cylinder, using the cheaper night-rate electricity (**3**). A double-element heater that has a single thermostat is called a twin-element heater; one with a thermostat for each element is known as a dual-element heater.

Side-entry elements are of identical length. One is positioned near to the bottom of the cylinder, and the other a little above half way up (**4**).

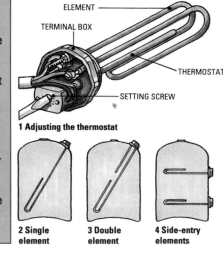

1 Adjusting the thermostat

2 Single element

3 Double element

4 Side-entry elements

WIRING AN IMMERSION HEATER

HEATING WATER ON THE NIGHT RATE

If you agree to have a special meter installed, the Electricity Company will supply you with cheap-rate power for seven hours sometime between mid-night and 8.00 a.m., the exact period being at the discretion of the Company. This scheme is called Economy 7. Provided you have a cylinder that is large enough to store hot water for a day's requirements, you can benefit by heating all your water during the Economy 7 hours. Even if you heat your water electrically only in summer, the scheme may be worthwhile. For the water to retain its heat all day, you must have an efficient insulating jacket fitted to the cylinder or a cylinder already factory-insulated with a layer of heat-retaining foam.

If your cylinder is already fitted with an immersion heater, you can use the existing wiring by fitting an Economy 7 programmer, a device that will switch your immersion heater on automatically at night and heat up the whole cylinder. Then if you occasionally run out of hot water during the day, you can always adjust the programmer's controls to boost the temperature briefly, using the more expensive daytime rate.

You can make even greater savings if you have two side-entry immersion heaters or a dual-element one. The programmer will switch on the longer element – or the bottom one – at night, but if the water needs heating during the day then the upper element is used.

You can have a similar arrangement without a programmer by wiring two separate circuits for the elements. The upper element is wired to the daytime supply, while the lower one is wired to its own switchfuse unit and operated by the Economy 7 time switch during the hours of the night time tariff only. A setting of 75°C (167°F) is recommended for the lower element, and 60°C (140°F) for the upper one. If your water is soft or your heater elements are sheathed in titanium or incoloy, you can raise the temperatures to 80°C (175°F) and 65°C (150°F) respectively without reducing the life of the elements.

To ensure you never run short of hot water, leave the upper unit switched on permanently. It will only start heating up if the thermostat detects a temperature of 60°C (140°F) or less, which should happen very rarely if you have a large, properly insulated cylinder.

The circuit

Immersion heaters are mostly rated at 3kW – but although you can wire most 3kW appliances to a ring circuit, an immersion heater is regarded as using 3kW continuously, even though rarely switched on all the time. A continuous 3kW load would seriously reduce a ring circuit's capacity, so immersion heaters must have their own radial circuits.

The circuit needs to be run in 2.5mm² two-core-and-earth cable protected by a 15amp fuse. Each element must have a two-pole isolating switch mounted near the cylinder; the switch should be marked 'WATER HEATER' and have a neon indicator (1). A 2.5mm² heat-resistant flexible cord runs from the switch to the immersion heater.

If the cylinder is situated in a bathroom, the switch must be inaccessible to anyone who is using the washbasin or the bath or shower. If this precludes a normal water-heater switch, use a 20amp ceiling-mounted pull-switch with a mechanical ON/OFF indicator.

Wiring side-entry heaters

For simplicity use two switches, one for each heater and marked accordingly.

Wiring the switches

Fix the mounting boxes to the wall, feed a circuit cable to each, and wire them in the same way. Strip and prepare the wires, then connect them to the 'Mains' terminals – red to L, black to N. Sheath the earth wire in a green-and-yellow sleeve and fix it to the common earth terminal (2). Prepare a heat-resistant flex for each switch. At each, connect the green-and-yellow earth wire to the common earth terminal and the other wires to the 'Load' terminals – brown to L and blue to N (2). Then tighten the flex clamps and screw on the faceplates.

Wiring the heaters

The flex from the upper switch goes to the top heater, and that from the lower switch to the bottom one. At each heater, feed the flex through the hole in the cap and prepare the wires. Connect the brown wire to one terminal on the thermostat (the other terminal on the thermostat is already connected to the wire running to an L terminal of the heating element). Connect the blue wire to the N terminal and the green-and-yellow wire to the E terminal (3), then replace the caps on the terminal boxes.

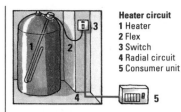

Heater circuit
1 Heater
2 Flex
3 Switch
4 Radial circuit
5 Consumer unit

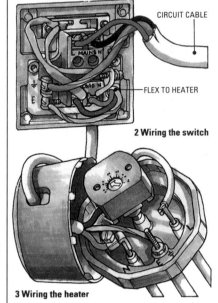

CIRCUIT CABLE

FLEX TO HEATER

2 Wiring the switch

3 Wiring the heater

Running the cable

Run the circuit cables from the cylinder cupboard to the fuse board; then, with the power switched off, connect the cable from the upper heater to a spare fuseway in the consumer unit. Although the consumer unit is switched off, the cable between the main switch and the meter will remain live – so take special care. Wire the other cable to its own switchfuse unit – or to your storage-heater consumer unit, if you have one – ready for connection to the Economy 7 time switch. Make the connections as described for a cooker circuit.

WIRING A DUAL-ELEMENT IMMERSION HEATER

Wire the immersion-heater circuit as described above, but feed the flex from both switches into the cap on the heater. Connect the brown wire from the upper switch to the L2 terminal on one thermostat and the other brown wire to the L1 terminal on the second thermostat (4). Connect the blue wires to their respective neutral terminals (4). Connect both earth wires to E terminal.

1 A 20amp switch for an immersion heater

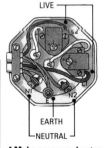

LIVE

EARTH
NEUTRAL

4 Make sure your heater is fitted with two thermostats as shown.

325

STORAGE HEATERS

The heart of a storage heater is a heat-retaining core, or block, that houses heating elements which are supplied with electricity during the off-peak night-time hours to take advantage of the cheap Economy 7 tariff. The storage core is insulated in such a way that it will give off heat gradually during the day. Heat emission is controlled in various ways.

With the earliest storage heaters it was not possible to control the rate of heat emission, and towards the end of the day emission tended to lessen. This is no longer a problem. Modern heaters have dampers to regulate the flow of air through the core and control the rate of heat loss. Some heaters have dampers that are automatically controlled by circuits that monitor the air temperature in the room.

Research has shown that a cold day is usually preceded by a proportionally cold night – and the more sophisticated storage heaters are designed to make use of this fact by storing just the right amount of heat during the night to meet the needs of the following day.

Fan-assisted storage heaters have a similar heat-retaining core, which is efficiently insulated to reduce heat loss to an absolute minimum. When the fan is switched on, it draws air into the heater to be warmed before flowing out into the room. Apart from a very small amount of radiant heat through the casing, heat emission occurs only when required, particularly if the fan is controlled thermostatically.

Storage heaters vary in size. Ratings of ones without fans range from 1.2kW to 3.4kW, and fan-assisted models are rated even higher (up to 6kW). A large area requires a heater with a big heat-retaining core able to store enough heat to warm it; and since cheap-rate power is supplied for only a few hours, a large core needs more powerful elements to charge it completely.

When you install storage heaters, you have to assemble them yourself. Follow the manufacturer's instructions exactly, and handle the heating elements and insulation with care. Make sure that slim heaters are fixed securely to the walls – but leave a 75mm (3in) gap all round so that the air can circulate. Use fibre wall plugs for the fixings, as plastic ones may be softened by the heat.

Drying clothes on a storage heater is likely to make a fusible link in the unit melt. Never assemble or dismantle old secondhand storage heaters – they may contain asbestos.

Outlets for storage heaters

The circuit cable for an ordinary storage heater should terminate at a 20amp double-pole switch with a flex outlet **(1)** that fits into a standard plastic or metal mounting box. A three-core heat-resistant flex connects the switch to the storage heater.

A fan-assisted heater needs a more complex circuit. The heating elements are supplied from a straightforward radial circuit using 4mm^2 cable, but the fan requires its own circuit for daytime use. Take a spur from a ring circuit to a fused connection unit that has a 3amp fuse, and run a 1.5mm^2 two-core-and-earth cable from the unit for the fan. The heater and fan circuits both terminate at a special dual switch **(2)** where fan and heater can be isolated simultaneously. Two lengths of heat-resistant flex run from the switch, one to the heater, the other to the fan. A dual switch can be surface-mounted or flush-mounted.

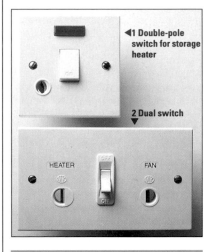

◀1 Double-pole switch for storage heater

2 Dual switch ▼

Electricity Company equipment

Because an Economy 7 storage-heater system uses cheap-rate power, you need a special meter that registers the number of units consumed during the night-time and daytime separately. You also need a time switch to connect the various circuits at the appropriate time.

This equipment is supplied by the Electricity Company, whom you should contact for advice as soon as possible if you plan to have storage heaters. At the same time make sure your present electrical installation is safe, especially the provision for earthing – otherwise the Company may refuse to connect the new circuits.

Storage-heater circuits

Unlike other kinds of electrical heating, all the storage heaters in a house are usually switched on at the same time – a procedure that would overload a ring circuit. You therefore have to provide an individual radial circuit for each heater. A separate consumer unit is installed to cope with the off-peak load.

It's wise to choose a consumer unit that is not only large enough to take all the heater circuits but has spare fuseways for possible additional heaters in the future. Make sure there is an extra fuseway to take the immersion-heater circuit, so your water can be heated at the off-peak rate too. A circuit for an ordinary storage heater up to 3.6kW should be wired with 2.5mm^2 two-core-and-earth cable with a 15amp circuit fuse or 16amp MCB.

Storage-heater circuits
1 Off-peak consumer unit
2 Day-time consumer unit
3 Radial circuits to heaters
4 20amp switch
5 Storage heater
6 Fan-assisted storage heater
7 Dual switch
8 Connection unit
9 Ring circuit

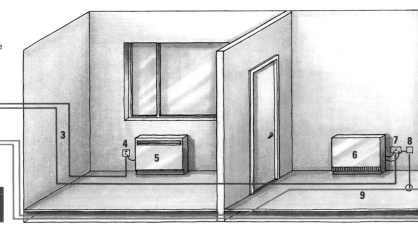

Wiring storage heaters

For ordinary storage heaters, mount a 20amp switch close to where you are planning to stand each heater. Run a single length of 2.5mm² two-core-and-earth cable from each switch to the site of the new consumer unit, taking the most economical route.

Feed a cable into the mounting box of each switch, then strip and prepare the wires and connect them up to the 'Mains' terminals: red to L, black to N. Sleeve the earth wire and connect it to the E terminal **(1)**.

Pass the flex from each heater through the outlet hole in the faceplate of its switch. Strip and prepare the wires, then connect them to the 'Load' terminals: brown to L, blue to N, and the green-and-yellow earth wire to E **(1)**. Tighten the cord clamp and fix the switch into its mounting box.

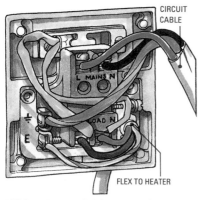

CIRCUIT CABLE

FLEX TO HEATER

1 Wiring a 20amp switch for a storage heater

Wiring fan-assisted heaters

When you wire a fan-assisted heater, mount a dual switch nearby and from its 'heater' side **(2)** run a 4mm² two-core-and-earth cable to the consumer unit.

Mount a fused connection unit near the switch and run a short length of 1.5mm² two-core-and-earth cable between the two, connecting to the 'Load' side of the connection unit and the 'Fan' side of the dual switch **(2)**.

Run a spur of 2.5mm² two-core-and-earth cable from the 'Mains' terminals on the connection unit **(2)** to either a junction box or a socket outlet on the nearest ring circuit.

Feed the fan and heater flex into the outlets in the faceplate of the dual switch and strip and prepare the wires. Connect each flex to its own part of the switch, which is clearly labelled **(2)**.

Tighten the cord clamps and screw the switch to its box.

WIRING THE CONSUMER UNIT

For ordinary storage heaters, fit a 15amp cartridge fuse or 16amp MCB for each heater circuit, and a similar fuse or MCB for an immersion-heater circuit if required. Mount the unit on an exterior-grade plywood board 9mm (⅜in) thick. Even if there's sufficient room, don't mount it on the Electricity Company's meter board.

Screw your board to the wall, using plastic or ceramic insulators to space it away, so that damp won't penetrate it. Get the insulators when you buy the consumer unit. Position the board close to the meter to keep the meter leads as short as possible. Screw the consumer unit to the board; run the circuit cables from the heaters into it one at a time; then prepare the wires for connection.

Each circuit is wired in the same way to a separate fuseway: the red wire to the terminal on the fuseway, the black one to the neutral block, and the earth wire to the earth block after sheathing it with a green-and-yellow sleeve.

Use 16mm² single-core cable for the meter leads. They must be insulated and sheathed in red for the live conductor and black for the neutral. Feed the leads into the consumer unit and connect them to their terminals –red to L, black to N – on the main isolating switch.

Next, connect a length of green-and-yellow 16mm² single-core cable to the earth block. Connect the other end to the consumer's earth terminal, and a further length of the same-size cable to the same earth terminal – this will be connected to the Electricity Company's earth by their representative.

Fit MCBs, or clip a fuse into each of the fuse carriers and insert the carriers into their fuseways. Label all of the circuits clearly so that in future you can tell which heater each one supplies.

Fit the cover on the consumer unit and test the circuits. Submit a signed test certificate to the Company, giving them three days' notice, and they will connect the unit to the meter and earth. Don't in any circumstances try to make these connections yourself.

● **Fuses and MCBs for fan-assisted heaters**
You will need to fit a 30amp circuit fuse or a 32amp MCB for each fan-assisted storage heater (see CIRCUITS: MAXIMUM LENGTHS).

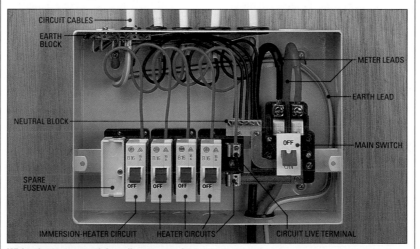

CIRCUIT CABLES

EARTH BLOCK

METER LEADS

EARTH LEAD

NEUTRAL BLOCK

MAIN SWITCH

SPARE FUSEWAY

IMMERSION-HEATER CIRCUIT　　HEATER CIRCUITS　　CIRCUIT LIVE TERMINAL

Wiring the consumer unit for ordinary storage heaters

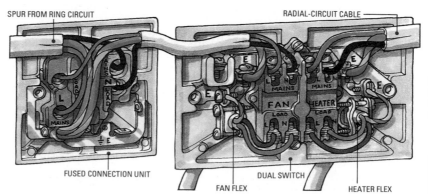

SPUR FROM RING CIRCUIT　　　　RADIAL-CIRCUIT CABLE

FUSED CONNECTION UNIT

FAN FLEX　　DUAL SWITCH　　HEATER FLEX

2 Wiring a dual switch
Connect a fused connection unit to the dual switch.

DOORBELLS, BUZZERS AND CHIMES

Chimes
A set of chimes has
two tubes, each tuned
to a different note.

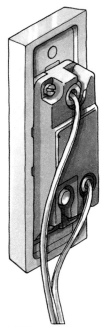

1 Wiring a bell push

Whether you choose a doorbell, a buzzer or a set of chimes, there are no practical differences that affect the way they are installed.

Bells

Most doorbells are of the 'trembler' type. When electricity is supplied to the bell – that is when someone presses the button at the door – it activates an electro-magnet which causes a striker to hit the bell. But as the striker moves to the bell it breaks a contact, cutting off power to the magnet, so the striker swings back, makes contact again and repeats the process, going on for as long as the button is depressed. This type of bell can be operated by battery or, if it is an AC bell, by a mains transformer which may be inside the unit or mounted separately.

Buzzers

A buzzer operates on exactly the same principle as a trembler bell, but in the buzzer the striker hits the magnet itself instead of a bell.

Chimes

A set of ordinary door chimes has two tubes or bars tuned to different notes. Between them is a solenoid, a wound coil that acts like a magnet when it is energized. When the button is pressed, a spring-loaded plunger inside the solenoid is thrown against one tube, sounding a note. When the button is released, the spring throws the plunger against the other tube, sounding the other note before returning to its point of rest. You can also buy chimes with a programmed microprocessor that gives a choice of tunes when operated by the bell push. Most chimes can be run from a battery or a transformer.

Bell pushes

Pressing a bell push completes the circuit that supplies power to the bell. It is in effect a switch that is operated by holding it in the 'on' position. Inside it are two contacts to which the circuit wires are connected. One contact is spring-loaded, touching the other when the button is depressed, to complete the circuit, and then springing back again when the button is released (1).

Illuminated bell pushes incorporate a tiny bulb, which enables you to see the bell push in the dark. These have to be operated from a mains transformer – as the power to the bulb, although only a trickle, is on continuously and would soon drain a battery. Luminous types glow at night without a power supply.

Batteries or transformer?

Some bells and chimes house batteries inside the casing, while other types incorporate a built-in transformer that reduces the 240-volt mains electricity to the very low voltages needed for this kind of equipment. For many doorbells or chimes you can use either method. Most of them take either two or four 1½ volt batteries, but some need a 4½ volt battery that is housed separately.

Transformers sold for use with doorbell systems have three low-voltage tappings – 3 volt, 5 volt and 8 volt – to cater for various needs. Usually 3 volt and 5 volt connections are suitable for bells or buzzers, and the 8 volt tapping is adequate for many sets of chimes.

However, some chimes require a higher voltage, and for these you will need a transformer with 4 volt, 8 volt and 12 volt tappings. A bell transformer must be designed in such a way that the full mains voltage cannot cross over to the low-voltage wiring.

Circuit wiring

The battery, bell push and bell are all connected by two-core insulated 'bell wire'. This fine wire is usually surface run, fixed with small staples, but it can be run under floors and in cupboards too. Bell wire is also used to connect a transformer to a bell and bell push.

Connect a BS 3535 Class 2 double-insulated transformer to a junction box or ceiling rose on a lighting circuit with 1mm² two-core-and-earth cable. As no earth is required for a double-insulated transformer, cut and tape back the cable's earth wire at the transformer end. Alternatively, run a spur from a ring circuit in 2.5mm² two-core-and-earth cable to an unswitched fused connection unit fitted with a 3amp fuse; and then run a 1mm² two-core-and-earth cable from the unit to the transformer's 'Mains' terminals. Or you could run 1mm² two-core-and-earth cable directly from a spare 5amp fuseway in your consumer unit.

INSTALLING A SYSTEM

The bell itself can be installed in any convenient position, so long as it is not over a source of heat. The entrance hall is usually best, as a bell there can be heard in most parts of the house. Keep the bell-wire runs as short as possible, especially for a battery-operated bell. With a mains-powered bell you will want to avoid long and costly runs of cable, so place the transformer where it can be wired simply. A cupboard under the stairs is a good place, especially if it is near the consumer unit.

Drill a small hole in the doorframe and pass the bell wire through to the outside. Fix the conductors to the terminals of the bell push, then screw it over the hole.

If the battery is housed in the bell casing, there will be two terminals for attaching the other ends of the wires. Either wire can go to either terminal. If the battery is separate from the bell, run the bell wire from the push to the bell. Separate the conductors, cut one of them and join each cut end to a bell terminal. Run the wire on to the battery and attach it to the terminals (1).

If you are wiring to a transformer, proceed as above but connect the bell wire to whichever two of the three terminals combine to provide you with the necessary voltage (2). Some bells and chimes require separate lengths of bell wire, one from the bell push and another from the transformer. Fix the wires to terminals in the bell housing, following manufacturer's instructions.

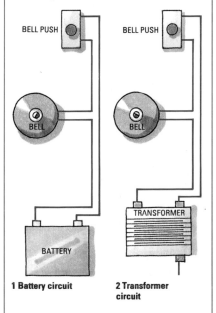

1 Battery circuit

2 Transformer circuit

APPLIANCES
TV AERIALS

WIRING
EXTRA AERIAL
SOCKETS
SEE ALSO

Many people operate only one television set from the aerial mounted on the roof of the house, relying on portable aerials for any additional sets. You can improve reception by extending the main aerial with additional sockets and, at the same time, provide for viewing a video-cassette recorder from any of your television sets.

One convenient arrangement is to connect the output socket from your VCR to a double aerial socket, which acts as a 'splitter', diverting the signal to two television sets. Each set will work independently of the other.

If you want to serve even more sets, you will probably have to substitute a multi-output amplifier in place of the splitter in order to boost the signal. An amplifier is wired in a similar way to the splitter socket, but must also be plugged into a 13amp socket.

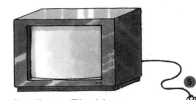

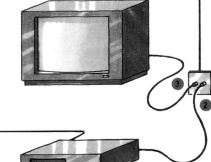

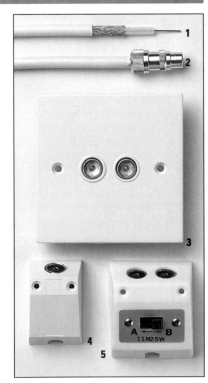

Extending your TV aerial
1 Cable from roof aerial plugs directly into VCR.
2 Output from VCR plugs into double splitter socket.
3 Aerial cable from first TV set plugs into splitter.
4 Coaxial cable runs from the back of the splitter to a single aerial socket.
5 Aerial cable from second TV set plugs into single socket.

CONNECTING COAXIAL PLUGS

Slide the plug's locking ring (1) onto the coaxial cable and strip about 25mm (1in) of the sheathing, taking care not to sever the copper strands beneath. Slide the cable gripper (2) onto the end of the sheathing, then unravel the copper strands and fold them down over the gripper. Cut off excess strands, leaving enough copper to cover the gripper.

Strip all but about 3mm (⅛in) of the polyethylene insulation (3) to reveal the single-core conductor (4). Bend a slight kink in the conductor and insert it in the plug pin (5). Ideally you should secure the conductor with a touch of solder on the tip of the pin, though kinking the conductor usually provides sufficient grip inside the hollow pin. Slide the plug body (6) over the whole assembly and secure it with the locking ring.

1   2   3   4   5   6

Wiring a coaxial plug

Cable and equipment

Aerial sockets are wired with coaxial cable that consists of a single-core solid-copper conductor insulated with polyethylene, which is surrounded by a braided conductor woven from many fine copper strands then sheathed in white, brown or black PVC. Most electrical suppliers stock the required 75ohm cable (1). Coaxial cable is either wired directly into the back of aerial sockets or fitted with special plugs (2) for insertion into the sockets.

Single and double aerial sockets are made with square faceplates (3) for attaching to standard plastic or metal mounting boxes. You can also buy small surface-mounted sockets (4) suitable for screwing to skirting boards.

A double socket can serve to split the incoming signal to two television sets, but if the signal is weak you may find reception is not satisfactory. In that case, either install a signal amplifier or use a switched splitter (5), which allows you to divert the full-strength signal to one set or the other at will.

It is simplest to install only 'female' sockets – those that have holes which accept 'male' coaxial plugs – and fit this type of plug only on all your aerial-extension cables.

Cable, plugs and sockets
1 Coaxial cable 2 Coaxial plug 3 Double-socket faceplate 4 Surface-mounted socket 5 Switched splitter socket

Running coaxial cable

Fit mounting boxes or screw sockets to the skirting in convenient positions for your VCR and television sets, then cut suitable lengths of coaxial cable to run from socket to socket. Although it's quite safe to leave coaxial cable as temporary unfixed 'leads', you can conceal cable runs under floorboards and inside wall cavities – in the same way as you would mains cable. Avoid taking the cable around tight bends.

Wiring the splitter

Prepare a length of coaxial cable to connect the back of the double socket that is to act as the splitter to the back of the single remote socket. Strip about 50mm (2in) of sheathing from the splitter end of the cable and fold back the braided copper strands. Strip about 32mm (1¼in) of insulation from the single-core conductor, then pass the conductor through both terminals (6) and tighten the terminal screws. Fold back the braided copper and trap it along with the cable under the metal clamp (6). Trim off excess copper strands, and then screw the faceplate to the mounting box. The remote socket is wired in a similar way.

6 Wiring a double socket as a splitter

329

INSTALLING
A TELEPHONE
EXTENSION

SEE ALSO

Details for:
Running cable	309–311
Mounting boxes	314–315

Although a telephone company such as British Telecom, Mercury Communications Ltd. or Kingston upon Hull Telephone Department must be employed to install the master socket that is connected to the incoming network cable, you are permitted to install extension cables and sockets yourself. All the necessary equipment is available from DIY outlets or from one of the telephone company's own shops.

You can install as many telephone extension sockets as you want – so long as the total 'Ringer Equivalence Number' (REN) in your house or flat does not exceed four. A telephone is normally allocated an REN of one, but it is advisable to check this before you decide which equipment to purchase. Telephones are made with either 'tone' or 'pulse' dialling, and modern phones can be switched from one to the other. However, the type of dialling does not affect the wiring of extension sockets.

Sockets and accessories
1 Single-socket faceplate
2 Surface-mounted socket
3 Socket doubler
4 Converter plug
5 British Telecom Linebox
6 Insertion tool

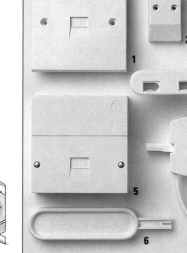

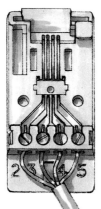

1 Connecting cable to blade terminals
There will be two identical wires per terminal in some sockets.

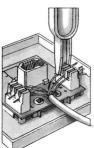

2 Insert wires into screw terminals

Telephone sockets

Single and double sockets designed to accept the small rectangular telephone plugs are made in the form of square faceplates (1) that fit standard electrical metal and plastic mounting boxes. Alternatively, use compact surface-mounted sockets (2). You can run two telephones – or a telephone and an answering machine – from a single socket, without additional wiring, simply by plugging in a 'socket doubler' (3). Run your extension from any master socket by means of a converter plug (4), which normally comes complete with several metres of cable. However, you can wire your extension cable directly into a British Telecom Linebox (5), which has a removable cover to provide customer access without disturbing the company's wiring.

Running the circuit

Fix the extension sockets where most convenient and run a length of cable from the existing master socket to each of the extension sockets. The cable can be pinned to the top of skirting boards or along picture rails and doorframes, using small plastic cable clips.

Alternatively, you can conceal the cable under the floorboards or within walls, provided that you do not follow exactly the same route used for any mains wiring. Both for safety's sake and in order to avoid interference on the line, you should maintain a minimum of 75mm (3in) between telephone cable and mains cables. At each socket, feed a loop of cable into the mounting box ready for connecting to the terminals.

Connecting to the sockets

At each socket, cut the loop of cable and strip the sheathing to expose the colour-coded conductors, then separate the conductors and connect them to the appropriate numbered terminals.

Telephone-socket terminals usually comprise two opposing brass blades that cut into the cable's insulation and make contact with the wire core as the conductor is forced between them with a special insertion tool. Lay the insulated conductor across its terminal, and press it firmly to the base of the terminal (1). Trim the end of the wire.

Other sockets are made with screw terminals, similar to those found in 13amp plugs. Strip about 6mm (¼in) of insulation from the end of each of the conductors, then insert the wire into the terminal and tighten the screw (2).

Sometimes, plastic cable ties are provided to secure the cable inside the socket in order to prevent strain on the actual connections.

TELEPHONE CABLE

Telephones, including extensions, are wired with special extra-low-voltage cable. This cable usually comprises six colour-coded conductors sheathed in PVC. However, four-core cable is often sold for running domestic telephone extensions, and is perfectly adequate provided you match the colour-coded conductors to any existing wiring (see chart below).

Socket terminals are numbered 1 to 6. Always match the same colour coding to the same number terminal in each socket. If you are using four-core cable, ignore terminals 1 and 6.

Number	Colour coding
Terminal 1	Green with white rings.
Terminal 2	Blue with white rings.
Terminal 3	Orange with white rings.
Terminal 4	White with orange rings.
Terminal 5	White with blue rings.
Terminal 6	White with green rings.

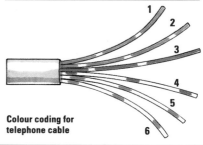

Colour coding for telephone cable

Connecting to the master socket

Plugging a converter plug into the master socket connects all your extensions to the telephone company network. To connect cable to a British Telecom Linebox, remove the front cover (3) and use the insertion tool to introduce the conductors into the bladed terminals, as described left.

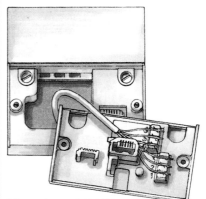

3 Connecting to a British Telecom Linebox

WIRING A SHOWER UNIT

An electrically heated shower unit is plumbed into the mains water supply. The flow of water operates a switch to energize an element that heats the water on its way to the shower spray-head. Because there is so little time to heat the flowing water, instantaneous showers use a heavy load, from 6 to 9.6kW. Consequently, an electrically heated shower unit has to have a separate radial circuit, which must be protected by a 30 milliamp RCD.

The circuit cable needs to be 10mm^2 two-core-and-earth, protected by a 40amp MCB or a 45amp fuse in a spare fuseway at the consumer unit or in a separate 45amp switchfuse unit. The cable runs directly to the shower unit, where it must be wired according to the manufacturer's instructions.

The shower unit itself has its own on/off switch, but there must also be a separate isolating switch in the circuit. This must not be accessible to anyone using the shower, so install a ceiling-mounted 45amp double-pole pull-switch that has a contact gap of at least 3mm, preferably with a neon 'on' indicator. Fix the backplate of the switch to the ceiling and, having sheathed the earth wires with a green-and-yellow sleeve, connect them to the E terminal on the switch. Connect the conductors from the consumer unit to the switch's 'Mains' terminal, and those of the cable to the shower to the 'Load' terminals (1).

The shower unit and all metal pipes and fittings must be bonded to earth.

Every lighting system needs a feed cable to supply power to all the lighting points, and a switch that can interrupt the supply to each point. There are two ways of meeting these requirements in your home: the junction-box system and the loop-in system. Your house may be wired with either one, though it is quite likely that there will be a combination of the two systems.

The junction-box system

With a junction-box system, a two-core-and-earth feed cable runs from a fuse-way in the consumer unit to a series of junction boxes, one for each lighting point. From the junction box, a separate cable runs to the light itself and another runs to its switch.

The loop-in system

In the loop-in system the ceiling rose takes the place of the junction box. The cable from the consumer unit runs into each rose and out again, then on to the next. The switch cable and the flex to the bulb are connected at the rose.

Combined system

The loop-in system is now more widely used since it entails fewer connections, as well as saving on the cost of junction boxes. However, lights located at some distance from a loop-in circuit are often run from a junction box on the circuit in order to save cable, and lights added after the circuit has been installed are often wired from junction boxes.

The circuit

Both the junction-box and the loop-in systems are, in effect, multi-outlet radial circuits. The cable runs from the consumer unit, looping in and out of the ceiling roses or junction boxes and terminating at the last one. Unlike the cable of a ring circuit, it doesn't return to the consumer unit.

Lighting circuits require 1mm^2 or 1.5mm^2 PVC-insulated-and-sheathed two-core-and-earth cable, and each circuit is protected by a 5amp circuit fuse or 6amp MCB. A maximum of twelve 100W bulbs or their equivalent can therefore use the circuit.

In the average two-storey house the usual practice is to have two separate lighting circuits – one for the ground floor and another for upstairs.

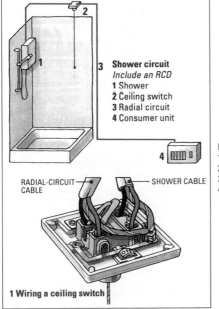

Shower circuit
Include an RCD
1 Shower
2 Ceiling switch
3 Radial circuit
4 Consumer unit

RADIAL-CIRCUIT CABLE — SHOWER CABLE

1 Wiring a ceiling switch

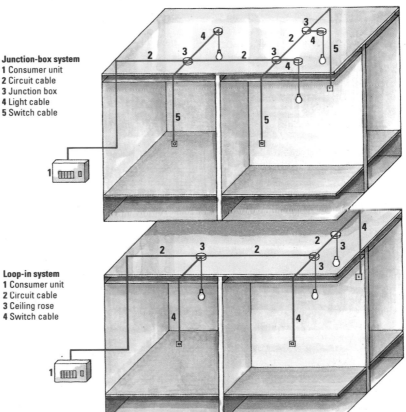

Junction-box system
1 Consumer unit
2 Circuit cable
3 Junction box
4 Light cable
5 Switch cable

Loop-in system
1 Consumer unit
2 Circuit cable
3 Ceiling rose
4 Switch cable

IDENTIFYING

THE

CONNECTIONS

SEE ALSO
Details for:
Lighting circuits   331

Loop-in system

A modern loop-in ceiling rose has three terminal blocks, which are arranged in a row. The live (red) conductors from the two cut ends of the circuit-feed cable run to the live central block, and the neutral (black) conductors run to the neutral block on one side. The earth conductors (green-and-yellow) run to a common earth terminal (1).

The live (red) wire from the switch cable is connected to the remaining terminal in the live central block. The electricity runs through this wire to the switch, then back to the ceiling rose via the black conductor – the 'switch-return wire' – which is connected to the third terminal block in the ceiling rose (the 'switch-wire block'). When the light is 'on', the switch-return wire is live – it

is therefore important to identify it by wrapping a piece of red tape round it to distinguish it from the other black wires, which are neutral. The earth conductor in the switch cable goes to the common earth terminal (1).

The brown (live) conductor from the flex of the pendant light connects to the remaining terminal in the switch block, while the blue conductor runs to the neutral block. If three-core flex is used, the green-and-yellow earth conductor runs to the common earth terminal (1).

If the circuit-feed cable terminates at the last ceiling rose on the circuit, then only one set of cable conductors is connected (2). The switch cable and the light flex are connected in the same way as those in a normal loop-in rose.

Junction-box system

The junction boxes on a lighting circuit normally have four unmarked terminals, for live, neutral, earth and switch connections. The live, neutral and earth conductors from the circuit-feed cable go to their respective terminals (3).

The live (red) conductor from the cable that runs to the ceiling rose has to be connected to the switch terminal; the black wire to the neutral terminal; and the green-and-yellow earth wire to the earth terminal (3).

The red wire from the switch cable is connected to the live terminal; the earth conductor to the earth terminal; and the black 'return' wire (see above) from the switch goes to the switch terminal

(3). This last conductor must be clearly identified by having a piece of red tape wrapped round it.

At the ceiling rose the live cable conductor is connected to one of the outer terminal blocks, and the neutral conductor to the other one. The central block is left empty. The earth conductor goes to the earth terminal (4).

The flex conductors are wired up to match those from the cable. The brown wire is connected to the same terminal block as the red conductor, and the blue wire goes to the block holding the black conductor. If the flex has a green-and-yellow earth wire, it is connected to the common earth terminal (4).

Checking an old light circuit

Having first switched off the power at the consumer unit, remove the circuit fuse and examine the ceiling roses and light switches for signs of deterioration.

In the majority of houses and flats built before World War II the wiring of the lighting circuits was carried out in rubber-insulated-and-sheathed cable. If the rubber sheathing has become dry and crumbly, it is no longer safe and the circuit must be rewired. If you detect any signs that the circuitry is out of date or merely suspect it may be dangerous, consult a professional electrician.

An old installation may have loop-in or junction-box lighting circuits, though the junction-box system is more likely. It may also lack earth conductors, which is another good reason for renewing it.

Old fabric-covered flex should be replaced

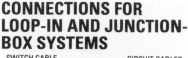

CONNECTIONS FOR LOOP-IN AND JUNCTION-BOX SYSTEMS

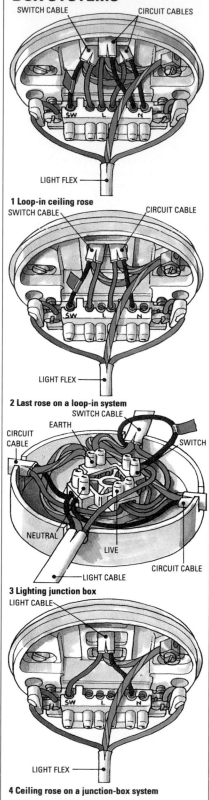

1 Loop-in ceiling rose

2 Last rose on a loop-in system

3 Lighting junction box

4 Ceiling rose on a junction-box system

LIGHT
FITTINGS

REPLACING A CEILING ROSE

Turn off the power at the consumer unit and remove the circuit fuse. Switching off at the wall is not enough.

Unscrew the cover of the rose and examine the connections, so that you can wire the new ones to operate in the same way. If it is a loop-in rose, identify the switch-return wire with red tape if it isn't already marked. If there's only one red and one black conductor, then the rose is on a junction-box system and will therefore have no switch cable.

In an old rose you may have to identify all the wires. If there are wires running into three terminal blocks, look first for the one with all red wires and no flex wires. That is the live block, containing live circuit-feed wires and a live switch wire. The neutral terminal block contains the black neutral circuit-feed wires and the blue flex wire. The third block will contain the brown flex wire plus a black conductor – the switch-return wire – which should be marked with red tape and may even be sheathed in red PVC.

All earth conductors will run to one terminal on the backplate. However, an old system may have no earth wires – in which case reconnect the other wires temporarily and get expert advice on rewiring the circuit.

Fixing the new rose

Disconnect the wires from the terminals and separate any that are twisted together, but identify them with tapes.

Unscrew the old backplate from the ceiling. Knock out the entry hole in the new backplate and thread the cables through it, then fix the backplate to the ceiling, using the old screws and fixing points if possible.

If the old fixings are not secure, nail a piece of wood between the joists above the ceiling (see right) and drill a hole through it from below for cable access. Screw the new rose backplate to the wood through the ceiling.

Make sure that the ends of all the conductors are clean and sound, then rewire the ceiling rose.

Slip the new cover over the pendant flex and connect the flex wires to the terminals in the rose, looping the wires over the rose's support hooks to take the weight off the terminals. Screw the cover onto the backplate, then switch on the power and test the light.

There is now a vast range of lighting fittings that can be used in the home, and though they may differ greatly in their appearance they can be grouped roughly into seven basic categories according to their functions.

Types of light fitting

Pendant lights

The pendant light is probably the most common light fitting. It comprises a lamp-holder with bulb, usually with some kind of shade, suspended from a ceiling rose by a length of flex. The flex is connected to the power supply through terminals inside the ceiling rose (see opposite).

Most decorative pendant-light fittings are designed to take several bulbs, and are consequently heavier than standard pendant lights. Because of its weight, this type of fitting is attached to the ceiling by a rigid tube. The flex that conducts the power to the bulbs passes through the tube to the lighting circuit.

Close-mounted ceiling lights

A close-mounted light fitting is screwed directly to the ceiling, without a ceiling rose, by means of a backplate housing the lampholder or holders. The fitting is usually enclosed by some kind of rigid light-diffuser, which is also attached to the backplate.

Recessed ceiling lights

With this type of light fitting, the lamp housing itself is recessed into the ceiling void, and the diffuser lies flush with, or projects only slightly below, the ceiling. Lights of this type are ideal for rooms with low ceilings; they are often referred to as downlighters.

Track lights

Several individual light fittings can be attached to a metal track which is screwed to the ceiling or wall. Because a contact runs the length of the track, lights can be fitted anywhere along it.

Fluorescent light fittings

A fluorescent light fitting uses a glass tube containing mercury vapour. The voltage makes electrons flow between electrodes at the ends of the tube and bombard an internal coating – which fluoresces, producing light.

Different types of coating make the light appear 'warmer' or 'cooler'. Choose either 'warm white' or 'daylight' for domestic purposes.

The light fitting, which includes a starter mechanism, is usually mounted directly on the ceiling – though, as they produce very little heat, fluorescent lights are also frequently fitted to the underside of cupboards above kitchen work surfaces.

Compact fluorescent lamps can be used in place of conventional bulbs and last up to eight times longer. The tube is folded to make a very small unit. They either have the control circuits built-in or are supplied with plug-in holders containing these controls. Make sure the light fitting can support the weight of a compact fluorescent lamp.

Wall lights

A light fitting adapted for screwing to a wall instead of a ceiling can be supplied from the lighting circuit in the ceiling void or from a spur off a ring circuit. Various kinds of close-mounted fittings or adjustable spotlights are the most popular wall lights.

SEE ALSO	
Details for:	
Lampholders	301
Switching off	302
Close-mounted light	334
Track light	334
Fluorescent light	335
Wall lights	339

Batten holders
A batten holder is a basic fitting with a lamp-holder mounted on a plate that fixes directly to the wall or ceiling. Straight, angled and swivel versions are available. Batten holders are for use in areas such as lofts or cellars where appearance is not important.

Fixing a platform
Skew-nail a board between the joists to support a ceiling rose.

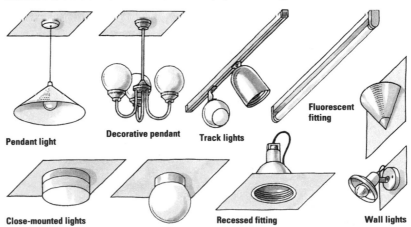

Pendant light

Decorative pendant

Track lights

Fluorescent fitting

Close-mounted lights

Recessed fitting

Wall lights

FITTING A CLOSE-MOUNTED LIGHT

1 BESA box
Use a BESA box, also known as a conduit box, to house the connections when a light fitting is supplied without a backplate. A metal box must be earthed.

Some close-mounted light fittings have a backplate that screws directly to the ceiling in place of a ceiling rose. To fit one, first switch off the power for the circuit at the consumer unit and take out the fuse, then remove the ceiling rose and fix the backplate to the ceiling.

If only one cable feeds the light, attach its conductors to the terminals of the lampholder and connect the earth wire to the terminal on the backplate.

As more heat will be generated in an enclosed fitting, slip heat-resistant sleeving over the conductors before attaching them to their terminals.

If the original ceiling rose was wired into a loop-in system, then you will find that a close-mounted light fitting won't accommodate all the cables. In which case, withdraw them into the ceiling void and wire them into a junction box screwed to a length of 100 x 25mm (4 x 1in) timber nailed between the joists; then run a short length of heat-resistant cable from the junction box to the new light fitting.

FITTING A PLASTIC BESA BOX

Fix a wooden platform between the ceiling joists to support the junction box and the BESA box.

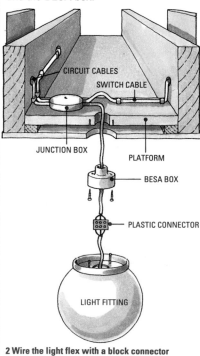

CIRCUIT CABLES
SWITCH CABLE
JUNCTION BOX
PLATFORM
BESA BOX
PLASTIC CONNECTOR
LIGHT FITTING

2 Wire the light flex with a block connector

Sometimes close-mounted lights are supplied without backplates.

Wiring Regulations recommend that all unsheathed wires and terminals must be enclosed in a non-combustible housing – so if you want to use a fitting without a backplate you must find a means of complying. The best way is to fit a BESA box (**1**), a plastic or metal box that is fixed into the ceiling void so as to lie flush with the ceiling.

Screw-fixing lugs on the box should line up with the fixing holes in the light fitting's cover plate, but check that they do so before buying the box. You will also need two machine screws of the right thread for attaching the light to the BESA box.

Check that there is no joist directly above where you wish to fit the light. If there is one, move the light to one side until it fits between two joists. Hold the box against the ceiling, trace round it, and carefully cut the traced shape out of the ceiling with a padsaw.

Cut a fixing board from timber 25mm (1in) thick to fit between the joists, and place it directly over the hole in the ceiling while an assistant marks out the position of the hole on the board from below. Then drill a cable-feed hole centrally through the marked-out shape of the ceiling aperture on the board. This hole must also be able to take any boss on the back of the BESA box. Position the box and screw it securely to the board.

Have your assistant press some kind of flat panel against the ceiling and over the aperture. Fit the BESA box into the aperture from above so that it rests on the panel; mark the level of the fixing board on both joists; and then screw a batten to each joist to support the board at that level.

Fix the board to the battens and feed the cable through the hole in the centre of the BESA box. The light fitting itself will probably have a plastic connector for attaching the cable conductors (**2**), and this may have three terminals – or, alternatively, a separate terminal for the earth conductor may be attached to the cover plate.

When the conductors are secured, fix the cover plate to the BESA box with the machine screws.

If the original ceiling rose was fed by more than one cable, connect them to a junction box in the ceiling void as described above left.

FITTING A DOWNLIGHTER

Decide where you want the light, check from above that it falls between joists, and then use the cardboard template supplied with all downlighters to mark the outline of the circular aperture in the ceiling. Drill a series of 12mm (½in) holes just inside the perimeter of the marked circle to remove most of the waste, then cut it out with a padsaw.

Bring a single lighting-circuit cable from a junction box through the opening and attach the cable to the downlighter, following the maker's instructions. You may have to fit another junction box into the void in order to connect the circuit cable to the heat-resistant flex attached to the light fitting.

Fit the downlighter into the opening and secure it there by adjusting the clamps that bear on the upper, hidden surface of the ceiling.

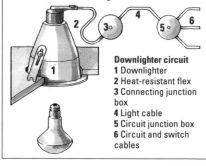

Downlighter circuit
1 Downlighter
2 Heat-resistant flex
3 Connecting junction box
4 Light cable
5 Circuit junction box
6 Circuit and switch cables

FITTING TRACK LIGHTING

Ceiling fixings are supplied with all track-lighting systems. Mount the track so that the terminal-block housing at one end is situated close to where the old ceiling rose was fitted. Pass the circuit cable into the fitting and wire it to the cable-connector provided.

If the circuit is a loop-in system, mount a junction box in the ceiling void to connect the cables.

Make sure that the number of lights you intend to use on the track will not overload the lighting circuit – which can supply a maximum of twelve 100W lamps or their equivalent.

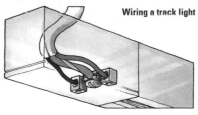

Wiring a track light

Fluorescent lights

Fluorescent light fittings are supplied with terminal blocks for connection to the mains supply.

Remove the ceiling rose and then screw the new light fitting to the ceiling, positioned so that the circuit cable can be fed into it conveniently. The terminal block will take only three conductors, so the fitting must be connected to a junction-box system, or a junction box must be installed in the ceiling void to accommodate loop-in wiring as for a close-mounted light (see opposite).

Fluorescent lights normally need earth connections, so they cannot be used on old systems that have no earth conductors.

You can mount a fluorescent unit by screwing directly into ceiling joists or into boards nailed between joists to provide secure fixings.

Wiring a fluorescent light fitting
A simple plastic block connector for the circuit cable is fitted inside a fluorescent light fitting.

FLUORESCENT LIGHTS UNDER CUPBOARDS

You can fit fluorescent lighting to the underside of wall-mounted kitchen cupboards to illuminate the work surfaces below, the power being supplied from a switched fused connection unit fitted with a 3amp cartridge fuse.

You can install a second fluorescent light fitting and supply its power by wiring it into the terminal block of the first one.

The type of switch most commonly used for controlling lighting is the plateswitch. This incorporates a switch mechanism mounted behind a square faceplate with either one, two or three rockers. Although that is generally adequate for domestic purposes, double faceplates that have as many as four or six rockers are also available.

A one-way switch simply turns a light on and off, but two-way switches are wired in pairs so that the light can be controlled from two places – typically, at the head and foot of a staircase. There is also an intermediate switch that allows a light to be controlled from three places.

Any switch can be flush-mounted in a metal box that is buried in the wall, or surface-mounted in a plastic box. Boxes 16 and 25mm (⅝ and 1in) deep are available to accommodate switches of different depths.

A narrow architrave switch can be used where there is not enough room for a standard switch. There are double versions that have two rockers, one above the other.

A dimmer switch is a device that not only turns the light on and off but also controls the intensity of illumination. In some versions a single knob serves as both switch and dimmer. Others have a separate knob for switching, so that the light level does not have to be adjusted every time the light is switched on.

A conventional switch cannot be mounted within reach of a washbasin, bath or shower unit. To comply with the Wiring Regulations, ceiling-mounted double-pole switches with pull-cords are therefore used in bathrooms.

Fixing switches and running cable

Lighting cable is either run underneath floorboards or within the hollow of cavity walls, or is buried in wall plaster. The mounting boxes and switches are fixed to various walls by exactly the same methods as used for sockets.

Light switches must be installed in relatively accessible positions, which normally means at about adult shoulder height for a wall switch and just inside the door of a room.

TYPES OF SWITCHES

Most light switches are made from white plastic, but you can buy more-interesting finishes to compliment your decorative scheme. Bright primary-coloured switches can look striking in a modern house, while brass antique-reproduction switches are attractive in a traditional interior.

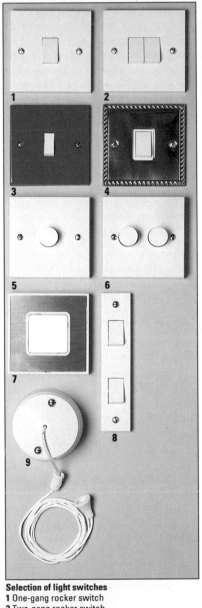

Selection of light switches
1 One-gang rocker switch
2 Two-gang rocker switch
3 Primary-coloured rocker switch
4 Reproduction antique switch
5 One-gang dimmer switch
6 Two-gang dimmer switch
7 Touch dimmer switch
8 Two-gang architrave switch
9 Ceiling switch

REPLACING
SWITCHES

Replacing a damaged switch is a matter of connecting the existing wiring to the terminals of the new switch so that it is connected in exactly the same way as it was in the old one.

Always turn off the power and remove the fuse before you take off the faceplate to inspect the wiring.

In the case of a surface-mounted switch, make sure that a new faceplate will fit the existing box – otherwise you will have to replace both parts of the switch.

If you are able to use the old box, use the old machine screws when you attach the new faceplate. You can then be certain of having screws that will match the old threads.

If you want to replace a surface-mounted switch with a flush-mounted one, remove the old switch, then hold the metal box over the position of the original switch and trace round it. Cut away the plaster to the depth of the box and screw it to the brickwork. Take great care not to damage the existing wiring while you are working.

Replacing a one-way switch

If you look at a one-way switch, you will find that it is serviced by a two-core-and-earth cable. The earth conductor, if there is one, will be connected to an earth terminal on the mounting box; and the red and black conductors will be connected to the switch itself.

A true one-way switch has only two terminals, one situated above the other, and the red or black conductors can be connected to either terminal (1). The back of the faceplate is marked 'top' to ensure that you mount the switch the right way up, so the rocker is depressed when the light is on. The switch would work just as well upside down – but the 'up for off' convention is a useful one, as it tells you whether the switch is on or off even when the bulb has failed.

Occasionally you may come across a light switch that is fed by a two-core-and-earth cable and operates as a one-way switch, yet has three terminals (2). This is a two-way switch that has been wired up for one-way function, something that's fairly common and perfectly safe. If the switch is mounted the right way up, then the red and black wires should be connected to the 'Common' and 'L2' terminals (2).

Replacing a two-way switch

A two-way switch will have at least one conductor in each of its three terminals. Without going into the complexities of two-way wiring at this stage, the most straightforward method of replacing a damaged two-way switch is to make a written note of which conductors run to which terminals before disconnecting the various wires.

Another way is to detach the wires from their terminals one at a time, then connect each one to the corresponding terminal on the new two-way switch before dealing with the next conductor.

Two-gang switches

A two-gang switch is the name for two individual switches mounted on a single faceplate. Each of the switches may be wired differently. One may be working as a one-way switch, and the other as a two-way (3). To transfer the wires from an old switch to the terminals of a new one, work on one switch at a time and use one of the methods for replacing a two-way switch described above.

Replacing a rocker switch with a dimmer switch

Examine the present switch in order to determine the type of wiring that feeds it, then purchase a dimmer switch that will accommodate the existing wiring. The manufacturers of dimmer switches provide instructions with them, but the connections are basically the same as for ordinary rocker switches (4).

Don't attempt to use a dimmer switch to control a fluorescent light.

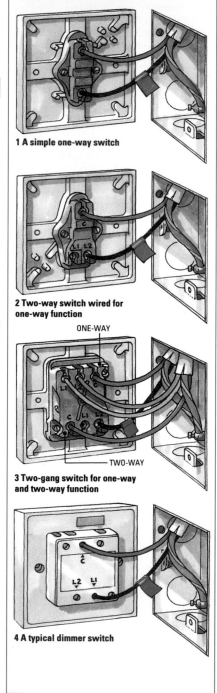

HOW SWITCHES ARE WIRED

It is very easy to replace a damaged switch or swap one for a switch of a different nature. The illustrations below show four common methods of wiring switches. If one of your switches appears to be wired differently, it is probably part of a two-way or three-way lighting system. Replace the switches as described left.

1 A simple one-way switch

2 Two-way switch wired for one-way function

3 Two-gang switch for one-way and two-way function

4 A typical dimmer switch

ADDING NEW SWITCHES AND CIRCUITS

When you want to move a switch or install one where none existed before, you will have to modify the circuit cables or run a new spur cable from the existing lighting circuit to take the power to where it is needed.

Replacing a wall switch with a ceiling switch

Light switches must be out of reach of anyone using a bath or shower. If your bathroom has a wall switch that breaks this rule, replace it with a ceiling switch that is operated by a pull-cord.

Turn the power off at the consumer unit and remove the old switch. If the cable running up the wall is surface-mounted or in a plastic conduit, you can pull it up into the ceiling void. It should be long enough to reach the point where the new switch is to be located.

If the switch cable is buried in the wall, trace it in the ceiling void and cut it. Then wire the part that runs to the light into a three-terminal junction box fixed to a joist or to a piece of wood nailed between two joists. Connect the conductors to separate terminals (1),

and from those terminals run matching 1mm² two-core-and-earth cable to the site of the ceiling switch.

Bore a hole in the ceiling to pass the cable through to the switch. Screw the switch to the joist if the hole is close enough; otherwise fix a support board between joists.

Knock out the entry hole in the backplate of the switch and pass the cable through it, then screw the plate to the ceiling. Strip and prepare the ends of the conductors, connecting the earth to the terminal on the backplate. Connect the red and black conductors to the terminals on the switch – either wire to either terminal (2). Finally, attach the switch to the backplate and make good any damage done to the plasterwork.

1 Link the switch cable with a junction-box

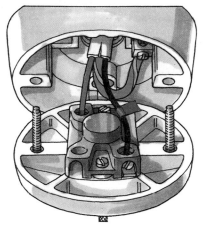

2 Wiring a ceiling switch

Adding a new switch and light

Switch the power off at the consumer unit and inspect your lighting circuit to check whether it is earthed. If there's no earth wire, get expert advice before installing new light fittings.

Decide where you want the light and bore a hole through the ceiling for the cable. Screw a ceiling rose to a nearby joist, or nail a board between two joists to provide a strong fixing for the rose.

Bore another hole in the ceiling right above the site of the new switch and as close to the wall as possible. Push twists of paper through both holes, so you can find them easily from above.

Screw the switch mounting box to the wall and cut a chase in the plaster for the cable up to the appropriate hole already bored in the ceiling.

Your new light fitting can either be supplied from a nearby junction box or ceiling rose that's already on the lighting circuit or, if it is more convenient that way, from a new junction box wired into the lighting-circuit cable.

From whichever of these sources you choose, run a length of 1mm² two-core-and-earth cable to the position of the new light – but do not connect the circuit until the whole of the installation is complete. Push the end of the cable through the hole in the ceiling and identify it with tape (1). Write 'Mains' on the tape to be absolutely sure.

The next step is to run a similar cable

from the switch to the same lighting point. Strip and prepare the cable at the switch – connecting the earth wire to the terminal on the mounting box – and connect the red and black conductors, either wire to either terminal if it is a one-way switch. If you are able to obtain only a two-way switch, connect the wires to its 'Common' and 'L2' terminals (see opposite). Now screw the switch to the mounting box.

Knock out the cable-entry hole in the ceiling rose, feed both cables through it, and screw the rose to the ceiling.

Take the cable marked 'Mains' and connect its red conductor to the live central block and its black one to the neutral block. Slip a green-and-yellow sleeve over the earth wire and connect it to the earth terminal.

Connect the red conductor of the switch cable to the live block, and the black wire to the switch-wire block: mark the black wire with red tape. Connect the switch earth wire to the common earth terminal. Screw the cover on the rose.

Make sure the power is turned off, and then connect the new light circuit to the old one at the rose or junction box. The new conductors will have to share terminals that have already been connected: red to live, black to neutral, and earth to earth (2). Finally, test and switch on the new circuit.

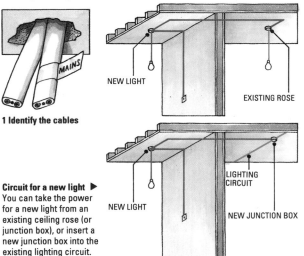

1 Identify the cables

NEW LIGHT

EXISTING ROSE

LIGHTING CIRCUIT

NEW LIGHT

NEW JUNCTION BOX

Circuit for a new light ▶
You can take the power for a new light from an existing ceiling rose (or junction box), or insert a new junction box into the existing lighting circuit.

NEW LIGHT CABLE

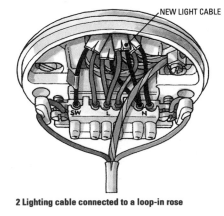

2 Lighting cable connected to a loop-in rose

ADDING TWO- OR THREE-WAY LIGHTING

Adding a two-way light

There are several situations in which a light should be controllable from two points. A hall light is best switched from both ends of the passageway, and a landing light must be controlled from the top and bottom of the stairs.

Installing a new two-way light is very similar to installing a one-way light, the only real difference being in the wiring of the switches.

First mount the ceiling rose and both two-way switches, then run 1mm² two-core-and-earth cable from the power source to the light and from the light to the nearest switch. Don't connect the new installation to the circuit till all the wiring has been completed.

Run a 1mm² three-core-and-earth cable from the first to the second switch. Then strip the conductors and prepare them for connecting to the switches, slipping insulating sleeves over the bare ends of the earth wires.

At the first switch you will have two cables to connect: the switch cable from the light and the one linking the switches. The switch cable has three conductors (red, black and green-and-yellow); the linking cable has four (red, yellow, blue and green-and-yellow). Take the two green-and-yellow wires, twist their bare ends together and connect them to the earth terminal on the mounting box (1).

Connect the red wire from the linking cable to the 'Common' terminal on the switch. Twist together the ends of the yellow wire and either the red or black switch-cable wire, and connect them to the 'L1' terminal. Twist together the ends of the blue wire and the remaining switch-cable wire, and connect them to the 'L2' terminal (1). Screw the switch's faceplate to the mounting box.

At the second switch, connect the linking cable's green-and-yellow wire to the earth terminal; its red wire to the 'Common' terminal; its yellow wire to 'L1'; and its blue wire to 'L2' (1). Screw the switch's faceplate to the box.

Make sure the power is switched off, and then connect the installation to the lighting circuit at either a ceiling rose or a junction box. Test the new installation.

Three-way lighting

You can control a light from three places by adding an intermediate switch to the circuit described above.

This intermediate switch interrupts the three-core-and-earth cable linking the other two. It has two 'L1' terminals and two 'L2' ones.

At its mounting box you will have two identical sets of wires – red, yellow, blue and green-and-yellow. Connect the green-and-yellow wires to the earth terminal of the box (2) and join the two red wires – which play no part in the intermediate switching – with a plastic block connector (2). Ease the block to one side, in order to clear the switch when you fit it.

Connect the blue and yellow wires of either cable to the 'L1' terminals on the new switch and those of the other cable to the 'L2' terminals (2). Screw the faceplate to the mounting box.

Two-way-lighting circuit (right)
1 Consumer unit
2 Light fitting
3 Lighting-circuit cable
4 Switch cable
5 Switch
6 Linking cable
7 Junction box

Three-way-lighting circuit (far right)
1 Consumer unit
2 Light fitting
3 Lighting circuit
4 Switch cable
5 Switch
6 Intermediate switch
7 Linking cable
8 Junction box

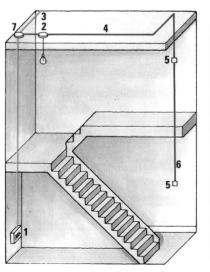

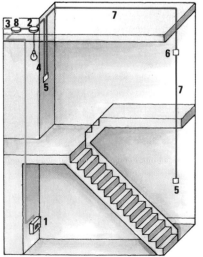

WIRING TWO-WAY AND THREE-WAY SWITCHES

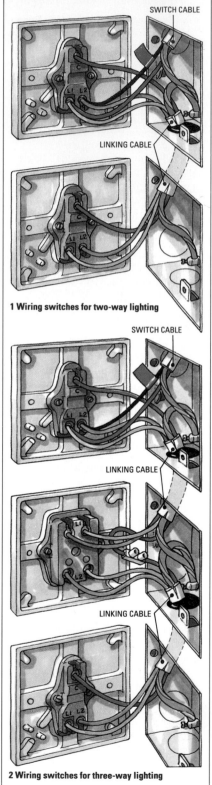

SWITCH CABLE

LINKING CABLE

1 Wiring switches for two-way lighting

SWITCH CABLE

LINKING CABLE

LINKING CABLE

2 Wiring switches for three-way lighting

ADDING
WALL LIGHTS

Many wall lights are supplied without integral backplates to enclose the wires and connections. In order to comply with the Wiring Regulations such a fitting must be attached to a non-combustible mounting such as a BESA box – a round plastic or metal box that's screwed to the wall in a recess chopped out of the plaster and brickwork.

Alternatively, you can use an architrave-switch mounting box. This is a slim box that leaves plenty of room on each side for the wall-plug fixings needed for the light fitting.

Both mounting boxes are fixed to the wall like a flush-mounted socket.

The basic circuit and connections

The simplest way to connect wall lights to the lighting circuit is via a junction box. The procedure is to complete the wall-light installation first, then switch off the electricity and connect the new installation with the junction box.

Wire up a one-way switch. All the wall lights in the room will be controlled by this switch, though if you choose lights that have integral switches they can be controlled individually too.

Next, run a 1mm^2 two-core-and-earth cable from the junction box, looping in and out of each wall-light mounting to the last one, where the cable ends.

Prepare the cut ends of the conductors for connection. At each of the lights, slip green-and-yellow sleeving over the earth wires and connect them to the earth terminal on the mounting box (1).

Connect up the red and black wires to a block connector inside each light fitting: the black conductors to the terminal holding the blue wire, and the red ones to the terminal holding the brown wire (1).

The last wall-light mounting will have one end of the cable entering it. Strip and prepare the ends of the wires, then connect them as described above.

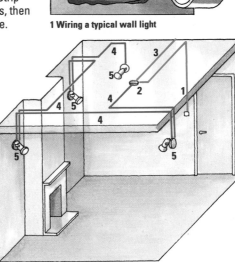

1 Wiring a typical wall light

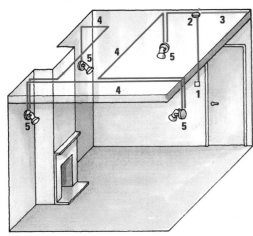

Basic wall-light circuit
The basic circuit and connections are as described above.
1 Switch
2 Junction box
3 Existing lighting circuit
4 Wall-light cable
5 Wall light

Replacing a ceiling light
You can dispense with a ceiling light in favour of wall lights, using the existing wiring and switch. Switch off the power, then remove the rose and connect up the wiring to a fixed junction-box.
1 Existing switch and cable
2 Junction box replaces rose
3 Existing lighting circuit
4 1mm^2 wall-light cable
5 Wall light

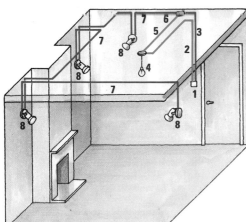

Ceiling light plus wall lights
If you want to retain your ceiling light, you can substitute a double-gang switch for the single one, and wire the present ceiling-light cable to one half of the switch and the new wall-lighting cable to the other half.
1 Double-gang switch
2 Old switch cable
3 New switch cable
4 Ceiling light
5 Existing lighting circuit
6 Junction box
7 1mm^2 wall-light cable
8 Wall light

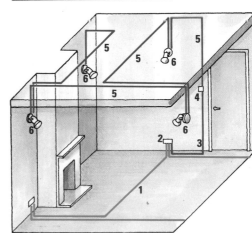

Using a spur
Wall lights can be wired to a ring circuit by means of a spur cable. Run a 2.5mm^2 two-core-and-earth spur from a nearby socket to a switched fused connection unit that has a 3amp fuse.
1 Ring circuit
2 Socket outlet
3 Spur cable
4 Fused connection unit
5 1mm^2 wall-light cable
6 Wall light

USING
ELECTRICITY
OUTDOORS

● **Cutting through electrical flex**
If you accidentally cut the flex that services a power tool, switch off and unplug the tool before you inspect it or touch the severed flex.

There are good reasons for extending your electrical installation outside the house. First, and most important, it is safer to run electric garden tools from a convenient, properly protected socket than to trail long leads from sockets inside the house – a practice that can lead to serious accidents.

A garage or workshop is also safer, and more efficient, if it is equipped with good lighting and its own circuit from which to run power tools.

Finally, well-arranged spot or floodlighting and waterfalls or fountains powered by electric pumps can add considerably to the charm of a garden or patio and extend its use in summer by providing a pleasing background for barbecues and outdoor parties.

SAFETY OUTDOORS

The need for absolute safety outdoors cannot be overemphasized. Damp conditions and the fact that users are likely to be in direct contact with the earth can result in fatal accidents if you don't follow the correct procedures.

● Install only light fittings specifically made for outside use.

● Use only cables recommended in the Wiring Regulations, and check their condition regularly.

● Protect all outside installations with residual current devices (RCDs), as they provide an almost instantaneous response to earth-leakage faults.

● Always disconnect the power before servicing electrical equipment and tools. Don't handle pool lighting or pumps unless the power has been switched off.

● Wear thick rubber-soled footwear when you use electric garden tools.

● Choose double-insulated power tools for extra protection.

Porch-light circuit
1 Loop-in circuit and switch cables
2 Ceiling rose
3 1mm² lighting cable
4 Junction box
5 Porch light
6 Switch cable
7 Porch-light switch

Fitting a porch light

A light that illuminates the front or back entrance to your home suggests a welcoming atmosphere to visitors and helps them to identify the house. It also enables you to view unexpected callers before you open the door.

Fit only a light specifically designed for outdoor use. The fitting should be weatherproof, and the lamp or bulb itself should be held in a moisture-proof rubber gasket or cup that surrounds the electrical connections.

If possible, position the porch light in such a way that the cable to it can be run straight through the wall or ceiling of the porch directly into the back of the fitting. But if you do have to run ordinary cable along an outside wall, it should be protected by being passed through a length of plastic conduit.

Wiring procedure
A porch light is installed by a procedure very similar to that for adding a new light indoors. Take your power from the nearest ceiling rose – probably in the entrance hall – and run it to a 5amp four-terminal junction box screwed to a board between ceiling joists.

From the junction box, run a 1mm² two-core-and-earth cable to a switch mounted near the door, and a similar cable to the light fitting itself. Using a large masonry drill, bore a hole through the wall where you plan to position the light. Cement a short length of plastic conduit into the hole, using a soft rubber grommet to seal each end of the tube. Run the cable through the conduit; wire it into the fitting, following the manufacturer's instructions; and then, with the power switched off, connect the new porch-light cable at the ceiling rose.

INSTALLING A SOCKET FOR GARDEN TOOLS

Many people plug garden tools into the nearest indoor socket – which often results in long extension leads trailing across the kitchen or living room out into the garden. A lead that is likely to cause someone to trip is dangerous – and, even more importantly, the Wiring Regulations stipulate that any socket outlet supplying mains power to garden tools or equipment must be protected by a residual current device (RCD) with a trip rating of 30 milliamps. This device automatically switches off the power as soon as it detects a fault, before anyone who is using the equipment can receive a fatal electric shock.

Sockets can be mounted outside the house provided that they are protected from the weather, although the special procedures involved are best left to a qualified electrician. But you can install a socket in a weatherproof workshop or garage, or lobby or conservatory that's part of the house by running a spur from a ring circuit. Mount it high enough to avoid being struck by a wheelbarrow or hidden by sacks or garden tools.

You can provide RCD protection in several ways. Perhaps the best method is to have a consumer unit with its own built-in residual current device or fit a separate RCD near the consumer unit so that it protects the whole ring circuit, including a spur for garden equipment. Alternatively, install a socket that incorporates an RCD (1). RCDs fitted in adaptors (2) or plugs provide some protection, but they do not satisfy the requirement in the Regulations for the socket itself to be protected.

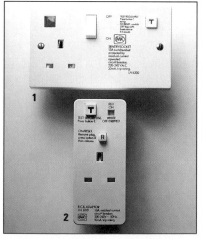

1 Socket with built-in RCD
2 Adaptor RCDs plug into any socket outlet

Any form of exterior lighting that illuminates the approaches to your house and garage allows you to move about your home with greater comfort and safety and, if it's controlled automatically, it saves you having to fumble with your door keys in the dark. However, probably higher on most people's list of priorities is the added security afforded by installing a system that will detect the presence of intruders and draw attention to their activities.

Dusk-to-dawn lighting

You cannot feel completely secure if you have to remember to switch on exterior lighting every evening. The simplest solution is therefore to install exterior light fittings that are controlled automatically by the ambient light level. Known as dusk-to-dawn lights, these fittings create permanently illuminated areas during the hours of darkness. A photocell detects a change in the level of daylight, switching the lamp on at the approach of darkness and off again early in the morning.

For larger properties, it may be more economical to install a single photocell that controls a number of ordinary exterior light fittings.

The circuit
From a junction box installed in your domestic lighting circuit (1), run a 1mm² two-core-and-earth cable to the light fitting (2) and another cable of the same size from the junction box to an ordinary wall switch (3). If you want to install more than one light fitting, run the cable from the junction box to each light in turn, using the single switch to control all of them.

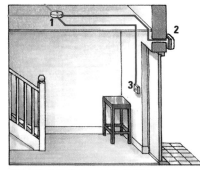

Wiring dusk-to-dawn security lighting
1 Junction box inserted in existing lighting circuit.
2 Light fitting with built-in photocell.
3 Wall switch.

Mounting the light fitting

Follow the manufacturer's fitting instructions, and make sure the light fitting is mounted high enough to prevent unauthorized interference. Drill the cable-access hole through the wall, and line it with a short length of plastic conduit (see opposite). At the same time, bore holes for wall plugs to take the fixing screws provided.

Pass a length of cable through the hole in the wall and into the back of the fitting. Screw the fitting to the wall.

Inside the fitting, cut the separate conductors to length, leaving enough slack to reach their separate terminals. Connect the black conductor to the neutral terminal and the red one to the live terminal – these may have internal wiring already connected to them (1). Fit green-and-yellow sleeving over the bare earth conductor and connect it to the earth terminal. If required, connect the internal wires running from the photocell; then fit the bulb or tube in the fitting and replace its cover.

Run the cable from the light fitting along the most convenient route back to where you plan to connect up to the lighting circuit – but do not cut the lighting cable at this stage.

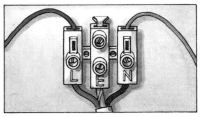

1 Wiring the light fitting

Mounting the light switch

Screw a plastic or metal mounting box to the wall for the switch and cut a chase in the plaster for the cable. Run the cable into the mounting box and connect the black and red conductors to the terminals of a simple one-way switch (2). Sleeve the earth conductor and connect it to the earth terminal in the mounting box. Screw the faceplate to the mounting box, then take the cable to the point in the lighting circuit where you plan to install the junction box.

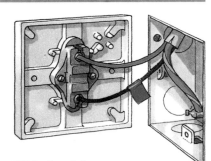

2 Wiring the switch

Connecting to the lighting circuit

Having first switched off the power at the consumer unit and removed the lighting-circuit fuse, cut the lighting cable in order to install a four-terminal junction box. Screw the box securely to a joist. The terminals are normally unmarked, so it's up to you to designate them as live, neutral, earth and switch.

Prepare the cut ends of the lighting-circuit cable and connect the live, neutral and earth conductors to their respective terminals (3).

Prepare the end of the cable running from the light fitting and connect its red conductor to the switch terminal (3). Connect its black conductor to the neutral terminal, and its sheathed earth conductor to the earth terminal.

Prepare the end of the cable running from the switch and then connect its red conductor to the live terminal, the sleeved earth conductor to the earth terminal, and its black conductor to the switch terminal (3). Identify this last conductor by wrapping a piece of red tape round it. Make sure that all the connections are secure, and then refit the cover of the junction box.

Finally, put the lighting-circuit fuse back in the consumer unit and switch the power supply on again.

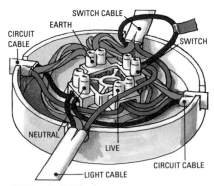

SWITCH CABLE
EARTH
CIRCUIT CABLE
SWITCH
NEUTRAL
LIVE
CIRCUIT CABLE
LIGHT CABLE

3 Wiring the junction box

SEE ALSO

Details for:	
Switching off	302
Running cable	309–311
Lighting circuits	331
Circuit lengths	346

● **Adjusting security lighting**
On some dusk-to-dawn light fittings, a screw is provided for adjusting the sensitivity of the photocell. Wait until it is getting dark; then, with the wall switch in the 'on' position, gradually turn the adjustment screw until the light comes on. The photocell will continue to operate your security lighting, provided the wall switch is left on permanently.

Exterior lighting connected to a passive infra-red detector illuminates only when the sensor picks up the body heat of someone within range. Because the detector is also fitted with a photocell, the lighting only operates at night. A passive infra-red system has two advantages over simple dusk-to-dawn lighting. A porch light, for example, switches on only as you or a visitor approaches the entrance, then switches off again after a set period. Consequently, you are not wasting electricity by burning a lamp continuously all night. Secondly, remote passive infra-red detectors can be positioned to detect movement of an intruder almost anywhere around your home and will switch on all your security lights or only those you think necessary. The effect is likely to startle intruders and hopefully deter them from approaching any further.

Light fittings and sensors

Because infra-red detectors are designed to be mounted about 2.5m (8ft) above ground level, light fittings made with integral detectors tend to be for porch lighting and are usually styled accordingly. However, because the lighting is operated for periods of no more than a few minutes at a time, remote detectors are often used to control powerful halogen floodlights. Floodlights are also available with built-in detectors to simplify the wiring.

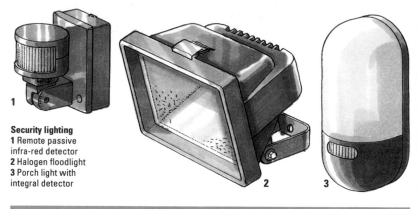

Security lighting
1 Remote passive infra-red detector
2 Halogen floodlight
3 Porch light with integral detector

Positioning detectors

Unless you position detectors carefully, your security lighting will be activated unnecessarily. This can be a nuisance to neighbours and, as with any security device that's constantly giving false alarms, you will soon begin to mistrust it and ignore its warnings.

Infra-red detectors have sensitivity controls so that they won't be activated by moving foliage or the presence of small animals. However, if your house is close to a footpath, you will need to adjust the angle of the detector so that the lights don't switch on every time a pedestrian passes by.

When fitting a remote detector, make sure it isn't aimed directly at a floodlight that it is controlling – or its photocell will try to switch off the light as soon as it illuminates, and the likely result will be a light that simply flickers and never fully illuminates the scene.

It is also important not to position an infra-red detector above a balanced flue from a boiler or any other source of heat that could activate the sensor.

The circuit

It is usually possible to wire infra-red security lighting in exactly the same way as dusk-to-dawn lighting. However, as some detectors are capable of controlling several powerful floodlights, you may not be able to run them from the domestic lighting circuit. In which case, you will need to run a 2.5mm^2 two-core-and-earth spur from a power circuit and control the lighting with a switched fused connection unit. Install a 3amp fuse in the connection unit for a combined rating of up to 720W, or a 13amp fuse for anything greater.

Wiring a remote sensor

Wire an individual light fitting that has an integral infra-red detector in the same manner as a dusk-to-dawn fitting unless the manufacturer's instructions suggest an alternative method.

To wire a remote sensor controlling light fittings mounted elsewhere, take the incoming cable from the junction box or fused connection unit into the back of the fitting and connect its red and black conductors to the 'Mains' terminals (1). Run a second cable of the same size from the 'Load' terminals (1) back through the wall and on to the first light fitting. Sleeve both bare copper earth conductors and connect them to the earth terminal (1).

Wire the first light fitting using the method described for a dusk-to-dawn fitting, then connect another cable to the same terminals and run it on to the second light fitting and so on.

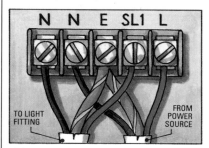

1 Wiring a remote sensor

Adjusting infra-red detectors

Having made all the connections, you need to set the infra-red detector's adjustment knobs or screws. One of them is for setting the photocell so that the system only operates during the hours of darkness. A second control dictates the period of time that the lights will remain on – three or four minutes should be sufficient to make any intruder feel conspicuous. Some sensors are fitted with a sensitivity control to avoid 'nuisance' operation.

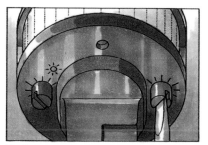

The final operation is to set the sensor's controls

Just a few outdoor light fittings can transform a garden dramatically. Spot or floodlights can emphasize particularly attractive features, at the same time providing functional lighting for pathways and steps, while strings of light bulbs woven through foliage afford attractive background illumination. The most impressive effects are produced with underwater lights, which can make small pools or fountains the focal points of a garden.

Extra-low-voltage lighting

A number of garden light fittings can be powered directly from mains electricity, though they need to be installed by a professional electrician. However, you can install light fittings or a complete lighting kit yourself if they connect up to an extra-low-voltage transformer.

Store the transformer under cover in a garage or workshop, close to a 13amp socket outlet, and connect it to the socket by an ordinary square-pin plug. The flex, which is normally supplied with the light fitting, is connected to the two 12 volt outlet terminals on the transformer. Carry out the connections to the lights following the instructions supplied by the manufacturer.

Unless the makers state otherwise, extra-low-voltage flex supplying garden lights can be run along the ground without further protection, but inspect it regularly and don't let it trail over stone steps or other sharp edges that could damage the PVC insulation if someone steps on it. If you have to add extra flex, use a waterproof connector.

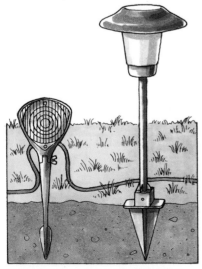

Typical extra-low-voltage garden light fittings

Pool lighting

Pool lights are normally submerged so as to have at least 18mm (¾in) of water above their lenses. Some are designed to float unless they are held below the surface by smooth stones placed carefully on the flex.

Submerged lights get covered by the particles of debris that float in all ponds. To clean the lenses without removing the lights from the water, simply direct a gentle hose over them.

Occasionally you will have to remove a light and wash the lens thoroughly in warm soapy water. Always disconnect the power supply before you handle the lights or take them out of the pond.

Run the flex for pool lighting under the edging stones via a drain made from corrugated plastic sheeting. The entire length of the flex can be protected from adverse weather by being run through a length of ordinary garden hose. Take the safest route to the power supply, anchoring the flex gently in convenient spots – but do not cover it with soil or grass in case someone inadvertently cuts through it with a spade or fork. Join lengths of low-voltage cable with waterproof connectors.

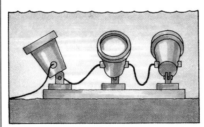

Stand underwater floodlights on a flat stone

Pumps

Electric pumps in garden pools provide fountains and waterfalls. A combination unit will send an adjustable jet of water up into the air, at the same time pumping water through a plastic tube to the top of a rockery to trickle back into the pool.

Some pumps run directly from the mains supply. To fit these, follow the manufacturer's instructions and consult an electrician. But there are also extra-low-voltage pumps that connect to a transformer shielded from the weather (see left). So you can disconnect the pump without disturbing the extra-low-voltage wiring to the transformer, join two lengths of cable with a waterproof connector. Conceal the connector under a stone or gravel beside the pool.

Most manufacturers recommend you take a pump from the water at the end of each season, clean it thoroughly, then return it to the water immediately. To avoid corrosion, don't leave it out of the water for very long without cleaning and drying it. Never service a pump without first disconnecting it from the power supply. During the winter, run the pump for an hour every week to keep it in good working condition.

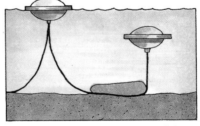

Place a stone on the cable to submerge a light

● **Extra-low-voltage**
This is the strictly correct term to describe equipment that runs on 50V or less. However, manufacturers and suppliers often use the term low-voltage to describe similar equipment.

Waterproof cable connector
A suitable cable connector is available from pump and lighting suppliers.

SEE ALSO
Details for:
Pond drain   471

Pump and lighting circuits
1 Socket outlet
2 BS3535 Type 3 isolating transformers
3 Plastic conduit
4 Waterproof connectors
5 Home-made drain
6 Pump cable
7 Lighting cable

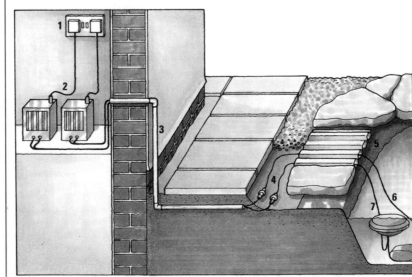

343

RUNNING POWER TO OUTBUILDINGS

The power supply to a separate workshop, garage or toolshed cannot be tapped from other domestic circuits.

The cable must run from a switchfuse unit or from its own fuseway in the consumer unit and pass safely underground or overhead to the outside location – where it has to be wired into a switchfuse unit from which the various circuits in the outbuilding can be distributed as required.

Types of cable permitted outdoors

Three types of cable can be used outside. The type you choose will depend on how you wish to run the cable.

Armoured cable
This two-core or three-core cable is insulated in the ordinary way but is also protected by a steel-wire armour, which is itself insulated with an outer sheath of PVC. In the two-core cable the wire armour provides the path to earth, but some authorities insist on three-core cable, which has an earth wire.

Armoured cable is expensive, and must be terminated at a special junction box at each end of its run where it can be connected to ordinary PVC-insulated cable. It is fitted with threaded glands for attaching it to the junction boxes. This type of cable needs no additional protection when buried in the ground.

Mineral-insulated copper-sheathed cable
The only other cable that can be buried without additional protection is mineral-insulated copper-sheathed (MICS) cable. This has bare copper conductors tightly packed in magnesium-oxide powder within a copper sheathing. The copper sheathing can act as the earth conductor, and is itself sheathed in PVC insulation. Because the mineral powder absorbs moisture, special seals must be fitted at the ends of the cable.

Like armoured cable, MICS cable is expensive and must be terminated at special junction boxes in order to use cheaper cable in the outbuilding itself.

PVC-insulated-and-sheathed cable
Ordinary PVC-insulated two-core-and-earth cable can be run underground to an outbuilding providing it is protected against damage by being enclosed in an impact-resistant plastic conduit. If it has to go round corners, elbow joints are cemented onto the ends of straight runs of conduit. The electrical cable itself can be continuous. This is a much cheaper way of taking power to an outbuilding than installing armoured or MICS cable.

PVC-insulated cable can also be run overhead quite safely under certain specified conditions (see below).

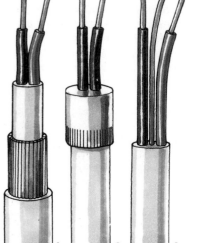

Outdoor cables
1 Armoured cable
2 Mineral-insulated copper-sheathed cable
3 PVC-insulated-and-sheathed cable

Ways of running outdoor cable

Protecting underground cable
Support paving slabs on bricks to protect a cable at the bottom of a trench.

Underground
Running cable underground is usually the best way of supplying electricity to an outbuilding.

You should bury the cable in a trench at least 500mm (1ft 8in) deep, or deeper still if the cable has to pass under vegetable plots or other areas where digging is likely to go on.

It's best to plan your cable run so as to avoid such areas wherever possible. But you can provide extra protection for the cable by laying housebricks along both sides of it to support a covering made from pieces of paving slab. You can also bury special black-and-yellow-striped tape to serve as a warning to anyone who happens to uncover the slabs at a later date.

Line the bottom of the trench with finely sifted soil or sand, lay the cable, and then carefully fill in.

Overhead
Ordinary PVC-insulated cable can be run from house to outbuilding provided that it is at least 3.5m (12ft) above the ground or 5.2m (17ft) above a driveway that's accessible to vehicles. The cable may not be used unsupported over a distance of more than 3m (10ft), though the same distance can be spanned by running the cable through a continuous length of rigid steel conduit suspended at a height of at least 3m (10ft) above the ground or 5.2m (17ft) above a driveway. The conduit itself must be earthed.

Over greater distances, the cable must be supported by a metal catenary wire stretched taut between the house and outbuilding. The supporting wire must be earthed. The cable is clipped to it or hung from slings.

PVC-insulated cable can also be run through conduit mounted on a wall.

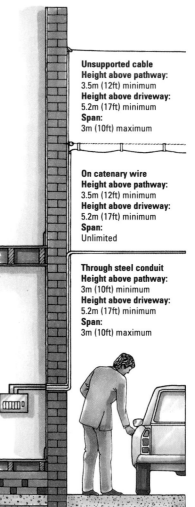

Unsupported cable
Height above pathway:
3.5m (12ft) minimum
Height above driveway:
5.2m (17ft) minimum
Span:
3m (10ft) maximum

On catenary wire
Height above pathway:
3.5m (12ft) minimum
Height above driveway:
5.2m (17ft) minimum
Span:
Unlimited

Through steel conduit
Height above pathway:
3m (10ft) minimum
Height above driveway:
5.2m (17ft) minimum
Span:
3m (10ft) maximum

Running cable overhead

A variety of equipment and cables can be used to run a circuit to an outbuilding. The method described here uses normal PVC-insulated cable and a switchfuse unit at each end of the circuit – but you can start in a spare fuseway in the consumer unit if one is available.

It is assumed that sockets and lighting are required in the outbuilding, so the lighting circuit is taken from the power cable via a junction box and an unswitched fused connection unit. Run the cable underground in impact-resistant plastic conduit, entering both buildings above the DPC and, if possible, beneath the floorboards.

House end of the circuit

Mount a 30amp switchfuse unit near the meter and then fit a 30amp circuit fuse. Install a residual current device between the unit and the meter.

Next, run 10mm^2 two-core-and-earth cable from the 'Load' terminals of the RCD to the 'Mains' terminals of the switchfuse unit. Connect the outgoing 4mm^2 cable to the 'Load' terminals (1) of the switchfuse unit.

Prepare one red and one black 16mm^2 PVC-sheathed-and-insulated cable for the meter leads and attach them to the 'Mains' terminals of the RCD.

Wire a 16mm^2 earth lead to the RCD (1) in readiness for connection to the consumer's earth terminal. Don't try to make the connections to the meter and Company's earth yourself – they must be made by the Electricity Company.

Outbuilding end of circuit

Run a 4mm^2 two-core-and-earth cable through conduit from the house to the outbuilding, terminating at a 30amp switchfuse unit mounted on the wall.

Connect up the incoming cable to the supply or 'Mains' terminals of the switchfuse unit and the outgoing 4mm^2 cable to its 'Load' terminals (2), then run this cable to the outbuilding's sockets.

Insert a 30amp junction box at some point along the power cable (3), and run a 4mm^2 spur from it to an unswitched fused connection unit fitted with a 3amp fuse; then run 1mm^2 two-core-and-earth cable from the connection unit to the light fitting and switch.

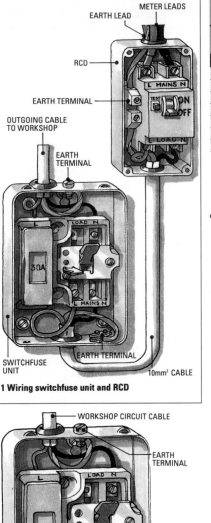

HOUSE END OF CIRCUIT

METER LEADS
EARTH LEAD
RCD
L MAINS N
EARTH TERMINAL
TEST ON OFF
OUTGOING CABLE TO WORKSHOP
EARTH TERMINAL
L LOAD N
L
LOAD N
30A
L MAINS N
SWITCHFUSE UNIT
EARTH TERMINAL
10mm^2 CABLE

1 Wiring switchfuse unit and RCD

● **Meter leads and earth lead**
If 16mm^2 cable is too thick for the terminals in the RCD, use 10mm^2 cable but keep the leads as short as possible.

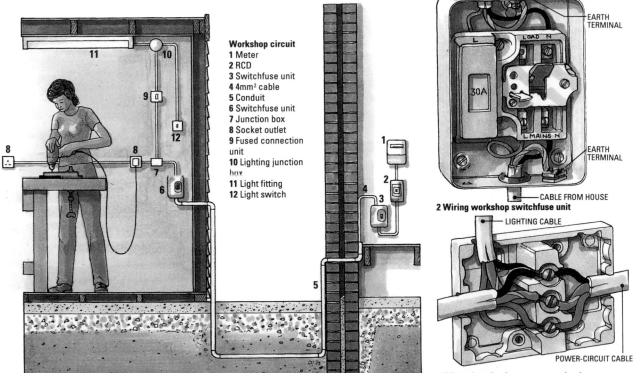

Workshop circuit
1 Meter
2 RCD
3 Switchfuse unit
4 4mm^2 cable
5 Conduit
6 Switchfuse unit
7 Junction box
8 Socket outlet
9 Fused connection unit
10 Lighting junction box
11 Light fitting
12 Light switch

WORKSHOP CIRCUIT CABLE
EARTH TERMINAL
L LOAD N
30A
L MAINS N
EARTH TERMINAL
CABLE FROM HOUSE

2 Wiring workshop switchfuse unit

LIGHTING CABLE
POWER-CIRCUIT CABLE

3 Wiring junction box on power circuit

345

COMPLETE WIRING

Planning ahead

As an amateur, before deciding to take on the complete rewiring of your house yourself, it is advisable to consider the time factor very carefully. When you are working on only one circuit, the rest of the household can function normally, but to renew all the circuits running to the house's consumer unit means that eventually every part of your home will be affected by the work.

A full-time professional can cope with all this in such a way that the level of inconvenience and disruption to the household is kept to a minimum. But the amateur, perhaps obliged to work only at weekends, will almost certainly have to think in terms of a time span lasting several weeks – especially since it is very important not to work hastily on such installations, as hurried work can lead to dangerous mistakes.

So unless you are very experienced and are able to make the installation a full-time commitment for a week or two, you would be well advised to employ a fully qualified electrician to undertake this time-consuming job.

He or she may perhaps be willing to work alongside you, enabling you to save considerably on the cost by doing some of the jobs that have nothing to do with electrical work – such as running cable under floors and channelling out plaster and brickwork.

Circuits: maximum lengths

The maximum length of a circuit is limited by the permitted voltage drop and the time it takes to operate the fuse or MCB in the event of an earth fault.

The method for calculation given in the Wiring Regulations is extremely complicated, but the table below will provide you with a simple method for determining the maximum cable lengths for common domestic circuits.

If necessary, split up your circuits so that none of the indicated cable lengths are exceeded. If your requirements fall outside the limits of this chart, then ask a professional electrician to make the calculations for you.

Rewirable fuses are not included as they are subject to special restrictions, which make them an unwise choice.

Most two-core-and-earth cables have a standard-size protective circuit conductor (earth wire). In each case, the chart shows the size of earth wire used in the calculations.

The maximum circuit lengths given in the chart are based on the assumption that you won't install any cables where the ambient temperature exceeds 30°C (86°F), that no more than two cables will be bunched together, and that you will not cover any of the cables with thermal insulation. The shower-circuit lengths assume that a 30 milliamp RCD is used in the circuit.

MAXIMUM LENGTHS FOR DOMESTIC CIRCUITS

TYPE OF CIRCUIT		Max. floor area	Cable size in mm²	Size of earth wire in mm²	USING FUSES		USING MCBs	
					Current rating of circuit fuse	Max. cable length using cartridge fuse	Current rating of MCB	Max. cable length using MCB
RING CIRCUIT		100sq m	2.5	1.5	30amp	60m	32amp	50m
RADIAL CIRCUIT		20sq m	2.5	1.5	20amp	35m	20amp	33m
		50sq m	4	1.5	30amp	38m	32amp	15m
COOKER with socket outlet			4	1.5	30amp	20m	32amp	15m
			6	2.5	30amp	38m	32amp	24m
IMMERSION HEATER up to 3kW			2.5	1.5	15amp	40m	16amp	38m
SHOWER up to 9.6kW			10	4	45amp	20m	40amp	20m
STORAGE HEATER			2.5	1.5	15amp	35m	16amp	30m
STORAGE FAN HEATER			4	1.5	30amp	24m	32amp	34m
FIXED LIGHTING excluding switch drops			1	1	5amp	95m	6amp	95m
			1.5	1	5amp	110m	6amp	110m

DESIGNING YOUR SYSTEM

Before discussing your requirements with a professional, you need to form clear ideas about the kind of installation you want. Although you may eventually decide between you to change some of the details, a proper specification can help the electrician considerably and will also enable you to avoid expensive additions and modifications.

Choosing the best consumer unit

It is worth installing the best consumer unit you can afford. Choose one that has cartridge fuses or miniature circuit breakers (MCBs), and make sure it has enough spare fuseways for possible additional circuits.

Residual current devices

Ask the electrician about the value of installing a residual current device (RCD). You could have one built into your consumer unit.

Power circuits

Ring circuits are better than radial circuits for supplying socket outlets. Provided that the floor area in question does not exceed 100sq m (120sq yds), you can have as many sockets as you like – so make sure your plan includes enough outlets to meet your present and likely future needs. Economizing on the cost of a few sockets now could cause you considerable inconvenience in the future, if you have to start adding spurs to the system.

Lighting circuits

Modern domestic lighting circuits are normally designed round a loop-in system; but remember that, if expedient, individual light fittings can be supplied from a junction box.

You should insist on a lighting circuit for each floor – so that you will never be left totally without electric lights if a fuse should blow.

In the interests of safety, make sure that you have two-way or three-way switches installed for lights in passage-ways and on landings and staircases.

Additional circuits

If you are having your whole house rewired, consider installing extra radial circuits for appliances such as immersion heaters and electrically heated showers.

CHAPTER 8

PLUMBING

PLUMBING –
UNDERSTANDING
THE SYSTEM

For many years, DIY enthusiasts have shown a preference for tackling their own plumbing repairs. As manufacturers responded to demand by supplying hardware especially designed for them, householders in turn became even more ambitious, stimulating a growing industry aimed directly at the DIY market. Almost every aspect of home-plumbing repair and improvement has been catered for with lightweight, attractive fittings which can be plumbed in quickly and confidently with traditional metal or modern plastic pipework.

The advantages of DIY plumbing

While plumbing materials are relatively expensive the price of professional labour constitutes the greater part of any plumber's bill, especially if the job has to be done outside normal working hours. Consequently, doing the work yourself can save a substantial sum and even just knowing how to stop a leak quickly can avoid the expense and disappointment of ruined decorations or even the replacement of rotted household timbers.There is also the cost of water itself – a dripping tap wastes gallons of water a day, and if it's a hot-water tap there is the additional expense of heating it. A few pence spent on a washer can save you pounds.

Direct and indirect cold-water systems

You should familiarize yourself with the plumbing system in your own house so that you can isolate the relevant sections and drain the water during an emergency, or prior to carrying out repairs and rerouting pipework.

Direct system
In many older properties, mains pressure is supplied to all cold-water taps and WCs. Hot water is fed indirectly from the storage cistern via the hot-water cylinder. One advantage with this direct system is that drinking water can be drawn from any cold-water tap in the house.

Indirect system
Most homes are plumbed with an indirect system. Water under mains pressure enters the house through a service pipe and proceeds via the rising main directly to the cold-water storage cistern, normally situated in the roof space. A branch pipe from the rising main delivers drinking water to the kitchen sink and possibly to a garden tap through another pipe. All other cold-

water taps and appliances are fed indirectly, that is, under gravity pressure only, from the storage cistern. The hot-water storage cylinder is also supplied with cold water from the same cistern. There it is heated either indirectly by the central-heating system or by electric immersion heaters, then drawn off from the top of the cylinder to hot-water taps in the bathroom, kitchen and some bedrooms.

An indirect system provides several advantages to the householder as well as the water authority. First, there is adequate water stored in the cisterns to flush sanitary ware during a temporary mains failure. Also, as the major part of the supply is under relatively low pressure, an indirect system is reasonably quiet. (High mains pressure can sometimes cause 'water hammer' as the water tries to negotiate tight bends.) A further advantage is that as few outlets are connected to the mains, there is less likelihood of impure water being siphoned back into the mains supply – an important consideration with regard to hygiene.

Drainage

Waste water is drained from either system in one of two ways. Up until the late 1940s or '50s, water was drained from baths, sinks and basins into a wastepipe which fed into a trapped gully at ground level. Toilet waste fed separately into a large-diameter soil pipe running directly to the underground main drainage network.

With a single-stack waste system, used on later buildings, all waste drains into a single soil pipe. The only possible exception is the kitchen sink which may still drain into a gully.

Rainwater usually feeds into a separate drain so that the house drainage system will not be flooded in the event of a storm.

PLUMBING REGULATIONS

Water Bylaws govern the way you can connect your plumbing system to the public water supply. The laws are intended to prevent the misuse, waste and contamination of water. Your local water supplier will provide you with the relevant information on inspection requirements and possible certification for new work and major alterations.

The Building Regulations on drainage are designed to protect health and safety. At present this aspect is controlled by the local authority, but there are proposals to have the supply and drainage controlled by a single independent body.

When making repairs or improvements to your plumbing, make sure that you do not contravene electrical Wiring Regulations. All metal plumbing must be bonded to earth. If you replace a section of metal plumbing with plastic, you may break the path to earth, so make sure that you reinstate the link. If you are in doubt, always consult a qualified electrician.

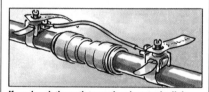

If you break the path to earth, reinstate the link
Bridge a plastic joint in a metal pipe with an earth wire and two clamps.

THE DIRECT SYSTEM

❶ Water supplier's stopcock

❷ Service pipe

❸ Main stopcock

❹ Rising main
Supplies water directly to cold-water taps and WCs as well as the storage cistern.

❺ Cold-water storage cistern

❻ Hot-water cylinder

❼ Wastepipe
Surmounted by hopper head, it collects water from basin and bath.

❽ Soil pipe
Separate pipe takes toilet waste to main drains.

❾ Kitchen wastepipe
Kitchen sink drains into same gully as wastepipe from upstairs.

❿ Trapped gully

PLUMBING
SYSTEMS

DIRECT AND
INDIRECT
SYSTEMS

SEE ALSO

Details for:
Wet central heating   405

Indirect system

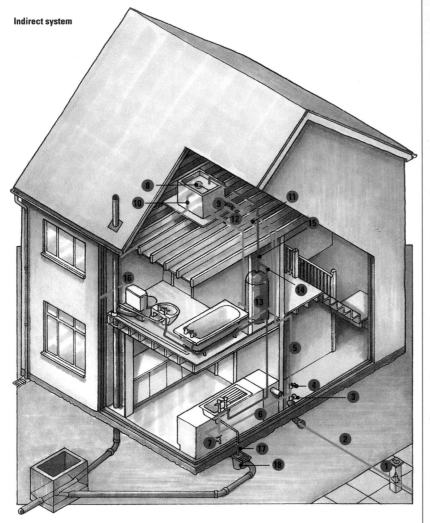

THE INDIRECT SYSTEM

① Water supplier's stopcock
The water company uses this stopcock to turn off the supply to the house. Make sure it can be located quickly in an emergency.

② Service pipe
From the supplier's stopcock onwards, the plumbing becomes the responsibility of the householder. The service pipe enters the house through a drainpipe packed with insulant to prevent water freezing.

③ Main stopcock
The water supply to the house itself is shut off at this point.

④ Draincock
A draincock here allows you to drain water from the rising main.

⑤ Rising main
Mains-pressure water passes to the cold-water cistern via the rising main.

⑥ Drinking water
Drinking water is drawn off the rising main to the kitchen sink.

⑦ Garden tap
The water supplier allows a garden tap to be supplied with mains pressure provided it is fitted with a check valve.

⑧ Float valve
This valve shuts off the supply from the rising main when the cistern is full.

⑨ Cold-water storage cistern
Stores from 230 to 360 litres (50 to 80 gallons) of water. Positioned in the roof, it provides sufficient 'head' or pressure to feed the whole house.

⑩ Overflow pipe
Also known as a warning pipe, it prevents an overflow by draining water to the outside of the house should the float valve fail to operate.

⑪ Cold-feed pipes
Water is drawn off to the bathroom and to the hot-water cylinder from the base of the cold-water storage cistern.

⑫ Cold-feed valves
Valves at these points allow you to drain the cold water in the feed pipe without having to drain the whole cistern as well. Alternatively, they may be placed in the airing cupboard.

⑬ Hot-water cylinder
Water is heated and stored in this cylinder.

⑭ Hot-feed pipe
All hot water is fed from this point.

⑮ Vent pipe
A vent pipe drains into the cistern to allow for expansion of heated water and to vent air from the system.

⑯ Single-stack soil pipe

⑰ Sink waste
Water from the sink drains into a trapped gully.

⑱ Trapped gully

● **Central heating**
Omitted for clarity.

Direct system

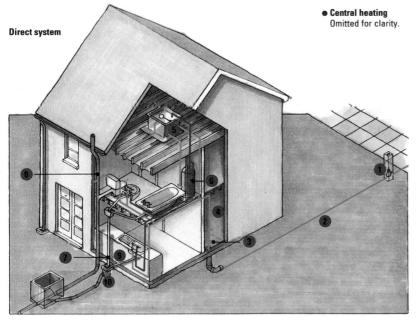

DRAINING
THE SYSTEM

You will have to drain at least part of any plumbing system before you can work on it and, if you detect a leak, you will have to drain the relevant section quickly, so find out where the valves, stopcock and draincocks are situated before you are faced with an emergency.

Draining cold-water taps and pipes

● Turn off the main stopcock on the rising main to cut off the supply to the kitchen tap. (And every other cold tap on a direct system.)
● Open the tap until the flow ceases.
● To isolate bathroom taps, close the valve on the appropriate cold-feed pipe from the storage cistern and open all

taps on that section. If you can't find a valve, rest a wooden batten across the cistern and tie the arm of the float valve to it. This will shut off the supply to the cistern so you can empty it by running all the cold taps in the bathroom. If you can't get into the loft, turn off the main stopcock, then run the cold taps.

Closing a float valve
Cut off the supply of water to a storage cistern by tying the float arm to a batten.

Draining hot-water taps and pipes

● Turn off immersion heaters or boiler.
● Close the valve on the cold-feed pipe to the cylinder and run the hot taps. Even when the water stops flowing, the cylinder will still be full.
● If there is no valve on the cold-feed pipe, tie up the float-valve arm, then turn on the cold taps in the bathroom to

empty the storage cistern. (If you run the hot taps first, the water stored in the cistern will flush out all your hot water from the cylinder.) When the cold taps run dry, open the hot taps. In an emergency, run the hot and cold taps together in order to clear the pipes as quickly as possible.

Draining a WC cistern

● To merely empty the WC cistern itself, tie up its float-valve arm (see above) and flush the WC.
● To empty the pipe that supplies the cistern, either turn off the main stopcock on a direct system, or, on an

indirect system, close the valve on the cold feed from the storage cistern. Alternatively, shut off the supply to the storage cistern and empty it through the cold taps. Flush the WC until no more water enters its cistern.

Draining the cold-water storage cistern

● To drain the storage cistern in the roof, close the main stopcock on the rising main, then open all the cold taps

in the bathroom (hot taps on a direct system.) Bail out the residue of water at the bottom of the cistern.

Draining the hot-water cylinder

● **Sealed central-heating systems**
A sealed system (see WET CENTRAL HEATING) does not have a feed-and-expansion tank – the radiators are filled from the mains via a flexible hose known as a filling loop. The indirect coil in the hot-water cylinder is drained as described right, but you might have to open a vent pipe that is fitted to the cylinder before the water will flow.

● If the hot-water cylinder springs a leak, or you wish to replace it, first turn off immersion heaters and boiler, then shut off the cold feed to the cylinder from the storage cistern (or drain the cold-water storage cistern – see above). Run hot water from the taps.
● Locate a draincock from which you can drain the water remaining in the cylinder. It is probably located near the base of the cylinder where the cold feed from the storage cistern enters but, if not, empty the cylinder from the draincock on the central-heating boiler. Attach a hose to the draincock and run it to a drain or sink that is lower than the cylinder. Turn the square-headed spindle on the draincock until you can hear water flowing.

● If the washer is baked onto the draincock seating, the water cannot be drained and you will have to disconnect the vent pipe and insert a hosepipe to siphon the cylinder.
● If the water is heated indirectly by a heat-exchanger, there will be a coil of pipework inside the hot-water cylinder that is still full of water. This pipework is drained via the stopcock on the boiler after you have shut off the mains supply to the small feed-and-expansion tank located in the roof space and switched off the electrical supply to the central-heating system.
● Once you have drained the cylinder completely, disconnect all its pipework, with rags or old towels to hand to mop up spillages.

ADDING EXTRA VALVES

You will have to drain off a substantial part of a typical plumbing installation even for a simple washer replacement unless you divide the system into relatively short pipe runs with valves.
● Install a gate valve on both the cold feed pipes running from the cold-water storage cistern. This will eliminate the necessity for draining off gallons of water in order to isolate pipes and appliances on the low-pressure cold- and hot-water supply.
● When you are fitting new taps, take the opportunity to fit miniature valves on the supply pipes just below the sink or basin. In future, you will be able to isolate an individual tap in moments when you have to repair it.

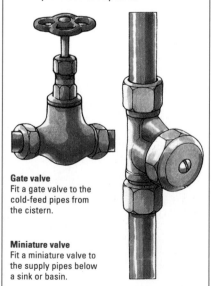

Gate valve
Fit a gate valve to the cold-feed pipes from the cistern.

Miniature valve
Fit a miniature valve to the supply pipes below a sink or basin.

DRAINING AND REFILLING THE WHOLE SYSTEM

Drain the complete plumbing system when you intend to leave the house unoccupied for a long period during the winter, otherwise you run the risk of a 'freeze up' which may burst pipes or force joints apart. Drain the system in the following order.

● Switch off the boiler or immersion heaters. Rake out a solid-fuel boiler and allow it to cool.

● Turn off the main stopcock on the rising main and run off the water from all cold and hot taps.

● If there is a draincock on the rising main, drain what water is left in the pipe from that point.

● Flush the WCs.

● Drain the hot-water cylinder.

● Don't bother to drain the water from the central-heating system, but make sure it contains antifreeze.

● Place a note prominently to remind yourself to fill the system before lighting the boiler or switching on the immersion heater.

● If very low temperatures are the norm in the area where you live, pour some salt into the WC pan to prevent the water from freezing in the trap. Treat other traps in a similar fashion.

Refilling the system

To refill the system, close all taps and draincocks, then open the main stopcock. As the system fills, check that float valves are operating smoothly. Air trapped in the system may cause taps to splutter for a while. If air does not clear naturally, flush it out with mains pressure (see below).

CURING AN AIRLOCK

Air trapped in the system can cause a tap to splutter or fail completely. The answer is to force the air out by using mains pressure.

Attach a length of hose between the affected tap and the cold-water tap at the kitchen sink. (Any cold-water tap on a direct system.) Leave both taps open for a short while and try the airlocked tap again. Repeat if necessary until the water runs freely. If you have used a long hose it will contain a lot of water, so drain it into the sink before moving it.

Every householder should master the simple techniques for coping with emergency repairs in order to avoid unnecessary damage to property as well as the high cost of calling out a plumber at short notice. All you need is a simple tool kit and a few spare parts.

Thawing frozen pipes

Insulate your pipework and fittings, particularly those in the loft or under the floor, to stop them freezing. If you leave the house unheated for a long time during the winter, drain the system (see left). Cure dripping taps so that leaking water does not freeze in your drainage system overnight.

If water will not flow from a tap during cold weather, or a cistern refuses to fill, a plug of ice may have formed in one of the supply pipes. The plug cannot be in a pipe supplying the taps or float valves that are working normally, so you should be able to trace the blockage quickly. In fact, freezing usually occurs first in the roof space.

As copper pipework transmits heat quickly, use a hairdryer to warm the suspect pipe, starting as close as possible to the affected tap or valve and working along it. Leave the tap open so that water can flow normally as soon as the ice thaws. If you cannot heat the pipe with a hairdryer, wrap it in a hot towel or hang a hot-water bottle over it.

Dealing with a nailed pipe

Unless you are absolutely sure where your pipes run, it is all too easy to nail through one of them when fixing a loose floorboard. You may be able to detect a hissing sound as water escapes under pressure, but more than likely you won't notice your mistake until a wet patch appears on the ceiling below or some problem associated with damp occurs at a later date. While the nail is in place, water will leak relatively slowly, so don't pull it out until you have drained the pipework and can repair the leak. If you pull out the nail by lifting a floorboard, put it back immediately.

If you plan to lay fitted carpet, you can paint pipe runs on the floorboards to avoid such an accident.

Patching a leak

During freezing conditions, water within a pipe turns to ice which expands until it eventually splits the walls of the tube or forces a joint apart. Copper pipework is more likely to split than lead, which can stretch to accommodate the expansion and thus survive a few hard winters before reaching breaking point. Patch copper or lead pipes as described right, but close up a split in lead beforehand, using gentle taps with a hammer. Repairing lead permanently is not easy, so hire a plumber as soon as you have contained the leak.

The only other reason for leaking plumbing is mechanical failure, either through deterioration or because a plumber failed to make a completely waterproof joint.

If possible, make a permanent repair by inserting a new section of pipe or replacing a leaking joint. (If it is a compression joint that has failed, try tightening it first.) However, you may have to make an emergency repair for the time being. Drain the pipe first unless it is frozen, in which case make the repair before it thaws.

Using a hose and clips

Cut a length of garden hose to cover the leak and slit it lengthwise so that you can slip it over the pipe. Bind the hose with two or three clips of the type that is used to attach hoses on a car engine. If you cannot obtain hose clips, twist wire loops around the hose with pliers.

Patching with epoxy putty

Epoxy putty is supplied in two parts which begin to harden as soon as they are mixed, giving you about 20 minutes to complete the repair. The putty adheres to most metals and hard plastic. Although it is better to insert a new length of pipe, epoxy putty will produce a fairly long-term repair.

Use abrasive paper or wire wool to clean a 25 to 50mm (1 to 2in) length of pipe on each side of the leak. Mix the putty thoroughly and press it into the hole or around a joint, building it to a thickness of 3 to 6mm ($\frac{1}{8}$ to $\frac{1}{4}$in). It will cure to full strength within 24 hours, but you can run low-pressure water immediately if you bind the putty with self-adhesive tape.

SEE ALSO	
Details for:	
Insulating pipes	267
Joining pipes	362–369
Compression joints	364

Thawing a frozen pipe
Play a hairdryer gently along a frozen pipe, working away from the blocked tap or valve.

Closing a split pipe
In an emergency, close a split by tapping the pipe with a hammer before you bind it. This works particularly well with lead pipe.

Binding a split pipe
Bind a length of hosepipe around a damaged pipe using hose clips.

Smoothing epoxy putty
When patching a hole with epoxy putty, smooth it with a damp, soapy cloth to give a neat finish.

351

REPAIRING A LEAKING TAP

SEE ALSO
Details for:
Spanners and
wrenches   505–506

A tap may leak for a number of reasons, but none of them is difficult to deal with. When water drips from a spout, for example, it is normally the result of a faulty washer and, if the tap is old, the seat against which the washer is compressed may be worn also. If water leaks from beneath the head of the tap when it's in use, the gland packing or O-ring needs replacing. When you are working on taps, insert the plug and lay a towel in the bottom of the sink or bath to catch small objects.

Replacing a washer

To replace the washer in a traditional bib or pillar tap, first drain the supply pipe, then open the valve as far as possible before you begin dismantling either of the taps.

If the tap is shrouded with a metal cover, unscrew it by hand or use a wrench, taping the jaws in order to protect the chrome finish.

Lift up the cover to reveal the headgear nut just above the body of the tap. Slip a narrow spanner onto the nut and unscrew it **(1)** until you can lift out the entire headgear assembly.

The jumper to which the washer is fixed fits into the bottom of the

headgear. In some taps the jumper is removed along with the headgear **(2)**, but in other types it will be lying inside the tap body.

The washer itself may be pressed over a small button in the centre of the jumper **(3)**, in which case, prise it off with a screwdriver. If the washer is held in place by a nut it can be difficult to remove. Allow penetrating oil to soften any corrosion, then, holding the jumper stem with pliers, unscrew the nut with a snug-fitting spanner **(4)**. (If the nut will not budge, replace the whole jumper and washer.) Fit a new washer and retaining nut, then reassemble the tap.

Removing a shrouded head from a tap
On most modern taps the head and cover is in one piece. You will have to remove it to expose the headgear nut. Often a retaining screw is hidden beneath the coloured hot/cold disc in the centre of the head. Prise out the disc with the point of a knife. If there's no retaining screw, simply pull the head off.

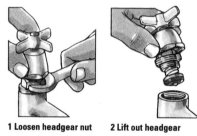

1 Loosen headgear nut   **2 Lift out headgear**   **3 Prise off washer**   **4 Or undo fixing nut**

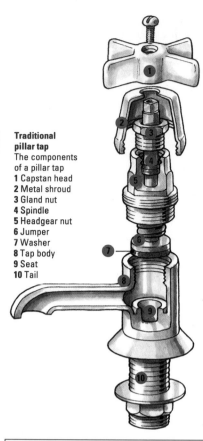

Traditional pillar tap
The components of a pillar tap
1 Capstan head
2 Metal shroud
3 Gland nut
4 Spindle
5 Headgear nut
6 Jumper
7 Washer
8 Tap body
9 Seat
10 Tail

Replacing a washer in a reverse-pressure tap

The distinctive reverse-pressure tap is like an upside-down version of a conventional tap – the washer is screwed upwards against the seat. This type of tap is no longer manufactured, but spare parts are still available to service the thousands of taps in use.

When you are replacing a washer, there is no need to cut off the water because an integral check valve closes automatically as the body is removed. Loosen the retaining nut (left-hand thread) above the tap body **(1)**, then unscrew the body itself as if you were

opening the tap. Water will run until the check valve operates, but continue to unscrew the body **(2)** until it drops into your hand.

Tap the nozzle on the floor **(3)**, not on a ceramic basin, then turn the body upside down to tip out the finned anti-splash device. Prise the combined jumper and washer from the end of the anti-splash device **(4)** and replace it.

Reassemble the tap in the reverse order, remembering that the body is screwed back clockwise when viewed from above.

Reverse-pressure tap

1 Loosen retaining nut   **2 Remove tap body**   **3 Tap nozzle on floor**   **4 Prise off jumper**

REPLACING A CERAMIC-DISC CARTRIDGE

In theory ceramic-disc taps are maintenance-free, but they are not without their problems and there is really no alternative to replacing the whole ceramic-disc cartridge.

Turn off the water and open the tap to drain it, then remove the handle or shroud to expose the top of the cartridge. Unscrew the cartridge with a spanner **(1)** and lift it out of the tap body **(2)**. If scale has built up in the tap body, turn on the water slightly to flush it out. Fit a new cartridge, making sure you fit the right one – they are handed and designated hot or cold. At the same time, ensure that the new sealing washer supplied is fitted into the bottom of the cartridge.

1 Unscrew the cartridge   **2 Lift it out of the tap**

REPLACING O-RINGS ON MIXER TAPS

Each valve on a mixer tap is fitted with a washer like a conventional tap, but in most mixers, the gland packing has been replaced by a rubber O-ring.

Having removed the shrouded head, take out the circlip holding the spindle in place (1). Remove the spindle and slip the old O-ring out of its groove (2). Replace it with a new one, using silicone grease as a lubricant, then reassemble the tap.

1 Remove circlip   **2 Roll ring from groove**

The base of a mixer's swivel spout is sealed with a washer or O-ring. If water seeps from that junction, turn off both valves and unscrew the spout, or remove the retaining screw (3) on one side. Note the type of seal and buy a matching replacement.

3 Remove screw to release mixer spout

MAINTAINING STOPCOCKS AND VALVES

Stopcocks and gate valves are rarely used, so their maintenance is often neglected – although it can cause a serious problem if they fail to work just when they are needed.

Make sure they are operating smoothly by closing and opening them from time to time. If the spindles move stiffly, lubricate them with a little penetrating oil. A stopcock is fitted with a standard washer, but as it is hardly ever under pressure it is unlikely to wear. However, the gland packing on both the gate valve and stopcock may need attention (see right).

Regrinding the seat

If a tap continues to drip after you have replaced the washer, it is probably the case that the seat is worn and water is leaking past the washer.

One way to cure this is to grind the seat flat with a special reseating tool rented from a hire company. Remove the headgear and jumper so you can screw the tool into the body of the tap.

1 Revolve the tool to smooth the seat

Curing a leaking gland

The head of a tap is fixed to a shaft or spindle which is screwed up or down to control the flow of water. The spindle passes through a gland, also known as a stuffing box, on top of the headgear assembly. A watertight packing is forced into the gland by a nut to prevent water leaking past the spindle when the tap is turned on. If water drips from under the head of the tap, the gland packing has failed and needs replacing.

Some taps incorporate a rubber O-ring which slips over the spindle to perform the same function as the packing (see left).

Replacing the gland packing

There is no need to turn off the supply of water to replace gland packing; just make sure the tap is turned off fully.

To remove a cross or capstan head, expose a fixing screw by picking out the

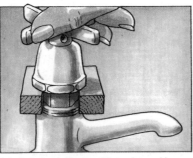

1 Jack the head off a tap with wooden packing

Adjust the cutter until it is in contact with the seat, then turn the handle to smooth the metal (1). Alternatively, cover the old seat with a nylon substitute that is sold with a matching jumper and washer (2). Drop the seating component over the old seat, replace the jumper and assemble the tap. Close the tap to force the seat into position.

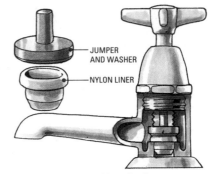

JUMPER AND WASHER

NYLON LINER

2 Repair a worn seat with a nylon liner

plastic plug in the centre of the head, or look for a screw holding it at the side. Lift off the head by rocking it from side to side, or tap it gently from below with a hammer.

If the head is stuck firmly, open the tap as far as possible, unscrew the cover and wedge wooden packing between it and the headgear (1). Closing the tap will then jack the head off the spindle.

Once you have removed the head and cover, try to seal the leak by tightening the gland nut. If that fails, remove the nut and pick out the old packing with a small screwdriver.

To replace the packing, use special fibre twine available from a plumbers' merchant or twist a thread from PTFE (polytetrafluorethylene) tape. Wind it around the spindle and pack it into the gland with a screwdriver (2).

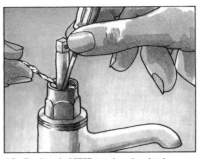

2 Stuff a thread of PTFE tape into the gland

GLAND PACKING

Gland packing
Older-style taps are sealed with a watertight packing around the spindle.

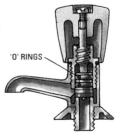

'O' RINGS

O-ring seal
Modern taps are sealed with rubber rings in place of the gland packing.

MAINTAINING
WC & STORAGE
CISTERNS

There is no reason why anyone should have to call out a plumber to service a WC cistern. Most of them are situated directly behind the WC pan so they are readily accessible, but even an old-style high-level cistern can be reached using a stepladder. Components are available from any plumbers' merchant and many DIY outlets.

The storage cistern (tank) in the loft is simply a container for cold water. Other than a leak, which is unlikely to occur with a modern cistern, the only problems to arise are as a result of float-valve failure. The float valve in a storage cistern is basically the same as that used for the WC cistern, but never replace it with a miniature float valve.

Miniature float valve
This type of float valve is designed for installing in WC cisterns only.

Tying up a float arm
Tie the arm to a batten placed across the cistern when you need to shut off the supply of water.

● **Maintaining a high-level cistern**
Before you begin to service a high-level cistern, place a folded towel over the WC seat and pan to protect them from falling spanners.

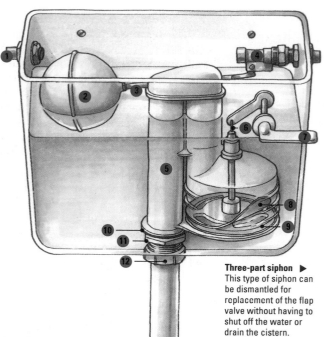

Direct-action cistern
The components of a typical direct-action WC cistern.
1 Overflow
2 Float
3 Float arm
4 Float valve
5 One-piece siphon
6 Wire link
7 Flushing lever
8 Flap valve
9 Perforated plate
10 Sealing washer
11 Retaining nut
12 Flush-pipe connector

Three-part siphon ▶
This type of siphon can be dismantled for replacement of the flap valve without having to shut off the water or drain the cistern.

DIRECT-ACTION WC CISTERN

Most modern WCs are washed down with direct-action cisterns. Water enters a cistern through a valve which is opened and closed by the action of a hollow float attached to one end of a rigid arm. As the water rises in the cistern, it lifts the float until the other end of the arm eventually closes the valve and shuts off the supply.

Flushing is carried out by depressing a lever which lifts a perforated plastic or metal plate at the bottom of an inverted U-bend tube (siphon). As the plate rises, the perforations are sealed by a flexible plastic diaphragm (flap valve) so that the plate can displace a body of water over the U-bend to promote a siphoning action. The water pressure behind the diaphragm lifts it again so that the contents of the cistern flow up through the perforations in the plate, over the U-bend and down the flush pipe. As the water level in the cistern drops, so does the float, opening the float valve to refill the cistern.

The few problems with this type of cistern are easy to solve. A faulty float valve or poorly adjusted arm allows water to leak into the cistern until it drips from the overflow pipe running to the outside of the house. Slow or noisy filling is often rectified by replacing the float valve. If the cistern will not flush until the lever is operated several times, the flap valve probably needs replacing.

Replacing the flap valve

If the WC cistern will not flush first time, take off the lid and check that the water level is up to the internal mark and that the lever is actually operating the mechanism. If it is working normally, replace the flap valve in the siphon. Before you service a one-piece siphon, shut off the water by tying up the float arm (see left), then flush the cistern.

Use a large wrench to unscrew the nut holding the flush pipe to the underside of the cistern (1). Move the pipe to one side. Release the remaining nut which clamps the siphon to the base of the cistern (2). A little water will run out as you loosen the nut, so have a bucket handy. (The siphon may be bolted to the base of the cistern instead of being clamped by one retaining nut.)

Disconnect the flushing arm and ease the siphon out of the cistern. Lift the diaphragm off the metal plate (3) and replace it with one of the same size. Reassemble the flushing mechanism in the reverse order and attach the flush pipe to the cistern.

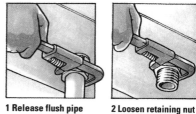

1 Release flush pipe **2 Loosen retaining nut** **3 Lift off flap valve**

Making a new link

If the flushing lever feels slack and the cistern will not flush, check that the wire link at the end of the flushing arm is intact. Retrieve broken pieces from the cistern and bend a new link from a piece of thick wire. If you have thin wire only, twist the ends together with pliers to make a temporary repair.

Curing continuous running water

If you notice water continuously running into the pan, turn off the supply and let the cistern drain. Check to see whether the siphon has split. If not, try changing the sealing washer.

Alternatively, water could be flowing from the float valve so quickly that the siphoning action is not interrupted. The solution is to fit a float-valve seat with a smaller water inlet (see opposite).

DIAPHRAGM VALVES

The pivoting end of the float arm on a diaphragm valve (known in the trade as a Part 2 valve) presses against the end of a small plastic piston which moves the large rubber diaphragm to seal the water inlet.

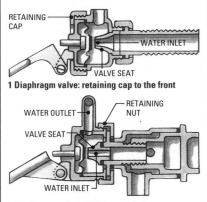

1 Diaphragm valve: retaining cap to the front

2 Diaphragm valve: retaining nut to the rear

Replacing the diaphragm

Turn off the water supply, then unscrew the large retaining cap. Depending on the model, the nut may be screwed onto the end of the valve (**1**) or behind it (**2**).

With the latter type of valve, slide out the cartridge inside the body (**3**) to find the diaphragm behind it. With the former, you will find a similar piston and diaphragm immediately behind the retaining cap (**4**).

Wash the valve before assembling it along with the new diaphragm.

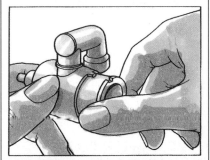

3 Slide out piston to release the diaphragm

4 Remove cap and pull float arm to find valve

A faulty float valve is responsible for most of the difficulties that arise with WC and water-storage cisterns. The water inlet inside the valve is traditionally sealed with a washer but modern valves are fitted with a large diaphragm instead, designed to protect the mechanism from scale deposits. The earlier valves are still available, but fit a diaphragm valve in a new installation to comply with Bylaws. If the inlet isn't sealed properly, water continues to feed into the cistern and escapes via the overflow. Since some overflow pipes can't cope with a full flow of mains water, repair a dripping float valve before the flow becomes a torrent.

Portsmouth-pattern valves

In a Portsmouth-pattern valve, a piston moves horizontally inside the hollow metal body. The float arm, pivoting on a split pin, moves the piston back and forth to control the flow of water. A washer trapped in the end of the piston finally seals the inlet by pressing against the valve seat.

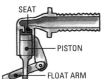

Portsmouth-pattern valve

Replacing a washer

If you have to force the valve closed to stop water dripping, replace the washer. Cut off the supply of water to the cistern and, although it is not essential, flush the cistern in case you drop a component into the water. Remove the split pin from beneath the valve and detach the float arm.

If there is a screw cap on the end of the valve body, remove it (**1**). You may have to apply a little penetrating oil to ease the threads and grip the cap with slip-joint pliers. Insert the tip of a screwdriver in the slot beneath the valve body and slide the piston out (**2**).

To remove the washer, unscrew the end cap of the piston with pliers. Steady the piston by holding a screwdriver in its slot (**3**). Pick the old washer out of the cap (**4**), but before replacing it clean the piston with fine wire wool. Some pistons do not have a removable end cap, and the washer must be dug out with a pointed knife. Take care when replacing this type of washer, which is a tight fit within a groove in the piston.

Use wet-and-dry paper wrapped around a dowel rod to clean inside the valve body, but take care not to damage the valve seat at the far end.

Reassemble the piston and smear it with a light coating of petroleum jelly. Rebuild the valve and connect the float arm. Restore the supply of water and adjust the arm to regulate the water level in the cistern.

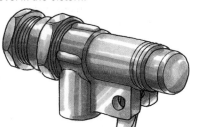

1 Take screw cap from the end of the valve

2 Slide the piston out with a screwdriver

3 Split the piston into two parts

4 Pick out the washer with a screwdriver

Croydon-pattern valve
Only old-fashioned cisterns will be fitted with this valve. The piston travels vertically to close against the seat. Replace the washer as described left.

Interchangeable valve seats
A plastic seat against which a washer or diaphragm closes has a large inlet for low-pressure water or a small inlet for mains or high pressure. Worn or damaged seats should be replaced.

RENOVATING VALVES AND FLOATS

SEE ALSO
Details for:
Supporting pipes   365

Thumb-screw adjustment
Some float arms are cranked, and the float is attached with a thumb-screw clamp. To adjust the water level in the cistern, slide the float up or down the rod.

Adjusting the float arm

Adjust the float to maintain the optimum level of water, which is about 25mm (1in) below the outlet of the overflow pipe.

The arm on a Portsmouth-pattern valve is usually a solid-metal rod. Bend it downward slightly to reduce the water level or straighten it to admit more water **(1)**.

The arm on a diaphragm valve has an adjusting screw which presses on the end of the piston. Release the lock nut and turn the screw towards the valve to lower the water level or away from it to allow the water to rise **(2)**.

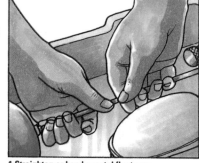

1 Straighten or bend a metal float arm

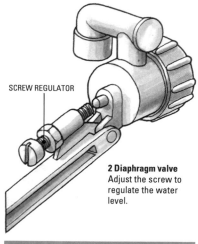

SCREW REGULATOR

2 Diaphragm valve
Adjust the screw to regulate the water level.

Replacing the float

Modern plastic floats rarely leak, but old-style metal floats eventually corrode and allow water to seep into the ball. The float gradually sinks until it won't ride high enough to close the valve.

Unscrew the float and shake it to test whether there is water inside. If you can't replace it for several days, lay the ball on a bench and enlarge the leaking hole with a screwdriver, then pour out the water. Replace the float and cover it with a plastic bag, tying the neck tightly around the float arm.

Curing noisy cisterns

Cisterns that fill noisily can be a real source of annoyance, particularly if the WC is situated right next to a bedroom. It was once permitted to screw a pipe into the outlet of a valve so that it hung vertically below the level of the water. It solved the problem of water splashing into the cistern, but water companies were alarmed at the possibility of water 'back-siphoning' through the silencer tube into the mains supply. Although rigid tubes are banned nowadays, you are permitted to fit a valve with a flexible plastic silencer tube because it will seal itself by collapsing should back-siphoning occur.

A silencer tube can also prevent water hammer – a rhythmic thudding that reverberates along the pipework. It is largely the result of ripples on the surface of the water in a cistern, caused by a heavy flow from the float valve. As the water rises, the float arm, bouncing on the ripples, hammers the valve and the sound is amplified and transmitted along the pipes. A flexible plastic tube will eliminate ripples by introducing water below the surface.

If the water pressure through the valve is too high, the arm oscillates as it tries to close the valve – another cause of water hammer. This can be cured by fitting an equilibrium valve. As water flows through the valve, some of it is introduced behind the piston or diaphragm to equalize the pressure on each side so that the valve closes smoothly and silently.

Before swapping your present valve, check that the pipework is clipped securely to cut down vibration.

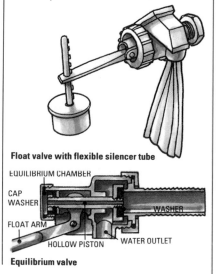

Float valve with flexible silencer tube

EQUILIBRIUM CHAMBER
CAP WASHER
WASHER
FLOAT ARM
HOLLOW PISTON   WATER OUTLET

Equilibrium valve

Renewing a float valve

Turn off the supply of water to the cistern and flush the pipework, then use a spanner to loosen the tap connector joining the supply pipe to the float-valve stem. Remove the float arm, then unscrew the fixing nut on the outside of the cistern and pull out the valve.

Fit the replacement valve and, if possible, use the same tap connector to join it to the supply pipe. Adjust and tighten the fixing nuts to clamp the replacement valve to the cistern, then turn the water supply back on and adjust the float arm.

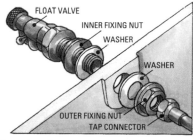

FLOAT VALVE
INNER FIXING NUT
WASHER
WASHER
OUTER FIXING NUT
TAP CONNECTOR

Renewing a float valve
Clamp a valve to the cistern with fixing nuts.

CHOOSING THE RIGHT PRESSURE

Float valves are made to suit different water pressures: low, medium and high (LP, MP and HP). It is important to choose a valve of the correct pressure or the cistern may take a long time to fill. Conversely, the water pressure may be so high that the valve leaks continuously. Those fed direct from the mains should be HP valves, whereas most domestic WC cisterns require an LP valve. If the head (the height of the cistern above the float valve) is greater than 13.5m (45ft), fit an MP valve. In rare cases where the head exceeds 30m (100ft), fit an HP valve. In an apartment using a packaged plumbing system (a storage cistern built on top of the hot-water cylinder), the pressure may be so low that you will have to fit a full-way valve to the WC cistern to get it to fill quickly. If you live in an area where water pressure fluctuates a great deal, fit an equilibrium valve (see left).

To alter the pressure of a modern valve, simply replace the seat inside it. If the valve is a very old pattern, you will have to swap it for another one of a different pressure.

A drainage system is designed to carry dirty water and WC waste from the various appliances to underground drains leading to the main sewer. The different branches of the waste system are protected by U-bend traps full of water to stop drain smells fouling the house. Depending on the age of your house, it will have a two-pipe system or a single stack. Because the two-pipe system has been in use for very much longer, it is still the more common of the two. Use similar methods to maintain either system.

MAINTAINING
A DRAINAGE
SYSTEM

SEE ALSO

Details for:	
Plumbing systems	349
Blocked soil pipe	359
Yard gully	359
Blocked drains	360

Two-pipe system

The wastepipes of older houses are divided into two separate systems. WC waste is fed into a large-diameter, vertical soil pipe that leads directly to the underground drains. To discharge drain gases at a safe height and to make sure that back-siphoning cannot empty the WC traps, the soil pipe is vented to the open air above the guttering.

Individual branch pipes, leading from upstairs washbasins and baths, drain into an open hopper which funnels the water into another vertical wastepipe. Instead of feeding directly into the underground drains, this wastepipe terminates over a yard gully – another trap covered by a grid. A separate wastepipe from the kitchen sink normally drains into the same gully.

The yard gully and soil pipe discharge into an underground inspection chamber, or manhole. These chambers provide access to the main drains for clearing blockages, and there will be one wherever the drain changes direction on its way to the sewer. At the last inspection chamber, just before the drain enters the sewer, there is an interceptor trap, the final barrier to drain gases and, in this case, sewer rats.

Single-stack system

Since the 1960s, most houses have been drained using a single-stack system. Waste from basins, baths and WCs is fed into the same vertical soil pipe or stack, which, unlike the two-pipe system, is often built inside the house. A single-stack system must be designed carefully to prevent a heavy discharge of waste from one appliance siphoning the trap of another, and to avoid the possibility of WC waste blocking other branch pipes. The vent pipe of the stack terminates above the roof and is capped with an open cage to prevent birds nesting in it.

The kitchen sink can be drained through the same stack, but it is still common practice to drain sink waste into a yard gully. Nowadays, wastepipes must pass through the grid, stopping short of the water in the gully trap so that even when the grid becomes blocked with leaves, the waste can discharge unobstructed into the gully. Alternatively, it will be a back-inlet gully with the wastepipe entering below ground level.

A downstairs WC is sometimes drained through its own branch drain to an inspection chamber.

RESPONSIBILITY FOR THE DRAINS

Where a house is drained individually, the whole system up to where it joins the sewer is the responsibility of the householder. However, where a house is connected to a communal drainage system which links several houses, the arrangement for maintenance, including the clearance of blockages, is not so straightforward.

If the drains were constructed prior to 1937, the local council is responsible for cleansing, but can reclaim the cost of repairing any part of the communal system from the householders. After that date all responsibility falls upon the householders collectively, so that they are required to share the cost of repair and cleansing of the drains up to the sewer, no matter where the problem occurs. Contact the Technical Services Department of your local council to find out who is responsible for your drains.

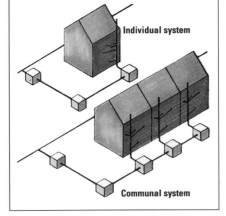

Individual system

Communal system

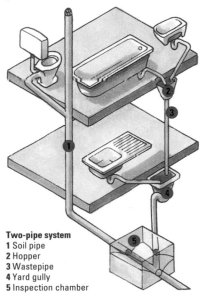

Two-pipe system
1 Soil pipe
2 Hopper
3 Wastepipe
4 Yard gully
5 Inspection chamber

Single-stack system
1 Interior soil pipe
2 All branch pipes run to stack
3 Inspection chamber

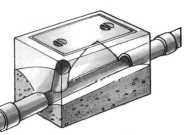

An inspection chamber where drains branch

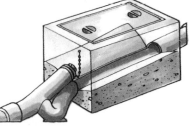

A chamber with interceptor trap

Prefabricated chamber
The inspection chambers of a modern drainage system may be cylindrical prefabricated units. There may not be an interceptor trap in the last chamber before the sewer.

CLEARING A BLOCKED WASTE SYSTEM

Don't ignore the early signs of an imminent blockage of the wastepipe from a sink, bath or basin. If the water drains away slowly, use a chemical cleaner to remove a partial blockage before you are faced with clearing a serious obstruction. If a wastepipe blocks without warning, try a series of measures to locate and clear the obstruction.

Cleansing the wastepipe

Grease, hair and particles of kitchen debris build up gradually within the traps and wastepipes. Regular cleaning with a proprietary chemical drain cleaner will keep the waste system clear and sweet-smelling.

If water drains away sluggishly use a cleaner immediately. Follow the manufacturer's instructions carefully, with particular regard to safety. Always wear protective gloves and goggles when handling chemical cleaners and keep them out of the reach of children.

If unpleasant odours linger after you have cleaned the waste, pour a little disinfectant into the basin overflow.

USING A PUMP TO CLEAR A BLOCKED SINK

If a plunger is ineffective in clearing a blocked waste outlet, use a simple hand-operated hydraulic pump. A downward stroke on the tool forces a powerful jet of water along the pipe to disperse the blockage. If it is lodged firmly, an upward stroke creates enough suction to pull it free.

Using the hydraulic pump
Block the sink overflow with a wet cloth. Fill the pump with water from the tap, then hold its nozzle over the outlet, pressing down firmly. Pump up and down until the obstruction is cleared.

Using a plunger

If one basin fails to empty while others are functioning normally, the blockage must be somewhere along its individual branch pipe. Before you attempt to locate the blockage, try forcing it out of the pipe with a sink plunger. Smear the rim of the rubber cup with petroleum jelly, then lower it into the blocked basin to cover the waste outlet. Make sure there is enough water in the basin to cover the cup. Hold a wet cloth in the overflow with one hand while you pump the handle of the plunger up and down a few times. The waste may not clear immediately if the blockage is merely forced further along the pipe, so repeat the process until the water drains away. If it will not clear after several attempts, try clearing the trap, or use a pump to clear the pipe (see left).

Clearing the trap

The trap, situated immediately below the waste outlet of a sink or basin, is basically a bent tube designed to hold water that seals out drain odours. Traps become blocked when debris collects at the lowest point of the bend. Place a bucket under the basin to catch the water, then use a wrench to release the cleaning eye at the base of a standard trap. Alternatively, remove the large access cap on a bottle trap by hand. If there is no provision for gaining access to the trap, unscrew the connecting nuts and remove the entire trap.

Let the contents of the trap drain into the bucket, then bend a hook on the end of a length of wire and use it to probe the section of wastepipe beyond the trap. (It is also worth checking outside to see if the other end of the pipe is blocked with leaves.) If you have had to remove the trap, take the opportunity to scrub it out with detergent before replacing it.

Cleaning the branch pipe

Quite often, a vertical pipe from the trap joins a virtually horizontal section of the wastepipe. There should be an access plug built into the joint so that you can clear the horizontal pipe. Have a bowl ready to collect any trapped water, then unscrew the plug by hand. Use a length of hooked wire to probe the branch pipe. If you locate a blockage which seems very firmly lodged, rent a drain auger from a tool-hire company to clear the pipework.

If there is no access plug, remove the trap and probe the pipe with an auger. If the wastepipe is constructed with push-fit joints, you can dismantle it.

Use a plunger to force out a blockage

Use hooked wire to probe a branch pipe

Unscrew the access cap on a bottle trap

Tubular trap
If the access cap to the cleaning eye is stiff, use a wrench to remove it.

Bottle trap
A bottle trap can be cleared easily because the whole base of the trap unscrews by hand.

CLEARING A STACK OR GULLY

If several fittings drain poorly, the vertical stack is probably obstructed. In autumn, the hopper, downpipe and yard gully may be blocked with leaves. The blockage may not be obvious when you empty a basin, but the contents of the bath will almost certainly cause an overflow. Clear the blockage urgently to avoid penetrating damp.

Cleaning out the hopper and drainpipe

Wearing protective gloves, scoop out the debris from the hopper, then gently probe the drainpipe with a cane to check that it is free. Clear the bottom end of the pipe with a piece of bent wire. If an old cast-iron wastepipe has been replaced with a modern plastic type, you may find cleaning eyes or access plugs at strategic points for clearing a blockage.

While you are on the ladder, scrub the inside of the hopper and disinfect it to prevent stale odours entering a nearby bathroom.

Unblocking a yard gully

Unless you decide to hire an auger, there is little option but to clear a blocked gully by hand. However, by the time it overflows the water in the gully will be quite deep, so try bailing some of it out with a small disposable container. Wearing rubber gloves, scoop out the debris from the trap until the remaining water disperses.

Rinse the gully with a hose and cleanse it with disinfectant. Scrub the grid as clean as possible or burn off accumulated grime from a metal grid with a gas torch.

If a flooded gully appears to be clear, and yet the water will not drain away, try to locate the blockage at the nearest inspection chamber.

Bail out the water, then clear a gully by hand

Unblocking the soil pipe

Unblocking the soil pipe is an unpleasant job and it's worth hiring a professional cleaning company, especially if the pipe is made of cast iron as it will almost certainly have to be cleared via the vent above the roof.

You can clean a modern plastic stack yourself because there should be a large hinged cleaning eye or other access plugs wherever branch pipes join the stack. If the stack is inside the house, lay polyethylene sheets on the floor and be prepared to mop up trapped sewage when it spills from the pipe.

Unscrew and open the cleaning eye to insert a hired drain auger. Pass the auger into the stack until you locate the obstruction, then crank the handle to engage it. Push or pull the auger until you can dislodge the obstruction to clear the trapped water, then hose out the stack. Wash and disinfect the surrounding area.

Use a hired auger to clear a soil stack

Unblocking a WC pan

If the water in a WC pan rises when you flush it, there is a blockage in the vicinity of the trap. A partial blockage allows the water level to fall slowly.

Hire a larger version of the sink plunger to force the obstruction into the soil pipe. Position the rubber cap of the plunger well down into the U-bend and pump the handle several times. When the blockage clears, the water level will drop suddenly, accompanied by an audible gurgling.

If the trap is blocked solidly, hire a special WC auger. Pass the flexible clearing rod as far as possible into the trap, then crank the handle to dislodge the blockage. Wash the auger in hot water and disinfect it before returning it to the hire company.

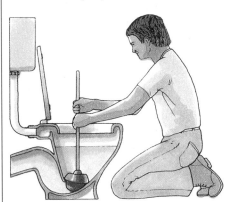

Use a 'Cooper's' plunger to pump a blocked WC

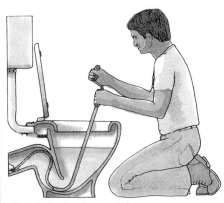

Alternatively, clear it with a WC auger

RODDING
THE DRAINS

The first sign of a blocked underground drain could be an unpleasant smell from an inspection chamber, but a severe blockage can cause sewage to back up until it begins to overflow from a gully or from beneath the cover of an inspection chamber. Before you resort to expensive professional jetting services, hire a set of drain rods – short, flexible rods made of plastic or wire, screwed end-to-end – to clear the blockage. Metal screws or a rubber plunger are threaded onto the rods.

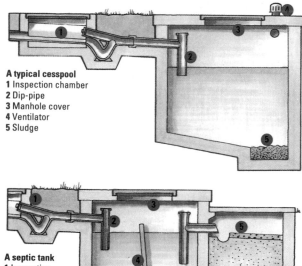

A typical cesspool
1 Inspection chamber
2 Dip-pipe
3 Manhole cover
4 Ventilator
5 Sludge

A septic tank
1 Inspection chamber
2 Dip-pipe
3 Manhole cover
4 Baffle
5 Filter chamber
6 Outlet

Rodding points
A modern drainage system is often fitted with rodding points to provide access to the drain. They are sealed with small oval or circular covers.

Locating the blockage

Lift the cover from the inspection chamber nearest the house. If it is stuck firmly, or the handles have rusted away, scrape the dirt from around its edges and prise it up with a garden spade.
● If the chamber contains water, check the one nearer the road or boundary. If that chamber is dry, the blockage is between the two chambers.
● If the chamber nearest the road is full, the blockage will be in the interceptor trap or in the pipe beyond, leading to the sewer.
● If both chambers are dry and yet either a yard gully or downstairs WC will not empty, check for blockages in the branch drains that run to the first inspection chamber.

Rodding a drain

Screw two or three rods together and attach a corkscrew fitting to the end. Insert the rods into the drain at the bottom of the inspection chamber in the direction of the suspected blockage. If the chamber is full of water, use the end of a rod to locate an open channel running across the floor, leading to the mouth of the drain.

As you pass the rods along the drain, attach further lengths until you reach the obstruction, then twist the rods clockwise to engage the screw. (Never twist the rods anti-clockwise or they will become detached.) Pull and push the obstruction until it breaks up, allowing the water to flow away.

Extract the rods, flush the chamber with clean water from a hose and replace the lid.

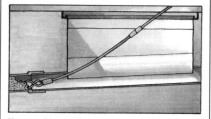

Use a corkscrew fitting to clear a drain

Clearing an interceptor trap

Screw a rubber plunger to the end of a short length of rods and locate the channel that leads to the base of the trap. Push the plunger into the opening of the trap, then pump the rods a few times to expel the blockage. (This is also a useful technique for clearing blocked yard gullies.)

If the water level does not drop after several attempts, try clearing the drain leading to the sewer. Access to this drain is through a cleaning eye above the trap. It will be sealed with a stopper which you will have to dislodge with a drain rod unless it is attached to a chain stapled to the chamber wall. Don't let the stopper fall into the channel and block the trap. Rod the drain to the sewer, then hose out the chamber before replacing the stopper and cover.

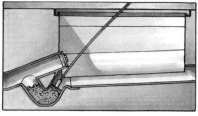

Rod an interceptor trap, using a rubber plunger

CESSPOOLS AND SEPTIC TANKS

Houses built in the country or on the outskirts of a town are not always connected to a public sewer. Instead, waste is drained into a cesspool or septic tank. A cesspool simply acts as a collection point for sewage until it can be pumped out by the local council, whereas a septic tank is a complete waste-disposal system in which sewage is broken down by bacterial action before the water is finally discharged into a local waterway or else distributed underground.

Cesspools

Building Regulations stipulate that cesspools should have a minimum capacity of 18cu m (4000 gallons) but many existing cesspools accommodate far less, and require emptying perhaps once every two weeks. It would be worth checking before you buy a country home to ensure it will cope with your needs. Water authorities estimate the disposal of approximately 115 litres (25 gallons) per person per day.

Most cesspools are cylindrical pits lined with brick or concrete. Modern ones are sometimes prefabricated in glass-reinforced plastic. Access is via a manhole cover.

Septic tanks

The sewage in a septic tank separates slowly, heavy sludge falling to the bottom to leave relatively clear water with a layer of scum floating on the surface. A dip-pipe discharges waste below the surface so that incoming water does not stir up the sewage. Bacterial action takes a minimum of 24 hours, so the tank is divided into chambers by baffles to slow down the movement of sewage through the tank.

The partly treated waste passes out of the tank through another dip-pipe into some form of filtration system that allows further bacterial action to take place. It may be another chamber containing a deep filter bed or, alternatively, the waste may flow underground through a network of drains which disperses the water over a wide area to filter through the soil.

The ability to install a run of pipework, make watertight joints and connect up to fittings are the basic requirements of plumbing. Without these skills, a householder is restricted to simple maintenance. When lead piping was universal, plumbing was a trade requiring years of experience, but modern materials and technology have made it possible for anybody who is prepared to master a few techniques to upgrade and extend household plumbing without having to hire a professional.

Metric and imperial pipes

Copper and stainless-steel pipes are now made in metric sizes, whereas a lot of pipework already installed in a house will be of the old imperial measurements. If you compare the equivalent dimensions (15mm – ½in, 22mm – ¾in and 28mm – 1in), the difference seems obvious, but metric pipe is measured externally while imperial pipe is measured internally. In fact, the difference is very small, but enough to cause some problems when joining one type of pipe to the other.

An exact fit is essential when making soldered joints. Imperial to metric adaptors are necessary when you are joining 22mm pipe to its imperial equivalent and, though they are not essential, adaptors are convenient when you are working with 28mm pipes or thick-walled ½in pipes. Adaptors are not required when you are using compression fittings, but when connecting 22mm to ¾in plumbing, slip an imperial olive onto the ¾in pipe.

You might experience some difficulty when joining to old pipework that has frozen in the past since this can cause the pipe to expand considerably.

Electro-chemical action

Joining pipes made from different metals can accelerate corrosion as a result of electrolytic action. If you live in a soft-water area, where this problem is often pronounced, use plastic pipe and connectors when joining to old pipework, but make sure that the metal pipework is still bonded to earth as required by the Wiring Regulations (see SUPPLEMENTARY BONDING).

TYPES OF METAL PLUMBING

Over the years, most household plumbing systems have undergone some form of improvement or alteration. As a result you may find any of a number of metals used, perhaps in combination, depending on the availability of materials at the time it was installed, or the preference of an individual plumber.

Copper

Half-hard tempered copper tubing is by far the most widely used material for pipework. This is because it is lightweight, solders well and can be bent easily – even by hand, with the aid of a bending spring. It is employed for both hot-water and cold-water pipes as well as central-heating systems. There are three sizes of pipe that are invariably used for general domestic plumbing: 15mm (½in), 22mm (¾in) and 28mm (1in).

Stainless steel

Stainless-steel tubing is not as common as copper, but is available in the same sizes. You may have to order it from a plumbers' merchant. Stainless steel offers few advantages to a DIY plumber. It is harder than copper so cannot be bent as easily and it is difficult to solder. For both reasons, it pays to use compression joints to connect stainless-steel pipes, but tighten them slightly more than you would when joining copper. Use push-fit connectors with collet clips for stainless-steel pipes.

Stainless steel does not react adversely with galvanized-steel (iron) pipework which might have been installed previously in the system (see ELECTRO-CHEMICAL ACTION, left).

Lead

Lead is never used for new plumbing, but thousands of houses still have a lead rising main connected to a modernized system. Lead plumbing still in use must be nearing the end of its life, so replace it whenever the opportunity arises. When drinking water lies in a lead pipe for some time, it absorbs toxins from the metal. If you have a lead pipe supplying your drinking water, always run off a little water before you use any.

Galvanized steel (iron)

Galvanized steel was used to provide strong pipework where lead might easily have been damaged. It can still be obtained, but there is no longer any point in using it for general plumbing, especially as the end of straight lengths have to be threaded before you can make a joint. Take care when joining copper to existing galvanized-steel pipes (see ELECTRO-CHEMICAL ACTION, left).

Cast iron

All old soil pipes are made of cast iron. The metal is prone to rusting – in fact, it is only the relatively thick walls of the pipes that have preserved them for so long. Should you need to replace one, ask for one of the plastic alternatives.

Brass

Because it machines and casts so well, brass is used to make compression joints, taps, stopcocks and a variety of other fittings. Corrosion-resistant brass is employed to avoid the electro-chemical action that would otherwise take place between the zinc content of brass and copper pipes.

Gunmetal

Gunmetal connectors are used for joining copper pipework to galvanized steel where standard brass fittings would be corroded. Gunmetal is often used for underground fittings, which tend to suffer most from corrosion.

Corrosion resistance
Look for the symbol that denotes a fitting made from brass that resists dezincification.

361

METAL PIPE JOINTS

SEE ALSO
Details for:
Metal plumbing   361
Soldering   504

As most domestic plumbing is carried out in copper, the methods described on the next few pages are primarily for joining copper pipes. You can use the same techniques for stainless-steel plumbing but, because it is harder than copper, you will find it easier to cut the metal with a hacksaw and use an active flux for soldering joints. Join copper to galvanized-steel or plastic plumbing with specially designed couplings.

Capillary & compression joints

It would be impossible to make strong, watertight joints by simply soldering two lengths of copper pipe end-to-end. Instead, plumbers use capillary or compression joints.

Capillary joints

Capillary joints are made to fit snugly over the ends of the pipe. The very small space between the pipe and sleeve is filled with molten solder which solidifies on cooling to hold the joint together and make it watertight. Capillary joints are neat and inexpensive but, because you need to heat the metal with a gas torch, there is a slight risk of fire attached when working in confined spaces under floors and in the loft.

Capillary joints
Solder is introduced to each mouth of the assembled end-feed joint (right) and flows by capillary action into the fitting. The rings pressed into the sleeves of an integral-ring fitting (far right) contain the exact amount of solder to make perfect joints.

Compression joints

Compression joints are very easy to use, but are more expensive than capillary joints. They are also more obtrusive, and you will find it impossible to manoeuvre a wrench where space is restricted. When the cap-nut is tightened with a wrench it compresses a ring of soft metal, known as an olive, to fill the joint between fitting and pipe.

Compression joint
This is the simplest and most widely used compression joint. The end of each pipe is cut square before the joint is assembled.

METAL JOINTS AND FITTINGS

Capillary and compression joints are made to connect pipes at different angles and in various combinations. There are adaptors for joining metric and imperial pipes and for connecting one material to another. You will have to consult manufacturers' catalogues to see every variation, but the examples below illustrate a range of typical joints and fittings.

Straight connectors
To join two pipes end-to-end in a straight line.
1 For pipes of equal diameter – *compression joint.*
2 Reducer to connect a 22mm (¾in) pipe to a 15mm (½in) pipe – *capillary joint.*

Bends or elbows
To join two pipes at an angle.
3 90 degree elbow – *compression joint.*

Tees
To join three pipes.
4 Equal tee to join three pipes of the same diameter – *capillary joint.*
5 Unequal tee to reduce size of pipe run when connecting a branch pipe – *compression joint.*
6 Off-set tee joins branch pipe to one side of main pipe run – *compression joint.*

Adaptors
To join dissimilar pipes.
7 Straight coupling to join 22mm and ¾in pipes – *compression joint.*
8 Copper to galvanized-steel connector – *compression joint* for copper, *threaded female coupling* for steel.

Fittings
Identical jointing systems are used to connect fittings.
9 Tank connector joins pipes to cisterns – *compression joint.*
10 Tap connector with threaded nut for connecting supply pipe to tap – *capillary joint.*
11 Bib-tap wall plate for fixing tap on outside wall – *compression joint* for supply pipe, *threaded female connector* for tap.
12 Bib tap has threaded tail to fit wall plate.
13 Gate valve to fit in straight pipe run – *compression joint.*
14 Draincock to empty a pipe run – *compression joint.*
15 Straight service valve for isolating a tap or float valve – *compression joint.*
16 Double-check non-return valve used for outside taps and other outlets where contamination of water supply is possible – *compression joint.*

SEE ALSO

Details for:
Pipe fittings 362

Soldering pipe joints is very simple once you have had a little practice. The fittings are quite cheap, so try out the techniques before you begin to install pipework. Your basic equipment is a gas torch to apply heat, some flux to clean the metal and solder to make the joint. Make sure the pipe is perfectly dry before you attempt to solder a joint.

CUTTING METAL PIPE

Calculate the length of pipe you need, allowing enough to fit into the sleeve of the joint at each end. Whatever type of joint you use, it is essential to cut the end of every length of pipe square.

To ensure a perfectly square cut each time, use a tube cutter. Align the cutting wheel with your mark and adjust the handle of the tool to clamp the rollers against the pipe (1). Rotate the tool around the pipe, adjusting the handle after each revolution to make the cutter bite deeper into the metal. A tube cutter makes a clean cut on the outside of the pipe, but use the pointed reamer on the tool to clean the burr from inside the cut end (2).

If you use a hacksaw, make sure the cut is square by wrapping a piece of paper with a straight edge around the pipe. Align the wrapped edge and use it to guide the saw blade (3). Remove the burr, inside and out, with a file.

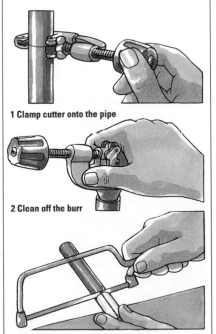

1 Clamp cutter onto the pipe

2 Clean off the burr

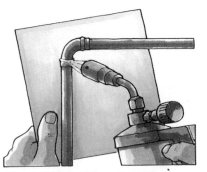

3 Wrap paper around a pipe to guide a saw

Gas torches

To heat the metal sufficiently for a soldered joint, most plumbers use a gas torch. Gas, liquefied under pressure, is contained in a disposable metal canister. When the control valve of the torch is opened, gas is vaporized to combine with air to make a highly combustible mixture. Once ignited, the flame is adjusted until it burns steadily with a clear blue colour.

Many professional plumbers use a propane torch which is connected by a hose to a metal gas bottle. The average householder does not need such expensive equipment, but if you happen to own a propane torch, perhaps for car repairs, you can use the same tool to solder plumbing joints.

Using integral-ring joints

Clean the ends of each pipe and the inside of the joint sleeves with wire wool or abrasive paper until the metal is shiny. Brush flux onto the cleaned metal and push the pipes into the joint, twisting them to spread the flux evenly. Make sure each pipe is up against the integral stop in the joint.

If you are using elbows or tees, mark the pipe and joint with a pencil to make sure they do not get misaligned during the soldering.

Slip a ceramic tile or a plumbers' fibreglass mat behind the joint to protect any flammable materials, then apply the flame of a gas torch over the area of the joint to heat it evenly (1). When a bright ring of solder appears at

Using end-feed joints

Clean and assemble an end-feed joint like an integral-ring type, then heat the area of the joint evenly. When the flux begins to bubble, remove the flame and touch the end of the solder wire to two

1 Heat the joint to melt the captive solder

Solder and flux

Solder is a soft alloy manufactured with a melting point lower than that of the metal it is joining. Plumbers' solder is sold as wound wire.

Copper must be spotlessly clean and grease-free to produce a properly soldered joint. Even when you have cleaned it mechanically with wire wool, copper begins to oxidize immediately so a chemical cleaner known as flux is painted onto the metal to provide a barrier against oxidation until the solder is applied. A non-corrosive flux in the form of a paste is the best one to use. On stainless-steel pipework use a highly efficient active flux, but wash it off with warm water after the joint is made or the metal will corrode.

each end of the joint, remove the flame and allow the metal to cool for a couple of minutes before disturbing it.

Repairing a weeping joint

When you fill a new installation with water for the first time, check every joint to make sure it is watertight. If you notice water 'weeping' from a soldered joint, drain the pipe and allow it to dry. Heat the joint and apply some fresh solder to the edge of each mouth. If it leaks a second time, heat the joint until you can pull it apart with gloved hands. Use a new joint or clean and flux all surfaces and reuse the same joint, adding solder as if you were working with an end-feed fitting (see below).

or three points around the mouth of each sleeve (2). You will know that the joint is full of solder when a bright ring appears around each sleeve. Allow it to cool. Mend a weeping joint as above.

Gas torches
A gas torch is used to heat soldered joints. A simple torch (top) is available from any DIY outlet. The propane torch (above) is used by professional plumbers.

2 Introduce solder to a heated end-feed joint

MAKING COMPRESSION JOINTS

SEE ALSO
Details for:
Plumbing adaptors   362
Wrenches   506

Using compression fittings is so straightforward that you will be able to make watertight joints without any previous experience.

Assembling a joint

Cut the ends of each pipe square and clean them, along with the olives, with wire wool. Dismantle a new joint and slip a cap-nut over the end of one pipe, followed by an olive (**1**). Look carefully to see if the sloping sides of the olive are equal in length. If one is longer than the other, that side should face away from the nut.

Push the pipe firmly into the joint body (**2**), twisting it slightly to ensure it is firmly against the integral stop. Slide the olive up against the joint body, then tighten the nut by hand.

The olive must be compressed by just the right amount to ensure a watertight joint. As a guide, use a pencil to mark one face of the nut and the opposing face on the joint body (**3**) then, holding the body steady with a spanner, use another spanner to turn the nut one complete revolution (**4**). Assemble the other half of the joint in exactly the same manner.

To make absolutely sure the joint is watertight, some plumbers prefer to wrap a single turn of PTFE tape over the olive before tightening the nut. However, a properly tightened compression joint should be watertight without it.

1 Slip an olive onto the pipe after the cap-nut

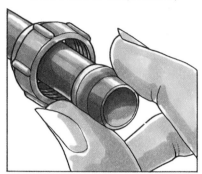

2 Clamp joint to pipe with the nut

3 Mark the nut and joint with a pencil

4 Tighten the joint with two spanners

Repairing a weeping joint

Having filled the pipe with water, check each joint for leaks. Make one further quarter turn on any nut that appears to be weeping.

Crushing an olive by overtightening a compression joint will cause it to leak. Drain the pipe and dismantle the joint. Cut through the damaged olive with a junior hacksaw, taking care not to damage the pipe. Remake the joint with a new olive, restore the supply of water and check for leaks once more.

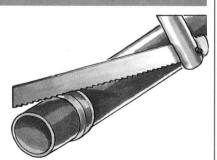

Saw through a damaged olive

MAKING COPPER-TO-STEEL CONNECTIONS

Galvanized-steel pipe is connected by threaded joints, so if you plan to extend old pipework using the same material you will need a pipe die to cut the threads on the end of each length of new pipe. You can hire this tool but it would be simpler to continue the run in copper, using an adaptor to connect one system to another. One end of the adaptor has a capillary or compression joint for the copper pipework; the other end has a male or female threaded connector for the galvanized steel.

Use two Stillson wrenches to unscrew the joint on the old pipework where you intend to connect up to copper. Grip the joint with one wrench and the pipe with the other, pushing and pulling in the direction the jaws face (**1**). If the joint is stiff, use penetrating oil or play the flame of a gas torch along it.

Threaded connections leak unless they are made watertight with plumbers' PTFE tape. Wrap the tape clockwise two or three times around the pipe to cover the threads (**2**), then engage and tighten the nut.

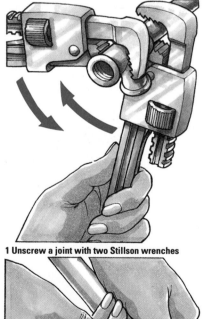

1 Unscrew a joint with two Stillson wrenches

2 Wrap plenty of PTFE tape over the threads

BENDING PIPES

MAKING COPPER-TO-LEAD CONNECTIONS

When replacing old lead plumbing with copper, a plumber would formerly make the connection to the lead rising main with solder and a blowlamp. It is illegal to make such joints nowadays, and it is also far simpler to use a special lead-to-copper compression joint. The connection can be made even with water still in the pipe.

Joints are manufactured to fit different size lead pipes and for 15 and 22mm (½ and ¾in) copper pipes. You can use the same joints for plastic plumbing provided you reinforce the plastic pipe with metal inserts. Although the connectors are specified according to the bore of lead pipework, measure the outside diameter of your rising main and ask a plumbers' merchant to provide a suitable compression joint.

Making the connection

Select a straight length of lead pipe that is as round as possible. It must also be in good condition: the O-ring inside the fitting will not make a watertight seal if the lead is dented or scored.

If possible, turn off the water. Cut the lead pipe with a hacksaw, chamfer the outside edge and remove the burr from inside. Dismantle the compression joint and check that the large thrust nut makes a good sliding fit on the pipe. You can scrape back a slightly oversize pipe to fit, keeping it as round as possible.

Slide the thrust nut onto the pipe, then the two metal rings and the rubber O-ring (**1**). Slide the threaded coupling body onto the end of the pipe and push it against the internal end stop. Tighten the coupling (**2**) until you feel resistance, but don't use excessive force.

The other end of the coupling body carries a conventional compression joint for the copper pipe.

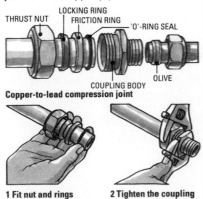

THRUST NUT — LOCKING RING — FRICTION RING — 'O'-RING SEAL — COUPLING BODY — OLIVE
Copper-to-lead compression joint

1 Fit nut and rings   **2 Tighten the coupling**

You can change the direction of a pipe run by using an elbow joint, but there are occasions when bending the pipe itself will produce a neater or more accurate result. If you want to carry a pipe over a small obstruction, such as another pipe for example, a slight kink in the pipe will be less of an obstruction to the flow of water and therefore create less noise than two elbows within a few centimetres of each other. It is also cheaper. You might also want to run pipes into a window alcove where the walls meet at an unusual angle. Bending the pipes accurately will allow you to fit the pipes neatly against the walls of the alcove.

Using a bending spring

A bending spring is the cheapest and easiest tool for making bends in small pipe runs. It is a hardened-steel coil spring that supports the walls of copper tube to stop it kinking. Most bending springs are made to fit inside the pipe, but some slide over it.

Slide the spring into the tube to support the area you want to bend. Hold the tube against your knee and bend it to the required angle. The bent tube will grip the spring, but slipping a screwdriver into the ring at one end and turning it anti-clockwise will reduce the diameter of the spring so that you can pull it out.

If you make a bend some distance from the end of a tube, you won't be able to withdraw the bending spring in the normal way; either use an external spring or tie a length of twine to the ring and lightly grease the spring with petroleum jelly before you insert it. Slightly overbend the tube and open it out to the correct angle to release the spring, then pull it out with the twine.

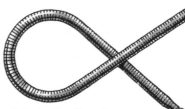

A plumbers' bending spring

Bend a pipe against your knee

Using a pipe bender

Although you can hire bending springs to fit the larger pipes, it is not easy to bend 22 or 28mm (¾ or 1in) tube over your knee, so it is well worth hiring a pipe bender to do the job.

Hold the pipe against the radiused former and insert the straight former to support it. Pull both levers towards each other to make the bend, then open up the bender to remove the pipe.

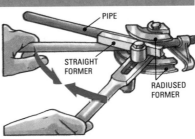

PIPE — STRAIGHT FORMER — RADIUSED FORMER
Use a pipe bender for larger tubing

Getting the bends in the right place

It is difficult to position two or more bends accurately along a single length of pipe. If you want to fit an alcove, for example, it is easier to bend individual lengths of pipe to fit each corner, then cut the tubes where they overlap and insert joints.

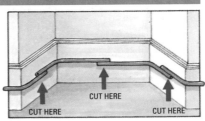

CUT HERE — CUT HERE — CUT HERE
Bend separate lengths of pipe to fit an alcove

● **Annealing pipe**
When you are working with large-diameter copper pipe, play the flame of a gas torch around the area of the intended bend until the metal is cherry red, then allow it to cool. The pipe will bend with minimal effort, using a bending spring.

Supporting pipe runs
Place a plastic or metal clip at 1m (3ft 3in) intervals along a horizontal run of 15mm (½in) pipe. Increase the spacing to every 1.5m (4ft 6in) on a vertical run. In the case of larger pipes, increase the spacing a little more.

Notching floor joists
When you run pipes under floorboards, notch each joist to receive the pipe. Cut the notch to align with the centre of a floorboard and drive a nail on each side when replacing the board.

365

PLASTIC PLUMBING

The introduction of plastics is probably the most innovative development in plumbing since copper was first used. Plastic plumbing is lightweight and extremely easy to construct. It does not burst when frozen, corrode or adversely affect other materials and, depending on the type of plastic, it can be used for hot and cold water, including central-heating pipework. Most plastic systems can be connected with adaptors to existing metal pipe.

Plastic pipe: standard sizes

Plastic pipes are made to more or less standard sizes, but there may be slight variation from one manufacturer's stock to another. As with metal pipework, most metric dimensions refer to the outside diameter of the tube and imperial dimensions to the inside, but not all manufacturers specify their pipes in the same way. Check that pipes and fittings are compatible with existing plumbing before you buy them. The following list is a guide to the available sizes of plastic pipe.

PLASTIC PIPEWORK	
General pipework	15mm (½in); 22mm (¾in); 28mm (1in)
Overflow pipes	21mm (¾in)
Wash basin wastepipes	32mm (1¼in)
Bath/sink wastepipes	40mm (1½in)
Soil pipe	110mm (4in)

Supporting pipe runs

Plastic pipework should be supported with clips or saddles similar to those used for metal pipe, but because it is more flexible you will have to space the clips closer together. Check with the manufacturers' literature to establish the exact dimensions.

If you plan to surface-run flexible pipes, consider ducting or boxing-in because it's difficult to make a really neat installation.

JOINTS AND FITTINGS FOR PLASTIC PLUMBING

Most plastic joints and fittings are similar to those used for metal plumbing, but in addition there are easy-flow swept bends and tees for drainage systems. These joints frequently have cleaning eyes or access plugs for removing blockages in the pipe. Joints and pipes are normally manufactured from the same material, but there are several specialized connectors available for joining plastic plumbing to taps, valves and existing metal plumbing.

You will have to browse through manufacturers' catalogues to see the huge variety of plastic joints for both supply and waste systems, but the selection below shows the main categories of joint with examples of the different types of coupling.

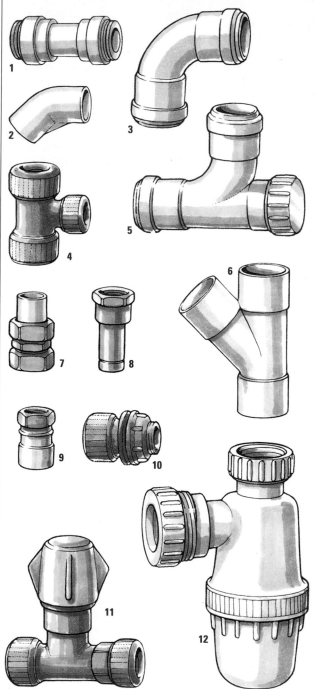

Straight connectors
To join two pipes end-to-end in a straight line.
1 For pipes of equal diameter – *push-fit:* supply.

Bends or elbows
To join two pipes at an angle.
2 45 degree elbow – *solvent weld:* supply.
3 Swept bend – *push-fit:* waste.

Tees
To join three pipes.
4 Unequal tee to join 15mm (½in) branch pipe to main pipe run – *push-fit:* supply.
5 Swept tee with access plug – *push-fit:* waste.
6 45 degree branch – *solvent weld:* waste.

Adaptors
To join dissimilar pipes.
7 Plastic to copper connector – *solvent weld* and *compression joint:* supply.
8 Plastic to galvanized-steel connector – *push-fit* and *threaded female coupling:* supply.

Fittings
Specialized connections are available to join plastic plumbing to fittings. All manufacturers supply items like taps and valves to match their particular range.
9 Tap connector with threaded nut for connecting supply pipe to tail of tap – *solvent weld:* supply.
10 Tank connector joins pipes to storage cisterns – *push-fit:* supply.
11 Stopcock – *push-fit:* supply
12 Bottle trap for sink or basin– *compression joint:* waste.

JOINING
PLASTIC PIPES

Plastics are complex materials, each one having its own properties. Consequently, a technique or material that is suitable for joining one plastic might be quite useless for another. To make sure joints are watertight, it is important to follow each manufacturer's instructions carefully, and to use the particular solvents and lubricants that are recommended. The examples below illustrate the common methods used to connect plastic plumbing.

Solvent-weld joints

Lengths of pipe are linked by simple socketed connectors. As they are assembled, a solvent is introduced to the joint which dissolves the surfaces of the mating components. As the solvent evaporates, the joint and pipes are literally fused together into one piece of plastic. Solvent-weld joints are sometimes used for supply pipes, but the technique is more commonly employed for waste systems.

Compression joints

So that they can be dismantled easily, sink, bath and washbasin traps are often connected to the pipework by means of compression joints that incorporate a rubber ring or washer to make the joint watertight.

Push-fit joints – waste systems

Because a waste system is never under pressure, a pipe run can be constructed by simply pushing plain pipes into the sockets of the joints. A captive rubber seal in each socket holds the pipe in place and makes the joint watertight.

Push-fit joints – supply systems

When the pipe is inserted, an O-ring seals in the water in the normal way and, depending on the model, a metal grab ring or a collet with stainless-steel teeth grips the tube securely to prevent water under mains pressure forcing the joint apart. Joints fitted with collets can be disconnected easily, but it is necessary to remove the retaining cap and crush the grab ring to dismantle the other type of push-fit joint.

Push-fit joints are more obtrusive than solvent-welded types, but the speed and simplicity with which you can assemble them more than compensate for this.

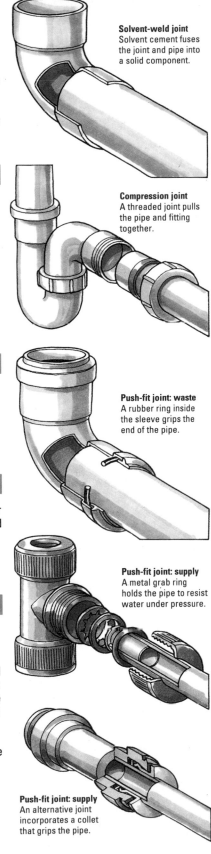

Solvent-weld joint
Solvent cement fuses the joint and pipe into a solid component.

Compression joint
A threaded joint pulls the pipe and fitting together.

Push-fit joint: waste
A rubber ring inside the sleeve grips the end of the pipe.

Push-fit joint: supply
A metal grab ring holds the pipe to resist water under pressure.

Push-fit joint: supply
An alternative joint incorporates a collet that grips the pipe.

TYPES OF PLASTIC

Plumbing manufacturers have a wide variety of plastics to draw upon, each with its own special characteristics.

Unplasticized polyvinyl chloride (uPVC)
A hard, rigid plastic used for waste systems and cold-water supply.

Modified polyvinyl chloride (PVC)
A similar plastic to uPVC, but it is slightly more flexible and therefore shock-resistant.

Chlorinated polyvinyl chloride (cPVC)
A versatile plastic suitable for hot and cold supply. It can even withstand the temperatures required for central-heating systems.

Polypropylene (PP)
This slightly flexible plastic with a somewhat greasy feel is used for waste systems. It is impossible to glue PP so it is never welded with solvent.

Acrylonitrile butadiene styrene (ABS)
A very tough plastic equally suited to hot and cold waste.

Polybutylene (PB)
A tough, flexible plastic used for hot and cold supply – even central heating. Available in standard lengths or continuous coils, PB resists bursting when frozen.

Cross-linked polyethylene (PEX)
Although it expands considerably when heated, PEX is used to make pipes that supply hot and cold water and for underfloor heating systems. However, it tends to sag so is unsuitable for surface running. A PEX pipe resists bursting when subjected to frost.

Medium-density polyethylene (MDPE)
This plastic is widely used for underground domestic supply pipes. The pipes, normally coloured blue, can be laid in continuous lengths, and are resistant to pressure and corrosion.

SEE ALSO

Details for:	
Solvent joints	368
Push-fit joints	368–369

● **Oxygen-diffusion barriers**
There is some concern that the small amount of oxygen drawn through the walls of plastic central-heating pipes contributes to the corrosion of the system. To prevent this happening, an oxygen-diffusion barrier is built into the walls of some pipe.

MAKING JOINTS IN PLASTIC WASTEPIPES

SEE ALSO
Details for:
Hacksaws   502–503
Files   506

While you should follow the detailed advice supplied with any specific make of pipe or fitting, the instructions below and on the facing page demonstrate the basic methods used to connect plastic pipework. Do not inhale solvent fumes, and never smoke when welding joints – some solvents give off fumes which become toxic when inhaled through a cigarette. Keep solvents away from children. Work carefully to avoid spilling solvent cement as it will etch the surface of the pipework and certain other plastics as well.

● **Making compression joints to traps**
Traps with compression joints are connected directly to a plain wastepipe. Just slip the threaded nut onto the pipe, followed by the washer and then the rubber ring. Push the pipe into the socket of the trap and tighten the compression nut.

JOINING PUSH-FIT WASTEPIPES

Cut the pipe to length and chamfer the end as for solvent-weld joints. Wipe the inside of the socket with the recommended cleaner and lubricate the pipe with a little of the silicone lubricant supplied with it.

Push the pipe into the joint right up to the stop and mark the edge of the socket on the pipe with a pencil (**1**).

Withdraw the pipe about 9mm (⅜in) (**2**) to allow the pipe to expand when subjected to hot water.

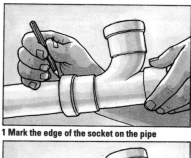

1 Mark the edge of the socket on the pipe

2 Withdraw the pipe about 9mm (⅜in)

Repairing a weeping joint
If a push-fit joint is leaking, the rubber seal has been pushed out of position, probably because the socket is out of line with the pipe. Dismantle the joint and check the condition of the seal.

While the sequence of illustrations right show large-diameter wastepipe, the methods described are identical when joining plastic supply pipe. Cut the pipe to length with a saw, allowing for the depth of the joint socket. To make sure your cut is square, wind a piece of notepaper round the tube, aligning the wrapped edge as a guide (**1**). Revolve the pipe away from you as you cut it. Smooth the end with a file (**2**).

Welding the joint
Push the pipe into the socket to test the fit, then mark the end of the joint on the pipe with a pencil (**3**). This will act as a guide for applying the solvent. You must key the outside of the pipe and the inside of the socket with fine abrasive paper before using some solvents. Check the manufacturer's instructions.

Before dismantling elbows and tees, scratch the pipe and joint with a knife (**4**) to help you align them correctly when you reassemble the components.

Use a clean rag to wipe the surface of the pipe and fitting with the recommended spirit cleaner. Paint solvent evenly onto both components (**5**) and immediately push home the socket. (Some manufacturers recommend that you twist the joint to spread the solvent.) Align the joint properly and leave it for 15 seconds.

The pipe is ready for use with cold water after one hour. Do not pass hot water through the system until at least four hours have elapsed, preferably longer, according to the manufacturer's recommendations.

Allowing for expansion
Plastic pipes expand when subjected to hot water, but this is only a problem over a straight run more than 3m (10ft) in length (or less if recommended by the manufacturer). Incorporate an expansion coupling with a push-fit rubber seal at one end that allows the pipe to slide in or out without putting other joints under load. Lubricate the end of the pipe with silicone grease before you insert it in the coupling.

Repairing a weeping joint
If a joint leaks when the system is filled with water, drain it again and allow it to dry out. Apply a little more solvent cement to the mouth of the socket, allowing it to flow into the joint by capillary action.

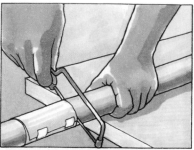

1 Use paper as a guide to keep the cut square

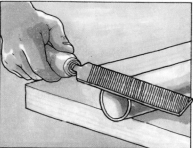

2 Smooth the end with a file

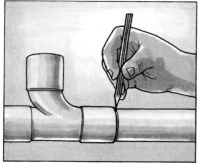

3 Assemble the joint and mark the socket

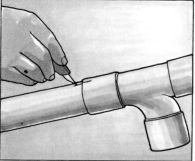

4 Scratch the pipe and joint to realign them

5 Paint solvent up to the pencil mark

MAKING JOINTS
IN PLASTIC
SUPPLY PIPES

Plastic supply pipes can be connected using solvent-weld joints as described opposite, but you may prefer to use the more convenient push-fit connectors shown below.

Using grab-ring push-fit joints

Cut polybutylene pipe to length with the special shears that are supplied by the manufacturer (1), or alternatively use a sharp craft knife. Provided you make the cut reasonably square, the joint will be watertight.

Push a metal support sleeve into the pipe (2), then use a fingertip to smear a little silicone lubricant around the end of the pipe and inside the socket (3).

Push the prepared pipe firmly into the socket a full 25mm (1in) (4). As the joint can revolve freely around the pipe after connection without breaking the seal, there is no problem when aligning tees and elbows with other pipe runs.

1 Cut pipe to length

2 Insert metal sleeve

3 Apply lubricant

4 Push pipe into joint

Dismantling a joint

If you need to dismantle a joint to alter a system, unscrew the cap by hand and pull out the pipe. Slide the rubber ring and washer along the pipe, then crush the metal grab ring with pliers (5) to remove it.

Drop a new grab ring into the socket, teeth facing into the fitting, and replace the washer, followed by the rubber ring.

Screw back the cap hand-tight, then use mole grips to turn it 2mm (⅛in) further. Overtightening will render the joint ineffective.

Connect to the pipe as described above. Never attempt to assemble the fitting like a compression joint or it will blow out under pressure.

Repairing a weeping joint
A supply push-fit joint may leak if the pipe is not pushed home fully or the O-ring is damaged.

5 Crush the metal grab ring to dismantle joint

Using collet-type push-fit joints

Push-fit joints that incorporate collets are particularly easy to assemble. Cut the end of the pipe square, push it into the socket until it comes up against the internal stop, then pull on the pipe to check that the joint is secure.

If you need to dismantle a joint, hold in the collet with your fingertips (1) and pull the pipe out of the socket.

Join metal pipes in the same way, but remove burrs and sharp edges to prevent tearing the O-ring. Provide extra grip by slipping a collet clip into the grooved collar (2).

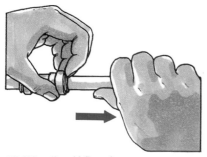

1 Hold in collet with fingertips

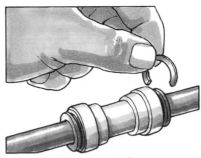

2 Slip collet clip into grooved collar

CONNECTING METAL TO PLASTIC PLUMBING

Use special adaptor couplings to connect most types of plastic pipe to copper or galvanized-steel plumbing. To join polybutylene pipe to copper, insert a metal support sleeve (see left), then use a standard brass compression joint. Alternatively, join copper pipes to a polybutylene run using a push-fit connector. Cut and deburr copper pipe carefully before pushing it into the joint.

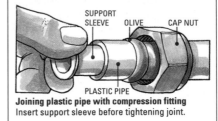

SUPPORT SLEEVE   OLIVE   CAP NUT

PLASTIC PIPE

Joining plastic pipe with compression fitting
Insert support sleeve before tightening joint.

Bending plastic pipes

It is possible to bend a rigid supply pipe by heating it gently. Pass the flame of a gas torch over the area you wish to bend. Keep the flame moving and revolve the pipe all the time. When the pipe is soft enough, bend it by hand on a flat surface (1) and hold it still until the plastic hardens again.

Flexible pipes are bent cold to a minimum radius of eight times the pipe diameter. Use a pipe clip at each side of the bend to hold the curve, or use a special corner clamp (2). Long, gentle curves can be made by threading flexible pipe around obstacles, and running it under floorboards is easy.

1 Bend the softened pipe on a flat surface

2 Hook flexible pipe into a metal clamp

Simply renewing an old WC or even replacing it with a more modern suite is a relatively straightforward operation, provided you can connect it to the existing branch of the soil pipe. However, if you plan to move the WC or perhaps install a second one elsewhere, you will have to break into the main soil pipe itself or run the waste directly into the underground drainage system. In either case, it would probably pay you to hire a professional plumber to make these connections.

Before you buy a replacement suite, remember to check that there is sufficient space to use the new equipment (see left) and that there is enough room to open and close the bathroom door. Don't forget to check the headroom if you plan to install a high-level cistern. It is important to check out soil-pipe connections in advance, but the supply pipe and overflow can usually be run without difficulty.

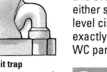

Space for a WC
You will need to allow a space in front of the pan of at least 600mm (2ft) square.

Types of cistern

From antique-style high-level cisterns to discreet close-coupled or concealed models, the choice is so wide that you are bound to find one that will suit your needs. Before buying, make sure that the equipment carries the British Standard Kite mark or complies with equivalent EC standards.

High-level cistern
If you simply want to replace an existing high-level cistern without having to modify the pipework, comparable cisterns are still available from plumbers' merchants.

Standard low-level cistern
Many people prefer a cistern that is mounted on the wall just above the WC pan. A short flush pipe from the base of the cistern connects to the flushing horn on the rear of the pan, while inlet and overflow pipes can be fitted to either side of the cistern. Most low-level cisterns are manufactured from exactly the same vitreous china as the WC pan itself.

Compact low-level cistern
Where space is limited, use a plastic cistern which is only 114mm (4½in) from front to back.

Concealed cistern
A low-level cistern can be completely concealed behind panelling. The supply and overflow connections are identical to those of other cisterns, but the flushing lever is mounted on the face of the panel. These plastic cisterns are utilitarian in character with no concession to fashion or style, and are therefore relatively inexpensive. Don't forget that you will need to provide access for servicing.

Close-coupled cisterns
A close-coupled cistern is bolted directly to the pan, forming an integral unit. Both the inlet and overflow connections are made at the base of the cistern. An internal standpipe rises vertically from the overflow connection to protrude above the level of the water in the cistern.

Floor-exit trap
S-traps are connected to a soil pipe that is then passed through the floor.

Wall-exit trap
The outlet from a P-trap connects to a soil-pipe branch located behind the pan.

Types of WC pan

When you visit a showroom you are confronted with many apparently different WC pans to choose from, but in fact there are two basic patterns: a washdown pan and a siphonic pan.

Siphonic pans
Siphonic pans need no heavy fall of water to cleanse them and are much quieter as a result. A single-trap pan has a narrow outlet immediately after the bend to slow down the flow of water from the pan. The body of water expels air from the outlet to promote the siphonic action. A double-trap pan is more sophisticated and exceptionally

quiet. A vent pipe connects the space between two traps to the inlet running between the cistern and pan. As water flows along the inlet, it sucks air from the trap system through the vent pipe. A vacuum is formed between the traps, and atmospheric pressure forces the water in the pan into the soil pipe.

Washdown pans
Washdown pans work by simple displacement of waste by fresh water falling from the cistern. They are inherently more reliable than siphonic pans, but they make considerably more noise when flushed.

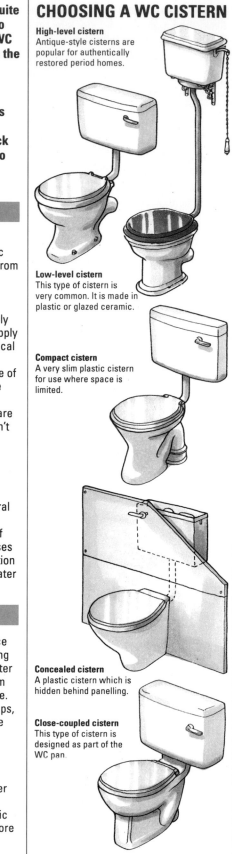

CHOOSING A WC CISTERN

High-level cistern
Antique-style cisterns are popular for authentically restored period homes.

Low-level cistern
This type of cistern is very common. It is made in plastic or glazed ceramic.

Compact cistern
A very slim plastic cistern for use where space is limited.

Concealed cistern
A plastic cistern which is hidden behind panelling.

Close-coupled cistern
This type of cistern is designed as part of the WC pan.

CHOOSING A WC PAN

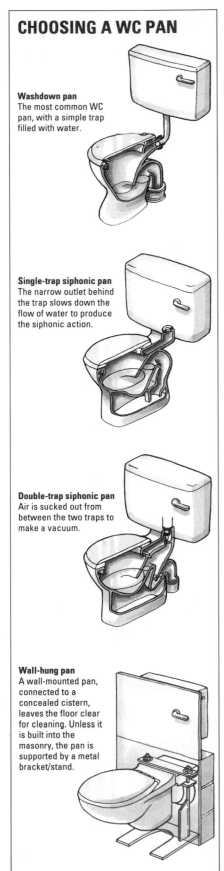

Washdown pan
The most common WC pan, with a simple trap filled with water.

Single-trap siphonic pan
The narrow outlet behind the trap slows down the flow of water to produce the siphonic action.

Double-trap siphonic pan
Air is sucked out from between the two traps to make a vacuum.

Wall-hung pan
A wall-mounted pan, connected to a concealed cistern, leaves the floor clear for cleaning. Unless it is built into the masonry, the pan is supported by a metal bracket/stand.

Cut off the water supply, then flush the cistern to empty it. If you are merely renewing a cistern, you will have to disconnect the supply and overflow pipes with a wrench and loosen the large nut connecting the flush pipe to the base of the cistern. These connections are often corroded and painted, so it is easier to hacksaw through the pipes close to the connections if you intend to replace the entire suite.

Having lifted the cistern off its support brackets, try freeing the fixing screws. In all probability they will be corroded, so lever the brackets off the wall with a crowbar.

Cut the overflow pipe from the wall with a cold chisel. Repair the plaster when you decorate the bathroom.

If the pan is screwed to a wooden floor, it will probably have a P-trap connected to a nearly horizontal branch soil pipe. Remove the floor-fixing screws and scrape out the old putty around the pipe joint. Attempt to free the pan by pulling it towards you while rocking it slightly from side to side.

If the joint is fixed firmly, smash the pan outlet just in front of the soil pipe with a club hammer (**1**). Protect your eyes with goggles. Stuff rags into the soil pipe to prevent debris falling into it, then chip out the remains of the pan outlet with a cold chisel (**2**). Work carefully to preserve the soil pipe.

Smash an S-trap in the same way, and if the pan is cemented to a solid floor, drive a cold chisel under its base to break the seal. Chop out the broken fragments as before and clean up the floor with a cold chisel.

REMOVING THE OLD WC

SEE ALSO

Details for:	
Turning off water	350
WC cistern	354
Chain-link cutter	503

1 Break the outlet of the pan with a hammer

2 Use a cold chisel to cut out the remnants

Cutting the soil pipe

If you break the soil pipe while chipping out the pan outlet, cut the pipe square with a hired chain-link pipe cutter. Clamp the chain of cutters around the pipe and work the shaft back and forth to sever it. Ratchet-action cutters enable you to work in a confined space. When you buy a push-fit pan connector (see below), make sure it is long enough to reach the severed pipe.

Pan to soil-pipe connection

Before you install the new suite, choose a push-fit flexible connector to join the pan to the soil pipe. There are connectors to suit most situations, even when the two elements are slightly misaligned. You will probably need an angled connector to join a modern horizontal-outlet pan to an old P-trap branch pipe. Make a note of the following dimensions when selecting a connector: the external diameter of pan outlet; the internal diameter of soil pipe; the distance between the outlet and pipe when the pan is installed.

CUT HERE

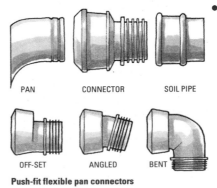

CUT HERE

Removing an appliance
If fittings are corroded, remove the appliance by cutting through the flush pipe, overflow and pan outlet.

Cutting a soil pipe
Use a chain-link cutter to cut a broken soil pipe square.

● **Lubricating connectors**
When installing plastic soil-pipe connectors, it pays to smear the surfaces lightly with a silicone lubricant.

PAN   CONNECTOR   SOIL PIPE

OFF-SET   ANGLED   BENT

Push-fit flexible pan connectors

371

INSTALLING
A NEW
WC SUITE

SEE ALSO

Details for:
Fused connection unit	320
Flex outlet	321
Float valves	355
Adjusting float valve	356
Tank connector	362, 366
Connecting pipes	362–369
Running pipework	365
Waste boss	376
Overflow unit	378

Tundish
A special funnel
known as a tundish
allows you to detect
an overflow from a
cistern.

● **Fixing a new WC pan
to the floor**
All manufacturers
advise against the old-
fashioned method of
cementing a WC pan
to a concrete floor. In
fact, guarantees are
usually invalidated if
cement or a strong
adhesive is used. If
you cannot screw the
pan in place (see
right), lay it on a bed of
flexible silicone
sealant.

● **Installing a new high-
level cistern**
A three-piece
adjustable flush pipe
allows you to hang a
high-level cistern to
one side of the pan. Fit
a flow restrictor in the
pan inlet if splashing
water is a problem.

INSTALLING A NEW WC SUITE

Push the plastic connector onto the pan
outlet. Check that the inside of the soil
pipe is clean and smooth, then slide the
pan to push the connector firmly into
the pipe.

Don't fix the pan yet, but drill fixing
holes in a concrete floor and plug them
(see left). Level the pan using scraps of
veneer or vinyl floorcovering. (Trim with
a knife when installation is complete.)

Connect the flush pipe and hold the
cistern against the wall to mark fixing
holes. Fix the cistern with non-corroding
screws and washers, making sure it is
level. You may have to use tap washers
as packing behind the cistern to provide
a clearance for the lid. Tighten the flush
pipe connection under the cistern.

Screw the pan to the floor. Fit rubber
washers under each screwhead and
tighten the screws carefully in rotation
to avoid cracking the pan. You can buy
kits that include all the necessary
washers and fixings for fitting WCs.

Run the new 15mm (½in) supply pipe
to the float valve, fit a tap connector
and tighten it with a wrench.

Attach a 21mm (¾in) overflow pipe
with the connector provided. Drill a hole
through the nearest outside wall where
an overflow will be detected promptly.
Slope the pipe a few degrees and let it
project from the outer face of the wall
at least 150mm (6in). When there is no
external wall nearby, run the pipe to a
combined waste and overflow unit on
the bath. Alternatively, fit a tundish (see
left) and run the overflow to the flush
pipe or via a trap to a drain. Turn on the
water supply and adjust the float valve.

Plumbing a WC
1 Overflow-pipe
connector
2 21mm (¾in) overflow
3 Cistern
4 Float valve
5 Tap connector
6 15mm (½in) supply
pipe
7 Flush-pipe connector
8 Flush pipe
9 Push-fit flexible
connector
10 WC-pan outlet
11 Flexible outlet
connector
12 Soil pipe

Typical pipe run
Red: Hot water
Blue: Cold water

Small-bore waste system

The siting of a WC is normally limited by
the need to use a conventional 110mm
(4in) soil pipe, and to provide sufficient
fall to discharge the waste into the soil
stack. By using an electrically driven
pump and shredder, you can discharge
WC waste through a 22mm (¾in) pipe
up to 50m (55yd) away from the stack.
The shredder will even pump vertically
to a maximum of 4m (4yd). You can run
the small-bore pipework through the
narrow space between a floor and
ceiling. Consequently, a WC can be
installed as part of an en-suite
bathroom, under the stairs or even in a
basement, provided the space is
adequately ventilated.

The unit accepts any conventional
P-trap WC pan. It is activated by
flushing the cistern, and switches off
about 18 seconds later. It must be wired
to a fused connection unit, but via a
suitable flex outlet if it is installed in a
bathroom. The wastepipe is connected
to the soil stack using any standard
32mm (1¼in) waste boss, provided the
manufacturer supplies a 22–32mm
(¾–1¼in) adaptor. A WC wastepipe
must be connected to the soil stack at
least 200mm (8in) above or below other
waste connections.

Before you install a small-bore waste
system, check that they are approved
by your local water supplier.

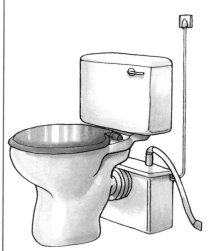

Small-bore waste system for a WC
The shredding unit fits neatly behind a P-trap WC
pan. When it is situated in a bathroom the unit
must be wired to a flex outlet as shown above;
otherwise it can be connected directly to a fused
connection unit.

FITTING A WASHBASIN

Whether you are modifying existing plumbing or running pipework to a new location, fitting a washbasin in a bathroom or guest room will present few difficulties provided you give some thought to how you will run the waste to the vertical stack. The waste must have a minimum fall or slope of 6mm (¼in) for every 300mm (1ft) of pipe run, and it should not exceed 3m (10ft) in length.

Choosing a washbasin

Wall-hung and pedestal washbasins are invariably made from vitreous china, but basins that are supported all round by a counter top are also available in pressed steel and plastic. Select the taps at the same time to ensure that the basin of your choice has holes at the required spacing to receive the taps, or no holes at all if the taps are to be wall-mounted.

Make sure the basin has sufficient space on each side or to the rear for soaps, shampoo and other toiletries, otherwise you will have to provide a separate shelf or cabinet.

Pedestal basins
The hollow pedestal provides some support to the basin and it conceals unsightly supply pipes.

Wall-hung basin
Older wall-hung basins are supported on large screw-fixed brackets, but a modern concealed mounting is just as strong provided the wall fixings are secure. Check that you can screw into the studs of a timber-frame wall or hack off the lath-and-plaster and install a mounting board. (Use the same method to secure an existing basin with loose wall fixings.)

If you want to hide supply pipes, consider some form of panelling.

Corner basin
Hand basins which fit into the corner of a room are popular because supply and wastepipes can be run conveniently through adjacent walls or concealed by boxing them in across the corner.

Recessed basin
A small hand basin can be recessed into a wall of a cloakroom or WC where space is limited.

Counter-top basins
In a large bathroom or bedroom you can fit a washbasin into a counter top as part of a built-in vanity unit. The cupboards below provide ample storage for towels and toiletries while hiding the plumbing at the same time.

CONCEALING PIPEWORK

The manufacturers of appliances and fittings are aware that most people find visible plumbing unattractive and, as a result, supply fitments such as sink units, panelled baths, shower cubicles, concealed cisterns and pedestal and counter-top basins, all of which are designed to hide their supply pipes and drainage. With careful selection and well-designed pipe runs, it should be possible to plumb your house without a single visible pipe. In practice, however, there are always situations where you have no option but to surface-run at least some pipes, especially when you cannot take them under floorboards. You can minimize the effect by taking care to group pipes together neatly and keep runs both straight and parallel. When painted to match the skirtings or walls, such pipes are barely visible.

Alternatively, you can construct ducting to conceal pipes completely. Make your own ducting with softwood battens and plywood to bridge the corner of a room, or construct a false skirting that is deep enough to contain the pipes. It pays to make at least part of the ducting removable to give you access to joints or other fittings in case you need to service them later. For total accessibility, use proprietary ducting made from PVC. This is manufactured in a range of sizes to contain grouped or individual pipes. With right-angle and tee-piece joints, you can construct a system of ducting to cover any new or existing installation. Optional foam liners are available to insulate hot-water and central-heating pipes.

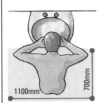

Space for a basin
Allow extra elbow room for washing hair. A space 1100mm (3ft 8in) x 700mm (2ft 4in) should be sufficient. To suit most people, position the rim of a basin 800mm (2ft 8in) from the floor.

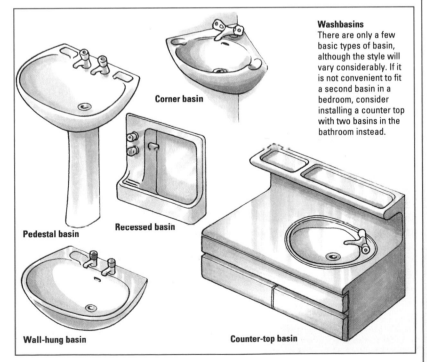

Washbasins
There are only a few basic types of basin, although the style will vary considerably. If it is not convenient to fit a second basin in a bedroom, consider installing a counter top with two basins in the bathroom instead.

Corner basin

Pedestal basin

Recessed basin

Wall-hung basin

Counter-top basin

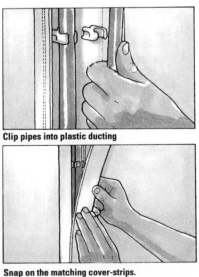

Clip pipes into plastic ducting

Snap on the matching cover-strips.

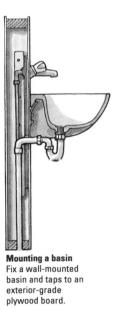

Mounting a basin
Fix a wall-mounted basin and taps to an exterior-grade plywood board.

SELECTING

TAPS FOR A

BASIN

SEE ALSO
Details for:
Repairing taps   352–353

The majority of taps are made of chromium-plated or enamelled brass, although there is a limited range of plastic-bodied taps. While the latter are not as durable as metal ones, they are much cheaper. All basin taps have a 15mm (½in) threaded inlet known as the tail for attaching the supply pipe.

Types of tap

Individual taps
The majority of washbasins are fitted with individual taps for hot and cold water. While capstan-head taps are still manufactured for use in period-style bathrooms, most modern taps have a shrouded head of metal or plastic. A lever-head tap turns the water from off to full on with one quarter turn only. This type is convenient for the elderly or disabled, who may have difficulty in manipulating taps.

Individual wall-mounted taps are called bib taps; those fixed directly to the basin itself are known as pillar taps.

Mixer taps
In a mixer tap, hot and cold water is directed to a common spout. Water is provided at the required temperature by the appropriate adjustment of the two valves . With a single-lever mixer tap, both flow rate and temperature are controlled by adjusting the one lever.

Washbasin mixer taps frequently incorporate a pop-up waste plug. A series of interlinked rods, operated by a button on the centre of the mixer, open and close the waste plug in the basin.

Normally, the body of the tap which connects the valves and spout rests on the upper surface of the basin; the tails protrude through holes in the basin to meet the supply pipes. A two-hole mixer has tails spaced 100mm (4in) apart. A three-hole mixer appears to have separate valves and spout, but they are in fact linked by a tube below the basin. The tube is cut so as to accommodate the distance between the holes in the basin, which may be spaced from 200 to 250mm (8 to 10in) apart. Both the inlets of a one-hole mixer pass through the same hole.

A mixer set can be mounted in its entirety on the wall above the basin. Alternatively, the valves can be mounted on the basin yet still divert hot and cold water to a spout mounted on the wall above.

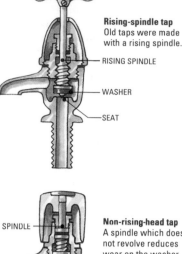

Shrouded-head tap

Lever-head tap

Two-hole mixer

Three-hole mixer

Single-lever mixer

Tap mechanisms

Over recent years there have been revolutionary changes in the design of taps, and these have not been limited to appearance. Entirely new thinking about the function of a tap has provided the consumer with taps that are easier to operate, more hard-wearing and simpler to maintain.

Rising-spindle taps
Within a traditionally designed tap, the entire spindle, jumper and washer move up and down, turning along with the head when you operate the tap.

Non-rising-head taps
Outwardly, these taps resemble a rising-spindle tap, but when the head turns it does not move up and down. Instead, it causes a threaded spindle and washer unit to rise vertically without turning. Because the washer is not twisted against the seat as the valve is closed, neither the washer nor seat wear as quickly as those in a conventional tap.

Ceramic-disc taps
In these, precision-ground ceramic discs replace the traditional washer. Instead of separating, one disc rotates on the other so that waterways through them gradually align with each other to allow water to flow. There is minimal wear as hard water-scale or other debris cannot interfere with the fit of the discs. If a problem develops, the whole mechanism is replaced.

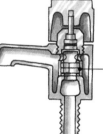

Rising-spindle tap
Old taps were made with a rising spindle.

RISING SPINDLE

WASHER

SEAT

Non-rising-head tap
A spindle which does not revolve reduces wear on the washer.

SPINDLE

WASHER

SEAT

Ceramic-disc tap
The traditional washer is replaced with rotating ceramic discs.

CERAMIC DISCS

SINGLE-LEVER MIXER TAPS

Neatness of appearance and convenience of operation make the single-lever ceramic-disc tap a popular choice for modern bathrooms. Moving the lever up and down turns the water on and off: swinging the lever from one side to the other gradually increases the temperature. Some taps are made with adjustable stops that limit the travel of the lever so that it cannot deliver water that is too hot for comfort.

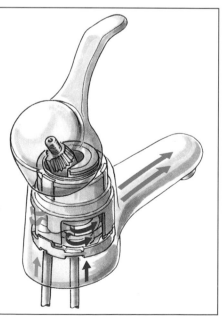

Multi-port cartridge
Adjusting the tap to the fully open mixed position provides maximum flow of water through both hot and cold ports.

REPLACING OLD TAPS

When replacing taps you will want to use the existing plumbing if possible, but it can be difficult to disconnect old, corroded fittings. Apply penetrating oil to the tap connectors and to the back-nuts that clamp the tap to the basin. While the oil takes effect, shut off the cold and hot water.

Applying heat with a gas torch can break down corrosion by expanding metal fittings, but wrap a wet cloth around nearby soldered joints or you may melt the solder. Take care that you do not damage a plastic waste and trap, and protect flammable surfaces with a ceramic tile. Try not to play the flame on to a ceramic basin.

It is not always possible to engage the nuts with a standard wrench. Instead, hire a special cranked spanner designed to reach into the confined spaces below a basin or bath. You can apply extra leverage to the spanner by slipping a stout metal bar or wrench handle into the other end.

Having disconnected the pipework, tap the bottom of the tap tails with a wooden mallet to break the seal of plumbers' putty underneath the taps. Clean the remnants of putty from around the holes in the basin, then fit new taps. If the tap tails are shorter than the originals, buy special adaptors designed to take up the gaps.

Releasing a tap connector
Use a special cranked spanner to release the fixing nut of a tap connector.

A cranked spanner fits basin and bath taps

Removing the old basin

Turn off the supply of water to an old basin before you disconnect it. If you want to use existing plumbing, loosen the compression nuts on the tap tails (see left) and trap; otherwise, cut through the waste and supply pipes at a point where you can most easily connect new plumbing **(1)**.

Remove any fixings holding the basin to its support brackets or pedestal and lift it from the wall. Apply penetrating oil to the bracket wall fixings in an attempt to remove them without damaging the plaster, but as a last resort lever the brackets off the wall. Take care not to break cast-iron fittings as they can be quite valuable.

1 Cut through old supply pipes with a hacksaw

Fitting new taps

Fit new taps to the basin before fixing it to the wall. Slip the plastic washer supplied with the tap onto its tail, then pass the tail through the hole in the basin. (If no washer is supplied, spread some silicone sealant around the top of the tail and beneath the base of the tap.)

With the basin resting on its rim, slip a second washer onto the tail then hand-tighten the back-nut to clamp the tap onto the basin **(2)**. Check that the spout faces into the basin, then tighten the back-nut carefully with a cranked spanner (see left).

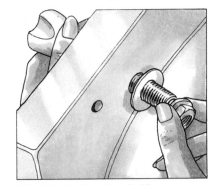

2 Slip the back-nut onto the tail of the tap

Fixing the basin to the wall

Have an assistant hold the basin to the wall at the required height while you check it is horizontal with a spirit level, then mark the fixing holes for the wall bracket **(3)**. Lay the basin to one side while you drill and plug the holes **(4)**.

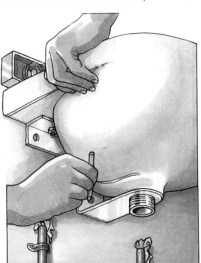

3 Mark the fixing holes on the wall

4 Drill and plug the holes

SEE ALSO	
Details for:	
Turning off water	350
Connecting pipes	362–369
Hacksaws	502–503
Gas torch	504
Spanners and wrenches	505–506

Pressed-metal basin
When you fit taps to a pressed-metal basin, slip built-up 'top-hat' washers onto the tails to cover the shanks. The basin itself may be supplied with a rubber strip to seal the joint with the counter top. It will need a combined waste and overflow like a bath.

● **Counter-top basin**
Manufacturers supply a template for cutting the hole in a counter top to receive the basin. Run mastic around the edge to seal a ceramic basin, and clamp it with the fixings supplied.

CONNECTING A WALL-HUNG BASIN

Once you have fitted the new taps and mounted the basin securely on the wall, finish the installation by connecting the trap and wastepipe, followed by the supply pipes for hot and cold water.

Plumbing a washbasin
1 Tap back-nut and washer
2 Flexible copper pipe
3 15mm (½in) supply pipe
4 Waste outlet (slot faces overflow)
5 Waste back-nut and washer
6 Bottle trap
7 32mm (1¼in) wastepipe

Typical pipe runs
Red: Hot water
Blue: Cold water

Fitting trap and wastepipe

Fit the waste outlet into the bottom of the basin as described for taps, using washers or a silicone sealant to form a watertight seal. The basin will probably have an integral overflow running to the waste, in which case ensure that the slot in the waste outlet aligns with the overflow. Tighten the back-nut under the basin while holding the outlet still by gripping its grille with pliers.

If you can use the existing wastepipe, connect the trap to the waste outlet and to the end of the pipe. A two-part trap provides some adjustment for aligning with the old wastepipe.

If necessary, run a new 32mm (1¼in) wastepipe, cutting a hole through the wall with a masonry drill and cold chisel. Run the pipe, with sufficient fall – 6mm (¼in) per 300mm (1ft) run – to terminate over the hopper on top of the vertical wastepipe. Fix the pipe to the wall with saddle clips.

Connecting the taps

You can run standard 15mm (½in) copper or plastic pipes to the taps and join them with tap connectors, but it is easier to use short lengths of flexible, corrugated copper pipe especially designed for tap connection. They can be bent by hand to allow for any slight misalignment there may be between the supply pipes and tap tails. Each pipe has a tap connector at one end and either a compression or capillary joint at the other.

Connect the corrugated pipes to the tap tails, leaving them hand-tight only, then run new branch pipework to meet them, or connect the corrugated pipes to the existing plumbing. Make soldered or compression joints to connect the pipes. Tighten the tap connectors with a cranked spanner.

Turn on the water supply and check the pipes for leaks. Drain the system to repair a weeping joint.

Connecting waste to soil pipe

Connect a basin wastepipe to a single-stack plastic soil pipe with a proprietary pipe boss. There are various ways of conecting a boss, one of the simplest of which is to clamp it with a strap.

Mark where the basin waste meets the soil pipe and cut a hole of the recommended diameter with a hole saw (**1**). Smooth the edge of the hole with abrasive paper.

Wipe both contacting surfaces with the manufacturer's cleaner, then apply gap-filling solvent cement around the hole. Strap the boss over the hole and tighten the bolt (**2**).

Insert the rubber lining in the boss in preparation for the wastepipe (**3**).

Lubricate the end of the pipe and push it firmly into the boss (**4**). Clip the pipe to the wall.

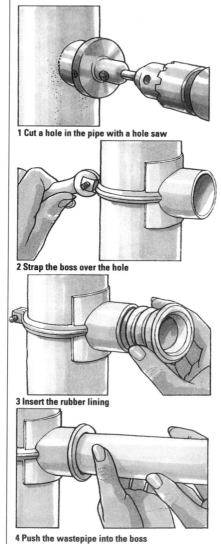

1 Cut a hole in the pipe with a hole saw

2 Strap the boss over the hole

3 Insert the rubber lining

4 Push the wastepipe into the boss

There are companies who will re-enamel your old bath, and some will even spray it *in situ*. If you own an antique cast-iron bath, it would be worth asking for quotations before you make up your mind to discard it. However, many an old bath has deteriorated so badly that it will prove to be more economical to replace it, and a cracked bath is completely beyond repair. If the bath is serviceable but you don't want it yourself, you may be able to sell it to a company that specializes in bath restoration.

Choosing a bath

You can buy reproduction or even restored Victorian baths in cast iron from specialist suppliers, but they are likely to be expensive. In practical terms, a cast-iron bath is far too heavy for one person to handle: even two people would have difficulty carrying one to an upstairs bathroom. Also, while a cast-iron bath can look splendid when left freestanding in a room, it can be virtually impossible to clean behind it, and panelling-in the curved and often tapering shape is rarely successful.

Nowadays, the majority of baths are made from enamelled pressed steel, acrylic or glass-reinforced plastic. Two people can handle a steel bath with ease and you could carry a plastic bath on your own. Although modern plastic baths are strong and durable, some are harmed by abrasive cleaners, bleach and especially heat. It is not advisable to use a gas torch near a plastic bath.

When it comes to style and colour there is no lack of choice in any material, although the more unusual baths are likely to be made of plastic. Nearly every bath comes with matching panels and optional features like hand grips and dropped sides to make it easier to step in and out. Taps do not have to be mounted at the foot of the

bath – many manufacturers offer alternative corner or side-mounting facilities. Some will even cut tap holes to your specification.

You can order bath tubs that double as jacuzzis, but the plumbing is somewhat complicated so you will need to have them professionally installed.

Rectangular bath

A standard rectangular bath is still the most popular and economical design. Baths vary in size from 1.5 to 1.8m (5 to 6ft) in length, with a choice of widths from 700 to 800mm (2ft 4in to 2ft 8in).

Corner bath

A corner bath occupies more actual floor area than a rectangular bath of the same capacity but, because the tub itself is turned at an angle to the room, it may take up less wall space. A corner bath always provides general shelf space for essential toiletries.

Round bath

A round bath would prove to be impractical in most bathrooms, but if you are converting a spare bedroom you may decide to make the bath a feature of the interior design as well as a practical appliance.

TYPES OF BATH

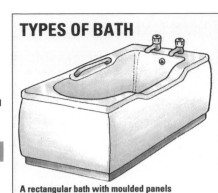

A rectangular bath with moulded panels

A bath shaped to fit the corner of a room

A circular bath fits flush with the floor

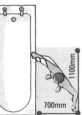

Access to the bath
Allow a space of 1100 x 700mm (3ft 8in x 2ft 4in) beside the bath to climb in and out safely, and for bathing younger members of the family.

SUPPORTING A PLASTIC BATH

A frame is supplied to cradle a flexible plastic bath. Without it, the bath would distort and possibly crack.

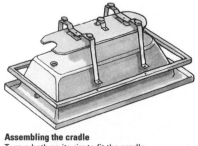

Assembling the cradle
Turn a bath on its rim to fit the cradle.

Selecting taps for a bath

In basic design and style bath taps are identical to basin taps, but they are proportionally larger with 22mm (¾in) tails. Individual hot and cold taps and mixers are made to fit a bath with hole centres 180mm (7⅛in) apart.

Some bath mixers are designed to supply water to a sprayhead, either mounted telephone-style on the mixer itself or hung from a bracket mounted on a wall above the bath.

RENOVATING BATH ENAMEL

You can buy two-part paints prepared specifically to restore the enamel surface of an old bath, sink or basin. To achieve a first-class result, the bath must be scrupulously clean and dry, so tape plastic bags over the taps to prevent water dripping into the bath and work in a warm atmosphere where condensation will not occur. Wipe the surface with a cloth dampened with white spirit to remove any grease, then paint the bath from the bottom upwards in a circular direction. This type of paint is self-levelling, so don't brush it out too much. Pick up runs immediately and work quickly to keep wet edges fresh.

For a professional finish, hire a company which will send an operator to spray the bath *in situ*. The process should take no longer than two to three hours. The bath is cleaned chemically before a grinder is used to key the surface and remove heavy stains. Chipped enamel can be repaired at the same time. Finally, surrounding areas are masked before the bath is sprayed.

377

PLUMBING
THE BATH

Waste/overflow units
A flexible tube takes any overflow water to the trap.

Compression unit
Runs to the cleaning eye on the trap.

Banjo unit
Slips over the tail of the waste outlet.

WC and bath overflow
Overflow from a WC joins the bath unit.

Shallow-seal trap
Use this type of trap when space is limited. It must discharge to a yard gully or hopper, not to a soil stack.

PLUMBING THE BATH

Once a bath is fitted close to the wall, it can be difficult to make the joints and connections, so fit the taps, overflow and trap before you remove the existing bath and push the new bath into position. Fit adjustable feet to the new bath or suspend a plastic bath in its cradle according to the manufacturer's instructions.

Plumbing a bath
1 Mixer
2 Mixer gasket
3 Mixer back-nut and washer
4 Flexible copper pipe
5 Overflow unit
6 Waste outlet
7 Waste back-nut and washer
8 Deep-seal trap to 40mm (1½in)
9 22mm (¾in) supply pipe

Fitting the taps

Fit individual hot and cold taps as for a washbasin. Fitting a mixer is again a similar procedure, but most units are supplied with a long sealing gasket which slips over both tails. Drop the tails through the holes in the rim, slip top-hat washers onto them and tighten both back-nuts to clamp the mixer securely to the bath.

Fit a flexible 22mm (¾in) copper pipe (similar to those used for washbasin taps) onto each tail. As an alternative you can attach short lengths of standard 22mm (¾in) copper or plastic pipe with tap connectors in preparation for jointing to the pipe run, but the flexible pipes allow for adjustment that will be necessary if the joints are slightly misaligned.

Fitting waste and overflow

Fit a combined waste and overflow unit. A flexible plastic hose takes water from the overflow outlet in the end of the bath to the waste outlet or trap. If you

use a 'banjo' unit, you must fit the overflow before the trap, but the flexible pipe of a compression-fitting unit connects to the trap itself (see left).

Spread a layer of silicone sealant under the rim of the waste outlet, or fit a circular rubber seal. Before inserting its tail into the hole in the bottom of the bath, seal the thread with PTFE tape. On the underside, add a plastic washer, then tighten the large back-nut, bedding the outlet down onto the sealant or rubber seal. Wipe off excess sealant.

Connect the bath trap (see left) to the tail of the waste outlet with its own compression nut. (Fit a banjo overflow unit at the same time.)

Pass the threaded boss of the overflow hose through the hole in the end of the bath. Slip a washer seal over the boss, then use a pair of pliers to screw on the overflow outlet grille.

If you are using a compression-fitting overflow, connect the nut located on the other end of the hose to the cleaning eye of the trap.

Removing the old bath

Turn off the water supply before you drain the system.

Have a shallow bowl ready to catch any trapped water, then use a hacksaw to cut through the old pipes. As the overflow from an old bath will almost certainly exit through the wall, saw through it at the same time.

If the bath has adjustable feet, lower them and push down on the bath to break the mastic seal between the rim and bathroom walls. Pull the bath away from the walls.

If a cast-iron bath is beyond restoration, it will be easier to break it up in the bathroom and carry it out in pieces. Wearing protective gloves, goggles and ear protectors, drape a dust sheet over the bath, then smash it with a heavy hammer.

Hack the old overflow from the wall with a cold chisel, fill the hole with mortar and repair the plasterwork.

Installing the new bath

Run new 22mm (¾in) supply pipes, or attach spurs to the existing ones, ready for connection to the flexible pipes already fitted on the bath taps.

If the bath has small feet, cut two boards to go under them to give them support and spread the point load over a wider area. Slide the bath into position and adjust the height of the feet with a spanner. Use a spirit level to check that the rim is horizontal.

Adjust the flexible tap pipes and join them to the supply pipes. Connect a 40mm (1½in) wastepipe to the trap and run it to the external hopper or soil stack as for a washbasin. Restore the water supply and check for leaks before you fix the bath panels.

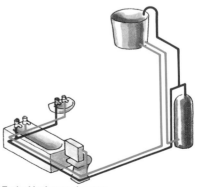

Typical bathroom pipe runs
Red: Hot water. **Blue**: Cold water.

CHOOSING

A SHOWER

SEE ALSO

Details for:	
Booster pumps	370
Shower units	380-381
Unvented cylinders	393

Panelling a bath

In all probability, your bath will be supplied with moulded polystyrene panels to hide the plumbing and facilitate cleaning.

You can panel a basic rectangular bath with a softwood framework covered with sheets of hardboard or plywood. The finish is a matter of personal choice. You can either paint a standard plain hardboard or apply a wallcovering to match or contrast with the bathroom decor; alternatively, use a melamine-faced board – giving a practical, easy-to-clean surface – or add a texture with an embossed hardboard. You could also continue the floorcovering up the panel, using an adhesive to attach carpet, vinyl or cork tiles. Stick ceramic tiles onto stiff exterior-grade plywood, but provide a small removable section of panelling so that you can service the plumbing.

When a bath does not fit against a wall at both ends, either continue the panelling around the exposed end, or make a fixed shelf of tiled exterior-grade plywood to fit behind the head or taps and run the panelling straight from wall to wall.

Make the framework of 50 x 25mm (2 x 1in) sawn softwood. Simple butt joints held together with timber connectors will suffice as the fixed sheet will make the frame rigid.

Scribe the sheet to fit under the rim of the bath and to fit the wall at each end, then pin and glue it to the framework. If pinning would spoil the appearance of the surface, use planed timber for the frame and attach the sheet with adhesive.

Screw a vertical batten to the wall at each end of the bath to support the panelled frame and then nail one or two softwood blocks to the floor for the frame to rest against. Fix the finished panel to the battens with brass screws and screw caps. Alternatively, use magnetic catches and fit small knobs or handles to the panel.

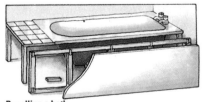

Panelling a bath
This example shows wall-to-wall panelling with a tiled shelf to fill the gap, but you can use a similar construction to fit any situation.

Soaking in a bathtub is very relaxing but taking a shower is more invigorating and hygienic, while using far less hot water – you can take several showers for the cost of one bath. Most shower cubicles occupy only a 750mm (2ft 6in) square of floor space, so it is quite possible to locate one somewhere other than the bathroom.

FIRST CONSIDERATIONS

The age-old problems of lack of pressure and erratic performance need no longer be endured. Improved shower technology has made available a variety of ideas for making showers more powerful and responsive. There is a shower for every type of plumbing system, but because most are superficially similar in appearance it is important to select the right shower from manufacturers' literature.

Pressure and flow rate

For many showers, flow rates and pressures are expressed in graph form. These are manufacturers' test-rig pressures and may vary in a real situation, depending on the design of isolating valves and, perhaps more importantly, the number and types of bends in the pipework. In general, it pays to avoid using 90 degree elbows – swept or formed bends ensure optimum shower performance.

It should be remembered that pressure and flow rate are two different things. A mains-fed electric shower, for example, is fed with water at a high pressure but employs a low flow rate so that there is sufficient time for the water to be heated before it emerges from the sprayhead. Conversely, a cistern-fed shower mixer may have a very high flow rate but, because the cistern is located at a relatively low level, water pressure may be low. A combination of high flow and pressure makes for a very pleasant shower, but it also uses a lot of water, so if economy is a priority a high-performance shower may not be your best choice.

Gravity-fed showers

In most homes, cold water is stored in a cistern and hot water is stored in a copper cylinder. Provided the bottom of the cold-water cistern is a minimum of 900mm (3ft) above the sprayhead, water pressure (the head) will be sufficient to provide a satisfactory shower. Hot-water pressure is unaffected by the position of the cylinder as it is supplied initially from the same cold-water cistern and therefore its pressure is the same as that of the cold-water supply. If necessary, water pressure can be boosted with an electric pump.

Mains-pressure showers

If your house is plumbed with a direct system, or it is more convenient to use mains pressure, there are several types of shower to choose from. The most obvious is an electric instantaneous shower. Buy a 9.2kW model for the best performance – low-powered showers are slow to heat cold water during the winter. It may be worthwhile installing a water softener if you live in a hard-water area.

Alternatively, you can store water in a combination unvented pressurized cylinder which will supply high-pressure hot and cold water to a shower without the need for a booster pump.

A thermal-store shower uses mains-fed water that passes through a rapid heat exchanger inside a cylinder.

If you have a gas instantaneous water heater or combination boiler operating under mains pressure, you can install a shower that is both powerful and safe, provided you include a pressure-equalizing valve in the system to stabilize pressure imbalances.

Drainage

Because a shower tray stands on the floor, it can be difficult to obtain the minimum fall of 6mm (¼in) per 300mm (1ft) run of wastepipe. You may be able to run the waste under floorboards, but only if the joists run in the same direction as the pipe. Sometimes it is necessary to raise the tray on a plinth.

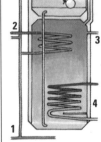

Thermal-store shower
Mains-fed water passes through a heat exchanger on its way to the shower.
1 Mains feed
2 To shower
3 Other outlets
4 Boiler connections

SHOWER
UNITS

Installing an independent shower cubicle with its own supply and waste system requires some previous experience of plumbing, but, if you utilize an existing bath as a shower tray, fitting a shower unit can involve little more than replacing the taps.

Bath/shower mixers

This type of shower is the simplest to install. It is connected like a standard bath mixer to the existing 22mm (¾in) cold and hot pipes, while the bath waste system takes care of the drainage. Once you have obtained the required temperature at the spout by adjusting the hot and cold valves, you lift a button on the mixer to divert the water, via a flexible hose, to the sprayhead. The sprayhead can be hand-held for washing hair, or hung from a wall-mounted bracket to provide a conventional shower. The only real disadvantage with this type of shower is that the controls are uncomfortably low to reach.

As the supply pipes are already part of the bathroom plumbing network, it is impossible to guard against fluctuating pressure unless the mixer is fitted with a thermostatic valve or you install a pressure-equalizing valve in the pipework. If the pressure is insufficient, fit a booster pump.

Don't fit a bath/shower mixer when cold water is supplied under mains pressure to the bath tap.

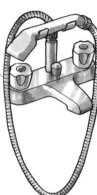

Bath/shower mixer
Fit this type of shower unit like an ordinary bath mixer.

Single-lever mixer
A manual mixer with single-lever control.

Manual shower mixers

A manual shower mixer can be mounted on the wall above a bathtub, but with its own supply of hot and cold water, or it can be situated in a separate shower cubicle. A manual mixer must have independent hot and cold supply.

Simple mixers have individual hot and cold valves, but most manual shower mixers have a single control which regulates the flow and temperature of the water. Single-lever ceramic-disc mixers offer exceptionally smooth operation and, having few moving parts, are not so prone to hard-water scaling.

You can choose a surface-mounted unit or a neater flush mixer with the pipe connections and shower mechanism concealed in the wall.

Thermostatic shower mixers

A thermostatic mixer is similar in design to a manual version, but another control is incorporated to preset the water temperature. If the flow rate drops on either the hot or cold supply, a thermostatic valve rapidly compensates by reducing the flow on the other side. This is primarily a safety measure to prevent the shower user being scalded should someone run a cold tap elsewhere. Consequently, you can supply a thermostatic shower with branch pipes from the bathroom plumbing, but try to join them as near as possible to the cold cistern and hot cylinder. The mixer cannot raise the pressure of the supply: you still need a booster pump if it is low. Neither will it compensate for the considerable difference in pressure between mains and gravity-fed water.

Thermostatic mechanisms are usually based on wax-filled cartridges or bimetallic strips. Brand new thermostatic valves respond extremely quickly to changes of temperature, but you can expect the rate to slow down as scale gradually builds up inside the mixer. Even when new, reaction time will be slower if the mixer is expected to cope with exceptionally hot water (over 65°C /149°F). At such high temperatures the hot-water ports are almost fully closed and the cold-water ones practically wide open so there is very little margin for further adjustment.

Most thermostatic mixers can be used with existing gravity-fed hot and cold supply, but it may be necessary to fit a booster pump. Check the manufacturer's literature carefully, since some showers perform well at low head pressures while others will be less than satisfactory.

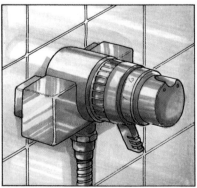

Thermostatic mixer
This unit prevents excessive fluctuations occurring in water temperature.

INSTANTANEOUS SHOWERS

An instantaneous electric shower is designed specifically for connection to the mains water supply, using one 15mm (½in) branch pipe from the rising main. Because the rising main passes through every floor of the house, you can install an instantaneous shower practically anywhere so long as drainage is feasible. Incoming water is heated within the unit so there is no separate hot-water supply to balance. The shower is thermostatically controlled to prevent fluctuations in pressure affecting the water temperature – in fact it switches off completely if there is a serious failure of pressure. You can even buy a shower with a shut-down facility: when you switch off, water continues to flow for a short period to flush hot water out of the pipework. This ensures that anyone stepping into the cubicle immediately after another user is not subjected to an unexpectedly hot start to their shower.

An instantaneous shower requires its own circuit from the consumer unit. A ceiling-mounted double-pole switch is connected to the circuit to turn the appliance on and off. With most instantaneous showers, all plumbing and electrical connections are contained in a single mixer cabinet that is mounted in the shower cubicle or over the bathtub. However, you can buy showers that comprise a slim flush-fitting control panel that is connected to a power pack installed out of sight in an adjacent cupboard, under the bath or anywhere convenient within a few metres of the shower cubicle.

Fit a stopcock or miniature isolating valve in the supply pipe to allow the shower to be serviced.

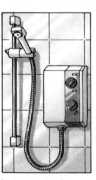

Instantaneous shower
Typical wall-mounted mixer cabinet and adjustable sprayhead.

Flush control panel
This type of panel is connected to a remote power pack.

Sprayheads

High-performance showers have propagated a new generation of sprayheads that offer a variety of spray patterns. As well as the standard shower spray, a simple adjustment is all that is required to produce an invigorating jet to wake you up in the morning or a soft bubbly stream that is ideal for small children. Some sprayheads can also be adjusted to deliver a very light spray while you soap yourself or apply shampoo. If you intend to upgrade an existing shower with an electric pump, it would be worth enquiring whether you could also substitute an adjustable sprayhead.

High-performance sprayhead

Cleaning a sprayhead

The accumulation of lime scale will gradually block the holes in the sprayhead and will eventually affect the performance of your shower. It is essential to clean the sprayhead, the frequency of cleaning depending on the hardness of the water in your locality.

Once you have removed the entire sprayhead from its hose, it is usually possible to unscrew the actual perforated plate from which the water escapes. Soak the plate in a proprietary descalant until the lime scale has dissolved, then rinse it thoroughly under running cold water.

Before you reattach the sprayhead, turn on the shower to flush any loose scale deposits from the flexible hose.

ELECTRICAL INSTALLATIONS

Electrical installations in a bathroom are potentially dangerous unless they conform to the current Wiring Regulations as compiled by the Institution of Electrical Engineers. Read the electrical section in this book as well as the manufacturers' instructions carefully to make sure you understand the requirements for wiring in a bathroom before you undertake the work. If you are in any doubt as to the procedure, or have had no previous experience, hire a qualified electrician.

Power showers

The pump-assisted 'power' shower is perhaps most people's concept of the ideal shower. The pump delivers water at a constant pressure and flow rate, eliminating the need for the minimum head normally required for a gravity-fed shower. Most power showers require a head of about 75 to 225mm (3 to 9in) to activate the pump when the mixer control is turned on. The pump boosts the pressure and flow rate of stored hot and cold water, but not mains-fed water. Ideally the cold supply should be taken directly from the storage cistern, not from branch pipes that feed other taps and appliances.

The hot-water supply can be connected to the cylinder by means of a Surrey or Essex flange. This helps eliminate the tendency for the pump to suck in air from the vent pipe.

If the water is heated by an electric immersion heater, make sure the cylinder is fed with a dedicated cold feed and that the cold-feed gate valve is fully open. This is to prevent the top of the cylinder running dry, perhaps burning out the heater. If the cylinder is heated from a boiler, make sure the water temperature is controlled by a thermostat. If the water is too hot the shower could splutter.

Power showers are frequently manufactured with the electrically driven pump built into the mixer cabinet that is mounted in the shower cubicle. However, some pumps are designed for remote installation, with hot and cold pipes running to the pump, then out again to the shower mixer. These freestanding pumps are also used to improve the performance of an existing installation. The usual location for this type of pump is next to the hot-water cylinder in an airing cupboard, and as low as possible so that the pump remains full of water. However, there are pumps that are designed to perform satisfactorily when mounted at a high level, even in the loft if that is the only option available. In such situations, a single-impeller pump is best.

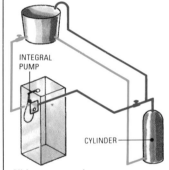

All-in-one power shower
The cold supply comes from the storage cistern, and the hot supply from the hot-water cylinder.

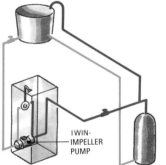

A separate booster pump
A typical installation with hot and cold supplies being fed through a twin-impeller pump.

High-level pump
If this is your only option, it is best to fit a single-impeller pump between the mixer and the sprayhead.

COMPUTER-CONTROLLED SHOWERS

Computerized showers allow for the precise selection of temperature and flow rates, using a touch-sensitive control panel. Most panels also include a memory programme so that each member of a family can select their own preprogrammed ideal shower. Far from being simply a gimmicky sales device, a computerized shower has real advantages for the disabled and for elderly people. The shower is exceptionally easy to operate and the control panel could even be mounted outside the cubicle so that you could operate the shower on behalf of someone else.

Touch-sensitive computerized panel

● **Water Bylaws**
If the shower is mounted in such a way that the sprayhead could dangle below the rim of the bath or shower tray, you must fit double-seal non-return valves in the supply pipes to prevent dirty water being siphoned back into the system.

CONSTRUCTING
A SHOWER
CUBICLE

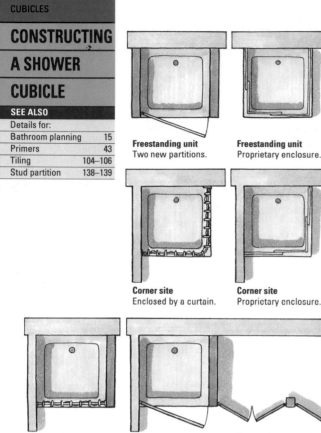

Freestanding unit
Two new partitions.

Freestanding unit
Proprietary enclosure.

Corner site
Enclosed by a curtain.

Corner site
Proprietary enclosure.

Corner site
Partition and curtain.

Corner site
Built-in cupboards.

Without doubt, the simplest way to acquire a shower cubicle is to install a factory-assembled cabinet, complete with tray and mixer, together with waterproof doors or a curtain to contain the spray from the sprayhead. Once you have run supply pipes and drainage, the installation is complete. However, the cabinets are expensive. The alternative is to construct a purpose-made shower cubicle to fit exactly the space you have allocated.

Choosing the site

When deciding upon the location of your shower, consider how you are going to build the cubicle walls.

Freestanding

You can place the shower tray against a flat wall and either construct a stud partition on each side or surround the tray with a proprietary enclosure.

Corner site

If you place the tray in a corner of a room, two sides of the cubicle are ready-made. Run a curtain around the tray or install a corner-entry enclosure with sliding doors. Alternatively, build a fixed side wall yourself and place a door or curtain across the entrance.

Built-in cupboards

Blend a shower cubicle into a bedroom by placing it into a corner as described above, then construct a built-in wardrobe unit between the shower and the opposite wall.

Concealing the plumbing

A shower with exposed pipework will work perfectly well, but it tends to spoil the appearance of the cubicle. One solution is to install a proprietary rigid-plastic pillar in the corner of the shower cubicle to conceal the pipework and house the mixer and adjustable sprayhead.

If you erect a stud partition on one side, you can run the plumbing between the studs. Screw and glue exterior-grade plywood on the inside of the frame as a mounting board for the shower mixer and sprayhead. You will find it easier if you connect the plumbing to the shower mixer before you panel the outside of the wooden framework with plasterboard.

Cover the plywood panel with ceramic tiles or, alternatively, use a melamine-faced board, attaching it to the framework with metal brackets. Prime the edges of the board and apply a mastic seal where it meets the wall and tray.

Proprietary unit to conceal plumbing
A typical shower kit includes the plastic corner pillar, shower set, tray and enclosure.

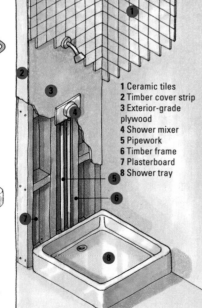

1 Ceramic tiles
2 Timber cover strip
3 Exterior-grade plywood
4 Shower mixer
5 Pipework
6 Timber frame
7 Plasterboard
8 Shower tray

Running plumbing through a partition
Conceal pipework in a simple timber partition covered with plywood and ceramic tiles.

SHOWER TRAYS

Shower trays are made from enamelled cast iron or steel, ceramics or fibreglass. Metal and ceramic trays are substantial but heavy, and may require two people to move them into position. Plastic trays are lightweight and cheap, but they do have a tendency to flex slightly in use so it is particularly important to seal the edges carefully with a flexible mastic instead of relying on grout. Whatever material you choose, you should have no problem finding a colour to match other bathroom appliances.

The majority of trays are between 750mm (2ft 6in) and 900mm (3ft) square. You can also buy trays that fit across the corner of a room to save floor space, or choose a larger rectangular tray that will give you more elbow room. Most trays are designed to stand on the floor with a surrounding apron about 150mm (6in) in height. Some have adjustable feet to level the tray, or even a metal underframe to raise it off the floor, providing a fall for the wastepipe. A plinth screwed across the front of the tray hides the underframe and plumbing while providing access to the trap for servicing. Some trays are intended to be flush with the floor.

A round waste outlet fits in the bottom of the tray. If possible, fit a space-saving, shallow-seal trap to the waste outlet.

Clipped corner tray

Square recessed tray

INSTALLING A GRAVITY-FED SHOWER

Use the procedure below as a guide to the stage-by-stage installation of a standard gravity-fed shower and cubicle. Ideally, run an independent cold supply from the storage cistern and, for the hot-water supply, take a branch pipe directly from the vent pipe above the cylinder. Fit isolating gate valves in both supplies. Follow the instructions on fitting plastic or copper supply pipes and drainage, and take note of the manufacturer's recommendations for the particular shower you are installing.

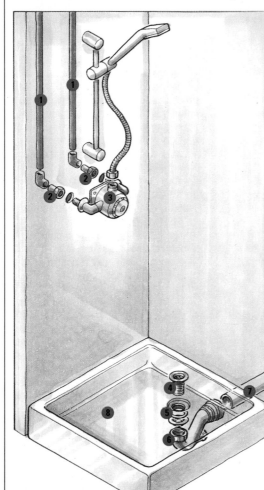

Plumbing a shower
1 15mm (½in) supply pipe
2 Connector (Push-fit joints are fairly common.)
3 Shower mixer
4 Waste outlet
5 Back-nut and washer
6 Shallow-seal trap (Use a deep-seal trap for a single-stack waste system.)
7 40mm (1½in) wastepipe
8 Shower tray

Typical pipe runs
Red: Hot water
Blue: Cold water

Fit the waste outlet in the shower tray and connect a shallow-seal trap as for a bath. Install the tray and run a 40mm (1½in) wastepipe to the outside hopper. Make sure there is access to the shower-tray trap. Some traps can be cleaned by lifting the grille and removing an insert (see far right). Use a deep-seal trap if you plan to connect the wastepipe directly to a waste stack with a strap boss.

To enclose a shower situated in a corner, construct a stud partition on one side and line the inner surface with exterior-grade plywood. Cut a hole in the board for a flush-fitting shower mixer, or drill holes for the supply pipes to a surface-mounted version.

Panel or plasterboard the outside of the stud partition and tile the inside of the cubicle with ceramic tiles, using waterproof adhesive and grout.

Assemble the shower mixer and sprayhead according to the instructions supplied by the manufacturer.

Connect the mixer to 15 or 22mm (½ or ¾in) pipes, running them back to the supply. Turn off the water and join the pipes to the supply. Turn the water on again, then test for leaks.

Enclose the shower by fitting a door or a shower rail and curtain.

Seal around the edges of the tray with a flexible mastic.

Instantaneous showers

If you want to install an instantaneous shower in the cubicle, run the electrical supply cable, and a single 15mm (½in) pipe from the rising main, through the stud partition. Fit an isolating valve. Drill two holes in the wall behind the shower unit for the pipe and cable. Join a threaded or compression connector to the supply pipe, whichever is appropriate for the water inlet built into the shower unit. Make the electrical connections to the shower as recommended by the manufacturer and read the instructions in this book for wiring a shower.

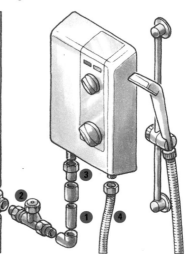

Plumbing an instantaneous shower
1 15mm (½in) pipe
2 Isolating valve
3 Tap connector from rising main
4 Hose to sprayhead

Enclosing the shower

Showers in cubicles and over bathtubs must be provided with some means of preventing water spraying out onto the floor. Hanging a plastic curtain across the entrance is the simplest and cheapest method, but it is not really suitable for a power shower. Fit a ceiling-mounted curtain track or a tubular shower rail.

Even when a curtain is tucked into the shower tray, water always seems to escape around the sides of the curtain, or at least drips onto the floor when it is drawn aside. Make a more satisfactory enclosure with metal-framed glass or plastic panels. Hinged, sliding or concertina doors operate within an adjustable frame fixed to the top edge of the tray and the side walls. Bed the lower track onto mastic to make a waterproof joint with the tray and, having completed the enclosure, run a bead of mastic between the framework and the tiled walls of the cubicle.

INSTALLING A GRAVITY-FED SHOWER

SEE ALSO

Details for:	
Tiling	104–106
Plasterboard	162–169
Wiring a shower	331
Turning off water	350
Connecting pipes	362–369
Leaking joints, metal	363, 364
Leaking joints, plastic	368, 369
Strap boss	376
Shallow-seal trap	378
Waste outlet	378

Shallow trap
Some shallow traps for showers have a lift-out chamber for easy cleaning.

383

INSTALLING POWER SHOWERS

If you are installing a brand-new power shower, it probably pays to opt for an all-in-one model with an integral pump. If you are merely unhappy with the performance of an existing shower, it is much cheaper and more convenient to plumb in a separate pump.

Whichever system you decide upon, check that your cold-water storage capacity is typically a minimum of 115 litres (25 gallons). Some manufacturers also recommend a hot-water cylinder with a minimum 161 litres (35 gallons) capacity. Don't connect a power shower to the mains water supply.

Both types of shower need an electrical supply to drive the pump. The pump is wired to a ring main by means of a fused connection unit installed outside the bathroom. As a means of isolating the pump, use a switched fused connection unit or, if you prefer, fit a separate ceiling-mounted double-pole switch inside the bathroom. Once connected the shower pump switches on automatically as soon as the shower valve is operated.

Typical pipe runs
Red: Hot water
Blue: Cold water

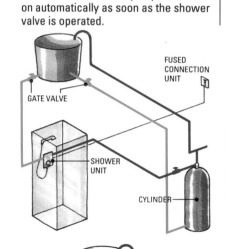

Power shower with integral pump

1 A single-impeller pump boosts ready-mixed water.

2 A twin-impeller pump can boost other outlets as well as a shower.

Fitting an all-in-one shower

To plumb a shower with an integral pump, you can run dedicated hot and cold supplies to the shower as for fitting a gravity-fed shower. Alternatively, connect the hot-water supply directly to the cylinder with a cylinder flange. An Essex flange is connected to the side of the cylinder (1) but, to avoid cutting into the cylinder wall, fit a Surrey flange that screws into the vent-pipe connection on top of the cylinder (2). Fit gate valves in the hot and cold supplies in order to isolate the shower for servicing.

The only appreciable drawback with an all-in-one shower is vibration. When mounting a mixer unit on a timber-frame wall, it pays to cushion it on rubber tap washers slid over the fixing screws.

All tiling and grouting should be completed before mounting the shower on the wall.

Installing the shower

Drain the cold-water cistern and drill a hole for a tank connector. Fit a gate valve close to the cistern and run the pipe to the shower unit.

Turn off the cold supply to the hot-water cylinder and open the hot taps in the bathroom to drain a small amount of water from the cylinder. Unscrew the vent-pipe connector (3) and catch any residue of water with an old towel.

Wrap PTFE tape around the threads of the Surrey flange and screw it into the cylinder. Connect the original vent pipe to the top of the flange and run the hot supply for the shower from the side connection (4).

Arrange the pipework at the shower end to receive connectors: make sure you have the hot and cold pipes on the correct side for the particular unit. Open the gate valves momentarily to flush the pipes.

Following the shower manufacturer's instructions carefully, run the electrical cable to the shower ready for connection. Unless you have had some experience with electrical wiring, have the unit wired by a qualified electrician.

Mount the shower unit with the screws provided, taking care not to bore into pipes or cable. Connect the pipes to the unit (this is often achieved by means of simple push-fit connectors) and connect the electrical cable to the terminal block inside the unit. Metal pipes must be bonded to earth.

Before you turn on the electricity to the pump, attach the shower hose (without sprayhead) and use the mixer controls to run the shower fully hot then fully cold to prime both supplies. Seal around the pipes with mastic to prevent water entering the wall cavity.

Fit the cover on the unit and mount the sprayhead rail on the wall.

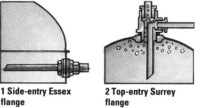

1 Side-entry Essex flange   2 Top-entry Surrey flange

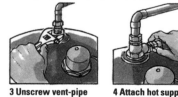

3 Unscrew vent-pipe connector   4 Attach hot supply for shower

Installing a booster pump

Fitting an electric pump can improve the performance of an existing shower. If you have access to the pipe running from the mixer to the sprayhead, you can install a single-impeller pump that boosts ready-mixed hot and cold water (1). If the pipework is embedded behind tiling, install a twin-impeller pump in the supply pipes before the mixer. You can use the same twin-impeller pump to boost the supply to other outlets in the bathroom also (2).

Positioning the pump

Place the pump somewhere convenient for servicing, perhaps on the floor of an airing cupboard or under the bath, but not where it will be splashed with water. Stand it on a resilient mat or pads to reduce the noise from vibration, and do not screw it to the floor. If possible, use flexible connectors to join pipes to the pump to prevent vibration being transmitted to rigid pipework.

Connect the pump to a switched fused connection unit (see top left). Once connected, the pump is activated automatically by flow switches.

The basic plumbing is identical to that described for installing an all-in-one shower. Flush the pipes before you switch on the pump.

Although a bidet is primarily for washing the lower parts of the body and genitals, it can double as a footbath for the elderly and for small children. Owing to the stringent requirements of the Water Bylaws, installing a bidet can be an expensive and time-consuming procedure. However, if you opt for the simpler version, it is just like plumbing a washbasin.

Over-rim-supply bidet

This type of bidet is simply a low-level basin. It is fitted with individual hot and cold taps or a basin mixer and has a built-in overflow running to the waste outlet in the basin. There's only one disadvantage with an over-rim bidet: the rim is cold when you sit astride it.

Rim-supply bidet

A more sophisticated bidet delivers warm water to the basin via a hollow rim. Consequently the rim is preheated and comfortable to sit on. A special mixer set with a douche spray is fitted to this type of bidet. It incorporates the normal hot and cold valves, but a control in the centre of the mixer diverts water from the rim to the sprayhead mounted in the bottom of the basin. Because the sprayhead is submerged when the basin is full, the Water Bylaws stipulate that a rim-supply bidet must take its cold water directly from the storage cistern and there must be no other connections to that pipe. Similarly, the hot-water supply must be completely independent and connected to the vent pipe immediately above the cylinder. Check with your water supplier before you install a bidet to make sure you comply with the bylaws.

INSTALLING A BIDET

When plumbing an over-rim-supply bidet, use exactly the same procedures, pipes and connectors described for plumbing a washbasin. Fit the taps, waste outlet and trap, then use a spirit level to position the bidet before fixing it to the floor with non-corrosive screws and rubber washers. Supply the taps with branch pipes from the existing bathroom plumbing and take the wastepipe to the hopper or stack.

Attach the bidet set and trap to a rim-supply appliance following the manufacturer's instructions. Screw the bidet to the floor before running 15mm (½in) supply pipes and a 32mm (1¼in) waste according to the Water Bylaws (see left). Connect the cold supply to the cistern at the same level as the existing supply pipe.

SEE ALSO	
Details for:	
Bathroom planning	15
Connecting pipes	362–369
Taps	374
Washbasin	375–376
Strap boss	376
Cistern supply	391

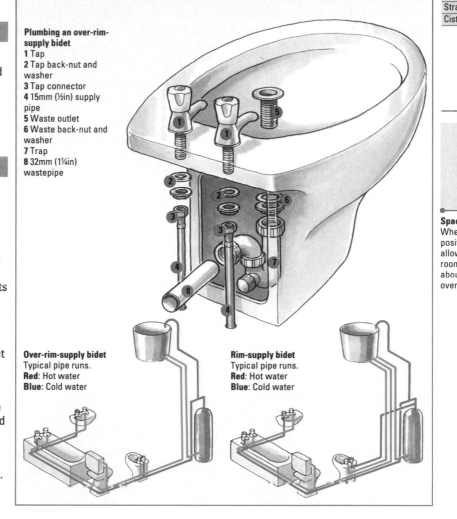

Plumbing an over-rim-supply bidet
1 Tap
2 Tap back-nut and washer
3 Tap connector
4 15mm (½in) supply pipe
5 Waste outlet
6 Waste back-nut and washer
7 Trap
8 32mm (1¼in) wastepipe

Space for a bidet
When planning the position of a bidet, allow enough knee room on each side – about 700mm (2ft 4in) overall.

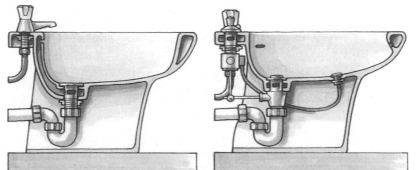

Over-rim-supply bidet
Typical pipe runs.
Red: Hot water
Blue: Cold water

Rim-supply bidet
Typical pipe runs.
Red: Hot water
Blue: Cold water

Over-rim-supply bidet (right)
This type of bidet is simple to install; follow the same procedure as for a washbasin.

Rim-supply bidet (far right)
The installation of this type of bidet is complicated by the submerged douche spray. Independent plumbing is essential, and you will need a special mixer set to comply with the Water Bylaws.

FITTING A NEW SINK

If your ambition is to re-create a period-style kitchen, you may want a reproduction Butler or Belfast fireclay sink complete with a teak draining board. Most of the original stoneware sinks were replaced years ago, usually by a stainless-steel sinktop incorporating a bowl and drainer in a single pressing. The durability of stainless steel is hard to beat, but many people dislike its 'institutional' association and prefer to introduce a touch of colour to their scheme. Good-quality resin (plastic) or enamelled sinks will withstand the inevitable wear and tear of daily use, but some of the cheaper varieties are just not up to the job.

Choosing a kitchen sink

Choose the sink to make the best use of available space, to suit the style of the kitchen, and according to how many labour-saving appliances you plan to install. Unless your kitchen is fitted with an automatic dishwasher, for example, the sink must be large enough to cope with a considerable volume of washing-up (don't forget to allow for larger items like baking trays, oven racks and freezer baskets). In addition, check that the bowl is deep enough to allow you to fill a bucket from the kitchen tap.

If space allows, select a unit with two bowls, primarily for washing and rinsing dishes but also to ensure that one bowl is always free for washing vegetables and salads even when the second is occupied by soaking dishes or laundry. If you plan to install a waste-disposal unit, one of the bowls must have a waste outlet of the appropriate size (see opposite), or choose a sink unit with a small bowl reserved especially for waste disposal. A double drainer is another useful feature, but if there is no room, allow at least some space to the side of the bowl to avoid piling soiled and clean crockery on a single drainer.

One-piece sinktops are made to modular sizes to fit standard kitchen base units, but many sinks are designed to be set into a continuous worktop, offering greater flexibility in size, shape and, above all, positioning. Moreover, you can set individual bowls or drainers into the worktop to suit yourself, and even add a second bowl at a later stage if the need arises. If you opt for this type of installation, choose a drainer equipped with its own waste outlet that drains surface water into the trap beneath the bowl.

Kitchen taps

Kitchen taps are comparable in style to those used for washbasins, and they incorporate similar mechanisms. A kitchen mixer, however, has an additional feature: drinking water is supplied to the sink from the rising main, whereas the hot water comes from the same storage cylinder that supplies all the other hot taps in the house. A sink mixer should have separate waterways to isolate one supply from the other until the water emerges from the spout, otherwise you need special check valves to prevent possible contamination of your drinking water. If you are fitting a double-bowl sink, choose a mixer with a swivelling spout.

Some sink mixers have an additional hot-rinse attachment with a lever-operated spray and detachable brush head for removing food scraps from crockery and saucepans. Alternatively, you can install an individual attachment supplied by a flexible hose that is plumbed into the hot-water pipe below the sink. Make sure the sink you choose is supplied with a hole in the rim to accept the attachment holder.

Individual kitchen taps resemble basin taps in every respect except for their extended pillars that make it possible to fill a bucket in the sink. Sink taps and mixers are provided with tails for connecting to the pipes.

Accessories for a kitchen sink

There is a range of accessories designed to fit most kitchen sinks, typically a hardwood or laminated-plastic chopping board that drops into the rim of the bowl or drainer, and a selection of plastic-dipped wire baskets for rinsing vegetables or draining crockery. Pump-action dispensers for soap and washing-up liquid rid the sink of plastic bottles and soap dishes.

SINK UNITS, TAPS AND ACCESSORIES

There is a wide variety of kitchen sinks, taps and accessories available for the domestic market. Steel, enamel, resin, double, single, plain and coloured: a bewildering choice confronts you when you are planning your kitchen. A cross section of popular sinks, accessories and taps is shown below to assist you with your decision.

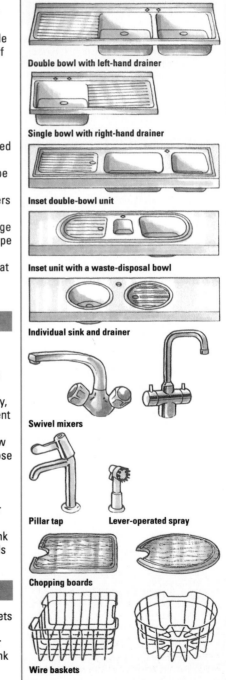

Double bowl with left-hand drainer

Single bowl with right-hand drainer

Inset double-bowl unit

Inset unit with a waste-disposal bowl

Individual sink and drainer

Swivel mixers

Pillar tap   **Lever-operated spray**

Chopping boards

Wire baskets

WASTE DISPOSAL

INSTALLING A SINK

The installation of a kitchen sink is essentially the same as fitting a washbasin or vanity unit. All except a ceramic sink will require a combined overflow/waste outlet like a bath. Fit a tubular trap to a sink because a bottle trap blocks too easily.

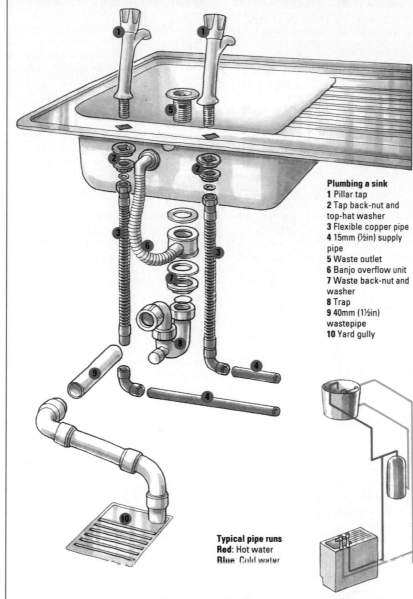

Plumbing a sink
1 Pillar tap
2 Tap back-nut and top-hat washer
3 Flexible copper pipe
4 15mm (½in) supply pipe
5 Waste outlet
6 Banjo overflow unit
7 Waste back-nut and washer
8 Trap
9 40mm (1½in) wastepipe
10 Yard gully

Typical pipe runs
Red: Hot water
Blue: Cold water

Fit the taps and the overflow/waste outlet to the new sink before you place it into position.

Turn off the water supply to the taps, then remove the old sink by dismantling the plumbing. Hack the old pipes from the wall unless you plan to adapt them.

Clamp the new sink to its base unit or worktop with the fittings provided, then run a 15mm (½in) cold supply from the rising main and a branch pipe of the same size from the nearest hot-water pipe. Connect the pipes to the taps with

flexible copper-tap connectors. If you prefer to use standard pipe and tap connectors, attach short spur pipes to each tap tail before you install the sink.

Fit the trap and run a 40mm (1½in) wastepipe through the wall behind the base unit to the yard gully. According to current Bylaws, the pipe should pass through the grid covering the gully but stop short of the water in the gully trap. You can quite easily adapt an existing grid by cutting out one corner with a sharp hacksaw.

Waste-disposal units

A waste-disposal unit provides a hygienic method of dealing with soft food scraps, reserving the kitchen wastebin for dry refuse and bones. The unit houses an electric motor which drives steel cutters that grind food scraps into a fine slurry to be washed into the yard gully or soil stack. A continuous-feed disposal unit is operated by a manual switch; scraps are then fed into it while the cold tap is running. To prevent it being switched on accidentally, a batch-feed model cannot be operated until a removable plug is inserted in the sink waste outlet.

Most disposal units are designed to fit an 89mm (3½in) outlet in the base of the sink bowl. A special cutter can be hired to adapt a standard stainless-steel or plastic sink.

With a sink waste outlet and seal in position, clamp a retaining collar to the outlet from under the sink. Bolt or clip the unit housing to the collar: every unit is supplied with individual instructions.

The waste outlet from the unit itself fits a standard sink trap (not a bottle trap) and wastepipe. If the wastepipe runs to a yard gully, make sure it passes through the covering grid (see left). Wire the unit to a switched, fused connection unit mounted above the worktop where it is out of the reach of children. Identify the switch to avoid accidental operation.

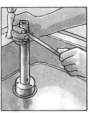

Cutting a hole for a waste-disposal unit
The supplier of the waste-disposal unit – or possibly a tool-hire company – will rent you a special cutter to convert an existing sink. The cutter cannot be used on a ceramic or enamel sink.

A typical waste-disposal unit
Waste-disposal units differ in design, but the illustration left shows the type of components that are used to clamp a unit to the sink.
1 Sink waste outlet
2 Gasket
3 Back-up ring
4 Collar
5 Snap ring
6 Unit housing
7 Cutters
8 Waste outlet
9 Trap

387

WASHING
MACHINES

Appliance valves
Typical valves used to
connect washing
machines or
dishwashers to the
water supply.

In-line valve

Right-angle valve

Tee-piece valve

PLUMBING A DISHWASHER AND WASHING MACHINE

The full potential of a dishwasher or washing machine as a labour-saving appliance is somewhat limited if you have to pull it out from under a worksurface before attaching flexible hoses to the kitchen sink. If at all possible, provide any automatic machine with permanent supply and waste systems. Dishwashers need a cold supply only, whereas washing machines may be hot-and-cold fill. Washing machines supplied with hot water provide a faster washing cycle and may be more economical to run, depending on how you heat your water. Any retailer will be happy to advise you.

The instructions supplied with the machine should state what water pressure is required. If the machine is installed upstairs, make sure the storage cistern is high enough to provide the required pressure. In a downstairs kitchen or utility room there is rarely any problem with pressure, especially if you can take the cold water from the mains supply at the sink. However, check with your water supplier if you want to connect more than one machine.

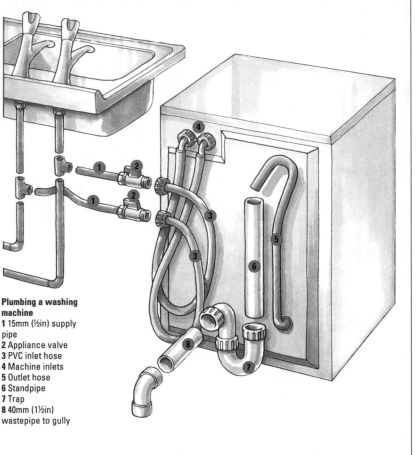

**Plumbing a washing
machine**
1 15mm (½in) supply
pipe
2 Appliance valve
3 PVC inlet hose
4 Machine inlets
5 Outlet hose
6 Standpipe
7 Trap
8 40mm (1½in)
wastepipe to gully

Running the supply

Washing machines and dishwashers are supplied with PVC hoses to link the water inlets at the back of each appliance to special miniature valves connected to the household plumbing. Using these valves, you can turn off the water to service a machine without

disrupting the supply to the rest of the house. There are a number of valves to choose from. Select the type which provides the most practical method of connecting to the plumbing, depending on the location of the machine in relation to existing pipework.

Self-bore valves

When 15mm (½in) cold and hot pipes run conveniently behind or alongside the machine, use a valve which will bore a hole in the pipe without your having to turn off the water and drain the system. Each valve is colour-coded for hot or cold, and has a threaded outlet for the standard machine hose. Self-bore valves are not approved by all water suppliers because the small disc of metal they cut from the pipe may restrict the flow of water. In practice, this hardly ever happens.

To fit a valve, screw the backplate to the wall behind the pipe. Place the saddle with its rubber seal over the pipe. Ensure that the holes in the seal and saddle are aligned before screwing the saddle to the backplate (**1**).

Make sure the valve is turned off, then screw it into the saddle (**2**). As you insert the valve, the integral cutter bores a hole in the pipe. With the valve in the vertical position, tighten the adjusting nut with a spanner (**3**). Connect the hose to the valve outlet (**4**).

1 Fit the saddle   **2 Insert the valve**

3 Tighten the nut   **4 Attach the hose**

Running branch pipes

If you have to extend the plumbing to reach the machine, take branch pipes from the hot and cold pipes supplying the kitchen taps. Terminate the branch pipes at a convenient position close to the machine and fit a small appliance valve (see left) that has a standard compression joint for connecting to the pipework and a threaded outlet for the machine hose. When you are fitting this type of valve, turn off the water and drain the system in the normal way. When the supply is restored, open the valve by turning the control level to align with the outlet.

Dishwashers and washing machines are supplied with an outlet hose which must be connected to a waste system to discharge dirty water into a yard gully or single waste stack, not into a surface water drain where detergents could pollute rivers.

Standpipe and trap

The standard method, approved by all water suppliers, employs a vertical 40mm (1½in) plastic standpipe attached to a deep-seal trap (see opposite). Most plumbing suppliers stock the standpipe, trap and wall fixings as a kit. The machine hose fits loosely into the open-ended pipe to avoid the possibility of dirty water being siphoned back into the machine. Check with the machine manufacturer's instructions on the position of the standpipe; in the absence of advice, ensure that the open end is at least 600mm (2ft) above the floor.

Cut a hole through the wall and run the wastepipe to the gully, or attach it to a drainage stack with a strap boss. Allow a minimum fall of 6mm (¼in) for every 300mm (1ft) of pipe run.

Draining to a sink trap

You can drain a washing machine to a sink trap that has a built-in spigot (1), but you should insert an in-line anti-siphon return valve in the machine's outlet hose. This is a small plastic device with a hose connector at each end (2). Drain a washing machine and dishwasher into a dual-spigot trap.

1 Sink trap with drainage spigot

2 An in-line anti-siphon hose valve

PREVENTING A FLOOD

Overflowing dishwashers and washing machines can cause a great deal of damage in a few minutes, particularly if the appliance is plumbed into an upstairs flat and the water can find its way through a multi-storey building. Most overflows occur simply because the water backs up the wastepipe and spills out over the standpipe or sink.

A sealed waste system overcomes this problem by doing away with the air gap through which the water overflows. The anti-vacuum function is formed instead by a fitting that incorporates a small air-inlet valve which stops the wastepipe siphoning the machine. The air inlet must be upright, so attach the fitting to a standard vertical standpipe, using a 40mm (1½in) plastic elbow. Push the machine's outlet hose onto the spigot and clamp it with a hose clip.

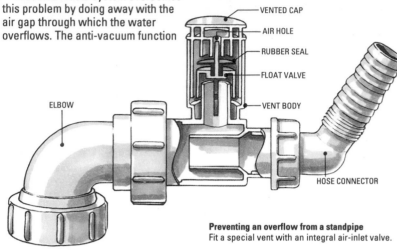

VENTED CAP
AIR HOLE
RUBBER SEAL
FLOAT VALVE
VENT BODY
ELBOW
HOSE CONNECTOR

Preventing an overflow from a standpipe
Fit a special vent with an integral air-inlet valve.

Anti-siphon devices

The standpipe-and-trap method of draining domestic appliances prevents back-siphonage by venting the pipe to the air, but there are other ways to deal with the problem. If an existing 36 or 40mm (1¼ or 1½in) wastepipe runs behind the machine, for example, you can attach a hose connector which incorporates a non-return valve to eliminate reverse flow. Connectors are available with short spigots (1) or can be attached to a standpipe.

Connecting to the wastepipe
Clamp the saddle over the wastepipe (2), then use the cutter supplied with the fitting to bore a hole in the pipe, with the saddle acting as a guide (3).

1 Short-spigot anti-siphon connector
This type of connector is clamped to a wastepipe that runs behind the machine.

2 Clamp the saddle over existing wastepipe

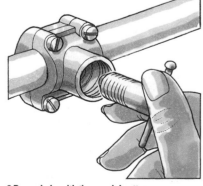

3 Bore a hole with the special cutter

WATER SOFTENERS

A typical domestic water softener

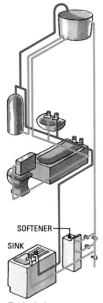

Typical pipe runs
A domestic system incorporating a softener.
Red: Hot water
Blue: Cold water

Water treated at the local waterworks should be rendered safe to drink, in that harmful impurities should be removed before it is supplied to our houses. However, minerals absorbed from the ground are still present, and it is the concentration of these that determines whether our water is hard or soft.

Rocky terrain gives rise to surface-run water which is naturally soft. However, in areas of the country where water runs through the ground rather than over it a much higher dissolved mineral content produces hard water. Mineral salts are deposited in the form of hard scale on the inside of pipes, cisterns and, especially, hot-water cylinders. If the concentration of minerals is very high, scale can eventually block pipework and insulate heating elements to such an extent that their efficiency is reduced by anything from 15 to 70 per cent. The more obvious effects of hard water are the scumming and discoloration of baths and basins, blocked sprayheads, blemished stainless-steel surfaces and furred-up kettles. Most people learn to live with them, but they can be reduced or even eliminated altogether by installing a water softener.

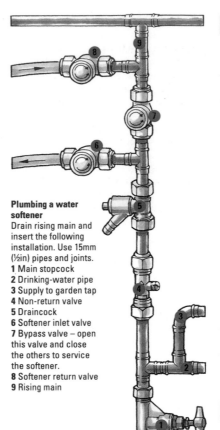

Plumbing a water softener
Drain rising main and insert the following installation. Use 15mm (½in) pipes and joints.
1 Main stopcock
2 Drinking-water pipe
3 Supply to garden tap
4 Non-return valve
5 Draincock
6 Softener inlet valve
7 Bypass valve – open this valve and close the others to service the softener.
8 Softener return valve
9 Rising main

FITTING A GARDEN TAP

A bib tap situated on an outside wall is convenient for attaching a hose for a lawn sprinkler or for washing the car. To comply with Bylaws, a double-seal non-return (check) valve must be incorporated in the plumbing to prevent contaminated water being drawn back into the system. Provide a means of shutting off the water and draining the pipework during winter, and keep the outside pipe run as short as possible.

Turn off the main stopcock and drain the rising main. Fit a tee joint (**1**) in the rising main to run the supply to the tap. Run a short length of pipe to a convenient position for another stopcock (**2**) and the non-return valve (**3**), making sure the arrows marked on both fittings point in the direction of flow. Fit a draincock (**4**) after this point. Run a pipe through the wall inside a length of plastic overflow (**5**) so that any leaks will be detected quickly and will not soak the masonry. Wrap PTFE tape

around the bib-tap thread before screwing it into a wallplate attached to the masonry outside (**6**).

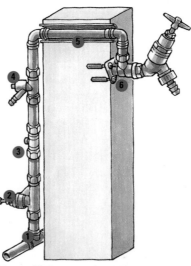

Pipes and fittings to supply a garden tap

Domestic water softeners

A water softener works on the principle of ion exchange. Incoming water flows through a compartment containing a synthetic resin that absorbs scale-forming calcium and magnesium ions and releases sodium ions in their place. After a period of about three or four days the resin is unable to absorb any more mineral salts, at which time the softener automatically flushes the compartment with a saline solution to regenerate the resin. Topping up with granular salt is required at intervals of perhaps two to three months. The softener is fitted with a timer so you can programme regeneration when water consumption is at its lowest, usually during the early hours of the morning.

The unit must be connected to the rising main at the point where the pipe enters the house, which could be under the stairs, in the cellar or utility room, but more than likely in the kitchen. For this reason, softeners designed for average domestic use fit under a standard kitchen worktop.

Installing a water softener

The installation of a water softener may appear to be fairly complicated because it involves a great deal of joint making, both to fit the valves and branch pipes that supply and bypass the softener, and to include certain fittings to comply with the Water Bylaws.

The bypass assembly allows for the unit to be isolated for servicing while maintaining the supply of water to the rest of the house. In addition, you must install a branch pipe before the assembly to supply unsoftened drinking water to the kitchen sink. Supply a garden tap from the same pipe – there is no need to waste softened water on the garden.

Install a non-return valve in the system to prevent the reverse flow of salty water. A pressure-reducing valve may also be required (check with your water supplier). You will need a draincock to empty the rising main. Some manufacturers supply an installation kit which includes all the necessary equipment.

You will have to provide drainage in the form of a standpipe and trap as for a washing machine.

Wire the water softener to a switched, fused connection unit that contains a 3amp fuse.

The cold-water storage cistern, normally situated in the roofspace, supplies the hot-water cylinder and all the cold taps in the house, other than the one used for drinking water in the kitchen. An old house may still be fitted with a heavy, galvanized-steel cistern which has probably been in service since the house was built. Eventually it will corrode and, although it can be patched up temporarily with an epoxy filler, it makes sense to replace it before a serious leak develops. A circular, 227 litre (50 gallon) capacity, polyethylene cistern is a popular choice as a replacement because it can be folded to pass through a narrow hatchway to the loft.

Complying with the Bylaws

Make sure the new cistern is supplied with a Bylaw 30 kit to keep the water clean. This is a requirement of the water supplier. The kit includes a close-fitting lid that excludes light and insects, and is fitted with a screened breather and a sleeved inlet for the vent pipe. In addition, there should be an overflow-pipe assembly that is screened to prevent insects crawling into the cistern, a reinforcing plate to stiffen the cistern wall around the float valve and an insulating jacket.

Removing the old cistern

Switch off water-heating appliances, then close the stopcock on the rising main and drain the cistern by opening the bathroom cold taps.

Bail out the remaining water in the bottom of the cistern, then use a spanner to dismantle the fittings connecting the float valve, distribution pipes and overflow to the cistern. Use a little penetrating oil if the fittings are stiff with corrosion. The cistern may have been built into the house before the roof was completed, so it is unlikely to pass through the loft hatch; just pull it to one side. Prepare a firm base for the new cistern by nailing stout planks across the joists or build a platform with 18mm (¾in) thick chipboard or plywood.

PLUMBING A NEW CISTERN

Connecting the float valve
A float valve shuts off the flow of water from the rising main when the cistern is full. Cut a hole for the float valve 75mm (3in) below the top of the cistern. Slip a plastic washer onto the tail of the float valve and pass it through the hole. Slide the reinforcing plate onto the tail, followed by another washer and a fixing nut, then tighten the fitting with the aid of two spanners.

Screw a tap connector onto the valve, ready for connecting to the 15mm (½in) rising main.

Connecting the distribution pipes
The 22mm (¾in) pipes running to the cylinder and cold taps are attached to the cistern with tank connectors – threaded inlets with a compression fitting for the pipework. Drill a hole for each tank connector about 50mm (2in) above the bottom of the cistern. Push a tank connector through each hole with one polyethylene washer on the inside. Wrap a couple of turns of PTFE tape around the threads and fit the other washer. Screw on the nut, holding the tank connector to stop it turning. Do not overtighten the nut or you will damage the washer and cause it to leak.

Take the opportunity to fit a gate valve to each distribution pipe so that you can cut off the supply of water without having to empty the cistern.

Connecting the overflow
Drill a hole 25mm (1in) below the level of the float-valve inlet for the threaded connector on the overflow-pipe assembly. Pass the connector through the hole, fit a washer and tighten its fixing nut on the inside of the cistern. Fit the dip pipe and insect filter.

Attach a 21mm (¾in) plastic overflow pipe to the assembly. Run the pipe to the floor then to the outside of the house, maintaining a continuous fall. The pipe must emerge in a conspicuous position so that an overflow can be detected immediately. Clip the pipe to the roof timbers.

Connecting the plumbing
Modify the rising main and distribution pipes to align with their fittings, then connect them with compression fittings. (Don't use soldered joints near a plastic cistern.) Clip all the pipework securely to the joists.

Open the main stopcock and check for leaks as the cistern fills. As the water level approaches the top, adjust the float arm to maintain the level 25mm (1in) below the overflow outlet.

Adapt the vent pipe from the hot-water cylinder to pass through the hole in the lid. Finally, insulate the cistern and pipework, but make sure there is no loft insulation under the cistern as this will prevent warmth rising from below.

Plumbing a cistern.
1 Float valve
2 Reinforcing plate
3 Tap connector
4 Rising main
5 Tank connector
6 Gate valve
7 22mm (¾in) distribution pipe
8 Pipe clip
9 Overflow-pipe assembly
10 Overflow pipe
11 Vent pipe

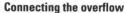

SEE ALSO	
Details for:	
Insulation	267, 272
Float valves	355–356
Adjusting float arm	356
Tap connector	356
Gate valve	362
Compression joint	364
Cylinder	392

Tank cutters
Hire a tank cutter to bore holes in a cistern for pipework. Some cutters are adjustable so that you can drill holes of different diameters. As an alternative, use a hole saw clamped to a drill.

Adjustable cutter

Hole saw

VENTED HOT-WATER CYLINDERS

Typical pipe runs
Red: Hot water
Blue: Cold water

Direct water heating by means of a boiler

Indirect water heating employs the central-heating boiler

The hot water in most houses is heated and stored in a large copper cylinder situated in the airing cupboard. Cold water is fed to the base of the cylinder from the storage cistern in the loft. As the water is heated it rises to the top of the cylinder, where it is drawn off via a branch from the vent pipe to the hot taps. The vent pipe itself runs back to the loft, where it passes through the lid of the cold-water storage cistern with its open end just above the level of the water.

When water is heated in the copper cylinder it rises to the top, where it is drawn off through the hot-water supply pipe. It is replaced by cold water at the base. The vent pipe provides a safe escape route for air bubbles or steam should the system overheat.

Heating causes the water in the cylinder to expand. The vent pipe accommodates some of this expansion, although much of the excess water is forced back up the cold-feed pipe into the cistern.

Methods of heating water

There are two different methods of heating the water in a vented hot-water cylinder: either directly, most usually by means of electric heaters, or indirectly by a central-heating system.

Direct heating

Water heating may be accomplished by means of electric immersion heaters only. A single-element or double-element heater is fitted in the top of the cylinder, or there may be two individual side-entry heaters. Alternatively the water may be heated in a boiler, the sole purpose of which is to provide hot water for the cylinder. A cold-water pipe runs from the base of the cylinder to the boiler, where the water is heated before returning to the top half of the cylinder. Both of these methods are known as direct systems. In practice, a boiler-heated cylinder is generally fitted with an immersion heater as well in order that hot water can be supplied independently during the summer months, when use of the boiler would make the room in which it is situated uncomfortably warm.

Indirect heating

When a house is centrally heated with radiators fed by a boiler, the water in the cylinder is normally heated indirectly by a heat exchanger. Hot water from the boiler passes through the exchanger, a coiled tube within the cylinder, where the heat is transmitted to the stored water. The heat exchanger is part of a completely self-contained system with its own feed-and-expansion tank, a small storage cistern in the loft which tops up the system. A vent pipe terminates open-ended over the same small cistern. The whole system is known as the primary circuit, and the pipes running from and back to the boiler are known as the primary flow and return. An indirect system is often supplemented with an immersion heater to provide hot water during the summer months.

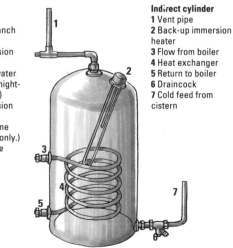

Direct cylinder
1 Vent pipe
2 Hot-water branch pipe
3 Lower immersion heater
(Provides hot water using cheaper night-rate electricity.)
4 Upper immersion heater
(Used for daytime top-up heating only.)
5 Cold-feed pipe
6 Draincock

Indirect cylinder
1 Vent pipe
2 Back-up immersion heater
3 Flow from boiler
4 Heat exchanger
5 Return to boiler
6 Draincock
7 Cold feed from cistern

HOT-WATER CYLINDERS

The capacity of domestic cylinders ranges from 114 litres (25 gallons) to about 227 litres (50 gallons), although there are bigger cylinders to meet the requirements of large families. A cylinder with a capacity of between 182 and 227 litres (40 and 50 gallons) will store enough hot water to satisfy the needs of an average family for a whole day. Many cylinders are made from thin, uninsulated copper and need a thick lagging jacket to reduce heat loss. However, there is a growing preference for factory-insulated cylinders covered with a layer of foamed polyurethane.

Changing a cylinder

You may wish to replace an existing cylinder because it has sprung a leak, or because a larger one will allow you to take full advantage of economical night-time electricity by storing more cheap hot water. A simple replacement can sometimes be achieved without modifying the plumbing, but you will have to adapt the pipework to fit a larger cylinder. If you plan to install central heating at some time in the future, you can plumb in an indirect cylinder with a double-element immersion heater and simply leave the heat-exchanging coil unconnected for the time being.

First drain the pipework and cylinder. Disconnect any immersion heaters from the electrical supply, then use a special spanner (available from a tool-hire outlet) to unscrew them. Disconnect all the pipework, springing it out of the way while you remove the cylinder.

Place the new cylinder in position and check the existing pipework for alignment. Modify the pipes as necessary then make the connections, using PTFE tape to make sure the threaded joints are watertight. Take the opportunity to fit a draincock to the supply pipe from the cistern.

With the fibre sealing washer in place, wrap PTFE tape around the thread of an immersion heater and screw it into the cylinder. Connect the immersion heater to the electrical supply, then fill the system and check for leaks before you attempt to heat the water. Check for leaks once again when the water is up to temperature and, if all is well, complete the job by lagging the cylinder and pipework.

THERMAL-STORE CYLINDERS

A thermal-store cylinder reverses the indirect principle. Water heated by a central-heating boiler passes through the cylinder and transfers heat via a highly efficient coiled heat exchanger to mains-fed water supplying hot taps and showers. An integral feed-and-expansion tank is normally built on top of the cylinder. When the system is working at maximum capacity, the mains-fed water is delivered at such a high temperature that cold water must be added via a thermostatic mixing valve plumbed into the outlet supplying taps and showers. As the cylinder is exhausted, less cold water is added. The thermal-store system provides mains-pressure hot water throughout the house, dispenses with the need for a loft cistern and increases the efficiency of the boiler.

A valve is needed to prevent the heat from the cylinder thermo-siphoning (gravity circulating) around the central-heating system. The valve can be motorized or a simple mechanical gravity check (non-return) valve which is opened by the force of the central-heating pump. As with all open-vented systems, the feed-and-expansion tank determines the head of water and radiators must be lower than the tank in order to be filled with water. When the tank is combined with the cylinder, it must be situated on the top floor of a house in order to provide central heating throughout the building. If this is impossible, install a tankless thermal-store cylinder and fit a conventional feed-and-expansion tank in the loft.

An unvented cylinder provides mains-pressure hot water throughout the house. This is achieved by connecting the cylinder directly to the rising main. Most manufacturers recommend a 22mm (¾in) incoming pipe, but in practice a 15mm (½in) main at high pressure is adequate. An unvented cylinder can be heated directly, using immersion heaters, or indirectly provided you are not using a solid-fuel boiler.

There are no storage cisterns, feed-and-expansion tanks or open-vent pipes associated with unvented cylinders. Instead, a diaphragm inside a pressure vessel mounted on top of the cylinder flexes to accommodate expanding water. If the vessel fails, an expansion-relief valve protects the system by releasing water via a discharge pipe.

There are several other safety devices associated with unvented cylinders. A normal thermostat should keep the water within the cylinder below 65°C (150°F). If the water should reach 90°C (195°F), a second thermostat will switch off the immersion heaters or shut off the water supply from the boiler. Finally, if the temperature should get as high as 95°C (205°F) a temperature-relief valve opens, discharging water outside.

Bylaws and Regulations

The installation of an unvented cylinder must satisfy Water Bylaws and Building Regulations. It must include all the necessary safety devices and be installed by a competent fitter such as those registered with the Institute of Plumbing, the Construction Industry Training Board or the Association of Installers of Unvented Hot Water Systems (Scotland and Northern Ireland). Have an installation serviced regularly by a similarly qualified fitter to ensure all the equipment is in good working order.

You must notify the water company and your local Building Control Office of your intention to install an unvented hot-water cylinder.

Thermal-store cylinder
1 Integral feed-and-expansion tank
2 Heat-exchanger
3 Supply pipe to hot taps/shower
4 Thermostatic mixing valve
5 Expansion vessel
6 Mains feed
7 Space-heating flow
8 Space-heating return
9 Boiler flow
10 Boiler return

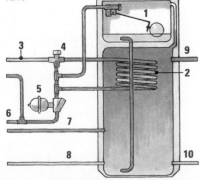

Unvented hot-water cylinder
1 Incoming mains water
2 Stopcock
3 Line strainer
4 Cold water to taps
5 Non-return (check) valve
6 Pressure limiter
7 Pressure vessel
8 Expansion-relief valve
9 Cold-water inlet
10 Immersion heater
11 Hot-water outlet
12 Temperature-relief valve
13 Tundish
14 Discharge pipe

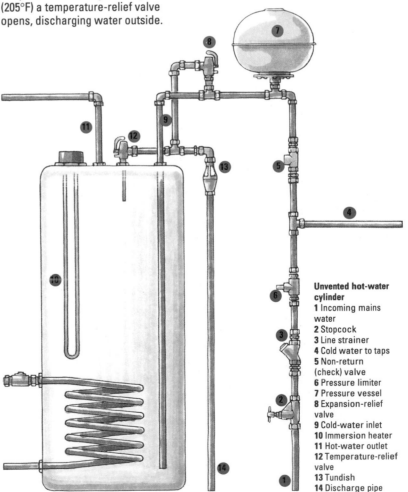

WATER
HEATERS

Most people are familiar with the small point-of-use instantaneous water heaters that are normally mounted above a sink or in a cupboard below a hand basin. It is also possible to install much larger instantaneous heaters which are powerful enough to heat bath water, service a shower and even provide central heating.

Direct-fired gas water heaters

High-output gas heaters provide instant hot water for the entire house.

Water drawn off by turning on a tap or shower is replaced with cold water introduced to the base of the tank by a dip tube. A thermostat senses the drop in temperature and ignites the gas burner in a chamber below the water tank. Heated gases rise through a flue that passes vertically through the centre of the tank, heating the surrounding water. The flue contains a baffle that slows down the passage of gases to achieve maximum heat exchange. The gases are finally dispelled to the outside via a vent which also draws fresh air into the burning chamber – a balanced-flue arrangement. Heated water rises to the top of the tank, where it is drawn off through a pipe on demand.

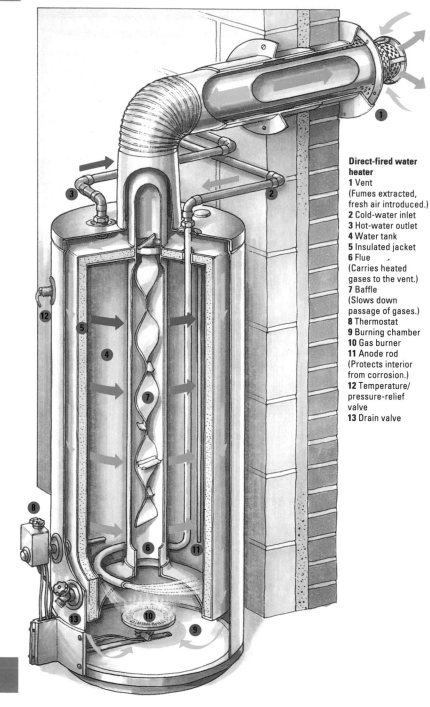

Direct-fired water heater

1 Vent
(Fumes extracted, fresh air introduced.)
2 Cold-water inlet
3 Hot-water outlet
4 Water tank
5 Insulated jacket
6 Flue
(Carries heated gases to the vent.)
7 Baffle
(Slows down passage of gases.)
8 Thermostat
9 Burning chamber
10 Gas burner
11 Anode rod
(Protects interior from corrosion.)
12 Temperature/pressure-relief valve
13 Drain valve

SMALL POINT-OF-USE HEATERS

Instantaneous water heaters provide hot water at the point it is required – beside the sink or washbasin. When you turn the tap, the flow of water activates a powerful electric heater, or ignites the burner in the case of a gas appliance. (Gas water heaters should be installed by a qualified fitter.)

Electric heaters are supplied with water from the rising main via 15mm (½in) pipework connected to the water inlet just below the tap with a standard compression fitting.

A 3kW model, suitable for a sink, is wired to a fused connection unit containing a 13amp fuse. The unit must be out of reach of anyone using the sink, so if necessary fit a flex outlet near the heater and run a cable from there to the connection unit.

A 7kW heater requires a 45 amp radial circuit similar to a shower, but in a kitchen you can use a wall-mounted double-pole switch to connect it instead of a ceiling-mounted switch.

Connecting a 3kW heater
1 Flex outlet
2 15mm (½in) supply pipe

CHAPTER 9

HEATING

OPEN FIRES

Traditional open fires are extremely popular, even if only to supplement central heating. Some people prefer to burn real fuel while others are content with fuel-effect gas fires that provide the comforting aspects of a real fire without the inconvenience. Neither form of heating is particularly efficient or cost effective compared with a glass-fronted room heater, but for many of us the warm glow from the hearth is justification enough.

How an open fire works

To burn properly, a fire needs a good supply of oxygen (1) and a means of escape for its smoke and gases (2). If either of these is cut off, the fire will be stifled and will eventually go out.

A domestic open fire is usually built on a barred grate (3), through which ash and debris fall into a removable tray. Oxygen is sucked up into the base of the fire to maintain combustion. As the fuel burns, it gives off heated gases, which expand and become lighter than the surrounding air, so that they rise (4). To prevent the gases and smoke drifting out and filling the room, a flue above the fire provides an escape route, taking them above roof level to

be discharged into the atmosphere.

As the hot gases rise, they induce suction at the bottom of the fire, which draws in the supply of oxygen that keeps it burning. For this reason, an open fire needs not only an effective chimney but also good ventilation in the room where it is burning, so that the air consumed by the fire is replenished continually. Sometimes the efficient draughtproofing of doors and windows can prevent a fire burning properly by denying it the constant supply of air that it needs. In such cases, ventilation must be provided by means of an airbrick or a window vent; underfloor ventilation is another possibility.

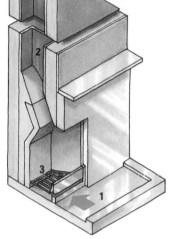

How a traditional open fire works
1 Air is sucked in as the gases rise.
2 Gases escape up the narrow flue.
3 The grate lets ash out and air in.
4 Gases vent to the air outside.

Sweeping chimneys

All solid fuels give off dust, ash, acids and tarry substances as they burn, and this combination of materials is carried up the chimney, where some of them are deposited as soot. If too much soot collects in a chimney, that effectively reduces its size internally, restricting the flow of gases and stopping the fire burning properly. The build-up of soot can even create a complete blockage, particularly at a bend, and cause the more serious hazard of a chimney fire.

To prevent soot building up, sweep your chimneys at least twice a year, once during the heating season and once at the end (to prevent acids in the soot attacking the chimney's lining and mortar joints during the summer). If a chimney is left unswept for long, smoke begins to billow into the room and soot occasionally drops into the fire.

Though it's seemingly a dirty job, you can sweep a chimney without making a great deal of mess, provided you take some care. Brushes with nylon bristles and 'canes' made from polypropylene are available for hire.

Remove any loose items from the hearth. If the room has a large rug or an unfitted carpet, roll it back and cover it with a dustsheet for protection. Drape a large old sheet or blanket over the fire surround, weighting it down along the

mantle shelf and leaning something heavy against each side to form a seal with the edges of the fire surround.

Screw the brush to the first cane and place it in the fireplace, then gather the sheet around the cane and weight down its edges on the hearth. Now screw on the next cane and push the brush up the flue. Continue screwing on lengths of cane and pushing the brush upwards until you feel resistance cease as the brush emerges from the top of the chimney pot. If the pot is fitted with a cowl, try to anticipate when the brush will emerge, so you avoid pushing the cowl off the chimney.

If the brush meets an obstruction in the flue, pull it back slightly, then push upwards again, working it up and down until you clear the blockage. Don't twist the canes to and fro: this may unscrew a joint and leave the brush irretrievably stuck up the chimney.

Pull the brush back down, unscrewing the canes as they appear, then pull out the brush and either shovel the heap of soot out of the grate or use a hired industrial vacuum cleaner.

Although using a brush and canes is the time-honoured method of sweeping a chimney, and also the most effective one, there are other ways of coping with the job (see left).

● **Fitting a gas fire**
All gas fires must be installed by a fitter registered with CORGI (Confederation of Registered Gas Installers), who needs to check that the flue, hearth and ventilation are adequate. Always sweep the chimney before installing a fire of any sort. Use a smoke pellet to test the draw and to see if there is any leakage through to other flues.

● **Vacuum sweeping**
You can have a chimney swept with a special vacuum cleaner. Its nozzle is inserted through a cover over the fire opening and sucks out the soot – a very clean method, but no use for heavy soot deposits or other obstructions.

● **Chemical cleaning**
There are chemicals that will remove light soot deposits and stop further sooting up. In liquid or powder form, they are sprinkled onto the hot fire and produce a non-toxic gas that causes soot to crumble away from the chimney walls.

Sweeping your chimney
Seal off the fireplace with an old sheet and feed the canes up under it.

MENDING A CRACKED FIREBACK

Years of intense heat eventually damage a fireback. Large cracks may mean a replacement, but fine ones can be repaired. First let the fireback cool for at least 48 hours, then brush away all soot and rake the cracks out with a trowel point, undercutting their sides to make an inverted V-shape. Brush out the dust and soak the area with water for better cement adhesion. With a small trowel, work fire cement into the cracks and trowel away the surplus; then go over it with a paintbrush and clean water for a smooth finish. Allow the cement to harden for a few days before lighting a fire.

You may be thinking of removing an old fireback because it is damaged and looks unsightly, and the exposed brick recess can be used to make an attractive niche for flowers, house plants and ornaments. But before doing so, it's worth considering whether a better alternative might be to replace the fireback and retain the functioning fireplace.

Removing an old fireback

If you plan to replace the old fireback, first of all you will need to measure the width across its mouth and order a new one. The standard sizes are 400mm (1ft 4in) and 450mm (1ft 6in), although larger ones are available.

Before proceeding to remove the old fireback, cover the floor with a dust-sheet and protect a tiled hearth with cardboard; then remove the grate (1). The grate may simply rest on the back hearth, or it may be screwed down and sealed to the fireback with asbestos rope and fire cement (2). If so, take out the screws and chip away the cement with a hammer and cold chisel to free

it. Next, break out the old fireback (3) with a hammer and chisel, starting at one corner. If cracks develop, exploit them to remove larger pieces. Take care not to damage the fire surround when you are breaking the cement seal (4) between it and the fireback. Don't touch the asbestos-braid packing (5) between the fireback and the surround unless it is in poor condition and needs replacing (see right).

Having removed the fireback, you will find a lot of rubble in the space behind it (6). Chop this out with a hammer and chisel until you have cleared the original brick-lined builder's opening.

Installing a new fireback

Although your new fireback will be supplied in one piece, you will have to install it in two pieces, divided horizontally, to allow for the expansion and contraction of the lower portion due to heat from the fire.

A recessed cutting line across the fireback shows where the two halves must be separated. This is done by tapping gently along the line with a bolster chisel and a hammer.

Mix a mortar of 4 parts vermiculite : 1 part lime, and trowel a layer of it round the rear edge of the back hearth (1) to make a bed for the lower portion of the fireback. Ease that portion into position, at the same time pulling it forward so that it lightly compresses the asbestos-rope packing at the edge of the fire surround. Check that the fireback is properly upright.

Cut out two pieces of corrugated cardboard to the shape of the fireback's lower portion, then place them directly behind it (2) and fill with the same mix of mortar that was used for bedding it on the hearth (3). To save on mortar, you can add brick rubble and pieces of the old broken fireback to the mix as an infill (4). Bring the mortar up level with the top edge of the fireback's lower portion (5), tamping down the mortar with a piece of wood as you go.

Trowel a layer of mortar along the top edge of the fireback's lower portion and set the upper portion in place on

top of it (6), making sure that the two halves are accurately lined up. Trowel off surplus mortar and finish the joint by brushing clean water over it.

Continue filling the space behind the fireback with the mixture of mortar and rubble – again tamping it down as you work – until the infill reaches the top. Now form a slope with the mortar, from the top of the fireback to the rear face of the chimney (7). This slope is called the 'flaunching', and the surface of the mortar must be made parallel with the slope of the rear edge of the loadbearing lintel that runs across the top of the fire opening. The two slopes have a narrow 'throat' between them, about 100mm (4in) wide, that takes the smoke from the fire into the flue itself. Trowel the flaunching smooth, and add any mortar that may be needed at the sides to avoid the formation of ledges that might collect soot.

Finally, seal the new fireback to the surround with fire cement (8) (see above right) and replace the grate. Use a little more fire cement to cover any asbestos packing visible at the sides.

SEALING THE FIREBACK

The cement seal between the fireback and the surround must be renewed when a new fireback is installed or if the seal is cracked or broken. Wearing a face mask, repair the joint by chipping away the old cement with a hammer and cold chisel, then rake out the debris to uncover the asbestos expansion joints. If these are sound, leave them; but if they are broken or crumbling, cover the floor with plastic sheet, then spray the asbestos with water, cut out the damp packing with a sharp knife, and seal it in a labelled plastic bag. Carefully fold the sheeting for disposal and pick up any asbestos dust with a damp sponge (not with a vacuum cleaner). Your local authority will advise on disposal. Repack with an asbestos-substitute, brush the joint with clean water, and trowel in fire cement to finish flush with the surround. Smooth off with a wet paintbrush.

SEE ALSO

Details for:
Fitting fire surround   400

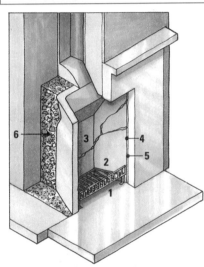

Taking out an old or damaged fireback
1 The grate may be fixed or freestanding.
2 The grate may be sealed with asbestos rope and fire cement.
3 The fireback will have to be broken out.
4 The surround is bonded to the fireback with cement.
5 Braided packing may need replacing.
6 Rubble to be cleared from the brick-lined builder's opening.

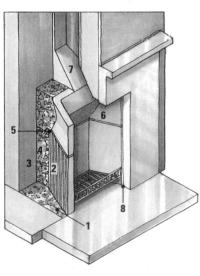

Installing a fireback
1 The back hearth supports the fireback.
2 Corrugated card leaves an expansion gap when it burns.
3 The rear space, to be filled with mortar.
4 Rubble gives the mortar bulk.
5 Level the mortar with the top edge of the fireback.
6 Upper section of fireback is set in place and infilled behind.
7 Mortar sloped to form flaunching.
8 Fireback has to be sealed to surround.

397

REMOVING A FIREPLACE

● **Thinking ahead**
Before you remove a fireplace, bear in mind that should you decide to reinstate a working fireplace in the future it may be necessary to enlarge your constructional hearth to meet current Building Regulations.

● **Saving a surround**
Fire surrounds can be very heavy, especially stone, slate or marble ones. In order to keep a surround intact, place an old mattress in front of it before you pull it from the wall – so minimum damage is done if it should fall.

When restoring an old house, you may want to remove a fireplace in order to reinstate one with authentic period styling. Or perhaps you want to change the use of a room and dispense with an unattractive modern fireplace altogether. Taking out an old fire surround and superimposed hearth is easy enough, but it does create a lot of dust and debris. Before you start, sweep the chimney, move all furniture as far from the fireplace as possible, roll back the carpet and cover everything with dustsheets.

Removing the hearth

Most superimposed hearths are laid after the fire surround has been fitted and so must come out first – but check beforehand that your surround has not been installed on top of the hearth.

Wearing safety goggles and heavy gloves, use a club hammer and bolster chisel to break the mortar seal between the superimposed hearth and the constructional hearth beneath it. Driving wooden wedges under the hearth will help to break the seal. Lever the hearth free with a crowbar or a strong garden spade and lift it clear. It will be heavy, so get someone to help you.

Instead of a superimposed hearth, some fireplaces have a tiled constructional hearth that lies flush with the surrounding floorboards. You can leave the tiles in place and run the floorcovering over them, or lift them out with a bolster chisel and fill flush with mortar.

Removing the surround

Most surrounds are fixed to the wall with screws driven through metal lugs, which are hidden by the plaster on the chimney breast. Chip away 25mm (1in) of plaster all round the surround to find the lugs, then expose them completely and take out the screws. If the screws are immovable, soak them for a few hours in penetrating oil, then try again. If that fails, drill out the screw heads. The surround will be heavy, so get help when levering it from the wall (see left).

Brick and stone surrounds
A brick or stone surround can be taken out a piece at a time, using a bolster to break the mortar joints. There may also be metal ties holding it to the wall.

Marble surrounds
Marble surrounds are made in sections, so remove the shelf first, then the lintel, and lastly the side jambs.

Wooden surrounds
A timber surround may be held by screws driven through its sides and top into battens fixed to the chimney breast inside the surround. The screw heads will be concealed by wooden plugs or filler. Chisel these out, then remove the screws and lift away the surround.

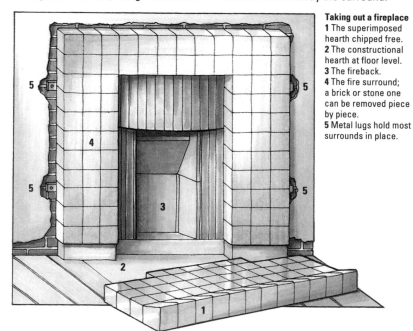

Taking out a fireplace
1 The superimposed hearth chipped free.
2 The constructional hearth at floor level.
3 The fireback.
4 The fire surround; a brick or stone one can be removed piece by piece.
5 Metal lugs hold most surrounds in place.

REPLACING CRACKED TILES

If you are able to find substitutes that match, replace cracked or broken tiles in a hearth or fire surround. Old tiles are stocked by most architectural salvage companies, or you may be lucky enough to retrieve an old fireplace that's been ripped out of a neighbouring house.

Break out the damaged tile, using a hammer and cold chisel, working from the centre outwards. Wear thick gloves and safety goggles, and protect nearby surfaces with dustsheets. Remove all traces of old adhesive or mortar, and vacuum up the dust.

If necessary, cut the replacement tile to fit, then butter its back with heat-resistant tile adhesive. Place the tile in position, taking care that the clearance is equal all round, and wipe off any excess adhesive. Leave the adhesive to set, and then apply colour-matched grout to the gaps. If you are replacing one tile only, don't buy a tub of special adhesive – use a paste mixed from cellulose filler and PVA glue, but wet the back of the tile first. If the location of the tile is very close to the fire opening, use fire cement instead.

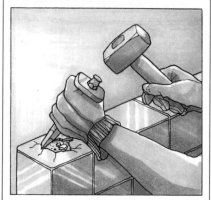

Chipping out a damaged tile
Start in the middle and work out towards the edges. Clean out all old mortar or adhesive.

Complete retiling
If a large number of tiles have been lost or damaged, then your best course may be to retile the surround and hearth completely. This is likely to be much less trouble than it sounds, as you will probably be able to buy appropriate modern tiles, instead of having to track down a supply of period ones.

Chop off the old tiles and clean up the surround with a bolster chisel, then proceed as you would when tiling a wall and window surround.

Having removed a fireplace , you can close the opening with a thin panel on a wooden frame or by bricking it up. Panelling the opening will make it easier to reinstate the fireplace at some time in the future. In either case, it is necessary to fit a ventilator in the centre of the opening just above skirting level. This provides a flow of air through the chimney to prevent condensation forming and seeping through the brickwork.

Making good the floor

If the floor is solid, all you need do after removing the fireplace is to bring the constructional hearth up level with the floor, using mortar or a self-levelling screed; and you can do the same with a boarded floor, if it is to be carpeted. But if you want exposed floorboards, chop back the concrete hearth with a hammer and cold chisel to make room for a new joist and floorboards.

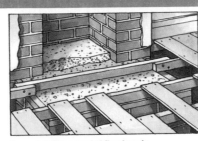

A new joist for extended floorboards

Sealing the opening with plasterboard

Make a panel from 9.5mm (⅜in) plaster-board nailed to a 50 x 50mm (2 x 2in) sawn-timber frame fixed inside the fire opening. Nail the frame in the opening with masonry nails, setting the battens back from the face of the brickwork, so the plasterboard, when nailed on, will lie flush with the surrounding plaster. Set the battens back a further 3mm (⅛in) if a plaster skim is to be added to the plasterboard. For papering, fix the plasterboard with its ivory side out; for a plaster skim the grey side should be showing. After decorating or plastering the panel, fit a plastic ventilator.

Panelling for a gas fire
If you are planning to close off the fire opening so that you can connect up the flue outlet for a gas fire, you will need to construct a similar timber frame, but the panel must be made from asbestos-free fire-resistant insulation board.

Make a cutout in the panel for the outlet of the gas fire; then fix the panel to the timber frame, using countersunk woodscrews and screw cups. Make good the plaster over the top of the panel, and seal the gas fire to it with a combination of asbestos-substitute packing and fire cement.

An inset frame to support plasterboard

An unused chimney must be ventilated

Sealing the opening with bricks

If you wish to brick up the fire opening, take out bricks from alternate courses at the edges of the opening so the new brickwork can be 'toothed in'. Provide ventilation for the chimney by fitting an airbrick centrally in the brickwork, just above skirting level. Plaster the brick-work and allow it to dry. Make sure that the plaster has dried thoroughly before you redecorate the wall. Finally, lever off the old pieces of skirting board from the ends of the chimney breast, and replace them with a full-length piece running from corner to corner.

One of the bricks must be an airbrick

INSTALLING A LOG-BURNING GRATE

To install a log-burning grate, you must first remove the old fireback and the rubble infill, then open out the fireplace to the original builder's opening. You can leave the bricks exposed if you like their appearance, or line the opening with fire brick, ordinary brick or stone.

Choose a grate that will fit the opening, leaving a gap of 50 to 75mm (2 to 3in) at each side. The best types have cast-iron firebacks that radiate more heat from the fire.

The original back hearth will be quite suitable as a level surface for the grate, but if you have taken out the old superimposed hearth you will have to install a new one. This is normally at least 50mm (2in) thick, and extends 300mm (1ft) in front of the grate and at least 150mm (6in) on each side of the fire opening – or to the width of any surround if this is greater.

The new superimposed hearth can be of brick, stone, or tiled concrete. Bed the hearth on mortar mixed with 3 parts sand : 1 part cement.

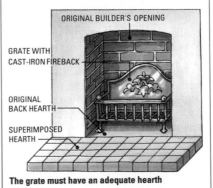

ORIGINAL BUILDER'S OPENING

GRATE WITH CAST-IRON FIREBACK

ORIGINAL BACK HEARTH

SUPERIMPOSED HEARTH

The grate must have an adequate hearth

CAPPING THE CHIMNEY

When you close off a fire opening, you should cap the chimney – to keep rain out while allowing an outlet that draws air through the vent in the room below. Either replace the chimney pot with a half-round ridge tile bedded in cement, or fit a proprietary cowl or cap.

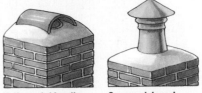

Half-round ridge tile   Commercial cowl

Reinstating a fireplace

Constructional hearth
Before reinstating a fireplace, it's essential to check that the constructional hearth complies with current Building Regulations.

Superimposed hearth
Minimum dimensions for an open fire. The width of the hearth should not be less than the width of the fire surround.

FITTING A TRADITIONAL SURROUND

Once ripped out without thought, today period fireplaces are much sought after and can cost hundreds of pounds – but fortunately it is possible to buy excellent reproduction inserts and surrounds that look completely authentic.

Most fire surrounds are held in place by lugs screwed to the wall, although some are fixed with mortar. A plaster surround can be held with dabs of bonding plaster. First remove a strip of plaster from around the fire opening, about 50mm (2in) wider all round than the surround.

Carefully position and plumb a cast-iron insert in the builder's opening. Most inserts simply stand on the back hearth; but some have lugs for screwing to the wall, in which case use heat-resistant wall plugs or expanding bolts to hold the insert. Fit lengths of asbestos-substitute packing as expansion joints where the insert touches the wall, and seal with fire cement. Fill behind the insert with mortar and rubble, or use a lightweight aggregate such as expanded clay or vermiculite. Form a throat with mortar, as described for installing a fireback.

Holding the surround in place, mark the wall for the screw holes and drill them. Use a spirit level to check that the surround is upright and the mantel horizontal; any adjustments can be made with small wooden wedges. An alternative fixing for plaster surrounds is to apply mortar or plaster to the wall and prop the surround against it with battens until the mortar or plaster sets.

Reinstate the constructional hearth or build a new one to the dimensions given (see left). Set a superimposed hearth on a bed of mortar and point the edges. Replaster the wall and fit new skirting boards between the hearth and the corners of the chimney breast.

Prop a lightweight surround while plaster sets

An astonishing number of beautiful fireplaces lie hidden beneath layers of paint. Stripping a painted fireplace may well reveal a tiled Victorian insert with brass trimmings, a veined-marble surround or elegant carving.

You may want to repaint some materials – especially cast iron, which tends to rust if left unprotected. Elementary care is all that is required to maintain the appearance of marble and slate, provided you mop up spilled coffee, fruit juices and spirits, which can stain absorbent materials. Always let the hearth and surround cool down before you clean them.

Stone

Stonework can be sponged with warm water that has a little detergent mixed into it. Remove the more stubborn stains with a stiff-bristle brush.

Marble and granite

These stones are easily damaged, so should be treated with care. Wash them regularly with warm soapy water and polish them with a chamois leather or good-quality wax polish. Patch small chips with a putty made from kaolin powder (china clay) and epoxy glue; rub down the filler, when hard, with silicon-carbide paper and touch in with lacquer.

Ceramic tiles

Wash ceramic tiles with warm water containing a little detergent. Refix any that are loose with adhesive.

Bricks

Scrub sooty deposits with a stiff-bristle brush. Dust bricks off occasionally with a soft brush. Paint a new brick surround with a proprietary sealer or cold-water wallpaper size to prevent 'dusting'. Repair any broken bricks with an epoxy adhesive, or cut them out and replace them with new ones, using fresh mortar.

Slate

Wash slate with warm water mixed with a little detergent, using a stiff-bristle brush. If the slate is unpolished, you can remove stubborn stains with an abrasive cleaner.

Unpainted metalwork

Wash this with warm soapy water, and take off stubborn tar and soot stains with methylated spirit. Clean up rusty cast-iron surrounds and inserts with wet-and-dry abrasive paper or emery cloth. Finish an insert with 'black lead' and paint the surround.

Woodwork

If the grain is exposed, maintain the finish with wax polish or varnish. Fill any cracks or gouges with a wood filler, tinted to match with a little wood dye. Alternatively, finish a wooden surround with solvent-based or acrylic paint.

Stone surround

Marble surround

Wood surround

Modern solid-fuel room heaters are highly efficient and, with the addition of a back boiler, can provide domestic hot water and central heating. The toughened-glass doors provide a view of the glowing fire.

Standing a heater on the hearth

You can buy room heaters designed to stand on the hearth, forward of the chimney breast. These radiate extra warmth from their casings, but their size tends to make them look obtrusive in small rooms, and you may find you need to extend your constructional hearth to the required 300mm (1ft) in front of the heater. If you have a superimposed hearth, extend it by the same amount.

A heater of this type has a flue outlet at its rear, which must be connected to the chimney. This is normally achieved by passing the outlet through a metal backplate that closes off the fire opening (1). The projecting end of the outlet must stop short of the fireback by at least 100mm (4in) (2). If necessary, remove the fireback to provide the clearance. If the void is very large, extend the outlet up into the main flue, with a seal all round, to provide a satisfactory updraught.

The closure plate should be of metal at least 1mm (18 gauge) thick. Fold its edges to form flanges through which fixing screws can be driven into the edges of the fire opening. Use heat-resistant wall plugs to hold the screws, and seal the joint between plate and opening with asbestos-substitute packing and fire cement.

1 A backplate closes off the fire opening

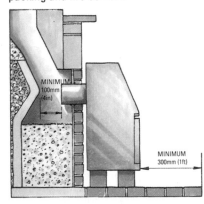

MINIMUM 100mm (4in)

MINIMUM 300mm (1ft)

2 Important measurements for a room heater

Standing a heater in the fire opening

Some room heaters are designed to stand in the fire opening. Installing one means first taking out the fireback and rubble infill to expose the builder's brick-lined opening. This type of heater has a vertical flue outlet, which must be connected to a closure plate set in the base of the chimney.

The closure plate can be of metal or precast concrete. To fit it, remove some bricks from the chimney breast just above the opening but below the load-bearing lintel. If the plate is of concrete, take out a course of bricks round the bottom of the chimney to support it properly. You can insert a metal plate into a chased-out mortar joint. Bed the plate on fire cement, sealing the edges above and below; check that the heater's outlet enters the chimney flue, and seal the plate joint with asbestos-substitute packing and fire cement.

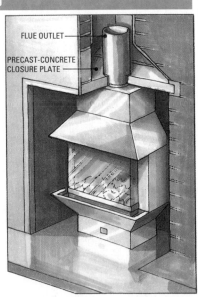

FLUE OUTLET

PRECAST-CONCRETE CLOSURE PLATE

A horizontal plate seals off the chimney

An inset room heater

To install an inset (built-in) room heater, you must first take out the fireback and the rubble infill behind it. The heater has its flue outlet mounted on top, to be connected to a chimney closure plate.

This type of appliance is designed to fill and seal the fire opening completely, so to install one you may have to modify your present fire surround or, if the opening is very large, even build a new one. The sides of the surround must be exactly at right angles to the hearth, as the front portion of the heater's casing has to be sealed to both. If the surround and the hearth form an odd angle, a good seal with the heater casing will be impossible. The seal is made with asbestos-substitute packing material.

Most inset heaters are screwed down to the back hearth, and some may need a vermiculite-based infill around the back of the casing (the infill has to be in place before the chimney closure plate is fitted and the flue outlet connected). Some models are supplied with their own fire surround, complete with a drop-in closure plate designed for easy installation.

Finish the job by making good the brickwork of the chimney breast and replastering it.

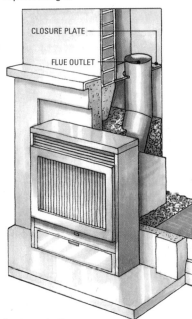

CLOSURE PLATE

FLUE OUTLET

Inset room heater
The top-mounted flue outlet connects to a horizontal closure plate in the chimney base. Some versions need an infill around the rear casing.

SEE ALSO

Details for:	
Lintels	126
Providing ventilation	396
Removing fireback	397

● **Sweeping the chimney**
The flue above a solid-fuel heater can usually be swept by passing a brush up through the heater itself. If not, you need a separate double-seal soot door fitted in the closure plate or in the chimney breast (on either the inside or outside).

● **Hearth for a freestanding heater**
For a freestanding room heater, the constructional hearth has to be at least 840mm (2ft 9in) square and 125mm (5in) thick. It must extend not less than 300mm (1ft) in front of an open heater, and at least 225mm (9in) in front of a closed one.

INSTALLING
FLUE LINERS

SEE ALSO
Details for:
Sweeping chimney   396

If your house was built before 1965, there is a good chance that its chimney is unlined and is simply a rectangular duct with brickwork that's either rendered with cement or even exposed. Over the years, the corrosive elements in the combustion gases rising from the fire eat into a chimney's mortar and brickwork and weaken it, allowing condensation to pass through and form damp patches on the chimney breast. In extreme cases, smoke may seep through too. Such problems are particularly prevalent where solid-fuel or wood-burning fires or appliances are in use.

Choosing a flue liner

You can deal with these problems by installing a flue liner, which protects the brickwork from the corrosive elements. A liner also reduces the 'bore' of the flue. This speeds up the flow of gases, preventing them from cooling and condensing; and the increased draught of air through the fire encourages more efficient combustion.

It is important to fit the type of liner that's appropriate to the kind of heating appliance being used, and it pays to have the liner installed professionally.

Flue linings take the form of tubes, either one-piece or in sections, and are made of metal or from other rigid non-combustible materials, such as pumice.

Installing a flexible flue liner

A popular type of liner is a one-piece flexible corrugated tube of stainless steel that is easily fed into a flue. Thin-wall tubes are sufficient for gas appliances, but they burn through in no time if they are connected to a solid-fuel or wood-burning stove. For these heaters, install a double-skinned liner with a smooth inner surface. Some installers recommend filling around the liner with lightweight insulation.

As it is necessary to get onto the roof in order to install most liners, you must expect to have scaffolding erected round the chimney (see above right). It is advisable to have the chimney swept before work begins.

The installer will chop away the flaunching surrounding the base of the chimney pot and lower the pot to the ground on a rope. The liner is fed into

the chimney from the top. A weighted line dropped down the chimney (**1**) is attached to the conical endpiece of the flue liner. An assistant pulls gently on the line from below while the liner is fed down into the chimney (**2**). When the conical endpiece emerges below, it is removed and the liner is connected to a closure plate set across the base of the chimney or to the flue outlet of the heating appliance. The joint is sealed with an asbestos-substitute packing and fire cement.

The chimney pot is replaced and additional mortar is shaped to match the original flaunching. If the liner is connected to a gas or oil-fired appliance, a top closure plate is bedded on mortar laid on the top of the chimney and a cowl is fitted (**3**).

ROOF ACCESS

Two units of scaffolding will make a half platform for a central or side chimney; four will provide an all-round platform.

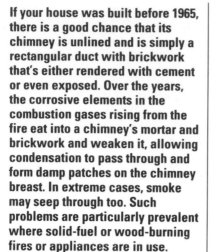

Scaffolding is essential for safe working

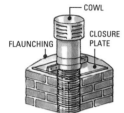

Approved cowl for gas

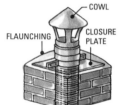

Approved cowl for oil

● **Casting a flue liner**
Professional installers can cast a flue liner *in situ*. A deflated tube is lowered into the chimney. It is inflated, and a lightweight infill is poured into the gap between the tube and chimney. When the infill has set, the tube is deflated and removed, leaving a smooth-bore flue.

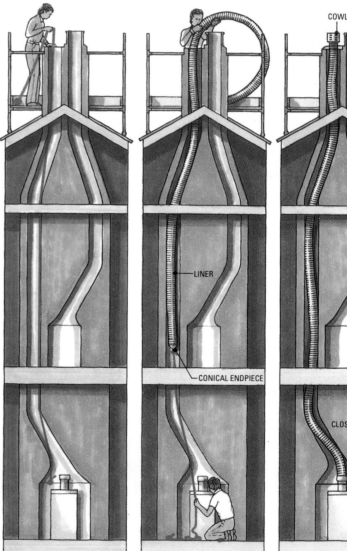

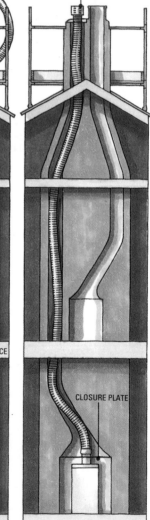

1 Weighted line is lowered   **2 Liner is fed into chimney**   **3 Top closure fitted with cowl**

INSTALLING A SECTIONAL FLUE LINER

A lightweight refractory-concrete or pumice liner is very durable, and is also suitable for all types of fuel. It is made in short sections, which are mortared together inside the flue. This type of liner is ideal for straight flues, although it can be adapted with standard elbow sections to fit offset flues. Most liners are made with interlocking joints, and some have locating collars too.

The installer will have to remove the chimney pot, and may also need to make holes at key points in the chimney to gain access to the flue. A strong support is required at the bottom of the flue to support the liner and insulation.

The sections of liner are lowered down the flue one at a time, with the top joint of each mortared to receive the next section. Once the liner is complete and any access openings have been rebuilt, the void around the liner is usually filled with lightweight concrete. However, that is not always considered necessary, since sectional liners have excellent insulating properties (your installer will advise you about this). Finally, the original chimney pot is put back or a cowl fitted, as appropriate.

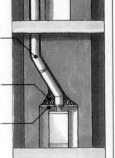

Remove chimney pot and flaunching before you begin installing.

Sections are joined with steel collars.

Where the chimney bends, break a hole through the masonry to feed flue sections into the lower parts of the chimney.

Use ready-made bends or cut straight sections with a masonry saw to make a mitre joint.

A lightweight cement fills the gap between the flue liner and chimney.

Fit closure plate into brickwork or fix it to angle-iron supports

If you have access to plenty of cheap wood, one of the most economical ways to heat a room is with a modern slow-combustion log-burning stove. Like freestanding solid-fuel room heaters, these can be stood on the hearth (when fitted with a rear flue outlet) or in the fireplace (with a top-mounted outlet). A good wood-burning stove can burn all day or night with one filling of logs. To get the full benefit of the heat that radiates from its casing, it is best to install the stove forward of the chimney breast. You can stand it on your present superimposed hearth – provided that it projects the required minimum of 300mm (1ft) in front of the stove and at least 150mm (6in) on each side of it. Otherwise, you will need to build a larger one. The hearth must be level and constructed of stone, brick or tiles. Also, make sure that your constructional hearth complies with current Building Regulations.

A log-burning stove is fitted with a flue pipe that can be passed through a horizontal plate that closes off the base of the chimney. The gap around the flue pipe is sealed with an asbestos-substitute packing and fire cement. The closure plate must be fireproof.

As burning wood produces heavy deposits of soot and tar, the stove's flue pipe must be connected to a double-skinned stainless-steel liner or the flue itself lined with lightweight concrete or pumice (see left).

Vertical flue outlet
This type of stove has its flue sealed into the opening of a horizontal closure plate in the base of the chimney.

Rear flue outlet
A rear flue outlet allows the stove to stand clear of the chimney breast.

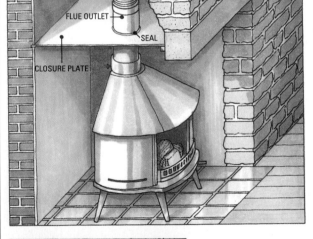

FLUE OUTLET

SEAL

CLOSURE PLATE

Vertical flue outlet
This type of stove has its flue sealed into the opening of a horizontal closure plate in the base of the chimney.

Rear flue outlet
A rear flue outlet allows the stove to stand clear of the chimney breast.

FLUE OUTLET

CLEANING EYE

CENTRAL
HEATING

Typically a central-heating system supplies heat from a single source either to selected rooms or to all the rooms in the house. This is a much more efficient arrangement than having an individual heater in each room – since with central heating there is just one appliance to be controlled, cleaned and maintained.

Central-heating systems can be divided into two basic types: dry and wet systems. With a dry system, heated air carries warmth to the rooms; with a wet system, the heat-carrying medium is water.

Dry central-heating systems

The heat source for the majority of warm-air central-heating systems is a large gas-fired furnace. Air is warmed by being passed relatively quickly over a metal heat exchanger containing hot gas fumes, which are eventually ducted to the flue. A fan embodied in the unit blows the warmed air through ducts to the rooms being heated. Each of these ducts ends in an adjustable damper that is used to regulate the temperature in the room by controlling the heat emission. Runs of ducting in this kind of system can be quite long.

A ducted warm-air system is the only dry heating system that is genuinely central – that is, with a central heating source – but there are a number of other electric heating systems that are broadly classed as central heating. Among them are underfloor and ceiling heating systems. These use elements built into the structure of the floor or ceiling to warm their surfaces, which in turn radiate heat into the room.

A house kept warm with individual electric storage heaters is also usually regarded as centrally heated, though each heater is a separate heat source. The individual heaters – like the central one in a ducted-air system – contain a number of firebricks, and these are heated by electric elements running on low-cost electricity during the night. The bricks give off their heat during the daytime, either by simple convection or with the aid of fans.

In recent years, storage heaters have undergone considerable improvements, both in terms of efficiency and control of heat emission. As a result, they are now much more sophisticated than the early versions that acquired such a poor reputation.

CENTRAL-HEATING SYSTEMS COMPARED

Wet systems

A wet system is by far the easiest kind of genuine central heating to install. Its small-bore copper or plastic pipes can be run through floor and ceiling voids with little trouble, and can be clipped unobtrusively along skirting boards and in corners. Panel radiators or skirting heaters take up very little room, and compact boilers are available that can make use of a fireplace and chimney, stand between kitchen units, or even be hung on a wall. In fact, there is a much wider choice of equipment for wet central heating than for any other kind.

Most installations use a small-bore two-pipe system (see right). Micro-bore heating also employs a two-pipe circuit, but the radiators are fed by 6–10mm (¼–⅜in) malleable-copper pipes. A micro-bore system is simpler to install than a standard two-pipe system; it also offers quicker warm-up and less heat loss from the pipes.

Dry systems

A ducted warm-air system is not really practical unless it's incorporated into a house when it is being built. Since the ducts that carry the air are generally some 150 x 200mm (6 x 8in) in cross section, installing them in an existing house would entail extensive structural work – and even if feasible, the result would probably be extremely unsightly.

Similarly, both underfloor and ceiling heating systems are best put in while a house is being built. To install either in a completed building would cause a great deal of disruption.

Of the dry-heating methods, room storage heaters offer the only system that can be installed in an existing house with minimal disruption. It is true that they must have their own meter, consumer unit and wiring, but these are easily fitted. Moreover, their cables can be run through walls and floor and ceiling voids even more easily than the pipes used for a wet system.

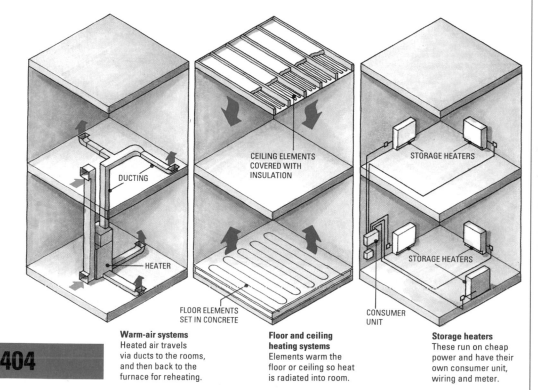

Warm-air systems
Heated air travels via ducts to the rooms, and then back to the furnace for reheating.

Floor and ceiling heating systems
Elements warm the floor or ceiling so heat is radiated into room.

Storage heaters
These run on cheap power and have their own consumer unit, wiring and meter.

HEATING
SYSTEMS

WET
CENTRAL
HEATING

SEE ALSO

The most popular form of central heating is the wet system in which water is heated by a boiler and pumped through small-bore pipes to radiators or convector heaters, where the heat from the water is released into the rooms. The water then circulates back to the boiler for reheating, in a continuing cycle.

The control of such a system can be extremely flexible. Thermostats and valves allow the output of the individual radiators or convectors to be adjusted automatically, and parts of the system can be shut down when rooms are not in use. In addition, the system can be used to heat your domestic hot-water supply as well as the house itself, and the boiler may be fuelled by gas, oil, electricity, bottled gas (propane), or a solid fuel such as anthracite.

Some older systems employ gravity circulation to heat the hot-water storage cylinder, while a mechanical pump is used to drive the water around the radiators. In other systems the pump propels the water to the cylinder and radiators via diverter valves.

Sealed central-heating systems

A sealed system offers an alternative to the traditional open-vented method. Water is fed into the system via a filling loop that is temporarily connected to the mains. The loop incorporates a non-return valve to prevent contamination of mains drinking water. In place of a feed-and-expansion tank, a pressure vessel containing a flexible diaphragm accommodates the expansion of the water as the temperature rises. Should the system become overpressurized, a safety valve discharges water.

A sealed central-heating system offers several advantages. There is less risk of corrosion. Because there is no tank or plumbing in the loft, radiators can form the highest part of the system; and smaller-than-average radiators can be used, since the system runs at a relatively high temperature.

On the negative side, sealed systems must have high-quality components, in order to prevent pressure loss due to leakage; and surface protection is necessary for the very hot radiators. The system also has to be completely watertight, since there is no automatic top up, and a special boiler with a high-temperature cut-out is required in case the ordinary thermostat fails.

Open-vented system
The water heated by the boiler (**1**) is driven by a pump (**2**) through the pipes to the various radiators or special convector heaters (**3**). These retain the hot water long enough for it to warm the rooms to the desired temperature; then it returns to the boiler to be reheated. A cistern known as a feed-and-expansion tank (**4**), situated in the loft, keeps the system topped up and receives any expansion of the water due to overheating. The hot-water cylinder is heated by gravity circulation (**5**). In the diagram red indicates the flow of water from the pump, and blue shows the return flow.

● **One-pipe systems**
A one-pipe system has a single large-bore pipe running around the perimeter of the house, forming a loop. The flow and return pipes of each radiator are connected to this large-bore pipe. The water is pumped round the loop, though the radiators work by gravity circulation. Larger radiators may be used at the end of the loop in order to compensate for heat loss. The cistern and hot-water circuits are the same as on a two-pipe system.

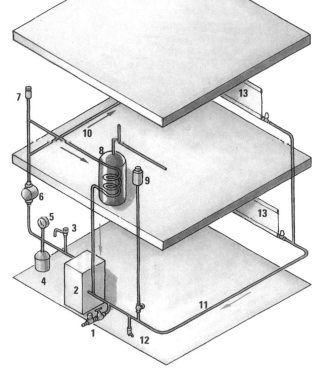

Sealed heating system
1 Filling loop with non-return valve
2 Boiler
3 Safety valve
4 Expansion vessel
5 Pressure gauge
6 Pump
7 Air release point
8 Hot-water cylinder
9 Topping-up bottle
10 Heating flow to radiators
11 Heating return to boiler
12 Draincock
13 Radiators

405

BOILERS
FOR CENTRAL
HEATING

● **Gas installers**
Gas boilers must always be installed by a competent fitter who is registered with CORGI (Confederation of Registered Gas Installers). Check that your installer has the correct public-liability insurance for working with gas.

Technological improvements have made it possible to make central-heating boilers that are much smaller than their predecessors, though just as efficient. The most popular fuels are gas and oil because, despite improvements in solid-fuel technology, the dirt and inconvenience associated with solid fuels cannot be totally overcome. Wood-burning boilers enjoyed a rise in popularity for a while; but realistically, wood as a fuel is best suited to room-heating stoves – perhaps with a small back boiler providing hot water rather than full central heating.

HEATING REQUIREMENTS AND BOILER CAPACITY

The heating requirement for each room is affected by the heat lost through the structure and also by the number of air changes due to ventilation. You can calculate your requirements using a purpose-made calculator known as a Mears wheel, which can be hired cheaply (complete with instructions) from a supplier of central-heating equipment. There are also software packages that enable you to make the calculations on a home computer.

The capacity of the boiler needed to satisfy your heat requirements can be calculated by adding up the heat output of all the radiators, plus an allowance of 3kW for the hot-water cylinder and an additional ten per cent for exceptionally cold weather.

Some plumbers' merchants will make all the calculations for you if you provide them with the dimensions of each room.

Ideal room temperatures
A central heating designer and installer normally aims at providing a system that will heat rooms to the temperatures shown below, assuming an outdoor temperature of -1°C (30°F).

ROOM TEMPERATURE	
Living room	21°C (70°F)
Dining room	21°C (70°F)
Kitchen	16°C (60°F)
Hall/landing	18°C (65°F)
Bedroom	16°C (60°F)
Bathroom	23°C (72°F)

Gas-fired boilers

Many gas-fired boilers have pilot lights that burn constantly and light the burners whenever heat is required. They may be operated manually or by a timer set to switch the heating on and off at selected times. It is also possible to link the boiler to a room thermostat, so that the heating is switched on and off to keep temperatures even throughout the house. Another thermostat, in the boiler itself, prevents the water overheating at any time.

An increasing number of boilers now have electronic ignition. With it, the pilot ignites only when the thermostat demands heat – then once the boiler reaches the required temperature, valves to the burner and pilot light close until the next time heat is called for.

Oil-fired boilers

Oil-fired boilers, which have the same efficient controls as gas boilers, are of two basic types: pressure-jet and vaporizing. This refers to whether the oil is reduced to tiny droplets or turned into vapour so that it will burn.

Since pressure-jet boilers are noisy, they are best housed in an outbuilding; vaporizing boilers are much quieter. With both types, you will need a large oil-storage tank sited outside, with easy access for delivery tankers.

Solid-fuel boilers

Solid-fuel heating also needs a suitable place for fuel storage; and the residual ash has to be removed every day.

The rate at which the fuel is burnt is usually controlled by a thermostatic damper, and sometimes by a fan. Instant switching on and off of the heat – as with oil-fired and gas boilers – is not possible with a solid-fuel boiler, and the system must have some means for the heat to escape in the event of the circulation pump failing; otherwise the water could boil in the appliance and damage it. This is usually arranged by means of a 'natural-convection' pipe circuit between the boiler and the heat exchanger in the domestic hot-water cylinder and a radiator in the bathroom, where the excess heat can be used to dry wet towels.

A solid-fuel boiler must be kept stoked if it is to continue burning: you can have one with a hopper feed that will top it up automatically.

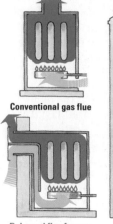
Conventional gas flue

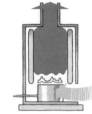
Balanced flue for gas

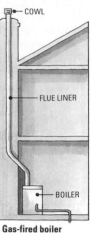
COWL
FLUE LINER
BOILER
Gas-fired boiler

Vaporizing boiler

Pressure-jet boiler

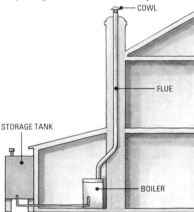
COWL
FLUE
STORAGE TANK
BOILER
Oil-fired boiler

Hopper-fed boiler

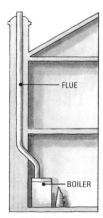
FLUE
BOILER
Solid-fuel back boiler   **Solid-fuel boiler**

POSITIONING A BOILER

A solid-fuel boiler must be connected to a chimney, but oil-fired or gas boilers may have a conventional or a balanced flue. Conventional-flue boilers can be connected to an existing chimney or to a new prefabricated one. Balanced-flue boilers do not need a chimney; instead, they are mounted on an external wall and the flue gases are passed outside through a short horizontal duct. The duct is split into two passages: one for the outgoing flue gases and the other for combustion air drawn into the boiler from outside. A fan-assisted boiler can be mounted up to 3m (9ft 9in) away from its fume-exhaust vent in the wall.

Boilers are often fitted with a tubular flue which can be swung through 360 degrees, so that the duct can run in any direction. It is possible to incorporate bends – but, due to the resistance they create, each bend reduces the effective length of the flue by 1m (3ft 3in).

Balanced-flue vents

There are strict regulations governing the siting of balanced-flue vents or 'terminals'. Some of the more obvious situations are listed below, but you can obtain the full list of requirements from a Building Control Officer. The figures in bold denote the minimum distances for natural-draught terminals; those in plain type are for fan-assisted ones.

● **300mm (1ft)**/300mm (1ft) below an openable window or other opening (such as an airbrick).
● **300mm (1ft)**/75mm (3in) below gutters or eaves.
● **600mm (2ft)**/200mm (8in) below a balcony.
● **300mm (1ft)**/300mm (1ft) above the ground, or a balcony or roof. Fit a guard if less than **2m (6ft 6in)**/2m (6ft 6in).
● **600mm (2ft)**/600mm (2ft) from an opposite wall.
● **600mm (2ft)**/300mm (1ft) from a corner.
● **1.5m (4ft 10in)**/1.5m (4ft 10in) vertically from another terminal.
● **300mm (1ft)**/300mm (1ft) horizontally from another terminal.

Back boilers

Some gas and solid-fuel boilers can be fitted as a 'back boiler' behind a radiant fire or room heater, usually sited in the living-room fireplace. With gas, the fire and the boiler are controlled separately, so you can operate one or both, as you wish, according to the season.

The hot water from a central-heating boiler is pumped along narrow pipes connected to radiators or convectors, mounted at strategic points to heat individual rooms and hallways. The standard radiator is a double-skinned metal panel, which is heated by the hot water flowing through it. Despite its name, a radiator delivers only a fraction of its output as radiant heat – the rest being emitted through natural convection as the surrounding air comes into contact with the hot surfaces of the radiator. As the warmed air rises towards the ceiling, cooler air flows in around the radiator, and this air in turn is warmed and moves upwards. As a result, a steady but very gentle circulation of air takes place in the room, and the temperature gradually rises to the optimum set on the room thermostat.

Panel and finned radiators

Radiators are available in a wide range of sizes. The larger they are, the greater their heat output – and heat output can be further increased by using radiators with two panels (mounted one behind the other). Most types of radiator have finned rear faces so as to help induce convected heat.

The handwheel valve at one end of the radiator turns the flow on or off; the lockshield valve at the other end is set to balance the system, then left alone.

An ordinary handwheel valve can be fitted at either end of a radiator, regardless of the direction of flow – whereas thermostatic valves are marked with arrows to indicate the direction of flow and must be fitted accordingly.

A bleed valve is fitted at one of the top corners to release air that gradually builds up, preventing the radiator from heating properly.

Single-panel radiator

Double-panel radiator

Finned radiator

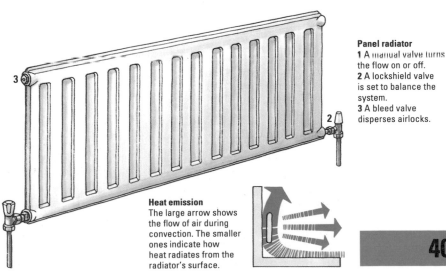

Panel radiator
1 A manual valve turns the flow on or off.
2 A lockshield valve is set to balance the system.
3 A bleed valve disperses airlocks.

Heat emission
The large arrow shows the flow of air during convection. The smaller ones indicate how heat radiates from the radiator's surface.

POSITIONING

HEATERS

Convectors

It is possible to fit convector heaters, instead of radiators, as part of a wet central-heating system.

Unlike radiators, convectors emit none of their heat in the form of direct radiation. The hot water from the boiler passes through a finned pipe inside the heater, the fins absorbing the heat and transferring it to the air around them. The warmed air escapes through a vent at the top of the appliance – and at the same time cool air is drawn in through the open bottom, to be warmed in turn.

Some convectors are designed for inconspicuous fixing at skirting level. Most models have a damper that can be set to control the airflow. With a fan-assisted heater, airflow is accelerated over the heating fins in order to speed up room heating.

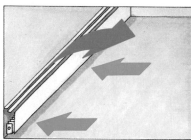

FINNED PIPE

DAMPER

Skirting convector

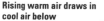

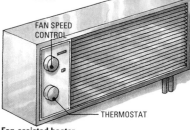

**Rising warm air draws in
cool air below**

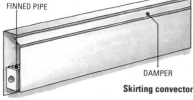

FAN SPEED
CONTROL

THERMOSTAT

Fan-assisted heater

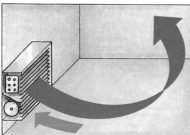

Airflow by fan-assisted convection

POSITIONING RADIATORS AND CONVECTORS

At one time, central-heating radiators and convectors were nearly always placed under windows, since the area around them tends to be the coldest part of a room, with draughts caused by warmed air cooling against the glass. However, if you've fitted double glazing to reduce heat loss and draughts, then you may prefer to place your heaters elsewhere – especially if your windows are hung with long curtains.

Finned radiators, which accelerate the convection process considerably, are another development that permits a greater degree of flexibility in the siting of heaters. Since this type of radiator warms a room relatively quickly, it can be positioned somewhere other than the coldest spot yet still keep the whole room at a comfortable temperature.

The shape of a room can also affect the siting of heaters and perhaps their number. For example, it is difficult to heat a large L-shaped room with just a single radiator at one end. In this type of situation it is probably best to consult a heating installer beforehand to help you decide upon the optimum number of heaters and their positions.

If possible, avoid hanging curtains or standing furniture in front of radiators and convector heaters. Both curtains and furniture absorb radiated heat, and curtains also tend to trap convected heat behind them.

Although convectors radiate almost no heat, you should never obstruct warm air leaving the appliance nor cool air being drawn into it.

The warm air rising from radiators will eventually discolour the paint or wallpaper above them. Fitting a narrow shelf about 50mm (2in) above a radiator prevents staining without inhibiting convection. It is even possible to box in a radiator without any loss of efficiency, provided that air is free to pass through the boxing at the top and bottom.

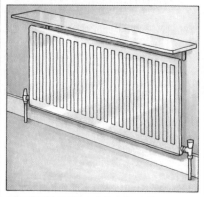

A shelf deflects warm air from the wall

UNDERFLOOR CENTRAL HEATING

Warming the floors in order to heat a building is by no means a new idea, but corrosion in metal pipes previously made the technique impractical as part of a wet central-heating system. However, now that it is possible to use continuous lengths of high-quality plastic pipe such as PEX in place of metal pipework, underfloor heating can be installed instead of radiators in an ordinary central-heating system.

Because the source of heat is spread over a wide area, the water passing through the underfloor pipes does not have to be heated to the high temperatures normally required by standard radiators. If underfloor heating is to be an integral part of a central-heating system that includes radiators, it therefore pays to incorporate a temperature-operated mixing valve. This makes use of some of the cooler water returning from the radiators to the boiler by diverting it through the underfloor pipes.

The underfloor circuit is run from a manifold, which can be isolated by valves to allow independent control and testing of the circuit.

A layer of insulation (now standard in new buildings) is laid down and covered by mesh, which serves as a key for the subsequent floor screed and assists in heat distribution through conduction. The heating pipes are placed over the mesh and stapled in position to hold them securely while a sand-and-cement screed is laid over the top. The screed must be allowed to dry out for a few weeks before the heating is turned on.

It is also possible to have piped heating of this kind installed beneath a suspended wooden floor.

HEATING
SYSTEMS

CONTROLS
FOR CENTRAL
HEATING

SEE ALSO

The various automatic control systems and devices available for wet central heating can, if used properly, provide useful savings in running costs by reducing wasted heat to a minimum.

Three basic devices

Automatic controllers can be divided into three basic types: temperature controllers (thermostats), automatic on-off switches (timers and programmers), and heating-circuit controllers (zone valves). These devices can be used individually or in combination to provide a very high level of control.

It must be added that they are really effective only with either oil-fired or gas boilers, since these can be switched on and off at will. When linked to solid-fuel boilers, which take time to react to controls, automatic control systems are much less effective.

ZONE CONTROL VALVES

There seems very little point in heating rooms that are not being used. In most households, for example, the bedrooms are unoccupied for the greater part of the day, and to heat them continuously is wasteful. One way of avoiding such waste is to divide your central-heating system into circuits, or 'zones' – the usual ones being upstairs and down-stairs – and to heat the whole house only when necessary. However, if you divide your house into zones, make sure the unheated areas are adequately ventilated to prevent condensation.

Control is provided by motorized valves linked to a timer or programmer that directs the heating water through selected pipes at predetermined times of day. Alternatively zone valves, linked to individual zone thermostats, can be used in order to provide separate temperature control.

A motorized zone control valve

Thermostats

All boilers incorporate thermostats to prevent overheating. An oil-fired or gas boiler will have one that can be set to vary heat output by switching the unit on and off; and some are also fitted with modulating burners, which adjust flame height to suit heating requirements. On a solid-fuel boiler, the thermostat opens and closes a damper that admits more or less air to the firebed to increase or reduce the rate of burning as required.

A room thermostat – 'roomstat' for short – is often the only form of central-heating control fitted. It is placed in a room where the temperature usually remains fairly stable, and works on the assumption that any rise or drop in the temperature will be matched by similar variations throughout the house. Room-stats control the temperature by means of simple on-off switching of the boiler – or the pump if the boiler has to run constantly in order to provide hot water.

The main drawback of a roomstat is that it makes no allowance for local temperature changes in other rooms – caused, for example, by the sun shining through a window or a separate heater being switched on. More sophisticated temperature control is provided by a thermostatic radiator valve, which can be fitted to the radiators instead of the standard manually operated valve. A temperature sensor opens and closes the valve, varying the heat output to maintain the desired temperature in the individual room. Thermostatic radiator valves need not be fitted in every room. You can use one to reduce the heat in a kitchen or a small bathroom, while a roomstat regulates the temperature in the rest of the house.

The most sophisticated thermostatic controller is a boiler-energy manager or 'optimizer'. This device collects data from sensors inside and outside the building in order to deduce the optimum running period of the central-heating system, so the boiler is not wastefully switched on and off in rapid cycles.

Timers and programmers

You can cut fuel bills substantially by ensuring that the heating is not on while you are out or asleep. A timer can be set so that the system is switched on to warm the house before you get up and goes off just before you leave for work, then comes on again shortly before you return home and goes off at bed time. The simpler timers provide two 'on' and two 'off' settings, which are normally repeated every day. A manual override enables you to alter the times for week-ends and other changes in routine.

More sophisticated devices, known as programmers, offer a larger number of on-off programmes – even a different one for each day of the week – as well as control of domestic hot water.

Timer

Roomstat

Programmer

Thermostatic radiator valve

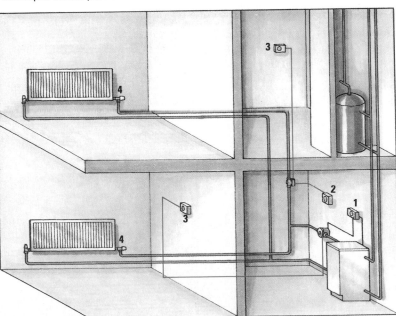

Heating controls
There are several ways to control central heating.
1 Programmer governs boiler and pump.
2 A timer is used to control a zone valve. You can also use one to regulate the boiler and pump, instead of a programmer.
3 A roomstat can be used to control the pump or zone valves.
4 A thermostatic radiator valve controls an individual heater.

HEATING-SYSTEM FAULTFINDER

Hissing or banging sounds from boiler or heating pipes.

This is caused by overheating due to:

- Blocked chimney (with solid fuel).
  Sweep chimney to clear heavy soot.

- Build-up of scale due to hard water.
  Shut down boiler and pump. Treat system with a descaler, then drain, flush and refill system.

- Faulty boiler thermostat.
  Shut down boiler. Leave pump working, to circulate water to cool system quickly. When it's cool, operate boiler thermostat control. If you do not hear a clicking sound, call in an engineer.

- Lack of water in system.
  Shut down boiler. Check feed-and-expansion tank in loft. If empty, the valve may be stuck. Move ball-valve float arm up and down to restore flow and fill system. If this fails, with valve in open position, check if mains water has been turned off by accident or (in winter) if supply pipe is frozen.

- Pump not working (with solid fuel).
  Shut down boiler, then check that the pump is switched on. If pump is not running, turn off power and check wired connections to it. If pump seems to be running but outlet pipe is cool, check for airlock by using bleed screw. If pump is still not working, shut it down, drain system, remove pump and check it for blockage. Clean pump or, if need be, replace it.

Radiators in one part of the house do not warm up.

- Timer or thermostat that controls zone valve is not set properly or is faulty.
  Check timer or thermostat setting and reset if need be. If this has no effect, switch off power supply and check wired connections. If that makes no difference, call in an engineer.

- Zone valve itself is faulty.
  Drain system and replace valve.

- Pump not working.
  See above.

All radiators remain cool, though boiler is operating normally.

- Pump not working.
  Check pump by listening or feeling for motor vibration. If pump is running, check for airlock by operating bleed valve. If this has no effect, the pump outlet may be blocked. Switch off boiler and pump, remove pump and clean or replace as necessary. If pump is not running, switch off and try manual restart. Look for large screw in the middle – removing or turning it will reveal another screw beneath. Turn this until the spindle feels free, then switch pump on again.

- Pump thermostat or timer is set incorrectly or is faulty.
  Adjust thermostat or timer setting. If that has no effect, switch off power and check wiring connections. If they are in good order, call in an engineer.

Single radiator does not warm up.

- The handwheel valve is closed.
  Open the valve.

- Thermostatic radiator valve is not set properly or is faulty.
  Check setting of valve and reset it if necessary. If this has no effect, drain system and replace valve.

- Lockshield valve not set properly.
  Remove lockshield cover and adjust valve setting until radiator seems as warm as those in other rooms. Have lockshield valve properly balanced when the system is next serviced.

- Radiator valves blocked by corrosion.
  Close both radiator valves, remove radiator and flush out.

Area at top of radiator stays cool while bottom is warm.

- Airlock at top of radiator is preventing water circulating fully.
  Bleed radiator to release trapped air.

Cool patch in centre of radiator while top and ends are warm.

- Deposits of rust at bottom of radiator are restricting circulation of water.
  Close both radiator valves, remove radiator and flush out.

Boiler not working.

- Thermostat set too low
  Check roomstat or boiler thermostat is set correctly.

- Timer or programmer not working.
  Check that the timer or programmer is switched on and set correctly. Have it replaced if the fault persists.

- Gas-boiler pilot light goes out.
  Relight pilot following the instructions supplied with the boiler (these are usually on the back of the front panel). If pilot fails to ignite, have it replaced.

Continuous drip from overflow pipe of feed-and-expansion tank in roof.

- Faulty ball valve or leaking float, causing valve to stay open.
  Shut off mains water supply to tank and bale it out to below level of valve. Remove valve and fit new washer. Alternatively unscrew leaking float from arm and fit new one.

- Leaking heat-exchanger coil in hot-water cylinder.
  In this case, dripping from the overflow will occur only if the feed-and-expansion tank is positioned below the cold-water cistern. Turn off boiler and mains water. Let system cool, then take dip-stick measurement in both cisterns. Don't use water overnight, then check again in morning. If level of water has risen in the feed-and-expansion tank and dropped in the other cistern, have the coil tested.

Water leaking from system.

- Loose pipe unions at joints, pump connections, boiler connections, etc.
  Turn off boiler (or close down solid-fuel appliance, raking out coals) and switch off pump, then tighten leaking joints. If this has no effect, drain the system and remake joints completely.

- Split or punctured pipe.
  Wrap rags around the damaged pipe temporarily, then switch off boiler and pump and make a temporary repair with hose or commercial leak sealant. Drain system and fit new pipe.

It is inadvisable to do so unnecessarily, but there may be times when you have to drain your wet central-heating system completely and refill it. This could be for routine maintenance, when dealing with a fault, or because you have decided to extend the system or upgrade the boiler. The job can be done fairly easily if you follow the procedures outlined here.

Draining the system

Before draining your central-heating system, cool the water by shutting off the boiler and leaving the circulation pump running. The water in the system will cool quite quickly.

Switch off the pump and turn off the mains-water supply to the feed-and-expansion tank in the loft by closing the stopcock in the feed pipe or by laying a batten across the cistern and tying the float arm to it to keep the ball valve shut.

The main draincock for the system will normally be in the return pipe near the boiler. Push one end of a garden hose onto its outlet and lead the other end of the hose to a gully or soakaway in the garden, then open the draincock. If you have no key for its square shank, use an adjustable spanner.

Water will drain from the system, but some will be held in the radiators by vacuum. To release the trapped water, start at the top of the house and carefully open the radiator bleed valves. Air will flow into the tops of the radiators, breaking the vacuums, and the water will drain out. Last of all, drain inverted pipe loops (see below).

Draining procedure
Turn off the mains supply to the cistern at the feed-pipe stopcock (**1**). If there is no stopcock, tie the ball-valve arm to a batten laid across the tank (**2**). With a hose on the main draincock (**3**) and its other end at a gully or soakaway outside, open the draincock and let the system empty. Release any water trapped in the radiators (**4**) by opening their bleed valves (**5**), starting at the top of the house. Be sure to close all draincocks before you refill the system.

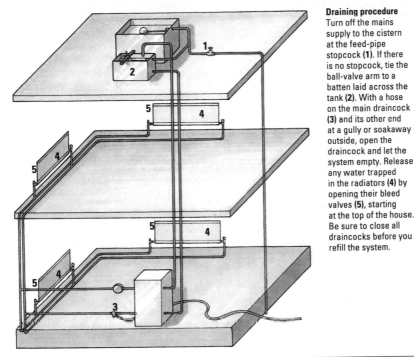

REFILLING THE SYSTEM

Before refilling the system, check that you have closed all the draincocks and radiator bleed valves. Restore the water supply to the feed-and-expansion tank in the loft. As the system fills up, air will be trapped in the tops of the radiators; so when the water stops running, bleed all the radiators, starting at the bottom of the house and working upwards. You may also have to bleed the circulating pump. Finally, check all the draincocks and bleed valves for signs of leakage, and tighten them if necessary.

Tightening a leaking draincock

CLEANING THE SYSTEM

After installing or modifying a central-heating system, flush the pipework with water to get rid of swarf and flux, which can induce corrosion or damage valves or the pump. To protect the pump during cleaning, it's best to remove it, bridging the gap with a short length of pipe. But it is much easier to turn the pump impeller with a screwdriver before running the system after flushing, in order to make sure it's clear. If you can feel resistance, drain the system and remove the motor, then clean and refit the impeller.

Descaling
If your system is old or badly corroded, a harsh cleaner or descaler may expose minor leaks sealed by corrosion – so use a mild cleanser, introduced into the system via the feed-and-expansion tank. Manufacturers' instructions vary, but in principle run the cleanser through the system for a week, with the boiler set to a fairly high temperature. Afterwards, turn off and drain the system, then refill and drain it several times – if possible, using a hose to run mains-pressure water through the system while draining it. Some cleansers must be neutralized before you can add a corrosion inhibitor.

If your boiler is making loud banging noises, treat it and the immediate pipework with a fairly powerful descaler, running the hot-water programme only.

INVERTED PIPE LOOPS

Often when fitting a central-heating system in a house that has a solid ground floor, installers run the heating pipes from the boiler into the ceiling void and drop them down the walls to the individual radiators. Each of these 'inverted pipe loops' has its own draincock. When you're draining the system, they must be drained separately after the main system has been emptied.

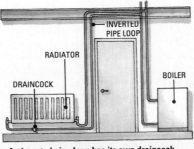

An inverted pipe loop has its own draincock

411

BOILER
MAINTENANCE

• **Servicing gas boilers**
Any maintenance that involves dismantling any part of a gas boiler must be carried out by a registered CORGI engineer, who should undertake all the necessary gas safety checks as part of the service. There is no point in attempting to service the boiler yourself if you are not qualified and equipped to do so – it can be dangerous and you will also be breaking the law.

The efficiency of modern oil-fired and gas boilers depends on their being checked and serviced annually. Because the mechanisms involved are so complex, the work must be done by a qualified engineer. With either type of boiler you can enter into a contract for regular maintenance with your fuel supplier or the original installer.

REDUCING CORROSION IN THE SYSTEM

Modern boilers and radiators are made from fairly thin materials, and if you fail to take basic anti-corrosion measures, the life of the system can be reduced to ten years or less. Corrosion may result from hard-water deposits or a chemical reaction between the water and the metal components of the system .

Lime scale
Scale builds up quickly in hard-water areas of the country. Even a thin layer of lime scale on the inner wall of a boiler's heat exchanger reduces its efficiency and may cause banging and dog-like howling within the system – and the scale can insulate sections of the heat exchanger to such an extent that it produces 'hot spots', leading to premature failure of the component.

Rust
Rust corrodes steel components, most notably radiators. Most rusting occurs within weeks of filling the system; but if air is being sucked in constantly, then rusting is progressive. Having to bleed radiators regularly is a sure sign that air is being drawn into the system.

Sludge
Magnetite (black sludge) clogs the pump and builds up in the bottom of radiators, reducing their heat output.

Electrolytic action
Dissimilar metals such as copper and aluminium act like a battery in the acidic water that is present in some central-heating systems. This results in the corrosion of the less-noble metal.

Testing your system for corrosion
Drain about half a litre (1 pint) of water from the boiler or a radiator. Orange water denotes rusting, and black the presence of sludge. In either case, treat immediately with corrosion inhibitor.

If there are no obvious signs of corrosion, compare the sample with tap water. Drop two plain steel nails into a screw-top glass jar containing some of the sample water, and place two similar nails in a jar of clean tap water. After a couple of days the nails in the tap water should rust; but if your heating system contains sufficient corrosion inhibitor, the nails in the sample jar will remain bright. If they show signs of corrosion, your system needs topping up with inhibitor. It is important to use the same product that is already present in the system; if you don't know what that is, drain and flush the system, then refill with fresh water and inhibitor.

If the test proves inconclusive, check the sample jar after a month or so; and if the nails have begun to rust, then the inhibitor needs topping up.

Adding corrosion inhibitor
You can slow down corrosion by adding a proprietary corrosion inhibitor to the water. This is best done when the system is first installed, but the inhibitor can be introduced into the system at any time, provided that the boiler is descaled before doing so. If the system has been running for some time, it is better to flush it out first by draining and refilling it repeatedly until the water runs clean. Otherwise, drain off about 20 litres (4 gallons) of water – enough to empty the feed-and-expansion tank and a small amount of pipework – then pour the inhibitor into the cistern and restore the water supply, which will carry the inhibitor into the pipes. About 5 litres (1 gallon) will be enough for most systems, but check the maker's instructions. Finally, switch on the pump to distribute the inhibitor throughout the system.

Reducing scale
You can use low-voltage coils to create a magnetic field that will prevent the heat exchanger of your boiler becoming coated with scale. However, unless you have soft water in your area, the only way to actually avoid hard water in the system is to install a water softener.

Phosphate balls are sometimes used to prevent the formation of scale in an instantaneous boiler. But unless the dispenser is regulated to release just the right amount, there is a danger of overdosing the system with phosphates.

Before fitting any device to reduce scale, it is essential to seek the boiler manufacturer's advice.

Gas-fired installations

British Gas offer a choice of servicing schemes for boilers. These normally cover their own installations, but the company will service systems put in by other installers on condition that a British Gas inspection of the installation is carried out first.

The simplest of the British Gas schemes provides for an annual check and adjustment of the boiler. If any repairs are found to be necessary, either at the time of the regular check or at other times during the year, then the labour and necessary parts are charged separately. But for an extra fee it is possible to have both free labour and free parts for boiler repairs at any time of year. British Gas will also extend the arrangement to include inspection of the whole heating system when the boiler is being checked, plus free parts and labour for repairs to the system.

You may find that your installer or a local firm of CORGI heating engineers offers a similar choice of servicing and maintenance contracts. The best course is to compare the schemes and decide which gives greatest value for money.

Oil-fired installations

Both the installers of oil-fired central heating systems and the suppliers of fuel oil offer servicing and maintenance contracts similar to those outlined above for gas-fired systems. The choice of schemes available ranges from a simple annual check-up to complete cover for parts and labour whenever repairs are necessary.

As with the schemes for gas, it pays to shop around and make a comparison of the various services on offer and the charges that apply.

Solid-fuel installations

If you have a solid-fuel system, it is important to keep the chimney and the flueway swept. The job, which should be done twice a year, is very similar to sweeping an open-fire chimney, access being through the front of a room heater that has a back boiler or through a soot door in the flue pipe or chimney breast.

When you have swept the chimney, clean out the boiler with a stiff brush and remove the dust and soot with a vacuum cleaner.

Lift out any broken fire bars and drop new ones in place.

HOW TO REMOVE A RADIATOR

You can remove an individual radiator without draining the whole system. Make sure you have plenty of rag for mopping up spilled water, plus a jug and a large bowl. The water in the radiator will be very dirty – so, if possible, roll back the floorcovering before you start.

Shut off both valves, turning the shank of the lockshield valve clockwise with a key or an adjustable spanner (1). Note the number of turns needed to close it, so that later you can reopen it by the same amount.

Unscrew the cap-nut holding either the handwheel valve or the lockshield valve to the adaptor in the end of the radiator (2). Hold the jug under the joint and open the bleed valve slowly to let the water drain out. Transfer the water from jug to bowl, and continue doing this until no more water can be drained.

Unscrew the cap-nut that holds the other valve onto the radiator, lift the radiator free from its wall brackets and drain any remaining water into the bowl (3). Unscrew the brackets if you plan to decorate the wall.

To replace the radiator, screw the brackets back in place, then hang the radiator on them and tighten the cap-nuts on both valves. Close the bleed valve and reopen both radiator valves (open the lockshield valve by the same number of turns you used when closing it). Last of all, use the bleed valve to release any air trapped in the radiator.

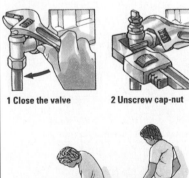

1 Close the valve   **2 Unscrew cap-nut**

3 Final draining
Lift radiator from brackets and drain off any remaining water.

Trapped air stops radiators heating up fully, and regular intake of air can cause corrosion. If a radiator feels cooler at the top than at the bottom, it's likely that a pocket of air has formed in it and is stopping full circulation of the water. Getting the air out – 'bleeding' – is a simple matter.

Bleeding a radiator

First switch off the circulation pump – and preferably turn off the boiler too, although that is not vital.

Each radiator has a bleed valve at one of its top corners, identifiable by a square-section shank in the centre of the round blanking plug. You should have been given a key to fit these shanks by the installer; but if not, or if you have inherited an old system, you can buy a key for bleeding radiators at any DIY shop or ironmonger's.

Use the key to turn the shank of the valve anticlockwise about a quarter of a turn. It shouldn't be necessary to turn it further – but have a small container handy to catch spurting water, in case you open the valve too far, plus some rags to mop up water dribbling from the valve. Don't be tempted to speed up the process by opening the valve further than necessary to let the air out – that is likely to produce a deluge of water.

You will hear a hissing sound as the air escapes. Keep the key on the shank of the valve – then when the hissing stops and the first dribble of water appears, close the valve tightly.

Blocked bleed valve
If no water or air comes out when you

attempt to bleed a radiator, check whether the feed-and-expansion tank in the loft is empty. If the tank is full of water, then the bleed valve is probably blocked with paint.

Close the inlet and outlet valve at each end of the radiator, then remove the screw from the centre of the bleed valve. Clear the hole with a piece of wire and reopen one of the radiator valves slightly to eject some water from the hole. Close the radiator valve again and refit the screw in the bleed valve. Open both radiator valves and test the bleed valve again.

Dispersing the air pocket in a radiator

Fitting an air separator

If you find you are having to bleed a radiator frequently, a large quantity of air is entering the system. This situation should be remedied before it leads to serious corrosion.

First check that the feed-and-expansion tank in the loft is not acting like a radiator and warming up when you run the central heating or hot-water circuit. This would indicate that hot water is being pumped through the vent pipe into the tank and taking air with it back into the system. Cure the problem by fitting an air separator in the vent pipe and link it to the cold feed that runs from the feed-and-expansion tank.

If the pump is fitted on the return pipe to the boiler, it may be sucking in air through the unions or even through leaking spindles on radiator valves.

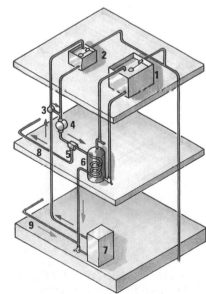

Heating system with air separator
1 Storage cistern
2 Feed-and-expansion tank
3 Air separator
4 Pump
5 Motorized valve
6 Hot-water cylinder
7 Boiler
8 Radiator flow
9 Radiator return

RADIATOR VALVES

VALVE HEAD

GLAND NUT

Leaking spindle
Tighten the gland nut with a spanner to stop a leak from a radiator-valve spindle. If the leak persists, undo the nut and wind a few turns of PTFE tape down into the spindle.

● **Resealing a cap-nut**
Drain the system and undo the leaking nut. Smear the olive with silicone sealant and retighten the cap-nut. Do not overtighten, or you may damage the olive. As an alternative to silicone, wind two turns of PTFE tape around the olive (not the threads).

Curing a leaking radiator valve

Water leaking from a radiator valve is probably seeping from around the spindle (see left). However, because water can run round and drip from a valve cap-nut, the nut often appears to be the source of the leak. Dry the valve, then hold tissues against various parts of it to ascertain exactly where the moisture is coming from. If it proves to be a nut that is leaking, try tightening it gently; if that is unsuccessful, undo and reseal it (see below left).

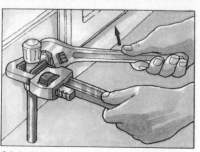
Grip leaky valve with wrench to tighten cap-nut

Replacing a worn or damaged valve

Make sure the new valve is exactly like the old one, or it may not align with the water pipe. Drain the system and lay rags under the valve to catch the dregs.

Hold the body of the valve with a wrench and use an adjustable spanner to unscrew the cap-nuts that hold the valve to the water pipe (1) and to the adaptor in the end of the radiator. Lift the valve from the end of the pipe (2); if you are replacing a lockshield valve, be sure to close it first, counting the turns so you can open the new valve by the same number to balance the radiator.

Unscrew the valve adaptor from the radiator (3). You may be able to use an adjustable spanner, or you may need an hexagonal radiator spanner, depending on the type of adaptor.

Fitting the new valve
Ensure that the threads in the end of the radiator are clean. Drag the teeth of a hacksaw across the threads of the new adaptor to roughen them slightly, then wind PTFE tape four or five times round them. Screw the adaptor into the end of the radiator and tighten with a spanner. Slide the valve cap-nut and a new olive over the end of the pipe and fit the valve (4) – but don't tighten the cap-nut yet. First, keeping the valve body firm with a wrench, align it with the adaptor and tighten the cap-nut that holds them together (5). Now tighten the cap-nut that holds the valve to the water pipe (6). Refill the system and check for leaks at the joints of the new valve; if need be, tighten the cap-nuts a little more.

REPLACING O-RINGS IN A BELMONT VALVE

The spindle of a Belmont radiator valve is sealed with O-rings, which you can replace without having to drain the radiator. On very old valves the rings are green, whereas the newer rings are red. Take the plastic head of the valve to a plumbers' merchant to discover which you need before you begin work.

Wrap an old towel around the valve body and undo the spindle (which has a left-hand thread). A small amount of water will leak out, but continue to remove the spindle until the pressure seals the valve automatically.

Two O-rings are housed in grooves in the spindle. Prise the rings off, using the tip of a small screwdriver, and then lubricate the spindle with a smear of silicone grease. Slide the new rings into position and replace the spindle.

O-rings are housed in grooves in the valve spindle

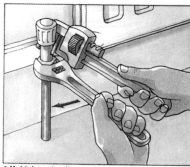
1 Hold the valve firm and loosen both cap-nuts

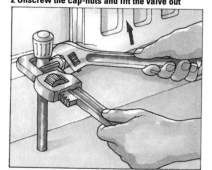
2 Unscrew the cap-nuts and lift the valve out

3 Remove the valve adaptor from the radiator

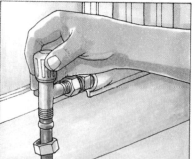
4 Fit new adaptor, then fit new valve to pipe

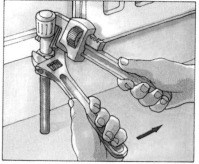
5 Connect valve to adaptor and tighten cap-nut

6 Tighten cap-nut holding valve to water pipe

Try to obtain a new radiator that is exactly the same model as the one you plan to replace. This will make the job relatively straightforward.

Simple replacement

Drain the old radiator and remove it from the wall, then unscrew both of the valve adaptors from the bottom with an adjustable spanner or, if necessary, a hexagonal radiator spanner. Unscrew the bleed valve, using the bleed key, and then the two blanking plugs from the top of the radiator, using a square or hexagonal radiator spanner (1).

Use wire wool to clean any corrosion from the threads of both adaptors and blanking plugs (2), then wind four or five turns of PTFE tape round the threads (3). Screw the plugs and adaptors into the new radiator; and then screw the bleed valve into its blanking plug.

Hang the new radiator on the wall brackets and connect the valves to their adaptors. Open the valves, then fill and bleed the radiator.

1 Removing the plugs
Use a radiator spanner to unscrew the two blanking plugs at the top of the radiator.

2 Cleaning the threads
Use wire wool to clean any corrosion from the threads of both blanking plugs and valve adaptors.

3 Taping the threads
Make the threaded joints watertight by wrapping four or five turns of PTFE tape round the plugs and adaptors before you screw them into the new radiator. Use a hacksaw blade to roughen the threads in order to encourage the tape to grip.

Replacement with a different-pattern radiator

Rather more work is involved in the replacement if you can't get a radiator of the same pattern as the old one. You will have to fit new wall brackets and alter the pipe runs.

Drain your central-heating system, then take the old brackets off the wall. Lay the new radiator face down on the floor and slide one of its brackets onto the hangers welded to the back of the radiator. Measure the position of the brackets and transfer these measurements to the wall (1). You need to allow a clearance of 100 or 125mm (4 or 5in) below the radiator.

Line up the new radiator brackets with the pencil marks on the wall, and mark the fixing-screw holes for them. Drill and plug the holes, then screw the brackets in place (2).

Take up the floorboards below the radiator and cut off the vertical portions of the feed and return pipes. Connect the valves to the bottom of the radiator and hang it on its brackets. Slip a short length of pipe into each of the valves as a guide for any further trimming of the pipes under the floor. Connect these lengths to the original pipes (3) with capillary or compression fittings, then connect the new pipes to the valves.

Finally, refill the system with water, and check all the new connections and joints for leaks.

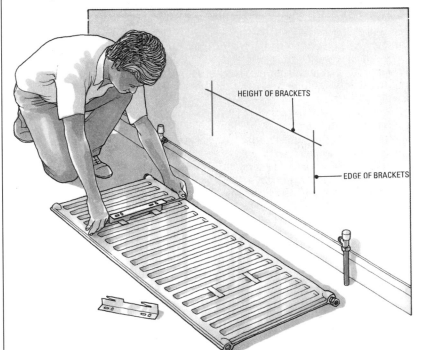

HEIGHT OF BRACKETS

EDGE OF BRACKETS

1 Transferring the measurements
Measure the positions of the radiator brackets and transfer the measurements to the wall. Double-check the results to make sure that the radiator is equidistant from the two pipes projecting from the floor.

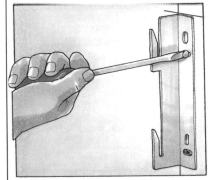

2 Securing the brackets
Screw the mounting brackets to the wall. Make sure they are on the right side of the line.

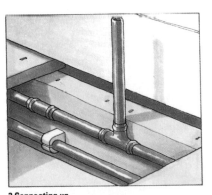

3 Connecting up
Connect the new section of pipework. The vertical pipe aligns with the radiator valve.

CIRCULATING PUMPS

Wet central heating depends on a steady cycle of hot water pumped from boiler to radiators then back to the boiler for reheating. If the pump is not working properly, the result is poor circulation or none at all. Adjusting or bleeding the pump may be the answer; otherwise, it may need replacing.

Bleeding the pump

If your radiators are not warming up properly although you can hear or feel the circulation pump running, it's likely that an airlock has formed in the pump and its impeller is spinning in air. The cure is to bleed the air from the pump: this is done in a similar way to bleeding a radiator, and there is a screw-in valve for the purpose in the pump's outer casing. The valve's position varies with different makes, but is usually marked.

Switch off the pump. Then, with a jug or glass jar handy to catch any water spillage, open the valve slightly with a screwdriver or vent key until you hear air hissing out. When the hissing stops and a drop of water appears, close the bleed valve fully.

Open the bleed valve with a screwdriver

Adjusting the pump

Two basic types of central-heating circulation pump are made: fixed-head and variable-head. Fixed-head pumps run at a single speed, forcing the hot water round the system at a fixed rate, whereas variable-head models can be adjusted to run at different speeds, circulating the water at different rates.

When a variable-head pump is fitted as part of a central-heating system, the installer balances the radiators, then adjusts the pump's speed so that each room reaches its optimum temperature. If you find your rooms are not as warm as you would like although you have opened the radiators' handwheel valves fully, try adjusting the pump speed – but first check that all your radiators show the same temperature drop between their inlets and outlets. You can obtain clip-on thermometers for this purpose

• **Bridging the gap**
You may find that a modern pump is smaller than the one you are replacing. There are converters designed to take up the gap between the existing valves.

from a plumbers' merchant, and will need to buy a pair of them.

Clip one thermometer to the feed pipe just below the radiator valve and the other to the return pipe below its valve **(1)**. The difference between the temperatures registered by the two should be about 11°C (20°F). If it is not, uncover the lockshield valve and close it further (to increase the difference) or open it more (to reduce the difference).

Having balanced the radiators, you can now adjust the pump. Switch the pump off and then increase the speed adjustment **(2)**, one step at a time, until the radiators are giving the overall temperatures you require. You may be able to work the adjustment by hand or you may need some special tool, such as an Allen key, depending on the make and model of your pump.

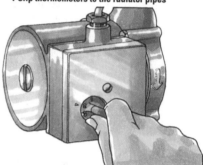

RETURN PIPE   FEED PIPE

1 Clip thermometers to the radiator pipes

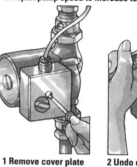

2 Adjust pump speed to increase temperatures

Replacing a worn pump

If you have to replace your circulation pump, make sure you buy one that is equivalent to the old pump. If in doubt, consult a professional installer.

First, turn off the boiler and close the isolating valves located on each side of the circulation pump. If there are no isolating valves, then you will have to drain down the whole system.

Identify the electrical circuit that controls the pump and remove the fuse of that circuit from the consumer unit, then take the cover plate off the pump and disconnect its wiring **(1)**.

You will need a bowl or bucket to catch the water left in the pump, plus some old rags for mopping up drips and spillage. Use an adjustable spanner to undo the nuts that hold the pump to the valves or the pipework **(2)**; have the

bowl or bucket ready to catch the water as it flows out.

Remove the old pump and fit the new one **(3)**, taking care to fit correctly any sealing washers that are provided, then tighten the retaining nuts. Take the cover plate off the new pump and feed in the flex, then connect up the wires to the pump's terminals **(4)** and replace the cover plate. If the pump is of the variable-head type (see above), set the speed control to the speed indicated on the old pump.

Open both isolating valves – or refill the system, if you had to drain it – then check the pump connections for leaks and tighten them if necessary. Open the pump's bleed valve to release any trapped air. Finally, replace the fuse in the consumer unit and test the pump.

1 Remove cover plate   **2 Undo connecting nuts**

3 Attach new pump   **4 Connect power flex**

Efficient control valves are vital to the working of a modern central-heating system, for it is through them that timers and thermostats adjust the level of heating to the programmed requirements of the householder. Worn or faulty control valves can seriously impair the reliability of the system and should therefore be replaced promptly.

Replacing a faulty valve

Be sure to buy a replacement valve that is of exactly the same pattern as the faulty one. If you are in any doubt, seek professional advice.

Drain down the system, then identify the electrical circuit that services the central-heating controls and remove its fuse from the consumer unit.

The electric flex from the valve will be connected to the terminals of a nearby junction box, which will also be linked to the heating system's other controls. Take the cover off the junction box and disconnect the wiring for the valve. When you do this, it is worth carefully noting the connections, so as to make reconnection easier.

You will probably find it's impossible to remove the old valve from the pipe run by simply unscrewing its cap-nuts, since you won't be able to pull the ends of the pipe free of their sockets in the valve. Instead, cut through the pipe on each side of the valve (1) and take out the section, complete with valve; then make up two pieces of pipe to fit on either side of the new control valve.

Assemble the valve with its olives and cap-nuts, pipes and joints, but only loosely at first, and fit the assembly into the pipe run (2). There should be sufficient play in the joints to allow the assembly to be sprung into place (freeing the original pipes from the clips on each side of the valve will help).

When the new pipes and valve are in place, connect them to the original pipework with compression or capillary joints, then tighten the valve cap-nuts. Hold the body of the valve firmly with a second spanner to prevent it turning (3).

Reconnect the flex to the terminals of the junction box and replace its cover plate, then put the fuse back in the consumer unit.

Refill the heating system and check the working of the valve by adjusting the timer or thermostat that controls it.

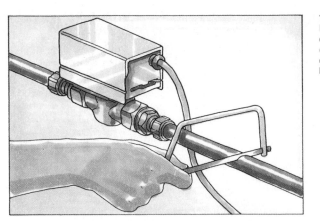

1 Removing the valve
If you are unable to disconnect the valve, cut through the pipe on each side with a hacksaw.

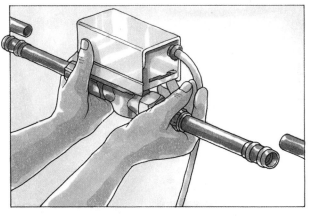

2 Fitting new valve
With the new valve connected to short sections of pipe, spring the assembly into the pipe run.

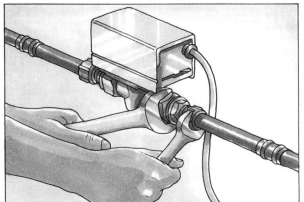

3 Closing the joints
Having connected the pipework, tighten the valve cap-nuts on each side with a pair of spanners.

Slip couplings
If you cannot spring pipework to locate a conventional soldered joint, use a slip coupling, which is free to slide along the pipe to cover the junction.

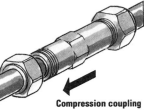

Compression coupling

Soldered coupling

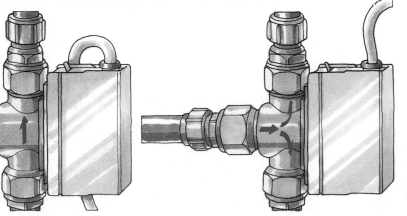

Two-port control valve
(Far left)
A two-port valve seals off a section of pipe-work when the water in it has reached the required temperature.

Three-port control valve
(Left)
This type of valve can independently isolate central heating or hot-water circuits.

417

STORAGE HEATERS

SEE ALSO
Details for:
Heater circuits   326–327

One good reason for the popularity of electric storage heaters is their use of cheap night-time power. Indeed, the Electricity Companies' special rate for off-peak power can be as little as half that charged for daytime supply, or even less. This cut-rate scheme is called Economy 7, referring to the seven hours of the night when the cheap rate is in force.

The night-time power heats up a core of firebrick or similar material in the storage heater, and the core releases the heat next day – a process of convection whereby cool air is drawn in at the bottom of the heater, to be warmed as it passes over the hot core and expelled from the top.

The refined lines of modern storage heaters look at home in any interior

Types of storage heater

The early storage heaters were bulky and space-consuming; and they emitted heat at a set rate, so the user had no control over the output. The heat stored during the night could be adjusted – but this involved making an estimate of the next day's heating requirements, and a sudden change of weather could leave the user with too much or too little heat.

Recent advances in storage-heater technology and design have improved their appeal considerably. Modern ones are slimmer – some are just 150mm (6in) deep – and may either be wall-mounted or freestanding. They also have better insulation and allow greater control of heat output. Adjustable dampers and fans (some thermostatically controlled) enable the modern units to be run at low levels in unoccupied rooms and opened up when needed – even late in the day, when the older type of storage heater would run out of stored heat.

Some units retain a residue of stored heat, which reduces overnight charging and cuts costs further. Others monitor room temperatures at night, assess the next day's heating needs (a cold night is normally followed by a cold day) and adjust the heat charge accordingly.

Positioning storage heaters

Like radiators, storage heaters should be placed below single-glazed windows to counter draughts and balance the room temperature. With double glazing, they can go anywhere that's convenient and, if possible, should be positioned to give the best heat spread. The heaters have individual circuits and a separate consumer unit, plus an off-peak meter to record their power consumption.

HOW MANY STORAGE HEATERS?

To work out the ideal number of storage heaters for your home really accurately, together with the optimum output, you would have to calculate your needs in the same way as when planning a wet central-heating system with radiators. With this process the heating requirements of each room have to be worked out in detail, and then heaters selected to meet those demands.

Ready-reckoner charts

However, installing storage heaters is a much easier undertaking than putting in a full central-heating system – in fact, it is a very common DIY job. Guides for the amateur are therefore provided by the Electricity Companies and by some manufacturers. These take the form of simple charts that help you to estimate each room's requirements on the basis of the floor area and number of outside walls. Although charts of this kind are not completely accurate, they at least help you to choose heaters from the sizes that are most commonly available.

Selecting the optimum number

But there is an even simpler method for deciding the optimum number of storage heaters for your home.

If your total night-time load (including water heating) exceeds 14.4kW, then the 60amp service-cable fuse will be overloaded – and, if that happens, your Electricity Company may insist on a hefty contribution towards the cost of reinstating the service. However, within this limit you can safely install one small (1.7kW), one medium-size (2.5kW) and two large (3.4kW) storage heaters.

Place one of the large heaters in the hall and the other in your main living room. (In a small flat, these may be the only storage heaters that are needed). The medium-size heater can be placed in your second most important downstairs room, and the small heater should supply adequate warmth for your main bedroom. You can then use convection heaters or 'direct' oil-filled radiators to heat any other rooms and to provide top-up heating for the principal rooms of your house or flat.

With this type of system something like 90 per cent of your total heating will be supplied at the cheap off-peak rate, and consequently your overall running costs will be reasonable.

WORKING OUTDOORS

PLANNING
A GARDEN

SEE ALSO
Details for:
Building Regulations 18–19

Designing a garden is not an exact science. Plants may not thrive in a particular spot even though you select the right soil conditions and amount of daylight, and shrubs and trees may never reach the size specified for them in a catalogue. Nevertheless, forward planning will produce a more satisfactory result than a haphazard approach which could involve expensive mistakes like laying a patio where it will be in shade for most of the day or building a boundary wall that is too high to meet with official planning approval. It is these permanent features you should concentrate on planning first, always, of course, considering how they will fit into the planted and turfed areas of the garden.

Deciding on the approach

Before you even put pencil to paper, get a feel for the type of garden you would like and ask yourself whether it would sit happily with the house and its immediate surroundings. Is it to be a formal garden, laid out in straight lines or geometric patterns – a style which often marries successfully with modern architecture? Or do you prefer the more relaxed style of a rambling cottage garden? If you opt for the latter, bear in mind that natural informality may not be as easy to achieve as you think, and your planting scheme will certainly take several years to mature into the established garden you have in mind. You may prefer a blend of both styles, where every plant, stone and pool of water is carefully positioned; a Japanese-style garden bears all the hallmarks of a man-made landscape yet conveys a sense of natural harmony.

There is no shortage of material from which to draw inspiration, for there are countless books and magazines devoted to garden design. As no two gardens are alike you probably won't find a plan that fits your plot exactly, but you may be able to adapt a particular approach or develop a small detail into your own design. Visiting other gardens is an even better way of getting ideas. Large country estates and city parks will have been designed on a much grander scale, but at least you will be able to see how a mature shrub should look or how plants, stone and water have been used in a rockery or water garden. Don't forget that your friends may also have had to tackle problems identical to yours; if nothing else, you might learn by their mistakes!

A convincing rockery
(Top left)
Once plants become established, a rockery should blend into a garden without a hint of artificiality. The effect relies on the careful positioning of stones during its construction.

A simple layout
(Top right)
Simplicity is often the best approach, but the proportions of the various elements must be carefully considered to avoid a boring result.

Cottage-style garden
(Bottom left)
The informal character of abundant flowers planted around natural-stone or brick paths and over a rustic trellis ideally complements traditional cottage architecture.

Consider the details
(Bottom right)
Good design does not rely on having a large garden. A successful combination of natural forms can be just as rewarding on a small scale.

SURVEYING THE PLOT

Measuring the plot
Measure your plot of land as accurately as you can. Include the diagonal measurements, because a garden that appears to be exactly rectangular or square may not in fact be so.

Slopes and gradients
Make a note of how the ground slopes. An accurate survey is not necessary, but at least jot down the direction of the slope and plot the points where it begins and ends. You can get some idea of the differences in level by using a long straightedge and a spirit level. Place one end of the straightedge on the top of a bank, for example, and measure the vertical distance from the other end to the foot of the slope.

Climatic conditions
Check the passage of the sun and the direction of prevailing winds. Don't forget that the angle of the sun will be higher in summer and a screen of deciduous trees will be less of a windbreak when they drop their leaves.

Soil conditions
Make a note of soil conditions. You can easily adjust soil content by adding peat or fertilizers. A peat or clay soil is not very stable, however, and will affect the type of footings and foundations you may want to lay.

Existing features
Plot the position of features you want to retain in your plan, such as existing pathways, areas of lawn, established trees and so on.

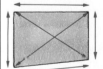

Measuring a plot
Note the overall dimensions including the diagonals to draw an accurate plan.

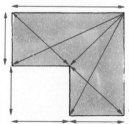

Gauging a slope
Use a straightedge and spirit level to measure the height of a bank.

A formal garden
(Top)
Sculptured box hedges used to create regular patterns in traditional knot-garden style.

Using textures
(Centre left)
Still water punctuated with rugged stones makes for a pleasing contrast of textures.

A sloping site
(Centre right)
Some of the most dramatic gardens are a result of having to contend with a sloping site. Here retaining walls are used to terrace a steep bank of colourful shrubs.

Japanese-style garden
(Bottom)
Well-chosen plants with carefully placed natural stones and pebbles give an overall effect of tranquility.

421

BASIC CONSIDERATIONS

Having surveyed your plot, it is worth taking the time to plan all aspects of the design of your garden. Practical problems will need careful thought.

Drawing a plan

Draw a plan of your garden on paper. It must be a properly scaled plan or you are sure to make some gross errors, but it need not be professionally perfect. Use squared paper to plot the dimensions, but do the actual drawing on tracing paper laid over the graph paper so that you can try out several ideas and adapt your plan without having to redraw it every time.

Make a garden plan on tracing paper

Plotting your design

Planning on paper is only the first stage. Gardens are rarely seen from above so it is essential to plot the design on the ground to check your dimensions and view the features from different angles. A pond or patio which looks enormous on paper can be pathetically small in reality. Other shortcomings, such as the way a tree will block the view from your proposed patio, become obvious once you lay out the plan full-size.

Plot individual features by driving pegs into the ground and stretching string lines between them. Scribe arcs on the ground with a rope tied to a peg, and mark the curved lines with stakes or a row of bricks. Use a garden hose to mark out less regular curves and ponds. If you can scrape areas clear of weeds, it will define the shapes still further.

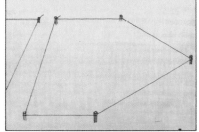

Mark out straight lines with pegs and string

Practical experiments

When you have marked out your design, carry out a few experiments to check that it is practicable. Will it be possible, for instance, for two people to pass each other on the footpath without having to step into the flowerbeds? Can you set down a wheelbarrow on the footpath without one of its legs slipping into the pond?

Try placing some furniture on the area you have marked out for a patio to make sure you can relax comfortably and even sit down to a meal with visitors. Most people build a patio alongside the house, but if you have to put it elsewhere to find a sunny spot, will it become a chore to walk back and forth for drinks and snacks?

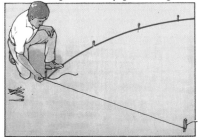

Use rope tied to a peg to scribe an arc

Siting ponds

Site a pond to avoid overhanging trees and in an area where it will catch at least half-a-day's sunlight. Check that you can reach it with a hose and that you can run electrical cables to power a pump or night-time lighting.

Common-sense safety

Don't make your garden an obstacle course. For example, a narrow path alongside a pond could be intimidating to an elderly relative, while low walls or planters near the edge of a patio could cause someone to trip.

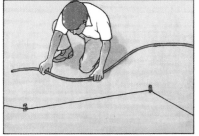

Try out irregular curves with a garden hose

Driveways and parking spaces

Allow a minimum width of 3m (9ft 9in) for a driveway, making sure there is enough room to open the car doors if you park alongside a wall. Remember that vehicles larger than your own might need to use the drive or parking space. Allow room for the turning circle of your car if possible and make sure that when you pull out into the road you will have a clear view of the traffic.

Consider the neighbours

There may be legal restrictions on what you can erect in your garden, but even if you have a free hand it is only wise to consult your neighbours if anything you plan might cause discomfort or inconvenience. A wall or even trees which are high enough to shade their favourite sunspot or block out the light to a window could be the source of argument for years to come.

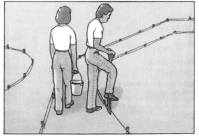

Make sure two people can pass on a path

SEE ALSO

Details for:	
Repairing cracks	46
Penetrating damp	257–259

As a permanent feature of your garden you will probably want to plant at least one tree. You will need to think carefully about your choice of trees and their position – they could be potentially damaging to the structure of the house if planted too near.

GROWING CLIMBERS

There is a widely held misconception that a climbing plant, especially ivy, will damage any masonry wall. If exterior rendering or the mortar between bricks or stonework is in a poor condition then an exuberant ivy plant will undoubtedly weaken the structure as its aerial roots attempt to extract moisture from the masonry. The roots invade broken joints or rendering and, on finding a source of nourishment for the main plant, expand and burst the weakened material, thus encouraging damp to penetrate. However, with sound bricks and mortar, ivy can do no more than climb by the aid of training wires and its own sucker-like roots which do not provide nourishment but are for support only. So long as the structure is sound and free from damp, there is some benefit from allowing a plant to clothe a wall in that its close-growing mat of leaves, mostly with their drip tips pointing downwards, acts as insulation and a watershed against the elements. Where ivy is permitted to flourish as a climber, it must be hard-pruned to prevent it penetrating between roof tiles or slates and clogging gutters and drainpipes. If any climber is allowed to grow unchecked, the weight of the mature plant may eventually topple a weakened wall.

Don't allow plants to get out of control

Cracks: subsidence and heave

Minor cracks in house plaster, rendering and even brickwork are often the result of shrinkage as the structure dries out. Such cracks are not serious and can be repaired during normal maintenance, but more serious structural cracks are due to movement of the foundations. Trees planted too close to a building can add to the problem by removing moisture from the site, causing subsidence of the foundations as the supporting earth collapses. Tree-felling can be just as damaging; the surrounding soil, which has become stabilized over the years, swells as it takes up the moisture which has been removed previously by the tree-root system. Upward movement of the ground, known as heave, distorts the foundations until cracks appear.

Siting trees

Tree roots search out moisture, which can result in an expensive repair or replacement of the house drainage system. Large roots can fracture rigid pipework or penetrate joints until the drain becomes blocked.

Before you plant a tree close to a building, find out the likely spread of the mature root system. As a rough guide, make sure there is a distance of at least two-thirds the mature height of a tree between it and nearby buildings. If an existing tree is likely to cause a problem, ask your local planning department for advice – the tree may be protected by a preservation order and you could be fined if you cut it down without permission. It may be possible to prune the branches and roots to lessen the likelihood of future damage.

Subsidence
A mature tree growing close to a house can draw so much water from the ground that the earth subsides, causing damage to the foundations.

Heave
When a mature tree is felled the earth can absorb more water, causing it to swell until it displaces the foundations of a building.

423

FENCES: CHOOSING

A fence is the most popular form of boundary marker or garden screen because of its advantages over other methods of dividing plots of land. A fence takes very little time to erect when compared with a wall and especially with a hedge, which takes years to establish. Most fencing components are relatively lightweight and are therefore easy to transport and handle on site.

Economics and maintenance

In the short term a fence is cheaper than a masonry wall, although one can argue that the cost of maintenance and replacement over a very long period eventually cancels out the saving in cost. Wood does have a comparatively short life because it is susceptible to insect infestation and rot when exposed to the elements, although a fence will last for many years if treated regularly with a preserver. If you are prepared to spend a little more money on plastic or concrete components, you can erect a virtually maintenance-free fence.

Chain-link fencing

Trellis fencing

Post-and-chain fence

Choosing your fencing

When you measure even a small garden you will be surprised by the overall length of fencing required to surround your property, so it is worth considering the available options carefully to make sure that you invest your money in the kind of fence that will be most suitable. Unless your priority is to keep neighbourhood children or animals out of your garden, the amount of privacy afforded by a fence is likely to be the most important consideration. There are a number of 'peep-proof' options, but you may have to compromise to some extent if you plan to erect a fence on a site exposed to strong prevailing winds. In that case you will need a fence which will provide a decent windbreak without offering such resistance that the posts will have worked loose within a couple of seasons of constant buffeting.

Planning and planning permission

You can build any fence up to 2m (6ft 6in) high without planning permission unless your boundary adjoins a highway, in which case you may not be able to erect a barrier higher than 1m (3ft 3in). In addition, there may be local restrictions on fencing if the land surrounding your house has been designed as an open-plan area. Even so, many authorities will permit low boundary markers such as a ranch-style or post-and-chain fence.

At least discuss your plans with your neighbours, especially as you will require their permission if you want to work from both sides when erecting a fence. Check the line of the boundaries to make certain that you do not encroach upon the neighbours' land. The fence posts should run along the boundary or on your side of the line, and before you dismantle an old fence make sure that it is indeed yours to demolish. If a neighbour is unwilling to replace an unsightly fence, or even to allow you to replace it at your expense, there is nothing to stop you erecting another fence alongside the original one provided it is on your property. It is an unwritten law that a good neighbour erects a fence with the post and rails facing his or her own property, but there are no legal restrictions which force you to do so.

TYPES OF FENCING

Chain-link fencing

Chain-link fencing is a utilitarian form of barrier constructed from wire netting stretched between fence posts. A true chain-link fence is made from strong galvanized or plastic-coated wire woven into a diamond-shape mesh, suspended from a heavy-gauge wire tensioned between the posts. You can make a cheap fence from soft wire netting or 'chicken wire', but it will not be durable and it will stretch if a large animal leans against it. Decorative wire fencing, which is available at many garden centres, is designed primarily for marking boundaries or supporting lightweight climbing plants. In fact, any chain-link fence will benefit from a screen of climbers or hedging plants.

Trellis fencing

A concertina-fold trellis formed from thin softwood or cedar laths joined together is virtually useless as a fence in the true sense, relying exclusively on the posts and rails for its strength. However, a similar fence made from split rustic poles nailed to stout rails and posts forms a strong and attractive barrier. Both types of trellis are ideally suited as plant supports for climbers.

Post-and-chain fencing

A post-and-chain fence is no more than a decorative feature which will prevent people inadvertently wandering off a path or pavement onto a lawn or flowerbed. They are constructed by stringing lengths of painted metal or plastic chain between short posts sunk into the ground.

TYPES OF FENCING

Closeboard fencing

A closeboard fence is made by nailing overlapping featherboard strips to horizontal rails. Featherboards are sawn planks which taper across their width from 16mm (⅝in) at the thicker side down to about 3mm (⅛in). The boards are 100mm (4in) or 150mm (6in) wide, and the best quality are made from cedar. However, softwood is the usual choice because of the high timber content of a closeboard fence. Although it is expensive, closeboard fencing forms a screen that is both strong and attractive. Because they are fixed vertically, the boards are quite difficult to climb from the outside – which makes them ideal for keeping children out!

Closeboard fencing

Prefabricated panel fencing

Fences made from prefabricated panels nailed between timber posts are very common, perhaps because they are particularly easy to erect. Standard panels are 1.8m (6ft) wide and range in height from approximately 600mm (2ft) to 1.8m (6ft); they are supplied in 300m (1ft) gradations. Most panels are made from interwoven or overlapping strips of larch sandwiched between a frame of sawn timber. The overlapping strip panels are usually designated 'larchlap', or, if the strips have a natural wavy edge, 'rustic larchlap'. You may also see them described as 'waney-edged', referring to where the thin strips of bark were, or may still be, attached to the planks.

A panel fence offers good value for money as a reasonably durable screen, but if privacy is a consideration choose the lapped type; interwoven strips will shrink to some extent in the summer, leaving gaps.

Panel fence

Interlap fencing

An interlap fence is made by nailing square-edged boards to the horizontal rails, fixing them alternately one side then the other. Spacing is a matter of choice. Overlap the edges of the boards for privacy, or space them apart for a decorative effect.

This is the type of fence to choose for a windy site as it is substantial yet the gaps between the boards allow the wind to pass through without exerting too much pressure. Because of its construction, an interlap fence is equally attractive from either side.

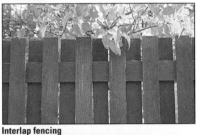
Interlap fencing

Picket fencing

The traditional low picket fence is still popular as a 'cottage-style' barrier at the front of the house where a high fence is unnecessary. Narrow, vertical 'pales' with rounded or pointed tops are spaced at 50mm (2in) centres. As they are laborious to build by hand, most picket fences are sold as ready-made panels constructed from plastic or softwood to keep down the cost.

Picket fencing

Ranch-style fencing

Low-level fences made from simple horizontal rails fixed to short, stout posts are the modern counterpart of picket fencing. Used extensively in some housing developments, this ranch-style fencing is often painted, although clear-finished or stained timber is just as attractive and far more durable. Softwoods and some hardwoods are used for this fencing; plastic ranch-style fences are also popular, both for their clean, crisp appearance and because they do not need to be repainted.

Ranch-style fence

Concrete fencing

A cast-concrete fence offers the security and permanence of a masonry wall and needs minimal maintenance. Interlocking horizontal sections are built one upon the other up to the required height. Each is supported by grooves cast into the sides of purpose-made concrete fence posts.

Concrete fencing

FENCE POSTS

Whatever type of fence you plan to erect, its strength and durability rely on good-quality posts set solidly in the ground. Buy the best posts you can afford, and erect them carefully. It is worth taking longer over its construction to avoid having to dismantle and repair a fence in the future.

TYPES OF POST

In some cases the nature of the fencing will determine the choice of post. Concrete fencing, for example, must be supported by compatible concrete posts, but, in the main, you can choose the material and style of post which suits the appearance of the fence.

Timber posts

Most fences are supported by square-section timber posts. Standard sizes are 75 and 100mm (3 and 4in) square, but 125, 150 and even 200mm (5, 6, 8in) square gate posts are available. Most timber merchants supply pretreated softwood posts unless you ask specifically for hardwood.

Concrete posts

A variety of 100mm (4in) square, reinforced-concrete posts exists to suit different styles of fence: drilled for chain-link fixings, mortised for rails and recessed or grooved for panels. Special corner and end posts are notched to accommodate bracing struts for chain-link fencing.

Metal posts

Angle-iron posts are made to support chain-link fences, and wrought-iron gates are often hung from plastic-coated tubular-steel posts. Angle-iron posts are very sturdy, but they do not make for an attractive fence.

Plastic posts

Extruded PVC posts are supplied with plastic fencing, together with moulded-plastic end caps and rail-fixing bolts and unions.

Preserving fence posts

Even when a timber fence post is pretreated to prevent rot, provide additional protection by soaking the base of each post in a bucket of chemical preserver for at least ten minutes and preferably longer.

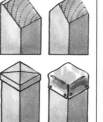

Capping fence posts
If you simply cut the end of a timber post square, the top of the post will rot relatively quickly. The solution is to cut a single or double bevel to shed the rainwater, or nail a wooden or galvanized-metal cap over the end of the fence post.

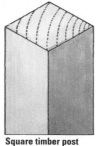

Square timber post

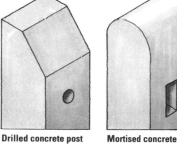

Drilled concrete post   **Mortised concrete post**

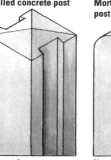

Grooved concrete post   **Notched end post**

Angle-iron post   **Tubular-steel post**

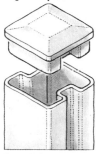

Capped plastic post

REMOVING OLD FENCE POSTS

Fixing posts in virgin soil is straightforward, but if you are replacing a fence you may want to put the new posts in the same position as the old. Remove the topsoil from around each post to loosen it. If one is bedded firmly, or sunk into concrete, lever it out with a stout batten. Drive large nails into two opposite faces of the post, about 300mm (1ft) from the ground. Bind a length of rope around the post just below the nails and tie the ends to the tip of the batten. Build a pile of bricks close to the post and use it as a fulcrum to lever the post out of the ground.

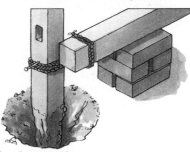

Levering a rotted fence post
Use a pile of bricks as a fulcrum to lift the post.

FIXING TO A WALL

If a fence runs up to the house, fix the first post to the wall with three expanding masonry bolts. Place a washer under each bolt head to stop the wood being crushed. Check that the post is vertical with a spirit level and drive packing between the post and wall to make any adjustments needed.

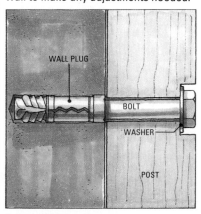

Bolting a post to a wall
If you are fitting a prefabricated panel against a wall-fixed post, counterbore the bolts so that the heads lie flush with the surface of the wood.

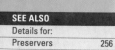

ERECTING FENCE POSTS

USING METAL SPIKES

Instead of anchoring fence posts in concrete, you can plug the base of each post into the square socket of a metal spike driven into firm ground. Use a 600mm (2ft) spike for fences up to 1.2m (4ft) high, and a 750mm (2ft 6in) spike for a 1.8m (6ft) fence.

Place a scrap of hardwood post into the socket to protect the metal, then drive the spike partly into the ground with a sledgehammer. Hold a spirit level against the socket to make certain the spike is upright (1), then hammer the spike into the ground until only the socket is visible. Insert the post and secure it by screwing through the side of the socket or by tightening clamping bolts (2), depending on the type of spike.

If you are erecting a panel fence, use the edge of a fixed panel to position the next spike (3).

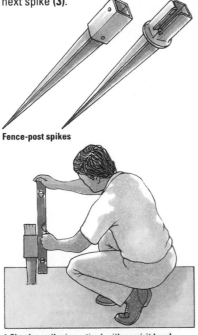

Fence-post spikes

1 Check a spike is vertical with a spirit level

2 Fix the post
3 Position next spike

The type of fence often dictates whether you erect all the posts first or one at a time along with the other components. When you are building a prefabricated panel fence, for example, fix the posts as you erect the fence – but complete the run of posts before you install chain-link fencing.

Marking out

Drive a peg into the ground at each end of the fence run and stretch a line between. If possible, adjust the spacing of the posts to avoid obstructions such as large tree roots. If one or more posts have to be inserted across a paved patio, lift enough slabs to dig the necessary holes. You may have to break up a section of concrete beneath the slabs using a cold chisel and hammer.

Erecting the posts

Digging the hole
Bury one quarter of each post to provide a firm foundation. For a 1.8m (6ft) high fence, dig a 600mm (2ft) hole to take a 2.4m (8ft) post. You can hire a post-hole auger to remove the central core of earth. Twist the tool to drive it into the ground (1) and pull it out after every 150mm (6in) to remove the soil. When you have reached a sufficient depth, taper the sides of the hole slightly so that you can pack hardcore and concrete around the post.

Anchoring the post
Ram a layer of hardcore (broken bricks or small stones) into the bottom of the hole to support the base of the post and provide drainage. Get someone to hold the post upright while you brace it with battens nailed to the post and to stakes driven into the ground (2). Use guy ropes to support a concrete post. Check with a spirit level that the post is vertical.

Ram more hardcore around the post, leaving a hole about 300mm (1ft) deep for filling with concrete. Mix some concrete to a firm consistency using the proportions 1 part cement : 2 parts sand : 3 parts aggregate. Use a trowel to drop concrete into the hole all round the post and tamp it down with the end of a batten (3). Build the concrete just above the level of the soil and smooth it to slope away from the post (4). This will help shed water and prevent rot. Leave the concrete to harden for about a week before removing the struts. To support a panel fence temporarily, wedge struts against the posts.

1 Dig the post hole   2 Brace the post   3 Fill with concrete   4 Slope the concrete

Supporting end posts

Chain-link fence posts must resist the tension of the straining wires. Brace each end post (and some intermediate ones over a long run) with a strut made from a length of fence post. Shape the end of the strut to fit a notch cut into the post (1) and nail it in place. Order special posts and precast struts for concrete components.

Anchor the post in the ground in the normal way, but dig a 450mm (1ft 6in) deep trench alongside for the strut. Wedge a brick under the end of the strut before ramming hardcore around the post and strut. Fill the trench up to ground level with concrete (2).

Support a corner post with two struts set at right angles. Where a fence adjoins a masonry wall, fix as described in the box opposite.

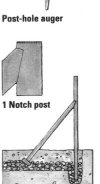

Post-hole auger

1 Notch post

2 Concreting end post

427

ERECTING A CHAIN-LINK FENCE

Set out a complete row of timber, concrete or angle-iron posts to support chain-link fencing, spacing them no more than 3m (10ft) apart. Brace the end posts with struts to resist the pull of the straining wires. A long run of fencing will need a braced intermediate post every 70m (225ft) or so.

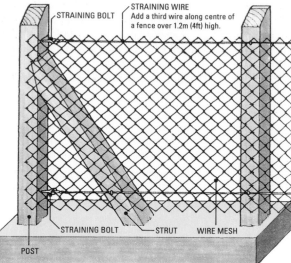

STRAINING BOLT

STRAINING WIRE
Add a third wire along centre of a fence over 1.2m (4ft) high.

Attaching the mesh
Staple each end link to the post. Unroll the mesh and pull it taut. Tie it to straining wires every 300mm (1ft) with galvanized wire. Fix to the post at the far end.

STRAINING BOLT — STRUT — WIRE MESH

POST

Staple mesh to post

Tie with wire loops

Chain-link fencing

Using timber posts

Support the chain-link fencing on straining wires (see right). As it is impossible to tension this heavy-gauge wire by hand, use large straining bolts to stretch it between the posts: one to coincide with the top of the fencing, one about 150mm (6in) from the ground, and the third midway between. Drill 10mm (³⁄₈in) diameter holes right through the posts, insert a bolt into each hole and fit a washer and nut, leaving enough thread to provide about 50mm (2in) of movement once you begin to apply tension to the wire (**1**).

Pass the end of the wire through the eye of a bolt and twist it around itself with pliers (**2**). Stretch the wire along the run of fencing, stapling it to each post and strut, but leave enough slack for the wire to move when tensioned (**3**). Cut the wire to length and twist it through the bolt at the other end of the fence. Tension the wire from both ends by turning the nuts with a spanner (**4**).

Standard straining bolts provide enough tension for the average garden fence, but over a long run of fencing (70m (225ft) or more) use a turnbuckle for each wire, applying tension with a metal bar (see left).

Using a turnbuckle
Apply tension by turning the turnbuckle with a metal bar.

KNUCKLE

SPIRAL

Joining wire mesh
Chain-link fencing is supplied in 25m (82ft) lengths. To join one roll to another, unfold the knuckles at each end of the first wire spiral, then turn the spiral anti-clockwise to withdraw it from the mesh. Connect the two rolls by rethreading the loose spiral in a clockwise direction through each link of the mesh. Bend the knuckle over at the top and bottom.

Using concrete posts

Fix straining wires to concrete posts using a special bolt and cleat (see right). Bolt a stretcher bar to the cleats when erecting the wire netting.

Tie the straining wire to intermediate posts with a length of galvanized wire passed through the predrilled hole.

Using angle-iron posts

Winding brackets are supplied with angle-iron fence posts to attach stretcher bars and to apply tension to the straining wires (see right). As you pass the straining wire from end to end, pass it through the predrilled hole in every intermediate post.

1 Insert a straining bolt in the end post

2 Attach a straining wire to the bolt
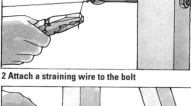
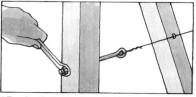
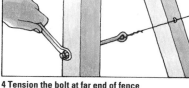

3 Staple the wire to the post and strut

4 Tension the bolt at far end of fence
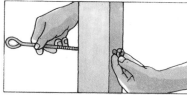
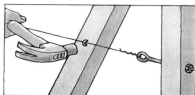

NOTCHED END POST   INTERMEDIATE POST

BOLTED CLEAT

STRETCHER BAR

STRAINING WIRES

STRUT

BOLTED CLEAT

Concrete fence posts
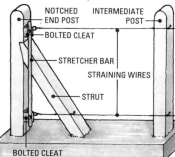

Cleat and stretcher bar   **Tie wire to post**
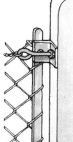

END POST

WINDING BRACKET

STRETCHER BAR

STRAINING WIRES

STRUT

WINDING BRACKET   INTERMEDIATE POST

Angle-iron posts
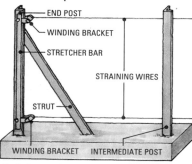

Winding bracket   **Pass wire through post**
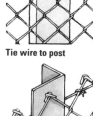

428

The featherboards used to panel the fence are nailed to triangular-section rails known as arris rails. The arris rails are mortised into the fence posts. Concrete, and some wooden, posts are supplied ready-mortised, but if you buy standard timber posts you will have to cut the mortises. The end grain of the featherboards is liable to rot, especially if they are in contact with the ground, so fix horizontal 150 x 25mm (6 x 1in) gravel boards at the foot of the fence and nail wooden capping strips across the tops of the featherboards. Space the fence posts no more than 3m (10ft) apart.

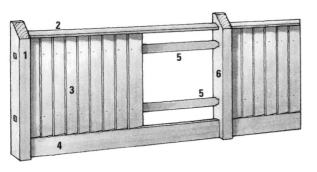

Closeboard fencing
1 End post
2 Capping strip
3 Featherboards
4 Gravel board
5 Arris rail
6 Intermediate post

REPAIRING A DAMAGED ARRIS RAIL

The arris rails take most of the strain when a closeboard fence is buffeted by high winds. Not surprisingly, they eventually crack across the middle or break where the tenon enters the mortise. Galvanized-metal brackets are available for repairing broken arris rails.

You can use end brackets to construct a new fence instead of cutting mortises for the rails. However, it will not be as strong as a fence built with mortise-and-tenon joints.

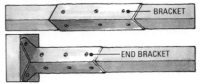

— BRACKET

— END BRACKET

Erecting the framework

If you are using plain wooden posts, mark and cut 50 x 22mm (2 x ⅞in) mortises for the arris rails about 150mm (6in) above and below the ends of the fixed featherboards. For fencing over 1.2m (4ft) high, cut mortises for a third rail midway between the others. Position the mortises 25mm (1in) from the front face of each post (the featherboarded side of the fence).

As you erect the fence, cut the rails to length and shape a tenon on each end with a coarse rasp or Surform file **(1)**. Paint preserver onto the shaped ends and into the mortises before you assemble the rails.

Erect the first fence post and pack hardcore around its base. Get someone to hold the post steady while you fit the arris rails and erect the next post, tapping it onto the ends of the rails with a mallet **(2)**. Check that the rails are horizontal and the posts are vertical before packing hardcore around the second post. Construct the entire run of posts and rails in the same way. If you cannot manoeuvre the last post onto tenoned rails, cut the rails square and fix them to the post with metal brackets (see box top right).

Check the whole run once more to ensure that the rails are bedded firmly in their mortises and the framework is true, then secure each rail by driving a nail through the post into the tenon **(3)** or drilling a hole and inserting a wooden dowel. Pack concrete around each post. Leave to harden for about a week.

Fitting the boards

Gravel boards
Some concrete posts are mortised to take gravel boards; fit them at the same time as the arris rails. If the posts are not mortised, bed wooden cleats into the concrete filling at the base of the post and screw the board to the cleat when the concrete is set.

To fit gravel boards to wooden posts, skew-nail treated wooden cleats at the foot of each post, then nail the boards to the cleats **(4)**.

Featherboards
Cut the featherboards to length and treat the end grain. Stand the first board on the gravel board with its thick edge against the post. Nail the board to the arris rails with galvanized nails set 18mm (¾in) from the thick edge. Place the next board in position, overlapping the thin edge of the fixed board by 12mm (½in). Check that it is vertical, then nail it in the same way. Don't drive a nail through both boards or they won't be able to move when they shrink. To space the other boards equally, make a spacer block from a scrap of wood **(5)**. Place the last board to fit against the next post and fix it, this time with two nails per rail **(6)**. When the fence is completed, nail capping strips across the tops of the featherboards, cut the posts to length and cap them.

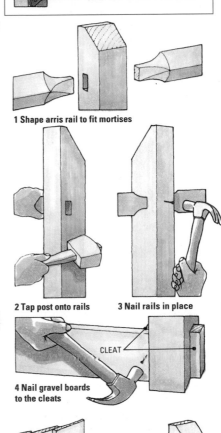

1 Shape arris rail to fit mortises

2 Tap post onto rails **3 Nail rails in place**

CLEAT

4 Nail gravel boards to the cleats

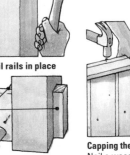

Capping the fence
Nail a wooden capping strip to the ends of the featherboards to shed rainwater.

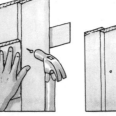

5 Use a spacer block to position featherboards **6 Fix last board with two nails**

429

ERECTING A
PANEL FENCE

To prevent a prefabricated panel rotting, either fit gravel boards as for a closeboard fence, or leave a gap at the bottom by supporting a panel temporarily on two bricks while you nail it to the fence posts.

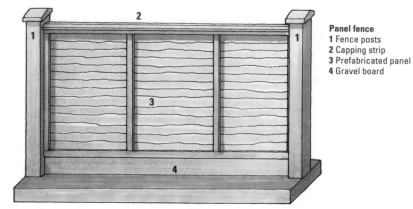

Panel fence
1 Fence posts
2 Capping strip
3 Prefabricated panel
4 Gravel board

Using timber posts

Pack the first post into its hole with hardcore, then get someone to hold a panel against the post while you skew-nail through its framework into the post (**1**). If you can work from both sides, drive three nails from each side of the fence. If the frame starts to split, blunt the nails by tapping their points with a hammer. Alternatively, use metal angle brackets to secure the panels (**2**). Construct the entire fence erecting panels and posts alternately.

Nail capping strips across the panels if they have not already been fitted by the manufacturer. Finally, cut each post to length and cap it.

Wedge struts made from scrap timber against each post to keep it vertical, then top up the holes with concrete. If you are unable to work from both sides, you will have to fill each hole as you build the fence.

1 Nail the panel through its framework

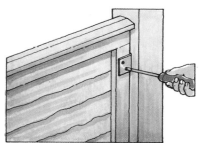

2 Or use angle brackets to fix panel to posts

Using concrete posts

Grooved concrete posts will support panels without the need for additional fixings (**3**). Recessed concrete posts are supplied with metal brackets for screw-fixing the panels (**4**).

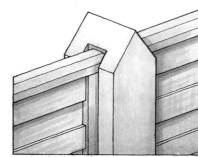

3 A grooved concrete post for a fence panel

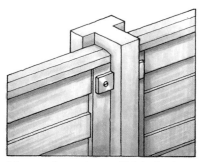

4 A recessed concrete post with fixing bracket

Building a panel fence
Posts and panels are erected alternately. Dig a hole for the post (**1**) and hold it upright with hardcore. Support a panel on bricks (**2**) and have a helper push it against the post (**3**) while you nail it (**4**). Fit gravel boards (**5**), capping strips (**6**) and cap the posts (**7**). Top up the holes with concrete (**8**) and allow it to set.

ERECTING A POST-AND-RAIL FENCE

A simple ranch-style fence is no more than a series of horizontal rails fixed to short posts concreted into the ground in the normal way. A picket fence is made in a similar way, but with vertical pales fixed to the rails.

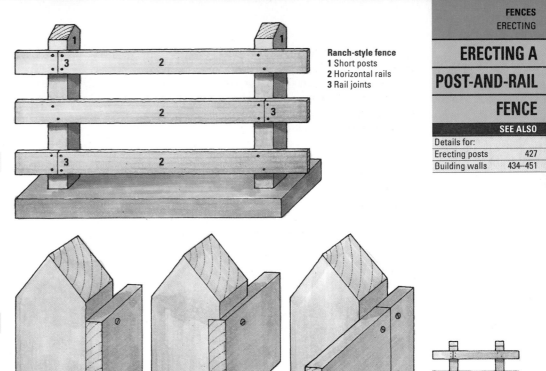

Ranch-style fence
1 Short posts
2 Horizontal rails
3 Rail joints

Fixing horizontal rails

You can simply screw the rails directly to the posts (**1**), but the fence will last longer if you cut a shallow notch in the post to locate each rail before you fix it permanently (**2**).

Join two rails by butting them over a post (**3**). Arrange to stagger these joints so that you don't end up with all the rails butted on the same post (**4**).

Fixing picket panels

When you construct a picket fence from ready-made panels, buy or make metal brackets for fixing two panels to a single post.

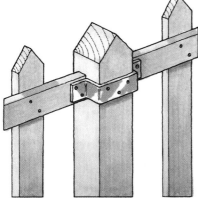

Use a metal bracket to fix picket-fence panels

1 Screw rail to post   **2 Or notch it first**   **3 Butt rails on posts**   **4 Stagger rail joints**

Supporting a rotted post

A buried timber post will quite often rot below ground level, leaving a perfectly sound section above. To save buying a whole new post, brace the upper section with a concrete spur.

Erecting a spur
Dig the soil from around the post and remove the rotted stump. Insert the spur and pack hardcore around it (**1**), then fill with concrete (**2**). Drill pilot holes for coach screws – woodscrews with hexagonal heads (**3**). Insert the screws with a spanner to draw the post tightly against the spur.

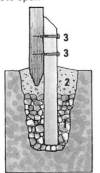

ERECTING FENCES ON SLOPING GROUND

Crossways slope
If a slope runs across the garden, so that your neighbour's garden is higher than yours, build brick retaining walls between the posts or set paving stones in concrete to hold back the soil.

Downhill slope
The posts must be set vertically even when you erect a fence on a sloping site. Chain-link fencing or ranch-style rails can follow the slope of the land if you wish, but fence panels should be stepped and the triangular gaps beneath filled with gravel boards or retaining walls.

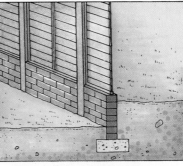

A retaining wall for a crossways slope

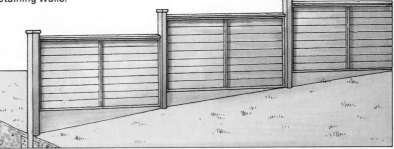

Step fence panels to allow for a downhill slope

● **Building plastic fences**
The basic construction of a plastic ranch-style fence is similar to one built from timber, but follow the manufacturer's instructions concerning the method for joining rails to posts.

431

GATES: CHOOSING

There are several points to consider when choosing a gate, not the least the cost. All gates are relatively expensive, but don't buy one merely because it is cheaper than another; a gate must be sturdy if it is to be durable. It must also be mounted on strong posts.

Choose a style of gate which matches the fence or complements the wall from which it is hung, with due consideration for the character of the house and its surroundings. If in doubt, aim for simplicity.

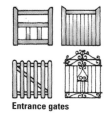

Side gates

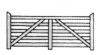

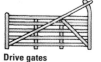

Entrance gates

Drive gates

GATES FOR DIFFERENT LOCATIONS

When you browse through suppliers' catalogues you will find gates grouped according to their intended location, because it is where it is to be sited that has most influence on the design of a gate and which dictates its function.

Side gates

A side gate is designed to protect a pathway next to a house from intruders. Side gates are invariably 2m (6ft 6in) high and are made from wrought iron or stout sections of timber. Wooden gates are heavy and are therefore braced with strong diagonal members to keep them rigid. With security in mind, choose a closeboarded or tongued-and-grooved gate as vertical boards are difficult to climb. When you hang a side gate, fit strong bolts top and bottom.

Entrance gates

An entrance gate is designed as much for its appearance as its function, but because it is in constant use, make sure it is properly braced with a diagonal strut running from the top of the latch stile down to the bottom of the hanging or hinge stile. If you hang a gate with the strut running the other way, the bracing will have no effect whatsoever.

Common fence structures are reflected in the style of entrance gates. Picket, closeboard and ranch-style gates are available, plus a simple and attractive frame-and-panel gate. With the latter style of gate, the solid timber or exterior-grade plywood panels keep the frame rigid. If the tops of both stiles are cut at an angle they will shed rainwater, reducing the likelihood of wet rot – a small, but important, feature to note when buying a wooden gate.

Decorative iron gates are often used for entrances, but make sure the style is not too ostentatious for the building or its location. A very elaborate gate might look ridiculous in the entrance of a simple modern house or a traditional country cottage.

Drive gates

First decide whether hanging a gate across a drive to a garage is a good idea. Parking the car in a busy road in order to open the gate can be a difficult manoeuvre unless you have enough room to set the gate back from the entrance, leaving enough space to pull the car off the road even when the gate is closed. Gates invariably open into the property, so make sure there is enough ground clearance for a wide gate if the drive slopes up. An alternative is to hang two smaller gates to meet in the centre. If you decide on a wide gate, choose a traditional five-bar gate for both strength and appearance.

Gate posts and piers

Gate posts and masonry piers have to take a great deal of strain, so they must be both strong and anchored securely in the ground.

Choose hardwood posts whenever possible, and select the section according to the weight of the gate: 100mm (4in) square posts are adequate for entrance gates, but use 125mm (5in) posts for 2m (6ft 6in) high gates. For a gate across a drive, choose 150mm (6in) or even 200mm (8in) square posts.

Concrete posts are a possibility, but unless you find a post predrilled to accept hinges and catch, you will have to screw them to a strip of timber bolted securely to the post.

Square or cylindrical tubular-steel metal posts are available with hinge pins, gate-stop and catch welded in place. Like metal gates, they must be protected from rust with paint unless they have been coated with plastic at the factory.

A pair of masonry piers is another possibility. Each pier should be a minimum of 328mm (1ft 1½in) square and built on a firm concrete footing. For large, heavy gates, the hinge pier at least should be reinforced with a metal rod buried in the footing and running centrally through the pier.

HARDWARE FOR GATES

A range of specialized hardware has been developed to allow for the considerable strain that a garden gate imposes on its hinges and catch.

Hinges

Strap hinges
Side gates and most wooden entrance gates are hung on strap hinges, or T-hinges. Screw the long flap horizontally to the gate rails and the vertical flap to the face of the post. Heavier gates need a stronger version bolted through the top rail.

Wide drive gates need a double strap hinge with a long flap bolted on each side of the top rail. These heavy-duty hinges are supported by bolts which pass through the gate post.

Hinge pins
Metal collars, welded to the hinge side of metal gates, drop over hinge pins attached to gate posts in a variety of ways: screw-fixed to timber posts; bolted through concrete; built into the mortar joints of masonry piers; welded to metal posts. The gate can be lifted off its hinges at any time unless you reverse the top pin or drill a hole and fit a split pin and washer.

Latches

Automatic latches
Simple wooden gates are fitted with a latch that operates automatically as the gate is closed. Screw the latch bar to the latch stile of the gate and use it to position the latch on the post.

Thumb latches
Cut a slot through a closeboard side gate for the latch lifter of a thumb latch. Pass the lifter bar (sneck) through the slot and screw the handle to the front of the gate. Screw the latch beam to the inner face so that the sneck releases the beam from the hooked keeper.

Ring latches
A ring latch works in a similar way to a thumb latch, but is operated from inside only by twisting the ring handle to lift the latch beam.

Chelsea catches
Bolt a Chelsea catch through a drive gate. The latch pivots on the bolt to drop into a slot in the catch plate screwed to the post.

Loop-over catches
When two wide gates are used in a drive entrance, one gate is fixed with a drop bolt located in a socket concreted into the ground. A simple U-shaped metal bar, bolted through the latch stile of the other gate, drops over the stile of the fixed gate.

Strap hinge

Heavy-duty strap hinge

Double strap hinge

LATCH BEAM

KEEPER

SNECK

Hinge pin

Automatic latch

Thumb latch

Ring latch

Chelsea catch

Loop-over catch

Materials for gates

Many wooden gates are made from relatively cheap softwood, but a wood such as cedar or oak is a better investment. Most so-called wrought-iron gates are made from mild-steel bar which must be primed and painted if it is to last any time at all.

Hang a heavy drive gate on a stout post

Gate posts are set in concrete like ordinary fence posts, but the post holes are linked by a concrete bridge to provide extra support.

Entrance-gate posts

Lay the gate on the ground with a post on each side. Check that the posts are parallel and the required distance apart to accommodate hinges and catch. Nail two horizontal battens from post to post and another diagonally to keep the posts in line while you erect them (**1**).

Dig a 300mm (1ft) wide trench across the entrance. Make it long enough to accept both posts. It need be no deeper than 300mm (1ft) in the centre, but dig an adequate post hole at each end: 450mm (1ft 6in) deep for a low entrance gate; 600mm (2ft) deep for a taller side gate. Set the battened gate posts in the holes with hardcore and concrete as for fence posts, using temporary battens to hold them upright until the concrete sets (**2**). Fill the trench with concrete at the same time and either level it flush with the pathway or allow for the thickness of paving slabs or blocks.

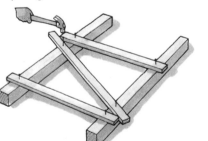

1 Nail temporary struts to the gate posts

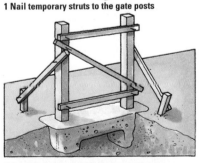

2 Support the posts until the concrete sets

Drive-gate posts

Hang wide farm-style gates on posts set in 900mm (3ft) deep holes (**3**). Erect the latch post in concrete like any fence post, but bolt a stout piece of timber across the base of the hinge post before anchoring it in concrete.

---

3 Drive-gate post
Bolt a balk of timber to the post to help support the weight of the gate.

433

MASONRY: BUILDING WALLS

Whatever structure you build with masonry, the basic techniques for laying brick, stone or concrete blocks remain the same. It pays to hire a professional builder when the structure is complicated or extensive, or if it will have to bear considerable loads or stress.

A stone-built retaining wall

A boundary wall of yellow brick

Facing blocks make attractive dividing walls

A decorative pierced-block screen

Amateur bricklaying

It is difficult to suggest when a particular job is beyond the level of skill or confidence of an amateur bricklayer as this differs from one individual to another. It would be foolhardy for anyone to attempt to build a two-storey house, for example, unless they had had a lot of experience and, possibly, professional tuition; even building a high boundary wall, which in terms of pure technique is simple, would be an arduous task if it were very long or had to allow for changes in gradient. The simple answer is to begin with low retaining or dividing walls and screens until you have mastered the skills of laying bricks and blocks solidly upon one another, and developed the ability to build a wall that is sound, straight and absolutely vertical.

WALLS FOR DIFFERENT LOCATIONS

Retaining walls

Raised planting beds are made by means of low 'retaining' walls, although a true retaining wall is designed to hold back a bank of earth, usually to terrace a sloping site. Provided it is not too high a retaining wall is quite easy to build, although strictly speaking it should slope back into the bank to resist the weight of the earth. You must also allow for drainage in order to reduce the water pressure behind the wall. Retaining walls are built with bricks, concrete blocks or stone, and are sometimes dry-laid with earth packed into the crevices for planting – it is a matter of personal choice.

Boundary walls

A brick or stone wall surrounding your property provides security and privacy while forming an attractive background to trees and shrubs. New brickwork complements a formal garden or modern setting, while second-hand materials or undressed stone blend well with an old, established garden. If you cannot quite match the colour of existing masonry, encourage the growth of lichen with a wash of liquid fertilizer or disguise the junction with a climbing plant. You will need to apply for local-authority approval if you want to build a wall higher than 1m (3ft 3in) adjoining a highway or 2m (6ft 6in) elsewhere.

Dividing walls

Many gardeners divide a plot of land with walls to form a visual break between patio and lawn, to define the edges of pathways, or simply to add interest to an otherwise featureless site. Dividing walls are often merely 'dwarf' walls, perhaps 600 to 750mm (2 to 2ft 6in) in height.

Use simple concrete block or brick walls to divide spaces inside your workshop or garage.

Screen walls

Screens are also dividing walls, which provide a degree of privacy without completely masking the garden beyond. They are built with decorative pierced blocks, often with solid-block or brick bases and concrete piers.

Structural walls

The walls of even a small building have to support the weight of a roof and, depending on the complexity of the structure, incorporate doorframes and window frames. In most cases a damp-proof course will have to be built into the walls to prevent rising damp; some walls are constructed with a cavity between two leaves of masonry to provide insulation and weatherproofing. A brick foundation for a glazed conservatory is no more difficult to build than a simple garden wall, but make certain you are familiar with building methods before you attempt to build a garage or similar outbuilding.

The names given to bricks refer to their district of origin, where a particular clay will impart a distinctive colour, or are simply chosen by the manufacturer to suggest the continuation of that tradition. Typical examples are London stocks, Pennines, Leicester reds, Blue Staffs and so on. What is important to the builder is the variety, quality and type of brick, and, particularly when matching existing masonry, the colour and texture.

The variety of brick

Facings
Facings are suitable for any type of exposed brickwork. They are water-resistant and frost-resistant. Being visible, facings are made as much for their appearance as their structural qualities and, as such, are available in a wide range of colours and textures. They are made to specific standards of strength and water-absorption and are uniform in size.

Commons
Commons are cheap general-purpose bricks used primarily for internal brickwork which is to be plastered, or rendered if used externally. They are not colour-matched as carefully as facings, but the mottled effect of a wall built with commons is not unattractive.

Although they could be damaged by frost if used on an exposed site, commons are sometimes employed for garden walling.

Engineering bricks
Engineering bricks are exceptionally dense and strong. You are unlikely to need them for the average wall, but, because they are impervious to water, they have been used to construct a damp-proof course in some houses.

The quality of brick

Internal quality
Internal-quality bricks would not be very durable if they were exposed to weathering. Most commons are of internal quality only, so check before you buy them for use in the garden.

Ordinary quality
Ordinary-quality bricks are suitable for most external uses. They may suffer, however, if used for a wall exposed to frequent driving rain and frost, or for a retaining wall which holds back earth that is poorly drained.

Special quality
Special-quality bricks will withstand extreme weathering and frost. Most types of facing brick are available in this quality; they are especially suitable for walls in coastal areas.

Seconds
Seconds are second-hand rather than second-rate bricks. They should be cheaper than new bricks, but demand can inflate the price. Using seconds might be the only way you can match the colour of weathered brickwork.

Types of brick

Solid bricks
The majority of bricks are solid throughout, either flat on all surfaces or with a depression known as a 'frog' on one face. When filled with mortar, the frog keys the bricks.

Cored or perforated bricks
Cored bricks have holes through them, providing the same function as the frog. A wall made with cored bricks must be finished with a coping of solid bricks.

Special shapes
Specially shaped bricks are made for decorative brickwork. Master bricklayers use the full range to build arches, chamfered or rounded corners and curvilinear walls. A number of shaped bricks are made for coping garden walls.

SEE ALSO
Details for:
Coloured and
textured brick   436
Laying bricks   442–447

BUYING BRICKS

Ordering bricks
Bricks are normally sold by the thousand, but builders' merchants are usually willing to sell them in smaller quantities. It is cheaper to order them direct from the manufacturer, but only if you buy a sufficient load to make the delivery charge economical.

Estimating quantities
The size of a standard brick is 215 x 102.5 x 65mm (8½ x 4 x 2½in), but dimensions may vary by a few millimetres, even within the same batch of bricks. Manufacturers normally specify a nominal size which includes an additional 10mm (⅜in) to each dimension to allow for the mortar joint.

To calculate how many bricks you need, allow about 58 bricks for every square metre (48 per sq yd) of single-skin walling. Add a five per cent allowance for cutting and breakages.

Storing bricks
When the bricks are delivered, stack them carefully on a flat, dry base. Cover the bricks with polyethylene sheet or a tarpaulin until you are ready to use them in order to prevent them becoming saturated with rain, which could cause staining as well as an increased risk of frost damage to the mortar and the bricks themselves.

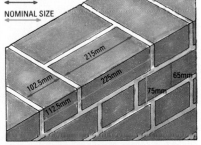

Nominal and actual size of bricks

Types of brick

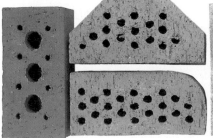
STANDARD CORED BRICK   BULLNOSE   DOUBLE-CANT COPING

STANDARD BRICK WITH FROG   SQUINT FOR SHAPED CORNER   HALF-ROUND COPING

THE COLOUR AND TEXTURE OF BRICKS

The popularity of brick as a building material stems largely from its range of subtle colours and textures, which actually improve with weathering. Weathered brick can be difficult to match by using a manufacturer's catalogue, so try to borrow samples from your supplier's stock or, if you have spare bricks, take one to the supplier to compare it with new bricks.

Colour

The colour of bricks is determined by the type of clay used in their manufacture, although it is modified by the addition of certain minerals and the temperature of the firing. Large manufacturers supply a wide variety of colours and there are also brindled (multi-coloured or mottled) bricks that are especially useful for blending with existing masonry.

Texture

Texture is as important to the appearance of a brick wall as colour. Simple rough or smooth textures are created by the choice of materials. Others are imposed upon the clay by scratching, rolling, brushing and so on. A brick may be textured all over or on the sides and ends only.

Brick colours and textures
A small selection from the extremely wide range of colours and textures.
1 Smooth blended
2 Handmade
3 Sand-faced yellow
4 Smooth blue engineering
5 Sand-faced grey
6 Smooth red stock
7 Wire-cut brindle
8 Textured multi-buff
9 Second London stock
10 Wire-cut blue
11 Red common
12 Coarse fletton
13 Moulded fletton
14 Dragwire multi-red

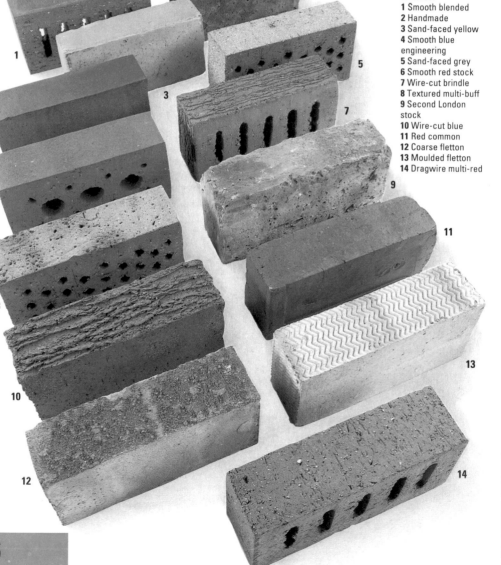

Pattern formed by projecting headers

Decorative combination of coloured bricks

Look out for second-hand moulded bricks

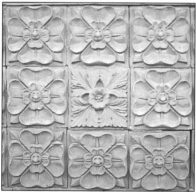

Sometimes whole panels are available

Weathered antique bricks are very attractive

SEE ALSO

Details for:
Blocks	438
Laying blocks	448–449

Cast-concrete building blocks are not as standardized as clay bricks, but describing them under the same specifications – that is, variety, quality and type – makes for a handy comparison when choosing which to use.

The variety of block

Structural blocks
Simple rectangular blocks, cement-grey or white in colour, are used as the structural core of a wall which will be rendered or plastered. Consequently, they are often made with a zig-zag key on the surface. As they are not intended to be visible, they have no aesthetic qualities at all. A wall can be built quickly with blocks because they are much larger than standard housebricks, and the cost will be relatively low.

Facing blocks
These are blocks with one decorative face and end for walls which are to be left exposed. They are often made to resemble natural stone by including crushed-stone aggregate. There is a range of colours to blend with the local stone in most areas of the country. Facing blocks are used for the external skin of cavity walls, backed by the cheaper structural blocks. They are also used for ornamental garden walling, for which matching coping slabs are available as a finishing touch.

Screen blocks
Screen blocks are pierced decorative building units for constructing a lightweight masonry trellis or screen. They are not bonded like brickwork or structural blocks and therefore require supporting piers made from matching pilaster blocks with locating channels to take the pierced blocks. Coping slabs finish the top of the screen and piers.

The quality of block

Loadbearing blocks
Structural blocks are used to construct the loadbearing walls of a building. Those made with lightweight aggregate are easier to handle, but when the loads are excessive, use stronger blocks made from dense concrete.

Non-loadbearing blocks
Non-loadbearing blocks are used to build internal, dividing partitions. They are either lightweight-aggregate blocks or low-density foamed-concrete blocks which are easy to cut to shape or chase for electrical wiring. Foamed blocks are also made in a loadbearing quality.

Decorative blocks
Screen blocks should not be used in the construction of loadbearing walls. However, they are capable of supporting a lightweight structure such as a timber-and-plastic carport roof.

Insulating blocks
Foamed blocks are often used for constructing the inner leaf of a cavity wall. They have good insulating properties and meet the minimum Building Regulation standards without the need for secondary insulation. Use ultra-light foamed blocks when improved insulation is required.

Types of block

Solid blocks
Solid blocks are constructed either with lightweight aggregate or with foamed concrete.

Cored blocks
To reduce their weight, large dense-concrete blocks are virtually hollow with supporting ribs between the outer skins. Stretcher blocks are used for the main part of the wall, while corner blocks are used when the end of a wall is exposed. The hollows can be reinforced with concrete. Solid-top blocks, partly hollowed out on the underside, are used to support joists.

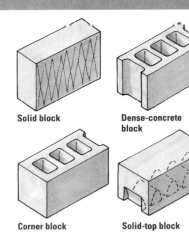

Solid block

Dense-concrete block

Corner block

Solid-top block

BUYING CONCRETE BLOCKS

Estimating quantities
Blocks are available in such a variety of sizes that in order to calculate the number required you must divide a given area of walling by the dimensions of a specific type. Blocks are sometimes specified in nominal sizes (also known as coordinating sizes), but with 10mm (⅜in) allowance for mortar on the length and height only. Block walls are normally constructed with one skin of masonry, so the thickness of a block remains as the actual size.

Available sizes
Structural blocks are normally 450mm (1ft 6in) long, with heights of 150 to 225mm (6 to 9in). Actual thicknesses range from 75 to 300mm (3 to 12in).

Although larger sizes are available, facing blocks are normally 100mm (4in) thick, with lengths of between 225 and 450mm (9in and 1ft 6in) and heights of between 75 and 150mm (3 and 6in).

Decorative screen blocks are invariably 300mm (1ft) square and 90mm (3½in) thick.

Storing blocks
When blocks are delivered have them unloaded as near as possible to the construction site to save time and reduce the possibility of damage in transit – they are quite brittle and chip easily. Stack them on a flat, dry base and protect them from rain and frost with a polyethylene sheet or tarpaulin.

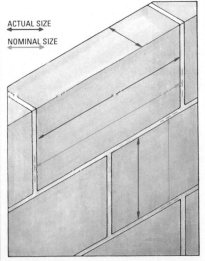

ACTUAL SIZE

NOMINAL SIZE

Sizes of structural blocks
The nominal size of a block refers to the length and height only. Thicknesses are always specified as an actual size.

BLOCKS AND STONES

Man-made blocks made from poured concrete are available in a variety of colours, shapes and sizes. Aesthetically, however, nothing can surpass quarried stone such as granite or sandstone. Whether it be roughly hewn or finely dressed, natural stone is durable and weathers well.

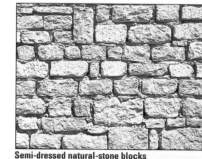

Semi-dressed natural-stone blocks

Split-stone walling

Dry-stone retaining wall

Knapped-flint boundary wall

Man-made concrete blocks

1 Solid dense concrete
2 Lightweight aerated
3 Lightweight aggregate
4 Pierced decorative
5 Solid decorative
6 Pitched-face reconstituted stone
7 Pilaster block
8 Pilaster coping
9 Multi-stone block
10 Screen coping
11 Split-face facing
12 Hewn-stone facing

CHOOSING NATURAL STONE

Practical considerations

In practical terms, the type of natural stone you choose for walling depends almost entirely on where you happen to live. In some parts of the country there are local restrictions governing the choice of building materials, and, in any case, a structure built from stone that is indigenous to the locality is more likely to blend into its surroundings. Buying stone from a local quarry also makes economical sense – transporting stone over long distances can be very costly.

Where to obtain stone

If you live in a large town or city, obtaining natural stone can be a real problem. You might be prepared to buy a few small boulders for a rockery from a local garden centre, but the cost of buying enough stone for even a short run of walling is likely to be prohibitive. If you don't want to use reconstituted stone – concrete facing blocks – your only alternative is to hire an open truck and drive to a quarry out of town.

Another source of materials, and possibly the cheapest way to obtain dressed stone, is to visit a demolition site. Prices vary considerably, but the cost of transport may be less than a trip to a quarry.

Estimating quantities

Most quarries sell stone by the tonne. When you have worked out the dimensions of the wall, telephone the nearest quarry for advice on quantity and a quote for the cost of the stone. Once you know the quantity you need you will be able to hire a truck of the appropriate capacity.

Types of stone

Limestone, sandstone and granite are all suitable materials for building walls. Flint and slate require specialized building methods and are often used in combination with other materials. Stone bought in its natural state is classed as random rubble (undressed); it is perfect for dry-stone walling in an informal garden setting. For a more regular form of masonry, ask for squared rubble (semi-dressed) stone which is cut into reasonably uniform blocks but with uneven surfaces, or ashlar (fully dressed stone with machine-cut faces). The cost of stone increases in proportion to its preparation.

SEE ALSO
Details for:
Cutting bricks   442

In the building of a wall, mortar is employed to bind together the bricks, concrete blocks or stones. The durability of a masonry wall depends upon the quality of the mortar used in its construction. If it is mixed correctly to the right consistency the mortar will become strong yet flexible, but if the ingredients are added in the wrong proportions it may be weak or, conversely, so hard that it is prone to cracking. If too much water is added to the mix the mortar will be squeezed out of the joints by the weight of the masonry, while if the mortar is too dry adhesion will be poor.

BRICKLAYERS' TERMS

Bricklayers use a number of specialized words and phrases to describe their craft and materials. Terms used frequently are listed below while others are described as they occur.

BRICK FACES *The surfaces of a brick.*
Stretcher faces The long sides of a brick.
Header faces The short ends of a brick.
Bedding faces The top and bottom surfaces.
Frog The depression in one bedding face.

COURSES *The individual, horizontal rows of bricks.*
Stretcher course A single course with stretcher faces visible.
Header course A single course with header faces visible.
Coping The top course designed to protect the wall from rainwater.
Bond Pattern produced by staggering alternate courses so that vertical joints are not aligned one above the other.
Stretcher A single brick from a stretcher course.
Header A single brick from a header course.
Closure brick The last brick laid in a course.

CUT BRICKS *Bricks cut with a bolster chisel to even up the bond.*
Bat A brick cut across its width, i.e. half-bat, three-quarter bat.
Queen closer A brick cut along its length.

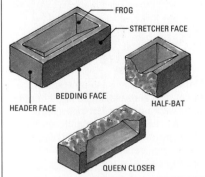

FROG
STRETCHER FACE
BEDDING FACE
HEADER FACE
HALF-BAT
QUEEN CLOSER

The ingredients of mortar

The ingredients of general-purpose mortar are cement, hydrated lime and sand, mixed with enough water to make a workable paste.

Cement is the hardening agent which binds the other ingredients together. The lime slows down the drying process and prevents the mortar setting too quickly. It also makes the mix flow well so that it fills gaps in the masonry and adheres to the texture of blocks or bricks. The sand acts as fine aggregate, adding body to the mortar, and reduces the possibility of shrinkage.

Use fine builders' sand for general-purpose mortar; if you want a paler mortar to bond white screen blocks, use silver sand.

Plasticizers
If you are laying masonry in a period of cold weather, substitute a proprietary plasticizer for the lime. Plasticizer produces aerated mortar in which the tiny air bubbles allow water to expand in freezing conditions, so reducing the risk of cracking. Premixed masonry cement, which has an aerating agent, is ready for mixing with sand.

Ready-mix mortar
Ready-mix mortar contains all the essential ingredients mixed to the correct proportions; you simply add water. It is a more expensive way of buying mortar but is convenient to use and available in small quantities.

Mixing mortar

Mortar must be used within two hours of mixing or discarded, so make only as much as you can use within that time. An average of about two minutes to lay one brick is a reasonable estimate.

Choose a flat site upon which to mix the materials – a sheet of plywood will do – and dampen it slightly to prevent it absorbing water from the mortar. Make a pile of half the amount of sand to be used, then add the other ingredients. Put the rest of the sand on top, and mix the dry materials thoroughly.

Scoop a depression in the pile and add clean tap water. Never use contaminated or salty water. Push the dry mix from around the edge of the pile into the water until it has absorbed enough for you to blend the mix with a shovel, using a chopping action. Add more water, little by little, until the mortar has a butter-like consistency, slipping easily from the shovel but firm enough to hold its shape if you make a hollow in the mix. If the sides of the hollow collapse, add more dry ingredients until the mortar firms up. Make sure the mortar is sufficiently moist; dry mortar won't form a strong bond with the masonry.

If mortar stiffens up while you are working, add just enough water to restore the consistency and dampen the mixing board again.

Proportions for masonry mixes

Mix the ingredients according to the prevailing conditions at the building site. Use a general-purpose mortar for moderate conditions where the wall is reasonably sheltered and a stronger mix for severe conditions where the wall will be exposed to wind and driving rain, or where the site is elevated or near the coast. If you are using plasticizer rather than lime, follow the manufacturer's instructions regarding the quantity you should add to the sand.

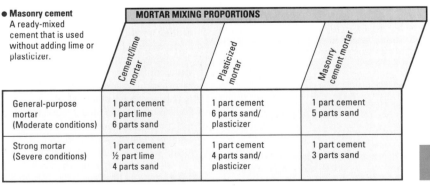

Correct consistency
The mortar mix should be firm enough to hold its shape when you make a depression in the mix.

● **Estimating quantity**
As a rough guide to estimating how much mortar you will need when building single-skin walls, allow approximately 1cu m (1⅓ cu yd) of sand (other ingredients in proportion) to lay: 3364 bricks; 1946 average concrete blocks; and 1639 decorative screen blocks.

● **Masonry cement**
A ready-mixed cement that is used without adding lime or plasticizer.

MORTAR MIXING PROPORTIONS	Cement/lime mortar	Plasticized mortar	Masonry cement mortar
General-purpose mortar (Moderate conditions)	1 part cement 1 part lime 6 parts sand	1 part cement 6 parts sand/ plasticizer	1 part cement 5 parts sand
Strong mortar (Severe conditions)	1 part cement ½ part lime 4 parts sand	1 part cement 4 parts sand/ plasticizer	1 part cement 3 parts sand

BONDING

BRICKWORK

DESIGNING A WALL FOR STABILITY

It is easy enough to appreciate the loads and stresses imposed upon the walls of a house or outbuilding, and therefore the necessity for solid foundations and adequate methods of reinforcement and protection to prevent them collapsing. It is not so obvious that even simple garden walling requires similar measures to ensure its stability. It is merely irritating if a low dividing wall or planter falls apart, but a serious injury could result from the collapse of a heavy bounr'ary wall.

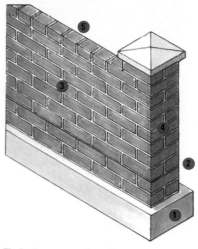

The basic structure of a wall
Unless you design and build a wall in the correct manner, it will not be strong and stable.

1 Footings
A wall must be built upon a solid concrete platform known as a strip footing. The dimensions of the footing vary according to the height and weight of the wall.

2 Damp-proof course
A layer of waterproof material 150mm (6in) above ground level stops water rising from the soil. It is not needed for most garden walling unless it abuts a building with a similar DPC. Not only does it protect the house from damp, but it reduces the likelihood of freezing water expanding and cracking the joints.

3 Bonding
The staggered pattern of bricks is not merely decorative. It is designed to spread the static load along the wall and to tie the individual units together.

4 Piers
Straight walls over a certain height and length must be buttressed at regular intervals with thick columns of brickwork known as piers. They resist the sideways pressure caused by high winds.

5 Coping
The coping prevents frost damage by shedding rainwater from the top of the wall where it could seep into the upper brick joints.

Mortar is extremely strong under compression, but its tensile strength is relatively weak. If bricks were stacked one upon the other so that the vertical joints were continuous, any movement within the wall would pull them apart and the structure would be seriously weakened. Bonding brickwork staggers the vertical joints, transmitting the load along the entire length of the wall. Try out the bond of your choice first by dry-laying just a few bricks before you embark upon the building work.

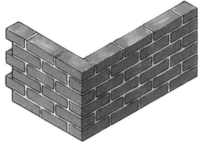

Stretcher bond
The stretcher bond is the simplest form of bonding and is used for single-thickness walls, including the two individual leaves of a cavity wall found in the construction of modern buildings. Half-bats are used to make the bond at the end of a straight wall, while a corner is formed by alternating headers and stretchers.

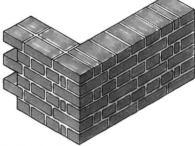

English bond
If you were to build a 215mm (8½in) thick wall by laying courses of stretcher-bonded bricks side by side, there would be a weak vertical joint running centrally down the wall. An English bond strengthens the wall by using alternate courses of headers. Staggered joints are maintained at the end of a wall and at a right-angle corner by inserting a queen closer before the last header.

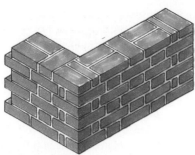

Flemish bond
The Flemish bond is another method used for building a solid, 215mm (8½in) thick wall. Every course is laid with alternate headers and stretchers. Stagger the joint at the end of a course and at a corner by laying a queen closer before the header.

Decorative bonds
Stretcher, English and Flemish bonds are designed to construct strong walls – decorative qualities are incidental. Other bonds, used primarily for their visual effect, are suitable for low, non-loadbearing walls only, supported by a conventionally bonded base and piers.

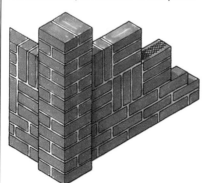

Stack bonding A basket-weave effect is achieved by stack-bonding bricks in groups of three. Strengthen the continuous vertical joints with wall ties.

Honeycomb bond Build an open, decorative screen using a stretcher-like bond with a quarter-bat-size space between each brick. Build the screen carefully to keep the bond regular, and cut quarter-bats to fill the gaps in the top course.

Stringent Building Regulations govern the size and reinforcement required for the footings to support high walls (and especially those that are structural). However, the majority of garden walls can be built upon concrete footings laid in a straight-sided trench.

Size of footings

The footing must be sufficiently substantial to support the weight of the wall, and the soil must be firm and well-drained to avoid possible subsidence. It is unwise to set footings in ground which has been filled recently, such as a new building site. Take care also to avoid tree roots and drainpipes. If the trench begins to fill with water as you are digging, seek professional advice before proceeding.

Dig the trench deeper than the footing itself so that the first one or two courses of brick are below ground level. This will allow for an adequate depth of soil for planting right up to the wall.

If the soil is not firmly packed when you reach the required depth, dig deeper until you reach a firm level, then fill the bottom of the trench with compacted hardcore up to the lowest level of the proposed footing.

RECOMMENDED DIMENSIONS FOR FOOTINGS

Type of wall	Height of wall	Thickness of footing	Width of footing
One brick thick	Up to 1m (3ft 3in)	150mm (6in)	300mm (1ft)
Two bricks thick	Up to 1m (3ft 3in)	225 to 300mm (9in to 1ft)	450mm (1ft 6in)
Two bricks thick	Over 1m up to 2m (Up to 6ft 6in)	375 to 450mm (1ft 3in to 1ft 6in)	450 to 600mm (1ft 6in to 2ft)
Retaining wall	Up to 1m (3ft 3in)	150 to 300mm (6in to 1ft)	375 to 450mm (1ft 3in to 1ft 6in)

Setting out the footings

For a straight footing, set up two profile boards made from 25mm (1in) thick timber nailed to stakes driven into the ground at each end of the proposed trench, but well outside the work area.

Drive nails into the top edge of each board and stretch lines between them to mark the front and back edges of the wall. Then drive nails into the boards on each side of the wall line to indicate the width of the footing and stretch more lines between them (1). When you are satisfied the setting out is accurate, remove the lines marking the wall but leave the nails so you can replace the lines when you come to lay the bricks.

Place a spirit level against the remaining lines to mark the edge of the footing on the ground (2). Mark the ends of the footing extending beyond the line of the wall by half the wall's thickness. Mark the edge of the trench on the ground with a spade and remove the lines. Leave the boards in place.

Turning corners
If your wall will have a right-angled corner, set up two sets of profile boards as before, checking carefully that the lines form a true right angle using the 3 : 4 : 5 principle (3).

Digging the trench
Excavate the trench, keeping the sides vertical, and check that the bottom is level, using a long, straight piece of wood and a spirit level.

Drive a stake into the bottom of the trench near one end until the top of the stake represents the depth of the footing. Drive in more stakes at about 1m (3ft) intervals, checking that the tops are level (4).

Filling the trench
Pour a foundation mix of concrete (see MIXING CONCRETE BY VOLUME) into the trench, then tamp it down firmly with a stout piece of timber until it is exactly level with the top of the stakes. Leave the stakes in place and allow the footing to harden thoroughly before building the wall.

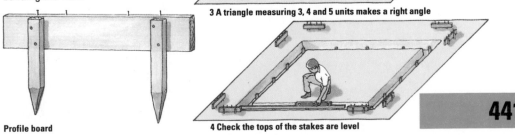

Profile board

SLOPING-SITE FOOTINGS

When the ground slopes gently, simply ignore the gradient and make the footing perfectly level. If the site slopes noticeably, make a stepped footing by placing plywood shuttering across the trench at regular intervals. Calculate the height and length of the steps using multiples of normal brick size.

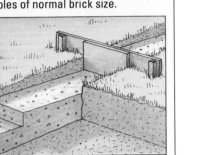

Support plywood shuttering with stakes

Section through a stepped footing
A typical stepped concrete footing with one of the plywood shuttering boards in place.

SEE ALSO
Details for:
Concrete mixes 455

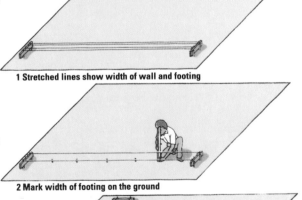

1 Stretched lines show width of wall and footing

2 Mark width of footing on the ground

3 A triangle measuring 3, 4 and 5 units makes a right angle

4 Check the tops of the stakes are level

LAYING BRICKS

BRICKLAYING TOOLS

While you can improvise a number of builder's tools, you will have to buy some of the more specialized tools that are used by bricklayers.

Tools for basic bricklaying
1 Club hammer 2 Spirit level 3 Bolster chisel
4 Pointing trowel 5 Brick trowel

Spreading a bed of mortar – throwing a line – requires practice before you can develop speed, so concentrate at first on laying bricks accurately. Mixing the mortar to exactly the right consistency helps to keep the visible faces of the bricks clean. In hot, dry weather dampen the footings and bricks, but let any surface water evaporate before you lay the bricks.

Bricklaying techniques

Hold the brick trowel with your thumb in line with the handle, pointing towards the tip of the blade (**1**).

Scoop a measure of mortar out of the pile and shape it roughly to match the dimensions of the trowel blade. Pick up the mortar by sliding the blade under the pile, setting it onto the trowel with a slight jerk of the wrist (**2**).

Spread the mortar along the top course by aligning the edge of the trowel with the centre line of the bricks. As you tip the blade to deposit the mortar, draw the trowel back towards you to stretch the bed over at least two to three bricks (**3**). Furrow the mortar by pressing the point of the trowel along the centre (**4**).

Pick up a brick with your other hand, but don't extend your thumb too far onto the stretcher face or it will disturb the builders' line (see right) every time you place a brick in position. Press the brick into the bed, picking up excess mortar squeezed from the joint by sliding the edge of the trowel along the wall (**5**).

With the mortar picked up on the trowel, butter the header of the next brick, making a neat 10mm (⅜in) bed for the header joint (**6**). Press the brick against its neighbour, scooping off excess mortar with the trowel.

Having laid three bricks, use a spirit level to check that they are horizontal. Make any adjustments by tapping them down with the trowel handle (**7**).

Hold the spirit level along the outer edge of the bricks to check that they are in line. To move a brick sideways without knocking it off its mortar bed, tap the upper edge with the trowel at about 45 degrees (**8**).

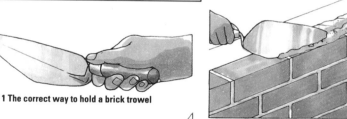

1 The correct way to hold a brick trowel

● **Cutting bricks**
To cut brick bats, use a bolster to mark the line on all faces by tapping gently with a hammer. Realign the blade on the visible stretcher face and strike the chisel firmly.

2 Scoop a measure of mortar onto the trowel

3 Stretch a bed of mortar along the course

4 Furrow the mortar with the trowel point

5 Push down brick and remove excess mortar

6 Butter the head of the next brick

7 Level the course of bricks with the trowel

8 Tap the bricks sideways to align them

BUILDING A STRETCHER-BONDED WALL

A single-width brick wall tends to look visually mean and, over a certain height, is also structurally weak unless it is supported with piers, or changes direction by forming right-angle corners. The ability to construct accurate right-angle corners is a requirement for building most structures, even simple garden planters. The main thing to remember is to keep checking and rechecking the alignment of the bricks.

Setting out the corners

Mark out the footings and face of the wall by stretching string lines between profile boards. When the footings have been filled and the concrete has set, use a plumb line or hold a level lightly against the line to mark the corners and the face of the wall on the footing (1). Join the marks with a pencil and straight batten, and check the accuracy of the corners with a builder's square. Stretch a line between the corner marks to check the alignment.

Building the corners

Build the corners first as a series of steps or 'leads' before filling between. It is essential that they form true right angles, so take your time.

Throw a bed of mortar, then lay three bricks in both directions against the marked line. Make sure that they are level in all directions, checking the diagonal by laying a spirit level between the end bricks (2).

Build the leads to a height of five stepped courses, using a gauge stick to measure the height of each course as you proceed (3). Use alternate headers and stretchers to form the actual point of the corner.

Use a level to plumb the corner, and check the alignment of the stepped bricks by holding the level against the side of the wall (4).

A stepped lead for a corner

1 Mark the face of the wall on the footing

2 Level the first course of bricks

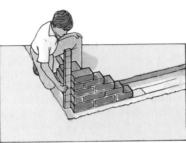

3 Check the height with a gauge stick

4 Check that the steps are in line

Building the straight sections

Stretch a builder's line between the corners so that it aligns perfectly with the top of the first course (5).

Lay the first straight course of bricks from both ends towards the middle. As you near the middle point, lay the last few bricks dry to make certain they will fit. If necessary, cut the central or 'closure' brick to fit. Mortar the bricks in place, finishing with the closure brick by spreading mortar onto both ends and onto the header faces of the bricks on each side (6). Scoop off excess mortar with the trowel.

Lay subsequent courses between the leads in the same way, raising the builder's line each time. To build the wall higher, raise the corners first by constructing leads to the required height, then fill the spaces between.

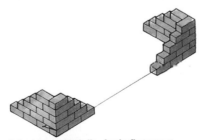

5 Stretch a builder's line for the first course

6 Carefully lay the last or closure brick

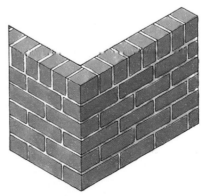

Coping the wall
You could finish the wall by laying the last course frog downwards, but a coping of half-bats laid on end looks more professional. Alternatively, use proprietary coping bricks or blocks.

● **Covering the wall**
Cover finished or partly built walls overnight with sheets of polyethylene or tarpaulin to protect the brickwork from rain or frost. Weight the edges of the covers with bricks.

● **Building a straight wall**
To build a straight wall without a corner, follow the procedure described left, building and loado straight stepped sections – at each end of the wall, then fill between with bricks.

443

POINTING

BRICKWORK

SEE ALSO
Details for:
Damp-proof course 257, 445
Engineering bricks   435

Pointing the mortar joints makes for a packed, watertight joint as well as enhancing the appearance of the wall. Well-struck joints and clean brickwork are essential if the wall is to look professionally built; for best results, the mortar must be shaped when it is just the right consistency.

The consistency of the mortar

If the mortar is still too wet the joint will not be crisp and you may drag mortar out from between the bricks. On the other hand, if it is left to harden too long, pointing will be hard work and you may leave dark marks on the joint.

Test the consistency of the mortar by pressing your thumb into a joint. If it holds a clear impression without sticking to your thumb the mortar is just right for pointing. Because it is so important that you shape the joint at exactly the right moment you may have to point the work in stages before you can complete the wall. Shape the joints to match existing brickwork or choose a profile that is suitable for the prevailing weather conditions.

How to make pointing joints

Flush joint
Having scraped the mortar flush with the edge of the trowel, stipple the joints with a stiff-bristle brush to expose the sand aggregate.

Rubbed (concave) joint
Buy a shaped jointing tool to make a rubbed joint, or improvise with a length of bent tubing. Flush the mortar first, then drag the tool along the joints. Finish the vertical joints, then do the horizontal ones. This is a utilitarian joint, ideal for a wall built with second-hand bricks which are not of a sufficiently good quality to take a crisp joint.

Shape the mortar with a jointing tool

V-joint
Produced in a similar way to the rubbed joint, the V-joint gives a very smart finish to new brickwork and sheds rainwater well.

Raked joint
Use a piece of wood or metal to rake out the joints to a depth of about 6mm (¼in), then compress them again by smoothing the mortar lightly with a lath or piece of rounded dowel rod. Raked joints do not shed water, so they are not suitable for an exposed site.

Weatherstruck joint
The angled weatherstruck joint is ideal, even in harsh conditions. Use a small pointing trowel to shape the vertical joints **(1)**. They can slope to the left or right, but be consistent throughout the same section of brickwork. Shape the horizontal joints allowing the mortar to spill out slightly at the base of each joint. Professionals finish the joint by cutting off excess mortar with a tool called a Frenchman, similar to a table knife but with the tip at 90 degrees. Improvise a similar tool with a strip of bent metal. Nail two scraps of plywood to a batten to hold it away from the wall. Align the batten with the bottom of the joint to guide the tool and make a neat, straight edge to the mortar **(2)**.

1 Shape a weatherstruck joint with a trowel

2 Remove excess mortar with a Frenchman

Brushing the brickwork
Let the shaped joints harden a little before you clean scraps of mortar from the face of the wall. Use a medium-soft banister brush, sweeping lightly across the joints so as not to damage them.

Flush joint

Rubbed joint

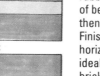

V-joint

Raked joint

Weatherstruck joint

● **Coloured mortar**
You can add coloured powders to your mortar mix. Make a trial batch to test the colour when dry. Rake out the joint and apply it carefully to avoid staining the bricks.

COPING FOR BRICK WALLS

The coping which forms the top course of the wall protects the brickwork from weathering and gives the wall a finished appearance. Strictly speaking, if the coping is flush with both faces of the wall it is called a capping; a true coping projects from the face so that water drips clear and does not leave a stain on the brickwork.

You can lay a coping of bricks with their stretcher faces across the width of the wall. Use the same type of brick as that employed in the construction of the wall, or engineering bricks – the water-resistant quality of the latter is an advantage and the colour contrasts pleasingly with regular brickwork. You can also obtain special coping bricks designed to shed rainwater

Stone or cast-concrete slabs are popular for garden walling. They are quick to lay and are wide enough to form low, bench-type seating.

On an exposed site, consider installing a damp-proof course under the coping to reduce the risk of frost attack. Use a standard bituminous-felt DPC or lay two courses of plain roof tiles with staggered joints and a brick coping above. Let the tiles project from the face of the wall, but run a sloping mortar joint along the top of the projection to shed water.

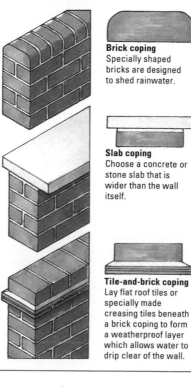

Brick coping
Specially shaped bricks are designed to shed rainwater.

Slab coping
Choose a concrete or stone slab that is wider than the wall itself.

Tile-and-brick coping
Lay flat roof tiles or specially made creasing tiles beneath a brick coping to form a weatherproof layer which allows water to drip clear of the wall.

When building new garden walls which intersect at right angles, either anchor them by bonding the brickwork (see below) or take the easier option and link them with wall ties at every third course. If the intersecting wall is over 2m (6ft 6in) in length, make the junction a control joint by using straight metal strips as wall ties.

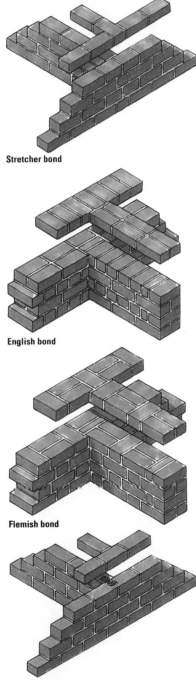

Stretcher bond

English bond

Flemish bond

Using a wall tie

Building up to an existing wall

When you build a new wall to intersect with the existing wall of a house you must include a damp-proof course to prevent water bridging the house DPC via the new masonry. You must also make a positive joint between the walls.

Inserting a DPC
Building Regulations require a damp-proof course in all habitable buildings to prevent rising damp. This consists of a layer of impervious material built into the mortar bed 150mm (6in) above ground level. When you build a new wall, its DPC must coincide with the DPC in the existing structure. Use a roll of bituminous felt chosen to match the thickness of the new wall.

Locate the house DPC and build the first few courses of the new wall up to that level. Spread a thin bed of mortar on the bricks and lay the DPC upon it with the end of the roll turned up against the existing wall (**1**). The next course of bricks will trap the DPC between the header joint and the wall. Lay more mortar on top of the DPC to produce the standard 10mm (⅜in) joint ready for laying the next course in the normal way. If you have to join rolls of DPC, overlap the ends by 150mm (6in).

Tying-in the new wall
The traditional method for linking a new wall with an existing structure involves chopping recesses in the brickwork at every fourth course. End bricks of the new wall are set into the recesses, bonding the two structures together (**2**). An alternative and much simpler method, however, is to screw to the wall a special stainless-metal channel which is designed to accept bricks or concrete blocks and provide anchoring points for standard wire wall ties. Channels are available for masonry units up to 215mm (8½in) thick.

Screw the channel to the old wall above the DPC with stainless-steel coachscrews and wall plugs, or use expanding bolts (**3**). While it is not essential, it is advisable to trap 1m (3ft 3in) of DPC felt behind the channel.

Mortar the end of a brick before feeding it into the channel (**4**). As the brick is pushed home, the mortar squeezes through the perforated channel to make a firm bond.

At every third course, hook a wall tie over the pressed lugs in the channel and bed it firmly into the mortar joint (**5**).

1 Lap the existing DPC with the new roll

2 You can tooth the wall into the brickwork

3 But it is easier to use a special channel

4 Locate the ends of the bricks in the channel

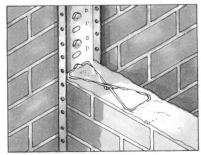

5 Hook wire wall ties over the pressed lugs

DPC on a sloping site
When the site slopes noticeably, the wall footing is stepped to keep the top of the wall level. If you include a DPC in the wall, that too must follow the line of the steps to keep it the required height above ground level.

BRICKWORK

PIERS

A pier is, strictly speaking, a freestanding column of masonry which may be used, for example, as a support for a porch or a pergola or as an individual gatepost. When a column is built as part of a wall, it is more accurately termed a pilaster. In practice, however, the word 'column' is often used to cover either description. To avoid confusion, any supporting brick column will be described here as a pier. Thorough planning is essential when building piers.

Structural considerations

Any freestanding straight wall over a certain length and height must be buttressed at regular intervals by piers. Sections of walling and piers must be tied together, either by a brick bond or by inserting metal wall ties in every third course of bricks. Any single-width brick wall, whatever its height, would benefit from supporting piers at open ends and gateways where it is most vulnerable; these will also improve the appearance of the wall. Piers over 1m (3ft 3in), and especially those supporting gates, should be built around steel reinforcing rods set in the concrete footings. Whether reinforcing is included or not, allow for the size of piers when designing the footings.

Designing the piers

Piers should be placed no more than 3m (9ft 9in) apart in walls over a certain height (see the chart below). The wall itself can be flush with one face of a pier, but the structure is stronger if it is centred on the pier.

Piers should be a minimum of twice the thickness of a 102.5mm (4in) thick wall, but build 328mm (1ft 1½in) square piers when reinforcement is required, such as for gateways, and to buttress 215mm (8½in) thick walls.

INCORPORATING PIERS IN A BRICK WALL		
Thickness of wall	Maximum height without piers	Maximum pier spacing
102.5mm (4in)	450mm (1ft 6in)	3m (9ft 9in)
215mm (8½)	1.35m (4ft 6in)	3m (9ft 9in)

BONDING PIERS

If you prefer the appearance of bonded-brick piers, construct them as shown below. It is easier, however, to use wall ties to reinforce continuous vertical joints in the brickwork, especially when building walls centred on piers.

Various types of galvanized-metal wall ties are available: wire bent into a butterfly shape (1); stamped-metal steel strips with forked ends, known as fish tails (2); and expanded-metal mesh cut in straight strips (3).

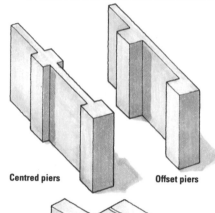

Centred piers   Offset piers

Bonding piers
While it is simpler to tie a wall to a pier with wall ties (see above right), it is relatively easy to bond a pier into a wall that is of single-brick width.

Colour key
You will have to cut certain bricks to bond a pier into a straight wall. Whole bricks are coloured with a light tone, three-quarter bats with a medium tone, and half-bats with a dark tone.

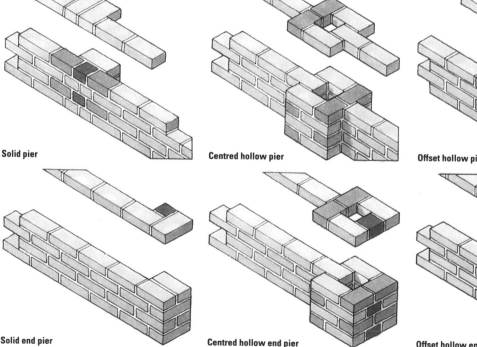
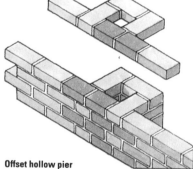
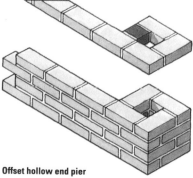

Solid pier   Centred hollow pier   Offset hollow pier

Solid end pier   Centred hollow end pier   Offset hollow end pier

BUILDING
PIERS

Mark out accurately the positions of piers and the face of the wall on the concrete footing. Lay the first course for the piers using a builder's line stretched between two stakes to align them **(1)**. Adjust the position of the line if necessary and fill in between with the first straight course, working from both ends towards the middle **(2)**. Build alternate pier and wall courses,

checking the level and the vertical faces and corners of the piers. At the third course, push metal wall ties into the mortar bed to span the joint between wall and pier **(3)**. Continue in the same way to the required height of the wall, then raise the piers to their required height **(4)**. Lay a coping along the wall and cap the piers with concrete or stone slabs **(5)**.

1 Lay pier bases
Stretch a builder's line to position the bases of the piers.

2 Lay first wall course
Use the line to keep the first course straight.

3 Lay pier ties
Join the piers to the wall by inserting wall ties into every third course. Put a tie into alternate courses for a gate-supporting pier.

4 Raise the piers
Build the piers higher than the wall to allow for a decorative coping along the top course.

5 Lay the coping
Lay coping slabs and cap the piers.

Incorporating control joints

Although it is not noticeable, a brick wall moves constantly as a result of ground settlement as well as expansion and contraction of the materials. Over short distances the movement is so slight that it has hardly any effect on the brickwork, but in a long wall it can crack the structure. To compensate for this movement, build unmortared, continuous vertical joints into a wall at intervals of about 6m (19ft 6in). Although these control joints can be placed in a straight section of walling, it is neater and more convenient to place them where the wall meets a pier. Build the pier and wall as normal, but omit the mortar from the header joints of the wall. Instead of inserting standard wall ties, embed a flat, 3mm (⅛in) thick galvanized strip in the mortar bed. Lightly grease one half of the strip with motor grease or petroleum jelly so that it can slide lengthwise to allow for movement yet still key the wall and pier together. When the wall is complete, fill the joint from both sides with mastic.

Adding reinforcement

Use 16mm (⅝in) steel reinforcing bars to strengthen brick piers. If the pier is under 1m (3ft 3in) in height, use one continuous length of bar **(1)**; for taller piers, embed a bent 'starter' bar in the footing, projecting a minimum of 500mm (1ft 8in) above the level of the concrete **(2)**. As the work proceeds, use galvanized wire to bind extension bars to the projection of the starter bar up to within 50mm (2in) of the top of the pier. Fill in around the reinforcement with concrete as you build the pier, but pack it very carefully so that you do not disturb the brickwork.

Making a control joint
Tie the pier to the wall with galvanized-metal strips when making a control joint (shown here before it is set in mortar). The mastic is squeezed into the joint between the wall and the pier.

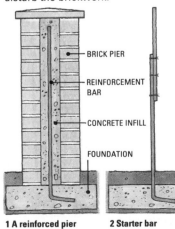

BRICK PIER

REINFORCEMENT BAR

CONCRETE INFILL

FOUNDATION

1 A reinforced pier   **2 Starter bar**

447

BUILDING WITH CONCRETE BLOCKS

The methods for laying concrete blocks are much the same as for building with bricks. Block walls need similar concrete footings and the same type of mortar, although heavy blocks should be laid with a firm mix to resist the additional weight of the freshly constructed wall. As blocks are made in a greater variety of sizes, you can build a wall of any thickness with a simple stretcher bond. However, don't dampen concrete blocks before laying them – wet blocks can shrink and crack the mortar joints as the wall dries out. When you are building decorative walls with facing blocks use any of the pointing styles described for bricks, but flush-joint a wall built with structural blocks which is to be rendered or plastered by rubbing the joints with sacking.

● **Building piers**
High, free-standing garden walls constructed from blocks must be supported by piers at 3m (9ft 9in) intervals.

CONTROL JOINTS

Walls over 6m (19ft 6in) long should be built with a continuous vertical control joint to allow for expansion. Place an unmortared joint in a straight section of wall or against a pier, and bridge the gap with galvanized-metal dowels as for brickwork. Fill the gap with mastic.

If you need to insert a control joint in a dividing wall, form the joint between the doorframe and wall. Fill the joints with mortar in the normal way, but rake them out to a depth of 18mm (¾in) round one end of the lintel and vertically to the ceiling on both sides of the wall. Fill the control joint flush with mastic.

Forming a control joint next to a door opening
Take the joint around the lintel and up to the ceiling on both sides of the wall.

Building a dividing wall

Building a non-loadbearing stud partition is the usual method employed for dividing up a large internal space into smaller rooms, but if your house is built on a concrete pad, a practical alternative is to use concrete blocks. If you install a doorway in the dividing wall, plan its position to avoid cutting away too many blocks. Allow for the wooden doorframe and lining as well as a precast lintel to support the masonry above the opening. Fill the space above the lintel with cut blocks or bricks to level the courses.

Screw galvanized pressed-metal channels to the existing structure to support each end of the dividing wall. Plumb them accurately or the new wall will be out of true. Lay the first course of blocks without mortar across the room to check their spacing and the position of a doorway if it is to be included. Mark the positions of the blocks before building stepped leads at each end as for brickwork. Check for accuracy with a spirit level, then fill in between the leads with blocks.

Build another three courses of blocks, anchoring the end blocks to the channels with wall ties in every joint. Leave the mortar to harden overnight before you continue with the wall.

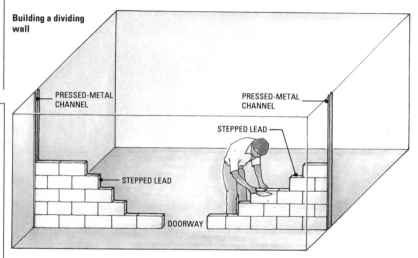

Building a dividing wall

PRESSED-METAL CHANNEL

PRESSED-METAL CHANNEL

STEPPED LEAD

STEPPED LEAD

DOORWAY

Building intersecting walls

Butt intersecting garden walls together with a continuous vertical joint between them, but anchor the structure as for brickwork with wire-mesh wall ties (**1**). If you build a wall with heavyweight hollow blocks, use stout metal tie bars with a bend at each end. Fill the block cores with mortar to embed the ends of the bars (**2**). Install a tie in every course.

1 **Wire-mesh wall ties for solid blocks** ▶
2 **Metal tie bar for hollow blocks**

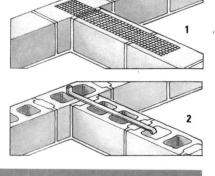

Cutting blocks

To cut a concrete block, use a bolster chisel and straightedge to score a line right round it. Deepen the line into a groove by striking the chisel sharply with a club hammer, working your way round the face of the concrete block until it eventually fractures along the chiselled groove.

Cutting a block
Use a bolster and club hammer to cut a block.

Basic bricklaying techniques and tools are used to build a pierced concrete screen, but because the blocks are stack-bonded – with continuous vertical joints – the wall must be reinforced vertically with 16mm (⅝in) steel bars, and horizontally with galvanized mesh if it is built higher than 600mm (2ft). Build the screen with supporting piers no more than 3m (9ft 9in) apart, using matching pilaster blocks. Alternatively, if you prefer the appearance of contrasting masonry, construct a base and piers from bricks or facing blocks.

Constructing the screen

Set out and fill the footings twice the width of the pilaster blocks. Embed pier-reinforcing bars in the concrete and support them with guy ropes until the concrete sets.

Lower a pilaster block over the first bar, setting it onto a bed of mortar laid around the base of the bar. Check the block is perfectly vertical and level, and that its locating channel faces the next pier. Pack mortar or concrete into its core, then proceed with two more blocks so that the pier corresponds to the height of two mortared screen blocks (1). Construct each pier in the same way. Intermediate piers will have a locating channel on each side.

Allow the mortar to harden overnight, then lay a mortar bed for two screen blocks next to the first pier. Butter the vertical edge of a screen block and press it into the pier locating channel. Tap it into the mortar bed and check it is level. Mortar the next block

and place it alongside the first. When buttering screen blocks, take special care to keep the faces clean by making a neat, chamfered bed of mortar on each block (3).

Lay two more blocks against the next pier, stretch a builder's line to gauge the top edge of the first course, then lay the rest of the blocks towards the centre, making sure the vertical joints are aligned perfectly. Before building any higher, embed a wire reinforcing strip running from pier to pier in the next mortar bed (4). Continue to build the piers and screen up to a maximum height of 2m (6ft 6in), inserting a wire strip into alternate courses. Finally, lay coping slabs on top of each pier and along the top of the screen (5).

If you don't like the appearance of ordinary mortar joints, rake out some of the mortar and repoint with mortar made with silver sand. A concave rubbed joint suits decorative screening.

1 Build the piers

2 Fit block to pier

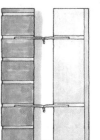

3 Butter edge of block

4 Lay a wire reinforcing strip into the mortar

5 Lay coping slabs along the wall

CAVITY WALLS

Cavity walls are used in the construction of habitable buildings to prevent the passage of moisture through the wall to the interior. This is achieved by building two independent leaves of masonry with a clear gap between them. The gap provides a degree of thermal insulation, but the insulation value increases appreciably if an efficient insulant is introduced to the cavity. The exterior leaf of most cavity walls is constructed with facing bricks. The inner leaf is sometimes built with interior-grade bricks, but more often with concrete blocks. Whatever type of masonry is used, both leaves must be tied together with wall ties spanning the gap. Cavity walls are likely to be loadbearing, so have to be built very accurately – hire a professional for this job. Make sure he or she includes a DPC in both leaves and avoids dropping mortar into the gap; if mortar collects at the base of the cavity, or even on one of the wall ties, moisture can bridge the gap and cause damp on the inside.

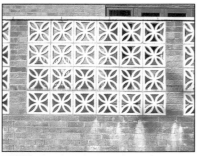

Cavity-wall construction
A section through a typical cavity wall built with an exterior leaf of bricks tied to an inner leaf of plastered concrete blocks.

Building a brick base and piers
You can construct a wall using a combination of bricks and screen blocks. Build a low base of bricks with reinforced piers spaced so as to accord with the size of the blocks. Build up the piers and the screen blocks together and tie them with reinforcing strips as described left, inserting standard wall ties in alternate courses to provide additional location and support.

BUILDING
WITH STONE

Constructing garden walling with natural stone requires a different approach to that needed for bricklaying or building with concrete blocks. A stone wall must be as stable as one built with any other masonry, but its visual appeal relies on the coursing being less regular; indeed, there is no real coursing when a wall is built with undressed stone or rubble.

Structural considerations

Stone walls don't necessarily require mortar to hold the stones together, although it is often used, especially with dressed or semi-dressed stone, to provide additional stability. As a result, many stone walls taper, having a wide base of heavy, flat stones and gradually decreasing in width as the wall rises.

This traditional form of construction was developed to prevent a wall of unmortared stones toppling sideways when subjected to high winds or the weight of farm animals. Far from detracting from its appearance, this informal construction suits a country-style garden perfectly.

Building a dry-stone wall

A true dry-stone wall is built without mortar, relying instead on a selective choice of stones and careful placement to provide stability. Experience is needed for perfect results, but there is no reason why you cannot introduce mortar, particularly within the core of the wall, and still maintain the appearance of dry-stone walling. You can also bed the stones in soil, packing it firmly into the crevices as you lay each course. This enables you to plant alpines or other suitable rockery plants in the wall, even during construction.

When you select the masonry, look out for flat stones in a variety of sizes and make sure you have some large enough to run the full width of the wall, especially at the base of the structure. These 'bonding' stones, placed at regular intervals, are important components which tie the loose rubble into a cohesive structure. Even a low wall will inevitably include some heavy stones. When you lift them, keep your back straight and your feet together, using the strong muscles of your legs to take the strain.

Constructing the wall

Assuming you are using soil as a jointing material, spread a 25mm (1in) layer over the footing and place a substantial bonding stone across the width to form the bed of the first course (1). Lay other stones about the same height as the bonding stone along each side of the wall, pressing them down into the soil to make a firm base. It is worth stretching a builder's line along each side of the wall to help you make a reasonably straight base.

Lay smaller stones between to fill out the base of the wall (2), then pack more soil into all the crevices.

Spread another layer of soil on top of the base and lay a second course of stones, bridging the joints between the stones below (3). Press them down so that they angle inwards towards the centre of the wall. Check by eye that the coursing is about level as you build

DESIGNING THE WALL

A dry-stone wall must be 'battered' – in other words, it must have a wide base and sides that slope inwards. For a wall about 1m (3ft 3in) in height (it is risky to build a dry-stone wall any higher) the base should be no less than 450mm (1ft 6in) wide. You should aim to provide a minimum slope of 25mm (1in) for every 600mm (2ft) of height.

Traditionally, the base of this type of wall rests on a 100mm (4in) bed of sand laid on compacted soil at the bottom of a shallow trench. For a more reliable foundation, lay a 100mm (4in) concrete footing, making it about 100mm (4in) wider than the wall on each side.

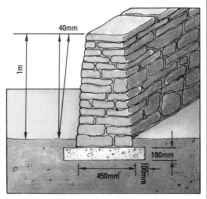

Proportions of a stone-built wall

the wall and remember to include bonding stones at regular intervals.

Introduce plants into the larger crevices or, alternatively, hammer smaller stones into the chinks to lock the large stones in place (4).

At the top of the wall, either fill the core with soil for plants or lay large, flat coping stones, firming them with packed soil. Finally, brush loose soil from the faces of the wall.

1 Lay a bonding stone at the end of the wall

2 Fill out the base with small stones

3 Lay a second course of stones

4 Fill the chinks

Retaining walls are designed to hold back a bank of earth, but don't attempt to cut into a steep bank and restrain it with a single high wall. Apart from the obvious dangers of the wall collapsing, terracing the slope with a series of low walls is a more attractive solution which offers opportunities for imaginative planting.

Choosing your materials

Bricks and concrete blocks are perfectly suitable materials to choose for constructing a retaining wall, provided it is sturdily built. It is best to support these walls with reinforcing bars buried in the concrete footing. Run the bars through hollow core blocks (1) or build a double skin of brickwork, rather like a miniature cavity wall, using wall ties to bind each skin together (2).

The mass and weight of natural stone make it ideal for retaining walls. The wall should be battered to an angle of 50mm (2in) to every 300mm (1ft) of height so that it virtually leans into the bank (3). Keep the height below 1m (3ft 3in) for safety. A skilful builder could construct a dry-stone retaining wall perfectly safely, but it pays to use mortar for additional rigidity.

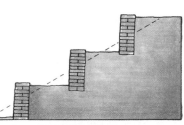
Terracing with retaining walls

1 A retaining wall of hollow concrete blocks

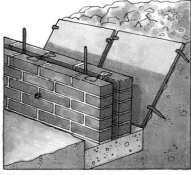
2 Use two skins of brick tied together

3 Lean a stone wall against the bank of earth

Constructing the wall

Excavate the soil to provide enough room to dig the footing and construct the wall. If the soil is loosely packed, restrain it temporarily with sheets of scrap plywood, corrugated iron or similar sheeting. Drive long metal pegs into the bank to hold the sheets in place (1). Lay the footing at the base of the bank and allow it to set before you begin building the wall.

Build a block or brick wall, using standard techniques. Lay uncut stones as if you were building a dry-stone wall, but set each course on mortar. If you

use regular stone blocks, select stones of different proportions to add interest to the wall, and stagger the joints. Bed the stones in mortar.

It is essential to allow for drainage behind the wall to prevent the soil becoming waterlogged. When you lay the second course of stones embed 22mm (¾in) plastic pipes in the mortar bed, allowing them to slope slightly towards the front of the wall. The pipes should be placed at about 1m (3ft) intervals and pass right through the wall, projecting a little from the face (2).

1 Hold back the earth with scrap boards

2 Set plastic pipes in the wall for drainage

FINISHING STONE WALLS

When the wall is complete, rake out the joints to give a dry wall appearance. An old paintbrush is a useful tool for smoothing the mortar in deep crevices to make firm, watertight joints. Alternatively, point regular stones with concave rubbed joints.

Allow the mortar to set for a day or two before filling behind the wall. Lay hardcore at the base to cover the drainage pipes and pack shingle against the wall as you replace the soil. Provide a generous layer of topsoil so that you can plant up to the wall.

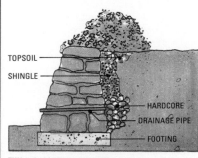

TOPSOIL
SHINGLE
HARDCORE
DRAINAGE PIPE
FOOTING

Filling behind a stone wall

For many people, paving of any kind is associated with the old 'back yard' environment, conjuring up an image of a concreted patch devoid of plants, trees and grass. In reality, introducing paving to a garden provides an opportunity to create contrasts of colour and texture which are intensified by sunlight and deep shade. A hard, unyielding surface is softened by the addition of foliage, while certain sculptural plants which recede into a background of soil and grass are seen to advantage against stone and gravel.

A paved patio
A paved area surrounded by stone or brick walls makes a perfect suntrap for swimming and relaxing.

Designing paved areas
The marriage of different materials offers numerous possibilities. It may be convenient to define areas of paving as paths, drives and patios, but they are only names to describe the function of those particular spaces in the garden. There is no reason why you cannot blend one area into another by using the same material throughout or employing similar colours to link one type of paving with another. On the other hand, you could take a completely different approach and deliberately juxtapose coarse and smooth textures or pale and dark tones to make one space stand out from the next.

Having so many choices at your disposal does have drawbacks; there is a strong temptation to experiment with any and every combination until the end result is a mishmash that is distracting to the eye. A few well-chosen materials which complement the house and its surroundings produce an effect which is much more appealing.

Working with concrete

Concrete might not be everybody's first choice for paving a garden, but it is a much more versatile material than is often realized. When cast into paving slabs, for example, it can be mistaken for natural stone, or it may be that the geometric pattern created by the combination of individual units attracts the eye while the material itself goes relatively unnoticed. Even ordinary concrete can be finished with a surprising variety of textures which dispel the drab image that concrete conjures up for many people.

THE INGREDIENTS OF CONCRETE

Concrete in its simplest form consists of cement and fine particles of stone – sand and pebbles – known as aggregate. The dry ingredients are mixed with water to create a chemical reaction with the cement which binds the aggregate into a hard, dense material. The initial hardening process takes place quite quickly. The mix becomes unworkable after a couple of hours depending on the temperature and humidity, but the concrete has no real strength for three to seven days. The hardening process continues for up to a month, or as long as there is moisture still present within the concrete. Moisture is essential to the reaction and consequently the concrete must not dry out too quickly during the first few days.

Cement

Standard Portland cement, sold in 50kg (110lb) bags from builders' merchants or DIY outlets, is used in the manufacture of concrete. In its dry condition it is a fine grey powder.

Sand

Sharp sand, a rather coarse and gritty material, constitutes part of the aggregate of a concrete mix. Don't buy fine builders' sand used for mortar, and avoid unwashed or beach sand, both of which contain impurities that could affect the quality of the concrete. Sharp sand is sold by the cubic metre (or cubic yard) from a builders' merchant, although it is perhaps more convenient to buy it in large plastic bags if you have to transport it by car or van.

Coarse aggregate

Coarse aggregate is gravel or crushed stone composed of particles large enough to be retained by a 5mm (¼in) sieve up to a maximum size of 20mm (¾in) for normal use. Once again, it can be bought loose by the cubic metre (cubic yard) or in smaller quantities packed in plastic sacks.

Pigments

Special pigments can be added to the concrete to colour it, but it is difficult to guarantee an even colour from one batch to another.

Combined aggregate

Naturally occurring sand-and-gravel mix, known as ballast, is sold as a combined aggregate for concreting. The proportion of sand to gravel is not guaranteed unless the ballast has been reconstituted to adjust the mix, and you may have to do it yourself. In any case, make sure it has been washed to remove impurities.

Dry-packed concrete

You can buy dry cement, sand and aggregate mixed to the required proportions for making concrete. Choose the proportion that best suits the job you have in mind. Concrete mix is sold in various size bags up to 50kg (110lb). Available from the usual outlets, it is a more expensive way of buying the ingredients, but is a simple and convenient method of ordering exactly the amount you will need. Before you add water to the mix, make sure the ingredients are mixed thoroughly.

Water

Use ordinary tap water to mix concrete, never river or sea water.

PVA admixture

You can buy a PVA admixture from builders' merchants to make a smoother concrete mix which is less susceptible to frost damage. Follow manufacturers' instructions for its use.

You can hire small mixing machines if you have to prepare a large volume of concrete, but for the average job it is just as convenient to mix it by hand. It isn't necessary to weigh the ingredients; simply mix them by volume, choosing the proportions that suit the job in hand.

Mixing by hand

Use large buckets to measure the ingredients, one for the cement and an identical one for the aggregate, in order to keep the cement perfectly dry. Different shovels are also a good idea. Measure the materials accurately, levelling them with the rim of the bucket. Tap the side of the bucket with the shovel as you load it with sand or cement so that the loose particles are shaken down.

Mix the sand and aggregate first on a hard, flat surface. Scoop a depression in the pile for the measure of cement, and mix all the ingredients until they form an even colour.

1 Mixing ingredients
Mix the ingredients by chopping the concrete mix with the shovel. Turn the mix over and chop again.

Form another depression and add some water from a watering can. Push the dry ingredients into the water from around the edge until surface water is absorbed, then mix the batch by chopping the concrete with the shovel **(1)**. Add more water, turn the concrete from the bottom of the pile and chop it as before until the whole batch has an even consistency. To test the workability of the mix, form a series of ridges by dragging the back of the shovel across the pile **(2)**. The surface of the concrete should be flat and even in texture, and the ridges should hold their shape without slumping.

2 Testing the mix
Make ridges with the back of the shovel to test the workability of the mix.

Mixing by machine

Make sure you set up the concrete mixer on a hard, level surface and that the drum is upright before you start the motor. Use a bucket to pour half the measure of coarse aggregate into the drum and add water. Add the sand and cement alternately in small batches, plus the rest of the aggregate. Keep on adding water little by little along with the other ingredients.

Let the batch mix for a few minutes, then tilt the drum of the mixer while it is still rotating and turn out a little concrete into a wheelbarrow so you can test its consistency (see above). If necessary, return the concrete to the mixer to adjust it.

MACHINE SAFETY

- Make sure you understand the operating instructions before turning on the machine.
- Prop the mixer level and stable with blocks of wood.
- Never put your hands or shovel into the drum while the mixer is running.
- Don't lean over a rotating drum when you inspect the contents. It is good practice to wear goggles when mixing concrete.

Storing materials

If you buy sand and coarse aggregate in sacks, simply use as much as you need for the job in hand and keep the rest bagged up until required. If you buy them loose, store them in piles, divided by a wooden plank if necessary, on a hard surface or on thick polyethylene sheets. Protect them from rain with weighted sheets of plastic.

Storing cement is more critical. It is sold in paper sacks which will absorb moisture from the ground, so pile them on a board propped up on battens. Keep cement in a dry shed or garage if possible, and if you have to store it outdoors cover the bags with sheets of plastic weighted down with bricks. Once the bag is opened cement can absorb moisture from the air, so keep a partly used bag in a sealed plastic sack.

READY-MIXED CONCRETE

If you need a lot of concrete for a driveway or large patio it may be worth ordering a delivery of ready-mixed concrete from a local supplier. Always contact the supplier well in advance to discuss your particular requirements. Specify the proportions of the ingredients and say whether you will require the addition of a retarding agent to slow down the setting time. (Once a normal mix of concrete is delivered, you will have no more than two hours in which to finish the job; a retarding agent can add up to two hours to the setting time.) Tell the supplier exactly what you need the concrete for and accept his advice. For quantities of less than 6cu m (8cu yd) you might have to shop around for a supplier who is willing to deliver without making an additional charge.

Talk over with the supplier any problems that may be involved in the delivery of the concrete. In order to avoid moving it too far by wheelbarrow, you will want it discharged as close to the site as possible, if not directly into place. However, the chute on a delivery truck can reach only so far, and if the vehicle is too large or heavy to drive onto your property you will need several helpers to move the concrete while it is still workable; a single cubic metre of concrete will fill 25 to 30 large wheelbarrows. If it takes longer than 30 to 40 minutes to discharge the load, you may have to pay extra.

SEE ALSO

Details for:
Calculating quantities	455
Cleaning equipment	455
Laying concrete	456–459

● **Professional mixing**
There are companies who will deliver concrete ingredients and mix them to your specifications on the spot. All you have to do is barrow the concrete and pour it into place. There is no waste as you only pay for the concrete you use. Telephone a local company for details on price and minimum quantity.

Storing sand and aggregate
Separate the piles of sand and aggregate with a wooden plank.

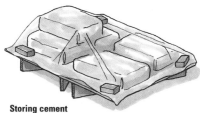

Storing cement
Raise bags of cement off the ground and cover them with plastic sheeting.

453

DESIGNING CONCRETE PAVING

● **Sloping floors**
Although you can build upon a perfectly flat base, it is a good idea to slope the floor towards the door of a garage or outbuilding that is to be scrubbed out from time to time. Alternatively, slope a floor in two directions towards the middle to form a shallow drain that runs to the door.

The idea of having to design simple concrete pads and pathways might seem odd, but there are important factors to consider if the concrete is to be durable. At the least, you will have to decide on the thickness of the concrete that is needed to support the weight of traffic and the angle of slope required to drain off surface water. When the area of concrete is large or of a complicated shape, you must incorporate control joints to allow the material to expand and contract. If a pad is for a habitable building, it must include a damp-proof membrane to prevent moisture rising from the ground. Even the proportions of sand, cement and aggregate used in the mix must be considered carefully.

Deciding on the slope

A freestanding pad can be laid perfectly level, especially when it is supporting a small outbuilding, but a very slight slope or fall prevents water collecting in puddles if you have failed to get the concrete absolutely flat. When a pad is laid directly against a house it must have a definite fall away from the building, and any parking area or drive must shed water to provide adequate traction for vehicles and to minimize the formation of ice. When concrete is laid against a building, it must be at least 150mm (6in) below the existing damp-proof course.

USE OF PAVING	ANGLE OF FALL
Pathways	Not required
Drive	1 in 40 25mm per metre 1in per yard
Patio Parking space	1 in 60 away from building 16mm per metre ⅝in per yard
Pads for garages and outbuildings	1 in 80 towards the door 12.5mm per metre ½in per yard

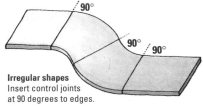

Irregular shapes
Insert control joints at 90 degrees to edges.

RECOMMENDED THICKNESSES FOR CONCRETE

The normal thicknesses recommended for concrete paving assume it will be laid on a firm subsoil, but if the soil is clay or peat, increase the thickness by about 50 per cent. The same applies to a new site where the soil might not be compacted. Unless the concrete is for pedestrian traffic only, lay a sub-base of compacted hardcore below the paving. This will absorb ground movement without affecting the concrete itself. A sub-base is not essential for a very lightweight structure like a small wooden shed, but as you might want to increase the weight at some time it is wise to install a sub-base at the outset.

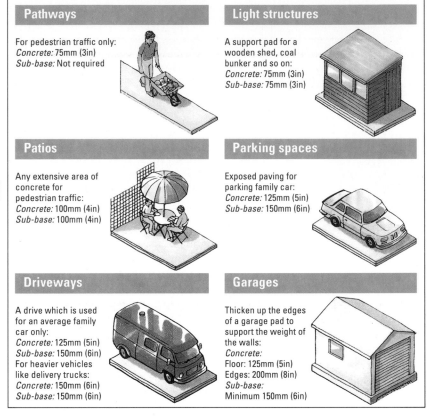

Pathways
For pedestrian traffic only:
Concrete: 75mm (3in)
Sub-base: Not required

Light structures
A support pad for a wooden shed, coal bunker and so on:
Concrete: 75mm (3in)
Sub-base: 75mm (3in)

Patios
Any extensive area of concrete for pedestrian traffic:
Concrete: 100mm (4in)
Sub-base: 100mm (4in)

Parking spaces
Exposed paving for parking family car:
Concrete: 125mm (5in)
Sub-base: 150mm (6in)

Driveways
A drive which is used for an average family car only:
Concrete: 125mm (5in)
Sub-base: 150mm (6in)
For heavier vehicles like delivery trucks:
Concrete: 150mm (6in)
Sub-base: 150mm (6in)

Garages
Thicken up the edges of a garage pad to support the weight of the walls:
Concrete:
Floor: 125mm (5in)
Edges: 200mm (8in)
Sub-base:
Minimum 150mm (6in)

Allowing for expansion

Changes in temperature cause concrete to expand and contract. If this movement is allowed to happen at random, a pad or pathway will crack at the weakest or most vulnerable point. A control joint, composed of a compressible material, will absorb the movement or concentrate the force in predetermined areas where it does little harm. Joints should meet the sides of a concrete area at more or less 90 degrees. Always place a control joint between concrete and a wall, and around inspection chambers.

Positioning control joints
The exact position of control joints depends upon the area and shape of the concrete.

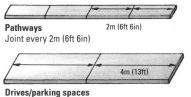

Pathways   2m (6ft 6in)
Joint every 2m (6ft 6in)

Drives/parking spaces
Joint every 4m (13ft)

Concrete pads
Joints no more than 4m (13ft) apart and around inspection chambers.

Divide a pad into equal bays if:
● Length is more than twice the width.
● Longest dimension is more than 40 x thickness.
● Longest dimension exceeds 4m (13ft).

Estimate the amount of materials you require by calculating the volume of concrete in the finished pad, path or drive. Measure the surface area of the site and multiply that figure by the thickness of the concrete.

Estimating quantities of concrete

Use the gridded diagram to estimate the volume of concrete you will need by reading off the area of the site in square metres (square yards) and tracing it across horizontally to meet the angled line indicating the thickness of the concrete. Trace the line up to find the volume in cubic metres (cubic yards).

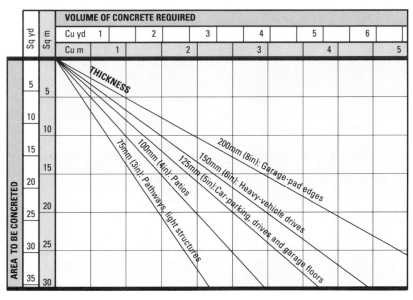

Estimating quantities of ingredients

Use the bar charts below to estimate the quantities of cement, sand and aggregate you will require to mix up the volume of concrete arrived at by using the chart above.

The figures are based on the quantity of ingredients required to mix one cubic metre of concrete for a particular type of mix, plus about 10 per cent in order to allow for wastage.

	CUBIC METRES OF CONCRETE	1.00	1.50	2.00	2.50	3.00	3.50	4.00	4.50	5.00
GENERAL-PURPOSE MIX										
	Cement (50kg bags)	7.00	10.50	14.00	17.50	21.00	24.50	28.00	31.50	35.00
plus	Sand (cubic metres)	0.50	0.75	1.00	1.25	1.50	1.75	2.00	2.25	2.50
	Aggregate (cubic metres)	0.75	1.15	1.50	1.90	2.25	2.65	3.00	3.40	3.75
or	Ballast (cubic metres)	0.90	1.35	1.80	2.25	2.70	3.15	3.60	4.05	4.50
FOUNDATION MIX										
	Cement (50kg bags)	6.00	9.00	12.00	15.00	18.00	21.00	24.00	27.00	30.00
plus	Sand (cubic metres)	0.55	0.80	1.10	1.40	1.65	1.95	2.20	2.50	2.75
	Aggregate (cubic metres)	0.75	1.15	1.50	1.90	2.25	2.65	3.00	3.40	3.75
or	Ballast (cubic metres)	1.00	1.50	2.00	2.50	3.00	3.50	4.00	4.50	5.00
PAVING MIX										
	Cement (50kg bags)	9.00	13.50	18.00	22.50	27.00	31.50	36.00	40.50	45.00
plus	Sand (cubic metres)	0.45	0.70	0.90	1.15	1.35	1.60	1.80	2.00	2.25
	Aggregate (cubic metres)	0.75	1.15	1.50	1.90	2.25	2.65	3.00	3.40	3.75
or	Ballast (cubic metres)	1.00	1.50	2.00	2.50	3.00	3.50	4.00	4.50	5.00

CALCULATING AREAS

Squares and rectangles
Calculate the area of rectangular paving by multiplying width by length:

Example:
2m x 3m = 6sq m
78in x 117in = 9126sq in or 7sq yd

Circles
Use the formula πr^2 to calculate the area of a circle. $\pi = 3.14$. r = radius of circle.

Example
3.14 x 2sq m = 3.14 x 4 = 12.56sq m
3.14 x 78sq in = 3.14 x 6084 = 19104sq in or 14.75sq yd

Irregular shapes
Draw an irregular area of paving on square paper. Count the whole squares and average out the portions to find the approximate area.

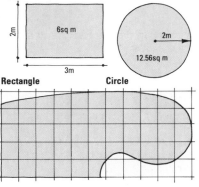

Rectangle   Circle

Square-up an irregular shape to calculate area

CLEANING TOOLS AND MACHINERY

Keep the shovel as clean as possible between mixing batches of concrete, and at the end of a working day wash all traces of concrete from your tools and wheelbarrow.

When you have finished using a concrete mixer, add a few shovels of coarse aggregate and a little water, then run the machine for a couple of minutes to scour the inside of the drum. Dump the aggregate, then hose out the drum with clean water.

Shovel unused concrete into sacks ready for disposal at a refuse dump and wash the mixing area with a stiff broom. Never hose concrete or any of the separate ingredients into a drain.

455

LAYING A
CONCRETE PAD

Laying a simple pad as a base for a small shed or similar structure involves all the basic principles of concreting: building a retaining formwork, as well as the pouring, levelling and finishing of concrete. Provided the base is less than 2m (6ft 6in) square, there is no need to include control joints.

Mixing concrete by volume

Mixing the ingredients by volume is the easiest and most accurate way in which to guarantee the required proportions. Whatever container you use to measure the ingredients – shovel, bucket, wheelbarrow – the proportions remain the same.

MIXING CONCRETE BY VOLUME			
Type of mix		Proportions	For 1cu m concrete
GENERAL PURPOSE			
Use in most situations including covered pads other than garage floors.	plus	1 part cement	6.4 bags (50kg)
		2 parts sand	0.448cu m
	or	3 parts aggregate	0.672cu m
		4 parts ballast	0.896cu m
FOUNDATION			
Use for footings at the base of masonry walls.	plus	1 part cement	5.6 bags (50kg)
		2½ parts sand	0.49cu m
	or	3½ parts aggregate	0.686cu m
		5 parts ballast	0.98cu m
PAVING			
Use for parking areas, drives, footpaths, and garage floors.	plus	1 part cement	8 bags (50kg)
		1½ parts sand	0.42cu m
	or	2½ parts aggregate	0.7cu m
		3½ parts ballast	0.98cu m

Excavating the site

Mark out the area of the pad with string lines attached to pegs driven into the ground outside the work area (**1**). Remove them to excavate the site, but replace them afterwards to help position the formwork which will hold the concrete in place.

Remove the topsoil and all vegetable matter within the site down to a level which allows for the combined thickness of concrete and sub-base. Extend the area of excavation about 150mm (6in) outside the space allowed for the pad. Cut back any roots you encounter and if there is any turf put it aside to cover the infill surrounding the completed pad. Level the bottom of the excavation by dragging a board across it (**2**), and compact the soil with a garden roller.

Erecting the formwork

Until the concrete sets hard it must be supported all round by formwork. For a straightforward rectangular pad, construct the formwork from 25mm (1in) thick softwood planks set on edge. The planks, which must be as wide as the finished depth of concrete, are held in place temporarily with stout 50 x 50mm (2 x 2in) wooden stakes. Second-hand or sawn timber is quite adequate. If it is slightly thinner than 25mm (1in), just use more stakes to brace it. If you have to join planks, butt them end to end, nailing a cleat on the outside (**3**).

Using the string lines as a guide, erect one board at the 'high' end of the pad, and drive stakes behind it at about 1m (3ft) intervals or less, with one for each corner. The tops of the stakes and board must be level and correspond exactly to the proposed surface of the pad. Nail the board to the stakes (**4**).

Set up another board opposite the first one, but before you nail it to the stakes, establish the crossfall with a spirit level and straightedge. Work out the difference in level from one end of the pad to the other. For example, a pad which is 2m (6ft 6in) long should drop 25mm (1in) over that distance. Tape a shim of timber to one end of the straightedge, and with the shim resting on the 'low' stakes, place the other end on the opposite board (**5**). Drive home each low stake until the spirit level reads horizontal, then nail the board flush with the tops of the stakes.

Erect the sides of the formwork, allowing the ends of the boards to overshoot the corners to make it easier to dismantle them when the concrete has set (**6**). Use the straightedge, this time without the shim, to level the boards across the formwork.

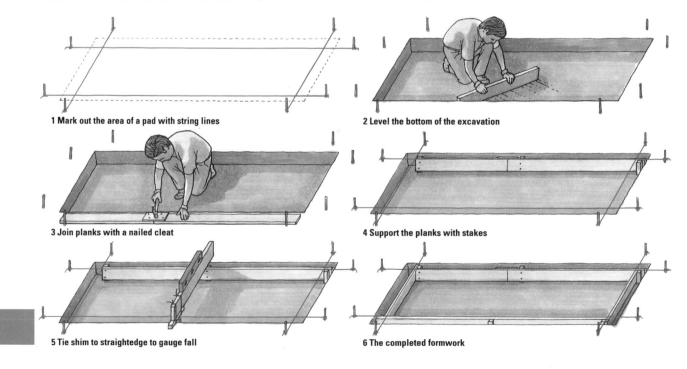

1 Mark out the area of a pad with string lines

2 Level the bottom of the excavation

3 Join planks with a nailed cleat

4 Support the planks with stakes

5 Tie shim to straightedge to gauge fall

6 The completed formwork

LAYING A CONCRETE PAD

Laying the sub-base

Hoggin, a mixture of gravel and sand, is an ideal material for a sub-base, but you can use crushed stone or brick provided you throw out any plaster, scrap metal or similar rubbish. Also remove large lumps of masonry as they will not compact well. Pour hardcore into the formwork and rake it fairly level before tamping it down with a heavy balk of timber (7). If there are any stubborn lumps, break them up with a heavy hammer. Fill in low spots with more hardcore or sharp sand until the sub-base comes up to the underside of the formwork boards.

Filling with concrete

Mix the concrete as near to the site as is practicable and transport the fresh mix to the formwork in a wheelbarrow. Set up firm runways of scaffold boards if the ground is soft, especially around the perimeter of the formwork. Dampen the sub-base and formwork with a fine spray and let surface water evaporate before tipping the concrete in place. Start filling from one end of the site and push the concrete firmly into the corners (8). Rake it level until the concrete stands about 18mm (¾in) above the level of the boards.

Tamp down the concrete with the edge of a 50mm (2in) thick plank that is long enough to reach across the formwork. Starting at one end of the site, compact the concrete with steady blows of the plank, moving it along by about half its thickness each time (9). Cover the whole area twice, then remove excess concrete, using the plank with a sawing action (10). Fill any low spots, then compact and level the concrete once more.

To retain the moisture, cover the pad with sheets of polyethylene, taped at the joints and weighted down with bricks around the edge (11). Alternatively, use wet sacking and keep it damp for three days by means of a fine spray. Try to avoid laying concrete in very cold weather, but if it is unavoidable, spread a layer of earth or sand on top of the sheeting to insulate the concrete from frost. You can walk on the concrete after three days, but leave it for about a week before removing the formwork and erecting a shed or similar outbuilding.

7 Level hardcore base with a heavy balk of timber

8 Pour the concrete, starting in the corners

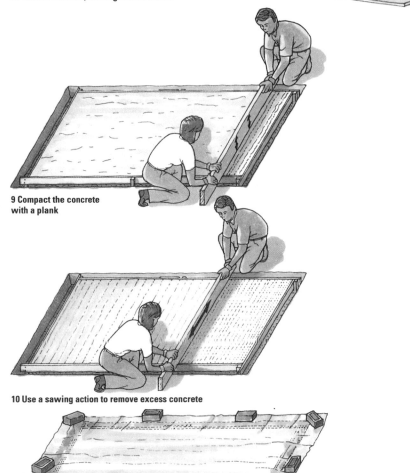

9 Compact the concrete with a plank

10 Use a sawing action to remove excess concrete

11 Cover the pad with weighted sheets of polyethylene

Extending a pad
If you want to enlarge a patio, simply butt a new section of concrete against the existing pad. The butt joint will form a control joint. To add a narrow strip, for a larger shed for example, drill holes in the edge of the pad and use epoxy adhesive to glue in short reinforcing rods before pouring the fresh concrete.

Finishing the edges
If any of the edges are exposed, the sharp corners might cause a painful injury. Radius the corners with a homemade edging float. Bend a piece of sheet metal over an 18mm (¾in) diameter rod or tube and screw a handle in the centre. Run the float along the formwork as you finish the surface of the concrete.

457

LAYING PATHS AND DRIVES

Paths and drives are laid and compacted in the same way as rectangular pads, using similar formwork to contain the concrete. However, the proportions of most paths and drives necessitate the inclusion of control joints to allow for expansion and contraction. You must install a sub-base beneath a drive, but a footpath can be laid on compacted soil levelled with sharp sand. Establish a slight fall across the site to shed rainwater. Don't use a vehicle on concrete for 10 days after laying.

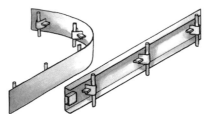

1 A water level made from a garden hose

2 Level the formwork using a datum peg

A sloping drive
If you build a drive on a sloping site, make the transition from level ground as gentle as possible. If the drive runs towards a garage, let the last 2m (6ft) slope up towards the door. Use a pole to impress a drain across the wet concrete at the lowest point.

458

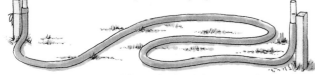

5 Support board with concrete and nails

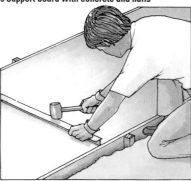

6 Make a dummy joint with T-section metal

Setting out paths and drives

Excavate the site, allowing for the thickness of sub-base and concrete. Level the bottom of the excavation as accurately as you can, using a board to scrape the surface flat.

Drive accurately levelled pegs into the ground along the site to act as datum points for the formwork. Space them about 2m (6ft 6in) apart down the centre of the pathway. Drive in the first peg until its top corresponds exactly to the proposed surface of the concrete. Use a long straightedge and spirit level or, better still, a home-made water level to position every other peg. To make the latter, push a short length of transparent plastic tubing into each end of an ordinary garden hose. Fill the hose with water until it appears in the tube at both ends. As long as the ends remain open, the water level at each end is constant so that you can establish a level over any distance, even around obstacles or corners. Tie one end of the hose to the first datum peg so that the water level aligns with the top of the peg. Use the other to establish the level of every other peg along the pathway (1). Cork each end of the hose to retain the water as you move it.

To set a fall with a water level, make a mark on one tube below the surface of the water and use that as a gauge for the top of the peg.

Erecting formwork

Construct formwork from 25mm (1in) thick planks as for a concrete pad. To check it is level, rest a straightedge on the nearest datum peg (2).

If the drive or path is very long, timber formwork can be expensive. It might be cheaper to hire metal 'road forms' (3). Straight-sided formwork is made from rigid units, but flexible sections are available to form curves.

If you want to bend wooden formwork, make a series of parallel saw cuts across the width of the plank in the area of the curve (4). The timber is less likely to snap if you place the saw cuts on the inside of the bend.

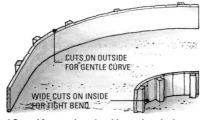

3 Curved and straight road forms

CUTS ON OUTSIDE FOR GENTLE CURVE

WIDE CUTS ON INSIDE FOR TIGHT BEND

4 Curved formwork made with wooden planks

Installing control joints

Install a permanent expansion joint every 2m (6ft 6in) for a footpath and every 4m (13ft) along a drive. Cut strips of rot-proofed hardboard or 12mm (½in) thick softwood to fit exactly between the formwork and to match the depth of the concrete. Before pouring, hold the control joints in place with mounds of concrete and nails on each side of the board driven into the formwork (5). Pack more concrete carefully on each side of the joints as you fill the formwork and tamp towards them from both sides so that they are not dislodged.

As the joints are permanent fixtures, make sure they are level with the surface of the concrete. Install similar joints in a patio or use an alternate-bay construction (see opposite page).

To prevent concrete cracking between joints on a narrow path, cut 18mm (¾in) deep grooves across the compacted concrete to form dummy joints alternating with the physical ones. The simplest method is to cut a length of T-section metal to fit between the formwork boards. Place it on the surface of the wet concrete and tap it down with a mallet (6). Carefully lift the strip out of the concrete to leave a neat impression. If the concrete should move, a crack will develop unnoticed at the bottom of the groove.

Place strips of thick bituminous felt between concrete and an adjoining wall to absorb expansion. Hold the felt in place with moulds of concrete, as described left, before pouring the full amount of concrete.

ALTERNATE-BAY METHOD OF CONSTRUCTION

It is not always possible to lay all the concrete in one operation. In such cases it is easier to divide the formwork crosswise with additional planks known as stop ends to form equal-size bays. By filling alternate bays with concrete, you have plenty of time to compact and level each section and more room in which to manoeuvre. It is a convenient way to lay a large patio which would be practically impossible to compact and level in one go, and it is the only method to use for drives or paths butting against a wall which makes it impossible to work across the width. Alternate-bay construction is often used for drives on a steep slope to prevent heavy, wet concrete from slumping downhill.

There is no need to install control joints when using bay construction, but you may want to form dummy joints for a neat appearance (see opposite).

Concreting alternate bays
Stand in the empty bays to compact concrete laid against a wall. When the first bays are set hard, remove the stop ends and fill the gaps, using the surface of the firm concrete as a level.

INSPECTION CHAMBERS

Prevent expansion damaging an inspection chamber by surrounding it with control joints. Place formwork around the chamber and fill with concrete. When set, remove the boards and place felt strips or preserver-treated softwood boards on all sides.

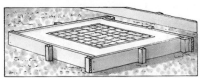

Surround an inspection chamber with formwork

The surface finishes produced by tamping or striking off with a sawing action are perfectly adequate for a skid-proof, workmanlike surface for a pad, drive or pathway, but you can produce a range of other finishes using simple handtools once you have compacted and levelled the concrete.

Float finishes
Smooth the tamped concrete by sweeping a wooden float across the surface, or make an even finer texture by finishing with a trowel (steel float). Let the concrete dry out a little before using a float or you will bring water to the top and weaken it, which will eventually result in a dusty residue on the hardened concrete. Bridge the formwork with a stout plank so that you can reach the centre, or hire a skip float with a long handle for large pads.

Make a smooth finish with a wooden float

Brush finishes
Make a finely textured surface by drawing a yard broom across the setting concrete. Flatten the concrete initially with a wooden float, then make parallel passes with the broom held at a low angle to avoid 'tearing' the surface.

Texture the surface with a broom

Brush-finishing concrete

Exposed-aggregate finish
Embedding small stones or pebbles in the surface makes a very attractive and practical finish, but you will need a little practice in order to do it successfully.

Scatter dampened pebbles onto the freshly laid concrete and tamp them firmly with a length of timber until they are flush with the surface (**1**). Place a plank across the formwork and apply your full weight to make sure the surface is even. Leave to harden for a while until all surface water has evaporated, then use a very fine spray and a brush to wash away the cement from around the pebbles until they protrude (**2**). Cover the concrete for about 24 hours, then lightly wash the surface again to clean any sediment off the pebbles. Cover the concrete again and leave it to harden thoroughly.

1 Tamp pebbles into fresh concrete

2 Wash the cement from around the pebbles

Exposed-aggregate finish

PAVING SLABS

SEE ALSO
Details for:
Brick pavers 463

If your only experience of paving slabs is the rather bland variety used for public footpaths, then cast-concrete paving may not seem a very attractive proposition for a garden. However, manufacturers can supply more pleasing products in a wide range of shapes, colours and finishes.

Colours and textures

Paving slabs are made by hydraulic pressing or casting in moulds to create the desired surface finish. Pigments and selected aggregates added to the concrete mix create the illusion of natural stone or a range of muted colours. Combining two or more colours within the same area of paving can be very striking.

1 Cobbles or sets
Large slabs resemble an area of smaller cobbles or sets. Careful laying and filling are essential for success. Sets are 'laid' either in straight rows or as curves.

2 Planter
Four planter stones laid in a square leave a circle in which to plant a tree or shrub.

3 Exposed aggregate
Crushed-stone aggregate has a very pleasing mottled appearance, either exposed to make a coarse gritstone texture or polished flat to resemble terrazzo.

4 Brushed finishes
A brush-finished slab, textured with parallel grooves as if a stiff broom had been dragged across the wet concrete, has a practical non-slip surface. Straight or swirling patterns are available.

5 Riven stone
The finish resembles that of natural stone. The best-quality slabs are cast from real-stone originals in a wide variety of subtle textures. If the texture continues over the edge of the slabs, they can be used for steps and coping.

SHAPES AND SIZES

Although some manufacturers offer a wider choice than others, there is a fairly standard range of shapes and modular sizes. You can carry the largest slabs single-handed, but it is a good idea to have an assistant when manoeuvring them carefully into place.

Square and rectangular
A single size and shape makes grid-like patterns or, when staggered, creates a bonded brickwork effect. Rectangular slabs can form a basket-weave or herringbone pattern. Alternatively, combine different sizes so as to create the impression of random paving.

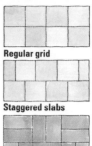
Regular grid

Staggered slabs

Basket-weave pattern

Herringbone pattern

Random paving

Hexagonal
Hexagonal slabs form honeycomb patterns. Use half slabs, running across flats or from point to point, to edge areas that are paved in straight lines.

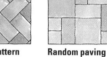
Half-hexagonal slabs

Hexagonal slab

Honeycomb pattern

Tapered slabs
Use tapered slabs as edging for ponds, around trees, and for curved paths or steps. Lay them head to toe to make straight sections of paving. Use right-handed or left-handed half slabs at the ends.

Full and half-tapered slabs

Straight section

Circular
Circular slabs make perfect individual stepping stones across a lawn or flower bed, but for a wide area fill the spaces between with cobbles or gravel.

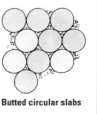
Butted circular slabs

LAYING
PAVING SLABS

Laying heavy paving slabs involves a good deal of physical labour, but in terms of technique it is no more complicated than tiling a wall. Accurate setting out and careful laying, especially during the early stages, will produce perfect results. Take extra care when you lay hexagonal slabs to ensure that the last few slabs fit properly.

CUTTING CONCRETE SLABS

Mark a line across a slab with a soft pencil or chalk. Using a bolster and hammer, chisel a groove about 3mm (⅛in) deep along the line (**1**). Continue the groove down both edges and across the underside of the slab. Place the slab on a bed of sand and put a block of wood at one end of the groove. Strike the block with a hammer while moving it along the groove until the slab splits (**2**). Clean up the edge with a bolster.

For a perfect cut, hire an angle grinder fitted with a stone-cutting disc. Using the grinder, score a deep groove as before. Tap along the groove with a bolster until the slab splits.

1 Cut a groove with a bolster chisel

2 Strike block over groove with a hammer

PROTECTING YOUR EYES

When cutting slabs with a chisel or an angle grinder, always protect your eyes with plastic goggles. An angle grinder throws up a great deal of dust, so wear a simple gauze facemask too as a safeguard.

Setting out the area of paving

Wherever possible, to eliminate the arduous task of cutting units to fit, plan an area of paving to be laid with whole slabs only. Use a straight wall as a datum line and measure away from it, or allow for a 100 to 150mm (4 to 6in) margin of gravel between the paving and wall if the location dictates that you have to lay slabs towards the house. A gravel margin not only saves time and money by using fewer slabs, but also provides an area for planting climbers and for adequate drainage to keep the wall dry. Even so, establish a 16mm per metre (⅝ in per yard) slope across the paving so that most surface water will drain into the garden. Any paving must be 150mm (6in) below a damp-proof course to protect the building.

As paving slabs are made to fairly precise dimensions, marking out an area simply involves accurate measurement, allowing for a 6 to 8mm (¼in) gap between slabs. Some slabs are cast with sloping edges to provide a tapered joint (**1**) and should be butted edge to edge. Employ pegs and string to mark out the perimeter of the paved area, and check your measurements before you excavate.

1 Tapered joint

Preparing a base for paving

Paving slabs must be laid upon a firm, level base, but the depth and substance of that base depends on the type of soil and the proposed use of the paving.

For straightforward patios and paths, remove vegetable matter and topsoil to allow for the thickness of the slabs, a 25mm (1in) layer of sharp sand and an extra 18mm (¾in) so that the paving will be below the level of surrounding turf and thus will not damage your lawn mower. Compact the soil with a garden roller, spread the sand with a rake and level it by scraping and tamping with a length of timber (**2**).

To support heavier loads, or if the soil is composed of clay or peat, lay a sub-base of firmly compacted hardcore – broken bricks or crushed stone – to a depth of 75 to 100mm (3 to 4in) before spreading the sand to level the surface.

If you plan to park vehicles on the paving, increase the depth of hardcore to 150mm (6in).

2 Level the sand base

Laying the paving slabs

Set up string lines again as a guide and lay the edging slabs on the sand, working in both directions from a corner. When you are satisfied with their positions, lift them one at a time and set them on a bed of mortar (1 part cement : 4 parts sand). Add just enough water to make a firm mortar. Lay a fist-size blob under each corner and one more to support the centre of the slab (**3**). If you intend to drive vehicles across the slabs, lay a continuous bed of mortar about 50mm (2in) thick.

Lay three slabs at a time with 6mm (¼in) wooden spacers between. Level each slab by tapping with a heavy hammer, using a block of wood (**4**). Check the alignment.

Gauge the slope across the paving by setting up datum pegs along the high side. Drive them into the ground until the top of each corresponds to the finished surface of the paving, then use the straightedge to check the fall on the slabs (**5**). Lay the remainder of the slabs, working out from the corner each time to keep the joints square. Remove the spacers before the mortar sets.

3 Lay blobs of mortar

4 Level the slabs

5 Check the fall with a spirit level

Filling the joints

Don't walk on the paving for two to three days until the mortar has set. If you have to cross the area, lay planks across the slabs to spread the load.

To fill the gaps between the slabs, brush a dry mortar mix of 1 part cement : 3 parts sand into the open joints (**6**). Remove any surplus material from the surface of the paving, then sprinkle the area with a very fine spray of water to consolidate the mortar. Avoid dry mortaring if heavy rain is imminent; it may wash the mortar out.

6 Fill the joints

461

LAYING
CRAZY PAVING

The informal nature of paths or patios laid with irregular-shaped paving stones has always been popular. The random effect, which many people find more appealing than the geometric accuracy of neatly laid slabs, is also very easy to achieve. A good eye for shape and proportion is more important than a practised technique.

Materials for crazing paving

You can use broken concrete slabs if you can find enough but, in terms of appearance, nothing compares with natural riven stone. Stratified rock which splits into thin layers of its own accord as it is quarried is ideal for crazy paving, and can be obtained at a very reasonable price if you can collect it yourself. Select stones which are approximately 40 to 50mm (1½ to 2in) thick in a variety of shapes and sizes.

Crazy paving made with broken concrete slabs

SETTING OUT AND LAYING A BASE

You can set out string lines to define straight edges to crazy paving, although they will never be as precisely defined as those formed with regular cast-concrete slabs. Alternatively, allow the stones to form an irregular junction with grass or shingle, perhaps setting one or two stones out from the edge.

Create an irregular edge to crazy paving

Laying the stones

Arrange an area of stones, selecting them for a close fit but avoiding too many straight, continuous joints. Trim those that don't quite fit with a bolster and hammer. Reserve larger stones for the perimeter of the paved area as small stones tend to break away.

Use a mallet or block of wood and a hammer to bed each stone into the sand (**1**) until they are all perfectly stable and reasonably level. Having bedded an area of about 1sq m (1sq yd), use a straightedge and spirit level to true up the stones (**2**). If necessary, add or remove sand beneath individual stones until the area is level. When the main area is complete, fill in the larger gaps with small stones, tapping them into place with a mallet (**3**).

Fill the joints by spreading more sand across the paving and sweeping it into the joints from all directions (**4**). Alternatively, mix up a stiff, almost dry, mortar and press it into the joints with a trowel, leaving no gaps.

Use an old paintbrush to smooth the mortared joints and wipe the stones clean with a damp sponge.

1 Bed the stones in the sand base

2 Check the level across several stones

3 Fill the gaps with small stones

4 Sweep dry sand into the joints

Laying stepping stones

Place individual stones or slabs across a lawn to form a row of stepping stones. Cut around the edge of each stone with a spade or trowel and remove the area of turf directly beneath. Scoop out the earth to allow for a 25mm (1in) bed of sharp sand plus the stone, which must be about 18mm (¾in) below the level of the surrounding turf. Tap the stone into the sand until it no longer rocks when you step on it.

Cut around a stepping stone with a trowel

Stepping stones preserve a lawn

PAVING WITH
BRICK SYSTEMS

BRICK PATTERNS

Concrete bricks have one surface face with chamfered edges all round, and spacers moulded into the sides to form accurate joints. Housebricks can be laid on edge or face down showing the wide face normally unseen in a wall.

Unlike brick walls, which must be bonded in a certain way for stability, brick paths can be laid to any pattern that appeals to you.

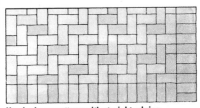

Herringbone pattern with straight edging

Angled herringbone with straight edging

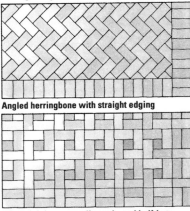

Whole bricks surrounding coloured half-bats

Staggered basket-weave pattern

Stretcher-bonded brickwork

Cane-weave pattern

Bricks make charming paths. The wide variety of textures and colours available offers endless possibilities of pattern, but do choose the type of brick carefully, bearing in mind the sort of use your paving can expect.

Materials for brick paving

Ordinary housebricks are often used for paths and small patios, even though there is the risk of spalling in freezing conditions unless they happen to be engineering bricks. The slightly uneven texture and colour are the very reasons why second-hand bricks are so much in demand for garden paving, so a little frost damage is usually acceptable.

Housebricks are not really suitable if the paved area is to be a parking space or drive, especially if it is to be used by heavy vehicles. For a durable surface, even under severe conditions, use concrete bricks instead. These are slightly smaller than standard housebricks, being 200 x 100 x 65mm (8 x 4 x 2½in). Red or grey are widely available and you can obtain other colours by special order.

Providing a base for brick paving

Lay brick footpaths and patios on a 75mm (3in) hardcore base covered with a 50mm (2in) layer of sharp sand. If you are laying concrete bricks for a drive, increase the depth of hardcore to 150mm (6in).

Fully compact the hardcore and fill all voids so that sand from the bedding course is not lost to the sub-base.

Provide a cross-fall on patios and drives as for concrete, and make sure that the surface of the paving is at least 150mm (6in) below a damp-proof course to protect the building.

Retaining edges

Unless the brick path is laid against a wall or some similar structure, the edges of the paving must be contained by a permanent restraint. Timber, treated with a chemical preserver, is one solution, constructed like the formwork for concrete. The edging boards should be flush with the surface of the path, but drive the stakes below ground so that they can be covered by soil or turf **(1)**.

As an alternative, set an edging of bricks in concrete. Dig a trench deep and wide enough to accommodate a row of bricks on end plus a 100mm (4in) concrete 'foundation'. Lay the bricks while the concrete is still wet, holding them in place temporarily with a staked board while you pack more concrete behind the edging. When the concrete has set, remove the board and lay hardcore and sand in the excavation.

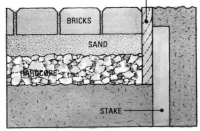

1 Wooden retaining edge

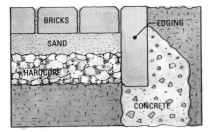

2 Brick retaining edge

Brick pavers
Clay brick pavers *(top row)* are made in a wide variety of colours and textures. Concrete pavers *(bottom row)* are less colourful but more shapes are available.

463

PAVING
WITH BRICKS

LAYING THE BRICKS

Having chosen your bricks, prepared the ground and set retaining edges you can start laying your paving. When bricks are first laid upon the sand they should project 10mm (⅜in) above the edging restraints to allow for bedding them in at a later stage (**1**). To level the sand for a path, cut a notched spreader to span the edging (**2**). If the paving is too wide for a spreader, lay levelling battens on the hardcore base and scrape the sand to the required depth using a straightedge (**3**). Remove the battens and fill the voids carefully with sand. Keep the sand bed dry at all times. If it rains before you can lay the bricks, either let the sand dry out thoroughly or replace it with dry sand.

Lay an area of bricks on the sand to your chosen pattern. Work from one end of the site, kneeling on a board placed across the bricks (**4**). Never stand on the bed of sand. Lay whole bricks only, leaving any gaps at the edges to be filled with cut bricks after you have laid an area of approximately 1 to 2sq m (1 to 2½sq yd). Concrete bricks have fixed spacers, so butt them together tightly .

Fill any remaining spaces with bricks cut with a bolster. If you are paving a large area you can hire an hydraulic guillotine (see left).

When the area of paving is complete, tamp the bricks into the sand bed by striking a stout batten with a heavy club hammer. The batten must be large enough to cover several bricks to maintain the level (**5**). For a professional finish, hire a powerful plate vibrator(**6**). Pass the vibrator over the paved area two or three times until it has worked the bricks down into the sand and flush with the outer edging. Vibrating the bricks will work some sand up between them; complete the job by brushing more sand across the finished paving and vibrating it into the open joints.

Plain concrete-brick drive and parking space

Mottled-brick garden path

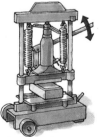
Cutting bricks
Hire an hydraulic brick-cutting guillotine to cut pavers.

1 Start by laying bricks 10mm above edging

2 Level the sand with a notched spreader

3 Or lay levelling battens on the hardcore

4 Lay the bricks to your chosen pattern

5 Tamp the bricks with a hammer and batten

6 A vibrator levels brick paving perfectly

Interlocking concrete pavers

Bricks laid to a herringbone pattern

Cobblestones and gravel are used more for their decorative quality than for functional paving for drives or pathways. Cobbles in particular are most uncomfortable to walk on and, although a firmly consolidated area of gravel is fine for vehicles, walking on a gravel footpath can be rather heavy going. Both materials come into their own, however, when used as a foil for areas of flat paving slabs or bricks, and to set off plants such as dwarf conifers and heathers.

Laying cobbles

Cobbles – large flint pebbles found on many a beach – can be laid loose, perhaps with larger rocks and plants. However, they are often set in mortar or concrete to create more formal areas.

Consolidate a layer of hardcore and cover it with a levelled layer of dry concrete mix about 50mm (2in) deep.

Press the cobbles into the dry mix, packing them tightly together and leaving them projecting well above the surface. Use a stout batten to tamp the area level (**1**), then lightly sprinkle the whole area with water, both to set off the concrete-hardening process and to clean the surfaces of the cobbles.

Large cobbles as a background to plants

1 Tamp the cobbles into a dry concrete mix

Laying gravel

If an area of gravel is to be used as a pathway or for motor vehicles, construct retaining edges of brick, concrete kerbs or wooden boards as for brick paths. This will stop gravel being spread outside its allotted area.

To construct a gravel drive, the sub-base and the gravel itself must be compacted and levelled to prevent cars skidding and churning up the material. Lay a 150mm (6in) bed of firmed hardcore topped with 50mm (2in) of very coarse gravel mixed with sand. Roll it flat. Rake an 18 to 25mm (¾ to 1in) layer of fine 'pea' gravel across the sub-base and roll it down to make it firm.

Making a gravel garden
To lay an area of gravel for planting, simply excavate the soil to accept a 25mm (1in) deep bed of fine gravel. Either set the gravel 18mm (¾in) below the level of the lawn or edge the gravel garden with bricks or flat stones. Scrape away a small area of gravel to allow for planting, then sprinkle the gravel back again to cover the soil right up to the plant.

Gravel-and-conifer garden ▶

COARSE GRAVEL AND SAND

HARDCORE   PEA GRAVEL

Rake pea gravel across the surface of a drive

WOODEN PATHWAYS

If you live in a rural district where large logs are plentiful or perhaps a mature tree has been felled in your garden, you can use 150mm (6in) lengths of sawn timber set on end to make a practical and charming footpath. Lay the logs together like crazy paving or use large pieces of wood as stepping stones. Hold wood rot at bay by soaking the sawn sections in chemical preserver.

Laying a log pathway
Excavate the area of the pathway to a depth of 200mm (8in) and spread a 50mm (2in) deep layer of gravel and sand mix across the bottom. Use concreting ballast – combined aggregate – or make up the mix yourself. Level the bed by scraping and tamping with a straightedge.

Place the logs on end on the bed, arranging them to create a pleasing combination of shapes and sizes (**1**). Work them into the sand until they stand firmly and evenly, then pour more sand and gravel between them (**2**). Brush the material across the pathway in all directions until the gaps between the logs are filled flush with the surface (**3**). If any logs stand proud so that they could cause someone to trip, tap them down with a heavy hammer.

If you want to plant between the logs, scrape out some sand and gravel and replace it with the appropriate soil.

1 Arrange the logs on end

2 Shovel sand-and-gravel mix between the logs

3 Brush more mix into the joints

● **Use a heavy roller**
A lightweight garden roller is fine for compacting earth or sand, but use one weighing about 100kg (2cwt) when levelling hardcore.

RESURFACING WITH TARMAC

SEE ALSO

Details for:

Edging   463

Laying a new path
Although cold-cure tarmac is primarily a resurfacing material, it can be applied to a new hardcore base that has been compacted firmly, levelled and sealed with a slightly more generous coat of bitumen emulsion.

● **Treating for heavy wear**
At entrances to drives and on bends, vehicle tyres cause more wear than normal. Treat these areas with an 18mm (¾in) rolled layer of cold-cure tarmac (see far right) before applying a dressing of stone chippings.

● **Double dressing**
If the surface you are dressing is in a very poor condition or exceptionally loose, apply a first coat of bitumen emulsion. Cover with chippings and roll thoroughly. Two days later sweep away loose chippings and apply a second coat of emulsion and finish with chippings as described right.

DRESSING WITH STONE CHIPPINGS

As an alternative to tarmac, completely resurface a path or drive with natural-stone chippings embedded in fresh bitumen emulsion. Chippings in various colours are available in 25kg (55lb) sacks which cover about 2.5sq m (3sq yd). Apply weedkiller and fill potholes as for tarmac (see right).

Bitumen emulsion sets by evaporation in about 12 hours, but until that time it is not completely waterproof so check the weather forecast to avoid wet conditions. You can lay emulsion on a damp surface, but not on an icy one.

Apply emulsion, available in 5, 25 and 200kg (11, 55 and 440lb) drums. A 5kg drum will cover about 7sq m (8sq yd), provided the surface is dense macadam or concrete. However, an open-textured surface will absorb considerably more bitumen emulsion.

Decant the emulsion into a bucket to make it easier to pour onto the surface, and brush it out, not too thinly, with a stiff broom as for laying tarmac (see right). Having brushed out one bucket of emulsion, spread the stone chippings evenly with a spade. Hold the spade horizontally just above the surface and gently shake the chippings off the edge of the blade (1). Don't pile them too thickly, but make sure the emulsion is covered completely. Cover an area of about 5sq m (6sq yd), then roll the chippings down. When the entire area is covered, roll it once more. If traces of bitumen show between the chippings, mask them with a little sharp sand and roll again. (See margin notes left for applying dressing to heavy-wear areas.)

You can walk or drive on the dressed surface immediately. One week later, gently sweep away surplus chippings. Patch any bare areas by re-treating them with emulsion and chippings.

1 Sprinkle a layer of chippings with a spade

Smarten up an old tarmac path or drive, or any sound but unsightly paved area, by resurfacing with cold-cure tarmac. It makes a serviceable surface and is ready to lay from the sack. Roll it flat with a garden roller; a light one will do, although you will have to make extra passes.

Choosing the materials

Choose between red or black tarmac. It is available in 25kg (55lb) sacks, which will cover about 0.9sq m (10sq ft) at a thickness of 12mm (½in). Each sack contains a separate bag of decorative stone chippings for embedding in the soft tarmac as an alternative finish. Cold-cure tarmac can be laid in any weather, but it is much easier to level and roll flat on a warm, dry day. If you have to work in cold weather, store the materials in a warm place the night before laying. While it is not essential, edging the tarmac with bricks, concrete kerbs or wooden boards will improve the appearance of the finished surface.

Preparing the surface

Pull up all weeds and grass growing between the old paving, then apply a strong weedkiller to the surface two days before you lay the tarmac. Sweep the area clean, and level any potholes; cut the sides vertical, remove dust and debris from the hole, then paint with bitumen emulsion supplied by the tarmac manufacturer. Wait for it to turn black before filling the hole with 18mm (¾in) layers of tarmac, compacting each layer until the surface is level.

Apply a tack coat of bitumen emulsion to the entire surface to make a firm bond between the new tarmac and the old paving. Mask surrounding walls, kerb stones and manhole covers. Stir the emulsion with a stick before pouring it from its container, then spread it thinly with a stiff-bristled broom. Try not to splash, and avoid leaving puddles, especially at the foot of a slope. Leave the tack coat to set for about 20 minutes and, in the meantime, wash the broom in hot, soapy water. Don't apply the tack coat when it is likely to rain.

Apply a tack coat of bitumen emulsion

Applying the tarmac

Rake the tarmac to make a layer about 18mm (¾in) thick (1), using a straightedge to scrape the surface flat. Press down any stubborn lumps with your foot. Spread the contents of no more than three sacks before the initial rolling. Keep the roller wet (2) to avoid picking up specks of tarmac. Don't run the roller onto grass or gravel or you may roll particles into the tarmac.

Spread and roll tarmac over the whole area, then achieve the final compaction by rolling it thoroughly in several directions. Lightly scatter the chippings (3) prior to the final pass.

You can walk on the tarmac immediately, but avoid wearing high-heeled shoes. Don't drive on it for a day or two, and if you have to erect a ladder on it spread the load by placing a board under the ladder. You should always protect tarmac from oil and petrol spillage, but take special care while the surface is fresh.

1 Level the tarmac

2 Keep the roller wet

3 Scatter chippings

BUILDING GARDEN STEPS

Designing a garden for a sloping site offers many possibilities for creating attractive changes of level by terracing areas of paving or holding planting beds in place with retaining walls. However, moving safely from one level to another requires at least one flight of steps.

Designing steps

If you are fortunate enough to own a large garden, and the slope is very gradual, a series of steps with wide treads and low risers can make an impressive feature. If the slope is steep, you can avoid a 'staircase' appearance by constructing a flight of steps composed of a few treads interposed with wide, flat landings, at which points the flight can change direction to add further interest and offer a different viewpoint of the garden. In fact, a shallow flight can be virtually a series of landings, perhaps circular in plan, sweeping up the slope in a curve.

For the steps to be both comfortable and safe to use, the proportion of tread (the part you stand on) to riser (the vertical part of the step) is important. As a rough guide, construct steps so that the depth of the tread (from front to back) plus twice the height of the riser equals 650mm (2ft 2in). For example, match 300mm (1ft) treads with 175mm (7in) risers, 350mm (1ft 2in) treads with 150mm (6in) risers and so on. Never make treads less than 300mm (1ft) deep or risers higher than 175mm (7in).

Garden steps built with natural stone

Using concrete slabs

Concrete paving slabs in their various forms are ideal for making firm, flat treads for garden steps. Construct the risers from concrete facing blocks or bricks, allowing the treads to overhang by 25 to 50mm (1 to 2in) to cast an attractive shadow line which also defines the edge of the step.

Measure the difference in height from the top of the slope to the bottom to gauge the number of steps required. Mark the position of the risers with pegs and roughly shape the steps in the soil as a confirmation (1).

Either lay concrete slabs, bedded in sand, flush with the ground at the foot of the slope or dig a trench for hardcore and a 100 to 150mm (4 to 6in) concrete base to support the first riser (2). When the concrete has set, construct the riser using normal bricklaying methods and check its alignment with a spirit level (3). Fill behind the riser with compacted hardcore until it is level, then lay the tread on a bed of mortar (4). Using a spirit level as a guide, tap down the tread until it slopes very slightly towards its front edge to shed rainwater and so prevent ice forming in cold weather.

Measure from the front edge of the tread to mark the position of the next riser on the slabs (5), and construct the step in the same way. Set the final tread flush with the area of paving, pathway or lawn at the top of the flight of steps.

Dealing with the sides

It is usually possible to landscape the slope at each side of the flight of steps, and turf or plant it to prevent the soil washing down onto the steps.

Alternatively, extend the riser to edge each tread or build a wall or planter on each side of the steps. Another solution is to retain the soil with large stones, perhaps extending into a rockery on one or both sides.

1 Cut the shape of the steps in the soil

2 Dig the footing for the first riser

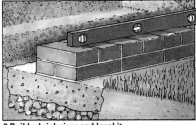
3 Build a brick riser and level it

4 Lay the tread on mortar

5 Mark the position of the next riser

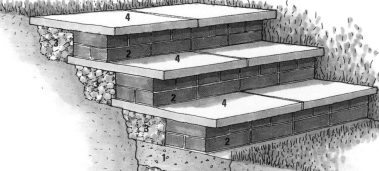

Concrete-slab steps
A section through a simple flight of garden steps built with brick risers and concrete-slab treads.
1 Concrete footing
2 Brick-built riser
3 Hardcore infill
4 Concrete-slab tread

● **Dealing with slippery steps**
Algae will grow in damp conditions, especially under trees, and steps can become dangerously slippery if it is allowed to build up on the surfaces. Brush with a solution of 1 part household bleach : 4 parts water. After 48 hours, wash with clean water and repeat if the fungal growth is heavy. You can also use a proprietary fungicidal solution, but follow manufacturers' instructions carefully.

BUILDING GARDEN STEPS

Casting new steps in concrete needs such complicated formwork that the end result hardly justifies the amount of effort required, especially when better-looking steps can be constructed from cast-concrete slabs and blocks. Nevertheless, if you have a flight of concrete steps in your garden you will want to keep them in good condition. Like other forms of masonry, concrete suffers from spalling, where frost breaks down the surface and flakes off fragments of material. It occurs a great deal along the front edges of steps where foot traffic adds to the problem. Repair broken edges as soon as you can – not only are they ugly, but the steps arc not as safe as they might be.

Building up broken edges

Wearing safety goggles, chip away concrete around the damaged area and provide a good grip for fresh concrete. Cut a board to the height of the riser and prop it against the step with bricks **(1)**. Mix up a small batch of general-purpose concrete, but add a little PVA bonding agent to help it stick to the step. Dilute some bonding agent with water, say 3 parts water : 1 part bonding agent, and brush it onto the damaged area, stippling it into the crevices. When the surface becomes tacky, fill the hole with concrete mix flush with the edge of the board **(2)**. Radius the front edge slightly with a home-made edging float, running it against the board **(3)**.

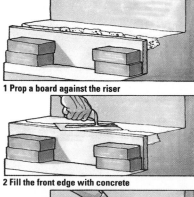
1 Prop a board against the riser

2 Fill the front edge with concrete

3 Run an edging float against the board

Building curved steps

To build a series of curved steps, choose materials which will make the job as easy as possible. You can use tapered concrete slabs for the treads, designing the circumference of the steps to suit the proportions of the slabs. Alternatively, you can construct the treads from crazy paving, selecting fairly large stones for the front edge. Use bricks laid flat or on edge to build the risers. Set the bricks to radiate from the centre of the curve, and fill the slightly tapered joints with mortar.

Use a length of string attached to a peg driven into the ground as an improvised compass to mark out the curve of each step. Tie a batten to the string to help you gauge the front edge of the lower steps **(1)**. Roughly shape the soil and lay a concrete foundation for the bottom riser. Build risers and treads as for regular concrete-slab steps, using the improvised string compass as a guide.

Building circular landings

To construct a circular landing, build the front edge with bricks and paving as for a curved step. When the mortar has set, fill the area of the landing with compacted hardcore and lay gravel up to the level of the tread **(2)**.

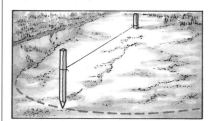
1 Mark the edge with an improvised compass

2 Circular landings made with bricks and gravel

Making log steps

For an informal garden, build steps from lengths of sawn timber soaked in a chemical preserver. Try to construct risers of a fairly regular height, otherwise someone might stumble if they are forced to break step. As it is not always possible to obtain uniform logs you may have to make up the height of the riser with two or more slimmer logs.

Cut a regular slope in the earth bank and compact the soil by treading it down. Drive stakes cut from 75mm (3in) diameter logs into the ground, one at each end of a step **(1)**. Place one heavy log behind the stakes, bedding it down in the soil **(2)**, and pack hardcore behind it to construct the tread of the step **(3)**. Shovel a layer of gravel on top of the hardcore to finish the step.

If large logs are in short supply, build a step from two or three slim logs, holding them against the stakes with hardcore as you construct the riser **(4)**.

Log-built garden steps

1 Drive a stake at each end of a step

2 Place a log behind the stakes

3 Fill behind the log with hardcore

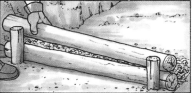
4 Make up a riser with two slim logs

SEE ALSO

Details for:	
Installing pond liners	470–471
Building a waterfall	473

There is nothing like still or running water to enliven a garden. Waterfalls and fountains have an almost mesmeric fascination and the sound of trickling water has a delightfully soothing effect. Even a small area of still water will support all manner of interesting pond life and plants, with the additional bonus of the images of trees, rocks and sky reflected in its placid surface.

Garden pond
A well-planted water garden surrounded by flowering shrubs looks like a natural pond.

Pond liners

It is not by chance that the number of garden ponds has greatly increased over recent years; their popularity is largely due to the emergence of easily installed rigid and flexible pond liners, making it possible to create a complete water garden by putting in just a few days' work.

In the past it was necessary to line a pond with concrete. While it is true that concrete is a very versatile material, there is always the possibility of a leak developing through cracks caused by ground movement or the force of expanding ice. There are no such worries with rigid and flexible liners. In addition to the labour and expense involved in building formers for a concrete pond, it must be left to season for about a month, during which time it must be emptied and refilled a number of times to ensure that the water will be safe for fish and plant life. However, you can introduce plants to a pool lined with plastic or rubber as soon as the water itself has matured, which takes no more than a few days.

Ordering a flexible liner

Use a simple formula to calculate the size of liner you will need. Disregard the design, planting shelves and so on that you have planned; simply take the overall length and width of the pond and add twice the maximum depth to each dimension to arrive at the size of the liner. If possible, adapt your design to fall within the nearest stock liner size.

POND DIMENSIONS	
Length – 3m	9ft 9in
Width – 2m	6ft 6in
Depth – 450mm	1ft 6in
SIZE OF LINER	
3m + 0.900m = 3.9m	9ft 9in + 3ft = 12ft 9in
2m + 0.900m = 2.9m	6ft 6in + 3ft = 9ft 9in

CHOOSING A POND LINER

The advantages of proprietary pond liners over concrete are fairly clear, but there are still a number of options to choose from, depending on the size and shape of the pond you wish to create and how much you propose to spend.

Rigid liners

Regular garden-centre visitors will be familiar with the range of preformed plastic pond liners. The best liners are those made from rigid glass-reinforced plastic (fibreglass), which is very strong and resistant to the effects of frost or ice. Provided they are handled with a reasonable degree of care and installed correctly, rigid plastic pond liners are practically leak-proof.

Rigid pond liner
Rigid liners are moulded using glass-reinforced plastic.

Semi-rigid liners

Semi-rigid liners, made from vacuum-formed plastic, are cheaper than those made from fibreglass, but the range of sizes is very limited. However, they make ideal reservoirs or header pools for the top of a cascade or waterfall. Rectangular or irregular-shaped liners are available in rigid or semi-rigid plastic, and a very acceptable water garden can be created with a carefully selected series of pond liners linked together by watercourses.

Flexible liners

For complete freedom of design, choose a flexible-sheet liner designed to hug the contours of a pond of virtually any shape and size. Another advantage is that a pond made with even the most expensive sheet liner is cheaper to construct than a rigid-plastic liner of equivalent size; it is also guaranteed to last longer.

Polyethylene liners, once the only type of flexible liner on the market, are relatively fragile and should be considered only for temporary pools; even then, they should be lined with a double thickness of material. PVC liners, especially those reinforced with nylon, are guaranteed for up to 10 years of normal use, but if you want your pond to last for 50 years or more, choose a synthetic-rubber membrane based on butyl. Not all butyl liners are of the same quality, so buy one from a reputable manufacturer offering a 20-year written guarantee if you want the best product. Black and stone-coloured butyl liners are made in a wide range of stock sizes up to 6.5 x 10.75m (22 x 35ft); larger liners can be supplied to order.

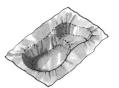

Flexible liners
The better-quality flexible liners are made from butyl.

469

DESIGNING A POND

A pond must be sited correctly if it is to have any chance of maturing into an attractive, clear stretch of water. Never place a pond under deciduous trees – falling leaves will pollute the water as they decay, causing fish to become ill and even die. Laburnum trees are especially poisonous.

Positioning for sunlight
Although sunlight promotes the growth of algae, which causes ponds to turn a pea-green colour, it is also necessary to encourage the growth of other water plants. An abundant growth of oxygenating plants will compete with the algae for mineral salts and, aided by shade cast from floating and marginal plants, will keep the pond clear.

Size and shape
The proportion of the pond is important in creating harmony between plants and fish. It is difficult to maintain the right conditions for clear water in a pond less than 3.75sq m (40sq ft) in surface area, but the volume of water is even more vital. A pond up to about 9sq m (100sq ft) in area should be 450mm (1ft 6in) deep. As the area increases you will have to dig deeper to about 600mm (2ft) or more, but it's rarely necessary to go below 750mm (2ft 6in).

The profile of the pond must be designed to fulfil certain requirements. To grow marginal plants, you will need a 225mm (9in) wide shelf around the edge of the pond, 225mm (9in) below the surface of the water. This will take a standard 150mm (6in) planting crate with ample water above, and you can always raise the crate on pieces of paving or bricks. The sides of the pond should slope at about 20 degrees to prevent soil collapse during construction and to allow the liner to stretch without promoting too many creases. It will also allow a sheet of ice to float upwards without damaging the liner. Judge the angle by measuring 75mm (3in) inwards for every 225mm (9in) of depth. If the soil is very sandy, increase the angle of slope slightly for extra stability.

Accommodating a sloping site
On a sloping site build up the low side with earth, turfing up to the paving surround. Cut back the higher side and build a low retaining wall, or bed stones against the earth to create a rockery.

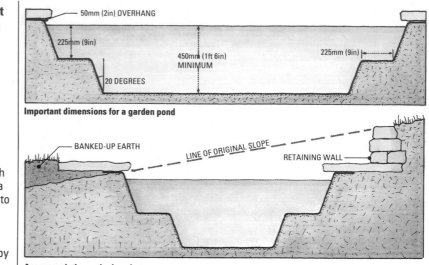

Important dimensions for a garden pond

Accommodating a sloping site

Installing a rigid liner

Stand a rigid liner in position and prop it up with cardboard boxes, both to check its orientation and to mark its perimeter on the ground. Use a spirit level to plot key points on the ground (**1**) and mark them with small pegs. You will need to dig outside this line, so absolute accuracy is not required.

As you move the topsoil, either take it away in a wheelbarrow or pile it close by, ready to incorporate into a rockery. Lay a straightedge across the top and measure the depth of the excavation (**2**), including marginal shelves. Keep the excavation as close as possible to the shape of the liner, but extend it by 150mm (6in) on all sides. Compact the base and cover it with a 25mm (1in)

deep level of sharp sand. Lower the liner and bed it firmly into the sand. Check that the pool stands level (**3**) and wedge it temporarily with wooden battens until the back-fill of soil or sand can hold it.

Start to fill the liner with water from a hose and, at the same time, pour sifted soil or sand behind the liner (**4**). There is no need to hurry as it will take some time to fill, but keep pace with the level of the water. Reach into the excavation and pack soil under the marginal shelves with your hands.

When the liner is firmly bedded in the soil, either finish the edge with stones as for a flexible liner (see opposite) or re-lay turf to cover the rim of the liner.

1 Mark the perimeter of the liner

2 Measure the depth of the excavation

3 Make sure the liner stands level

4 Infill with sifted soil or sand

CONSTRUCTING

A POND:

FLEXIBLE LINER

SEE ALSO	
Details for:	
Cutting slabs	461
Pumps	472

Excavating the pond

Mark out the shape of the pond on the ground. A garden hose is useful for trying out curvilinear shapes. Excavate the pond to the level of the planting shelf, then mark and dig out the deeper sections (**1**). Remove sharp stones and roots from the sides and base to make sure they won't puncture the liner.

The top of the pond must be level, and the surrounding stone or concrete slabs must be 18mm (¾in) below the turf. For both reasons, cut back the turf to accommodate the stones and then drive wooden datum pegs into the exposed surround every metre or so (3 to 4 ft). Level the tops of all the pegs using a straightedge (**2**) and check the level across the pond as well. Remove or pack earth around the pegs until the compacted soil is level below the pegs.

When the surround is level, remove the pegs and spread a 12mm (½in) layer of slightly damp sand over the base and sides of the excavations (**3**).

Installing a flexible liner

Drape the liner across the excavation with an even overlap all round and hold it in place with bricks while you fill the pond with water from a hose (**4**). It will take several hours to fill a large pond, but check it regularly, moving the bricks as the liner stretches. A few creases are inevitable around sharp curves, but you will lose most of them by keeping the liner fairly taut and easing it into shape as the water rises. Turn off the water when the level reaches 50mm (2in) below the edge of the pond. Cut off surplus liner with scissors, leaving a 150mm (6in) overlap all round (**5**). Push 100mm (4in) nails through the overlap into the soil so that the liner cannot slip while you place the edging stones.

Building the surround

Lay flat stones dry at first, selecting those which follow the shape of the pond with a reasonably close fit between them. Let the stones project over the water by about 50mm (2in) to cast a deep shadow line and reflection. Using a bolster, cut stones to fit the gaps behind the larger edging stones. Lift the stones one or two at a time and bed them on two or three strategically placed mounds of mortar mixed with 1 part cement : 3 parts soft sand (**6**). Tap the stones level with a mallet and fill the joints with a trowel. Smooth the joints flush with an old paintbrush. Do not drop mortar in the water or you will have to empty and refill the pond before you introduce fish or plants.

INCORPORATING A DRAIN

The recommended water level for a pond is about 50mm (2in) below the edging stones, but in exceptional circumstances, such as a heavy storm, or if you forget to turn off the water when topping up, the water can rise fast enough to spill over and flood the garden. As a precaution, build a drain beneath the edging stones to allow excess water to escape; this will also provide a means of running electric cable into the pond to power a pump or lighting. Cut corrugated-plastic sheet into two strips 150mm (6in) wide and long enough to run under the edging stones. Pop-rivet the strips together to make a channel about 25mm (1in) deep (**1**). Scrape earth and sand from beneath the liner to accommodate the channel (**2**), then lay edging stones on top to hold it in place. Dig a small soakaway behind the channel and fill it with rubble topped with fine gravel or turf up to the level of the stones.

1 Drain components

2 Place finished drain beneath edging stones

● **Preventing punctures**
A cushion of sand normally prevents a pool liner being punctured, but on very stony ground it pays to install additional protection in the form of polyester matting, which is available from garden centres.

1 Dig the excavation as accurately as possible

2 Level the edge using datum pegs

3 Line the excavation with damp sand

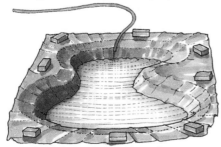

4 Stretch the liner by filling the pond

5 Cut the flexible liner to fit

6 Lay edging stones to complete the pond

471

MAKING A RAISED-EDGE POND

If you want a more formal pond you can build a raised edge using bricks or concrete facing blocks. An edging about 450mm (1ft 6in) high serves as a deterrent for small children while also providing seating. If you prefer a low wall, say 225mm (9in) high, create planting shelves at ground level, digging the pond deeper in the centre. Place planting crates on blocks around the edge of a deep raised pond.

Building the pond

Lay 100 to 150mm (4 to 6in) concrete footings to support the walls, which are constructed from two skins of masonry set apart to match the width of flat coping stones. Allow for an overhang of 50mm (2in) over the water's edge and lap the outer wall by 12 to 18mm (½ to ¾in). To save money, build the inner wall from plain concrete blocks or cheap common bricks, reserving more expensive decorative bricks or facing blocks for the outer skin of the wall. Raised ponds can be lined with a standard flexible liner, or you can order a prefabricated fitted liner to reduce the amount of creasing at the corners. Trap the edge of the liner underneath the coping stones.

Raised-edge pond
A well-designed and well-constructed pond which is attractively integrated into a sloping site.

Partly excavated pond

Fully raised pond built with a cavity wall

ALTERNATIVE POND EDGING

Edging a pond with flat stones provides a safe and attractive footpath for tending to water plants and fish, but a more natural setting is often required, particularly for small header pools in a rockery. Incorporate a shelf around the pond as for marginal plants, but this time for an edging of rocks. If you place them carefully there is no need to mortar them. Arrange rocks behind the edging to cover the liner (1).

To create a shallow, beach-like edging, slope the soil at a very shallow angle and lay large pebbles or flat rocks upon the liner. You can merge them with a rockery or let them form a natural water line (2).

To discourage neighbourhood cats poaching fish from a pond, create an edging of trailing plants. Without a firm foothold, no cat will attempt to reach into the water. Bed a strip of soft wire netting in the mortar below flat edging stones. Cut the strip to overhang the water by about 150mm (6in) as a support for the plants (3). Once the plants are established they will disguise the nature of the pool liner.

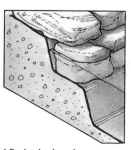

1 Rock-edged pond

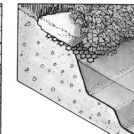

2 Pebble-strewn shelf

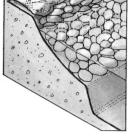

3 Wire edge holds plants

Pumps and fountains

Small submersible pumps for fountains and waterfalls are operated either directly from the mains electrical supply or through a transformer which reduces the voltage to 24 volts. Mains electricity and water can be fatal, so consult a qualified electrician if you plan to use a mains-operated pump. An extra-low-voltage pump is perfectly safe and can be installed and wired simply.

Place the pump in the water and run its electric cable beneath the edging stones, preferably via a homemade drain, to a waterproof connector attached to the extension lead of a transformer installed inside the house. This permits removal of the pump for servicing without disturbing the extension cable or transformer. Run the pump regularly, even in the winter, to keep it in good working order, and clean both the pump and its filter according to the manufacturer's instructions.

There are so many waterfall pumps and fountain kits available that you should consult manufacturers' catalogues to find one that best suits your purpose. Place a submersible waterfall pump close to the edge of the pond so that you can reach it to disconnect the hose running to the waterfall when you need to service the pump. Stand fountain units on a flat stone or propped up on bricks so that the jet is vertical. Plant water lilies some distance away from a fountain as falling water will encourage the flowers to close up.

Extra-low-voltage waterfall pump and transformer

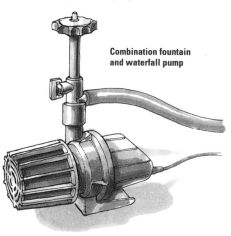

Combination fountain and waterfall pump

BUILDING A ROCKERY AND WATERFALL

SEE ALSO

Details for:	
Obtaining stone	438
Pond liners	469

A waterfall, complemented by a rockery planted with alpines or graceful shrubs and trees such as Japanese maple or dwarf conifers, adds a further dimension to a water garden. The technique for building a series of watercourses is not as complicated as it may appear, and at the same time you can also cover much of the groundwork needed for your rockery.

Materials

You will be surprised at the amount of soil produced by excavating a pond. To avoid waste and the trouble of transporting it to a local dump, use it to create your pool-side rockery. If you include a small reservoir on the higher ground you can pump water into it from the main pond to be returned via a trickling waterfall.

Obtaining a sufficient number of stones to give the impression of a real rocky outcrop can work out extremely expensive if you buy them from a garden centre. A cheaper way is to use hollow-cast reproduction rocks, which will eventually weather-in quite well. However, your best option is to buy natural stone direct from a local quarry. Real rocks can be very heavy, so have them delivered as close to the site as possible and hire a strong trolley to facilitate moving individual stones about the garden.

A rockery and waterfall are built as one operation, but for the sake of clarity they are described separately here.

AVOIDING STRAIN

Lifting stones
Keep your back straight when lifting heavy stones (right). Use a rope to lift and place large rocks (below).

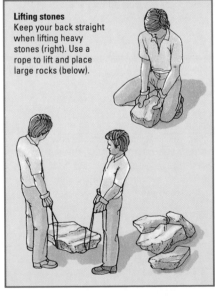

Creating a waterfall

So that the waterfall can discharge directly into the main pond, form a small inlet at the side of the pond by leaving a large flap of flexible liner. Build shallow banks at each side of the inlet and line it with stones (1). Create a stepped watercourse ascending in stages to the reservoir. Line the watercourse with off-cuts of flexible liner, overlapping them on the face of each waterfall. Tuck the edge of each lower piece of liner under the edge of the piece above, and hold them in place with stones. To retain water in small pools along the watercourse, cut each step with a slope towards the rear (2) and place stones along the lip for the desired effect (3). A flat stone will produce a sheet of water, a layer of pebbles a rippling cascade.

As the construction work progresses, test the watercourse by running water from a garden hose as it is difficult to adjust the angle of stones once the watercourse has been completed.

Bury the flexible hose from the waterfall pump in the rockery, making sure there are no sharp bends which would restrict the flow of water. Cut the hose so that it emerges at the edge of the reservoir and cover it with a flat stone (4) to hold and hide it.

A rigid-plastic reservoir will have a lip moulded in one edge which allows water to escape down the watercourse. If you construct a reservoir with flexible liner, however, you will have to shape the edge to form a low point and support a flat stone over the opening to hide the liner (5).

Cascades and waterfalls
This cross section shows a series of cascades and waterfalls running from reservoir to pond.
1 Pond inlet.
2 Watercourse step.
3 Overhanging stone creates a sheet of water.
4 Hose from pump.
5 Reservoir outlet.
6 Reservoir.

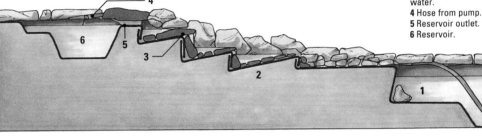

Constructing a rockery

Select and place each stone in a rockery to create an illusion of layers of rock. Stones placed haphazardly at odd angles tend to resemble a spoil heap rather than a natural outcrop. Take care not to strain yourself when lifting rocks. Keep your feet together and use your leg muscles to do the work, keeping your back as straight as possible. To move a particularly heavy rock, slip a rope around it (see left).

Lay large, flat rocks to form the front edge of the rockery, placing soil behind and between them to form a flat, level platform. Compact the soil to make sure there are no air pockets which will damage the roots of plants. Lay subsequent layers of rock set back from the first, but not in a regular pattern. Place some to create steep embankments, others to form a gradual slope of wide steps. Pockets of soil for planting alpines or other small rockery plants will form naturally as you lay the stones, but plan larger areas of soil for specimen shrubs or dwarf trees.

Building a rockery
A rockery should have irregular rock 'steps' along its front edge.

Incorporating a bog garden

An area of wet, boggy soil where specialized waterside plants can flourish complements a pond perfectly. When you excavate the pond, make a wide planting shelf covered with the flexible liner. Place a row of stones to form the edge of the pond, dividing the bog area from the deep water. Bed the stones in 50mm (2in) of mortar. When the mortar has set, neutralize its lime content by painting on a solution of waterproofing powder available from pond specialists. Follow the manufacturer's instructions for its use.

Incorporate the bog garden into a rockery by lining the perimeter with stones, then fill the area with soil. The liner underneath the soil will retain sufficient moisture to keep the garden permanently damp, but make the planting bed deep enough to ensure that the plants will not be waterlogged.

BOG GARDEN

POND

Bog garden
Construct a bog garden next to a pond for waterside plants.

473

CHOOSING A SWIMMING POOL

SEE ALSO
Details for:
Official approval   18–19

Owning a private swimming pool is no longer the exclusive privilege of the rich and famous. Several specialist companies offer reasonably priced pool kits which you can install yourself. It is worth hiring professional help for deep excavations and to remove soil from the site, and anything but the most basic heating equipment should be installed by a qualified tradesperson. Most authorities do not insist on planning permission for the building of a private pool in your garden, but it is required if you erect an enclosure over the pool. Once a pool is filled it requires very little water for topping up and maintenance, but you may find it advantageous to have a water meter fitted by your local water authority prior to the installation of your swimming pool.

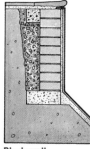

Sunken-pool kits
Vinyl liners are used with block-built walls or a frame-and-panel construction.

Block-wall construction

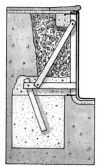

Frame-and-panel walling

● **Tiled concrete pools**
For a top-quality permanent pool, hire a professional contractor to install a reinforced-concrete structure. Hollow pool walls, constructed with cast-concrete sections, are filled with vibrated concrete, rendered and lined with polished marble or mosaic tiles.

A self-assembly pool
Swimming pools made from self-assembly kits are just as attractive as professionally installed pools, but are a fraction of the cost.

Siting a swimming pool

The size and shape of a swimming pool is largely dictated by the area of your garden, but it should be positioned away from trees so that it benefits from the sun and does not collect falling leaves. Most people prefer to install a pool reasonably close to the house so that the facilities of the latter can be used to supply water, electricity and heating, and an existing building such as a garage can be utilized to house the pool filtration plant. It is normally easier to install a pool on a level site, but you can partially bury one in a sloping bank and fill in the lower area with the excavated soil.

Above-ground pool kits

Above-ground pools are cheap and easy to erect. Most are circular or oval in plan, and are constructed by bolting together galvanized-steel panels and frame members. A heavy-duty vinyl liner and wide coping strips complete the basic pool. Above-ground pools are the least likely to be contaminated by wind-blown leaves and other debris, and they can be dismantled and moved when you buy another house. Young children cannot fall into the water once you have removed the steps. With some modification you can partially bury an above-ground pool and bank the excavated soil around the sides.

Sunken-pool kits

Sunken pools can be built in a wide range of shapes and sizes from prefabricated panels similar to those used for above-ground pools. The wall panels, anchored in concrete, line the perimeter of the pool to a depth of about 1m (3ft 3in). A deeper hopper-shaped excavation at one end of the pool is rendered with a sand-and-cement mix before a fitted vinyl liner is installed. The pool walls are back-filled with gravel to balance the water pressure, and an edging of shaped coping stones is bedded in mortar. Similar pools are built using standard concrete blocks laid on a concrete footing to construct the walls. The walls and floor are rendered to present a smooth face to the vinyl liner. You could hire a local builder to construct and render the walls and floor, then back-fill and line the pool yourself.

A swimming-pool liner will last for years but, should one become damaged accidentally, it can be patched without emptying the pool.

SWIMMING-POOL ACCESSORIES

Some accessories, such as diving boards, water chutes and underwater lights, merely add to your enjoyment of the pool. Others are absolutely essential to keep the water pure.

Skimmer and filter
A pump-operated skimmer built into the side of a pool sucks lightweight floating debris into a filter housed outside the pool. The filtered water is returned to the pool via a separate inlet. The entire unit is supplied with most pool kits.

Pool vacuum cleaner
You will need a special vacuum cleaner to remove the heavier debris that sinks to the bottom of the pool. Its hose connects to the pool-side skimmer.

Leaf net
Buy a net attached to a long pole to periodically remove floating leaves which might clog the filter.

Pool cover
Lightweight woven covers are available for both above-ground and sunken pools to keep leaves, twigs and other windblown debris out of the water during the winter months.

Test equipment
Chlorine or other chemicals must be added to the water at regular intervals to kill harmful bacteria and algae. The water must be analysed in order to maintain an effective chemical balance. Pool kits are supplied with simple test equipment which allows you to analyse water samples yourself.

Heating the water
Floating thermal blankets, which are removed prior to swimming, provide the cheapest means of raising the water temperature. They are essential to reduce the cost of heating the water by more sophisticated equipment. You can install a heat exchanger which uses heat produced by the house central-heating boiler or a separate boiler provided exclusively for the pool, although both methods are expensive. Solar panels or mats provide free heat, but installation costs are high. A heat pump which extracts heat from the surrounding air, even during a cloudy day, is probably the most effective way to heat a swimming pool.

Ever since the Victorian well-to-do used them to raise exotic plants and relax in, conservatories have been a desirable addition to any house. Today, with double glazing and efficient modern heating, they are used to extend the home to provide not only an indoor garden, but living and dining rooms, studios, workrooms and sometimes kitchens. Conservatories are made in a wide range of standard sizes and styles. They are available in kit form for self-build or are supplied and erected for you.

The materials used for the construction of conservatories may include traditional softwood framing combined with dwarf masonry walls, hardwood timber frames and panels, or aluminium or uPVC plastic framing in traditional and modern styles. The roof may use traditional glass panes or modern double or triple-wall polycarbonate plastic sheet. Double-glazed toughened-glass sealed units are generally used for the windows and doors.

Study the range of designs to choose a conservatory that will suit the style of the house. A decorative 'Victorian-style' conservatory will be acceptable for an ornate or period house but may look out of place with a modern one. However, a plain modern-style conservatory can sometimes look at home with an old house. The proportions of the design and the quality of the building materials and construction details are important factors to consider.

From a practical point of view, traditional softwood frames will need periodic painting and hardwood frames occasional treatment with a coloured wood preserver. Aluminium frames are factory finished and like uPVC conservatories should require little or no decorative maintenance.

The period style of the conservatory complements the character of the house

Choosing the site

Although formal planning permission and Building Regulation approval are usually not required for conservatories under 30sq m (323sq ft) in most areas, it is sensible to discuss your proposed development with the local authorities. Before committing to your preferred design, check the manufacturer's specification to establish the size of the conservatory in relation to your site, any problems with drainage and possibly the proximity of trees or other garden features. Quite apart from practical matters, which can also include the ease of access from the house and ventilation, the choice of location should also take into consideration the direction of the sun.

A conservatory built on a south-facing wall will benefit from available sunshine all year round and would provide a pleasant environment in the winter months. However, in high summer it will be hot and will require good ventilation and shading to be comfortable. A west-facing conservatory will provide a bright room which will receive less direct sunlight and be comfortable to sit in during the afternoons and evenings. East-facing conservatories will catch only the morning sunlight. A north-facing one will not receive direct sunlight and for much of the winter require efficient heating while providing an attractive, comfortable environment in the summer. If you use a corner site your options are increased.

Heating and ventilation

Conservatories are particularly susceptible to changes in the elements and need to have a controlled environment if they are not to be too hot in summer and cold in winter. The large expanse of glass will quickly absorb the natural heat from the sun but can equally quickly lose any heat in cold wintery weather.

Double glazing is essential to retain the heat gained from sunlight, particularly if the conservatory is to be used all year round. Ideally low-emissivity glass should be used, as this reflects the absorbed heat back into the room. However in winter months when the sun's rays are weak and outside temperatures are usually low it will be necessary to provide internal heating. This is usually provided by an extension to the house central-heating system or electric-powered heaters.

In high summer the heat can rise to uncomfortable levels. To help overcome this fit blinds at the windows and to the underside of the roof. Special heat-reflective types are available. These not only add shade and an elegant finish to the interior, they also contribute to reducing heat loss in winter. Conservatory suppliers can provide made-to-measure blinds to fit your particular requirements.

However effective blinds may be, it is essential to have good ventilation, not only to combat heat in summer but also to reduce condensation in winter. Most conservatories are supplied with opening windows or top vents, and roof ventilators, to provide cross-ventilation. Roof ventilators are normally manually operated but temperature-controlled automatic systems are available as optional extras.

BUILDING
CONSERVATORIES

Although conservatories are relatively light structures it is essential that a suitable base is constructed. Erecting one on an existing patio is unlikely to be acceptable. Suppliers will specify a typical base for their products, but as site conditions can vary you should consult your local Building Control Officer. Problems associated with the base covering underfloor ventilation, the level of the DPC, or drains running below the base may also need to be discussed. A concrete base is usually recommended, but a special metal-frame platform that requires less site preparation may be a possible alternative.

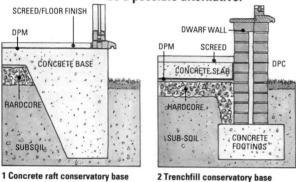

1 Concrete raft conservatory base
2 Trenchfill conservatory base

Components of a conservatory
1 Concrete footings
2 Dwarf cavity wall
3 Damp-proof membrane
4 Damp-proof course
5 Cavity insulation
6 Blinded hardcore
7 Concrete slab
8 Insulation board
9 Sand-and-cement screed
10 Double glazed frames
11 Hipped glazed roof
12 Flashing

Types of concrete base

A typical base specification has a 100mm (4in) thick slab of concrete, which may or may not be screeded, laid over a minimum of 100mm (4in) of well compacted hardcore and with adequately deep footings to suit the ground conditions. This can be constructed as a concrete raft which combines the footings (1), or more often, a trenchfill concrete foundation supporting masonry walls which contain the concrete slab (2).

The base must incorporate a continuous damp-proof membrane and a damp-proof course that is linked into the house DPC.

Constructing a base

A typical trenchfill type is described here. Start by marking out with chalk the finished floor level on the house wall. Using profile boards, set out the area of the base foundations following closely the dimensions given by the conservatory manufacturer. Check the house wall is vertical with a plumb bob held at side-frame height. If it leans outwards, set the base dimensions from the plumb line, not the wall.

The width of the footings should be 300mm (1ft) for a wall of single-brick construction, or 450mm (1ft 6in) for a cavity wall with a 50mm (2in) cavity. A minimum depth of 500mm (1ft 8in) set two or three brick courses below ground level should be suitable for most sites. Dig out the trenches and pour in concrete to the required level.

Excavate the area within the footings to allow for the thickness of the floor covering, floor screed, concrete slab, insulation board if required, and sand-blinded hardcore. Lay the perimeter bricks up to at least 150mm (6in) above ground level. Lay a bedding of well compacted hardcore in the excavation and cover with up to 50mm (2in) of levelled sand. Lay a polyethylene DPM over the sand with the edges of the sheet overlapping the walls all round (the inner skin of a cavity wall), and turned up the house wall at the back. Insulation board can now be laid (see right). Lay the concrete slab to a minimum of 100mm (4in).

Lay a damp-proof course on the walls and tie it into the house DPC, then complete the brickwork. Finally, after erecting the framing, complete the base by laying a sand-and-cement screed followed by the floor covering when fully dry. If flooring panels are to be laid over insulation boards the screed can be omitted.

Erecting the frame
It is essential the sill is set level and the modular frames are mounted squarely.

Erect the frame units following the detailed instructions provided by the manufacturer. Any gaps at the junctions with the house wall should be filled with silicone mastic. The roof wall rafter should also be sealed and covered with flashing. A traditional lead flashing or a self-adhesive type can be used. The flashing should be tucked into a mortar joint or a groove cut in the wall about 100mm (4in) to 150mm (6in) up the wall and pointed or filled with mastic. The lower edge should be dressed over the top edge of the wall rafter.

If the conservatory is built against a cavity wall that is subjected to driving rain it may be necessary to fit cavity trays into the wall above the roof line prior to erecting the frame.

INSULATING A BASE

The Building Regulations require a new floor to be insulated, but this does not apply for a conservatory under 30sq m (323sq ft) unless it is used as a habitable room. However it would be sensible to include insulation in any case as it will help conserve energy.

Expanded-polystyrene insulation board can be incorporated in the base or laid over it. The extra thickness of the insulation, up to 50mm (2in), will need to be taken into account when excavating the ground for the concrete slab.

For a screeded floor the insulation can be placed under the concrete slab (1), or under a screed not less than 65mm (2½in) thick (2). The insulation in either case is turned up the wall to prevent cold bridging.

1 Insulation under concrete slab

2 Insulation under screed

CHAPTER 11

TOOLS & SKILLS

WOODWORKING TOOLS

SEE ALSO
Details for:
Joints   491-493

A TOOL KIT IS PERSONAL

If you talk to people who make a living using tools, you will find that they guard them jealously, are loath to lend them and even less likely to borrow them. Tools are very personal. The way a person uses or sharpens a tool, even his or her working stance, will shape and modify it until it works better for its owner than in other hands. This is particularly noticeable with old wooden tools. If you examine the sole of a well-used wooden jack plane, for example, you will see that it has worn unevenly to suit the style of one person. Even the handle of a new plane feels unfamiliar after the feel of a plane you have used for years.

When it comes to building up a kit, the choice of tools is equally personal. No two professionals' tool kits are identical, and each might select different tools to do the same job. The tools shown and described on these pages will enable you to tackle all but the more specialized tasks involved in repairing, maintaining, extending and decorating your home and garden, although the final choice is yours.

No one buys a complete kit of tools all at once. Apart from the considerable cost, it makes more sense to buy tools as you need them. You may prefer to do your own decorating yet hire a professional for electrical work, in which case you are better off spending your money on good-quality brushes, rollers or scrapers than spreading it thinly on a wider range of cheaper tools. Consequently we have listed the essential tools for each 'trade' under specific headings – plumber's tool kit, decorator's tool kit and so on. But a great many tools are common to all trades, and you will find that you can gradually add to your tool kit as you tackle a growing range of activities.

Although even hand tools are expensive, it is worth buying the best you can afford, for top-quality tools are always a wise investment. Not only will they perform well, but they will last a lifetime provided that they are used, stored and maintained properly. Power tools are especially expensive, so unless you plan to use them regularly it may be more economical to hire them. Make sure that hired tools are in good condition and ask for a set of written instructions or a demonstration before you leave the hire shop.

It's impossible to produce first-class work with cutting tools that are blunt ; they are also more dangerous than sharp ones. Keep the blades in good condition, and discard disposable ones when they no longer cut smoothly and easily. You can sharpen and maintain hand tools yourself, but it is advisable to have power tools serviced professionally.

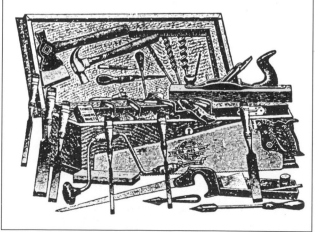

WOODWORKER'S TOOL KIT
A full woodworking tool kit is enormous, but for general home maintenance you can make do with a fairly limited one. The most essential tools are listed in the page margin as a guide to building up a basic kit.

TOOLS FOR MEASURING AND MARKING

Take care of your measuring and marking tools. If they are thrown carelessly into a tool box, try squares can be knocked out of true and gauges will become blunt and inaccurate.

Tape measure and folding rule
A folding boxwood rule is the traditional cabinet-maker's tool, but a modern retractable steel tape measure is more versatile.

Choose a tape that is about 5m (16ft) long, and which can be locked open at any point so that even a large workpiece can be measured single-handedly.

Avoid letting the spring-loaded tape snap back into its case, or the hook riveted to the end of the tape will eventually work loose.

Try square
A try square is used for checking the accuracy of jointed corners and planed timber, and also for marking out workpieces that are to be cut 'square'.

Choose a try square that has the blade and stock (handle) cut from a single L-shaped piece of metal – one with a straight blade riveted to the stock may lose its accuracy. Some try squares are made with the top of the stock cut at 45 degrees for marking out mitre joints. It's worth buying the largest square you can afford: they are available with blades up to 300mm (1ft) long.

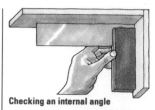

Checking an internal angle

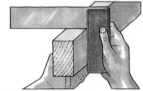

Checking planed timber
View the work against the light to check you are planing square.

Combination square
A combination square is a very versatile tool. Essentially it is a try square, but instead of a fixed blade it has a calibrated rule that slides in the stock to make a blade of any length up to 250mm (10in). This serves as a useful depth gauge. The head has an angled face for marking mitres and incorporates a small spirit level for checking vertical and horizontal surfaces.

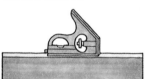

Checking horizontals
Remove the blade and place the stock face on the horizontal surface.

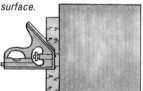

Checking verticals
Place the blade against a vertical face and read the spirit level to check for accuracy.

Sliding bevel
A sliding bevel is used like a standard try square, but its blade can be adjusted to check or mark any angle.

Marking knife

Before sawing timber, mark the cutting line with a knife – which is more accurate than a pencil and will prevent the fibres of the wood breaking out when you saw across the grain. The blade of a marking knife is ground on one side only; the flat face is run against the square or bevel.

Marking gauge

With a marking gauge you can score a line parallel to an edge. Slide the stock along the beam until it is the required distance from the pin. Press the face of the stock against the edge of the timber and, with the pin touching the wood's surface, push the tool away from you to scribe the line.

Cutting gauge

If you try to score a line across the grain with a marking gauge, the pin tends to tear the surface, whereas a cutting gauge – which has a small sharp blade – is ideal for the purpose. The blade is held in place by a removable wedge.

Mortise gauge

This type of gauge has two pins, one fixed and the other movable, for marking the parallel sides of mortise-and-tenon joints. First set the points to match the width of the mortise chisel, then adjust the stock to place the mortise the required distance from the edge of the wood. Mark the limits of the mortise with a try square (1), then score the two lines with the gauge (2). With the same setting, mark the tenon on the rail.

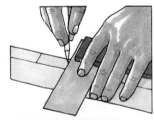

1 Mark the limits of the mortise

2 Score the lines

SAWS

Don't try to make do with just one or two saws in your kit. The right tool for the job will make for fast and accurate work.

HANDSAWS

Handsaws, with their flexible unsupported blades, are used to convert solid timber and man-made boards. All handsaws are similar in appearance, but each type is made with different-shaped teeth that are designed for a specific purpose.

Ripsaw

The ripsaw is designed for 'ripping down' – sawing solid timber along its length. Each of its teeth is like a tiny chisel that slices the timber along its grain. Alternate teeth are 'set' (bent outward in opposite directions) so that the 'kerf' (the groove cut in the timber) is slightly wider than the thickness of the blade. If saws were not set, they would jam in the kerf.

Crosscut saw

Unlike ripsaw teeth, which are filed square with the face of the blade, crosscutting teeth are filed at an angle to form points that score lines along both sides of the kerf before the wood in between is removed. This allows the saw to cut across the grain of solid timber without tearing the fibres.

Panel saw

The teeth of a panel saw are set and shaped like those of a crosscut saw but, being smaller and closer together, they cut a finer kerf. The saw is used for cutting man-made boards such as plywood and hardboard.

1

2

Using handsaws

Hold the saw with your forefinger extended towards the tip of the blade. This will help to keep the blade in line with your forearm and produce a straight cut.

To saw down the length of a board, support it on sawhorses. Start at one end using short, backward strokes only, while steadying the saw blade with the tip of your thumb against its flat face (1). Lengthen your stroke once you have established the kerf, and continue cutting with slow, regular strokes, using the full length of the blade. Move the sawhorses as need be to provide a clear path for the blade. As you approach the end of the board, turn it round and start a fresh cut from that end, sawing back to meet the original kerf.

When crosscutting, support the work with your free hand (2) and finish the cut with slow, gentle strokes to avoid breaking off the last uncut layer of wood.

STORING SAWS

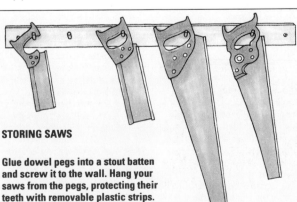

Glue dowel pegs into a stout batten and screw it to the wall. Hang your saws from the pegs, protecting their teeth with removable plastic strips.

BACKSAWS

The blade of a backsaw is stiffened with a heavy metal strip folded over its top edge. The relatively fine teeth make it ideal for cutting joints.

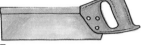

Tenon saw

A tenon saw has small teeth shaped and set like those of a crosscut saw. It is the perfect saw for general-purpose woodworking and joinery.

Dovetail saw

Because the tails and pins of a dovetail joint run with the grain, the teeth of a dovetail saw are like miniature ripsaw teeth. Use this saw for fine cabinet-making.

Gent's saw

This cheap alternative to a dovetail saw has a straight handle.

Using backsaws

Support the work in a vice or on a bench hook, and hold the saw at a shallow angle to establish the kerf. As the cut progresses, gradually level the blade until you are sawing parallel to the face of the wood.

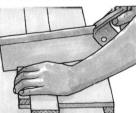

Using a bench hook

A bench hook is a simple jig, used when crosscutting narrow sections of wood with a backsaw. Steady the 'hook' against the front edge of the bench, then clamp the work firmly against the top block with one hand.

SEE ALSO

Details for:
Sharpening saws 480–481

Using a mitre box
A mitre box has slots set at 45 degrees to guide the saw blade when you are cutting mitre joints. There are also slots set at 90 degrees to guide the blade when cutting square butt joints.

● **Essential tools**
Tape measure
Combination square
Marking knife
Marking gauge
Crosscut saw
Tenon saw

WOODWORKING TOOLS

FRAME SAWS

A frame saw is fitted with a very slim blade for cutting curves. To stop the blade bending, it is held taut by the strong metal frame.

Coping saw

A coping saw is the most useful frame saw. Its teeth are coarse enough to cut fairly thick timber, yet it can cope with thin boards.

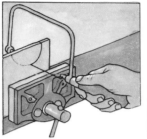

Using a coping saw
The blade is held between pins that swivel so you can turn it in the direction of the cut, swinging the frame out of the way.

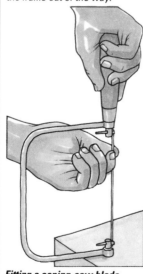

Fitting a coping-saw blade
A coping saw's blade needs to be replaced if it breaks or when it gets blunt. Loosen the handle with a few anticlockwise turns. Hook the new blade into the pin furthest from the handle, then press the frame down on the bench and locate the other end of the blade. Tension the blade by turning the handle clockwise. Make sure that the teeth point away from the handle and that the two pins are aligned so that the blade is not twisted.

Fret saw

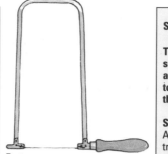

A fret-saw blade is so fine that the spring of the frame is able to keep it under tension. The blade is held at each end by a thumb-screw and plate, with the teeth pointing towards the handle.

Using a fret saw
Hold the wood over the edge of the workbench so you can saw with the blade upright, pulling on it from below.

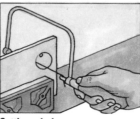

Cutting a hole
Use a frame saw to cut a large hole in a piece of wood. Having marked out the hole, drill a small one inside the outline. Pass the blade through the small hole, then connect it to the saw frame. Cut out the hole, adjusting the angle of the blade to the frame as required, then dismantle the saw in order to free the blade.

Padsaw or keyhole saw

A padsaw is designed for cutting holes in panels. Having a blade that is wider than a coping saw's, it's easier to use on straight cuts, although the unsupported blade bends easily. As there's no frame to restrict its movement, a pad-saw can be used for jobs such as cutting the slot for a letter box.

SHARPENING SAWS

To cut properly saws must be sharpened carefully with special tools, so you may prefer to have them sharpened professionally, especially any that are finer than a tenon saw. If you want to keep them in tip-top condition yourself, you will need to buy a saw file for sharpening the teeth and a saw set for bending the teeth to the required angle.

Saw-sharpening tools
A saw file is double-ended and triangular in section. Strictly speaking, its length should relate precisely to the spacing of the saw's teeth, but in practice you can use one file about 150mm (6in) long for handsaws and another, 100mm (4in) long, for a tenon saw. You can also buy a file guide, which locates over the saw's teeth and keeps the file at a constant angle while in use.

Closing the handles of a saw set squeezes the saw tooth between a plunger and an angled anvil, which you set first to correspond with the number of tooth points per 25mm (1in) on the saw blade (**1**). To set the anvil, close the handles and release the locking screw at the end of the tool. Turn the anvil till the required setting number on its edge aligns with the plunger, then tighten the locking screw.

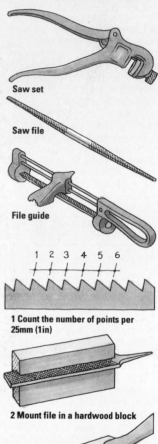

Saw set

Saw file

File guide

1 Count the number of points per 25mm (1in)

Topping a saw
*Topping restores all of a saw's teeth to the same height. It is not absolutely essential every time a saw is sharpened, but a light topping will produce a spot of bright metal on each point that will help you to sharpen the teeth evenly. Near the top edge of a block of hardwood, plane a groove that will grip a smooth flat file (**2**). Clamp the saw, teeth uppermost, between two battens held in a vice and, with the wood block held against the flat of the blade, pass the file two or three times along the tops of the teeth (**3**) so that each one shows a tiny spot of bright metal.*

2 Mount file in a hardwood block

3 Top the saw with the file

Setting the teeth
*Adjust the saw set to the right number of points (see above) and, starting at one end of the saw, place the set over the first tooth facing away from you. Align the plunger with the centre of the tooth. Hold the set steady and squeeze the handles together (**4**). Set every other tooth – those facing away from you – then turn the saw round and set those in between.*

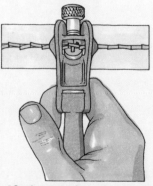

(Continued in next column)

4 Set the saw teeth

WOODWORKING TOOLS

SHARPENING SAWS

Sharpening a ripsaw

Clamp the blade between two battens with its teeth projecting just above the edges of the wood. Starting next to the handle, place the saw file against the front edge of the first tooth facing away from you, and settle the file snugly into the gullet (the space between the teeth). Holding the file square to the flat of the blade (5), make two or three strokes until the edge of the tooth is shiny right up to its point and half of the bright topping spot has disappeared. File alternate teeth in this way, then turn the saw round and sharpen those in between until the bright spots are completely removed.

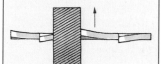

5 Filing ripsaw teeth

Sharpening a crosscut saw

Use the same method, but hold the file at an angle of 60 to 70 degrees to the flat of the blade (6). Lower the file handle slightly.

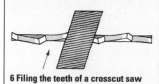

6 Filing the teeth of a crosscut saw

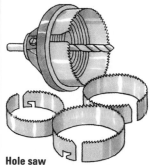

Hole saw

You can buy a set of hole saws for cutting perfectly round holes of different diameters. These clip into a backing plate clamped to a twist drill that fits into the chuck of a power drill. Place the tip of the twist drill at the centre of the required hole, set the power tool to a slow speed and push the revolving saw against the wood. Always place a piece of scrap timber behind the work to stop the saw breaking out the back.

POWER SAWS

Power saws are invaluable for cutting heavy structural timbers and large man-made boards. Battery-powered saws are made, but they are rarely available to the DIY market.

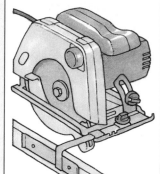

Portable circular saw

When you buy or hire a circular saw, choose one with a 190mm (7½in) blade. Its motor will be powerful enough to give a blade speed that can cut thick timber and man-made boards without straining the saw or scorching the work. You can buy blades designed specifically for ripping or crosscutting, but for general use choose a universal blade. This will cut efficiently along and across the grain, and is equally suitable for sawing timber and man-made boards. There are also special blades and abrasive discs for cutting metal and stone.

On a good portable circular saw, you can adjust the angle of the blade for cutting bevels.

Making straight cuts

Circular saws have removable fences to guide their blades parallel to the edge of the work, but these are often too small to be of much use. You can extend the fence by screwing a batten to it. Alternatively, clamp a strip of wood onto the work itself to guide the edge of the sole plate; by clamping the strip at various angles across the wood, you can crosscut boards or planks at those angles.

Sawing by eye

When accuracy of cut is not too important you can use the saw freehand, guiding a notch in the sole plate along a line marked on the work. Place the tip of the sole plate on the work and align the notch with the line. Switch on, let the blade run up to speed, then advance the saw steadily.

Reciprocating saws

With their powerful motors, and blades up to 300mm (1ft) long, these saws are especially useful for such jobs as cutting openings in stud partitions.

Portable power jigsaw

Portable jigsaws are primarily for making curved cuts in timber and man-made boards. Although they generally have guide fences for straight cutting, the fences are rarely sturdy enough to stop the blade wandering. Discard jigsaw blades when they become blunt, and keep some spares handy. As the blades are fairly cheap, it's worth buying some of the special ones for cutting plastics, metal, plasterboard and even ceramics.

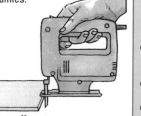

Using a jigsaw

Rest the front of the sole plate on the edge of the work, squeeze the trigger, and then advance the moving blade into the work along the marked cutting line. Don't force or twist the blade or it will break. Let the blade come to rest before you put the saw down.

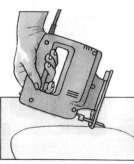

1 Preparing to plunge-cut

Cutting holes with a jigsaw

The simplest way to cut a large hole in a panel is first to drill a starter hole into which you can insert the jigsaw blade, but you can start by 'plunge cutting'.

First tilt the jigsaw onto the front edge of its sole plate, with the tip of the blade just above the surface of the work (1); then switch on the saw, and gradually lower the blade into the wood until it is upright and the sole plate is flat on the surface.

CIRCULAR-SAW SAFETY

A circular saw is perfectly safe to use provided that you follow the manufacturer's handling and fitting instructions carefully, and observe the following rules:

● Always unplug a circular saw before you adjust or change the blade.
● Don't use a blunt blade. Have it sharpened professionally.
● Fit new blades according to manufacturers' instructions. Check that the teeth at the bottom of the blade are facing in the direction of the cut.
● All circular saws must have a fixed blade guard and a lower guard that swings back as the cut proceeds. Never use the saw without these guards in place, and always make sure that the lower guard closes automatically when the blade clears the work.
● The work must be securely held, either on sawhorses or a workbench.
● Never have the electrical flex in front of the saw blade.
● Never force the blade into a cut. If it jams, back off a little until it returns to full speed.
● Never put a portable circular saw down before the blade has stopped spinning.
● Never wear loose clothing, or a necktie or necklace, as any of these could easily become entangled in the machine.

Saw bench

You can clamp a portable circular saw upside down under a saw-bench attachment and cut wood by passing it across the blade, which projects through the flat bed.

WOODWORKING TOOLS

PLANES AND SPOKESHAVES

Unless timber is to be used for framing, as in a stud partition or a bath panel, it must be planed to remove the marks of saw teeth. Planes are also used for reducing wood to size and shape. Wooden planes are still made, and many antique ones are for sale at reasonable prices, but most people find modern metal planes easier to adjust for the exact thickness of shaving they require.

BENCH PLANES

Bench planes are general-purpose tools for smoothing wood to make joints between boards or to level the surface of several boards glued together. Bench planes are all similar in design, differing only in the length of the sole.

Jointer plane

This is the longest bench plane, with a sole as much as 600mm (2ft) long. The jointer is designed for truing up the long edges of boards that are to be butted and glued together. It is also useful for levelling large flat panels, since the long sole bridges minor irregularities till the blade shaves them down – whereas a plane with a shorter sole would simply follow the uneven surface.

Jack plane

A jack plane 350 to 375mm (1ft 2in to 1ft 3in) long is a good all-purpose tool. If you can afford only one bench plane, choose a jack plane, which is light enough to cope with most planing without tiring you.

● Essential tools
Jack plane
Block plane

Smoothing plane

A finely set smoothing plane is used for putting the final surface on a piece of timber after it has been reduced to size with a jack plane or jointer plane.

1 Checking the blade angle

Adjusting a bench plane

Before you use a bench plane, adjust the angle and depth of the blade. Check the angle by sighting down the sole of the plane from the toe (1), and use the lateral-adjustment lever behind the blade to set the cutting edge so that it projects an equal amount across the width of the sole. Use the knurled adjusting nut in front of the handle to set the depth to take off a fine shaving.

STORING PLANES

Never put a plane sole-down on the bench during work – always lay it on its side. Similarly, a plane should always be stored on its side, even when the blade is withdrawn. For long-term storage, dismantle and clean the plane, and grease all bare-metal parts lightly to prevent rusting.

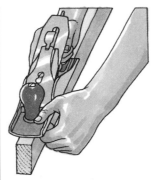

Planing a square edge

Keep the plane flat on the edge of the work by holding the toe down with the thumb of your free hand and pressing the fingers against the side of the wood to guide the tool along.

Planing a wide flat surface

To plane a wide surface as flat as possible, first work across it diagonally, following the general direction of the grain. Finish by working parallel to the grain, taking off very fine shavings.

Block plane

The blade of a block plane is mounted at a shallow angle so that its edge can slice smoothly through the end grain of timber. Since it is small and lightweight (you can hold the tool in the palm of one hand), a block plane is also ideal for all kinds of fine trimming and shaping.

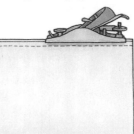

Trimming end grain

Cut a line all round the work with a marking knife, then set the workpiece vertically in a vice. To prevent the wood splitting, form a chamfer down to the line on one side by planing towards the centre. Plane the end square, working from the other side down to the marked line until you have removed the chamfer.

Using a shooting board

You can trim end grain with a bench plane on its side, running on a shooting board. The blade must be sharp and finely set. The work is held against the stop.

Shoulder plane

A shoulder plane is not a tool you need for everyday use – but, as its blade spans the whole width of its squarely machined body, it is ideal for trimming the square shoulders of large joints and rebates. With the body removed, the exposed blade can trim a rebate right up to a stopped end.

Power plane

A power plane is particularly useful for smoothing and shaping large structural timbers, and also for trimming door bottoms in order to accommodate new carpet. When the tool is fitted with a guide fence, its revolving cutter block can be used for planing rebates. Most power planes can be fixed upside down in a bench-mounted frame so that you can pass timber across the cutters using both hands.

Spokeshaves

A spokeshave is a miniature plane for shaping curved edges. Use one that has a flat base to shape convex curves, and one with a bellied base when shaping concave curves. When using either tool, shape the curve from two directions so as to work with the grain all the time. Sharpen a spokeshave cutter as you would the blade of a plane.

Adjusting the cutter

Use the two adjusting screws to produce a fine setting, then turn the central locking screw to 'fix' the spokeshave's cutter.

Using a spokeshave

With a handle in each hand and your thumbs on the back edges of the handles, push the tool away from you. Rock it backwards or forwards as you work, to produce a continuous shaving.

SEE ALSO

Details for:
Routers   484

MOULDING PLANES

Woodworkers often need to cut grooves in wood, both with and across the grain, and to plane rebates or mouldings along the edges of workpieces.

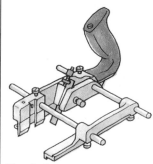

Plough plane
A plough plane takes narrow blades for cutting grooves. You can only use it in the direction of the grain.

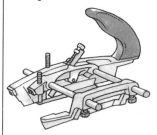

Combination plane
A combination plane can be used, with a variety of shaped blades, to cut grooves or rebates and a number of moulding profiles. It has a pair of vertically adjusting blades – called 'spurs' – that cut parallel lines ahead of the main blade, in order to prevent tearing the wood fibres when a groove or housing is planed across the grain. The plane can also be used to cut tongue-and-groove joints along the edges of boards.

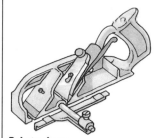

Rebate plane
A rebate plane is similar to a bench plane, but its blade spans the whole width of the sole. With its depth gauge and guide fence set to the required dimensions, the plane will cut any number of identical rebates.

1 Starting a moulding

Using moulding planes
Whether you are using a plough, combination or rebate plane, follow the maker's instructions for setting the depth gauge and guide fence, which together control the position of the blade relative to the surface and edge of the wood.

Hold the guide fence against the edge of the workpiece at the far end and make short strokes to begin the moulding (1) – and then move backwards, making longer and longer strokes till the depth gauge rests on the surface of the wood. Finish with one continuous pass along the length of the workpiece.

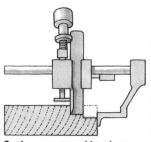

Cutting an extra-wide rebate
If you need to cut a rebate wider than a standard blade, first plane a rebate on the outer edge, then adjust the guide fence to make a second cut that will make up the required width.

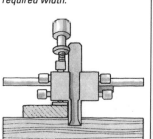

Cutting a housing
When using a moulding plane to cut a housing (a groove across the grain), remove the guide fence and clamp a batten across the workpiece in order to guide the body of the plane.

SHARPENING PLANES

To keep its sharp cutting edge, a plane blade must be honed on a flat oilstone. Choose one with a medium grit on one side to remove metal quickly and fine grit on the other side for the final honing of the edge.

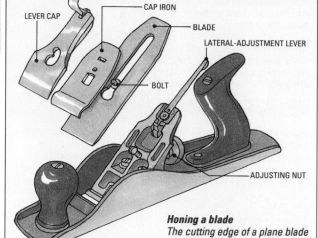

LEVER CAP — CAP IRON — BLADE — LATERAL-ADJUSTMENT LEVER — BOLT — ADJUSTING NUT

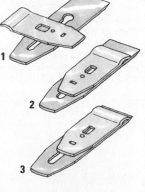

1
2
3

Removing and replacing a blade
The blade of a bench or block plane is clamped in place by a metal lever cap. Slacken the lever to remove the cap and lift the blade out of the plane. The blade of a bench plane has a cap iron bolted to it to break and curl the shavings as they are trimmed from the wood. Undo the fixing bolt with a screwdriver and remove the cap iron before you sharpen the blade.

When you replace the cap iron, place it across the blade (1), then swivel it until the two are aligned (2). Don't drag the iron across the cutting edge, but slide it to within 1mm (¹⁄₁₆in) of it (3).

Honing a blade
The cutting edge of a plane blade will have been ground to an angle of about 25 degrees. The object of sharpening it on an oilstone is to hone the leading edge only to about 30 degrees.

Hold the blade against the stone at the correct angle and rub it to and fro to produce a sharp edge. A wide blade must be held at an angle across the stone so that the whole edge is in contact with it (1). Keep the stone lubricated with a little oil while you work.

Honing creates a burr along the cutting edge. Remove it by laying the back face of the blade flat on the stone (2) and making several passes along the surface.

1 Hone the cutting edge

2 Remove the burr

Using a honing guide
If you want to be certain that you are honing a blade to the correct angle, clamp it in a honing guide and roll the guide to and fro on the surface of the stone to sharpen the blade.

Repairing a chipped cutting edge
If you chip the cutting edge of a plane blade (against a nail, for example), regrind it on a bench grinder. Hold the blade against the tool rest and move the cutting edge from side to side against the revolving wheel until it is straight and clean. Use only light pressure and dip the blade into water regularly to cool it. Finally, sharpen the ground edge by honing it on an oilstone.

● **Essential tools**
Combination oilstone

WOODWORKING TOOLS

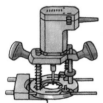

Hand router

Power router

Power-router bits
1 Grooving bit
2 Edge-moulding bit

● **Essentials tools**
Firmer chisels
3 to 25mm (⅛ to 1in)
Bevel-edge chisels
12 to 25mm (½ to 1in)
Gouges
Select sizes as required
Mortise chisels
Select sizes as required

ROUTERS

A hand router is used to finish the bottom of a sawn housing after most of the waste has been cut out with a chisel. A power router is a sophisticated tool that replicates the various tasks performed by a combination plane. It will follow a curved edge as easily as a straight one, and the cutter revolves so fast that it produces as clean a cut across the grain as with it.

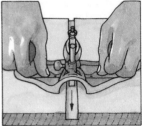

Using a hand router
To pare the bottom of a housing, hold one handle of the router in each hand and push it away from you, as you would a plane.

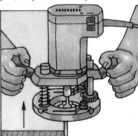

Using a power router
Always let the bit run up to full speed before you allow it to come into contact with the work, and always lift it clear of the groove or moulding before you switch off. Since the bit revolves clockwise, you have to feed the machine against the rotation when moulding an edge – so the cutter pulls itself into the wood.

Router cutters and bits
Hand-router cutters have square shafts that clamp into the tool and are adjusted vertically to set the chisel-like cutting edges at the required depth.

Power-router bits fit into a chuck at the base of the tool and need to be adjusted until they project through the baseplate. A grooving bit has two symmetrical cutting edges that run down to the bottom. An edge-moulding bit has a cylindrical pilot tip below shaped cutting edges; this runs against the edge of the work to stop the cutter biting too deeply.

Always follow the manufacturer's instructions when fitting and adjusting router bits and cutters.

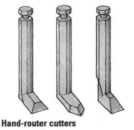

Hand-router cutters

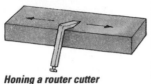

Honing a router cutter
Hone blunt hand-router cutters on an oilstone. Position the stone so the cutter's shaft will clear the bench, then rub the cutter from side to side on the stone.

Cutting grooves and housings
To cut a groove parallel to an edge, fit and set the adjustable guide fence (1) or run the edge of the baseplate against a batten clamped to the work (2). To cut a wide groove, use two parallel battens to guide the bit along the outer edges (3), then remove the waste from the centre.

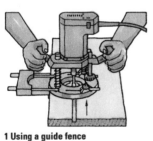

1 Using a guide fence

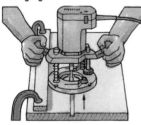

2 Using a guide batten

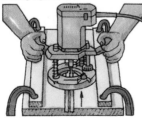

3 Cutting a wide groove

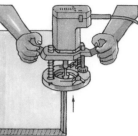

Cutting edge mouldings
Rest the baseplate of the router on the upper surface of the work and, when the bit has run up to full speed, feed it against and along the edge of the timber.

If you need to mould all four edges of a rectangular piece of wood, shape the end grain first, then run the router along each side of the workpiece.

SHARPENING POWER-ROUTER BITS

Although it is possible to grind and hone power-router bits yourself, they must be perfectly symmetrical. It is therefore generally better to have them sharpened professionally.

CHISELS AND GOUGES

Chisels are general-purpose woodcutting tools, but are used mostly to remove the waste from joints or to pare and trim them to size. The size of a chisel refers to the width of its cutting edge. Although chisels range in width from 3mm (⅛in) to 50mm (2in), a selection of sizes up to 25mm (1in) should be sufficient for most woodworking purposes.

Gouges are similar to wood chisels, but their blades are curved in cross section for such work as cutting the shoulders of a joint to fit against a turned leg or scooping out the waste from a 'finger pull' on a drawer front or sliding cupboard door.

Wood chisels and gouges have handles made of boxwood or impact-resistant plastic.

Firmer chisel
A firmer chisel has a strong, flat, rectangular-section blade for chopping out waste wood. It is strong enough to be driven with a mallet or hammer – though you should never use a hammer on a wooden tool handle.

Bevel-edge chisel
A bevel-edge chisel is used for paring – especially for trimming undercuts such as dovetail joints or housings. The bevels enable you to work the blade in spaces that would be inaccessible to a firmer chisel. However, a bevel-edge chisel is not as strong as a firmer chisel and may break if it is used for heavy work. If a little extra force is needed to drive the chisel forward, use your shoulder or the ball of your hand.

Mortise chisel
A mortise chisel has a thick blade, rectangular in section, for chopping and levering the waste out of mortise joints. Because this type of chisel is often driven with a mallet, a shock-absorbent leather washer is fitted between the blade and the ferrule.

Chopping out waste wood
Don't chop out too much waste in one go – the wood will split or the chisel will be driven over the line of the joint, resulting in a poor fit. Remove the waste a little at a time, working back to the marked line. Use a mallet at first, but finish off by hand.

Paring with a chisel
Finish a joint by paring away very thin shavings with a bevel-edge chisel. Control the blade with finger and thumb, steadying your hand against the work, while applying pressure to the tip of the handle with the other hand.

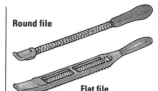

In-cannel gouge

Out-cannel gouge

Gouges

The cutting edge of an in-cannel gouge is formed by grinding the inside of the curved blade. This type of gouge is used for trimming rounded shoulders.

An out-cannel gouge is ground on the outside, so that the blade will not be driven into the wood when it is being used to scoop out shallow recesses.

STORING CHISELS

You can make a rack for chisels and gouges by gluing spacer blocks between two strips of plywood, leaving a slot for the blades. Screw the rack to the wall behind your workbench, so the tools are within easy reach.

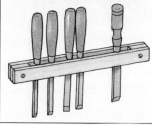

RASPS AND SURFORMS

Rasps are coarse files used for shaping free curves in wood.

Traditional rasps have teeth formed in the solid metal to wear away the wood, whereas modern Surform files have hollow blades pressed out to form a great many cutting edges. Surform files stay sharp for a long time; they also remove wood very quickly and do not get clogged up like rasps, as the shavings fall through their hollow blades.

Cabinet rasp

Flat rasp

Round rasp

Rasps

Traditional rasps are available in various degrees of coarseness, designated bastard, second-cut and smooth. Their names refer to their shapes: a cabinet rasp is half-round, with one flat and one curved face; a flat rasp has two flat faces and one cutting edge; a round rasp is circular in section, tapering towards the tip.

Round file

Flat file

Surform files

A round Surform file has a detachable handle and thumb-grip at the tip. A flat Surform has a disposable blade that fits into a hollow metal frame.

Using a rasp

A rasp cuts only on the forward stroke. Control its tip with your finger tips as you work, and never use one without first fitting a handle. Holding the bare pointed tang is very dangerous.

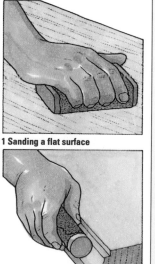

Cleaning a rasp

When a rasp becomes clogged with wood fibres, clear the teeth with a fine wire brush made for the purpose.

SANDERS AND ABRASIVES

Abrasive papers are used for smoothing wood after it has been shaped with rasps or Surform files. Always sand in the direction of the grain. Tiny scratches made by cross-grain sanding may not appear until the work has been clear-varnished or polished. Though flat surfaces are often sanded smooth, you can get a better finish with a cabinet scraper.

Sanding by hand

Abrasive papers – still widely referred to as 'sandpapers' – are graded by the size and spacing of the grit. There are coarse, medium and fine grits, but they are also designated by number (the higher the number, the finer the grit). On 'open-coat' papers the particles are spaced wide apart to reduce clogging. The more tightly packed 'close-coat' papers produce a finer finish.

TYPES OF ABRASIVE

Yellow flint or glasspaper is cheap and relatively soft. Use it for the first stages of sanding, especially on softwoods.

Garnet paper is much harder than glasspaper and wears more slowly. It is a reddish colour and comes in very fine grades. Use it on hardwoods.

Silicon-carbide paper (usually known as wet-and-dry paper) is most widely used for smoothing paintwork – but you can also use it dry to produce an extra-smooth finish on hardwoods.

Using abrasive papers

Fold the sheet of paper over the edge of a bench and tear it into convenient strips. To smooth flat surfaces or square edges, wrap a strip of paper round a cork sanding block (1); on curves, use your finger tips to apply the paper. To sand mouldings, wrap a strip of abrasive paper round a dowel (2) or shaped block.

As the work proceeds, use progressively finer grades of paper. Before the final sanding, dampen the wood with water to raise the grain. When the wood is dry, sand it with a very fine abrasive for a perfect finish.

To sand end grain, first rub the grain with your fingers: the wood feels rougher in one direction than the other. Sand the grain in the smoother direction only, not to and fro.

When the grit gets clogged with wood dust, clear it by tapping the paper against the bench, or use a fine wire brush.

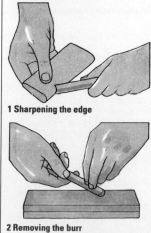

1 Sanding a flat surface

2 Sanding a moulding

SHARPENING CHISELS AND GOUGES

Sharpen a chisel as you would a plane blade – but hone it across the whole surface of the oilstone in a figure-of-eight pattern to avoid uneven wear on the stone.

Honing an out-cannel gouge

Stand to the side of the oilstone and rub the bevel of the gouge along the stone from end to end in a figure-of-eight pattern (1). At the same time, rock the blade from side to side to hone the curved edge evenly. Remove the burr from the inside of the cutting edge with a slipstone (2) – a small oilstone shaped to fit a variety of gouge sizes.

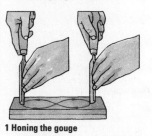

1 Honing the gouge

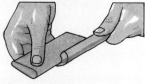

2 Removing the burr

Honing an in-cannel gouge

Sharpen the bevel on the inside of an in-cannel gouge by honing with a slipstone (1), then remove the burr by holding the back of the blade flat on an oilstone and rocking it from side to side while sliding it up and down the surface of the stone (2).

1 Sharpening the edge

2 Removing the burr

WOODWORKING TOOLS

SEE ALSO
Details for:
Preparing wood	53
Sharpening planes	483
Cabinet scraper	486

● **Essential tools**
Combination oilstone
Slipstone
Range of abrasives
Sanding block
Rasps or Surform files
(choose a Surform file in preference to a solid rasp, but buy as required)

WOODWORKING TOOLS

POWER SANDERS

Power sanders ease the chore of sanding large surfaces but rarely produce a surface good enough for a clear finish – so a final sanding by hand is needed.

Belt sander

A belt sander has a continuous loop of abrasive paper passing round a revolving drum at each end. A flat plate between the two drums presses the moving abrasive against the wood.

Using a belt sander

Switch on the machine and lower it gently onto the work, then make forward and backward passes with the sander, holding it parallel to the grain. The machine's weight provides enough pressure to do the work, especially when the abrasive band is fresh. Cover the surface with overlapping passes, but don't let the sander ride over the edges of the work or it will round them over. Lift the sander from the surface before you switch it off, and don't put the tool aside before the belt comes to a stop.

Change to a finer-grade belt to remove the marks left by the previous sanding. Always follow the manufacturer's instructions when changing the belt.

Finishing sander

A finishing sander produces a surface that needs only a light hand sanding before you apply a clear polish. On this type of sander, a strip of abrasive paper is stretched across a flat rubber pad that is moved by the motor in a tight, rapid orbital pattern. Use only light pressure – otherwise the paper will leave tiny swirling marks on the wood. A cordless finishing sander is convenient for working outdoors.

Rubber-disc sander

Disc sander

The simplest disc sander is a flexible rubber pad with a central shaft that is gripped in the chuck of an electric drill. An abrasive-paper disc is bolted to the face of the pad. This type of sander is not suitable for fine woodwork, since it inevitably leaves swirling scratch marks that have to be removed with a finishing sander or cabinet scraper before a clear finish can be applied. However, it is a handy tool for cleaning up old floorboards.

Using a rubber-disc sander

With the drill running, flex the edge of the rubber disc against the wood. Keep the sander moving along the work to avoid deep scratching.

Foam drum sander

This flexible plastic-foam drum covered by an abrasive-paper band is driven by a central shaft that fits into the chuck of a power drill. The drum deforms against irregularly curved workpieces.

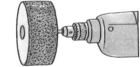

Orbital disc sander

This power tool – sometimes called a random orbital sander – has a sanding disc that moves eccentrically and simultaneously rotates, leaving the surface of the wood virtually scratch-free. The flexible backing pad copes with curved surfaces.

WOOD SCRAPERS

Scrapers provide wood with the smoothest finish. They take off fine shavings, whereas abrasive papers leave minute scratches on the surface.

Cabinet scraper

This is a simple rectangle of thin steel used for scraping flat surfaces. Curved-edge versions are used for working mouldings and carved wood.

Using a cabinet scraper

Hold the scraper in both hands, pressing it into a slightly curved shape with your thumbs Tilt the scraper away from you and work diagonally across the surface in two directions to scrape the wood flat. Finally, scrape lightly in the direction of the grain.

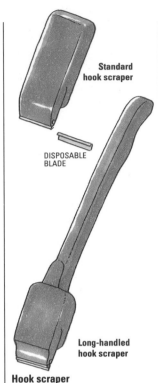

Standard hook scraper

DISPOSABLE BLADE

Long-handled hook scraper

Hook scraper

A hook scraper's disposable blade slides into a clip at the end of a wooden handle. Simply pull the scraper towards you along the grain of the wood, applying light pressure.

SHARPENING A CABINET SCRAPER

A cabinet scraper is sharpened by raising a burr along its edge. Straight and curved scrapers are both sharpened the same way, although it's harder to turn an even burr along a curved edge.

First, draw-file the edge of the scraper and hone it perfectly square on an oilstone (1). To raise the burr, hold the scraper flat on a workbench, then stroke the edge firmly several times with the curved back of a gouge (2). This stretches the metal along the edge of the scraper, which produces the burr.

Turn the burr to project from the face of the scraper by holding the scraper upright on the bench and stroking the burred corner with the gouge held at an angle to the face (3).

1 Hone the edge square

2 Raise the burr

3 Turn the burr over

● **Essential tools**
Flat cabinet scraper

DRILLS AND BRACES

The versatile electric drill is the only essential power tool for a tool kit. However, it has not yet completely replaced the brace and the hand drill.

Brace

A brace is designed for boring holes that have a relatively large diameter. The bit is driven into the wood by the turning force on the handle, plus pressure on the head of the tool.

A good-quality brace has a ratchet so you can turn the bit in one direction only when working in a confined space where a full turn of the handle isn't possible.

1 Tightening the chuck

Brace bits

Brace bits have a square-section tang that fits into the jaws of the tool's chuck.

To fit a bit, grip the chuck in one hand and turn the handle of the brace clockwise to open the jaws. Drop the bit into the chuck, then tighten the chuck on the bit by turning the handle in the anticlockwise direction **(1)**.

Auger bit

An auger bit has helical twists along its shank that remove the waste as the bit bores into the wood. Being the same diameter as the cutting tip, the twisted shank keeps the bit straight when you are boring deep holes. A tapered lead screw helps to draw the bit into the timber, and knife-edge spurs cut the perimeter of the hole before the bit enters the wood.

Expansive bit

This bit has an adjustable spurred cutter for boring holes of up to 75mm (3in) in diameter.

Centre bit

This type of bit is fast-cutting because it has no helical twists to create friction, but it tends to wander off line.

It's best for drilling man-made boards, in which the holes are never very deep. Its relatively short shank makes it useful for working in confined spaces.

Using a brace

When using a brace, don't let the bit burst through the back of the work and split the wood. As soon as the lead screw emerges, turn the work over and complete the hole from the other side.

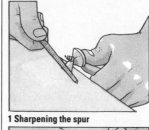

Hand drill

For small-diameter holes use a hand drill (sometimes called a wheelbrace). Some models have a cast body enclosing the drive mechanism to keep gear wheels and pinions free from dust.

Using a hand drill

Centre the drill bit on the work. This is easier if the centre for the hole has been marked with a bradawl puncture. Give the bit a start by moving the handle to and fro until the bit bites into the wood, then crank the handle to drive the bit clockwise.

Twist drills

Use standard twist drills with a hand drill. To fit a twist drill, open the tool's chuck by turning it anticlockwise. Insert the bit, and then turn the chuck clockwise to tighten it. Check that a very small twist drill is centred accurately between the chuck's three jaws.

SHARPENING TWIST DRILLS

It is possible to sharpen a blunt twist drill on a bench grinder, but it takes practice to centre the point. An electric sharpener centres the point automatically. Insert the tip of the drill in the appropriate hole in the top of the machine and switch on for a few seconds to grind one cutting edge – then rotate the drill one half turn to position the other edge and repeat the process.

SHARPENING BRACE BITS

Brace bits are sharpened with fine needle files. Put an edge on a spur by stroking its inside face with a flat file (1), then rest the point of the bit on a bench and sharpen the cutting edge with a triangular file (2).

1 Sharpening the spur

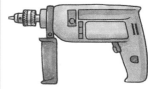

2 Sharpening the edge

Power drill

A power drill is likely to be the most useful and versatile item in your tool kit. Buy a good-quality drill that has a relatively powerful motor – 500 to 600W – and a lightweight plastic body that will protect you from electric shock.

Cordless power drill

Drills powered by rechargeable batteries are quiet-running and convenient, doing away with the need for an extension lead in order to reach a remote work site or the top of a ladder. Choose a cordless drill that has a variable-speed facility for inserting wood-screws and a hammer action for drilling masonry.

SELECTING USEFUL FEATURES

Before you buy an electric drill, make sure it has all the features that you are likely to require.

● Variable speed

With a variable-speed drill, you are able to select the ideal speed for drilling different materials. A slow speed uses the drill's power to produce more torque (turning force) for drilling into masonry or metal; a high speed produces a clean cut when drilling wood. You can select a maximum speed with a dial, or run the tool at any convenient speed by varying the pressure on the trigger.

A variable-speed facility is essential if you want to use a power drill for driving screws.

● Trigger lock

A trigger-lock button sets the drill for continuous running when it is used to drive attachments.

● Chuck size

The chuck's size refers to the maximum diameter of drill shank it can accommodate. A 10mm (⅜in) chuck is adequate for most purposes, though there are drills with a chuck size of 16mm (⅝in). You can drill holes of a diameter greater than the chuck size by using special bits with cutters that are larger than their shanks.

● Percussion or hammer action

Operating a switch converts most electric drills from smooth rotation to a hammer action that delivers several hundred blows per second to the revolving chuck. This action is only used when drilling into brick or stone; the hammer vibration helps by breaking up hard particles ahead of specially toughened masonry bits. Helical flutes along the shank of the bit clear the debris from the hole.

● Reverse rotation

If you want to use a screwdriver bit with your power drill, make sure its rotation can be reversed, so you can take screws out as well as being able to insert them.

● Handgrips

A power drill normally has a pistol-grip handle and a second handgrip for steadying the drill. Some manufacturers provide an extra handle that bolts onto the rear of the drill to enable you to exert maximum pressure directly behind the bit.

WOODWORKING TOOLS

SEE ALSO	
Details for:	
Bench grinding	483
Power-drill bits	488
Safety tips	488

● **Essential tools**
Set of twist drills
Power drill

WOODWORKING TOOLS

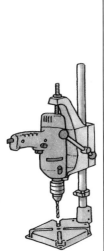

Using a drill stand
To bore holes that are absolutely square to the face of the work, mount your power drill in a vertical drill stand.

● **Essential tools**
Set of spade or power-bore bits
Countersink bit
Claw hammer
Cross-peen hammer
Pin hammer
Carpenter's mallet
Pincers
Nail set

POWER-DRILL BITS

A variety of bits can be used in a power drill, depending on the kind of hole you want to bore.

Twist drills
You can use standard twist drills of any size up to the maximum opening of the chuck. To bore larger holes, use reduced-shank twist drills.

Power-bore bit

Spade bit

Power-bore and spade bits
With power-bore and spade bits you can drill holes up to 38mm (1½in) in diameter. Both produce minimal friction. Place the sharp lead point of the bit on the centre of the hole before squeezing the trigger of the drill.

Countersink bit
To sink the head of a counter-sunk woodscrew flush with the surface of the work, make a tapered recess in the top of the clearance hole with a 'rose' or countersink bit. These bits can be used with a hand drill or a brace, but a high-speed power drill forms a neater recess.

Unless you use a drill stand (see left), the countersink bit will 'chatter' if the hole has already been drilled, producing a rough recess. When using a power drill without a stand, it's best to make the countersink recess first, then drill the hole itself in the centre.

Screwdriver bits
With slotted-head or cross-head screwdriver bits, you can use your electric drill as a power screwdriver. The drill must be capable of slow speeds.

Plug cutter
This special bit cuts cylindrical plugs of wood for concealing the heads of screws sunk below the surface of the work.

Dowel bit
This is a twist drill with a sharp lead point and cutting spurs that help to keep it on line when you are boring holes for dowel joints.

Drill and countersink bit
This bit makes the pilot hole, clearance hole and countersink recess for a woodscrew in a single operation. As it is matched to one specific screw size, it is only worth purchasing when you are planning to use a fair number of identical screws.

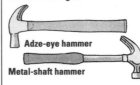

Fitting a power-drill bit
Turn the chuck anticlockwise to open its jaws, and insert the bit. Close the jaws on the bit and tighten the chuck with the key supplied with the drill. Remove the key before you switch on.

USING A POWER DRILL SAFELY

● **Choose a drill with a plastic non-conducting body.**
● **Always unplug a drill before fitting bits, accessories or attachments.**
● **Remove the chuck key before switching on the drill.**
● **Don't wear loose clothing or a necktie or necklace while using a drill.**
● **Use a proper purpose-made extension lead if you need to extend the drill's flex.**
● **Never lift the drill by its flex.**

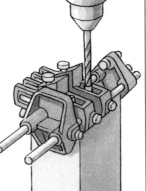

Dowelling jig
A dowelling jig clamped to the work ensures alignment of dowel holes and also keeps the drill bit perpendicular to the work.

HAMMERS AND MALLETS

Driving in a nail is so simple that one hammer would seem to be as effective as another, but using one that is the right shape and weight for a job makes for easier, trouble-free work.

A mallet has its own specific uses, and should never be used for hammering nails.

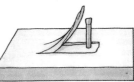

Adze-eye hammer

Metal-shaft hammer

Claw hammer
This is a heavy general-purpose hammer, and probably the most useful one to have in a basic tool kit. The claw at the back of the head is for levering out nails. In order to cope with the leverage, the hammer head has to be fixed firmly to a strong shaft.

The traditional adze-eye head has a deep, square socket driven and wedged onto a tough but flexible hickory shaft. However, an all-metal claw hammer is an even better tool. Its tubular-steel shaft won't bend or break; the head can't work loose; and the rubber grip is both comfortable and shock-absorbing.

Cross-peen hammer
For tasks that are too delicate for a heavy claw hammer, use a medium-weight cross-peen hammer. Its wedge-shaped peen is for setting (starting) a nail held between finger and thumb.

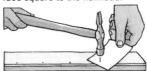

Pin hammer
A small, lightweight pin hammer is the perfect tool for tapping in fine panel pins and tacks.

Using a hammer
Set a nail in wood with one or two taps of the hammer until it stands upright without support, then drive it home with firm steady blows, keeping your wrists straight and the hammer face square to the nailhead.

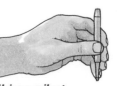

Using a nail set
A nail set is a punch with a hollow-ground tip used for sinking nails below the surface of the wood. Nail sets are made in several sizes for use with large and small nails. Having driven the nail almost flush, hold the set upright between thumb and fingertips and place its tip on the protruding nailhead, then tap the tool with your hammer. With a heavy hammer very little force is needed to sink the nail.

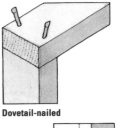

Blind nailing
To hide a nail fixing, lift a flap of wood with a gouge, sink the nail with a nail set, then glue the flap and cramp it flat.

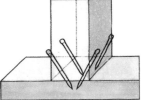

Dovetail-nailed

Skew-nailed

Making a strong nailed joint
The grip between the nails and the wood is usually enough to hold the joint together, but for stronger fixings drive the nails in at an angle. When angled nails fix wood onto the end grain of another member, the technique is called dovetail-nailing: when they pass through the side of a section it's called skew-nailing.

◄ *Hammering small nails*
If the nail is very small, either set it with the hammer peen or push it through a piece of thin card to steady it. Just before you tap the nail flush with the wood, tear the card away.

WOODWORKING TOOLS

SEE ALSO
Details for:
Oilstone	483
Centre punch	502

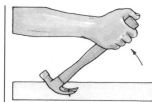

Removing a bent nail
If you bend a nail while driving it in with a claw hammer, lever it out by sliding the claw under the nailhead and pulling back on the end of the shaft. The hammer's curved head will roll on the wood without doing too much damage, but you can protect the work by placing a piece of thick card or hardboard under the hammer head. A thick packing of this kind will also give you extra leverage for removing a long nail.

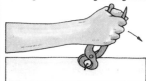

If a nailhead is too small to catch in a claw hammer, lever it out with carpenter's pincers. Grip the nail with the jaws resting on the wood, squeeze the handles together, and roll the pincers away from you. As with a claw hammer, cardboard or hardboard packing will protect the wood.

Sanding a hammer head
You are more likely to bend nails if your hammer head is greasy. Rub the hammer's face on fine abrasive paper for a better grip.

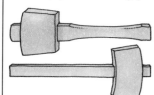

Carpenter's mallet
A carpenter's mallet is for driving a chisel or gouge into wood. Its striking faces are angled so as to deliver square blows to the end of the chisel. Tighten a loose mallet head by tapping the top of the tapered shaft on a bench.

Soft-faced mallet
Though you can use a hardwood carpenter's mallet to knock joints together or apart, a soft-faced rubber, plastic or leather mallet is less likely to mark the wood.

SCREWDRIVERS

A woodworker's tool kit needs to include a number of screwdrivers because it is important to match the size of the driver to the screw. If you use a screwdriver with a tip that is slightly too big or too small, it is likely to slip out of the slot as you turn it, damaging both the screw and the surrounding wood.

Pump-action screwdriver
A straight thrust of the tool causes the tip of a pump-action screwdriver to revolve. The spring-loaded shaft moves in and out of a hollow handle, which contains a ratchet mechanism that controls the direction of rotation. Interchangeable cross-head and flat-tipped bits fit into a chuck at the end of the shaft.

Cabinet screwdriver
A cabinet screwdriver has a shaft that is ground on two sides to produce a flat, square tip. It may have a hardwood handle, strengthened with a metal ferrule, or a plastic one moulded onto the shaft.

Cross-head screwdriver
Always use a matching cross-head screwdriver to drive screws that have cruciform slots. If you try to use a flat-tip screwdriver instead, that invariably damages the head of the screw.

Ratchet screwdriver
Using a ratchet screwdriver, you can insert and remove screws without having to adjust your grip on the handle of the driver.

You can select clockwise or anticlockwise rotation, or lock the ratchet and use the tool like an ordinary fixed screwdriver.

Power screwdriver
A cordless electric screwdriver, which takes interchangeable bits, is especially convenient for working in confined spaces.

HONING A FLAT TIP

When worn, a screwdriver tip no longer grips screws properly. To reshape the tip, hone it on an oilstone, then file the end square.

Inserting a woodscrew
You may split the wood if you drive in a screw without boring a hole for it first. To make a starter hole for a small screw, place the flat tip of a bradawl **(1)** across the grain of the wood, then press it in and twist. To guide a large screw, drill a pilot hole, followed by a clearance hole for the shank **(2)**. For the pilot hole, use a drill bit slightly narrower than the thread of the screw, but drill the clearance hole fractionally larger than the screw's shank.

Use a countersink bit to make recesses to accommodate the heads of countersunk screws.

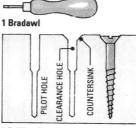

1 Bradawl

2 Drilling for screws

Lubricating a screw
If a screw is a tight fit in the hole you have drilled for it, withdraw it slightly and put a little grease on its shank.

Getting old screws out
Before attempting to extract a painted-over screw, scrape the paint from the slot with the end of a hacksaw blade – or, for the best results, place a corner of the screwdriver tip in the slot **(1)** and tap it sideways until it fits snugly, then extract the screw.

When a screw's slot has been completely stripped, remove the head with a power drill. Mark the centre of the head with a metal punch, then use progressively larger drill bits to remove the metal in stages.

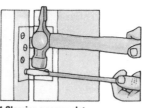

1 Clearing a screw slot

CRAMPS

Cramps are for holding glued joints together while the adhesive sets. They are also used to assemble structures temporarily to see if they work or fit, and for holding small workpieces on a bench while you are working on them.

Sash cramp
A sash cramp is a long metal bar with a screw-adjustable jaw at one end. Another jaw, known as the tail slide, is free to move along the bar, but can be fixed at any convenient point by inserting a metal peg in one of a series of holes along the cramp. Sash cramps are for clamping large glued frames, and it's worth having a couple of medium-size ones in your tool kit. You can hire additional ones when needed.

Cramp heads
If you need a very long sash cramp, hire a pair of cramp heads. Use a 75 x 25mm (3 x 1in) softwood rail as a cramp bar, locating the heads on it by plugging their pegs into holes drilled through the wood.

G-cramp
A screw-adjusted G-cramp grips the work between the adjustable shoe and the cast-metal frame. You need at least one 150mm (6in) and one 300mm (1ft) G-cramp.

Frame and mitre cramps
The four plastic corner blocks of a simple frame cramp hold the glued corners of a mitred frame while a cord is pulled taut around the blocks in order to apply equal pressure to all four joints.

A mitre cramp holds one joint at a time. Made of cast metal, it clamps the two mitred members against a right-angle fence.

Web cramp
A web cramp acts like a frame cramp. Use one to form a tourniquet around a large frame. The nylon webbing is tensioned by adjusting a ratchet mechanism with a spanner or screwdriver.

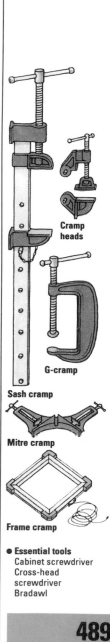

Cramp heads

G-cramp

Sash cramp

Mitre cramp

Frame cramp

● **Essential tools**
Cabinet screwdriver
Cross-head screwdriver
Bradawl

WOODWORKING TOOLS

SEE ALSO
Details for:
Sash cramps   489

1 Sash cramps square to jointed frame

2 Sash cramps set at angle to frame

Clamping a jointed frame
Prepare and adjust your sash cramps before you glue and assemble a jointed frame. If you waste time adjusting them after the joints are glued, the adhesive may begin to stiffen before you can close the joints properly. Set the tail slides to accommodate the frame and make sure that the adjustable jaws will have enough movement to tighten the joints. Place the cramps in line with the joints, using softwood packing strips to protect the work from the metal jaws. Apply pressure gradually, first with one cramp, then the other, until the joints are tightly closed **(1)**.

Check that the frame is square by measuring both diagonals. If they aren't equal, set the cramps at a slight angle to the frame so as to pull it square by squeezing the long diagonal **(2)**.

Clamping boards together
To clamp several glued boards edge to edge, use at least three sash cramps. Place one of the cramps on top of the assembly to prevent the boards bowing under pressure from the other two. A long sash cramp will bend as you tighten it, so protect the wood by inserting strips of hardboard packing between the sash bars and the work.

Lay a straightedge across the clamped boards to check that the panel is flat. If it isn't, correct the distortion by slackening or tightening the cramps as need be. If a board is misaligned, tap it back into position by placing a softwood block across the joint and striking the block firmly with a heavy hammer.

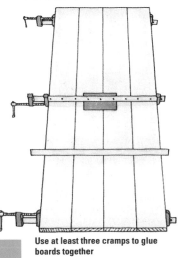

Use at least three cramps to glue boards together

BENCHES AND VICES

A woodworking bench must be strong and rigid. Heavy timbers and man-made boards put a considerable strain on a bench, and the stress imposed by sawing and hammering will eventually weaken a poorly constructed one.

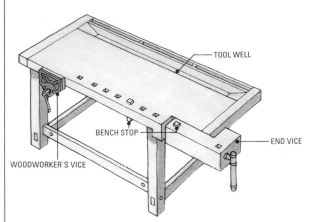

TOOL WELL

BENCH STOP

WOODWORKER'S VICE

END VICE

Woodworker's bench
The hardwood underframe of a traditional woodworker's bench is constructed with large double-wedged mortise-and-tenon joints. The longer rails are usually bolted to the rigid end-frames so that the bench can be dismantled to facilitate removal. The thick hardwood worktop is normally of short-grain beech. A storage recess, or tool well, keeps the worktop free of tools so you can lay large boards on it.

Better-quality benches have an end vice, built onto one end of the worktop, for clamping long sections of timber between metal pegs called bench stops.

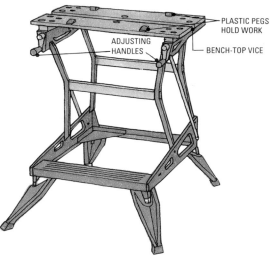

PLASTIC PEGS HOLD WORK

ADJUSTING HANDLES

BENCH-TOP VICE

Portable bench
A portable workbench can be folded away between jobs. The two halves of the thick plywood worktop are in effect vice jaws, operated by adjusting handles at the ends of the bench. Because the handles work independently, the jaws can hold tapered work-pieces. Plastic pegs fit into holes in the worktop to hold work laid flat on it; they can be arranged to hold very irregular shapes.

Clamp-on vice ▶
This lightweight vice can be clamped temporarily to the edge of any worktop. Although not as good as a proper woodworker's vice, it is a lot cheaper.

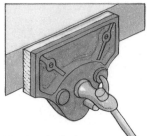

Woodworker's vice
A feature of most benches is a large woodworker's vice. This is normally screwed to the underside of the worktop, close to one leg, so that the top will not flex when you are working on wood held in the vice. Wooden linings (pads) must be fixed inside the jaws to protect the work from the metal edges. A quick-release lever on the front of the vice lets you open and shut the jaws quickly, turning the handle only for final adjustments.

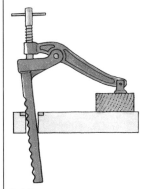

Holdfast
A holdfast is a bench-mounted cramp for holding a workpiece firmly against the worktop. The notched shaft of the cramp is slipped into a metal collar that is let into the bench.

When pressure is applied with the cramp's tommy bar, the shaft rocks over to lock in the collar, and the shoe at the end of the pivoting arm bears down on the workpiece. A pair of holdfasts, one at each end of the bench, is ideal for clamping long boards.

WOODWORKING JOINTS

BASIC WOODWORKING JOINTS

Craftsmen have invented countless ingenious ways of joining pieces of timber. Some are as decorative as they are practical, but for general joinery and home maintenance only a few basic woodworking joints are needed.

BUTT JOINTS

When you cut a piece of wood square and butt it against its neighbour you need some kind of mechanical fixing to hold the joint together, as the end grain doesn't glue strongly enough for adhesive alone to be used.

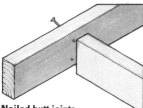

Nailed butt joints
When you nail-fix a butt joint, drive the nails in at an angle, to clamp the two pieces together.

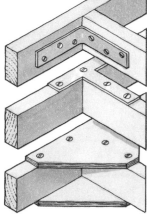

Bracket and plate fixing
Screwed-on metal right-angle or T-brackets make strong, though not very attractive, butt joints.
  Similarly, you can reinforce a butt joint by nailing or screwing a plywood plate across it.

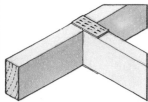

Timber connectors
The sharp pointed teeth of metal timber connectors hammered onto a butt joint will grip the wood like a bed of nails.

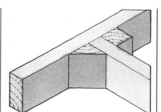

Corner blocks
Pin and glue, or screw, a square or triangular block of wood in the angle between two components.

OVERLAP JOINT

You can make a simple overlap joint by laying one square-cut board across another and fixing them with nails or screws.

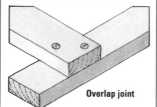

Overlap joint

Making an overlap joint
Clamp the components together accurately with a G-cramp, and drill pilot and clearance holes for the screws. Remove the cramp, apply glue, and then screw the components together.

HALVING JOINTS

Halving joints can be adapted to join lengths of wood at a corner or T-joint, or where components cross one another.

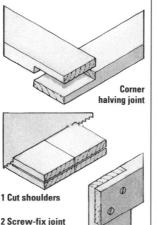

Corner halving joint

1 Cut shoulders

2 Screw-fix joint

Cutting a corner halving joint
To join two pieces of wood at a corner, cut identical tongues in their ends as for a T-halving joint – but clamp the components side by side and cut their shoulders simultaneously (1). Reinforce the glued joint with screws (2).

Cutting a T-halving joint

Lay the crossrail on the side rail (1) and mark the width of the housing on it with a marking knife, extending the lines halfway down each edge of the rail. With a marking gauge set to exactly half the thickness of the rails, score the centre lines on both rails (2). Mark the shoulder of the tongue on the crossrail (3), allowing for a tongue slightly longer than the width of the side rail. Hold the crossrail at an angle in a vice (4) and saw down to the shoulder on one edge, keeping to the waste side of the line. Then turn the rail round and saw down to the shoulder on the opposite edge. Finally, saw down square to the shoulder line (5) and remove the waste by sawing across the shoulder line (6).
  To cut the housing in the side rail, saw down both the shoulder lines to the halfway mark, then make several sawcuts across the waste (7). Pare out the waste with a chisel down to the marked lines, working from both sides (8). Glue and assemble the joint; and when it has set, plane the end of the tongue flush with the side rail.

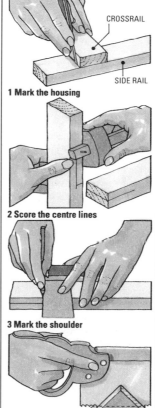

CROSSRAIL

SIDE RAIL

1 Mark the housing

2 Score the centre lines

3 Mark the shoulder

4 Saw with the rail at an angle

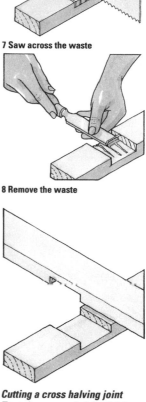

5 Saw square to the shoulder

6 Saw across the shoulder line

7 Saw across the waste

8 Remove the waste

Cutting a cross halving joint
To make a cross halving joint, cut two housings (as described above) of equal size. Clamp the two components together, side by side, and saw both sets of shoulders simultaneously. Then separate the components and remove the waste with a chisel.

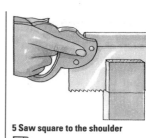

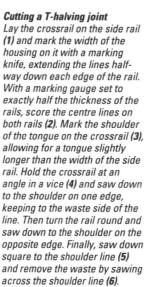

Edge-to-edge cross halving joint

WOODWORKING
JOINTS

LAP JOINT

This is a simple joint for joining two wide boards at a corner.

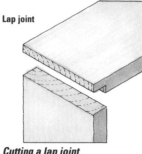

Lap joint

Cutting a lap joint

Cut the square-ended board first and use it to mark out the width of the rebate on the other board **(1)**. Set a marking gauge to about half the timber's thickness and mark out the tongue **(2)**. Cut out the rebate with a tenon saw, then glue and dovetail-nail the joint.

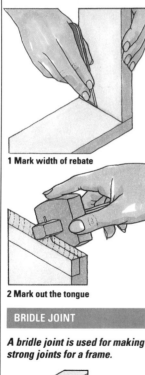

1 Mark width of rebate

2 Mark out the tongue

BRIDLE JOINT

A bridle joint is used for making strong joints for a frame.

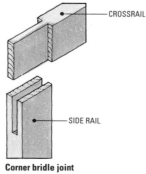

CROSSRAIL

SIDE RAIL

Corner bridle joint

Cutting a corner bridle joint

To make a corner bridle joint, cut equal-size tongues, two on the side rail and one centred on the crossrail. Mark them out with a mortise gauge, making all three slightly longer than the width of the rails. Cut the waste away from both sides of the crossrail tongue with a tenon saw, as described for a T-halving joint. To form the side-rail tongues, saw down to the shoulder on both sides keeping to the waste side of the two marked lines **(1)**, then chop out the waste with a narrow firmer chisel or mortise chisel. Glue and assemble the joint and, when the glue has set, plane the ends of the over-long tongues flush with the rails.

1 Saw down to the shoulder

CROSSRAIL

UPRIGHT

T-bridle joint

When a crossrail joins an upright rail or leg, cut two tongues on the upright, as for a corner bridle joint, and a housing on each side of the crossrail, as for a T-halving joint. The depth of the housings must, of course, be equal to the thickness of the tongues.

HOUSING JOINTS

Housing joints are often used for shelves and similar structures. A through housing can be seen from both sides of the structure, while a stopped housing is not visible from the front.

Through housing   **Stopped housing**

Cutting a through housing

Square the end of one board and use it to mark out the width of the housing on the other board **(1)**, then with a marking gauge set to about a third of the board's thickness, mark the depth of the housing on both edges **(2)**. Saw along both sides of the housing **(3)**, keeping just on the waste side of the two lines, then chisel out the waste, working from both edges of the board **(4)**. A router is the ideal tool for levelling the bottom of the housing; otherwise, pare it flat with the chisel.

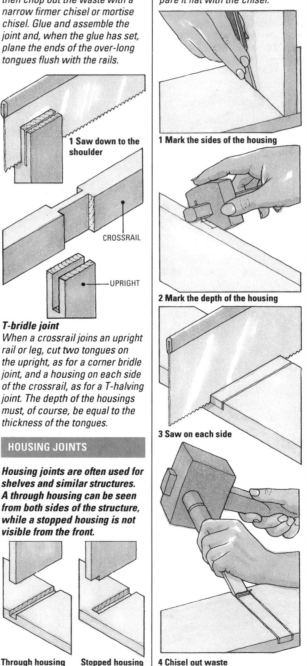

1 Mark the sides of the housing

2 Mark the depth of the housing

3 Saw on each side

4 Chisel out waste

Cutting a stopped housing

First, mark out the housing as described left – but stop about 18mm (¾in) short of the front edge. To give the saw clearance, remove about 38mm (1½in) of the housing at the stopped end, first with a drill and then with a chisel **(1)**. Saw down both sides of the housing and pare out the waste to leave a level bottom. In the front corner of the other board, cut a notch **(2)** to fit the stopped housing, so the two edges lie flush when assembled.

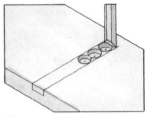

1 Chop out saw clearance

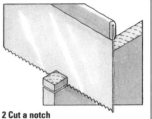

2 Cut a notch

DOWEL JOINTS

Dowel joints are strong and versatile. They can secure butt-jointed rails, mitred frames and long boards butted edge to edge. Use dowels that are about one third the thickness of the wood.

Dowelled butt joint

Dowelled mitre joint

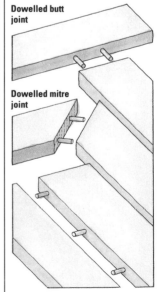

Dowelled edge-to-edge joint

WOODWORKING

JOINTS

Cutting a dowel joint

When joining boards edge to edge, cut dowels about 38mm (1½in) long; otherwise, saw the dowels to a length equal to two-thirds the width of the rails. File chamfers on both ends of each dowel and saw a groove along each one **(1)** so air and surplus glue can escape when the joint is assembled. To save time, buy ready-cut and chamfered dowels that are grooved all round.

If you are using a dowelling jig, then you won't need to mark the centres of the dowel holes. Otherwise, set a marking gauge to the centre line on both rails **(2)**, drive panel pins into the edge of the side rail to mark dowel-hole centres, then cut them to short sharp points with pliers **(3)**. Line up the rails, push them together for the metal points to mark the end grain of the crossrail **(4)**, and then pull out the cut panel pins.

Using a power drill, with the appropriate dowel bit, bore the holes to a depth just over half the length of the dowels; then glue and assemble the joint. Drilling accurate dowel holes is much easier if the drill is mounted in a vertical drill stand.

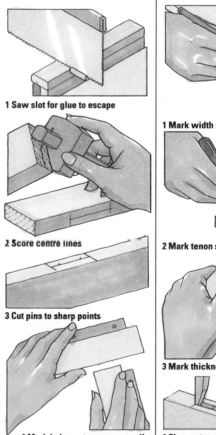

1 Saw slot for glue to escape

2 Score centre lines

3 Cut pins to sharp points

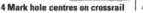

4 Mark hole centres on crossrail

MORTISE & TENON JOINTS

A mortise and tenon is a strong joint for narrow components – and essential for chair and table frames. A through tenon can be wedged for extra strength, but a stopped tenon is neater.

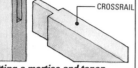

Stopped mortise and tenon
— SIDE RAIL
— CROSSRAIL

Cutting a mortise and tenon

Mark the width of the mortise, using the crossrail as a guide **(1)**, and mark the shoulder of the tenon all round the crossrail **(2)** so that the tenon's length will be two-thirds of the side rail's width. Set a mortise gauge to one third of the crossrail's thickness and mark both mortise and tenon **(3)**.

Cut the tenon as for the tongue of a T-halving joint. Remove the waste from the mortise with an electric drill (preferably mounted in a drill stand), then square up its ends and sides with a chisel **(4)**. Glue and assemble the joint.

1 Mark width of mortise

2 Mark tenon shoulder

3 Mark thickness of joint

4 Chop out remaining waste

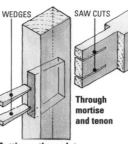

WEDGES SAW CUTS

Through mortise and tenon

Cutting a through tenon

When a tenon is to pass right through a side rail, cut it slightly longer than the width of the rail and saw two slots through it. Glue and assemble the joint, then drive glued hardwood wedges into the sawcuts to expand the tenon in the mortise. When the glue has set, plane the wedges and tenon flush with the rail.

MITRE JOINT

Mitre joints are used for joining corners of frames. They are also especially useful for decorative mouldings and skirting boards.

Mitre joint

Cutting a mitre joint

A right-angled mitre joint is made by sawing the ends of two rails to 45 degrees in a mitre box, then butting them together. Trim the mitres with a finely set plane on a shooting board and assemble the glued joint in a mitre cramp. If the meeting faces of the rails are fairly large, glue alone will hold them together, but you can reinforce a mitre joint by sawing two slots across the corner and gluing strips of veneer into them **(1)**. Plane the veneers flush with the rails after the glue has set.

1 Inserting veneer strips

SCARF JOINT

A scarf joint is used for joining two lengths of timber end to end.

Scarf joint

Making a scarf joint

Clamp the two lengths side by side, their ends flush, and mark out the angled cut. The span of a scarf joint should be four times the width of the timber **(1)**. Saw and plane both lengths down to the marked line simultaneously, then unclamp them. Glue the two angled faces together, securing them with battens and G-cramps while the glue sets **(2)**.

If the scarf joint is likely to be subjected to a great deal of stress, you can reinforce it with plywood plates screwed to both sides of the rails **(3)**.

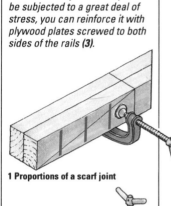

1 Proportions of a scarf joint

2 Clamp joint with G-cramps

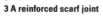

3 A reinforced scarf joint

BUILDING
TOOLS

Using a pointing hawk
A pointing hawk makes the filling of mortar joints very easy. Place the lip of the hawk just under a horizontal joint and scrape the mortar into place with a jointer.

Continental-pattern trowels

● **Essential tools**
Brick trowel
Pointing trowel
Plasterer's trowel
Mortar board
Hawk
Spirit level
Try square
Plumb line

BUILDER'S TOOL KIT

A specialist builder – such as a plasterer, joiner or bricklayer – needs only a limited set of tools, whereas the amateur is more like a one-man general builder, who has to be able to tackle all kinds of construction and repair work, and therefore requires a much wider range of tools than the specialist.

The tool kit suggested here is for renovating and improving the structure of your home and for such tasks as erecting or restoring garden structures and laying paving. Electrical work, decorating and plumbing call for other sets of tools.

FLOATS AND TROWELS

For a professional builder, floats and trowels have their specific uses – but in home maintenance a repointing trowel may often be the ideal tool for patching small areas of plaster, or a plasterer's trowel for smoothing concrete.

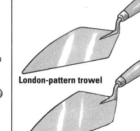

London-pattern trowel

Canadian-pattern trowel

Brick trowels
A brick trowel is for handling and placing mortar when laying bricks or concrete blocks. A professional might use one with a blade as long as 300mm (1ft) – but such a trowel is too heavy and unwieldy for the amateur, so buy a good-quality brick trowel with a fairly short blade.

The blade of a *London-pattern trowel* has one curved edge for cutting bricks, a skill that takes much practice to perfect; the blade's other edge is straight, for picking up mortar. This type of trowel is made in right-handed and left-handed versions, so be sure to buy the right one for you. A right-handed trowel has its curved edge on the right when you are holding the tool.

A *Canadian-pattern trowel* is symmetrical, so it's convenient when people with different left-hand and right-hand preferences want to share the one trowel.

Pointing trowel
A pointing trowel is designed for repairing or shaping mortar joints between bricks. The blade is only 75 to 100mm (3 to 4in) long.

Jointer
Use a jointer to shape the mortar joints between bricks. Its narrow blade is dragged along the mortar joint and the curved front end used for shaping the verticals.

Frenchman
A Frenchman is a specialized tool for scraping off excess mortar from brickwork jointing. You can make one by heating and bending an old table knife or a metal strip.

Wooden float
A wooden builder's float is for applying and smoothing cement renderings and concrete to a fine, attractive texture. The more expensive ones have detachable handles, so their wooden blades can be replaced when they wear. Similar floats made from plastic are also available.

Plasterer's trowel
A plasterer's trowel is a steel float for applying plaster and cement renderings to walls. It is also dampened and used for 'polishing', stroking the surface of the material when it has firmed up. Some builders prefer to apply rendering with a heavy trowel and finish it with a more flexible blade – but one has to be quite skilled to exploit such subtle differences.

BOARDS FOR CARRYING MORTAR OR PLASTER

Any convenient-sized sheet of 12 or 18mm (½ or ¾in) exterior-grade plywood can be used as a mixing board for plaster or mortar. A panel about 1m (3ft) square makes an ideal mixing board, while a smaller spot-board, about 600mm (2ft) square, is convenient for carrying the material to the actual work site. Screwing some battens to the underside of the boards makes them easier to lift and carry.

You will also need a small lightweight hawk for carrying pointing mortar or plaster. Make one by nailing a block of wood underneath a plywood board so you can plug a handle into it.

A home-made hawk

LEVELLING AND MEASURING TOOLS

You can make some levelling and measuring tools yourself – but don't skimp on essentials, such as a good spirit level and a robust tape measure.

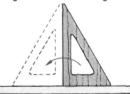

VIAL

Spirit level
A spirit level is a machine-made straightedge incorporating special glass tubes or vials that contain a liquid. In each vial an air bubble floats. When a bubble rests exactly between two lines marked on the glass, then the structure on which the level is held is known to be properly horizontal or vertical, depending on the orientation of the vial.

Buy a wooden or lightweight aluminium level, 600 to 900mm (2 to 3ft) long. A well-made one is very strong, but treat it with care and always clean mortar or plaster from it before they set.

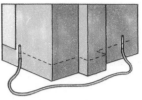

Water level
You can make a water level by plugging short lengths of transparent plastic tubing into the two ends of a garden hose; fill the hose with water till it appears in both tubes. Since water level remains constant, the levels in the tubes are always identical and can therefore be used for marking identical heights, even over long distances and round obstacles and bends.

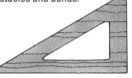

Builder's square
A large set square is useful when you set out brick or concrete-block corners. The best squares are stamped out of sheet metal, but you can make a serviceable one by cutting out a thick plywood right-angled triangle with a hypotenuse of about 750mm (2ft 6in). Cut out the centre of the triangle to reduce the weight.

Checking a square
Accuracy is important, so check the square by placing it against a straight batten on the floor. Draw a line against the square to make a right angle with the batten, then flop the square to see if it forms the same angle from the other side.

Try square
Use a try square for marking out square cuts or joints on timber.

Making a plumb line
Any small heavy weight hung on a length of fine string can act as a plumb line for judging whether a structure or surface is vertical.

BUILDING

TOOLS

Bricklayer's line

This is a nylon line used as a guide for laying bricks or blocks level. It is stretched between two flat-bladed pins that are driven into vertical joints at the ends of a wall, or between line blocks that hook over the bricks at the ends of a course. As a substitute, you can stretch string between two stakes driven into the ground outside the line of the wall.

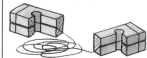

Steel pins and line
Buy the special flat-bladed pins, or make your own by hammering flats on 100mm (4in) nails.

Line blocks
The blocks grip the corners of the bricks at the end of a course; the line passes through their slots.

Plasterer's rule

This is simply a straight length of wood used for scraping plaster and rendering undercoats level.

Straightedge

Any length of straight rigid timber can be used to check whether a surface is flat, or (in conjunction with a spirit level) to see whether two points are at the same height.

Gauge stick

For gauging the height of brick courses, calibrate a softwood batten by making sawcuts across it at 75mm (3in) intervals – which is the thickness of a brick plus its mortar joint.

Tape measure

An ordinary retractable steel tape measure is adequate for most purposes; but if you need to mark out or measure a large plot, hire a wind-up tape – which can be up to 30m (100ft) in length.

Marking gauge

A marking gauge has a sharp steel point for scoring a line on timber parallel to the edge. Its adjustable stock acts as a fence and keeps the point a constant distance from the edge.

HAMMERS

Several types of hammer are useful on a building site.

Claw hammer

Choose a strong claw hammer for building stud partitions, nailing floorboards, making doorframes and window frames, and putting up garden fencing.

Club hammer

A heavy club hammer is used for driving cold chisels and for a variety of demolition jobs. It is also useful for driving large masonry nails into walls.

Sledgehammer

Hire a sledgehammer if you have to break up hardcore or paving. It's also the best tool for driving stakes or fence posts into the ground, though you can make do with a club hammer if the ground is not too hard.

Mallet

A carpenter's wooden mallet is the proper tool for driving a wood chisel. But you can use a hammer instead if the chisel has an impact-resistant plastic handle.

SAWS

Every builder needs a range of handsaws, but consider hiring a power saw when you have to cut a lot of heavy structural timbers – especially if you plan to rip floorboards down to width, which is a very tiring job when done by hand.

Special saws are available for cutting metal, and even for sawing through masonry.

Panel saw

All kinds of man-made building boards are used in house construction, so it is worth investing in a good panel saw.

It can also be used for cutting large structural timbers to the required lengths.

Tenon saw

This is a good saw for accurately cutting wall studs, floorboards, panelling and joints. The metal stiffening along the top of the blade keeps it rigid and prevents the saw from wandering off line.

Padsaw

Also called a keyhole saw, this small saw has a narrow tapered blade for cutting holes in timber.

Coping saw

A coping saw has a frame that holds a fairly coarse but very narrow blade under tension for cutting curves in wood.

Floorboard saw

If you prise a floorboard above its neighbours, you can cut across it with an ordinary tenon saw – but the curved cutting edge of a floorboard saw makes it easier to avoid damaging the boards on either side.

Hacksaw

The hardened-steel blades of a hacksaw have fine teeth for cutting metal. Use one to cut steel concrete-reinforcing rods or small pieces of sheet metal.

Sheet saw

A hacksaw's frame prevents its use for cutting large metal sheets – but a sheet saw has a replaceable hacksaw blade bolted to the edge of a flat blade that can pass through the sheet like a handsaw. It will also cut corrugated plastic sheeting and roofing slates.

Universal saw

A universal or general-purpose saw is able to cut wood, metal, plastics and building boards. The short frameless blade has a low-friction coating.

This type of saw is particularly useful for cutting secondhand timber, which may contain nails or screws that would blunt the blade of an ordinary woodsaw.

POWER SAWS

A *circular saw* will accurately rip timber or man-made boards down to size. As well as saving you the effort of hand-sawing large timbers, a sharp power saw produces such a clean cut that there is often no need for planing afterwards.

A *power jigsaw* is able to cut curves in timber and boards. It is equally useful for cutting holes in fixed wall panels and for sawing through floorboards.

A *reciprocating saw* is a two-handed power saw that has a long pointed blade. It is powerful enough to saw sections of heavy timber, and can even cut through a complete stud partition.

Masonry saw
Masonry saws closely resemble handsaws for wood, but their tungsten-carbide teeth cut brick, concrete blocks and stone.

DRILLS

A powerful electric drill is invaluable to a builder. A cordless version is useful when you have to bore holes outdoors or in lofts and cellars that lack convenient electric sockets.

Power drill

Buy a good-quality power drill, plus a range of twist drills and spade or power-bore bits for drilling timber. Make sure the drill has a percussion or hammer action for drilling walls. For masonry you need special drill bits tipped with tungsten carbide. The smaller ones are matched to the size of standard wall plugs; there are also much larger ones that have reduced shanks, so they can be used in a standard power-drill chuck. The larger bits are expensive, so it pays to hire them. Percussion bits are even tougher than masonry bits, and have shatter-proof tips.

Brace

A brace is the ideal hand tool for drilling large holes in timber. In addition, when fitted with a screwdriver bit, it provides the necessary leverage for inserting or extracting large woodscrews.

Drilling masonry for wall plugs
Set the drill to hammer action and low speed. Wrap tape round the bit to mark the depth to be drilled, allowing for slightly more depth than the length of the plug, as dust will pack down into the hole as the plug is inserted. Drill the hole in stages, partly withdrawing the bit at times in order to clear the debris.

To protect paintwork and floorcoverings from falling dust, tape a paper bag just below the position of the hole before starting drilling.

● **Essential tools**
Straightedge
Tape measure
Claw hammer
Club hammer
Panel saw
Tenon saw
Hacksaw
Padsaw
Power drill
Masonry bits
Brace and bits

495

BUILDING TOOLS

ADDITIONAL BUILDER'S TOOLS
The following tools would be a useful addition to a builder's tool kit, especially when carrying out major repairs and improvements:

Crowbar
A crowbar, or wrecking bar, is for demolishing timber framework. Force the flat tip between the components and use the leverage of the long shaft to prise them apart. Choose a crowbar that has a claw at one end for removing large nails.

Slater's ripper
To replace individual slates you must cut their fixing nails without disturbing the slates overlapping them, and for this you need a slater's ripper. Pass the long hooked blade up between the slates, locate one of the hooks over the fixing nail, and pull down sharply to cut it.

● **Essential tools**
Glass cutter
Putty knife
Cold chisel
Bolster chisel
Spade
Shovel
Rake
Wheelbarrow
Cabinet screwdriver
Cross-head screwdriver
Jack plane

GLAZIER'S TOOLS

Glass is such a hard and brittle material that it can only be worked with specialized tools.

Glass cutter
A glass cutter does not actually cut glass, but merely scores a line in it. This is done by a tiny hardened-steel wheel or a chip of industrial diamond mounted in the pen-like holder. The glass breaks along the scored line when pressure is applied to it.

Beam compass cutter
A beam compass cutter is for scoring circles on glass — when, for example, you need to cut a round hole in a window pane in order to fit a ventilator. The cutting wheel is mounted at the end of an adjustable beam that turns on a central pivot attached to the glass by suction.

Spear-point glass drill
A glass drill has a flat tungsten-steel tip shaped like a spearhead. The shape of the tip is designed to reduce friction that would otherwise crack the glass, but it does need lubricating with oil, paraffin or water during drilling.

Hacking knife
A hacking knife has a heavy steel blade for chipping old putty out of window rebates in order to remove the glass. Place the point between the putty and the frame, then tap the back of the blade with a hammer.

Spearpoint knife

Clipped-point knife

Straight knife

Putty knife
The blunt blade of a putty knife is for shaping and smoothing fresh putty. You can choose between spearpoint, clipped-point and straight blades according to your personal preference.

CHISELS

As well as chisels for cutting and paring wood joints, you will need some special ones when working with masonry.

Cold chisel
Cold chisels are made from solid-steel hexagonal-section rod. They are primarily for cutting metal bars and chopping the heads off rivets, but a builder will use one for cutting a chase in plaster and brickwork or for chopping out old brick pointing.

Slip a plastic safety sleeve over the chisel to protect your hand from a misplaced blow with a club hammer.

Plugging chisel
A plugging chisel has a narrow, flat 'bit' (tip) for cutting out old or eroded pointing. It's worth hiring one when you have a large area of brickwork to repoint.

Bolster chisel
The wide 'bit' of a bolster chisel is designed for cutting bricks and concrete blocks. It is also useful for levering up floorboards.

WORK GLOVES

Wear strong work gloves whenever you are carrying paving slabs, concrete blocks or rough timber. Ordinary gardening gloves are better than none, but they won't last very long on a building site. The best work gloves have leather palms and fingers, although you may prefer a pair with ventilated backs for comfort in hot weather.

DIGGING TOOLS

Much building work requires some kind of digging – for laying strip foundations and concrete pads, sinking rows of post holes, and so on. You probably have the basic tools in your garden shed; the others you can hire.

Pickaxe
Use a medium-weight pickaxe to break up heavily compacted soil – especially if it contains a lot of buried rubble.

Mattock
The wide blade of a mattock is ideal for breaking up heavy clay soil, and it's better than an ordinary pickaxe for ground that's riddled with tree roots.

Spade
Buy a good-quality spade for excavating soil and mixing concrete. One with a stainless-steel blade is best, but alloy steel lasts reasonably well. Choose a strong hardwood shaft split to form a D-shaped handle that is riveted with metal plates to its crosspiece. Make sure that the hollow shaft socket and blade are forged in one piece.

Although square spade blades seem to be more popular, many builders prefer a round-mouth spade with a long pole handle for digging deep holes and trenches.

Shovel
You can use a spade for mixing and placing concrete or mortar, but the raised edges of a shovel retain it better.

Garden rake
Use an ordinary garden rake for spreading gravel or levelling wet concrete, but be sure to wash it before any concrete sets on it.

Post-hole auger
Hire a post-hole auger to sink narrow holes for fence and gate posts. You drive it into the ground like a corkscrew, then pull out the plugs of earth.

Wheelbarrow
Most garden wheelbarrows are not strong enough for building work, which generally involves carting heavy loads of rubble and wet concrete.

Unless the tubular underframe of the wheelbarrow is rigidly strutted, the barrow's thin metal body will distort and may well spill its load as you are crossing rough ground.

Check, too, that the axle is fixed securely – a cheap barrow can lose its wheel as you are tipping a load into an excavation.

SCREWDRIVERS

Most people gradually acquire an assortment of screwdrivers over a period of time, as and when need arises. Alternatively, buy a power screwdriver with a range of bits or buy screwdriver bits for your power drill.

Cabinet screwdriver
Buy at least one large flat-tip screwdriver. The fixed variety is quite adequate, but a pump-action one, which drives large screws very quickly, is useful when you assemble big wooden building structures.

Cross-head screwdriver
Choose the size and type of cross-head screwdriver to suit the work in hand. There is no 'most-useful size', as each driver must fit a screw slot exactly.

PLANES

Sophisticated framing may call for moulding or grooving planes, but most household joinery needs only skimming to leave a fairly smooth finish.

Jack plane
A jack plane, which is a medium-size bench plane, is the most versatile general-purpose tool.

DECORATING
TOOLS

DECORATOR'S TOOL KIT

Most home owners collect a fairly extensive kit of tools for decorating their houses or flats. Although traditionalists will want to stick to tried-and-tested tools and to materials of proven reliability, others may prefer to try recent innovations aimed at making the work easier and faster for the home decorator.

TOOLS FOR PREPARATION

Whether you are tiling, painting or papering, make sure the surface to which the materials will be applied is sound and clean.

Straight scraper

Serrated scraper

Wallpaper and paint scrapers

The wide stiff blade of a scraper is for removing softened paint or soaked paper. The best scrapers have high-quality steel blades and riveted rosewood handles. One with a blade 100 to 125mm (4 to 5in) wide is best for stripping wallpaper, while a narrow one, no more than 25mm (1in) wide, is better for removing paint from window frames and doorframes.

A serrated scraper will score impervious wallcoverings so that water or stripping solution can penetrate faster – but take care not to damage the wall itself.

Vinyl gloves

Most people wear ordinary household 'rubber' gloves as protection for their hands when washing down or preparing paintwork – but tough PVC work gloves are more hard-wearing and will protect your skin against many harmful chemicals.

WOODWORKING TOOLS

As well as the decorating tools described here, you will need a basic woodworking tool kit for repairing damaged floorboards or window frames and for jobs such as installing wall panelling or laying parquet flooring.

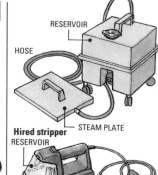

RESERVOIR

HOSE

STEAM PLATE

Hired stripper
RESERVOIR

STEAM PLATE

Lightweight stripper

Steam wallpaper stripper

To remove wallpaper quickly (especially thick wallcoverings), either buy or hire an electric steam-generating stripper.

All steam strippers work on similar principles – but follow any specific safety instructions that come with the machine.

Using a steam stripper

Fill the stripper's reservoir with water and plug the tool into a socket outlet. Hold the steaming plate against the wallpaper until it is soft enough to be removed with a scraper. You will find that some wallcoverings take longer to soften than others.

Straight-sided shavehook

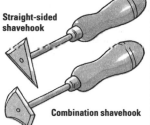

Combination shavehook

Shavehook

This is a special scraper for removing old paint and varnish. A straight-sided triangular shavehook is fine for flat surfaces, but one with a combination blade can be used on concave and convex mouldings too. You pull a shavehook towards you to remove the softened paint.

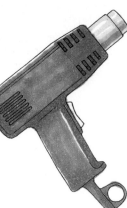

Hot-air stripper

The gas blowtorch was once the professional's tool for softening old paint that required stripping, but the modern electric hot-air stripper is much easier to use. It is as efficient as a blowtorch, but there's less risk of scorching woodwork. With most strippers, you can adjust the temperature. The interchangeable nozzles are shaped to concentrate the heated air or direct it away from window panes.

Filling knife

A filling knife looks like a paint scraper, but has a flexible blade for forcing filler into cracks in timber or plaster. Large areas of damaged wall should be patched with a plasterer's trowel.

Handbrush

Cup brushes

Wire brushes

You can use a handbrush with steel-wire 'bristles' to remove flaking paint and particles of rust from metalwork before repainting it. However, the job is easier if you use a rotary wire cup brush fitted into the chuck of an electric drill, wearing goggles or safety glasses to protect your eyes.

Mastic guns

Non-setting mastic, which is permanently flexible, is used to seal joints between materials with different rates of expansion that would eventually crack and eject a rigid filler. You can buy mastic that you squeeze direct from a plastic tube, but it's more easily applied from a cartridge clipped into a spring-loaded gun.

Tack rag

A resin-impregnated cloth called a 'tack rag' is ideal for picking up particles of dust and hard paint from a surface that's prepared for painting. If you can't get a tack rag, use a lint-free cloth dampened with white spirit.

Dusting brush

A dusting brush has long soft bristles for clearing dust out of mouldings and crevices just before painting. You can use an ordinary paintbrush, provided that you keep it clean and dry.

WET-AND-DRY PAPER

Wet-and-dry abrasive paper is used for smoothing new paintwork or varnish before applying the final coat. It consists of silicon-carbide particles glued to a waterproof backing paper. Dip a piece in water and rub the paintwork until a slurry of paint and water forms. Wipe it off with a cloth before it dries; then rinse the paper clean and continue.

● **Essential tools**
Wallpaper scraper
Combination shavehook
Filling knife
Hot-air stripper
Wire brush

DECORATING

TOOLS

Paint kettle
To carry paint to a work site, decant a little into a cheap, lightweight plastic paint kettle.

● **Essential tools**
Flat brushes
12, 25 and 50mm
(½, 1 and 2in)
Wall brush
150mm (6in)

12mm (½in)   25mm (1in)   50mm (2in)

Flat paintbrush
The filling is set in rubber – or pitch or resin – and bound to the wooden or plastic handle with a pressed-metal ferrule. You will need several sizes, up to 50mm (2in), for painting, varnishing and staining woodwork.

PAINTBRUSHES

Some paintbrushes are made from natural animal hair. Hog bristle is the best, but it is often mixed with inferior horsehair or oxhair to reduce cost.

Synthetic-bristle brushes are generally the least expensive, and are quite adequate for the home decorator.

Bristle types
Bristle is ideal for paintbrushes since each hair tapers naturally and splits at the tip into even finer filaments that hold paint well. Bristle is also tough and resilient. Synthetic 'bristle' (usually made of nylon) is designed to resemble the characteristics of real bristle, and a good-quality nylon brush will serve most painters as well as a bristle one.

Choosing a brush
The bristles of a good brush – the 'filling' – are densely packed. When you fan them with your fingers they should spring back into shape immediately. Flex the tip of the brush against your hand to see if any bristles work loose. Even a good brush will shed a few bristles at first, but never clumps. The ferrule should be fixed firmly to the handle.

One-knot paintbrush
The bristles of a one-knot paintbrush are bound to a cylindrical handle with string or wire or a metal ferrule.

The grouping of the bristles makes them very resilient – but when flexed against a surface, they will fan out like those of the commoner flat paintbrush.

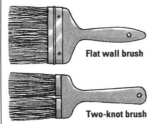

Flat wall brush

Two-knot brush

Wall brush
To apply emulsion paint by brush, use a 150mm (6in) flat wall brush or a two-knot brush of the kind favoured by continental painters and decorators.

Cutting-in brush
The filling of a cutting-in brush, or 'bevelled sash tool', is cut at an angle so that you can paint moulded glazing bars right up into the corners and against the glass. Most painters make do with a 12mm (½in) flat brush.

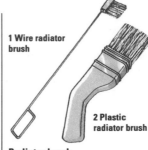

1 Wire radiator brush

2 Plastic radiator brush

Radiator brush
Unless you take a radiator off the wall for decorating, you will need a special brush to paint the back of it and the wall behind it. There are two types of radiator brush: the one has a standard flat paintbrush head at right angles to a long wire handle (**1**); the other is like an ordinary paintbrush but has an angled plastic handle (**2**).

Banister brush
A household banister brush gives excellent results when used for painting rough or rendered walls.

Paint shield

Glass scraper

Paint shield and scraper
There are various plastic and metal shields for protecting glass when you are painting window frames and glazing bars. If the glass does get spattered, it can be cleaned with a blade clipped into a special holder.

STENCIL AND GRAIN-EFFECT TOOLS

Stencil brush
A stencil brush has short stiff bristles. The paint is stippled through or around a cut-out template that defines the shape to be painted.

Graphers
You can buy special brushes for creating wood-grain effects with paint or varnish. A 'mottler' has a dense soft filling of squirrel hair for lifting bands or streaks of colour to simulate figured hardwoods. A 'pencil grainer' has a row of fine brushes mounted in one handle for drawing patterns of parallel lines.

Stencil brush

Mottler

Pencil grainer

CLEANING PAINTBRUSHES

● **Water-based paints**
As soon as you finish working, wash the bristles with warm soapy water, flexing them between your fingers to work the paint out of the roots. Then rinse the brush in clean water and shake out the excess. Smooth the bristles and slip an elastic band round their tips to hold the shape of the filling while it is drying.

Holding the shape of a brush

● **Solvent-based paints**
If you are using solvent-based paints, you can suspend the brush overnight in enough water to cover the bristles, then blot it with kitchen paper before you resume painting.

When you have finished painting, brush out excess paint onto newspaper, then flex the bristles in a bowl of thinners. Some finishes need special thinners – so check for this on the container. Otherwise, use white spirit or a chemical brush cleaner. Wash the dirty thinners from the bristles with hot soapy water, then rinse the brush.

Soaking a brush

● **Hardened paint**
If paint has hardened on a brush, soften it by soaking the bristles in brush cleaner. It will then become water-soluble and will wash out easily with hot water. If the old paint is very stubborn, dip the bristles in some paint stripper.

STORING PAINTBRUSHES

Before storing, fold soft paper over the filling and secure it to the ferrule with an elastic band.

DECORATING
TOOLS

PAINT PADS

Paint pads help inexperienced decorators to apply paints and wood dyes quickly and evenly. They are not universally popular, but no one would dispute their usefulness for painting large flat areas. Paint pads should not drip paint provided that they are loaded properly.

Standard pads
There is a range of rectangular paint pads for decorating walls, ceilings and flat woodwork. These standard pads have short mohair pile on their painting surfaces and are generally made with D-shape handles.

Edging pad
An easy way to paint a straight edge – between a wall and a ceiling, for example – is to use an edging pad with small wheels or rollers that guide it parallel to the adjacent surface.

Sash pad
A sash pad has a small mohair sole for painting the glazing bars of sash windows. Most sash pads incorporate plastic guides to stop them straying onto the glass.

POWER ROLLER

With a power roller you can paint continuously for as long as the batteries last – about five hours. Paint is delivered from the portable reservoir, via a flexible hose, to the roller head. Because you don't have to keep reloading the roller, you can work very quickly, covering about 1sq m (1sq yd) per minute. To wash the roller, connect its hose to a tap and flush water through the roller head.

PAINT HOSE
POWER PACK/ PAINT CONTAINER
CONTROL HANDLE
SHOULDER STRAP
ROLLER HEAD

CLEANING PAINT PADS

Before dipping a new pad into paint for the first time, brush it with a clothes brush to remove any loose nylon filaments.

● When you finish painting, blot the pad on old newspaper, then wash it in the appropriate solvent – water, white spirit or brush cleaner, or any special thinners recommended by the paint manufacturer. Squeeze the foam and rub the pile with gloved fingertips, then wash the pad in hot soapy water and rinse it.

● A new paint pad that has just been used for the first time may appear to be stained by paint even after it has been washed. However, the colour will not contaminate the next batch of fresh paint.

Pad tray
Pads and trays are normally sold as sets; but if you buy a separate tray, get one with a loading roller that distributes paint evenly onto the sole of a pad drawn across it.

PAINT ROLLERS

A paint roller is the ideal tool for painting a large area of wall or ceiling quickly. The cylindrical sleeves that actually apply the paint are interchangeable, and slide onto a revolving sprung-wire cage fitted to the cranked handle of the roller. The sleeves are very easy to swap or remove for washing.

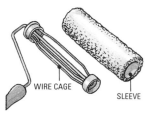

WIRE CAGE
SLEEVE

Sizes of roller sleeves
Sleeves for standard paint rollers are 175mm (7in) or 225mm (9in) long, but it is also possible to buy 300mm (1ft) rollers.

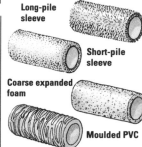

Long-pile sleeve

Short-pile sleeve

Coarse expanded foam

Moulded PVC

Types of roller sleeves
You can buy roller sleeves of various materials to suit different surface textures and kinds of paint. Most sleeves are made of *sheepskin* or *synthetic fibres* cropped to different lengths. A sheepskin sleeve can hold more paint than one that is made from synthetic fibre, but costs about 25 per cent more.

Choose a *long-pile sleeve* for emulsion or masonry paint on rough or textured surfaces. A *medium-pile sleeve* is best for emulsion or satin-finish oil paints on smooth surfaces. It is also ideal for applying solid emulsion. For gloss paints, use a *short-pile sleeve*.

Cheap *plastic-foam sleeves* are unsatisfactory both for oil paints and emulsions. They leave tiny air bubbles in the painted surface, and the foam often distorts as it dries after washing. But they are cheap enough to be thrown away after use with finishes such as bituminous paint that would be difficult to remove even from a short-pile sleeve.

Use a *coarse expanded-foam sleeve* for applying textured paints and coatings. There are also *moulded PVC rollers* with embossed surfaces to pattern high-build textured coatings.

Extending a pad or roller
If your paint pad or roller has a hollow handle, you can plug it onto a telescopic extension handle to enable you to reach a ceiling from the floor.

CLEANING A ROLLER

Remove most of the excess paint by running the roller backwards and forwards across some old newspaper. If you are planning to use the roller next day, apply a few drops of the appropriate thinners to the sleeve and then wrap it in plastic. Otherwise, clean, wash and rinse the sleeve before the paint has time to dry.

● **Water-based paints**
If you've been using emulsion or acrylic paint, flush most of it out under running water, then massage a little liquid detergent into the pile of the sleeve and flush it again.

● **Solvent-based paints**
To remove solvent-based paints, pour some thinners into the roller tray and slowly roll the sleeve back and forth in it. Squeeze the roller and agitate the pile with gloved hands. When the paint has dissolved, wash the sleeve in hot soapy water.

Roller tray
A paint roller is loaded from a sloping plastic or metal tray, the deep end of which acts as a paint reservoir. Load the roller by rolling paint from the deep end up and down the tray's ribbed slope once or twice, so as to get even distribution on the sleeve.

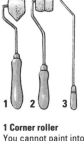

1   2   3

1 Corner roller
You cannot paint into a corner with a standard roller, so unless there are to be different adjacent colours, paint the corner first with a shaped corner roller.
2 Pipe roller
A pipe roller has two narrow sleeves, mounted side by side, which locate over the cylindrical pipework to paint it.
3 Radiator roller
This is a thin roller on a long wire handle for painting behind radiators and pipes.

● **Essential tools**
50 and 200mm (2 and 8in) standard pads
Sash pad
Large roller and selection of sleeves
Roller tray

DECORATING TOOLS

Spraying reinforced paints
Hire a special gravity-fed spray gun to apply reinforced masonry paint and 'Tyrolean' finishes. The material is loaded into a hopper on top of the gun.

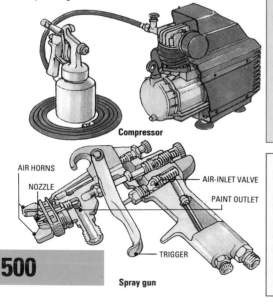

Compressor

AIR HORNS
NOZZLE
AIR-INLET VALVE
PAINT OUTLET
TRIGGER

Spray gun

PAINTSPRAYING EQUIPMENT

Spraying is so fast and efficient that it's worth considering if you plan to paint the outside walls of a building. The equipment is expensive to buy, but it can be rented from tool-hire outlets. You can spray most exterior paints and finishes if they are thinned properly, but tell the hire company which paint you intend to use, so they can supply the right spray gun with the correct nozzle. Acquire goggles and a respirator at the same time.

Preparation

As far as possible, plan to work on a dry and windless day. Also, allow time to mask off windows, doors and pipework.

Follow the setting-up and handling instructions supplied with the equipment; and if you are new to the work, practise beforehand on an inconspicuous section of wall.

Compressor-operated spray

With this equipment, the paint is mixed with compressed air to emerge as a fine spray. Some compressors deliver air to an intermediate tank and top it up as the air is drawn off by the spray gun, but most hired compressors supply air directly to the gun.

The trigger opens a valve to admit air, and at the same time opens the paint outlet at the nozzle. The paint is drawn from a container, usually mounted below the gun, and mixes with air at the tip. Most guns have air-delivery horns at the sides of the nozzle to produce a fan-shaped spray.

Airless sprayer

In an airless sprayer, an electric pump delivers the paint itself at high pressure to the spray gun. The paint is picked up through a plastic tube inserted in the paint container, and the pump forces it through a high-pressure hose to

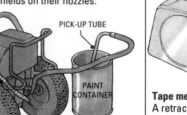

SPRAY GUN
FILTER
PRESSURE REGULATOR
HIGH-PRESSURE HOSE
PICK-UP TUBE
PAINT CONTAINER

Airless spray equipment

a filter and pressure regulator, which is adjustable to produce the required spray pattern.

The paint leaves the nozzle at such high pressure that it can penetrate skin. Most spray guns of this kind therefore have safety shields on their nozzles.

USING SPRAYERS SAFELY

Follow safety recommendations supplied with the sprayer, and take the following precautions:

- Wear goggles and a respirator when spraying.
- Don't spray indoors without proper extraction equipment.
- Atomized oil paint is highly flammable, so extinguish any naked lights and never smoke when you are spraying.
- Never leave the equipment unattended, especially where there are children or pets.
- If the gun has a safety lock, always engage it whenever you are not actually spraying.
- Unplug the equipment and release the pressure in the hose before trying to clear a blocked nozzle.
- Never aim the gun at yourself or anyone else. If you should accidentally spray your skin at close quarters with an airless gun, then seek medical advice immediately.

CLEANING A SPRAY GUN

Empty out any paint that is left in the container and add some thinners. Spray the thinners until they emerge clear, then release the pressure and dismantle the spray nozzle. Clean the parts with a solvent-dampened rag and wipe out the container.

COMMON SPRAYING FAULTS

Streaked paintwork
An uneven, streaked finish will result if you do not overlap the passes of the gun.

Patchy paintwork
Coverage won't be consistent if you move the gun in an arc. Keep it pointing directly at the wall and moving parallel to it.

Orange-peel texture
A wrinkled paint film resembling the texture of orange peel is usually caused by spraying paint that is too thick. Alternatively, if the paint seems to be of the right consistency, you may be moving the gun too slowly.

Runs
Runs will occur if you apply too much paint – probably through holding the gun too close to the surface you are spraying.

Powdery finish
This is caused by paint drying before it reaches the wall. The remedy is to hold the gun a little closer to the wall's surface.

Spattering
If the pressure is too high, the finish will look speckled. To avoid spattering, lower the pressure till the finish is satisfactory.

Spitting
A partly clogged nozzle will make the gun splutter. Clear the nozzle with a stiff bristle from a brush – never use wire – and then wipe it with a rag dampened in thinners.

PAPERHANGER'S TOOLS

You can improvise some of the tools needed for paperhanging. However, even purpose-made equipment is inexpensive, so it's worth having a decent kit.

Tape measure
A retractable steel tape is best for measuring walls and ceilings in order to estimate the amount of wallcovering you will need.

Plumb bob and line

Retractable plumb line

Plumb line
Any small weight suspended on fine string can be used to mark the position of one edge of a strip of wallpaper. Hold the end of the line close to the ceiling, allow the weight to come to rest, and then mark the wall at points down the length of the line.

A purpose-made plumb line has a pointed metal weight called a plumb bob. The more-expensive versions have a string that retracts into a hollow plumb bob containing coloured chalk, so the string is coated with chalk every time it is withdrawn. With the string stretched taut, snap it like a bowstring to leave a chalk line on the wall.

Paste brush
Use either a wide wall brush or a short-pile roller to apply paste to the back of wallcoverings.

Clean either tool by washing it in warm water.

DECORATING
TOOLS

PASTING TABLE

You can paste wallcoverings on any flat surface, but a purpose-made pasting table provides a much more convenient working surface. It stands higher than the average dining table, but is only 25mm (1in) wider than a standard roll of wallpaper – which makes it easier to spread paste without getting it onto the worktop. The underframe folds flat and the top is hinged, enabling the table to be carried from room to room and stowed in a small space.

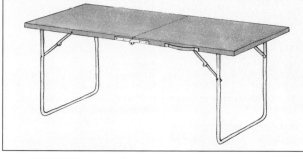

Paperhanger's brush
This is used for smoothing wall-coverings onto a wall or ceiling. Its bristles should be soft, so as not to damage delicate paper, but springy enough to provide the pressure to squeeze out air bubbles and excess paste. Wash the brush in warm water when you finish work to prevent paste hardening on the bristles.

Seam roller
Use a hardwood or plastic seam roller to press down the seams between strips of wallpaper – but don't use one on embossed or delicate wallcoverings.

Rubber   Felt

Smoothing roller
There are rubber rollers for squeezing trapped air from under wallcoverings, but use a felt one on delicate or flocked papers.

Paperhanger's scissors
Any fairly large scissors can be used for trimming wallpaper to length, but special paperhanger's scissors have extra-long blades to achieve a straight cut.

Craft knife
Use a knife to trim paper round light fittings and switches, and to achieve perfect butt joints by cutting through overlapping edges of paper. The knife must be extremely sharp to avoid tearing the paper, so use one with disposable blades that you can change as soon as one gets blunt. Some craft knives have short double-ended blades clamped in a metal or plastic handle. Others have long retractable blades that are snapped off in short sections to leave a new sharp point.

TILING TOOLS

Most of the tools in a tiler's kit are for applying ceramic wall and floor tiles, but others are used for laying soft tiles and vinyl sheeting.

Spirit level
You will need a spirit level for setting up temporary battens to align a field of tiles both horizontally and vertically.

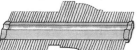

Profile gauge
A profile gauge is used for copying the shape of door mouldings or pipework to provide a pattern so you can fit soft floorcoverings.

As you press the steel pins of the gauge against the object you wish to copy, they slide back, replicating the shape. When you want to copy another shape, you press the needles against a flat surface to reposition them in a straight line.

Serrated trowel
Make a ridged bed for ceramic tiles by drawing the toothed edge of a plastic or steel tiler's trowel through the adhesive.

Tile cutter
A tile cutter has either a pointed tungsten-carbide tip or a steel wheel – like a glass cutter's – for scoring the glazed surface of ceramic tiles. The tile snaps cleanly along the scored line.

Tile saw
A tile saw has a bent-metal frame that holds a thin wire rod under tension. The rod is coated with particles of tungsten-carbide, which are hard enough to cut through ceramic tiles. As the rod is circular in section, it will cut in any direction, making it possible to saw straight and curved lines with equal ease.

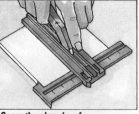

Grout spreader
This tool has a hard-rubber blade mounted in a plastic handle. It is used for spreading grout into the gaps between ceramic tiles.

Nibblers
It is impossible to snap a very narrow strip off a ceramic tile. Instead score the line with a tile cutter, then break off the waste little by little with tile nibblers. They resemble pincers, but have sharper jaws of tungsten-carbide that open automatically when you relax your grip on the spring-loaded handles.

TILE-CUTTING JIGS

A jig makes it much easier to cut and fit tiles for the border around a field of tiles. With the one tool, you can measure the gap and cut the tiles to infill the border.

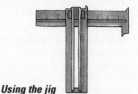

Using the jig
To measure the size of a border tile, slide the jig open until one pointer is against the adjacent wall and the other is against the edge of the last full tile (1). The jig automatically makes an allowance for grouting.

Fit the jig over the tile to be cut and use a tile cutter to score the glaze through the slot in the jig (2). The cutter comes with a pair of pliers with angled jaws for snapping the tile in two. Centre the scored line in the pliers' jaws, and squeeze the handles until the tile breaks cleanly (3).

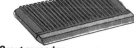

1 Measure the margin

2 Score the glazed surface

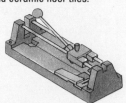

3 Snap the tile with special pliers

Floor-tile jig
Hire or buy a sturdy jig for marking and cutting quarry tiles and ceramic floor tiles.

● **Essential tools**
Steel tape measure
Plumb line
Paste brush
Paperhanger's brush
Seam roller
Scissors
Craft knife
Pasting table
Spirit level
Serrated trowel
Tile cutter and jig
Nibblers
Tile saw
Squeegee

PLUMBING TOOLS

PLUMBER'S AND METALWORKER'S TOOL KIT
Although plastics have been used for drainage for some time, the advent of plastics suitable for mains-pressure and hot water has affected the plumbing trade more radically. However, brass fittings and pipework made of copper and other metals are still extensively used for domestic plumbing, so the plumber's tool kit is still basically for working metal.

EQUIPMENT FOR REMOVING BLOCKAGES

You don't have to get a plumber to clear blocked appliances, pipes or even main drains. All the necessary equipment can be bought or hired.

Sink plunger

Plunger
This is a simple but effective tool for clearing a blockage from a sink, washbasin or bath trap. A pumping action on the rubber cup forces air and water along the pipe to disperse the blockage. When you buy a plunger, make sure the cup is large enough to cover the waste outlet.

It is possible to hire larger plungers for clearing blockages from WC traps.

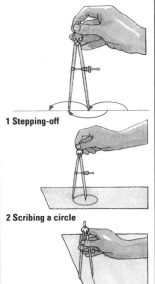

Hydraulic pump
A blocked wastepipe can be cleared with a hand-operated hydraulic pump. A downward stroke creates a powerful jet of water that should push the obstruction clear. If, however, the blockage is lodged firmly, an upward stroke creates enough suction to pull the obstruction out of place.

WC auger
The short coiled-wire WC auger designed for clearing WC and gully traps is rotated by a handle in a hollow, rigid shaft. The auger has a vinyl guard to prevent the WC pan getting scratched.

- **● Essential tools**
  Sink plunger
  Scriber
  Centre punch
  Steel rule
  Try square
  General-purpose
  hacksaw

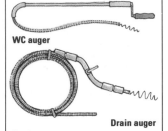
WC auger

Drain auger

Drain auger
A flexible coiled-wire drain auger will pass through small-diameter wastepipes to clear blockages. Pass the corkscrew-like head into the wastepipe till it reaches the blockage, clamp the cranked handle onto the other end, and then turn it to rotate the head and engage the blockage. Push and pull the auger till the pipe is clear.

RODS

PLUNGER   CORKSCREW   SCRAPER

Drain rods
You can hire a complete set of rods and fittings for clearing main drains and inspection chambers. Rods come in 1m (3ft 3in) lengths of polypropylene with threaded brass connectors.

The clearing heads comprise a double-worm corkscrew fitting, a 100mm (4in) rubber plunger and a hinged scraper for clearing the open channels in inspection chambers.

MEASURING AND MARKING TOOLS

Tools for measuring and marking metal are very like those used for wood but they are made and calibrated for greater accuracy because metal parts must fit with precision.

Scriber
For precise work, use a pointed hardened-steel scriber to mark lines and hole centres on metal. However, use a pencil to mark the centre of a bend, as a scored line made with a scriber may open up when the metal is stretched on the outside of the bend.

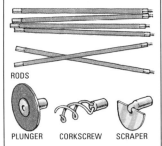

Spring dividers
Spring dividers are like a pencil compass, but both legs have steel points. These are adjusted to the required spacing by a knurled nut on a threaded rod that links the legs.

Using spring dividers
Use dividers to step-off divisions along a line (1) or to scribe circles (2). By running one point against the edge of a workpiece you can scribe a line parallel with the edge (3).

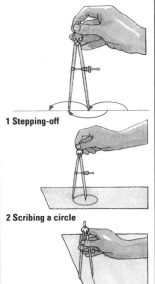

1 Stepping-off

2 Scribing a circle

3 Parallel scribing

Centre punch
A centre punch is for marking the centres of holes to be drilled.

Using a centre punch
With its point on dead centre, strike the punch with a hammer. If the mark is not accurate, angle the punch towards the true centre, tap it to extend the mark in that direction, and then mark the centre again.

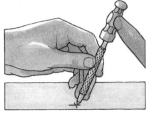
Correcting a misplaced centre mark

Steel rule
You will need a long tape measure for estimating pipe runs and positioning appliances, but use a 300 or 600mm (1 or 2ft) steel rule for marking out components when absolute accuracy is important.

Try square
You can use a woodworker's try square to mark out or check right angles; however, an all-metal engineer's try square is precision-made for metalwork. The small notch between blade and stock allows the tool to fit properly against a right-angled workpiece even when the corner is burred by filing. For general-purpose work, choose a 150mm (6in) try square.

METAL-CUTTING TOOLS

You can cut solid bar, sheet and tubular metal with an ordinary hacksaw, but there are tools specifically designed for cutting sheet metal and pipes.

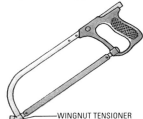
WINGNUT TENSIONER

General-purpose hacksaw
A modern hacksaw has a tubular-steel frame with a light cast-metal handle. The frame is adjustable to accommodate replaceable blades of different lengths, which are tensioned by tightening a wingnut.

CHOOSING A HACKSAW BLADE

You can buy 200, 250 and 300mm (8, 10 and 12in) hacksaw blades. Try the different lengths till you find the one that suits you best. Choose the hardness and size of teeth according to the type of metal you are planning to cut.

PLUMBING
TOOLS

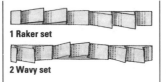

1 Raker set

2 Wavy set

Size and set of teeth

A coarse hacksaw blade has 14 to 18 teeth per 25mm (1in); a fine one has 24 to 32. The teeth are set – bent sideways – to make a cut wider than the blade's thickness, to prevent it jamming in the work. Coarse teeth are 'raker set' **(1)**, with pairs of teeth bent to opposite sides and separated by a tooth left in line with the blade to clear metal waste from the kerf (cut). Fine teeth are too small to be raker set and the whole row is 'wavy set' **(2)**. Use a coarse blade for cutting soft metals like brass and aluminium, which would clog fine teeth, and a fine blade for thin sheet and the harder metals.

Hardness

A hacksaw blade must be harder than the metal it is cutting, or its teeth will quickly blunt. A flexible blade with hardened teeth will cut most metals, but there are fully hardened blades that stay sharp longer and are less prone to losing teeth. However, being rigid and brittle, they break easily. Blades of high-speed steel are expensive and even more brittle than the fully hardened ones, but they will cut very hard alloys.

Fitting a hacksaw blade

With its teeth pointing away from the handle, slip the new blade onto the pins at each end of the hacksaw frame. Apply tension with the wingnut. If the new blade tends to wander off line as you cut, tighten the wingnut.

If you have to fit a new blade after starting to cut a piece of metal, it may jam in the kerf because its set is wider than that of the old worn blade – so start a fresh cut on the other side of the workpiece and work back to the kerf you began with.

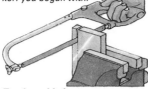

Turning a blade

Sometimes it's easier to work with the blade at right angles to the frame. Rotate the square-section spigots a quarter turn before fitting the blade.

1 Turn first kerf away from you

Sawing metal bar

Hold the work in an engineer's vice, with the marked cutting line as close to the jaws as possible. Start the cut on the waste side of the line with short strokes until the kerf is about 1mm (¹⁄₁₆ in) deep; then turn the bar 90 degrees in the vice, so that the kerf faces away from you, and cut a similar kerf in the new face (1). Continue in this way until the kerf runs right round the bar, then cut through the bar with long steady strokes. Steady the end of the saw with your free hand, and put a little light oil on the blade if necessary.

Sawing rod or pipe

As you cut a cylindrical rod or tube, rotate it away from you till the kerf runs right round the rod or tube before you sever it.

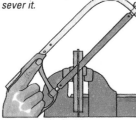

Sawing sheet metal

To saw a small piece of sheet metal, sandwich it between two strips of wood clamped in a vice. Adjust the metal to place the cutting line close to the strips, then saw down the waste side with steady strokes and the blade angled to the work. To cut a thin sheet of metal, clamp it between two pieces of plywood and cut through all three layers at once.

Sawing a groove

To cut a slot or groove wider than a standard hacksaw blade, fit two or more identical blades in the frame at the same time.

Junior hacksaw

Use a junior hacksaw for cutting small-bore tubing and thin metal rod. The simplest ones have a solid spring-steel frame that holds the blade under tension.

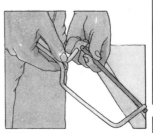

Fitting a new blade

To fit a blade, locate it in the slot at the front of the frame and bow the frame against a workbench until the blade fits in the rear slot.

Engineer's vice

A large engineer's or metal-worker's vice has to be bolted to the workbench, but smaller ones can be clamped on. Slip soft fibre liners over the jaws of a vice to protect workpieces held in it.

Cold chisel

Plumbers use cold chisels for hacking old pipes out of masonry. They are also useful for chopping the heads off rivets and cutting metal rod. Sharpen the tip of the chisel on a bench grinder.

Straight snips

Universal snips

Tinsnips

Tinsnips are used for cutting sheet metal. **Straight snips** have wide blades for cutting straight edges. If you try to cut curves with them, the waste usually gets caught against the blades; but it is possible to cut a convex curve by progressively removing small straight pieces of waste down to the marked line. **Universal snips** have thick narrow blades that cut a curve in one pass and will also make straight cuts.

Using tinsnips

As you cut along the marked line, let the waste curl away below the sheet. To cut thick sheet metal, clamp one handle of the snips in a vice, so you can apply your full weight to the other one.

Try not to close the jaws completely each time, as it can cause a jagged edge on the metal. Wear thick gloves when you are cutting sheet metal.

SHARPENING SNIPS

Clamp one handle in a vice and sharpen the cutting edge with a smooth file. File the other edge and finish by removing the burrs from the backs of the blades on an oiled slipstone.

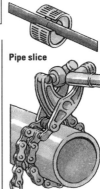

Sheet-metal cutter

Tinsnips tend to distort a narrow strip cut from the edge of a metal sheet. However, the strip remains perfectly flat when removed with a sheet-metal cutter. The same tool is also suited to cutting rigid plastic sheet, which cracks if it is distorted by tinsnips.

Tube cutters

A tube cutter slices the ends off pipes at exactly 90 degrees to their length. The pipe is clamped between the cutting wheel and an adjustable slide with two rollers, and is cut as the tool is moved round it. The adjusting screw is tightened between each revolution. A pipe slice, which works like a tube cutter, can be operated in confined spaces.

Chain-link cutter

Cut large-diameter pipes with a chain-link cutter. Wrap the chain round the pipe, locate the end link in the clamp, and tighten the adjuster until the cutter on each link bites into the metal. Work the handle back and forth to score the pipe, and continue tightening the adjuster intermittently until the pipe is severed.

Sheet-metal cutter

Tube cutter

Pipe slice

Chain-link cutter

● **Essential tools**
Junior hacksaw
Cold chisel
Tinsnips
Tube cutter

PLUMBING
TOOLS

● **Essential tools**
High-speed twist
drills
Variable-speed
power drill
Bending spring
Soft mallet
Soldering iron
Gas torch

DRILLS AND PUNCHES

Special-quality steel bits are made for drilling holes in metal. Cut 12 to 25mm (½ to 1in) holes in sheet metal with a punch.

Twist drills

Metal-cutting twist drills are similar to the ones used for wood but are made from high-speed steel and their tips are ground to a shallower angle. Use them in a power drill at slow speeds.

Mark the metal with a centre punch to locate the drill point, and clamp the work in a vice or to the bed of a vertical drill stand. Drill slowly and steadily, and keep the bit oiled. To drill a large hole, make a small pilot hole first to guide the larger drill bit.

When drilling sheet metal, the bit can jam and produce a ragged hole as it exits on the far side of the workpiece. As a precaution, clamp the work between pieces of plywood and drill through all three layers.

Hole punch

Use a hole punch to make large holes in sheet metal. Having first marked out the circumference of the hole on the metal with spring dividers, lay the work on a piece of scrap softwood or plywood. Place the punch on the marked circle and tap it with a hammer, then check the alignment of the punched ring with the scribed circle. Reposition the punch and, with one sharp hammer blow, cut through the metal. If the wood crushes and the metal is slightly distorted, tap it flat again with the hammer.

Tank cutter

Use a tank cutter to make holes for pipework in plastic or metal storage cisterns.

METAL BENDERS

Thick or hard metal must be heated before it can be bent successfully, but soft copper piping and sheet metal can be bent while cold.

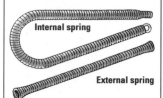

Internal spring

External spring

Bending springs

You can bend small-diameter pipes over your knee, but their walls must be supported with a coiled spring to prevent them buckling.

Push an internal spring inside the pipe, or slide an external one over it. Either type of spring must fit the pipe exactly.

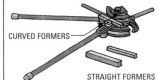

CURVED FORMERS

STRAIGHT FORMERS

Tube bender

With a tube bender, a pipe is bent over one of two fixed curved formers that are designed to give the optimum radii for plumbing and support the walls of the pipe during bending. Each has a matching straight former, which is placed between the pipe and a steel roller on a movable lever. Operating this lever bends the pipe over the curved former.

Soft mallet

Soft mallets have heads made of coiled rawhide, hard rubber or plastic. They are used in bending strip or sheet metal, which would be damaged by a metal hammer.

To bend sheet metal at a right angle, clamp it between stout battens along the bending line. Start at one end and bend the metal over one of the battens by tapping it with the mallet. Don't attempt the full bend at once, but work along the sheet, increasing the angle gradually and keeping it constant along the length until the metal lies flat on the batten. Tap out any kinks.

PIPE-FREEZING EQUIPMENT

To work on plumbing without having to drain the system, you can form temporary ice plugs in the pipework. The water has to be cold and not flowing.

Using freezing equipment

You can buy a kit containing an aerosol of liquid freezing gas, plus two plastic-foam 'jackets' to wrap round the pipework at the points where you want the water to freeze. Pierce a small hole through the wall of each jacket and bind it securely to the pipe (1); then insert the extension tube through the hole (2) and inject the recommended amount of gas. It takes about five minutes for the ice plug to form in a metal pipe, and up to 15 minutes in a plastic one. If the job takes more than half an hour to complete, you will need to inject more gas.

Alternatively, hire jackets with cylinders of carbon dioxide; or an electric freezer connected to two blocks that you clamp over the pipework. An electric freezer will keep the water frozen until you finish the job and switch off.

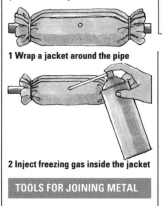

1 Wrap a jacket around the pipe

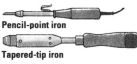

2 Inject freezing gas inside the jacket

TOOLS FOR JOINING METAL

You can make permanent watertight joints with solder, a molten alloy that acts like a glue when it cools and solidifies.

Mechanical fixings such as compression joints, rivets, and nuts and bolts are also used for joining metal.

SOLDERS

Solders are designed to melt at relatively low temperatures, but they will not work in the presence of water. When working on hot-water and cold-water plumbing, use a lead-free solder. It has a slightly higher melting point than the old lead solder and makes stronger joints.

FLUX

To be soldered successfully, a joint must be perfectly clean and free of oxides. Even after the metal has been cleaned with wire wool or emery, oxides form immediately, making a positive bond between the solder and metal impossible. Flux is therefore used to form a chemical barrier against oxidation.

Corrosive or 'active' flux, applied with a brush, dissolves oxides but must be washed from the surface with water as soon as the solder solidifies, or it will go on corroding the metal.

A 'passive' flux, in paste form, is used where it is impossible to wash the joint thoroughly. Though it does not dissolve oxides, it excludes them adequately for soldering copper plumbing joints and electrical connections.

Another alternative is to use wire solder containing flux in a hollow core. The flux flows just before the solder melts.

To remove flux from a central-heating system, fill it with water and let it heat up, then switch off and drain the system. This should be repeated a couple of times.

Soldering irons

For successful soldering, the work has to become hot enough for the solder to melt and flow – otherwise it solidifies before it can completely penetrate the joint. A soldering iron is used to apply the necessary heat.

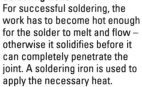

Pencil-point iron

Tapered-tip iron

Use a low-powered pencil-point iron for soldering electrical connections. To bring sheet metal up to working temperature, use a larger iron with a tapered tip.

Tinning a soldering iron
The tip of a soldering iron has to be 'tinned' to keep it oxide-free. Clean the cool tip with a file; then heat it to working temperature, dip it in flux, and apply a stick of solder to coat it evenly.

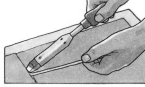

Using a soldering iron
Clean the mating surfaces of the joint to a bright finish and coat them with flux, then clamp the joint tightly between two wooden battens. Apply the hot iron along the joint to heat the metal thoroughly, then run its tip along the edge of the joint, following closely with a stick of solder. The solder flows immediately into a properly heated joint.

Gas torch
Even a large soldering iron cannot heat thick metal fast enough to compensate for heat loss from the joint, and this is very much the situation when you solder pipework. Although the copper unions have very thin walls, the pipe on each side dissipates so much heat that a soldering iron cannot get the joint itself hot enough to form a watertight soldered seal. Use a gas torch with an intensely hot flame to heat the work quickly.

The torch runs on liquid gas contained under pressure in a disposable metal canister that screws onto the gas inlet. Open the control valve and light the gas released from the nozzle, then adjust the valve until the flame roars and is bright blue. Use the hottest part of the flame – about the middle of its length – to heat the joint.

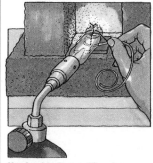

Hard soldering and brazing
Use a gas torch for brazing and hard soldering. Clean and flux the work – if possible with an active flux – then wire or clamp the parts together. Place the assembly on a fireproof mat or surround it with firebricks. Bring the joint to red heat with the torch, then dip a stick of the appropriate alloy in flux and apply it to the joint. When the joint is cool, chip off hardened flux, wash the metal thoroughly in hot water, and finish the joint with a file.

Fireproof mat
Buy a fireproof mat from a plumber's merchant to protect flammable surfaces from the heat of a gas torch.

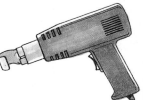

Hot-air gun
Some hot-air guns designed for stripping old paintwork can also be used for soft soldering. You can vary the temperature of an electronic gun from about 100 to 600°C. A heat shield on the nozzle reflects the heat back onto the work.

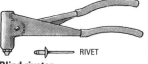
RIVET

Blind riveter
Join thin sheet metal with a blind riveter, a hand-operated tool with plier-like handles. It uses special rivets with long shanks that break off, leaving slightly raised heads on both sides of the work.

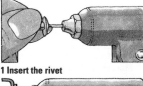
1 Insert the rivet

2 Squeeze the handles

Using a riveter
Clamp the two sheets together and drill holes right through the metal, matching the diameter of the rivets and spaced regularly along the joint. Open the handles of the riveter and insert the rivet shank in the head (1). Push the rivet through a hole in the work and, while pressing the tool hard against the metal, squeeze the handles to compress the rivet head on the far side (2). When the rivet is fully expanded the shank will snap off in the tool.

SPANNERS AND WRENCHES

A professional plumber uses a great variety of spanners and wrenches on a wide range of fittings and fixings. However, there is no need to buy them all, since you can hire ones that you need only occasionally.

Open-ended spanner
A set of open-ended spanners is essential for a plumber or metal-worker. Pipes generally run into a fitting or accessory, and the only tool you can use is a spanner with open jaws. The spanners are usually double-ended – perhaps in a combination of metric and imperial sizes – and the sizes are duplicated within a set to enable you to manipulate two identical nuts simultaneously (for example, on a compression joint).

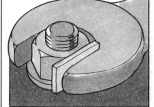

Achieving a tight fit
A spanner must be a good fit, or it will round the corners of the nut. You can pack out the jaws with a thin 'shim' of metal if a snug fit is otherwise not possible.

Ring spanner
Being a closed circle, the head of a ring spanner is stronger and fits better than that of an open-ended one. It is specially handy for loosening a corroded nut, provided that you are able to slip the spanner over it.

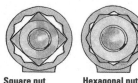
Square nut   **Hexagonal nut**

Choosing a ring spanner
Choose a 12-point spanner. It is fast to use and will fit both square and hexagonal nuts. You can buy combination spanners with a ring at one end and an open jaw at the other.

Box spanner
A box spanner is a steel tube with hexagonal ends. The turning force is applied with a tommy bar slipped through holes drilled in the tube. Don't use a very long bar: too much leverage may strip the thread of the fitting or distort the walls of the spanner.

Adjustable spanner
Having a movable jaw, an adjustable spanner is not as strong as an open-ended or ring spanner, but is often the only tool that will fit a large nut or one that's coated with paint. Make sure the spanner fits the nut snugly by rocking it slightly as you tighten the jaws; and grip the nut with the roots of the jaws. If you use just the tips, they can spring apart slightly under force and the spanner will slip.

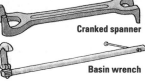
Cranked spanner

Basin wrench

Cranked spanner and basin wrench
A cranked spanner is a special double-ended wrench for use on tap connectors.

A basin wrench, for the same job, has a pivoting jaw that can be set for either tightening or loosening a fitting.

Radiator spanner
Use a simple spanner of hexagonal-section steel rod to remove radiator blanking plugs. One end is ground to fit plugs that have square sockets.

● **Essential tools**
Blind riveter
Set of open-ended spanners
Small and large adjustable spanners

PLUMBING
TOOLS

Stillson wrench
The adjustable toothed jaws of a Stillson wrench are for gripping pipework. As force is applied, the jaws tighten on the work.

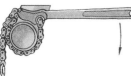

Chain wrench
A chain wrench does the same job as a Stillson wrench, but can be used on very large-diameter pipework and fittings. Wrap the chain tightly round the work and engage it with the hook at the end of the wrench, then lever the handle towards the toothed jaw to apply turning force.

Strap wrench
With a strap wrench you can disconnect chromed pipework without damaging its surface. Wrap the smooth leather or canvas strap round the pipe, pass its end through the slot in the head of the tool, and pull it tight. Levering on the handle rotates the pipe.

● **Essential tools**
Plier wrench
Second-cut and smooth flat files
Second-cut and smooth half-round files

Plier wrench
A plier wrench locks onto the work. It grips round stock or damaged nuts, and is often used as a small cramp.

1 Adjusting the wrench   **2 Releasing the wrench**

Using a plier wrench
Squeeze the handles to close the jaws while slowly turning the adjusting screw clockwise until they snap together (1). Release the tool's grip on the work by pulling the release lever (2).

FILES

Files are used for shaping and smoothing metal components and removing sharp edges.

CLASSIFYING FILES

The working faces of a file are composed of parallel ridges, or teeth, set at about 70 degrees to its edges. A file is classified according to the size and spacing of its teeth and whether it has one or two sets.

Single-cut file

Double-cut file

A *single-cut file* has one set of teeth virtually covering each of its faces. A *double-cut file* has a second set of identical teeth crossing the first at a 45-degree angle. Some files are single-cut on one side and double-cut on the other.

The spacing of teeth relates directly to their size: the finer the teeth, the more closely packed they are. Degrees of coarseness are expressed as number of teeth per 25mm (1in). Use progressively finer files to remove marks left by coarser ones.

File classification

Bastard file – Coarse grade (26 teeth per 25mm), used for initial shaping.
Second-cut file – Medium grade (36 teeth per 25mm), used for preliminary smoothing.
Smooth file – Fine grade (47 teeth per 25mm), used for final smoothing.

CLEANING A FILE

Soft metal tends to clog file teeth. When a file stops cutting efficiently, brush along the teeth with a fine wire brush, then rub chalk on the file to help reduce clogging in future.

Needle files

FLAT FILE | HAND FILE | HALF-ROUND FILE | ROUND FILE | SQUARE FILE | TRIANGULAR FILE

Flat file
A flat file tapers from its pointed tang to its tip, in both width and thickness. Both faces and both edges are toothed.

Hand file
Hand files are parallel-sided but tapered in their thickness. Most of them have one smooth edge for filing up to a corner without damaging it.

Half-round file
This tool has one rounded face for shaping inside curves.

Round file
A round file is for shaping tight curves and enlarging holes.

Square file
Square files are used for cutting narrow slots and smoothing the edges of small rectangular holes.

Triangular file
Triangular files are designed for accurately shaping and smoothing undercut apertures of less than 90 degrees.

Needle files
These are miniature versions of standard files and are all made in extra-fine grades. Needle files are used for precise work and to sharpen brace bits.

FILE SAFETY

Always fit a wooden or plastic handle on the tang of a file before you use it.

1 Fitting a file handle

2 Knock a handle from the tang

If an unprotected file catches on the work, then the tang could be driven into the palm of your hand. Having fitted a handle, tap its end on a bench to tighten its grip (1).

To remove the handle, hold the blade of the file in one hand and strike the ferrule away from you with a block of wood (2).

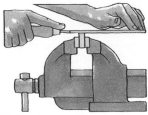

Using a file
When using any file, keep it flat on the work and avoid rocking it during forward strokes. Hold it steady, with the fingers of one hand resting on its tip, and make slow firm strokes with the full length of the file.

To avoid vibration, hold the work low in the jaws of a vice or clamp it between two battens.

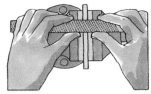

Draw filing
You can give metal a smooth finish by draw filing. With both hands, hold a smooth file at right angles to the work and slide the tool backwards and forwards along the surface. Finally, polish the workpiece with emery cloth wrapped round the file.

PLIERS

Pliers are for improving your grip on small components and for bending and shaping metal rod and wire.

Engineer's pliers
For general-purpose work, buy a sturdy pair of engineer's pliers. The toothed jaws have a curved section for gripping round stock and also have side cutters for cropping wire.

Slip-joint or waterpump pliers
The special feature of slip-joint pliers is a movable pivot for enlarging the jaw spacing. The extra-long handles give a good grip on pipes and other fittings.

FINISHING METAL

Before painting or soldering it, always make sure that metal is clean and rust-free.

Wire brush
Use a steel-wire hand brush to clean rusty or corroded metal.

Wire wool
Wire wool is a mass of very thin steel filaments. It is used to remove file marks and to clean oxides and dirt from metals.

Emery cloth and paper
Emery is a natural black grit which, when backed with paper or cloth, is ideal for polishing metals. There's a range of grades from coarse to fine. For the best finish, use progressively finer abrasives as the work proceeds.

1 Glue paper to a board

2 Clean a pipe with an emery strip

Using emery cloth and paper
To avoid rounding the crisp edges of a flat component, glue a sheet of emery paper to a board and rub the metal on it (*1*).

To finish round stock or pipes, loop a strip of emery cloth over the work and pull alternately on each end (*2*).

Buffing mop
Metals can be brought to a shine by hand, using a liquid metal polish and a soft cloth; but for a really high gloss, use a buffing mop in a bench-mounted power drill or grinder.

Using a buffing mop
After applying a stick of buffing compound – a fine abrasive with wax – to the revolving mop, move the work from side to side against the lower half, keeping any edges facing downwards.

Reseating tool
If the seat of a tap has become so worn that even fitting a new washer won't produce a perfect seal, use a reseating tool to grind the seat flat.

Remove the tap's headgear and jumper, then screw the cone of the reseating tool into the body of the tap. Turn the knurled adjuster to lower the cutter onto the worn seat, and then turn the tommy bar to regrind the metal.

WOODWORKING TOOLS

A plumber needs a set of basic woodworking tools in order to lift floorboards, notch joists for pipe runs, and attach pipe clips.

● **Essential tools and materials**
Engineer's pliers
Wire brush
Wire wool
Emery cloth and paper

507

ELECTRICAL TOOLS

Torch
Keep a torch handy for checking your consumer unit when a fuse blows on a lighting circuit. You may also need artificial light when working on connections below floorboards or in the loft, and a torch that stands unsupported is particularly helpful.

Electrician's skate

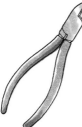

Diagonal cutters

● **Essential tools**
Terminal screwdrivers
Wire cutters
Wire strippers
Power drill and bits
Torch
General-purpose tools

508

ELECTRICIAN'S TOOL KIT
You need only a fairly limited range of tools to make electrical connections, but an extensive general-purpose tool kit is required for making cable runs and for fixing electrical accessories and appliances to the structure of the house.

SCREWDRIVERS

Buy good screwdrivers for tightening electrical terminals. Cheap ones are practically useless, being made from such soft metal that the tips soon twist out of shape.

Terminal screwdriver
A terminal screwdriver has a long, slim cylindrical shaft that is ground to a flat tip.

For turning screw terminals in sockets and larger appliances, buy a screwdriver with a plastic handle and a plastic insulating sleeve on its shaft.

Use a smaller screwdriver with a very slim shaft to work on ceiling roses or to tighten plastic terminal blocks in small fittings.

Cabinet screwdriver
You will need a woodworking screwdriver to fix mounting boxes to walls.

SKATE

A skate is made with a cutting disc that severs the joint between tongue-and-groove floorboards. Run the tool back and forth with one foot.

WIRE CUTTERS

Use wire cutters for cropping cable and flex to length.

Electrician's pliers
These are engineer's pliers with insulating sleeves shrunk onto their handles. Use them for cropping circuit conductors and for twisting their ends together.

Diagonal cutters
Diagonal cutters will crop thick conductors more effectively than electrician's pliers – although you may need a junior hacksaw to cut meter leads.

WIRE STRIPPERS

There are various tools for cutting or stripping the plastic insulation that covers cables and flexible cords.

Wire strippers

Multi-purpose tool

Wire strippers
To remove the insulation from cable and flex, use a pair of wire strippers with jaws shaped to cut through the covering without damaging the wire core. There is a multi-purpose version that can both strip the insulation and crop conductors to length.

Sharp knife
A knife with sharp disposable blades is best for slitting and peeling the sheathing encasing cable and flex.

DRILLS

When you run circuit wiring, you need a drill with several special-purpose bits for boring through wood and masonry.

Auger
Some electricians employ a long wood-boring auger to drill through the wall head plate and noggings when they're running a switch cable from an attic down to its mounting box.

Power drill
A cordless power drill is often ideal for boring cable holes through timbers and for making wall-plug fixings. As well as standard masonry bits for wall fixings, you will need a much longer version for boring through brick walls and clearing access channels behind skirting boards.

If you shorten the shaft of a wide-tipped spade bit, you can use it in a power drill between floor joists instead of hiring a special joist brace.

TESTERS

Even when you have turned off the power at the consumer unit, use a tester to check that the circuit is safe to work on.

Electronic mains tester
Be sure to buy an electronic two-prong tester that is intended for use with mains voltage – similar devices are sold in auto shops for 12volt car wiring only.

Always check that the tester is functioning properly before and after you use it by testing it on a circuit you know to be live.

Following the manufacturer's instructions, place one probe on the neutral terminal and the other one on the live terminal to be tested. If the bulb illuminates, the circuit is live; if it does not illuminate, try again between the earth terminal and each of the live and neutral terminals. If the bulb still doesn't light up (and you've checked the tester), you can assume the circuit is not live.

Continuity tester
A continuity tester will test whether a circuit is complete or an appliance is properly earthed. Alternatively, buy a multi-tester that combines the functions of continuity testing and mains-voltage testing (see above).

Using a continuity tester
Switch off the power at the consumer unit before making the following test. To find the two ends of a buried disconnected cable, twist the black and red conductors together at one end, and then apply the tester's probes to the same conductors at the other end (1). Depress the circuit-testing button on the tester. The bulb should light up and, with some testers, there may also be an audible signal. Untwist the conductors. Make the test again – and if the bulb does not illuminate, the two ends don't belong to the same cable.

To check whether a plug-in appliance is safely earthed, apply one probe to the earth pin of the plug – the longest of the three – and touch an unpainted part of the metal casing of the appliance with the other probe (2). Depress the test button – if the earth connection is good,

then the bulb will illuminate.

Don't try to use the appliance if the bulb illuminates when you apply the probe to either of the plug's other pins (3). (Make sure the plug fuse is working.) Have a suspect appliance overhauled by an electrician.

You cannot test a double-insulated appliance, as it has no earth connection in the plug.

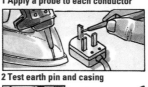

1 Apply a probe to each conductor

2 Test earth pin and casing

3 Test one other pin and casing

GENERAL-PURPOSE TOOLS

Every electrician needs tools for lifting and cutting floorboards, for fixing mounting boxes, and for cutting cable runs.

Claw hammer
For nailing cable clips to walls and timbers.

Club hammer
For use with a cold chisel.

Cold chisel
For cutting channels in plaster and brickwork in order to bury cables or mounting boxes.

Bolster chisel
For levering up floorboards.

Padsaw or power jigsaw
For cutting through floorboards close to skirtings.

Floorboard saw
This is the best tool for cutting across a prised-up board, though a tenon saw can be used instead.

Spirit level
For checking that mounting boxes are fixed horizontally.

Plasterer's trowel or filling knife
Either tool can be used for covering concealed cable with plaster or other kinds of filler.

Spanner
A small spanner is needed for making the earth connection in some appliances, and also for supplementary earth bonding.

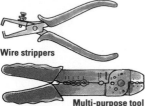

REFERENCE & INDEX

SOFTWOODS & HARDWOODS

SEE ALSO
Details for:
T & G boards   89

TIMBER AND MAN-MADE BOARDS

Timber is classified in two main groups, softwood and hardwood, according to the type of tree it comes from. Softwoods are from the evergreen coniferous trees like firs and pines, hardwoods from the deciduous broad-leaved ones. Most softwoods are in fact softer than most hardwoods, but that is not invariably the case.

Some hardwoods, particularly from tropical rainforests, are now endangered species and you should check the product labelling or ask the salesman to ensure it has come from a sustainable source.

SOFTWOODS

Softwoods generally stocked by suppliers are referred to as 'pine', 'whitewood' or 'redwood'. Most of the wood you see in a timber yard is softwood as it is by far the cheaper and more widely used for structural house timbers, floorboards, stairs and the simpler kinds of domestic furniture.

Buying softwood

Most softwood is available in rough and smooth versions called, respectively, sawn and planed. The rough unplaned surface of sawn timber means that it is suitable only for jobs where it will be out of sight. Where appearance is important you need planed wood – that is, of course, sawn and planed – which has been through a planing machine and is relatively smooth. But here a confusion can arise. Planed timber, or 'PAR' (planed all round), is always slightly thinner and narrower than its nominal dimensions. Machine planing takes about 3 to 6mm (⅛ to ¼in) off the width and thickness, but the loss is not uniform and so the wood is always referred to in terms of its nominal size, the size before planing. You have to take this into account when you plan jobs involving planed wood. However, some pre-packed planed wood sold in DIY stores is now labelled in finished sizes.

Timber yards use the metric system, but assistants in the yards are experts at instant conversion between the systems and will advise you if you think and work in imperial measures.

Choosing softwood

A number of defects can be found in softwood such as shakes, which are splits or cracks, and should be avoided, especially when a job's appearance is important. For this reason it is always best to pick out the wood yourself. Never order by phone unless you specify a clear selected grade.

Knots

Knots can look attractive in pine boards, but they must be 'live' knots – the glossy brown ones. 'Dead' knots, the black ones, will shrink and are likely to drop out, leaving unsightly holes that weaken the wood.

Warping

Distorted wood is another common problem. Look along the edges of each board to check that it is not bowed or twisted.

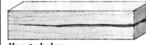

End shakes

These are splits in the ends of boards, and can be cut off, but you should not be charged for split sections.

Heart shakes

These are splits that occur along radial lines in the log. When these are combined at the centre of the tree they are known as star shakes.

Cup shakes

These occur parallel to the annual rings - the layers of new wood that grow each year. Typically a board cut from the centre of the tree may have the central 'ring' split away from the rest along its length.

Surface checking

This is when many fine cracks appear on the timber's surface. Very fine ones may be removed by planing, or filled if the work is to be painted; wood with wider ones should be rejected.

Other defects

Watch out for rough patches that have escaped the saw and planer such as remaining bark, damage from rough handling in the yard and water staining.

Cutting to size

At extra cost, a timber yard with modern woodworking machinery can cut wood to size for you. However, standard stock is usually cut to length by a busy yard worker using a handsaw, so for best results buy it a little over length and cut your own wood to the exact size required.

Most yards will cut a plank to the length you want unless it leaves too small an offcut to be sold, in which case you will have to buy the whole plank.

Seasoning softwood

Softwood is usually seasoned by kiln drying, but as it is often exposed to damp in the yard, it is best to let it dry out indoors for a week or so, preferably in the room where it is to be used, and lying flat, not propped against a wall or furniture.

Standard sizes and sections

Planed softwood comes in a range of standard thicknesses and widths, from small sections of a nominal 12 x 25mm (½ x 1in) to planks 75mm (3in) thick x 225mm (9in) wide. It can also be bought tongued and grooved for flooring or matchboarding and machined into a variety of sectional shapes known as mouldings for such uses as architraves, glazing bars, skirting boards and picture rails.

HARDWOODS

Hardwoods are much more expensive than softwoods and must usually be sought from specialist timber merchants. They are mainly used with a clear finish to display their attractive grain.

Ordering hardwoods

Some hardwoods, such as oak and ash, are typically stocked in timber yards, but a wider range is available from specialist suppliers. The commonly stocked hardwoods are cut to order and, like softwoods, are listed in nominal sizes. Specialists will also sell you whole planks as cut from the log, ready seasoned for you to convert into smaller sizes with the necessary machinery.

Hardwoods are relatively knot free but can suffer from warping, shakes and checks. The figure and colour of the wood can vary from tree to tree of the same species and according to how it is cut from the log, so try to check its appearance before it is machined for you.

If you need to match up a hardwood with one already used in your house, check it carefully as they are not always what they seem. Wood dyes are often used to improve the colour of a wood or change its appearance to resemble another species. Light-coloured beech, for example, is commonly stained darker to simulate mahogany.

Working with hardwoods

In order to work hardwoods, which are generally somewhat harder than softwoods, tools need to be sharpened more often and honed to a fine cutting edge.

Screw fixings require drilled pilot holes. The acidic nature of oak causes steel screws to stain the wood black. If you are screwing into oak, use brass or plated screws.

The dust created when machining hardwoods can be unpleasant if inhaled, and it is good practice to wear a suitable face mask or respirator when working with these woods.

Some hardwoods such as teak are naturally oily and joints need to be glued with a synthetic-resin adhesive to give best results.

Hardwood veneers

Veneers are thin slices of wood cut from the log in various ways and sold as single leaves or in bundles. Expensive hardwoods have been used in veneer form for centuries to cover cheaper woods. Today a wide range is available for laying onto man-made boards to create a luxurious-looking and stable material. Pre-veneered boards are also available in a limited range of hardwoods.

MAN-MADE BOARDS

Five man-made boards are widely used by woodworkers – plywood, chipboard, blockboard, hardboard and fibreboard.

Plywood

Plywood is a sheet material made by bonding a number of thin wood veneers together under high pressure. The veneers, or plies, may be of the same thickness throughout or the core veneers may be thicker than the face veneers. To maintain stability, veneers are typically laid in an odd number with their grain direction alternating: the grain of the two face veneers runs parallel with the longer edges of the board. Most plywood is made entirely from birch or pine, but you can also buy boards faced with quality hardwoods or melamine.

The type of glue used in its manufacture determines whether plywood is suitable for interior or exterior use. Best-quality plywood is used extensively for manufacturing furniture, while the cheaper grades are mostly used for building work such as shuttering for concrete.

Plywood sizes

Available thicknesses range from 4 to 18mm (⅛ to ¾in) and there are several sheet sizes, the most common standard size being 2440 x 1220mm (8 x 4ft).

Chipboard

Chipboard is a relatively cheap material commonly used to make modern cabinet furniture. The board is manufactured by gluing small softwood chips together under pressure. There are several grades, including standard and moisture-resistant types for flooring and roofing.

Standard chipboard, which is sanded smooth on both sides, can be filled and primed for painting. It also makes a good substrate for veneer. There are also several proprietary brands of chipboard faced with timber or melamine veneers.

Extra thick melamine-faced boards are made especially for kitchen worktops.

Chipboard sizes

Standard chipboard sheets measure 2440 x 1220mm (8 x 4ft) and are available 9, 12, 15 and 18mm (⅜, ½, ⅝ and ¾in) thick.

Melamine-faced and veneered chipboard is available as 15mm (⅝in) thick planks that range from 150 to 600mm (6in to 2ft) wide, and either 1820 or 2440mm (6 or 8ft) long. They are used extensively for shelving and DIY cabinet-making.

Blockboard

Blockboard comprises a core of rectangular-section wood battens sandwiched between two double layers of pressure-bonded veneer. It is used where structural strength and stability are required, such as for an unsupported span of worktop or shelving to take heavy loads.

Blockboard is an excellent material for veneering but, where appearance is important, any exposed edges need to be covered with solid-wood lippings. Lippings may be applied before or after veneering. For painting, the outer veneers of blockboard need only light sanding, but the edges need filling or lipping.

Blockboard sizes

Blockboard is usually sold as 2440 x 1220mm (8 x 4ft) sheets, 18 or 25mm (¾ or 1in) thick.

Hardboard

Hardboard is a dense, thin, sheet material made from compressed softwood pulp. It has less structural strength than other man-made boards, but it is relatively cheap and very stable.

Types of hardboard

Standard hardboard is brown in colour and 3.2mm (⅛in) thick, with one smooth shiny side and one textured. Other types include *Duo-faced hardboard* – having a smooth surface on both sides; *Perforated hardboard* – pierced with a regular pattern of round or decoratively shaped holes; *Textured hardboard* – with a decorative moulded surface; *Oil-tempered hardboard* – a moisture-resistant type; *Flame-retardant hardboard* - more resistant to fire; and *Pre-finished* – with a white finish or printed wood-grain effect.

Uses and sizes

Standard hardboard is relatively light, easy to cut and ideal for small sliding doors, cabinet backs and drawer bottoms, and as underlay for floorcoverings. Textured and pre-finished boards are used for wall panelling. The standard sheet measures 2440 x 1220mm (8 x 4ft), but many suppliers stock subdivisions of this size.

Fibreboards

Like hardboard, these are made from compressed wood fibre in various densities. Soft types are used for insulation, pinboard and wall sheathing .

Medium-density fibreboard (MDF) is a hard, dense material which has similar properties to solid wood. The boards have fine smooth surfaces on both sides, and the edges machine well, making them easy to finish with paint or veneer. It is an excellent material for furniture-making. MDF is made in a range of thicknesses from 6 to 25mm (¼ to 1in) or more, and a sheet size of 2440 x 1220mm (8 x 4ft).

SEE ALSO
Details for:
Preparing boards   54

Man-made boards
1 Plywood
2 Chipboard
3 Blockboard
4 Standard hardboard
5 Perforated hardboard
6 Textured hardboard
7 Medium-density fibreboard

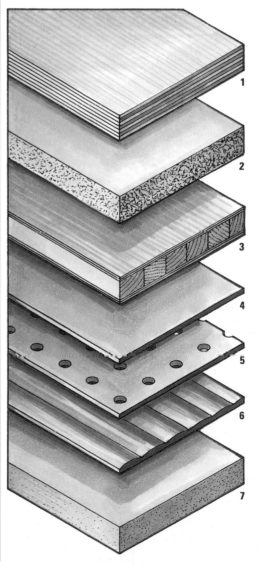

MOULDINGS & ADHESIVES

Moulding sections
1 Astragal
2 Double astragal
3 Half astragal
4 'D' shape
5 Flat corner
6 Cushion corner
7 Broken ogee
8 Quadrant
9 Half round
10 Hockey stick
11 Reeded
12 Parting bead
13 Staff bead
14 Triangle
15 Scotia
16 Architrave
17 Dado
18 Picture rail
19 Skirting

MOULDINGS

Softwoods and hardwoods are used to make mouldings. The cheaper softwoods are generally used for the larger joinery mouldings such as skirtings and architraves, although some are made in hardwood. Small sections for dowelling, picture framing, quadrant and scotia mouldings, and decorative cover mouldings are usually made from hardwoods. Period-style mouldings are more ornate than modern designs and reproduce the profiles of the past. If you need to replace wooden mouldings and cannot find the right profile to match, it is possible to have any shape machined by specialists. Simply supply them with a pattern or sample piece.

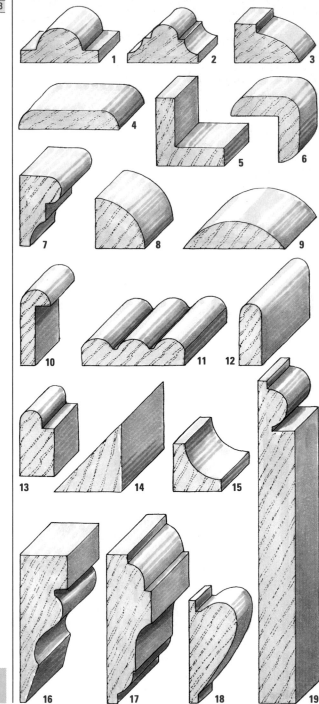

ADHESIVES

Modern adhesives are greatly superior to the old glues they have supplanted, having very powerful bonding properties. Though there is no true 'universal adhesive' that will stick anything to anything, you can bond most materials to others with the right adhesive.

There is now an impressive range of adhesives for specific purposes, including low-odour, solvent-free general-purpose types; those discussed here relate to the procedures dealt with in this book.

Woodworking
To glue wood and man-made boards for use indoors, apply a polyvinyl (PVA) woodworker's glue to one or both of the mating surfaces. Clamp or weight the work and wipe off any excess glue squeezed from the joint with a damp cloth. The joint can be handled within 30 minutes and the bond is complete in 24 hours.

For outdoor work, use an exterior PVA glue, a waterproof powdered synthetic-resin glue that you mix with water to use, or a two-part (resorcinol and urea) adhesive whose parts are applied separately to the faces being glued. The latter sets when the faces come together. All these glues require the work to be clamped or weighted during the setting period.

For interior work where clamping or weighting is not possible (fixing wall panels to a batten frame, for example), use a synthetic rubber-based contact adhesive. Apply it to both mating surfaces, allow it to become touch-dry, then press the surfaces together by hand. The bond is almost instantaneous.

Fixing melamine laminates
Contact adhesives were developed for fixing melamine laminates to wood and other surfaces. No cramps or weights are needed, though pressure improves the bond. The newer contact adhesives allow some repositioning of the laminates; with the older ones the instant bond meant that laminates placed wrongly could not then be moved. Consequently, it pays to choose a contact adhesive with what's called 'slideability'. Apply the adhesive to both surfaces, let it become touch-dry, then press them firmly together.

Fixing floorcoverings
Flooring adhesives must be versatile enough to fix a wide range of coverings – cork, vinyl, linoleum and many others – to such surfaces as floorboards, concrete, cement screed and hardboard underlays. They must also be able to withstand regular floor washing and the spillage of various liquids. Such multi-purpose flooring adhesives are made from synthetic resin or latex. They will stick virtually any covering to any floor surface. They are semi-flexible and will not crack or fail due to slight movement of the covering.

Fixing ceiling tiles
Expanded-polystyrene ceiling tiles and larger panels are fixed with a synthetic latex-based 'non-flamm' adhesive to plaster, plasterboard, hardboard and timber surfaces. This thick adhesive has gap-filling properties that allow the material to be fixed effectively to quite uneven surfaces, and the tiles or panels can be adjusted after they are stuck in place.

Fixing ceramic tiles
Ceramic wall tiles are usually fixed with a white adhesive that is available ready-mixed or in powder form. Some are dual-purpose for use as an adhesive and grout. Ordinary 'thin-bed' adhesives are for tiling on fairly flat surfaces, and there are 'thick-bed' ones for use on rough and uneven surfaces. Use a water-resistant version for kitchens and bathrooms. Epoxy-based grouts resist mould growth and help keep kitchens and bathrooms germ-free.

Ceramic floor tiles are usually laid with a cement-based tile adhesive. Thick tiles are sometimes laid on a sand-and-cement mortar to which a special builder's adhesive – PVA bonding agent – is added to improve adhesion, a method also used for sand-and-cement renderings and concrete repairs.

Gluing metals
Metals can be glued with epoxy-resin adhesives, which produce such a powerful bond that they have replaced welding and riveting in some industries. The adhesives are in two parts, a resin and a hardener, and most require both parts to be mixed together, then used within a certain time after mixing.

ADHESIVES

An acrylic-based adhesive has two parts that are applied separately to the mating faces. These glues impose no time limit as they are dormant until the faces meet, when a chemical bonding reaction begins.

Epoxy-resin adhesives are also generally suitable for joining glass, ceramics, glass fibre and rigid plastic. However, some products will not join all of these materials, so ensure that you get the right adhesive for the job.

Cyanoacrylates

The cyanoacrylates, or 'super glues', come close to being universal adhesives that will stick anything. They rapidly bond a great many materials, including human skin, and so need great care when handling (see Adhesive Solvents, right).

Usually supplied in tubes with fine nozzles, super glues must be used sparingly. Most are thin liquids, but a gel type is also made. They are commonly employed in joining small objects of metal, glass, ceramic, glass fibre and rigid plastic.

Glue guns

An electric 'hot-melt' glue gun is loaded with a rod of solid glue that melts under heat and discharged as a liquid onto the work when the gun is activated . The components are pressed or clamped together and the glue bonds as it cools. Glue guns are useful for accurate spot-gluing, and there is a choice of glue rods for use with various materials. The glues cool and set within 20 to 90 seconds.

Cold gun-applied adhesive for fixing wallboards and ceiling tiles is supplied in cartridges fitted with nozzles. When you squeeze the gun's trigger, a ram pushes on the base of the cartridge and forces out the glue.

Polyurethane-foam adhesive

Available in pressurized cans, this glue is used for fast and clean application when bonding a range of building materials. Some expand rapidly for use as gap fillers.

ADHESIVE SOLVENTS

When using an adhesive you will inevitably get some where you don't want it, usually on your hands. So have the right solvent handy for the glue in question and use it promptly, as the more the glue has set the harder it is to remove. Once a glue has set hard it might be impossible to dissolve it.

ADHESIVE	SOLVENT
PVA woodworking glue	Clean water
Synthetic-resin	Clean water
Two-part acrylic	Methylated spirit
Rubber-based contact glue	Acetone
Rubber-resin	Petrol
Synthetic-latex	Clean water
Epoxy-resin	Acetone or methylated spirit; liquid paint stripper if hard (not on skin)
Cyanoacrylates (Super glues)	Special manufacturer's solvent
PVA tile adhesive	Clean water
Polyurethane foam	Special manufacturer's solvent

BRAND-NAME GUIDE TO ADHESIVES

Unless a manufacturer prints the type of glue on its container, it can be difficult to identify the adhesive you need. The brand names listed below are intended to help you recognize a type of glue. This is not necessarily a list of recommended products.

PVA adhesives
Bostik Wood Adhesive Rapide
Brummer Wood Adhesive
Clam 7
Dunlop Wood Glue
Evo-Stik Wood Adhesive
Evo-Stik Wood Adhesive waterproof
Evo-Bond Building Adhesive
Humbrol Extra Bond
Humbrol Cascorez
Loctite Wood Bond Rapid
Unibond Universal PVA
Polycell Super Bond

Contact adhesives (rubber-based)
Bostik Contact
Dunlop Powerfix
Dunlop Thixofix
Clam 3
Evo-Stik Impact
Evo-Stik Time bond
Evo-Stik 528
Evo-Stik Safe 80

Epoxy-resin adhesives
Araldite (3 versions)
Bostik Epoxy
Humbrol Superfast Epoxy
Loctite Tough Bond
Plastic Padding Super Epoxy
JB Weld

Synthetic-resin adhesives
Humbrol Carpenters' Wood Glue
Humbrol Cascamite
Humbrol Cascophen
Aerolite

Two-part acrylic adhesives
Loctite Multi-bond

Rubber-resin and synthetic-latex adhesives
Bostik Panel & Coving Adhesive
Clam 9
Dunlop Flooring Adhesive
Evo-Stik 873 Flooring Adhesive
Evo-Stik 863 Ceiling Tile Adhesive
Evo-Stik Panel Adhesive (Gun-O-Prene)
Unibond Unilast
Unibond Flooring Adhesive
Unibond Wallboard Adhesive
Vallance Wall Panel

Cyanoacrylates (super glues)
Bostik Superglue
Hermetite Super Glue Plus
Humbrol Wonderbond
Loctite Super Glue-3
Supergluematic
Vallance UPVC Superglue

PVA tile adhesives
Evo-Stik Wall Tile Adhesive
Dunlop PVA Wall Tile Adhesive
Clam Ceramic Tile Adhesive

Polyurethane-foam adhesives
Mangers PFA (3 types)
Dunlop Gap Filling Foam
Humbrol Multipurpose Foam

Use this chart as a guide for gluing the materials on the left to those across the top.	WOOD AND MAN-MADE BOARDS	MASONRY	PLASTER	METAL	STONE	GLASS	CERAMIC	RIGID PLASTIC/ FIBRE GLASS
WOOD/MAN-MADE BOARDS	1,2,3,5,10	5, 10	5, 10	4	5	4, 8	8	8
METAL	4, 8			4, 7, 8	4, 7	4, 7, 8	4, 7 ,8.	7, 8
SYNTHETIC LAMINATES	3	3	3		3			
FLOORCOVERINGS	5, 6	5, 6			5, 6		5, 6	
CEILING TILES/PANELS	6,10	6,10	6,10		6,10			
CERAMIC	8, 9	9	9	8	9	4, 7, 8	4, 7, 8	8
STONE		4			4	4		
GLASS	3, 4	4	4	4, 7, 8	4	4, 7, 8	4, 7, 8	4, 8
RIGID PLASTICS/GLASS FIBRE	8, 10			10	10	4, 8	8	4, 7, 8

KEY TO TYPES OF ADHESIVES
1 PVA woodworking glue
2 Synthetic resin/Resorcinol and urea
3 Rubber-based contact
4 Epoxy-resin
5 Rubber-resin
6 Synthetic-latex
7 Cyanoacrylates
8 Acrylic
9 PVA tile adhesive
10 Polyurethane foam

NAILS

● **Preventing
split wood**
A blunt nail punches
its way through
timber instead of
forcing the fibres
apart. To avoid
splitting, if that
seems likely, blunt
the point of a nail
with a light hammer
blow.

● **Removing a
dent from wood**
If you dent wood
with a misplaced
hammer blow, put a
few drops of hot
water on the dent
and let the wood
swell. When it is dry
smooth it with
abrasive paper.

● **Key to diagram**
Red symbols
superimposed on the
nails and pins
represent their cross
section.

FIXINGS

**A crucial aspect of any
assembly or construction is
choosing the right method of
fixing. In addition to the time-
honoured variety of nails and
screws for woodwork, and nuts,
bolts and rivets for metal work,
there are nowadays a number of
patent devices that speed and
simplify many jobs.**

NAILS

Nails provide a cheap and simple
though relatively crude method
of fixing for a variety of timber
structures. They are useful for
holding glued joints together and
can be used decoratively when
applied to upholstery. There are
many types of nail for general
use and for specific purposes.
Choose the right kind and size of
nail for a good fixing.

Round plain-head wire nail
Rough general carpentry. Bright
steel or galvanized finish. 20 to
150mm (¾ to 6in).

Round lost-head wire nail
Joinery. Head can be punched in
and concealed. Bright steel
finish. 40 to 75mm (1½ to 3in).

Lath nail
Fixing laths and thin battens.
Galvanized finish. 25 to 40mm
(1 to 1½ in).

Ring-shank nail
For extra secure fixings. Bright or
stainless steel. 20 to 100mm
(¾ to 4in).

Square twisted plain-head
General purpose. Twisted shank
gives extra grip. Bright steel or
sherardized. 20 to 100mm
(¾ to 4in).

Cut clasp nail
Carpentry and fixing wood to
masonry. Black iron. 25 to 200mm
(1to 8in).

Cut floor brad
Nailing floorboards to joists.
Black iron. 40 to 75mm
(1½ to 3in).

Oval wire nail
Carpentry. Can be punched in
and concealed. Less likely to
split the wood than round wire
nails. Bright steel. 25 to 150mm
(1 to 6in).

Oval lost-head
An oval brad, but small head
gives neater finish. Bright steel.
25 to 150mm (1 to 6in).

Plasterboard nail
Fixing plasterboard to battens.
Jagged shank for good grip.
Bright steel, sherardized or
galvanized. 30 to 40mm
(1¼ to 1½ in).

Panel pin
Cabinet work and fine joinery
(with glue). Bright steel. 15 to
50mm (⅝ to 2in).

Veneer pin (moulding pin)
Applying veneers and small
mouldings. Bright steel. 15 to
50mm (⅝ to 2in).

Hardboard panel pin
Fixing hardboard and light
plywood. Diamond-shaped head
is driven in flush with board.
Coppered. 20 to 40mm
(¾ to 1½in).

Corrugated fastener
Making rough mitre and butted
framing joints.

Clout (slate) nail
Fixing slates and roofing
materials. Galvanized or bright
steel, aluminium or copper. 20 to
100mm (¾ to 4in).

Felt nail or large-head clout nail
Attaching roofing felt, webbing
etc. Bright steel or galvanized.
12 to 50mm (½ to 2in).

Roofing nail or drive screw
Fixing corrugated sheet to
timber. Spiral shank gives extra
grip. Used with shaped washers.
Galvanized. 65 to 115mm (2½ to
4½in).

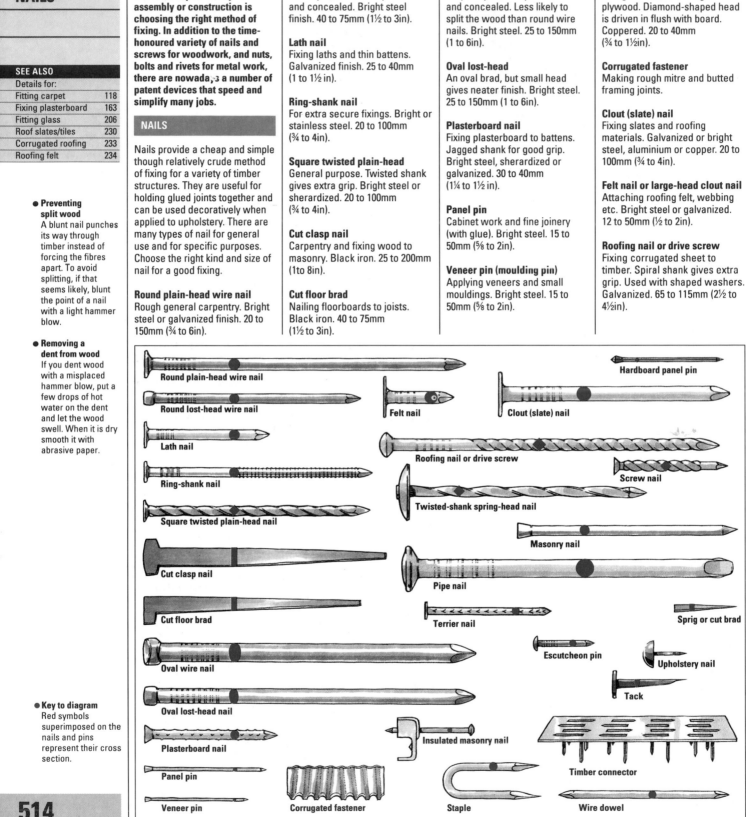

Twisted-shank spring-head nail
Fixing sheet materials and man-made boards. Galvanized. 65mm (2½ in).

Masonry nail
Fixing wood to masonry. Hard bright steel. 23 to 85mm (⅞ to 3⅜in).

Escutcheon pin
Fixing keyhole plates etc. Brass. 15 or 20mm (⅝ or ¾in).

Terrier nail
Barbed nail for extra strong wood-to-wood fixings. Made with countersunk head from 25 to 65mm (1 to 2½in), and flat head 30 to 80mm (1⅛ to 3⅛in).

Pipe nail
Chisel-tipped for holding down pipes to masonry. Galvanized. 75 to 100mm (3 to 4in).

Sprig or cut brad
Glazing, picture framing and fixing linoleum. Black iron. 12 to 20mm (½ to ¾in).

Timber connector
Making rough mitre and butted wood joints.

Staple
Rough carpentry and fixing fencing wire. Bright steel or galvanized. 10 to 40mm (⅜ to 1½ in).

Wire dowel
Hidden fixing in woodwork, one point entering each component. Bright steel. 40 to 50mm (1½ to 2in).

Upholstery nail
Upholstering furniture. Domed decorative head. Brass, bronze, chromed or antique. 3 to 12mm (⅛ to ½ in).

Tack
Attaching fabric to wood; carpeting. Blued, galvanized or coppered. 6 to 30mm (¼ to 1¼in).

Insulated masonry nail
Securing electric cable and micro-bore pipe to masonry. Nail is driven through a plastic cable grip. Various shapes and sizes.

Screw nail
Pilot-pointed nail with an helical-threaded shank and countersunk head. Fixing hardboard, plywood and sheet materials. Bright steel. 12 to 50mm (½ to 2in).

SCREWS

Screws are manufactured with a small range of head shapes suited to various purposes and in a choice of materials and finishes. Screws are usually made of mild steel, but hardened steel is also used.

Corrosion-resistant screws are made from stainless-steel and brass and others are plated with chromium, zinc and brass. There are also sherardized, bronzed and japanned screws.

Screw fixing
For anything other than rough work, use screws in preference to nails when joining wooden components together or attaching other materials to wood. Screws provide a strong clamping force, and they can be removed to allow components to be removed or adjusted without damage to the parts. When combined with the correct glue, screws can be used to clamp the joint tight without the need for extra cramps.

Screw threads
The traditional woodscrew has a plain 'full' shank below the head and acts as a dowel. The shank is about one third the length of the screw, the remainder being threaded and ending with a gimlet point.

More modern screws have a modified thread that may be single or double. They have a sharp point that makes starting easier and a shank that's smaller in diameter than the thread so that the smaller screws, at least, require no pilot hole to be drilled. Some screws are threaded along their entire length – they can be driven in quickly with little risk of splitting the wood.

Screwheads
There are six basic head shapes:
Countersunk head, for work where the screw must be recessed flush with the surface or below it.
Roundhead, or domed, usually used with sheet material that is too thin for countersinking.
Raised head, a combination of domed and countersunk, often used for attaching metal items like door furniture to wood.
Mirror screws, countersunk screws with threaded centre holes for attaching decorative domes, are for holding up fixed wall mirrors and the like.

Pan head and flange head, similar to roundhead screws but mainly used for self-tapping types for joining sheet metals.
A further subdivision of all these screws is between those with slotted heads and those with cross-slotted heads, which need special cross-section screwdrivers. The latter type provide improved grip and are ideal for use with power screwdrivers.

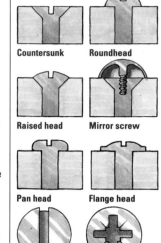

Countersunk	**Roundhead**
Raised head	**Mirror screw**
Pan head	**Flange head**
Slotted head	**Cross-head**

Sizes and gauges
All screws are described in terms of their length, given in millimetres or inches, and their shank diameter, or gauge (swg), expressed as a simple number from 1 to 20. The thicker the screw the higher its gauge number. Gauges in most general use are 4, 6, 8 and 10. Some are now given in metric sizes only.

The length of a screw is the distance between its pointed tip and the part of the head that lies flush with the work surface. Woodscrews are available in lengths from 6 to 150mm (¼ to 6in), but not every combination of length, head shape and material is available, let alone stocked in every gauge. Generally the widest choice is to be found within gauges 6 to 12.

Cups, sockets and caps
Countersunk and raised-head screws may be used with metal screw cups, which improve their clamping force and also make for a neat appearance. Plastic sockets with snap-on caps are also available to conceal the heads of screws, as well as

simple plastic caps that plug into flush-mounted cross-head screw heads.

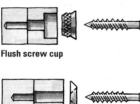

Flush screw cup

Surface screw cup

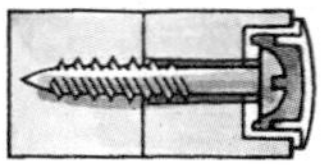

Plastic socket and cap

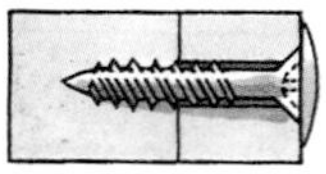

Plastic cap

Types and uses
The machine-made gimlet-point woodscrew has changed little since it was developed in the last century. However, since the introduction of man-made boards and electric-powered screwdrivers, manufacturers have produced new thread and head forms.

Unhardened woodscrews
The traditional woodscrew, with its single-helix thread, is made in the widest range of sizes, head types and materials. It is suitable for most woods and is particularly suited for fixing metal fittings such as hinges, locks and catches. This type of screw requires a pilot hole and shank-clearance hole to be drilled prior to fitting.
Length: 9 to 150mm (⅜ to 6in)
Diameter/gauge: 2 to 18swg

Hardened-steel woodscrews
Countersunk or roundhead screws are available with twin steep-pitch threads for fast insertion. They can be used with all types of solid wood and man-made boards. The hardened metal makes it possible to drive into a range of relatively soft materials without the need for pilot holes.
Length: 12 to 100mm (½ to 4in)
Diameter/gauge: 3 to 12swg

SEE ALSO

Details for:
Thermal plasterboard 275
Countersink bits 488
Inserting screws 489
Screwdrivers 489
Drilling masonry 495

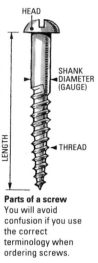

Parts of a screw
You will avoid confusion if you use the correct terminology when ordering screws.

SCREWS &
WALL FIXINGS

Chipboard screws
This is a hardened-steel screw, primarily used for chipboard, but suitable as a general-purpose woodscrew. Made with counter-sunk heads only, chipboard screws have a single-helix thread. Pilot holes are required for all materials other than softwoods or low-density man-made boards, using small-diameter screws.
*Length: 12 to 100mm (½ to 4in)
Diameter/gauge: 3 to 6mm
(⅛ to ¼in)*

Carcass screws
This hardened-steel screw with a coarse single-helix thread is designed to be driven into the edge of chipboard without splitting it. Although not always necessary, a pilot hole should be drilled for easy installation.
*Length: 45mm (1¾in)
Diameter/gauge: 8swg*

Drywall screws
A special range of hardened screws with twin threads are made for fixing plasterboard or fibreboard to wooden or metal furring battens. Each screw has a sharp point for drilling its own hole and a bugle-shaped countersunk head enabling it to bed down into the board material.
*Length: 25 to 50mm (1 to 2in)
Diameter/gauge: 3.5 and 4.2mm
(⅜ and ⁵⁄₃₂in)*

Security screws
These are countersunk screws with special 'slots' that permit the screw to be driven into the work but reject the tip of the screwdriver when the action is reversed in an attempt to remove the screw. The latest type has twin threads and is made for cross-head screwdrivers.
*Length: 18 to 50mm (¾ to 2in)
Diameter/gauge: 6 to 12swg*

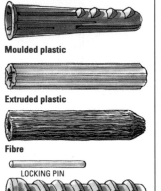

Coach screws
Coach screws, made from unhardened steel, are used for heavy-duty applications such as building a workbench. They have a square head and are driven into the work with a spanner. Large washers prevent the heads cutting into the timber.
*Length: 25 to 150mm (1 to 6in)
Diameter/gauge: 6 to 12mm
(¼ to ½ in)*

Self-tapping screws
Self-tapping screws are designed to cut their own thread in materials such as thin sheet metal and plastics. The screws are made from case-hardened steel, and are normally available in four head forms: countersunk, raised head, pan head and flange head, either slotted or cross-head. Hexagonal-head screws are available for insertion using spanners.
*Length: 6 to 63mm (¼ to 2½in)
Diameter/gauge: 4 to 14swg*

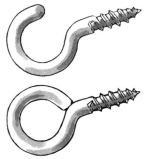

Screw hooks and eyes
Made of steel, screw hooks and eyes have a conventional woodscrew thread for fixing to a wall or panel.
Plain or shouldered screw hooks are made in various sizes with round or square-shaped hooks, either bright-plated or plastic-coated.
Screw eyes are available in a range of sizes to provide fixing points for cords, chains etc.

To make secure fixings to any but solid wooden surfaces involves the use of various fixing aids. These range from the simple plug to take a woodscrew in a hole drilled in brick or masonry, up to fairly elaborate heavy-duty devices complete with bolts. There are also special products for making fixings to hollow walls.

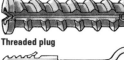

Moulded plastic

Extruded plastic

Fibre

LOCKING PIN

Threaded plug

Clothesline fixing

Wall plugs
There are lightweight to medium-duty **moulded-plastic wall plugs** to take a range of standard woodscrews, generally from No 4 to No 14. Some are colour-coded for easy recognition. A wall plug is pushed into the drilled holes and the screw then driven into the plug, which expands to grip the sides of the hole tightly.

There are also **extruded-plastic plugs**, simply straight tubes, which accommodate only the thread of the screw and so must be cut shorter than the depth of the hole. These are cheaper than moulded plugs but less convenient, as are the traditional fibre ones which serve the same purpose.

Threaded plugs are for use in walls of crumbly material like aerated concrete blocks. These plugs have a coarse thread on the outside and are screwed into the soft material to provide a socket for screws. One plastic type uses a locking pin for extra security. Another is supplied with a universal drill bit for making the hole, fitting the plug and driving the screw. There is also an all-metal plug with a coarse thread

and a sharp point that cuts its own hole in a plasterboard wall. Heavy-duty nylon wall plugs are supplied with coach screws or with screw hooks for use as clothesline attachments etc.

Expansion bolts
These are for making very rugged fixings. There are various designs, but all work on one basic principle: a bolt is screwed into a segmental metal or plastic shell and engages the thread of an expander. As the bolt is tightened, the expander forces the segments apart to grip the sides of the hole. Some expansion bolts have built-in hooks and eyes.

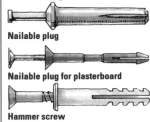

Nailable plug

Nailable plug for plasterboard

Hammer screw

Nailable plugs
These can be used to speed up jobs in which a great many fixings have to be made. There are two types: one is simply a flanged expansion sleeve with a masonry nail. The other consists of a ready-assembled wall plug and 'hammer screw'. Both are simply hammered into masonry, but the hammer screw can be removed with a screwdriver. These plugs are often used for fixing battens, frames, wall linings and skirting boards.

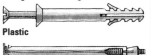

Plastic

Metal-sleeved frame fixing

Frame fixings
These are designed to speed up screw-fixing by eliminating the need to mark out and pre-drill the fixing holes. Supplied with a plated screw or bolt, these long fittings may use a plastic plug or a split metal sleeve.

Position the item to be fixed and drill right through it into the wall, then insert the frame fixing and tighten the screw. Typical uses are attaching battens, wall plates, doorframes, window frames and fitted furniture.

Fixings for hollow walls

There are many variations on each of several devices for making fixings to hollow walls of plasterboard on studs, lath and plaster and so on. All of them work on the principle of opening out behind the panel and gripping it in some way.

Special wall plugs, plastic toggles and *collapsible anchors* all have segments that open out or fold up against the inside of the panel.

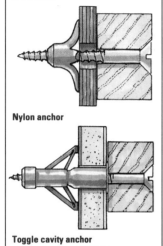

Nylon anchor

Toggle cavity anchor

Plastic collapsible anchor

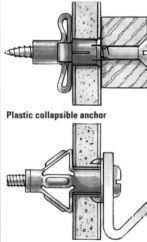

Metal collapsible anchor

A *rubber anchor* is supplied with a steel bolt which, when tightened, draws up an internal nut to make the rubber bulge out behind the panel.

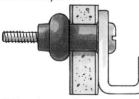

Rubber-sleeve anchor

Metal gravity toggles and *spring toggles* have arms that open out inside the cavity. A gravity toggle has a single arm, pivoted near one end so that its own weight causes it to drop. A spring toggle has two spring-loaded arms that fly open when they are clear of the hole and a bolt that draws them tight up against the panel.

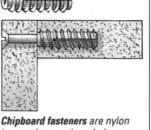

Gravity toggle

Spring toggle

A nylon strap toggle has an arm that is held firmly behind the panel by a thin plastic strap while the screw is driven into its pilot hole. The strap is cut off after installation.

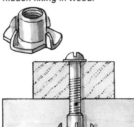

Nylon strap toggle

Some anchors will remain in their holes if their screws have to be removed. Others, such as nylon anchors and spring toggles are all lost in the cavity if their screws are removed. The rubber anchor can be removed and used again.

None of these devices should be used for fixings meant to take a heavy load. Instead locate the timber studs and fix directly into them. Even for moderate loads the larger spring and gravity toggles should be used on lath-and-plaster walls rather than plug-type devices.

KNOCK-DOWN FITTINGS

Woodscrews in their various forms provide a simple and effective fastener for all manner of assemblies. However, there are times when the material requires reinforcement or even an alternative mechanical fitting to hold the parts together. Knock-down fittings allow components to be easily put together and also taken apart.

Chipboard fasteners are nylon inserts that are threaded externally and driven into a hole in the face or edge of chipboard to give a secure fixing for woodscrews.

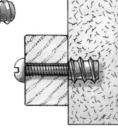

Screw sockets are metal inserts that are threaded internally to receive a bolt and provide a neat hidden fixing in wood.

A *tee nut* is used to provide a strong bolt fastening in wood. The metal nut is pressed into the back of a hole drilled in the component. Projecting prongs bite into the wood to provide a secure fixing.

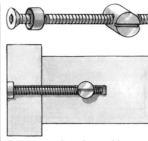

Steel *cross dowels* provide a strong fixing for the ends of rails where they meet side panels or frames. The dowel is housed in a stopped hole drilled in the underside of the rail. A threaded hole through the side of the dowel receives a bolt. The clearance hole for the bolt is drilled in the end of the rail.

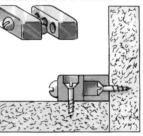

Block-joints are used to join panels at right angles to one another. Made in various patterns they are basically plastic blocks made in two halves that are screwed to the panels and bolted together. Moulded dowels in one half locate in holes in the other for accurate alignment.

SEE ALSO	
Details for:	
Inserting screws	489
Screwdrivers	489
Drilling masonry	495

GLOSSARY

A

Accessory
An electrical component permanently connected to a circuit – a switch, socket outlet, fused connection unit etc.

Aggregate
Particles of sand or stone mixed with cement and water to make concrete, or added to paint to make a textured finish.

Airlock
A blockage in a pipe caused by a trapped bubble of air.

Anthropometry
The comparative study and technique of sizes and proportions of the human body.

Appliance
A machine or device powered by electricity. or A functional piece of equipment connected to the plumbing such as a basin, sink, bath etc.

Architrave
The moulding around a window or door.

Arris
The sharp edge at the meeting of two surfaces.

B

Back-siphonage
The siphoning of part of a plumbing system caused by the failure of mains water pressure.

Balanced flue
A ducting system that allows a heating appliance, such as a boiler, to draw fresh air from, and discharge gases to, the outside of a building.

Ballast
Naturally occurring sand-and-gravel mix used as aggregate for making concrete.

Baluster
One of a set of posts supporting a stair handrail.

Balustrade
The protective barrier alongside a staircase or landing.

Banisters
See balustrade.

Batt
A short cut length of glass-fibre or mineral-fibre insulant.

Batten
A narrow strip of wood.

Batter
The slope of the face of a wall that leans backwards or tapers from bottom to top.

Blind
To cover with sand.

Blown
To have broken away, as when a layer of cement rendering has parted from a wall.

Bore
The hollow part of a pipe or tube. or To drill a hole.

Burr
The rough raised edge left on a workpiece after cutting or filing.

Buttercoat
The top layer of cement render.

C

Came
The grooved strip of lead which holds the glass in a leaded light or stained-glass window.

Cap-nut
The nut used to tighten a fitting onto pipework.

Casing
The timber lining of a door or window opening.

Catenary wire
A length of wire cable suspended horizontally between two points.

Cavity wall
A wall of two parallel separate masonry skins with an air space between them.

Chamfer
A narrow flat surface along the edge of a workpiece – normally at an angle of 45 degrees to adjacent surfaces. or To plane the angled surface.

Chase
A groove cut in masonry or plaster to accept pipework or an electrical cable. or To cut or channel such grooves.

Circuit
A complete path through which an electric current can flow.

Concave
Curving inwards.

Conductor
A component, usually a length of wire, along which an electric current will pass.

Convex
Curving outwards.

Cornice
The continuous horizontal moulding between walls and ceiling in a room.

Counterbore
To cut a hole which allows the head of a bolt or screw to lie below a surface. or Such a hole.

Countersink
To cut a tapered recess which allows the head of a screw to lie flush with a surface. or The tapered recess itself.

Coving
A pre-fabricated moulding used to make a cornice.

Cup
To bend as a result of shrinkage, specifically across the width of a piece of wood.

D

Dado
The lower part of an interior wall – usually defined with a moulded wooden rail (the dado rail) at about waist height.

Damp-proof course
A layer of impervious material which prevents moisture rising from the ground into the walls of a building.

Damp-proof membrane
A layer of impervious material which prevents moisture rising through a concrete floor.

Datum point
The point from which measurements are taken.

DPC
See damp-proof course.

DPM
See damp-proof membrane.

Drip groove
A groove cut or moulded in the underside of a windowsill to prevent rainwater running back to the wall.

Drop
A strip of wallpaper measured and cut to length ready for pasting to a wall.

E

Earth
A connection between an electrical circuit and the earth (ground). or A terminal to which the connection is made.

Eaves
The edges of a roof that project beyond the walls.

Efflorescence
A white powdery deposit caused by soluble salts migrating to the surface of a wall or ceiling.

End grain
The surface of wood exposed after cutting across the fibres.

Extension
A room or rooms added to an existing building.

Extension lead
A length of electrical flex for temporarily connecting the short permanent flex of an appliance to a wall socket.

F

Face edge
In woodworking, the surface planed square to the face side.

Face side
In woodworking, the flat planed surface from which other dimensions and angles are measured and worked.

Fall
A downward slope.

D

Fascia
A strip of wood which covers the ends of rafters and to which external guttering is fixed.

Feather
To wear away or smooth an edge until it is undetectable.

Fence
An adjustable guide to keep the cutting edge of a tool a set distance from the edge of a workpiece.

Flashing
A weatherproof junction between a roof and a wall or chimney, or between one roof and another.

Flaunching
A mortared slope at the top of a fireback or round a chimney pot.

Flute
A rounded concave groove.

Footing
A narrow concrete foundation for a wall.

Frass
Powdered wood produced by the activity of woodworm.

Frog
The angled depression in one face of some housebricks.

Furring battens
See furring strips.

Furring strips
Parallel strips of wood fixed to a wall or ceiling to provide a framework for attaching panels.

Fuse board
Where the main electrical service cable is connected to the house circuitry. or The accumulation of consumer unit, meter etc.

G

Galvanized
Covered with a protective coating of zinc.

Gel
A substance with a thick jelly-like consistency.

Going
The horizontal measurement between the top and bottom risers of a stair or the depth of one tread.

Grain
The general direction of wood fibres. or The pattern produced on the surface of timber by cutting through the fibres. See also end grain and short grain.

Grommet
A ring of rubber or plastic, lining a hole to protect electrical cable from chafing. A blind grommet incorporates a thin web of plastic or rubber that seals the hole until the web is cut to provide access for a cable.

Groove
A long narrow channel cut in plaster or wood in the general direction of the grain. *or* To cut such channels.

Grounds
Strips of wood fixed to a wall to provide nail-fixing points for skirting boards, door casings etc. See also pallets.

Gullet
The notch formed between two saw teeth.

H

Hardcore
Broken bricks or stones used to form a sub-base below paving, foundations etc.

Head
The height of the surface of water above a specific point – used as a measurement of pressure; for example, a head of 2m. *or* The top horizontal member of a wooden frame.

Head plate
The top horizontal member of a stud partition.

Heave
An upward swelling of level ground caused by excess moisture.

Helical
Spiral shaped.

Hoggin
A fine ballast, usually with a clay content, used to form a sub-base for concrete pads or paving.

Hone
To finely sharpen a cutting edge.

Horns
Extended door or window stiles, designed to protect the corners from damage while in storage.

Housing
A long narrow channel cut across the general direction of wood grain to form part of a joint.

I

Insulation
Materials used to reduce the transmission of heat or sound. *or* Nonconductive material surrounding electrical wires or connections to prevent the passage of electricity.

J

Jamb
The vertical side member of a doorframe or window frame.

Joist
A horizontal wooden or metal beam such as an RSJ, used to support a structure such as a floor, ceiling or wall.

K

Kerf
The groove cut by a saw.

Key
To abrade or incise a surface to provide a better grip when gluing something to it.

Knurled
Impressed with a series of fine grooves designed to improve the grip, for instance a knurled knob or handle.

L

Lath and plaster
A method of finishing a timber-framed wall or ceiling. Narrow strips of wood are nailed to the studs or joists to provide a supporting framework for plaster or tiles.

Lead
A stepped section of brickwork or blockwork built at each end of a wall to act as a guide to the height of the intermediate coursing.

Lintel
A horizontal beam used to support the wall over a door or window opening.

M

Marine plywood
Exterior-grade plywood.

Mastic
A nonsetting compound used to seal joints.

Microporous
See moisture-vapour permeable.

Mitre
A joint formed between two pieces of wood by cutting bevels of equal angle at the ends of each piece. *or* To cut the joint.

Moisture-vapour permeable
Used to describe a finish which allows moisture to escape from timber, allowing it to dry out, while protecting the wood from rainwater or damp.

Mono-pitch roof
A roof that slopes in one direction only.

Mortise
A rectangular recess cut in timber to receive a matching tongue or tenon.

Mouse
A small weight used to pass a line through a narrow vertical space.

Mullion
A vertical dividing member of a window frame.

Muntin
A central vertical member of a panel door.

N

Needle
A stout wooden beam used with props to support the section of a wall above an opening prior to the installation of a rolled steel joist or lintel.

Neutral
The section of an electrical circuit which carries the flow of current back to source. *or* A terminal to which the connection is made. *or* A colour composed mainly of black and white.

Newel
The post at the top or bottom of a flight of stairs which supports the handrail.

Nogging
A short horizontal wooden member between studs.

Nosing
The front edge of a stair tread.

O

Outer string
See string.

Oxidize
To form a layer of metal oxide as in rusting.

P

Pallet
A wooden plug built into masonry to provide a fixing point for a door casing.

Pare
To remove fine shavings from wood with a chisel.

Pargeting
The internal render of a chimney.

Party wall
The wall between two houses over which each of the adjoining owners has equal rights in law.

Penetrating oil
A thin lubricant which will seep between corroded components and ease them.

Phase
The part of an electrical circuit which carries the flow of current to an appliance or accessory. Also known as live.

Pile
Raised fibres which stand out from a backing material, for instance in a carpet.

Pilot hole
A small-diameter hole drilled prior to the insertion of a woodscrew to act as a guide for its thread.

Pinch rod
A wooden batten used to gauge the width of a frame or opening.

PME
See protective multiple earth.

Point load
The concentration of forces on a very small area.

Primer
The first coat of a paint system to protect the workpiece and to reduce absorption of subsequent undercoats and top coats.

Profile
The outline or contour of an object.

Protective multiple earth
A system of electrical wiring in which the neutral part of the circuit is used to take earth-leakage current to earth.

PTFE
Polytetrafluoroethylene – used to make tape for sealing threaded plumbing fittings.

Purlin
A horizontal beam that provides intermediate support for rafters or sheet roofing.

R

Rafter
One of a set of parallel sloping beams that form the main structural element of a roof.

Ratchet
A device that permits movement in one direction only by restricting the reversal of a toothed wheel or rack.

RCD
See residual current device.

Rebate
A stepped rectangular recess along the edge of a workpiece, usually as part of a joint. *or* To cut such recesses.

Render
A thin layer of cement-based mortar applied to exterior walls to provide a protective finish. Sometimes fine stone aggregate is embedded in the mortar. *or* To apply the mortar.

Residual current device
A device which monitors the flow of electrical current through the live and neutral wires of a circuit. When an RCD detects an imbalance caused by earth leakage, it cuts off the supply of electricity as a safety precaution.

Reveal
The vertical side of an opening in a wall.

Riser
The vertical part of a step.

Rising main
The pipe which supplies water under mains pressure, usually to a storage cistern in the roof.

Rolled steel joist
A steel beam usually with a cross section in the form of a capital letter I.

519

GLOSSARY

RSJ
See rolled steel joist.

Rub joint
Glued wood rubbed together and held by suction until it sets.

Rubber
A pad of cotton wool wrapped in soft cloth used to apply stain, shellac polish etc.

S

Sash
The openable part of a window.

Score
To scratch a line with a pointed tool. See also scribe.

Scratchcoat
The bottom layer of cement.

Screed
A thin layer of mortar applied to give a smooth surface to concrete etc. or A shortened version of screed batten.

Screed batten
A thin strip of wood fixed to a surface to act as a guide to the thickness of an application of plaster or render.

Scribe
To copy the profile of a surface on the edge of sheet material which is to be butted against it; to mark a line with a pointed tool. See also score.

Set
A small rectangular paving block.

Sheathing
The outer layer of insulation surrounding an electrical cable or flex.

Short circuit
The accidental rerouting of electricity to earth which increases the flow of current and blows a fuse.

Short grain
When the general direction of wood fibres lies across a narrow section of timber.

Sill
The lowest horizontal member of a stud partition. or The lowest horizontal member of a frame that surrounds a door or window.

Sleeper wall
A low masonry wall used as an intermediate support for ground-floor joists.

Soakaway
A pit filled with rubble or gravel into which water is drained.

Soffit
The underside of a part of a building such as the eaves, an archway etc.

Softwood
Timber cut from coniferous trees.

Sole plate
Another term for a stud-partition sill. or A wooden member used as a base to level a timber-framed loadbearing wall.

Spalling
Flaking of the outer face of masonry caused by expanding moisture in icy conditions.

Spandrel
The triangular infill below the outer string of a staircase.

Staff bead
The innermost strip of timber holding a sliding sash in a window frame.

Stile
A vertical side member of a door or window sash.

Stopper
A wood filler which matches the colour of the timber.

String
A board which runs from one floor level to another, into which staircase treads and risers are jointed. The one on the open side of a staircase is an outer string, and the one against the wall is a wall string.

Stud partition
An interior timber-framed dividing wall.

Studs
The vertical members of a timber-framed wall.

Subsidence
A sinking of the ground caused by the shrinkage of excessively dry soil.

Supplementary bonding
The connecting to earth of electrical appliances and exposed metal pipework in a bathroom or kitchen.

T

Tamp
To pack down firmly with repeated blows.

Template
A cut-out pattern of paper, wood, metal etc, to help shape a workpiece accurately.

Tenon
A projecting tongue on the end of a piece of wood which fits in a corresponding mortise.

Terminal
A passive conductor for an electrical connection.

Thinner
A solvent such as turpentine, used to dilute paint or varnish.

Thixotropic
A property of some paints which have a jelly-like consistency until stirred or applied, at which point they become liquefied.

Top coat
The outer layer of a paint system.

Torque
A rotational force.

Transom
A horizontal dividing member of a window frame.

Trap
A bent section of pipe below a bath, sink etc. It contains standing water to prevent the passage of gases.

Tread
The horizontal part of a step.

U

Undercoat
A layer or layers of paint used to obliterate the colour of a primer and to build a protective body of paint prior to the application of a top coat.

V

Vapour barrier
A layer of impervious material which prevents the passage of moisture-laden air.

Vapour check
See vapour barrier.

W

Wall plate
A horizontal timber member placed along the top of a wall to support the ends of joists and to spread their load.

Wall string
See string.

Wall tie
A strip of metal or bent wire used to bind sections of masonry together.

Waney edge
A natural wavy edge on a plank, which might still be covered by tree bark.

Warp
To bend or twist as a result of damp or heat.

Water closet
A lavatory that is flushed by water. or A room containing such a lavatory.

Water hammer
Vibration in plumbing caused by fluctuating water pressure.

WC
See water closet.

Weathered
Showing signs of exposure to the weather. or Sloped so as to shed rainwater.

Weep hole
A small hole at the base of a cavity wall to allow absorbed water to drain to the outside.

Workpiece
An object in the process of being shaped, produced or otherwise worked upon. Sometimes referred to as 'work'.

constructing footings 441
DPCs 445
erecting fences 431
garden steps 467
gardens 421
ponds 470
terracing 451
sludge 412
small-bore waste system 372
smoke detectors 250
snow boards 241
sockets
aerials 329
assessing condition 312-13
extending ring circuits 317, 318
fitting & replacing 314-16
flex extenders 300
flush 91, 315
outdoor 340
shaver 322
surface-mounted 91, 314
telephones 330
trailing 300
soffit linings 167
soffit vents 285
softwoods 510
soil 421, 450
soil pipes 348, 349, 357, 359, 371, 376
solar-control glass 203
solder & soldering 363, 504-5
solid floors
damp-proofing 264
fixing floorboards 179
ground floors 122, 123, 177
laying 186-7
laying pipes 186
painting 65
repairing 49, 186
running cable 310, 311
solid-fuel boilers 406, 407, 412
solid-fuel room heaters 401
solid strutting 177
solvent-based paints 63, 69
cleaning paintbrushes 498
masonry 64, 65
metalwork 87, 88
woodwork 76, 77, 78
solvent-weld joints 367, 368
solvents, adhesives 513
sound insulation 266, 277, 281-2
space
assessing potential 14-16
manipulating 30-1
spades 496
spalling 46, 49, 468
spanners 505
spattering 71
specifications 20
insulation 266
spikes, fence post 427
spiral balances 201, 212
spiriting-off 85
splitters 329
spokeshaves 482
sponge stippling 71
spray guns 66, 500
sprayheads, showers 381
spurs
fence posts 431
spur cables 307, 317, 339
stack bonding 440
stacks, unblocking 359
staining, woodwork 76, 77, 82-3
stainless-steel pipes 361
stains, masonry 45
stairs & staircases 218-26
balusters & balustrades 220, 224-6
carpeting 118
creaking 221
headroom 14

lighting 38
painting 81
repairing 221-4
types & construction 218-20
stairwells 42, 98
standpipe-and-tap drainage 389
steam strippers 52, 497
steelwork
lintels 126, 131, 133, 202
pipes 361, 364
preparation 60
stencilling 74
stepladders 40, 41
stepped footings 441
stepping stones 462
steps
aligning floors 136
garden 467-8
staircases see stairs & staircases
stippling 71-2
stone 438
chippings 173, 466
cleaning 400
fireplace surrounds 398, 400
lifting stones safely 473
lintels 126
paving 462
pond edgings 471, 472
roofing 229
sub-sills 210
tiles 101, 102, 108
walls 124, 450-1
stopcocks 348, 349, 353
stoppers 53
storage
assessing potential 16
building materials 162, 173, 435, 437, 453
tools 479, 482, 485, 498
under-stair 220
storage cisterns see cold-water storage cisterns
storage heaters 292, 302, 326-7, 404, 418
stretcher bond 440, 445
strings 219
strip flooring 114, 115
strip footings 441
stripping
cable 308, 508
chemical strippers 59
flex 299, 508
industrial 59
metalwork 60, 61
mouldings 58
painted masonry 48
spilled paint from masonry 45
wallcoverings 52, 497
woodwork 58-9
structural condition, assessing house condition before purchase 12
structural walls see loadbearing walls
stud-partition walls 125
constructing 137-40
cutting openings 127, 128
filling openings 129
hanging wall fixtures 141, 145
removing 135
running services 141
staggered 140
studio flats 36
sub-contractors 20
sub-floors 114
subsidence 123, 423
Super glues 513
superimposed hearths 400
supplementary bonding 296
surforms 485
surveying, garden plots 421

surveyors 17
suspended-ceiling systems 147, 150
suspended ceilings 147, 149, 282
suspended floors 122, 123, 176-7
sweeping chimneys 396, 401
swimming pools 474
switched connection units 320
switches 91, 294
assessing condition 312-13
in-line 300
light switches 91, 335-8, 341
storage heaters 326-7
time 246, 292
switchfuse units 323, 324

T

tables, pasting 95, 501
tack rags 53, 497
tacks, carpet 118
tank cutters 391, 504
tapes 168, 169, 239
taps
baths 377
draining 350
fitting & replacing 375, 376, 378
garden 390
kitchen sinks 386
leaking, repairing 352-3
seats & glands 353
types 374
washbasins 374-5
washers 352
see also by type eg ceramic-disc taps
tarmac 466
telephone extensions 330
television-aerial sockets 329
terminals 299
terracing 451
texture 28
bricks 436
paving slabs 460
textured coatings 64, 65, 75
textured paints 67, 69
textured renderings 175
TGV boards 89
thermal-insulation plasterboard 162, 275
thermal-store showers 379
thermostatic radiator valves 407, 409
thermostatic shower mixers 380
thermostats 292, 409
thinners 63, 64, 69, 78, 87
thistle plasters 153, 155
thixotropic paints 63, 67, 77, 78
through rooms 130-6
tile cutters 106
tile-cutting jigs 106, 112, 501
tile nibblers 106, 501
tiles & tiling 62, 101-13
adhesives 105, 108, 110, 111, 112, 512
bedding down 113
cleaning 62, 400
cutting 106, 108, 110, 112, 113, 232, 501
fireplace surrounds 398, 400
floors 57, 62, 109-13
preparation 62
preparing for plastering 154
removing 62, 104
renovating & repairing 104, 398, 400
ridge 231, 233
roof 229-31, 232, 233
setting out 104, 109, 112, 113
tile sections 101
tile vents 285-6
tools 106, 112, 501
types of tiles 101-3

walls 62, 104-8
see also by type eg quarry tiles
timber see wood & woodwork
timber-faced cork 114
timber fence posts 426, 428, 429, 430, 431
timber-framed houses 123
time, planning 22
time switches 246, 292
timers, central-heating systems 409
tinsnips 503
toilets see WCs
tone 26-7
tongue-and-groove boards 89, 114, 115, 181, 183, 310
tools
bricklaying 442
building 494-6
decorating 497-501
digging 496
electrician's 508
glazier's 496
paperhanger's 500-1
plumbing & metalworking 502-7
tiling 501
woodworking 478-90
see also by type eg brushes
toughened glass 203
track lighting 333, 334
trailing sockets 300
transformers 328
traps
basins 376
baths 378
clearing 358, 360
fitting 368, 376, 378, 389
kitchen sinks 387, 389
showers 383
standpipe-and-trap drainage 389
WCs 370
see also by type eg bottle traps
treads 219, 222-3
trees 423
trellis fences 424
trenches, wall footings 441
trickle ventilation 283
triple glazing 277
trowels 494, 501
trunking 289
trussed roofs 123, 227
tubular traps 358
tundish 372
turnbuckles 428
two-pipe waste systems 348, 357
Tyrolean finish, render 175

U

U-values 266
undercloaks 286
undercoat plasters 153, 155
underground cables 344
underlay
carpet 116, 117, 118
roofs 230
universal tiles 101
up-and-over garage doors 198-9
upper floors 176, 177
urea-formaldehyde foam 275
urethane 264

V

V-joints 444
vacuum sweeping, chimneys 396
valleys 228, 231
valley flashing 238
valley gutters 240
valves
adding to plumbing 350

527